A GUIDE TO GLOBAL PRIVATE INTERNATIONAL LAW

This book provides a substantial overview of the discipline of private international law viewed from a global perspective.

The guide is divided into four key sections: theory; institutional and conceptual framework issues; civil and commercial law; and family law.

The chapters are written by leading experts. They address specific areas/aspects of private international law, consider the existing global solutions, and assess the potential to improve or create new ones. Where appropriate, the chapters are co-authored by experts from different legal perspectives in order to achieve as balanced a picture as possible.

The range of contributions includes authors from Europe, North America, Latin America, Africa, Asia and Oceania. It is an essential resource for academics, practitioners and students alike.

Volume 32 in the series Studies in Private International Law

Studies in Private International Law

Recent titles in the series

The Nature and Enforcement of Choice of Court Agreements: A Comparative Study
Mukarrum Ahmed

Cross-Border Litigation in Europe
Edited by Paul Beaumont, Mihail Danov, Katarina Trimmings and Burcu Yuksel

Forum (Non) Conveniens in England: Past, Present, and Future
Ardavan Arzandeh

Commercial Issues in Private International Law: A Common Law Perspective
Edited by Vivienne Bath, Andrew Dickinson, Michael Douglas and Mary Keyes

Jurisdiction and Cross-Border Collective Redress: A European Private International Law Perspective
Alexia Pato

Rethinking Judicial Jurisdiction in Private International Law
Milana Karayanidi

Economic Sanctions in EU Private International Law
Tamás Szabados

Clawback Law in the Context of Succession
Jayne Holliday

Place of Performance: A Comparative Analysis
Chukwuma Okoli

Private International Law in Nigeria
Chukwuma Okoli and Richard Oppong

Planning the Future of Cross Border Families: A Path Through Coordination
Edited by Ilaria Viarengo and Francesca Villata

The Private International Law of Authentic Instruments
Jonathan Fitchen

The Hague Judgments Convention and Commonwealth Model Law: A Pragmatic Perspective
Abubakri Yekini

A Guide to Global Private International Law
Edited by Paul Beaumont and Jayne Holliday

A Guide to Global Private International Law

Edited by
Paul Beaumont
and
Jayne Holliday

• HART •
OXFORD • LONDON • NEW YORK • NEW DELHI • SYDNEY

HART PUBLISHING

Bloomsbury Publishing Plc

Kemp House, Chawley Park, Cumnor Hill, Oxford, OX2 9PH, UK

1385 Broadway, New York, NY 10018, USA

29 Earlsfort Terrace, Dublin 2, Ireland

HART PUBLISHING, the Hart/Stag logo, BLOOMSBURY and the Diana logo are trademarks of Bloomsbury Publishing Plc

First published in Great Britain 2022

A catalogue record for this book is available from the British Library.

A catalogue record for this book is available from the Library of Congress.

Library of Congress Control Number: 2022930762

ISBN: HB: 978-1-50993-207-8
ePDF: 978-1-50993-210-8
ePub: 978-1-50993-209-2

Typeset by Compuscript Ltd, Shannon

SERIES EDITOR'S PREFACE

As I am one of the editors of this book I do not need to say much in this preface.

It is a privilege to be the series editor for Hart Studies in Private International Law. One of the aims of the series is to publish high-quality books on private international law. Hopefully this book achieves that aim. I know that the editors have tried very hard to pick excellent authors and to meticulously review and edit each chapter. They are both devoted to the cause of global private international law and want the book to make a major contribution to its growing success. I hope you will enjoy reading it.

Paul Beaumont, University of Stirling

PREFACE

Many of the usual matters mentioned in a preface can be found in the first chapter of this book. So, all that needs to be said here is how much we appreciate the hard work of the authors and reviewers in writing and improving the chapters of this book, especially in the context of a global pandemic. We are also very grateful for the team at Hart Publishing for all their various inputs into trying to make this book a success.

We hope that the book will prove very useful not only as a work of reference but also as a textbook for any courses that exist or may come into being with a focus on global private international law. We also hope that the Hague Conference on Private International Law (HCCH) including its Members and its Secretariat will find some of the ideas for the refinement and development of global private international law helpful. We pray for a constructive use of 'consensus' decision-making at the HCCH so that new legislative instruments can be worked on and adopted, new soft law instruments can be created, and existing Conventions can be the subject of excellent guidance on their interpretation. We hope and pray that members of the HCCH and other States will devote more of the time of their civil servants and legislatures to becoming parties to more HCCH Conventions and to implementing them fully and properly.

Global justice (for people and businesses) can only be achieved by the 'progressive unification of private international law' (the aim of the HCCH) and this requires a strong (time and resources intensive) commitment to making this happen by States. Those States need to send able and expert (in private international law) people to represent them at the HCCH, and they need to engage with stakeholders (notably academics, judges and lawyers) to make global private international law an ever-greater reality – beginning in their own State.

Paul Beaumont and Jayne Holliday
University of Stirling
20 August 2021

CONTENTS

PART VI
CONCLUSION

LIST OF CONTRIBUTORS

Nadia de Araujo
Professor of Law, Pontifical Catholic University of Rio de Janeiro

Ardavan Arzandeh
Associate Professor of Law, National University of Singapore

Maria Caterina Baruffi
Professor of International Law, University of Bergamo

Paul R Beaumont
Professor of Private International Law, University of Stirling

Giacomo Biagioni
Associate Professor of European Law, University of Cagliari

Ronald Brand
Chancellor Mark A Nordenberg University Professor, University of Pittsburgh School of Law

Janeen Carruthers
Professor of Private Law, University of Glasgow

Adeline Chong
Associate Professor of Law, Singapore Management University

Giuditta Cordero-Moss
Professor of Law, University of Oslo

Mihail Danov
Associate Professor of Law, University of Exeter

Albert Font i Segura
Associate Professor of Law, University Pompeu Fabra Barcelona

Pietro Franzina
Professor of International Law, Catholic University of the Sacred Heart, Milan

Francisco Garcimartín Alférez
Professor of Private International Law, University Autónoma Madrid

Richard Garnett
Professor of Law, University of Melbourne

David Goddard
Judge of the Court of Appeal of New Zealand

Susanne Gössl
Professor of Private International Law, Christian-Albrechts University of Kiel

Chiara Goetzke
Research Associate, Max Planck Institute for Comparative and International Private Law, Hamburg

Uglješa Grušić
Associate Professor in Law, University College London

Jonathan Harris QC (Hon)
Professor of International Commercial Law, King's College London and Barrister, Serle Court, London.

Trevor Hartley
Emeritus Professor of Law, London School of Economics

Michael Hellner
Professor of Private International Law, Stockholm University

Paul Herrup
Attorney, US Department of Justice

Jayne Holliday
Lecturer in Private International Law, University of Stirling

Costanza Honorati
Professor of Private International Law and of EU Law, University of Milano-Bicocca

Maria Hook
Senior Lecturer in Law, University of Otago

Mary Keyes
Professor of Law, Griffith University

Ruth Lamont
Senior Lecturer in Child and Family Law, University of Manchester

Matthias Lehmann
Professor of Private Law, Private International and Comparative Law, University of Vienna

Jan Lüttringhaus
Professor of Civil Law and Insurance Law, Leibniz University Hanover

Brooke Marshall
Lecturer in Law, University of New South Wales

Laura Martínez-Mora
Secretary (Lawyer), Hague Conference on Private International Law (HCCH)

Lucian C Martinez
Attorney, US Department of Justice

David McClean
Emeritus Professor of Law, University of Sheffield

Johan Meeusen
Professor of Law, University of Antwerp

Ralf Michaels
Director, Max Planck Institute for Comparative and International Private Law, Hamburg; Chair in Global Law, Queen Mary University of London, and Professor of Law, Hamburg University

Reid Mortensen
Professor and Head of School of Law, University of Southern Queensland

Máire Ní Shúilleabháin
Associate Professor of Law, University College Dublin

Carmen Otero García-Castrillón
Professor of Private International Law, Complutense University of Madrid

Ignacio Goicoechea and Brody Warren
For the Permanent Bureau of the Hague Conference on Private International Law (HCCH)

Marta Pertegás Sender
Professor of Law, Universities of Antwerp and Maastricht

Marta Requejo Isidro
Professor of Private International Law, University of La Laguna and Legal Secretary, Advocate General Campos's Chambers, Court of Justice of the European Union

Nieve Rubaja
Professor of Private International Law, University of Buenos Aires

Verónica Ruiz Abou-Nigm
Senior Lecturer in International Private Law, University of Edinburgh

Sara Sánchez
Assistant Professor of Law, IE Law School

Rhona Schuz
Professor of Law, Academic College of Law and Science, Israel

Symeon C Symeonides
Alex L Parks Distinguished Professor of Law, Willamette University College of Law

Koji Takahashi
Professor of Law, Doshisha University

Sophia Tang
Professor, Wuhan University, International Law Institute; Associate Dean, Wuhan University, Academy of International Law and Global Governance.

Paul Torremans
Professor of Intellectual Property Law, University of Nottingham

Karen Vandekerckhove
Head of Unit, EU Commission and Collaborator in Private International Law, Catholic University Louvain-la-Neuve

Lara Walker
Associate Professor of Law, University of Warwick

Matthias Weller
Professor of Law, University of Bonn

Abubakri Yekini
Lecturer in Law, University of Manchester

PART I

Introduction

1

Introduction

JAYNE HOLLIDAY AND PAUL BEAUMONT

The title of this book – *A Guide to Global Private International Law* – indicates that the purpose of the book is to help law students, lawyers, judges and academics to become initiated into private international law at the worldwide level. Traditionally private international law is seen as a branch of domestic law and more recently it has become an important part of EU law for the Member States of the European Union. However, for over 125 years the Hague Conference on Private International Law (HCCH) has been trying to bring about global private international law through binding public international law (multilateral treaties described in the HCCH as Conventions) and more recently soft law instruments (including Principles, Good Practice Guides to the Conventions, Practical Guides and Handbooks, and recommendations of Review Special Commissions). The aim of this book is to support the only aim of the Hague Conference on Private International Law to 'work for the progressive unification of private international law' (Article 1 of the Statute of the HCCH).

The HCCH is the only global international organisation dedicated to private international law. It has 90 Members (89 States and the EU) and many other States are Parties to some of their Conventions. Its mission is to gradually increase the amount of private international law that is the same (or at least operates within a common framework) in as much of the globe as possible. In the twenty-first century, the HCCH operates by consensus and therefore the task of developing global private international law in new instruments can be slow and painstaking (the work on the Judgments Convention 2019 began in 1992 and the Maintenance Convention 2007 took five years to negotiate). Furthermore, it can take many years for a significant number of States to become Parties to HCCH Conventions. Nevertheless, in successful cases more States are Parties to the Conventions than are Members of the HCCH (Child Abduction 1980 has 101 parties and Intercountry Adoption 1993 has 104). However, it is a vital effort to gradually achieve fair and efficient cross-border access to justice in all areas of private law for all types of natural (children and adults) and non-natural persons (companies, partnerships, associations, non-governmental organisations, governments, etc). The ability to arrive at true global consensus has been demonstrated in the new millennium in a wide range of matters. In the core areas of international commercial law (Choice of Court Agreements Convention 2005 and Principles on Choice of Law in International Commercial Contracts 2015), in a general treaty on the recognition of foreign judgments in most non-family private law (Judgments Convention 2019) and, building on hugely successful earlier Conventions on family law – particularly concerning children (Child Abduction 1980, Intercountry Adoption 1993 and Child Protection 1996) – in the increasingly high volume issue of securing maintenance for spouses and children across borders (Maintenance Convention 2007).

The *Guide* sets out to cover systematically all areas of private international law, considering the scope of the existing unification of private international law at the global level. The authors of each substantive chapter aim to identify the challenges to unification, problems with the content and interpretation of unifying laws and whether there are any remaining gaps to be rectified. In areas of private international law where there is no global unification (or the HCCH Convention is clearly unsuccessful), the authors consider whether it is possible to resolve these problems through the creation of unified rules (given the need for consensus amongst the Members of the HCCH) and, where they believe it is possible, offer ideas for global solutions. These ideas can be for a new Convention or for a soft law solution.

It is already clear that successful global private international law exists for Child Abduction 1980, Intercountry Adoption 1993, Service of documents relating to litigation 1965, and Taking of Evidence relating to litigation 1970. Four of the 41 chapters in the book cover these matters. There are HCCH Conventions which have not yet achieved enough State Parties to be regarded as 'global' private international law but may still get there (Child Protection 1996, Maintenance 2007, Form of Wills 1961, Choice of Court 2005, Divorce 1970, Trusts 1985, Adult Protection 2000, and Judgments 2019). Eight chapters in the book cover these matters. There is one significant soft law instrument independent of any Convention (Principles on Choice of Law in International Commercial Contracts 2015) which may prove to be globally influential and one chapter in the book discusses it. There are three legislative projects in the HCCH which might yield new Conventions and/or soft law instruments (parentage/surrogacy, family agreements involving children, and jurisdiction – especially conflicts of jurisdiction). Three chapters in the book cover these matters. There are 12 chapters in the book covering topics where HCCH Conventions do not exist or have no realistic prospect of becoming global (application of foreign law, contract jurisdiction, tort jurisdiction, tort applicable law, unjustified enrichment, property, companies, competition, intellectual property, maritime law, collective redress, and matrimonial property). One chapter of the book focuses on private international law of arbitration where there is a very successful global Convention that was negotiated under the auspices of the UN (the New York Convention on Arbitration 1958) and another chapter focuses on private international law of bankruptcy and insolvency where model laws have been adopted in the United Nations Commission on International Trade Law (UNCITRAL) with some success. Finally, nine chapters in the book are not on specific subject matters but rather concern cross-cutting aspects of private international law. These cross-cutting matters help the reader understand the discipline of private international law.

The book has brought together private international law scholars from all over the world (27 men, 25 women and one international secretariat). The authors range from three of the long-established 'greats' in the field – both in their contributions to scholarship and law-making (Trevor Hartley, David McClean and Symeon Symeonides); through 15 who have been at the cutting edge of the practical development of global private international law as well as making significant contributions to scholarship (Nadia de Araujo, Paul Beaumont, Ron Brand, Giuditta Cordero-Moss, Pietro Franzina, Francisco Garcimartín Alferez, Richard Garnett, David Goddard, Michael Hellner, Paul Herrup, Mary Keyes, Laura Martínez-Mora, Permanent Bureau of the HCCH, Marta Pertegás and Karen Vandekerckhove); to 17 of the well-established and highly respected commentators in the field (Maria Caterina Baruffi, Giacomo Biagioni, Janeen Carruthers, Albert Font i Segura, Jonathan Harris, Costanza Honorati, Matthias Lehmann, Ralf Michaels, Johan Meeusen, Reid Mortensen, Carmen Otero García-Castrillón, Marta Requejo Isidro, Rhona Schuz, Koji Takahashi, Sophia Tang, Paul Torremans and Matthias Weller); and finally to 18 of the rising stars of private international law (Ardavan Arzandeh, Adeline Chong,

Mihail Danov, Susanne Goessl, Chiara Goetzke, Uglješa Grušić, Jayne Holliday, Maria Hook, Ruth Lamont, Jan Lüttringhaus, Brooke Marshall, Mickey Martinez, Máire Ní Shúilleabháin, Nieve Rubaja, Veronica Ruiz Abou-Nigm, Sara Sánchez, Lara Walker and Abubakri Yekini).

Quite often authors have been brought together to give different perspectives on the topics they are writing about (eg, Uglješa Grušić, Paul Herrup and Mickey Martinez straddling the common law/civil law divide and the academic/State practice divide to analyse States/governments in private litigation); to make sure both common law and civil law perspectives are understood (eg, Susanne Gössl and Ruth Lamont on connecting factors, Ron Brand and Karen Vandekerckhove on contract jurisdiction, Adeline Chong and Jan Lüttringhaus on unjust(ified) enrichment, Janeen Carruthers and Matthias Weller on property, Albert Font i Segura and Jayne Holliday on Succession, Ardavan Arzandeh and Matthias Lehmann on conflicts of jurisdiction and Costanza Honorati and Mary Keyes on parental responsibility); or to pair people at different stages in their careers to bring fresh insights tempered by experience (Nadia de Araujo and Brooke Marshall on taking of evidence, Paul Beaumont and Nieve Rubaja on family agreements, Maria Caterina Baruffi and Jayne Holliday on child abduction, Francisco Garcimartín Alferez and Sara Sánchez on bankruptcy and insolvency, Paul Beaumont and Lara Walker on maintenance and Paul Beaumont and Abubakri Yekini on pragmatism); or to bring together people with similar expertise and experience (eg, David Goddard and Paul Beaumont on recognition and enforcement of judgments, Paul Beaumont and Mary Keyes on choice of court agreements, Máire Ní Shúilleabháin and Jayne Holliday on divorce, Koji Takahashi and Sophia Tang on collective redress and Carmen Otero García-Castrillón and Mihail Danov on competition).

The editors are very grateful for the significant help they received in reviewing the draft chapters by the authors from their editorial advisory board (Mary Keyes, Ralf Michaels and Symeon Symeonides) and from a number of other anonymous colleagues (both authors of other chapters in the book and, very generously, some who were not authors in the book, ie, Laura Carballo, Christopher Forsyth, Philippe Lortie, Barry Rodger and Hans van Loon).

The book is divided into six parts. The first part is this introductory chapter. Part II is on private international law theory. There is no attempt here to consider all the theories of private international law. Rather the book adopts the pragmatic theory of private international law. The chapter on pragmatism by Abubakri Yekini and Paul Beaumont (chapter 2) explains the origins of the philosophical theories of pragmatism and brings insights from those origins to a new theory of global private international law. The rest of part II analyses some of the key components of the private international law toolbox: characterisation, connecting factors, renvoi and preliminary questions, and public policy and mandatory provisions. Characterisation is one of the fundamental building blocks of private international law. In some jurisdiction cases (eg, where the jurisdictional basis is confined to a particular type of legal dispute – contract, tort, unjustified enrichment, movable property, marriage, divorce, matrimonial property, maintenance, custody, access, etc) and in all applicable law cases, it is necessary to decide which 'branch' of law the dispute or the particular issue to be decided falls into before applying the correct jurisdiction or applicable law rule. Ralf Michaels (chapter 3) brings his massive erudition on comparative law and private international law to bear, along with the hard work of one of his assistants at the Max Planck Institute in Hamburg – Chiara Goetzke – in their analysis of characterisation in the context of uniform global private international law. Susanne Gössl and Ruth Lamont (chapter 4) focus largely on the global personal connecting factor of habitual residence – developed by the HCCH – with very interesting ideas on the balance between objective facts and the intention of the relevant person or persons. They advocate greater weight should be given to intention than in the case law of the Court of Justice of the European Union on habitual residence in cross-border family law while noting the admirable tendency of some of the leading courts in the world (notably the Supreme Courts in Canada, the UK and US) to try to forge a uniform meaning for habitual residence in the Hague Child Abduction Convention 1980. Maria Hook's chapter on renvoi and preliminary questions (chapter 5) brilliantly and succinctly explains these difficult, but still significant, private international law building blocks which are relevant in nearly all Hague Conventions. The recent significance of renvoi is particularly notable in relation to custody rights under the Hague Child Abduction Convention and to substantive validity of choice of court agreements under the Hague Choice of Court Agreements Convention 2005. Preliminary questions are the subject of serious analysis in the Hague Choice of Court Agreements Convention, Judgments Convention 2019 and the Maintenance Convention 2007.

Global private international law relies on the basic concept of mutual trust of one Contracting State in the ability of another Contracting State to a Convention (treaty) to rule on the merits of a cross-border case. Where the law applicable to a cross-border legal issue is agreed globally – as in the Hague Principles on Choice of Law in International Commercial Contracts 2015 – States are indicating a willingness to apply any law chosen by the parties to resolve their commercial contract dispute. However, this is balanced by each State's ability to protect its vital interests through applying the overriding mandatory provisions of its law, or the law of another State with a strong connection to the dispute, or by the use of public policy refusing to apply a particular provision of foreign law which is contrary to its fundamental interests (including human rights) in the instant case. Furthermore, public policy is a standard ground in Hague Conventions for the refusal of the recognition and enforcement of a foreign judgment which otherwise should be enforced (see Divorce 1970, Intercountry Adoption 1993, Child Protection 1996, Adult Protection 2000, Choice of Court 2005, Maintenance 2007, Judgments 2019). In each of these Conventions the policy is to trust the ability of the foreign court (the court of origin) to decide the merits of the dispute even if that court applied a different law to resolve it from the court where recognition and enforcement is sought (the court addressed) would have done had they been deciding the case *ab initio*. Public policy is a safety valve that will only be used rarely to allow the court addressed to decide that in this case the foreign judgment is manifestly contrary to their State's fundamental interests and values. As public policy and mandatory rules are such important building blocks in private international law, the chapter (chapter 6) was entrusted to one of the lifetime leaders in the field (Trevor Hartley) who was the co-rapporteur on the Choice of Court Convention 2005.

Part III is on institutional and framework issues connected to developing global private international law. The 'institutional' issues are covered in two chapters on the Hague Conference on Private International Law. Paul Beaumont and Marta Pertegás (chapter 7) bring the perspectives of two senior academics in the field. The former being a long-standing negotiator at the Hague for the UK and EU (including on the Statute 2005, Choice of Court, Maintenance and Judgments) and the latter being a former First Secretary in the Permanent Bureau of the HCCH who had a significant role to play in leading the Permanent Bureau's work on the Principles on Choice of Law in International Commercial Contracts and starting the renewed work on the Judgments Convention 2019. One of their heartfelt pleas is that the HCCH and its Members should not undervalue the work of specialist private international law academics in developing new global instruments and in reviewing the operation of the Hague *acquis*. It must not become a bureaucratic organisation – either in the Permanent Bureau or in the various fora where private international law is developed in the HCCH (notably Experts' and Working Groups, Special Commissions, the Council, and Diplomatic Sessions). We are delighted that the Permanent Bureau agreed to write a chapter for the book (chapter 8). It focuses on two of the tools that the

HCCH has created to help ensure strong engagement by States and public authorities in the work of the HCCH. First, a 'national organ' creates a focal point in the government of each Member State of the Conference to take responsibility for that State's involvement in the HCCH. Second, many of the successful Hague Conventions utilise the concept of 'Central Authorities' to take on specific administrative responsibilities to make the operation of a Convention successful in that State and to ensure cross-border cooperation between those States. The Permanent Bureau gives insights into best practice for national organs and central authorities. We are particularly grateful to the Secretary General, Dr Christophe Bernasconi, for authorising the Permanent Bureau to write this chapter and for supporting the writing of this chapter by his hard-working attaché, Brody Warren, and the excellent representative of the Latin American and Caribbean Regional Office, Ignacio Goicoechea.

The framework issues relate to all types of cross-border litigation. Richard Garnett (chapter 9) analyses the crucial divide between substance and procedure. When private international law rules require a court to apply foreign law to resolve a dispute it is only the foreign substantive law which should be applied not the foreign procedural law. Where the line should be drawn is not always clear but Garnett's pre-eminence in this field enables him to do so using up-to-date case law and scholarship. Marta Requejo Isidro (chapter 10) records the failure of the HCCH in recent years to reach consensus on adopting a new instrument in the field of application of foreign law. In some systems foreign law must be proved by the parties and is treated as an issue of fact whereas in other systems courts are required to know the foreign law and to apply it as a matter of law. Harmonising such divergent approaches to law and procedure in a cross-cutting instrument will not happen globally for the foreseeable future but the Child Abduction Convention 1980 creates a special rule to limit the difficulties in proving the relevant foreign law from the country of the child's habitual residence (Article 14). This example could be followed in future instruments on other subject matters. Private international law does apply to States, governments and international institutions when they are not acting in their 'sovereign' capacity. The dividing line is tricky to establish but the transatlantic team of Uglješa Grušić, Paul Herrup and Lucian Martinez (chapter 11) do an excellent job of distilling some very clear principles in their case studies. David McClean (chapter 12) was the pre-eminent jurist on the Hague Service Convention 1965 and therefore it is a thrill to have his chapter explaining how this key part of the global private international law *acquis* works. Cross-border litigation can only work if it is possible to successfully serve litigation-related documents abroad. With goodwill, following the soft law guidance provided by the HCCH, the Service Convention still operates well in the modern digital world. Finally, the Australian/Brazilian partnership of Brooke Marshall and Nadia de Araujo (chapter 13), have done a brilliant job of encapsulating how the other key building block of the Hague *acquis* on the process of cross-border litigation, the Taking of Evidence Convention 1971, is working. The next Review Special Commission on the Service and Evidence Conventions is scheduled for the first half of 2023 and the revisions of the Practical Handbooks on each of the Conventions are part of the work plan for the Permanent Bureau.

Part IV is on each of the areas of civil or commercial law (excluding family law). It begins with a chapter (chapter 14) on applicable law in contract by Symeon Symeonides that focuses on party autonomy but also discusses mandatory rules, public policy and choice of applicable law in tort. Symeonides brings to bear his brilliant lifetime work on comparative law in relation to private international law of contract. In relation to party autonomy the global framework for applicable law in contract is provided for by the Principles on Choice of Law in International Commercial Contracts 2015. The next chapter on contract jurisdiction (chapter 15) brought together two of the Transatlantic protagonists from the early stages of the negotiations on the Judgments

Convention 2019. Karen Vandekerckhove has a PhD in private international law from Belgium and was for many years a key member of and then leader of the private international law unit in the EU Commission. Ron Brand is a leading academic and a long-standing member of the US delegation in The Hague going back to the original Judgments Convention negotiations in the 1990s. Paul Beaumont enjoyed negotiating then with Ron for a direct contract jurisdiction rule that would work on both sides of the Atlantic (combining the US activity-based jurisdiction with the largely contractual place of performance-based jurisdiction in Europe and many other parts of the world) but never quite managing to succeed. In the 2010s the focus shifted to only having to agree an indirect contract jurisdiction rule and negotiators, including Karen, Ron and Paul, had more room for manoeuvre because no State (or states in the US) will have to amend their contract jurisdiction rule to comply with the 2019 Convention. Instead, the 2019 Convention may have a more subtle, long-term effect on direct jurisdiction rules. Once the Convention has been adopted by a significant number of States there will be an incentive to align the direct jurisdiction rules with the indirect rules of the Convention to increase the number of judgments which will circulate abroad.

Johan Meeusen (chapter 16) analyses the lack of progress on developing global private international law on the law applicable to companies paying particular attention to the position in Europe and the US. There is a long-standing divide between States that focus on the law of incorporation and those that focus on the real seat of the company (whether that is its place of central administration or its principal place of business). This divide has largely been solved globally in the context of the jurisdiction rules for where a company can be sued (in the indirect jurisdiction rule in the 2019 Convention on 'habitual residence' of non-natural persons taking the idea from the identical rules on 'residence' determining the territorial scope of the 2005 Choice of Court Convention obligations) by allowing judgments to circulate if the non-natural person had its place of incorporation, or its central administration, or its principal place of business in the State where the judgment was given. Agreeing global rules on the private international law of competition has proved very difficult: it is an area completely excluded from the 2005 Choice of Court Convention. However, at least a toehold has been created by the 2019 Judgments Convention due to the good offices of China. China informally negotiated with other key partners a compromise to get competition rules relating to hard-core cartels into the scope of the Convention (having opposed any competition rules being included) and then when consensus was lacking on this point in the plenary of the Diplomatic Session persuaded the remaining sceptical States to accept the compromise. Mihail Danov and Carmen Otero García-Castrillón (chapter 17) rightly show how limited the toehold created by the 2019 Convention is. They do come up with interesting arguments for further work to be pursued in The Hague in this area.

Like contract, tort is given two chapters, one on applicable law and the other on jurisdiction. Paul Beaumont enjoyed working with Michael Hellner negotiating the EU's Rome II Regulation on the Law Applicable to Non-Contractual Obligations in the EU Council Working Party in the 2000s. At the time the Council and European Parliament reached agreement that Rome II should not override the obligations of those EU Member States who were already parties to the Hague Traffic Accidents Convention 1971 and the Hague Products Liability Convention 1973. Those two Conventions have not been very successful and there is no prospect, due to the constraints of EU law, of any EU Member States that are not already party to them becoming Parties to those Conventions. Michael Hellner (chapter 18) considers if this dilemma can be solved by creating new global private international law on the law applicable to torts (or at least on traffic accidents and products liability) at the HCCH. Reid Mortensen in the chapter on tort jurisdiction (chapter 19) does an excellent job of a comparative law analysis of tort jurisdiction rules.

On the basis of that analysis, he considers whether the relatively narrow indirect tort jurisdiction rule in the Judgments Convention 2019 could provide a good basis for the tort jurisdiction rule in a future instrument that might be agreed on direct jurisdiction in the HCCH. Perhaps, as a first step, it might be possible to agree to use the tort indirect jurisdiction rule in the 2019 Convention as a rule for guiding the determination of acceptable, or appropriate, or prioritised bases of jurisdiction in a future Convention on conflicts of jurisdiction in the HCCH under the current Jurisdiction Project.

Unjustified enrichment is a virgin area for the development of global private international law. Adeline Chong and Jan Lüttringhaus (chapter 20) do an excellent historical and comparative law job of framing the issues in this complex field of law to set the scene for some very interesting ideas as to how global private international law could be created.

Janeen Carruthers and Matthias Weller (chapter 21) discuss an area with very little global harmonisation – private international law of property – and bring to bear a helpful comparative law perspective. One notable feature in this area is the extent to which the law of the place of the property is a very significant connecting factor for the law applicable to movables and immovables in many States. Additionally, the courts of the State where an immovable is situated are the only acceptable forum for a judgment on a right *in rem* in relation to that property under the Judgments Convention 2019. Only a judgment from such a forum can be recognised and enforced under the Convention and there is a prohibition, even under national law, against the recognition and enforcement of a judgment on a right *in rem* in relation to immovable property if it comes from a court that is not a court of the Contracting State where the immovable property is situated. On the other hand, succession is an area with one relatively successful Hague Convention on Formal Validity of Wills 1961 and the other on the Law Applicable to Succession 1989 which is currently not ratified by any State and has no prospect of becoming successful. Albert Font i Segura and Jayne Holliday (chapter 22) explain the former Convention (advocating for a Review Special Commission on it at the HCCH) and consider ideas for future development of legislative work on succession at the HCCH focusing particularly on the law applicable to clawback in the context of succession. Trusts is an area where we are very happy to see the writer of the leading monograph on the Hague Trusts Convention 1985 holding the pen for the trusts chapter in this book. Jonathan Harris (chapter 23) considers some of the case law on the Trusts Convention decided since writing his monograph, to give ideas about how the uniform interpretation of the Convention can be enhanced. It is timely that the HCCH Permanent Bureau prepared a report on the Convention (Prel Doc No 15 of December 2020) for the HCCH Council on General Affairs and Policy (CGAP) meeting in March 2021. The CGAP mandated the Permanent Bureau to continue its work in relation to the Convention and to leverage the thirtieth anniversary of the entry into force of the Convention (1 January 2022) when planning research activities, publications and events.

The book then moves on to four subject areas where the HCCH has not in the past played a major role, but other international organisations have done so or could be expected to do so. The areas of insolvency and bankruptcy are the subject of several soft law instruments created in UNCITRAL and further work is ongoing there on applicable law. It is encouraging to read in the Conclusions and Decisions of the CGAP of March 2021 that cooperation between the UNCITRAL Secretariat and the Permanent Bureau of the HCCH is mandated on the development of a new instrument on the law applicable to insolvency. Francisco Garcimartín Alferez and Sara Sánchez (chapter 24) skilfully unpack the various UNCITRAL soft law instruments that make up global private international law in this field. We are delighted that Paul Torremans (chapter 25), the co-author of the leading English language monograph on private international law of intellectual property, explains the limited coverage of intellectual property in the Choice of Court Convention and the even more limited coverage in the Judgments Convention 2019. These exclusions were driven by extensive lobbying of a number of Members of the HCCH by groups representing intellectual property stakeholders and the resulting lack of consensus amongst the States negotiating those Conventions to cover intellectual property issues more comprehensively. Torremans analyses the CLIP Principles (Principles on Conflict of Laws in Intellectual Property) that have been agreed in the field by specialist academics, and advocates for persisting with efforts to develop global private international law of intellectual property perhaps with the World Intellectual Property Organization (WIPO) taking the lead assisted by the HCCH. It is good to see from the Conclusions and Decisions of the CGAP of March 2021 that cooperation between WIPO and the HCCH is progressing on future work on private international law of intellectual property by the preparation of a questionnaire on the topic. Giuditta Cordero-Moss (chapter 26) brings her enormous knowledge of international commercial arbitration to bear in lucidly explaining global private international law of arbitration, noting that many of the key rules have been harmonised by the UN through the highly successful New York Convention, backed up by the UNCITRAL Model Law. She is a strong advocate for the significance of private international law in arbitration battling against the more extreme anti-private international law position adopted by those favouring complete delocalisation of arbitration. Finally, Veronica Ruiz Abou-Nigm (chapter 27) brings her undoubted expertise in the field of private international law of maritime law to bear to show that the specialised Conventions in the field of maritime law are incomplete and/or unsuccessful in developing private international law rules. She puts forward ideas as to how this could begin to be rectified by the HCCH taking a bigger role in this field in collaboration with some or all of the specialised international bodies dealing with maritime law.

Paul Beaumont combines with Mary Keyes (chapter 28) to analyse the jurisdictional aspects of the Hague Choice of Court Convention 2005 and then with David Goddard (chapter 29) to discuss recognition and enforcement of foreign judgments under that Convention and the Hague Judgments Convention 2019. Keyes and Beaumont build on and refine Beaumont's earlier work, continuing the dialogue with Brand and Herrup, in analysing the best interpretation of the 2005 Convention on what constitutes an 'agreement' under the Convention. Is it something that has an autonomous meaning which might in rare cases be different from the combination of the Convention's rules on formal validity and applicable law rule on substantive validity? What role should the manifest injustice exception to the duty of non-chosen courts to decline jurisdiction in favour of the chosen court play in this context? It is good to note that in March 2021 the CGAP supported the proposal to dedicate Edition 2021 of HCCH abridged to the Choice of Court Convention and the circulation of a questionnaire to elicit reasons as to why more States have not become party to the Convention. Goddard and Beaumont show that the Judgments Convention 2019 enhances the treatment of choice of court agreements by complementing the 2005 Convention. The core of the 2005 Convention only covers exclusive choice of court agreements whereas the 2019 Convention covers all other types of choice of court agreement (providing a non-exclusive indirect jurisdictional rule for them). The 2019 Convention also provides a ground for refusal of recognition of a foreign judgment coming from a Contracting State to that Convention if it is contrary to a choice of court agreement whether that agreement falls within the scope of the 2005 Convention or the 2019 Convention. In the latter case such a judgment will only be contrary to the choice of court agreement if it has derogating effect and not just prorogating effect, eg, in relation to multiple exclusive choice of court agreements where the parties can litigate in two or more States but not in any non-chosen States. Hopefully many States will become Parties to both Conventions and thereby create a strong framework for private international commercial law alongside compliance with the Hague Principles from 2015. This area of the HCCH's work is in the very capable hands of First Secretary João Ribeiro-Bidaoui. See, eg, his excellent article on uniform treaty interpretation: 'The international obligation of the uniform and autonomous interpretation of private law Conventions: consequences for domestic courts and international organisations' (2020) 67 *Netherlands International Law Review* 139.

To conclude part IV of the book there are two chapters on areas where global private international law is limited or non-existent: conflicts of jurisdiction and collective redress. Ardavan Arzandeh and Matthias Lehmann (chapter 30) combine common law and civil law perspectives to consider potential global private international law dealing with reducing the harms caused to access to justice by parallel proceedings in different States. They note the important work achieved on this in the first phase of the Judgments Convention negotiations between 1992 and 2001. They also give some ideas as to how this work might be built upon in the current work at the HCCH on the Jurisdiction Project. This chapter is particularly timely because that work is initially focusing on conflicts of jurisdiction given the remit given to the Working Group in 2021. Koji Takahashi and Sophia Tang (chapter 31) deal with the increasingly important topic of collective redress. It is a vital method for ensuring, eg, where many people make small losses from the actions of the same defendant, that justice can be secured. They expose the weaknesses of the Judgments Convention 2019 from the perspective of dealing with collective redress actions and give some very insightful ideas for future work on this topic at the HCCH.

Part V is on family law. Máire Ní Shúilleabháin and Jayne Holliday (chapter 32) show that the Hague Divorce Convention 1970, despite only having 20 Contracting States, is still fit for purpose. The drafters (including some of the greats of private international law – Graveson, Von Mehren, Anton, Bellet and Goldman – and a famous dean from Harvard (Griswold)) did an excellent job of future proofing the Convention when it was negotiated in the 1960s. Recently the HCCH Permanent Bureau has shown a renewed interest in the Convention and is preparing a questionnaire on it as part of a process of understanding how it is operating in Contracting States and why other Members of the HCCH have not become Parties to it. The authors have some very interesting ideas for points of interpretation that could be clarified in a future Review Special Commission on the Convention. They also advocate that the HCCH should explore a new Convention on conflicts of jurisdiction in relation to divorce and other personal status matters.

In the area of child protection and children's rights the HCCH has four excellent Conventions (Child Abduction, Intercountry Adoption, Child Protection and Maintenance (Child Support)). Maria Caterina Baruffi and Jayne Holliday (chapter 34) write about the Hague Child Abduction Convention 1980. With over 100 Contracting States the 1980 Convention has greatly improved access to justice for parents and children caught up in the tragedy of cross-border child abductions (usually by one parent without the consent of the other parent). Its simplicity – the prompt return of the abducted child to their habitual residence before the abduction so that the courts there can determine the long-term custody and access arrangements for the child – has stood the test of time and also the swings in the percentages of mothers or fathers being the abductors. This simplicity has a lot to do with the ability of its key drafters (Alexander (Sandy) Anton – Paul Beaumont's mentor in the 1980s and 1990s – Elizabeth Perez Vera, Adair Dyer and Georges Droz). Baruffi and Holliday give insights into the key provisions in the Convention showing how the extensive case law on this Convention (much of which is made available through the HCCH's vital and excellent INCADAT database) gives some excellent examples of the development of uniform interpretation (eg, on custody rights, habitual residence, the hearing of the child and on what constitutes a grave risk of harm to the child). The very last of these has also been greatly helped by the efforts of the person then responsible for this Convention in the Permanent Bureau, Gérardine Goh Escolar – now the Deputy Secretary General, in helping to steer the successful adoption by consensus of the Members of the HCCH of the Guide to Good Practice on Article 13(1)(b) of the 1980 Convention. The Guide, published in 2020, is a vital tool for courts to use to give a uniform interpretation to this exception to the requirement to return the abducted child to its habitual residence when this would create a grave risk of physical or psychological harm or an otherwise intolerable situation for the child.

Costanza Honorati and Mary Keyes (chapter 33) combine their well-known talents in private international law from civil law and common law perspectives to bring an insightful analysis of the key provisions in the Hague Child Protection Convention 1996 relating to parental responsibility. They point out how that Convention heavily influenced the various versions of the Brussels II Regulation in the EU which applies to parental responsibility matters between EU Member States (apart from Denmark). All EU Member States are Parties to the Child Protection Convention as it is part of the EU *acquis* (like the Hague Conventions on Child Abduction 1980, Choice of Court 2005 and Maintenance 2007) and the Child Protection Convention (like the other Conventions just noted) applies to cases involving an EU Member State and a non-EU Contracting State to that Convention. Honorati and Keyes give convincing arguments about how the application of the Child Protection Convention could be improved by learning from some of the developments in EU law arising from the amendments to and interpretation of the Brussels II regime.

We are delighted that the Secretary (a diplomatic lawyer level position) in the Permanent Bureau with responsibility for the highly successful Hague Intercountry Adoption Convention 1993 (over 100 Contracting States) agreed to write the chapter on adoption. Laura Martínez-Mora (chapter 35) packs the chapter full of the insights gained from her understanding of the everyday operation of and strategic overview of the strengths and weaknesses of the Convention. She is in the vanguard of ensuring its continued improvement as she leads the preparations for the next Review Special Commission meeting in June 2022.

Paul Beaumont and Lara Walker (chapter 36) build on their extensive writings on the Hague Maintenance (Child Support) Convention 2007 to explain some of its key provisions. They analyse the practice of the Convention through the lens of States' answers to the questionnaire prepared for the Review Special Commission on the Convention to be held between March and June 2022. This Convention is already a success given it is in force in a significant number of States including Brazil, the EU, Turkey, the UK, Ukraine and the US. It is welcome that in March 2021 the CGAP mandated the Permanent Bureau to make arrangements for online events before the Special Commission meeting, namely, a general information session for Contracting and non-Contracting Parties, bilateral meetings for Contracting and non-Contracting Parties, and an information session on iSupport. Furthermore, the practical ability of the Convention to secure a good flow of money from maintenance debtors to maintenance creditors across borders should be enhanced by the fact that the CGAP in March 2021 invited States to implement the iSupport software with a view to standardising and generating savings in their child support operations. The persistence and hard work of the First Secretary, Philippe Lortie, responsible in the Permanent Bureau for the Maintenance Convention 2007, has much to do with the creation and development of iSupport and the chances of maximising cross-border maintenance flows as a result of it and the work of the Experts' Group on international transfer of maintenance funds.

We are delighted that Rhona Schuz, a leading author on private international law of family law, agreed to write the chapter (chapter 37) on matrimonial property. There is a Hague Convention in this field but it has not been a success. Schuz gives a very interesting comparative law analysis of the different types of matrimonial property systems and also of the diverse rules on determining the law applicable to matrimonial property disputes. Aware of the difficulty of reaching consensus on any hard law rules in this area, Schuz suggests that the HCCH might begin by seeking to develop a soft law instrument.

The HCCH has been working for several years on family agreements involving children. Two members of the HCCH Experts' Group on this topic, Paul Beaumont and Nieve Rubaja, combine to write the chapter on this topic (chapter 38). They explain how the existing HCCH Conventions (1980, 1996 and 2007) operate to encourage and enable family agreements in child abduction cases, cross-border parental responsibility (custody and access) cases, and in cross-border maintenance cases. They also show how those Conventions are not always easy to operate in relation to comprehensive family ('package') agreements, notably because they have different direct or indirect jurisdiction rules and in many Contracting States the cases under these Conventions are heard in different courts. Beaumont and Rubaja set out the arguments that the Experts' Group has put forward for a new Convention in the Hague creating a 'one stop shop' for family agreements, thereby encouraging such agreements by making it cheaper and easier to make them enforceable, and to be sure they will be recognised and enforced in other Contracting States in one court process. This also increases respect for party autonomy – by allowing a wider choice of forum to make the family agreement enforceable than currently permitted by the Hague Conventions – and should reduce the weight on courts of family law cases in many jurisdictions.

Pietro Franzina (chapter 39) does an excellent job of explaining the key features of the Hague Adult Protection Convention 2000. Although it has only a modest number of Contracting States there is no doubt that it is fit for purpose. The task remains to persuade more States to invest in the protection of the rights of their vulnerable adults. The fact that increasing numbers of vulnerable adults have cross-border interests should prompt States to become parties to the Convention. As always important work can be done on explaining how the Convention should operate. In March 2021 the CGAP noted the progress made on the draft Practical Handbook on the Operation of the Adult Protection Convention and mandated the Permanent Bureau to establish a Working Group to continue its development. This Working Group will meet online and will comprise experts with experience on the operation or implementation of the Convention. The CGAP agreed to provisionally reschedule the first meeting of the Special Commission on the practical operation of the Adult Protection Convention to the second half of 2022.

Giacomo Biagioni (chapter 40) traces the development of the HCCH's work on parentage and surrogacy. He is broadly supportive of the traditional private international law solutions for legal parentage discussed by the HCCH Experts' Group on the Parentage/Surrogacy Project in their possible proposed new private international instrument on legal parentage. However, he strongly encourages the Experts' Group to not just create a separate Protocol on legal parentage established as a result of international surrogacy arrangements (as they are considering doing) but to create a regulatory solution to these controversial issues inspired by the radical regulatory solution in the Hague Intercountry Adoption Convention 1993 that has proved to be incredibly successful in a wide range of sending and receiving countries as well as in countries with limited (or at times no) enthusiasm for intercountry adoptions.

Part VI is a concluding chapter where we will highlight the ideas from the book which we hope the HCCH will take forward in their future work plans, either on their own or in collaboration with other international organisations.

PART II

Theory

2

Pragmatism and Private International Law

ABUBAKRI YEKINI AND PAUL BEAUMONT

> [T]he modern legal mind has come to realize that the complexity of contemporary conflicts problems requires a toolbox approach – the more tools the better – rather than a single tool or method; that no single theory or school of thought has all the right solutions to all conflicts problems, but each school has something valuable to contribute; and that, rather than choosing a single school or method wholesale, it is better to draw the best ideas from each and properly combine them into a workable system.[1]

I. Introduction

Private international law is the branch of law that seeks to resolve conflicts arising from cross-border relationships and the potential application of conflicting normative systems to a given case. Scholars differ on the objectives of private international law and the methods for resolving conflictual problems.[2]

This chapter presents a pragmatic theory of private international law for the development of the subject globally, primarily by the Hague Conference on Private International Law (HCCH). It builds on earlier work by Kegel[3] and by Beaumont and McEleavy[4] that outlined the importance of the discipline's ability to separate conflicts justice from substantive justice (the latter being protected where necessary by exceptions – public policy and overriding mandatory rules – to

[1] SC Symeonides, 'Private International Law: Idealism, Pragmatism, Eclecticism General Course on Private International Law' (2017) 384 *Hague Collected Courses* 350.

[2] J Basedow, 'Methods of Private International Law' in J Basedow et al (eds), *Encyclopedia of Private International Law*, Vol I (Edward Elgar 2017) 1401–02; G Rühl, 'Methods and Approaches in Choice of Law: An Economic Perspective' (2006) 24 *Berkeley Journal of International Law* 801, 801–12.

[3] G Kegel, 'Fundamental Approaches' in *International Encyclopaedia of Comparative Law, Vol III, Private International Law* (Martinus Nijhoff 1986) 12–16.

[4] P Beaumont and P McEleavy, *Anton's Private International Law*, 3rd edn (W Green/Thomson Reuters 2011) paras 2.87–2.99. For earlier attempts to build on this approach see L Walker, *Maintenance and Child Support in Private International Law* (Hart Publishing 2015) esp 6–8, who incorporates human rights into a pragmatic approach to private international law; and J Holliday, *Clawback Law in the Context of Succession* (Hart Publishing 2020) esp 28–30, 109-110 and 164, who follows Walker on human rights and develops pragmatic theory by emphasising the importance of comprehensive comparative law work on the substantive law underlying the area of private international law (in this case the law on clawback of lifetime gifts by a person to third parties as part of the succession process in relation to that person) as part of the process of developing a new private international law instrument globally or regionally.

the normal, objective conflicts justice rules).[5] The pragmatic approach emphasises the empirical study of the effectiveness of a variety of private international law solutions and of the underlying substantive law differences in order to design the best private international law solutions. This chapter makes a new contribution to the theory of pragmatism of private international law. First, it goes back to the work of the founders of pragmatism as an intellectual idea,[6] sets out some pragmatic goals for global private international law, and then develops the pragmatic method for global private international law relying on multilateralism, comparativism and empiricism.

II. Pragmatic Movements

The pragmatism movement began in the United States in the late nineteenth century when Charles S Peirce (1839–1914) and a few other philosophers such as William James (1842–1910) started the Metaphysical Club in 1872. Other prominent members of the Club include Oliver Wendell Holmes Jr (1841–1935).[7] The members of the Club met regularly to exchange ideas on topical issues of that time. They were puzzled by the dogmatic approach to philosophical thoughts, such as continental rationalism and German idealism amongst others, that had taken over the social, political and intellectual space in the United States.

Charles S Peirce and his colleagues evolved a new approach to analysing ontological and epistemological issues, focusing on the theory of truth and the foundation of knowledge. Their goal was to build a bridge between those philosophies that hold that true knowledge is grounded in reason (eg, rationalism) and those which hold that true knowledge is only derivable from facts and observation (eg, British empiricism).[8]

The classical pragmatists offered what may be considered as a new perspective to the nature of truth and knowledge. Like other philosophical movements, the early proponents differed considerably in their ideas. Perhaps, this may be attributed to their different callings. Peirce was a mathematician, James was a psychologist and also had a medical degree, Holmes practised as a lawyer and judge. Their respective backgrounds influenced their propositions. Nevertheless, the common theme amongst them was that true knowledge is not entirely derived from *a priori* propositions or beliefs. Rather, it is something that is inextricably linked with human practices and experience. Truth is discovered with actions and sensory experience. To say a proposition, idea, theory, or belief is true means that it has been tested and verified to be useful concerning practical matters of human experience. For James, an idea is true if it helps us 'to get into satisfactory relation with other parts of our experience'.[9] Otherwise, if a proposition or belief has no practical usefulness, then it is no true proposition or belief. Thus, as recorded in

[5] For the distinctions between these two concepts, see SC Symeonides, 'Material Justice and Conflicts Justice in Choice of Law' in P Borchers and J Zekoll (eds), *International Conflict of Laws for the Third Millennium: Essays in Honor of Friedrich K Juenger* (Transnational Publishers 2001) 125–40; R Banu, 'Conflicting Justice in Conflict of Laws' (2020) 53 *Vanderbilt Journal of Transnational Law* 461, 471–93.

[6] See A Yekini, *The Hague Judgments Convention and Commonwealth Model Law: A Pragmatic Perspective* (Hart Publishing 2021) ch 3.

[7] R Siltala, *Law, Truth, and Reason* (Springer Netherlands 2011) 97; T Grey, 'Holmes and Legal Pragmatism' (1989) 41 *Stanford Law Review* 787, 864.

[8] Grey, ibid, 799.

[9] W James, *Pragmatism: A New Name for Some Old Ways of Thinking* (Longmans Green & Co 1908) 58.

one of James' titles, the pragmatists began a movement which shifted philosophical reasoning away from conceptions and abstractions to practical results, and from logic to life.[10]

The pragmatic theory suggests that truths – ideas and propositions – must have a practical value. The next question is how a truth seeker arrives at a true position. In other words, how do we determine that a given proposition or belief works? This takes us to the second aspect of pragmatism which is its methodology. The major disagreement amongst the classical pragmatists lies in how to determine what works or the method of enquiry about truths. For Peirce, for a proposition to be meaningful, it must be verified to be true or false based on an objective or scientific process. Propositions must have effects that have practical bearings (ie, solutions to practical problems) and those effects are verifiable by empiricism.[11] Peirce's pragmatism implies that any abstract ideas which have no conceivable practical effects are meaningless and mere deception. On the other hand, James is a pluralist who believes that no singular method of enquiry is absolute. James thought that certain phenomena have practical effects that cannot be verified through a scientific process. Thus, he posited that beyond the field of scientific enquiry, issues concerning religious, moral and other ethical questions could be verified by subjective means such as experience, opinions and beliefs provided they have a value for real life.[12]

III. Pragmatism and Law

From the sophists' era, rationality and logical thoughts had been part of civilisation. Many centuries before the emergence of philosophical pragmatism, rationalism which has always been a dominant philosophy had a great influence on legal theory. Its influence on the development of law could be seen in the activities of the Glossators who attempted to systematise and render the Justinian Code (Roman law) intelligible for students and practitioners.[13] Legal rationalism further gained prominence in the enlightenment era due to the pre-eminence of science. In this same period, particularly in the late eighteenth and nineteenth centuries, many legal theorists considered law to be 'rational knowledge obtained through concepts'.[14] Building on this rationalistic approach, law was essentially thought to be autonomous, logically ordered and rationally determinate.[15] Foundational premises are derivable from natural law, Roman law, codes or precedents as the case may be. From these premises, a body of rules can be derived. The preoccupation of many classical legal theorists was the formulation of abstract concepts and ideas to extract and analyse rules. For instance, in an attempt to treat law in a scientific manner, through which general principles can be derived, taught and applied by judges to varieties of cases, Georg Friedrich

[10] See the lecture he delivered in 1898 titled 'Philosophical Conceptions and Practical Results' published in W James, *Collected Essays and Reviews* (Longmans Green & Co 1920).

[11] CJ Misak, *Truth and the End of Inquiry: A Peircean Account of Truth* (Oxford University Press 2004) 9–10; AJ Ayer, *The Origins of Pragmatism* (Macmillan 1968) 29–40 gives a sophisticated exposition and critique of Peirce's view on the centrality of the scientific method to his theory of truth.

[12] Grey (n 7) 791; Siltala (n 7) 98–99.

[13] A Padoa-Schioppa, *A History of Law in Europe: From the Early Middle Ages to the Twentieth Century* (Cambridge University Press 2017) 73–81.

[14] D Canale et al (eds), *A Treatise on Legal Philosophy and General Jurisprudence: A History of Philosophy of Law in the Civil Law World, 1600–1900* (Springer 2009) 189.

[15] PN Cox, 'An Interpretation and (Partial) Defense of Legal Formalism' (2003) 36 *Indiana Law Review* 57, 59–60; DZ Epstein, 'Rationality, Legitimacy, and the Law' (2014) 7 *Washington University Jurisprudence Review* 1, 7.

Puchta came up with the *Science of Pandects* in Germany. This systemic study and analysis of Roman law opened the way for the development of law by judges and legal theorists through dogmatic and conceptual constructions.[16] A somewhat similar experience could be observed in the United States where Christopher Columbus Langdell pioneered a scientific approach to the study of law at Harvard in the late nineteenth century through his casebook method.[17]

Legal rationalism inevitably led us to legal formalism. Legal formalism gives credence to foundational principles and doctrines from which other lower-level rules and ideas are derived. The function of a judge in the administration of justice is to discover and apply the law to the established facts. Reason and logic play a vital role in decision-making as they provide an objective means of analysing the legitimacy and validity of decisions. The quality of a judicial decision, for instance, would be assessed by the extent to which it is rational, logical and in conformity with universal *a priori* principles, doctrines, concepts, or rules established by codes or precedents. Both in the Anglo-common law and civil law systems, broadly speaking, judges were not expected to rationalise based on set values or other policy considerations outside the well-established rules.[18]

It is no coincidence that one of the early jurisconsults to challenge legal formalism in the nineteenth century was Oliver Wendell Holmes who was also one of the members of the Metaphysical Club pragmatists. In 1881, Holmes published his famous book, *The Common Law*,[19] where he derided legal formalism. Holmes disagreed with the prevalent view of the pre-eminence of logic in the judicial decision-making process. According to him, law 'cannot be dealt with as if it contained only the axioms and corollaries of a book of mathematics'.[20] There is more to law than syllogism. Laws must grow organically taking into consideration the necessities of the time, social policy and other non-legal norms like history, economics and practical experience.

Holmes was not standing alone. There were a few other legal scholars who called for a paradigm shift in legal theorising and the judicial decision-making process. Rudolf von Jhering and Roscoe Pound also advocated against mechanical jurisprudence.[21] Justice Benjamin Cardozo in various writings and lectures argued that the common law rules are a 'working hypothesis' and precedents are often tested and re-examined based on emerging circumstances.[22] While these scholars might not have described themselves as legal pragmatists, they called for a paradigm shift away from the mechanical application of law without regard for social facts and practical legal problems.[23]

What then is legal pragmatism? Brian Tamanaha notes that legal pragmatism gained prominence as one of the offshoots of the struggle against legal formalism. It initially represents a meeting point for scholars from law and economics, critical legal studies and others who identified with no school of thought.[24] Today, there are as many legal pragmatists as there are variations

[16] H Hofmann, 'From Jhering to Radbruch: On the Logic of Traditional Legal Concepts to the Social Theories of Law to the Renewal of Legal Idealism' in D Canale et al (eds), *A Treatise on Legal Philosophy and General Jurisprudence: A History of Philosophy of Law in the Civil Law World, 1600–1900* (Springer 2009) 301.

[17] GJ Postema, *Legal Philosophy in the Twentieth Century: The Common Law World*, Vol 11 (Springer 2011) 48–49.

[18] G Mousourakis, *Comparative Law and Legal Traditions: Historical and Contemporary Perspectives* (Springer 2019); K Zweigert and H Kötz, *Introduction to Comparative Law*, 3rd edn (Oxford University Press 1998) 256–75.

[19] OW Holmes, *The Common Law* (William S Hein & Company 1881).

[20] Ibid, 1.

[21] R von Jhering, *Law as a Means to an End* (The Boston Book Company 1913); R Pound, 'Mechanical Jurisprudence' (1908) 8 *Columbia Law Review* 605.

[22] D Lind, 'The Mismeasurement of Legal Pragmatism' (2012) 4 *Washington University Juridical Review* 213, 252–53.

[23] BZ Tamanaha, *Law as a Means to an End: Threat to the Rule of Law* (Cambridge University Press 2006) 61–68.

[24] Ibid, 127.

in what pragmatism itself means. However, like the pragmatism of Peirce and James, certain core principles unify them. Legal pragmatism in its general outlook is a theory that disavows purely *a priori* and rationalistic approaches to the legal and judicial decision-making process. Legal pragmatists hold the view that law is to be contextualised, should be instrumental, and should take full account of experience.[25] As Thomas C Grey has said: 'A pragmatic legal theorist will embed questions about law in a context and address them for a purpose, and so may reach different and apparently inconsistent answers as context and purpose vary'.[26] Laws are required to solve practical problems that the citizenry face in their daily pursuits; civil and commercial transactions, social engagements, and so on. In formulating policies or making laws, legislators and judges must consider the practical effects of these laws and whether they meet the needs of the time. Laws are often made with regard to a specific context. For instance, the concept of territorialism was developed at a time when we had hard borders and every State needed to defend its sovereignty against external interference. A pragmatist judge must consider these contexts when addressing territorialism in this age where globalisation continues to shrink State borders. Where this is taken for granted, the courts will be turning out rulings that have no bearing with the concrete problems that litigants submit for adjudication. This, in our view, summarises what pragmatists mean when they say laws should be contextual, instrumental and experience-based. On this note, the connection between legal pragmatism and philosophical pragmatism is established.

Legal scholarship on legal pragmatism often focuses more on legal reasoning and the judicial process rather than the policy or law-making processes. For instance, most of the works of Richard Posner on pragmatism are on judicial pragmatism. Posner sought to detach legal pragmatism from philosophical pragmatism by introducing what he refers to as 'everyday pragmatism'. His view of pragmatic adjudication can be broadly summarised as a common-sense approach to judicial decision-making. He argued that in resolving disputes placed before courts, judges should be guided by facts and consequences of their decisions rather than conceptualisms and generalities.[27] Accordingly, a pragmatic judge is one who makes the 'most reasonable decision … all things considered'.[28]

Posner's view on legal pragmatism was essentially anti-theoretical.[29] While other legal pragmatists agree that law and judicial decision-making should be driven by contextualism and instrumentalism, they are of the considered view that they should not necessarily be a just-do-it approach with no theoretical basis or methodology.[30] We agree that legal pragmatism needs not to be a just-do-it approach to law-making or judicial reasoning. The founders of philosophical pragmatism did not conceive it as anti-theoretical. Indeed, James has this to say on this point:

> Theories thus become instruments, not answers to enigmas, in which we can rest. We don't lie back upon them, we move forward, and, on occasion, make nature over again by their aid. Pragmatism unstiffens

[25] Ibid; TC Grey, 'Freestanding Legal Pragmatism' (1996) 18 *Cardozo Law Review* 21, 22.

[26] Grey (n 7) 805.

[27] RA Posner, 'Legal Pragmatism' (2004) 35 *Metaphilosophy* 147, 150.

[28] RA Posner, *Law, Pragmatism, and Democracy* (Harvard University Press 2005) 64.

[29] However, he later conceded that legal pragmatism is not averse to all forms of theory. Rather 'it is friendlier to some forms of theory than legal formalism is, namely, theories that guide empirical inquiry, such as economics'. See Posner (n 27) 152. He further demonstrated his position by applying the efficiency theory from his law and economics background as a normative argument to justify legal pragmatism. See further RA Posner, 'Pragmatic Adjudication' (1996) 18 *Cardozo Law Review* 1, 11–12.

[30] Grey (n 25) 38 (argues that pragmatism 'is a theoretical middle way between grand theorizing and anti-intellectual business-as-usual').

> all our theories, limbers them up and sets each one at work. Being nothing essentially new, it harmonizes with many ancient philosophic tendencies. It agrees with nominalism for instance, in always appealing to particulars; with utilitarianism in emphasizing practical aspects; with positivism in its disdain for verbal solutions, useless questions, and metaphysical abstractions … As the young Italian pragmatist Papini has well said, it lies in the midst of our theories, like a corridor in a hotel. Innumerable chambers open out of it. In one you may find a man writing an atheistic volume; in the next someone on his knees praying for faith and strength; in a third a chemist investigating a body's properties. In a fourth a system of idealistic metaphysics is being excogitated; in a fifth the impossibility of metaphysics is being shown. But they all own the corridor, and all must pass through it if they want a practicable way of getting into or out of their respective rooms.[31]

Therefore, legal pragmatism is not averse to theories. Rather, it extracts from every theory what works best for a given practical problem. Seen in this light, pragmatism is no different from other socio-legal thoughts and movements such as realism and law and economics. The major difference is this: while scholars in law and economics consider issues from cost and benefit perspectives for instance, a pragmatist is not so constrained. He considers a diverse set of data and applies those suited for identified legal problems.

IV. A Pragmatic Theory of Private International Law

Legal scholars have regarded private international law as a very technical field due to the primacy of highly sophisticated rules that have been developed over the years to resolve conflictual problems. Little wonder William Prosser describes private international law specialists as 'eccentric professors who theorise about mysterious matters'.[32] For centuries, the rules have developed into a dogmatic approach where judges are simply required to select applicable laws based on some pre-defined connections without any interest in the substantive result of the law chosen. This approach, which was formulated and popularised by Savigny became the dominant approach in continental Europe and many other States. The approach was challenged in the twentieth century by prominent scholars from the United States who opposed a dogmatic and mechanical solution to private international law disputes.[33] As is well known, this challenge led to what might be considered as the greatest debate in private international law post-Savigny: the conflicts-justice and material justice dichotomy. Kegel remained the foremost defender of the conflicts justice approach after Savigny. From the other side of the Atlantic, we had scholars like Currie who promoted a government interest analysis approach and others who can be broadly classified as pro-material justice. The latter is led by Leflar who argued that courts should be able to choose the law that would produce a just and better result amongst the potentially applicable laws.[34] Thus, private international law like other areas of law is also caught in the web of dogmatic or result-driven approaches to legal theorising and judicial decision-making. The question that follows is what has pragmatism to offer private international law?

The above excerpt from James is quoted at length to demonstrate the inclusive strand of pragmatism upon which we intend to build our pragmatic theory of private international law.

[31] James (n 9) 53–54.

[32] WL Prosser, 'Interstate Publication' (1953) 51 *Michigan Law Review* 959, 971.

[33] R Michaels, 'Private International Law and the Question of Universal Values' in F Ferrari and DP Fernández Arroyo (eds), *The Continuing Relevance of Private International Law* (Edward Elgar 2019) 156–57.

[34] Symeonides (n 5); Michaels, ibid, 157–58.

We shall discuss pragmatism as a theory and method of private international law. This involves a synthesis of the core of philosophical pragmatism and legal pragmatism. To this end, we agree with Tamanaha that law is a means to an end.[35] The core of our pragmatic theory is that private international law must address the practical challenges that cross-border litigants face and as such it must be practical, value-driven and deliver desired results. A pragmatic theory necessarily has a pluralist outlook in substance and in its methods since it stands for no particular result but rather any or a combination of results that are found to be useful. It is anti-theoretical to the extent that it is not preoccupied with abstractions and conceptions. Rather, it is open to, and ready to explore different theories and techniques that deliver on pragmatic goals. The pragmatic goals are likewise not etched in fixed abstracts and concepts. They are identified through empiricism and practical experiences.

As mentioned in the preceding section, legal pragmatism is often considered from the prism of the judicial decision-making process. While the brand of pragmatism we seek to establish in this chapter can be applied to the judicial decision-making process, our primary focus is the legislative process. In most jurisdictions, civil law, common law and others, the primary responsibility of law-making rests squarely on the legislators. This is more apparent in private international law where the laws are largely codified. Judges are required to apply laws as formulated by the legislators or treaty makers. When the law needs to be reformed it is also the latter's responsibility. The subsequent sections shall expand on this theory and its application in practice.

A. Pragmatic Goals

One of the major tasks of the legislators is to determine the nature of the problems posed by private international law disputes and what the needs of cross-border litigants are. The nature of these problems should determine the objectives and goals which the lawmakers should pursue. Having a clear picture of the practical problems will enable law reformers, judges and legal commentators to experiment with the efficacy or otherwise of the extant or proposed legal solutions. Without having a firm grasp on what the problems are, it is difficult to determine whether the law works or not and if other options would have worked better.

Pragmatism dictates that there is no one-size-fits-all approach to looking at issues. In designing a legal framework for any branch of private international law, the goals are not necessarily the same since the nature of the problems differs from one branch to another. While some problems may be peculiar to specific private international areas, others may be a common theme in all private international law disputes.

The cross-border nature of private international law disputes and the practical problems that have been recorded from the menu of cases in court readily suggest some general or common problems. These problems are issues that cross-border litigants deal with in real life. They are practical and not theoretical, real not imagined. Litigants need access to justice in an appropriate forum; they need legal certainty as to the law applicable to their transactions; they need to be able to enforce fairly obtained judgments in other countries; they need protection against litigation in unforeseeable or inconvenient jurisdictions; they need simple, efficient and cost-effective mechanisms to make cross-border litigation work (eg, reliable service of documents and taking of evidence); they expect a high degree of respect for their prior agreements on where litigation should take place and which law should govern their disputes (party autonomy); and when the

[35] Borrowing from the title of Tamanaha, see above (n 23).

parties have not previously agreed on these questions they expect that the private international laws on jurisdiction, applicable law and recognition and enforcement of judgments will broadly satisfy their reasonable and legitimate expectations. States need to be able to protect some fundamental aspects of their sovereignty and essential legal principles and they need to be able to make appropriate use of their judicial resources. The list is not exhaustive.[36]

The problems highlighted above engage issues concerning legal certainty, mutual trust (the presumption that a foreign jurisdiction and a foreign law are in principle acceptable to resolve disputes – subject only to limited exceptions like public policy and overriding mandatory rules), legitimate expectations of parties, party autonomy, efficiency and access to justice. Other scholars have also identified these issues as substantive values of various national laws.[37] Thus, a pragmatic private international theory looks beyond the conflicts justice and material justice debate. As a value-driven approach, it takes cognisance of the inherent values of both concepts as well as those enumerated above. While these items do not constitute an exclusive list, they should, however, form the broad goals of private international law frameworks whether national, bilateral, regional or multilateral.

B. The Pragmatic Method

The next task is to carefully select theories that reflect the enumerated goals and to use techniques that can balance the goals so that the resulting framework is best suited to address the underlying problems. In this way, pragmatism is not devoid of theory. Neither is it a just-do-it approach to law-making or judicial decision-making.

Pragmatism endorses methodological pluralism. There is no one perfect way of delivering a pragmatic private international law framework. Rather, pragmatists are open to any method (eg, multilateralism) that offers useful ideas that can deliver a framework that works. It also entails that even if a specific method is adopted, a pragmatist should be able to mix and match concepts from different legal traditions to arrive at a practical solution.

This chapter has a particular focus on pragmatism in the context of developing global private international law. It identifies three methods – multilateralism, comparativism and empiricism – that are crucial to creating excellent global private international law consistent with the pragmatic goals identified above.

i. Multilateralism

Private international law is traditionally seen as a branch of domestic law. The traditional approach in many jurisdictions is to develop private international rules or frameworks unilaterally. Both judicial and academic discussions are focused on the private international law of each country.[38] This approach often leads to uncertainty and unpredictable results as litigants are faced with diverse national rules. Since States will often act in self-interest, it is inevitable that national responses, in some cases, may be parochial.[39] This may lead to reciprocal treatment

[36] Symeonides (n 1) 338–39, has also considered the goals of contemporary private international law to include international uniformity, national interests and values, conflicts justice, material justice, legal certainty and flexibility.

[37] Michaels (n 33) 157–60.

[38] Kegel (n 3) 12.

[39] For the relationship between unilateralism and multilateralism as private international law methods and especially the non-parochial use of unilateralism, see Symeonides (n 1) 131–94.

from other States with the attendant consequences of the denial of access to justice or expensive and time-consuming cross-border litigation because of the non-cooperative attitude of States. This approach can lead to unpragmatic results in most cases for litigants and States as both are affected by inefficient legal frameworks or absence of coordination amongst States. Private international law benefits from having its own international organisation, the HCCH, dedicated to the 'progressive unification of the rules of private international law'.[40] It further serves as a platform through which the tension arising from the competing values/goals of private international law are harmonised. Eighty-nine Member States and the EU are committed to achieving this objective and therefore believe in playing their parts to bring about the gradual multilateralisation of the rules of private international law.

In the HCCH many of the lawyers in the Secretariat, those representing the Members and those involved as experts are pragmatists.[41] While keeping tabs on the pragmatic goals, they adopt different techniques to deliver a workable framework. Many are devoted experts and technicians[42] but at the same time realists (in the ordinary sense), who are problem-solvers. They are open minded and ready to adapt, refine and remix legal theories and concepts to arrive at concrete results. While pursuing private justice and private interests, they are not unaware of the political undertones of cross-border issues. Thus, the pragmatic negotiators engage various doctrines in aggregating or balancing States' interests and policies in order to arrive at the optimum result that can be achieved by consensus.[43] As Ralf Michaels once suggested, doctrinal and political approaches to private international law are not mutually exclusive.[44] This is the hallmark of pragmatism. It can deliver a framework that prioritises private justice and yet is acceptable to the State and regional economic integration organisation (REIO) actors that are needed to drive the framework. This method has delivered several useful conventions on evidence, service, recovery of maintenance, choice of court agreements, and foreign judgments, amongst others.

ii. Comparativism

One of the legacies of James's pragmatism is his views on pluralism. In his preface to *The Will to Believe*, James rejected the monist view of the universe because 'there is no possible point of view from which the world can appear an absolutely single fact'.[45] In an epistemological context, it also means that no single point of view represents an absolute knowledge of any phenomenon. Put differently, there are other reasonable and valid points of view about any idea different from those we hold, and those views should be respected. The interest of a pragmatist should therefore lie in the 'cash value' from other points of view. James's pluralism reflects comparative law and its values. Hence, it is our second prescribed pragmatic method for private international law. Its relevance to the field of private international law is its transnational nature and

[40] Art 1 of the Statute of the Hague Conference, available at: www.hcch.net/en/instruments/conventions/full-text/?cid=29. See Marta Pertegás and Paul Beaumont, 'The Hague Conference on International Law', ch 7 in this book.

[41] On the importance of ensuring that enough genuine 'experts' on private international law are involved in the HCCH through the Permanent Bureau and in all levels of decision-making, see Pertegás and Beaumont (ch 7).

[42] R Michaels, 'Post-critical Private International Law: From Politics to Technique' in H Muir-Watt and DP Fernández Arroyo (eds), *Private International Law and Global Governance* (Oxford University Press 2014) 66.

[43] See PR Beaumont, 'Reflections on the relevance of public international law to private international law treaty making' (2009) 340 *Hague Collected Courses* 19–20 and 55–61.

[44] Michaels (n 42).

[45] W James, *The Will to Believe and other Essays in Popular Philosophy* (Longmans Green & Co 1912).

this ordinarily makes it a perfect selection for private international law disputes which are also inherently transnational.[46]

Comparative law methodology is relatively new in legal scholarship when compared with other prevalent doctrinal or dogmatic legal methods.[47] Its emergence towards the end of the nineteenth century was facilitated by the burgeoning cross-border trade and commerce of the new European States and the divergent laws and policies arising from the implementation of national codes. Coincidentally, pragmatism made an inroad into private international law scholarship through comparative law.[48] The German comparatist, Ernst Rabel has been credited as the leader of this pragmatic movement in private international law.[49]

Comparative law methodology is an integral part of a pragmatic theory of private international law. It is useful in policy and law-making, as well as judicial reasoning. To start with policymakers, negotiators and legislators, the use of comparative law exposes them to many solutions to a given set of problems that are available in different legal systems. In this regard, Rabel's functional methodology can be used to solve many practical problems that cross-border litigants face. Whether they are on national assignments or negotiating an international treaty, functional comparative law enables legislators to move beyond theoretical conceptions and abstractions by focusing on how similar problems have been treated elsewhere, the results that have been achieved and the utility of those results. It allows them to pick from the best results or to come up with a new solution.

Legislators who are working on the development of private international law should have adequate time and resources to carry out an extensive macro-comparative inquiry to further identify the underlying circumstances which make some solutions work better in one legal system and not the other. Thus, they should not confine themselves to a mere black letter law comparative study.

At the global level, an extensive comparative study becomes a preparatory work upon which treaty makers can build an effective and efficient system of private international law that can work in harmony with the divergent (both in terms of procedure and substantive law) national systems.[50] They can also build bridges across the seemingly irreconcilable concepts and conceptions of various national legal systems, or develop a brand new legal framework which takes cognisance of the concrete legal problems of cross-border transactions by mixing and matching from different national concepts.[51] This will culminate in the universal adoption of best rules.

[46] For general works on comparative law in private international law, see A Delic, 'The Role of Comparative Law in the Development of Modern Private International Law (1750–1914)' in I van Hulle and R Lesaffer (eds), *International Law in the Long Nineteenth Century (1776–1914)* (Nihjoff, 2019); R Michaels, 'The Functional Method of Comparative Law' in M Reimann and R Zimmermann (eds), *The Oxford Handbook of Comparative Law* (Oxford University Press 2006); R Michaels, 'Comparative Law and Private International Law' in J Basedow et al (eds), *Encyclopedia of Private International Law*, Vol I (Edward Elgar 2017); HP Glenn, 'Comparative Legal Reasoning and the Courts' in M Andenas and D Fairgrieve (eds), *Courts and Comparative Law* (Oxford University Press 2015); K Zweigert and H Kötz, *The Method of Comparative Law*, 3rd edn (Oxford University Press 1998).

[47] P Mäntysaari, *User-friendly Legal Science A New Scientific Discipline* (Springer 2017) 2; J Basedow, 'Comparative Law and its Clients' (2014) 62 *American Journal of Comparative Law* 821, 829.

[48] Beaumont and McEleavy (n 4) para 2.88.

[49] Beaumont and McEleavy, ibid; Basedow (n 47) 832–33.

[50] Lord Reed, 'Comparative Law in the Supreme Court of the United Kingdom' (Centre for Private Law, University of Edinburgh, 2017), available at: www.supremecourt.uk/docs/speech-171013.pdf.

[51] Michaels, 'The Functional Method of Comparative Law' (n 46) 376–77; O Elias, 'Globalisation and private international law: reviewing contemporary local law' (2001) 36 *Amicus Curiae* 6. See also Holliday (n 4) and Albert Font i Segura and Jayne Holliday, 'Succession', ch 22 in this book, showing the vital need to do careful comparative law research on substantive law, in relation to tricky issues where the characterisation of an issue (in this case clawback of lifetime gifts to third parties) varies amongst States, before developing harmonised private international law rules at a regional or global level.

Michaels has described this as the systematising, evaluative and universalising functions of comparative methodology.[52] In the Hague Judgments Convention 2019 'place of performance', 'purposeful availment' and 'substantial connection' were blended to deliver an acceptable indirect jurisdictional rule for contracts, thereby ending the US/EU divide which stalled previous attempts.[53] Article 5(2) of the Hague Choice of Court Convention 2005 eliminated the practical problems arising from the common law allowing the chosen court to decline jurisdiction and Articles 5 and 6 eliminated the 'Italian torpedo' tactics in civil law systems by allowing the chosen court to proceed without waiting for the non-chosen first seised court.[54] The summary return mechanism of the 1980 Child Abduction Convention was conceived as a pragmatic and original solution to the problem of cross-border child abduction when the harmonisation of traditional private international law could not be agreed and would not provide the expeditious remedy needed.[55]

Comparative law methodology can also assist national judges in the progressive development of private international law frameworks as part of evolving a uniform global interpretation of harmonised private international law rules in accordance with the rules provided by the Vienna Convention on the Law of Treaties.[56] Uniform interpretation is a key objective of the Hague Conventions. The clearest example of its success to date is in the Child Abduction Convention where leading courts have been guided by the official explanatory report to the Convention, academic analysis informed by careful studies of the *travaux préparatoires*, and by the case law interpreting the Convention (notably by the leading courts in the world).[57]

Insofar as national private international law rules are open to judicial development, judges can borrow from the best foreign legal solutions (including international treaties that have not yet been ratified by their State). Many of the useful techniques of private international law such as characterisation,[58] renvoi and preliminary questions,[59] connecting factors,[60] public policy and mandatory provisions,[61] amongst others, can be developed in similar ways by different legal systems. They are already broadly adopted and assimilated into most national legal systems today and the process of comparative methodology can increase the high-quality use of the private international law toolbox in specific cases.[62]

iii. Empiricism

Empirical legal studies just like comparative methodology are new and evolving.[63] Empiricism is the tool of a pragmatist and it is indispensable in any pragmatic theory. If pragmatism is about

[52] Michaels, ibid, 373–78 and Holliday (n 4) 35–52, 69–74 and 164–67.

[53] See Art 5(1)(g), discussed in ch 15 in this book.

[54] See ch 28 in this book.

[55] See ch 34 in this book.

[56] On the tools for uniform interpretation of Hague Conventions, see Beaumont (n 43) 22–33.

[57] The HCCH has created an excellent database to aid the interpretation of the Convention, INCADAT, available at: www.incadat.com/en. Some of the leading courts in the world, notably the US, Canadian and UK Supreme Courts strive for uniform interpretation of the Convention taking full account of the Perez-Vera explanatory report, leading legal scholarship and case law from sister courts, see P Beaumont, 'Uniform Interpretation of Habitual Residence in the Hague Child Abduction Convention – US Supreme Court helped by Beaumont and McEleavy', available at: privateinternationallaw.stir.ac.uk/news/.

[58] See ch 3 in this book.

[59] See ch 5 in this book.

[60] See ch 4 in this book.

[61] See ch 6 in this book.

[62] Michaels, 'Comparative Law and Private International Law' (n 46) 418.

[63] LB Nielsen, 'The Need for Multi-Method Approaches in Empirical Legal Research' in P Cane and HM Kritzer (eds), *The Oxford Handbook of Empirical Legal Research* (Oxford University Press 2010) 957; FL Leeuw and H Schmeets, *Empirical Legal Research: A Guidance Book for Lawyers, Legislators and Regulators* (Edward Elgar 2016) 6.

delivering legal solutions that work, it goes without saying that there is a need for the experimentation of laws to determine whether they are fit for purpose. Arguably, evidence-based legislation or treaties will produce better results than those which are derived from overarching principles or personal prejudices.[64] Empiricism is required to identify the concrete problems cross-border litigants face. It is required in designing the appropriate framework. Still, it is further required to assess the operation of that framework to see whether it works.[65]

Legal empiricism may come in many forms. Comparative law enquiry is a form of empiricism. In the Anglo-American jurisdictions, it is not unusual for lawyers and judges to do a critical assessment of a line of authorities when faced with important legal issues. This is a form of judicial empiricism. One way or the other, it is possible to have an insight into the practical legal problems through this analysis and it is often discovered whether the law works or not, although having formed an opinion on the practicality or otherwise of the extant laws, judges may defer to the legislature for the appropriate legal changes.[66] This is to avoid judicial legislation and the uncertainty that often attends it.

It is preferred that empirical legal research should be carried out on behalf of governments and international organisations (legislators) by expert non-governmental bodies (usually academics). This will deliver pragmatic results compared with judicial empiricism. For instance, legislators have the time and resources to ensure painstaking empirical research is done. They can commission experts who can devote enough time and energy to dig out the problems associated with the law. Unlike judicial officers who are not specially trained in empirical research, academic experts or specially commissioned bodies are well suited to do a thorough and scientific investigation.

Private international law has several stakeholders who need to be consulted to determine the impact of a given law in real life. Some of the issues to be investigated involve the perception of litigants on procedural matters, whether they have access to practical justice, the functioning of central authorities and how simple and effective does the process appear to the administrators and users, whether litigants' legitimate expectations concerning their transactions are met, the disposition of States to proposed legal solutions amongst others. Thus, apart from the litigants, the judicial and administrative officials, government legal departments, relevant regulatory agencies, and international organisations all may need to be consulted in a proper empirical study.[67] These highlighted issues are often complex. Diverse data, both quantitative and qualitative, are therefore required to produce an objective truth about the law in practice.[68] This objective truth is desired for setting legislative goals, the design of the legislation, and its subsequent reviews.[69]

[64] M Partington, 'Empirical Legal Research and Policy-making' in P Cane and HM Kritzer (eds), *The Oxford Handbook of Empirical Legal Research* (Oxford University Press 2010) 1004; X Kramer, 'Empirical legal studies in private international law' (2015) *Nederlands Internationaal privaatrecht* 195, 195.

[65] Partington, ibid.

[66] See *Rubin v Eurofinance* [2012] All ER (D) 258. The Irish Supreme Court in *Re Flightlease (Ireland) Ltd* [2012] IESC 12, shared a similar sentiment while noting that adopting the Canadian real and substantial connection test for recognition and enforcement of foreign judgments would amount to judicial legislation.

[67] For instance, see some of the recent empirical research on private international law as listed in Kramer (n 64).

[68] Nielsen (n 63) 956–57.

[69] The HCCH has limited resources but it has benefited from some very important empirical studies on how Conventions are operating in practice which are then discussed at Review Special Commissions, notably on Child Abduction (see the excellent statistical analyses prepared by Nigel Lowe and his team since 1999, available at: www.hcch.net/en/instruments/conventions/publications1/?dtid=32&cid=24).

V. Conclusion

Since the beginning of the twentieth century, private international law has continued to evolve owing to the rapid change in the ways cross-border transactions occur. As time changes, the objectives of private international law and the needs of the end-users of the law change as well. Certain theoretical frameworks that were developed in the formative years to resolve conflictual disputes might have met the need of that time, but human experience dictates that at some point in time, those frameworks would have outlived their usefulness. Hence, the need for a fresh look at how private international law responds to cross-border disputes.

Conflicts justice was widely adopted as the appropriate response to cross-border disputes. The American conflict revolution brought in new perspectives in the twentieth century. The central debate amongst private international law scholars then became (and still is) whether private international law should be neutral and thus should simply select the jurisdiction and law which should govern a given legal relationship or whether the preferred approach should be a policy and result-oriented approach.

Our view is that private international law has something to learn from legal and philosophical pragmatism. It is easy to conflate legal pragmatism with any or all legal movements that promote a result-oriented approach to legal theorising. While such schools or movements have many things in common with pragmatism, what makes pragmatism stand out is its pluralist outlook and the openness to engage any theory, idea or solution that focuses on practical legal problems.

Pragmatic private international law theory is emerging. It seeks to build a framework that can potentially be applied to all aspects of the field. The debate today is beyond conflicts justice and material justice. While pragmatism acknowledges that there are inherent values in both, other values are also engaged in cross-border disputes. The focus today, therefore, is to identify through empirical methods the state of the law, the problems posed by current laws and practices, the relevant values that are engaged, and how these values are to be balanced in order to deliver the best response to the identified problems.

To this end, conflicts justice will be adopted because of its inherent values and material justice will be integrated because of its inherent values. The same attitude is maintained towards other values such as party autonomy, legal certainty and predictability, efficiency, State interests, access to justice and others that have been enumerated in this chapter. Pragmatism dictates that legislators and judges should tolerate and be open to fresh and better ideas that can potentially work better than what is available in their legal traditions or systems. This openness will lead to dialogues, coordination and harmonisation of thoughts preferably through multilateral solutions. This pragmatic approach which focuses on practical and realistic solutions will better address the numerous challenges of private international law today.

3

Characterisation

CHIARA GOETZKE AND RALF MICHAELS*

I. Introduction

The first step in a private international law analysis is characterisation. Choice of law rules designate different laws as applicable for different categories, which implies that, in order to determine the applicable law, the appropriate choice of law rule must be selected.[1] The same is true for different bases of jurisdiction. The process by which this is done is called characterisation, though different names like classification or qualification also exist.[2]

It is unsurprising, then, that characterisation is a core concern in private international law. Many judicial opinions in the field concern primarily the question how issues should best be characterised; much scholarly literature does the same. In addition, scholars ask more generally how characterisation should best be achieved – according to the categorisations of the *lex fori* or of the *lex causae*, or in some other way – and what policy considerations matter.[3] Not much can be added to the literature in this chapter. However, most discussions do not distinguish between characterisation issues in domestic private international law and those in international uniform instruments on private international law.[4] Where the latter is at stake, experiences of the former are often merely transposed. This seems hasty. Closer inspection reveals that characterisation within international instruments creates peculiar challenges that deserve both a different treatment and specific scholarly attention.[5] This will be the focus of this chapter.

II. The Characterisation Problem

A. Characterisation is not Merely Statutory Construction

At least where dealing with written choice of law rules,[6] characterisation is, at heart, a simple process of statutory construction. To apply Article 4(1) Rome II Regulation, one must determine

* Special thanks for very valuable suggestions go to Hans van Loon.

[1] There was, and to some extent still is, dispute over what is the object of characterisation: legal issues, legal rules, legal relations, or legal claims. We ignore this dispute because it is of no practical relevance for our questions here.

[2] EG Lorenzen, 'The Qualification, Classification, or Characterization Problem in the Conflict of Laws' (1941) 50 *Yale Law Journal* 743.

[3] For a good recent debate, see J Holliday, *Clawback Law in the Context of Succession* (Hart Publishing 2020) 75 ff.

[4] By international instruments we mean both global or regional private international law conventions (like the Hague Conventions) and supranational law like EU private international law. Obviously, these categories are different, and where those differences matter we point them out.

[5] For excellent analysis, see S Bariatti, 'Classification (characterization)' in J Basedow et al (eds), *Encyclopedia of Private International Law*, Vol 1 (Edward Elgar 2017) 357–65.

what is meant by 'a non-contractual obligation arising out of a tort/delict'. Characterisation is, then the process of determining the proper category for legal issues, and thus also the delimitation between different categories – between contract and tort, between family law and succession law, between substance and procedure.

Insofar as the task is one of determining the appropriate legal category and defining the scope of these categories, characterisation is not specific to private international law. Appropriate categories must also be found in domestic law; the delimitation of categories like substance and procedure is also important in the application of rules of domestic law. Indeed, some scholars have suggested that there is nothing peculiar to characterisation in private international law as opposed to internal law, and therefore the same kinds of arguments should be available. This would make characterisation no more than a specific application of general approaches to statutory interpretation, at least in civil law countries. But this is not correct. At least one thing is peculiar about characterisation in private international law: its objects include foreign legal rules.

That difference is most visible where the question is whether a foreign substantive rule belongs to the category of a specific choice of laws rule of the forum. Unlike conflict of norms rules – the rules that designate the applicable legal rules within one legal system (commercial law versus general contract law, administrative law versus private law, etc) – conflict of laws rules operate between legal systems.[7] It is therefore not possible in the same way to resolve characterisation problems with reference to actual or desired coherence within a system, because more than one system is at stake: the foreign rule belongs to a different system. Sometimes, that foreign system may use other ways to divide between categories – between tort/delict and contract, between substance and procedure – than the forum. Sometimes, foreign rules and legal institutions may even be unknown to the forum altogether, like the floating charge or the trust for traditional civil law systems.

However, problems can exist even where internal law rules of the forum are at stake. True, the legal categories of private international law rules are often based on categories also used in internal law – tort, civil procedure, matrimonial property. However, insofar as the relevant policies in private international law differ from those in internal law, the relevant categories may differ as well. A rule may be characterised as substantive for the purpose of determining the applicable law, even though it is understood as a matter of procedural law in other areas, as is the case, frequently, for rules on limitation.

B. The Characterisation Problem as a Problem of Conflicts of Laws

In a general sense, characterisation has existed as long as the discipline of private international law and at least since the distinction between *statuta realia* and *statuta personalia* made it necessary to allocate legal issues to one of these two categories.[8] Nonetheless, the 'discovery'[9]

[6] This is always the case for international conventions and EU regulations. Some of the early discussions on characterisation, held in an environment with few or no legislated private international law rules, are in this regard no longer very relevant.

[7] See R Michaels and J Pauwelyn, 'Conflict of Norms or Conflict of Laws? Different Techniques in the Fragmentation of Public International Law' (2012) 22 *Duke Journal of Comparative & International Law* 349.

[8] See NE Hatzimihail, 'Bartolus and the Conflict of Laws' (2007) 60 *Revue hellénique de droit international* 11 ff.

[9] H Dölle, *'Juristische Entdeckungen' in: Ständige Deputation des deutschen Juristentages (ed), Verhandlungen des 42. Deutschen Juristentages 1957*, Vol 2 (Mohr 1958) 19 ff; H Weber, *Die Theorie der Qualifikation: Franz Kahn, Etienne Bartin und die Entwicklung ihrer Lehre bis zur universalen Anerkennung der Qualifikation als allgemeines Problem des internationalen Privatrechts* (1890–1945) (Mohr 1986) 3.

of characterisation had to wait until the late nineteenth century, when private international law had sufficiently matured as a discipline and was understood by many as a matter of domestic law. The discovery was made in Germany by Franz Kahn in 1890 and, in ignorance of Kahn's earlier piece, in France by Etienne Bartin in 1897.[10]

Notably, the specific problem they discovered was not a mere problem of statutory interpretation but a problem emerging immediately from the tension between the domestic character of law and the transnational character of the relevant situation: the characterisation problem described the situation that the laws of different States would characterise the same situation differently. Bartin developed his theory of 'qualification' in explicit response to a judicial opinion in which that problem had arisen: a widow's rights to her deceased husband's property was characterised as a matter of property law under Maltese law, but as a matter of succession law under French law.[11] And Kahn even described the entire problem as one of different characterisations which he called 'latent conflicts of laws': for him, the main problem was 'the territorially different nature of legal relations'.[12] Characterisation, then, is a real problem between laws.

Bartin and Kahn agreed not only on the short-term solution to the problem – characterisation according to the categories of *lex fori* – but also, and arguably more importantly, on the long-term solution: unification of private international law rules, which would do away with latent conflicts of laws. That solution, unachievable in their time, has now been reached in many areas for which uniform instruments exist. One might think, therefore, that the characterisation problem as a special problem of private international law would have disappeared with such unification; all that would remain would be the general problem of statutory construction.[13] This is not the case. Vis-à-vis third countries, characterisation problems in unified private international law are largely similar to those in domestic private international law. And even within the group of countries whose private international law rules are unified, characterisation problems can arise. But characterisation within unified private international law presents some idiosyncratic challenges.

C. Traditional Responses to the Characterisation Problem

How should one characterise? In general, two different types of approach can be distinguished. Approaches of the first type determine the rule of characterisation based on the domestic substantive laws involved – be it the *lex fori* or the *lex causae*. Approaches of the second type attempt to transcend these domestic laws.

The leading approach to characterisation belongs to the first approach and suggests characterisation according to the *lex fori*. In a narrow sense, this would mean that the categories of the forum's substantive law should be used. Such an approach runs into three well-known problems.

[10] F Kahn, 'Gesetzeskollisionen – Ein Beitrag zur Lehre des internationalen Privatrechts' (1891) 30 *Jherings Jahrbücher* 1 (republished in Kahn, *Abhandlungen zum internationalen Privatrecht*, Vol 1 (Duncker & Humblot 1928) 1–123) §§ 23 ff; E Bartin, 'De l'impossibilité d'arriver à la suppression définitive des conflits de lois' (1897) 24 *Journal du droit international* 225–55, 466–95, 720–38 (republished as 'La théorie des qualifications en droit international privé' in E Bartin, *Etudes de droit international privé* (A Chevalier-Marescq 1899) 1–82). *cf* Weber, ibid; P Beaumont and P McEleavy, *Anton's Private International Law*, 3rd edn (W Green/SULI 2011) 90–97.

[11] *A v Bartholo*, 24 December 1889, Cour d'App, d'Alger (1891) 18 *Clunet* 1171; B Ancel and Y Lequette, *Les grands arrêts de la jurisprudence française de droit international privé*, 5th edn (Dalloz 2006) no 9, 70 ff; *cf* AH Robertson, *Characterization in the Conflict of Laws* (Harvard University Press 1940) 158–63.

[12] Kahn, *Abhandlungen* (n 10) 92 (Latente Gesetzeskollisionsnormen; territorial verschiedene Natur der Rechtsverhältnisse).

[13] *cf* G Cuniberti, 'Should European Teachers Focus on European Private International Law?' in J von Hein, EM Kieninger and G Rühl (eds), *How European Is European Private International Law?* (Intersentia 2019) 355, 360–61.

First, it cannot determine the precise rules of the foreign law that must be applied, because those rules exist within different categories. Second, it must fail for institutions of foreign law that are unknown to the forum and thus do not belong to any category. Third, it cannot account for policy differences between private international law and substantive law.

The first and second of these problems are ostensibly solved by characterisation according to the *lex causae*.[14] That approach is rarely defended generally today. It runs into problems of circularity, given that we cannot know what the *lex causae* is before we have determined the applicable law, but we cannot determine the applicable law without prior characterisation. And it may lead to the unfortunate situation that more than one law would be applicable, or that none of them would be. It works reasonably well only where the applicable law rules are relatively clear, as for example in the matter of real property, where the determination of what counts as real property can be safely left to the *lex rei sitae*.

Given these shortcomings of characterisation methods based on *lex fori* or *lex causae* (and skipping over attempts at compromise)[15] other methods have been put forward to transcend specific domestic laws altogether. Ernst Rabel suggested characterising using a comprehensive comparative law approach (a method that can be found already in Kahn).[16] If categories in private international law rules must be open towards phenomena in all existing legal orders, so he argued, then in turn all legal orders should be considered when determining the meaning of the legal categories. Thus, their meaning should be found through a comparative law analysis. The method has been called impractical for judges, although at least as a desideratum it appears almost unavoidable: a legal category (like 'tort' or 'marriage') that should 'bundle' together (in the words of Klaus Schurig)[17] the relevant rules from all legal systems in the world must by necessity be comparative.

Today, the leading approach is a *lex fori* characterisation, however, with significant modifications that move it from the first type of approach to the second that transcends internal law. The *lex fori* approach is modified so as to account for the specific requirements of private international law. This is sometimes called autonomous characterisation, where the autonomy sought is that from internal law.[18] Such autonomous characterisation uses functional categories and teleological policies of the forum to determine potentially applicable foreign legal rules. In reality, this is not very different from comparative characterisation.[19] It makes it necessary to designate, in foreign legal systems, the functional and/or teleological equivalents to domestic institutions.[20] There is almost universal agreement on some kind of functional-teleological autonomous characterisation as described above, regardless of the denomination.

An additional reason exists for widespread agreement on a modified *lex fori* approach: the theoretical problem of characterisation has declined in practical importance. Private international law rules have become far more detailed than they once were and many characterisation issues are now resolved by the lawmaker. Where characterisation is still needed, it is no longer (if it ever was) a matter of finding the 'true nature' of a legal institution, but rather of determining,

[14] M Wolff, *Private International Law*, 2nd edn (Clarendon Press 1950) 148.

[15] JD Falconbridge, 'Renvoi, Characterization and Acquired Rights' (1939) 17 *Canadian Bar Review* 369.

[16] E Rabel, 'Das Problem der Qualifikation' (1931) 5 *Zeitschrift für ausländisches und internationales Privatrecht* 241, 282.

[17] K Schurig and G Kegel, *Internationales Privatrecht: Ein Studienbuch*, 9th edn (CH Beck 2004) 313–16; C v Bar and P Mankowski, *Internationales Privatrecht*, Vol 1, 2nd edn (CH Beck 2003) 638–39; P Mankowski, 'Das Bündelungsmodell im Internationalen Privatrecht' in R Michaels and D Solomon (eds), *Liber amicorum Klaus Schurig* (Sellier 2012) 159–79.

[18] Schurig and Kegel, ibid, 336.

[19] B von Hoffmann and K Thorn, *Internationales Privatrecht*, 9th edn (CH Beck 2007) § 6 Rn 27.

[20] R Michaels, 'Internationales Privatrecht als Rechtsvergleichung – Die kollisionsrechtlich-vergleichende Methode' in N Jansen (ed), *Rechtsgeschichte und Rechtsvergleichung – Festschrift Reinhard Zimmermann* (Mohr 2022).

pragmatically, the proper category or really the proper law – one can speak of a move from ontology through epistemology to pragmatism. Because characterisation is pragmatic, methodological debates are no longer very relevant for practical questions.

III. Peculiarities of Unified Private International Law

With regard to unified private international law, the same is true, though some differences exist. For example, a true *lex fori* approach would be incompatible with the need to interpret unified rules uniformly: it would be unacceptable if the courts in each Contracting State were allowed to interpret the terms in treaties harmonising private international law rules differently. A modified approach that bases characterisation on the policies of each respective forum would run into similar concerns.

Admittedly, uniform private international law sometimes allows for, or even encourages, such an approach where it aims at a minimum level of uniformity only. Some EU rules on private international law, eg, relating to consumer protection, may leave EU Member States free (or even encourage them) to expand the notion of consumer in their (private international) laws beyond that found in the Brussels Ia and Rome I Regulations (where a consumer is a natural person, who is acting outside the scope of an economic activity (trade, business, craft, liberal profession)).[21]

Where uniformity is sought, what would be possible for certain cases would be a comparative characterisation asking for uniformity between the relevant laws. The House of Lords proposed such an approach, albeit in application of a domestic statute and not as a matter of interpretation of the Hague Evidence Convention because the Statute applied to cases beyond those covered by the Convention, when it found that a request for evidence is a 'civil or commercial matter' if it is so under the laws of the requesting and requested State.[22] But this approach breaks down where legal systems disagree.

In principle, there is agreement that characterisation for uniform private international law must happen in a uniform and autonomous fashion, as is the case for unified law more generally.[23] Uniformity and autonomy are connected. A uniform interpretation requires that the provisions are interpreted without taking recourse to the national law of the Contracting States.[24] Thus, only an autonomous interpretation and consequently also an autonomous characterisation achieves the aim of unification.[25] This is what the Vienna Convention on the Law of Treaties requires for the interpretation of international treaties; it is also in accordance with the purposes of legal unification. Uniformity of characterisation follows from the purpose of unified law which is unification not just of texts but also of results. Autonomy from domestic categories

[21] See Library of the European Parliament, Library Briefing: The notion of 'consumer' in EU law (06/05/2013), available at: www.europarl.europa.eu/RegData/bibliotheque/briefing/2013/130477/LDM_BRI(2013)130477_REV1_EN.pdf A broader notion of consumer is found in the Package Travel Directive.

[22] *In re State of Norway's Application* [1990] 1 AC 723, 804, Lord Goff of Chieveley giving the unanimous judgment of their Lordships. Those words are used in the Hague Evidence Convention and in the relevant UK statute which implemented that Convention into UK law. However the Statute also covers cases not covered by the Convention (eg, intra-UK and those involving non-Convention States) and the same words were used in previous UK statutes on the same topic that were not implementing the Hague Evidence Convention.

[23] FM Wilke, *A Conceptual Analysis of European Private International Law: The General Issues in the EU and its Member States* (Intersentia 2019) 118–19.

[24] Ibid, 118.

[25] C Heinze, 'Bausteine eines Allgemeinen Teils des europäischen Internationalen Privatrechts' in D Baetge, J von Hein and M von Hinden (eds), *Die richtige Ordnung: Festschrift für Jan Kropholler zum 70. Geburtstag* (Mohr Siebeck 2008) 108–09.

and policies is necessary to effectuate the specific private international law policies underlying the uniform instrument.

Despite the general agreement on this, characterisation in unified private international law creates special problems. For characterisation within uniform instruments, courts face two discrepancies: that between domestic and unified law, and that between substantive and private international law policies. This can create frictions. Take, for example, the characterisation of § 1371 paragraph 1 of the German Civil Code (essentially a problem similar to that in the *Bartholo* case):

> If the property regime is ended by the death of a spouse, the equalisation of the accrued gains is effected by the share of the inheritance on intestacy of the surviving spouse being increased by one quarter of the inheritance; it is irrelevant here whether the spouses in the individual case have made accrued gains.

Under German domestic private international law rules, it was long unclear whether the rule should be characterised as one of succession or of matrimonial property, until the Federal Court of Justice decided, in 2015, in the latter sense, invoking a functional-teleological interpretation of the provision.[26] By then, the EU Succession Regulation had entered into force,[27] and in its realm the Court of Justice of the European Union (CJEU) considered § 1371 to fall under the scope of the Regulation, implying a characterisation as succession and not matrimonial property that is excluded from the Regulation's scope (Article 1(2)(d)).[28] The Court based its reasoning in part on a different assessment of the purpose of § 1371, in part on consideration of the policies underlying the Regulation.

IV. Characterisation Rules in International Instruments

It turns out, then, that characterisation does not necessarily become easier once private international law is unified: although private international law rules are unified, neither substantive laws nor the system of courts applying these rules are unified. Thus, uniform conflict of laws rules alone cannot solve the characterisation problem. To mediate remaining problems, drafters have found ways to reduce the situations in which characterisation creates problems.

A. Rules on Method

One such way could be a rule providing for the proper method of characterisation. National codifications sometimes contain such explicit rules on characterisation,[29] but the effect on judges tends to be limited because abstract methods are often too crude for specific problems. The same is true, in principle, for international instruments. Article 6 of the Bustamante Code appears to provide an unusual exception: its explicit reference to each Member State's own method of

[26] BGH 13 May 2015 – IV ZB 30/14, BGHZ 205, 289 = Neue Juristische Wochenschrift 2015, 2185.

[27] Regulation (EU) No 650/2012 on jurisdiction, applicable law, recognition and enforcement of decisions and acceptance and enforcement of authentic instruments in matters of succession and on the creation of a European Certificate of Succession [2012] OJ L201/107.

[28] C-558/16 *Mahnkopf* EU:C:2018:138.

[29] See Wilke (n 23) 117–18; S Symeonides, 'Codification and Flexibility in Private International Law' in KB Brown and DV Snyder (eds), *General Reports of the XVIIIth Congress of the International Academy of Comparative Law* (Springer 2011) 167–90.

characterisation seems to endorse *lex fori* characterisation that would undermine the goal of uniformity.[30] In reality, the provision provides little more than that Contracting States are free to apply their own private international law rules for matters not regulated by the Code.[31]

Recital 11 of the Rome II Regulation provides explicitly that the concept of non-contractual obligations should be understood as an autonomous concept – a rule providing for autonomous characterisation. Other recitals do so for specific concepts and rules.[32] But uniform texts require autonomous and uniform interpretation anyway, as argued above, so it seems questionable whether there is much value in drafting a provision that explicitly states the characterisation method. Inserting a provision that requires an autonomous interpretation according to the aims of the Convention would thus be unnecessary and only declaratory.[33]

B. Specific Rules on Characterisation[34]

Some rules provide concrete criteria of characterisation. An example can be found in the Hague Trusts Convention.[35] This Convention does not provide a precise definition of a 'trust' but gives, in its Article 2 (a 'gateway provision') a number of characteristics of the institution based on a rough comparison of common characteristics of trusts in common law jurisdictions. Article 11(1) then stipulates that a 'trust' validly created in accordance with the law thus designated must be recognised *as a trust*. Therefore, any jurisdiction bound by the Convention which does not have the trust in its legal system, may not characterise the trust as a contract, foundation, usufruct etc (or a combination of such institutions of its own laws), but *must* characterise the trust as a trust. What that means is set out in paragraphs 2 and 3 of Article 11 and the following provisions, which may be seen as the ingredients of the Convention's autonomous trust concept. The recognition of these minimum effects is, however, subject to, in particular, the broad provisions of Article 15.

A somewhat comparable technique is used in the Hague Intercountry Adoption Convention.[36] Article 2(2) provides that the instrument applies only to adoptions which create a permanent parent–child relationship. (It thereby excludes, in particular, the provision of care to children by way of *kafalah*, which found its place in the 1996 Hague Convention on Protection of Children.) But the Convention does not define the notion of adoption, and does not formally distinguish, within that broad notion, between 'strong' or 'full' adoptions and 'simple' or 'limited' adoptions. Article 26(1) provides a characterisation rule, and requires States Parties to examine the effects of the adoption under the laws of the State where the adoption was made. If under those laws, the pre-existing parent–child relationship is terminated ('strong' adoption), this effect must be recognised by all States Parties. Moreover (paragraph 2) they must give the child rights equivalent to those resulting from ('strong') adoptions in each recognising State Party. By contrast, if the adoption made in the State of origin is a 'simple' adoption, paragraph 1(c) does not apply, but the recognising State is free to apply 'any provision more favourable to the child' (paragraph 3).

[30] 'En todos los casos no previstos por este Código, cada uno de los Estados contratantes aplicará su propia calificación a las instituciones o relaciones jurídicas que hayan de corresponder a los grupos de leyes mencionados en el artículo 3'.

[31] See J Samtleben, *Internationales Privatrecht in Lateinamerika* (Mohr Siebeck 1979) 179–80, 219–20.

[32] Examples from EU law in Wilke (n 23) 120, fn 787.

[33] Similarly HJ Sonnenberger, 'Randbemerkungen zum Allgemeinen Teil eines europäisierten IPR' in Baetge et al (eds) (n 25) 227, 240.

[34] This section is based on input from Hans van Loon.

[35] Convention of 1 July 1985 on the Law Applicable to Trusts and on their Recognition, available at: www.hcch.net/en/instruments/conventions/full-text/?cid=59.

[36] Convention of 29 May 1993 on Protection of Children and Cooperation in Respect of Intercountry Adoption, available at: https://www.hcch.net/en/instruments/conventions/full-text/?cid=69.

C. Rules Determining the Result of Characterisation

Other rules provide not for the process but for the result of characterisation. Recital 11 of the Rome II Regulation provides that '[t]he conflict-of-laws rules in this Regulation should also cover non-contractual obligations arising out of strict liability'. This is a rule prescribing not the (autonomous) method of characterisation but instead the result of the characterisation process. A similar example can be found in Article 5 of the Hague Form of Wills Convention, which provides that form rules that depend on personal conditions or qualifications of a testator or witness 'shall be deemed to pertain to matters of form'.[37] Similarly, Article 12(1) of the Rome I Regulation explicitly defines the 'scope of the law applicable' and provides that it includes, among other things, rules on 'prescription and limitation of actions' (Article 12(1)(d)).[38] This rule takes precedence over Article 1(3), which excludes 'procedure' from the scope of the Regulation. Moreover, it prescribes the result of the characterisation process. Hence, even when the foreign applicable law considers prescription to be a procedural and not a substantive matter, the foreign prescription rules will be applied.

Such private international law rules that determine what substantive rules are covered are effectively characterisation rules.[39] More precisely, they are rules that make judicial characterisation unnecessary. Such non-exclusive lists of issues included within a category have been called 'characterization by example'.[40] That seems misleading, however: there is not much that judges can learn from the listed issues with regard to those not explicitly listed. By including certain issues, the drafter resolves potentially difficult questions, but the list need not, and usually does not, lead to a coherent whole.

D. More Specific Categories

A more comprehensive tool to reduce the need for characterising is to make categories and rules in private international law texts more specific.[41] One example concerns *culpa in contrahendo*.[42] It was long disputed whether *culpa in contrahendo* should be characterised as contractual or delictual (or perhaps quasi-contractual). The Hague Principles on Choice of Law in International Commercial Contracts explicitly include pre-contractual obligations in their scope (Article 9(1)(g)), thereby resolving, within their scope, this complex question.[43] By contrast, prior to the enactment of the Rome II Regulation, the CJEU had characterised *culpa in contrahendo* as delictual within the realm of the Brussels I Regulation;[44] similarly, the drafters of the Rome I

[37] See Albert Font i Segura and Jayne Holliday, 'Succession', ch 22 in this book for a discussion of the Hague Form of Wills Convention.

[38] For precedents, see Art 8(8) of the Hague Convention of 4 May 1971 on the Law Applicable to Traffic Accidents, and Art 8(9) of the Hague Convention of 2 October 1973 on the Law Applicable to Products Liability.

[39] Wilke (n 23) 120.

[40] See, eg. Sonnenberger (n 33) 239–40. This is called 'characterization by example' by Wilke (n 23) 120 (citing AL Calvo Caravaca and J Carrascosa González, *Derecho Internacional Privado*, Vol 1 (Editorial Comares 2016) 471: 'calificación ejemplificativa'); '(specific) characterization rules' by A Metzger, 'Characterisation' in J Basedow, K Hopt, R Zimmermann and A Stier (eds), *Max Planck Encyclopedia of European Private Law*, Vol 1 (Oxford University Press 2012) 167, 169.

[41] R Baratta, 'The Process of Characterization in the EC Conflict of Laws: suggesting a flexible Approach' (2004) VI *Yearbook of Private International Law* 155, 168.

[42] DM Vicente, 'Culpa in contrahendo' in *Encyclopedia of Private International Law* (n 5) 491–98.

[43] Welcomed for this reason by JA Moreno Rodríguez, 'Advocating party autonomy in private international law – the 2015 Choice of Law Principles' in T John, R Gulati and B Köhler (eds), *The Elgar Companion to the Hague Conference on Private International Law* (Edward Elgar 2020) 349–53.

[44] C-334/00 *Tacconi v Wagner* [2002] ECR-I 7357.

Regulation had excluded from its scope 'obligations arising out of dealings prior to the conclusion of a contract' (Article 1(2)(i)). Now, that question of characterisation is made redundant through Article 12 of the Rome II Regulation, which provides a specific applicable law rule and thereby resolves the former characterisation problem through legislative fiat.

However, that very rule also demonstrates some of the problems of more specific categories. The legislative decision strikes an odd compromise: the rule is contained in an instrument for non-contractual obligations, but the primary connecting factor is the same as for contractual obligations, suggesting an implicit contractual characterisation (Article 12(1)).[45] A contractual obligation of course requires that at least a potential contract can be recognised; where that is not the case, the law switches to an applicable law rule that seems more grounded in tort (Article 12(2)). The result is a somewhat artificial distinction. Moreover, the rule is inflexible because it does not allow for differentiations according to whether the action arises in relation to a contract or not.[46] And it leads to discrepancies with the law of jurisdiction, where delictual characterisation is likely still good EU law.[47] The resulting lack of coherence demonstrates some of the shortcomings of substituting specific rules for broader categories: the process of characterisation can, if done properly, lead to results that are both appropriate to the specific case and consistent with policy decisions made elsewhere in the instrument. Specific rules may prevent this.

E. Inclusion and Exclusion Rules

One more legislative tool serves as a substitute for characterisation: inclusion and exclusion rules. By determining which issues are, and which are not, governed by a private international law instrument, the drafters can determine characterisation results at least indirectly. For example, Article 1(2)(i) of the Rome I Regulation states that 'obligations arising out of dealings prior to the conclusion of a contract' are excluded from the scope of the Regulation, whereas Article 2(1) of the Rome II Regulation includes them. The question of whether to characterise these obligations as contractual or non-contractual is hence solved.

Such happy coincidence of explicit inclusion in one, exclusion from all other instruments, conforms with the ideal of internal consistency in EU law; the same is true, *mutatis mutandis*, for internationally unified private international law. Similar principles ought to govern where the drafters are not as comprehensive. Thus, the exclusion of certain issues from one instrument should normally imply their inclusion in another instrument.[48] Similarly, the inclusion in one instrument implies the exclusion from another.

Moreover, internal consistency requires, at least typically, that characterisation should normally be done the same way among different instruments, including for matters of applicable law and for jurisdiction. What counts as a tort for the purpose of the Rome II Regulation should do so also for the purpose of Article 7(2) of the Brussels Ia Regulation; what counts as a contract for the Hague Principles should be a contract also for the Hague Judgments Convention. Of course, there are limits to both principles, given that different instruments may pursue different policies; an interpretation 'unconnected to the scheme and objectives pursued by that regulation' is impossible.[49]

[45] L Tichy, 'Art 12' in P Mankowski and U Magnus (eds), *ECPIL – Rome II Regulation* (Otto Schmidt 2019).

[46] See N Hage-Chahine, '*Culpa in Contrahendo* in European Private International Law: Another Look at Article 12 of the Rome II Regulation' (2012) 32 *Northwestern Journal of International Law & Business* 451.

[47] See *Tacconi* (n 44) and P Mankowski, 'Art 7' in U Magnus and P Mankowski (eds), *ECPIL – Brussels Ibis Regulation* (Otto Schmidt 2016).

[48] Bariatti (n 5) 361–62.

[49] Case C-45/13 *Andreas Kainz v Pantherwerke AG* EU:C:2014:7 [20].

In a world in which supranational and international regulation of private international law is not comprehensive, inclusion and exclusion rules have different effects, however. Inclusion rules clearly have the effect of including an issue within the category or categories that are regulated by the respective instrument. Article 2(1) of the Rome II Regulation, eg, includes 'any consequence arising out of tort/delict, unjust enrichment, *negotiorum gestio* or *culpa in contrahendo*' as falling within the notion of 'damage' under the Regulation. This implies first the decision that the matter is no longer regulated by domestic private international law and it implies secondly the exclusion of that law from other international instruments on applicable law. The argument is not that a legal rule is essentially either a tort rule or a contract rule – most contested questions concern legal rules that are arguably in between – but that the law, by including it in one category, decides to exclude it from the other category.

Exclusion rules, by contrast, are less clear. An exclusion could mean applicability of a different international instrument, but will more often leave the matter to domestic private international law regimes. The question for them is how free domestic courts are to develop their own approach.

Sometimes an exclusion rests on the explicit policy decision that a certain matter does not belong among the categories dealt with in the instrument. In that case a court is barred from simply applying that instrument by analogy, and arguably even from using a similar kind of reasoning and the same connecting factors. The decision in an international instrument that a matter is not one of tort is binding on States party to it and bars them from treating the same matter as one of tort.

In other cases, however, an exception rule may merely signal that no agreement on this topic could be achieved during the drafting process of the uniform instrument. This is the case, eg, for the exclusion of 'non-contractual obligations arising out of violations of privacy and rights relating to personality, including defamation' from the Rome II Regulation (Article 1(2)(g))[50] and of 'defamation' and 'privacy' from the Hague Judgments Convention (Article 2(1)(k) and (l)),[51] and of 'intellectual property' from the Hague Judgments Convention.[52] In such a case, domestic legislators and courts are free to fill the gap as they want – including by using the same connecting factor as that used by the international instrument and thereby treating the matter, as a result, as though it had been included. When the CJEU decided that non-judicial divorces do not fall within the scope of the Rome III Regulation, it based that on the argument that the EU legislator had not considered them during the drafting process and significant changes to the Regulation would be necessary that only that legislator could undertake.[53] This leaves a gap that States can fill as they want, including by expanding the scope of the Rome III Regulation, as was done in Germany.[54] Of course, such a decision has no strong precedential value for the courts of other States Parties to the instrument, because the policy of uniformity encompassed in the instrument does not apply to matters outside its scope. If, however, most other States follow the example, this may be a good basis on which to revise the characterisation issue on the international sphere.

[50] I Bach, 'Art 1 Rome II' in P Huber (ed), *Rome II Regulation Pocket Commentary* (Sellier 2011) Art 1 no 53.

[51] See David Goddard and Paul Beaumont, 'Recognition and Enforcement of Judgments in Civil or Commercial Matters', ch 29 in this book.

[52] See Paul Torremans, 'Intellectual Property', ch 25 in this book.

[53] C-372/16 *Sahyouni* EU:C:2017:988.

[54] Art 17 (2) EGBGB.

V. Autonomous Characterisation

Private international law rules are always, and necessarily, to some extent unfinished.[55] This means that even fixed characterisation rules will be unable to provide a solution to every characterisation problem. This is true even among the States Parties to the instrument, whose laws evolve; it is true even more so vis-à-vis third States. Where no explicit legislative solutions exist, or where those are insufficient, courts must engage in characterisation. What seems clear, save for rare exceptions,[56] is that such characterisation must be autonomous, meaning: independent of the domestic law of the forum. What is less clear is what exactly that implies.

A. Treaty Interpretation

A first approach to characterisation is not specific to private international law but exists for all uniform texts: statutory or treaty interpretation. Terms in international instruments are analysed with regard to their text and their context, their legislative history and the policies underlying the entire instrument in order to shed light on the proper interpretation. Thus, detailed analysis of the legislative history of the EU Succession Regulation shows that the drafters agreed on inclusion of clawback of lifetime gifts to third parties within the scope of the Regulation whereas the matter had been fudged at the HCCH in relation to the Succession Convention 1989.[57] Inclusion of § 1371 of the German Civil Code within the EU Succession Regulation is justifiable with the objective of the European Certificate of Succession to 'include full information relating to the surviving spouse's rights regarding the estate'. Such process, then, is appropriate; it does not, however, raise many considerations that are specific to private international law.

B. A Modified *lex fori* Approach?

Should characterisation follow a modified *lex fori* approach, in analogy to developments for characterisation in domestic courts? A literal *lex fori* approach allowing each court to refer to its own law's categories and policies would undermine uniformity. This is not the case when EU or international law is treated as the relevant *lex fori*. EU private international law would then characterise following the categories of substantive EU law; international instruments would follow along categories of substantive international law.

The solution has some charm, but it runs into counter-arguments. Some of those are known from debates in domestic law: substantive law does not provide categories for legal institutions from other legal systems, especially third States, and policy differences between substantive law and private international law may make categories of the former inadequate for problems of the latter.

Private international law rules in EU and international law create additional challenges.[58] Among the most important may be this: international and EU instruments on private international law are often more comprehensive than the respective substantive law areas. They will

[55] K Schurig, *Kollisionsnorm und Sachrecht* (Duncker & Humblot 1981) 170 f.
[56] For Art 6 of the Bustamante Code see pages 36–37.
[57] Holliday (n 3) 87 ff.
[58] Bariatti (n 5) 359–60.

contain private international law rules for areas in which no unified substantive law exists, and often even could not exist, due to a lack of competence. In fact, the purpose of uniform private international law instruments is often to achieve harmony precisely in those areas in which substantive unification is impossible. In such cases, no modified *lex causae* exists that could guide characterisation.

C. Comparative Characterisation

In those situations where there is no unified substantive law to fall back on, comparative characterisation as proposed by Rabel becomes attractive.[59] Comparative law is crucial when formulating common principles of EU law; it also plays a predominant role in the drafting of private international law texts.[60] International instruments are typically drafted with input from representatives of many legal systems; they are, in this sense, already results of a comparative process. Moreover, they will normally not be accepted by States that do not see their own substantive law adequately dealt with. It is therefore appropriate that the characterisation process regularly happens through a comparative law analysis.[61]

This is certainly appropriate where Member State laws are at stake: comparative law is necessary to do justice to the Member States' legal orders. But it frequently helps even with regard to third States: the amount of comparative law material that the Member States' legal orders present that reflects both civil and common law traditions can help also with foreign legal systems belonging to these traditions. It does not help, of course, where third State laws are different, as is the case with the aforementioned non-judicial divorce: here, more comparative law would have been useful and desirable. Of course, this brings to the fore the desirability of unification of private international law at the global level.[62]

D. Functional-Teleological Characterisation

While a comparative approach brings out a common understanding of the States Parties, it is not well geared towards an explicit regulatory role for private international law. Where the private international law instrument itself has a specific purpose, that purpose will influence characterisation. One example is 'measures of protection' for the purpose of protecting the child, introduced in the 1961 Hague Convention on the Protection of Children. This concept was expressly coined as a *functional autonomous* concept to avoid the characterisation issues to which the 1902 Guardianship Convention had famously led in the International Court of Justice *Boll* case (1958),[63] but also to achieve a sufficiently high level of protection. It achieved its objective only partially, however, because the Convention maintained a distinction between measures

[59] See above (n 16).

[60] See R Michaels, 'Comparative Law' in *Max Planck Encyclopedia of European Private Law* (n 40) 297, 300.

[61] Thus for EU private international law see G Rühl, 'Rechtsvergleichung und europäisches Kollisionsrecht: 'Die vergessene Dimension' in R Zimmermann (ed), *Zukunftsperspektiven der Rechtsvergleichung* (Mohr Siebeck 2016) 103, 121.

[62] See H van Loon, 'Remarks on the needs and methods for governance in the field of private international law – at the global and regional levels' in F Cafaggi and H Muir-Watt (eds), *Making European Private Law: Governance Design* (Edward Elgar 2008) 197–208.

[63] See Rapport explicatif by W de Steiger, Bureau Permanent de la Conférence de La Haye, *Actes et Documents de la Neuvième Session*, Tome IV, Protection des Mineurs, 224.

for the purpose of protection, and measures relating to parental responsibility, governed by different applicable law rules (Articles 2 and 3), which in practice led to difficulties. This issue has now been resolved by the 1996 Hague Child Protection Convention, which aligns the applicable law rules (Articles 15, 16 and 17) and thereby makes characterisation decisions between the concepts unnecessary.

Even beyond such explicit goals, uniform private international law instruments can be interpreted in accordance with their general regulatory role and potential. Formulation of the Sustainable Development Goals 2030 enables a comprehensive regulatory policy on the international realm that should also be able to shape private international law.[64]

VI. Institutional Aspects: Judges, Legislators and Professors

So much for how characterisation is in fact dealt with, and how it should be dealt with, in international instruments. This leaves the question what institutions should be given that task: judges, legislators, or professors?[65]

A. Legislative Solutions

Are legislative solutions to the characterisation process desirable? The answer is ambivalent. On the one hand, drafting clear and explicit rules can facilitate the process of characterisation to a great extent. In many cases in which experience has shown that a certain set of facts are difficult to subsume under common legal categories, it can make sense for the drafters of a uniform instrument to counteract these difficulties by drafting detailed provisions that clearly define the scope of the legal categories. Where the drafting process of an international instrument includes representatives from many legal orders, the chances are that the drafters will be aware of potential characterisation problems that may arise within their jurisdiction or those of other (potentially) Contracting States. In this way, both clarity and uniformity can be enhanced.

On the other hand, such legislative decisions come at the cost of a loss of flexibility. This can be a problem for a legal institution like *culpa in contrahendo* which, in reality, is an umbrella for many different issues, some more contractual, others less so. A fixed rule like Article 12 of the Rome II Regulation does not allow for nuanced differentiation between such cases. Moreover, fixed rules are problematic for unanticipated legal institutions, an especially pertinent problem for unification that is not yet truly global where the applicability of a third State's law is at stake. Drafters cannot possibly consider every potentially applicable substantive law, including those of States not involved in the drafting process.

B. Judicial Solutions

Development of private international law has always been left, to a significant degree, to courts.[66] There are several reasons for this. Private international law, more so than domestic law, creates an

[64] See R Michaels, V Ruiz Abou-Nigm and H van Loon (eds), *The Private Side of Transforming our World: UN Sustainable Development Goals 2030 and Private International Law* (Intersentia 2021).
[65] A quip on RC Caenegem, *Judges, Legislators and Professors* (Cambridge University Press 1987).
[66] Thus for EU PIL instruments: Baratta (n 41) 169.

array of unforeseen, indeed unforeseeable, specific fact patterns. Conflicts of law rest on tensions that cannot be resolved through systemic coherency arguments: they occur between, not within, legal systems, and there is always a tension between international and domestic uniformity of result. Private international law rules are necessarily unfinished, in need of further development and of sensitivity to the demands of the specific case.

When these courts are national courts, this is not an optimal solution. Judges are often overwhelmed by private international law in general; this sense is exacerbated when that private international law rests in instruments outside domestic law. National courts have a natural tendency to use domestic categories they know and the methods of private international law they have studied in their domestic context, creating the risk of inconsistencies.[67]

Within the EU, this problem is countered through the existence of the CJEU. Whenever Member States' courts are unsure of the interpretation of an EU private international law (PIL) instrument, Article 267 of the Treaty on the Functioning of the European Union allows, and sometimes requires them, to ask for a preliminary ruling by the CJEU on a matter that is necessary for the outcome of the case before the national court. The interpretation outcome is binding for courts in all Member States and thus ensures a uniform interpretation of the PIL Regulations.

Uniform interpretation of international treaties is harder to achieve. Domestic courts may look at foreign courts' decisions to achieve consistency, however, difficulties in accessing foreign court decisions and possible language barriers can impede that. In some areas help comes from databases.[68] The Hague Conference provides such information in collection of decisions, including the INCADAT database.[69]

C. The Role of Academics and Institutions

These shortcomings in both legislators and courts raise the importance of academics. Academics can help with characterisation problems in various ways. International commentaries that provide not only detailed discussion of PIL instruments but also compile materials from different States Parties facilitate comparative characterisation and also uniformity.[70]

In the EU context, the European Group of Private International Law (GEDIP), an unofficial but influential group of highly regarded private international law scholars,[71] could play a role here, in view of the fact that it combines a number of leading private international law scholars from various countries. Traditionally, GEDIP focuses largely on legislative proposals. But it seems conceivable that it could also engage in matters of characterisation, to provide a well-reasoned focal point for courts faced with similar issues. That role would be similar to that of the UN Convention on Contracts for the International Sale of Goods (CISG) Advisory Council that provides opinions on the interpretation of the CISG.[72]

[67] See P Beaumont et al (eds), *Cross-Border Litigation in Europe* (Hart Publishing 2017) 822–23.

[68] See most notably in relation to the Hague Child Abduction Convention 1980 by the Canadian and US Supreme Courts, noted by Maria Caterina Baruffi and Jayne Holliday, 'Child Abduction', ch 34 in this book.

[69] See CS Bruch and MM Durkin, 'The Hague's Online Child Abduction Materials' (2011) 28 *GPSolo* 12–13, 44; N Lowe, 'A supra-national approach to interpreting the 1980 Hague Child Abduction Convention: a tale of two European courts' [2012] *International Family Law* 48–52, 170–79.

[70] See R Michaels, 'Kommentare zum transnationalen Privatrecht: Grenzen der Entnationalisierung eines nationalen Modells' in D Kästle-Lamparter, N Jansen and R Zimmermann (eds), *Juristische Kommentare: Ein Internationaler Vergleich* (Mohr Siebeck 2020) 395–416.

[71] K Siehr, 'GEDIP' in *Encyclopedia of Private International Law* (n 5) 835: 'The aims of GEDIP are that European scholars of private international law regularly observe the developments of European PIL, exchange information and make proposals in annual sessions'.

[72] I Schwenzer, 'The CISG Advisory Council' [2012] *Nederlands Tijdschrift voor Handelsrecht* 46; see also C Legros, 'The CISG Advisory Council: A Model to Improve Uniform Application of the CMR' (2017) 9 *European Journal of Commercial Contract Law* 27.

At the global level, Article 8(1) of the Statute of the Hague Conference provides for the establishment of special commissions to study the operation in practice of Hague Conventions; such commissions sometimes recommend proper interpretations in recommendations and conclusions. The Hague Conference on Private International Law (HCCH) provides guidance on the interpretation of its instruments in the explanatory reports on each Convention, and in Guides to Good Practice, Practical Handbooks, etc.[73] Such interpretations are not binding – the HCCH is neither a party to nor an adjudicator on its own Conventions. But they should serve as well-reasoned focal points for courts to take account of when addressing characterisation issues in relation to HCCH Conventions.

Altogether, international instruments provide specific opportunities for characterisation that is on the one hand explicitly comparative and on the other explicitly regulatory. Such processes are best done in cooperation between courts and academics. Lawmakers should indeed interfere where it is possible to resolve difficult characterisation issues or where the implications of specific policy decisions are important. Beyond that, a very detailed regulation of specific issues threatens to deprive private international law of its necessary flexibility in view of new and unexpected situations and undermine the chance for a successful comprehensive international system.

[73] See Marta Pertegás and Paul Beaumont, 'Hague Conference on Private International Law', ch 7; and HCCH Permanent Bureau, 'National Organs and Central Authorities under HCCH Conventions', ch 8 in this book.

4

Connecting Factors

SUSANNE L GÖSSL AND RUTH LAMONT

I. Introduction

A connecting factor (or 'reference point'; German: *Anknüpfungsmoment*, French: *facteur de rattachement*) in private international law is a factor that attaches the disputed case to a place for a certain legal purpose, mainly to determine the applicable law or to establish jurisdiction.[1] There are several different connecting factors in private international law, depending on the legal relationship that is in question; eg, property issues are often referred to the *lex rei sitae*, ie, the law/jurisdiction of the place where a chattel or immovable is located;[2] tort law usually refers to the place a tort occurred;[3] whereas in contract law the parties' choice of law is key.[4]

Usually, connecting factors are supposed to create legal certainty, thus, the connecting factor should be easy to determine from an *ex ante* perspective. To create this legal certainty, two approaches exist, depending on the nature of the dispute in question: First, it can be achieved by allowing the parties to choose the forum or the law applicable, thus, the connecting factor is the parties' choice.[5] Second, it can be achieved by using factual, objective elements that are also easy to determine for third parties, therefore called 'objective' connecting factors.[6] As choice of law and choice of courts are the topics of separate chapters,[7] we deal with 'objective' connecting factors.

II. Outline and Focus of the Chapter

A. Personal Connecting Factors

We will emphasise connecting factors that relate to a person in a dispute. We are going to develop a concept that is feasible for a private international law rule from a global perspective. In our

[1] See, eg, H-P Mansel, 'Connecting factor' in J Basedow et al (eds), *Encyclopedia of Private International Law*, Vol I (Edward Elgar 2017); F Vischer, 'Connecting Factors' in K Lipstein and R David (eds), *International Encyclopedia of Comparative Law: Volume III, Private International Law, Part 1* (Mohr Siebeck 2011) 4-1.

[2] See Janeen M Carruthers and Matthias Weller, 'Property', ch 21 in this book; also, eg, Mansel, ibid, I; Vischer, ibid, 4–16.

[3] See Michael Hellner, 'Tort: Applicable Law', ch 18 in this book.

[4] See Symeon C Symeonides, 'Law Applicable to Contracts', ch 14 in this book; and J Basedow, 'Choice of law' in J Basedow et al (eds), *Encyclopedia of Private International Law*, Vol I (Edward Elgar 2017).

[5] See H-P Mansel, 'Party Autonomy, Legal Doctrine on Choice of Law, and the General Section of the European Conflict of Laws' in S Leible (ed), *General Principles of European Private International Law* (Wolters Kluwer 2016) 148.

[6] Mansel (n 1) II 1a and 2.

[7] See Symeon C Symeonides, 'Law Applicable to Contracts', ch 14 in this book; and Paul Beaumont and Mary Keyes, 'Choice of Court Agreements', ch 28 in this book.

opinion, this focus is reasonable, as the determination of such a connecting factor is one of the most difficult and most highly disputed aspects of private law in a global context. Legal traditions differ, sometimes tremendously, on which should be preferred.[8] Furthermore, these personal connecting factors are highly relevant in several different cross-border situations. They create a link between an individual and the laws of a country, identifying the personal law of the individual. Ideally, the connecting factor should identify a country with which that individual has a significant association so that the personal law is one which may be expected to govern their personal relationships and a court should be competent to decide the case. Assuming jurisdiction on an appropriate basis is normally a requirement for recognition of the judgment by a foreign legal system. Usually, this personal connection is required in family and succession law and questions of personal status,[9] but it is also relevant in other conflict of law rules. For example, habitual residence, a person-related connecting factor, is the fallback connecting factor in European Union (EU) contract law if the contract is lacking a choice of law (Article 4, Rome I Regulation)[10] and it is the main connecting factor in EU tort law if both parties share a habitual residence (Article 4(2), Rome II Regulation).[11]

While this personal connecting factor traditionally is understood as an 'objective' connecting factor, it also becomes part of a new 'subjective' tendency to allow the parties a so-called 'limited' choice of law, ie, a choice of law between a few listed jurisdictions.[12]

B. Nationality, Domicile and Habitual Residence

Traditionally, under national private international family law rules, there has been a split between the civil and common law systems regarding the connecting factor. Civil law systems – and some systems in the Middle East and Asia[13] – seek to connect individuals to a legal system primarily through use of their nationality,[14] even though nationality then faces many follow-up questions, particularly in the treatment of multinationals or stateless persons.[15] By contrast, common law systems maintained the concept of domicile that had been used in civil law countries before the rise of nationality in the nineteenth century.[16] A person's domicile is equated to their 'long-term home' and is attributed at birth (domicile of origin) and can be later changed by the person (domicile of choice) on the basis of presence in a country that they intend to make their

[8] See, eg, the Latin American Código Bustamante, Art 7, that leaves the notion explicitly unresolved; broadly J Basedow, *The Law of Open Societies: Private Ordering and Public Regulation in the Conflict of Laws* (Brill Nijhoff 2015) 482 et seq.

[9] See Albert Font i Segura and Jayne Holliday, 'Succession', ch 22; and chs 32–40 on family law, in this book.

[10] Reg 593/2008 on the law applicable to contractual obligations [2008] OJ L177.

[11] Reg 864/2007 on the law applicable to non-contractual obligations [2007] OJ L199.

[12] eg, Arts 6 et seq Hague Protocol of 23 November 2007 on the Law Applicable to Maintenance Obligations; see Mansel (n 5); to such an approach in Australia see Basedow (n 8) para 374 et seq, 387 et seq.

[13] According to Basedow (n 8) 311 with fn 743.

[14] P Mankowski, 'Dual and Multiple Nationality, Stateless Persons, and Refugess' in S Leible (ed), *General Principles of European Private International Law* (Wolters Kluwer 2016) 189; E Rabel, *The Conflict of Laws: A Comparative Study, Vol I: Introduction: Family Law*, 2nd edn (University of Michigan Law School 1958) 120 et seq.

[15] Basedow (n 8) para 402 et seq; Mankowski (n 14) 189 et seq.

[16] Domicile came into the common law world from continental Europe via the mixed legal system of Scotland to the common law system of England and Wales, see part III of P Beaumont and J Holliday, 'Some Aspects of Scots Private International Law of Succession Taking Account of the Impact of the EU Succession Regulation' in F Villata et al (eds), *EU Cross-Border Succession Law* (Edward Elgar 2021) (original version is available as Working Paper 2015/6 at: www.abdn.ac.uk/law/research/working-papers-455.php).

long-term home.[17] Domicile of choice of an individual relies on the interpretation of the intentions in residing in a particular location and doubts over the purpose of a period of residence may prevent its acquisition even after a long period of residence.[18] A great strength of the concept of domicile is that it may change immediately after a person moves to a country with a clear intention to stay there for the long term.

The development of international agreements on various aspects of private international family law both through the Hague Conference on Private International Law (HCCH), and more recently through the European Union (EU), has led to the adoption of habitual residence as a global connecting factor.[19] Newer codifications, eg, the Chinese Private International Law codification[20] and the Uruguayan Ley General de Derecho Internacional Privado[21] use habitual residence (*Jing Chang Ju Suo Di*; *residencia habitual)* as the main connecting factor regarding a person.[22]

C. Habitual Residence as a Global Connecting Factor

Habitual residence is intended to create a factual and responsive connection between an individual and a country. A global connecting factor for personal law should combine approaches of different systems. Habitual residence seems to be preferable to domicile and nationality, but its success depends on a common understanding that learns from the strengths and weaknesses of its predecessors.

Habitual residence has its basis in a factual assessment of the practical links with a particular jurisdiction but, particularly where there has been a recent move between jurisdictions and the links are tenuous, emphasis should be placed on the intention of the individual in moving, as some jurisdictions already do.[23] The relevance of a party's subjective intentions to determining their factual habitual residence, rather than focusing solely on their objective links to a country, then forms a key aspect of the interpretation of habitual residence. We suggest that clear subjective intention has an important role to play in modern private international law (as it does in determining a domicile of choice) and should be regarded as an essential element of the broad contextual assessment of habitual residence.

This applies especially in relationships that have a personal basis. As long as the persons involved are the only parties to a possible dispute, the parties' intention does not create legal uncertainty. On the contrary, it may even enhance certainty for them, as they know their intentions, while it might be hard to predict which factual elements a court might consider as important. Thus, at least as long as third and vulnerable parties are not involved, an emphasis on clear intention will satisfy the general need of every connecting factor to create legal certainty.

[17] Rabel (n 14) 117 et seq, 150 et seq.

[18] *In the Estate of Fuld (No 3)* [1968] P 675, 684–85.

[19] J Harris and L Collins (gen eds), *Dicey, Morris and Collins on the Conflict of Laws*, 15th edn (Sweet & Maxwell) 6.4.

[20] Act of the People's Republic of China on Application of law in Civil Relations with Foreign Contacts, which came into effect as of 7 January 2013.

[21] Ley General de Derecho Internacional Privado C/619/2020 N° 130.

[22] See Tong Xue, 'Neue Regeln des Obersten Volksgerichts: Die erste Justizielle Interpretation des chinesischen IPR-Gesetzes' [2012] *IPRax* 206; Weizuo Chen, 'China' in J Basedow et al (eds), *Encyclopedia of Private International Law*, Vol I (Edward Elgar 2017) 1; Artícolo 14 A Ley General de Derecho Internacional Privado.

[23] For details see below.

D. Outline

This contribution will consider the connecting factors used in the Conventions promulgated by the HCCH on international family law and how habitual residence has been utilised in Conventions covering both adults and children (section III). It will then discuss the approach of EU private international law to connecting factors, focusing on the influential role of the Court of Justice of the European Union (CJEU) in providing a uniform interpretation across Member States and beyond (section IV). Reflecting on the importance of effective connecting factors that take account of circumstances, we will address the position of refugees under the Geneva Refugee Convention of 1951 (section V). In this context, the regard paid to subjective intentions is important in determining the connecting factor between refugees and a legal system for the resolution of their personal status. Afterwards, we will also refer to some national courts that have not limited habitual residence to a mere factual notion (section VI). Finally, we will conclude that habitual residence should have a central role in global private international law regarding personal relationships but understood – different from the EU approach – as not merely factual but including subjective elements (section VII).

III. Connecting Factors in HCCH Family Conventions

The HCCH provides a global forum for the promulgation of agreements on international family law rules.[24] The benefit of consistency created by these agreements is evident in encouraging cooperation between countries and increased recognition of foreign judgments. The HCCH has also been an important forum for the cooperation and interaction of judges with an international family law remit, sharing experience and approaches to the interpretation and application of the Conventions and developing consistency in practice.

In seeking to create agreements that countries with a range of legal traditions can accede to and implement, the HCCH has sought to use a connecting factor that can be agreed upon to encourage accession. In doing so, it has effectively promoted habitual residence as the most important modern connecting factor without the links to the traditions of the civil or common law systems of nationality and domicile.[25] Habitual residence has been adopted for Conventions affecting both children and adults in a range of contexts.[26]

A. HCCH Conventions Affecting Children

The Hague Convention on jurisdiction, applicable law, recognition, enforcement and cooperation in respect of parental responsibility and measures for the protection of children 1996 (Children's Convention 1996) aims to provide a comprehensive international instrument for disputes relating to children. Habitual residence is adopted as the central connecting factor under Article 5 as the basis of primary jurisdiction. The place of the child's habitual residence has jurisdiction over decisions relating to parental responsibility. All the other grounds of jurisdiction are exceptions to this basic principle. For example, if habitual residence cannot be established in the case of

[24] See: www.hcch.net/.
[25] Vischer (n 1) 4–17 et seq.
[26] ibid 4–28.

internationally displaced or refugee children then presence may be used, and under Article 11 emergency measures may be taken in relation to a child based on their presence in a territory, but only on a temporary basis. Under Article 23 recognition of a judgment may be refused if jurisdiction was not based on one of the grounds under Chapter II.[27]

The Hague Convention on the Civil Aspects of International Child Abduction 1980 (Abduction Convention 1980) also adopts habitual residence as a key connecting factor. Under Article 3 of the Convention, a child must have been removed or retained away from their habitual residence in breach of rules of custody under the law of that country for the return mechanism created by the Convention to operate. This has led parents to argue over the habitual residence of the child, seeking to avoid return under the 1980 Convention.[28] Parents' migration may alter their child's habitual residence without them being aware of the implications for the child's subsequent legal status. It is the use of habitual residence in this Convention that has led to a globalised discussion over the interpretation of habitual residence and how the concept applies to children. The Perez-Vera Report on the interpretation of the Convention states only that habitual residence is a 'well-established concept' and is a 'pure question of fact'.[29] In seeking consistency in interpretation to ensure that the return mechanism applies in the same circumstances throughout the signatory States, there have been efforts to determine how habitual residence should apply to children.[30]

The increasingly mobile lives of families led to many children having connections to more than one jurisdiction and determining their habitual residence can be affected by a range of factors.[31] On a practical level, infants do not have an awareness of their residence beyond the people who provide primary care for them. Older children do have a much greater awareness, but they do not have the ability to control their place of residence as an adult would, or it is at least highly circumscribed. In identifying the habitual residence of a child, the determination will take place in the context of their family life. This will focus on links to family locally, integration in the country including language usage, education and friendship groups, medical and social support networks. However, the extent to which the parents' intentions in locating a child in a specific country should influence the child's habitual residence has been of particular concern. The high number of State Parties to the 1980 Abduction Convention and the volume of cases conducted nationally has meant that the interpretation of habitual residence has been focused on this context, identifying potentially different approaches in practice between jurisdictions.

Schuz has identified the emergence of different models regarding the relationship between the child's habitual residence and that of the parents: the parental intention (or parental rights model) and the child-centred model.[32] She identifies that the parental intention model assumes that the parent has the right to determine the place of the child's habitual residence focusing on the subjective intention of the parent, whereas the perspective of the child and their factual connections are the focus of the child-centred model. She identifies that many courts combine the two approaches, accounting for both the factual connections of the child, and the subjective intentions of the parents.[33] Vivatvaraphol has discussed this split in interpretative approach within the

[27] See Costanza Honorati and Mary Keyes, 'Parental Responsibility, Custody and Access', ch 33 in this book.

[28] See, eg, *KL (A Child) (Abduction: Habitual Residence)* [2013] UKSC 75; and Maria Caterina Baruffi and Jayne Holliday, 'Child Abduction', ch 34 in this book.

[29] Explanatory Report on the 1980 HCCH Child Abduction Convention, available at: www.hcch.net/en/publications-and-studies/details4/?pid=2779.

[30] See recently, *Monasky v Taglieri* [2020] 18-935, [2020] 140 S Ct 719 (US Supreme Court).

[31] *M (Children: Habitual Residence: 1980 Hague Child Abduction Convention* [2020] EWCA Civ 1105.

[32] R Schuz, 'Disparity and the Quest for Uniformity in Implementing the Hague Abduction Convention' (2014) 9 *Journal of Comparative Law* 1, 6.

[33] Ibid, 8.

US circuit courts, identifying that the parental intention model tends to be used more in common law jurisdictions. She argues that, in the absence of guidance in the text of the Convention, the focus should be on objective evidence of the child's integration and acclimatisation in a particular country.[34] In the Australian context, Easteal et al have argued for a checklist of factors for determining a child's habitual residence, including: parental intention, family and social ties, length of time in the country, community involvement to promote predictability, and a child-centred focus.[35] Most States have moved towards a hybrid approach, including parental intention as a factor in the assessment of the overall links of the child to a particular State.[36]

B. Hague Conventions Affecting Adults

Habitual residence has also been adopted as the primary connecting factor by the HCCH in Conventions affecting adults. This may raise fewer issues in practice than for children. In particular, giving weight to intention may be less of a concern where an adult is able to determine their residence, and may be regarded as a desirable realisation of party autonomy over the governance of their personal relationships.

The HCCH Maintenance Convention 2007 is designed to make the recovery of maintenance abroad a much more practical, fair and efficient process. The Convention refers to habitual residence in determining the jurisdiction for the recognition of a judgment from abroad. Articles 18 and 20 contain broad jurisdictional links for the recognition of a maintenance decision with the aim of maximising the circumstances in which a maintenance order will be recognised and prevent the need to establish a new decision on migration. Duncan recognises that habitual residence of either the respondent or the creditor in the State of origin of the judgment is likely to be the principal base of subsequent recognition. However, he highlights that, for some States, the creditor's residence alone in the State of origin is not a sufficient link for recognition of a maintenance judgment, and a reservation is therefore possible under the terms of the Convention.[37]

The Hague Convention on the International Protection of Adults 2000 is designed for safeguarding incapacitated adults who are not able to protect their own interests. It covers jurisdiction, applicable law and the recognition and enforcement of measures. Article 5 of the Protection of Adults Convention defines the primary ground of jurisdiction as the habitual residence of the adult concerned. The supplementary grounds of jurisdiction are exceptions to this primary ground and emergency measures may be adopted on the basis of presence in the jurisdiction under Article 10, but it is clear that the habitual residence court is expected to resume primary jurisdiction as soon as possible as the measures should be only temporary in effect. The applicable law is also identified as the law of the forum which will normally be the adult's habitual residence.[38] The Convention provides further evidence of the shift towards habitual residence as the central connecting factor in private international family law. Long argues that it is the

[34] T Vivatvaraphol, 'Back to Basics: Determining a Child's Habitual Residence in International Child Abduction Cases under the Hague Convention' (2009) 77 *Fordham Law Review* 3325, 3360–65.

[35] P Easteal, J Favaloro and F Thornton, 'Hague Convention on the Civil Aspects of International Child Abduction: The consideration of habitual residence in Australian courts' (2016) 6 *Family Law Review* 194, 207.

[36] S Bookman, 'The new Canadian test for habitual residence in the Hague Convention' [2018] *International Family Law* 222 discussing the decision of the Supreme Court of Canada in *Office of the Children's Lawyer v Balev* 2018 SCC 16.

[37] W Duncan, 'The New Hague Child Support Convention: Goals and Outcomes of the Negotiations' (2009) 43 *Family Law Quarterly* 1, 11–12; Paul Beaumont and Lara Walker, 'Maintenance', ch 36 in this book.

[38] Art 13. See generally on vulnerable adults, Pietro Franzina, 'The Protection of Adults', ch 39 in this book.

underlying influence of the principle of securing the best interests of the adult that informs the choice of habitual residence as a connecting factor:

> Habitual residence is chosen because the state of residence is better placed to assess the factual life situation of the vulnerable person since it is physically closer to her or him. Other grounds of jurisdiction are established only when the authorities of those countries are deemed better prepared to assess the interests of the adult.[39]

She points out that habitual residence as a connecting factor originated in international conventions designed to provide protection of individuals, particularly children and vulnerable adults.[40] As the connecting factor which focuses on factual links to a country, it enables assessment on the entirety of the circumstances of the individual as they change over time along with their purpose.

C. Interim Conclusion

Habitual residence has developed as the main connecting factor in Hague Conventions affecting children and adults alike. Uncertainty remains how to interpret that concept. The historical origins to find a compromise between the intention-focused concept of domicile and the factual-focused concept of nationality have led to reliance on a concept that is mainly factual. As the concept has no historical model that could give inspiration for a clear interpretation, different national scholars and courts tend to 'charge' the concept with requirements they know from their respective systems. It remains unclear how far the concept should be understood as merely factual or the extent to which a person's intention can be deemed relevant as well. The recent trend is clearly towards a hybrid approach which takes account of intention alongside objective evidence but the weight that should be given to intention in different contexts has not been clarified or agreed.

IV. The Influence of EU Cross-Border Family Law

A. The Global Relevance of EU Cross-Border Family Law

Even though this book focuses on global and not EU private international law it seems wise to take account of the concept of habitual residence as interpreted by the Court of Justice of the European Union (CJEU). First, it is one of the few courts that can and does interpret private international law concepts on a supranational level. Second, the CJEU case law is noticed and discussed in countries other than EU Member States.[41] It influences academic discussion and courts all over the world. An interesting pattern of interpretation of the concept of habitual residence has evolved over the last two decades oscillating between a more subjective, intent-focused and a more objective, factual-based understanding.

[39] J Long, 'Rethinking Vulnerable Adults' Protection in the Light of the 2000 Hague Convention' (2013) 27 *International Journal of Law, Policy and the Family* 51, 59.

[40] Ibid, 65.

[41] eg, for the Eurasian Union see M Karliuk, 'The Influence of CJEU Judgments on the Legal Order of the Euroasian Economic Union' in A Reich and H-W Micklitz (eds), *The Impact of the European Court of Justice on Neighbouring Countries* (Oxford University Press 2020) 68 et seq; for Switzerland, see F Maiani, 'CJEU Citations in the Case Law of the Swiss Federal Supreme Court: A Quantitative/Qualitative Analysis' in Reich and Micklitz, ibid, 105 et seq.

B. Habitual Residence in EU Cross-Border Family Law: Overview

In EU cross-border family law, habitual residence has evolved to be the main and central connecting factor.[42] The Brussels IIa[43] and Brussels IIb Regulations[44] provide a wide range of possibilities to determine jurisdiction, nevertheless, almost all rules refer to the habitual residence of either both spouses, or the child, or at least the respondent (Articles 3(1)(a), 6(a), 8 et seq, Brussels IIa). Under Brussels IIa, further connecting factors to constitute jurisdiction are domicile and nationality (Article 3(1)(b), 6(b)), demonstrating the intention of the EU to accommodate both civil and common law traditions. Brussels IIb, on the other hand, eliminated reference to domicile. The spouses' nationality remains as an additional connecting factor in Article 3(b), but habitual residence (of the child or the spouses) moves closer to the centre. Furthermore, in Regulations regarding family or inheritance matters,[45] the main connecting factor to determine jurisdiction and applicable law (if there is no choice of law) is habitual residence – of the deceased, or the common habitual residence or most recent common habitual residence of the spouses.

C. Habitual Residence in CJEU Case Law

In the context of the Brussels IIa Regulation, the CJEU interpreted the concept of habitual residence several times.

i. Starting Point: Physical Presence

The starting point and essential element to determine habitual residence always is physical presence in the State in question.[46] Furthermore, other factors have to show 'that that presence is not in any way temporary or intermittent and that the residence [of the child] reflects some degree of integration in a social and family environment'.[47]

[42] See, eg, SL Gössl, 'Art 8 Rome III' in B Gsell, S Lorenz and W Krüger (eds), *beck-online.GROSSKOMMENTAR zum Zivilrecht* (Beck 2020) para 15; R Lamont, 'Habitual Residence and Brussels II bis: Developing Concepts for European Private International Family Law' (2007) 3 *Journal of Private International Law* 261, 262; P Rogerson, 'Habitual Residence: The New Domicile?' (2000) 49 *ICLQ* 86.

[43] Reg 2201/2003 concerning jurisdiction and the recognition and enforcement of judgments in matrimonial matters and the matters of parental responsibility [2003] OJ L338.

[44] Reg 2019/1111 on jurisdiction, the recognition and enforcement of decisions in matrimonial matters and the matters of parental responsibility, and on international child abduction [2019] OJ L178.

[45] Reg 650/2012 on jurisdiction, applicable law, recognition and enforcement of decisions and acceptance and enforcement of authentic instruments in matters of succession [2012] OJ L201; Reg 1103/2016 implementing enhanced cooperation in the area of jurisdiction, applicable law and the recognition and enforcement of decisions in matters of matrimonial property regimes [2016] OJ L183; Reg 1104/2016 implementing enhanced cooperation in the area of jurisdiction, applicable law and the recognition and enforcement of decisions in matters of the property consequences of registered partnerships [2016] OJ L183; Reg 2010/1259 implementing enhanced cooperation in the area of the law applicable to divorce and legal separation [2010] OJ L343.

[46] See C 523/07 *A* [2009] para 38; C 497/10 PPU *Mercredi* [2010] para 49; C-499/15 *W, V v X* [2017] paras 60–62; C 111/17 PPU *OL v PQ* [2017] para 43; C 512/17 *HR* [2018] para 41; C-393/18 PPU *UD v XB* [2018] para 59 et seq, esp 63, 70.

[47] See *A* (n 46) para 38; C 376/14 PPU *C v M* [2014] para 51; *OL v PQ* (n 46) para 42; *HR* (n 46) para 41.

ii. (Minor) Relevance of the Parties' Intention

The parties' or parents' intent to settle in that State was initially regarded as an important factor to determine a high degree of integration.[48] Initial inspiration was probably derived from the case law regarding habitual residence in the context of social security law.[49] Nevertheless, in *C v M* the Court had held that such an intent could not be relevant in cases where the parents could not be sure that a change of the child's residence would be permanent.[50] Furthermore, in *A* and in *OL v PQ*, the Court narrowed the parents' intent to a 'manifested' intent, eg, manifested by 'certain tangible steps such as the purchase or lease of a residence in the host Member State'.[51] Subsequently, the Court concluded in *OL v PQ* that 'the intention of the parents cannot as a general rule by itself be crucial to the determination of the habitual residence …, but constitutes an "indicator" capable of complementing a body of other consistent evidence'.[52] Furthermore, even in the case that a mother was coerced by the father to change the country and give birth there, thus, where the child was placed in a country against the will of the mother (and principal care giver), habitual residence had to be determined independently of this intentional factor. As the physical presence of the child was never in the country of the mother's intention, a habitual residence could not be established there.[53]

Thus, while the parents' intention initially was regarded as one important factor to determine the habitual residence, it then was downgraded to an indicator that could only complement other already consistent evidence but not form such evidence in itself. In the same decision, *OL v PQ*, the Court affirmed that direction by stating that the initial intent of the parent cannot take precedence over other facts, such as a continuous residence in another State.[54] Thus, habitual residence is strictly narrowed down to a factual concept.[55] Subjective factors, especially the parties' intention, can only confirm an already determined factual result, but cannot be used to question it.[56] Consequently, legal preliminary questions, especially the exercise of custody rights, do not influence the determination of habitual residence.[57] This interpretation is also justified by the objective of Brussels IIa to create legal certainty and ensure a quick and effective procedure.[58]

iii. Relevance for Other Regulations

The decisions based on a factual understanding of habitual residence were linked, inter alia, with the best interests of the child, a very regulation-specific argument. Nevertheless, the other arguments can be generalised and extended to other regulations, especially regarding legal certainty and the principle of proximity as basic principles of EU private international law. As some first decisions in the context of the Succession Regulation and the Insolvency Regulation[59] show,

[48] *A* (n 46) para 40; *Mercredi* (n 46) para 50; *C v M* (n 47) para 52.
[49] C-90/97 *Swaddling* [1999] ECR I-2801 I-1075; see also Lamont (n 42) 264 et seq.
[50] *C v M* (n 47) para 55.
[51] *A* (n 46) para 40; *OL v PQ* (n 46) para 46; see also *HR* (n 46) para 46.
[52] *OL v PQ* (n 46) para 47.
[53] *UD v XB* (n 46) para 61 et seq.
[54] *OL v PQ* (n 46) para 51.
[55] Ibid, para 51; C-85/18 PPU *CV v DU* [2018] para 49.
[56] See, eg, *HR* (n 46) para 61, 64 et seq.
[57] *OL v PQ* (n 46) para 52 et seq; *HR* (n 46) para 65.
[58] *OL v PQ* (n 46) para 56 et seq.
[59] Reg 2015/848 on insolvency proceedings [2015] OJ L141.

the CJEU confirmed the importance of these core elements defining the concept of habitual residence: focusing on a factual, physical approach that follows the principles of legal certainty and proximity.[60]

D. Interim Conclusion

Regarding the question whether habitual residence focuses merely on factual issues or also takes into consideration the intent of the parties, the CJEU's reasoning in the case law involved some manoeuvring. The CJEU initially proposed to regard the parties' intention as the core element of habitual residence. In the course of several decisions, the court finally decisively reached the conclusion that the parties' intention is one of the least important factors to determine habitual residence. Each decision confirms more strongly that habitual residence is a question of fact. In academic literature, this approach has been questioned. As habitual residence also reflects the autonomy of the people involved (in the case of children exercised by their parents), the intention of the parties to settle at a certain place should receive more attention.[61]

V. Geneva Refugee Convention Interpretation

The Geneva Refugee Convention of 1951 and its 1967 Protocol are mainly important for questions of asylum law. Nevertheless, Article 12 contains an important private international law rule: Paragraph 1 provides that 'The personal status of a refugee shall be governed by the law of the country of his domicile or, if he has no domicile, by the law of the country of his residence'. Furthermore, paragraph 2 provides for the respect of rights vested under an earlier applicable law. The drafters of the Convention explicitly did not choose nationality as a connecting factor as they regarded the refugee as a person who had intentionally broken with the home country and also should not be forced to accept the law of a country that made them flee.[62]

As the Convention does not define the concept of 'domicile', the general agreement seems to be that the definition belongs to the *lex fori*. Consequently, common law jurisdictions use the concept of domicile as known by their legal systems while civil law jurisdictions translate 'domicile' into their understanding of habitual residence.[63] This creates uncertainty for a refugee, being treated as 'domiciled' in different ways, depending on the jurisdiction. A more consistent approach and a consistent way to interpret the connecting factor 'domicile' would be feasible.

[60] See C-253/19 *MH, NI v OJ, Novo Banco SA* [2020] para 27 et seq; C-80/19 *EE* [2020] para 37 et seq.

[61] eg, M-P Weller and B Rentsch, '"Habitual Residence": A Plea for "Settled Intention"' in S Leible (ed), *General Principles of European Private International Law* (Wolters Kluwer 2016) 171 et seq; see also, Gössl, (n 42) para 20.

[62] JC Hathaway, 'Reconciling Refugee Autonomy to Private International Law: Keynote address to the conference on "Families Beyond Borders: Migration with or without Private International Law?" Ghent University March 28, 2019', paras 12–14.

[63] See, eg, *Alam v Minister of Home Affairs* (2012) 3414/2010 12 ZAECPEHC (High Court of South Africa) (*domicile*); similar in Australia in *Armstead v Armstead* [1954] Vic LR 733 (Supreme Court of Victoria) 734, cited after Hathaway, ibid, para 34; as to the Belgium practice, see J Verhellen, 'Cross-Border Portability of Refugees' Personal Status' (2017) 31 *Journal of Refugee Studies* 427, 436 et seq; in general, S Arnold, 'Der Flüchtlingsbegriff der Genfer Flüchtlingskonvention im Kontext des Internationalen Privatrechts' in C Budzikiewicz et al (eds), *Migration und IPR* (Dialog Internationales Familienrecht Band 1 Nomos 2018) 25 et seq; C Budzikiewicz, 'Der gewöhnliche Aufenthalt von Flüchtlingen als Anknüpfungspunkt im Internationalen Privat- und Privatverfahrensrecht' in C Budzikiewicz et al (eds), *Migration und IPR* (Dialog Internationales Familienrecht Band 1 Nomos 2018) 99; different (only common law domicile) Hathaway, ibid, para 19.

Furthermore, a connecting factor that reconciles both common law and civil law approaches and, furthermore, puts the refugee and the refugee's autonomy at the centre of attention, should not neglect the refugee's intention.[64]

VI. National Courts

To conclude, some national courts interpreting the concept of habitual residence have also taken the stance that the parties' intention should not only have a minor but a more prominent role to determine the concept of habitual residence. All agree that at least some kind of physical presence is still the starting point.

For example, the Austrian Supreme Court (OGH) decided that the intention of a person should have a 'considerable weight' (*erhebliches Gewicht*) in determining habitual residence.[65] Similarly, the German Supreme Court (BGH) held that the habitual residence of a newborn was never established at the place of birth (Ukraine) but only in Germany, as all possible parents involved agreed on the fact that the newborn should later live in Germany. Thus, even though the BGH in the same decision initially affirmed that habitual residence is a factual concept and referred to the CJEU case law regarding Brussels IIa, the Court finally focused on the intention of the (possible) parents to exclude Ukraine as the country of habitual residence.[66]

In the US Supreme Court case of *Monasky v Taglieri*,[67] Justice Ginsburg confirmed that habitual residence of a child is not supposed to be limited to certain elements but requires an overall assessment of the facts and the intentions of the parties. Finally, English law has increasingly emphasised focusing on the entire circumstances of the child to determine habitual residence but still regards intention as an important element, especially where the physical presence has only been for a short period.[68]

VII. Discussion

This contribution has examined connecting factors and highlighted the importance of habitual residence as the primary connecting factor especially in private international family law. Both in the HCCH and the EU, it has been consistently adopted as the primary connecting factor for the assumption of jurisdiction in cross-border disputes affecting both children and adults. On the other hand, nationality and domicile have steadily lost importance on the global stage – an important development for a truly global private international law that should not remain stuck in an approach originating from either the common or the civil law tradition.

[64] Similarly Hathaway, ibid, para 37 et seq; see also Verhellen, ibid, 437.

[65] [2009] 1Ob115/09g, [2009] Zak 360 (OGH); [2015] 6Ob194/14v, [2015] iFamZ 146 (OGH); but see also (2012) 5Ob104/12y; 5Ob201/12p unalex AT-825 (OGH); to the Austrian Habitual Residence, see recently, B Lurger, 'Die erblasste Schöne "IPRG" und die Herausforderungen der Zukunft' in F Heindler (ed), *Festschrift 40 Jahre IPRG* (IGKK/IACPIL Jan Sramek Verlag 2020) 100.

[66] [2019] XII ZB 530/17, [2019] FamRZ 892 (BGH); to habitual residence under German law see SL Gössl, 'Art 14 EGBGB' in K Johannsen, D Henrich and C Althammer (eds), *Familienrecht: Scheidung, Unterhalt, Verfahren: Kommentar*, 7th edn (2020) para 11 et seq.

[67] *Monasky v Taglieri* (n 30).

[68] *Re LC* [2014] UKSC 1; Lamont (n 42) 264; R Schuz, 'Habitual Residence of the Child Revisited: A Trilogy of Cases in the UK Supreme Court' (2014) 26 *Child and Family Law Quarterly* 342, 350 et seq.

Some courts from civil and common law jurisdictions differ from the autonomous EU approach regarding the weight they put on the intention of the parties to determine habitual residence. While the CJEU limits intention to a factor that can only complement an already consistent body of (factual) evidence, some national courts see the parties' intention as an important factor. It cannot overcome the lack of any physical presence. Nevertheless, it is not only a complementing factor but has at least the same weight as a longer period of stay in confirming or (where there is no period of presence) negating the habitual residence of a person.

As a global connecting factor for personal relationships we propose to use the already widely accepted habitual residence. Whilst habitual residence is mainly described as based on a factual assessment of the links the individual has to a particular country, we demonstrate how important intention can be in determining habitual residence. This has highlighted the continuing influence of different legal traditions on the interpretation of globalised concepts in private international family law.

Intention creates uncertainty for third parties in that it is subjective and potentially whimsical, but to give due regard to intention enhances the autonomy of the parties – and enhances their personal legal certainty. As domestic family laws seek increasingly to enhance individual autonomy in decision-making, it is appropriate that account should be taken of individual choices and the reasons for them in an international family law context, including connecting factors. Parties should be able to influence their family rights and obligations, rather than having them entirely imposed upon them.

We recognise that personal intention cannot be the only factor in the determination of habitual residence and is part of a contextual assessment. Nevertheless, it should not be interpreted as strictly factual. Instead, the party's intention to settle or not settle at a certain place should have an equally relevant weight to determine the place where she or he is habitually resident. In case of vulnerable parties, importance should be placed on the question of what the 'real' intention of the party is – a refugee, for example, might be vulnerable but their actions will have very clear intentions. As an autonomous subject she or he is able to form a clear and personal intention.[69]

The same logic can potentially be applied to adults in the context of the Hague Convention on the International Protection of Adults 2000. Where an intention can be evinced by the subject, this can be accounted for in determining habitual residence where relevant, but if the adult concerned lacks capacity or cannot convey an intention effectively, a factual assessment may be conducted in the context of the care arrangements of the individual. This issue also arises for children: the child may not yet have the capacity to form an intention, but the parents' intention may form part of the factual assessment and the older the child is, the more relevant their opinions will be to the determination of habitual residence. In these cases, it seems more feasible to require an overall assessment of the case, including the facts but also possible intentions, to determine the habitual residence of the child or the person involved.

VIII. Final Conclusions

1. Habitual residence seems the most feasible connecting factor to determine the law of the person in a truly global private international law, as it does not stem from either the common or the civil law traditions but can combine elements of both legal traditions and seems to be accepted in other jurisdictions as well.

[69] Verhellen (n 63) 437.

2. The most important Hague Conventions use habitual residence as a central connecting factor. There is a lack of global consistency in interpreting the concept and the extent to which habitual residence should be limited to a mere factual notion, or can also include intentional elements.
3. In EU private international law habitual residence is also one of the central connecting factors. The CJEU understands the concept as mainly factual while the parties' intention plays a subordinate – if any – role.
4. The Geneva Refugee Convention uses the concept of 'domicile' as the main connecting factor but does not define it. Therefore, national courts interpret 'domicile' as 'domicile' (common law courts) or 'habitual residence' (civil law courts), referring to their national understandings of the notion.
5. While the CJEU understands habitual residence merely factually, in implementing EU private international family law, national courts have also put some importance on the intention of the parties.
6. Habitual residence in general should not be limited to a factual understanding. Instead, intention should have at least equal importance in determining the concept. This reflects the growing acceptance in substantive law that legal issues relating to the person, eg, family law issues, should focus on the autonomy of the persons involved. Private international and domestic law should correspond in that notion, thus regarding the parties' intention also as central to determine the connecting factor.
7. An exception should be made for children or adults lacking capacity to form a clear intention. In these cases, an overall assessment of the facts and the intentions of the parents/guardians should be made to determine habitual residence.

5

Renvoi and Preliminary Questions

MARIA HOOK

I. Introduction

This chapter considers the role of two concepts – the doctrine of renvoi, and the problem of the preliminary (or incidental) question – in the unification of private international law. The concepts are distinct. They each have their own methodology and body of law. Yet they tend to be relevant in similar circumstances, and they both raise the question whether the conflict of laws rules of the *lex causae* should be applied. For example, when determining the validity of a marriage, a court may consider answering the question *not* by reference to the internal law of the *lex causae* but by reference to the law identified by the applicable law rules of the *lex causae* (renvoi). Similarly, when determining the validity of a marriage for the purposes of determining a party's entitlement to inherit as a wife, the court may consider dispensing with its own conflict of laws rules on status altogether, in order to apply the conflict of laws rules of the law governing the succession (incidental question).

Although there is no agreed rationale for the use of these concepts, they are both associated with the aim of harmonious decision-making. By applying the conflict of laws rules of the *lex causae*, the court adopts an approach that is more likely to accord with the approach that would have been taken in the foreign court. This raises interesting questions in the context of the unification of private international law. Is there any need (or room) for rules on renvoi and the incidental question in uniform choice of law instruments, the very purpose of which is to avoid inconsistent decision-making? That is the main question to be answered in this chapter.

II. Renvoi

A. The Doctrine of Renvoi

Private international law involves many questions of great methodological complexity. One such question is whether applicable law rules, when they identify a foreign *lex causae*, refer to the internal law of the *lex causae*, or whether the reference includes the applicable law rules of that law. For example, the forum's applicable law rules may call for the application of the *lex situs*, the law of Country X; but a court in Country X would apply not its own law but the law of the domicile, which is the law of the forum. In these circumstances, the forum court might give effect to the applicable law rules of Country X and apply its own substantive law. This strategy is known as renvoi.

Some legal systems embrace renvoi; some reject it; and many fall somewhere in the middle.[1] There are a number of (often interrelated) 'versions' of renvoi. There is single renvoi (where the court applies the internal law designated by the foreign law's applicable law rules); double renvoi (where the court applies the law designated by the foreign law's applicable law rules, including the applicable law rules of that law); the foreign court theory of renvoi (where the court puts itself in the shoes of the foreign court and applies not only the foreign court's applicable law rules, but also its theory of renvoi); and renvoi that allows for one – or both – of remission (a reference back to the law of the forum) and transmission (a reference to the law of a third State). Moreover, the reasons that have been relied upon to justify the doctrine range widely. They include the protection of sovereignty and comity, international harmony of decision-making and, when used flexibly, its general potential to support the aims of the conflict of laws. It is no exaggeration to say that the doctrine reflects 'the most famous dispute in conflicts law'.[2]

If States agree on the unification of applicable law rules, then there is usually no need for renvoi, because there is no longer a conflict of applicable law rules.[3] However, the problem of renvoi may still arise where the uniform applicable law rule identifies the law of a non-Contracting State. More generally, unified rules of renvoi may serve one of three functions:[4]

- First, in the absence of uniform applicable law rules, a general rule of renvoi may be relied upon to increase the chances of uniform decision-making.
- Second, uniform applicable law rules may be combined with a rule of renvoi allowing reference to be made to applicable law rules of Contracting States.
- Third, uniform rules of applicable law may be usefully complemented by rules that either provide for or exclude the application of renvoi in relation to the law of non-Contracting States.

B. Unifying Renvoi Instead of Applicable Law Rules

In the absence of uniform applicable law rules, a general rule of renvoi may be relied upon to increase the chances of uniform decision-making. The idea is that, by taking a uniform approach to the resolution of conflicts between applicable law rules, courts are ultimately more likely to apply the same substantive law to a case.

There is currently no general international rule on the application or exclusion of renvoi.[5] Attempts to introduce such a rule were made many decades ago, culminating in the Hague Renvoi Convention.[6] A preliminary draft of the Convention provided for a general regulation of renvoi.[7] The final draft, however, was limited to conflicts between rules of domicile and nationality. There was at the time a significant divide between States that relied on domicile, and States that relied

[1] See R Garnett and M Sonnentag, 'Renvoi' in J Basedow et al (eds), *Encyclopedia of Private International Law*, Vol I (Edward Elgar 2017) 1537.

[2] E Rabel, *The Conflict of Laws* (University of Michigan Press 1945) 70.

[3] See, eg, JG Sauveplanne, 'Renvoi' in K Zweigert and K Drobnig (eds), *International Encyclopedia of Comparative Law* (Brill 1991) [19].

[4] For a detailed overview of the use of renvoi in international instruments, see A Davì, 'Le renvoi en droit international privé contemporain' (2010) 352 *Hague Collected Courses* 254–358; ED Graue, 'Rück- und Weiterverweisung (renvoi) in den Haager Abkommen' (1993) 57 *Rabels Zeitschrift* 26.

[5] *cf* the relevant principles identified by Institut de Droit International, 'Taking Foreign Private International Law to Account' (Session of Berlin 1999).

[6] Convention of 15 June 1955 relating to the settlement of the conflicts between the law of nationality and the law of domicile (not in force).

[7] Sauveplanne (n 3) [21].

on nationality as a personal connecting factor. There was no hope of reaching a general consensus on which connecting factor should prevail; and the best option was to enhance uniform decision-making through the introduction of a shared approach to renvoi in relation to those connecting factors. Despite its relatively modest aim, the Convention was ultimately unsuccessful and never came into force.[8]

C. Renvoi by Virtue of Applicable Law Rules of Contracting States

In some rare cases, uniform applicable law rules allow for renvoi by designating the applicable law rules of the law of a Contracting State.

i. A Conflict between Uniform Applicable Law Rules

The most obvious scenario that might create a need for this form of renvoi would be where a Contracting State has agreed to overlapping – but inconsistent – applicable law rules, with the result that one agreement must take precedence over the other. There has been some discussion of such a scenario in the context of EU law. For example, if a French court is bound to give effect to the Hague Convention on Traffic Accidents[9] over the Rome II Regulation,[10] but a German court would apply French law pursuant to the Regulation, would it be appropriate for the German court to give effect to the French renvoi (thus applying the Hague Convention)?[11] This situation is analogous to renvoi vis-à-vis non-Contracting States, which is discussed below.

ii. A Uniform Applicable Law Rule Designating the Applicable Law Rules of the lex causae *of a Contracting State*

An altogether different scenario is where the uniform applicable law rule is the same in both Contracting States, but the rule nevertheless leaves room for the application of the country's own applicable law rules. There seem to be three distinct rationales that have been relied upon to justify this form of renvoi.

As a compromise solution: An early example is Article 1 of the Hague Marriage Convention 1902.[12] It provided that the capacity to marry was governed by the spouse's national law. However, it also required that, where the national law expressly provided for the application of another law (eg, the law of domicile or the law of the place of marriage), a renvoi to that law had to be followed. This rule had been included at Switzerland's insistence, because Switzerland's applicable law rules would have given effect to the law of the place of marriage. It offered a compromise solution that opened the way for Switzerland's accession to the Convention.

However, combining a uniform applicable law rule with the possibility of renvoi from the law so identified affords only a modest role to that country's applicable law rules. Here, the solution led to the rather curious result that the law of the place of marriage was only applicable where the spouses were Swiss nationals.[13] Even though the Swiss seemed to consider Article 1 a diplomatic

[8] Belgium and the Netherlands were the only States to ratify the Convention.

[9] Convention of 4 May 1971 on the Law Applicable to Traffic Accidents.

[10] Reg 864/2007 on the law applicable to non-contractual obligations [2007] OJ L199/40.

[11] The answer provided by the Regulation is 'no': Art 24. See more generally, J von Hein, 'Renvoi in European Private International Law' in S Leible (ed), *General Principles of European Private International Law* (Kluwer 2016) 245.

[12] Convention of 12 June 1902 Governing Conflicts of Laws Concerning Marriage.

[13] See A Overbeck, 'The Hague Conference and Swiss Private International Law' [1993] *Netherlands International Law Review* 93, 100.

success,[14] it was a small victory, and the price – a complex and confusing applicable law rule – not insignificant. There must be better solutions for ensuring a uniform applicable law approach that is palatable to countries with differing applicable law rules. The introduction of escape clauses may be one of them.

Operating *in favorem*: A more recent example of an international provision that accepts a renvoi from a Contracting Party's own applicable law rules is Article 3(a) of the Hague Child Abduction Convention.[15] It states that rights of custody are referred to 'the law of the State' – not the *internal* 'law of the State' – in which the child was habitually resident immediately before the removal or retention. This omission was apparently deliberate, opening the door to the doctrine of renvoi.[16] The Explanatory Report notes that 'the spirit of the Convention appears to point to the choice of the one which, in each particular case, would [recognise] that custody had actually been exercised'.[17] This would ensure that the Convention – the operation of which depends on the existence of rights of custody – would be given as wide a scope as possible. In other words, Article 3 was supposed to operate '*in favorem*' a finding that the applicant had rights of custody.[18]

This approach has serious flaws.[19] In particular, there is a question whether the same result could not be brought about through a more straightforward applicable law rule of alternative reference (eg, submitting the issue of custody rights to either the law of habitual residence or the law of domicile, depending on which law leads to the existence of such rights). Such rules of alternative reference are increasingly common in modern private international law.

If, for whatever reason, a renvoi *in favorem* rule is considered preferable to a rule of alternative reference, its intended effect should be made express.[20] In particular, Article 3(a) is not drafted in a way that ensures that the renvoi will operate *in favorem*, with the result that an English court once applied renvoi to *defeat* the applicant's rights of custody.[21]

Serving a jurisdictional function: A third example is the selection of the choice of law regime of the *forum prorogatum* to determine the substantive validity of exclusive choice of court agreements in the Hague Choice of Court Convention 2005.[22] The Convention provides that the substantive validity of such an agreement is determined under the law of the chosen State, which includes that State's applicable law rules.[23] This approach ensures that courts apply the applicable law rules of the same country. It seems to perform a jurisdictional function: it recognises that it is the courts of the chosen State that would be best placed to determine the validity of the agreement.[24]

D. Renvoi vis-à-vis Non-Contracting States

The most important function of renvoi in international instruments is to clarify the operation of uniform rules of applicable law vis-à-vis non-Contracting States. If using a uniform applicable

[14] Ibid, 100.
[15] Convention of 25 October 1980 on the Civil Aspects of International Child Abduction.
[16] E Pérez-Vera, 'Explanatory Report on the 1980 Hague Child Abduction Convention' [66], available at: hcch.net.
[17] Ibid, [70].
[18] See K Beevers and J Pérez Milla, 'Child Abduction: Convention 'Rights of Custody' – Who Decides? An Anglo-Spanish Perspective' (2007) 3 *Journal of Private International Law* 201, 226.
[19] But see R Schuz, *The Hague Child Abduction Convention* (Hart Publishing 2013) 170.
[20] Beevers and Pérez Milla (n 18) 226–27.
[21] *Re JB (Child Abduction) (Rights of custody: Spain)* [2003] EWHC 2130, [2004] 1 FLR 796.
[22] Convention of 30 June 2005 on Choice of Court Agreements.
[23] Arts 5, 6 and 9. T Hartley and M Dogauchi, *Explanatory Report on the Convention of 30 June 2005 on Choice of Court Agreements* (Permanent Bureau of the Hague Conference on Private International Law 2005) [125], available at: hcch.net.
[24] See P Beaumont, 'Hague Choice of Court Agreements Convention 2005: Background, Negotiations, Analysis and Current Status' (2009) 5 *Journal of Private International Law* 125, 139–40 (noting that the approach avoids 'a party

law rule leads to the identification of the law of a non-Contracting State, and the applicable law rules of that State point to a different applicable law, the question arises whether the Contracting State should give effect to the renvoi. Thus, uniform applicable law rules tend to be accompanied by rules that either exclude or accept renvoi vis-à-vis non-Contracting States.

The most common approach adopted by the modern Hague Conventions has been to exclude the application of renvoi.[25] For example, Article 12 of the Hague Maintenance Protocol provides that 'the term "law" [in the Protocol] means the law in force in a State other than its choice of law rules';[26] and a provision to the same effect is contained in Article 17 of the Hague Trusts Convention.[27] There are general provisions excluding the application of renvoi in the EU in the Rome I Regulation,[28] the Rome II Regulation[29] and the Rome III Regulation.[30]

However, there are also some Conventions that expressly provide for renvoi. The Hague Succession Convention states, in Article 4, that if the applicable law

> is that of a non-Contracting State, and if the choice of law rules of that State designate, with respect to the whole or part of the succession, the law of another non-Contracting State which would apply its own law, the law of the latter State applies.[31]

The EU similarly recognises renvoi in relation to matters of succession.[32]

Another example of an express inclusion of renvoi can be found in the Hague Convention on the Protection of Children.[33] Although Article 21(1) generally excludes renvoi, Article 21(2) provides for renvoi in relation to the law governing the attribution or extinction of parental responsibility. Thus, Article 21(2) states that if the law governing parental responsibility is that of a non-Contracting State 'and if the choice of law rules of that State designate the law of another non-Contracting State which would apply its own law, the law of the latter State applies'. However, 'if that other non-Contracting State would not apply its own law, the applicable law is that designated by [the Convention]'.

Finally, the Hague Principles on Choice of Law in International Commercial Contracts enable parties to agree that the chosen law includes an express reference to renvoi.[34] Thus, Article 8 provides that '[a] choice of law does not refer to rules of private international law of the law chosen by the parties unless the parties expressly provide otherwise'.

i. Rationale for Renvoi vis-à-vis Non-Contracting States

There are competing views as to the desirability of including renvoi vis-à-vis non-Contracting States, which may prove a sticking point in future projects to create uniform applicable law rules. Broadly speaking, there are two schools of thought.

running to a forum that does not like such agreements and getting them struck down there on the basis of some spurious forum rule on consent'). The jurisdictional function of renvoi is considered further below (nn 45 and 46).

[25] For a detailed overview of the use of renvoi in international instruments, see Davì (n 4) and Graue (n 4).

[26] Protocol of 23 November 2007 on the Law Applicable to Maintenance Obligations.

[27] Convention of 1 July 1985 on the Law Applicable to Trusts and on their Recognition.

[28] Art 20 Reg 593/2008 on the law applicable to contractual obligations [2008] OJ L177/6.

[29] Art 24 Reg 864/2007 on the law applicable to non-contractual obligations [2007] OJ L199/40.

[30] Art 11 Reg 1259/2010 implementing enhanced cooperation in the area of the law applicable to divorce and legal separation [2010] OJ L343/10.

[31] Convention of 1 August 1989 on the Law Applicable to Succession to the Estates of Deceased Persons (not in force).

[32] Art 34 Succession Regulation 650/2012 [2012] OJ L201/107.

[33] Convention of 19 October 1996 on Jurisdiction, Applicable Law, Recognition, Enforcement and Co-operation in Respect of Parental Responsibility and Measures for the Protection of Children.

[34] Principles on Choice of Law in International Commercial Contracts (19 March 2015).

The first school of thought is that inclusion of renvoi is generally undesirable. The main argument is that renvoi would undermine the very uniformity that international instruments seek to establish – ie, the uniform application of applicable law rules by Contracting States.[35] The problem here is *not* that the application of renvoi would lead to inconsistent decision-making. Because all Contracting States would give effect to the renvoi, they would, ultimately, apply the same law to the dispute. Rather, the problem seems to be that the application of renvoi undermines the overall success of the chosen applicable law rule.[36] If Contracting States are happy to defer to the applicable law rules of non-Contracting States, it seems that a global convergence of applicable law will be less likely. Another argument is that renvoi would interfere with the certainty and predictability of applicable law, and that it would place an unnecessary burden on courts (or administrative authorities) and parties.[37]

The second school of thought is that the inclusion of renvoi may be appropriate in certain circumstances.[38] Domestic rules of renvoi vary in scope and content, so there would likely be some disagreement as to what these circumstances are. Nevertheless, it is possible to identify two guiding considerations.

The first is that renvoi should only be included if its application is consistent with the policy of the applicable law rule. For example, renvoi has been considered incompatible with an applicable law rule designed to facilitate divorce,[39] and with a carefully crafted applicable law rule designed to uphold maintenance obligations.[40] There is also a tension between partial renvoi and the principle of unity of succession (which is reflected in Article 4 of the Hague Succession Convention).[41] If the aim is to achieve a particular substantive result, it is usually preferable to rely on alternative applicable law rules rather than a renvoi *in favorem*.[42] On the other hand, a limited form of renvoi may be consistent with the principle of party autonomy where parties have expressly provided for it. This is recognised in the Hague Principles on Choice of Law in International Commercial Contracts, but not in the Hague Trusts Convention, which does not enable the settlor of a trust to select the whole of the chosen law,[43] or the Hague Succession Convention.

The second consideration is that, in some areas more than others, uniformity of decision vis-à-vis non-Contracting States continues to be an important goal. These areas include matters of status and property.[44] Another way of looking at the same problem is to say that uniformity of decision is particularly important where the forum court seeks to 'recognise, support or supplement the subject-matter jurisdiction of the court of the lex causae'.[45] For example, there may be a need to defer to the courts of the *lex causae* if those courts have the exclusive power to enforce a judgment or if the *lex causae* is treated as the source of a person's status. In that sense, renvoi may serve a jurisdictional function.[46]

[35] See the references cited by von Hein (n 11) 242; W Chen and G Goldstein, 'The Asian Principles of Private International Law: objectives, contents, structure and selected topics on choice of law' (2017) 13 *Journal of Private International Law* 411, 424–25; Sauveplanne (n 3) [19].

[36] See Davì (n 4) 255–56.

[37] Chen and Goldstein (n 35) 425; von Hein (n 11) 243.

[38] See, eg, von Hein (n 11) 243; recital 57 of the EU Succession Regulation.

[39] von Hein, ibid 251.

[40] A Bonomi, 'Explanatory Report on the Protocol of 23 November 2007 on the Law Applicable to Maintenance Obligations' [175], available at: hcch.net.

[41] D Waters, 'Explanatory Report on the 1989 Hague Succession Convention' [57]–[59], available at: hcch.net.

[42] von Hein (n 11) 231; but *cf* Garnett and Sonnentag (n 1) 1543. *cf* also above the discussion regarding the Hague Child Abduction Convention.

[43] For criticism of the latter, J Harris, *The Hague Trusts Convention* (Hart Publishing 2002) 388–89.

[44] See Garnett and Sonnentag (n 1) 1541 (in relation to status).

[45] M Hook and J Wass, *The Conflict of Laws in New Zealand* (LexisNexis 2020) [4.54].

[46] *cf* the argument that renvoi serves a function that is similar to the doctrine of forum (non) conveniens: A Briggs, 'In Praise and Defence of *Renvoi*' (1998) 47 *ICLQ* 877.

There has been criticism of the exclusion of renvoi from Article 7 of the Hague Trusts Convention. Without renvoi, the claimant has 'an incentive to forum shop and sue in the state where the law applicable on the substance is more favourable to him', and the court may reach a decision that is inconsistent with the law of the country where the trust would need to be enforced.[47] The inclusion of renvoi in the Hague Succession Convention (and, indeed, the EU Succession Regulation) was intended to address similar concerns.[48] Thus, the Explanatory Report to the Hague Succession Convention asks:[49]

> If two non-Contracting States are able to reach a point where there is unity between them as to which law shall apply, why destroy that unity in the name of the Convention which proclaims unity as its object?

Ultimately, the decision for or against renvoi may require the balancing of a range of competing considerations. It is no longer correct simply to say that the exclusion of renvoi is '[the] solution … of all the modern conventions'.[50] Rather, there are some areas of law, and some connecting factors, where the policies underlying the uniform applicable law rule may support the application of renvoi vis-à-vis non-Contracting States.[51] In some cases, the most appropriate solution may be to combine a rule of renvoi with one or several exceptions, to allow courts to take account of the most important competing considerations. This approach has been adopted in Article 34 of the EU Succession Regulation.[52]

ii. What Kind of Renvoi?

If there are grounds for including renvoi, the next question is what *kind* of renvoi should be adopted. National practice varies widely, recognising forms of single renvoi, double renvoi, remission and/or transmission and approaches based on the foreign court theory. Uniform rules of applicable law usually specify the particular form of renvoi that is to be followed. Although this may reduce flexibility, it ensures uniformity of decision-making (at least as between Contracting States), and it means that the rule is much more accessible and easier to apply. Whatever approach is adopted, it must be consistent with the particular reasons that have been identified as justifying the renvoi.

There are two main points that a uniform rule of renvoi could usefully address.[53] First, at what point does the renvoi end? For example, Article 4 of the Hague Succession Convention provides for renvoi to the extent that the State designated by the renvoi 'would apply its own law'. If the law of that country would lead to a different law being applicable, the applicable law is the internal law of the non-Contracting State identified by the uniform applicable law rule in Article 3. Article 21(2) of the Child Protection Convention follows the same approach (but makes it even more explicit). The rationale behind this particular solution appears to be that there is little value in recognising renvoi unless it leads to uniformity of decision as between the two non-Contracting States.[54] This reasoning has been criticised as arbitrary.[55]

[47] Harris (n 43) 388.
[48] Waters (n 41) [57]–[59]; see recital 57 to the Succession Regulation.
[49] Waters, ibid, [59].
[50] A Overbeck, 'Explanatory Report on the 1985 Hague Trusts Convention' [160], available at: hcch.net.
[51] *cf* von Hein (n 11) 273, in relation to EU Law.
[52] A Davì, 'Article 34: Renvoi' in A-L Calvo Caravaca et al (eds), *The EU Succession Regulation: A Commentary* (Cambridge University Press 2016) [9]–[17].
[53] *cf* Davì, ibid, [21] ff.
[54] Davì, ibid, [5].
[55] von Hein (n 11) 254–55.

Second, does the renvoi allow for remission as well as transmission? Both Article 4 of the Hague Succession Convention and Article 21(2) of the Child Protection Convention are limited to transmission (that is, they allow for renvoi identifying the law of a non-Contracting State, but they do not give effect to renvoi identifying the law of a Contracting State). For example, Article 21(2) states that 'if the choice of law rules of [the non-Contracting State] designate the law of another non-Contracting State … the law of the latter State applies'. The exclusion of remission was not without controversy,[56] and a different approach has since been adopted in the EU Succession Regulation, Article 34(1)(a) of which provides that a remission to the law of a Member State will be accepted. This solution is said to combine 'the general benefits of coordination' with 'the possibility of applying the substantive law of the forum State or that of another Member State', which may be easier to ascertain and apply than the law of a third country.[57]

III. Preliminary Question

A. The Problem of the Preliminary Question

It is well accepted that the process of identifying the applicable law starts with characterisation of the issue. A dispute may raise several issues, in the sense that there is more than one issue that must be characterised and that attracts its own distinct applicable law rule. Ordinarily, this does not create any difficulty. For example, parties may have a dispute that covers both the formal validity of a contract and the consequences of its breach, and the court will simply apply the law governing the formal validity of contracts to the former, and the law governing the contract more generally to the latter.

In some cases, however, the issues are so closely interconnected that it could – potentially – be inappropriate to characterise the issues separately in the normal fashion. This occurs where one issue logically depends on the other. For example, to determine whether a claimant is entitled to succeed to their deceased wife's property, it may be necessary first to determine whether the claimant was the spouse of the deceased. In such cases it may – in some circumstances – be inappropriate to apply the forum's applicable law rules to both issues. This problem is generally known as the problem of the 'incidental question' or 'preliminary question'.[58]

In such cases, the court is faced with two main options: applying its own conflict of laws rules to the incidental issue, in the way that it usually would; or applying the conflict of laws rules of the law governing the main issue, so that it determines the dispute as a court in that country would. In other words, the question is: in determining whether the claimant is a spouse for the purposes of a claim in succession governed by a foreign *lex causae*, does the court apply its own conflict of laws rules, or does it apply the conflict of laws rules of the *lex causae*? This chapter refers to these two competing options as the *lex fori* approach and the *lex causae* approach for ease of reference.[59]

[56] P Lagarde, 'Explanatory Report on the 1996 Hague Child Protection Convention' [116], available at: hcch.net; see Davì (n 4) 280 ff, fn 575.

[57] Davì (n 52) [5].

[58] L Collins (ed), *Dicey, Morris and Collins on the Conflict of Laws*, 14th edn (Sweet & Maxwell 2006) [2-049].

[59] This terminology is used more widely: see, eg, S Gössl, 'Preliminary Questions in EU Private International Law' (2012) 8 *Journal of Private International Law* 63; and L Carballo Piñeiro and A Bonomi, 'Incidental (preliminary) question' in J Basedow et al (eds), *Encyclopedia of Private International Law*, Vol I (Edward Elgar 2017) 912.

B. Relevance of the Problem

There has been limited engagement with the *lex causae* approach in doctrine. In fact, with the exception of Germany, courts have rarely raised the issue of the incidental question (at least not explicitly).[60] Many scholars consider that there is no justifiable basis for treating incidental questions any differently from 'ordinary' issues: they argue that the *lex causae* approach is unprincipled and unnecessarily complicated, and that there should be only one substantive answer to an incidental issue in the courts of the forum.[61] More generally, it seems to be accepted that, if the *lex causae* approach deserves any recognition at all,[62] it is largely confined to questions of status and should be applied with flexibility.[63]

One may legitimately wonder, therefore, whether international drafters should bother to concern themselves with the problem of the incidental question.[64] In this author's view, the answer is 'yes'. The problem continues to give rise to debate. Traditionally, reasons that have been relied upon as justifying a *lex causae* approach include:[65]

- International harmony (the importance of treating the incidental issue in the same way as the court of the *lex causae*).
- The need to give 'full effect' to the applicable law rule governing the main issue (by prioritising the closer connection of the *lex causae* to the incidental issue).[66]
- Substantive policy (the ability to apply the conflict of laws rules of the *lex causae in favorem*, in order to achieve a particular result such as the recognition of a marriage).
- The territoriality of status (the idea that a person may be a spouse in one country but not in another because a person has as many statuses as there are countries).[67]

Moreover, in the particular context of unification, the *lex causae* approach has been identified as a useful tool to achieve international harmony as between Contracting States.[68] Here, the problem of the incidental question may arise where:

- the *lex causae* is that of a non-Contracting State to a uniform applicable law rule on an incidental issue (eg, the law of succession is the law of B, but country B is not a Contracting State to a uniform conflict of laws rule on the validity of marriage); or
- the uniform applicable law rule concerns an issue that may depend on the resolution of an incidental question (eg, there is a uniform applicable law rule designating the law of country B as the law governing the succession, but the claimant's entitlement depends on their status).[69]

[60] T Schmidt, 'The Incidental Question in Private International Law' (1992) 233 *Hague Collected Courses* 396. For an overview of the incidental question generally, see Carballo Piñeiro and Bonomi, ibid.

[61] See Carballo Piñeiro and Bonomi, ibid, 915–16.

[62] See, eg, P Torremans et al, *Cheshire, North & Fawcett on Private International Law*, 15th edn (Oxford University Press 2017) 54.

[63] See the review of cases in AE Gotlieb, 'The Incidental Question Revisited – Theory and Practice in the Conflict of Laws' (1977) 26 *ICLQ* 734; see Collins (n 58) [2-049].

[64] *cf* G Mäsch, 'Preliminary Question' in S Leible (ed), *General Principles of European Private International Law* (Kluwer 2016).

[65] See generally, Carballo Piñeiro and Bonomi (n 59) 917–21.

[66] Collins (n 58) [2-050].

[67] Hook and Wass (n 45) [4.37]; *cf* the argument that marriage is not an 'all-purpose concept': WLM Reese, 'The Hague Convention on Celebration and Recognition of the Validity of Marriages' (1979) 20 *Virginia Journal of International Law* 25, 30. It is unclear whether this theory reflects modern ways of thinking about family relationships (see, eg, A Bucher, 'La dimension sociale du droit international privé' (2009) 341 *Hague Collected Courses* 246).

[68] See, eg, the references cited in D Solomon, 'Die Anknüpfung von Vorfragen im Europäischen Internationalen Privatrecht' in J Bernreuther et al (eds), *Festschrift für Ulrich Spellenberg* (Sellier 2010) 355, 366–67.

[69] See also Schmidt (n 60) 387.

C. Where the Uniform Applicable Law Rule Designates the Law of an Issue that may Arise Incidentally

Where an international instrument provides for uniform conflict of laws rules on an issue that may arise incidentally, there is a question whether the rules are – or should be – applicable to such incidental issues. In practice, this question is most likely to arise where the uniform conflict of laws rule relates to a question of status. For example, validity of marriage is an issue that, more often than not, arises incidentally in the context of another claim, such as a claim for rights of succession or maintenance. If a uniform applicable law rule on the validity of marriage applies in all cases, including cases where the issue arises incidentally, then the marriage will be treated the same for all purposes. A couple will be either married or unmarried, regardless of whether the question arises in its own right or whether it is asked for the purposes of succession, maintenance or some other matter that may be governed by a foreign law.

As between Contracting States, there is every reason to adopt an expansive approach and to apply the rule even where the issue arises incidentally. In fact, it should be immaterial whether the issue arises incidentally or not. If all Contracting States apply the same rule governing the validity of the marriage, and the issue arises in the context of a succession claim governed by the *lex causae* of a Contracting State, then the problem of the incidental question disappears.

Things are not so straightforward where the *lex causae* is the law of a non-Contracting State, because then the conflict of laws rule applied by that State may differ from the uniform rule. Here, the question arises whether Contracting States may, or should, adopt the *lex causae* approach, with the result that courts would refer the issue to the conflict of laws rules of the *lex causae* of the non-Contracting State. For example, to determine whether the claimant is a spouse entitled to succeed to property under the law of a non-Contracting State, they would apply the conflict of laws rules of the law governing succession. The result would be that a couple might be married for some purposes but not others. Here, the usual arguments in favour of the *lex causae* approach come into play.

These arguments must be balanced against the usual arguments against the *lex causae* approach – and in particular, in this context, the benefits of adopting an indivisible approach to questions of status across all Contracting States. Thus, under the *lex fori* approach, courts in Contracting States will apply the same law to determine the parties' status, regardless of what the claim is and whether it is governed by the *lex causae* of a non-Contracting State. The *lex causae* approach may also undermine wider goals of international convergence, providing little incentive to non-Contracting States to move towards adoption of the uniform applicable law rule. Thus, Article 11 of the Hague Divorce Convention provides that, where a State must recognise a divorce under the Convention, it 'may not preclude either spouse from remarrying on the ground that the law of another State does not recognise that divorce'.[70]

In light of these arguments, it is possible that the *lex causae* approach could still play a limited role in international instruments dealing with questions of status. An interesting compromise in this regard was struck by Article 12 of the Hague Marriage Convention.[71] Article 12(1) provides, as a general rule, that the Convention's rules 'shall apply even where the recognition of the validity

[70] Convention of 1 June 1970 on the Recognition of Divorces and Legal Separations. See the *Explanatory Report* by P Bellet and B Goldman [54], available at: on hcch.net.

[71] Convention of 14 March 1978 on Celebration and Recognition of the Validity of Marriages. Reese referred to it as 'ingenious': Reese (n 67) 33.

of a marriage is to be dealt with as an incidental question in the context of another question' (adopting a *lex fori* approach); but Article 12(2) sets out an important exception to the rule, which is that the Convention's rules 'need not be applied where that other question, under the choice of law rules of the forum, is governed by the law of a non-Contracting State'. The effect of this latter provision is to clarify that the uniform rules need not be applied where the issue arises incidentally and the main question is governed by the *lex causae* of a non-Contracting State. This exception could be applied flexibly, allowing for the kind of case-by-case assessment that the *lex causae* approach seems to require.[72]

D. Where the Uniform Applicable Law Rule Designates the *lex causae* of the 'Main' Question

Where an international instrument provides for uniform conflict of laws rules on an issue that may depend on the resolution of an incidental question, there is a question whether the instrument should clarify the approach to be taken to the incidental question. For example, the Hague Maintenance Protocol provides for a uniform applicable law rule for determining rights and obligations of maintenance;[73] but a person's entitlement to maintenance depends on the nature of their relationship with the respondent (eg, whether the person is the respondent's child or spouse). So if the nature of the relationship is in dispute, but the instrument does not provide a separate uniform applicable law rule to govern this incidental question, then what is the court to do? Should it apply its own conflict of laws rules (adopting the *lex fori* approach), or should it apply the conflict of laws rules of the law that has been designated as being applicable by the uniform applicable law rule (adopting the *lex causae* approach)?

So far, international instruments have avoided answering the question directly. For example, Article 1(1) of the Hague Maintenance Protocol provides that it 'shall determine the law applicable to maintenance obligations arising from a family relationship, parentage, marriage or affinity'.[74] Neither has the EU tackled the question.[75]

The result is a considerable degree of uncertainty, and at least one author has concluded that 'there is no clear way of resolving it any time soon'.[76] As a minimum, future instruments should make it clear whether they set out to regulate the problem of the incidental question, to avoid the kind of lingering confusion that has formed part of the discourse on the Maintenance Conventions.[77] Beyond that, there appear to be three broad options:

- avoidance of the problem of the incidental question by including the incidental issue within the scope of the applicable law rule designating the *lex causae* (this may be referred to as the 'absorption' approach);[78]
- express adoption of the *lex fori* approach; or
- express recognition of a residual role for the *lex causae* approach.

[72] But see s 88F of the Marriage Act 1961 (Aust), which provides for a *lex fori* approach.
[73] Protocol of 23 November 2007 on the Law Applicable to Maintenance Obligations.
[74] *cf* recital 21 to the EU Maintenance Regulation 4/2009 [2009] OJ L7/1.
[75] See, eg, the Succession Regulation and Art 1(2) of the Rome III Regulation.
[76] L Walker, *Maintenance and Child Support in Private International Law* (Hart Publishing 2015) 76.
[77] See M Verwilghen, 'Explanatory Report on the 1973 Hague Maintenance Conventions' [124], available at: hcch.net.
[78] Schmidt (n 60) 387.

i. Absorption Approach

The first option refers to the application of the *internal* law of the *lex causae* to the incidental issue. In effect, the instrument would clarify that questions of status fall within the scope of the uniform applicable law rule. There is precedent for this solution. Article 1(1) of the 1956 Hague Maintenance Convention provided that '[t]he law of the habitual residence of the child shall determine whether, to what extent, and from whom the child may claim maintenance'; and courts relied on this provision – and a similar provision in Article 10 of the 1973 Hague Maintenance Convention – to apply the internal law of the country of habitual residence to questions of parentage.[79] In fact, a provision to that effect was almost included in the 1973 text.[80] The absorption approach received favourable attention in subsequent discussions, especially insofar as parentage was concerned.[81] The Explanatory Report to the Maintenance Protocol notes that 'there is nothing to prevent [courts from] reemploying' the solution.[82] However, the Report also concludes that the solution is not binding on Contracting States (despite Article 11(a) largely recreating Article 10 of the 1973 Convention). State practice remains mixed, and academic commentary, too, is divided.[83]

Would there be merit in an instrument endorsing this absorption approach? There has been limited principled discussion of this question.[84] An obvious concern is that the policies underlying the respective conflict of laws rules – the conflict of laws rule on status and the applicable law identifying the *lex causae* – would be quite different. This would mean that characterising questions of status as falling within the rule of the *lex causae* may be a rather arbitrary exercise.[85] Moreover, the approach could undermine efforts to apply uniform conflict of laws rules on questions of status.

ii. Lex fori *versus* lex causae *Approach*

This leaves a choice between the *lex fori* approach and the (whole of the) *lex causae* approach. This choice is often framed as one between internal (domestic) consistency and international harmony.[86] If the former approach is adopted, a person's status will be the same domestically for all purposes, regardless of whether the main question (such as the existence of maintenance obligations) is governed by foreign law or not; but in the context of resolving the main question, the person's status may differ from country to country. If the latter approach is adopted, then for the purposes of the particular 'main' question, a person's status will be the same in all States that have adopted the uniform applicable law rule (eg, all Contracting Parties to the Hague Maintenance Protocol would apply the conflict of laws rules of the particular *lex causae* that has been designated as applicable by the Protocol).

[79] Verwilghen (n 77) [127]; Schmidt (n 60) 388–92.

[80] Verwilghen, ibid, [127].

[81] Conclusions of the 1995 Special Commission on the operation of the Hague and New York (1956) Conventions on maintenance obligations (Prel Doc 10, May 1996) [29], [30]; Report on the First Meeting of the Special Commission on the International Recovery of Child Support and other Forms of Family Maintenance (Prel Doc 5, March 2003) [124]; Parentage and International Child Support Responses to the 2002 Questionnaire and an Analysis of the Issues (Prel Doc 4, April 2003) [33].

[82] Bonomi (n 40) [24].

[83] Schmidt (n 60) 390–93.

[84] See Schmidt, ibid; Solomon (n 68) 360 ff.

[85] See Solomon, ibid, 364–65.

[86] Gössl (n 59); Solomon, ibid, 367–68. Both authors argue in favour of a *lex fori* approach.

More generally, the choice would have to engage with the wider debate about the relevance of the incidental question. For example, if there were still support for the proposition that questions of status are somehow territorial and divisible, a limited *lex causae* approach may well be justifiable. Similarly, a *lex causae* approach may be desirable in cases involving party autonomy (where the *lex causae* is the result of a choice of law). Perhaps there would be scope for a flexible solution that requires courts to select one of the two approaches in the context of the particular case, by reference to a non-exhaustive list of relevant considerations.

Given the controversial nature of this question, agreement may be impossible. In these circumstances, an appropriate compromise may be to leave Contracting States to apply the *lex causae* approach as they see fit (which would be consistent with Article 12 of the Hague Marriage Convention). After all, the problem arises only in cases where the conflict of laws rules of the *lex causae* differ from those applicable in the forum court. The more harmonisation (or unification) there is of applicable law rules for issues that are likely to arise incidentally (eg, the validity of marriage), the less likely it is that courts will need to worry about their approach to the incidental question. From this perspective, therefore, the unification of conflict of laws rules on questions of status would be a priority.

6

Public Policy and Mandatory Provisions

TREVOR HARTLEY

I. Introduction

This chapter is concerned with public policy and mandatory provisions. It explores their function in comparative private international law and in the multilateral solutions adopted in the Hague Conference on Private International Law. Its aim is to consider how these concepts should be used in order to develop global private international law.

II. The Concept of an Escape Mechanism

Public policy and mandatory provisions are both escape mechanisms. To understand them, we must first consider the structure of a legal rule. The basic idea of a legal rule is to lay down a system that makes it possible to begin with the facts of a case and to end up with a legal conclusion. Private international law is concerned with one segment of this process: deciding whether the court has jurisdiction; determination of the applicable law; and deciding whether or not to recognise a foreign judgment. The decision-maker starts with facts and ends up with a legal conclusion.

The decision-making process is based on policies and principles on the one hand and legal rules on the other. Policies and principles are concerned with objectives – what the law is seeking to achieve – and with the methods by which this is to be done. They are not normally applied directly to the facts: only the legal rules are. However, the policies and principles help to mould the legal rules and influence the way they are applied to the facts.

In private international law, the policies and principles are normally based on the interests of the parties and seek to do justice to them. They seek to give effect to the reasonable expectations of the parties, especially where they have based their conduct on such expectations. The specific legal rules – eg, regarding applicable law – are to a large extent based on this policy.

In many legal systems, the legal rules applicable in private international law are largely designed to be applied in an objective and value-free way in order to secure legal certainty – in order to make it possible, that is, to predict the outcome of a legal decision with reasonable certainty. In applicable law, one starts with a legal category – eg, substantive validity of a marriage – and uses a predetermined connecting factor – eg, the domicile of the parties – to indicate the applicable law. The system has the outward appearance of clockwork, producing a predetermined result.

However, legal certainty and predictability of outcome can come at too high a price. In some situations, the result may be unacceptable. For this reason, an escape mechanism is needed, some special rule that allows the court to abort the normal process and reach an outcome more acceptable to its values.

For example, assume that a man and a woman go through a ceremony of marriage within the territory of the forum. The marriage is entirely valid under the law of the forum. However, the couple are both domiciled in another country – let us call it the Republic of Ruritania – and under the law of that country the marriage is void as to its substance because the parties are of different races. If the applicable-law rule of the forum for the substantive validity of a marriage is that it must comply with the law of the domicile of the parties, the outcome, if the normal procedure is followed, would be that the courts of the forum would have to declare the marriage void. However, most Western countries would today regard such an outcome as unacceptable. So, the doctrine of public policy can come to the rescue: it can operate to prevent the application of the racist rule of the law of Ruritania. The court can hold the marriage valid.

Public policy thus constitutes a device, intended to apply only in exceptional circumstances, which allows the court to change track, to take into account considerations that would not normally be relevant – usually, the content of the applicable law. The decision-making procedure is changed, or at least a new loop is added. The essence of this new loop is that the applicable law is scrutinised to ensure that it complies with the fundamental values of the forum.

In its purest form, public policy is based solely on the content of a legal rule. It is because that content is unacceptable that public policy decrees that it will not be applied. In this form, it is only applied negatively – that is, to block the application of a rule of law that would otherwise be applicable. However, in common law countries, public policy has been applied positively to require the application of a rule of law that would not otherwise be applicable. Most often, this would be a rule of forum law; but it can also be a rule of foreign law.

An example of the positive application of the law of a foreign State would be the English case of *Regazzoni v Sethia*.[1] This case concerned a contract, between an English company and a Swiss resident, for the sale of jute. Delivery was to be in Italy. Although the contract did not say so, both parties knew that the jute would come from India and that it would be re-exported to South Africa. The applicable law was English law, under which the contract was valid. However, it was invalid under Indian law since the export of jute from India to South Africa was illegal under Indian law.[2] The House of Lords applied public policy to hold the contract invalid.

It is generally recognised that public policy is a much narrower concept as applied in private international law than in domestic law.[3]

The concept of a mandatory provision is also a form of escape mechanism. Mandatory provisions are provisions that have to be applied – despite the fact that they are not part of the normal applicable law – because their application in the particular circumstances of the case is regarded as essential by a particular country for safeguarding its public interests.[4]

Article 9(1) of the Rome I Regulation contains a definition of an 'overriding mandatory provision' as follows:

> Overriding mandatory provisions are provisions the respect for which is regarded as crucial by a country for safeguarding its public interests, such as its political, social or economic organisation, to such an

[1] [1958] AC 301; [1957] 3 WLR 752; [1957] 3 All ER 286 (HL).

[2] This was an expression of India's opposition to the policy of apartheid practised in South Africa at the time.

[3] See, eg, the Commentary to the Hague Principles of Choice of Law in International Commercial Contracts 2015, point 11.25 and Symeon Symeonides, 'Law Applicable to Contracts', ch 14 in this book.

[4] See Symeonides, ibid.

> extent that they are applicable to any situation falling within their scope, irrespective of the law otherwise applicable to the contract under this Regulation.

Mandatory provisions have been adopted in international instruments on the basis of ideas developed by writers in civil law countries.[5] In such instruments – which generally restrict the concept of public policy to its negative application – they play much the same role as public policy does in the common law when it is positively applied.

III. When Public Policy Applies

In international instruments on private international law, public policy most often applies in the field of applicable law, where it may be used to block the application of a rule of foreign law that would otherwise be applicable. It can also apply as a ground for not recognising and enforcing a foreign judgment that would otherwise be recognised and enforced; and it may apply as a ground for not giving effect to a foreign choice of court agreement.

A. Applicable Law

Under the Hague Principles of Choice of Law in International Commercial Contracts 2015, it is provided by Article 11(3):

> A court may exclude application of a provision of the law chosen by the parties only if and to the extent that the result of such application would be manifestly incompatible[6] with fundamental notions of public policy (*ordre public*) of the forum.

This is an example of the negative application of public policy: it excludes the application of a provision of law that would otherwise be applicable.

There is a similar provision in Article 21 of the Rome I Regulation:[7]

> The application of a provision of the law of any country specified by this Regulation may be refused only if such application is manifestly incompatible with the public policy (*ordre public*) of the forum.

The Report on the equivalent provision in the Rome Convention (by Professor Giuliano and Professor Lagarde) states that a court may refuse to apply a provision on this ground only if its *application* in the case would lead to a consequence contrary to the public policy of the forum, not if the foreign law is merely in the *abstract* contrary to the forum's public policy.[8] The Commentary on the Hague Principles makes a similar point.[9]

[5] See, in particular, LI de Winter, 'Dwingend Recht bij Internationale Overeenkomsten' (1964) 11 *Nederlands Tijdschrift voor Internationaal Recht* 329; see also J Schultsz, 'Dutch Antecedents and Parallels to Article 7 of the EEC Contracts Convention of 1980' (1990) 54 *RabelsZ* 267. For Dutch cases in which the principle was considered by the court (though not in the end applied) see *The Alnati, Hoge Raad* (Dutch Supreme Court) 13 May 1966, [1966] *Schip en Schade* 50; [1977] *Ned Jur* No 3 16; Schultsz, ibid 273 et seq; *CEP v Sensor Nederland*, Pres Rb Den Haag, 17 September 1982, *Rechtspraak van de Week/Kort Geding* 1982, No 167; Schultsz, ibid 279–81.

[6] The phrase 'manifestly incompatible' is standard in recent international instruments: see, eg, the Hague Agency Convention (1978) Art 17; the Rome Convention (1980) Art 16; and the Rome I Regulation (2008) Art 21.

[7] See also Art 26 of the Rome II Regulation.

[8] [1980] OJ C282/1 at 38.

[9] See point 11.26.

B. Recognition and Enforcement of Judgments

Public policy can also constitute a ground for refusing to recognise or enforce a foreign judgment that would otherwise be recognised or enforced. Thus Article 7(1)(c) of the Hague Convention of 2019 on the Recognition and Enforcement of Foreign Judgments in Civil or Commercial Matters provides that recognition or enforcement may be refused if

> recognition or enforcement would be manifestly incompatible with the public policy of the requested State, including situations where the specific proceedings leading to the judgment were incompatible with fundamental principles of procedural fairness of that State and situations involving infringements of security or sovereignty of that State.

This is similar to the provisions on public policy in the context of applicable law quoted above, but it makes clear that the procedure that resulted in the judgment may also give rise to issues of public policy.[10]

C. Choice of Court Agreements

The 2005 Hague Convention on Choice of Court Agreements contains two provisions on public policy.[11] Article 6(c) provides that a court of a Contracting State other than that of the chosen court must suspend or dismiss proceedings to which an exclusive choice of court agreement applies unless 'giving effect to the agreement would lead to a manifest injustice or would be manifestly contrary to the public policy of the State of the court seised'. Here public policy would almost invariably relate not to the content of the choice of court agreement itself but to the consequences of giving effect to it. An example would be where one of the parties would not get a fair trial in the designated court.

The second provision is Article 9(e), which provides that recognition or enforcement of a judgment given under a choice of court agreement may be refused if it would be 'manifestly incompatible with the public policy of the requested State, including situations where the specific proceedings leading to the judgment were incompatible with fundamental principles of procedural fairness of that State'. This is similar to the provision discussed above in the Hague Judgments Convention 2019.

IV. When Mandatory Rules Apply

Mandatory rules apply to decide the substance of a case regardless of the content of the applicable law. A striking feature of their formulation in many international instruments is the difference between the treatment of mandatory rules of forum law and of those of foreign law.

[10] See F Garcimartín and G Saumier, *Explanatory Report on the 2019 HCCH Judgments Convention* (HCCH 2020) 59–60, available at: assets.hcch.net/docs/a1b0b0fc-95b1-4544-935b-b842534a120f.pdf.

[11] See T Hartley and M Dogauchi, *Explanatory Report on the Convention of 30 June 2005 on Choice of Court Agreements* (Permanent Bureau of the Hague Conference on Private International Law 2005) paras 153 and 189–90, available at: www.hcch.net/en/publications-and-studies/details4/?pid=3959. Some common law countries have similar rules. For Canada, see *Douez v Facebook Inc*, 2017 SCC 33 discussed in LW Harris, 'Understanding Public Policy Limits to the Enforceability of Forum Selection Clauses after *Douez v Facebook*' (2019) 15 *Journal of Private International Law* 50.

Thus Article 11(1) of the Hague Principles of Choice of Law in International Commercial Contracts, which deals with the mandatory rules of the forum, provides:

> These Principles shall not prevent a court from applying overriding mandatory provisions of the law of the forum which apply irrespective of the law chosen by the parties.

On the other hand, Article 11(2), which deals with mandatory rules of foreign law, states:

> The law of the forum determines when a court may or must apply or take into account overriding mandatory provisions of another law.

There is no requirement to apply foreign mandatory rules: the forum is merely *permitted* to do so if its law so requires.[12]

This difference between forum law and foreign law is also to be found in the Rome I Regulation. Mandatory provisions of forum law are dealt with in Article 9(2), which states simply and clearly that 'Nothing in this Regulation shall restrict the application of the overriding mandatory provisions of the law of the forum'.

Mandatory provisions of foreign law are dealt with in Article 9(3). This is very different. It provides:

> Effect may be given to the overriding mandatory provisions of the law of the country where the obligations arising out of the contract have to be or have been performed, in so far as those overriding mandatory provisions render the performance of the contract unlawful. In considering whether to give effect to those provisions, regard shall be had to their nature and purpose and to the consequences of their application or non-application.

As under the Hague Principles, this never *requires* the application of foreign mandatory provisions. It merely *permits* it and then only in limited circumstances. This means that, both where the Hague Principles are adopted and where Rome I applies, the outcome of a case can depend on which court is hearing it.

What would happen if the case of *Regazzoni v Sethia* (discussed above)[13] came before a court applying Rome I? There was a contract for the sale of jute to be delivered in Italy. Although not stated in the contract, both parties knew that the jute could come only from India. They also knew that the buyer intended to re-export it to South Africa. Under Indian law the export of jute in these circumstances was illegal. We assume that there was an express or implied choice of law in favour of the law of England, under which the contract was valid and legal. Under Rome I, Article 9(3), a court other than an Indian court could apply Indian law in these circumstances only if 'the obligations arising out of the contract have to be or have been performed' in India and only if Indian law renders the performance of the contract unlawful. Could one say that one of the obligations arising out of the contract had to be performed in India? This raises a problem because the contract did not stipulate where the jute was to come from (though both parties knew that it could only come from India).

The limited scope of Article 9(3) of Rome I (mandatory provisions of a foreign legal system) may be illustrated by the decision of the Court of Justice of the European Union (CJEU) in *Republik Griechenland v Nikiforidis*.[14] This case arose out of the austerity measures adopted in

[12] A similar distinction is found in the Hague Trusts Convention 1985 Art 16. A State by reservation can even preclude any possibility of applying the mandatory rules of a State other than those of the forum or the applicable law, see Jonathan Harris, 'Trusts', ch 23 in this book. Art 11 of the Hague Securities Convention 2006 only permits the application of some mandatory rules of the forum and not of any other law apart from the applicable law.

[13] (n 1).

[14] Case C-135/15, EU:C:2016:774.

the financial crisis in Europe. Mr Nikiforidis was a teacher at a Greek school in Germany. He was paid by the Greek Government. The EU required Greece to cut its deficit and Greece passed laws to do this, including reducing the salaries of public employees. The Greek Government reduced Nikiforidis's salary and he sued Greece in Germany. The Bundesarbeitsgericht (Federal Labour Court) referred questions to the CJEU including the meaning of Article 9 of Rome I. His contract of employment was governed by German law, and the forum and his place of work were both in Germany. Was the German court precluded by Article 9 from applying any law other than German law?

The CJEU said that Article 9 permitted application of mandatory provisions only if they form part of the law of the forum (Germany) or the law of the place of performance (Germany). So there was no way in which the Greek provisions could be applied as law.[15] This was unfortunate since it was unjust that an austerity measure applicable to all State employees should not be applied to Mr Nikiforidis just because he worked outside Greece. A different result could probably have been reached under the doctrine of the positive application of public policy[16] and under the American doctrine of interest analysis (discussed below).

V. The Doctrine of Overriding Statutes: Another Mechanism with Similar Effects

In many common law countries, rules of forum law can, if contained in a statute, be applied under another doctrine, that of an 'overriding statute'.[17] The doctrine of overriding statutes is based on the fact that, in most common law countries, applicable law is not entrenched or otherwise given a special status. Conflicts rules can be set aside by a statute, just like any other rule of common law (or of an earlier statute). Consequently, if a statute provides – expressly or by implication – that it is to override the normal applicable-law rules, it will do so. This means that the provision in question must be a mandatory rule in the sense explained above.[18]

The Australian case of *Freehold Land Investments v Queensland Estates*[19] is an example. Queensland legislation, the Auctioneers, Real Estate Agents, Debt Collectors and Motor Dealers Acts 1922 to 1961, required estate agents to be licensed, and provided that unlicensed estate agents had no legal right to their fees. The developers of land in Queensland engaged a firm of Hong Kong estate agents, Golden Acres, to find buyers for the land. It seems that they were hoping to attract Chinese buyers. Golden Acres was licensed in Hong Kong but not in Queensland. They found some buyers but the developers refused to pay the agreed commission because Golden

[15] The CJEU said that they could be taken into account as a matter of fact, insofar as this was provided for by a substantive rule of the law that was applicable to the contract under the Rome I Regulation. However, the German courts did not do this: see S Francq, 'Public Policy and Overriding Mandatory Rules as Mirrors of the EU System of Thought and Integration' in J von Hein, E-M Kieninger and G Rühl (eds), *How European is European Private International Law?* (Intersentia 2019) 305, 322, fn 70.

[16] *cf Lemenda Trading Co v African Middle East Petroleum Co* [1988] 3 WLR 735.

[17] Much of the original thinking on this topic was done by JHC Morris. See, eg, Morris, 'The Scope of the Carriage of Goods by Sea Act 1971' (1979) 95 *LQR* 59. Morris's ideas were challenged by FA Mann (see (1979) 95 *LQR* 346) but were upheld by the English courts: *The Hollandia (The Morviken)* [1982] QB 872, especially Lord Denning MR 880–84. This case went on appeal to the House of Lords but no further challenges were made to Morris's approach: [1983] AC 565.

[18] On the dangers of applying the doctrine of an overriding statute more widely than this, see M Hook, 'The "statutist trap" and subject matter jurisdiction' (2017) 13 *Journal of Private International Law* 435. The author accepts the legitimacy of the approach, provided it is confined to cases where the statute is intended to have overriding mandatory force: ibid, 441.

[19] (1970) 123 CLR 418 (High Court of Australia).

Acres was not licensed in Queensland. The law governing the contract between the developers and Golden Acres appeared to be that of Hong Kong. However, the highest court in Australia ruled that the statute overrode the normal applicable law rules.

The problem here is the interpretation of the statute. If it does not expressly say when it is to apply in an international context, how is one to decide whether it is intended to do so in a particular case? Thus, in the *Queensland Estates* case, when was the rule in the statute intended to apply? Was it applicable when the land was in Queensland, or when the buyer came from Queensland? The statute contained no express provision on the point, but the court held that it applied when the estate agent *acted* in Queensland. Golden Acres had carried out activities as an estate agent in Queensland, so the statute applied and it could not claim commission.

The doctrine applies only to *forum* statutes, not to *foreign* statutes. If the *Queensland Estates* case had come before a court in Hong Kong, and if it had considered that the applicable law was Hong Kong law, there would have been no question of applying the Queensland legislation as an overriding statute. As we shall see below, however, this *is* possible under the American doctrine of interest analysis.

Where forum law is involved, the doctrine is similar to that of a mandatory provision. For example, a case like *Freehold Land Investments v Queensland Estates* would be decided in almost exactly the same way under Rome I or the Hague Principles.[20] The court would first have to consider whether the rule that an unlicensed estate agent cannot claim commission constituted a mandatory provision. If it did, it would be 'applicable to any situation falling within [its] scope'. The court would then have to decide what its scope was. This would entail exactly the same exercise as that performed by the High Court of Australia. If it concluded that it applied to any estate agent who acted as such within the territory in which the statute applied, it would then be applicable.

The *Ingmar* case[21] is an example of a similar case decided by the CJEU. The English court had to decide whether UK legislation, the Commercial Agents (Council Directive) Regulations 1993, implementing an EU directive, the Commercial Agents Directive,[22] applied in the case. The Directive and the Regulations gave a commercial agent the right to claim compensation on the termination of the agency, even if there was no provision for this in the contract.

The case concerned a contract between a UK company, Ingmar, and an American company, Eaton Leonard Technologies (ELT), under which Ingmar was to act as agent for ELT in the UK and Ireland. The contract contained an express choice of the law of California. The relationship subsequently came to an end and Ingmar sued ELT in England for compensation. ELT argued that the UK legislation implementing the Directive could not apply in view of the choice of California law. Ingmar said that the provision granting a right to compensation was what today would be called a mandatory provision and should be applied, irrespective of any choice of law, whenever the agent operated in an EU Member State. The English court asked the CJEU whether this was a correct interpretation of the Directive. The CJEU said it was. The English court then awarded the agent compensation.[23] This case must have been decided under the English doctrine of an overriding statute.[24]

[20] The position would be similar under an instrument based on the Hague Principles of Choice of Law in International Commercial Contracts 2015: see Art 11(1) of the Principles.

[21] Case C-381/98 *Ingmar* [2000] ECR I-9305.

[22] Council Directive 86/653/EEC, [1986] OJ L382/17.

[23] See *Ingmar GB Ltd v Eaton Leonard Inc* [2001] CLC 1825 (QBD).

[24] For another case on the Commercial Agents Directive where the overriding mandatory provisions of the forum (Belgium) going beyond the terms of the Directive were applicable, see Case C-184/12 *Unamar* EU:C:2013:663.

The doctrine of an overriding statute can also be applied to jurisdictional questions. *The Hollandia (The Morviken)*[25] is an example. This concerned a contract for the carriage of goods by sea from a UK port to a port in a foreign country. The bills of lading contained a choice of law clause applying Dutch law and a choice of court clause giving exclusive jurisdiction to the courts of the Netherlands. The contract also exempted the carrier from liability for damage to the goods above a rather small sum (approximately £250 per package). The goods were damaged and the cargo owners sued the carriers in England.

The background to this case consisted of two international Conventions. The first, the International Convention for the Unification of Certain Rules of Law relating to Bills of Lading, was signed in Brussels in 1924. It provided that the bill of lading could not exempt the carrier below a specified minimum sum (equivalent to approximately £250) from liability for damage to, or loss of, the goods. The Netherlands was a Party to this Convention and the provisions of this Convention were part of the law of that country. The UK was also a Party.

Subsequently, however, the provisions of this Convention were amended at a conference held in Visby, Sweden. These were adopted by the Brussels Protocol 1968. One of the amendments was that the minimum liability was increased from approximately £250 per package to approximately £11,000 per package. The UK ratified the Brussels Protocol and it was enacted into UK law by the Carriage of Goods by Sea Act 1971. This applied the new rules to all shipments out of a port in the UK. At the time, the Netherlands had not adopted the new rules. The result was that the lower level of liability applied under Dutch law and the higher level under UK law.

The level of liability specified in the bills of lading was the minimum that was legal under Dutch law. It was far below the minimum in UK law. The carriers argued that the English courts should give effect to the choice of court agreement and decline jurisdiction. The cargo owners would then have had no choice but to sue in the Netherlands, where the court would uphold the low level of liability.

The House of Lords held that the proceedings should not be stayed. The UK statute provided that the new rules were to have the force of law in the UK. The Rules provided that any clause in a contract of carriage lessening the liability of the carrier below the minimum permitted by the Rules would be null and void. The House of Lords held that since the choice of court agreement would have the practical effect of lessening the liability of the carrier, it was null and void in the UK.

This case was decided in 1982 before either the Brussels Convention[26] or the 2005 Hague Convention on Choice of Court Agreements became applicable in the UK.[27] If it had been decided when the Hague Convention, but no other relevant instrument, was applicable and the case was not excluded from the scope of the Hague Convention,[28] the same result could have been reached on the basis of Article 6(c) of the Convention (discussed above). This, it will be remembered, provides that a court in a Contracting State other than that of the designated court is not obliged to suspend or dismiss the proceedings if this would be manifestly contrary to its public policy.

VI. How Strong an Interest?

Since a conflict of interests can be just as much a problem as a conflict of laws, any system of public policy (or mandatory rules) must have some way of resolving such conflicts. Attention must be given to the strength of a country's interest.

[25] [1983] AC 565 (HL).
[26] The Brussels Convention 1968 came into force in the UK in 1987.
[27] The 2005 Convention became applicable in the UK in 2015.
[28] The 'carriage of passengers and goods' is excluded from the scope of the Convention: Art 2(2)(f).

There are various ways in which this may be done. One is connection, the extent to which a person or set of facts is *connected* with the country of the forum. A country has a greater interest in protecting a person from an unfair rule when that person is connected in some way with the country of the forum than when he or she is not. For example, a country might be more willing to apply public policy to refuse to apply a racist rule of foreign marriage law if the marriage was celebrated in the territory of the forum, or the parties subsequently settled there, than if there was no connection with the forum.[29]

Another way is the degree of conflict. If one takes the policy of preventing child marriage as an example, the *extent* to which the party is below the minimum age is an important factor. If, for example, the minimum age of marriage under the law of the forum is 16, public policy should not be engaged at all if a party is only 15: here the normal applicable law rule should apply. It is only if a party is considerably below 16 that the forum should consider the application of public policy. Here, however, the precise age at which public policy will come into play might also depend on whether there is a significant connection with the forum.[30]

VII. The American Theory of Interest Analysis

Interest analysis is a theory developed by a group of academics among whom Brainerd Currie was pre-eminent.[31] The idea was that applicable-law problems should be solved by considering the interests of the countries concerned, not just in exceptional circumstances, but as the basic applicable-law mechanism for use, at least in theory, in *all* cases.

Under interest analysis, instead of thinking in terms of broad, abstract categories, such as the substantive validity of a contract, the court must focus on a particular rule of law, a rule that applies in a particular country. For example, if the state of Massachusetts has a rule of law that a contract of suretyship is invalid if it is concluded by a married woman, the court must consider whether Massachusetts has an interest in the application of that rule in the case before it.[32] If the surety is a married woman domiciled in Massachusetts, and the person with whom she concludes the contract is domiciled in the state of Maine, a state which does not have a similar rule, the court must consider the interest of each state in the application of its law as regards this question. To do this, it must determine the purpose of the law of each state – what it seeks to achieve – and decide whether that purpose requires its application in the case.

This gives rise to several problems. One is to decide what the purpose of the rule is; a second is to decide whether that purpose requires the application of the rule in the case before the court; and a third is to decide what happens if each state requires the application of its rule to the case before the court.

It is fairly easy to conclude that the purpose of a rule that married women cannot conclude contracts of suretyship is to protect married women from their own rashness.[33] On the other hand, one might think that the purpose of a rule that a person who is a guest in another person's

[29] Nevertheless, in very strong cases, public policy might be applied even if there is no connection.

[30] For a critical account of recent Swedish legislation that runs counter to the principles suggested in the above paragraphs, see M Bogdan, 'Some critical comments on the new Swedish rules on non-recognition of foreign child marriages' (2019) 15 *Journal of Private International Law* 247.

[31] See, in particular, B Currie, 'Married Women's Contracts: A Study in Conflict-of-Laws Method' [1958] *University of Chicago Law Review* 227.

[32] This example is given because it was the issue in a case decided in 1878, *Millikin v Pratt* 125 Mass 374, the case on which Currie based his analysis, ibid.

[33] This was what Currie concluded in the article, ibid.

car cannot sue the driver for injuries if the car is involved in an accident, common in the United States and Canada in the post-war period, is to protect drivers from 'ungrateful' guests. In fact, however, such laws (known as 'guest statutes') were passed to protect insurers from fraudulent claims. It was thought that if the 'guest' was a friend or family member of the driver, the latter might deliberately exaggerate his bad driving in order to help the victim, knowing that the damages would be paid by the insurance company. This example shows that the apparent purpose of a law may not always be its real purpose.

A more difficult problem is to decide when the purpose of the law requires its application in a given case. It seems to be generally accepted that a law of the forum giving effect to basic moral principles should be applied in all cases, irrespective of whether or not the facts have any connection with the territory of the forum. It can hardly be doubted, for example, that courts in Western countries would refuse to apply a foreign law permitting slavery even if the case had no connection with their territory. Consequently, once it is decided that the issue falls into this category, the application of the foreign law will be automatically rejected.

There are other cases, however, in which a country would be regarded as having an interest in the application of its law only if there was a significant connection between the facts and its territory. It was into this category that Currie thought that a married woman's contract of suretyship fell. In the example given above, he considered that Massachusetts had an interest in the application of its rule only when the married woman was domiciled in Massachusetts.

The third problem is what happens if both the countries concerned have an interest in the application of their law. In the example of the married woman's contract of suretyship, it could be said that Massachusetts would have an interest in the application of its rule because the woman was domiciled in Massachusetts; however, Maine would have an interest in the application of its rule (that such contracts were valid) because the creditor was domiciled in Maine. Maine would want to ensure that a contractor domiciled in Maine would be paid the money owing to him.

According to Currie, there is no solution in such a case. The courts of each state would apply the law of their state: if the case came before a court in Massachusetts, the contract of suretyship would be invalid; if the case came before a court in Maine, it would be valid. Later writers, however, have said that the courts of each state should balance the interests of the two states. They should consider which state's interests would be the more impaired if its law were not applied.[34] This has been adopted by some courts.[35]

In other cases, however, a careful analysis will show that only one state has an interest in the application of its law. If a woman domiciled in Maine concludes a contract of suretyship with a creditor domiciled in Massachusetts, Massachusetts would have no interest in the application of its rule that contracts of suretyship concluded by married women were invalid, while Maine would regard such contracts as valid. Both could agree, therefore, that the contract would be upheld. This is what Currie called a 'false conflict'.

Interest analysis comes in various forms and has been applied in different ways in different states. One form, which has been codified in the Restatement of the Law Second Conflict of Laws, has been applied in a number of cases.[36] The question when a court can depart from a choice of law made by the parties is dealt with in §187(2) of the Restatement. §187(2)(b) lays down three requirements for the application of a provision of the law of a state other than that of the chosen law. The first is that the application of the chosen law must be contrary to a fundamental policy

[34] See WF Baxter, 'Choice of Law and the Federal System' (1963) 16 *Stanford Law Review* 1, 18–19. For another approach, see D Cavers, *The Choice-of-Law Process* (University of Michigan Press 1965).

[35] See, eg, *Bernhard v Harrah's Club* 128 Cal Rptr 215 (Supreme Court of California, 1976).

[36] The Restatement is not binding on courts in the United States, but it is nevertheless followed quite often.

of the state of the other law; the second is that the state of that other law must have a materially greater interest than the state of the chosen law in the determination of the question at issue; and the third is that, under the general applicable-law provisions laid down in the Restatement, the law of that other state must be the law that would have applied in the absence of an effective choice.[37]

The case of *Newcomb v Daniels, Saltz, Mongeluzzi & Barrett*[38] shows how this provision is applied. The case concerned a rule of New Jersey law limiting the fees that attorneys could charge a client. Newcomb, a resident of New Jersey, had been injured in an industrial accident in New Jersey. Mongeluzzi, a member of the defendant law firm, approached him in his home in New Jersey and offered to obtain compensation for him on the basis of a contingent fee of 40 per cent. Newcomb accepted the offer. Mongeluzzi was admitted to practise in both New Jersey, where a contingent fee of 40 per cent was unlawful,[39] and in Pennsylvania, where it was lawful.

Proceedings were brought in Pennsylvania and the case was settled for $1 million. Newcomb refused to give 40 per cent of this to the law firm. He hired new attorneys and brought proceedings in a court in New Jersey. The New Jersey court decided the case on the assumption that the parties had chosen the law of Pennsylvania to govern the fee agreement. It applied interest analysis as set out in §187(2)(b). It held that even if the parties intended Pennsylvania law to apply, the New Jersey rule should govern because the application of Pennsylvania law would be contrary to a fundamental policy of New Jersey and that New Jersey had a materially greater interest in the application of its law than Pennsylvania. It said that the purpose of the New Jersey rule was to protect clients negotiating fee arrangements from the greater knowledge and bargaining power of their attorneys. Although Pennsylvania would have an interest in protecting its citizens from overreaching attorneys, it considered that Pennsylvania's interest would not apply where the client was a New Jersey citizen injured in New Jersey who negotiated his contingent fee contract in New Jersey with a New-Jersey-licensed attorney. So the attorney was entitled to no more than what was permitted by New Jersey law.

VIII. Interest Analysis Compared with Conventional PIL Theories

How does interest analysis compare with the conventional PIL theories discussed previously? If we compare §187(2)(b) of the Restatement with Article 11 of the Hague Principles or with Article 9 of Rome I, we see some interesting differences. The first is that, under the Restatement, mandatory rules of forum law and mandatory rules of foreign law are dealt with in the same way and in the same provision, §187(2). Under the conventional PIL instruments, on the other hand, they receive very different treatment. Another difference is that the Restatement provides that the interests of the two states in the application of their law to the issue in question must be balanced: the law of the other state will be applied only if it has a materially greater interest.

The application of §187(2)(b) to mandatory rules of the forum was illustrated above.[40] The reasoning of the American court is not very different from what the reasoning would be of a court

[37] The law that would apply in the absence of an effective choice is set out in §188 of the Restatement. It is the law of the state which, with respect to the particular issue before the court, has the most significant relationship to the transaction and the parties. The Restatement provides guidelines for the determination of this law.

[38] 847 F Supp 1244 (DNJ 1994); affirmed 67 F 3d 292 (3rd Cir, 1995); cert denied 516 US 1117; 116 S Ct 921; 133 L Ed 2d 850 (US Supreme Court, 1996).

[39] The maximum fee under New Jersey law would have been approximately half of what had been agreed.

[40] See the discussion of *Newcomb v Daniels, Saltz, Mongeluzzi & Barrett* (n 38).

applying Article 11(1) of the Hague Principles or Article 9(2) of Rome I, though the American court had to consider more issues before applying the law of the forum.

Where the law of a foreign state is in issue, the position is different. Article 11(2) of the Hague Principles gives the court *carte blanche* to do whatever it wants. Article 9(3) of Rome I permits foreign law to be applied if certain conditions are satisfied, but it never requires the application of the foreign law. Under the Restatement, on the other hand, the same requirements apply in both situations.

Some examples will now be given of the application of §187(2)(b) to the law of a foreign country. The first is *Triad Financial Establishment v Tumpane Co.*[41] Tumpane was a US company incorporated in New York with its main office in Washington State. Triad was a Liechtenstein entity controlled by a certain Mr Khashoggi, a Saudi citizen. Tumpane wanted to obtain a military contract with the Government of Saudi Arabia. It engaged the services of Mr Khashoggi as a go-between and agreed to pay him a commission if it obtained the contract. The parties chose the law of New York as the governing law of this contract.[42] Tumpane obtained the contract but refused to pay the commission. The reason was that a Saudi decree, passed after the contract with Mr Khashoggi had been concluded, prohibited such arrangements with retroactive effect. The Saudi decree had been passed because it was thought that such contracts led to bribery and corruption.[43] Mr Khashoggi sued Tumpane before a federal district court in New York. The court held that the contract between Tumpane and Triad was contrary to a fundamental policy of Saudi Arabia and that Saudi Arabia had a materially greater interest in the matter than New York. It therefore applied the Saudi decree as from the date when it was adopted. This case could probably be decided the same way under Article 9(3) of Rome I: the place of performance of the contract with Mr Khashoggi appeared to have been Saudi Arabia and the Saudi decree made performance of the contract illegal.

The next case is *Business Incentives Co v. Sony Corporation of America.*[44] Sony was a New York corporation. Business Incentives was a New Jersey company. It concluded a contract with Sony to act as its sales agent in New Jersey (originally also in New York). The contract, which contained a choice of law clause designating the law of New York, gave either party the right to terminate the contract on 15 days' notice. Subsequently Sony terminated the contract. Business Incentives then sued it for compensation in New York, relying on a New Jersey statute and New Jersey common law. The New York court referred to §187(2)(b) of the Restatement and held that the relevant provisions of New Jersey law applied.

This case resembles the *Ingmar* case, discussed above.[45] The crucial difference, however, is that in *Ingmar* the action was brought in the agent's country, while in *Business Incentives* it was brought in the other party's country. It is difficult to see how the same result could have been reached under Article 9(3) of Rome I: performance of the contract was not illegal under the law of New Jersey. New Jersey law was just invoked to obtain compensation for the agent. This shows that the result in *Ingmar* would have been different under Rome I if the company had been British and the agent had operated in a non-EU State which had a law similar to the EU Commercial Agents Directive.

[41] 611 F Supp 157 (Northern District of New York, 1985).
[42] The contract contained a choice of court clause but the New York court read this as a choice of law clause.
[43] For a similar English case, see *Lemenda Trading Co v African Middle East Petroleum* Co [1988] 3 WLR 735.
[44] 397 F Supp 63 (Southern District of New York, 1975).
[45] (n 21).

IX. Public Policy and Mandatory Provisions in International Instruments

The purpose of international instruments dealing with private international law is to unify the law internationally so as to increase certainty and ensure that the result will be the same irrespective of the court in which proceedings are brought. However, by their very nature, the theories of public policy and mandatory provisions introduce – and are intended to introduce – an element of unpredictability. The whole idea behind them is that in some situations certainty and predictability have to be sacrificed in order to protect important values and interests of one of the countries involved. Moreover, if a distinction is drawn between the application of forum law and that of foreign law, the result will necessarily be different depending on which court is hearing the case.

How is this to be reconciled with the objectives of certainty and predictability? In general, there is not a great deal that can be done except by using restrictive language. Thus, most international instruments insert a word like 'manifestly' in the phrase 'contrary to public policy'. For example, Article 11(3) of the Hague Principles says that a provision of the law chosen by the parties may be refused application 'only if and to the extent that the result of such application would be manifestly incompatible with fundamental notions of public policy (*ordre public*) of the forum'. Similar language is used in other instruments.[46]

X. Conclusion

The theories of public policy and mandatory provisions by their very nature run counter to the ideal of certainty and predictability. However, they are essential in any system of private international law. The important issues are to ensure that they are not applied too widely and that the interests of foreign countries are not forgotten.

[46] See Art 7 of the Hague Convention of 1961 on the Conflicts of Laws Relating to the Form of Testamentary Dispositions; Art 10 of the Hague Convention of 1970 on the Recognition of Divorces and Legal Separations; Art 18 of the Hague Convention 1985 on the Law Applicable to Trusts and on their Recognition; Art 24 of the Hague Convention of 1993 on Protection of Children and Co-operation in Respect of Intercountry Adoption (which also requires the court to take into account the best interests of the child when applying public policy); Arts 22 and 23(2)(d) of the Hague Convention of 1996 on Jurisdiction, Applicable Law, Recognition, Enforcement and Co-operation in Respect of Parental Responsibility and Measures for the Protection of Children (which again require the best interests of the child to be taken into account); Arts 21 and 22(2)(c) of the Hague Convention of 2000 on the International Protection of Adults; Arts 6(c) and 9(e) of the 2005 Hague Convention on Choice of Court Agreements; Art 11(1) of the Hague Securities Convention 2006; Art 22(a) of the Hague Convention of 2007 on the International Recovery of Child Support and Other Forms of Family Maintenance; and Art 7(1)(c) of the Hague Convention of 2019 on the Recognition and Enforcement of Judgments.

PART III

Institutional and Framework Issues

7

Hague Conference on Private International Law

MARTA PERTEGÁS AND PAUL BEAUMONT

I. Introduction

The Hague Conference on Private International Law (the Hague Conference or the HCCH) is regarded as the pivotal institution of global private international law. The Hague Conference forms the cradle of global private international law and, for more than 125 years, it has developed a growing body of private international law for the world. As such, the HCCH is the institutional incarnation of what this book is all about.

This chapter, drawing on the long-term experience with the Hague Conference of its authors,[1] takes stock on the relevance of this institution for global private international law. They critically assess how the HCCH's mandate, which is 'to work for the progressive unification of the rules of private international law',[2] came into place, has evolved and is fulfilled to date. Furthermore, they offer some recommendations about the role of the Hague Conference in the further progressive unification of private international law.

II. The HCCH as the Cradle of Global Private International Law

The Hague Conference's first session was held in 1893, long before it achieved the stature of an intergovernmental organisation with the adoption of its Statute in 1951,[3] when a limited number of like-minded diplomats met in The Hague, in the Netherlands, upon the invitation of the Dutch Government, on the initiative of Tobias Asser (a prescient Dutch jurist who was awarded the Nobel Peace Prize in 1911). The pioneering ideas on international cooperation of this Dutch academic and diplomat resonated in the minds of the small group of civil law States participating in the first session (Austria-Hungary (by 1925 two Member States of Austria and Hungary), Belgium, Denmark, France, Germany, Italy, Luxembourg, the Netherlands, Portugal, Romania, Russia, Spain and Switzerland). This first session of the Hague Conference

[1] Respectively, as a Member of the Hague Conference's Secretariat from 2008 to 2017 and as a delegate on behalf of the United Kingdom and the European Union since 1996. The authors thank Elgar for authorising the use of a shorter entry on the Hague Conference, published in the *Encyclopedia of Private International Law* in 2017, as the basis for this chapter: see M Pertegás, 'Hague Conference on Private International Law' in J Basedow et al (eds), *Encyclopedia of Private International* Law, Vol 1 (Edward Elgar 2017) 870–75.

[2] Statute of 15 July 1955 of the Hague Conference on Private International Law, Art 1.

[3] H van Loon, 'The Hague Conference on Private International Law: Asser's vision and an evolving mission' (2012) *Nederlands Internationaal Privaatrecht* 358; Bureau Permanent de la Conférence (ed), *Célébration du Centenaire de la*

was continued by five more sessions prior to the First World War and the Interbellum (in 1894, 1900, 1904, 1925 and 1928). Sweden and Norway joined as early as the second session, in 1894, Japan followed as the first non-European State in 1904, and Czechoslovakia, Latvia, Poland, the Serbo-Croat-Slovene State and the United Kingdom joined in 1925. The UK joining in 1925 as the first common law State was very significant. The Hague Conference did not exist as an international organisation but as a series of intermittent conferences (hence the somewhat odd name that the Organisation has kept to date) where international conventions, initially for the central part of the continent of Europe and progressively for other like-minded States, were concluded.[4]

The lack of an institutional permanent framework was not an impediment to the conclusion of international conventions by the Hague Conference from its inception. The first successful Hague Convention, the Convention on Civil Procedure was adopted, together with an additional Protocol, by the second session in 1894. It was signed on 14 November 1896, and the Convention entered into force on 23 May 1899, coinciding with the first Hague Peace Conference. The success of this first Convention laid the groundwork for the conclusion of five family law Conventions at the Conference's third and fourth sessions in 1900 and 1904.[5]

In 1951, the founding Statute of the Hague Conference was signed by the governments of 16 States (the Federal Republic of Germany, Austria, Belgium, Denmark, Spain, Finland, France, Italy, Japan, Luxembourg, Norway, the Netherlands, Portugal, the United Kingdom, Sweden and Switzerland). They provided the Conference with a founding charter, which entered into force on 15 July 1955 and, as a result, the Hague Conference became a permanent intergovernmental organisation, equipped with a Secretariat referred to as the *Permanent* Bureau to underscore the importance of continuity.

The adoption of this multilateral founding Statute as the institutional basis for the Conference reinforced its pivotal position for the development of global private international law. The States 'which participated in one or more Sessions of the Conference' were invited to accept the Statute (as set out by Articles 2 and 15 of the Statute). In 2001, a liberal interpretation of that Statute enabled the Russian Federation to become a Member of the Organisation (the Russian Federation being the successor of the Russian Empire, which had participated in the first four Sessions from 1893 to 1904). It also made it possible for Brazil to return to the Organisation in 2001, based on its prior membership between 1972 and 1978. Any other State 'the participation of which is from a juridical point of view of importance for the work of the Conference' may become a Member, provided they secure a majority of the votes cast by the Members of the Organisation (Statute Article 2(2)).[6] In practice, all States that have expressed their willingness to join the

Conférence de la Haye de droit international privé 19 mai 1993 (Permanent Bureau 1995); G Droz, 'Démembrement d'États et succession aux Conventions de La Haye' in B Audit and YEJJ Loussouarn (eds), *L'internationalisation du droit: mélanges en l'honneur d'Yvon Loussouarn* (Dalloz 1994); G Droz, 'La Conférence de la Haye de Droit International Privé en 1980: Évolution et Perspectives' (1980) 168 *Hague Collected Courses* 127; D McClean, 'The Contribution of the Hague Conference to the Development of Private International Law in Common Law Countries' (1992) 233 *Hague Collected Courses* 267; A Struycken, 'Coordination and Co-operation in Respectful Disagreement – General Course on Private International Law' (2004) 311 *Hague Collected Courses* 401; MH van Hoogstraten, 'La codification par traités en droit international privé dans le cadre de la Conférence de la Haye' (1967) 122 *Hague Collected Courses* 337–425.

[4] CCA Voskuil, 'Preface' in TMC Asser Institute (ed), 'The Influence of the Hague Conference on Private International Law. Selected Essays to Celebrate the 100th Anniversary of the Hague Conference on Private International Law' (1993) 40 *Netherlands International Law Review*, Issue 1.

[5] A von Overbeck, 'La contribution de la Conférence de la Haye au développement du droit international privé' (1992) 233 *Hague Collected Courses* 13.

[6] See H van Loon, 'Conférence de La Haye de Droit International Privé' entry in *Répertoire International* (Dalloz, 2011) 41, available at: online database Dalloz.fr, with an extensive bibliography; for an overview of the results of the first three decades of the Hague Conference as an intergovernmental organisation, see Droz (1980) (n 3).

Hague Conference have been accepted by the other Members. As such, the membership of the Hague Conference has steadily increased from 16 founding States to a membership of 89 States and one regional economic integration organisation, the European Union (EU), in 2021. This transformation from a European dominated organisation to a truly global one was an aspiration[7] of the Conference as early as 1980 when there were only 29 Member States.[8]

The admission of an international organisation as a Member of the Conference required a modification of the Statute (adopted in 2005, approved in 2006 and entered into force on 1 January 2007). According to the current Article 3 of the Statute, a Regional Economic Integration Organisation (REIO) may submit an application for membership to the Secretary General. Given the exclusive competence of the EU for all areas of private international law for which it has adopted legislation,[9] the EU (the European Community as it then was) took the important step to become a full Member of the Conference (previously an Observer). By doing so, the EU gave an important signal that, besides the creation of uniform private international law for the EU, it has the broader objective of contributing to global unification projects affirming the unique position of the Hague Conference to do so. The EU became the first (and so far, the only) REIO in the membership of the Hague Conference. The modification of the Statute to allow the EU to become a Member included a change in the voting system in the HCCH from simple majority of the Member States to consensus of the Members. This was insisted upon by Members like the United States who were worried that the HCCH was being dominated by the voting power of the EU and its allies in Europe under the simple majority system.[10] The evidence of HCCH negotiations in the period after consensus has been adopted is that it generally ensures more inclusive negotiations that take full account of global legal diversity, for instance by working on pragmatic outcomes compatible with both the common law and civil law traditions rather than favouring the civil law in the way that a simple majority system is inclined to do given the preponderance of civil law Members. It is very significant that the four Conventions, one Protocol and one instrument on Principles adopted since 2002 have all been adopted by consensus without ever resorting to voting.[11]

The European roots of the Hague Conference remain very visible more than 125 years after its origins. There is, of course, the institutional linkage of the Hague Conference with its host State, the Netherlands. As host State, the Chairman of the Netherlands Standing Committee on Private International Law presides over the Diplomatic Sessions of the Hague Conference (which are funded by the Dutch Government) and the Dutch Government maintains certain important prerogatives, such as the appointment of the Secretary General and the Secretaries of the

[7] See G Droz and A Dyer, 'The Hague Conference and the Main Issues of Private International Law for the Eighties' (1981) 3 *Northwestern Journal of International Law & Business* 155, 156.

[8] Ibid, 210.

[9] Art 3(2) TFEU (Treaty on the Functioning of the European Union (consolidated version)) [2012] OJ C326/47).

[10] See PR Beaumont, 'Reflections on the Relevance of Public International Law to Private International Law Treaty Making' (2009) 340 *Hague Collected Courses* 9–62, 56. Beaumont explains (at 58) that a correct purposive and historic interpretation of the limitation on the use of consensus 'to the furthest extent possible' in Art 8(2) of the Statute and the then Art 1A of the Rules of Procedure must be 'to strengthen the obligation to arrive at consensus before resorting to the exceptional use of majority voting'. The current Rules of Procedure (see: www.hcch.net/en/governance/rules-of-procedure) were approved by the Members during the 2020 meeting of the CGAP. The Rules (entered into force on 6 March 2020) reinforce the 'exceptional' nature of voting, see Rule IIH (3) and (4) as follows, and confirm that if voting ever does occur it will be by a simple majority of the votes cast:

> 'Consensus principle
>
> 3. To the furthest extent possible, all decisions shall be taken by consensus.
>
> Voting at meetings
>
> 4. If exceptionally it is not possible to reach consensus, decisions shall be taken by a vote. If a decision must be taken by a vote, then that decision shall be made by a majority of the votes cast by delegations'.

[11] The first Convention adopted without voting was the Securities Convention in 2002.

Hague Conference (Statute Articles 4 and 5), upon presentation by the Standing Government Committee. Beyond the institutional linkage with the host State, it is significant that around a half of the current membership (in 2021) is composed of European States, which in turn means that a large percentage of the Hague Conference's budget depends on their contributions. The HCCH has kept the same system of distribution of expenses (similar to the States' class of contribution in the system of the Universal Postal Union) from its inception until now. This very much begs the question whether its financial regulations are in line with the twenty-first-century economic and geopolitical weight of its Members.

In the past quarter of a century, the institutional and budgetary ties with European States contrasted with the huge expansion of EU private international law. For a significant number of Members of the Hague Conference, the main unification hub for private international law was in Brussels rather than The Hague.[12] Consequently, the HCCH had to have a much clearer global focus. Attempts to adapt the institutional and budgetary structure to this new truly global mandate proved very cumbersome and have achieved limited results so far.[13]

III. The Hague Conference as a Contemporary Intergovernmental Organisation

The Hague Conference is more than the sum of its Members: as an influential intergovernmental organisation, it may deliver on its mandate by a myriad of techniques, ranging from the conclusion of Conventions, to more indirect activities influencing the progressive unification of private international law.[14]

A. Function and Competences

The Hague Conference is charged with drawing up and servicing multilateral treaties in the field of private international law.

The focus of the Hague Conference on private international law is understood as the rules on applicable law, international jurisdiction, recognition and enforcement of judgments and related aspects of judicial and administrative cooperation. This focus distinguishes its mandate from that of other intergovernmental organisations operating in the field of the unification or harmonisation of questions of private law, such as UNIDROIT or UN agencies such as UNCITRAL or UNICEF.

Uniform private law is about the unification of substantive law while uniform private international law is about unifying rules on jurisdiction, applicable law, recognition and enforcement

[12] For an analysis on the progressive impact of 50 years of EU private international law in the work of the Hague Conference, see M Pertegás, 'El proceso de codificación del DIPr en la Unión Europea y su interacción con otros procesos de codificación: La Haya' in C Esplugues Mota (ed), *Cincuenta años de derecho internacional privado en el diván* (Tirant Lo Blanch Ed 2019) 175–94.

[13] The current Financial Regulations were approved in 2015 after lengthy negotiations but failed to revisit the distribution of the Hague Conference budget among its membership. See: hcch.net under 'Governance' and then 'Financial regulations'.

[14] See, for a plea for pragmatism in the work of the Hague Conference by its first Secretary General, van Hoogstraten (n 3) 344; and about the indirect influence in the national codifications of private international law, K Siehr, 'National Private International Law and International Instruments' in J Fawcett (ed), *Reform and Development of Private International Law: Essays in Honour of Sir Peter North* (Oxford University Press 2002) 335–47.

of judgments, recognition of legal concepts, documents and status, and creating frameworks for administrative and judicial cooperation.[15] Experience with real-life negotiations and project management at the Hague Conference shows that the distinction can be blurred in practice. The HCCH cooperates with other international organisations whose focus is primarily on the unification of private law, notably UNCITRAL, UNICEF, UNIDROIT and WIPO. Sometimes officials representing the Members at the Hague Conference (as delegates, experts, secondees, etc) interact with many international organisations and actively contribute to their respective work programmes without fully appreciating the different techniques used to pursue international cooperation and (legal) coordination. For example, in the United States, the Office of the Assistant Legal Adviser for Private International Law is responsible for all international instruments 'governing private transactions that cross international borders' and, as such, oversees the work of all international and regional institutions active in this very vast area of the law.[16] The portfolios of the officials working in this US office (and its counterparts in other States around the world) span over dozens (if not more) of international organisations. Another problem for the private international law purity of the HCCH is that States may be interested in becoming Members or acceding to its Conventions for reasons that only remotely relate to private international law as such. Over the past decades, there have been States connecting with the HCCH to consolidate their international status (for instance, in cases of State secession or post-war situations). There is also the growing tendency of acceding States to possess no or very rudimentary private international law rules in their domestic legal systems. It is thus essential for the Permanent Bureau to adapt to the practical constraints of a much wider and more varied audience than in the origins of its international treaty-making. Conversely, it is important that the Permanent Bureau and the Chair of the Council on General Affairs and Policy (CGAP) convey to the Members the importance of inviting subject matter experts to be part of their delegations at experts' groups, working groups, Special Commissions and Diplomatic Sessions. It would be remiss of Members not to involve private international law experts who are often willing to lend their time and efforts to the development of their area of expertise. The involvement of such experts is crucial for States where civil servants frequently rotate over different subject areas and/or whose portfolio covers a very wide range of areas within (international) law leading to a limited expertise in private international law.

One could say that, over the decades, the Hague Conference gained stature as an international organisation and possibly lost focus on *traditional* private international law.

i. The Hague Conference's Geopolitical Relevance

The Hague Conference is a truly international organisation, thanks to its growing and diversified membership and its firm embedding in the networks of international cooperation.

There are clear signals that the Hague Conference has owned its position in the current dynamics of global governance.[17] For instance, the Organisation operates in multiple networks, both within the public and the private sector, with diplomatic bodies, caseworkers and judicial

[15] The 15th edn of *Cheshire* refers to this division as 'the two possible ways in which this lack of unanimity among the various systems of private international law may be ameliorated': P Torremans (ed), *Cheshire, North & Fawcett's Private International Law*, 15th edn (Oxford University Press 2017) 9.

[16] See: www.state.gov/bureaus-offices/bureaus-and-offices-reporting-directly-to-the-secretary/office-of-the-legal-adviser/office-of-the-assistant-legal-adviser-for-private-international-law/.

[17] See H van Loon, 'The present and prospective contribution of global private international law unification to global legal ordering' in F Ferrari and D Fernández Arroyo (eds), *Private International Law: Contemporary Challenges and Continuing Relevance* (Edward Elgar 2019) 214–34.

and administrative institutions. A like-minded 'international family'[18] has given way to a less engaged and more amorphous community of Hague Conference actors. To facilitate the interaction, the Hague Conference 'profile' reflects its closer relationships with public administrations, the diplomatic community and the private sector, as well, sadly, as the increasing disengagement of academic subject-specific experts.

In the same vein, the Hague Conference's *acquis* is increasingly presented and promoted in the light of broader objectives of the international community. To illustrate this idea, one could refer, eg, to the efforts of linking the results of the Judgments Project to the multilateral trading system, but also to the presentation of the 1996 Child Protection Convention in the framework of 'an international cooperation system for the civil protection of children'[19] or the interpretation of the 1980 Child Abduction Convention in the broader schemes of human rights instruments or migration law.[20]

ii. The Hague Conference's Diversification of Outputs

The widening of the Hague Conference's membership coincided with a progressive weakening of its treaty-making hallmark in the 2010s after an earlier decline from the over-productivity of the 1970s to a sensible level between the 1980s and the 2000s.[21] Acknowledging that the mere adoption of Conventions does not suffice for a tangible unification of private international law, the Conference progressively shifted to more 'fieldwork' in order to ensure the real impact of its Conventions (particularly its more successful Conventions like Child Abduction, Intercountry Adoption, Service and Evidence), including in States that often lack the (legal) infrastructure necessary for their implementation and operation.

IV. Organisation and Working Methods

A. Institutional Structure

Since its establishment as a permanent international organisation, the bulk of the Conference's activities is coordinated by a Secretariat – the Permanent Bureau. The main office is in The Hague and two regional offices were set up for Latin America in Buenos Aires (2005) and one for the Asia-Pacific region in Hong Kong, SAR of China (2012). The plans to secure a permanent presence in the African continent have not materialised yet.

According to the Statute, the Permanent Bureau is composed of a Secretary General and four Secretaries (although the number of Secretaries has varied and can be amended by the Council), as well as a staff of international civil servants (Statute Article 5). The Permanent Bureau is responsible for the preparation and the organisation of Diplomatic Sessions, as well

[18] See the frequent references to the HCCH as an 'international family' in formal addresses at the opening of Diplomatic Conferences or Special Commissions. For instance, the address of the former Prime Minister of The Netherlands Ruud Lubbers, *Proceedings of the Seventeenth Session, Vol 1* (The Hague 1995) 18.

[19] See I Goicoechea and F Castro, 'Building an international cooperation system for the civil protection of children' in Permanent Bureau (ed), *A Commitment to Private International Law* (Intersentia 2013) 214.

[20] PR Beaumont, 'The Jurisprudence of the European Court of Human Rights and the European Court of Justice on the Hague Convention on International Child Abduction' (2008) 335 *Hague Collected Courses* 9–104.

[21] The HCCH adopted the following numbers of Conventions per decade: 1950s 8; 1960s 6; 1970s 11 (+ 1 Protocol); 1980s 5; 1990s 2; 2000s 4 (+ 1 Protocol); 2010s 1 (+ 1 Principles).

as Special Commissions, for both the development of Hague Conference instruments and the effective implementation and operation of the Conventions (Statute Articles 5 and 6). The Permanent Bureau has evolved from a substance-oriented 'scientific secretariat'[22] to a project management hub. Ideally, the Permanent Bureau should offer both subject matter expertise and project management skills, to facilitate in-house research required for any subject taken up by the Conference and the various activities to support the efficient operation of the Conventions. The Permanent Bureau should ensure that a number of its diplomatic level staff and senior legal officers are recruited from academia so that the tradition of the greats like Georges Droz and William Duncan is not lost. Furthermore, the HCCH should continue to encourage academic participation in its work by bidding with academic and other experts to do empirical and comparative research to embed a pragmatic approach to the development of private international law.[23]

For its traditional treaty-making functions, the Statute of the Hague Conference refers to the Ordinary Session of the Hague Conference as the high-level meeting to be held, in principle, every four years. The Conference may also be convened in Extraordinary Session if necessary (Statute Article 4(7)). Each Session (also referred to as the Diplomatic Session) is concluded by the adoption of a Final Act which contains the official version of the Convention or Conventions concluded during that Session.

The CGAP is composed of all Members of the Conference and 'has charge of the operation of the Conference' (Statute Article 4). A CGAP meeting is held every year around March. At this meeting, CGAP decides which topics are to be placed on, kept on, or removed from the Conference's Agenda and determines which actions are needed for the development of ongoing projects, including the establishment of Special Commissions (Statute Article 8).

The Council of Diplomatic Representatives is the organ with primary responsibility for financial and budgetary matters. The annual budget of the Conference is submitted to this Council for approval.

The CGAP may set up Special Commissions 'to prepare draft Conventions or to study all questions of private international law which come within the purpose of the Conference' (Statute Article 8). Special Commissions are composed of subject matter experts appointed by Members, as well as observers representing other interested intergovernmental organisations or NGOs, which examine draft Conventions and other normative instruments. The functions of Special Commissions have evolved from just preparing new instruments, to also reviewing the spread and effective implementation of existing Conventions (a practice that started in the 1970s and led to the inclusion of a review clause in the 1993 Intercountry Adoption Convention and subsequent Conventions).

i. Working Methods

To prepare possible new instruments, the first step is for a topic to be included on the Agenda/Work Programme of the Hague Conference by the Diplomatic Session or CGAP (upon request

[22] In the words of its former Secretary General Hans van Loon: H van Loon, 'The Global Horizon of Private International Law' (2015) 380 *Hague Collected Courses* 9–108, 30.

[23] One example of this was the partnership of the HCCH in a bid led by the German Institute for Youth Human Services and some key academics to gain EU funding to do empirical and analytical work on the early implementation and application of the Hague Maintenance Convention 2007, see P Beaumont, B Hess, L Walker and S Spancken (eds), *The Recovery of Maintenance in the EU and Worldwide* (Hart Publishing 2014), especially the foreword by William Duncan. On the importance of comparative and empirical work for a pragmatic approach to global private international law see Abubakri Yekini and Paul Beaumont, 'Pragmatism and Private International Law', ch 2 in this book.

by a Member, another international organisation, or further to a suggestion made by the Permanent Bureau).[24] Normative work on new Conventions and on non-binding legal instruments like Principles remains the Strategic Priority No 1 of the HCCH.[25] There is no doubt that the requirement of reaching consensus before an item can be considered by an Experts' Group makes it difficult to start a new normative project[26] and it can be even more difficult to get it to the stage where a Special Commission is empowered to draft a Convention or prepare new Principles.[27] As Judge Moller often said in Hague meetings, 'the best can be the enemy of the good'. Some Members can insist on moving forward on a topic only if they are committed to the possibility of ratifying any Convention or adopting any Principles that might emerge from the work. However, in order for the HCCH to fulfil its 'purpose' which is 'to work for' the 'progressive unification' of the 'rules of private international law' (Article 1 Statute) it seems to us that Members should allow discussion to progress in Experts' Groups and Working Groups if even a significant number of Members want to take the matter forward and to allow a Special Commission to be formed even if only a majority of Members envisage the possibility of ratifying a resultant Convention or implementing the resulting Principles into their law. This should not be done by resorting to majority voting but rather by Members adopting a more constructive (and less self-interested) approach to consensus decision-making.

Once an issue is on the Work Programme for the HCCH, the Permanent Bureau conducts preliminary studies on that topic, by consulting widely with experts and practitioners in the relevant field, from a comparative law perspective and, increasingly, about the feasibility of achieving international consensus on a new instrument. These preliminary studies will guide the Members of the Hague Conference in determining the further stages in the elaboration of a draft Convention. The Permanent Bureau may, for instance, be charged with the elaboration of an introductory memorandum or checklist of issues to be addressed by a limited number of experts (either appointed by States or by the Permanent Bureau depending on the project's mandate) in meetings of an Experts' Group. While there is historically no clear-cut distinction between an Experts' Group and a Working Group, the 2020 revision of the Rules of Procedure has defined the role of the former as 'exploratory bodies that may research, analyse or consider any matter within their mandate' and the role of the latter as 'bodies that develop proposed solutions which can take forms such as, but not limited to, draft provisions, principles or guides'.[28]

Work will then primarily shift to a Special Commission, which will be convened in a series of meetings until a preliminary draft Convention is ready. For instance, the most recently adopted

[24] The Agenda or Work Programme of the Conference is decided upon by a Diplomatic Session or CGAP as the only bodies in the HCCH who can take this type of 'decision' (see Art IIH(1) of the Rules of Procedure). The agenda for meetings of a Diplomatic Session and CGAP are set by the Permanent Bureau in consultation with the chair of the meeting and all Members have a right to propose the addition of any item to the agenda for discussion (see Art IIC of the Rules of Procedure).

[25] See the HCCH Strategic Plan for 2019–2022, available at: assets.hcch.net/docs/bb7129a9-abee-46c9-ab65-7da398e51856.pdf.

[26] The private international law issues surrounding same sex and opposite sex partnerships and same-sex marriages and divorces have been on the Agenda of the HCCH for many years, but no consensus is possible to even establish a working group or experts' group to take these matters forward.

[27] The normative project on Family Agreements has not been able to move from the Experts' Group's examination of a Guide to the existing Hague *acquis* on family agreements in the Child Abduction, Child Protection and Maintenance Conventions to the stage of trying to prepare a new normative instrument making it easier to make family agreements involving children enforceable across borders.

[28] See section III.E. The distinction was made a reality for the first time in the Jurisdiction Project in 2021 when the Experts' Group evolved into a Working Group with a mandate to draft provisions of a future binding instrument, see CGAP Conclusions, paras 7–9, available at: assets.hcch.net/docs/94e2d886-1cbf-4250-b436-5c1899cb942b.pdf.

Hague Convention, the 2019 Judgments Convention, was developed in a series of four meetings of the Special Commission. A rapporteur (or co-rapporteurs) will be appointed among the experts of the Special Commission and will be charged with the elaboration of a draft Report on the preliminary draft Convention. Members are consulted on the preliminary draft Convention in the light of the draft Report in preparation for discussions at the Diplomatic Session. It will be this Session that formally negotiates and adopts a Convention. For decades, until 1988, the Ordinary Session of the Hague Conference was held every four years to complete the Conventions under preparation. Diplomatic Sessions were held to conclude Conventions in 1993, 1996, 2002, 2005 and 2007 (and the Protection of Adults Convention was adopted in 1999 by a Special Commission of a diplomatic character). There was, however, a lapse of almost 12 years between the Diplomatic Sessions in 2007 and 2019.

Acknowledging that consensus-based treaty-making is difficult to achieve, the HCCH has broadened its toolbox of normative work. It opted for the elaboration of its first non-binding instrument, The Hague Principles on Choice of Law in International Commercial Contracts, in 2015 without requiring the intervention of a Diplomatic Session. The Principles were formally adopted by the CGAP. Since the adoption of the first self-standing non-binding instrument of the HCCH, the development of other non-binding instruments expressly features as a possibility in the directions of its Strategic Plan for 2019–2022 but this possibility has not been realised.[29]

For work on existing instruments (referred to as 'post-Convention' work in HCCH parlance), the Permanent Bureau is charged by the CGAP with very diverse tasks, ranging from the preparation of publications, such as Practical Guides on the operation of a Convention or the compilation of case law databases on the application of HCCH Conventions, to individualised programmes to assist a given State with the implementation of a Convention. The limited size of the HCCH Secretariat (approximately 25 FTEs) requires prioritisation of competing requests of the Members. Ideally, the broader HCCH international community at large, with active participation of the Members and/or through alliances with other international institutions, should contribute more to making existing Conventions work effectively. In many ways the most important task is making the Review Special Commissions on the practical operation of Conventions work well and this requires full cooperation from the Members.[30] Alliances with research institutions may facilitate the development of online global repositories on the application of Conventions. For implementation guidance, the one-on-one cooperation between an experienced Contracting State and a candidate Contracting State may be more effective than a resource-intensive implementation guide by the Permanent Bureau. Overseeing this broad range of activities is not an easy task for the CGAP and the individual Members and other entities may influence the Work Programme and the priorities through voluntary contributions. In addition to these challenges, there is an ongoing debate on the beneficiaries of these post-Convention services: only HCCH Members or also non- (but potential) Members?

[29] See HCCH Strategic Plan 2019–2022 (n 25). The diversification of HCCH normative outputs goes back to the Final Act of the 14th Session: *Proceedings of the 14th Session of the HCCH* (The Hague, National Publishing House, Tome I) 159.

[30] eg, Art 54(2) of the Maintenance Convention 2007 imposes obligations on Contracting States to provide information for these Reviews, see para 670 of the explanatory report, available at: assets.hcch.net/docs/09cfaa7e-30c4-4262-84d3-daf9af6c2a84.pdf, but it is clear that not all Contracting States are complying with this obligation in relation to the forthcoming Review Special Commission, see Paul Beaumont and Lara Walker, 'Maintenance', ch 36 in this book.

V. Contribution to Global Private International Law

The permanence, leaning on more than 125 years of history, of the Hague Conference gives weight to the notion of global private international law. Private international law is a multilayered system of rules where some of the HCCH instruments have global recognition.

The most prominent candidates for such global status are the most widely ratified Hague Conventions. Out of the 39 Conventions concluded by the Hague Conference as an intergovernmental organisation, the most widely ratified ones are, in this order, the 1961 Apostille Convention,[31] the 1993 Intercountry Adoption Convention,[32] the 1980 Child Abduction Convention,[33] the 1965 Service Convention,[34] the 1970 Evidence Convention,[35] the 1996 Child Protection Convention,[36] the 2007 Maintenance Convention[37] and the 1961 Form of Wills Convention.[38] Some of these Hague Conventions deal with the determination of applicable law, some with jurisdiction, some with the recognition and enforcement of foreign judgments, some with matters of administrative and judicial cooperation and one (1996) with all four of these. It is clear, however, that the most successful instruments in terms of their global reach are those that put in place mechanisms for international administrative or judicial cooperation between authorities (for the replacement of legalisation with an apostille, to facilitate service of documents and taking of evidence across borders, to regulate intercountry adoption, to deal urgently with the civil aspects of child abduction, to help children be protected internationally by regulating the system in cross-border cases of how their parents take responsibility for looking after them and their property, and to help children and their parents to get maintenance across international borders). As such, in terms of widely ratified instruments, the contribution of the Hague Conference principally relates to the institutionalisation and servicing of international cooperative networks in administrative or judicial matters.

However, the number of Contracting Parties to Hague Conventions is not the only valid indicator of the Conference's influence. Hague Conventions may, for instance, provide blueprints for domestic or regional codifications. As such, the rules on international recognition, of Conventions such as the 1970 Divorce and the 1985 Trusts Convention, proved to be very influential in the progressive acceptance of the recognition of foreign divorces and trusts, respectively. Without securing a high number of ratifications, such Conventions have catalysed significant domestic legal reforms in many jurisdictions.[39] More generally, the work of the Hague Conference has been

[31] See Status of Convention of 5 October 1961 Abolishing the Requirement of Legalisation for Foreign Public Documents (121 Contracting Parties), available at: www.hcch.net/en/instruments/conventions/status-table/?cid=41.

[32] See Status of Convention of 29 May 1993 on Protection of Children and Co-operation in Respect of Intercountry Adoption (104 Contracting Parties), available at: www.hcch.net/en/instruments/conventions/status-table/?cid=69.

[33] See Status of Convention of 25 May 1980 on the Civil Aspects of International Child Abduction (101 Contracting Parties), available at: www.hcch.net/en/instruments/conventions/status-table/?cid=24.

[34] See Status of Convention of 15 November 1965 on the Service Abroad of Judicial and Extrajudicial Documents in Civil and Commercial Matters (79 Contracting Parties), available at: www.hcch.net/en/instruments/conventions/status-table/?cid=17.

[35] See Status of Convention of 18 March 1970 on the Taking of Evidence Abroad in Civil and Commercial Matters (64 Contracting Parties), available at: www.hcch.net/en/instruments/conventions/status-table/?cid=82.

[36] See Status of Convention of 19 October 1996 on Jurisdiction, Applicable Law, Recognition, Enforcement and Co-operation in Respect of Parental Responsibility and Measures for the Protection of Children (53 Contracting Parties), available at: www.hcch.net/en/instruments/conventions/status-table/?cid=70.

[37] See Status of Convention of 23 November 2007 on the International Recovery of Child Support and other Forms of Family Maintenance (43 Contracting Parties), available at: www.hcch.net/en/instruments/conventions/status-table/?cid=131.

[38] See Status of Convention of 5 October 1961 on the Conflicts of Laws Relating to the Form of Testamentary Dispositions (42 Contracting Parties), available at: www.hcch.net/en/instruments/conventions/status-table/?cid=40.

[39] See, for instance, the influence of HCCH work in the PIL Act of the Dominican Republic of 2014 (Act Nr 544-14 of 15 October 2014) which preceded the admission of the Dominican Republic to the HCCH in 2020. More generally about

a primary source of inspiration for private international law reform on a smaller scale, either in the EU, for Commonwealth States[40] or for South-East Asian States within ASEAN. Some innovations introduced in Hague Conventions that eventually did not secure a wide ratification, were transferred to EU private international law, such as the pivotal role of habitual residence as the main connecting factor and several other ideas from the Hague Succession Convention in the EU Succession Regulation.[41] Even successful Conventions like that on the formal validity of wills can influence regional codification. The EU Succession Regulation defers to that Convention for EU Member States who are Party to it while incorporating largely the same rules into the Regulation for EU Member States who are not Party to it.[42] An example, from a Convention that hopefully will become successful, is the inclusion of rules on the substantive validity of choice of court agreements in the Brussels Ia Regulation, in line with the 2005 Choice of Court Convention and beyond the EU's obligations as a Party to that Convention because the rules are applied to cases outside the scope of application of the Convention.

Hague Conventions can attain a significant global status of a commonly accepted international legal standard even before their entry into force. The 'mere' conclusion of the 2019 Judgments Convention was welcomed by the legal community as a milestone in international dispute settlement in civil and commercial matters. For the Hague Conference, the adoption of this Convention revitalised its treaty-making function, rebuilt trust in the Judgments Project despite its extraordinary duration, and created a companion Convention to help boost commitment to the 2005 Choice of Court Convention.[43]

After all, the influence of the Hague Conference also stems from its networks and the wide variety of materials collected over intense preparations and negotiations. A Hague Conference publication of great comparative and explanatory value is the Collection of Proceedings (nearly 50 volumes available on the HCCH website) which compile the preliminary documents, preliminary draft Conventions and minutes of discussions, as well as the Explanatory Reports on the texts adopted (the last of which since 2002 have added weight as the Members had the opportunity to suggest changes before the final version was published).[44] As Hague Conference normative outputs diversify, as discussed above, the ways in which the influence of Hague Conference work may be measured change. The 2015 Choice of Law Principles are a soft-law instrument but still

the relevance of HCCH work for Latin America, see A Boggiano, 'The Contribution of the Hague Conference to the Development of Private International Law in Latin America – Universality and genius loci' (1992) 233 *Hague Collected Courses* 99. For further details on the Divorce Convention see Máire Ní Shúilleabháin and Jayne Holliday, 'Divorce', ch 32 in this book; and on the Trusts Convention, see Jonathan Harris, 'Trusts', ch 23 in this book.

[40] See the new Commonwealth Model Law on recognition and enforcement of foreign judgments which was heavily influenced by the early drafts of the 2019 Hague Judgments Convention, see A Yekini, *The Hague Judgments Convention and Commonwealth Model Law: A Pragmatic Perspective* (Hart Publishing 2021); and the paper by David McClean, 'The Commonwealth Perspective', available at: privateinternationallaw.stir.ac.uk/projects/ahrc-research-network/workshop-i/commonwealth/.

[41] This borrowing from the Hague was not always done well, notably in relation to clawback of lifetime gifts to third parties, see J Holliday, *Clawback Law in the Context of Succession* (Hart Publishing 2020) 2–4 and 75–151.

[42] See EU Succession Regulation 650/2012 [2012] OJ L201/107, Arts 27 and 75(1) and recital 52. See also Albert Font i Segura and Jayne Holliday, 'Succession', ch 22 in this book.

[43] It was encouraging to see Israel sign the 2005 and 2019 Conventions together in March 2021. For more on these two Conventions see chs 28 and 29 in this book on 'Choice of Court Agreements' by Paul Beaumont and Mary Keyes and 'Recognition and Enforcement of Judgments in Civil or Commercial Matters' by David Goddard and Paul Beaumont.

[44] See, eg, the Securities Convention Explanatory Report (2017, 2nd edn) Int-78, available at: assets.hcch.net/docs/d1513ec4-0c72-483b-8706-85d2719c11c5.pdf, and the foreword to and paras 7–8 of the Judgments Convention Explanatory Report (2020), available at: assets.hcch.net/docs/a1b0b0fc-95b1-4544-935b-b842534a120f.pdf. However, there can still be examples where the *Proceedings* can provide a helpful corrective to the explanatory report, see, on the permitted scope of subject matter declarations under the Choice of Court Convention, P Beaumont, 'The revived Judgments Project in The Hague' [2014] *Nederlands Internationaal Privaatrecht* 532 and the Judgments Convention Explanatory Report, ibid, para 337 and fn 243.

influential for the further development of a core value in private international law, ie, party autonomy.[45]

Another welcome characteristic of the Hague Conference's *oeuvre* is its adaptability to the changing needs of societies. The diversification of working methods, as sketched above, ensures the adaptation of 'dated' Conventions to the twenty-first-century realities that people and businesses face every day. Recommendations, Good Practice Guides and other instruments ensure the transition to the current needs of a globalised and digital society. For instance, the issuance and recognition of electronic apostilles is promoted on the 'basis' of the 1961 Apostille Convention, a Convention which preceded the age of electronic communication. Another example is the active promotion of taking of evidence by video-link using a pre-internet 1970 Convention.[46]

VI. Looking Ahead: The Hague Conference as an Evolving Forum for Global Private International Law

The Hague Conference is set to continue fulfilling its mandate for the progressive unification of the rules of private international law in a progressively broader context and with a wider range of available techniques than when it was created as an intergovernmental organisation.

The Members of the Conference must take their responsibility seriously to become Parties to, and implement properly, all the established core *acquis* of the Conference outlined above (Apostille, Adoption, Abduction, Service, Evidence, Child Protection, Form of Wills, and Maintenance), and to widen and deepen the *acquis* by ratifying and implementing the older Conventions produced by the Conference that are still highly relevant and workable (Divorce, Access to Justice, and Trusts) and the newer Conventions that have not yet been widely ratified but which provide a great basis for unifying private international law (Adults, Choice of Court, and Judgments). The Permanent Bureau should do all it can to encourage the Members and indeed non-Members to adopt these Conventions and implement the Hague Principles on Choice of Law in International Commercial Contracts. The widening of the Hague instruments' application is as important a goal as the further growth in the Organisation's membership. Hopefully the *acquis* will expand in the coming years to cover international jurisdiction (at least on parallel proceedings), parentage issues and family agreements.

Indeed, the outreach of the HCCH continues to increase, expanding the Organisation's geographic reach to all continents of the world and diversifying its influence through a toolbox of legal techniques and actions. In the spirit of Tobias Asser's visionary idea of cultivating trust and respect through law and legal institutions, the Hague Conference's footprint is essential as a permanent legal structure for international cooperation. In its more than centennial trajectory, the Hague Conference has known successes and setbacks. As an international organisation, it is obviously not immune to changing trends in international cooperation, the challenged role of intergovernmental organisations and, more generally, the ups and downs of a multilateral governance system.

[45] See D Girsberger, T Kadner Graziano and JL Neels, *Choice of Law in International Commercial Contracts* (Oxford University Press 2021) and Symeon Symeonides, 'Law Applicable to Contracts', ch 14 in this book.

[46] The Hague Conference embraces the use of modern technologies for a better operation of its Conventions and other relevant work. See further C Bernasconi, M Celis and A Kunzelmann, 'Of Luddites and Luminaries: the Use of Modern Technologies Under the Hague Legal Co-operation Conventions' in Permanent Bureau (ed), *A Commitment to Private International Law* (Intersentia 2013) 31–45; and Permanent Bureau, 'National Organs and Central Authorities under HCCH Conventions', ch 8 and Brooke Marshall and Nadia de Araujo, 'Taking of Evidence', ch 13 in this book.

However, private international lawyers can hardly imagine what global private international law would mean without the presence and operation of the Hague Conference. Importantly, the HCCH has evidenced resilience and responsiveness in critical times of its trajectory so far. Fostering its adaptability to the evolving realities of the world and capitalising on its rich *acquis*, the Hague Conference should consolidate its calling as the world's laboratory of global private international law.

8

National Organs and Central Authorities under HCCH Conventions

IGNACIO GOICOECHEA AND BRODY WARREN*

I. Introduction

In the previous chapter, we have seen how the HCCH has transformed from a small group of like-minded States to a global organisation. The pursuit of universality has led the Organisation to expand its activities, recognising that its mandate encompasses both the traditionally emphasised normative element, as well as non-normative work to support the effective implementation and practical operation of its Conventions.[1] This expansion has highlighted the importance of the role played by authorities at the national level.

This chapter explores National Organs[2] designated by HCCH Members and Central Authorities[3] designated by Contracting Parties to HCCH Conventions.[4] The authors first present the historical origins and key functions of National Organs, before outlining challenges faced and offering suggestions of how best to address them. The authors then consider Central Authorities and how their development was influenced by the negotiation of HCCH Conventions. This is followed by an examination of the key functions of Central Authorities, presenting challenges and outlining good practices to overcome them.

II. National Organs

A. Origins

HCCH founder Tobias Asser's vision for the role and functions of the Organisation was such that it already encompassed activities in which its Members would necessarily be implicated, giving

* For the Permanent Bureau of the Hague Conference on Private International Law (HCCH).

[1] See also, HCCH Permanent Bureau, *HCCH Strategic Plan 2019–2022* (The Hague 2019), available at: assets.hcch.net/docs/bb7129a9-abee-46c9-ab65-7da398e51856.pdf (HCCH Strategic Plan).

[2] Throughout this chapter, the term 'National Organ' includes the 'Contact Organ' designated by the European Union, the only Regional Economic Integration Organisation (REIO) to have joined the HCCH at the time of writing. See also (n 7) below.

[3] As distinct from 'Competent Authorities' under various HCCH Conventions. See, however (n 51) below.

[4] For ease of reference, unless otherwise specified, the term 'HCCH Conventions' comprises both Conventions and other instruments adopted by the HCCH.

rise to the need to have national bodies to discharge these responsibilities. As early as the first 'Hague Conference' in 1893, Asser suggested that States should establish 'Committees' to assist in preparing for future conferences.[5] In 1897, following the success of the first two sessions in 1893 and 1894, he addressed Queen Emma of the Netherlands, suggesting the continuation of the work and recommending the institution of a permanent committee. Her Majesty followed Asser's recommendation, enacting a Royal Decree establishing the 'Government Committee for the Preparation of Measures to be Taken to Promote the Codification of Private International Law'.[6] As founding chair of this Committee, Asser played an important role in shaping its operation. He decided to have the Committee publish not only the Convention texts, but relevant legislation and jurisprudence, to better monitor the application of the Conventions.[7] This emphasis on national authorities' involvement in monitoring the practical operation of Conventions demonstrates that Asser's early vision may have extended to what has become the modern role of Special Commission meetings.

In the 1950s, when the HCCH became a permanent organisation, the National Organ entity was enshrined in the Statute.[8] The text simply refers to 'facilitating communications between Members of the Conference and the Permanent Bureau', leaving Members considerable freedom to determine the organisation and functions of their National Organ. For the Netherlands, the Standing Government Committee was the natural candidate for designation as the Dutch National Organ, and the Committee continued to operate as originally conceived by Asser. In the absence of supplementary guidance from the Statute, the organisation of National Organs varies among HCCH Members, however Members have almost exclusively designated an office either at the Ministry of Justice or Ministry of Foreign Affairs.[9]

B. Key Functions

In fulfilling the mandate in its Statute, the core work of the HCCH broadly consists of identifying new topics; developing new instruments; implementing Conventions (including their incorporation into domestic legal systems); and supporting, monitoring and reviewing the practical operation of these Conventions. Importantly, each of these activities has both a national dimension (Members' domestic activities), and an international dimension (Members' direct participation in the work of the Organisation, facilitated by its Permanent Bureau).

In practice, Members are necessarily implicated in both the national and international dimensions and National Organs therefore have a central, coordinating role, discharging responsibilities in respect of the four key activities outlined below.

i. Identification of New Topics

The normative work of the HCCH begins with the identification of needs in the international community that could be addressed by a new instrument. Topics are proposed to the Council

[5] CCA Voskuil, 'Tobias Michael Carel Asser' in Institut de droit international, *Livre du centenaire, 1873–1973 Evolution et perspectives du Droit international* (Karger 1973) 11–31, 25–26.

[6] Hereafter, 'Standing Government Committee'. See Statute of the HCCH, Art 4(4) and Royal Decree (*Koninklijk Besluit*) of 20 February 1897, Government Gazette (*Staatscourant*) 1897, No 46.

[7] Voskuil (n 5) 26.

[8] Statute of the Hague Conference on Private International Law, Art 7(1). The Statute was adopted during the Seventh Session in 1951 and entered into force on 15 July 1955. Amendments were adopted on 30 June 2005, during the Twentieth Session, to allow for the possibility of REIOs to become Members. Art 7 was therefore amended to include a reference to a 'contact organ', to fulfil the National Organ role for an REIO.

[9] Approximately 95% of National Organs designated by the current HCCH Members.

of General Affairs and Policy by Members, other international organisations or the Permanent Bureau. This Council, comprising the entire HCCH Membership, considers the proposal, with Members expressing their positions as to whether the topic should be included in the Work Programme of the Organisation.[10]

This first key activity requires the active involvement of National Organs, as the primary voice for the Member they represent. To ensure National Organs are aware of any possible needs as they arise, they may need to liaise with other public institutions and members of civil society. The various topics presented for consideration may call for different levels of technical knowledge in their analysis, which requires the National Organ to consult other agencies and academic experts, to coordinate the national position.

ii. Development of New Conventions

As described in the previous chapter, the negotiation of new Conventions at the HCCH is a long and resource-intensive process, often prolonged by the Organisation's consensus-based decision-making model. In broad terms, States designate experts to follow each project, from the initiation of an Experts' or Working Group, through a series of Special Commission meetings, until the text of the draft instrument is sufficiently advanced to justify the convocation of a Diplomatic Session to adopt it.

The entire process can take several years, with much of the work being carried out between meetings, the so-called 'intersessional work', by experts and delegates in coordination with the Permanent Bureau. An important task of National Organs is therefore to follow and contribute to this work, responding to questionnaires, analysing and commenting on draft texts and proposals, and participating in preparatory calls and meetings.

Experts' and Working Groups generally comprise a limited number of specialists representing diverse regions and legal traditions, to ensure the work has the necessary legitimacy and to increase the potential global impact. At the level of Special Commissions and Diplomatic Sessions, participation is open to all Members, the rationale being that broader representation increases ownership of the project and is more likely to lead to widespread acceptance of the final instrument. National Organs are responsible for coordinating Member participation throughout the entirety of the normative process and in doing so, play a key role in shaping the content and trajectory of these projects.

iii. Incorporation and Implementation of Conventions

Before joining an HCCH Convention, many States will initiate a formal study to assess the impact of the instrument on the domestic legal system. In practice, the National Organ is often called upon to organise this initial study, a technical task requiring specialised knowledge, both of the relevant topic and the broader private international law context. National Organs do not always have the resources or expertise to conduct this work, so may rely on the support of external experts and stakeholders.

Even once a technical analysis has been conducted, additional challenges must be overcome. National Organs may need to prepare draft legislation and compile accompanying documentation for the consideration of the legislature. They also have an important monitoring role, following public consultations on the instrument and its consideration by parliamentary or congressional committees. Throughout the process, National Organs have a responsibility to engage with the

[10] For further discussion on this point, see the previous chapter.

relevant institutions, reiterating the importance of the instrument and working to allay any concerns, because urgent political priorities dominate the legislative agenda and a private international law instrument is easily sidelined.

Once the instrument has received the necessary legislative and executive approvals, the National Organ is typically the best-placed authority to oversee the preparation and deposit of the instrument of ratification or accession with the treaty depositary,[11] including any declarations, reservations or designations of authorities. Correct execution of these steps saves time and helps to ensure the smooth entry into force of the instrument.

Even after having completed these steps, the work of the National Organ is far from over. It may need to oversee the adjustment of domestic regulations or procedures, as well as promotional activities. Raising awareness of the instrument among both those who will apply it and those who will benefit from it is fundamental to its success.

iv. Supporting, Monitoring and Reviewing the Operation of Conventions

International conventions are living instruments, moulded by interpretation and practice developed throughout their lifetime. The HCCH approach is unique in nurturing the evolution and progressive implementation of its instruments, ensuring their continued relevance by maintaining their ability to fulfil their objectives. A key element of this approach is the convocation of Special Commissions to review the practical operation of HCCH Conventions, each of which meets periodically, depending on the Organisation's Work Programme.

The rotation usually results in multiple Special Commission meetings being held each year, to which National Organs are invited, together with the relevant Central Authority. In some States, the National Organ acts as the Central Authority for multiple Conventions.[12] In this capacity, National Organs must respond to technical questionnaires, review preliminary documentation, and attend the Special Commission meetings, or at minimum coordinate this preparatory work and attendance with relevant authorities.

At these meetings, Special Commissions adopt conclusions and recommendations to encourage uniform interpretation, promote good practices and provide guidance to the Council on General Affairs and Policy in relation to latest developments and possible future work. In addition, Special Commissions respond to other needs that arise, developing supplementary tools, either directly or together with smaller groups of experts and the Permanent Bureau. These tools are aimed at improving the operation of a given Convention and may include Handbooks, Guides to Good Practice, Country Profiles, implementation checklists and statistical or case law databases. National Organs are always involved in the development of these tools, whether at the drafting, review or approval stages.

Finally, National Organs have a responsibility to promote the autonomous interpretation[13] and smooth operation of HCCH Conventions. This involves the dissemination of Special Commission conclusions and recommendations, as well as Handbooks, Guides to Good Practice and other tools.

[11] For HCCH Conventions, the Treaties Division of the Ministry of Foreign Affairs of the Kingdom of the Netherlands.

[12] eg, the Australian National Organ acts as Central Authority for the both the Convention of 15 November 1965 on the Service Abroad of Judicial and Extrajudicial Documents in Civil or Commercial Matters (Service Convention) and Convention of 18 March 1970 on the Taking of Evidence Abroad in Civil or Commercial Matters (Evidence Convention); the Panamanian National Organ acts as Central Authority for the Convention of 25 October 1980 on the Civil Aspects of International Child Abduction (Child Abduction Convention).

[13] For a detailed analysis of this topic, see J Ribeiro-Bidaoui, 'The International Obligation of the Uniform and Autonomous Interpretation of Private Law Conventions: Consequences for Domestic Courts and International Organisations' (2020) 67 *Netherlands International Law Review* 139.

C. Challenges and Opportunities

Despite their best efforts, National Organs face a number of challenges in performing the functions within their purview. Managing responsibility for multiple organisations and projects is complicated by a lack of resources, the demand for technical expertise and the need to coordinate among stakeholders, all of which may be compounded by the political invisibility of the discipline.[14]

The sections that follow briefly present these challenges and outline good practices, including examples of approaches adopted in particular States, which may prove useful for other Members when establishing or strengthening the operation of their National Organs.

i. Resources and Expertise

As mentioned above, some National Organs act as a Central or Competent Authority under a specific HCCH Convention, sometimes in addition to responsibility for other international instruments and organisations.[15] Other National Organs are responsible for matters relating to both private and public international law,[16] or in some cases, for all legal matters of the relevant institution.[17]

The difficulties facing National Organs are particularly evident in the context of HCCH meeting participation. Where possible, it is advisable that the National Organ coordinate a delegation comprising representatives with subject matter expertise, as well as those with an understanding of the broader policy goals and experience in international negotiation. However, with limited resources, it is challenging to organise large delegations to attend meetings in The Hague. Many National Organs must therefore rely on their Embassies for support, Embassies which are required to cover multiple organisations with a small number of officials and are frequently not in a position to dedicate time to follow a highly technical meeting over several days.

In this context, it is worth noting the recent trend towards meetings in online or 'hybrid' formats which are less resource-intensive for States. Even as in-person meetings resume, the possibility of remote participation will undoubtedly facilitate the engagement of more experts in the work of the HCCH, further advancing its strategic goals of inclusiveness and universality.[18] While this may ease some of the resourcing pressures, it will not eliminate them completely.

In addition, faced with myriad topics with a private international law dimension, National Organs often lack the requisite specialised technical expertise. In response, some States have sought the support of academia, which has the dual benefit of drawing on the rich expertise in the academic community while alleviating resourcing pressures.

The National Organ of the Netherlands is composed of academics, judges and legal practitioners and is responsible for preparing measures to be taken to promote the codification of private international law, performing the duties required by the HCCH Statute, and advising the government and legislature.[19] In Germany and Canada, the National Organs both benefit

[14] See also, HCCH Permanent Bureau, 'Latin American Meeting on the Implementation and Operation of the Hague Conventions on Legal Co-operation and International Child Protection' (Report of 125th Anniversary Celebrations, Buenos Aires, 13–15 August 2018) 4, available at: assets.hcch.net/docs/cf581a8c-2c4b-4aec-ba5c-eb83ffdb5e19.pdf.

[15] eg, in Australia, France and Hungary.

[16] eg, in Georgia, the Russian Federation, Argentina, Mexico, Paraguay and Turkey.

[17] eg, in Chile, Peru and the Philippines.

[18] HCCH Strategic Plan (n 1) 7.

[19] The Committee remains as established by Royal Decree in 1897 (n 6). Its composition and operation was codified in the Law of 14 February 1998, Official Gazette (*Staatsblad*) No 208.

from the advice of relevant academic bodies. The German Council of Private International Law is an autonomous body comprising a limited group of private international law professors, which advises the German Ministry of Justice and Consumer Protection.[20] In the case of Canada, the Department of Justice benefits from a group of federal, provincial and territorial officials, advising on aspects of private international law projects, including the need for additional work.[21]

In the United States of America (US), Mexico, Paraguay and Argentina, the National Organs are the legal adviser offices of their respective Ministries of Foreign Affairs, each with an external advisory committee to advise them on private international law matters. In the cases of Mexico, Paraguay and Argentina, the relevant commissions are made up of a team of recognised private international law academics who provide advice as required.[22] Members are designated by the respective Ministries of Foreign Affairs and their work is honorary. In the case of the US, the Advisory Committee on Private International Law (ACPIL)[23] consists of representatives of government agencies, professional organisations and private international law experts from academia and the private sector. The Legal Adviser of the State Department typically serves as Chair of ACPIL, and the Committee establishes study groups to provide advice on specialised subjects of private international law. In light of these experiences, National Organs should consider drawing on the academic and technical expertise within their State to enhance the performance of their functions.

ii. Effective Coordination

Due to the diverse nature of their responsibilities, National Organs should regularly consult other domestic authorities and stakeholders. This enables better prioritisation of projects and instruments, as well as better coordination of a position in the national interest. Consultation and coordination are greatly facilitated where there are established mechanisms to do so.

For example, in the US, ACPIL holds public meetings for open discussion of private international law matters. In Canada, the National Organ develops annual reports on its activities and priorities, which are presented at the annual meeting of the Uniform Law Conference of Canada (ULCC),[24] bringing together government lawyers and analysts, private lawyers and law reform bodies.

The Peruvian Ministry of Foreign Affairs has developed another model. Together with the Ministry of Justice, it founded an Intersectoral Commission on Private International Law,[25] the objective of which is to study the work of the HCCH, with a view to incorporating it into

[20] Notice (*Mitteilung*), 'Deutscher Rat für Internationalis Privatrecht' (1953) 18 *Zeitschrift für ausländisches und internationales Privatrecht* 597.

[21] Department of Justice of Canada, 'Activities and priorities of the Department of Justice in International Private Law' (Report, ULCC Annual Meeting, Québec, 12–16 August 2018).

[22] In Mexico, the Commission of External Advisors on Private International Law (Comisión de Asesores Externos de la Secretaría de Relaciones Exteriores en materia de Derecho Internacional Privado) was established by Agreement (*Acuerdo*) of 29 November 2012; In Argentina, the Advisory Commission on Private International Law (Comisión Asesora del Ministerio de Relaciones Exteriores y Culto en materia de Derecho Internacional Privado) was established by Resolution (*Resolución*) 253/2019 of 15 May 2019; and in Paraguay 'the Legal Advisor's Office's *Ad Honorem* Working Group on PIL' (Grupo de Trabajo Ad Honorem de la Asesoría Jurídica en materia de Derecho Internacional Privado) was created by Resolution 503 of 2 December 2020.

[23] Established pursuant to Title 22, United States Code, ss 269g, 2651a and 2656, see: www.facadatabase.gov/FACA/apex/FACAPublicCommittee?id=a10t0000001gzpOAAQ.

[24] See 'Activities and priorities of the Department of Justice in International Private Law' (n 21) 7. Reports presented to other Annual Meetings are available at: www.ulcc.ca/en/annual-meetings.

[25] 'Comisión Intersectorial de Derecho Internacional Privado para estudiar los temas tratados en HCCH', established by Ministerial Resolution (Resolución Ministerial) 227-2004-PCM of 5 August 2004.

national legislation. The Commission is responsible for the coordination of the Peruvian position with respect to any (draft) international instruments in the field of private international law. Meetings of the Intersectoral Commission are convoked by the National Organ.

Broad consultation also facilitates the participation of national delegations in HCCH meetings. The more comprehensive the domestic level coordination, the more effective the participation of the national delegation in the work of the HCCH.

iii. Visibility of Private International Law

An examination of the increase in Contracting Parties of the 'core'[26] HCCH Conventions reveals that it takes on average, approximately 25 years to reach 40 Contracting Parties, equivalent to less than half of the current HCCH Membership. Moreover, each individual Member is, on average, party to fewer than half of these 'core' Conventions. These figures are cause for concern, because the Members invest in the Organisation and its work to generate global solutions to contemporary needs, but it is apparent that Members are not maximising the return on their investment.

The delays in States joining HCCH Conventions are indicative of a lack of priority afforded to the development of private international law. The discipline suffers from a considerable lack of awareness among governments and the wider community, which affects its political prioritisation and ultimately, the ability of National Organs to perform their functions. To address this challenge, National Organs should consistently seek to position the work of the HCCH in the context of broader policy goals, such as the protection of human rights and access to justice.

In the case of the HCCH 'Children's Conventions'[27] there is a clear relationship between the Conventions and the protection of human rights. The 1989 United Nations Convention on the Rights of the Child has several articles which are reinforced by the application of HCCH Conventions, including in relation to child abduction (Article 11), adoption (Article 21), recovery of child support (Article 27(4)), and preventing the abduction, sale and trafficking of children (Article 35).[28] National Organs can utilise these connections, partnering with public and private sector stakeholders in the area of child protection to raise the profile of the Conventions.

Similarly, while access to justice is identified as a high priority of many political agendas, its international dimension lacks visibility among national policymakers. Multiple HCCH Conventions contribute to facilitating international access to justice in the context of dispute resolution, when parties, information and evidence are dispersed across multiple jurisdictions.[29]

In addition to improving access to justice, these instruments contribute to the establishment of a robust legal framework for those operating across borders. The resulting legal certainty

[26] This term refers to a group of HCCH Conventions and instruments, prioritised based on their recent adoption, popularity or relevance.

[27] Child Abduction Convention (n 12); Convention of 29 May 1993 on Protection of Children and Co-operation in Respect of Intercountry Adoption (1993 Adoption Convention); Convention of 19 October 1996 on Jurisdiction, Applicable Law, Recognition, Enforcement and Co-operation in Respect of Parental Responsibility and Measures for the Protection of Children (1996 Child Protection Convention); Convention of 23 November 2007 on the International Recovery of Child Support and Other Forms of Family Maintenance (2007 Child Support Convention).

[28] See, for a detailed analysis of this topic, I Goicoechea, 'Implementing the CRC through the HCCH's Children Conventions' in F Prus (ed), *Family Law: Challenges and Developments from an International Perspective* (UIA-LexisNexis 2020) 89–99.

[29] Service and Evidence Conventions (n 12); Convention of 5 October 1961 Abolishing the Requirement of Legalisation for Foreign Public Documents (1961 Apostille Convention); Convention of 25 October 1980 on International Access to Justice (1980 Access to Justice Convention); Convention of 30 June 2005 on Choice of Court Agreements (2005 Choice of Court Convention); Convention of 2 July 2019 on the Recognition and Enforcement of Foreign Judgments in Civil or Commercial Matters (2019 Judgments Convention); and Principles on Choice of Law in International Commercial Contracts (2015 Choice of Law Principles).

and predictability creates a climate more conducive to international trade, commerce and investment.[30] National Organs should therefore consider partnerships with national chambers of commerce, bar and notary associations, and other stakeholders in the commercial field to advocate the commercial advantages of private international law instruments.

Finally, National Organs should not underestimate the power of leveraging partnerships with international organisations. Initiatives such as the United Nations 2030 Agenda for Sustainable Development encourage States to take all necessary steps to promote the rule of law and effective access to justice worldwide,[31] and can therefore be persuasive tools in raising the profile of private international law.

III. Central Authorities

A. Origins

While the first reference to a 'Central Authority' in the text of an HCCH Convention appears in the 1965 Service Convention,[32] the origins of the Convention provide a clearer picture of how the renowned Central Authority mechanism came to be.

Long before the Central Authority there was the '*autorité compétente*' or 'Competent Authority', a term which dates back to the First Session in 1893 and the adoption of the Convention of 14 November 1896 on Civil Procedure.[33] Its two successor Conventions, the Convention of 17 July 1905 on Civil Procedure and the Convention of 1 March 1954 on Civil Procedure, developed the notion, calling for the active designation of an authority to receive requests for service and evidence.[34]

The transmission of requests under these three Conventions was carried out via diplomatic and consular channels,[35] as the natural preference of the continental civil law systems which made up the majority of the States represented at the earlier Sessions of the Hague Conference.[36] However, by 1960, post-war economic prosperity had given rise to an unprecedented increase in the volume and importance of cross-border trade and commerce.[37] Coupled with the surge in transnational migration,[38] this placed additional strain on diplomatic channels. The inadequacy

[30] The benefits of these instruments have been recognised by international organisations such as the International Chamber of Commerce and the World Bank Group. See, eg, International Chamber of Commerce, 'ICC urges governments to ratify Hague Choice of Court Convention' (Media Release, 18 October 2007); World Bank Group, *Investing Across Borders* (World Bank 2010).

[31] United Nations General Assembly, *Transforming our World: The 2030 Agenda for Sustainable Development*, UN Doc A/RES/70/1 (21 October 2015, adopted 25 September 2015) 25–26, 'Goal 16'. See also, World Justice Project, *Rule of Law Index*, 14, 27, 'Civil Justice'.

[32] Art 2.

[33] See, eg, references to the '*autorité compétente*' in Arts 1 and 9.

[34] See, 1905 and 1954 Conventions, Arts 1 and 9.

[35] See, eg, references to '*la voie diplomatique*' in Arts 1 and 6 of the 1896, 1905 and 1954 Conventions.

[36] Japan, the first State not from Continental Europe to participate, was represented at the Fourth Session in 1904. ('Liste des Pays représentés à la Conférence et de leurs Délégués' in *Actes de la Quatrième Conférence de La Haye pour le droit international privé* (Van Langenhuysen Frères, 1904) XIII–XIV). The United Kingdom was the first State with a common law tradition to participate, when it was represented at the Fifth Session of the Conference in 1925 ('Liste des Pays représentés à la Conférence et de leurs Délégués' in *Actes de la Cinquième session* (Imprimerie Nationale, 1926) 9–11).

[37] See, on this point, 'Post-war reconstruction and development in the Golden Age of Capitalism' in *World Economic and Social Survey 2017: Reflecting on seventy years of development policy analysis* (United Nations Department of Economic and Social Affairs, 2017) UN Doc E/2017/50/Rev.1, 23–48.

[38] Just months after the Seventh Session in October 1951, which saw the adoption of what would become the 1954 Civil Procedure Convention, the Provisional Intergovernmental Committee for the Movement of Migrants from Europe

of what was then the default system eventually led to what would become a three-stage revision of the 1954 Civil Procedure Convention, beginning with service abroad.[39]

The establishment of 'the Central Authority system' was identified as one of the cornerstones of the negotiation of the 1965 Service Convention,[40] conceived to facilitate the direct communication of requests between designated authorities, without resorting to the burdensome, protracted and often costly formalities of traditional diplomatic and consular channels. While the duties and responsibilities of these earlier Central Authorities may not have been complex,[41] the mechanism proved to be revolutionary, its simplicity key to its effectiveness. It had the added benefit of accommodating the needs of different legal traditions, including common law systems, which was of increasing importance at the time of the Tenth Session.[42] It was therefore no surprise when, four years later, Central Authorities were again entrusted with the primary channel of transmission under the 1970 Evidence Convention.[43]

The Service and Evidence Conventions soon gained international significance, having attracted early interest from non-European States.[44] As a result, the first ever meeting of a Special Commission on the practical operation of an HCCH Convention was convened in 1977 to discuss the Service Convention,[45] marking the beginning of what would become the post-Convention work of the HCCH, a fundamental element of its operations today.[46]

A second Special Commission meeting was held in 1978 to discuss the Evidence Convention.[47] The reports of both the 1977 and 1978 Special Commissions meetings demonstrate that there was already a desire to further develop the Central Authority mechanism, foreshadowing the growth of an enhanced legal cooperation network.[48] The effectiveness of Central Authorities

was born 'out of the chaos and displacement of Western Europe following the Second World War'. This Committee, following a series of name changes, would eventually become the International Organization for Migration of today. See, International Organization for Migration, 'IOM History', available at: www.iom.int/iom-history.

[39] 'Signification des Actes judiciaries et extrajudiciaires à l'étranger' in *Actes et documents de la Neuvième session* (Imprimerie Nationale 1961) Tome I: Matières diverses 163–75, 169, 175.

[40] The delegates accepted the establishment of the Central Authority system as one of three basic principles identified to best realise the revision of the 1954 Civil Procedure Convention. V Taborda Ferreira, 'Rapport explicatif' in *Actes et documents de la Dixième session* (Imprimerie Nationale 1965) Tome III: Notification 363, 363–64.

[41] The role of the Central Authority as established in the Service Convention is primarily to receive, consider and direct incoming requests. See Arts 2–5.

[42] The United Kingdom was a founding Member of the Organisation in 1955; Ireland joined later the same year. The United States of America had previously been represented at the Eighth and Ninth Sessions, and deposited its instrument of acceptance of the Statute during the Tenth Session, finalising its Membership. See, 'Status Table' of the Statute of the Hague Conference on Private International Law, available at: www.hcch.net/en/instruments/conventions/status-table/?cid=29; 'Liste des Pays représentés à la Conférence et de leurs Délégués' in *Actes de la Huitième session* (Imprimerie Nationale, 1957) 1–4 and in *Actes et documents de la Neuvième session* (note 39) 11–14 and in *Actes et documents de la Dixième session* (note 40) Tome I: Séances plénières 11–12. See, for further discussion on this point, GAL Droz, 'A Comment on the Role of the Hague Conference on Private International Law' (1994) 57 *Law and Contemporary Problems* 3, 4–6.

[43] Art 2.

[44] Four of the first five States to join the Service Convention were non-European, and the United States was among the first to join the Evidence Convention. See, 'Status Table' of the Service Convention, available at: www.hcch.net/en/instruments/conventions/status-table/?cid=17 and 'Status Table' of the Evidence Convention, available at: www.hcch.net/en/instruments/conventions/status-table/?cid=82.

[45] HCCH Permanent Bureau, Report on the Work of the Special Commission on the Operation of the Convention of 15 November 1965 on the Service Abroad of Judicial and Extrajudicial Documents in Civil or Commercial Matters (1977).

[46] HCCH Strategic Plan (n 1) 5.

[47] HCCH Permanent Bureau, Report on the Work of the Special Commission on the Operation of the Convention of 18 March 1970 on the Taking of Evidence Abroad in Civil or Commercial Matters (1978).

[48] See, eg, discussions in relation to a future practical handbook and the willingness of Central Authorities to take a more active role in managing and handling requests, in both the *Report of the 1977 Special Commission* (n 45) 9, §2 and *Report of the 1978 Special Commission* (n 47) 2–3, §1 and 7, §8.

was therefore at the forefront of minds ahead of the Fourteenth Session in 1980 and both Conventions concluded at that Session established comparatively more developed Central Authority mechanisms.[49]

The continued success of the Central Authority model is evidenced by its incorporation in numerous HCCH Conventions adopted throughout the decades that followed, namely: the 1993 Adoption; 1996 Child Protection; 2000 Adults; and 2007 Child Support Conventions. While the scope of functions and responsibilities varies, the consistent inclusion of Central Authorities, in particular in international family law instruments, demonstrates confidence in their efficacy and a conscious effort to position them at the heart of international legal cooperation.

Since the Fourteenth Session, the only HCCH instruments which do not provide for the designation of a Central Authority are those without any mechanisms for administrative or judicial cooperation.[50] In fact, so important has the notion of legal cooperation between Central Authorities become, that it has influenced the development of the 1961 Apostille Convention. While it pre-dates the Service Convention, the role of Competent Authorities under the Apostille Convention has developed in a manner not unlike that of the early iterations of Central Authorities.[51]

B. Key Functions

Since their inception, the primary responsibility of Central Authorities and a key advantage of the mechanism has been the receipt and direction of requests submitted under the relevant Convention. The diversion of requests for judicial assistance away from diplomatic channels and towards specialised Central Authorities proved successful, yet the Central Authorities of today represent far more than a simple streamlining of requests for international judicial assistance.

The increasing importance of the role of Central Authorities over the last half century has been accompanied by an expansion of their key responsibilities. Noting that many of the obligations of Central Authorities are unique to the Convention under which they are designated, the discussion of tasks and responsibilities specific to each Convention is reserved for subsequent chapters.[52] There are, however, some general observations to be made about the functions of Central Authorities.

Earlier in this chapter, the functions of National Organs were illustrated in the context of four key activities of the HCCH. The latter two activities, concerning the implementation and operation of HCCH Conventions, necessarily involve Central Authorities. Many observations made above in relation to National Organs therefore apply equally to Central Authorities. However, in

[49] See, eg, Access to Justice Convention (n 29) Arts 3 and 8; Child Abduction Convention (n 12) Arts 8–11.

[50] Convention of 1 July 1985 on the Law Applicable to Trusts and on their Recognition; 2005 Choice of Court Convention (n 29); Convention of 5 July 2006 on the Law Applicable to Certain Rights in Respect of Securities held with an Intermediary; 2019 Judgments Convention (n 29); and the 2015 Choice of Law Principles (n 29).

[51] While their Convention responsibilities are essentially limited to the issuance and facilitation of the verification of Apostilles, Competent Authorities have taken on a more active role, communicating and cooperating to resolve difficulties, and coming together regularly at Special Commission meetings. Some Contracting Parties even have a de facto 'Central Authority' which, by virtue of internal law or practice, supervises the functions of the Competent Authorities designated under the Convention. This is particularly the case in States where notaries are the designated Competent Authorities, such as Brazil and Tunisia.

[52] See chs 12, 13 and 33–36 in this book.

contrast to National Organs, Central Authorities have the benefit of numerous HCCH publications specifically addressing establishment and operation of these authorities, outlining their key obligations and responsibilities.[53]

i. *Incorporation and Implementation of Conventions*

In keeping with fundamental notions of private international law, the structure and organisation of Central Authorities is left to the State in question.[54] This provides Contracting Parties with great flexibility and independence, enabling them to adapt the organisation of their Central Authorities to legal, political and socio-cultural realities, delegating functions and responsibilities as appropriate.

Therefore, with respect to incorporation and implementation, while the Central Authority comes into formal existence only upon its designation as such, its work may begin much sooner. Prior to a State's accession or ratification, consideration must be given to the most appropriate 'Central Authority' and how it will be organised.

Once the State has joined the Convention, Central Authorities play a key role preparing for its entry into force, promoting the Convention and training personnel, activities which are best coordinated with the National Organ. To ensure consistency in procedures and interpretation, in particular in the early stages of implementation, Central Authorities should develop internal guidelines, which will also facilitate the induction of new staff at later stages.

ii. *Supporting, Monitoring and Reviewing the Operation of Conventions*

The most important of the auxiliary responsibilities conferred upon Central Authorities is that of supporting, monitoring and reviewing the operation of the relevant instrument. First, while their level of involvement differs for each Convention, all Central Authorities should seek to ensure efficiency and expediency in processing requests. Second, Central Authorities have a responsibility to cooperate with their counterparts in other States and to promote this same spirit of cooperation among domestic authorities. In the context of international family law, these responsibilities are expressly articulated as obligations,[55] yet they remain desirable objectives for Central Authorities under all HCCH Conventions.

In the context of monitoring and reviewing, the first-hand experience of Central Authorities provides an invaluable insight into good practices and operational difficulties. For this reason, Special Commissions have long adopted conclusions and recommendations based on the experience of Central Authorities, whether to increase efficiencies, mitigate adverse effects of divergent practices or to facilitate the use of technology.[56] An essential element of a Central Authority's role

[53] See, eg, HCCH Permanent Bureau, *Guide to Good Practice under the 1980 Hague Child Abduction Convention: Part I – Central Authority Practice* (Jordan Publishing 2003); HCCH Permanent Bureau, 'Chapter 4 – Institutional Structures: Central Authorities and Accredited Bodies' in *Guide to Good Practice No 1: The Implementation and Operation of the 1993 Intercountry Adoption Convention* (Jordan Publishing 2008); HCCH Permanent Bureau, *Practical Handbook on the Operation of the Service Convention*, 4th edn (2016) paras 111 et seq.

[54] See also, Taborda Ferreira (n 40) 367.

[55] See, eg, Child Abduction Convention (n 12) Arts 2, 7 and 10; Adoption Convention (n 27) Arts 6–9; Child Support Convention (n 27) Arts 6 and 7.

[56] See, eg, *Report of the 1977 Special Commission* (n 45); *Report of the 1978 Special Commission* (n 47); HCCH Permanent Bureau, 'Annex IV: C&Rs of the SC' in *Guide to Good Practice on the Use of Video-Link under the Evidence Convention* (2020) 173–78.

is therefore to actively participate in meetings of the Special Commission convened to review the practical operation of the relevant instrument. As early as the 1979 Special Commission meeting, participation of Central Authority staff was recognised to be 'notable progress in the development of international judicial co-operation'.[57] After the conclusion of the meeting, Central Authorities have a responsibility to apply, implement and publicise these conclusions and recommendations in their home State.

The role of Central Authorities is much more than supporting, monitoring and reviewing the operation of HCCH Conventions; they are the 'engine rooms' without which the Conventions would not operate. Their expertise and insights therefore make them a primary source of information for domestic stakeholders and the public. As such, Central Authorities should ensure adequate provision of materials and services, including the promotion of HCCH publications and supplementary tools.

C. Challenges and Opportunities

In the same way that some of their primary functions overlap with those of National Organs, Central Authorities face many of the challenges outlined in the first part of this chapter. However, just as for National Organs, experience offers good practices to assist in overcoming the challenges faced by Central Authorities.

i. Resourcing and Competence

The ability of a Central Authority to effectively execute its functions under the relevant Convention is determined not by the obligations enshrined in the text, but in the proper establishment and adequate resourcing of the authority itself. First, it is important that, from its establishment, the Central Authority has the necessary legal power to carry out the tasks required of it. Second, States should ensure their Central Authorities are afforded sufficient resources, including qualified staff to oversee operations.

Unfortunately, in the broader context of the lack of visibility of private international law noted above, the practical reality is often an understaffed and under-resourced office, inundated with the sheer volume of cases, requests, negotiations, consultations and publications.

However, there are ways to overcome these challenges. States have adopted various approaches to mitigate resourcing difficulties, often by striking a balance between centralisation and decentralisation. For example, many States have sought to consolidate responsibility for multiple HCCH Conventions within a single unit or department,[58] while delegating or outsourcing some Central Authority responsibilities, either by designating multiple Central Authorities[59] or utilising 'competent' or 'additional' authority mechanisms, where permitted by the relevant Convention.[60]

[57] *Report of the 1978 Special Commission* (n 47) 7, §8.

[58] This trend was already evident as early as the 1977 Special Commission meeting, with many of the designated Central Authorities being the same for both the Service and Evidence Conventions. See *Report of the 1977 Special Commission* (n 45) 10. For example, in the case of Brazil, the Ministry of Justice plays the role of Central Authority under all HCCH Conventions to which it is a Party (and for which the designation of a Central Authority is required), with responsibility for most conferred upon a single department.

[59] eg, as Canada has done under the Service Convention.

[60] eg, as Australia has done under the Evidence Convention.

ii. Developing Expertise

When Central Authorities lack resources, there are limited opportunities for staff to fully develop a sufficient level of expertise. Some States have sought to address this by streamlining Central Authority responsibilities, providing the office with greater oversight while encouraging staff to acquire specialist knowledge operating as a Central Authority under a select few instruments. As mentioned above in the context of National Organs, other States have sought to supplement their expertise with input from academics, legal professionals and other stakeholders.

In the case of the family law Conventions, the higher burden placed upon Central Authorities means they are necessarily more implicated in the management of files, their staff gaining more intimate knowledge of the operation of the Conventions and in many cases, enjoying a closer relationship with the Permanent Bureau. While this same level of involvement is not formally required under the civil procedure Conventions, more active case management from within Central Authorities could have a demonstrably positive effect on the operation of the Conventions.

Once the requisite level of expertise has been developed, maintaining it becomes equally important. Central Authorities should therefore work to encourage stability among staff and, where possible, continuity among the experts with which the Central Authority engages.

iii. Progressive Implementation

The 'progressive implementation' of HCCH Conventions presents both a challenge and opportunity for Central Authorities.[61] The principle requires that Central Authorities regularly review practices and procedures, making adjustments as appropriate. This enables them to improve efficiencies and adapt to the changing needs of a changing population in an ever-changing world.

To ensure Central Authorities are aware of developments and challenges both within their State and abroad, it is important for them to consult other Convention actors. This may involve liaising with competent authorities domestically or leveraging international cooperation opportunities, such as during Special Commission meetings or through the HCCH International Hague Network of Judges. Authorities are also encouraged to exchange experiences on an *ad hoc* basis. Establishing personal contacts and building relationships leads to increased trust between authorities and may facilitate the resolution of any difficulties that may arise.

In addition, the periodic review of practices and procedures by Central Authorities informs the work of the Permanent Bureau and can lead to further post-Convention work, including the development of targeted resources.[62] In this way, Central Authorities shape the practical operation of the HCCH Conventions, benefiting not only their own State, but the entire network of Contracting Parties.

IV. The Continuing Legacy of National Organs and Central Authorities

National Organs and Central Authorities have long been fundamental to the operation of the HCCH and its Conventions. This has led not only to the recognition of legal cooperation as the

[61] For a discussion of the principle of 'progressive implementation', see 'Chapter 3 – Key Operating Principles' in *Guide to Good Practice No 1* (n 53) paras 114 et seq.

[62] eg, the practical experience of States under the Evidence Convention led to development of the *Guide to Good Practice on the Use of Video-Link under the Evidence Convention* (HCCH Permanent Bureau 2020).

newest pillar of the private international law, but to the realisation that the operation of a global legal cooperation network requires support. The ability of the HCCH to fulfil its global mandate is therefore intrinsically linked to the effectiveness of National Organs and Central Authorities.

National Organs play an essential role in policy decisions, including in relation to ongoing normative work, and in the coordination of their State's consideration of a particular Convention or instrument. They are involved in the subsequent implementation and operation of HCCH Conventions and promotional work, together with Central Authorities designated under the Conventions. Central Authorities are necessarily more implicated in the practical operation of HCCH Conventions, and their active involvement is crucial to the continuing relevance and success of these instruments. As illustrated throughout this chapter, an investigation of their respective origins reveals how their functions have evolved over time.

While their roles differ, National Organs and Central Authorities face many common challenges with respect to prioritisation, resources and expertise, all of which are compounded by a lack of visibility of private international law in government and the wider community. Irrespective of their size, composition or organisation, these institutions must be provided with the necessary resources to perform the many essential functions conferred upon them, just as their creators intended.

9

Substance and Procedure

RICHARD GARNETT

I. Introduction

The distinction between substance and procedure forms part of all major systems of private international law.[1] Matters of procedure are governed by the law of the forum and matters of substance are subjected to the law of the cause of action or obligation, selected by application of the appropriate applicable law rule of the forum.

The distinction between substance and procedure must also be analysed against the wider context of private international law, whose objectives include the pursuit of uniformity of outcome in decisions of national courts and the discouragement of forum shopping.[2] Such aims are compromised when national systems to determine the law applicable to a cross-border case allow too wide a scope for the operation of forum law at the expense of foreign rules. Arguably, a narrow and limited definition of procedure focusing on the idea of the conduct or regulation of court proceedings is more consistent with these concerns.[3] Also, when considering whether a procedural classification is justified, it is important to consider other methods of reference to forum law such as public policy and overriding mandatory rules. Either of these categories may be a more principled basis for applying forum law.[4] Finally, there may be scope in some cases to apply procedural rules of a country other than the forum, although the current approaches to substance and procedure do not explicitly acknowledge this.[5]

This chapter suggests that while common law and civil law views of what is substantive and what is procedural have traditionally diverged, more recently the gap between the positions has been closing. This topic therefore provides an important example of emerging harmonisation in private international law.

II. Background

The rule that forum law governs procedural matters (*lex fori regit processum*) is of ancient origin, dating back in civil law countries to the thirteenth century.[6] The original definition of procedure

[1] See generally, R Garnett, *Substance and Procedure in Private International Law* (Oxford University Press 2012).
[2] *Neilson v Overseas Projects Corp (Vic) Ltd* (2005) 223 CLR 331, [89]–[91] (Gummow and Hayne JJ).
[3] Garnett (n 1) ch 2.
[4] Ibid, ch 3.
[5] Ibid, 2–3.
[6] Ibid, 6.

was those norms which the judge used to conduct the proceeding. Such rules were distinguished from those employed to resolve the merits of the dispute before the court which were governed by the law of the relevant obligation. Civil law writers continued to follow the distinction which is now the universally admitted position in civil law countries.[7]

Common law countries, by contrast, originally gave a much wider scope to the concept of procedure, determining that it included all aspects of relief and enforcement in a suit (the remedy).[8] Under this approach, it was only matters involving the abrogation of 'the right' as opposed to the remedy, which were considered substantive and so could be governed by the law of the obligation and potentially, foreign law.

The consequence, therefore, was that a greater range of matters were referred to the law of the forum under the common law interpretation of procedure than under the more restrictive civil law view. The distinction remains important as it is arguable that the right-remedy analysis of substance and procedure continues to apply in some common law jurisdictions. By contrast, two key EU and UK instruments on applicable law grant a wide field of operation to the law of the obligation, see Article 12 of the Rome I Regulation[9] and Article 15 of the Rome II Regulation.[10] Those instruments are more consistent with the narrow civil law view of procedure.

III. General Principles

The strict common law/civil law dichotomy referred to above has been eroded in Australia and Canada who have developed an approach that is similar to the traditional civil law view. Matters affecting the mode, conduct or regulation of court proceedings are classified as procedural but matters affecting the existence, extent or enforceability of the rights and duties of the parties to an action are substantive.[11] This approach may also now apply in Hong Kong.[12]

The effect of this reformulation of the distinction in Australian and Canadian law has been to reduce the number of issues which are regarded as procedural and subjected to forum law. In other Commonwealth jurisdictions, however, including England and Wales (hereafter England), Singapore and New Zealand, the traditional right-remedy approach has been generally maintained,[13] although in England the impact of EU law has altered the position in contractual and non-contractual obligations covered by the Rome I and II Regulations.

In the USA perhaps the most widely accepted view is that taken in the 1971 Restatement (Second) of Conflict of Laws.[14] Under that Restatement no attempt is made to classify issues according to whether they are substantive or procedural, but instead the focus is on defining the

[7] eg, for France, see B Audit, *Droit International Privé*, 3rd edn (Economica 2005) [14].

[8] *Huber v Steiner* [1835] 2 Bing 202, 210.

[9] Regulation (EC) No 593/2008 of the European Parliament and of the Council of 17 June 2008 on the law applicable to contractual obligations [2008] OJ L177/6 (Rome I); see M McParland, *The Rome I Regulation on the Law Applicable to Contractual Obligations* (Oxford University Press 2015).

[10] Regulation (EC) No 864/2007 of the European Parliament and of the Council of 11 July 2007 on the law applicable to non-contractual obligations [2007] OJ L199/40 (Rome II); see A Dickinson, *The Rome II Regulation* (Oxford University Press 2008).

[11] *John Pfeiffer Pty Ltd v Rogerson* (2000) 203 CLR 503 [99]; in *Tolofson v Jensen* (1994) 120 DLR (4th) 289, 321 the Supreme Court of Canada described procedural matters as those that 'make the machinery of the forum court run smoothly'.

[12] *First Laser Ltd v Fujian Enterprises (Holdings) Co Ltd* (2012) 15 HKCFAR 569 [95].

[13] See, eg, for England, *Harding v Wealands* [2007] 2 AC 1; for Singapore, *Star City Pty Ltd v Tan Hong Woon* [2002] 1 SLR (R) 306 (Sing CA) but *cf Goh Suan Hee v Teo Cher Teck* [2010] 1 SLR 367 [21]. In New Zealand, commentators have advocated abandoning the traditional approach: M Hook and J Wass, *The Conflict of Laws in New Zealand* (LexisNexis 2020) 329.

[14] American Law Institute, Restatement of the Law, Second: Conflict of Laws, 1971.

scope of operation of forum law in respect of individual issues. Significantly, however, in determining whether forum law should govern, the Restatement adopts criteria similar to the recent Australian/Canadian approach; eg, a provision of forum law will not be applied where its purpose is found to 'affect the decision of the issue' or 'the ultimate result'.[15] Where, by contrast, a provision merely concerns 'the conduct of the trial', then forum law should be applied.

A similar trend to that in the US Second Restatement can be seen in the EU and UK Rome I and II Regulations referred to above. While the drafters excluded matters relating to evidence and procedure from the scope of the Regulations (Article 1(3) Rome I and Rome II Regulations), the overall approach involves subjecting specific issues directly to the applicable law of the obligation.

In applying the substance-procedure distinction courts have also had to examine important questions of classification. First, it is generally accepted that when characterising an issue as substantive or procedural, the law of the forum applies, not the law of the cause of action.[16] Hence, in the case of 'self-characterising' provisions, where the legislature expressly states that a provision in a statute is substantive or procedural, the prevailing view, at least among Australian courts, is that where such a provision forms part of the law of the cause of action, it is to be ignored and forum law principles of classification are to be applied to determine its effect.[17] Second, courts have generally adopted a holistic, rather than provision-specific, approach to characterising foreign legislative 'codes' as substantive or procedural.[18]

IV. The Principles Applied

In considering the application of the substance-procedure distinction to specific issues the primary focus will be on decisions of common law countries (for reasons of accessibility) with some reference to international instruments. While the narrow 'mode or conduct of court proceedings' view is advocated in this chapter, where decisions reflect the right-remedy approach, this will be noted. The impact of EU law, principally through the Rome I and II Regulations, will also be addressed, where a growing alignment with the Australia/Canada position can be discerned. Finally, attention will be drawn to those issues where foreign procedural rules should be applied.

A. Service and Jurisdiction

The manner of effecting service of originating process on a defendant is procedural and governed by forum law.[19] Where however service out of the jurisdiction on a foreign defendant is involved, the laws of most common law jurisdictions[20] and international instruments[21] allow service to

[15] Ibid, §122 comment a.

[16] *Leroux v Brown* (1852) 12 CB 801; *Huntington v Attrill* [1893] AC 150.

[17] *Hamilton v Merck & Co Inc* (2006) 66 NSWLR 48 [44] (Spigelman CJ, with whom Handley and Tobias JJA agreed); *Nalpantidis v Stark* (1996) 65 SASR 454, 459; *Alvear v Chetwynd Park Pty Ltd* [2014] VSC 214 [20].

[18] *Harding v Wealands* (n 13) [11] (Lord Woolf), [42], [48] (Lord Hoffmann) *cf* [73]–[77] (Lord Rodger); *Chomos v Economical Mutual Insurance Co* (2002) 216 DLR (4th) 356; *Hamilton v Merck & Co Inc*, ibid, [61], [67]–[69] (Spigelman CJ).

[19] Garnett (n 1) 71.

[20] For England see CPR r 6.40(3)(c).

[21] See, eg, Hague Convention of 15 November 1965 on the service abroad of judicial and extrajudicial documents in civil or commercial matters 658 UNTS 163 Art 19; Council Regulation EC 1393/2007 of 13 November 2007 on the service in the Member States of judicial and extrajudicial documents in civil or commercial matters Art 7(1).

be performed by any method permitted under the law of the country in which service is to be performed. Yet, service in a foreign country cannot involve conduct that is contrary to the law of such country.[22] This topic is an example of the forum applying foreign procedural rules.

Questions relating to the jurisdiction of a country's courts are also considered procedural. In the case of a choice of court agreement, however, the law applicable to such an agreement determines its scope and validity,[23] while its ultimate effect on the jurisdiction of the forum is resolved by forum law.[24]

B. Parties to Litigation

The question of whether a claimant or defendant has separate legal personality or capacity to sue or be sued is generally accepted as substantive, as it directly affects the parties' rights and is governed by the law of the entity's domicile or country of formation.[25] European civil law countries take the same approach.[26] By contrast, the question of whether the claimant or defendant is the type of entity that can be a party to litigation in the forum is procedural and governed by forum law, given its proximity to the conduct of court proceedings.[27] So, therefore, while the question of whether a company has been dissolved is a matter for the law of the country of incorporation,[28] the issue of whether a dissolved company can sue in the forum is governed by the law of the forum.[29]

The question of whether the claimant or defendant is the proper party to litigation is governed by the law of the cause of action. Consequently, the right of a claimant to sue directly the tortfeasor's liability insurer is substantive and governed by the law of the country creating such obligation.[30] This position also applies under EU law[31] and in European civil law countries.[32]

The statutory right of a tortfeasor to recover contribution from another tortfeasor arising from a primary wrong is widely viewed as substantive,[33] as it relates to the rights and liabilities of the parties. This position also applies under UK and EU law.[34] A claimant's right to subrogation is also substantive and governed by the law of the obligation under national law rules[35] and also under EU and UK law,[36] as is the issue of vicarious liability[37] and the question of whether a right to sue for damages survives the death of the victim and passes to his or her estate.[38]

[22] For England see CPR r 6.40(4). See generally *Humpuss Sea Transport Pte Ltd (in liq) v PT Humpuss Intermoda Transportasi TBK* [2015] 4 SLR 625.

[23] *Hamlyn & Co v Talisker Distillery* [1894] AC 202; *Shanghai Turbo Enterprises Ltd v Liu Ming* [2019] 1 SLR 779 [81] (Sing CA); Convention of 30 June 2005 on Choice of Court Agreements Art 6(a).

[24] *Global Partners Fund Ltd v Babcock & Brown Ltd (in liq)* (2010) 79 ACSR 383; *Shanghai Turbo Enterprises Ltd v Liu Ming*, ibid.

[25] *Chaff and Hay Acquisition Committee v JA Hemphill & Sons Pty Ltd* (1947) 74 CLR 375; *Maritime Investment Holdings Inc v Underwriting Members of Syndicate 1183 at Lloyds* [2015] EWHC 2190 (Comm) [7].

[26] See Garnett (n 1) 119 for references.

[27] L Collins and J Harris (gen eds), *Dicey, Morris and Collins on the Conflict of Laws*, 15th edn (Sweet & Maxwell 2012) 208; *7722656 Canada Inc v Financial Services Authority* [2013] EWCA Civ 1662 [75] (Lewison LJ dissenting).

[28] *Banque Internationale de Commerce de Petrograd v Goukassow* [1923] 2 KB 682 (CA).

[29] *Cirque du Soleil Inc v Volvo Group Canada Inc* (2015) 126 OR (3d) 234 [17].

[30] *Mapfre Mutualidad Compania de Seguros y Reaseguros SA v Keefe* [2016] 1 WLR 905 [80] (CA).

[31] Rome II Reg Art 18.

[32] See Garnett (n 1) 124 for references.

[33] *Sweedman v Transport Accident Commission* (2006) 226 CLR 362.

[34] Rome II Reg Art 15(b).

[35] *West Tankers Inc v Ras Riunione Adriatica Di Sicurta Sp A* [2005] EWHC 454 (Comm).

[36] Rome II Regulation Art 19.

[37] *The Halley* (1886) LR 2 PC 193; for UK and EU law, see Rome II Reg Art 15(g).

[38] Restatement (Second) §124 comment a; for UK and EU law, see Rome II Reg Art 15(e).

An issue which has divided common law courts is the status of a statutory derivative action, ie, a claim brought by a minority shareholder on behalf of a company for a wrong done to the company. The more widely accepted and better reasoned view is that the right to bring a derivative action is substantive, being intrinsically related to the rights and obligations of the parties and governed by the law of the place of incorporation.[39]

C. Judicial Administration

Issues concerning the constitution and competence of courts, the rules governing how an action is commenced, standing to sue,[40] the form and requirements of pleadings,[41] court powers to manage and conduct the proceedings (including joining additional parties or causes of action),[42] and the rules governing dismissal for abuse of process are procedural according to either the narrow or wide views of procedure.

Also widely acknowledged as procedural are the right to a jury trial or a public hearing, whether a party has a right to appeal,[43] and any statutory duty on a claimant to give notice to the defendant before commencing proceedings (at least where a failure to do so does not extinguish the cause of action).[44] The right to recover costs and legal expenses is also best classified as procedural as a tool in the management and control of the litigation process.[45]

Questions relating to the administration and distribution of a debtor's[46] or a deceased person's[47] assets, including issues of priority between creditors,[48] are also procedural matters governed by the law of the forum. The rationale for this view is practicality and efficiency, especially where the administration involves large numbers of claims by creditors from different jurisdictions. By contrast, EU law provides[49] that: 'the law applicable to the succession' should govern questions relating to the administration of the estate and the ranking of creditors.[50]

Authority in common law countries is however split on the nature and status of the right of the creditor who makes a claim to a fund (eg, relying on a maritime lien). Some English[51] decisions have regarded such a right as procedural and not applicable where it arises under the law of the cause of action. Canadian and US courts, by contrast, favour a substantive classification on the basis that the recognition of foreign security interests has little to do with the conduct of

[39] *Konamaneni v Rolls Royce Industrial Power (India) Ltd* [2002] 1 WLR 1269; *Hausman v Buckley* 299 F 2d 696 (2nd Cir, 1962); *East Asia Satellite Television (Holdings) Ltd v New Cotai LLC* [2011] 4 HKC 115 [37] (HKCA).

[40] *Breffka & Hehnke GmbH & Co KG v Navire Shipping Co Ltd* [2012] EWHC 3124 (Comm) [66]; C-396/13 *Sähköalojen ammattiliitto ry v Elektrobudowa Spółka Akcyjna* EU:C:2015:86 [20].

[41] eg, whether alternative claims may be brought arising out of the same facts: *Kazakhstan Kagazy Plc v Zhunus* [2017] EWHC 3374 (Comm) [144].

[42] *E Hofmann Plastics Inc v Tribec Metals Ltd* 2013 QCCA 2112 [15] ('joinder serves to streamline the judicial procedure'); Restatement (Second) §127 comment a (4).

[43] *Julia Farr Services Inc v Hayes* (2003) 25 NSWCCR 138; Restatement (Second) §127 comment a (9).

[44] *Hamilton v Merck & Co Inc* (n 17).

[45] *Somers v Fournier* (2002) 60 OR (3d) 225 [17]–[18]; *Labuda v Langford* [2001] ACTSC 126 [6]; *Hyde v Sara Assicurazioni SpA* [2014] EWHC 2881 (Ch) [33]; *Re the Enforcement of a United States Judgment for Damages* (Bundesgerichtshof Case IX ZR 149/91) [1994] IL Pr 602.

[46] *Re Melbourn* (1870) LR 6 Ch App 64.

[47] *Shenken v Phoenix Life Ltd* [2015] CSOH 96 [14].

[48] *The Ioannis Daskalelis* [1974] SCR 1248; *The Halcyon Isle* [1981] AC 221, 230–31; *The Betty Ott* [1992] 1 NZLR 655; *The Andres Bonifacio* [1993] 3 SLR(R) 71 [35] (Sing CA).

[49] EU Succession Regulation (650/2012) [2012] OJ L201/107.

[50] Recital 42; Art 23.

[51] *The Halcyon Isle* (n 48) 238.

court proceedings but impacts significantly on the rights and liabilities of the parties.[52] This latter view is to be preferred.[53]

Under EU and UK law, where a maritime lien arises in the context of a contract, it would likely be one of 'the consequences of a breach'[54] or if in the context of a non-contractual obligation, it would arguably be a 'measure … to ensure the provision of compensation'.[55]

The form and requirements of a judgment and meaning of any of its terms fall within the rubric of the forum's power of management and control of its proceedings and should be determined by the law of the country where the judgment was rendered.[56] This rule applies even in proceedings for recognition of such judgment in a foreign country – in which case foreign procedural rules are applied. The methods of enforcing a court's orders must however be those of the court in which enforcement is sought.[57]

D. Evidence

The law of evidence is partly procedural and partly substantive. The issue as to what are the material facts in a given case to prove, such as whether a contract exists, is substantive and governed by the law of the obligation. By contrast, the matter of how the facts in issue are to be proved, including the methods of proof which may be used (whether by oral or documentary evidence), is procedural.

The question of admissibility of evidence has been traditionally regarded as procedural in common law countries.[58] So, eg, a foreign law requirement that a document be stamped before being admitted into evidence is not applicable in the forum.[59] European civil law countries however take the view that if a document is formally valid according to the law of the place of its execution (*lex loci actus*) then it should be admitted into evidence in the forum.[60] EU and UK law under Article 18(2) of the Rome I Regulation take a more expansive approach, providing that a contract or an act intended to have legal effect may be proved by any mode of proof recognised by either the law of the forum, the law of the obligation or the law of the place of execution under which that contract or act is formally valid.

Common law countries that still apply the right-remedy view of substance and procedure have also drawn a distinction between extrinsic evidence relied upon to interpret a document and such evidence which adds to or varies the document's terms. The first situation is classified as an issue of interpretation of the instrument and governed by the law of the cause of action, but the second case is seen as an issue of admissibility of evidence and governed by forum law.[61] The consequence of this view is that the common law parole evidence rule – by which oral evidence

[52] See, eg, *The Strandhill* [1926] SCR 680; *Bominflot Inc v the MV Heinrich S* 465 F 3d 1013 (4th Cir, 2006).

[53] A hybrid approach now applies in Australia: the right must exist under the law of the cause of action *and* amount to a maritime lien under forum law: *The Ship 'Sam Hawk' v Reiter Petroleum Inc* (2016) 246 FCR 337.

[54] Rome I Reg Art 12(1)(c).

[55] Rome II Reg Art 15(d).

[56] *Martyn v Graham* [2003] QDC 447.

[57] *John Pfeiffer Pty Ltd v Rogerson* (n 11) [192] (Callinan J); *Martin v Nadel* [1906] 2 KB 26, 29 (garnishee order).

[58] *Bain v Whitehaven and Furness Junction Railway* (1850) 3 HLC 1; *Re Metal Storm Ltd (in liq) (Recrs and Mgrs Apptd) (No 2)* [2019] NSWSC 1682 [7].

[59] *Rothwells Ltd (in liq) v Connell* (1993) 119 ALR 538; *Herd v Haines* [2020] NZCA 396 [31], although in the latter case the court noted that a different result would ensue where the effect of non-stamping would be to render the document null and void.

[60] See Garnett (n 1) 193 for references.

[61] *Korner v Witkowitzer* [1950] 2 KB 128; *BQP v BQQ* [2018] 4 SLR 1364 [122].

may not be admitted to contradict the terms of a subsequent written agreement – will apply to a contract governed by the law of a civil law country where no such rule exists. By contrast, under the narrower 'mode or conduct of court proceedings' view of procedure, the issues of both interpretation and variation are considered substantive given their equally clear impact on the rights and liabilities of the parties as they determine the meaning and existence of the terms of an agreement.[62]

The issue of burden of proof was originally considered by common law countries to be procedural,[63] but more recently there has been a movement in favour of a substantive classification, driven by the fact that the question of which party bears the burden of proof can have a plainly outcome determinative effect in certain cases.[64] An example is where a claimant can provide no evidence of a right which he or she claims, yet under the law of the obligation which creates the right, the burden of proof would rest on the person denying the right to prevent the claimant succeeding. The substantive analysis is also adopted by most courts and commentators in the US.[65] Under the EU and UK Rome I and II Regulations, the applicable law of the obligation will apply to the extent that it contains, in the law of the obligation, rules which determine the burden of proof.[66]

Presumptions are treated in the same manner as the burden of proof[67] at least where they are not linked to the court's proceedings or fact-finding processes, in which case a procedural view will be adopted.[68]

A statutory provision which requires that, for a transaction to be enforceable, it must be evidenced in writing has long been regarded as procedural in common law countries that apply the right-remedy view of substance and procedure.[69] Yet under the narrower 'mode or conduct of court proceedings' view of procedure, such an issue is considered substantive as it clearly affects the rights of the parties and the outcome of litigation.[70]

The question of whether a witness is competent or compellable to testify is clearly procedural and governed by forum law on either of the above tests of substance and procedure. Also, issues such as the weight or value to be given to admitted evidence, rights to disclosure,[71] summonses against third parties, expert reports,[72] the method by which witness evidence is to be received and whether examination of witnesses may occur[73] are all procedural matters.

The Rome I[74] and II[75] Regulations suggest that this view would also apply under EU and UK law by providing that any mode of proof must be capable of being administered by the forum.

[62] M Davies, A Bell, P Brereton and M Douglas, *Nygh's Conflict of Laws in Australia*, 10th edn (LexisNexis 2020) 410; *Filter Solutions Ltd v Donaldson Australia Pty Ltd* [2006] NZHC 762.

[63] *The Roberta* (1937) 58 Lloyd's Rep 159, 177.

[64] *Fiona Trust and Holding Corporation v Privalov* [2010] EWHC 3199 (Comm) [94]; A Briggs, *The Conflict of Laws*, 2nd edn (Clarendon Press 2008) 234.

[65] Restatement (Second) of Conflict of Laws §133.

[66] Rome I Reg Art 18(1); Rome II Reg Art 22(1).

[67] *Re Cohn* [1945] Ch 5 (presumption as to order of death); *Henry v Henry Estate* (2014) 325 Man R (2d) 1 [43] (HC Beard JA, concurring) (presumption of paternity); *Fiona Trust and Holding Corporation v Privalov* (n 64) [98] (presumption that payment of bribe in relation to a contract causes loss); Rome I Reg Art 18(1); Rome II Reg Art 22(1).

[68] *Zoya Ltd v Ahmed* [2016] EWHC 1981 (Ch) [79] (evidential presumption).

[69] *Leroux v Brown* (n 16); *Naraji v Shelbourne* [2011] EWHC 3298 (QB).

[70] *Miller Farm Equipment (2005) Inc v Shewchuk* (2009) 335 Sask R 111 [56]; *Tipperary Developments Pty Ltd v the State of Western Australia* [2009] 38 WAR 488.

[71] *Secretary of State for Health v Servier Laboratories Ltd* [2013] EWCA Civ 1234 [99]; but a court retains a discretion not to order disclosure where a party may be at risk of prosecution under foreign law.

[72] *Wall v Mutuelle de Poitiers Assurances* [2014] EWCA Civ 138.

[73] Ibid.

[74] Art 18(2).

[75] Art 22(2).

E. Legal Professional Privilege

The traditional view of lawyer–client privilege is that it is a question of admissibility of evidence and governed exclusively by forum law.[76] In more recent decisions, however, commentators have questioned this view on the basis that the recognition of privilege may affect the outcome of a case.[77] Some English, Australian, Singaporean and Hong Kong judges have adopted a 'hybrid' position, where privilege is accepted as substantive but governed by forum law on the basis of local public policy, due to its link to the administration of justice.[78]

Significantly, international instruments show some flexibility in terms of applicable law. Article 11 of the Hague Evidence Convention[79] allows a party to resist disclosure in the context of a request for oral testimony or production of documents where a privilege exists under the law of the requesting or requested States or where there is a duty or obligation not to provide evidence under either or both laws. Article 14 of the EU Evidence Regulation[80] is to the same effect.

F. Estoppel

Classification of the doctrine of estoppel is complex. Issue estoppel arises where a particular matter has been decided in earlier proceedings and a party is precluded from raising it in subsequent proceedings and cause of action estoppel (*res judicata*) prevents a subsequent suit being brought on the same cause of action. In respect of both such estoppels it is universally accepted that such matters are procedural and governed by the law of the forum of adjudication.[81]

In the context of issue and cause of action estoppel based on a *foreign judgment*, however, common law courts have accepted that the law of the country in which the judgment was rendered should also be applied to determine whether the judgment was 'final and conclusive' and so eligible for recognition in the forum.[82] Further, according to recent English authority, for an issue estoppel to exist in respect of a foreign judgment, the law of the country of rendition must have a similar doctrine and regard the issue relied upon to form the estoppel as having preclusive effect.[83] To that extent, therefore, both the law of the forum and the law of the country of rendition (as a foreign procedural rule) apply. The same result also applies in the case of *Henderson v Henderson* estoppel, ie, where a party is precluded in subsequent proceedings from raising a cause of action or issue which they could and should have raised in earlier proceedings.[84]

[76] *Kennedy v Wallace* (2004) 142 FCR 185; *Bourns Inc v Raychem Corporation* [1999] 3 All ER 154; *Rochester Resources Ltd v Lebedev* [2014] EWHC 2185 (Comm).

[77] J McComish, 'Foreign Legal Professional Privilege: A New Problem for Australian Private International Law' (2006) 28 *Sydney Law Review* 297, 311, 320; Garnett (n 1) 236.

[78] *Stewart v Australian Crime Commission* (2012) 206 FCR 347 [53] (Besanko J); *Re the RBS Rights Issue Litigation* [2016] EWHC 3161 (Ch) [171]; *CIFG Special Assets Capital I Ltd v Polimet Pte Ltd* [2016] 1 SLR 1382 [56] (Sing HC); *Super Worth International Ltd v Commissioner of the ICAC* [2016] 2 HKC 416 [20] (HKCA).

[79] Hague Convention of 18 March 1970 on the taking of evidence abroad in civil or commercial matters, 847 UNTS 241.

[80] Council Regulation (EC) No 1206/2001 of 28 May 2001 on cooperation between the courts of the Member States in the taking of evidence in civil or commercial matters [2001] OJ L174/1.

[81] *Carl-Zeiss Stiftung v Rayner and Keeler Ltd (No 2)* [1967] 1 AC 853; *First Laser Ltd v Fujian Enterprises (Holdings) Co Ltd* (n 12) [97].

[82] *Carl-Zeiss Stiftung v Rayner and Keeler Ltd (No 2)*, ibid; *Bellezza Club Japan Co Ltd v Matsumura Akihiko* [2010] 2 SLR 342 [15]; *Zheng Zhenxin v Chan Chun Keung* [2018] HKCFI 2284 [47].

[83] *Mad Atelier International BV v Manes* [2020] EWHC 1014 (Comm).

[84] *PCH Offshore Pty Ltd v Dunn (No.2)* (2010) 273 ALR 167.

Other estoppels, such as estoppel by representation of existing fact, estoppel by convention,[85] promissory and proprietary estoppel, are generally regarded as substantive, given their close connection to the rights and liabilities of the parties.[86] The closely related doctrine of waiver is also best considered substantive.

G. Statutes of Limitation

The traditional common law approach to limitation questions was based on the right-remedy view of substance and procedure. Where a limitation provision merely 'barred the remedy' such as where it was expressed in terms such as 'an action shall not be brought except within X time period' it was considered procedural and not applicable in the forum where it was part of a foreign law of the cause of action. Such a view no longer applies in the UK after the Foreign Limitation Periods Act 1984 (FLPA), New Zealand after the Limitation Act 2010,[87] Singapore after the Foreign Limitation Periods Act 2013[88] and Australia[89] and Canada[90] who now treat all limitation provisions as substantive and applicable as part of the law of the cause of action. Such an approach is consistent with the European civil law view of limitation periods.[91]

The rationale is that all statutes of limitation, whether barring the remedy or right, have a direct impact on the rights and liabilities of the parties to the litigation in that they determine whether an action may proceed. Limitation is an example of a topic where the common law right-remedy view has been abandoned, even in jurisdictions that apply this approach to other issues. The law of the cause of action also determines whether a party has a right to an extension of time and the event which causes the limitation period to commence running.[92] The same approach applies under EU and UK law for contractual and non-contractual obligations.[93]

Note, however, that forum law may still apply where the effect of applying a foreign limitation provision would be to cause the claimant or defendant undue hardship[94] or where it would be otherwise manifestly contrary to public policy.[95] English and Singaporean courts have found, however, that something more than the fact that the forum's limitation period is more generous than the foreign provision is required to establish hardship, such as where the claimant was misled by the defendant as to the operation of the provision.[96] The foreign limitation provision must give the claimant, if acting with diligence, a reasonable opportunity to pursue the claim.[97] Where a claimant has knowledge of the foreign time bar, within the applicable limitation period, there is no undue hardship.[98]

[85] *First Laser Ltd v Fujian Enterprises (Holdings) Co Ltd* (n 12) [105].
[86] See Garnett (n 1) 219–21 for references.
[87] s 55(2).
[88] s 3(1).
[89] *John Pfeiffer Pty Ltd v Rogerson* (n 11).
[90] *Tolofson v Jensen* (n 11).
[91] See, eg, for France, Audit (n 7) [445].
[92] Garnett (n 1) 270 citing references.
[93] Rome I Reg Art 12(1)(d); Rome II Reg Art 15(h).
[94] FLPA s 2(2); Foreign Limitation Periods Act 2013 (Sing) s 4(2); Limitation Act (2010) (NZ) s 56(2).
[95] FLPA s 2(1); Rome I Art 21; Rome II Art 26.
[96] *Harley v Smith* [2010] EWCA Civ 78 [55]; *Jones v Trollope Colls Cementation Overseas Ltd* (*The Times*, 26 January 1990).
[97] *Alseran v Ministry of Justice* [2019] QB 1251 [828]; *L v Murphy* [2016] EWHC 3102 [54]; *Bank of St Petersburg OJSC v Arkhangelsky* [2014] EWCA Civ 593; *Recovery Vehicle 1 Pte Ltd v Industries Chimiques du Senegal* [2020] SGCA 107.
[98] *Recovery Vehicle 1 Pte Ltd v Industries Chimiques du Senegal*, ibid, [137]; *Arab Monetary Fund v Hashim* [1996] 1 Lloyd's Rep 589.

H. Remedies: Non-Monetary Relief

The position in common law countries has long been that a claimant can only obtain remedies which are available under forum law.[99] The rationale for this view is that remedies are part of the court's machinery for resolving disputes and it is not practical for the forum to have to implement foreign remedies alien to the forum's traditions and processes. The form of the remedy sought in litigation is therefore universally regarded as a matter of procedure.[100] Arguably, however, forum law should not apply to all aspects of remedies or else the application of foreign law on matters of liability will be undermined. The better view therefore is that where the remedy sought exists under forum law and the law of the cause of action, it is for the latter law to determine whether such relief may be granted on the facts of the case.[101]

English and Hong Kong courts have also had to consider the situation where the precise remedy sought in relation to a cause of action governed by foreign law does not exist under such law. In such circumstances, at common law, the court will consider the nature of the liability under foreign law and grant the remedy an English court would provide for English liability analogous to that under the foreign law.[102] So where, for example, a foreign law does not recognise the remedy of constructive trust for unjust enrichment, this is no bar to such relief being granted where the foreign law imposes analogous obligations to disgorge a benefit or fiduciary duties.[103]

The Rome I and II Regulations may however be more restrictive on this issue. Article 15(d) of Rome II provides that the law of the obligation applies to 'a measure designed to prevent or terminate injury or damage' and Article 12(1)(c) of Rome I provides that the applicable law applies to 'the consequences of a … breach of obligations'. While in both cases any remedy sought must be 'within the limits conferred by the forum's procedural law', it is not clear that a court may grant a remedy under forum law which does not exist under the law of the obligation.

i. *Interim Relief*

The traditional position in common law countries is that the availability of all interim measures, such as interlocutory injunctions, freezing or search orders and anti-suit injunctions, is procedural and hence governed by forum law. The absoluteness of this procedural classification in all cases must however be questioned.

First, in the case of anti-suit injunctions, where the injunction is sought only to protect the processes of the forum court, a procedural analysis is warranted but where enforcement of contractual or equitable rights is involved, a substantive classification is arguably more appropriate.[104] Second, where an interlocutory injunction is sought to restrain a breach of contract or a tort, the law of the obligation will be applied to determine whether a breach has occurred at least to the level of an arguable case. Once this is shown, principles of forum law are then applied to determine whether the injunction will be granted on the facts.[105]

[99] *John Pfeiffer Pty Ltd v Rogerson* (n 11) [99].
[100] *Phrantzes v Argenti* [1960] 2 QB 19.
[101] *Shanghai Electric Group Co Ltd v PT Merak Energi Indonesia* [2010] SGHC 2.
[102] *Cox v Ergo Versicherung AG* [2014] AC 1379 [19], [21]; *Fiona Trust and Holding Corporation v Privalov* (n 64) [158]; *Kuwait Oil Tanker Co SAK v Al Bader* [2000] 2 All ER (Comm) 271; *First Laser Ltd v Fujian Enterprises (Holdings) Co Ltd* (n 12) [66].
[103] *First Laser Ltd v Fujian Enterprises (Holdings) Co Ltd* (n 12).
[104] Such a conclusion would apply even more strongly in the case of a *final* injunction in respect of contractual or equitable rights.
[105] *Modern Computer Systems Inc v Modern Banking Systems Inc* 871 F 2d 734 (8th Cir, 1989); *Vital State Canada Ltd v Dreampak LLC* 303 F Supp 2d 516 (DNJ 2003).

In the case of interlocutory injunctions, the position under the Rome I and II Regulations would likely be different in requiring application of the law of the obligation to all aspects of the case.[106] Such orders would fall under Article 15(d) of Rome II, which provides that the law of the obligation applies to 'a measure designed to prevent or terminate injury or damage' and Article 12(1)(c) of Rome I as part of 'the consequences of a … breach'.[107]

Freezing and search orders, while 'enforcement mechanisms'[108] may nevertheless fall within the scope of Article 15(d) of the Rome II Regulation which applies the law of the obligation to 'measures … to ensure the provision of compensation'. The law of the obligation would then apply to the grant of the remedy, provided that remedy also existed under the law of the forum.

ii. Final Relief

In common law countries, final non-monetary relief such as orders for specific performance, rescission, declarations and injunctions, have historically been regarded as procedural because they originated in the medieval equitable jurisdiction based on conscience.[109] Such a classification is also consistent with the right-remedy view of substance and procedure. More recent commentary[110] and most US courts[111] however assert that the availability of final non-monetary relief, being intricately connected with the merits of the case, should be classified as substantive and governed by the law of the cause of action.

This latter view also applies under the Rome I and II Regulations.[112] Under Article 12(1)(c) of Rome I, the law of the obligation applies to 'the consequences of a total or partial breach of obligations' (which would include all final remedies in relation to contracts). Likewise, Article 15(d) of Rome II applies the law of the obligation to a measure designed to prevent or terminate injury or damage.

iii. Damages

In the area of damages for tort and contract, the distinction between substance and procedure has arisen frequently. In common law jurisdictions it is well established that the issue of available heads of damages (economic loss, physical injury) are classified as substantive and governed by the law of the cause of action.[113] Questions of remoteness of damage are similarly treated.[114]

It is also universally accepted that the right to claim interest on a contractual debt is substantive and governed by the law applicable to the contract.[115] A substantive classification also generally

[106] *OJSC TNK-BP Holding v Lazurenko* [2012] EWHC 2781 (Ch).

[107] McParland (n 9) 755; L Merrett, 'Commercial Remedies in International Cases' in G Virgo and S Worthington (eds), *Commercial Remedies* (Cambridge University Press 2017) 511.

[108] Merrett, ibid, 512.

[109] *National Commercial Bank v Wimborne* (1978) 5 BPR 11,958, 11,982; *Blue Steel Investments LLC v Hegco Canada Inc* (2013) 562 AR 1 (specific performance procedural).

[110] A Briggs, 'Conflict of Laws and Commercial Remedies' in A Burrows and E Peel (eds), *Commercial Remedies Current Issues and Problems* (Oxford University Press 2003) 271, 275; T Yeo, *Choice of Law for Equitable Doctrines* (Oxford University Press 2004) [4.24]–[4.27].

[111] See, eg, *Allegheny Energy Inc v DQE Inc* 171 F 3d 153, 159 (4th Cir, 1999).

[112] Merrett (n 107) 508; but *cf Actavis UK Ltd v Eli Lilly & Co* [2015] EWCA Civ 555 (conditions required to be satisfied for grant of a negative declaration are procedural).

[113] *Boys v Chaplin* [1971] AC 356, 379; *Breavington v Godleman* (1988) 169 CLR 41.

[114] *J D'Almeida Araujo Lda v Sir Frederick Becker & Co Ltd* [1953] 2 KB 329.

[115] *Mount Albert Borough Council v Australian Temperance and General Mutual Life Assurance Society* [1938] AC 224 (PC).

applies in the case of the right to pre-judgment interest, ie, interest by way of damages dating from the time of accrual of the cause of action,[116] although some English courts[117] maintain that the issue is procedural.

The question of deductibility from an award of damages of benefits already received by the claimant now appears to be accepted as substantive by most common law countries.[118]

All common law jurisdictions also accept that where general tort law recovery has been abolished by statute and replaced by a 'no fault' administrative scheme then such a scheme is substantive and applicable as part of the law of the cause of action.[119] Such a view would almost certainly be shared by European civil law jurisdictions.

Perhaps the most difficult and contentious question in relation to damages concerns quantification and assessment. English courts have long regarded the issue of assessment of damages as wholly procedural. Such an approach not only embraces the computational aspect of assessment but also the situation where the legislature imposes a limitation on damages. So, eg, if a foreign law of the cause of action restricted damages for non-economic loss an English court could ignore such a limitation on the ground that it is procedural.[120] The English approach must however now be read in light of Article 15(c) of Rome II and Article 12(1)(c) of Rome I (discussed below).

While Canadian[121] and Malaysian[122] courts take a similar approach to the English common law position, in Australia this view has been rejected with the High Court declaring that 'all questions about the … amount of damages that may be recovered … be treated as substantive issues'.[123] According to this approach, any issue regarding the assessment of damages is determined by the law of the cause of action. The Singapore Court of Appeal has expressed sympathy for the Australian position without conclusively endorsing it.[124]

In applying the Australian test, the forum court may receive evidence from foreign experts as to the likely ranges of recovery if the matter went to trial in the foreign country.[125] All jurisdictions would agree, however, that the forum cannot apply a rule under foreign law which requires a body such as a jury or special assessor to conduct an assessment as this would be beyond its procedural powers.[126]

Article 15(c) of the Rome II Regulation provides that the applicable law of the non-contractual obligation 'shall govern in particular … the existence, nature and the assessment of damage or the remedy claimed' and Article 12(1)(c) of the Rome I Regulation uses similar language in relation to contract. The effect of such provisions is that the available heads of damages and limitations or caps on damages are subjected to the law of the obligation. Further, all questions relating to the award of pre-judgment interest including the right to claim such interest and at what rate, are also so classified.[127] The issue of deductibility of benefits would also likely fall within Article 15(c) of the Rome II Regulation as a matter relating to the assessment of damages.

[116] *Somers v Fournier* (n 45) [28].

[117] Interpreting s 35A of the Senior Courts Act: *Maher v Groupama Grand Est* [2010] 1 WLR 1564; *JSC BTA Bank v Ablyazov* [2013] EWHC 867 (Comm) [26].

[118] *Cox v Ergo Versicherung AG* (n 102).

[119] *McMillan v Canadian Northern Railway Co* [1923] AC 120; *Amaca Pty Ltd v Frost* (2006) 67 NSWLR 635; *Sandhu v Vuong* 2016 BCSC 1490.

[120] *Harding v Wealands* (n 13); *Naraji v Shelbourne* (n 69) [179].

[121] *Somers v Fournier* (n 45) [51] (Ont CA); *Das v George Weston Ltd* 2018 ONCA 1053 [94].

[122] *Scandinavian Bunkering (Singapore) Pte Ltd v MISC Bhd* [2015] 3 MLJ 753 (Fed Ct).

[123] *John Pfeiffer Pty Ltd v Rogerson* (n 11) [100].

[124] *Goh Suan Hee v Teo Cher Teck* (n 13) [16], [21]–[22].

[125] Garnett (n 1) 333.

[126] *Re T & N Ltd* [2005] EWHC 2990 (Ch) [83].

[127] *XP v Compensa Towarzystwo SA* [2016] EWHC 1728 (QB) [67]; *cf Troke v Amgen* [2020] EWHC 2976 (QB) (discretionary right to interest under foreign law is procedural).

The more complex question under EU and UK law is whether all issues relating to the assessment of damages are referred to the law applicable to the obligation. Since both Article 15(d) of Rome II and Article 12(1)(c) of Rome I provide that the forum is only obliged to act within the limits of its procedural powers, a forum court would not apply a rule under foreign law which requires a body such as a jury to conduct an assessment. Yet, in assessing damages under the law of the obligation a court could again receive evidence from foreign experts as to likely ranges of recovery.[128] The position under EU and UK law is therefore similar to that which applies in Australia.

V. Conclusion

The substance and procedure distinction remains highly significant in private international law. Historically civil law and common law jurisdictions took differing positions on where to draw the line between substantive and procedural matters, with the common law taking a more expansive view of procedure. The gap between the two views has however narrowed in recent times, due to three factors. First, in Australia, Canada, Hong Kong and the United States a more limited concept of procedure based on court process or 'machinery' has been adopted which more closely mirrors the civil law position. This new approach aims to deter forum shopping and encourage uniformity of outcome between national courts through limiting the scope of the law of the forum. Second, the impact of the Rome I and II Regulations has legislatively allocated more matters to the applicable law of the obligation in the EU and the UK. Finally, international instruments such as the Hague Service, Evidence and Choice of Court Conventions and the EU Service and Evidence Regulations have created autonomous principles on certain issues.

While it would be premature to suggest that there has been a global unification of the principles in this area of private international law, there is undoubtedly evidence of increasing convergence.

[128] The court may refer to the 'practices, conventions and guidelines' used by judges to calculate damages under the applicable law: *Wall v Mutuelle de Poitiers Assurances* (n 72) [24].

10

Application of Foreign Law

MARTA REQUEJO ISIDRO

I. Introduction

The world may well be territorially and legally fragmented: human interactions know no borders. Private International Law (PIL) was born, and continues to exist, out of the need to ensure that rational solutions are given to disputes involving foreign elements. The application of a foreign law does not only belong to the set of imaginable 'rational solutions': it is actually the essential one. It is also one hard to put into practice for a number of reasons, starting with the very simple fact that total ignorance or imperfect knowledge of foreign law – 'a natural consequence of the training of the judges in the law of their own country' – is the rule.[1]

The difficulties in the application of foreign law are not a trivial matter. They may lead to the unjust determination of a case; to the failure of legitimate expectations of the parties; even further, to the violation of a fundamental right.[2] In addition, cross-border relationships are not exceptional or anecdotic occurrences. On the contrary, thanks to globalisation and the related phenomena, the presence of a foreign element is a normal condition of private relationships; foreign law must be applied, taken into account or, at least, consulted, more and more often. Even if the Covid-19 crisis has shaken the fundaments of the world as we know it, return to an era of closed borders and limited cross-border interaction is highly improbable.

Continuous scholarly and institutional attention paid to application-of-foreign law issues does not come as a surprise. Two approaches may be distinguished: one addresses the procedural treatment of foreign law; it focuses in particular on the absence, both worldwide and at the regional level, of a shared set of rules governing the application of foreign law. The other concentrates on ways to get knowledge of the foreign law applicable in a given case. They are not mutually exclusive: the reason to prefer one or the other with a view to achieving some degree of international agreement is purely practical, as evidenced by the evolution of the works at the Hague Conference from 2006 to 2015 in relation to the topic. After a global expert meeting in February 2007, it was concluded that any attempt to harmonise the rules for the procedural treatment of foreign law was unlikely to succeed. Therefore, the project shifted from that perspective to one focused on providing access to foreign legal systems.[3]

[1] GS Alexander 'The Application and Avoidance of Foreign Law in the Law of Conflicts: Variations on a Theme of Alexander Nekam' (1975) 70 *Northwestern University Law Review* 602, 604, quoting I Zajtay 'The Application of Foreign Law' (1972) 3 *International Encyclopedia of Comparative Law* 14-1–14-13.

[2] See *ad ex* ECtHR, judgment of 6 April 2004, Application no 75116/01 *Karalyos and Huber v Hungary and Greece*.

[3] See the Conclusions and Recommendations (Report of the Conference 'Access to Foreign Law in Civil and Commercial Matters', Brussels, 2012), available at: assets.hcch.net/upload/foreignlaw_concl_e.pdf, point 4.

In 2015, the Hague Conference abandoned the topic with the understanding that it could be revisited at a later stage. To date, it has not come back to the agenda.[4] In the meantime, a few initiatives of geographically limited reach are slowly taking off. The following pages outline the *status quo* and give an insight on experiences gained at regional levels; they also provide some conclusions. Should the Conference works be resumed, they may be a starting point for reflection.

II. The Procedural Treatment of Foreign Law

A. The Enduring Impasse

The academic and institutional interest in the procedural treatment of foreign law has never waned.[5] A particular emphasis has been put on the EU, as a regulatory environment with a unique degree of unification of the conflict of laws rules in civil and commercial matters.[6] After 2010, publically funded studies analysed in-depth and comparatively most questions relevant to the topic:[7] whether the conflict of laws rules are compulsory or not; who bears the burden of proof; what is to be proven; means of proof; reactions to the lack of proof or insufficient proof of the contents of the foreign law; review by upper courts; costs, etc. Some years later, a similar kind of exercise including jurisdictions outside the EU was undertaken under the auspices of the International Academy of Comparative Law.[8]

The research confirmed that multilateral conflict of laws rules remain a common tool for the determination of the law applicable to cross-border settings, and that legal systems privileging a different approach do not completely escape from the need to ascertain the contents of foreign law.[9] The studies coincided as well in their assessment of the historical divide between systems considering foreign law as law (thus to be applied *ex officio* and subject to the *iura novit curia* principle), and systems where it is characterised as a fact (thus to be pleaded by the interested party). While the conceptual distinction still exists, it is commonly acknowledged that no jurisdiction brings the theoretical approach to its final consequences. In practice, this entails the absence of a clear frame for the application of a foreign law: taking the example of the EU, scholars speak of a 'significant level of inconsistency … in Europe between the

[4] For a summary of the works see P Lortie and M Groff, 'The Evolution of the Work on Access to Foreign Law at the Hague Conference on Private International Law' in Y Nishitani (ed), *Treatment of Foreign Law: Dynamics Towards Convergence?* (Springer 2017) 615.

[5] M Jäanterä-Jareborg 'Foreign Law in National Courts a Comparative Perspective' (2003) 304 *Hague Collected Courses* 181; S Geeroms, *Foreign Law in Civil Litigation: A Comparative and Functional Analysis* (Oxford University Press 2004); S Lalani, 'A Proposed Model to Facilitate Access to Foreign Law' (2011) 13 *Yearbook of Private International Law* 299; R Hübner, *Ausländisches Recht vor deutschen Gerichten* (Mohr Siebeck 2014); J Verhellen, 'Access to foreign law in practice: easier said than done' (2016) 12 *Journal of Private International Law* 281; J-P Ancel et al, *L'application du droit étranger: cycle de conferences* (Société de Législation Comparée 2018).

[6] See M Requejo Isidro 'The application of European Private International Law and the ascertainment of foreign law' in J von Hein, EM Kieninger and G Rühl (eds), *How European is European Private International Law?* (Intersentia 2019) 139, with further references.

[7] Such as the research study contracted out by the European Commission to the Swiss Institute of Comparative Law in 2009, entitled *The Application of Foreign Law in Civil Matters in the EU Member States and its Perspectives for the Future.*

[8] Y Nishitani (ed), *Treatment of Foreign Law: Dynamics Towards Convergence?* (Springer 2017); Y Nishitani, 'Proof and Information about Foreign Law' in M Schauer and B Verschraegen (eds), *General Reports of the XIXth Congress of the International Academy of Comparative Law* (Springer 2017) 165.

[9] No legal system is based on strict unilateralism. Theories espousing policy analysis require knowledge of the foreign law as (at least in theory) a differentiated step prior to the decision on its application. The law-finding process may also be an element in jurisdiction-selecting decisions, eg, *forum (non) conveniens* motions and the like.

theoretical position embraced by States and the role assigned to the parties',[10] leading to non-predictable consequences for the parties. The panorama is not much different in jurisdictions outside the EU.[11]

Moreover, the research carried out confirmed that the application-of-foreign-law process encounters severe difficulties, remains time-consuming and costly to the detriment of the good administration of justice, and ends up much too often with the non-application, or the misapplication,[12] of the foreign law. As the need to access and to apply foreign law is not confined to litigation before the courts, non-judicial authorities and lawyers are confronted with the same troubles.

To this setting, the lack of common rules on the application of foreign law adds further negative impacts. From a systemic point of view, the final goal of the progressive global unification of private international law is jeopardised, or directly lost: the uniform rules do not lead to equally uniform decisions. In addition, the absence of shared solutions creates uncertainties and increases management cost, which in turn deter the economic operators from entering into cross-border transactions.

B. The Failure of the Wide-Ranging Normative Approach

Would it be possible to solve the application-of-foreign-law puzzle at the normative level? When the question was considered at the Hague Conference, it did not take long to conclude that any attempt to harmonise the approaches to the procedural treatment of foreign law was unlikely to succeed.[13] Normative solutions have not been endorsed either in the privileged legal environment of the EU. A more modest legislative intervention helps minimise the occasions where the application of foreign law is required.

i. Mandatory Application of the Conflict of Laws Rules

Ideally, to sort out the problems linked to the application of a foreign law and guaranteeing, at the same time, the consistent operation of unified conflict of laws rules, a common set of rules should be adopted, prompting, as point of departure, the *ex officio* application of the conflict of laws rules.[14] A proposal in this sense was made for the EU PIL Regulations at a conference held in Madrid in February of 2010, which led to the so-called 'Madrid Principles'.[15] To date, the 'Madrid Principles' are just an academic attempt to address the foreign law difficulties, and will likely remain so.

[10] C Esplugues Mota 'Harmonization of Private International Law in Europe and Application of Foreign Law: The 'Madrid Principles' of 2010' (2011) 13 *Yearbook of Private International Law* 281.

[11] See for the US, LE Teitz in D Fernández Arroyo and F Ferrari (eds), *Private International Law: Contemporary Challenges and Continuing Relevance* (Edward Elgar 2019) ch 16.

[12] While there are no recent broad surveys on the wrong application of a foreign law, scholars continue to report examples: see D Foxton, 'Foreign Law in Domestic Courts' (2017) 29 *Singapore Academy of Law Journal* 194, 209.

[13] 'Feasibility Study on the Treatment of Foreign Law – Report on the meeting of 23–24 February 2007', prepared by the Permanent Bureau, Prel Doc No 21 A of March 2007 for the attention of the Council of April 2007 on General Affairs and Policy of the Conference. See as well, P Beaumont, 'When Should EU Private International Law Require that Foreign Law be Applied?' in J von Hein, EM Kieninger and G Rühl (eds), *How European is European Private International Law?* (Intersentia 2019) 177, 181 – a comprehensive instrument on proof of foreign law is not needed.

[14] C Trautmann, *Europäisches Kollisionsrecht und ausländisches Recht im nationalen Zivilverfahren* (Mohr Siebeck 2011) Part 2.

[15] The Principles can be found in Annex to Esplugues Mota (n 10).

ii. Foreign-Law-Avoidance Strategies

In the history of private international law, the belief in the parity of national substantive laws has to be contrasted with homeward trend theories. The preference for the *lex fori* may be due to substantive policy reasons and require the examination of the contents of the foreign law prior to its exclusion; it may also be a simple, pragmatic solution to avoid the difficulties inherent in the application of a foreign law.[16]

But, just like the suggestions in favour of the mandatory application of foreign law, the parallelism between *forum* and *ius* is seldom authorised in general terms. Where it is the reasons are mainly substance- (and not procedure-) related: the *lex fori in foro proprio* is a principled solution in the EU Succession Regulation[17] as well as in the EU Insolvency Regulation.[18] Where the *lex fori* is adopted for the sake of simplicity, it is typically just one possibility among others, and depends on a choice by the parties, either of the applicable law itself, or of the courts of the country of the applicable law.[19] In addition, the parties may have the freedom to choose the *lex fori* after the proceedings have commenced, hence for the determination of the specific matters under dispute, as in Article 7 of the Hague Maintenance Protocol.[20]

iii. A Flexible, Tailor-Made Approach: The Unique Case of the Hague Convention on Child Abduction (1980 Convention)

In any process, late justice is not justice; but even in this regard not all disputes are equal. Certain procedures require fast action, lest they become completely useless. At the cross-border level insolvency and child abduction are well-known examples.

Many legal orders respond to the need for speed by establishing urgent or preferential procedures, characterised, among other things, by severe time limits for the different procedural acts. Should foreign law be ascertained, one would expect specific provisions facilitating access to it. Article 14 of the 1980 Convention corresponds to this very idea. Because the removal (or retention) of a child is only wrongful if it is in breach of custody rights attributed under the law of the State where the child was habitually resident immediately before the removal or retention, the competent authorities of requested States must take that law into consideration when deciding whether a child should be returned. Article 14 was adopted to allow the competent authorities to take judicial notice of foreign law (or of judicial or administrative decisions rendered in application of that law), directly, ie, without recourse to the specific procedures for the proof of that law or for the recognition of foreign decisions which would otherwise be applicable.[21] By way of complement, Article 15 provides for the possibility of requesting from the authorities of the

[16] See for instance, on Art 7 of the Hague Protocol of 23 November 2007 on the Law Applicable to Maintenance Obligations, A Bonomi, *Explanatory Report to the Protocol of 23 November 2007 on the Law Applicable to Maintenance Obligations* 115, says it responds 'to the benefits in terms of simplicity that arise from application of the law of the forum'.

[17] Reg 650/2012 [2012] OJ L201/27.

[18] Reg 2015/848 [2015] OJ L141/19.

[19] eg, Art 5 of the Succession Regulation.

[20] E-M Kieninger, 'Ascertaining and Applying Foreign Law' in S Leible (ed), *General Principles of European Private International Law* (Wolters Kluwer 2016) 358.

[21] See Explanatory Report on the 1980 HCCH Child Abduction Convention (Offprint from the Acts and Documents of the Fourteenth Session (1980), tome III, Child abduction), para 69, 110 ff; Guide to Good Practice Child Abduction Convention, Part II – Implementing Measures, Chapter 6.5.1, both available at: www.hcch.net/en/publications-and-studies/details4/?pid=2781.

child's habitual residence a declaration on the wrongful nature of the removal, amounting to a definitive ruling on foreign law.[22]

Article 14 has been successfully used in practice;[23] Article 15 has met more difficulties. A questionnaire circulated among Contracting States prior to the Sixth Meeting of the Special Commission on the Practical Operation of the 1980 Convention, held in 2011, revealed, among other things, that the possibility to get a declaratory judgment in the sense of Article 15 is unknown to some legal systems; where it exists, the delay in receipt of the decision or determination may make it no longer useful in the return proceedings, or that those proceedings are substantially delayed in flagrant breach of a principal purpose of the Convention.[24] The problems are indeed not insurmountable, but require action from the Contracting States.[25]

III. Access to Foreign Law (and Making One's Law Available)

The reciprocal sharing of the knowledge about the content of the laws of different countries is a sensible solution to the problems experienced in the treatment of cross-border civil and commercial relationships. This can be done in two (complementary) ways: (a) through cooperation, providing information on law upon request; (b) making law generally accessible to the public.

A. Administrative and Judicial Cooperation

Cooperation between administrative authorities of different jurisdictions for the application of a foreign law is the classical form of cooperation, usually set up by a convention and, more rarely, unilaterally.[26] Many bilateral conventions providing for reciprocal assistance in legal matters refer expressly to exchanges of information regarding substantive law – although they do not usually establish a procedure for the purpose,[27] or could be interpreted in that way. PIL multilateral Conventions done at The Hague regarding specific family matters include rules to the

[22] Both provisions are drafted in a way that would allow for direct application in the Contracting States. To check whether specific implementing rules have nevertheless been adopted see the country profiles, available at: www.hcch.net/es/instruments/conventions/publications1/?dtid=42&cid=24.

[23] See, among others, the decisions of 17 April 2020, *MBR v YR*, of the District Court in Tel Aviv-Yaffo serving as Court of Civil Appeals (esp paras 10 and 11 of the Discussion and Ruling); of 7 February 2002, of the Paris Court of Appeal (n 2001/21768); of 3 May 2001, *Armiliato v Zaric-Armiliato*, of the United States District Court for the Southern District of New York (Art 14 referred to, but not needed in this case as the proof of foreign law was clear in accordance with US law); of 18 August 1994, of the Outer House of the Court of Session (Scotland), *Bordera v Bordera* 1995 SLT 1176, in which Lord Coulsfield relied on proof of foreign law in the usual way but referred to Art 14 of the Convention (source and further references: INCADAT, available at: www.incadat.com/en).

[24] A *Discussion paper on the operation of Article 15 of the 1980 Child Abduction Convention* by the Permanent Bureau was released in August 2017 for the purposes of the Seventh Meeting of the Special Commission, summarising the findings of the survey and including recommendations for an improved application of the provision, available at: www.hcch.net/en/publications-and-studies/details4/?pid=6545&dtid=57. See also the interesting *obiter dicta* on Art 15 by Lord Coulsfield in *Bordera*, ibid.

[25] As acknowledged by the Conclusions and Recommendations adopted by the Special Commission on the practical operation of the 1980 and 1996 Hague Conventions in October 2017, available at: www.hcch.net/en/publications-and-studies/details4/?pid=6545&dtid=57.

[26] See for instance, Art 36 of the 2015 Spanish Ley de cooperación jurídica internacional, which is binding only on the Spanish authorities; in addition, it is subject to a de facto reciprocity on the side of the requesting State.

[27] See for instance, the Conventions on civil cooperation signed between France and Tunisia, of 28 June 1972, Art 25; France and Cameroon, of 21 February 1974, Art 61; Spain and Morocco, of 30 May 1997, Art 33 ff.

same effect.[28] Furthermore, multilateral Conventions have been adopted in some regional organisations: the best known are the 1969 London Convention on information on foreign law, Council of Europe, and the 1979 Montevideo Convention on proof of and information on foreign law, Organization of American States.[29]

The availability of support from judicial authorities – or from other legal professionals such as notaries – is a more recent, developing cooperative formula: promising, but not unbounded.

i. Administrative Cooperation: An Unavoidable Second Best

On the basis of international agreements, administrative authorities act as intermediaries for the purposes of obtaining information about foreign law in civil and commercial matters.[30]

A thorough evaluation of administrative cooperation would be impossible here. Limited to the two main multilateral Conventions,[31] the summary would be that they share a reputation of little success, which may nonetheless need to be reviewed.[32] It is frequently said that they are not well known; the claim of poor performance of the requesting and the replying authorities, and of tardy answers which, in addition, are formulated in abstract terms, is not uncommon.[33] In fact, to the extent that no in-depth, comprehensive, and up-to-date study has been devoted to the application in practice of the London and Montevideo Conventions,[34] any assessment is based on incomplete data and, therefore, partial. Moreover, a fair evaluation should take into account that the blame for the malfunction of the Conventions cannot be put exclusively on their authors, or on their wording. For instance, to this day not all the Contracting States have indicated to the Council of Europe Secretariat the mailing address of the receiving agency under the London Convention (or, even worse, who the responsible body for these purposes is).

[28] Hague Convention of 2 October 1973 Concerning the International Administration of the Estates of Deceased Persons, Art 5; Hague Convention of 25 October 1980 on the Civil Aspects of International Child Abduction, Arts 7(e), 8(f); Hague Convention of 29 May 1993 on Protection of Children and Co-operation in Respect of Intercountry Adoption, Art 7(2)(a); Hague Convention of 19 October 1996 on Jurisdiction, Applicable Law, Recognition, Enforcement and Co-operation in Respect of Parental Responsibility and Measures for the Protection of Children, Art 30(2); Hague Convention of 13 January 2000 on the International Protection of Adults, Art 29(2).

[29] Both are open to ratification by non-Member States. The Convention of 22 January 1993 on Legal Assistance and Legal Relations in Civil, Family, and Criminal Matters (the Minsk Convention), is usually referred to as well, but only one provision is actually devoted to the application of foreign law.

[30] The substantive scope of application of the London Convention was extended in 1979 to the field of criminal law and procedure via an additional Protocol, while the Montevideo Convention is not expressly limited to civil and commercial matters.

[31] Data on the actual working of the specific provisions in the Hague Conventions mentioned above (n 28) are available through the responses to the questionnaires concerning the practical operation of the different Conventions, published online, generally per country. Not surprisingly, the experiences vary considerably from one country to another.

[32] For a positive opinion see S-D Jastrow 'Zur Ermittlung ausländischen Rechts: Was leistet das Londoner Auskunftsübereinkommen in der Praxis?' [2004] *Praxis des Internationalen Privat- und Verfahrensrechts* 402; F Mélin, 'La cooperation internationale dans la recherché du droit étranger : les méthodes classiques' in J-P Ancel et al, *L'application du droit étranger: cycle de conferences* (Société de Législation Comparée 2018) 39, 55–59.

[33] Lalani (n 5), with further references; the author proposes a model to facilitate access to foreign law building on the strengths and weaknesses of the Conventions. Verhellen (n 5) 293–94. See also the Feasibility Study on the Treatment of Foreign Law – Summary of the Responses to the Questionnaire, Prel Doc No 9 A of March 2008, for the attention of the Council of April 2008 on General Affairs and Policy of the Conference, 10–12.

[34] See BJ Rodger and J Van Doorn, 'Proof of Foreign Law: The Impact of the London Convention' (1997) 46 *ICLQ* 151, which covered 21 Contracting States; and the questionnaire circulated in 2007 by the Permanent Bureau of the Hague Conference, in which 31 States took part ('Feasibility Study on the Treatment of Foreign Law – Questionnaire', drawn up by the Permanent Bureau, Prel Doc No 25 of October 2007 for the attention of the Council of April 2008 on General Affairs and Policy of the Conference). A survey on best practices in relation to the European Convention on Information on Foreign Law was electronically published on 30 April 2002 covering Germany, the UK and Slovakia. It does not seem to be available any longer.

From a principled perspective, the (relative)[35] ineffectiveness of these Conventions should not lead to the rejection of administrative cooperation as such, but rather trigger efforts to improve it. Administrative cooperation was for a long time the only realistic alternative to cumbersome diplomatic and consular channels. Today, it coexists with other forms of communication, which may prove better suited: whether this is the case depends on factors such as the foreign law at stake, the kind of information needed, the complexity of the questions, together with more prosaic elements like the proficiency of the requesting judge in a foreign language. Moreover, the lack of an accurate answer can be the consequence of an inaccurate query, a flaw that would affect negatively every form of cooperation.

ii. Judicial Cooperation: Scope and Limits

Besides classical (administrative) cooperation, the possibility of getting information about a foreign law from a provider used to apply that very law is slowly gaining ground; empirical evidence shows that the management of the requests in the framework of judicial networks can be swifter and quicker than administrative cooperation.[36] The fact that both the requesting authority and the one providing support are judges seems to be a psychological element favouring this type of cooperation.[37]

Assistance can be obtained through the contact points and the liaison judges of a judicial network, or (less common) by way of a direct communication between the judge or court seised, and a judge active in the State of the applicable law.

a. Judicial Networks

Judicial networks are in fashion. In the area of international judicial cooperation in civil and commercial matters, the International Hague Judicial Network (IHJN), and the European Judicial Network in Civil and Commercial Matters (EJN) are the most representative ones.[38]

1. The IHJN, counting 133 Members from 84 States, enables direct communication between liaison judges or a judge and another authority sitting in another country. The creation of the Network was proposed at the 1998 De Ruwenberg Seminar for Judges on the international protection of children, organised by the Permanent Bureau of the Hague Conference;[39] it is now managed and supported by the Permanent Bureau.

The Network has proven to be especially useful in international family matters, above all in cases of child abduction. The practical operation of the 1980 Convention was the main reason for establishing the Network; however, it does not need to be confined to that field.[40] On the other

[35] The London Convention has been ratified by 47 States, ie, almost one-fourth of the current existing jurisdictions. The Montevideo Convention is much more limited in this regard, with only 12 Parties.

[36] M Menne 'Die Arbeit der deutschen Verbindungsrichter im internationalen Familienrecht' [2019] *Zeitschrift für europäisches Privatrecht* 472, 483.

[37] Ibid, 485.

[38] Another one is the Ibero-American Network for Judicial Assistance (IberRED), established in October 2004 with a view to facilitating judicial assistance in the Ibero-American sphere. IberRED is composed of national correspondents from the Supreme Courts and Supreme Courts of Justice, the Judicial Councils, the Public Ministries and the Ministries of Justice or Central Authorities of the countries belonging to the Ibero-American Community of Nations. They are entrusted with tasks of active intermediation, streamlining, strengthening, simplifying and facilitating traditional mechanisms of international judicial cooperation.

[39] See: assets.hcch.net/docs/88af493b-a5b1-4a5c-9af1-992784063331.pdf.

[40] Conclusions and Recommendations of the Conference Celebrating the 20th Anniversary of the International Hague Network of Judges (24–26 October 2018), available at: assets.hcch.net/docs/69f03498-8a72-4ffe-aa44-30fc70493859.pdf, para 10.

hand, regarding the ascertainment of foreign law in particular, the Network can utilise the freedom provided by Article 14 of the 1980 Convention.[41]

2. At the EU level, Council Decision No 2001/470/EC,[42] set up a European Judicial Network for civil and commercial matters: a flexible, non-bureaucratic structure to improve, simplify and expedite effective cooperation between national judicial authorities in civil and commercial matters, through contact points in each Member State. A 2009 amendment makes the EJN a tool to get information on the national laws of EU Member States.[43] Under Article 5(2)(c), the contact points shall supply information to facilitate the application of the law of another Member State that is applicable under a Union or international instrument.

The European Commission's Report (2016) mentions no practice of the contact points or of the liaison judges in relation to the application of foreign law. According to the underlying study[44] the first objective of the EJN – namely, improving and facilitating effective judicial cooperation between the Member States in civil and commercial matters – seems to have been fulfilled very well, so it cannot be excluded that this kind of communication did take place.[45]

b. Judge-to-Judge *ad hoc* Communication

Answers given by contact points are of a theoretical nature; they lack the practical value of a response by an equivalent jurisdiction.[46] The alternative of formalised direct contacts between judges, exchanging queries on the applicable foreign law with a view to get an answer tailored to the case at hand, is worth exploring – although it should be acknowledged at the outset that the option remains academic.[47]

To date, no EU rule imposes judicial direct cooperation regarding the application of foreign law. Neither does any instrument of the Hague Conference. According to the 2007 Feasibility Study, the mechanism received little support from the experts, who rather expressed concerns: the model could affect domestic procedural law, result in judges' liability, and put the parties' right of due process at risk. They also listed practical obstacles – language barriers, workload of judges, formalities to be followed when posing questions – against this method, especially when compared with the informal judicial cooperation within the networks.[48]

The referral of a question of law to a foreign judge or court was already possible in the nineteenth century in some jurisdictions; it was never really exploited.[49] Today, it is foreseen in a few common law countries. In addition to the certification of questions of state law from federal

[41] See section II.B.iii above and ibid, para 11.

[42] [2001] OJ L174/25.

[43] Decision No 568/2009 [2009] OJ L168/35. Representatives of professional associations of legal practitioners may join the network; however, only judges are allowed to refer a request on the applicable law in relation to a specific case: E Bennett, 'Not only encouraged but essential: judicial collaboration in international family disputes' [2013] *International Family Law* 845, 850.

[44] Evaluation of the activities of the European Judicial Network in civil and commercial matters, JUST/2013/JCIV/FW/0103/A4, available at: op.europa.eu/en/publication-detail/-/publication/a877dc52-3f93-472b-a81f-9b7c5d810718.

[45] See Menne (n 36) 483: in 2017, the 17 German contact points processed a total of 131 inquiries; the four German liaison judges handled a total of 242 inquiries in 2017–135 inquiries in the EJN and 107 inquiries in the IHJN.

[46] GEDIP, 20ème réunion (2010), available at: www.gedip-egpil.eu/reunionstravail/gedip-reunions-20-fr.htm; Jäanterä-Jareborg (n 5) 321.

[47] See for instance, Jäanterä-Jareborg, ibid, 323.

[48] Feasibility Study on the Treatment of Foreign Law. Report on the meeting of 23–24 February 2007, Prel Doc No 21 A of March 2007 for the attention of the Council on General Affairs and Policy of the Conference, 5. See as well GEDIP, 20ème reunion (n 46).

[49] Such as the UK, under the British Law Ascertainment Act 1859 and the Foreign Law Ascertainment Act 1861.

courts in the US, which is confined to the legal systems of the sister states,[50] a rule has been adopted at the Supreme Court of New South Wales in Australia[51] and in Singapore[52] for international settings. How useful the option is in practice is unclear. Only a 2009 case of the Supreme Court of Singapore is known to date: the parties were ordered to refer a question of English law to the foreign court;[53] the Commercial Court in London answered the question.[54] It seems that a couple of further decisions exist originating in the UK.[55]

Memoranda of understanding (MoU) on references on questions of law between two jurisdictions, whereby each jurisdiction (or court) will provide an answer to a question of law submitted by the other, have been entered into in Singapore and Australia.[56] In practice, the MoUs have not been very successful: only one case has been reported from Australia so far,[57] and none from Singapore. An explanation may be the cumbersome character of the cooperation's design: both MoUs require that separate proceedings are conducted before the foreign court.

B. Making One's Law Available in the Time of Information and Communication Technologies

i. The (Unachieved) Trend Towards 'Open Law'

As a rule, legal acts are published. Publication is a common requirement for their entering into force; it may also determine the moment from which the act will be binding.

To the extent that the publication is made on paper in journals distributed within the territory of the State, and in the (or a) local language, it hardly helps authorities, legal practitioners or parties to a litigation in other countries seeking access to the foreign legal materials. However, the use of paper is no longer the norm. The Report of the Meeting of Experts on Global Co-operation on the Provision of Online Legal Information on National Laws, held in October 2008 under the auspices of the Hague Conference,[58] correctly highlighted the worldwide development of computerisation of legal information and the increasing trend towards rendering this material

[50] M Requejo Isidro 'Quelle communication des juges dans l'application de la loi etrangère?' in S Menétrey and B Hess (eds), *Les dialogues des juges en Europe* (Larcier 2014) 323, 328 ff, on the attempts to extend the procedure to international litigation.

[51] See s 125 Supreme Court Act 1970 (NSW), as amended by the Uniform Civil Procedure Rules (Amendment No 34) 2010.

[52] Rules of Court (Cap 322, R 5, 2014 Rev Ed) O 110 r 29(1)(a). 61 Rules of Court (Cap 322, R 5, 2014 Rev Ed) O 110 r 29(1)(b).

[53] *Westacre Investments Inc v The State-Owned Company Yugoimport SDPR (Jugoimport-SDPR)* [2009] 2 SLR (R) 166.

[54] *Westacre Investments Inc v Yugoimport SDPR* [2008] EWHC 801 (Comm).

[55] Another example of an ad hoc referral of a question of law from an English court to one in Switzerland is *Von Mitchke-Collande v Kramer* [2005] EWHC 977. In *Faraday Reinsurance Co Ltd v Howden North American Inc* [2012] EWCA 980, support was sought for proceedings opened in Pennsylvania.

[56] In Australia, the MoU between the Singapore Supreme Court and the New South Wales Supreme Court; and the one signed by Chief Justice Jonathan Lippman (Court of Appeals, New York State), and Justice James Spigelman (Supreme Court New South Wales). In Singapore, the *Westacre* experience triggered the MoU between the Singapore Supreme Court and the New South Wales Supreme Court already alluded to, plus two further MoUs on references of questions of law: in 2015, with the Dubai International Financial Centre Courts; in 2017, with the Supreme Court of Bermuda. In 2015 a similar MoU was signed by the Chief Justice of Singapore and the Chief Judge of the State of New York.

[57] *Marshall v Fleming* [2013] NSWSC 566. In addition, in 2014 the NSW Court of Appeal held that the provisions of the MoU on the appointment of the referee ran against the NSW rules of procedure: Nishitani, 'Proof and Information about Foreign Law' (n 8) 191.

[58] Report of the Meeting of Experts on Global Co-Operation on the Provision of Online Legal Information on National Laws (The Hague, 19–21 October 2008), Prel Doc No 11 B of March 2009 for the attention of the Council on General Affairs and Policy of the Conference, para 8.

accessible – to some extent against no payment. It was also acknowledged, though, that such a development poses in itself some challenges and would benefit from supportive forms of international cooperation. The Experts formulated some 'Guiding principles to be considered in developing a future instrument' concerning free access to legal materials in e-form, facilitating republication and reuse, integrity, identification of the origin, preservation, citations, translations, knowledge-based systems, and support and cooperation.[59] They also suggested that the Hague Conference could become a platform for cooperation with legal information institutes and governments, to facilitate access to foreign law and play a coordinating role in the various ongoing efforts to establish standards for online legal resources. The work could lead to a 'Hague portal on accessing foreign law' that would guide users to accredited (standards-based) legal information providers.[60]

Unfortunately, the proposal of the Experts was not accepted by the Hague Conference. Today, the digitisation of legal information has become the norm,[61] but this has not necessarily translated into an improved availability of legal materials for foreigners. While scholars claim free access to legal information should be recognised as a right,[62] official – governmental – sites' primary objective is not providing a service to foreign operators. As a consequence, their specific needs are not taken into account.

Much is still to be done to make legal information freely available to the legal professionals of a foreign origin: in terms of scope, official publications are often restricted to the primary sources of law; case law is not always accessible free of cost, nor are secondary (interpretative) materials;[63] language; helping understanding the taxonomy of the legal materials, etc. Efforts made by institutes for legal information,[64] or other scholarly initiatives[65] do not succeed in filling the gaps. On the contrary, fragmented information from many different sources populating the net, of dubious reliability and not subject to quality standards, is counterproductive.[66]

ii. *Information Sheets and 'Country Profiles'*

A first glimpse into a given foreign law can be achieved via information sheets such as those published on the EU e-justice portal. As a rule, a link to the national acts themselves is available. The duty to inform is imposed on the Member States by the EU;[67] however, the accuracy of the information depends on each Member State; there is no quality control, and non-compliance or poor compliance prompt no sanction. As a consequence, the information thus obtained may be taken as a starting point, but further research is required.

[59] Accessing the Content of Foreign Law and the Need for the Development of a Global Instrument in this Area – A Possible Way Ahead, March 2009, Prel Doc No 11 A of March 2009 for the attention of the Council of March/April 2009 on General Affairs and Policy of the Conference, Annex.

[60] Ibid, para 4.

[61] Entailing important consequences: for instance, since EU Council Regulation 216/2013, only the electronic editions of the Official Journal published after 1 July 2013 have legal force.

[62] L Ebenezer Mitee 'The Right of Public Access to Legal Information: A Proposal for Its Universal Recognition as a Human Right' [2017] *German Law Journal* 1429.

[63] Illustrating the many different practices in Europe, M van Opijnen, G Peruginelli, E Kefali and M Palmirani, 'Online publication of court decisions in Europe' [2017] *Legal Information Management* 136.

[64] The first LII was created in 1992 at the Cornell Law School. Others followed; the group was semi-formalised in 2002 with the signing of the Declaration on the Free Access to Law in Montreal, available at: www.worldlii.org/worldlii/declaration/montreal_en.html.

[65] Amateur legal databases on PIL national law and case law set up and supported by voluntary contributors, often in the context of research projects benefiting from governmental or institutional funding.

[66] On the other hand, the costs of making and maintaining reliable public databases would be simply enormous and difficult to explain to taxpayers, even in the context of a regional economic integration organisation such as the EU, as correctly pointed out by Beaumont (n 13) 178.

[67] See for instance, Regulation 2016/1103, recital 67, Art 63; Regulation 2016/1104, recital 65, Art 64.

In a similar vein, the Hague Conference website has a dedicated area for 'Country Profiles' regarding some of its Conventions.[68] There, information of a general character is provided on the law of each State in connection with the application of the Convention at hand: eg, implementing legislation and a description of the national laws concerning the subject matter of the Convention.[69]

iii. INCADAT: The Success of a Database Based on Voluntary Contributions

Any reference to publicly accessible databases on national legal materials would be incomplete without mentioning INCADAT.[70] INCADAT is a free and comprehensive tool for researching cases, case summaries and legal analysis of the application of the 1980 Hague Child Abduction Convention; it also provides additional material relevant to this area of law. The database, hosted by the Permanent Bureau of the Hague Conference, is sponsored by the German Federal Ministry of Justice and Consumer Protection and the law firm Miles & Stockbridges PC. It is regularly updated, and available in English, French and Spanish. As of June 2020, INCADAT comprises more than one thousand cases from all over the world.

It should be noted that INCADAT is possible thanks to a network of correspondents working on a voluntary basis; as a result, the database is neither exhaustive, nor intended to replace official sources. Moreover, the Permanent Bureau does not guarantee the accuracy, completeness or up-to-date nature of the information provided; translations are not official. INCADAT cannot be the final point of any research to ascertain foreign law as applied in practice; it remains nevertheless an invaluable resource.

IV. Future Outlook

The conclusions reached in 2012 in Brussels[71] on the non-feasibility of a Convention unifying the procedural treatment of foreign law, remain valid. So does the consensus on the need to facilitate access to foreign law. The chances to get some agreement are, however, still not good. The work at the HCCH concerning a future instrument did not get far in spite of the enthusiasm revealed by the reporting documents. The Conference has no plans to resume the topic.

Against this background, and in the light of the elaborations above, it may be sensible to 'think small'. *De lege ferenda*, a step-by-step strategy based on exploring and developing already available tools on the occasion of each new legislative project, could help fill the gaps and pave the way for a more far-reaching accord.

A. The Procedural Treatment of Foreign Law

The reluctance to endorse a mandatory (or, conversely, facultative) character of the conflict of laws rules may be easier to surmount if the question is addressed separately in the frame of subject-specific conventions. The workability of foreign-law-avoidance proposals depends in any event on the subject matter at stake.

[68] Among others, the 1980 Child Abduction Convention, the 1993 Adoption Convention, and the 2007 Child Support Convention.

[69] See for instance, the 'Country Profiles' available in the Child Support Section on the HCCH website, available at: hcch.cloudapp.net/smartlets/sfjsp?interviewID=hcchcp2012&t_lang=en.

[70] See: www.incadat.com/es.

[71] (n 3).

The negotiators of each individual Hague instrument on PIL should consider incorporating tailor-made solutions for the proof of the designated foreign law, following the example of Articles 14 and 15 of the 1980 Child Abduction Convention. For this purpose, exploring national rules and practices and whether they fit for specific matters – and/or restricted to a particular context – could be worthwhile.[72] By way of example, relying on the knowledge of the foreign law by the intervening authority may be acceptable in non-contentious procedures (as opposed to contentious ones).[73] In addition, there is no reason to limit the check of the legal systems to the procedural treatment of foreign law. To put the burden of proof of the foreign law on the party who is 'best placed' to cope with it,[74] or an *ex officio* ascertainment of the contents of foreign law when the interested party is structurally weak,[75] could be examples.

B. Access to Foreign Law (and Making One's Law Available)

Consensus of the HCCH Members on supplying information about their own laws in a dedicated site, administered by the Conference, can be reachable if restricted to the material scope of a specific Convention. An example in this sense is Article 57 of the 2007 Child Support Convention: it sets out a number of requirements on Contracting States to describe their laws concerning maintenance obligations, and how they give effect to certain key provisions of the Convention in their national laws, which are gathered into 'Country Profiles' and published by the Permanent Bureau.[76] Both ends of the informational procedure should be considered: a rule for making available legal materials would be impractical without one allowing them to be used as a means of evidence before (or by) a judge.[77]

In addition, a study on the feasibility of a database of national case law following the INCADAT model – ie, open to sponsorship and voluntary contributions – could be envisaged for future PIL instruments.[78]

Additionally, the transferability of experiences at The Hague in family matters – in particular, the possibility of extending the activity of IHJN – to other areas of law, is worth exploring. In case of a positive answer, the Hague Conventions should refer explicitly to the network as a tool to get information about foreign law. How actors other than judges could profit from the network services deserves thought.

Moreover, the traditional cooperative formulae should not be given up, but improved. No matter how sophisticated and well organised a system providing free online access to law, there will always be a need for some form of administrative cooperation. In this regard, a reasonable step could be to test the potential of new technologies of communication, and to authorise their use expressly in the text of the Conventions.[79]

[72] It goes without saying that the objective would not be limiting the means of proof, but rather facilitating the evidentiary process in light of the particularities of the subject matter.

[73] See in Spain Art 36 of the Reglamento Hipotecario (Decreto de 14 de febrero de 1947), as well as Art 168.4 of the Reglamento Notarial (Decreto de 2 de junio de 1944).

[74] So that the burden of proof is on the party to whom the evidence is available, or on the one better situated to furnish it easily and promptly.

[75] Such as a tourist, should the ongoing works at the Conference incorporate conflict of law provisions.

[76] See above, section III.B.ii.

[77] Along the lines of Art 14 of the Hague Abduction Convention.

[78] For instance for legal parentage, currently under examination at the Conference. The fact that the topic is relatively new would make it easier to set up the database.

[79] See the Preamble to the 2007 Child Support Convention which says: 'Seeking to take advantage of advances in technologies and to create a flexible system which can continue to evolve as needs change and further advances in technology create new opportunities'.

C. The Hague Conference, Meeting Point and Help-Desk

The Hague Conference supports judicial dialogue in a number of ways; the task should continue with a dedicated focus on the application of foreign law. Judicial seminars and training on the cooperation tools could be organised or promoted by the Permanent Bureau. The publication of guidelines on complex aspects, such as how to formulate questions on the applicable law, would also be helpful.

The creation of a global network of institutions and experts for complex questions on foreign law, facilitated by the Permanent Bureau, was mentioned in 2012 but left for study at a later stage; it was never taken up. The value of establishing mechanisms to identify experts to assist in the ascertainment and understanding of the foreign law was also acknowledged. Both initiatives should be resumed; to the extent that they focus on technical devices, they should not be hindered by political considerations.

11

States as Litigants in International Matters before Domestic Courts*

UGLJEŠA GRUŠIĆ, PAUL HERRUP AND LUCIAN MARTINEZ

I. Introduction

States regularly litigate matters with an international character in domestic courts. We use the term 'State' as defined in the 2004 UN Convention on Jurisdictional Immunities of States and Their Property.[1] By 'State', therefore, we mean bodies that exercise governmental authority.

State participation in international litigation in domestic courts raises a number of questions. In what capacity and under what conditions do States participate in such litigation? How does State participation affect the legal framework of international litigation in domestic courts? To what extent do the approaches and solutions in domestic laws converge or diverge? We address these questions in this chapter. Consistent with the structure and aims of this volume, we provide an overview of current global approaches and solutions in selected areas to provide a foundation for considering the scope of existing unification at the international level, the problems with such unification, and the prospect of further development of unifying law.

Before proceeding, we offer some preliminary observations. We generally approach the topic empirically. Thus, we largely ignore the doctrinal divisions that separate current academic discourse into subjects of private law and public law, domestic or international. The legal realities of international litigation in domestic courts with States as parties are not bounded by these *a priori* classifications and concepts.

The topic is broad and cannot be thoroughly covered in a short chapter. We, therefore, approach these questions using a case study method. We have selected four case studies, which allow us to examine some of the typical scenarios and key legal problems raised when States participate in international litigation in domestic courts.

This chapter is divided into six sections. Following this introduction, we briefly set out our case study method. We then discuss the case studies in three sections, with a particular focus on how State participation in international litigation in domestic courts affects the application of the rules of jurisdiction, applicable law and recognition and enforcement of foreign judgments. We conclude by joining the threads of analysis from these sections and assessing the prospect of deeper unification at the international level.

* The content of this chapter expresses the personal views of its authors and does not represent the views or positions of any institution with which they are affiliated.

[1] (New York, 2 December 2004), not yet in force, Art 2(1)(b).

II. Case Study Method

The case study method illuminates aspects of our subject. We have considered these factors in selecting our case studies: (1) the capacities in which States participate in international litigation in domestic courts; (2) the nature of international elements involved; and (3) the legal problems raised.

States can participate in different capacities in international litigation in domestic courts, eg, as claimants acting on their own behalf, claimants acting on behalf of citizens, defendants, *amici curiae*, bearers of sovereign authority intervening with the aim of protecting sovereign interests such as foreign relations interests, etc. We focus on two basic capacities in which States participate in international litigation in domestic courts, namely as claimants and defendants. When a State participates in litigation in a foreign court, an international element is automatically present. A State, however, more frequently participates in litigation in its own courts, in which case the rules of international law are potentially engaged only if there is an international element on the part of the other party to the litigation or in the State activity in question. If a State is sued in a foreign court, issues of State immunity must be considered. If a State is a claimant in foreign litigation, the problem of enforcement of what may be classified as sovereign rights may arise. If a State is sued in its own courts and the State activity in question may be classified as an external exercise of sovereign authority, the courts may have to grapple with the application of various domestic exclusionary doctrines in matters of foreign affairs, national defence, security and intelligence matters before considering applicable rules of international law. If a State is a claimant in domestic litigation with the aim of regulating the activities of foreigners or activities taking place on another State's territory, the courts may have to address the limits of the State's powers to adjudicate, prescribe and enforce its laws. Our chosen case studies are designed to raise these different scenarios and problems.

The first two case studies concern claims relating to commercial activity or employment contracts. The current approach, and continuing trend, in practice regarding litigation against foreign States starts from the position that such jurisdiction normally cannot be exercised unless the claim meets certain criteria constituting exceptions to the general rule of non-jurisdiction, prominently including 'commercial activity' and claims arising from employment contracts.

The third case study concerns personal damages suffered by civilians in the context of a foreign military operation. Although cases of this kind are not as frequent as commercial and employment cases with States as parties, this case study allows us to explore an area of complex and delicate interplay between considerations of the immunity a State has in foreign and its own courts and some of the applicable law issues that arise when a cause of action is advanced against a State for damage caused by the State's external exercise of sovereign authority.

The fourth case study falls within a broad topic of enforcement of laws with regulatory dimensions, which spans areas ranging from cross-border cooperation in criminal and taxation matters to cross-border protection of State secrets. This case study explores the limits of a State's prescriptive and enforcement jurisdiction and domestic law doctrines giving effect to those limits.

These four case studies deal with many problems raised by the participation of States in international litigation in domestic courts. Some issues are, however, not discussed, eg, the service of documents on States, the issuing of executive certificates as evidence of executive acts in the field of foreign affairs and the recognition of States and governments for the purposes of international litigation in domestic courts.

III. Cases Relating to Commercial Activity or Employment Contracts

We begin by considering four models that suggest templates for resolving litigation in domestic courts against foreign States.[2] The first treats litigation with State defendants no differently from litigation between private parties, with no concession to the State's presence. We know of no legal system that has chosen such a pure, private system. The second creates an entirely independent and autonomous system, both procedural and substantive, for adjudication of claims involving sovereigns or denies that they are justiciable. The absolute theory of foreign State immunity, which generally denies the ability of municipal courts to proceed in litigation involving foreign States, illustrates such a system. Whilst this was the dominant approach historically, the trend now is towards so-called restrictive theories, which usually start with absolute immunity, then identify exceptions to it.

More common are hybrids, which divide into two groups based on starting point. The first begins with the general template of private litigation, then makes limited accommodation to aspects of the special situation of States. The second starts from an independent State regime, then introduces limited private law analogues in either substantive law or procedure. Many countries actually deploy both models, depending upon the area of application. Thus, applicable law analysis and certain aspects of remedial and enforcement jurisdiction,[3] such as the types of assets amenable to enforcement measures, tend to depart from a private litigation template, then make adjustments to that model. On the other hand, the fundamental regimes governing the availability of jurisdiction to adjudicate[4] claims against foreign States tend to begin with a special regime of immunity rules.

We draw heavily on codifications of State immunity law, whether free-standing or within codes of private international law or civil procedure. The variations in provisions of the codifications or relevant procedural rules generally capture the spectrum of solutions contained in the case law. We refer to the following laws of 27 States and two treaties (one global and one regional): **Argentina**, Law No 24488 on Jurisdictional Immunity of Foreign States in Argentinian Courts (Arg); **Armenia**, Civil Procedure Code, Article 432 (Arm); **Australia**, Foreign Sovereign Immunities Act (Aus); **Bangladesh**, Code of Civil Procedure, sections 83–87 (Bangl); **Belgium**, Code Judiciaire, Article 1412 ter – quinquies (Bel); **Canada**, State Immunity Act (Can); **Czech Republic**, Private International Law Act, section 7 (Czech); **France**, Civil Procedure Code, Articles 643, 683–88 (Fr); Civil Enforcement Procedures Code, Article L111-1 (Fr); **Hungary**, Private International Law Act, sections 82–87 (Hung); **India**, Code of Civil Procedure, sections 83–87 (India); **Israel**, Foreign States Immunity Law (Isr); **Japan**, Act on the Civil Jurisdiction of Japan with respect to a Foreign State (Jap); **Kazakhstan**, Civil Procedure Code, Articles 427–50 (Kaz); **Kyrgyz Republic**, Civil Procedure Code, Article 390 (Kyr); **Malawi**, Immunities and Privileges Act (Malawi); **Moldova**, Civil Procedure Code, Article 457 (Mold); **Pakistan**, The State Immunity Ordinance (Pak); **Russian Federation**, Federal Law on the

[2] This is our focus in this section. Affirmative claims in this area generally proceed under the same rule and procedures as in private litigation.

[3] By remedial jurisdiction, we mean the legal power of a court to issue certain remedies or direct certain steps, whether provisional or incorporated in a final judgment. In the context of the established limitations on remedies and provisional measures that a court may impose on a State, we must treat remedial jurisdiction as separate from and antecedent to jurisdiction to enforce, which begins from issuance of a remedy in a final judgment.

[4] By jurisdiction to adjudicate, we mean the legal power of a court to proceed to resolution of a case presented to it.

Jurisdictional Immunities of Foreign State and the Property of a Foreign State in the Russian Federation (Rus); **Singapore**, State Immunity Act (Sing); **South Africa**, Foreign States Immunities Act (S Afr); **Spain**, Law on International Legal Cooperation in Civil Matters (Sp 1); Law on Privileges and Immunity of Foreign States (Sp 2); **Tajikistan**, Civil Procedure Code, Article 390 (Taj); Economic Procedure Code, Article 230 (Taj); **Tunisia**, Code of Private International Law, Articles 19–25 (Tun); **Turkey**, Act Concerning Private International Law and Procedural Law, Article 49 (Turk); **Ukraine**, Private International Law Act, Article 49 (Ukr); **United Kingdom**, State Immunity Act (UK); **United States of America**, Foreign Sovereign Immunities Act (US); **Uzbekistan**, Code of the Republic of Uzbekistan about Administrative Legal Proceedings, Article 362 (Uzb); **UN,** Convention on the Jurisdictional Immunities of States and Their Property (UN); **Council of Europe**, Convention on State Immunity (Eur).

A. Claims Relating to Commercial Activity

Disputes arising from commercial transactions are often considered the quintessential example of private litigation involving sovereigns. However, the sovereign State's presence as a party introduces new factors and complexities that differentiates this litigation from purely private litigation.

States generally come to these cases in three distinct postures. They may be:

1. Market competitors trading on their own account like other competitors in that market: eg utilising a separate legal person with its own sue and be sued authority but the State has an ownership interest in it or otherwise directs substantial control.
2. Market participants supporting their internal operations: eg, buying paper for their bureaucrats or boots for their military, or contracting private firms to operate prisons.
3. As regulators using commercial mechanisms for regulatory ends: eg, transacting in commodities markets to smooth price swings, or renegotiating bond payments to regulate budget or external debt levels.

i. Jurisdiction

a. Jurisdiction to Adjudicate

We briefly examine three illustrative topics regarding jurisdiction to adjudicate State commercial disputes: (1) the meaning of commercial activity, and specifically the nature/purpose distinction; (2) the required link between the conduct attributed to the State and the claim against it; and (3) the required territorial nexus between the conduct and the forum State. Whilst national solutions to each topic vary, those solutions tend to yield recognisably similar results.

The Nature/Purpose Distinction

Even presuming a general exception to the rule of non-jurisdiction for commercial claims, there is no uniform international definition of 'commercial activity', or which activities implicate the exception. Courts employ various devices to guide this determination, such as evaluating either the nature or the purpose of the activity. At one end of the spectrum, the US requires that an act's commercial character be determined by its nature, without reference to its purpose.[5] At the other, Russia's statute provides that, in deciding whether a foreign State's commercial act stems from the

[5] US 1603(d).

exercise of sovereign authority, the court shall consider both the act's nature and purpose.[6] The UN Convention stakes a middle ground, looking primarily to the transaction's nature, but taking into account its purpose if the parties to the transaction have so agreed or if, in the practice of the State of the forum, that purpose is relevant to determining the character of the transaction.[7] This intermediate position seems to capture the approach of most courts, most of the time.

The different approaches to the nature/purpose distinction yield quite different results for each general posture of State commercial activity. In the first (State as market competitor), application of either or both criteria will likely result in the activity being deemed commercial. In the second (State entering a commercial market to procure goods and services to maintain its operations), the activity will likely be found commercial if nature only is analysed, but there may be considerably more leeway to determine that it is not commercial if purpose is considered (eg, military procurement). The third (State uses commercial mechanisms to achieve sovereign ends) almost certainly will be found non-commercial under a purpose test. Here, the outcome of a nature-only test can be difficult to predict and will depend on the courts' appreciation of the relationship between the activity giving rise to the claim and the underlying State conduct.

The Required Connection between the Commercial Activity and the Claim

Exercising jurisdiction to adjudicate under the commercial activity exception requires not only that the activity in question be 'commercial', but that there be a specified nexus between the State's activity and the claim. Many States refer to a 'relation' or 'connection' between the activity and the claim.[8] This criterion encompasses a broad swathe of claims, possibly up to allegations of 'but-for' causation (the claim would not have arisen as a factual matter but for some antecedent commercial activity of the State). The US occupies another point on the spectrum. The claim against the foreign State must be 'based upon' a commercial activity of that State.[9] A claim is based upon a commercial activity if the commercial activity provides those elements of the claim that, if proven, would entitle the plaintiff to relief under its theory of the case.[10] Accordingly, at least formally, US courts have a broader conception than other courts of when an activity is commercial by excluding consideration of purpose but likely will narrow the scope of activity subject to jurisdiction due to tighter nexus requirements.

Territorial Nexus

The exercise of jurisdiction to adjudicate also is regulated by a nexus requirement of the activity to the territory of the forum. Many States apply a variant of the private international law rule that the activity or obligation requires performance on the territory of the forum.[11]

b. Remedial Jurisdiction

International law and practice significantly restrict the remedies that a court can order against a foreign State as opposed to private litigants. This is particularly true of conduct-based remedies and non-compensatory monetary awards, as opposed to compensatory money damages.

[6] Rus 74. See also, Kaz 435.
[7] UN 2(2).
[8] See, eg, Can 5.
[9] US 1605(a)(2).
[10] *Saudi Arabia v Nelson* 502 US 349 (1993).
[11] See, eg, Rus 7.3 (performance on territory or consequences connected to territory); US 1605(a)(2) (activity or, in some circumstances, direct effects of activity, on territory); Tun 20.

Most State immunity codifications explicitly limit the availability of performance-based orders or coercive measures against States. These limitations range from an outright prohibition of performance-based orders (although sometimes permitting restraints on commercial property rather than on State conduct)[12] to restrictions on non-compensatory money awards.[13]

ii. Applicable Law

The area of applicable law in State litigation generally starts from the regime governing private litigation in the forum State, as opposed to starting in many respects from rules of international law and practices specific to States. However, certain limitations contained in private litigation regimes bulk larger when a State is a party, most notably mandatory law and public policy considerations.

iii. Recognition and Enforcement

Generally, most States pay most commercial judgments, except default judgments or judgments seen as violating accepted limitations on jurisdiction. States generally have good practical reasons to accept efficient and fair dispute resolution mechanisms in claims arising from their commercial transactions: if their private commercial partners believe they have no judicial recourse, they will cover the increased risk of loss with higher prices. This attitude is reflected in the 2019 Hague Convention on the Recognition and Enforcement of Foreign Judgments in Civil and Commercial Matters (HCREFJ),[14] whose scope specifically includes State litigation, albeit with some exceptions and a declaration mechanism.[15]

However, when a State does not voluntarily satisfy a judgment, issues of recognition or enforcement of the judgment arise. This subsection focuses on municipal enforcement regimes and examines the treatment of States in the availability of enforcement actions against State assets, and the types of assets amenable to enforcement measures.

Although most systems do not formally restrict a judgment holder's ability to bring an enforcement action against State assets, several either bar enforcement measures against State assets entirely or require prior approval by the government of the forum or consent of the foreign State.[16]

Even when it is possible to enforce on State assets, the types of assets amenable to enforcement measures are limited in the absence of a waiver. The majority rule restricts enforcement measures to property in use, or intended for use, for commercial purposes,[17] though it is often joined with a provision explicitly identifying sets of assets as not 'commercial', such as central bank assets, assets of armed forces, or cultural property.[18] However, at least regarding judgments arising from foreign States' commercial activity, the US narrows the set of assets dramatically compared with other countries, by requiring that the property is or was used for the commercial activity upon which the claim was based.[19]

[12] See, eg, Rus 19; Can 11; Mal 15(1); Pak 14; S Afr 14(1)(a); Sp 2 17.1.
[13] See, eg, UK 13(2)(a); generally Uzb 362 (unless State consent); US 1606.
[14] (The Hague, 2 July 2019), not yet in force.
[15] Arts 2(1)(n)–(q), 2(4), 2(5), 19.
[16] Eur 23; Arm 432; Fr L111–1.2; Kyr 390(1) (consent by foreign State, taking various forms); India 81(3) (consent by government of India).
[17] UK 13(4); Aus 34; Hung 85; Isr 17; Jap 18; Kaz 442, Rus 15.3.
[18] See, eg, UN 21; Sp 2 20.1; Kaz 443; Rus 16; Hung 85; Can 12(b); Bel 1412.
[19] US 1610(a)(2).

B. Claims Relating to Contracts of Employment

Most codifications treat employment litigation separately from the general run of commercial litigation. The primary areas where the rules differ from those applicable to general commercial transactions are jurisdiction to adjudicate and remedial jurisdiction.

i. Jurisdiction

a. Jurisdiction to Adjudicate

Although jurisdiction to adjudicate a claim arising from an employment contract with a foreign State generally is available, the exercise of that jurisdiction is restricted and qualified. These restrictions balance two very strong, competing values: each State's interest to provide a local forum for employment claims, versus not infringing the foreign State's rights to structure, organise and administer their own operations, particularly regarding diplomatic and consular establishments.

First, such jurisdiction is to adjudicate claims relating to contracts of employment, not any claim conceivably related to 'employment' writ large.[20] Claims arising from a foreign State's decision not to renew an employment contract generally escape the local courts' jurisdiction to adjudicate.[21]

Second, the claim must relate to a contract of employment between a foreign State and an individual employee. It must be brought by or on behalf of natural persons, although representative actions are not necessarily precluded if the claims could be brought by each claimant individually.[22] Thus, structural or collective questions such as the amenability under local law of the workforce of a foreign State to unionisation, have been ruled outside the jurisdiction.[23]

Third, jurisdiction to adjudicate claims brought by specified classes of individuals is restricted. Thus, there is no jurisdiction to adjudicate claims brought by diplomatic or consular officers, or others who might claim international law privileges or immunities, or by an employee who was a citizen of the foreign State when the proceedings began, unless the claimant permanently resides in the forum.[24]

Fourth, jurisdiction is restricted based upon the function performed by the employee. Although the precise formulation and field of application differ locally, there generally is no jurisdiction over employment claims of a person specifically recruited to perform sovereign functions.[25]

Fifth, jurisdiction has a temporal dimension. A prerequisite to jurisdiction over claims arising from a contract is existence of a contract. Consequently, pre-contract claims such as those relating to recruitment generally fall outside the scope of jurisdiction.[26]

Sixth, there is a territorial nexus requirement. The standard criterion is performance-based; performance of the employment contract, in whole or in part, must be in the territory of the forum.[27]

[20] See, eg, Arg 2(d); Aus 12; Hung 84; Jap 4; Kaz 440 (by implication); Mal 6; Pak 6; Rus 8; Sing 6; Sp 2 10; UK 4; UN 11; Eur 5.

[21] See, eg, Jap 4; Kaz 440; Rus 8, Sp 2 10; UN 11.

[22] See, eg, Arg 2(d); Aus 12; Hung 84; Jap 4; Kaz 440; Mal 6; Pak 6; Rus 8; Sing 6; Sp 2 10; UK 4; UN 11; Eur 5.

[23] See, eg, *Re: Canada Labour Code* [1992] SCR 50.

[24] See, eg, Arg 2(d); Aus 12; Mal 6; Pak 6; Rus 8; Sing 6; Sp 2 10; UK 4; UN 11; Eur 5.

[25] See, eg, Arg 2(d); Aus 12; Jap 4; Pak 6; Rus 8; Sing 6; Sp 2 10; UN 11.

[26] See, eg, Arg 2(d); Aus 12; Hung 84; Jap 4; Kaz 440; Mal 6; Pak 6; Rus 8; Sing 6; Sp 2 10; UK 4; UN 11; Eur 5; but see Isr 10.

[27] See, eg, Arg 2(d); Aus 12; Hung 84; Jap 4; Kaz 440; Mal 6; Pak 6; Rus 8; Sing 6; Sp 2 10; UK 4; UN 11; Eur 5.

Seventh, a choice of forum clause may oust the jurisdiction of a forum not chosen, provided that clause is valid and enforceable under the law of the forum.[28] Note, however, that the 2005 Hague Convention on Choice of Court Agreements (HCCCA)[29] excludes from scope such agreements as they apply to employment relations.[30]

b. Remedial Jurisdiction

The importance of remedial jurisdiction, as opposed to jurisdiction to adjudicate, comes to the fore in employment litigation involving foreign States. Two examples suffice: demands for reinstatement and demands for certain damages available under local law, particularly so-called moral damages.

Given the general prohibition of conduct-based remedies against States, a court cannot order reinstatement, even if that remedy is available under local employment law.[31] This also reflects the view that the forum should not interfere with the foreign State's right to structure its internal operations.

Similarly, rules that generally allow only compensatory damages also apply in employment claims, regardless of local law in purely private litigation. Even if local law classifies moral damages as compensatory, since they effectively compensate for dignitary torts such as damage to reputation or loss of self-esteem, they are best handled under separate rules of immunity for torts or delicts.

ii. Applicable Law

Generally, litigation arising from employment contracts proceeds under the law specified in the contract (which often incorporates rules from administrative manuals or employee handbooks), or under the law of the place where the employee habitually carried out their work in the absence of a choice of law agreement, or if such a choice of law agreement is ineffective under the forum's employment law. Even if foreign law applies, eg, because the forum is the defendant's forum and the applicable law is the law of the place where the employee carried out their employment, it yields to the extent of any inconsistency with mandatory forum law. Public policy may also significantly limit use of foreign law in employment litigation.

iii. Recognition and Enforcement

Recognition and enforcement of employment judgments generally follow the regime applicable to judgments in claims relating to commercial transactions. One wrinkle is worth noting: at least for judgments brought across national borders for recognition or enforcement, HCREFJ generally applies to judgments in employment matters, in contrast to the provisions of HCCCA, which addresses both jurisdiction to adjudicate and recognition and enforcement of international cases, but which excludes employment matters from its scope.[32]

[28] See, eg, Arg 2(d); Aus 12; Hung 84; Jap 4; Kaz 440; Mal 6; Pak 6; Rus 8; Sing 6; Sp 2 10; UK 4; UN 11; Eur 5.
[29] (The Hague, 30 June 2005), entered into force 1 October 2015.
[30] Art 2(1)(b).
[31] See, eg, Arg 2(d); Aus 29; Hung 84; Jap 4; Kaz 440; Mal 6; Pak 6; Rus 8; Sing 6; Sp 2 10; UK 4; UN 11; Eur 5.
[32] HCCCA, Art 2(1)(b). However, HCREFJ, has limited grounds for indirect jurisdiction where the judgment is against the employee, see Art 5(2).

C. Conclusion

Cases relating to foreign States' commercial activities and their employment contracts with the forum State's citizens and residents highlight many of the unique considerations present when a sovereign State is party to what would otherwise be purely private litigation, particularly jurisdiction to adjudicate and remedial jurisdiction. These factors emerge especially in claims arising from contracts of employment. Certain restrictions that aim to balance the forum State's interest in providing for adjudication of such claims against the foreign State's right to structure its operations limit the exercise of jurisdiction to adjudicate in this area. Similarly, the general prohibition on injunctive remedies against States limits certain remedies, such as reinstatement, otherwise available under the forum's employment law. Applicable law principles in State litigation generally part from the forum State's private litigation regime. When a State does not voluntarily satisfy a judgment, issues arise concerning enforcement and recognition of the judgment, including limitation of, or an absolute bar on, enforcement against sovereign assets.

IV. Foreign Military Operations and Personal Damages Suffered by Civilians

Traditionally, compensation for personal damages suffered by civilians during armed conflict is treated as an inter-State matter. Individual claims before domestic courts are a relatively recent phenomenon and have come in two main waves. The first comprised individual claims for compensation for personal damages suffered before and during the Second World War, the best known of which were brought in Germany, Greece, Italy, Japan and the US. The second comprised individual claims for compensation for personal damages suffered during the armed conflicts in former Yugoslavia, Afghanistan, Iraq and the US 'war on terror', which were brought mainly in the allegedly wrongdoing States. These claims raise complex issues concerning jurisdiction, applicable law and recognition and enforcement.

A. Jurisdiction and Recognition and Enforcement

Civilian victims of armed conflict have tried to obtain compensation for personal damages from the allegedly wrongdoing States in the courts of those States and in the courts of the States in which those damages were suffered.

The International Court of Justice has confirmed that State immunity precludes individual claims before the courts of the States in which personal damages were suffered.[33] The European Court of Justice and the European Court of Human Rights have held that proceedings for alleged torts by occupying military forces fall outside the subject matter scope of the Brussels Convention[34] and that State immunity precludes the enforcement of judgments resulting from such proceedings.[35]

[33] *Jurisdictional Immunities of the State (Germany v Italy: Greece Intervening)*, Judgment, ICJ Rep (2012) (3 February) 99.
[34] Case C-292/05 *Lechouritou v Germany* [2007] ECR I-1519.
[35] *Kalogeropoulou v Greece and Germany*, App no 59021/00 (ECtHR, 12 December 2002).

Civilian victims of armed conflict are also unlikely to be able to bring proceedings before the courts of the allegedly wrongdoing State. Most domestic laws have developed exclusionary doctrines that preclude the bringing of individual claims for compensation for personal damages suffered during armed conflict before domestic courts. Despite a 1993 resolution of the Institute of International Law calling for the exercise of the jurisdiction to adjudicate these issues,[36] State practice shows that the resolution was merely a call for normative reform.

Domestic exclusionary doctrines form a spectrum. At the one end are States like Germany, Italy, Japan and the US, whose laws preclude the bringing of individual claims for compensation for personal damages suffered during armed conflict before domestic courts, typically on one or more of the following grounds: separation of powers; non-recognition of right to compensation by international humanitarian law; inapplicability of tort law; waiver of individual claims through peace treaties; statute of limitation.[37] This is not to say that the laws of these States generally preclude compensation of personal damages suffered during armed conflict. Indeed, compensation may be available through other dispute resolution mechanisms, including those established by international treaties, domestic administrative schemes, or on an *ex gratia* basis, and diplomatic protection. The laws of these States, however, preclude individual claims for compensation for personal damages suffered during armed conflict presented in domestic courts against the forum State as defendant. At the other end of the spectrum is the Netherlands, whose courts have awarded damages to victims of the Srebrenica genocide after expressly denying the existence of exclusionary doctrines in Netherlands law.[38] The UK stands in the middle: individual claims for compensation for personal damages suffered during armed conflict can be brought under either the Human Rights Act (HRA) 1998, which allows UK courts to hear claims for the violation of certain rights guaranteed by the European Convention on Human Rights (ECHR), or tort law. The biggest obstacles to the successful bringing of claims under the HRA 1998 are the limited extraterritorial reach of ECHR rights and the justification of compliance with international humanitarian law.[39] With respect to tortious claims, the fact that UK armed forces commit allegedly tortious acts jointly with another State's armed forces does not bar the claims;[40] where the military operation in question is lawful under English public law, however, the government can avoid tortious liability by pleading the defence of Crown act of State.[41]

B. Applicable Law

If the claimant can bring a justiciable claim, the problem of applicable law arises. The laws of the Netherlands and the UK represent two different approaches. After initial uncertainty, Netherlands

[36] 'The Activities of National Judges and the International Relations of Their State' (Milan, 1993), available at: www.idi-iil.org/app/uploads/2017/06/1993_mil_01_en.pdf, Art 2.

[37] Germany: the *Distomo* case, III ZR 245/98, 26 June 2003, Bundesgerichtshof; 2 BvR 1476/03, 15 February 2006, Bundesverfassungsgericht; *Sfountouris v Germany* App no 24120/06 (ECtHR, 31 May 2011); the *Varvarin* case, III ZR 190/05, 2 November 2006, Bundesgerichtshof; BvR 2660/06, 2 BvR 487/07, 13 August 2013, Bundesverfassungsgericht; the *Kunduz* case, III ZR 140/15, 6 October 2016, Bundesgerichtshof; Italy: *Presidency of the Council of Ministers v Marković*, Case no 8157, 8 February 2002, Corte di Cassazione; *Marković v Italy* (2007) 44 EHRR 52; Japan: SH Bong, 'Compensation for Victims of Wartime Atrocities: Recent Developments in Japan's Case Law' (2005) 3 *Journal of International Criminal Justice* 187; US: B Stephens et al, *International Human Rights Litigation in US Courts*, 2nd edn (Martinus Nijhoff Publishers 2008); JE Pfander, *Constitutional Torts and the War on Terror* (Oxford University Press 2017).

[38] *Netherlands v Nuhanović and Mustafić*, NL:HR:2013:BZ9225, NL:HR:2013:BZ9228, 6 September 2013, Hoge Raad; *Netherlands v Mothers of Srebrenica*, NL:HR:2019:1284, 19 July 2019, Hoge Raad.

[39] See *Al-Waheed v MoD* [2017] UKSC 2.

[40] *Belhaj v Straw* [2017] UKSC 3.

[41] *Rahmatullah v SoS* [2012] UKSC 48; *Alseran v MoD* [2017] EWHC 3289 (QB).

courts have settled on the application of the Netherlands Civil Code to the issue of liability of the Netherlands for personal damages caused to civilians in overseas military operations.[42] But Netherlands courts also apply the rules of conventional and customary international law to decide on the existence of two elements of the cause of action under the Netherlands Civil Code, namely the attribution to the Netherlands of the actions of Netherlands soldiers operating abroad as part of a multinational force and the wrongfulness of the conduct of Netherlands soldiers.[43] With respect to claims brought in UK courts under the HRA 1998, the Act provides the cause of action, which consists in the violation of an ECHR right by a UK public authority. The rules of conventional and customary international law are, therefore, relevant for deciding on individual claims for compensation for personal damages suffered during armed conflict brought under the Act. With respect to tortious claims brought in UK courts to which the defence of Crown act of State does not apply (eg, because the military operation in question is unlawful under English public law), English courts apply the *lex loci delicti* to substantive issues pursuant to the Private International Law (Miscellaneous Provisions) Act 1995.[44]

C. Conclusion

The customary international law rules of State immunity, as interpreted by international courts, preclude civilian victims of armed conflict from bringing proceedings against the allegedly wrongdoing State in the courts of another State and enforcing any judgment resulting from such proceedings. The chances of success of individual claims for compensation for personal damages brought by civilian victims of armed conflict in the courts of the allegedly wrongdoing State primarily depend on whether the *lex fori* has developed exclusionary doctrines and, only where such doctrines do not exist or are not applicable, on the rules of international law. Any unification of the rules of private international law should respect this. States are unlikely to give up the power to decide whether and, if so, under what conditions, individual claims for compensation for personal damages suffered during armed conflict against the forum State are allowed. A model is offered by EU private international law, whose 2012 Recast of the Brussels I Regulation and the Rome II Regulation provide that they do not apply to 'the liability of the State for acts and omissions in the exercise of State authority (*acta iure imperii*)'.[45] The attempt by the Institute of International Law to contribute to development of the law in this area by asking domestic courts not to decline competence on the basis of political question and similar doctrines has so far not succeeded.

V. Cross-Border Enforcement of Regulatory Laws

States often advance their interests through legislation. Some interests advanced in this way are shared with other States, eg, the fight against international and transnational crimes, fraud and tax evasion, protection of market competition and the environment, preservation of cultural heritage, etc. Regulatory laws can be enforced variously. One means relevant to our discussion is procedures under which a State brings a claim seeking relief on behalf of citizens.

[42] *Mothers of Srebrenica* (n 38).
[43] Ibid; *Nuhanović and Mustafić* (n 38).
[44] *Belhaj v Straw* [2014] EWCA Civ 1394.
[45] Brussels Ia Regulation, Art 1(1); Rome II Regulation, Art 1(1). See also HCREFJ, Art 2(1)(n) and (o).

Typical examples of such procedures are actions in the US under which a public body seeks relief on behalf of the public/victims under anti-trust,[46] environmental protection,[47] or securities,[48] legislation. Employing such procedures in cross-border contexts raises several international law questions concerning States' jurisdiction and cross-border cooperation in the enforcement of regulatory laws.

A. Jurisdiction

From the perspective of public international law, two questions that arise are whether, in a cross-border context, a State has jurisdiction to prescribe and, even if it has prescriptive jurisdiction, whether that State has jurisdiction to adjudicate and enforce its laws. Under public international law, the legality of the exercise of State power is traditionally viewed as depending on the existence of a territorial, personal or another genuine connection.[49] To keep the exercise of regulatory authority within the limits set by public international law, many States have developed domestic law rules defining the limits of State power. Presently, however, jurisdictional rules of public international law and most domestic law rules defining the limits of State power are unsettled, particularly with respect to the limits of prescriptive jurisdiction and extraterritorial application of domestic laws. The leading judgment of the International Court of Justice on the topic of jurisdiction in public international law, *SS 'Lotus'*,[50] now a century old, 'represents the high water mark of *laissez-faire* in international relations, and an era that has been significantly overtaken by other tendencies'[51] and has notoriously given rise to different interpretations. US law, which has the most developed domestic law rules defining the limits of State power, has been undergoing significant changes in the recent past. The US Supreme Court has emphasised the presumption against extraterritorial application of US regulatory laws in recent judgments.[52]

B. Cross-Border Cooperation in the Enforcement of Regulatory Laws

Cross-border cooperation in the enforcement of regulatory laws takes many forms. For example, the regulating State may seek assistance from another State with the taking of evidence located on the latter State's territory. Or a public body seeking relief on behalf of the public/victims under domestic regulatory laws may, after obtaining a judgment in its favour in the regulating State, seek to enforce the judgment in another State. Under public international law, jurisdiction to enforce is territorial. Thus, the regulating State cannot, absent an agreement with other States, exercise enforcement powers on other States' territory. The question, therefore, arises whether the taking of evidence at the request of a foreign State or the enforcement of a foreign judgment applying a foreign State's regulatory laws falls foul of the rule that one State's courts do

[46] Clayton Act, §4C, 15 USC §15c.

[47] Clean Water Act, §311(f), 33 USC §1321(f)(5); Comprehensive Environmental Response, Compensation, and Liability Act, §107(f)(1), 42 USC §9607(f)(1).

[48] Sarbanes-Oxley Act, §308(a), 15 USC §7246(a).

[49] *SS 'Lotus' (France v Turkey)*, Judgment (1927) PCIJ Series A, No 10; *Nottebohm (Liechtenstein v Guatemala)*, 2nd Phase Judgment, ICJ Rep 1955 (6 April) 4.

[50] *SS 'Lotus'*, ibid.

[51] *Arrest Warrant of 11 April 2000 (Democratic Republic of the Congo v Belgium)*, Joint Separate Opinion of Judges Higgins, Kooijmans and Buergenthal (2002) ICJ Rep 3 (14 February) 78.

[52] *Morrison v National Australia Bank* 561 US 247 (2010); *Kiobel v Royal Dutch Petroleum* 569 US 108 (2013).

not enforce the penal, revenue and other public law of another.[53] If the regulating State and the State addressed are bound by supranational instruments on cooperation in civil and commercial matters,[54] the question arises whether the taking of evidence at the regulating State's request or the enforcement of a judgment of the regulatory State's courts falls within the subject matter scope of those instruments.

There is evidence that the old taboo that categorically prohibits giving effect to foreign public law is crumbling. For example, some non-US courts have held that US actions by a public body seeking relief on behalf of citizens are civil claims and, consequently, US judgments given on such claims can be recognised and enforced. An important consideration underpinning the recognition and enforcement of these judgments is that the regulatory laws at issue are aimed at the protection of interests shared among most, if not all, States, such as environmental protection,[55] protection of consumers and investors and the fight against transnational fraud.[56] In addition, the Institute of International Law adopted a resolution to similar effect.[57]

C. Conclusion

Cases concerning cross-border enforcement of regulatory laws show that the classifications of 'public international law' and 'private international law' are fluid and contestable. Public international law sets some limits on States' exercise of regulatory authority, which many States have further developed by domestic law rules delimiting State power. These rules and judgments applying them evidence State practice, which, in turn, may affect the development of public international law.

The quick breakdown of academic classifications in practice suggests that we need new concepts to adequately describe that practice. In the field of cross-border enforcement of regulatory laws, jurisdiction is a key concept, referring both to the power of domestic forums to hear and decide disputes and the powers of a State to prescribe and enforce its laws.

Where regulatory laws protect States' shared interests, there tends to be cross-border cooperation to enforce them. Two questions arise: should States cooperate to enforce regulatory laws that do not promote shared interests? The evidence suggests they do not.[58] And should one State's organs be able to apply other States' regulatory laws? Courts have considered and applied foreign public law.[59] Nevertheless, the possibilities for applying foreign regulatory laws are limited since regulatory claims are seldom accorded an applicable law category in their own right.[60]

[53] L Collins (gen ed), *Dicey, Morris and Collins on the Conflict of Laws*, 15th edn (Sweet & Maxwell, 2012) para 5R-019.

[54] eg, Hague Convention on the Taking of Evidence Abroad in Civil or Commercial Matters; HCREFJ.

[55] *US v Ivey* (1996) 30 OR (3rd) 370 (Ontario CA).

[56] *USSEC v Peever* 2013 BCSC 1090; *Evans v European Bank Ltd* [2004] NSWCA 82; *USSEC v Manterfield* [2009] EWCA Civ 27.

[57] 'Public Law Claims Instituted by a Foreign Authority or a Foreign Public Body' (Oslo, 1977), available at: www.idi-iil.org/app/uploads/2017/06/1977_oslo_01_en.pdf, pt I.

[58] But see C-49/12 *The Commissioners for Her Majesty's Revenue & Customs v Sunico ApS* EU:C:2013:545 (cross-border enforcement of tax laws within the framework of the Brussels I Regulation).

[59] See the Institute of International Law's Wiesbaden resolution ('The Application of Foreign Public Law' (Wiesbaden, 1975), available at: www.idi-iil.org/app/uploads/2017/06/1975_wies_04_en.pdf; and international instruments like the Inter-American Convention on the Law Applicable to International Contracts (Mexico City, 1994), not yet in force) that have jettisoned the public law bar.

[60] But see the Swiss Federal Act on Private International Law, Art 137; Rome II Regulation, Art 6(3)(a) (both provisions concern acts restricting free competition and potentially allow the courts to apply foreign anti-trust laws).

International efforts to achieve a unified approach of national laws to the 'public law taboo', eg, through the work of the Institute of International Law, have had little impact. Nevertheless, State practice evidences the taboo's diminishing importance and a growing willingness to cooperate in the enforcement of regulatory laws protecting shared interests when the regulating State stays within the limits of its powers to prescribe and enforce its laws. There might, therefore, be some scope for unification at the international level in the cross-border enforcement of regulatory laws.

VI. General Conclusion

Having provided empirical surveys through our case studies, we turn to a brief consideration of the prospects of international unification. Our assessment follows the tradition of the Hague Conference. Is a proposed instrument desirable and feasible? If both, should it be a binding, multilateral instrument, or a model law or principles available for adoption by individual countries?

In the case of State litigation arising from commercial transactions and employment contracts, State practice shows a substantial commonality in results, albeit with limited variations that often reflect important local values and policies. A binding, multilateral instrument to achieve incremental uniformities appears neither feasible nor particularly desirable. However, the international regime in these case areas is still developing, and many courts without a tradition of adjudication could benefit from guidance provided by a model law or international principles.

In the case of State litigation concerning personal damages suffered by civilians in the context of a foreign military operation, State practice also shows a substantial commonality in results. Litigation is largely precluded by the customary international law rules of State immunity and domestic exclusionary doctrines in matters of foreign affairs, national defence, security and intelligence matters. Only where the allegedly wrongdoing State is sued in its own courts and domestic exclusionary doctrines do not exist or are not applicable do the rules of international law come into play. In the few countries whose courts have applied the rules of international law in this context, the application has not been uniform. This suggests that unification in this field is undesirable and not feasible. International instruments unifying private international law in civil and commercial matters should respect this by including an *acta iure imperii* exclusion.

In the case of State litigation concerning cross-border enforcement of regulatory laws, State practice shows that States tend to observe public international law limits of State power and are increasingly willing to cooperate in the enforcement of regulatory laws protecting shared interests. Presently, however, jurisdictional rules of public international law and most domestic law rules defining the limits of State power are unsettled. Given the importance of protecting shared interests and a degree of convergence of State practice, international unification appears desirable and possibly feasible in the form of a model law or international principles.

12

Service of Process

DAVID McCLEAN

I. Introduction

A. Meaning and Purpose

'Process' for our purposes is primarily what may be called more precisely 'originating process'. That is the document, known by a variety of names such as writ, summons, petition, citation, application or claim form, that marks the beginning of legal proceedings. Some international instruments, notably the Hague Convention of 15 November 1965 on the Service Abroad of Judicial and Extrajudicial Documents in Civil or Commercial Matters (the Service Convention), also deal with the service of a wider category, 'judicial and extra-judicial documents'.

Everywhere, the document constituting originating process serves two purposes; in a significant number of States the service of the document serves a third purpose.

The first purpose is simply to notify the court. The court on receiving or issuing the document will typically assign a number to the case and register it in its books (real or electronic). This purely administrative action cannot in itself raise any issue of private international law.

The second is to alert the defendant, respondent or other interested party, so providing the opportunity for the recipient of the document to take whatever steps are prescribed in the law of the State of issue, the potential *lex fori*, to admit the claim, indicate an intention to dispute it, or perhaps to challenge the validity of the document itself. Notice to a defendant is required by natural justice and, where a judgment is to be recognised or enforced in a State other than its State of origin, want of notice may be a ground for the refusal of recognition or enforcement. So, for example, Article 7(1)(a)(i) of the Hague Convention of 2 July 2019 on the Recognition and Enforcement of Foreign Judgments in Civil or Commercial Matters (the Judgments Convention), the most recent international instrument on the subject, provides that:

> Recognition or enforcement may be refused if the document which instituted the proceedings or an equivalent document, including a statement of the essential elements of the claim was not notified to the defendant in sufficient time and in such a way as to enable them to arrange for their defence, unless the defendant entered an appearance and presented their case without contesting notification in the court of origin, provided that the law of the State of origin permitted notification to be contested.[1]

[1] See, to similar effect, Art 45(1)(b) of Reg (EU) No 1215/2012 of the European Parliament and of the Council of 12 December 2012 on jurisdiction and the recognition and enforcement of judgments in civil and commercial matters [2012] OJ L351/1 (Brussels Ia).

As the Explanatory Report[2] makes clear, this provision protects the defendant by ensuring the most basic principle of procedural justice: the right to be heard, in response to a document that contains the essential elements of the claim to which the defendant is to respond. A defendant who entered an appearance and presented their case in the court of origin without contesting notification cannot rely on this defence in the requested State; the policy here is that any challenge is made at the first opportunity and before the court best capable of addressing it. If the law in the State of origin does not permit challenges, the condition does not apply.

Under the same Article of the Judgments Convention, the interests of the requested State are protected: recognition or enforcement may be refused if the document was notified to the defendant in the requested State in a manner that was incompatible with fundamental principles (not merely the general legal provisions) of the requested State concerning service of documents.[3]

B. Service as a Basis for Jurisdiction

In a number of States in the common law tradition, service of process has a third function. It is a basis for the jurisdiction of the court issuing the document. As an authoritative book states the position at common law:

> When process cannot legally be served upon a defendant, the court can exercise no jurisdiction over him. In proceedings *in personam* the converse of this statement holds good, and whenever a defendant can be legally served with process, then the court, on service being effected, has jurisdiction to entertain a claim against him.[4]

This requires some further explanation. The starting assumption made by the common law is that any person within the territory of the State is within the jurisdiction of the courts of that State. Whether a person is so present is established by the service of process upon that person at some place within the State. Although aspects of the decision continue to be controversial, that this was consistent with the Due Process requirements of the US Constitution was affirmed by Scalia J in the United States Supreme Court in *Burnham v Superior Court of California, County of Marin*:[5]

> Among the most firmly established principles of personal jurisdiction in American tradition is that the courts of a State have jurisdiction over non-residents who are physically present in the State. The view developed early that each State had the power to hale before its courts any individual who could be found within its borders, and that once having acquired jurisdiction over such a person by properly serving him with process, the State could retain jurisdiction to enter judgment against him, no matter how fleeting his visit.[6]

The 'person' will very commonly be a corporation or other business association and in such cases Rules of Court prescribe how service is to be effected (typically on a company officer) and other

[2] F Garcimartín and G Saumier, *Explanatory Report on the 2019 HCCH Judgments Convention* (HCCH 2020) paras 247–54. Compare the equivalent provision in Art 9(c) of the Choice of Court Convention, and T Hartley and M Dogauchi, *Explanatory Report on the Convention of 30 June 2005 on Choice of Court Agreements* (Permanent Bureau of the Hague Conference on Private International Law 2005) para 185 ff.

[3] Art 7(1)(a)(ii). *cf* Art 13(1) of the Service Convention: service under that instrument can only be refused if compliance would infringe the sovereignty or security of the requested State.

[4] Dicey, Morris and Collins, *The Conflict of Laws*, 15th edn (Sweet & Maxwell 2012) para 11-003.

[5] 495 US 604, 610–11 (1990).

[6] This is only one strand in the principles governing the jurisdiction of the courts in the US, principles developed primarily in inter-state cases; they cannot be dealt with here.

provisions may interpret the notion of the 'presence' of a company by reference to its incorporation or its having a place of business in the state.

This principle has been extended in England and many Commonwealth States to apply to service not within the territory of the State but, with the leave of the court whose jurisdiction is invoked, anywhere in the world. The origins of this are to be found in section 18 of the Common Law Procedure Act 1852 which was limited to cases in which the cause of action arose in England (a difficult phrase, not used in the current legislation in England) or which concerned a breach of a contract made in England. The principle has been much extended and now applies to many types of case. It has been 'normalised' to the extent that it is now expressed in England not in primary legislation but in a Practice Direction attached to the Civil Procedure Rules.

Jurisdiction based solely on the service of process, whether within or out of the jurisdiction, is widely regarded as unsatisfactory, as exorbitant. It was excluded by the Brussels Convention of 1968 so far as defendants domiciled in a Contracting State were concerned,[7] and current EU law is to the same effect.[8] The work on a Convention dealing with jurisdiction undertaken by the Hague Conference revealed the same opposition to this type of jurisdiction. Article 18 of the interim text of a preliminary draft Convention produced in 2001 dealt with 'prohibited grounds of jurisdiction'. This insisted that the application of a rule of jurisdiction provided for under the national law is prohibited if there is no substantial connection between that State and either the dispute or the defendant, and listed objection 'in particular' to a range of rules including 'the service of a writ upon the defendant in that [the forum] State'.[9]

C. Differences in Approach

This divergence between States in the common law tradition and other States reflects another difference as to the nature of the service of process. All States see the exercise of the judicial function as part of the sovereign power of the State. Some, by extension, see the commencement or invocation of the judicial function as equally a State matter. Common lawyers do not. An aggrieved person, individual or corporate, has the right of access to the court. The claimant is responsible for taking the necessary steps to get the issues before the court, and that includes serving process and also obtaining the necessary evidence to present to persuade the court of the justice of the claim. The fact that the State may provide some assistance, by providing process-servers, sheriffs or marshals to effect service within the jurisdiction and by issuing letters of request to a foreign court in some cases involving evidence abroad, does not affect the basic understanding.

A clear demonstration of this is the attitude of States to the service of foreign process within their own territory by the simple expedient of sending the document by post. The common law approach sees no possible objection; it is an efficient and inexpensive way of getting the necessary information to the defendant. Other States have traditionally objected strongly to what they see as an interference with their judicial sovereignty. Article 10(a) of the Service Convention allows service by post 'provided the State of destination does not object'. As at 1 September 2020, there were 78 Parties to the Convention. Of the 16 Commonwealth States, the great majority did not object to service by post; the only exceptions were Malta, India and Sri Lanka.

[7] Art 3: 'Persons domiciled in a Contracting State may be sued in the courts of another Contracting State only by virtue of the rules set out in Sections 2 to 6 of this Title'.

[8] Brussels 1a, Art 5(1).

[9] Interim Text, available at: assets.hcch.net/docs/e172ab52-e2de-4e40-9051-11aee7c7be67.pdf.

Other common law jurisdictions also allowing service by post were the Hong Kong SAR, Ireland and the United States. Of the remaining 59 Parties, just under a half (27) allowed service by post.

D. A Preliminary Question

When is service of process abroad needed? The obvious answer, 'Whenever the defendant is out of the jurisdiction', is not quite right. A better answer is, 'Whenever the defendant cannot be served within the jurisdiction'. The difference between those two answers is significant.

In the law of many States it is possible to take steps within the jurisdiction that amount to service on the absent defendant (individual or corporate). Some provisions to this effect are uncontroversial: a potential defendant based abroad may have provided an address for service within the jurisdiction, perhaps at the office of a lawyer. Establishing a place of business within the jurisdiction may enable a company to be served there, even if the company is regarded as having a nationality, residence or domicile abroad. But there are practices that are much more controversial.

One is the system of *notification au parquet* which was found in a number of European States: this allowed legally effective service on a defendant resident abroad to be made by leaving the relevant document at the office of the *parquet*, the local public prosecutor, in the forum State. Although the *parquet* was then expected to take steps to bring the document to the attention of the defendant, service was already complete and time began to run for various purposes regardless of the date upon which the defendant received actual notice of the proceedings.[10]

In the law of some of the United States, there is the notion of an 'involuntary agent' to be found in the relevant state and on whom good service may be made against the foreign principal. This was central to a controversial decision of the US Supreme Court in *Volksvagenwerk AG v Schlunk*.[11] Service of process concerning a claim brought in the courts of Illinois arising out of a motor vehicle accident was effected on Volkswagen of America, a New Jersey corporation which did business in Illinois and had a registered address for service there. The plaintiffs sought to join the German parent company, Volkswagen AG, as co-defendant; although no service had been attempted on that company it was held that Volkswagen of America was its parent company's agent by operation of law. Under the Service Convention, to which the US was Party, the rules of the Convention apply 'in all cases, in civil and commercial matters, where there is occasion to transmit a judicial or extra-judicial document for service abroad'.[12] The US Supreme Court held that this was *not* a case in which there was occasion to transmit a document for service abroad, so the Convention did not apply.

The issue, essentially whether the Service Convention was mandatory, was repeatedly discussed at Special Commissions of the Hague Conference held to review the operation of the Convention, and both the meetings in 2003 and 2009 accepted that the Convention had 'a non-mandatory but exclusive character'.[13] More fully:

> The language [of art 1] 'where there is occasion to transmit' is understood as meaning that the Service Convention is non-mandatory in the sense that it is a matter for the *lex fori* to determine whether a

[10] *cf* the practice discussed in the celebrated English case of *Buchanan v Rucker* (1808) 9 East 192 where the court of Tobago gave judgment against a merchant formerly resident in Dunkirk but then resident in London, the summons having been validly 'served' under the local law by nailing up a copy at the Tobago court house door.

[11] 486 US 694 (1988).

[12] Convention, Art 1.

[13] See para 12 of the Conclusions and Recommendations of the 2009 Special Commission, available at: assets.hcch.net/upload/wop/jac_concl_e.pdf.

document must be transmitted for service abroad. The use of the word 'shall' is understood as meaning that the Service Convention is exclusive, in the sense that once the law of the forum has determined that a document must be transmitted abroad for service, the channels of transmission expressly available or otherwise permitted under the Hague Service Convention are the *only* channels that may be used.[14]

II. The Hague Service Convention

How is service of process across national boundaries to be effected? The Service Convention is the most important international instrument answering this question. Its geographical coverage is impressive: 43 States in Europe; 13 in Asia; 14 in the Americas, including the Caribbean; six in Africa; and two in Oceania. All but four of the G20 Member countries are Parties to the Service Convention.[15] It represents a significant step in the gradual simplification of international service procedures, a process necessitated by the enormous increase in international trade and in the movement of persons across national boundaries. The earlier Hague Convention on the subject, part of the Convention on Civil Procedure of 1905, had as the primary channel for the transmission of documents the 'indirect consular channel', involving service by an authority in the requested State at the request of the consul of the requesting State. This often involved the Foreign Office or equivalent ministry of the State of origin and the whole process could be unacceptably slow.

The main innovation in the Service Convention was the creation of the system of Central Authorities.[16] Each Contracting State must designate such a Central Authority to receive requests for service from other Contracting States;[17] the expectation, borne out in practice, was that this would involve not the creation of some new agency but the designation as Central Authority for the purposes of this Convention of some existing office or ministry. Most Contracting States have designated their Ministries of Justice, the busier having specialist offices within the Ministry; others have placed the Central Authority within the courts service; relatively few have retained the Foreign Ministry.[18] While the United States Department of Justice acts as Central Authority it has 'outsourced' the main practical functions to a private company, ABC Legal, based in Seattle. Composite and Federal States may appoint more than one Central Authority or other, additional authorities.[19]

The Convention provides that the request is initiated by an 'authority or judicial officer competent under the law of the State in which the documents originate'.[20] Some countries, including the United Kingdom, have chosen to provide that outgoing requests must be forwarded through the Central Authority; the case for using a Central Authority as a transmitting agency rests on the argument that the familiarity of its officers with the system of the Convention and with

[14] Preliminary Document 10 for the Special Commission of 2009, para 6. *cf Australian Information Commission v Facebook Inc* [2020] FCA 531 (substituted service allowed as service under the Hague Convention in the United States and Ireland thought to be impossible because of the Covid-19 pandemic). An unsuccessful application was made to set aside the order in respect of service in the US, but on grounds not here relevant.

[15] The exceptions are Indonesia, Saudi Arabia, Singapore and South Africa. See the status table for the Convention, available at: www.hcch.net/en/instruments/conventions/status-table/?cid=17. There are 78 Contracting Parties to the Convention as at 1 December 2020.

[16] The indirect consular channel remains available (Convention, Art 9) but is now little used.

[17] Convention, Art 2(1).

[18] Argentina, Colombia, Costa Rica, Japan, Mexico and Venezuela. See also Botswana (Minister of State in the Office of the President), Iceland (District Commissioner of Suðurnes) and Sweden (County Administrative Board of Stockholm).

[19] Convention, Art 18.

[20] Ibid, Art 3(1).

the practice of other countries would ensure that requests would be handled expeditiously and without any need to refer a request back for clarification. Other States allow local court officials or *huissiers* to act. Private parties may not themselves originate requests, but a party's lawyer may do so if the law of the State of origin so allows. A number of States have made declarations specifying those (including practising lawyers) who may initiate requests.[21]

The Convention prescribes in some detail the documentation to be used, the extent to which translations may be required, and the actual mode of service to be employed in the State of destination. Various Model Forms are annexed to the Convention; they can be completed online. The 'Request for Service' is in three parts. The actual request is set out in the first part, which gives the relevant addresses and which may specify a particular mode of service. The second, printed on the reverse of the first, is a Certificate either that service was effected on a stated date or that service has proved impossible for stated reasons; the Certificate will be tendered in proof of service in any proceedings in the State of origin, and the law of that State will determine whether its contents can be challenged or whether the absence or incomplete nature of the Certificate is fatal. The third is a Summary of the document to be served, which is served with the document itself.[22] Unless the Contracting States concerned have agreed to dispense, in dealings between their two countries, with this requirement,[23] all three parts of the Request must be completed either in the language of the State of destination or in French or English.[24]

Article 5 of the Convention provides:

> The Central Authority of the State addressed must itself serve the document or shall arrange to have it served by an appropriate agency, either *a)* by a method prescribed by its internal law for the service of documents in domestic actions upon persons who are within its territory, or *b)* by a particular method requested by the applicant, unless such a method is incompatible with the law of the State addressed.
>
> Subject to sub-paragraph *(b)* of the first paragraph of this Article, the document may always be served by delivery to an addressee who accepts it voluntarily.

If the document is to be served under Article 5 by any method other than that of simple delivery, the Central Authority may require the document to be written in, or translated into, an official language of the State of destination.[25] If a translation is required, the whole document must be translated including any appended material treated by the law of the State of origin as an essential part of the document. Some countries always require the document to be translated. Others have some flexibility, being prepared to serve documents in any language which the addressee is likely to understand; a short document addressed to a commercial firm in English or in a language similar to that of the State of destination (eg, a document in Norwegian for service in Sweden) will be accepted, but a long document addressed to a private individual in a relatively obscure language will not.[26]

The Convention allows modes of service other than the use of Central Authorities. Mention has already been made of service by post,[27] to which many States have registered an objection.

[21] Under Art 21 of the Convention, States should inform the Ministry of Foreign Affairs of the Netherlands about the authority or judicial officer designated as being able to transmit the documents under Art 3 of the Convention. Amongst other forwarding authorities Canada lists 'the members of the law societies of all provinces and territories'; Ireland 'practising solicitors'; the Russian Federation 'notaries and advocates'; Turkey 'notaries'; and the United States 'any court official, any attorney, or any other person or entity authorized by the rules of the court'.

[22] See Convention, Arts 3, 5(4) and 6.

[23] Ibid, Art 20(b).

[24] Ibid, Art 7(2).

[25] Ibid, Art 5(3).

[26] See, eg, the flexibility allowed by the Finnish declaration in relation to Art 5, available at: www.hcch.net/en/instruments/conventions/status-table/notifications/?csid=400&disp=resdn.

[27] Convention, Art 10(a).

The same is true of two other modes of service. The first is from official to official, the text of the Convention preserving

> the freedom of judicial officers [*officiers ministériels* in the French text], officials or other competent persons of the State of origin to effect service of judicial documents directly through the judicial officers, officials or other competent persons of the State of destination.[28]

This is used, almost exclusively, in those countries with the institution of *huissier* to allow direct communication from *huissier* to *huissier*.

Subject to the same rights of objection, 'any person interested in a judicial proceeding' may effect service directly through the judicial officers, officials or other competent persons of the State of destination.[29] This enables an approach by a party directly to a competent local court official, eg, in the State of destination. Many Contracting States have indicated their objection to its use, and communication via the Central Authority is much easier and more likely to be successful.

Finally, Article 19 of the Convention provides:

> To the extent that the internal law of a Contracting State permits methods of transmission, other than those provided for in the preceding Articles, of documents coming from abroad, for service within its territory, the present Convention shall not affect such provisions.[30]

A. Safeguards

In most if not all legal systems, the plaintiff may obtain a default judgment if the defendant fails to put in an appearance or defence within a stated time. This assumes that the writ or other originating process was duly served. How does the use of the Service Convention affect the position? Article 15(1) provides that a default judgment must not be given until it is established either that the document was served by a method prescribed by the internal law of the State addressed for the service of documents in domestic actions upon persons who are within its territory, or it was actually delivered to the defendant or to his residence by another method provided for by the Convention. The service or the delivery must have been effected in sufficient time to enable the defendant to defend.

Those provisions proved very controversial in the negotiation of the Convention. The compromise reached allowed Contracting States to adopt additional rules in Article 15(2). These allow the judge in the State of origin to

> give judgment even if no certificate of service or delivery has been received, if all the following conditions are fulfilled –
>
> (a) the document was transmitted by one of the methods provided for in this Convention,
>
> (b) a period of time of not less than six months, considered adequate by the judge in the particular case, has elapsed since the date of the transmission of the documents,
>
> (c) no certificate of any kind has been received, even though every reasonable effort has been made to obtain it through the competent authorities of the State addressed.

[28] Ibid, Art 10(b).

[29] Ibid, Arts 10(c), 21(2)(a).

[30] This form of minimum harmonisation promotes greater liberality in methods of service. The United States in its notification pursuant to Art 31 of the Convention states: 'The United States has no objection to the informal delivery of such documents by members of diplomatic or consular missions in the United States, through the mails or by private persons if that would be effective under applicable law, provided no compulsion is used'. See notification, available at: www.hcch.net/en/instruments/conventions/status-table/notifications/?csid=428&disp=resdn.

This option has been taken by a significant majority of Contracting States including most of the large ones[31] and should be favoured as being more conducive to efficient adjudication in international cases. Whichever set of rules has been adopted, nothing in Article 15 prevents a court in the State of origin from taking, in case of urgency, any provisional or protective measures.[32]

Article 16 gives some protection to a defendant against whom a default judgment has been entered. A judge must have the power to allow an appeal to be heard, notwithstanding the expiry of the normal time limit, if the defendant, without any fault on his part, did not have knowledge of the document in sufficient time to defend, or knowledge of the judgment in sufficient time to appeal, and has disclosed a *prima facie* defence to the action on the merits. Application to proceed in this way must be made within a reasonable time after the defendant has knowledge of the judgment;[33] most Contracting States have taken advantage of a power to fix a time limit, which cannot be less than one year from the date of the judgment.[34] The declarations provided for in Articles 15 and 16 are interesting examples of the flexibility of Hague Conventions, permitting diversity within an acceptable range of options, and extending beyond the traditional realm of private international law into partial harmonisation of procedural issues.

B. Extra-Judicial Documents

Chapter II of the Convention, consisting solely of the brief Article 17, applies the provisions of the Convention to extra-judicial documents 'emanating from authorities and judicial officers of a Contracting State'. The cited words are important. Without them the phrase 'extra-judicial documents' would appear almost unlimited in scope. A 1977 Special Commission of the Hague Conference did, however, suggest that Central Authorities should serve extra-judicial documents not emanating from an authority or from a judicial officer if the documents were of a type which normally would call for the intervention of an authority in their countries.[35]

[31] Art 15(2) declarations have been made by 52 Contracting States: Andorra, Argentina, Australia, Austria, Belgium, Botswana, Bulgaria, Canada, China, Croatia, Cyprus, Czech Republic, Denmark, Estonia, France, Germany, Greece, Hungary, Iceland, India, Japan, Korea, Latvia, Lithuania, Luxembourg, Marshall Islands, Monaco, Montenegro, Netherlands, Nicaragua, Norway, Pakistan, Portugal, Moldova, North Macedonia, Russia, Saint Vincent and the Grenadines, San Marino, Serbia, Seychelles, Slovakia, Slovenia, Spain, Sri Lanka, Tunisia, Turkey, Ukraine, United Kingdom, United States of America, Venezuela and Viet Nam. See: www.hcch.net/en/instruments/conventions/status-table/?cid=17.

[32] Convention, Art 15(3).

[33] Ibid, Art 16(1)(2).

[34] The following Contracting States (44) have made a declaration fixing a time limit to bring an action reviewing the default judgment (time limit in brackets if not a year): Andorra, Argentina, Australia (but the court has discretion to extend the time limit beyond a year), Austria, Belgium, Bulgaria, Canada (with an exceptional cases exception permitted for the rules of the court seised), China, Croatia, Cyprus, Denmark, Estonia (3 years), France, Germany, Hungary, Iceland, India, Israel, Kazakhstan, Kuwait (the trial judge can make it longer than a year), Lithuania, Luxembourg, Marshall Islands, Mexico (discretion to judge to go beyond a year), Monaco, Montenegro (some dubiety about the scope of the declaration), Netherlands, Nicaragua, Norway (3 years), Pakistan (Pakistan law limitation period), Portugal, Moldova, North Macedonia, Romania, Serbia, Seychelles, Slovenia, Spain (16 months), Tunisia, Turkey (one year from the delivery of the decision), Ukraine, United Kingdom (for Scotland only), United States of America ('an application under Article 16 will not be entertained if it is filed (a) after the expiration of the period within which the same may be filed under the procedural regulations of the court in which the judgment has been entered, or (b) after the expiration of one year following the date of the judgment, whichever is later') and Venezuela (period specified in Venezuelan law). See: www.hcch.net/en/instruments/conventions/status-table/?cid=17.

[35] See the Report on the Work of the 1977 Special Commission at E, available at: assets.hcch.net/upload/scrpt14_77e.pdf.

C. Costs

The general principle as to the cost of effecting service is that the authorities of the State of destination seek no reimbursement of any costs they incur. However, the applicant must pay or reimburse costs occasioned by the use of the services of a judicial officer (*officier ministériel*) or of a person competent under the law of the State of destination or by the use of a particular method of service.[36] 'Simple delivery' (*remise simple*) is always free of charge.

III. European Union Arrangements

Since 2001 there have been arrangements for the service of process as between the Member States of the European Union.[37] These draw on the Hague Service Convention, but take account of the geographical proximity of the EU Member States. In particular, instead of the system of Central Authorities which is central to the Hague Convention, the EU arrangements reflect the belief that 'efficiency and speed in judicial procedures in civil matters means that the transmission of judicial and extrajudicial documents is to be made direct and by rapid means between local bodies designated by the Member States'.[38]

Member States are required to establish two types of authority. The first is a 'central body' which, unlike the Central Authorities of the Hague system, will only exceptionally be involved in the actual processes of service. The central body is responsible for (a) supplying information to the 'transmitting agencies'; (b) seeking solutions to any difficulties which may arise during transmission of documents for service; and (c) forwarding, 'in exceptional cases', at the request of a transmitting agency, a request for service to the competent 'receiving agency'.[39]

The operational agencies are the transmitting and receiving agencies designated by the Member States. They are specified 'public officers, authorities or other persons' competent either to transmit or receive documents, or to carry out both functions.[40] In some Member States, all local courts or judicial officers may act in both capacities; others designate a single transmitting agency. The relevant information is published on the website of the European Judicial Network in Civil and Commercial Matters.

Subject to various conditions, some other modes of service may be used. Unless the State of destination objects, service may be effected by diplomatic or consular agents directly on the addressee, without the application of any compulsion.[41] The indirect consular channel, using consular or diplomatic channels to forward judicial documents to the receiving agency of another Member State is permitted 'in exceptional circumstances'.[42] The postal channel is always available, but any Member State may specify 'the conditions under which' it will accept service of

[36] Convention, Art 12.

[37] Originally contained in Council Regulation (EC) No 1348/2000 of 29 May 2000 on the service in the Member States of judicial and extrajudicial documents in civil or commercial matters [2000] OJ L160/37; then in European Parliament and Council Regulation (EC) No 1393/2007 of 13 November 2007 on the service in the Member States of judicial and extrajudicial documents in civil and commercial matters (service of documents) and repealing Council Regulation (EC) 1348/2000 [2007] OJ L324/79. With effect from July 2022, this will be replaced by Regulation (EU) 2020/1784 of the European Parliament and of the Council of 25 November 2020 on the service in the Member States of judicial and extrajudicial documents in civil or commercial matters (service of documents) (recast) [2020] OJ L405/40.

[38] Reg 1393/2007, recital (6).

[39] Reg 1393/2007, Art 3; Reg 2020/1784, Art 4. A federal or composite state may designate more than one central body.

[40] Reg 1393/2007, Art 2; Reg 2020/1784, Art 3.

[41] Reg 1393/2007, Art 13; Reg 2020/1784, Art 17.

[42] Reg 1393/2007, Art 12; Reg 2020/1784, Art 16.

judicial documents by post by registered letter with acknowledgement of receipt or equivalent.[43] In language following that of the Hague Convention, the arrangements preserve the freedom of any person interested in a judicial proceeding to effect service of judicial documents directly through the judicial officers, officials or other competent persons of the Member State addressed, where such direct service is permitted under the law of that Member State.[44] The provisions of Articles 15 and 16 of the Service Convention on default judgments and related matters are reproduced in full, with only minimal changes of terminology.[45]

A single terse provision states that 'extrajudicial documents may be transmitted for service in another Member State in accordance with the provisions of this Regulation'.[46]

Regulation 2020/1784 introduced a number of new provisions taking advantage of technical developments provided by digitalisation and the use of IT technology. Subject to certain conditions, service may be effected directly on a person who has a known address for service in another Member State by any electronic means of service available under the law of the forum Member State for the domestic service of documents.[47]

Further provisions, which will not come into effect until 2025,[48] provide for the creation of a decentralised IT system, defined[49] to mean a network of national IT systems and interoperable access points, operating under the individual responsibility and management of each Member State, that enables the secure and reliable cross-border exchange of information between the national IT systems. Documents to be served, requests, confirmations, receipts, certificates and communications carried out between transmitting agencies and receiving agencies, between those agencies and the central bodies, or between the central bodies of different Member States, must be transmitted through the decentralised IT system. If that is not possible due to the disruption of the decentralised IT system or exceptional circumstances, the transmission must be carried out by the swiftest, most appropriate alternative means, taking into account the need to ensure reliability and security.[50]

IV. Inter-American Arrangements

Although some provisions as to Letters Rogatory requesting service of process were contained in earlier Conventions between Latin American States, they were not understood by the US courts; the result of one particular influential decision,[51] was that for many years a plaintiff in a Latin American State had no means of serving process on a defendant in the United States. The United States pressed for the adoption of the Service Convention, at least as the basis for some new inter-American arrangements. Although the Hague Conference is now much more active in Spanish-speaking states, the absence of any authentic Spanish text of the Hague Conventions and the Latin American attachment to the letters rogatory procedure made this unacceptable.

[43] Reg 1393/2007, Art 14; Reg 2020/1784, Art 18.
[44] Reg 1393/2007, Art 15; Reg 2020/1784, Art 20(1).
[45] Reg 1393/2007, Art 19; Reg 2020/1784, Art 22.
[46] Reg 1393/2007, Art 16; Reg 2020/1784, Art 21.
[47] Reg 2020/1784, Art 19.
[48] Reg 2020/1784, Arts 25 and 37(2).
[49] Reg 2020/1784, Art 2(2).
[50] Reg 2020/1784, Art 5. For the use of qualified electronic seals or qualified electronic signatures, where needed, see Art 5(3).
[51] *Re Letters Rogatory out of the First Civil Court of City of Mexico* 261 F 652 (SD NY, 1919).

Finally, the Organization of American States convened an Inter-American Specialized Conference on Private International Law (CIDIP from its Spanish title, Conferencia Especializada Inter-Americana sobre Derecho Internacional Privado) which produced six conventions, including the Inter-American Convention on Letters Rogatory signed in Panama on 30 January 1975 (the Inter-American Convention). This Convention retained something of the laconic style of drafting of its Latin American predecessors, and like them applied in principle to both the service of documents and the taking of evidence. It found little favour in the United States, but there was however considerable interest in securing some workable arrangement. As a result, the US delegation at the Second Inter-American Specialized Conference on Private International Law (CIDIP 2), held in 1979, secured the adoption of an Additional Protocol, limited to service of documents but containing a fuller treatment of that topic, drawing inspiration from some aspects of the Service Convention. Of the total of 18 States now Party to the Inter-American Convention, all but four have ratified the Protocol.[52]

A. The Inter-American Convention

The Inter-American Convention applies to letters rogatory, issued in conjunction with proceedings in civil and commercial matters held before a judicial or other adjudicatory authority of one of the States Parties to this Convention, that have as their purpose (inter alia) 'the performance of procedural acts of a merely formal nature, such as service of process, summonses or subpoenas abroad'.[53]

The actual transmission of letters rogatory to the authority to which they are addressed is governed by Article 4 which allows six possible modes of transmission. These involve action by diplomatic or consular agents, by the Central Authority designated for the purposes of the Convention in either the State of origin or that of destination, by 'the interested parties', or 'through judicial channels'. This last phrase presumably means that action to transmit a letter rogatory is to be taken by the staff of the court of origin. The clarity of the phrase is not advanced by the inclusion in Article 7 of the statement that 'courts in border areas of States Parties' (meaning, presumably, areas close to a common frontier between States of origin and destination) 'may directly execute the letters rogatory contemplated in this Convention'. It appears from the context that this is not intended as a limitation on the use of 'judicial channels' but rather as a preliminary observation before a specific provision that in such border cases legalisation is not required. Legalisation is required in other cases unless the letters rogatory are transmitted through consular or diplomatic channels or through the Central Authority;[54] a letter rogatory legalised by a competent consular or diplomatic agent is 'presumed to be duly legalized in the State of origin'.[55]

When transmitted, the letter must be accompanied by certain other documents, intended for delivery to the person on whom the process, summons or subpoena is to be served, and all must

[52] Nicaragua which signed but never ratified the Inter-American Convention is a Party to the Service Convention. Five States Parties to the Protocol and one (Costa Rica) Party only to the Inter-American Convention are also Parties to the Service Convention.

[53] Convention, Art 2.

[54] Ibid, Art 6.

[55] Ibid, Art 5(a). See also Art 18 which obliges States Parties to inform the General Secretariat of the Organization of American States as to their legal requirements as to the legalisation and translation of letters rogatory.

be translated into the official language of the State of destination.[56] The other required documents are:

a. An authenticated copy of the complaint with its supporting documents, and of other exhibits or rulings that serve as the basis for the measure requested.
b. Written information identifying the authority issuing the letter, indicating the time limits allowed the person affected to act upon the request, and warning of the consequences of failure to do so.
c. Where appropriate, information on the existence and address of the court-appointed defence counsel or of competent legal aid societies in the State of origin.[57]

The execution of letters rogatory is governed by the law of the State of destination, though special procedures or formalities requested by the issuing authority may be observed if to do so would not be contrary to that law.[58]

Article 12 of the Convention specifies that costs and other expenses must be borne by the interested parties. The State of destination is given a discretion (though the Convention does not specify by which organ of the State the discretion is to be exercised) to execute a letter rogatory which does not indicate the person to be held responsible for the costs and expenses; the point here is that there is a discretion to refuse to execute letters in such circumstances. In addition, the Convention contains an express provision allowing a State of destination to refuse to execute a letter rogatory that is manifestly contrary to public policy (*ordre public*).[59]

The Inter-American Convention contains no material comparable to that on safeguards for defendants in Articles 15 and 16 of the Service Convention. It does however provide expressly[60] that execution of letters rogatory does not imply ultimate recognition of the jurisdiction of the authority issuing the letter rogatory or a commitment to recognise or enforce any judgment.

B. The 1979 Additional Protocol

Although in form supplementary to the Inter-American Convention, the Protocol actually creates an alternative treaty regime. It applies to 'procedural acts (pleadings, motions, orders and subpoenas) that are served and requests for information that are made by a judicial or administrative authority of a State Party to a judicial or administrative authority of another State Party and are transmitted by a letter rogatory from the Central Authority of the State of origin to the Central Authority of the State of destination'.[61]

This definition makes mandatory as between Parties to the Protocol the use of Central Authorities both for the outward transmission and inward receipt of letters rogatory. The obligation to designate a Central Authority is dealt with in Article 2 and the duties of the receiving Central Authority are set out in detail in Article 4.

There are elaborate provisions in Articles 3 and 4 of the Protocol as to the appropriate documentation, and these provisions are very obviously inspired by provisions of the Service Convention. In particular three forms are prescribed, which to minimise translation problems

[56] Ibid, Arts 5(b), 8, 18.
[57] Ibid, Art 8.
[58] Ibid, Art 10.
[59] Ibid, Art 17.
[60] Ibid, Art 9.
[61] Protocol, Art 1.

are required to be printed either in all four official languages of the Organization of American States (English, French, Portuguese and Spanish) or at least in the languages of the States of origin and destination. The forms are of the Letter Rogatory itself, which follows the functional layout of the Hague 'Request' rather than the formal, almost supplicatory, style of a traditional letter rogatory; a statement of Essential Information for the Addressee, corresponding to the Hague 'Summary of the Document to be Served'; and a Certificate of execution or non-execution again on the model of the corresponding Hague document.

The translation requirements are considerably lightened. The only document which need be translated is the complaint or pleading that initiated the action in which the letter rogatory was issued. Attached documents and the actual rulings ordering that a letter rogatory be issued are to be supplied, but need not be translated. Legalisation is not required, as the Inter-American Convention already provided for the exclusion of this requirement when transmission was through a Central Authority.[62]

Article 5 declares that 'the processing of letters rogatory by the Central Authority of the State Party of destination and its judicial or administrative authorities shall be free of charge'. However, many countries in the Americas require the costs of judicial acts to be borne by the interested parties, and the Protocol reflects this by allowing a State of destination to seek payment from the party seeking execution of the letter rogatory of charges payable under its local law.[63]

C. The Medellin Treaty

As in the European Union, other regional organisations are seeking to make use of the latest digital technology in this context. The Medellin Treaty of 25 July 2019, negotiated under the auspices of the Conference of Ministers of Justice of the Ibero-American Countries, provides for the use of Iber@, a secure transmission system as a transmission channel between Central Authorities. The use of this system is not made mandatory but it is hoped that Iber@ will become the principal means of communication under the applicable Inter-American arrangements. It came into force on 31 August 2021 for Andorra, Cuba and Spain.[64]

V. The CIS Convention

The Commonwealth of Independent States (CIS) established after the dissolution of the Soviet Union adopted a Convention on Legal Assistance and Legal Relations in Civil, Family and Criminal Matters in Minsk in 1993; it was amended in 1998. It has 10 States Parties.

Under the Convention, judicial and other competent authorities of the Contracting States communicate with each other through their Central Authorities, in each case the relevant Ministry of Justice. Assistance provided under the Convention is at no charge to the applicant.[65] Many types of assistance are covered, including the service of documents. The requesting State addresses letters rogatory to the judicial authorities of the requested State. There are detailed provisions as to the information that must be included.[66] In executing the request for legal assistance

[62] Convention, Art 6.
[63] Protocol, Art 6.
[64] The signatory States are Argentina, Brazil, Colombia, Chile, Paraguay, Portugal and Uruguay.
[65] Convention, Art 2.
[66] Ibid, Art 7.

the requested State applies its own national legislation; however, upon request of the requesting authority, it may apply the procedural rules of the requesting State insofar as they are not incompatible with the law of the State addressed. The documents must be in the official language of the State addressed or in the Russian language or translated into those languages; however, a document not in those languages may be served by a simple delivery upon an addressee who accepts it voluntarily. The Convention also allows the diplomatic or consular agents of the State of origin to serve documents upon their citizens without any form of coercion.

VI. Other Conventions and Arrangements

The Conventions already examined cover some 90 States, but that leaves many that are Party to no multilateral arrangements. There is a whole network of bilateral Conventions on civil procedure that supplement the multilateral ones. Until the negotiation of the Service Convention, the United Kingdom favoured bilateral arrangements which could be tailored to the specific features of the two legal systems concerned. Some 22 such Conventions were agreed, many allowing service by post, and they were commonly extended to other Commonwealth States. Australia, one such State, has additional bilateral treaties with Korea and Thailand. The Russian Federation is Party to some 32 bilateral arrangements in addition to the Minsk Convention and Japan has 16 agreements with other States, seven of which are not Party to the Hague Convention. Singapore's Rules of Court contain specific provisions about service in Brunei and Malaysia. Obtaining information about such provisions is notoriously difficult. In many common law States, the plaintiff will make use of local process-servers, hoping that such service will be good; in other cases there may be no alternative to the use of letters rogatory and the diplomatic or consular channels, which may entail very great delays.

VII. Conclusion

The Hague Service Convention remains the most widely applicable international instrument. Successive reviews by Special Commissions of the Hague Conference have reaffirmed its utility. It has stood the test of time remarkably well, but there have been many technological developments since 1965. To some extent, recommendations of Special Commissions, such as those of the 2014 Special Commission on the use of electronic means of transmission,[67] can help ensure the most effective use of that Convention but almost 60 years after its negotiation there seems to be a need to revisit it and explore how the various regional arrangements can be brought into a global system.

[67] Recommendations 36–39.

13

Taking of Evidence

BROOKE MARSHALL AND NADIA DE ARAUJO*

I. Introduction

In cross-border litigation, most matters of evidence are, as the medieval rule commands, questions of procedure governed by the law of the forum.[1] Where, however, the testimony of a person or documents in their possession are located in a foreign State, comity and pragmatism require regard to be had to the law of that foreign State.[2] In such circumstances, there is the potential for a conflict of laws; one exacerbated by the distinct approaches which civil law and common law systems take to evidence and its collection.[3] In the former, evidence is mostly written; which evidence is to be gathered and how that is done is primarily a function of a trial judge or court officer.[4] In the latter, evidence is primarily oral; which evidence is obtained and presented to the court is largely an issue for the parties.[5] The potential for conflict is further exacerbated by the fact that the taking of evidence in common law countries is generally accompanied by a process, unknown to civil ones, which 'may lead to the discovery of evidence'.[6] It is amplified by the division between the courts of Commonwealth common law countries and those in the United States, as to the permissible subjects and objects of that process.

The Convention of 18 March 1970 on the Taking of Evidence Abroad in Civil or Commercial Matters (the Convention) seeks to limit the potential for conflicts to arise by creating cooperative procedures and reducing the 'formal and technical obstacles' of the letters rogatory system which preceded it.[7] The Convention provides for the application of the procedural laws of the place from which the evidence is sought, while accommodating certain procedural laws of the forum, at the latter's request. The Convention also facilitates the prevention of its misuse, allowing Contracting

* The law is stated as at November 2020. This chapter was subject to external peer review. We thank Caio Freitas and Jack Dennis for research assistance, and Amy Campbell, Barrister-at-Law, Professor Fleur Johns and Professor Michael Legg for their valuable comments on several issues.

[1] See generally, Garnett, 'Substance and Procedure', ch 9 in this book, text accompanying (n 6) and section IV.

[2] R Garnett, *Substance and Procedure in Private International Law* (Oxford University Press 2012) [8.01].

[3] See generally, D McClean, 'Judicial Cooperation: Resolving the Differing Approaches' in VR Abou-Nigm and MBN Taquela (eds), *Diversity and Integration in Private International Law* (Edinburgh University Press 2019) 128–31.

[4] D McClean, *International Co-operation in Civil and Criminal Matters*, 3rd edn (Oxford University Press, 2012) 4–5. References to the approach of 'common law' and 'civil law' jurisdictions in this chapter are necessarily very general.

[5] Ibid.

[6] L Collins, 'The Hague Evidence Convention and Discovery: A Serious Misunderstanding' (1986) 35 *ICLQ* 765, 768.

[7] Ibid, 774.

States to declare that it shall not be used for pre-trial document 'discovery' undertaken on their territories.[8]

This chapter examines whether the Convention adequately responds to the problems it was designed to address. It first explores how the Convention treats the issue of the taking of foreign evidence. It then identifies several uncertainties which persist in the Convention framework. The chapter suggests that residual confusion as to what is evidence, as opposed to discovery, continues to affect the Convention and that problems of a practical nature, chiefly delay, explain why a number of common law States continue to interpret the Convention as non-mandatory, preferring to rely on their internal law processes for the taking of evidence abroad.

II. Foreign Evidence and the Convention

This section sets out the Convention's scope before explaining the key procedures it provides for the taking of evidence abroad.

A. Scope

The Convention is intended to facilitate the taking of *evidence* for use in court *proceedings, commenced or contemplated*.[9] Although the Convention does not define the term 'obtain evidence', there is common law and civil law support for the view that this means the collection of material to prove or disprove facts in, or expected to be in, issue.[10]

The Convention only applies to *civil and commercial matters*.[11] However, as in other HCCH conventions, this term is not defined. Thus, countries may interpret it in a broad manner (generally the case in common law States) or more restrictively, as usually happens in civil law States.[12] Considering possible issues that could arise from this divergence, the 2014 Special Commission recommended that the term be 'interpret[ed] liberally and in an autonomous manner', consistently with the Hague Convention of 15 November 1965 on the Service Abroad of Judicial and Extrajudicial Documents in Civil or Commercial Matters (the 1965 Service Convention).[13]

The Convention's scope is also limited to the taking of (testimonial or documentary) evidence and to requests for performing other judicial acts within the territory of the Requested Contracting States. Though *other judicial acts* is also not defined, the Convention does not apply to cases of service of judicial and extrajudicial documents or to recognition and enforcement of judicial foreign decisions.[14] In these cases, the requesting State might benefit from the Service

[8] In the sense of material designed to lead to the discovery of evidence rather than evidence sought during the pre-trial discovery phase: Permanent Bureau of the Hague Conference on Private International Law, *Practical Handbook on the Operation of the Evidence Convention*, 3rd edn (HCCH 2016) [325]; see section II.A below.

[9] Convention on the taking of evidence abroad in civil or commercial matters (adopted 18 March 1970, entered into force 7 October 1972) 847 UNTS 231 (Convention) Art 1.

[10] *British American Tobacco Australia Services Ltd v Eubanks for the United States of America* (2004) 60 NSWLR 483, [33]. See also, from a civil law perspective, E Fongaro, *La loi applicable à la prevue en droit international privé* (LGDJ 2004) 1.

[11] Art 1.

[12] Permanent Bureau, *Handbook* (n 8) 76–77.

[13] 'Conclusions and Recommendations of the Special Commission on the practical operation of the Hague Service, Evidence and Access to Justice Conventions (20–23 May 2014)' ('Conclusions and Recommendations 2014') [40], available at: www.hcch.net/en/publications-and-studies/details4/?pid=6405&dtid=2.

[14] Art 1.

Convention or the 2019 Convention on Recognition and Enforcement of Foreign Judgments in Civil and Commercial Matters.[15] That said, the use of the Service Convention to serve a subpoena, a judicial act, for the purposes of obtaining discovery will be met with a refusal by the Central Authorities of those States that have made an Article 23 declaration[16] under the Evidence Convention,[17] at least in terms that would preclude it.[18] It is also likely to be met with a refusal by the Central Authorities of those States which have made no declaration but from whose perspective the Convention is mandatory,[19] given that a subpoena for the taking of evidence is a judicial act within the Convention's scope.[20]

B. Procedures

The Convention provides for the taking of evidence abroad through a Requested Court, via a Letter of Request, in chapter I and directly by consuls or commissioners in chapter II.

i. Letters of Request: Chapter I

Where evidence is sought under chapter I of the Convention, a court (or other judicial authority)[21] in one Contracting State must[22] transmit a Letter of Request to the relevant body of the Contracting State in which the witness is found,[23] known as the 'Central Authority'.[24] That Central Authority will then send the letter to the competent authority within its State[25] to execute the letter, so that the evidence can be obtained from the witness.

a. Transmission

Each Contracting State nominates a Central Authority charged with the receipt and transmission of letters of request.[26] Alternatively, the Convention allows courts of Requesting States to bypass the Central Authority of the Requested State and send requests directly to the 'judicial authority' of the Requesting State if they make a declaration allowing for court-to-court transmission.[27] Surprisingly few States have made such a declaration,[28] even though many allow

[15] Convention on the Recognition and Enforcement of Foreign Judgments in Civil or Commercial Matters (adopted 2 July 2019), available at: www.hcch.net/en/instruments/conventions/specialised-sections/judgments.
[16] See section II.A below.
[17] See generally, M Davies et al, *Nygh's Conflict of Laws in Australia*, 10th edn (LexisNexis Butterworths 2020) [11.35].
[18] M Legg and J Kang, 'Accessing Third Party Documents in a Foreign Jurisdiction by Subpoena: The *Ceramic Fuel Cells Ltd (in liq) v McGraw-Hill Financial Inc* Class Action' (2017) 41 *Melbourne University Law Review* 392, 409–410.
[19] See section II.B below.
[20] See *Gloucester (Sub-Holdings 1) Pty Ltd v Chief Commissioner of State Revenue* [2013] NSWSC 1419, [56].
[21] Although the Convention does not define 'judicial authority', the Commission in charge of its drafting decided that 'all courts of arbitration were excluded' by that term: PW Amram, 'Rapport Explicatif de M Ph W Amram' in Bureau Permanent (ed), *Actes et documents de la onzième session 7 au 26 octobre 1968: tome IV, Obtention des preuves à l'étranger* (Imprimerie Nationale 1970) 202, 216.
[22] The fact that States may make a declaration under Art 27(a), to depart from the procedure established by Art 2, strongly suggests that transmission of the Letter through a Central Authority is obligatory for evidence collected via ch I.
[23] Art 11(1).
[24] See The Hague Permanent Bureau, 'National Organs and Central Authorities under HCCH Conventions', ch 8 in this book.
[25] Art 2(1).
[26] Ibid.
[27] Arts 27(a), 28(a). For Federal States and States with territorial units or administrative regions, see Art 24.
[28] At the time of writing, only Denmark and Mexico had made a declaration.

for this via other instruments to which they are Party.[29] The Convention is silent as to how letters of request are to be transmitted – as at 2016, only a minority of Contracting Parties accepted the transmission of letters electronically,[30] though it is reasonable to expect this to have changed since the 2020 COVID-19 pandemic. The letter should generally specify the questions to be put to the witness or, with particularity, the subject matter of the examination, as well as any documents to be inspected,[31] in addition to a number of basic matters.[32] A model Letter of Request is available on the Hague Conference website.

b. Execution

The Convention obliges the competent authority of the Requested State to 'execute' (ie, give effect to) the letter. The identity of this authority differs among Contracting States and need not be a judge.[33] That authority will obtain the evidence, in accordance with its own law.[34] This means that the law of the Requested State will determine, inter alia, how the witness is prepared and examined, including as to whether the witness can be cross-examined by the competent authority of the Requested State, as well as whether the witness may appear before that authority remotely via audio or video link.[35] The law of the Requested State will also regulate the production of documents, including as to whether non-parties must produce them.[36] If, however, according to the law of the Requested State the court itself cannot take the evidence, eg, in England and Wales,[37] the 'Requested authority' of the Requested State must obtain the consent of the Requesting authority before appointing a person to take the evidence.[38]

Equally, the competent authority of the Requested State must apply any special method or procedure requested by the Requesting State (at the latter's cost),[39] unless it is 'incompatible' with the law of the Requested State – because of a 'constitutional inhibition or some absolute statutory prohibition'[40] – or impossible in light of its practice or procedures, or practical difficulties.[41] Special methods or procedures which are regularly requested include the taking of testimony in a particular form, or on oath or affirmation,[42] engaging a stenographer to take a transcript, and

[29] See, eg, Regulation (EU) 2020/1783 of the European Parliament and of the Council of 25 November 2020 on cooperation between the courts of the Member States in the taking of evidence in civil or commercial matters (taking of evidence) (recast) [2020] OJ L405/1 (Recast EU Evidence Regulation) Art 3(1).

[30] Permanent Bureau, *Handbook* (n 8) [145].

[31] Art 3(f)(g); ibid [128].

[32] eg, Art 3(a)–(d) and the translation requirements in Art 4.

[33] In the United Kingdom, it is the Master of the court (a judge). Even in civil law countries, such as France, competent authorities include persons designated as commissioners by the French government. See, eg McClean (n 4) 95. The nature of a 'competent authority' was discussed by the 1978 Special Commission, concluding that the term includes 'not only courts and judges …, but likewise other persons (commissioners, notaries public, *notaires*, lawyers) insofar as these persons are given [in] the specific case under their laws attributes of a judicial authority'. Permanent Bureau, *Report on the work of the Special Commission on the operation of the Convention of 18 March 1970 on the Taking of Evidence Abroad in Civil or Commercial Matters* (HCCH, 1978) [5], available at: www.hcch.net/en/publications-and-studies/details4/?pid=3308&dtid=2.

[34] Art 9(1).

[35] Permanent Bureau, *Handbook* (n 8) [213].

[36] ibid [214].

[37] McClean (n 4) 95 (noting that barristers are regularly appointed as examiners).

[38] Art 14(3).

[39] Art 14(2).

[40] Amram (n 21), 208. See also McClean (n 4) 97.

[41] Art 9(2).

[42] Permanent Bureau, *Handbook* (n 8) [137], [220].

asking that a judge of the Requesting State examine the witness, or that the witness be subject to cross-examination by the parties' lawyers[43] or an examiner.[44] The Requested State can refuse to execute the letter if doing so would prejudice its sovereignty or security[45] or if documents are requested for the purposes of pre-trial discovery.[46] Once taken, the competent authority forwards the evidence to the Requesting Court.[47]

Although the methods in chapter I are traditionally understood as facilitating the indirect taking of evidence, some Contracting States will accede to a Convention request for the direct taking of evidence via video-link.[48] This allows for a judge or the parties' lawyers, physically present in the Requesting State, to examine or cross-examine the witness, physically present in the Requested State, via video-link. As at November 2019, some Requested States allowed this as a 'special' method or procedure under the Convention,[49] while other Requested States allowed it under their internal law, as permitted by the Convention.[50] Some Requested States still did not allow it at all, considering chapter II to be the only permissible form of direct evidence-taking in line with the Convention.[51] It should be noted that, where the Convention is applied,[52] it is not enough that the internal law of the *Requesting* State allows for the direct taking of evidence via video-link;[53] it is the internal law of the *Requested* State that must allow it.[54]

c. Witnesses' Rights and Obligations

An unwilling witness shall be compelled to give evidence under the law of the Requested State.[55] A witness may invoke privileges or duties or obligations not to give evidence either under the laws of the Requesting State, if specified in the letter of request, or under the laws of the Requested State.[56] A witness can rely on the laws of a third State, only to the extent that the Requested State has specified this in a declaration.[57] This would allow, for instance, a Swiss witness requested to give evidence in the Netherlands (the Requested State) to invoke a duty of confidentiality under Swiss banking law, in circumstances where Switzerland is not the Requesting State.[58]

[43] Ibid [220].
[44] Ibid [231].
[45] Art 12(b).
[46] Again, in the sense that the material is sought in order to lead to the discovery of evidence. A State cannot refuse to execute a request merely because it seeks evidence during the phase called pre-trial discovery. See section II.A.
[47] Art 13.
[48] cp Recast EU Evidence Regulation, Art 20, which expressly provides for this possibility.
[49] Art 9(1), (2).
[50] Art 27(b).
[51] Permanent Bureau, *Guide to Good Practice on the Use of Video-Link under the Evidence Convention* (HCCH 2020) 47–49. See also M Mercedes Albornoz and S Paredes, 'No Turning Back: Information and Communication Technologies in International Cooperation Between Authorities' (2021) 17 *Journal of Private International Law* 224, text accompanying fns 19–25.
[52] Whether the Convention *must* be applied is considered in section II.B below.
[53] eg, Federal Court of Australia Act 1976 (Cth) s 47A.
[54] Art 27(b); Permanent Bureau, 'The Mandatory/Non-Mandatory Character of the Evidence Convention (Preliminary Document no 10 of December 2008)' (2008) ('Mandatory/Non-Mandatory 2008') [30]–[33], available at: assets.hcch.net/upload/wop/2008pd10e.pdf.
[55] Art 10; Amram (n 21) 208.
[56] Art 11(a)(b). See, eg, *Renfield Corp v E Remy Martin & Co SA* 98 FRD 442, 443–44 (D Del 1982).
[57] Art 11(2). At the time of writing, Bulgaria, Estonia and the Netherlands had each made declarations.
[58] See McClean (n 4) 99.

ii. Consuls and Commissioners: Chapter II

Unlike the Convention's letter of request procedure, which cannot be excluded, the possibility in chapter II of the Convention for evidence to be taken by consuls or commissioners is optional. Several Contracting States have made a reservation excluding it, in whole or in part.[59]

a. Consul

In chapter II,[60] the Convention provides for the taking of evidence by consular agents and diplomatic officers. Article 15 sets some conditions which shall be met by the officer or agent and by the request. Therefore: (a) the consul may only act within the territory in which they exercise their functions; (b) there shall be no use of compulsion against the person from whom the evidence is to be taken, except when 'appropriate assistance' is requested to the competent authority of the State of execution;[61] (c) the consul can only take evidence of nationals from the State which they represent in the State of execution; and (d) the evidence required is in aid of a proceeding already commenced in the courts of the State that they represent (and not in aid of 'contemplated' judicial proceedings). Unlike the general rule set by Article 1, the consul can only take *evidence* and cannot practise any other 'judicial act' ordinarily performed by the competent authority of the Requested State.

Moreover, Article 15 enables Contracting States to declare that a consul may take evidence only after the competent authority, designated by the Requested State, has granted permission on a case-by-case basis.[62] At the time of writing, Andorra, Australia, Denmark, Iceland, Kazakhstan, Liechtenstein, Norway, Portugal, Sweden and Switzerland follow this exception.

When issuing the permission, the designated authority can, according to Article 19, lay down conditions for the taking of evidence. Some examples are given by the provision itself, such as defining a time and place where the consul may act; or requiring that reasonable advance notice is given of the place, date and time of the taking of the evidence so that a representative of the authority can be present.[63]

The Convention enables a consul to collect evidence, fulfilling the same conditions as Article 15, from nationals of the State where they exercise their functions and of third States.[64] However, in this case, the general rule is that prior permission must be given by the competent authority of the State of execution. The authority may grant general permission for the taking of all evidence in a given case or specific permission for the taking of certain evidence only, depending on the particularities of the case. Yet, a Contracting State may declare that evidence can be

[59] Art 33. For a breakdown, see HCCH, *Table reflecting applicability of Articles 15, 16, 17, 18 and 23 of the Hague Evidence Convention* (June 2017), available at: assets.hcch.net/docs/627a201b-6c7a-4dc2-86ad-c1da582447d4.pdf.

[60] Arts 15–22.

[61] However, this possibility is only available in the territory of Contracting States, which made a declaration in that regard pursuant to Art 18. At the time of writing, Armenia, Belarus, Cyprus, Czech Republic, Greece, India, Italy, Kazakhstan, Serbia, Slovakia, the UK and the USA had made declarations.

[62] The 'competent authority', referred to in ch II of the Convention, may not be the same as the one referred to in Art 1. The Contracting States which have not made a declaration excluding the application of ch II specifically informed the competent authority to execute requests pursuant to each chapter of the Convention. See further HCCH, 'Authorities – 20: Convention of 18 March 1970 on the Taking of Evidence Abroad in Civil or Commercial Matters' (HCCH), available at: www.hcch.net/en/instruments/conventions/authorities1/?cid=82.

[63] According to the Convention's Explanatory Report, the presence of a representative of the authority at the examination by the consul may be justified for different reasons, including the wish to protect the person against examination, which violates the sovereignty and security of the State of execution (as in Art 12), or which does not comply with the privileges or duties of the witness (as in Art 11): Amram (n 21) 213–14.

[64] Art 16.

taken without prior permission.[65] Finland, the Netherlands and the United States have made the declaration. In other countries such as Germany, Singapore, Spain, the United Kingdom and the Czech Republic, permission is not required in some circumstances or is subject to reciprocity.

Pursuant both to Article 15 and 16, the consul will apply the law of the Requesting State in the proceeding for taking the evidence, to the extent that it is compatible with the law of the State of execution (including the permissibility of video-link) and does not violate its sovereignty and security.[66] Also, the request for a person to appear or to give evidence shall comply with administrative rules provided by Article 21, which encompass, among others, language requirements and the need to inform the person that they may be legally represented and not compelled to appear or to give the evidence.

b. Commissioner

The Convention also allows the taking of evidence by a commissioner, who could be appointed by the court of the State of origin or by the courts of the State of execution.[67]

The commissioner will have to fulfil all the same conditions, set by Article 16, when taking the evidence from persons located in the State where they exercise their functions. The commissioner is not authorised to use compulsion against the witness, except when an application is made to the competent authority in the State of execution, and the evidence must be in aid of a proceeding already commenced in the courts of the State of origin.

Moreover, the general rule is that permission should be sought from the competent authority of the State of execution, which will determine the conditions under which the evidence will be taken. Contracting States may declare otherwise, as in Article 16. No such permission is required in France, the United States, Spain (under certain circumstances) and in the United Kingdom (subject to reciprocity).

As in the case of Articles 15 and 16, the commissioner will apply the law of the State of origin to the extent that is compatible with the law of the State of execution.[68] In all methods provided by chapter II, video-link may be used to facilitate the taking of evidence and the presence and participation not only of the witness, but also of the parties, their representatives and of the judicial personnel or authority of the State of origin and the State of execution. However, in the cases where the State of execution made a declaration that prior permission is required, 'such presence or participation will be subject to any conditions specified when permission is granted'.[69]

c. Witnesses' Rights and Obligations

In all cases under Articles 15–17, the persons from whom the evidence must be taken shall be legally represented.[70] According to Article 21(c), an unwilling witness is not compelled to give evidence unless the consul or the commissioner has applied to the competent authority of the State of execution and that State has made a declaration pursuant to Article 18.

[65] See McClean (n 4) 101. See also Amram (n 21) 212.
[66] Art 12.
[67] Art 17. This is a well-known practice in the United States, especially in its 'relations with France and United Kingdom', whereby foreign judges are appointed to collect evidence in their own languages and under their own procedures: McClean (n 4) 102.
[68] Art 21(a), (d).
[69] Permanent Bureau, *Video-Link* (n 51) 68.
[70] Art 20.

Also, Article 21(e) permits the witness to invoke privileges or duties not to testify, as provided under the law of the State of execution or the law of the State of origin.

III. Uncertainties and Interpretative Inconsistencies

A long-standing uncertainty attending the Convention is the extent to which it is relevant to discovery as distinct from evidence (section II.A). A related interpretative uncertainty, still reflected in inconsistent State practice, is whether or not the Convention is mandatory (section II.B).

A. Contours of Article 23

There appears to be some residual confusion among Contracting States as to how the distinction between what is properly evidence (*toute acte d'instruction*) for the purposes of the Convention and what is discovery is to be drawn. This misunderstanding continues to lead some States to apply Article 23 of the Convention to refuse the execution of letters of request even where they are 'sufficiently substantiated' and where the 'production of documents … are specified in the request, or otherwise reasonably identified'.[71]

As is well known, the possibility of States making an Article 23 declaration arose out of a UK proposal based on a fear that, despite the scope of the Convention being limited to evidence,[72] it might nonetheless be used to facilitate US pre-trial discovery,[73] especially directed at *non-parties*.[74] At the time the Convention was drafted, when a Commonwealth common lawyer spoke of US pre-trial discovery, they were typically referring, disapprovingly, to a *particular aspect* of US discovery,[75] namely the practice of parties *taking oral testimony (in the form of depositions)* from *potential non-party witnesses* which could be used to identify *potentially relevant* documents that may then lead to the identification of evidence.[76] Broadly speaking, standard discovery or disclosure in Commonwealth jurisdictions then referred, and continues to refer, to the process of parties collecting documents *from each other* which are *directly relevant* to the issues raised by the pleadings or in the affidavits.[77] This latter process is also known as *inter partes* disclosure (sometimes called *inter partes* discovery) and can occur at several stages of the litigation. Non-standard discovery or disclosure in Commonwealth jurisdictions was and is, however, also possible in certain circumstances. If those apply, this means that parties may also collect *potentially relevant* documents *from each other*, which may then lead to the identification of evidence.[78]

Accordingly, at the time the Convention was drafted, a key distinction between US-style discovery and Commonwealth-style discovery, was that US-style discovery applied to the

[71] Special Commission, 'Conclusions and Recommendations 2014' (n 13) [18].

[72] See section I.A above.

[73] See H van Loon, 'Embracing Diversity – The Role of the Hague Conference in the Creation of Universal Instruments' in VR Abou-Nigm and MBN Taquela (eds), *Diversity and Integration in Private International Law* (Edinburgh University Press 2019) 39.

[74] Collins (n 6) 775; *cf* Amram (n 21) 204 which refers only to *inter partes* disclosure.

[75] Documentary discovery addressed to parties was, and is, another aspect.

[76] Collins (n 6) 776.

[77] There is more nuance to this which cannot, for reasons of space, be explained here. See M Legg, 'Discovery – A Comparative Approach to Reform' in M Kumar and M Legg (eds), *Ten Years of the Civil Procedure Act 2005 (NSW): A Decade of Insights and Guide to Future Litigation* (Thomson Reuters 2015) 104–06.

[78] See ibid, 105–06.

obtaining of potentially relevant documents from *non-parties*,[79] identified via an oral deposition, whereas Commonwealth-style discovery, at least under English law, in all but the most exceptional cases, did not.[80] It is this distinction which explains why the United Kingdom worded its declaration under Article 23 in the terms that it did.[81] In formulating its declaration in what has been described as 'qualified' terms due to the express reference to 'documents' and without reference to oral depositions, the UK did not intend to suggest that the Convention could nonetheless be used to facilitate the taking of depositions designed to point to documents which could then lead to the discovery of evidence, from non-party witnesses.[82] Nor did it intend to suggest, according to Collins, that the Convention could be used to facilitate *inter partes* disclosure.[83] A number of Contracting States formulated their declarations in the same terms as the United Kingdom;[84] others transposed the language of Article 23.[85]

Although, in principle, the distinction between evidence and discovery for the purposes of the Convention is clear, in practice it is sometimes less easy to draw. Both common law and civil law authority supports the view that this determination is to be made by considering, inter alia, the terms of the letter of request, including the breadth or generality of the order which the applicant proposes the Requested Court should make.[86] The legislation implementing the Convention into UK law provides that an order shall not require a person to state *which* documents, relevant to the proceedings, are in their control or to produce any documents 'other than particular documents specified in the order'.[87] In practice, this means that a request for 'monthly bank statements for the year 1984 relating to [the witness'] current account' would succeed, because it is a request for evidence, whereas a request for 'all [of the witness'] bank statements for 1984' would fail, because it is a request for discovery.[88] How relevant the information sought is to the issues in the foreign proceedings is important to determining whether that information is evidence or discovery, although the Requested Court should generally rely on the Requesting Court's determination of this issue.[89] The stage at which the information is sought is

[79] AF Lowenfeld, 'International Litigation and the Quest for Reasonableness' (1994) 245 *Hague Collected Courses* 196–97.

[80] Collins (n 6) 769–72.

[81] Ibid 775.

[82] *British American Tobacco* (n 10) [27]. But see Permanent Bureau, 'Conclusions and Recommendations Adopted by the Special Commission on the Practical Operation of the Hague, Apostille and Evidence, Service Conventions (28 October to 4 November 2003)' (November 2003) ('Conclusions and Recommendations 2003') [35], available at: assets.hcch.net/docs/0edbc4f7-675b-4b7b-8e1c-2c1998655a3e.pdf which states that 'the scope of the provision [Art 23] should not be extended to oral testimony' by which it presumably means 'should not be extended to oral testimony *that is in the nature of evidence*', given that oral testimony that is in the nature of evidence falls within the scope of the Convention.

[83] Collins (n 6) 775, 784.

[84] Cyprus, Denmark, Finland, Norway and Sweden. By the time of the US proposal, there was no public suggestion or any document indicating that the US delegation was proposing a convention to obtain anything different from evidence in the strict sense: ibid 774. However, 'perhaps as part of an effort to extend the scope of the Convention', the US persuaded some countries to change their declaration, to reflect the more restrictive terms of the United Kingdom's. The US delegation later revealed that 'unless American litigants could obtain assistance from the Contracting States during the pre-trial stage of a civil suit in the United States, the Convention would turn into a one way street as far as the United States was concerned': ibid 781–82.

[85] eg, Andorra, Armenia, Brazil, Bulgaria, Croatia, Germany, Greece, Portugal and Spain.

[86] eg, *(Brazil) STJ AgInt na CR 14548/EX* [2020], where the Superior Court of Justice granted the *exequatur* to a letter of request from the US because (a) the requested documents were extensively identified and (b) the letter explained the relevance of the evidence to the foreign proceeding. For a French perspective, see K Mehtiyeva, *La notion de cooperation judiciaire* (LGDJ, 2020) 70–71.

[87] Evidence (Proceedings in Other Jurisdictions) Act 1975 (UK) s 4.

[88] *Re Asbestos Insurance Coverage Cases* [1985] 1 WLR 331 (HL) 337–38 (Lord Fraser).

[89] *Atlantica Holdings Inc v Sovereign Wealth Fund Samruk-Kazyna JSC* [2019] EWHC 319 (QB), [2019] 4 WLR 62, [53].

also relevant, though the fact that it is sought at the procedural stage described as 'discovery', is not alone decisive.[90]

In sum, the Convention is not intended to be used for US-style discovery to obtain documents or depositions from non-party witnesses, where a Contracting State has made an Article 23 declaration in the same terms and spirit as the United Kingdom. Nor is it intended to be used for non-standard (ie, broad) discovery of documents between the parties, where a Contracting State has made an Article 23 declaration. (That is, in circumstances where the forum court has personal jurisdiction over the parties, but the purpose of that process is to collect potentially relevant documents which may lead to the identification of evidence rather than collect documents directly relevant to the facts in issue.) *Pace* Collins, however, the Convention would appear to apply to *standard inter partes* disclosure or discovery (ie, to the collection of documents directly relevant to the facts in issue), because that process is, for the purposes of the Convention, the obtention of 'evidence'.[91] The view that the Convention applies to the *inter partes* discovery of documents directly relevant to the facts in issue, in part, explains why the US Supreme Court in *Société Nationale Industrielle Aérospatiale v United States District Court for the Southern District of Iowa* arrived at the conclusion that the Convention has a non-mandatory character: if the Convention were mandatory, reasoned the Court, the ordinary pre-trial discovery of documents, where the court has personal jurisdiction over the *parties*, would always be subject to other Contracting States' authorities.[92]

IV. The Convention's Character: The Only, the First or the Last Resort?

An unresolved debate since 1985 is whether the Convention *must* be applied whenever *evidence* within its scope is to be taken or obtained abroad.[93] States are divided as to whether a Contracting State court may, for instance, use its internal law to subpoena an unwilling party or non-party witness, resident in another Contracting State, seeking to compel them to give evidence in the forum or to produce documentary evidence situate outside the forum, notwithstanding the jurisdictional challenges subpoenas may present.[94] Though the Recast EU Evidence Regulation, by which numerous civil law countries are bound, is non-mandatory[95] and thus does not prevent these possibilities,[96] countries which tend to view the Convention as mandatory[97] are nonetheless overwhelmingly civil law systems. Countries which tend to view the Convention as

[90] See *Gredd v Arpad Busson* [2003] EWHC 3001 [27] adopted in *British American Tobacco* (n 10), [42].

[91] *cf* Collins (n 6) 784.

[92] See *Société Nationale Industrielle Aérospatiale v United States District Court for the Southern District of Iowa* 482 US 522, 536–37, 539–40 (1987).

[93] For detailed analysis, see Permanent Bureau, 'Mandatory/Non-Mandatory' 2008' (n 54) [8].

[94] In both the private international law and public international law sense. As to the former, see generally HM Malek (ed), *Phipson on Evidence*, 19th edn (Sweet & Maxwell 2018) [8–34]; *Ives v Lim* [2010] WASCA 136 [18]; *Ceramic Fuel Cells Ltd (in liq) v McGraw-Hill Financial Inc (No 2)* (2016) 245 FCR 362 [30]–[34]. As to the latter, see generally A Mills, 'Private Interests and Private Law Regulation in Public International Law Jurisdiction' in S Allen et al (eds), *The Oxford Handbook of Jurisdiction in International Law* (Oxford University Press 2019) 331–32, 346–47; Opinion of Advocate General Jääskinen, Case C-170/11 *Lippens v Kortekaas* EU:C:2012:311, paras 29, 65.

[95] Case C-332/11 *ProRail BV v Xpedys NV* EU:C:2013:87, paras 43–46, 55 (interpreting the predecessor Regulation).

[96] *Lippens* (n 94), [39], followed in Cour de cassation, Belgique, 25.04.2013, aff *Fortis Luxembourg Vie c GR*, n° C.11.0103.F/1, 32–33; Cour de cassation, Belgique, 26.04.2018, *Banque de Luxembourg c AC, ADL*, n° C.16.0192.N/1 [6].

[97] See Suisse, Tribunal fédéral, 02.02.2017, 5A 566/2016 [2.1]; Permanent Bureau, *Handbook* (n 8) [20] (providing a survey of State practice).

non-mandatory are generally common law systems.[98] Those States which consider it to be mandatory have enacted blocking statutes, penalising a person for seeking or transmitting evidence without the State's permission, to try to force other Contracting States to use the Convention.[99] Those States which consider the Convention to be non-mandatory have sought to bypass its mechanisms in favour of internal law,[100] relying on an interpretation of the Convention which allows for this.[101]

Principles of treaty interpretation do not resolve the deadlock. Chapter I of the Convention provides that 'a judicial authority of a Contracting State *may* ... request the competent authority of another ... to obtain evidence'.[102] Similarly, chapter II provides that 'a diplomatic officer or consular agent ... *may*' and 'a commissioner ... *may*' take evidence.[103] The ordinary meaning[104] of the permissive term 'may'[105] could indicate either that the Convention is optional or that the mechanisms in chapters I and II are alternatives but that States must use either one.[106] Purposive interpretation supports both possibilities.[107] On the one hand, the fact that a purpose of the Convention is to facilitate the taking of evidence, not to hamper it, supports a non-mandatory interpretation.[108] On the other, the fact that an objective of the Convention was to 'reconcile' divergent approaches to the taking of evidence[109] tells in favour of its mandatory application.[110] Contextual interpretation is equally unhelpful: there appears to be nothing to indicate that the Contracting Parties had made an agreement regarding the interpretation of this point at the time the Convention was concluded.[111] Moreover, the minutes of the Special Commission meetings among Contracting Parties, at which this issue was discussed, clearly show the Contracting Parties have not subsequently reached an agreement regarding the interpretation of the Convention on this point.[112] Subsequent practice by Contracting States' courts is divided[113] and recourse to the *travaux préparatoires* to the Convention does nothing to resolve the ambiguity.[114] Finally, the Convention's French version, which uses the term '*peut*', discloses no difference in meaning with the English and thus does not assist either.[115]

[98] Permanent Bureau, *Handbook* (n 8) [20].

[99] ibid [26].

[100] ibid [254] noting that 'Delays may cause States to lose faith in the effectiveness of the Convention, and may prompt parties to seek alternative solutions to obtaining evidence abroad outside the Convention'.

[101] States rationalising their behaviour by reference to the international law norm from which they seek to depart is a long-standing practice.

[102] Art 1.

[103] Arts 15–17.

[104] Vienna Convention on the Law of Treaties (opened for signature 23 May 1969, entered into force 27 January 1980) 1155 UNTS 331 (VCLT) Art 31(1).

[105] Arts 1, 15–17; '*peut*' in the French version.

[106] See also, G Bermann, 'The Hague Evidence Convention in the Supreme Court: A Critique of the *Aérospatiale* decision' (1989) 63 *Tulane Law Review* 525, 531.

[107] VCLT (n 104) Art 31(1).

[108] Permanent Bureau, 'Mandatory/ Non-Mandatory 2008' (n 54) [40]–[41].

[109] Special Commission, 'Rapport de la Commission speciale établi par M Ph W Amram' in Bureau Permanent (ed), *Actes et documents de la onzième session 7 au 26 octobre 1968: tome IV, Obtention des preuves à l'étranger* (Imprimerie Nationale 1970) 55.

[110] M Seibl, 'Evidence, procurement of' in J Basedow et al (eds), *Encyclopedia of Private International Law*, Vol I (Edward Elgar 2017) 718. But see Permanent Bureau, 'Mandatory/ Non-Mandatory 2008' (n 54) [38]–[39].

[111] *cf* VCLT (n 104) Art 31(2)(a), (b).

[112] Ibid, Arts 31(1), (3)(a). See, eg, Permanent Bureau, 'Conclusions and Recommendations 2003' (n 82) [37]; Permanent Bureau of the Hague Conference on Private International Law, 'Conclusions and Recommendations of the Special Commission on the Practical Operation of the Hague, Apostille, and Taking of Evidence and Access to Justice Conventions (2 to 12 February 2009)' (February 2009) ('Conclusions and Recommendations 2009') [53], available at: assets.hcch.net/upload/wop/jac_concl_e.pdf.

[113] *cf* VCLT (n 104) Arts 31(1), (3)(a), (b).

[114] *cf*, ibid, Art 32.

[115] *cf*, ibid, Art 33(4).

The Conclusions of the 2009 Special Commission record that this 'point of difference between Contracting Parties … has not been an obstacle to the effective operation of the Convention'.[116] One may query the extent to which that is so, given that one determinant for the effective operation of any Convention must be the extent to which it is used. In 1989, the Special Commission recommended a principle of first resort: recourse should first be had to the provisions of the Convention when evidence abroad is being sought.[117] This seems to be an eminently sensible approach in theory,[118] but it has not yielded much success in practice. Indeed, recent case law suggests the Convention is instead used as a last resort:[119] if evidence can be directly taken via video-link under the laws of both the forum and foreign State, some Contracting States' courts will administer an oath or affirmation from the forum, swear in an interpreter in the forum and have the witness give evidence from the foreign country via video-link; it is only if this is not possible that recourse to the Convention will be had.[120]

The best solution to the deadlock may ultimately be to resolve the underlying causes for it. Chief among them, for common lawyers, is the issue of delay in the Convention's procedures.[121] Others are the desire of common law counsel and judges to question the witness, without the presence or aid of judges or interpreters in another Contracting State, and to control the process, eg, to give directions to the witness about how they give their evidence to ensure its integrity.[122] From a civil law perspective, a key cause of a proliferation of blocking statutes, to try to force compliance with their mandatory interpretation of the Convention, is related to the uncertainty canvassed in the previous section. It is to ensure that any material obtained in their territories is properly evidence rather than broad discovery and that such material is obtained only with their permission.[123] Given recent developments in US law, which narrow the circumstances in which a US court can exercise personal jurisdiction (a prerequisite for an order of discovery under internal law), it has been argued that US courts will seek to rely on the Convention more often.[124] If that is right, it will reduce the significance of the mandatory/non-mandatory debate in the United States, but it will make the need to distinguish between evidence and discovery under the Convention more acute.

V. Conclusion

The taking of evidence abroad is one of the most controversial fields in international judicial cooperation. The 1970 Evidence Convention began as a proposal of the US delegation to the

[116] Permanent Bureau, 'Conclusions and Recommendations 2009' (n 112) [53].

[117] Permanent Bureau, *Handbook* (n 8) [25].

[118] *cf Aérospatiale* (n 92) 533–34, 548–49 (rejecting it by a narrow 5:4 majority). The majority of the Court considered that international comity requires that courts should instead conduct a case-by-case analysis by reference to a number of factors, including sovereignty interests, the likelihood that recourse to the Convention 'will prove to be effective', the level of intrusiveness of the discovery procedure, and the need to protect foreign litigants from unnecessary or burdensome discovery requests: 482 US 522, 542–46 (1987). See generally GB Born, 'The Hague Evidence Convention Revisited: reflections on its role in US civil procedure' (1994) 57 *Law and Contemporary Problems* 77, 78–80.

[119] eg, *Motorola Solutions Inc v Hytera Communications Corporation Ltd* [2020] FCA 539 [2]–[4], [20].

[120] eg, *Auken Animal Husbandry Pty Ltd v 3RD Solution Investment Pty Ltd* [2020] FCA 1153.

[121] eg, *Motorola Solutions* (n 119) [2].

[122] One party's lawyer, acting as an interpreter in the foreign court, is obviously inappropriate and would justify the forum court appointing its own interpreter (eg, *Auken* (n 120) [55]). But that is quite different from an independent interpreter being engaged by the foreign Contracting State and present alongside the witness, as the Convention contemplates.

[123] See also, Mehtiyeva (n 86) 72.

[124] D Zambrano, 'A Comity of Errors: the Rise, Fall, and Return of International Comity in Transnational Discovery' (2016) 34 *Berkeley Journal of International Law* 157, 163–64, 192–93.

Hague Conference on Private International Law and has become one of the HCCH's most widely adopted instruments.[125] The Convention's modest goal, upon its inception, was to establish a more 'efficient' method for the taking of evidence abroad than the system of letters rogatory.[126] The loftier goal of the Convention was to bridge the gap between common law and civil law States' perspectives regarding cross-border evidence collection.

While there is a little doubt that the Convention has already achieved the first goal, attainment of the second remains a pursuit in progress. First, the difference between evidence, in the strict sense, and discovery of material which may lead to the identification of evidence remains problematic. Misunderstanding and misinterpretation of Article 23 of the Convention, and what is in form, though not in substance, a qualified declaration made by the UK and adopted by other States, make it a persistent issue.

Second, Contracting States disagree over the Convention's terms. While most civil law countries tend to interpret the Convention's methods for taking of evidence within their territory as mandatory, many common law countries perceive the Convention as an instrument to facilitate cooperation between States, not as one excluding recourse to internal practices where they are more expeditious.

Responsibility for remedying these issues falls to the Contracting States. Requesting States' judicial authorities ought to be sensitive to the concept of what evidence is and is not under the Convention and to the precise terms in which their letters are expressed. Equally, Requested States' Central Authorities should be cautious about rejecting a request that is in form, but not in substance, a 'pre-trial discovery' request.[127] A preference to use internal procedures in lieu of the Convention because of delays in processing Convention requests can be dealt with by technology: electronic transmission methods, court-to-court transmission,[128] and the direct taking of evidence via video-link under or through the Convention[129] each hold promise. The Hague Conference's Permanent Bureau is facilitating the use of these technologies.[130] Other problems are, perhaps, more intractable. Reluctance on the part of courts to examine witnesses in the presence of foreign judges or through the mouthpiece of a foreign interpreter, may suggest a lack of trust in other Contracting States' institutions on which the Convention depends. Conversely, reluctance on the part of governments to allow for a foreign judge to examine a witness directly under the Convention, via video-link, may reflect a concern based on sovereignty which only serves to encourage the infringement of that sovereignty: the more Requested States impose obstacles to the use of technology under the Convention, the more Requesting States will turn towards their internal procedures for the taking of evidence via video-link, relying on a non-mandatory interpretation of the Convention, as justification.

Notwithstanding, there is hope that the Convention will help to foster internationalism, tolerance and the administration of justice, and that comprehension of its procedures, coupled with technology, might help.

[125] At the time of writing, it had 63 Contracting States: HCCH, 'Status Table – 20: Convention of 18 March 1970 on the Taking of Evidence Abroad in Civil or Commercial Matters' (HCCH, 4 March 2020), available at: www.hcch.net/en/instruments/conventions/status-table/?cid=82.

[126] McClean (n 4) 74.

[127] (In the sense of Art 23). See Permanent Bureau, *Handbook* (n 8) [66]; Collins (n 6) 769.

[128] See above (nn 27–30).

[129] See above (nn 49–50, 66).

[130] Permanent Bureau, *Video-Link* (n 51); Permanent Bureau, 'Use of Information Technology in the Transmission of Requests under the Service and Evidence Conventions (Preliminary Document no 9 of January of 2019)', available at: assets.hcch.net/docs/97d961a9-4356-4fca-bdd9-00451a81716a.pdf; HCCH Council on General Affairs and Policy, 'Council on General Affairs and Policy (5–8 March): Conclusions and Recommendations Adopted by Council' (2019) [40], available at: assets.hcch.net/docs/c4af61a8-d8bf-400e-9deb-afcd87ab4a56.pdf.

PART IV

Civil and Commercial Law (Excluding Family Law)

14

Law Applicable to Contracts

SYMEON C SYMEONIDES

I. Introduction

Most contemporary legal systems have adopted two principal methods for determining the law applicable to contracts. The first recognises the parties' power to choose that law in advance, within specified parameters and limitations. This method is referred to (hereinafter) as 'party autonomy' and is discussed in section II. The second method operates when the parties have not validly chosen that law, or in systems that do not recognise their power to do so. In such a case, the applicable substantive law is determined through objective connecting factors specified in the forum's private international law rules. Section III briefly describes this method.[1]

II. Party Autonomy

A. Introduction

The term 'party autonomy' is a shorthand expression for the notion that parties to a multistate contract should be allowed, within certain parameters and limitations, to agree in advance on which law will govern their contract. After a slow start in the nineteenth century,[2] this notion became a universal principle of private international law (PIL) or conflicts law. In 1991, the Institut de Droit International characterised it as one of the 'fundamental principles' of PIL that has been 'enshrined as a freedom of the individual' in several conventions and UN resolutions.[3]

[1] Because of the prevalence and importance of party autonomy in contemporary practice, section II is much longer than section III. Moreover, because of the strict length limitations of this chapter, much of the following discussion is not documented with citations to sources. For full documentation of the assertions made in the text, the reader is kindly referred to SC Symeonides, *Codifying Choice of Law Around the World: An International Comparative Analysis* (Oxford University Press 2014) 109–70 (Symeonides, *Codifying*); SC Symeonides, *Oxford Commentaries on American Law: Choice of Law* (Oxford University Press 2016) 343–552 (Symeonides, *Oxford Commentaries*); SC Symeonides, 'The Scope and Limits of Party Autonomy in International Contracts: A Comparative Analysis' in F Ferrari and DP Fernández Arroyo (eds), *Private International Law: Contemporary Challenges and Continuing Relevance* (Edward Elgar 2019) (Symeonides, 'Scope').

[2] For a comprehensive discussion of the history and theoretical foundations of party autonomy, see SC Symeonides, 'The Story of Party Autonomy' in D Girsberger, J Neels and T Kadner Graziano (eds), *The Hague Principles and Beyond* (Oxford University Press 2020).

[3] Institut de Droit International, Basel Resolution ('The Autonomy of the Parties in International Contracts between Private Persons or Entities') (1991).

Two recent surveys confirm the near universality of this principle, showing a higher than 90 per cent following in the countries surveyed.[4] Today, party autonomy enjoys the status of a self-evident proposition. It has been characterised as 'perhaps the most widely accepted private international rule of our time'[5] and a 'fundamental right'[6] that belongs to 'the common core' of nearly all legal systems'.[7]

Although virtually all modern legal systems espouse the principle of party autonomy, they often disagree in defining its exact modalities, parameters, scope and limitations. For example, although most systems recognise an implied choice of law,[8] they differ in defining it. While some codifications leave it to the court to determine how to infer a choice of law agreement, other codifications contain more specific as well as slightly different requirements, such as whether the court's inference must be based on the terms of the contract or may also be based on the surrounding circumstances.[9] Similarly, although most systems allow parties to choose the applicable law only in international or multistate contracts, some systems additionally require that the State of the chosen law possess a certain geographical or other relationship with the contract or the parties.[10]

The requirement for a geographic nexus to the chosen State is only one tool for 'policing' party autonomy. The use of the word 'policing' suggests that party autonomy is not unfettered. It is constrained for reasons similar to those that limit 'freedom of contract' in domestic law. For example, in contracts involving presumptively weak parties, such as consumers or employees, 'an unfettered freedom to choose a law may be a freedom to exploit a dominant position'.[11] Consequently, most domestic laws 'curtail th[is] freedom',[12] and this curtailment usually extends to the multistate arena.

Various systems delineate the scope of party autonomy and police its exercise differently. SubSection B discusses the differences in delineating the permissible scope of party autonomy. SubSection C discusses the various public policy limitations that constrain the exercise of party autonomy within its delineated permissible scope.

[4] The first survey shows that 96 of the 98 PIL codifications enacted since 1960 have endorsed this principle. See Symeonides, *Codifying*, 114–15, 149–51 (as updated). Ecuador and Guinea-Conakry are the two exceptions. The second survey shows that 152 of the 161 countries surveyed follow the same principle. See Allen & Overy, *Global Litigation Survey* (2015), available at: www.allenovery.com/news/en-gb/articles/Pages/Global-Litigation-Survey-2015-Published.aspx (updated by this author). The remaining holdouts are Bolivia, Colombia, Cuba, Eritrea, Nepal, Saudi Arabia, UAE, Uruguay and Zimbabwe.

[5] RJ Weintraub, 'Functional Developments in Choice of Law for Contracts' (1984) 187 *Hague Collected Courses* 239, 271.

[6] E Jayme, 'Identité culturelle et intégration: Le droit international privé postmoderne' (1995) 251 *Hague Collected Courses* 147.

[7] O Lando, 'The EEC Convention on the Law Applicable to Contractual Obligations' (1987) 24 *CML Rev* 159, 169.

[8] An implied choice of law differs from a hypothetical choice, which most systems do not recognise. See, eg, Restatement (Second) § 187, comment a (stating that it 'does not suffice to demonstrate that the parties, if they had thought about the matter, would have wished to have the law of a particular state applied').

[9] For documentation, see Symeonides, *Codifying*, 120–21. Most recent codifications expressly allow parties to choose a law for only part of the contract, to choose different laws for different parts of the contract, or to make or change a choice of law after the initial contract. See ibid, 122–23. In other countries, general principles of contract law seem to permit these choices, even in the absence of statutory authorization. By contrast, no codification addresses the more difficult question (on which judicial practice differs significantly) of how to treat an agreement that choses a law that invalidates the contract, in whole or in part. See ibid, 123–24. The space limitations of this volume do not allow discussion of these differences here.

[10] For documentation, *see* Symeonides, *Codifying*, 116–20.

[11] A Briggs, *Agreements on Jurisdiction and Choice of Law* (Oxford University Press 2008) 37.

[12] Ibid.

B. The Scope of Party Autonomy

i. Exemptions from Scope

Some legal systems narrowly delineate the scope of party autonomy by:

1. Excluding certain contracts, in whole or in part, such as consumer contracts, employment contracts, insurance contracts and other contracts involving presumptively weak parties and having specified connections with the enacting State.
2. Excluding certain contractual issues, such as capacity, consent and form.
3. Confining party autonomy to contractual, as opposed to non-contractual, issues.
4. Otherwise limiting what 'law' the parties may choose, ie:
   a. substantive, as opposed to procedural law,
   b. substantive or internal, as opposed to PIL, and
   c. State law, as opposed to non-State norms.

The following discussion is limited to the exemptions listed in items (3) and (4), above.[13] Before proceeding, it should be noted that the scope of *party autonomy* differs from the scope of a choice of law *clause*, although in many cases the two may be coextensive. The first is a question of contractual *power*, which is conferred by the relevant legal system. The second is a matter of contractual *will*, which can never exceed the scope of the conferred power. It depends on whether, considering the wording of the clause, the parties have exercised all or only part of the conferred power. For example, in a system that does not allow parties to choose the applicable law for non-contractual issues, a choice of law clause whose wording encompasses those issues is unenforceable to that extent. Conversely, in a system that allows such a choice, the question of whether the clause encompasses non-contractual issues – or, for that matter, all or only some contractual issues[14] – depends on the wording of that clause.

ii. Contractual and Non-Contractual Issues

Party autonomy was born in the law of contracts but, in recent years, has migrated to other fields in which advance planning is important, such as marital property, trusts, succession and family law. The question here is to what extent a similar extension into the law of torts has occurred or is warranted. The answer depends on whether the choice of law agreement is concluded before or after the tort occurs.

Post-dispute agreements are unproblematic, and most systems allow them, at least tacitly.[15] However, pre-dispute agreements are inherently problematic because the parties' positions can be unknowable or unequal. The parties usually do not contemplate a future tort, nor do they know who will injure whom, or the nature or severity of the injury. An unsophisticated party (or a party in a weak bargaining position) may sign a choice of law agreement, even if it is more likely to become the victim rather than the tortfeasor. Thus, pre-dispute agreements may exploit weak parties.

[13] For detailed discussion and documentation of the exemptions listed in items (1)–(3), above, see Symeonides, 'Scope', 103–15.

[14] Today, many legal systems expressly provide that parties may choose a law for only part of a contract, or they may choose different laws for different parts of a contract. See Symeonides, *Codifying*, 122.

[15] See ibid, 99–100.

Most PIL codifications enacted in the last 50 years, and all those enacted before, do not authorise pre-dispute agreements encompassing tort issues. A few recent codifications authorise *only* post-dispute agreements.[16] Article 14 of the Rome II Regulation allows enforcement of pre-dispute choice of law agreements for non-contractual claims but only if 'all parties are pursuing a commercial activity',[17] thus excluding consumers and employees.[18]

In the United States, section 187 of the Restatement (Second) authorises choice of law agreements for the parties '*contractual* rights and duties'.[19] If taken literally, this language would exclude non-contractual rights and duties. However, a more logical conclusion is that the drafters did not consider this question, which was virtually unthinkable when they drafted the Restatement in the 1960s.[20] In the absence of clear guidance, many courts assume that the parties possess the power to agree on the law that will govern a future tort between them and then determine whether the parties have exercised that power by examining the wording of the choice of law clause. For example, courts have held that a clause that subjects 'the agreement' or 'the contract' to the chosen law does not encompass non-contractual claims, whereas a clause subjecting the parties' 'relationship' or 'any and all disputes' between them includes non-contractual claims. Under this test, which is not consistently followed, most cases held that the choice of law clause did not encompass non-contractual claims, but some reached the opposite conclusion.[21]

iii. Substantive versus Procedural Law

All choice of law codifications and conventions discussed here limit the scope of party autonomy to the chosen State's substantive law and exclude its procedural law.[22] This is consistent with the principle that the law of the forum governs matters of procedure, a principle that prevails over the principle of party autonomy. Because of this hierarchy: (1) an inbound choice of law clause *may not exclude* the forum's procedural law; and (2) an outbound clause *may not include* the chosen State's procedural law.[23]

However, the line between substance and procedure is not always clear or drawn in the same way in all systems. For example, most common law systems characterise statutes of

[16] Among them are the codifications of Belgium (Art 101), Bulgaria (Art 113.1), China (Art 47), Germany (Art 42), Hungary (Art 63), Japan (Art 21), Monaco (Art 84), North Macedonia (Art 33.3) and Turkey (Art 34.5). The codifications of Estonia, South Korea, Lithuania, Russia, Switzerland, Taiwan, Tajikistan, Tunisia and Ukraine also do likewise but limit such agreements to the law of the forum. The codifications of Armenia, Austria, Belarus, Kyrgyzstan and the Dutch Torts Act of 2001 authorise such agreements, but without any express limitation as to their timing and without limiting them to the law of the forum. For citations, see Symeonides, 'Scope', 117–18.

[17] Reg 864/2007, Art 14.1(b). This provision also requires pre-dispute agreements to be 'freely negotiated', but this requirement must also apply to post-dispute agreements. Art 14 applies to all non-contractual claims within the scope of Rome II other than those arising from unfair competition, restrictions to competition, and infringement of intellectual property rights, see Arts 6(4) and 8(3). For this issue and more generally on applicable law in tort, see Michael Hellner, 'Tort: Applicable Law', ch 18 in this book.

[18] For a critique of Art 14, especially its failure to protect small commercial actors, such as franchisees, see Symeonides, 'Scope', 118–20.

[19] Restatement (Second) § 187(2) (emphasis added).

[20] By contrast, the two American PIL codifications – Louisiana and Oregon – address this question and declare unenforceable pre-dispute choice of law agreements encompassing non-contractual issues. See Symeonides, 'Scope', 117.

[21] For extensive discussion and critique of the case law, see Symeonides, *Oxford Commentaries*, 393–400.

[22] eg, Rome I exempts from its scope – and thus from the scope of choice of law clauses – 'the rules of evidence and procedure'. Reg 593/2008, Art 1(3). This provision contains an exception (through a cross-reference to Art 18) regarding the burden of proof. Similarly, Art 9(1)(f) includes 'burden of proof and legal presumptions' within the scope of the law applicable pursuant to a choice of law clause.

[23] An inbound clause is one that chooses the law of a State that ends up being the forum, whereas an outbound clause is a clause that chooses another State.

limitation as procedural,[24] but civil law systems characterise them as substantive. Consistent with this characterisation, Rome I includes within the scope of the applicable law, which may be chosen contractually or judicially, 'the various ways of extinguishing obligations, and prescription and limitation of actions'.[25] The Hague Sales Convention, the Mexico City Convention, and the Hague Contracts Principles, as well as several national codifications, contain similar provisions.[26]

iv. Substantive Law versus PIL

When the parties choose the 'law' of a certain State to govern their contract, is the choice limited to the internal or substantive law of the chosen State or does it also encompass its PIL rules? The simplistic answer is that the choice is limited to the internal law. However, a more complete answer should distinguish between contractual power and contractual intent, as well as 'inbound' and 'outbound' choice of law clauses.

The exclusion of the chosen State's PIL should be understood as a presumption that conforms to the likely intent of the parties, and thus can be rebutted by contrary agreement, rather than as an ironclad rule constraining the parties' power. A choice of law clause resolves in advance the law question and is intended to reduce uncertainty. It is unreasonable to assume that parties who agree to such a clause intended to reintroduce that question through the back door and, with it, the uncertainties of a potential renvoi. However, if – for whatever reason – the parties expressly chose a State's 'whole law,' ie, including its PIL, it would be inconsistent with the very principle of party autonomy to honour only part of that choice. Several codifications take this position by adopting a presumptive rule that can be rebutted by contrary intent, whereas other codifications paternalistically restrict the parties' power to include in their choice the PIL rules of the chosen State.[27]

There is, however, one scenario in which the question is one of contractual power rather than contractual intent. It involves inbound clauses in which the parties expressly *excluded* the chosen State's PIL rules – as many parties increasingly do. In such a case, the exclusion cannot displace that PIL rule of the forum State by which the court determines the validity of the choice of law clause. For example, if the forum State is an EU Member State, an inbound choice of law clause cannot displace Article 3 of Rome I. Otherwise, all inbound clauses would be automatically enforceable without any scrutiny by the forum court.

v. State Law versus Non-State Norms

The final question is whether, *outside the realm of arbitration*,[28] Contracting Parties are limited to choosing the law of a State or whether they may also choose rules promulgated by non-State entities (hereinafter non-State norms). In the vast majority of countries, the answer is negative – a choice of non-State norms is not recognised as a true choice of law, although it may be treated

[24] In the United States, 28 states continue to follow the traditional procedural characterisation. For documentation and discussion of the relevant case law, see Symeonides, *Oxford Commentaries*, 401–05, 528–31. More generally on substance and procedure, see Richard Garnett, 'Substance and Procedure', ch 9 in this book.

[25] Rome I, Art 12(1)(d).

[26] For citations, see Symeonides, *Codifying*,137, fns 161–62.

[27] See Symeonides, 'Scope', 122, 124–25.

[28] In the last three decades, the use of non-State norms in arbitration has become routine. See Giuditta Cordero-Moss, 'Arbitration', ch 26 in this book.

as an *incorporation* of these norms as contractual terms.[29] The first international instrument to answer the above question in the affirmative is Article 3 of the Hague Contracts Principles of 2015. Referring to these norms as 'rules of law' – a prevalent misnomer – Article 3 provides that: 'The law chosen by the parties may be rules of law that are generally accepted on an international, supranational or regional level as a neutral and balanced set of rules, unless the law of the forum provides otherwise'.[30] This Article introduces two important qualifiers for non-State norms.

The first focuses on their attributes, requiring: (a) a 'set of rules', ie, fairly complete and comprehensive; (b) 'neutral and balanced'; and (c) 'generally accepted' as such 'on an international, supranational, or regional level'.[31] While norms drafted by impartial intergovernmental organisations, such as UNIDROIT or UNCITRAL, or academic commissions, tend to meet these qualifications, norms drafted by commercial organisations or groups, such as credit card associations, commodity merchants, or internet service providers would not qualify.

The second qualifier is that these norms will not be treated on an equal footing with State law if the law of the forum 'provides otherwise', eg, by *not* treating these norms as law. Although this qualifier is self-evident since the Principles themselves are 'soft law', its addition was necessary to gain the acquiescence of delegations (such as the EU) that had taken a negative stance on this matter.[32]

C. Limitations to Party Autonomy within its Delineated Scope

In addition to differences in delineating the scope of party autonomy, various legal systems also differ in the substantive limitations they impose on its exercise. These limitations fall under the rubric of public policy and they depend on the answers to two basic questions. The first is *which State's* public policy limitations should provide the yardstick for policing party autonomy? That State is referred to hereinafter as the State of the *lex limitativa*. The second question is which precise *level* or threshold of public policy should be used in this policing?

i. *Determining the* lex limitativa

In theory, the search for the State of the *lex limitativa* encompasses three candidate States:

1. The chosen State.
2. The State whose law would have been applicable if the parties had not chosen a law (hereinafter the (objective) *lex causae*).
3. The forum State.[33]

[29] For citations, see Symeonides, 'Scope', 126–27. Paraguay (2015 and Uruguay (2020) have statutorily endorsed the choice of non-State norms in cases that end up in litigation. Bahrain also allows the choice of the 'law of international trade and customs' (Art 4). The Mexico City Convention and the Venezuelan codification arguably take a favourable position towards non-State norms, but the argument is not beyond question. See Symeonides, *Codifying*, 142–44. A Chilean preliminary draft (Art 53.1) would allow the choice of non-State norms as defined in the Hague Principles, which are discussed in the text.

[30] Art 3 of the Hague Principles on Choice of Law in International Commercial Contracts (approved on 19 March 2015), available at: www.hcch.net/index_en.php?act=conventions.text&cid=135 ('Hague Contracts Principles').

[31] For detailed explanations regarding the meaning of the quoted terms, see Hague Contracts Principles, comments 3.4–3.13.

[32] For the background to Art 3 and the compromises that produced it in the 2012 negotiations, see SC Symeonides, 'The Hague Principles on Choice of Law for International Contracts: Some Preliminary Comments' (2013) 61 *American Journal of Comparative Law* 873, 893–94. Obviously, the 'unless' clause does not apply to arbitration.

[33] In some cases, these three States, or any two of them, will coincide, or will impose the same limits on party autonomy. The following discussion focuses on cases in which these States, or their limits, do not coincide.

Of the three candidates, the chosen State must be eliminated for a variety of reasons, including the possibility of leading to circular or 'bootstrapping' results.[34] This leaves the States of the *lex fori* and the *lex causae*. The *lex fori* is relevant because party autonomy operates only to the extent that the *lex fori* is willing to permit through its choice of law rules. The *lex causae* is relevant because, when party autonomy operates, it displaces the *lex causae*.

When the application of the chosen law exceeds the public policy limitations of *both* the *lex fori* and the *lex causae*, the choice of law clause is unenforceable.[35] Difficulties arise when the chosen law exceeds the limits of the *lex fori* but not the *lex causae*, or vice versa.

The positions of the various systems on this issue are clustered into three groups: (1) those that assign the role of the *lex limitativa* to the *lex fori*; (2) those that assign the role of *lex limitativa* primarily to the *lex causae*; and (3) those that follow a combination of the two positions.

a. Group 1: *lex fori* (Exclusively)

Most legal systems assign the role of the *lex limitativa* exclusively to the *lex fori*. This group consists of: (1) all the old codifications that recognise party autonomy; (2) nearly half (34 of 72) of the codifications adopted in the last 50 years; and (3) three international conventions.[36] These codifications do not impose a public policy limitation *specifically* addressing party autonomy. Instead, they contain a general *ordre public* exception, not limited to contracts, which authorises the court to refuse to apply a *foreign* law that is repugnant to the forum's public policy.[37] Some of those codifications[38] and two Conventions[39] contain an additional, albeit partly overlapping, exception in favour of the 'mandatory rules' of the *lex fori*.

The motivating logic of these systems is that, because only the forum legislator can decide whether to allow party autonomy, only *that* legislator can delineate the limits of that autonomy – the limits of other States are irrelevant. Consequently, party autonomy is prohibited when it exceeds the public policy limits of the forum State, but not when it violates the limits of another State, including the State whose law would have been applicable if the parties had not chosen a law, ie, the *lex causae*.

b. Group 2: *lex causae* (Primarily)

American law follows a different logic, which takes into account the interests of the State of the *lex causae*. Without questioning that the systemic decision to allow party autonomy rests with the forum legislator, American law focuses on the undeniable fact that the implementation of that decision, ie, the decision to honour the parties' choice, displaces the *lex causae*. The question

[34] This does not mean that the public policy of the chosen law is *irrelevant*. Rather it means that it becomes *part* of the parties' choice as opposed to acting as an *external limitation* of that choice. In other words, it cannot act as the *lex limitativa*. When the parties choose the law of State X, that choice automatically includes that State's public policy and the parties cannot exclude it. For example, if the chosen law invalidates a part of the contract, the contract will be invalid to that extent. On the other hand, if the contract does not implicate the public policy of State X, the choice of law clause will not necessarily survive unscathed. Its enforceability will depend on whether it remains within the public policy limits of the *lex fori* or the *lex causae*, depending on which of these laws the forum uses as the *lex limitativa*, as described below.

[35] Conversely, when the application of the chosen law would not exceed the limitations of either the *lex fori* or the *lex causae*, the chosen law will be applied without problems.

[36] See Symeonides, *Codifying*, 149–51.

[37] See ibid, fn 211 (citing 26 codifications).

[38] See ibid, fn 213 (citing eight codifications).

[39] See the 1986 Hague Convention on the Law Applicable to Contracts for the International Sale of Goods, Arts 17 and 18; and the 2006 Hague Convention on the Law Applicable to Certain Rights in Respect of Securities Held with an Intermediary, Arts 11(1) and 11(2).

then becomes whether the parties' power to make that choice should be unlimited or whether it should remain within the public policy limits of the *lex causae*. American law takes the latter position: parties cannot evade certain public policies of the *lex causae* merely by choosing the law of another State. Thus, American law assigns the primary role of policing party autonomy to the *lex causae* and only a secondary and almost rarely used role to the *lex fori*. Under this regime:

1. If the parties' choice exceeds a specified public policy threshold of the State of the *lex causae*, the choice is unenforceable, even if it remains within the public policy limits of the forum State.
2. If the parties' choice does not exceed the public policy threshold of the *lex causae*, the choice is enforceable, unless it exceeds a *significantly higher* public policy threshold of the forum State.

The Louisiana and Oregon codifications state this position expressly, the Uniform Commercial Code (UCC) does so obliquely,[40] and the Restatement (Second) does so in a black letter section. Section 187(2)(b) of the Restatement (Second), which is followed in most US states, provides that the state whose public policy may defeat the parties' choice of law is not the forum state *qua* forum, but rather the state whose law would, under section 188, govern the particular issue if the parties had not made an effective choice (ie, the *lex causae*).[41] However, unlike the Louisiana and Oregon codifications, the Restatement (Second) also assigns a residual but highly exceptional role to the public policy of the forum. Section 90 of the Restatement (Second), which is not limited to contracts, preserves the traditional *ordre public* exception of the *lex fori* as the last shield against entertaining 'a foreign cause of action the enforcement of which is contrary to a *strong* public policy of the forum'.[42] The accompanying Restatement comments explain that this exception should be employed only 'rarely'.[43] The comments quote Judge Cardozo's classic standard, which applies the exception only when the foreign law 'would violate some fundamental principle of justice, some prevalent conception of morals, some deep-seated tradition of the commonweal'.[44] The Restatement recognises the difference between the two public policies by stating that the public policy contemplated by section 187 'need not be as strong as would be required to justify the forum in refusing to entertain suit upon a foreign cause of action under the rule of § 90'.[45]

c. Group 3: Intermediate Solutions and Combinations

Between these extremes are several combinations between the standards of the *lex fori* and those of another state, which may be either the state of the *lex causae* or a third state.

Rome I

The Rome Convention enunciated the most widely followed model of such a combination,[46] which the Rome I Regulation preserved with slight modifications. Under Rome I, the chosen

[40] For citations and discussion, see Symeonides, 'Scope', 134.

[41] In addition, the Restatement provides that the state of the *lex causae* must have 'a materially greater interest' than the chosen state in the determination of the particular issue, ibid § 187(2)(b). In most cases, a conclusion that a state is the state of the *lex causae* is based on a conclusion that that state has a 'materially greater interest' in applying its law.

[42] Restatement (Second) § 90 (emphasis added).

[43] Ibid § 90 comment c.

[44] Ibid (quoting *Loucks v Standard & Oil Co of NY* 120 NE 198, 202 (NY 1918)).

[45] Ibid, § 187 comment g.

[46] See Convention on the Law Applicable to Contractual Obligations, Arts 3(3), 5(2), 6(1), 7 and 16 [1980] OJ L266/1.

law must always remain within the limitations imposed by the *ordre public* and the 'overriding mandatory provisions' of the *lex fori*.[47] However, in consumer and employment contracts the chosen law must also remain within the limitations imposed by the 'simple' mandatory rules of the *lex causae*.[48] In all other contracts, the chosen law must remain within the limitations of the 'simple' mandatory rules of the country in which 'all other elements relevant to the situation' (other than the parties' choice) are located.[49]

Other Systems

Several national PIL codifications outside the EU follow the Rome model, at least to the extent they protect consumers and employees through the mandatory rules of the *lex causae*.[50]

At least a dozen of the codifications that subject the chosen law to the limits of the *ordre public* and mandatory rules of the *lex fori* provide in addition that the court 'may' apply or 'take into account' the mandatory rules of a 'third country' that has a 'close connection'.[51] The State of the *lex causae* almost always has such a connection. However, because of the discretionary phrasing of the relevant Articles, there is no guarantee that the mandatory rules of that State will be applied, or even 'taken into account'.

The Hague Principles

The Hague Principles recognise that some legal systems assign the role of the *lex limitativa* exclusively to the *lex fori* (Group 1, above) and some assign that role primarily to the *lex causae* (Group 2, above). For this reason, Article 11 contains separate paragraphs for each group:

(a) Paragraphs 1 and 3 restate the practice of the *lex fori* systems. Paragraph 1 preserves the application of the overriding mandatory rules of the *lex fori*,[52] while paragraph 3 restates the classic *ordre public* exception in favour of the 'fundamental notions of public policy (*ordre public*)' of the forum state.[53]

(b) Paragraphs 2 and 4 restate and accommodate the practice of the *lex causae* systems.[54] Paragraph 2 allows the forum state to 'apply or take into account' the overriding mandatory rules of a third state,[55] and Paragraph 4 allows the forum state to 'apply or take into account the public policy (*ordre public*)' of the state of the *lex causae*.[56]

[47] See Rome I, Art 21 (*ordre public*); Art 9(2) ('overriding mandatory provisions' of the *lex fori*); Art 9(3) (allowing courts to 'give effect' to the 'overriding mandatory provisions' of the place of performance 'in so far as' those provisions 'render the performance of the contract unlawful').

[48] See ibid, Arts 6(2) and 8(1).

[49] See ibid, Art 3(3). *cf* ibid, Art 3(4) (mandatory rules of EU law); ibid, Art 11(5) (mandatory rules of the *lex rei sitae*).

[50] See Symeonides, *Codifying*, 155, fn 225 (citing 11 codifications).

[51] See ibid, fn 226 (citing 15 codifications); The Mexico City Convention follows a variation of the above position. Art 18 reiterates the classic *ordre public* exception in favour of the *lex fori*, while Art 11 preserves the application of the mandatory rules of the *lex fori* but also allows the application of the mandatory rules of a third State with which the contract has 'close ties'. See also Hague Convention on the Law Applicable to Agency, Arts 16 and 17. Article 9(3) of Rome I is similar to these articles except that it is limited to the State of performance. It allows courts to 'give effect' to the 'overriding mandatory provisions' of the place of performance 'in so far as' those provisions 'render the performance of the contract unlawful'. See on this point and more generally, Trevor Hartley, 'Public Policy and Mandatory Provisions', ch 6 in this book.

[52] Hague Contracts Principles, Art 11(1).

[53] Ibid, Art 11(3).

[54] As the proponent of these two provisions, the author takes full responsibility for them.

[55] Ibid, Art 11(2) ('The law of the forum determines when a court may or must apply or take into account overriding mandatory provisions of another law').

[56] Ibid, Art 11(4) ('The law of the forum determines when a court may or must apply or take into account the public policy (*ordre public*) of a State the law of which would be applicable in the absence of a choice of law').

ii. The Triggering Thresholds and Gradations of Limitations to Party Autonomy

Another disagreement among various legal systems is defining the threshold above which the parties' choice will be held unenforceable. If any difference between the *lex limitativa* and the chosen law would defeat the parties' choice, then party autonomy would become a specious gift. As one court noted, '[t]he result would be that parties would have the right to choose the application of another state's law only when that state's law is identical to [the *lex causae*]'.[57]

Accepting the old distinction between *ordre public interne* and *ordre public international*, most systems agree on the need for a higher threshold of public policy for multistate contracts than for domestic contracts. This fine conceptual distinction suggests courts should be more tolerant towards private volition in multistate contracts than in domestic contracts. But there is much less of a consensus in defining this threshold or applying it in practice. Emphatic but unquantifiable adjectives such as 'fundamental' public policy[58] or 'overriding' mandatory rules[59] reflect these differences.

a. The Ordre Public of the *lex fori*

Theoretically, the highest threshold is posed by the forum *ordre public*, when properly applied. The international literature has developed a consensus, which is reflected in many recent codifications, regarding the proper application of this exception:

> First, as noted above, *ordre public* in this context refers to the 'international' or 'external' public policy rather than the forum's 'internal' public policy. The idea is that multistate contracts are entitled to more tolerant treatment than domestic contracts. The codifications of Peru (Art 2079), Portugal (Art 22), and Uruguay (Art 5) express this concept by specifically referring to the forum's 'international' public policy, the Quebec codification (Art 3081) refers to *ordre public* 'as understood in international relations', and the codifications of Tunisia (Art 36) and Romania (Art 9) refer to the *ordre public* 'in the sense of private international law'.[60]
>
> Second, *ordre public* in this context contemplates a strongly held public policy. Some codifications express this notion by referring to 'fundamental principles',[61] 'fundamental values',[62] or 'those principles of the social and governmental system of the [forum state] and its law, whose observance must be required without exception'.[63]
>
> Third, what is to be compared with the forum's public policy is the 'effect', 'result', or 'consequences' of the *application* of the chosen law in the particular case, rather than the chosen law in the abstract.[64]
>
> Fourth, the application of the chosen law must produce a result that is clearly or 'manifestly' incompatible with the forum's public policy.[65]

[57] *Cherokee Pump & Equip Inc v Aurora Pump* 38 F3d 246, 252 (5th Cir, 1994).

[58] See Restatement (Second) § 187(2)(b).

[59] See Rome I, Art 9(2)–(3).

[60] The articles shown in parentheses are articles of a Civil Code or a PIL codification. For full citations, see Symeonides, *Codifying*, xxxv.

[61] German codification Art 6; Belarusian codification Art 1099; Kyrgyzstani codification Art 1173; North Korean codification Art 13; Mexican codification Art 15.1.II; Portuguese codification Art 22; Ukrainian codification Art 12; Uzbekistani codification Art 1164.

[62] Liechtenstein codification Art 6; Tunisian codification Art 36 ('fundamental choices'); Venezuelan codification Art 8 ('essential principles').

[63] Slovak codification Art 36.

[64] Virtually all codifications contain words to this effect. For citations to 48 codifications, see Symeonides, *Codifying*, 157, fn 237.

[65] The majority of codifications and conventions contain words to this effect. See ibid, fn 238. See also ibid for lower thresholds set in China, Iran, UAE and Yemen.

b. The 'Overriding' Mandatory Rules of the *lex fori*

Rome I distinguishes between 'overriding' and 'simple' mandatory rules. The latter are rules that 'cannot be derogated from by agreement',[66] while the former are rules that the enacting State regards as 'crucial … for safeguarding its public interests, such as its political, social or economic organisation, to such an extent that they are applicable … irrespective of the law otherwise applicable'.[67] Obviously, the two definitions contemplate a much higher threshold for applying the 'overriding' rather than the 'simple' mandatory rules.[68] Rome I ensures that the chosen law may not violate the overriding mandatory rules of the *lex fori* by providing that '[n]othing in this Regulation shall restrict the[ir] application'.[69]

Twenty-four codifications outside the EU and four conventions expressly authorise the application of the overriding mandatory rules of the forum State. Although these codifications do not use the word 'overriding', they use phraseology that contemplates an equally high threshold as that of Rome I. They provide that these mandatory rules apply 'directly'[70] and 'irrespective of',[71] 'regardless of',[72] or 'notwithstanding'[73] the law designated by the codification's choice of law rules, including rules that allow a contractual choice of law.

Eighteen codifications outside the EU also authorise the application of the overriding mandatory rules of a 'third' State that has a 'close' (but not necessarily a closer or the closest) connection with the case.[74] In this context, the 'third' State is a State other than the forum or the chosen State. More likely, it will be the State of the *lex causae*, but it can also be another State, ie, a fourth State. Although the overriding mandatory rules of that State must embody at least the same high level of public policy as those of the forum State, their application is not assured. While the forum's mandatory rules apply automatically, the application of foreign mandatory rules is always discretionary: the court 'may' apply or 'take into account' the mandatory rules of the third State after considering the 'nature' and 'purpose' of those rules and the 'consequences of their application or non-application'.[75]

c. The Public Policy of the *lex causae*

Group 2 systems, which use the public policy of the *lex causae* as the *lex limitativa*, also contemplate a high-level policy. The Louisiana codification conveys this by referring to 'strongly held'[76] policies of the *lex causae*, the Restatement (Second) uses the qualifier 'fundamental',[77] and the Oregon codification refers to an 'established fundamental' policy.[78]

[66] Rome I, Arts 3(3)–(4), 6(2) and 8(1).

[67] Ibid, Art 9(1). The 'overriding' mandatory rules are also known as 'internationally mandatory' or 'super mandatory' rules, while the 'simple' mandatory rules are sometimes referred to as 'domestic' or 'internal' mandatory rules.

[68] See ibid, recital 37 ('The concept of "overriding mandatory provisions" should be distinguished from the expression "provisions which cannot be derogated from by agreement" and should be construed more restrictively').

[69] Ibid, Art 9(2).

[70] Chinese codification Art 5.

[71] Rome I, Art 9(1); Rome II, Art 16; Belgian codification Art 20; Dutch codification Art 7; Italian codification Art 17; South Korean codification Art 7; North Macedonian codification Art 14; Swiss codification Art 18.

[72] Belarusian codification Art 1100(1); Kyrgyzstani codification Art 1174(1); Lithuanian codification Art 1.11(2).

[73] Bulgarian codification Art 46(1); Venezuelan codification Art 10; Mexico City Convention Art 11.

[74] See Symeonides, *Codifying*, 149–51 (Table 3.3). *cf* Rome I, Art 9(3) (quoted at n 47 above) which focuses on the law of the place(s) of performance.

[75] Dutch codification Art 7(3). With the exception of Rome I, similar language exists in all provisions discussed here.

[76] See La Civ Code Art 3540 comment f ('by definition, only strongly held beliefs of a particular state qualify for the characterization of "public policy"').

[77] Restatement (Second) § 187(2).

[78] Or Rev Stat § 15.355(1)(c).

However, although the word 'fundamental' suggests a high threshold, the examples the Restatement provides – statutes that make certain contracts illegal, and statutes intended to protect one party from 'the oppressive use of superior bargaining power'[79] – suggest a lower threshold than the classic *ordre public*.[80] Moreover, the Restatement states that this 'fundamental' policy 'need not be as strong' as that of the traditional *ordre public* exception,[81] which, under Cardozo's classic test, applies only in exceptional cases where the applicable foreign law is 'shocking' to the forum's sense of justice and fairness.[82]

d. The 'Simple' Mandatory Rules

The lowest threshold for defeating party autonomy is posed by the 'simple' mandatory rules, namely those that 'cannot be derogated from by agreement'.[83] Rome I employs this threshold in two categories of contracts:

(a) Contracts in which 'all other elements' other than the parties' choice are 'located in a country other than the country whose law has been chosen'.[84] In these contracts, the parties' choice 'shall not prejudice' the simple mandatory rules of that other country.[85]
(b) Consumer or employment contracts in which the parties chose the law of a state other than the state of the *lex causae*. In these contracts, the parties' choice of another law may not deprive the consumer or the employee of the protection of the simple mandatory rules of the *lex causae*.[86]

In the latter case, a 'passive' consumer or employee may enjoy the protection of whichever of the two laws is more favourable and sometimes the protection of both laws for different aspects of the contract. Although this may be too generous, the other Contracting Party can avoid this generosity by not deviating from the *lex causae*. Unfortunately, Rome I compensates for this generosity towards consumers and employees by providing little or ineffective protection to other presumptively weak parties, such as passengers and franchisees.[87]

e. No Threshold

At the opposite end of the spectrum, some US states have enacted statutes that uphold *inbound* choice of law clauses without examining whether they conflict with the public policy of any other state. The first and most notorious statute to this effect was § 5-1401 of New York's General Obligations Law. It provides that a New York choice of law clause in a contract whose value exceeds $250,000 is enforceable in New York, 'whether or not' the contract 'bears a reasonable relation to [New York]', and regardless of whether the enforcement of the clause would conflict with the public policy of another state.[88] A companion statute provides for the enforcement of inbound forum-selection clauses in contracts covering at least a million dollars.[89] In an effort to

[79] Restatement (Second) § 187 comment g.
[80] Or Rev Stat § 15.355(2). This provision defines 'fundamental policy' as one that 'reflects objectives or gives effect to essential public or societal institutions beyond the allocation of rights and obligations of parties to a contract at issue'.
[81] Restatement (Second) § 187 comment g.
[82] See *Loucks v Standard Oil Co of NY* 120 NE 198, 201–02 (NY 1918).
[83] Rome I, Arts 3(3), 3(4), 6(2) and 8(1).
[84] Rome I, Art 3(3); see also ibid, Art 3(4); Rome Convention, Art 3(3).
[85] Outside the EU and UK, similar rules are found in the codifications of Albania (Art 45.4); South Korea (Art 25.4); Quebec (Art 3111); and Serbia (draft Art 136.6).
[86] See Rome I, Arts 6(2) and 8(1). Outside the EU and UK, similar rules for consumer contracts exist in the codifications of about a dozen States. See Symeonides, *Codifying*, 160.
[87] For discussion of this issue, see Symeonides, *Codifying*, 166–68; Symeonides, 'Scope', 145.
[88] NY Gen Obl L § 5-1401(1). The statute exempts employment and consumer contracts, and certain contracts for which the UCC does not allow choice of law clauses. See ibid, § 5-1401(2).
[89] See ibid, § 5-1402.

compete for legal and banking business, California, Delaware, Florida, Illinois and Texas have enacted similar statutes ensuring enforcement of inbound choice of law and forum selection clauses in high-value commercial contracts.[90]

III. Law Applicable in the Absence of Contractual Choice

A. Introduction

This section summarises the applicable law rules used in cases in which the forum State (1) does not recognise the parties' power to choose the applicable law, or (2) recognises that power but the parties did not validly exercise it. The summary is limited to contracts in general, as opposed to (a) particular contracts, such as contracts of sale, services, agency, employment, insurance, etc, or (b) particular issues in a contract, such as form, capacity, or consent.[91]

i. The Traditional Method

The traditional method consists of rules based on a single, fixed connecting factor, such as the *locus contractus*, the *locus solutionis*, or both. For example, 11 US states continue to follow the *lex loci contractus* rule of the First Restatement, although they often evade it in practice.[92] The *lex loci contractus* rule is also followed in other countries, including Afghanistan (Article 27), Algeria (Article 18), Angola (Article 42.2), Brazil (Article 9), Cape Verde (Article 42.2), Central African Republic (Article 44), Costa Rica (Article 17(1)), Cuba (Article 17), Egypt (Article 19), Gabon (Article 55), Guinea-Bissau (Article 42.2), Jordan (Article 20), Mauritania (Article 10), Mozambique (Article 35), Qatar (Article 22), Rwanda (Article 14), Sudan (Article 13) and UAE (Article 19). In some of these countries, the law of the parties' common domicile or the law chosen by the parties displaces the *lex loci contractus*.

The *lex loci solutionis* rule was never as popular as the *lex loci contractus*, but remains the default law in some countries, including Argentina (Article 2652), Guatemala (Article 30), Iran (Article 968), Nicaragua (Article 14), Peru (Article 2095), and certain African countries that were previously British colonies.[93]

ii. The Rome Model

The model established by the Rome Convention is the most popular model internationally. Article 4 of the Convention provides: (1) that in the absence of a valid choice of law by the parties and subject to certain exceptions,[94] the substance of a contract is governed by the law of the

[90] See Cal Code Civ Proc § 410.40; Del Code, Tit 6 § 2708; 735; Fla Stats §§ 685.101, 685.102; Il Stats §§105/5-5, 105/5-10; Tex Bus & Comm Code Ann § 271.005.

[91] eg, many civil codes treat contractual capacity alongside capacity to enter into other juridical acts and usually subject it to the law of the domicile, residence, or nationality, even if they follow the *lex loci contractus* rule for the substance of the contract. Likewise, many civil codes apply the *lex loci contractus* to the form of the contract, even if they apply another law to the substance of the contract.

[92] See SC Symeonides, *Choice of Law in Practice: A Twenty-Year Report from the Trenches* (Brill-Nijhoff 2020) 31, 33–34 (listing Alabama, Florida, Georgia, Kansas, Maryland, New Mexico, Oklahoma, Rhode Island, South Carolina, Tennessee and Virginia).

[93] See RF Oppong, *Private International Law in Commonwealth Africa* (Cambridge University Press 2013) 131–48.

[94] The exceptions apply to consumer contracts (Art 5); employment contracts (Art 6); and issues of form (Art 9); capacity (Art 11); and consent (Art 8(2)).

'most closely connected' country; and (2) that this country is presumed to be the country where the party who is to effect the 'characteristic' performance of the contract has its habitual residence, central administration, or place of business. This presumption is inapplicable if the characteristic performance cannot be determined and is disregarded when the contract is 'more closely connected' with another country.

Article 4 of Rome I broadly preserved this scheme, despite changes in sequencing and drafting technique. The Article begins with a list of rules for eight different types of contracts (paragraph 1) (though it does not always follow the habitual residence of the characteristic performer approach) and then subjects all other contracts and contracts comprising more than one of the types in paragraph 1 to the law of the habitual residence of the party who is 'required to effect the characteristic performance of the contract' (paragraph 2). Paragraph 3 introduces an exception for cases in which the contract is 'manifestly more closely connected' with another country, and paragraph 4 provides that, if the applicable law cannot be determined under paragraphs 1 or 2, the contract is governed by the law of the 'most closely connected' country.

Rome I is in force in all EU Member States except Denmark, which follows the Rome Convention. In addition, the Rome model (Convention or Regulation) has been followed, with or without modifications,[95] in the majority of non-EU countries that have recently codified or recodified their PIL, including: Albania (Article 46), Armenia (Article 1285), Azerbaijan (Article 25), Belarus (Article 1125), (China (Article 41), Georgia (Article 36), Kazakhstan (Article 113), South Korea (Article 26), Kyrgyzstan (Article 1199), Moldova (Article 1612), Monaco (Article 69), Mongolia (Article 49), Montenegro (Article 39), North Macedonia (Article 22), Norway (Draft Article 4), Quebec (Articles 312–13), Russia (Article 1211), Serbia (Draft Article 137), Switzerland (Article 117), Taiwan (Article 20), Tajikistan (Article 1219), Tunisia (Article 62), Turkey (Article 24.4), Ukraine (Article 32), UK (kept Rome I as part of retained EU law post-Brexit); Uruguay (Article 48), Uzbekistan (Article 1190) and Vietnam (Article 683).

iii. The Closest Connection

Even countries that have not adopted the Rome model have adopted some version of the 'closest connection' concept (or the 'proximity principle'). For example, the Mexico City Convention (Article 9) and the codifications of the Dominican Republic (Articles 60.2 and 61), Macau (Article 41) and Venezuela (Article 30) call for the application of the law of the State with which the contract is most closely connected although they employ factors other than the characteristic performance. The same is true of the 'closest and most real connection', the relevant test in English, Scots and Northern Irish law (in the rare cases not covered by Rome I) and in most Commonwealth countries, which predates the Rome model.[96]

iv. The American Approaches

In the United States, the most prevalent model is that of the Restatement (Second), which is followed in 24 jurisdictions.[97] Section 188 provides that contractual issues are governed by the

[95] eg, some codifications omit the presumptive rules or the escape clause of Rome I, but all codifications adopt the concepts of the 'closest connection' and 'characteristic performance'.

[96] See Dicey, Morris & Collins, *The Conflict of Laws*, 15th edn (Sweet & Maxwell 2012) 1176–78; J-G Castel, *Canadian Conflict of Laws*, 4th edn (Butterworths 1997) 590–92; *Anton's Private International Law*, 2nd edn (W Green/SULI 1990) ch 10 and 3rd edn (W Green/SULI 2011) para 10.51; BA Marshall, 'Reconsidering the Proper Law of the Contract' (2012) 13 *Melbourne Journal of International Law* 505.

[97] For a list, see Symeonides, *Oxford Commentaries*, 146–47.

law of the state which, 'with respect to [the particular] issue, has the most significant relationship to the transaction and the parties under the principles stated in § 6'.

A superficial reading might lead to the conclusion that this is just another iteration of the 'closest connection' test, especially because the process of identifying this state includes consideration of geographical contacts, such as the place of contracting, negotiation and performance of the contract, the location of its subject matter, and the parties' domicile.[98] However, such a conclusion would be inaccurate because the search for the most significantly related state must be conducted 'under the principles stated in § 6', which require consideration of non-geographical factors, such as the policies and interests of the involved states. Moreover, this search must be conducted on an issue-by-issue basis, rather than for the contract as a whole, thus entailing the possibility of *dépeçage*.

A similar non-geographical issue-by-issue analysis is present in all other modern American approaches, such as interest analysis and Leflar's better-law approach. They also appear in the Louisiana codification, which calls for the application of the law of the state 'whose policies would be most seriously impaired if its law were not applied to [the particular] issue',[99] and the Oregon codification, which calls for the application of the 'most appropriate' law for the particular issue.[100]

IV. Conclusions

By focusing on the differences on the scope and limitations of party autonomy in various legal systems, this chapter may leave the impression that they are hopelessly apart. Such an impression would be inaccurate. It is therefore appropriate to conclude by reiterating the statement made at the beginning that party autonomy has become a universal PIL principle in contracts, around which most systems have converged. There is reason to expect that the Hague Principles will facilitate further convergence by enticing the few remaining systems to adopt party autonomy.

With the exception of countries that have emulated the model of the Rome Convention or Rome I Regulation, there is less of a convergence for cases in which the parties do not choose the applicable law. However, the availability of party autonomy suggests that the lack of uniformity in those cases is less problematic. In any event, there is reason to doubt the effectiveness of efforts to eliminate the remaining differences at the international level.[101] For example, only one of the three Hague Conventions on sales of goods – an important but narrow contract – has garnered the necessary number of ratifications or accessions to enter into force.[102] One can safely surmise that a convention covering all contracts would have even less success, at least for now.[103] If this assessment is correct, then the commendable efforts of the Hague Conference can be put to better use on other subjects for which the need for uniformity or approximation is more obvious.

[98] Restatement (Second) § 188(2).

[99] La Civ Code Art 3537.

[100] Or Rev Stat § 15.360.

[101] Even at the regional level, unification is difficult, eg, the Inter-American Convention on the Law Applicable to International Contracts (Mexico City Convention) has never entered into force because only two countries have ratified it.

[102] See Convention of 15 June 1955 on the law applicable to international sales of goods (in force in eight countries). The other two Conventions are the Convention of 15 April 1958 on the law governing transfer of title in international sales of goods (one ratification), and the Convention of 22 December 1986 on the Law Applicable to Contracts for the International Sale of Goods (two ratifications). The dramatic success of the 1980 United Nations Convention on Contracts for the International Sale of Goods (92 ratifications) may partially explain this phenomenon, although CISG is a substantive law Convention.

[103] The only other Hague Convention dealing with a contract is the Convention of 14 March 1978 on the Law Applicable to Agency, which is in force in four countries.

15

Contract Jurisdiction

RON BRAND AND KAREN VANDEKERCKHOVE

I. Introduction

Jurisdiction in contract cases involving parties from different States can exist through a number of methods. Sophisticated parties to cross-border contracts will usually include a carefully drafted choice of forum clause, whether that choice is for arbitration or litigation. Global respect for party autonomy in the twenty-first century means that international contractual disputes should always be decided by the forum freely chosen by the parties in advance of the dispute, unless restrictive laws prohibit such a choice from being made.

While parties normally have the ability to exercise party autonomy in choosing the forum for a contractual dispute, that freedom is not always exercised, however, and resort must be had to default rules of jurisdiction. Even then, many cases involving contract claims will not be brought under a rule of jurisdiction specifically limited to contract claims. For example, national rules of exclusive jurisdiction may dictate that the particular issue (eg, validity of an intellectual property right) may be determined only in the courts of a single State. Moreover, common rules on general jurisdiction in the courts of the State in which the defendant is present through domicile, habitual residence, or some other formula, exist in every modern legal system in the world. Such rules of general jurisdiction combine with the presence of the defendant (and thus the likelihood of the presence of the defendant's assets as well) to make recognition and enforcement of any resulting judgment a local matter, thus often rendering general jurisdiction an attractive default jurisdiction option in many cases in which no mutual choice of forum occurs in advance. Many legal systems also provide for jurisdiction over a non-local defendant when that defendant has a local branch, agency, or establishment through which the contractual arrangement either arose or was to be performed. Alternative rules of non-general jurisdiction, other than one designed specifically for contract cases, may also be available.[1] This makes it likely that only a subset of cases brought on contract claims will actually be brought in reliance on a true 'contract jurisdiction' provision. Nevertheless, the direct jurisdiction rule for contract cases is important to the structure of many systems of jurisdiction rules, whether national or regional.

Agreeing upon a default rule of contract jurisdiction has proved to be one of the most difficult issues in the international effort to harmonise rules of jurisdiction. While a growing consensus has been built with regard to party autonomy in determining the forum having jurisdiction over a contract dispute (see the 1958 United Nations Convention on the Recognition and Enforcement

[1] Joining of multiple defendants; joined contract and tort claims; exorbitant jurisdiction such as transient jurisdiction cases, etc.

of Foreign Arbitral Awards (New York Convention) and the 2005 Hague Convention on choice of court agreements), it has not been possible so far to reach international consensus over an appropriate direct jurisdiction rule for a contract dispute in a situation where parties have not chosen the court to hear their dispute, and the case is not brought in the home court of the defendant.

Regional harmonisation does exist, however, especially in the European Union and in the EFTA States, where consensus has been reached in the Lugano Convention among the 27 European Union Member States, Iceland, Norway and Switzerland on binding jurisdiction rules, including in contract matters. Agreement may also be demonstrated among Commonwealth States for purposes of indirect jurisdiction through their Model Law on the Recognition and Enforcement of Foreign Judgments.[2] There is, however, no similar instrument dealing with direct jurisdiction in the Commonwealth. Direct jurisdiction rules for contract cases exist in the statutes of many US states but those rules are affected by the gloss of the Due Process clauses of the US Constitution, making the system within the United States different from that within the European Union or the Lugano Convention. At a wider, global level, consensus has been reached on an indirect jurisdiction filter in the 2019 Hague Convention on the recognition and enforcement of foreign judgments in civil and commercial matters (Judgments Convention). This Convention was developed under the auspices of the Hague Conference on Private International Law. Following the mandate by the 2016 Council on General Affairs and Policy of the Hague Conference, expert work has started on matters relating to direct jurisdiction, with a preliminary focus on parallel proceedings and related actions (see the 2020 Hague General Affairs Council conclusions).

This chapter will focus on a general default jurisdiction rule in matters relating to contract, excluding specific contract matters such as the carriage of goods and passengers for which special rules exist.[3] We will begin with a discussion of the international legal framework now represented by the 2019 Hague Judgments Convention, which provides the clearest example of global thinking on contract jurisdiction, and follow with thoughts about the possibilities for global harmonisation of a default rule of direct jurisdiction for contract cases.

II. The 2019 Judgments Convention: Global Convergence on a Rule for Indirect Jurisdiction

A. Background to the 2019 Convention

The international organisation in which States most often deal with questions of international jurisdiction in civil matters is the Hague Conference on Private International Law, which has been in existence since 1893, but concluded its current Statute in 1955.[4] A rule of indirect contract jurisdiction could have been included in the 1971 Hague Convention on the recognition and enforcement of foreign judgments in civil and commercial matters.[5] That Convention did contain seven indirect jurisdiction rules as gateway provisions for judgments that would circulate under

[2] Available at: thecommonwealth.org/sites/default/files/key_reform_pdfs/D16227_1_GPD_ROL_Model_Law_Rec_Enf_Foreign_Judgements.pdf.

[3] See, for instance, Art 33 of the 1999 Montreal Convention for the unification of certain rules for international carriage by air.

[4] Statute of the Hague Conference on Private International Law, available at: www.hcch.net/en/instruments/conventions/full-text/?cid=29.

[5] Available at: www.hcch.net/en/instruments/conventions/full-text/?cid=78.

its terms, but none was a rule on contract jurisdiction.[6] The failure of the 1971 Convention to include an indirect jurisdiction rule for contract cases presaged the current difficulty in finding global consensus on such a rule, whether direct or indirect.

The Hague Conference revisited questions of both direct and indirect jurisdiction in the early 1990s, when it placed on its agenda the negotiation of a global Convention on jurisdiction and the recognition and enforcement of judgments.[7] A Preliminary Draft Convention text was prepared in October 1999,[8] with revisions at the first part of a split Diplomatic Conference in June 2001,[9] but conclusion of a comprehensive jurisdiction and judgments Convention became beyond reach. The focus of the negotiations was changed to a more manageable Convention on Choice of Court Agreements, which was concluded in June of 2005.[10]

The Choice of Court Convention is effectively a Convention for contract jurisdiction – when that jurisdiction is well planned through party agreement. It provides that a court chosen in an exclusive choice of court agreement shall have exclusive jurisdiction,[11] that a court not chosen shall defer to the chosen court,[12] and that the courts of all Contracting States shall recognise and enforce judgments from a court chosen in an exclusive choice of court agreement.[13] It thus supplements a consent-based jurisdictional rule with a strong rule on recognition and enforcement of resulting judgments.

The Choice of Court Convention was not, however, the end of the effort to deal with jurisdiction and recognition of judgments in global conventions at the Hague Conference. In October 2011, the Council on General Affairs and Policy of the Hague Conference established an Experts' Group to consider the resumption of the Judgments Project.[14] This resulted in a focus first on the recognition of judgments and led to the conclusion, on 2 July 2019, of the 2019 Convention on the Recognition and Enforcement of Foreign Judgments in Civil or Commercial Matters.[15] While the Judgments Convention contains only indirect rules of jurisdiction, and thus does not govern jurisdiction in the court of origin for any case, its provisions are useful indications of current global coalescence on what is considered to be appropriate in defining jurisdiction generally.

The basic structure of the Judgments Convention is contained in its Articles 4–7. Article 4(1) provides the operative rule of the Convention, which requires that each Contracting State shall recognise and enforce judgments from other Contracting States and permits refusal only on

[6] Ibid, Art 10. A direct jurisdiction rule is applied in the court of origin, in which the original judgment is rendered. An indirect jurisdiction rule is used by the court addressed when it is asked to grant recognition and enforcement. In this way, indirect jurisdiction rules are used by the court addressed to test the jurisdiction of the court of origin in order to determine the qualification of the judgment for recognition and enforcement in the court addressed. The recognising court indirectly applies these jurisdictional tests to consider the legitimacy of the resulting judgment for recognition and enforcement purposes.

[7] Final Act of the Eighteenth Session of the Hague Conference on Private International Law, 19 October 1996, 21.

[8] Informational note on the work of the informal meetings held since October 1999 to consider and develop drafts on outstanding items, drawn up by the Permanent Bureau, Hague Conference on Private International Law, Prel Doc No 15 (May 2001) (containing the text of the Preliminary Draft Convention).

[9] Hague Conference on Private International Law, Commission II, Jurisdiction and Foreign Judgments in Civil and Commercial Matters, Summary of the Outcome of the Discussion in Commission II of the First Part of the Diplomatic Conference, 6–20 June 2001, Interim Text.

[10] The text of the Final Act of the Twentieth Session, and a documentary history of the Choice of Court Convention project, are available on the Hague Conference website at: www.hcch.net/index_en.php?act=conventions.text&cid=98.

[11] Ibid, Art 5.

[12] Ibid, Art 6.

[13] Ibid, Art 8 (subject to an explicit list of bases for non-recognition found in Art 9). The Convention is discussed in more detail in Paul Beaumont and Mary Keyes, 'Choice of Court Agreements', ch 28 in this book.

[14] See: www.hcch.net/en/projects/legislative-projects/judgments.

[15] Available at: www.hcch.net/en/instruments/conventions/full-text/?cid=137. The Convention is discussed in more detail in David Goddard and Paul Beaumont, 'Recognition and Enforcement of Judgments in Civil or Commercial Matters' ch 29 in this book.

those grounds expressly set out in the Convention. Article 5 then determines which judgments are 'eligible for recognition and enforcement' under the Convention by providing a list of bases of jurisdiction on which a judgment may have been founded. If the facts before the court of origin could have satisfied any one of the jurisdictional tests in the Article 5(1) list, then the judgment is eligible for recognition and enforcement under the Convention. Article 7 provides the general bases for non-recognition of a judgment, even if that judgment meets the requirements of Article 5. The Article 7 list tracks closely the grounds for non-recognition found in the 2005 Hague Choice of Court Convention, which grounds are generally familiar in national law throughout the world and include such concerns as fraud, lack of proper notice, the existence of inconsistent judgments, and inconsistency with the public policy of the recognising State.

B. The Contract Jurisdiction Rule in Article 5(1)(g) of the 2019 Convention

The structure of the Judgments Convention makes Article 5(1) key to its operation. Paragraph 5(1)(g) provides the rule of indirect jurisdiction specifically addressing contract cases. That provision reads as follows:

> Article 5 Bases for recognition and enforcement
>
> A judgment is eligible for recognition and enforcement if one of the following requirements is met –
>
> …
>
> (g) the judgment ruled on a contractual obligation and it was given by a court of the State in which performance of that obligation took place, or should have taken place, in accordance with
>
> (i) the agreement of the parties, or
> (ii) the law applicable to the contract, in the absence of an agreed place of performance,
>
> unless the activities of the defendant in relation to the transaction clearly did not constitute a purposeful and substantial connection to that State.

The focus of the rule in Article 5(1)(g) is on the place of performance of the contractual obligation at stake. This focus presents a compromise between two existing types of connection in contract matters, ie, place of performance and carrying on activities. The connection to the place of performance is considered in many jurisdictions to be the key criterion; it is, for instance, one element in the evaluation whether a defendant is or has been carrying on activities in a given place.

Under Article 5(1)(g), a judgment ruling on a contractual obligation will be recognised and enforced under the Convention if it was given by a court of the State in which performance of the obligation in question took place or should have taken place. The place of performance of the obligation is determined either by the agreement of the parties or, if no such agreement exists, on the basis of the law applicable to the contract. If the resulting connection points to a State where the defendant did not purposefully and substantially carry on activities, it may be set aside as an insufficient connection to warrant recognition and enforcement of the judgment. The rule applies within the scope of application of the Convention, which excludes, among other matters, the carriage of goods and passengers (Article 2(1)(f)) and intellectual property (Article 2(1)(m) of the Convention).

The characterisation of a matter as a matter of contract and how contract matters should be delimited from other matters (such as tort) is left to the courts of the State where recognition and enforcement is sought. The characterisation by that court may differ from that made by the court of origin; it may be hoped that with time, the interpretation and application of the rule may lead to a common understanding of what should be considered a 'contract' under the Convention. The role of the Hague Conference in monitoring the application of the Convention and in organising an exchange of experience among Contracting States will be important in this respect.

The rule of Article 5(1)(g) must be seen in the general context of the Convention. In particular, it is important to take into account that the provision provides for recognition and enforcement of judgments emanating from a contract forum which is alternative to four other important possible fora, ie, the courts of the State where the defendant is habitually resident (Article 5(1)(a)); the courts of the State where the defendant maintained a branch, agency, or other establishment insofar as the claim arose out of the activities of that branch, agency, or establishment (Article 5(1)(d));[16] the courts designated in a non-exclusive choice of court agreement (Article 5(1)(m)); or the courts of the State designated in an exclusive choice of court agreement and thus covered by the 2005 Choice of Court Convention. A claimant in a contract matter therefore may consider, to the extent available, all of these fora, which may or may not coincide, if they want to ensure subsequent cross-border recognition and enforcement of the resulting judgment. The defendant bringing a counterclaim in such a case will also benefit from subsequent recognition and enforcement of the ruling on their counterclaim, to the extent that the counterclaim arose out of the same transaction or occurrence as the original claim. However, the defendant, claimant on a counterclaim, is protected against a ruling on the counterclaim against them if they were required under the law of the State of origin to file the counterclaim in order to avoid preclusion under the law of that State (see Article 5(1)(l) of the Convention).

i. The Place of Performance of the Contractual Obligation in Dispute

As the indirect jurisdictional basis which will ensure circulation of a judgment, in matters of contract, Article 5(1)(g) connects to the place of performance of the contractual obligation. The connection to the place of performance of the contractual obligation at stake means that the appropriate jurisdiction may vary depending on the basis of the dispute between the parties.[17] For instance, in a contract for the sale of goods, if the dispute concerns a claim for payment by the seller, the proper jurisdiction is with the courts of the State where payment was or should have been made. If, on the other hand, the dispute concerns a delayed delivery, jurisdiction shall lie with the courts of the State where the delivery took or should have taken place. As such, the indirect allocation of jurisdiction differs to a certain extent from the EU and Lugano Convention systems, which for certain types of contract connects to a single place of performance whatever the contractual obligation in dispute.[18]

It is interesting to note that the Judgments Convention does not retain other possible connecting factors in matters relating to contract, such as the place of signature of the contract. The place of signature or making of the contract exists as a connecting factor for direct jurisdiction in matters of contract in a number of States around the world.[19] Early in the judgments project

[16] Arguably the claim must be based primarily on the branch's activities; it should not only merely be connected to the activities of the branch.

[17] See F Garcimartín and G Saumier, *Explanatory Report on the 2019 HCCH Judgments Convention* (HCCH 2020) para 181, available at: www.hcch.net/en/publications-and-studies/details4/?pid=6797&dtid=3.

[18] This is the case for contracts for the sale of goods and the provision of services, see Art 7(1)(b) of Regulation 1215/2012 of 12 December 2012 on Jurisdiction and the Recognition and Enforcement of Judgments in Civil and Commercial Matters (Recast) (the so-called 'Brussels Ia Regulation') [2012] OJ L351/1; and Art 5(1)(b) of the Lugano Convention on Jurisdiction and the Recognition and Enforcement of Judgments in Civil and Commercial Matters [2009] OJ L147/5.

[19] In New Zealand, for instance, jurisdiction of the courts may be established in a contract case against a foreign defendant when the contract was made in New Zealand (see Rule 6.27(2)(b)(i) of the New Zealand High Court Rules 2016,

at the Hague Conference, the place of signature of a contract was considered to constitute an insufficient connecting factor for purposes of establishing jurisdiction, although no consensus was reached on the matter. Even more, it was preliminarily listed as a prohibited ground of jurisdiction on the draft Convention's list of prohibited grounds of jurisdiction. The *rationale* for this prohibition was that the place where a contract is signed may be of a purely accidental nature, and if there are no other connecting factors it will not be a sufficient connection on which to base a contract forum.[20]

ii. *Determination of the Place of Performance*

The place of performance of a contractual obligation is determined first by the express designation of such place by the parties. If the parties have agreed upon the place of performance of the obligation, that place is relevant to verify compliance with the jurisdictional filter, whether or not the obligation was actually performed at that place. Any dispute as to whether parties have validly agreed on the place of performance should be resolved on the basis of the law applicable to the contract, as designated by the private international law rules of the requested State.[21]

If the parties have not agreed on the place of performance, the place will be determined under the law governing the contract, which may itself be designated by the parties in a choice of law clause.[22] The law governing the contract, including the validity of a choice of law, will be determined by application of the conflict of laws rules of the requested State.[23] The Explanatory Report to the Convention explains the operation of the latter rule (Article 5(1)(g)(ii) of the Convention) on the basis of the following example: X brings a claim against Y in State A. The basis of the claim is Y's failure to pay for certain goods delivered to Y in State B. The contract was concluded by telephone and the parties did not designate the place of payment. In this case, if X obtains a favourable judgment based on that claim, it will be recognised and enforced under sub-paragraph (g), if in accordance with the law governing the contract, the place of payment was State A. The law of the requested State, including its private international law rules, will determine which law governs that contract.[24]

If the obligation at stake is a negative obligation, ie, an obligation not to do something (eg, an obligation not to compete), the applicable law will need to determine where that negative obligation needed to be performed.[25] Alternatively, recourse may be had to the general rule in Article 5(1)(a) or to Article 5(1)(d).

Questions may arise as well, in the absence of an agreed place of performance, when there is no material place of performance, for instance in the case of performance of contractual obligations purely online (eg, contracts for the online supply of digital content or digital services such

as last updated on 1 July 2020, available at: legislation.govt.nz/regulation/public/2016/0225/latest/DLM6951554.html). Similar rules exist in other countries, such as the United Kingdom (England and Wales and Northern Ireland) and Kenya, in cases where the defendant is served abroad (see the overview included in the Comparative Study on Jurisdictional Gaps and their Effects on the Judgments Project prepared by Jones Day in the context of the preparation of the 2019 Hague Judgments Convention).

[20] P Nygh and F Pocar, Report on the preliminary draft convention on jurisdiction and foreign judgments in civil and commercial matters adopted by the Special Commission at the end of its fifth meeting on 30 October 1999 and submitted to the Diplomatic Conference (Nineteenth Session) 83, available at: assets.hcch.net/docs/638883f3-0c0a-46c6-b646-7a099d9bd95e.pdf.

[21] See Explanatory Report (n 17) para 182.

[22] Ibid, para 183.

[23] Ibid, para 184.

[24] Ibid, para 185.

[25] The Explanatory Report to the Convention mentions that the solution in such a situation was left open for further analysis by courts and legal scholars, see ibid, para 186.

as i-cloud services). In such situations, the applicable law may provide for various solutions, eg, referring to the habitual residence of the service provider or of the recipient. Alternatively, again, recourse may be had to the general rule in Article 5(1)(a) or to Article 5(1)(d). It is important to note, in this regard, that judgments given against consumers on the basis of contracts concluded by the consumer, are excluded from the scope of application of Article 5(1)(g) (see below).

iii. Several Places of Performance

In case the dispute giving rise to the judgment concerns several obligations which must be performed at different places, the connection must be made for each obligation separately.[26] A claimant anticipating future recognition and enforcement abroad of the judgment may wish to avoid a division of the dispute into different claims to be brought before different courts; they may wish to opt for bringing all claims before one court, ie, the court of the State where the defendant is habitually resident (Article 5(1)(a)) or the courts of the State where the defendant maintained a branch, agency, or other establishment insofar as the claim arose out of the activities of that branch, agency, or establishment (Article 5(1)(d)). If the claimant nevertheless chooses to bring the claims on all obligations before the courts of the State where only one of them was performed, the judgment will still be eligible for recognition and enforcement to the extent that it concerns the obligation that was (to be) performed in the forum State (Article 9).

iv. Purposeful and Substantial Connection to the State of Origin

Like other provisions of Article 5(1), paragraph (g) relies on the connection between the forum State and the cause of action. As explained in the Explanatory Report, this single connection test may in certain cases point to a place that is arbitrary, random or insufficiently related to the transaction between the parties, which might be considered unfair to the defendant. In such situations, an additional safeguard is provided in Article 5(1)(g), with the jurisdiction being sufficient for recognition and enforcement purposes 'unless the activities of the defendant in relation to the transaction clearly did not constitute a purposeful and substantial connection to that State'. This protects a defendant against the recognition of a judgment rendered in a situation where the place of performance would create only a very loose link between the State concerned and the defendant. This could be the case, for instance, with contracts performed online, where the connection with the State of origin may be merely virtual and therefore insufficient to justify circulation of the judgment under the Convention.[27]

The basic contract jurisdiction rule in many legal systems requires only a connection between the forum State and the claim, on the theory that a court in a State connected to the claim is competent to hear the case and have the results be effective against all parties, whether they have connections to the State or not. In other legal systems, particularly that of the United States, there is a different approach to concepts of due process, and jurisdiction will not exist unless there is some connection as well with the defendant and that connection is more than tenuous. Both types of system find jurisdiction to exist when the defendant performs an act in the forum State and the claim arises out of that act. By ensuring that the connection between the forum State and the claim may need to be strengthened by a connection between the forum State and the defendant, Article 5(1)(g) is designed to provide convergence with all of the legal systems of countries that might become parties to the Judgments Convention.

[26] Ibid, para 186.
[27] Ibid, para 187.

The safeguard connection to the defendant required by Article 5(1)(g) applies whether or not the place of performance is designated in the contract, and whether or not it is necessary to resort to rules of private international law to determine the place of performance. Even a contract in which the place of performance is clear could result in jurisdiction in the courts of the State of that performance not being sufficient for purposes of the Convention in order to result in recognition and enforcement based solely on Article 5(1)(g), insofar as such a place would be arbitrary, random or insufficiently related to the transaction between the parties.

The drafting of the safeguard language in Article 5(1)(g) implies a burden on the judgment debtor at the stage of recognition and enforcement of the judgment both to raise the question of a connection between the forum State and the defendant/judgment debtor, and to demonstrate the absence of a purposeful and substantial connection. Because that language is in a Convention on the recognition and enforcement of judgments, and not a Convention on direct jurisdiction, it has no impact on rules of direct jurisdiction in any State. It simply brings together very different concepts of contract jurisdiction in States that may become parties to the Judgments Convention in order to facilitate a system of judgments recognition and enforcement that accounts for those differences.

C. The Special Rule on Consumer Contracts and Individual Employment Contracts

In many States protective policies exist in relation to jurisdiction and the recognition and enforcement of judgments given in matters concerning contracts concluded by consumers or employees.[28] The Hague Judgments Convention therefore provides for a special regime for the cross-border recognition and enforcement of judgments in these matters, incorporating the minimum floor for recognition and enforcement on which the negotiating States could agree.

The rule in Article 5(2) provides no limitations on the recognition and enforcement of judgments given against the trader or the employer and of judgments given in favour of the consumer or employee. However, as regards the recognition and enforcement of judgments given against the consumer or the employee, recognition and enforcement may not be based on the Convention if jurisdiction was based on the defendant's consent to the jurisdiction of the forum court unless the consent was given before the court (Article 5(2)(a)) or if the jurisdiction was based on a failure on the part of the defendant to contest the jurisdiction of the court in due time. Furthermore, the judgment against a consumer/employee will not be recognised and enforced if the court's jurisdiction was based on the place of performance of the contractual obligation concerned, to the extent that this place would differ from the consumer/employee's habitual residence (in which case recognition and enforcement would be ensured under Article 5(1)(a)). Most importantly, recognition and enforcement of a judgment given against a consumer or employee is not provided for under the Convention if the jurisdiction of the court of origin was based on a choice of court agreement between the parties (Article 5(2)(b)).

[28] In many States, it is considered that these policies aim at providing easy and close access to justice for consumers and individual employees which may not be circumvented by choice of court agreements concluded prior to the dispute or by the normal operation of contract jurisdiction rules. In other States, no such special protections exist or protections are laid down in substantive (versus procedural) law only. For a view in favour of the latter approach, see RA Brand, 'The Unfriendly Intrusion of Consumer Legislation into Freedom to Contract for Effective ODR' in M Piers, H Storm and J Verhellen (eds), *Liber Amicorum Johan Erauw* (Intersentia 2014) 365, prior draft, available at: papers.ssrn.com/sol3/papers.cfm?abstract_id=2520035.

This would exclude jurisdiction based, for instance, on a choice of court included in click-wrap agreements frequently used in online transactions.

III. Contract Rules for Direct Jurisdiction

A. The EU/EFTA Approach: The Brussels Ia Regulation and the Lugano Convention

An integrated regime with uniform jurisdiction rules, including on contract matters, exists in the European Union, and in certain States of the European Free Trade Association (Switzerland, Iceland and Norway). Since the 1968 Brussels Convention, the European Union has established uniform contract jurisdiction rules with a triple aim. These rules, now embodied in the Brussels Ia Regulation 2012 for intra-EU matters and for EU/EFTA matters in the Lugano Convention 2007,[29] ensure that parties know before the courts of which Member State they may sue or may be sued in matters relating to contract. At the same time, the uniform rules prevent that defendants domiciled in a European Union Member State or Lugano Contracting State in a contract dispute are brought before the courts of other Member States on the basis of unacceptably wide jurisdiction rules (so-called 'exorbitant' jurisdiction rules). Finally, the uniform direct jurisdiction rules, and the principle of mutual trust, obviate the need for the State where recognition and enforcement of the judgment in a contract dispute is sought, to verify the exercise of jurisdiction by the forum court, thus removing one of the most important obstacles to and greatly facilitating cross-border recognition and enforcement of judgments.

The main elements of the EU/EFTA regime on contract jurisdiction are a strong protection of party autonomy (choice of court or forum selection agreements), the allocation of jurisdiction in the absence of a choice of court agreement, and special protection of consumers, employees and insured. The contract jurisdiction rule exists as an alternative to the main rule of general jurisdiction, ie, that proceedings against a party should be brought before the courts of the State where that party is domiciled, and to other special jurisdiction alternatives such as jurisdiction based on the activities of a branch of the defendant.

If parties to a contract have agreed that a court or the courts of a Member State of the European Union are to have jurisdiction to settle any disputes which have arisen or which may arise in connection with a particular legal relationship, including a contractual relationship, then that court or those courts shall have jurisdiction, unless the agreement is null and void as to its substantive validity under the law of that Member State. The designated jurisdiction is considered to exclude the jurisdiction of any other court in the European Union, unless the parties have agreed otherwise.[30] As such, exclusive choice of court agreements have the double function of both conferring jurisdiction on the chosen court and depriving jurisdiction for other courts that may otherwise have exercised jurisdiction.[31] The regime has been further strengthened in the 2012 revision of the Regulation, by preventing litigants from

[29] For full references, see above (n 18). Both instruments have the same contract jurisdiction rule but do have slightly different regimes for choice of court because Brussels Ia reversed the *lis pendens* rule and added an applicable law rule on substantive validity in relation to exclusive choice of court agreements, whereas the Lugano Convention has not yet been revised to take account of these developments within the EU. The EU regime is described below.

[30] See Art 25 Brussels Ia.

[31] See TC Hartley, *The Modern Approach to Private International Law. International Litigation and Transactions from a Common-Law Perspective* (Martinus Nijhoff 2007) 111–12.

delaying the resolution of the dispute in the agreed forum by first seising a court not chosen by the parties.

When parties have not designated the court(s) to hear their contract dispute, jurisdiction exists in the courts of the Member State where the contractual obligation in dispute was or should have been performed, in accordance with the private international law rules of the forum State.[32] The contract rule for direct jurisdiction in the European Union and in the Lugano Convention is similar to the rule for indirect jurisdiction in the 2019 Hague Judgments Convention set out above. The EU/EFTA rules differ from the Convention, however, in two situations. In the case of a sale of goods, for jurisdiction purposes, the place of performance of all contractual obligations relating to that sale is considered to be the place where the goods were (or should have been) delivered; and in the case of a provision of services, the contract is considered to be performed at the place where the services were (or should have been) delivered.[33]

The above rules do not apply to consumer, individual employment and insurance contracts, for which protective jurisdiction rules apply, providing, in principle, that the consumer, the employee, or insured can only be sued before the courts of the Member State where they are domiciled.[34]

The uniform application of the above rules is ensured through rulings issued by the Court of Justice of the European Union, which answers questions of interpretation referred to it by the national courts of the Member States. To date, the Court has given more than 300 rulings on the Brussels Ia Regulation and its predecessors in general; many of these rulings concern the interpretation and application of the contract jurisdiction rule.[35]

B. The Commonwealth Approach in its Model Law

The Commonwealth model law on foreign judgments provides for a rule of indirect jurisdiction in contract matters very similar to that in the Brussels Ia Regulation. Its Article 5(1)(g) provides that 'a court in the State of origin of the judgment is deemed to have had jurisdiction if the proceedings related to a contractual obligation that was or should have been performed in the State of origin'. The explanatory text accompanying the model law does not elaborate on the provision; it limits itself to noting that this paragraph, among a number of others, 'include material not found in existing Commonwealth statutes, but which reflect an international consensus and correspond to grounds familiar in Commonwealth legislation on service out of the jurisdiction'.[36]

[32] Art 7(1)(a) Brussels Ia.

[33] Art 7(1)(b) Brussels Ia.

[34] ss 3, 4 and 5 of Chapter II of Brussels Ia. The exercise of these jurisdiction rules is subject to review at the recognition and enforcement stage to ensure that weaker parties are protected, see Art 35(1) of the Lugano Convention and Art 45(1)(e) of Brussels Ia.

[35] For instance, important interpretative guidance exists regarding the question to what extent a dispute regarding several obligations under one contract may be brought before the courts of a single State (Case 266/85 (*Shenavai v Kreischer* [1987] ECR 239) or must be brought before the courts of the different States where the relevant obligations are or should have been performed (Case C-420/97 *Leathertex v Bodetex* [1999] ECR I-6747; how to deal with several relevant places of performance within a single State (Case C-386/05 *Color Drack v Lexx* [2007] ECR I-3699) or in different States (in case of air transport, Case C-204/08 *Rehder v Air Baltic* [2009] ECR I-6073; in case of a contract of carriage of goods, Case C-88/17 *Zurich Insurance plc and Metso Minerals Oy v Abnormal Load Services (International) Ltd*) EU:C:2018:558). For a critical analysis of some of the CJEU case law on contract jurisdiction, advocating the old Brussels Convention rule of place of performance of the obligation in question, see P Beaumont and B Yüksel, 'Cross-border Civil and Commercial Disputes Before the Court of Justice of the European Union' in P Beaumont, M Danov, K Trimmings and B Yüksel (eds), *Cross-Border Litigation in Europe* (Hart Publishing 2017) 499, 513–24.

[36] Model Law on the Recognition and Enforcement of Foreign Judgments (n 2).

C. The US Approach in a Federal System

The starting point in any question of personal jurisdiction is very similar in the United States to that in other countries, and generally includes a rule of contract jurisdiction that looks rather similar to those found in systems like the European Union. Whether a case is brought in a state or federal court in the United States, the starting point in the personal jurisdiction analysis normally will be the state 'long-arm' statute. This is the statute setting out the basic rules of personal jurisdiction for the state. Under Federal Rule of Civil Procedure 4, even in a case brought in a federal district court, the state statute will generally govern the question of personal jurisdiction.[37]

State long-arm statutes differ, but generally can be categorised as list-type provisions, providing specific bases of jurisdiction, and constitutional limits statutes, providing that a court in the state can exercise personal jurisdiction to the limits of the Due Process Clause.[38] It is the list-type statute that can look very similar to those found in other countries. For example, the New York long-arm statute provision on contract jurisdiction states:

> Personal Jurisdiction by Acts of Non-domiciliaries
>
> (a) Acts which are the basis of jurisdiction. As to a cause of action arising from any of the acts enumerated in this section, a court may exercise personal jurisdiction over any non-domiciliary, or his executor or administrator, who in person or through an agent:
>
> (1) transacts any business within the state or contracts anywhere to supply goods or services in the state.[39]

Similarly, the Pennsylvania long-arm statute states:

> § 5322. Bases of personal jurisdiction over persons outside this Commonwealth
>
> (a) GENERAL RULE. – A tribunal of this Commonwealth may exercise personal jurisdiction over a person (or the personal representative of a deceased individual who would be subject to jurisdiction under this subsection if not deceased) who acts directly or by an agent, as to a cause of action or other matter arising from such person:
>
> (1) Transacting any business in this Commonwealth. Without excluding other acts which may constitute transacting business in this Commonwealth, any of the following shall constitute transacting business for the purpose of this paragraph:
>
> …
>
> (iii) The shipping of merchandise directly or indirectly into or through this Commonwealth.[40]

Unlike the system of jurisdictional rules in other countries, in the United States the question of personal jurisdiction over a defendant has been infused with a constitutional dimension. Through the Due Process Clauses of both the Fifth and Fourteenth Amendments to the US Constitution, the assertion of jurisdiction by federal and state courts has been limited by analysis of the relationship between the forum state and the defendant. Thus, the Due Process Clauses

[37] Jurisdiction in the federal courts is governed by Rule 4(k) of the Federal Rules of Civil Procedure. This Rule provides three principal jurisdictional authorisations:

> (1) Rule 4(k)(1)(A) authorises a district court to borrow the jurisdictional powers of state courts in the state where it is located;
> (2) Rule 4(k)(1)(C) confirms the availability of any applicable federal statute granting personal jurisdiction; and
> (3) Rule 4(k)(2) grants district courts personal jurisdiction to the limits of the [Fifth Amendment] due process clause in certain federal question cases.

[38] For an example of a constitutional limits statute, see Cal Civ Proc Code Ann § 410.10 ('A court of this state may exercise jurisdiction on any basis not inconsistent with the Constitution of this state or of the United States').

[39] New York Civ Prac L & R § 302 (McKinney's 2010).

[40] 42 Pa Cons Stat Ann § 5301.

restrict the extent to which courts may exercise jurisdiction over a defendant, and the application of the state long-arm statute must be followed by a determination that the jurisdiction asserted, even though consistent with the long-arm statute, does not reach beyond the limits of personal protection afforded by the Due Process Clauses.[41] This is the element that makes it more difficult for the United States to find common ground on global jurisdictional rules. In international negotiations, including the Judgments Convention, it has been discussed under the rubric of 'activity based jurisdiction,' reflecting the jurisprudence of the US Supreme Court in interpreting and applying the Due Process Clauses of the Fifth and Fourteenth Amendments of the US Constitution to jurisdiction questions. Thus, the defendant is considered to have been given due process where that defendant's activities within the forum state are significant enough to justify the exercise of the power of the courts of that state over the defendant – thus satisfying the US constitutional requirement of due process in dealing with that defendant's life, liberty, or property.

D. Looking Forward: Is Convergence on a Contract Rule for Direct Jurisdiction Possible?

A comparison of the systems of the European Union and the United States in relation to rules of contract jurisdiction shows the challenges in arriving at an acceptable default rule of direct jurisdiction in matters of contract. In the US, the connection necessary to justify the exercise of jurisdiction must exist primarily between the defendant and the forum, but also requires a connection to the claim, largely through the activity of the defendant within the forum state. This is usually measured on the basis of a purposeful activity carried out by the defendant in the forum state which has given rise to the claim at stake, subject to further due process control. In Europe, on the other hand, contract jurisdiction is based on a connection between the cause of action and the forum. Jurisdiction tied to the place of performance of the contract or even to the place of performance of the obligation in dispute is considered fair and appropriate *per se* for both parties. Once this link between the claim and the forum exists, no *additional* link between the defendant and the forum must be shown and no additional test as to the appropriateness of the jurisdiction from a due process perspective is needed; the defendant's rights of the defence can still be verified under public policy or as a matter of proper service of process, but these are not considered part of the verification of the foreign court's jurisdiction.[42]

As the Explanatory Report to the 2019 Judgments Convention points out, the rule in Article 5(1)(g) is the result of a compromise between these two approaches.[43] It remains to be seen whether this compromise could form a sufficient basis for further work on a rule of direct jurisdiction. Apart from the Member States of the European Union and the States Party to the Lugano Convention, no State has so far agreed to replace its own domestic contract jurisdiction rule for international cases. Taking into account the benefits of common rules for international legal certainty and supporting international trade, and the desire for a comprehensive multilateral and rule-based international dispute resolution system, the Hague Conference is continuing work to determine whether it is possible to find common ground on this and other bases of jurisdiction in cross-border cases.

[41] For a more detailed discussion of the development of the application of the Due Process Clauses to questions of personal jurisdiction, see RA Brand, *International Business Transactions Fundamentals* (Wolters Kluwer 2019) 289–321.

[42] The application of the public policy test is explicitly prohibited in regard to the rules of jurisdiction (see Art 45(3) of Brussels Ia and Art 35(3) of the Lugano Convention).

[43] See Explanatory Report to the Convention (n 17) para 180.

16

Companies

JOHAN MEEUSEN

I. Introduction

Devoting a chapter to companies in a book on the global unification of private international law shows optimism and ambition. At first sight, the achievements as regards any international, let alone global unification in this field have been remarkably few when compared with other areas of the law that are pertinent for international commerce and trade, such as international arbitration, international sales or international contracts more generally. Still, there is no doubt that international unification would benefit this field, and hence cross-border trade and investment. But while there are some interesting achievements with respect to jurisdiction and recognition and enforcement of judgments, attempts at unification of corporate applicable law rules have failed.

A closer look at the current state of international and regional unification, and the reasons for its failures and successes, can shed further light on the way forward.

II. *Lex societatis*

Corporate applicable law rules determine the *lex societatis*, which typically governs all aspects of a company's legal status, including its formation and dissolution, legal capacity, internal organisation and capital structure, membership and management matters.[1] The major challenge for any unification attempt in this field is the persistent international divergence between the two widely followed applicable law connecting factors.[2]

According to the incorporation theory, which is generally considered to be a liberal and flexible theory that follows an essentially contractual approach and prioritises party autonomy, a company is governed by the law of the country of incorporation. It has its origin in the common law jurisdictions but has been introduced more and more in civil law systems, such as continental European ones. Despite its increasing popularity, its adversaries accuse the incorporation theory of being open to abuse and fraud, in particular through the circumvention of the pertinent rules

[1] See, eg, the scope attributed to the *lex societatis* in the Member States of the European Union: LSE Enterprise, *Study on the Law Applicable to Companies. Final Report* (Brussels, European Commission, 2016) 144 ff.

[2] See for more details, FJ Garcimartín Alférez, 'Cross-Border Listed Companies' (2007) 328 *Hague Collected Courses* 9, 47–58 and P Paschalidis, *Freedom of Establishment and Private International Law for Corporations* (Oxford University Press 2012) 3–14.

and interests of the legal system that companies are closely connected with, from an economic and social perspective, through the location of their headquarters or business activities. For the incorporation theory, no such economic ties with the country of incorporation are, in principle, required.

According to the real seat theory, a company is governed by the law of the country where its 'real seat' is located. This real seat is usually concretised as the place where the company's central management and control are situated. This theory is inspired by territorialism and the traditional concept of the (presumed) closest connection and prioritises the public interests involved, including the protection of third parties. It is also subject to criticism however, for causing legal uncertainty because of the allegedly vague connecting factor and disproportionally restricting party autonomy and cross-border business operations.

It is obvious that bridging the gap between these divergent applicable law approaches constitutes the main challenge for the unification of private international law, but at the same time also its main cause for failure due to the very sensitive character of the choices to be made.

III. (Attempts at) International Unification of Private International Law for Companies

International agreement on corporate conflict of laws can stem from different sources. Bilateral treaties of all sorts, eg, have covered the so-called mutual recognition of companies.[3] Ambitious free trade agreements include provisions on the right of establishment of companies which may impact conflict of laws.[4] International, multilateral unification of corporate private international law has mainly been aimed at by the Hague Conference on Private International Law (HCCH). The Hague Conventions in this field have not been an overall success.

A. Applicable Law

The Hague Convention concerning the recognition of the legal personality of foreign companies, associations and institutions, concluded on 1 June 1956, constituted a first major unification attempt with respect to corporate applicable law, but has never entered into force due to a lack of sufficient ratifications.[5]

While the Convention has – though subject to reservation – a large material scope as regards the entities covered,[6] its subject matter is limited to the recognition of their legal personality, without a more far-reaching applicable law unification.[7] Its recognition system is based on the

[3] R Drury, 'The Regulation and Recognition of Foreign Corporations: Responses to the "Delaware Syndrome"' (1998) 57 *CLJ* 165, 181. See, eg, the bilateral treaties on mutual recognition concluded between the USA and Germany and France respectively (see C Kessedjian, *Droit du commerce international* (Presses Universitaires de France 2013) 121).

[4] KE Sørensen, 'Free Movement of Companies under the New EU Free Trade Agreements' (2016) 13 *European Company Law* 46, 46–55.

[5] For more information on this Convention, see: www.hcch.net/en/instruments/conventions/full-text/?cid=36. While the Convention was drawn up in French only, an unofficial English translation has been published in (1952) 1 *American Journal of Comparative Law* 277.

[6] Companies, associations and foundations.

[7] H Batiffol, 'La reconnaissance des personnes morales étrangères à la septième Conférence de droit international privé de La Haye (1951)' (1948–52) *Trav Com Fr DIP* 137, 145–46; Y Loussouarn, 'La Convention de La Haye sur la reconnaissance des personnes morales étrangères' [1958–59] *Trav Com Fr DIP* 67, 67–69.

incorporation theory, subject to exceptions however for those States that follow the real seat theory (in this case the company's central administration).

The lack of success cannot be explained by any excessive ambition of the Convention drafters or the bold or innovative character of its provisions. The Convention rested on a deliberate[8] but unconvincing compromise between the incorporation and real seat theories and failed to create a sufficient additional value for countries adhering to either of these.[9] This is not only true for the Convention's main rules on recognition, but for its provisions on seat transfers and mergers.[10] The limitation of the Convention's subject matter to the recognition of legal personality is the clearest evidence of 'shocking disagreement' and 'bitter dispute'.[11] A more far-reaching unification fully covering the corporate applicable law rules was an unrealistic undertaking.[12]

Interestingly, two international academic initiatives that took place around the same period managed to go further and develop proposals that also included uniform rules on the determination of the *lex societatis*. Both searched for an appropriate compromise between the two dominant applicable law theories. In 1960, the International Law Association adopted its Draft Convention on Conflicts of Law relating to companies. A company would be governed by the law of the country where it is incorporated. But in the absence of an 'effective connection' between a company and the country in which it is incorporated, the country of its 'place of central administration', ie, its real seat, as well as other real seat countries would be free to apply the law of the place of central administration.[13] In 1965, the Institut de Droit International adopted a resolution on 'Companies in Private International Law' whereby a company is governed by the law of the place of incorporation and must be recognised in all other States as a corporate person. But if the company's 'actual seat' – which conforms to the traditional concept of the real seat – and its principal business activities are elsewhere, the recognition of the company as a corporate person may be refused if its constitution is not in accordance with the law of the country of the actual seat. The same is true when such company has 'no real connection' with the law of the country of incorporation.[14]

B. Jurisdiction and Recognition and Enforcement

The failure of the 1956 Hague Convention contrasts with the success that the HCCH achieved as regards jurisdiction and recognition and enforcement through its 2005 Choice of Court Convention which was concluded on 30 June 2005 and entered into force on 1 October 2015. It has 32 Contracting States, mainly from Europe (following to a large degree from the European Union's accession) but also encompassing Mexico and Singapore, making it the most important international instrument that unifies, to a certain extent, private international law rules with

[8] Loussouarn, ibid, 69.
[9] J Borg-Barthet, *The Governing Law of Companies in EU Law* (Hart Publishing 2012) 6.
[10] Batiffol (n 7) 144.
[11] OA Borum, 'Scandinavian View on the Notion of Recognition of Foreign Companies' in *De conflictu legum: bundel opstellen aangeboden aan Roeland Duco Kollewijn en Johannes Offerhaus ter gelegenheid van hun zeventigste verjaardag* (Sijthoff 1962) 82, 83.
[12] Loussouarn (n 7) 69; G van Hecke, 'Le Droit International des Sociétés et les travaux de la 7ième Conférence de Droit international privé' (1952) 51 *Revue pratique des Sociétés, civiles et commerciales* 161, 162–64.
[13] The Draft Convention's text is published in (1960) 49 *Int'l Ass'n Rep Conf* 62, 93.
[14] The French text of the Resolution is authoritative; the English text is a translation. Both texts are published at the Institute's website: www.idi-iil.org/fr/sessions/warsaw-1965/?post_type=publication. See for more details the preliminary report by the Resolution's reporter van Hecke, 'Les sociétés anonymes en droit international privé' 250–51, as well as TC Drucker, 'Companies in Private International Law' (1968) 17 *ICLQ* 28.

respect to companies. It applies in international cases to exclusive choice of court agreements concluded in civil or commercial matters and governs both jurisdiction on the basis of such agreements and the recognition and enforcement of judgments given by courts designated in such agreements.

The Convention is pertinent for companies, but in a limited way only as it does not apply to the validity, nullity or dissolution of legal persons nor to the validity of decisions of their organs (Article 2(2)(m)). Legal persons are however included in the concept of 'parties' that conclude choice of court agreements. An entity or person other than a natural person is considered 'resident' – which is important to define the international nature of the case for the Convention's jurisdiction rules – in the State where it has its statutory seat, under whose law it was incorporated or formed, where it has its central administration, or where it has its principal place of business (Article 4(2)).

These residence criteria, which are quite similar to the ones used in EU law (see below), appear to be inspired by the desire to include companies' activities as broadly as possible under the Convention's scope.[15] As the Convention's Explanatory Report clarifies, these terms were chosen in order 'to cover all points of view', of both common and civil law systems, for jurisdictional purposes.[16] This explanation, together with the exclusion in Article 2(2)(m), makes clear that the Convention drafters' purpose was, quite understandably, to include civil and commercial litigation involving legal persons as much as possible within its scope of application, in a similar way to disputes involving natural persons.

The Choice of Court Convention avoids the truly sensitive issues of international company law. The same, cautious approach characterises the recent Hague Convention on the recognition and enforcement of foreign judgments in civil or commercial matters, which was concluded on 2 July 2019 but has not yet entered into force. This 'Judgments Convention' has long been awaited, and it is hoped it will become more successful than the earlier 1971 Hague Convention on the same subject.[17] The 1971 Convention has entered into force in five countries only; this limited success is allegedly due to the complexities that result from its bilateralisation mechanism and its interaction with a supplementary Protocol.[18]

According to its Article 2(1)(i), the 2019 Judgments Convention excludes the validity, nullity, or dissolution of legal persons or associations of natural or legal persons as well as the validity of decisions of their organs from its scope. It defines the 'habitual residence' of a legal person as a defendant, which is pertinent as a general jurisdictional basis for determining the judgments eligible for recognition and enforcement (Article 5(1)(a)),[19] through alternative references to the location of the statutory seat, the central administration or the principal place of business of the legal person, or to the State under whose law it was incorporated or formed (Article 3(2)).

[15] Kessedjian (n 3) 108.

[16] T Hartley and M Dogauchi, *Explanatory Report to the Convention of 30 June 2005 on Choice of Court Agreements* (Permanent Bureau of the Hague Conference on Private International Law 2005) paras 119–23. See further on choice of court, Paul Beaumont and Mary Keyes, 'Choice of Court Agreements', ch 28 in this book.

[17] On the Judgments Convention 2019, see David Goddard and Paul Beaumont, 'Recognition and Enforcement of Judgments in Civil or Commercial Matters', ch 29 in this book.

[18] PA Nielsen, 'The Hague 2019 Judgments Convention – from failure to success?' (2020) 16 *Journal of Private International Law* 1, 2–3; H van Loon, 'Towards a global Hague Convention on the Recognition and Enforcement of Foreign Judgments in Civil or Commercial Matters' (2020) 38 *Nederlands Internationaal Privaatrecht (NIPR)* 4, 6–8.

[19] See also Art 5(1)(d): 'eligibility for recognition and enforcement of a judgment if the defendant maintained a branch, agency or other establishment without separate legal personality in the State of origin at the time that person became a party to the proceedings in the court of origin, and the claim on which the judgment is based arose out of the activities of that branch, agency, or establishment'.

IV. (Attempts at) Regional Unification of Private International Law for Companies

Within Europe, several attempts have been undertaken to achieve the unification of (aspects of) private international law for companies but only the European Union (EU) has been partially successful.

The Council of Europe's European Convention on the Establishment of Companies (1966), which aimed at non-discrimination for the companies covered, has not entered into force, having been ratified by Luxembourg only.

In what is now the European Union, Article 220 of the original EEC Treaty (1957) empowered the Member States, so far as necessary, to enter into negotiations with each other to secure for the benefit of their nationals the mutual recognition of companies, the retention of legal personality in the event of cross-border transfer of their seat and the possibility of cross-border mergers. Today, the EU Treaties provide several relevant legal bases for Union action, with respect to both private international law as a component of the EU's 'area of freedom, security and justice' (Articles 67(4) and 81 of the Treaty on the Functioning of the European Union (TFEU)) and companies' right of establishment within the internal market (as recognised by Articles 49 and 54 TFEU). The EU's harmonisation of international company law has however remained limited and disappointing, in particular with respect to applicable law. The Court of Justice of the European Union (CJEU) has, through its interpretation of companies' right of establishment, contributed to the unification of corporate applicable law in the EU. Substantial progress has also been made as regards jurisdiction and recognition and enforcement.

The US legal system of course doesn't rest upon regional integration as envisaged in this chapter, but it provides, due to its federal character, an interesting comparative perspective. Recent developments narrowed the gap between EU and US corporate conflict of laws.

A. Applicable Law

Although the harmonisation of corporate applicable law has often been on the EU's agenda,[20] the EU has not yet adopted any general corporate applicable law legislation, comparable to its Rome I and II Regulations on contract and tort.

The most far-reaching attempt in this respect dates back to 29 February 1968, when the then six Member States signed a Convention on the mutual recognition of companies and bodies corporate. Like the 1956 Hague Convention, this Convention limits itself to the recognition of foreign companies and rests on a compromise between the real seat and incorporation theories. The Convention adopts the incorporation theory as the principal rule for recognition, but allows Member States to declare that they will not (completely) follow this with respect to companies with their central administration outside the EU, if they have no genuine link with its economy, as well as with regard to companies with their central administration on their territory (but in this

[20] See HP Mansel and K Thorn, 'Europäisches Kollisionsrecht 2017: Morgenstunde der Staatsverträge?' (2018) 38 *IPRax* 121, 129 and *Study on the Law Applicable to Companies* (n 1) 294–95. See also the European Council's 'Stockholm Programme' [2010] OJ C115/1, in particular 13 and 16, and the Commission's Action Plan implementing this Stockholm Programme, (COM)2010 171 final, 25.

case limited, in principle, to the essential provisions of its legislation). The Convention has been severely criticised as complicated, ambiguous and falling short of ensuring uniformity.[21] As the Netherlands refused to ratify it, it never entered into force.

To many, the Convention's failure was a great disappointment, which even appeared to increase the distrust between the respective proponents of the real seat and incorporation theories.[22] Possibly, the drafters of the Convention were too timid, as they tried to steer a middle course between existing national approaches to applicable law instead of boldly elaborating a new model for companies that would fit the precise business challenges of economic integration in the EU.[23] Several academic proposals go in that direction. In 2016, GEDIP presented its Draft rules on the law applicable to companies and other bodies: a set of universal corporate applicable law rules which were essentially based upon the incorporation theory but also integrated some nuances and safeguards.[24] A similar preference for the incorporation theory characterised a recent LSE study for the European Commission[25] and, earlier, the proposals by the influential Deutscher Rat für Internationales Privatrecht.[26]

These proposals have not managed to remedy all underlying political conflicts and clear the path for the initiation of pertinent EU legislation. In the absence of such harmonisation, the unification of corporate conflict of laws within the EU has made important progress nevertheless as a result of the CJEU's interpretation of the Treaty provisions on the right of establishment. Divergences between the Member States' non-harmonised corporate applicable law rules may obviously impact companies' right of establishment in the internal market, as laid down in Articles 49 and 54 TFEU. In a series of judgments, from *Avoir fiscal* and *Segers* in the mid-1980s[27] to *Polbud*,[28] the CJEU has examined possible obstructions to companies' freedom of movement.

The Court's approach is characterised by a combination of the recognition of Member State autonomy to decide, as the company's home State, the applicable law rule that determines its *lex societatis* with limitations to this autonomy regarding both companies governed by its *lex societatis* that wish to exercise their outbound freedom of establishment and companies governed by a foreign *lex societatis* that wish to exercise their inbound freedom of establishment. The freedom of establishment under Article 54, read together with Article 49 TFEU, consists in the prohibition of both discrimination and non-discriminatory restrictions, mutual recognition and a distinction between the admissibility of inbound and outbound restrictions respectively that has gradually softened. Of course, this case law cannot serve as a substitute for legislative harmonisation nor has it resulted in a fully consistent 'doctrine' of EU cross-border company law. Still, it has greatly impacted the Member States' corporate applicable law rules as the scope

[21] E Stein, 'Conflict-of-Laws Rules by Treaty: Recognition of Companies in a Regional Market' (1969–70) 68 *Michigan Law Review* 1327, 1344–45.

[22] See, eg, the very critical reactions, in Dutch academic doctrine, to Arts 3 and 4 of the Convention, which were called 'unacceptable', even 'a monstruous construction' and testifying of 'an obsession for the priority of one's own national law' (WCL van der Grinten, 'Erkenning van Vennootschappen en Rechtspersonen in de Europese Economische Gemeenschap' (1966) 14 *Sociaal-Economische Wetgeving* 201, 205–06). With a sense for understatement, J van Rijn van Alkemade called the Convention 'not exactly a milestone of international legal development' ('Het Brusselse verdrag inzake erkenning van vennootschappen en rechtspersonen' (1968) 11 *TVVS* 189, 195).

[23] See the criticism by Stein (n 21) 1352–54.

[24] See: www.gedip-egpil.eu/documents/Milan%202016/GEDIPs%20Proposal%20on%20Companies.pdf.

[25] *Study on the Law Applicable to Companies* (n 1).

[26] HJ Sonnenberger (ed), *Vorschläge und Berichte zur Reform des europäischen und deutschen internationalen Gesellschaftsrechts* (Mohr Siebeck 2007) 69 and 82–83.

[27] 270/83 *Commission v French Republic* ('Avoir fiscal') EU:C:1986:37; 79/85 *DHM Segers* EU:C:1986:308.

[28] C-106/16 *Polbud* EU:C:2017:804.

of freedom of establishment under the TFEU is very broad and stretches from the recognition of legal personality to cross-border seat transfers, conversions and mergers.[29]

The incorporation theory, with its focus on party autonomy, flexibility and commercial freedom, is considered a better fit with the intra-EU freedom of movement than the stricter, territorially inspired real seat theory. Still, the CJEU has systematically refused to consider the latter theory, at least if applied unilaterally, to be incompatible with the EU Treaties. Take, eg, the *Polbud* judgment, in which the CJEU confirmed that companies' right of establishment extends to cross-border conversion through the sole transfer of the registered office and so enhanced regulatory competition in the internal market.[30] While this far-reaching interpretation of the right of establishment undoubtedly has a negative impact on the political attractiveness of the real seat theory, the Court nevertheless emphasised the compatibility of both the real seat and incorporation theories with EU law.[31]

This consistent confirmation of the compatibility of the traditional corporate applicable law approaches used in the Member States with companies' freedom of establishment, rests on a remarkable interpretation of Article 54 TFEU which the CJEU first developed in *Daily Mail*. Article 54 refers to the location of a company's registered office, central administration or principal place of business within the Union as the delimitation factor for the scope *ratione personae* of freedom of establishment. According to the Court, however, this provision takes into account the variety in Member States' legislation as regards the connecting factor for applicable law purposes. In the absence of harmonisation, the definition of the connecting factor that determines the *lex societatis* falls within the power of each Member State, and Article 54 is interpreted as having placed on the same footing the registered office, the central administration and the principal place of business of a company or firm as such connecting factors.[32] This quite diplomatic interpretation has allowed the CJEU to play it safe and avoid the evaluation of the compatibility with EU law of the Member States' divergent applicable law approaches. All of the Member States' corporate applicable law rules are considered to have a Treaty basis and hence to be, per se, compatible with EU law. What remains to be checked, of course, are the potentially restrictive effects of their *application* to corporate mobility in the internal market, and that examination has been the subject of many CJEU judgments.

The direct impact of the CJEU's judgments consists in the compulsory adaptation, due to the supremacy of EU law, by the Member States of their corporate applicable law rules. When applying their rules, they must avoid any restriction of companies' freedom of establishment. The *Polbud* case not only impacts the application of the real seat theory but has important consequences as well for States adhering to the incorporation theory, as they are traditionally hesitant to accept reincorporation with continuing legal personality through the mere relocation of the statutory seat or registered office.[33] Another example is the *Überseering* case, which obliged a

[29] For an overview of the CJEU's case law, see J Meeusen and M Myszke-Nowakowska, 'International Company Law in the European Internal Market: Three Decades of Judicial Activity' in L Nemer Caldeira Brant (ed), *XI Anuário Brasileiro de Direito Internacional – Vol II* (CEDIN 2016) 92, 92–135.

[30] See for more details, J Meeusen, '*Polbud*: new perspectives for corporate mobility in the internal market' in B Hess, E Jayme and HP Mansel (eds), *Europa als Rechts- und Lebensraum. Liber amicorum für Christian Kohler zum 75. Geburtstag am 18. Juni 2018* (Verlag Ernst und Werner Gieseking 2018) 313, 319–27.

[31] *Polbud* (n 28) para 34.

[32] 81/87 *ex parte Daily Mail and General Trust plc* EU:C:1988:456, paras 20–21; C-210/06 *Cartesio* EU:C:2008:723, para 106; and *Polbud* (n 28) para 34.

[33] J Kokott and S Jund, 'Les sociétés peuvent-elles circuler librement au sein du marché intérieur? L'apport de la jurisprudence de la Cour de justice' in P Paschalidis and J Wildemeersch (eds), *L'Europe au présent! Liber amicorum Melchior Wathelet* (Bruylant 2018) 523, 542–43. For more details on the Member States' approach to reincorporation see *Study on the Law Applicable to Companies* (n 1) 215 ff.

Member State that adhered to the real seat theory (Germany) to recognise the legal capacity, and consequently the capacity to bring legal proceedings, of a company validly incorporated according to the law of its home State (the Netherlands) and exercising its freedom of establishment in the host State to which it had transferred its real seat (central administration).[34] The *Überseering* judgment entails the obligation for any Member State that applies the real seat theory to determine the *lex societatis*, not on the basis of a multilateral applicable law rule, but on the basis of a unilateral applicable law rule that solely determines the *lex societatis* for the companies formed in accordance with its own law. For all companies incorporated in accordance with the law of another Member State, their *lex societatis* and legal personality as determined according to that law, must be recognised. The Court said that 'a necessary precondition for the exercise of the freedom of establishment is the recognition of those companies by any Member State in which they wish to establish themselves'.[35]

The unification achieved by the CJEU is only 'functional' as its ambition is not to develop the Member States' private international law regimes. It is not possible for a court to introduce a complete and coherent 'system' of applicable law rules. The CJEU only interprets the Treaty provisions on companies' right of establishment, ensuring that it is not restricted (eg, by the Member States' non-harmonised private international law rules) for those companies governed by it. The inevitable consequence is that the development of the EU Member States' private international law regimes, insofar as the freedom of establishment is affected, is not so much determined by objectives that are proper to conflict of laws, but rather by the objectives of EU integration. This is very well illustrated by the CJEU's judgment in *Centros*.[36] When analysed from a traditional conflict of laws perspective, this judgment could be subject to criticism for essentially prohibiting the application of the law which was most closely connected. Judged from the perspective of freedom of establishment, however, the judgment makes more sense. The Court's recourse to the logic of the internal market, rather than that of private international law, may be regretted by conflicts scholars. Yet, they might welcome the upside of this approach: an unprecedented partial unification of private international law for (currently) 27 States.

The CJEU's interpretation of companies' freedom of establishment has increased the attractiveness of the incorporation theory. Through its case law, culminating in *Polbud*, the CJEU has transformed the internal market into a so-called market for corporate charters, governed by regulatory competition. Apart from the direct obligations that follow from the pertinent Treaty provisions, this may inspire Member States to voluntarily adapt their corporate applicable law rules to strengthen their own position in that market, or even beyond. While the popularity among the Member States of the incorporation theory gradually increased to the disadvantage of the real seat theory,[37] the CJEU's case law has intensified this evolution. Belgium, eg, recently replaced its traditional adherence to the real seat theory by a strict, very liberal statutory seat approach to promote Belgian company law in the international competition for corporate charters, which was explained by the Belgian government as an inevitable consequence of the freedom of establishment as interpreted by the CJEU.[38] Other EU Member States may follow suit, and so strengthen *de facto* the regional unification of corporate applicable law.

[34] C-208/00 *Überseering* EU:C:2002:632.

[35] *Überseering*, ibid, para 59.

[36] C-212/97 *Centros* EU:C:1999:126.

[37] The strong position which the incorporation theory currently enjoys within the EU has been clearly identified: *Study on the Law Applicable to Companies* (n 1) 117 ff.

[38] See for more details, R Houben and J Meeusen, 'The competition for corporate charters: Belgium wants a (bigger) piece of the pie' (2020) 29 *Zeitschrift für Europäisches Privatrecht* 11, 25–46.

It must be added, though, that a complete 'victory' of the incorporation theory is very unlikely, as concerns will remain about the precise balance between liberalisation and party autonomy on the one hand and countervailing legitimate public interests on the other. A first important element is that the EU has, through so-called company directives, harmonised to a certain extent relevant Member States' substantive law provisions. And even apart from legislative intervention, the internal market does not rest upon a model of absolute liberalisation. Even in its liberal *Polbud* judgment, the CJEU still recognised, subject to the requirement of proportionality, the importance of the objectives of protecting the interests of creditors, minority shareholders and employees of the company concerned and of preventing or penalising fraud.[39]

Although it has a reputation of liberalism in corporate conflict of laws, similar debates remain in the United States. The traditional US preference for the incorporation theory with respect to a company's 'internal affairs', see the Restatement (Second) of Conflict of Laws and the enormous popularity of incorporation in Delaware, is not absolute either. States often take recourse to so-called 'qualification statutes', according to which foreign corporations doing business there are obliged to register, and typically to provide the host state with particular information, pay a fee and consent to its jurisdiction.[40] From a constitutional perspective, a qualification statute is accepted insofar as its scope is limited to the foreign corporation's involvement in intrastate commerce in the host state.[41] Moreover, states such as California and New York have adopted 'outreach legislation' which regulates particular aspects of the internal affairs of so-called 'pseudo-foreign companies' and hence treats them in certain respects as domestic corporations.[42] In particular since its judgment in *CTS Corp v Dynamic Corp of America*, where the US Supreme Court appeared to grant constitutional status to the incorporation theory and emphasised that the corporate free market system depends at its core upon the fact that a corporation 'except in the rarest situations' is governed by the law of a single jurisdiction,[43] the application of forum law to a foreign corporation's internal affairs is controversial. Still, academic doctrine accepts that the host state can exercise well-tailored control over foreign companies that have substantial contacts with it.[44]

B. Jurisdiction and Recognition and Enforcement

The regional unification of private international law for companies in the EU also encompasses, through the Brussels Ia Regulation,[45] jurisdiction and recognition and enforcement going further than the international unification by the pertinent Hague Conventions.

[39] *Polbud* (n 28) paras 54 and 61.

[40] C Kersting, 'Corporate Choice of Law – A Comparison of the United States and European Systems and a Proposal for a European Directive' (2002) 28 *Brooklyn Journal of International Law* 1, 16 ff; P Hay, PJ Borchers and RD Freer, *Conflict of Laws, Private International Law, Cases and Materials*, 15th edn (Foundation Press 2017) 1142.

[41] Kersting, ibid, 22–24.

[42] R Drury, 'A European Look at the American Experience of the Delaware Syndrome' (2005) 5 *Journal of Corporate Law Studies* 1, 16 ff; Kersting, ibid, 25ff; Hay, Borchers and Freer (n 40) 1161–63.

[43] 481 US 69 (1987).

[44] Kersting (n 40) 31–36; EF Scoles, P Hay, PJ Borchers and SC Symeonides, *Conflict of Laws*, 4th edn (Thomson West 2004) 1233; Hay, Borchers and Freer (n 40) 1170–71.

[45] Regulation (EU) No 1215/2012 of the European Parliament and of the Council of 12 December 2012 on jurisdiction and the recognition and enforcement of judgments in civil and commercial matters (recast). Reference should be made to the Lugano Convention, which is very similar to the Brussels I Regulation (44/2001) and applies to the EU States, Iceland, Switzerland and Norway (Convention on jurisdiction and the recognition and enforcement of judgments in civil and commercial matters, Lugano, 30 October 2007; [2007] OJ L339/3). On 8 April 2020, the UK deposited its application

In the same vein as the 2005 Choice of Court Convention and the 2019 Judgments Convention, the Brussels Ia Regulation applies to natural and legal persons, including companies. This means that the latter are subject to the same rules as natural persons. As a result, the Brussels Ia Regulation applies to much litigation in civil and commercial matters that involves companies, eg, concerning typical claims of a contractual or tortious nature but as well on more particular issues such as the precise characterisation and effects of a choice of forum clause in a company's statutes.[46] Article 7(5) is a special jurisdictional rule regarding disputes arising out of the operations of a branch, agency or other establishment, granting jurisdiction to the courts for the place where the branch, agency or other establishment is situated.

The Brussels Ia Regulation grants a central place to the defendant's domicile, which (in principle) determines the applicability of the Regulation's jurisdiction rules and also constitutes a key criterion for jurisdiction itself. Article 63 gives an autonomous definition of a company's domicile, according to which a company is domiciled at the place where it has its statutory seat, central administration or principal place of business.[47] While this means that a company could have up to three domiciles in the sense of this Regulation,[48] the autonomous definition is consistent with the global approach in the 2005 and 2019 Hague Conventions and forms the basis for an important progressive unification of jurisdiction rules in actions against companies.

Further, Article 24(2) of the Brussels Ia Regulation holds a rule of exclusive jurisdiction with respect to a company's organisational, or internal, affairs. In proceedings which have as their object, ie, principal subject matter,[49] the validity of the constitution, the nullity or the dissolution of companies, or the validity of the decision of their organs, exclusive jurisdiction belongs with the courts of the Member State in which the company has its seat. If the exclusive jurisdiction is violated, recognition and enforcement can be refused (Article 45(1)(e)(ii) and Article 46). Somewhat surprisingly, and subject to criticism,[50] the seat in the sense of Article 24(2) is not defined autonomously, eg, by reference to the definition of Article 63, which would fit the exclusive character of the jurisdiction through the concentration of litigation.[51] Article 24(2) explicitly mentions that the court must apply its rules of private international law to determine the seat. Contrary to what would be the possible effect of an autonomous definition, such reference enhances the chances for the competent court to apply its *lex fori*.[52]

Although the EU's positive jurisdiction rules are absent in the US, which just has constitutional limits on jurisdiction rules that can be applied by the states, their respective approaches to jurisdiction have recently grown closer.

The US Supreme Court considers an individual's domicile as the paradigm forum for the exercise of so-called 'general jurisdiction' and stated in *Goodyear* that 'for a corporation, it is an equivalent place, one in which the corporation is fairly regarded as at home'.[53] In that same

to accede to the Lugano Convention, see: www.eda.admin.ch/dam/eda/fr/documents/aussenpolitik/voelkerrecht/autres-conventions/Lugano2/200414-LUG_en.pdf. On 28 June 2021, the EU notified the Convention's depository that it was not in a position to give its consent to invite the UK to accede to the Lugano Convention.

[46] C-214/89 *Powell Duffryn plc* EU:C:1992:115.

[47] Compare the quite similar concretisation of a company's (habitual) residence in the 2005 and 2019 Hague Conventions mentioned above. Art 63(2) further adds that for the purposes of Ireland, Cyprus and (former Member State) the United Kingdom, 'statutory seat' means the registered office or, where there is no such office anywhere, the place of incorporation or, where there is no such place anywhere, the place under the law of which the formation took place.

[48] TC Hartley, *International Commercial Litigation*, 2nd edn (Cambridge University Press 2015) 27–28.

[49] C-144/10 *Berliner Verkehrsbetriebe* EU:C:2011:300, para 44.

[50] Paschalidis (n 2) 22–23.

[51] See MV Benedettelli, 'Conflicts of Jurisdiction and Conflicts of Law in Company Law Matters Within the EU "Market for Corporate Models": Brussels I and Rome I after *Centros*' (2005) 16 *European Business Law Review* 55, 60.

[52] See P Mankowski, 'Artikel 24 Brüssel Ia-VO' in T Rauscher (ed), *Europäisches Zivilprozess- und Kollisionsrecht EuZPR/EuIPR – Band I* (Verlag dr. Otto Schmidt KG 2016, 4th edn) 614, 650–51.

[53] 564 US 915 (2011).

judgment, a unanimous Supreme Court introduced a new standard for general jurisdiction, as stated in the opinion of Justice Ginsburg: 'A court may assert general jurisdiction over foreign ... corporations to hear any and all claims against them when their affiliations with the State are so "continuous and systematic" as to render them essentially at home in the forum State', which was clarified by a reference to Brilmayer's identification of the corporation's place of incorporation and principal place of business as the paradigm bases of general jurisdiction. In the subsequent judgment in *Daimler*, the Supreme Court confirmed the 'at home' test, but added in a footnote that it did not foreclose the possibility that 'in an exceptional case' a corporation's operations in a forum other than its formal place of incorporation or principal place of business may be so substantial and of such a nature as to render the corporation at home in that state.[54] In spite of this exception, which the Court has not yet further explained, the new test serves to limit the number of available fora.[55] Taken together with the Supreme Court's quite narrow approach to specific jurisdiction, it is clear that the options for plaintiffs in corporate litigation have been reduced.[56]

This new US standard for general jurisdiction, and hence the rejection of the former, very broad 'doing business' jurisdiction ground which found no equivalent in EU law and had been subject to harsh criticism from an international perspective,[57] brings the US approach much closer to the EU rules on jurisdiction with respect to corporations.[58] Certainly, the two regimes are not identical, and further differences could perhaps stem from the search for alternative general jurisdiction grounds which the US Supreme Court would still be willing to accept.[59] It is remarkable that the Supreme Court in *Daimler* referred to the pertinent EU jurisdiction ground of corporate domicile as understood in the Brussels Ia Regulation and explicitly linked the concerns of international comity to the due process demands of 'fair play and substantial justice', which it had earlier developed as the crucial standard in *International Shoe*.[60] It referred to the risks which an expansive view of general jurisdiction may entail for the success of negotiations of international agreements on the reciprocal recognition and enforcement of judgments – an unmistakable reference to the then pending negotiations on the Hague Judgments Convention and an equally clear recognition of the importance of international unification in this field, in spite of the constraints imposed by the US Constitution.[61]

V. Outlook: From Unification to Coordination, and from Rules to Principles

The global unification of private international law for companies is not a success story. The international unification of corporate applicable law rules has failed, while some, but only limited

[54] 571 US 117 (2014).

[55] See K Roosevelt, *Conflict of Laws*, 2nd edn (Foundation Press 2015) 186–87 and the critical observations by SC Symeonides, 'Choice of Law in the American Courts in 2017: Thirty-First Annual Survey' (2018) 66 *American Journal of Comparative Law* 1, 8–9 after the Supreme Court's continued restrictive approach in *BNSF Ry Co v Tyrrell* 137 SCt 1549 (2017).

[56] LJ Silberman, '*Daimler AG v Bauman*: A new era for judicial jurisdiction in the United States' (2014–15) 16 *Yearbook of Private International Law* 9 and 12–14.

[57] See, eg, FK Juenger, 'A Shoe Unfit for Globetrotting' (1994–95) 28 *UC Davis Law Review* 1027, 1040–41.

[58] *cf* H Muir-Watt, 'Le droit international privé au service de la géopolitique: les enjeux de la nouvelle Convention de La Haye du 2 juillet 2019 sur la reconnaissance et l'exécution des jugements étrangers en matière civile ou commerciale' (2020) 109 *Revue critique de droit international privé* 427, 444.

[59] See, in particular, the very controversial 'consent-by-registration' jurisdiction: courts sometimes admit it on basis of compliance with States' qualification or registration statutes but academic doctrine often rejects it as unconstitutional. See, for more information on this topic and further references, Silberman (n 56) 19–22.

[60] 326 US 310 (1945).

[61] *cf* FK Juenger, 'American Jurisdiction: A Story of Comparative Neglect' (1993–94) 65 *University of Colorado Law Review* 1, 22–23.

results have been achieved with respect to jurisdiction and recognition and enforcement through the HCCH. A certain measure of regional unification has been achieved by the EU.

The lack of global unification is probably due to reasons germane to the field of company law, and its international aspects. Company law finds its roots in societal and economic approaches that differ from country to country and have been linked to the national cultural identity of each State.[62] Companies obviously fulfil a major societal role, especially economic. Their legal governance affects the very diverse interests of a great variety of stakeholders. Apart from the obvious interests of shareholders, managers and employees, other private interests (eg, of creditors, consumers and affiliated companies) and major public (governmental) interests are at stake as well. National policy choices, which can differ over time, carry great weight, which tends to impede unification.

The absence of a convincing conciliation between the real seat and incorporation theories obviously constitutes a major obstruction for any international unification of corporate applicable law.[63] The failure of several initiatives, resting upon a principled choice for the incorporation theory with exceptions inspired by the real seat theory, shows that a convincing balance between the interests involved is hard to find.[64]

It does not seem realistic to build any hopes for global unification upon the growing popularity of the incorporation theory. It started as a logical complement to the post-war process of economic reconstruction, liberalisation of cross-border investment and trade and the emergence of multinational enterprises.[65] But so many decades of European economic integration, with a prominent spot for companies' freedom of establishment, have not even convinced all EU Member States to abandon the real seat theory.[66] Within the EU, the increasing focus on regulatory competition in this domain, as stimulated in particular by the CJEU's judgments in *Centros* and *Polbud*, together with the ever-growing recognition of party autonomy will certainly further stimulate the attractiveness of the incorporation theory. But as the failed attempts of corporate applicable law harmonisation in the EU illustrate, even (mere) regional unification in a context of far-reaching economic integration and mutual trust is not feasible.

Although liberalisation and party autonomy obviously are values that are recognised far beyond the EU, these European experiences do not point towards any swift international consensus in favour of unification on the basis of the incorporation theory. There are two reasons for this. First, the rivalry between the two dominant applicable law approaches has become a conflict between symbols which are practically impossible to conciliate. The reality, however, is much more nuanced as many countries adhere to a mixed approach. Countries that follow the real seat theory, eg, permit, under certain conditions, the cross-border transfer of the company seat, while many countries that adhere to the incorporation theory are concerned about excessive liberalisation and have developed safeguards against abuse and fraud (eg, rules on 'pseudo-foreign companies').[67] While the search for a convincing balance between the various interests at stake is difficult and delicate within a single, national system of company law, this is even more so in an international context where symbols matter. Second, one must not be misled by the CJEU's case law on companies' right of establishment, which entails extensive 'judicial harmonisation'

[62] M Koutsias, 'Corporate domicile and residence' in P Stone and Y Farah (eds), *Research Handbook on EU Private International Law* (Edward Elgar 2017) 344, 377–78.

[63] Drury (n 3) 182–83.

[64] Ibid, 193–94.

[65] See Stein (n 21) 1335; GA van Hecke, 'Nationality of Companies Analysed' (1961) 9 *Nederlands Tijdschrift voor Internationaal Recht* 223, 227–28.

[66] See *Study on the Law Applicable to Companies* (n 1) 117 ff.

[67] See Garcimartín Alférez (n 2) 55–58.

of corporate conflict of laws and has given a boost to the incorporation theory. The functional character of this development within the framework of the internal market should not be lost sight of. The CJEU's very liberal interpretation of cross-border reincorporation in *Polbud* may be justified by the requirements of the internal market, but quite different concerns are at stake at a global level.

There is currently no miracle solution that would create global consensus on the adoption of a single applicable law rule. As the HCCH's and EU's experiences demonstrate, even nuanced solutions that search for a compromise between the real seat and incorporation theories or that assign only a limited scope to uniform rules, are unable to generate sufficient agreement.

Within the EU, the recognition of companies' right of establishment has been paired with tolerance for the Member States' divergent applicable law rules. Member States accept that while they may maintain in principle their own, often long held applicable law approach, they are obliged under EU law to adapt its application to the requirements of the internal market. This essentially means that they are prepared to accept a coordination of their own applicable law approach with that of the other Member States, in particular through mutual recognition and the prohibition, subject to justification under precise conditions, of discriminatory and non-discriminatory restrictions.

This search for coordination, rather than unification, could be a promising path at the international level. Why indeed not lower the ambitions to a more realistic level, one that would be within reach, and aim at agreement on a number of 'principles of coordination' to enhance smooth cross-border corporate activities?

Academic doctrine has proposed a very interesting set of such principles for the EU's internal market.[68] As to this technique, inspiration could also be drawn from the Hague Principles on Choice of Law in International Commercial Contracts which, as the Preamble mentions, may be used as a model for national, regional, supranational or international instruments.

Such Principles could be an interesting instrument to reach some international consensus on corporate applicable law. Putting the focus first on practical solutions, adopted on the basis of reciprocity, coupled with flexibility as to the precise principles that interested States would adopt, could be the basis for a step-by-step approach to generate trust and reach international agreement.

At the basis of these Principles should be the idea that whatever approach States follow with respect to the valid constitution of companies governed by their own law, it is only the cross-border action of these companies that is of interest to other States. Moreover, the Principles should recognise that the involvement of companies in another State's legal system can be more or less extensive: access to its courts, the capacity to conclude contracts, the transfer of its real seat or that of its statutory seat – all raise different concerns and therefore may be subject to different legal treatment.

One should not be naive. The identification of such principles of coordination inevitably rests on a political assessment of priorities, typically those of party autonomy and economic gain on the one hand and those of the general interest and the protection of all parties involved on the other. Moreover, such assessment will probably be different in a context of narrow economic cooperation, as opposed to more traditional international collaboration in the field of private international law which typically puts international harmony and legal certainty first. Nevertheless, the search for flexible and practical Principles could be an attractive and effective alternative to yet another attempt to reach agreement on unified, binding rules of corporate applicable law.

[68] See the four 'Community Law Criteria for the Coordination of the Company Laws of the Member States' as proposed by Benedettelli (n 51) 65–66.

17

Competition Law Enforcement: Private International Law and Access to Effective Legal Remedies in Cross-Border Cases

MIHAIL DANOV AND CARMEN OTERO GARCÍA-CASTRILLÓN

I. Introduction

Competition law is 'one of the most commonly deployed instruments to regulate the operation of markets and is a standard feature of economic policy in developed and developing countries alike'.[1] Its aims include safeguarding consumers' welfare and ensuring that markets function efficiently.[2] In comparison with Private International Law (PIL), competition law might be regarded as a relatively new legal discipline. Some recent comparative datasets show that many countries have now adopted competition laws.[3] Could an appropriate level of international cooperation ensure that various legitimate regulatory objectives and interests are adequately pursued and sufficiently safeguarded in cross-border competition law cases? What should be the role of PIL[4] and the Hague Conference on PIL (HCCH)?

In spite of some recent waves of national protectionism and populism,[5] cross-border trade continues to be actively promoted by the World Trade Organisation (WTO)[6] as well as by multilateral[7] and bilateral[8] trade agreements, including the recent EU-UK Trade and Cooperation Agreement.[9] The legal framework facilitating cross-border trade incentivises companies to adopt a multinational governance structure to efficiently optimise their international economic

[1] A Bradford et al, 'Competition law gone Global: Introducing the comparative competition law and enforcement datasets' (2019) 16 *Journal of Empirical Studies* 411, 411–12.

[2] FH Easterbrook, 'Limits of Antitrust' (1984) 63 *Texas Law Review* 1. See also Communication from the Commission Notice Guidelines on the application of Article 81(3) of the Treaty [2004] OJ C101/97 [33].

[3] Bradford et al (n 1).

[4] M Danov, 'Global Competition Law Framework: A Private International Law Solution Needed' (2016) 12 *Journal of Private International Law* 77.

[5] R Eatwell and M Goodwin, *National Populism: The Revolt Against Liberal Democracy* (Penguin 2018).

[6] Final Act embodying the results of the Uruguay Round of Multilateral Trade Negotiations, available at: www.wto.org/english/docs_e/legal_e/legal_e.htm.

[7] eg, Canada, Mexico and United States Free Trade Agreement (NAFTA); Brunei, Indonesia, Malaysia, Philippines, Singapore, Thailand. Vietnam, Laos, Myanmar and Cambodia Southeast Asian States Free Trade Area (ASEAN).

[8] eg, EU–Canada Comprehensive Trade and Economic Agreement (CETA); EU–Mexico Trade Agreement.

[9] Trade and Cooperation Agreement between the European Union and The European Atomic Energy Community, of the One Part, and the United Kingdom of Great Britain and Northern Ireland, of the Other Part [2021] OJ L149/10 (EU–UK Trade and Cooperation Agreement).

activities. Transnational supply chains are established by companies to maximise efficiencies and profits.

If some multinational companies decide to engage in anti-competitive business practices, they can use their transnational supply chains to adversely affect the process of competition across the globe.[10] The relationship between the rules facilitating market access and the effectiveness of the relevant competition policies was reflected in the EU–UK Trade and Cooperation Agreement title XI – 'Level Playing Field for Open and Fair Competition and Sustainable Development', with a specific chapter on 'Competition Policy'.[11] These developments signify the importance of the issues in relation to competition law enforcement and cooperation in cross-border cases.[12]

The connection between PIL and competition law needs to be thoroughly considered to facilitate injured parties' access to legal remedies in cross-border cases. In order to safeguard national and regional regulatory interests – whilst facilitating injured parties' access to justice in such cases – it is essential for the international community to attain an adequate level of cooperation with regard to competition law matters. PIL rules may be central to the effective enforcement of national/regional competition laws, not least because very many economic activities are transnational in nature, with the relevant infringements causing harm in different jurisdictions.

States should cooperate with a view to effectively regulating the competition law aspects of cross-border economic activities,[13] but there is a notable lack of an appropriate multilateral mechanism.[14] Even if certain international norms are agreed, they are not compulsory.[15] Whilst it is universally established that anti-competitive practices should be deterred,[16] there is no multilateral mechanism to facilitate international cooperation. Instead, there are some bilateral agreements facilitating cooperation between the national competition authorities[17] and recently one example of some substantive law principles and provisions in place.[18]

More importantly, the definition of 'enforcement activities'[19] provided in bilateral agreements indicates that international cooperation is limited to collaborations between public-administrative competition authorities (ie, regulators) in different jurisdictions. Cooperation is primarily in the area of 'Global Administrative Law',[20] eg, the EU–UK Trade and Cooperation Agreement's cooperation arrangements, involve 'the European Commission or the competition authorities of the Member States, on the one side, and the United Kingdom's competition authority or authorities,

[10] cp: *Motorola Mobility LLC v AU Optronics Corp* 775 F3d 816, 824 (7th Cir, 2015) and *The LCD Appeals* [2018] EWCA Civ 220.

[11] See Chapter two of Title XI of Part Two of the EU–UK Trade and Cooperation Agreement. See specifically Art 359(1) from the EU–UK Trade and Cooperation Agreement.

[12] See Arts 360 and 361 from the EU–UK Trade and Cooperation Agreement.

[13] WTO working group on competition at the Singapore Ministerial Declaration (13 December 1996, WT/MIN(96)/DEC) and OECD Council Recommendation concerning Cooperation between Member Countries on Anticompetitive Practices affecting International Trade (27 July 1995, OECD/LEGAL/0280).

[14] C Otero García-Castrillón, 'Private Parties WTO (Bilateralist) Competition Regime' (2001) 35 *Journal of World Trade Law* 99.

[15] eg, The 1980 United Nations Set of Multilaterally Agreed Equitable Principles and Rules for the Control of Restrictive Business Practices (UN Set).

[16] The UN Set: Section D – Principles and Rules for enterprises, including transnational corporations.

[17] eg, Agreement between the Government of the United States of America and the Commission of the European Communities regarding the application of their competition laws (US/EC Agreement) [1995] OJ L95/47. The relevant agreements within the EU are listed. See the European Commission, 'Bilateral relations on competition issues', available at: ec.europa.eu/competition/international/bilateral/index.html.

[18] See Arts 358 and 359 from the EU–UK Trade and Cooperation Agreement.

[19] eg, Art I(2) C) of the US/EU Agreement.

[20] JP Terhechte, *International Competition Enforcement Law Between Cooperation and Convergence* (Springer 2011) 77.

on the other side'.[21] The Agreement has no appropriate mechanism for judicial cooperation in antitrust matters.[22]

There is a major gap in the existing framework for cross-border judicial cooperation on allocation of jurisdiction, avoiding parallel proceedings and the recognition and enforcement of judgments in relation to competition claims. Devising an appropriate framework for judicial civil cooperation is central to facilitating access to justice.[23] The allocation of adjudicatory and regulatory jurisdiction and coordination of related proceedings would be at the heart of any system for judicial cooperation in relation to competition law matters.

The territorial scope of competition law has been analysed from the perspective of States' jurisdiction to prescribe.[24] Regulatory jurisdiction is associated with the universally accepted territoriality principle. In order to attain certain territorial objectives, the well-known effects doctrine was advanced in line with 'Curries' governmental interest analysis'.[25] The effects test provides the basis for the regulatory jurisdiction of individual legal orders to interplay with the territorial scope of the relevant national/regional competition laws.[26] A major feature of competition law provisions is that they often apply extraterritorially.[27]

The extraterritorial application of competition law may be legitimately justified because the conduct of an undertaking based in one jurisdiction may often adversely affect the trade (and the process of competition as well as consumers' welfare) in another jurisdiction.[28] Extraterritoriality is a common attribute of competition laws in more than 60 jurisdictions.[29] Extraterritorial effect is accepted in public-administrative proceedings before regulators[30] as well as in antitrust damages proceedings before national courts.[31]

In some systems adjudicatory jurisdiction in a cross-border competition law dispute can be retained where the court is *forum conveniens* or declined where it is *forum non conveniens*.[32] Adjudicatory jurisdiction 'is not a separate type of jurisdiction, but merely an emanation of the international jurisdiction to legislate ... a state's right of regulation is exercised by legislative jurisdiction which includes adjudication'.[33] A specific feature of competition law is that such

[21] See Art 361(2) from the EU–UK Trade and Cooperation Agreement.

[22] cp: the EU–UK Trade and Cooperation Agreement's Part Three: Law Enforcement and Judicial Cooperation in Criminal Matters. See also, Communication from the Commission to the European Parliament and the Council, Assessment on the application of the United Kingdom of Great Britain and Northern Ireland to accede to the 2007 Lugano Convention, COM(2021) 222 final.

[23] Prel Doc No 2 of December 2018, 'The possible exclusion of anti-trust matters from the Convention as reflected in Article 2(1)(p) of the 2018 draft Convention', 22nd Diplomatic Session of The Hague Conference on Private International Law. cp: Terhechte (n 20) 17.

[24] C Otero García-Castrillón, 'El alcance extraterritorial del derecho de la competencia y su utilización como medida comercial' (2001) *Gaceta Jurídica de la Unión Europea y de la Competencia* 34.

[25] HH Kay, 'A defense of Currie's governmental interest analysis' (1989) 215 *Hague Collected Courses* 9–204.

[26] *LCD Appeals* (n 10) [91]. See also *Timberlane Lumber Co v Bank of America* 549 F2d 597, 610 (9th Cir, 1976); Joined cases 89, 104, 114, 116, 117 and 125 to 129/85 *Ahlström Osakeyhtiö v Commission* EU:C:1988:447; C-413/14 P *Intel v Commission* EU:C:2017:632 [49]; Arts 3(1)(b) and 26 of the Treaty on the Functioning of the European Union (TFEU).

[27] Bradford et al (n 1) 423.

[28] EM Fox, 'Linked-In: Antitrust and the Virtues of a Virtual Network' (2009) *The International Lawyer* 151, 154; FW Papp, 'Competition law and extraterritoriality' in A Ezrachi (ed), *Research Handbook on International Competition Law* (Edward Elgar 2012) 21, 22.

[29] This amounts to over 50% of Bradford's datasets (n 1) 423.

[30] *Intel* (n 26). See also J Basedow, 'Conflicts of Economic Regulation' (1994) 42 *American Journal of Comparative Law* 432.

[31] *LCD Appeals* (n 10).

[32] *F Hoffmann-La Roche Ltd v Empagran* (2004) 542 US 155, 165 (Sup Ct (US)); *Iiyama UK Ltd v Samsung Electronics Co Ltd* [2016] EWHC 1980 (Ch); and *Iiyama UK Ltd v Schott AG* [2016] EWHC 1207 (Ch).

[33] FA Mann, 'The doctrine of international jurisdiction revisited after twenty years' (1984) 186 *Hague Collected Courses* 67.

adjudicatory jurisdiction may be exercised by regulators in public enforcement proceedings (ie, administrative adjudication)[34] as well as by national courts in private antitrust damages proceedings (ie, judicial adjudication). Since the precise determination of whether specific conduct is to be classified as anti-competitive is often to be ascertained by national/regional regulators applying their own competition laws, the distinction between the adjudicatory jurisdiction and the regulatory jurisdiction has been blurred in public enforcement proceedings.

PIL has an important role to play in promoting international cooperation and closing the regulatory gap in relation to judicial cooperation in a global context. PIL offers a suitable method[35] to systematically deal with issues of regulatory and adjudicatory jurisdiction, whilst avoiding parallel proceedings and facilitating private parties' access to legal remedies in cross-border competition law cases. A new model for international cooperation will be advanced by drawing a clear distinction between adjudicatory jurisdiction for a competent forum to determine a cross-border competition law dispute and regulatory jurisdiction for a legal order to regulate the competition law aspects of transnational economic activities.[36] If such a distinction is systematically put forward in a multilateral PIL instrument, the desired level of judicial cooperation could be achieved. Such a convention should enable an adjudicator to assume jurisdiction and apply several sets of competition laws (ie, regulatory regimes) when determining whether there is an infringement as well as when ascertaining the legal remedies (eg, assessing damages).[37]

This chapter sets out a research agenda to identify appropriate PIL solutions to promote access to justice. The focus is on competition law infringements with an international element. Since such infringements may cause harm to consumers and businesses in different jurisdictions, PIL will help to provide legal remedies. Although competition law includes merger control to safeguard the relevant market structure,[38] this chapter only considers rules prohibiting anti-competitive practices (transnational cartel agreements and serious abuses of dominant positions). State aid, subsidies and 'unfair competition'[39] are not discussed as being outside the UN Set of Principles on Competition.[40]

II. Main Limitations of the New Hague Judgments Convention (and the HCCH)[41]

The cross-border judicial cooperation gap is reflected in the multilateral PIL framework in the competition law arena. Appropriate and specific rules, which allocate adjudicatory jurisdiction – whilst considering the aspects of regulatory jurisdiction – in cross-border competition law cases in a global context, are yet to be drafted.

[34] JD González Campos, 'Les liens entre la compétence judiciaire et la competence legislative en droit international privé' (1977) 156 *Hague Collected Courses* 280.

[35] B Currie, 'Notes on Methods and Objectives in the Conflict of Laws' in B Currie, *Selected Essays on the Conflict of Laws* (Duke University Press 1963). See also K Roosevelt, 'Brainerd Currie's Contribution to Choice of Law: Looking Back, Looking Forward' (2015) Faculty Scholarship at Penn Law 1702, available at: scholarship.law.upenn.edu/faculty_scholarship/1702.

[36] Otero García-Castrillón (nn 14 and 24).

[37] M Danov, *Private International Law and Competition Litigation in a Global Context* (Hart Publishing 2023). *Deutsche Bahn AG & Others v MasterCard Incorporated* [2018] EWHC 412 (Ch).

[38] eg, Council Regulation (EC) No 139/2004 of 20 January 2004 on the control of concentrations between undertakings (EC Merger Regulation).

[39] Art 10bis(3) of the Paris Convention for the Protection of Industrial Property.

[40] Sections B and D of the UN Set (n 15).

[41] These aspects are further dealt with in Danov (n 37).

Competition law matters are excluded from the substantive scope of the 2005 Choice of Court Convention.[42] Nonetheless, the Service Convention[43] applies 'in all cases, in civil or commercial matters, where there is occasion to transmit a judicial or extrajudicial document for service abroad'.[44] Likewise, the Evidence Convention[45] and the Convention on Access to Justice[46] are applicable in competition law cases.

The Convention of 2 July 2019 on the Recognition and Enforcement of Foreign Judgments in Civil or Commercial Matters (Judgments Convention)[47] signals a new approach, with two significant features. First, it shows that PIL multilateral instruments can be used 'to promote effective access to justice for all and to facilitate rule-based multilateral trade and investment … through judicial co-operation'.[48] Second, although the Judgments Convention appears to make an important step in furthering the coverage of competition law cases, its application in cross-border competition law cases may be less than straightforward. Article 2(1)(p) states that:

> This Convention shall not apply to … anti-trust (competition) matters, except where the judgment is based on conduct that constitutes an anti-competitive agreement or concerted practice among actual or potential competitors to fix prices, make rigged bids, establish output restrictions or quotas, or divide markets by allocating customers, suppliers, territories or lines of commerce, and where such conduct and its effect both occurred in the State of origin.

The finalised text, being the only acceptable compromise,[49] is difficult to reconcile with the transnational nature of the instrument because it only applies with regard to judgments in relation to competition law infringements where the 'conduct and its effect both occurred in the State of origin'.[50]

If both the conduct and its effect had materialised in the same jurisdiction, then the defendant would most probably have assets in the State of origin (as long as this was the place where the infringement had occurred as well as the place where the damage had occurred).[51] The fact that the specific type of 'anticompetitive conduct [which is included] within the scope of the Convention is restricted to cases with a *significant link* to the State of origin'[52] indicates that the impact of the Judgments Convention will be somewhat limited. It is a relatively safe prediction that it would be rather unusual for injured parties to seek to recognise and enforce a judgment abroad under the Judgments Convention, not least because the 'significant link'[53] requirement would mean that the defendants would often have assets in the State of origin. Thus, the Judgments Convention has limited ability to facilitate injured parties' access to remedies in cross-border competition law cases.

By excluding many competition law matters from its scope, the drafters of the Judgments Convention left a number of important PIL competition law issues to be addressed in the future as part of another (more specific) instrument. During the negotiations, a specifically designated

[42] Art 2(2)(h) of the Convention on the Choice of Court Agreements of 30 June 2005.

[43] Convention on the Service abroad of Judicial and extrajudicial documents in civil or commercial matters of 15 November 1965.

[44] Ibid, Art 1.

[45] Convention on the Taking of Evidence Abroad in Civil or Commercial Matters of 18 March 1970.

[46] Convention on International access to Justice of 25 October 1980.

[47] The full text of the Judgments Convention, which is not in force yet, is available at: www.hcch.net/en/instruments/conventions/full-text/?cid=137.

[48] Ibid, Preamble.

[49] F Garcimartín and G Saumier, *Explanatory Report on the 2019 HCCH Judgments Convention* (HCCH 2020) [69].

[50] Art 2(1)(p). See also, Garcimartín and Saumier (n 49) [72].

[51] cp: *Cooper Tire & Rubber Company* [2009] EWHC 2609 (Comm), [2010] EWCA Civ 864.

[52] Garcimartín and Saumier (n 49) [72] – emphasis added by the authors.

[53] Ibid.

group of experts 'discuss[ed] the possible exclusion of antitrust (competition) matters'[54] and their report[55] discussing 'the different types of anti-trust matters and some of their unique features'[56] may provide a basis for future work with a view to addressing the remaining PIL issues at The Hague.

The types of antitrust matters which need to be considered are correctly identified.[57] However, the report does not sufficiently distinguish between the regulatory aspects of competition laws and the enforcement activities of various regulators and/or adjudicators:

> The *regulation* and *enforcement* of competition laws can then be broken down into three main categories: (i) merger control by a regulator; (ii) public enforcement actions in respect of competition law breaches; and (iii) private enforcement actions in respect of competition law breaches.[58]

It is essential for any future PIL initiative in the area to draw a clear distinction between the regulation of economic activities through competition laws, and the enforcement of the relevant competition laws in public-administrative and/or private proceedings (ie, public and/or private enforcement). In a PIL context, it should not be forgotten that competition regulation has an evidently public (as opposed to private)[59] nature that even leads to the characterisation of competition law as forming part of the national/regional public policy (imperative).[60]

In spite of the public dimension of competition laws, it is well established that 'private enforcement of [such] public rules is a highly efficient strategy of enforcing [them]'.[61] In other words, once national policymakers decide that the competition law aspects of cross-border economic activities are to be regulated, then an 'optimal institutional design'[62] (which strikes an appropriate balance between public and private enforcement strands) is normally advanced. That said, the various national enforcement (public and/or private) modes should make no difference to the regulatory nature of competition law rules.

Effective international cooperation in a multilateral PIL instrument has to successfully accommodate diverse sets of national enforcement regimes. Given the correlation between public and private enforcement, there is an important preliminary question: is a decision adopted by a regulatory authority (as opposed to a judgment rendered by a court) covered by the definition of 'judgment'?[63] The report suggests that this is 'unlikely'.[64] However, its wording seems to indicate that, despite being improbable for regulatory decisions to be covered by the Convention, this possibility cannot be absolutely excluded.

The problem was exacerbated by the *Revised Preliminary Explanatory Report*[65] which was using the concept of 'enforcement orders'.[66] Since there was no definition of enforcement order for those purposes, there was a level of ambiguity whether a decision of a national/regional

[54] Prel Doc No 2 of December 2018 (n 23) [59].

[55] Ibid.

[56] Ibid, [3].

[57] Ibid, [4].

[58] Ibid, [9] – emphases added by the authors.

[59] T Büthe and W Mattli, *The New Global Rulers: The Privatization of Regulation in the World Economy* (Princeton University Press 2013).

[60] Overriding mandatory provisions of the law of the forum within the meaning of the EU Rome I/II Regulations, eg, C-126/97 *Eco Swiss* [1999] ECR I-3055; Case 38/98 *Renault v Maxicar* [2000] ECR I-2973.

[61] A Shleifer, 'Understanding Regulation' (2005) 11 *European Financial Management* 439, 446.

[62] Ibid, 443.

[63] Art 3(1)(b) of the Convention and Prel Doc No 2 of December 2018 (n 23) [15].

[64] Prel Doc No 2 of December 2018 (n 23) [15].

[65] Preliminary Document No 10 of May 2018, 'Judgments Convention: Revised Preliminary Explanatory Report', available at: assets.hcch.net/docs/7cd8bc44-e2e5-46c2-8865-a151ce55e1b2.pdf.

[66] Ibid, para 28.

regulator establishing a cross-border competition law infringement would be classified as a *declaratory* or enforcement order. The Explanatory Report appears to endeavour to clarify the matter by stating:

> Whether a judgment relates to civil or commercial matters is determined by the nature of the claim or action that is the subject of the judgment. The nature of the court of the State of origin or the mere fact that a State was a party to the proceedings are not determinative factors.[67]

This clarification is welcome. The question whether particular conduct 'constitutes an anti-competitive agreement'[68] is an important classification issue. The matter must be classified as either 'civil or commercial' or 'administrative'[69] – irrespective of the nature of the adjudicator (regulator or court) that deals with the dispute.

However, a level of ambiguity remains because the Explanatory Report goes on to state that, '[i]n any event, since the Convention only applies in civil or commercial matters, any judgment resulting from anti-trust (competition) authorities exercising governmental or sovereign powers is excluded'.[70] Would decisions of the EU Commission finding cross-border EU competition law infringements, which are binding on all EU Member States courts,[71] be within the scope of the Judgments Convention? The EU Commission would hardly be exercising any 'governmental or sovereign powers'[72] when it determines whether there is a breach of EU competition law. A more appropriate test would be for the scope of the Convention to be dependent on whether the adjudicator/regulator is exercising judicial functions (or whether it is imposing administrative penalties) when dealing with antitrust matters.

A more nuanced approach is important, not least because, eg, a decision of the EU Commission *finding an infringement* is 'immune from challenge'[73] in follow-on private damages proceedings[74] in EU Member States. A judgment of an EU Member State's court, awarding antitrust damages in a private suit, in reliance on a decision of the EU Commission declaring that there was an anti-competitive agreement, should be recognised and enforced under the Judgments Convention.[75] The 'object'[76] of the relevant private enforcement proceedings would be to compensate the injured parties for the harm caused by the anti-competitive agreement. Such a damages award would be within the scope of the Judgments Convention because the action would principally be concerned with the assessment of the individual[77] or aggregate[78] damage which had resulted from the anti-competitive agreement.

But, if a similar line of reasoning is adopted when interpreting Article 2(2) which sets out an exception to the matters excluded by Article 2(1) of the Judgments Convention (ie, an exception to the exception), then the following questions would be bound to arise: would the

[67] Garcimartín and Saumier (n 49) [28].
[68] Art 2(1)(p).
[69] Art 1(1).
[70] Garcimartín and Saumier (n 49) [73] and also [37].
[71] Art 16 of Council Regulation 1/2003.
[72] Garcimartín and Saumier (n 49) [28].
[73] *The Secretary of State for Health v Servier Laboratories* [2019] EWCA Civ 1096 [74]. See also: C-234/89 *Delimitis* [1991] ECR I-935; C-344/98 *Masterfoods v HB Ice Cream* EU:C:2000:689 [57]; T-474/04 *Pergan Hilfsstoffe für industrielle Prozesse v Commission* EU:T:2007:306 [73]; and *Secretary of State for Health*, ibid [28].
[74] In follow-on actions, the claimants rely on a regulator's decision on the infringement of competition law rules. Such a decision facilitates the task of claimants and courts, not least because the issues concerning the existence of the infringement and the identity of the infringing undertakings are dealt with.
[75] Prel Doc No 2 of December 2018 (n 23) [46].
[76] Art 2(2) Judgments Convention.
[77] *BritNed Development v ABB* [2018] EWHC 2616 (Ch) conf'd [2019] EWCA Civ 1840.
[78] *Merricks v Mastercard Incorporated & Anor* [2020] UKSC 51.

'conduct that constitutes an anti-competitive agreement',[79] which had been established by the regulator, be regarded as a preliminary issue? Or would the 'conduct that constitutes an anti-competitive agreement'[80] be regarded as the 'object'[81] of antitrust damages proceedings? If the answer to the first question is in the affirmative, then the scope of the Judgments Convention could be easily broadened by some national judges to cover judgments awarding antitrust damages regarding conduct that constitutes an abuse of a dominant position as long as the breach had been established by a regulator in a prior set of public-administrative proceedings.

The fact that such important questions were not considered in the report[82] prepared for the Diplomatic Session indicates that the HCCH did not fully reflect how the competition law enforcement model is functioning in the EU.[83] To strengthen the role of the HCCH, a new PIL solution which presupposes a comprehensive in-depth analysis, taking account of how the enforcement regimes are functioning in different jurisdictions, is needed. As part of this process, the following challenges need to be addressed.

III. Challenges Concerning International Cooperation in Cross-Border Cases

The Judgments Convention is an initial attempt to facilitate the recognition and enforcement of certain competition law judgments. This might set the scene for future judicial cooperation in competition law matters. Such cooperation is central to the effective enforcement of competition law in cross-border cases and facilitating injured parties' access to legal remedies in such cases.

There are two major challenges which require PIL solutions in view of the fact that not only are substantive competition laws different, but so too are the enforcement regimes and procedural rules reflecting different national/regional legal traditions and policy choices.[84] In particular, a comparative dataset reiterates that the various national/regional competition laws pursue different objectives.[85] Striking an appropriate balance between the different (but legitimate) regulatory interests is the first major challenge which must be addressed by an appropriately functioning regime for international cooperation.[86]

The second major challenge is to devise a mechanism which enables different national regulators/adjudicators to cooperate in cross-border cases. The fact that competition laws may be enforced in public-administrative proceedings before national/regional regulators as well as in legal proceedings before national courts adds another layer of complexity. It seems obvious that the enforcement proceedings (be they public/administrative or private) should be more coherently coordinated than they are at present. Achieving an appropriate level of cooperation is

[79] Art 2(2) Judgments Convention.
[80] Ibid.
[81] Ibid.
[82] Prel Doc No 2 of December 2018 (n 23).
[83] cp: M Danov, F Becker and P Beaumont (eds), *Cross-border EU Competition Law Actions* (Hart Publishing 2013).
[84] WF Schwartz, 'Overview of the Economics of Antitrust Enforcement' (1980) 68 *Georgetown Law Journal* 1075; S Shavell, 'The Optimal Structure of Law Enforcement' (1993) 36 *Journal of Law and Economics* 255; RP McAfee, HM Mialon and SH Mialon, 'Private v public antitrust enforcement: A strategic analysis' (2008) 92 *Journal of Public Economics* 1863; WPJ Wils, 'The relationship between public antitrust enforcement and private actions for damages' (2009) 32 *World Competition* 3, 18, available at: papers.ssrn.com/sol3/papers.cfm?abstract_id=1296458; K Huschelrath and S Peyer, 'Public and private enforcement of competition law: A differentiated approach' (2013) 36 *World Competition* 585.
[85] Bradford et al (n 1) 418 – '*Figure 3*: Comparative Competition Law Dataset – main variables'.
[86] AT von Mehren, 'Special substantive rules for multistate problems: Their role and significance in contemporary choice of law methodology' [1974] *Harvard Law Review* 347.

complex because, whilst national competition authorities (ie, regulators) impose fines to punish and deter competition law infringers (safeguarding public interests),[87] civil courts (ie, national adjudicators) award legal remedies (eg, compensation for damage caused to injured parties), be it in follow-on or in stand-alone actions.[88]

On the one hand, both public and private enforcement modes respond to the need to protect the public interest in general (administrative action) and the private interests of the directly affected parties (civil jurisdiction).[89] On the other hand, different national/regional enforcement regimes strike a different balance between public and private enforcement modes. How should an appropriate level of international cooperation between the diverse national enforcement regimes be achieved? The response to this question is particularly important in cases where there is a parallel (or subsequent) set of proceedings (involving regulators and courts) concerning the same cross-border competition law infringement taking place in different jurisdictions.[90]

It is desirable for policymakers to coordinate enforcement proceedings before different administrative and judicial authorities in different jurisdictions. Achieving a level of judicial cooperation in antitrust matters is difficult, as The Hague report[91] acknowledged, because competition laws may be publicly and privately enforced. A sufficiently flexible model is needed to ensure that the enforcement of national/regional competition laws in international situations is effective, irrespective of the relevant enforcement modes (ie, publicly or privately initiated proceedings). An enhanced model of international cooperation between different national/regional regulators and national courts should be advanced, particularly to deter anti-competitive conduct and provide redress for multiple injured parties in several jurisdictions.[92]

IV. PIL Mechanisms and International Cooperation in Cross-Border Competition Law Cases

There are two major aspects which need to be dealt with in a new global PIL mechanism. Above all, '*the international jurisdiction to adjudicate*'[93] is central for courts and/or regulators to ascertain whether there is anti-competitive conduct. The rules allocating adjudicatory jurisdiction in cross-border competition law within the EU which have been discussed by courts[94] and commentators,[95] strongly indicate that it is very important for these issues to be dealt with in a

[87] Administrative decisions may be subject to judicial control.

[88] Civil claims that do not rely on a previous (administrative) decision ascertaining a breach of competition law. In these cases, the courts have to decide whether there has been a competition law infringement and, if that is the case, what legal remedies should be awarded.

[89] eg, Reg 1/2003 on the implementation of the rules on competition laid down in Arts 101 and 102 of the TFEU. cp: the US Sherman Act, 26 Stat 209 (1890); the US Clayton Act, 38 Stat 730 (1914); and the US Federal Trade Commission Act, 38 Stat 717 (1914).

[90] R Nazzini, *Competition Enforcement and Procedure*, 2nd edn (Oxford University Press 2016).

[91] Prel Doc No 2 of December 2018 (n 23) [59].

[92] R Mulheron, 'Asserting personal jurisdiction over non-resident class members: comparative insights for the United Kingdom' (2019) 15 *Journal of Private International Law* 445.

[93] Mann (n 33) 67. See also KM Meessen, 'Drafting Rules on Extraterritorial Jurisdiction' in KM Meessen (ed), *Extraterritorial Jurisdiction in Theory and Practice* (Kluwer 1996) 226; and Otero García-Castrillón (n 24).

[94] eg, C-352/13 *Cartel Damage Claims (CDC)* EU:C:2015:335; *Provimi Limited* [2003] EWHC 961 (Comm); *SanDisk Corporation* [2007] EWHC 332 (Ch); *Cooper Tire & Rubber Company* [2009] EWHC 2609 (Comm), [2010] EWCA Civ 864; *Toshiba Carrier UK Ltd and Other* [2011] EWHC 2665 (Ch), [2012] EWCA Civ 169.

[95] eg, M Danov, *Jurisdiction and Judgments in Relation to EU Competition Law Claims* (Hart Publishing 2010); J Basedow, S Francq and L Idot (eds), *International Antitrust Litigation: Conflict of Laws and Coordination* (Hart Publishing 2012); Danov, Becker and Beaumont (n 83).

global context. The case for an appropriate and nuanced approach to issues of jurisdiction was advanced by Justice Scalia:

> It is important to distinguish two distinct questions …: whether the District Court had jurisdiction, and whether the Sherman Act reaches the extraterritorial conduct alleged here. On the first question, I believe that the District Court had subject-matter jurisdiction over the Sherman Act claims against all the defendants (personal jurisdiction is not contested).
>
> …
>
> The second question … has nothing to do with the jurisdiction of the courts. It is a question of substantive law turning on whether, in enacting the Sherman Act, Congress asserted regulatory power over the challenged conduct … If a plaintiff fails to prevail on this issue, the court does not dismiss the claim for want of subject-matter jurisdiction – want of power to adjudicate; rather, it decides the claim, ruling on the merits that the plaintiff has failed to state a cause of action under the relevant statute.[96]

Justice Scalia identifies two separate issues which would need to be addressed in the US proceedings. One might go a step further in a global context and ask: how should regulatory and adjudicatory jurisdiction in cross-border cases be defined in a multilateral PIL instrument? What criteria should be used to ascertain whether a national/regional adjudicator is to be regarded as competent? How can parallel proceedings be avoided? Should the adjudicatory jurisdiction be dependent on the applicable law (*forum legis*)? Should an appropriate adjudicator be expected/entitled to apply foreign 'public' competition law (regulating cross-border economic activities)?

To answer these questions, some analogies could be drawn from the EU PIL rules and their application in cross-border EU competition law cases. However, in a global context there would be an additional issue concerning the question which set of public competition laws, and how, should be used to regulate the competition law aspects of transnational economic activities. Regulatory jurisdiction would normally not be the most contentious issue in cases where a breach of EU competition law has been pleaded. Since the core provisions in this area have public policy character,[97] EU Member State courts would have to apply them as 'overriding mandatory provisions of the law of the forum'.[98]

The question how foreign regulatory interests should be factored into domestic proceedings needs to be addressed by the international community. In this context, States are not constrained by international norms and are free to decide whether to take into consideration the possible foreign contacts of a competition law case. A negative response would imply the direct application of national laws (*Unilateralism*).[99] An affirmative answer would imply that the major interest/contact of a third State should be taken into consideration before applying national law (Balance of interests – *Multilateralism*).[100] Diverse approaches may be advanced

[96] *Hartford Fire Insurance Co v California* 113 SCt 2891, 2917–18 (1993).

[97] *Eco Swiss and Renault* (n 60).

[98] Art 9(2) Rome I; Art 16 Rome II.

[99] *Hartford Fire Insurance* (n 96); WS Dodge, 'Extraterritoriality and Conflict-of-Laws Theory: An Argument for Judicial Unilateralism' (1998) 39 *Harvard International Law Journal* 101; and PR Trimble, 'The Supreme Court and International Law: The Demise of Restatement Section 403' (1995) 89 *American Journal of International Law* 53. US Antitrust Guidelines use a concept of *comity* based in *Hartford* whereby its application will be necessary only when foreign law forces a behaviour not compatible with US norms.

[100] *Timberlane Lumber Co* (n 26) and *Mannington Mills, Inc v Congoleum Corp* 595 F2d 1987 (3rd Cir, 1979) adopt the balance of interests doctrine. A Lowenfeld, 'Conflict, Balancing of Interests and the Exercise of the Jurisdiction to Prescribe: Reflections on the *Insurance Antitrust Case*' (1995) 89 *American Journal of International Law* 42; and A Lowenfeld 'Jurisdictional Issues Before National Courts: The Insurance Antitrust Case' in KM Meessen (ed), *Extraterritorial Jurisdiction in Theory and Practice* (Kluwer 1996) 11, '*conflict is not just about commands, but about interests, values and priorities*'. See more Otero García-Castrillón (nn 14 and 24).

by different policymakers.[101] How should an appropriate balance between different regulatory interests with a view to ascertaining the appropriate and effective legal remedies in cross-border competition law cases be struck?

It is widely recognised that the doctrine of positive comity could have a role to play in public-administrative proceedings by encouraging '[c]ooperation regarding anticompetitive activities in the territory of one Party that adversely affect the interests of the other Party'[102] and some solutions along this line have been advanced as to judicial proceedings.[103] Problems, however, may arise in cross-border competition cases where several (or indeed all) the regulators take action, reaching different conclusions about the anti-competitive nature of the cross-border economic activities.[104] There may be even bigger problems in cases where appropriate adjudicators decline to exercise jurisdiction on the ground that they have no regulatory jurisdiction[105] despite the fact that the countries, which have regulatory jurisdiction, lack sufficient resources and appropriate expertise to deal with cross-border competition law cases.[106]

V. Access to Legal Remedies in Cross-Border Cases: Adjudicatory Jurisdiction and Regulatory Jurisdiction[107]

A major problem in competition law cases is that the global supply chains may be used to spread the antitrust harm across the globe.[108] Establishing adjudicatory jurisdiction before an appropriate forum could be central to effective access to legal remedies, particularly for private parties. The lack (or the existence) of regulatory jurisdiction might impact on the closely related jurisdiction to adjudicate by making the seised courts less appropriate to deal with the dispute.[109] The problems concerning the correlation between the regulatory jurisdiction and the adjudicatory jurisdiction on the one hand, and the injured parties' access to legal remedies, on the other, need to be thoroughly considered at the HCCH.

The weaknesses of the current regime for international cooperation were exposed in the anti-competitive agreement in relation to the Liquid Crystal Displays (LCDs) which was, inter

[101] Dodge (n 99) 147–49; Otero García-Castrillón, ibid.

[102] Art V of the US/EU Agreement. P Demaret, 'L'extraterritorialité des lois et les relations transatlantiques: Une question de Droit ou de diplomatie?' (1985) 21 *Revue Trim Droit Eur* 1, 26–27. See also A-M Slaughter, 'Government networks: the heart of the liberal democratic order' in GH Fox and BR Roth (eds), *Democratic Governance and International Law* (Cambridge University Press 2000) 199, 215.

[103] In order to protect their own interests, States tend to take into consideration the interests of other States. Though comity is not expressly mentioned, it is present when taking decisions so that it has been said that it is implicit in the system. The 'balance of interests' and the 'rule of reason' can be considered as legal principles (not just political). SW Waller, 'The Twilight of Comity' (2000) 38 *Columbia Journal of Transnational Law* 566. See more Otero García-Castrillón (nn 14 and 24).

[104] Statement of the Federal Trade Commission Regarding Google's Search Practices In the Matter of Google Inc FTC File Number 111-0163, 3 January 2013, available at: www.ftc.gov/sites/default/files/documents/public_statements/statement-commission-regarding-googles-search-practices/130103brillgooglesearchstmt.pdf, 2. cp: Case AT.39740, *Google Search (Shopping)*, Antitrust Procedure – Council Reg 1/2003 – Commission Decision of 27.6.2017 relating to proceedings under Art 102 of the TFEU and Art 54 of the Agreement on the European Economic Area, C(2017) 4444 final [341].

[105] eg, *Motorola Mobility* (n 10). See section V below.

[106] Bradford et al (n 1) 423–34; PM Horna, 'David & Goliath: How young competition agencies can succeed in fighting cross-border cartels' (2017) University of Oxford Centre for Competition Law and Policy, Working Paper CCLP (L) 45, available at: www.law.ox.ac.uk/sites/files/oxlaw/david_goliath_-_how_young_competition_agencies_can_succeed_in_fighting_cross-border_cartels_-_cclp_l_45.pdf; Fox (n 28) 154.

[107] These aspects are further dealt with in Danov (n 37). cp: Otero García-Castrillón (nn 14 and 24).

[108] eg, *Motorola Mobility* (n 10).

[109] Ibid, 825–27. See also the US Foreign Trade Anti-trust Improvements Act.

alia, investigated by the EU Commission.[110] In this case, the Commission established that '[t]he infringement had a global character both from the geographic and product point of view, with the parties generally aiming at increasing and/or maintaining the prices for LCD panels for TV and IT application'.[111] The infringers had a 'joint world-wide market share of around [65–80 per cent] in large LCD panels',[112] which was subject to various enforcement proceedings before the EU regulators,[113] EU[114] and UK courts,[115] US courts[116] and the competent adjudicators in Japan, South Korea, Taiwan and Canada.[117]

The parties[118] to the anti-competitive agreement were well-known groups of companies: Samsung, LPL, AUO, CMO, CPT Groups[119] and *HannStar* companies. This meant the global nature of the infringement was beyond doubt. The aggregate damage caused to consumers (who would normally absorb the cartel induced surcharge) was arguably significant. Indeed, the evidence before the EU regulator demonstrated that:

> The participating undertakings, … engaged in a *single, complex and continuous cartel infringement* in respect of LCD panels for IT and TV applications by a series of linked and interacting efforts that lasted from 5 October 2001 until February 2006, with the objective of increasing and maintaining prices of LCD panels for IT and TV applications at world-wide and EEA level. Throughout the period of the infringement those companies were competitors and were aware of the arrangements and the decisions taken which were implemented.[120]

An analysis of this case from a PIL perspective demonstrates that the scope of the regulatory jurisdiction is a difficult issue in both public and private proceedings. The English and Welsh High Court judgments[121] strongly suggest that different views may be taken on the effects, for the jurisdictional purposes, of an anti-competitive agreement in the EU[122] which impacts, in turn, on the scope of the applicable competition laws.[123] It is even more troubling that the issues in relation to adjudicatory and regulatory jurisdiction in this cross-border competition law case remained despite the fact that the court proceedings in England and Wales were preceded by the public enforcement proceedings before the EU Commission.[124]

This is a good example of a case where the claimants' access to legal remedies was dependent on the preliminary issue of the 'territorial scope'[125] of EU competition law (regulatory jurisdiction) and its correlation with adjudicatory jurisdiction.[126] In other words, the regulatory jurisdiction could have an impact on the adjudicatory jurisdiction (ie, the appropriateness of the English courts to hear and determine the dispute in a sort of *forum legis*). A prolonged dispute on

[110] COMP/39.309, *LCD (Liquid Crystal Displays)*, C(2010) 8761 final.
[111] Ibid, [402].
[112] Ibid, [51].
[113] Ibid.
[114] T-91/11 *InnoLux Corp v Commission* EU:T:2014:92; C-231/14 P, *InnoLux Corp v Commission* EU:C:2015:451.
[115] *Schott AG* (n 32); Iiyama UK (n 32); *LCD Appeals* (n 10).
[116] *AT & T Mobility LLC v AU Optronics Corp* 707 F3d 1106 (9th Cir, 2013); *Motorola Mobility* (n 10).
[117] See the Particulars of the Claim [47] quoted in *Nokia Corporation v AU Optronics Corporation & Others* [2012] EWHC 731 (Ch) [39].
[118] Ibid, [13]–[35].
[119] *Samsung Electronics Co Ltd and Samsung Electronics Taiwan Co Ltd; LG.Philips LCD Co, Ltd and LG Philips LCD Taiwan Co, Ltd; AU Optronics Corporation; Chimei InnoLux Corporation and Chunghwa Picture Tubes.*
[120] COMP/39.309, *LCD (Liquid Crystal Displays)*, C(2010) 8761 final [283] – emphasis added.
[121] *Samsung Electronics* (n 32); *Schott AG* (n 32).
[122] *LCD Appeals* (n 10) [20-25]. See also *Samsung Electronics* (n 32) [51–53]. cp: *Schott AG* (n 32) [140]–[141].
[123] *LCD Appeals* (n 10) [95], [104], [107], [119–21] and [128–32].
[124] *Schott AG* (n 32) [132].
[125] *LCD Appeals* (n 10) [61]–[100].
[126] *Schott AG* (n 32) [171].

such an important pre-trial issue inevitably generates a level of delay, inflating the litigation costs and having significant implications for injured parties' access to (any) legal remedies in cross-border cases. This would be so even when the related proceedings are being dealt with by different judges applying the same PIL regime as well as the same set of competition laws within the same jurisdiction. How is this problem to be addressed globally?

A case for international cooperation is strengthened by the interrelation between the transnational corporate structure (which is necessary to facilitate cross-border economic activities for multinational groups of companies) and the ineffective enforcement of national competition laws in some jurisdictions. The latter aspect might be successfully exploited by strategic defendants to impede the claimants' access to effective remedies. The point can be deduced from *Motorola Mobility*.[127] In this case, the US Court of Appeals held:

> Domestic corporate purchasers are not without remedy when buying component parts from foreign vendors. First, the US parent could buy directly from the foreign vendor and preserve the right to sue as a direct purchaser (while trading off the benefits the company gained from operating through a foreign subsidiary). *Or, if a US parent doesn't think that antitrust laws are sufficiently, or fairly, enforced in a given country, they certainly don't have to set up a subsidiary there* ... So, an adverse ruling in Motorola *would not eliminate every* avenue of damage redress for component price-fixing.[128]

Such an approach, which – despite acknowledging the inadequacy of the available remedies and the ineffectiveness of the relevant national enforcement regime – allows the US courts to decline jurisdiction, would inevitably deny some injured parties' access to effective legal remedies. Given the global nature of the economic activities, it does not appear to be a satisfactory solution for a national court to decline jurisdiction on the ground of comity[129] and go on to say that a company should not have set up its subsidiaries in jurisdictions where competition laws are not effectively enforced.[130] National courts should rather consider, before declining to exercise jurisdiction, whether there is a 'real risk ... that substantial justice would be unavailable'[131] in the appropriate forum. As part of a new model for cooperation, could foreign regulators be involved with the relevant court proceedings with a view to better balancing comity considerations?

VI. Concluding Remarks

Injured parties' access to effective legal remedies in cross-border competition law cases is a major issue which should be dealt with in a global context. PIL has an important role to play in coordinating regulatory and adjudicatory jurisdiction. International cooperation is much needed with a view to systematically addressing the relevant PIL issues. Coordination of enforcement proceedings between the national courts and the regulators across the globe is as important as ever. Existing mechanisms do not consider how to ensure that cross-border competition cases are centralised before an appropriate forum whilst facilitating injured parties' access to legal remedies.

An appropriate research agenda globally must address how to ensure that multiple injured parties are able to access effective legal remedies in cross-border competition law cases. It is

[127] *Motorola Mobility* (n 10).
[128] Ibid, 827 – emphasis added.
[129] Ibid, 825–27.
[130] Ibid, 827.
[131] *Vedanta Resources PLC and another v Lungowe and others* [2019] UKSC 20 [89]. See also *LCD Appeals* (n 10) [97].

high time for PIL scholars to consider how to answer some important questions.[132] How could the HCCH 'work for the progressive unification of the rules of private international law' in the field of competition law?[133] If different national judges respond to certain key questions inconsistently, then there would potentially be a high level of uncertainty/ambiguity in cross-border competition cases. Since these deficiencies may be exploited by strategic litigants with a view to generating delay (and inflating litigation costs), the Judgments Convention will not, on its own, sufficiently facilitate injured parties' access to remedies in cross-border cases.

The EU model for public-administrative and judicial cooperation in competition cases needs to be thoroughly studied. It should be noted that, beyond advancing a framework for public-administrative cooperation on competition law with third States, the EU has reached a high degree of harmonisation in competition law enforcement. PIL plays a significant role particularly regarding private parties' remedies within the EU. The research should analyse the way in which the current PIL framework is functioning within the EU and how the bilateral relations with the UK will be organised. If the European Commission's position that 'the European Union [should] not … give its consent to the accession of the United Kingdom to the 2007 Lugano Convention' prevails in the EU,[134] a new framework which uses PIL governance techniques should be advanced by the UK/EU policymakers to promote judicial cooperation in cross-border competition law cases. The HCCH should have a significant role in this context.

In the light of the diverse legal orders represented in the HCCH and the search for effective and efficient legal tools, alternatives to international treaties may be considered. Model laws,[135] which set out principles or even guides (addressing predominantly procedural issues concerning parallel and consecutive related proceedings), can be a feasible and successful approach. Such a soft legal instrument could set the scene for a more effective framework for international cooperation which would provide injured parties better access to adequate and effective regulatory and compensatory remedies, generating broader societal impacts. In other words, once such model laws have been successfully advanced, an appropriate regime for judicial cooperation on competition law enforcement may be devised. It would be important to consider issues of regulatory and adjudicatory jurisdiction including the interaction between regulators and courts.

Moreover, given the public interest safeguarding role of competition law, promoting an appropriate level of international cooperation is linked to the question: how could a PIL mechanism be advanced to safeguard the interests of claimants and defendants, as well as the various legitimate regulatory interests, by involving foreign regulators in the proceedings before appropriate national courts?

[132] M Kahler and DA Lake, 'Economic Integration and Global Governance: Why So Little Supranationalism?' in W Mattli and N Woods (eds), *The Politics of Global Regulation* (Princeton University Press 2009) 242. See also RH Graveson, 'Problems of Private International Law in Non-Unified Legal Systems' in RH Graveson, *Comparative Conflict of Laws: Selected Essays* (Vol 1, North-Holland Publishing 1977) 305, 337; M Danov and P Beaumont, 'Measuring the Effectiveness of the EU Civil Justice Framework: Theoretical and Methodological Challenges' (2015/2016) 17 *Yearbook of Private International Law* 151; AA Foer, and JW Cuneo, 'Toward an effective system of private enforcement' in AA Foer, and JW Cuneo (eds), *The International Handbook on Private Enforcement of Competition Law* (Edward Elgar 2010) 611.

[133] Art 1 of the HCCH Statute.

[134] Communication from the Commission (n 22) 5.

[135] cp: The UNCTAD Model Law on Competition – TD/RBP/CONF.5/7.

18

Tort: Applicable Law

MICHAEL HELLNER

I. Existing Unification

A. Background

At present there is no global convention of a general nature on the law applicable to torts. There is also no active work carried out with the purpose of drafting such a convention. However, for specific torts private international law has been unified on a global level within the framework of the Hague Conference on Private International Law (HCCH) in the form of the 1971 Convention on the Law Applicable to Traffic Accidents[1] and the 1973 Convention on the Law Applicable to Products Liability.[2] What is more, regionally within the European Union unification has taken place in the form of the 'Rome II Regulation' on the Law Applicable to Non-contractual Obligations.[3] There is a plethora of other instruments that also contain rules on applicable law in tort.[4]

Private international law in the area of tort has always been one (or two) steps behind that of contract. There are a number of reasons for this and one might start by going back to Friedrich Carl von Savigny (1779–1861) who in his seminal work *System des häutigen Römischen Rechts, Achter Band* concluded that obligations in tort were so closely related to criminal law that they generally belonged to what he referred to as 'Gesetze von streng positiver, zwingender Natur' – today, we would speak of internationally mandatory rules – for which nothing remains but the application of the *lex fori*.[5]

Over time, the focus of tort law has shifted from deterrence to compensation,[6] thus linking tort law more to the victim than the State seeking to deter. What is more, the number of cross-border torts has risen due to the increase in mobility and international trade as well as

[1] Convention of 4 May 1971 on the Law Applicable to Traffic Accidents.

[2] Convention of 2 October 1973 on the Law Applicable to Products Liability.

[3] Regulation (EC) No 864/2007 of the European Parliament and of the Council of 11 July 2007 on the law applicable to non-contractual obligations (Rome II) [2007] OJ L199/40.

[4] Some of these Conventions are listed in the 'Notifications under Article 29(1) of Regulation (EC) No 864/2007 on the law applicable to non-contractual obligations (Rome II)', [2010] OJ C343/7.

[5] FC von Savigny, *System des häutigen Römischen Rechts, Achter Band* (Veit und Comp 1849) 278–80. This book is available in the original language in facsimile at: www.deutschestextarchiv.de/book/view/savigny_system08_1849?p=1.

[6] For a North American perspective, see GE White, *Tort Law in America: An Intellectual History* (Oxford University Press 1980) 178 f. See also, Proposal for a Regulation of the European Parliament and the Council on the law applicable to non-contractual obligations ('Rome II') COM(2003) 427 final, 12.

technological developments. In the mid-nineteenth century there were no cars that caused traffic accidents in foreign countries, there was no international press and of course no internet to cause cross-border libel suits, there were very few consumer products manufactured in one country and sold in another and the law of products liability was still in its infancy, there were few factories that could cause pollution in other countries and there were no international cartels.[7]

Due to greater diversity between national substantive laws, unification of applicable law rules for tort has time and again proven to be more difficult than the harmonisation of applicable law rules for contract. In 1968, in the context of the HCCH, it was concluded that 'the field of torts was too wide and heterogeneous to be dealt with in one single convention' and it was decided to first proceed with work on a Convention on traffic accidents and afterwards products liability.[8]

In the context of the EU, work on a Convention on the law applicable to contractual and non-contractual obligations commenced at the same time but in 1978 a decision was taken to exclude non-contractual obligations from scope.[9] Not until 1998 did work on an instrument on the law applicable to torts – or as it were, 'non-contractual obligations' (which arguably is a wider concept) – recommence.[10] Initially a convention was conceived but after the coming into force of the Treaty of Amsterdam on 1 May 1999, which authorised the EU to adopt regulations and directives in the area of private international law, work continued on an EU Regulation – the Rome II Regulation.[11]

These three major unifications in the area of the private international law of tort will be the focus of this chapter.

B. The Hague Conventions

i. General Observations

As has already been pointed out, special commissions of the Hague Conference in 1967 and 1968 held that the field of torts was 'too wide and heterogeneous to be dealt with in one single convention'. It was therefore decided to first focus on traffic accidents[12] and afterwards move on to products liability.[13] On 4 May 1971 a Convention on the law applicable to traffic accidents was concluded and it came into force on 3 June 1975. On 2 October 1973 it was followed by a Convention on the law applicable to products liability, which came into force on 1 October 1977. The two Conventions can be described as 'medium successes' with 21 States Parties to the Traffic Accidents Convention and 11 States Parties to the Products Liability Convention.[14]

The risk, and advantage, of conventions covering specific subject matters is that they tend to become more detailed. The 'operative part' – that is the part of the Convention that is not devoted

[7] And if there were, they were not necessarily illegal. See, eg, DJ Gerber, *Law and Competition in Twentieth-Century Europe: Protecting Prometheus* (Oxford University Press 1998) 16–42 for the development of competition law in Europe in the 19th century.

[8] EW Essén, *Convention on the Law Applicable to Traffic Accidents. Explanatory Report* (Essén Report) 1.

[9] The result of the work was the 1980 Rome Convention on the law applicable to contractual obligations, see the explanatory report by M Giuliano and P Lagarde (Giuliano/Lagarde Report) [1980] OJ C282/1, 7.

[10] On 22–23 July 1998 the first meeting of the Council working party was held.

[11] (n 3).

[12] The increase in international traffic was given as a reason, see EW Essén, 'Tillämplig lag vid internationella trafikolyckor' [1969] *Nordisk Försäkringstidskrift* 217.

[13] See Essén Report (n 8) 1.

[14] See: www.hcch.net/en/instruments/conventions/status-table/?cid=81 for an updated status table for the Traffic Accidents Convention; and www.hcch.net/en/instruments/conventions/status-table/?cid=84 for the Product Liability Convention.

to general questions such as scope of the applicable law, public policy, entry into force, reservations, accessions etc – of the Traffic Accidents Convention consists of four Articles (Articles 3–6).[15] The Products Liability Convention also contains four 'operative' Articles (Articles 4–7).[16]

ii. The Traffic Accidents Convention

The point of departure of the Convention is, as could be expected, the *lex loci delicti*. According to Article 3, the law applicable shall be 'the internal law of the State where the accident occurred'. The Convention does not explicitly make the distinction between *lex loci delicti commissi* and *lex loci damni* but this distinction is of little relevance when it comes to traffic accidents.[17] Traffic accidents are not so-called distance delicts and almost always the event giving rise to the damage and the damage itself occur in the same country.[18] Should, by way of extreme exception, act and effect occur in different countries, the wording indicates that the *lex loci delicti commissi* applies.[19]

The general rule in Article 3 is conventional. However, a distinguishing feature of the Convention is that it introduces a relatively complex system of exceptions to the general rule in Article 4 including that of the State of registration of the vehicle(s) involved in the accident. Article 5 contains a specific rule concerning damage to goods.

The Convention has been criticised for its complexity and for the fact that different laws are applicable to the liability vis-à-vis different victims. There is also no explicit rule on party autonomy, leading to uncertainty as to its admissibility.[20] Moreover, there is no rule allowing for an exception in favour of the law applicable to a contractual relationship between the tortfeasor and the victim if there is one.[21] Such could be the case if there is a contract for the transportation of persons, such as international bus transport.

iii. The Products Liability Convention

The Products Liability Convention utilises four different connecting factors to determine the applicable law: the place of injury; the place of the habitual residence of the person directly suffering damage; the principal place of business of the person claimed to be liable; and the place where the product was acquired by the person directly suffering damage. The choice between the different connecting factors is determined through a complex interplay of rules contained in Articles 4–7 of the Convention. The complexity of the rules reflects the complexity of international products liability litigation.

First, products liability cases will often have multiple defendants. The underlying substantive law rules often impose liability on several different persons along the chain of manufacture and distribution of any product and a victim might bring an action against a producer,

[15] Admittedly, this delineation between rules of a general nature and specific rules is debatable.

[16] Again, one could discuss the delineation. For instance, Arts 2 and 3, containing definitions and scope could of course be seen as operative.

[17] Presupposing that indirect damages do not give rise to an independent applicable law.

[18] Essén Report (n 8) 3.

[19] See CI Nagy, 'The Rome II Regulation and Traffic Accidents: Uniform Conflict Rules with Some Room for Forum Shopping – How So?' (2010) 6 *Journal of Private International Law* 93, 99.

[20] See TK Graziano, 'Traffic accidents' in J Basedow et al (eds), *Encyclopedia of Private International Law*, Vol 2 (Edward Elgar 2017) 1717, 1719.

[21] See A Staudinger, 'Das Konkurrenzverhältnis zwischen dem Haager Straßenverkehrsübereinkommen und der Rom II-VO' in D Baetge, J von Hein and M von Hinden (eds), *Die richtige Ordnung: Festschrift für Jan Kropholler zum 70. Geburtstag* (Mohr Siebeck 2008) 691, 697.

a quasi-producer[22] and the importer, as well as the supplier (typically a seller) depending on the circumstances of the case and the applicable law.[23]

Second, products liability cases also often involve multiple applicants since a defect may be inherent in all products of a particular type and thus cause injury to many individuals. The victims may choose to bring individual actions but may also, if this is possible under the law of the forum, bring a collective action.

Third, products liability cases are often distance delicts since the harmful event giving rise to the damage – for instance the manufacture of a product – and the damage itself – for instance bodily harm caused by the consumption of the product – frequently take place in different States.

Fourth, the various parties in the chain of manufacture and distribution cannot always foresee and/or control distribution of the product and thus indirectly possible places of injury.

Fifth, there is a difference between injury caused to a person who has somehow acquired the defective product and the so-called innocent bystanders who do not have any contractual relationship with the person claimed liable. In the latter case an action in contract would not be possible.

The interplay between the various connecting factors is quite complex, perhaps overly so.[24] On the other hand, it can also be said that the complexity of the applicable law rules only reflects the complexity of international products liability cases and that it serves to ensure that the law of a State with which there is a strong connection is applied.[25]

C. The Rome II Regulation

i. *Outline and Background*

The 'Rome II Regulation' on the law applicable to non-contractual obligations[26] is an example of regional unification of the law applicable to torts within the framework of the EU. It follows from this that the Regulation applies in 26 States[27] and that in spite of its regional character it applies in more States than both Hague Conventions.[28] According to its Article 3 it is to be given universal application and applies even when the law specified by the Regulation is not the law of a Member State.

The Regulation is applicable to 'non-contractual obligations', which is a wider concept than tort. The Regulation distinguishes between 'torts/delicts', which are covered in chapter II and 'unjust enrichment, *negotiorum gestio* and *culpa in contrahendo*', which are the subject of chapter III.

It should be noted that the applicable law rules in the Rome II Regulation, like those in the two Hague Conventions, are traditional in nature in that they are multilateral applicable law rules that

[22] Defined in Art 3(1) of the EU Products Liability Directive as 'any person who, by putting his name, trademark or other distinguishing feature on the product presents himself as its producer', see [1985] OJ L210/29.

[23] Examples given from Art 3 of the EU Products Liability Directive.

[24] An indirect criticism of the complexity of the Convention can be read into the Commission's desire to keep the rule on products liability in the Rome II Regulation 'simple and predictable' and to 'avoid [it] being unnecessarily complex', see COM(2003) 427 final, 14.

[25] JJ Fawcett, 'Products Liability in Private International Law: A European Perspective' (1993) 238 *Hague Collected Courses* 9, 147.

[26] (n 3).

[27] The EU has 27 Member States but due to an exception Denmark is not bound by the Regulation.

[28] What is more, the UK has decided to maintain its rules as part of its national law even after Brexit. see The Law Applicable to Contractual Obligations and Non-contractual Obligations (Amendment etc) (EU Exit) Regulations 2019, SI 2019/834.

could lead to the application of the law of either the forum or of another State.[29] What is more, the rules are also traditional in that they are based on objective, physical connecting factors such as 'law of the country in which the damage occurs' or the habitual residence of the parties rather than taking into account the content of the different laws.[30]

The rules of the Regulation give greater weight to foreseeability than flexibility. The regulation also eschews a 'one-size-fits-all solution' and provides specific rules for several specific torts, namely products liability, unfair competition and antitrust, environmental damage, infringement of intellectual property rights and industrial action. Finally, the applicable law has been given a wide scope and the Regulation is generally negative to the 'issue-by-issue analysis' more prevalent in US private international law.[31]

It should also be noted that Article 28(1) provides that in those Member States that are bound by them, the two HCCH Conventions on traffic accidents and products liability take precedence. This reduces the practical value of the Rome II Regulation in two important areas.

ii. General Rule

The EU legislator opted for the law of the place in which the damage occurs or the *lex loci damni*. Article 4(1) of the Rome II Regulation reads as follows:

> 1. Unless otherwise provided for in this Regulation, the law applicable to a non-contractual obligation arising out of a tort/delict shall be the law of the country in which the damage occurs irrespective of the country in which the event giving rise to the damage occurred and irrespective of the country or countries in which the indirect consequences of that event occur.

As follows from the wording both the *lex loci delicti commissi* and the laws of countries in which indirect damage has occurred are excluded from application. The latter exclusion is clearly influenced by the case law of the Court of Justice of the European Union (CJEU) regarding the interpretation of the rule on jurisdiction for torts in Article 7(2) of the Brussels Ia Regulation and its predecessors.[32]

As for the choice of the *lex loci damni* over the *lex loci delicti commissi* the Commission's proposal for a Rome II Regulation indicates that the solution was chosen because it was in line with more recent codifications in the Member States[33] and in most cases corresponds to the injured party's habitual residence but yet maintains the balance between the various interests at stake. For this reason the habitual residence of the victim was not chosen (although it does appear as a connecting factor in the special rule for products liability) and neither was the victim given

[29] A unilateral applicable law rule defines its own territorial scope whereas a multilateral applicable law rule makes the applicable law dependent on a particular connecting factor, see, eg, SC Symeonides, 'The American Choice-of-Law Revolution in the Courts: Today and Tomorrow' (2002) 298 *Hague Collected Courses* 9, 357 ff and M Bogdan and M Hellner, *Svensk internationell privat- och processrätt*, 9th edn (Norstedts Juridik 2020) 46.

[30] For a discussion of jurisdiction-selecting rules versus content-oriented rules, see SC Symeonides, 'Rome II and Tort Conflicts: A Missed Opportunity' (2008) 56 *American Journal of Comparative Law* 173, 181. The European Parliament suggested that 'the policies underlying the foreign law to be applied and the consequences of applying that law' should be taken into account when determining the applicable law, see P6_TC1-COD(2003)0168. See also Y Nishitani, 'The Rome II Regulation from a Japanese Point of View' (2007) 9 *Yearbook of Private International Law* 175, 177.

[31] See Second Restatement on the Conflict of Laws § 145 and M Hellner, 'Private International Enforcement of Competition Law: The Application of Foreign Competition Law (2002) 4 *Yearbook of Private International Law* 257, 290 f.

[32] See C-220/88 *Dumez* EU:C:1990:8; C-364/93 *Marinari* EU:C:1995:289; C-168/02 *Kronhofer* EU:C:2004:364.

[33] Contradicting that statement as over-simplified, see A Dickinson, *The Rome II Regulation: The Law Applicable to Non-contractual Obligations* (Oxford University Press 2008) 297.

a choice between the *lex loci damni* and the *lex loci delicti commissi* (except in cases of environmental damage).[34]

iii. Specific Torts

The original 1972 draft Convention on the law applicable to contractual and non-contractual obligations did not provide for specific applicable law rules for specific torts. Its Article 10 adopted a 'one-size-fits-all' approach. In the end, more than 30 years later, an approach with specific rules for specific torts was chosen. In the negotiations the pros and cons of having specific rules were discussed and also what types of torts merited a specific rule as well as the content of those specific rules.[35]

The drawback of having specific rules for specific torts is that it introduces an extra element of characterisation. For instance, is the tort of 'passing off' an intellectual property infringement (Article 8), unfair competition (Article 6) a general tort (Article 4) or an act of unjust enrichment (Article 10)?[36] The advantage of specific rules is that it allows for further refinement and what may be perceived to be a better and more balanced solution for a particular type of tort and also for greater clarity. One could probably also speak of a trend in private international law in moving from a few general rules to increased precision.[37]

In the end, the result of negotiations is that the Rome II Regulation provides for specific rules for five different types of torts: products liability (Article 5), unfair competition and anti-trust (Article 6), environmental damage (Article 7), infringement of intellectual property rights (Article 8) and industrial action (Article 9). The Commission's original proposal also contained a specific rule for the law applicable to violations of privacy and rights relating to the personality. However, due to widespread disagreement regarding the content of this rule it was deleted and it was decided to exclude the entire matter from the scope of the Regulation.[38] Article 9 on the law applicable to non-contractual obligations arising out of industrial action was added during negotiations after a Swedish proposal to that effect was approved.[39] It should be noted that a proposal for a particular rule on the law applicable to traffic accidents did not meet with approval.[40]

In comparison with the rules contained in the Hague Conventions on the law applicable to traffic accidents and products liability, the Rome II Regulation constitutes a simplification. For traffic accidents, there is no special rule and hence the general rule in Article 4 is applicable. It is arguably much simpler than Articles 3–6 of the 1971 Convention. This author has yet to hear the argument that the added complexity of the Hague Convention constitutes an added value.[41]

As concerns products liability, the ambition of the Commission was to find a simpler solution than the one found in the 1973 Hague Convention.[42] Arguably, this held true for the

[34] COM(2003) 427 final, 11.

[35] The author was a member of the Swedish delegation to the Council working party in which the proposal for a Rome II Regulation was discussed.

[36] The Regulation provides that Art 8 takes precedence over Art 10 but does not solve the question of the relationship between Arts 6 and 8. Art 4 is explicitly subsidiary to special rules.

[37] Rolando Quadri once referred to legislation on private international law, as 'vere selve di rami secchi' (real forests of dry branches) due to their lack of detail in comparison to substantive law in *Lezioni di diritto internazionale privato* 5th edn (Liguri editore 1969) 7.

[38] At one point in time there were nine different proposals, see M Hellner, *Rom II-förordningen: tillämplig lag för utomobligatoriska förpliktelser* (Norstedts Juridik 2014) 64.

[39] See Dickinson (n 33) 471; Hellner, ibid, 188 f.

[40] See Council Document 9009/04 ADD8, 18.5.2004 with proposals from the Swedish delegation.

[41] eg, Nagy (n 19) 107 is critical of the Hague Convention.

[42] See COM(2003) 427 final, 14.

Commission's original proposal but in negotiations the products liability rule was transformed beyond recognition and Article 5 of the Rome II Regulation is just as complex as Articles 4–7 of the Hague Convention.[43] But then applicable law for products liability *is* complex due to the fact that the person claimed to be liable often has acted in another country than the place of injury and that place might be very difficult to foresee and even harder to control.[44] Moreover, an additional complexity is that in cases of products liability there is under the substantive law of many countries often concurrent liability in contract and tort.[45] The Rome II Regulation takes this into account in Article 5(2), which under certain circumstances allows for the application of the law applicable to the contract but the Hague Convention does not.[46] The point of departure is that for such cases the 1955 Hague Convention on the law applicable to international sales of goods would apply.[47]

iv. Party Autonomy

A novelty in relation to the two Hague Conventions is that the Rome II Regulation explicitly provides for party autonomy. Party autonomy in the area of non-contractual obligations is a relatively new phenomenon in private international law and the Commission's original proposal only allowed for a choice of law after a dispute had arisen.[48] However, during the negotiations that led to the adoption of the Regulation a compromise was found, which under certain conditions allows the parties to choose the applicable law in advance. It follows from Article 14 of the Rome II Regulation that a choice of law agreement is valid if it is either entered into after the event giving rise to the damage occurred or at an earlier point in time if all the parties are pursuing a commercial activity and the agreement was 'freely negotiated'.

For obvious reasons, choice of law agreements are much less common in the area of tort than in the area of contract. After all, prior to the event giving rise to the damage, the parties might never have met and after that they are often less inclined to agree. The most typical situation will be parties that are in a contractual relationship with each other and have a choice of law clause in their contract. By way of exception that clause will explicitly refer to non-contractual obligations that may arise between the parties, eg, excluding product liability. However, more often there will be a general clause along the lines of 'disputes arising out of this agreement shall be decided according to X law'. Whether such a clause also covers obligations arising between the parties that are non-contractual by their legal nature but clearly connected to the agreement is a question of interpretation of the contract. Examples of such non-contractual obligations that might arise between parties to a contract are claims in tort for misrepresentation and other fraudulent behaviour or damage caused to the person or property of one contract party by the

[43] A word count is perhaps not the most accurate way of determining complexity but reveals that Art 5 of the Rome II Regulation consists of 237 words (1,331 characters) and Arts 4–7 of the 1973 Hague Convention of 261 words (1,431 characters). The fact that the rules in the Hague Convention are dispersed in four different Articles adds six words and 29 characters.

[44] See TK Graziano, 'Products liability' in J Basedow et al (eds), *Encyclopedia of Private International Law*, Vol 2 (Edward Elgar 2017) 1413.

[45] See TK Graziano, *Gemeineuropäisches Internationales Privatrecht: Harmonisierung des IPR durch Wissenschaft und Lehre* (am Beispiel der außenvertraglichen Haftung für Schäden) (Mohr Siebeck 2001) 258.

[46] See H Duintjer Tebbens, *International Product Liability: A Study of Comparative and International Legal Aspects of Product Liability* (Sijthoff & Noordhoff 1980) 356 f for criticism.

[47] See WLM Reese, *Convention on the Law Applicable to Products Liability. Explanatory Report* (Reese Report) 13 (257).

[48] See COM(2003) 427 final, 36. See also Dickinson (n 33) 540 f and M Hellner, 'Choice of Law by the Parties in Rome II: Rationale of the Differentiation between Consumer and Commercial Contracts' (2019) 6 *Oslo Law Review* 67, 68 for background. See also Symeon Symeonides, 'Law Applicable to Contracts', in ch 14 in this book at I.B.ii.

other contract party (or persons for whom the party is responsible) in the course of fulfilling the contract.

A choice of law by the parties takes precedence over an objective applicable law. However, this is not the case if an action in tort is brought based on a violation of competition law (Article 6) or an infringement of intellectual property rights (Article 8). Due to the strong governmental interests involved in the application of the law provided for by Articles 6 and 8 respectively a choice of law clause will not be upheld.

II. A Hague Convention on the Law Applicable to Torts?

A. Likelihood

It is submitted that for a number of reasons it is unlikely that the Hague Conference on Private International Law will commence work on a Convention on the law applicable to torts in the foreseeable future. To begin with, conventions on applicable law are not the most successful Hague Conventions. Of the 39 Conventions and Protocols adopted[49] since 1954 only 16 are Conventions (or Protocols) exclusively devoted to applicable law. What is more, four Conventions contain applicable law rules in addition to rules on jurisdiction and/or recognition and enforcement.[50]

Of the 16 Conventions exclusively devoted to applicable law five have not entered into force and are unlikely ever to do so. Only eight of the applicable law Conventions have attracted more than 10 ratifications and three have attracted more than 20 ratifications: (1) the 1961 Convention on the Conflicts of Laws Relating to the Form of Testamentary Dispositions (42 Contracting Parties); (2) the 2007 Protocol on the Law Applicable to Maintenance Obligations (30 Contracting Parties);[51] and (3) the 1971 Convention on the Law Applicable to Traffic Accidents (21 Contracting Parties).

These numbers can be compared with the three most successful Conventions of the Hague Conference, viz. (1) the 1961 Apostille Convention (120 Contracting Parties); (2) the 1993 Convention on Protection of Children and Co-operation in Respect of Intercountry Adoption (103 Contracting Parties); and (3) the 1980 Convention on the Civil Aspects of International Child Abduction (101 Contracting Parties). All of them deal with international judicial cooperation, not applicable law.

There are simply not as compelling reasons to ratify conventions on applicable law as there are to ratify conventions on recognition and enforcement or international judicial cooperation. All applicable law conventions provide for universal application of their rules, ie, that the rules of the convention apply independent of any requirement of reciprocity and even if the applicable law is that of a non-Contracting State. Hence, the only added value in ratifying an applicable law convention is contributing to international legal uniformity and experience shows that this has not been sufficient. After all, there is nothing that prevents a State from copying the rules of a convention into its own law. By not ratifying a convention it maintains the freedom to make the adjustments that it would prefer.

What is more, a large majority of the States that do ratify applicable law conventions are Member States of the European Union and those States have already unified their applicable law

[49] The 2015 Principles on Choice of Law in International Commercial Contracts not included.

[50] The number of conventions and protocols given here does not take into account that some of them have become largely obsolete due to the adoption of later instruments.

[51] Only three States are not bound through their membership of the European Union. The EU is counted as a Contracting Party in addition to the individual Member States. Denmark is a Member State of the EU but not bound by the protocol.

rules for tort in the form of the Rome II Regulation. It is unlikely that the Member States would be willing to prioritise work on a general convention on the law applicable to tort unless there were strong indications that many non-Member States were very interested in commencing work on such a project. So far, there appears to be no such general interest. There have been no recent initiatives taken to put applicable law for torts on the Hague Conference list of future legislative projects, although applicable law for environmental damages and unfair competition were previously on the list of possible projects.

Finally, there is still great diversity between national substantive laws on tort. Hence, the main reason for not pursuing further work on a general convention on the law applicable to tort in the late 1960s still exists.

On the other hand, a situation where the two Hague Conventions on traffic accidents and products liability take precedence over the Rome II Regulation in some Member States of the EU, but not in all, is unsatisfactory. Proposals have ranged from denunciation by those Member States who are bound by the Conventions to an EU initiative for a modernisation of those two Conventions including the insertion of an 'REIO clause' allowing the EU to become a Party.[52] If such a proposal is to come it is likely that it would be coordinated with a future revision of the Rome II Regulation. Preparatory work for a review has commenced.[53]

B. Could the Rome II Regulation Serve as the Basis for a Hague Convention?

i. General Observations

Generally speaking, harmonisation of private international law is a good thing and enhances legal certainty as well as reducing the risk of conflicting judgments and forum shopping.[54] There is no reason why the Rome II Regulation could not serve as a basis for a future Hague Convention. The Regulation is in reality an international convention binding 26 States, just in another legal form, and few of the operative applicable law rules are EU specific.[55]

The fact that one fundamental reason for an international convention is international uniformity in courts' decision making would call for traditional bilateral applicable law rules that – to use North American terminology – are of a 'jurisdiction-selecting', character rather than being 'result-oriented'.[56] However, as has been pointed out, even within the context of traditional applicable law rules there can be room for rules that are geared towards a particular outcome.[57] One very clear example is Article 18 of the Rome II Regulation, according to which,

> [t]he person having suffered damage may bring his or her claim directly against the insurer of the person liable to provide compensation if the law applicable to the non-contractual obligation or the law applicable to the insurance contract so provides.[58]

[52] The acronym REIO stands for Regional Economic Integration Organisation.

[53] Currently the British Institute of International and Comparative Law is carrying out a study on the application of the Rome II Regulation with the purpose of supporting the Commission in a future review.

[54] However, applicable law is only one factor of many that triggers forum shopping.

[55] See E Guinchard, 'Unfinished business: Rome II in Practice and the Need for a Hague Convention on Non-contractual Obligations: Brief Reflections on the French Supreme Court's First Decision on Rome II' (2015) 40 *European Law Review* 100, 108 f.

[56] The negative influence on international uniformity caused by 'result-oriented' rules and the ensuing forum shopping was recognised already by DF Cavers, 'A Critique of the Choice-of-Law Problem' (1933) 47 *Harvard Law Review* 173, 200. His answer to the problem was greater uniformity in rules on forum.

[57] See Symeonides (n 30) 182.

[58] See C-240/14 *Prüller-Frey* EU:C:2015:567.

The desire to increase foreseeability should lead to rules that are geared in the direction of foreseeability rather than flexibility, albeit with some room for exceptions.[59]

ii. Scope

The Rome II Regulation has a very wide scope and covers the law applicable to 'non-contractual obligations', which is wider in scope than 'torts' and also includes unjust enrichment, *negotiorum gestio* and *culpa in contrahendo*.[60] There are some important exclusions from scope in Article 1(2), most notably any non-contractual obligation arising out of a family relationship, nuclear damage and violations of privacy and rights relating to personality. Although it is desirable to maintain as wide a scope as possible for a global convention on the law applicable to torts, it is to be expected that should work on such an instrument ever commence there will be more exclusions from scope than in the Rome II Regulation. One indication would be the 2019 HCCH Judgments Convention, which, just like the Rome II Regulation in its Article 2 excludes family law matters, nuclear damage and defamation and privacy (the exclusion is slightly differently worded than in Rome II). In addition, transboundary marine pollution, intellectual property and many antitrust matters are excluded from scope.[61] At least the two latter are relatively common in practice and if such an exclusion were carried over to a global convention on applicable law it would necessitate complementary EU rules, or the existence of two parallel systems, which is a possible but not very attractive solution.

iii. Party Autonomy

The trend in private international law in general, including torts, has been to allow the parties a right to agree on the applicable law so long as there is no compelling reason to limit that freedom.[62] Allowing party autonomy also fits well with the overarching aim of increasing legal certainty and predictability. However, party autonomy is not always appropriate and the prevailing reasons to limit it are either a desire to protect the weaker party or certain State interests.

Article 14 of the Rome II Regulation recognises party autonomy if the choice of law agreement was entered into *after* the 'event giving rise to the damage occurred'. It protects weaker parties in that a choice of law agreement entered into in advance will only be upheld if all the parties 'are pursuing a commercial activity' and if the agreement was 'freely negotiated before the event giving rise to the damage occurred'. States' interests in the application of their national laws are protected through Articles 6(4) and 8(3), voiding any choice of law for a non-contractual

[59] Symeonides (n 30) 180 argues that any overly rigid system that fails to lead to 'sensible, rational, and fair decisions in individual cases' will be ignored by judges. However, it is submitted that while this, due to the specifics of the legal culture and the position of judges, might hold true in an American context it is less likely to happen in other parts of the world.

[60] The latter could be characterised as a tort, unjust enrichment, quasi-contract or simply *sui generis*, see H Edlund, 'Culpa in Contrahendo: Tortious Liability, Breach of Contract or an Autonomous Legal Instrument?' (2019) 30 *European Business Law Review* 815. Whether Art 2(1) of the Rome II Regulation serves to exclude other non-contractual obligations than those three is a different story, see P Beaumont and P McEleavy, *Anton's Private International Law*, 3rd edn (W Green/SULI 2011) 613; Hellner (n 38) 50.

[61] Art 2 of the 2019 Judgments Convention also excludes 'activities of armed forces' and 'law enforcement activities'. Although not explicitly excluded from the scope of the Rome II Regulation, it follows from the limitation of scope to 'civil and commercial matters' and its interpretation in the case law of the CJEU that the activities of armed forces and police would be excluded from scope, see C-292/05 *Lechouritou and Others* EU:C:2007:102.

[62] See TK Graziano, 'Freedom to Choose the Applicable Law in Tort – Articles 14 and 4(3) of the Rome II Regulation' in W Binchy and J Ahern (eds), *The Rome II Regulation on the Law Applicable to Non-Contractual Obligations: A New Tort Litigation Regime* (Martinus Nijhoff 2009) 113, 114 f for an overview of developments in national PIL codifications up to that time.

obligation arising out of unfair competition, an act restricting free competition or an intellectual property infringement. In addition, Article 16 provides for the application of overriding (internationally) mandatory rules of the forum.

One major advantage of Article 14 is that it allows the parties to submit all their obligations, both contractual and non-contractual, to one and the same law and minimises the importance of the characterisation of a claim as one or the other.[63] All in all, the solutions in the Rome II Regulation are balanced and could certainly serve as a template for a Hague Convention. Having said this, there is room for improvement. For instance, the expression 'an agreement freely negotiated' fails to express what is actually meant and should be replaced by 'individually negotiated' or something along those lines and the limitation to parties pursuing a commercial activity is too wide and excludes non-commercial parties that are not weaker such as non-governmental organisations or even government authorities.

iv. The General Rule

The choice of the *lex loci damni* was chosen for the reason that it was perceived to favour the victim of a tort since the place where the damage occurs often coincides with his or her habitual residence. This solution was also chosen because it was seen as 'a compromise between the two extreme solutions of applying the law of the place where the event giving rise to the damage occurs and giving the victim the option'.[64]

However, the solution chosen is not necessarily particularly beneficial to the victim. First of all, it is often more difficult to determine the place where the damage occurred than that of the event giving rise to the damage, thus causing legal uncertainty.[65] Second, since indirect damage does not give rise to an independent applicable law, the rule necessitates the distinction between direct and indirect damage. This distinction is often far from self-evident, which again leads to legal uncertainty. Third, when damage occurs in several States, according to the 'mosaic principle' multiple laws apply. These difficulties are the same in the context of jurisdiction and have been recognised in the 2019 HCCH Judgments Convention,[66] according to which only judgments from the State of origin of the act or omission causing harm are entitled to recognition.[67]

It is submitted that giving the victim a choice between the law of the place of acting or the place of damage is not an 'extreme' solution but one that would lead to the most effective administration of justice without putting an undue burden on the tortfeasor. After all, there is a strong connection between the tort and the place of acting and, what is more, this place often coincides with the tortfeasor's habitual residence. Giving the applicant a choice would make it possible to avoid the mosaic principle, which could be particularly beneficial in the case of collective action.[68]

As for the application of the law of the common place of residence – Article 4(2) – it should be considered whether this rule should not be made optional for the victim. Although the rule has merit in many cases in which the connection to the State where the damage occurred is

[63] Art 4(3) and several other provisions of the Regulation have the same aim.

[64] COM(2003) 427 final, 12.

[65] Although, as the case law of the CJEU concerning the interpretation of Art 7(2) of the Brussels Ia Regulation shows, difficulties may arise in determining both.

[66] Convention of 2 July 2019 on the Recognition and Enforcement of Foreign Judgments in Civil or Commercial Matters. See the F Garcímartin and G Saumier, *Explanatory Report on the 2019 HCCH Judgments Convention* (HCCH 2020) 102.

[67] Art 5(1)(j).

[68] See on this in the context of environmental damage, C Bernasconi, 'Civil Liability Resulting from Transfrontier Environmental Damage: A Case for the Hague Conference?' Prel Doc No 8 of May 2000 for the Meeting of the HCCH Council on General Affairs and Policy 43.

fortuitous, in some cases it does not and could lead to one victim of a tort being less compensated than another victim who does not share a habitual residence with the tortfeasor.[69]

The possibility given in Article 4(3) to make an exception if there is a manifestly closer connection between the tort and another State should be kept. This facilitates application of one and the same law to actions in contract and actions in tort and reduces the cost of litigation.

V. Specific Torts

The fact that the Rome II Regulation contains specific rules for certain types of torts is both a blessing and a curse. It is a blessing in that it has given the legislator a possibility to fine-tune the rules for different torts with the intention of serving justice. It is a curse in that it creates problems of delimitation and adds to complexity as one and the same action could be characterised as several different torts. It is, by way of example, possible to imagine one and the same act as restricting free competition as well as constituting unfair competition, both of which are subject to slightly different rules in Article 6.[70]

It is submitted that now that 'Pandora's Box' has been opened, it would be very difficult to close it again. Moreover, since reforming the Conventions on the law applicable to traffic accidents and products liability would be one of the motives for commencing work on a Hague Convention on the law applicable to torts in general, it would be very difficult to argue for the deletion of special rules for those two areas.

The Rome II Regulation could serve as a starting point, with the addition of a special rule on traffic accidents. However, ever since the Hague Conference started working on a consensus basis rather than voting, the likelihood for the adoption of rules on controversial matters such as antitrust and industrial action has decreased. What is more, some of the rules in the Rome II Regulation are more or less EU specific and cannot just be transferred to a global convention. For instance, Article 8(2) concerns the law applicable to the infringement of a unitary EU intellectual property right and is unlikely to fit in a global convention. Likewise, Article 6(3)(b) on the law applicable to restrictions of competition allows the claimant to base his or her claim on the law of the forum if that is in a Member State whose market has been directly and substantially affected by the restriction of competition. This rule presupposes that the rules on jurisdiction are unified and perhaps also common antitrust rules.

C. Conclusions

The transformation of the HCCH from a largely European and North American organisation to a global organisation working under consensus rather than majority voting has made it quite unlikely that it would become the forum of a general convention on the law applicable to torts. The States that are interested in the unification of applicable law are mainly to be found in the EU and it is not to be expected that they would substitute their regional unification in the form of the Rome II Regulation for HCCH rules, which, given the consensus working methodology, may be watered down and/or rendered very complex in negotiations. What is more, most of the States that would have contributed to the – from an EU perspective – unfavourable result, would

[69] Admittedly, the rule could of course work the other way around.

[70] *Cf* recital 9 to Council Regulation (EC) No 1/2003 on the implementation of the rules on competition laid down in Articles 81 and 82 of the Treaty [2003] OJ L1/1, which foresees a parallel application of rules against the restriction of competition and rules against unfair competition.

not accede to a future convention anyway since they are not interested in acceding to applicable law conventions.

However, it is conceivable that the EU would take the initiative for a most welcome modernisation of the two HCCH Conventions on the law applicable to traffic accidents and products liability. Important aspects of their modernisation would include a simplification (here, the author remains pessimistic – the consensus methodology may lead to more complex solutions), the introduction of explicit rules on party autonomy, and regard to the interplay with choice of law in contract.

19

Tort: Jurisdiction

REID MORTENSEN

I. Tort and Tort Jurisdiction

Since the early twentieth century, the substantive law of tort[1] has grown to address the risks posed by industrialisation and the greater exposure to harm brought by transport accidents, mechanised workplaces, unsafe goods, pollution and environmental damage. The jurisdiction of civil courts to deal with tort claims has grown with it. *Actor sequitur forum rei* – the principle of litigating where the defendant is found – has long been superseded as the only credible basis of adjudicative jurisdiction in tort.

This chapter gives an account of the development of 'special' – or 'long-arm' or 'specific' – jurisdiction in tort claims. These are jurisdictions that are assumed when defendants are not 'at home' in the place of the forum court – whether because, in the civil law, they are not domiciled in that place;[2] in the common law, they were not in the place when served with a writ or when doing business there; or they have not voluntarily submitted to the forum court's jurisdiction. I therefore concentrate on the development of tort jurisdictions that rest on some ground other than the defendant's close connection with the place where the court is located. This analysis covers special tort jurisdictions across three families of the civil and common law – the European, American and Commonwealth models of jurisdiction. These jurisdictional models are introduced in section II. An attempt is then made in section III to compare them by reference to the grounds on which a court assumes special tort jurisdiction: ie, when it is the court for the place of the tort (the *forum delicti*), the place where damage was suffered (the *forum damni*) or, for the American model only, a place with which the defendant has sufficient minimum contacts. That comparison reveals points of convergence and divergence between the three models that, in section IV, suggest a possible direction for unifying the special tort jurisdictions of the civil and common law worlds.

Three preliminary observations are made. First, it is not possible in this chapter to cover the whole field of tort. This account tends to address the lines of special jurisdiction articulated by the highest courts in each model and, in these courts, personal injuries, product liability and defamation claims predominate. Second, section IV's suggestion to unify special tort jurisdictions may

[1] The term 'tort' is used throughout, even when the country or system being discussed uses alternative terms or language for non-contractual civil wrongs – such as 'delict'.

[2] For modern recognition of the preference that jurisdiction be grounded on domicile, see Article 4 Regulation (EU) No 1215/2012 of the European Parliament and of the Council of 12 December 2012 on jurisdiction and the recognition and enforcement of judgment in civil and commercial matters (recast) [2012] OJ L351/1 (Brussels I).

seem hopelessly naive, especially after the failed attempt to provide for common rules of adjudicative jurisdiction in the Hague Conference on Private International Law's (HCCH) Preliminary Draft Convention on Jurisdiction and Foreign Judgments in Civil and Commercial Matters.[3] Tort jurisdiction was one issue that was difficult to negotiate for the Preliminary Draft, but the greater concern about it related more to its easing of the enforcement of judgments – and especially of high damages awards from American tort proceedings.[4] However, the recent conclusion of the HCCH Convention on the Recognition and Enforcement of Foreign Judgments[5] gives a scheme that now addresses that greater concern – in part through Article 10 and its allowing for the reduction of damages awards to compensatory amounts. In the indirect special jurisdiction it recognises as supporting an internationally enforceable judgment, the Judgments Convention has a modest tort jurisdiction that could be used as a direct ground of jurisdiction in a future Convention.

Third, an account of special tort jurisdictions cannot escape the question of exorbitance. Just what amounts to an exorbitant jurisdiction is certainly open to contest, but it is no longer credible to claim that *actor sequitur forum rei* is the measure of an acceptable jurisdiction. In tort jurisdiction, there have been efforts at reducing claimants' 'venue risk' by easing their ability to sue where it is least expensive: usually, at home.[6] Where special jurisdictions rest on thick connections between the substance of the proceedings and the place of the forum court, they may be considered acceptable.[7] Having said that, an exorbitant jurisdiction arguably arises where it is based *merely* on a personal connection between the claimant and the place of the forum.[8]

II. The Context: European, American and Commonwealth Tort Jurisdictions

A. The European Model

The European model is represented by Article 7(2) of the Brussels Ia Regulation, which provides the uniform expression of the special tort jurisdiction for Member States of the European Union: 'A person domiciled in a Member State may be sued in another Member State … in matters relating to tort, delict or quasi-delict, in the courts for the place where the harmful event occurred or may occur'. The expression of this ground of jurisdiction has been relatively consistent since it was

[3] Preliminary Draft Convention on Jurisdiction and Foreign Judgments in Civil and Commercial Matters adopted by the Special Commission on 30 October 1999 (Preliminary Draft Convention).

[4] PR Beaumont, 'A United Kingdom Perspective on the Proposed Hague Judgments Convention' (1998) 24 *Brooklyn Journal of International Law* 75, 77–79, 109; P Borchers, 'A Few Little Issues for the Hague Judgments Negotiations' (1998) 24 *Brooklyn Journal of International Law* 157, 158.

[5] Convention on the recognition and enforcement of foreign judgments in civil or commercial matters (concluded at The Hague, 2 July 2019) (Judgments Convention).

[6] For an account of venue risk, see R Fentiman, *International Commercial Litigation* (Oxford University Press 2010) 52–55.

[7] See Lord Sumption's comments in *Abela v Baadarani* [2013] 1 WLR 2043, 2062.

[8] The 'place' in question is the one geographic territory under the one body of law. In a federation, the state or province is usually the 'place' in question, but for a federal court it is usually the nation as a whole: see *Adams v Cape Industries plc* [1990] Ch 433, 488. The claims of most Australian state courts to assume jurisdiction for events that take place in a different state are easily classified as exorbitant: R Mortensen, R Garnett and M Keyes, *Private International Law in Australia*, 4th edn (LexisNexis Butterworths 2019) 19, 50–51; A Dickinson, 'In Absentia: The Evolution and Reform of Australian Rules of Adjudicatory Jurisdiction' in M Douglas, V Bath, M Keyes and A Dickinson (eds), *Commercial Issues in Private International Law: A Common Law Perspective* (Hart Publishing 2019) 13, 41–44.

first stated in its predecessors: the Brussels Convention of 1968,[9] and the Brussels I Regulation of 2000.[10] The only change in expression was that the Regulation of 2000 added the words 'or may occur' to the ground of jurisdiction. This was just a clarification; the Court of Justice of the European Union (CJEU) had already held that proceedings to prevent a harmful event were within the Brussels Convention's special jurisdiction for torts.[11]

In *Handelskwekerij GJ Bier v Mines de Potasse d'Alsace*,[12] the CJEU extended the possibilities for a validly assumed special jurisdiction under Article 7(2) by holding that

> the expression 'place where the harmful event occurred' must be established in such a way as to acknowledge that the plaintiff has an option to commence proceedings either at the place where the damage occurred or the place of the event giving rise to it.[13]

As we will see,[14] the identification of both places has been further refined but, in a general sense, *Mines de Potasse d'Alsace* gives special jurisdiction to both the court for the place where the tort occurred and the court for the place where the damage was suffered.

B. The American Model

The common theme of American civil jurisdiction is the prior constitutional requirement that the assumption of jurisdiction must satisfy 'the minimum contacts test' of the Constitution's relevant due process clause; the Fourteenth Amendment's due process clause for state courts and, probably, the Fifth Amendment's due process clause for federal courts.[15] In *International Shoe Co v Washington*,[16] Stone J in the US Supreme Court confirmed that

> due process requires only that in order to subject a defendant to a judgment *in personam*, if he be not present within the territory of the forum, he have certain minimum contacts with it such that the maintenance of the suit does not offend 'traditional notions of fair play and substantial justice'.[17]

And where, say, a state court does assume special jurisdiction, there are two questions: whether the contacts with the state are related to the proceedings, and if so, whether those contacts meet the minimum that is juridically required to ensure that due process is given.[18]

International Shoe's minimum contacts test allowed a broader range of contacts than were traditionally contemplated by the common law for the assumption of jurisdiction to be considered constitutionally valid,[19] so American states subsequently explored the possibilities of broader special jurisdictions by legislation. Two patterns have emerged. The first is simply to appropriate the minimum contacts test as the sole determinant of jurisdiction. In California,

[9] Art 5(3) Convention on jurisdiction and the enforcement of judgments in civil and commercial matters, Brussels, 27 September 1968 [1998] OJ C27/1.

[10] Art 5 (3) Council Regulation (EC) No 44/2001 of 22 December 2000 on jurisdiction and the recognition and enforcement of judgment in civil and commercial matters [2001] OJ L12/1.

[11] Case C-167/00 *Verein für Konsumenteninformation v Henkel* [2000] ECR I-8129, 8141–43 [44]–[49]. See also, *Bonnier Media Ltd v Smith* 2003 SC 36.

[12] Case 21/76 [1976] ECR 1735.

[13] Ibid, 1747.

[14] See text to nn 76–91, 126–35 below.

[15] 5th and 14th Amendments Constitution (US).

[16] 326 US 310 (1945).

[17] Ibid, 316.

[18] ie, adopting the analysis in P Hay, PJ Borchers and SC Symeonides, *Conflict of* Laws, 5th edn (West Publishing Co 2010) 361.

[19] Ibid, 374. The Supreme Court departed from its previous position which (drawing on the common law) insisted on the presence of the defendant in the state: *Pennoyer v Neff* 95 US 714, 733 (1878).

a court 'may exercise jurisdiction on any basis not inconsistent with the requirements of the Constitution of this state or of the United States'.[20] This therefore constitutionalises every question of jurisdiction. New Jersey takes a similar approach,[21] its civil jurisdictions extending to the 'uttermost limits permitted by the United States Constitution'.[22] The second pattern demands a connection between the proceedings and the state that is, at least on its face, more substantial than minimum contacts. For instance, so far as cross-border tort claims are concerned, in New York the Civil Practice Law and Rules (CPLR) provide that

> a court may exercise personal jurisdiction over any non-domiciliary, or his executor or administrator, who in person or through an agent: …
>
> 1. transacts any business within the state or contracts anywhere to supply goods or services in the state; or
> 2. commits a tortious act within the state, except as to a cause of action for defamation of character arising from the act; or
> 3. commits a tortious act without the state causing injury to person or property within the state, except as to a cause of action for defamation of character arising from the act, if he (i) regularly does or solicits business, or engages in any other persistent course of conduct, or derives substantial revenue from goods used or consumed or services rendered, in the state, or (ii) expects or should reasonably expect the act to have consequences in the state and derives substantial revenue from interstate or international commerce.[23]

The New York CPLR can give the impression that there may be no special jurisdiction in defamation claims, but it has been held that paragraph 1 may capture claims in defamation.[24] Further, because the CPLR requires its own contacts with the state, the assumption of jurisdiction within its terms will usually be constitutionally valid – although the court must always conduct a minimum contacts enquiry.[25]

The CPLR centres special jurisdiction on the *forum delicti* or, subject also to having a commercial connection with the state, the *forum damni*. This is the most common pattern of American state jurisdiction – eg, Connecticut,[26] the District of Columbia,[27] Florida,[28] Georgia,[29] Indiana,[30] Massachusetts[31] and Virginia[32] provide rules of jurisdiction that parallel the CPLR, and even replicate the defendant's commercial connections with the state that qualify the *forum damni*'s jurisdiction. It gives rise to a relatively narrow, and limited, cross-border tort jurisdiction.[33] In form, at least, some states are even less ambitious: Illinois,[34] Michigan[35] and Texas[36] provide only for special jurisdiction in tort if the state court is the *forum delicti*. However, American special jurisdiction statutes can sometimes be generously interpreted. Despite the limited grounds of jurisdiction set out in statute, Texas courts have held that the only enquiry that they must

[20] § 4.10.10 Code of Civil Procedure (CA).
[21] R 4:4-4(e) New Jersey Rules of Court 2003 (NJ).
[22] *Avdel Corp v Mercure* 277 A 2d 207 (1971).
[23] § 302(a) Civil Practice Law and Rules (NY).
[24] *Legros v Irving* 327 NYS 2d 371, 373 (1971); *Best Van Lines Inc v Walker* 490 F 3d 239, 244–45 (2007).
[25] *Ingraham v Carroll* NY 2d 592, 596–97 (1997).
[26] § 52-59(a)(1)–(3) Connecticut Statutes (CT).
[27] § 13-423 (c)–(d) District of Columbia Code (DC).
[28] § 48.193 (1)(b), (f) Florida Statutes (FL).
[29] § 9-10-91 (2)–(3) Georgia Code (GA).
[30] R 4.4 Indiana State Trial Procedure (IN).
[31] Part III, Title II, Ch 223A, s 3 General Laws (MA).
[32] § 8.01-328.1 Code of Virginia (VA).
[33] Hay, Borchers and Symeonides (n 18) 356, 484.
[34] § 2-209(2) Code of Civil Procedure (IL).
[35] § 600.705 (2) Michigan Statutes (MI).
[36] § 17.042 (2) Civil Practice and Remedies Code (TX).

undertake when assuming jurisdiction is, 'is the exercise of jurisdiction consistent with the requirements of due process of law under the United States Constitution?'[37]

C. The Commonwealth Model

All Commonwealth special jurisdictions stem from the Common Law Procedure Act 1852 (UK), which allowed service of process outside England and Wales when there was 'a Cause of Action, which arose within the Jurisdiction'.[38] The development of special jurisdictions in England and Wales subsequently took place, for the most part, in the judge-made Supreme Court Rules of 1883 that gave power to allow service of defendants *ex iuris*.[39] A ground of jurisdiction specifically relating to tort claims was, though, relatively slow to develop,[40] and did not emerge until changes to the rules in 1920 allowed the court to exercise jurisdiction when the claim was 'founded on a tort committed within the jurisdiction'.[41] Similar rules of court were replicated throughout the Empire and Commonwealth. A significant expansion in tort jurisdiction, however, was introduced in 1970 in New South Wales, where the rules of court gave jurisdiction 'where the proceedings are founded on, or are for the recovery of, damage suffered wholly or partly in the State caused by a tortious act or omission wherever occurring'.[42] This development, too, was adopted by other Commonwealth courts. The leading example of the modern rule is in Practice Direction 6B for England and Wales, which relevantly provides:

> The claimant may serve a claim form out of the jurisdiction with the permission of the court … where … [a] claim is made in tort where –
>
> (a) damage was sustained, or will be sustained, within the jurisdiction; or
> (b) damage which has been or will be sustained results from an act committed, or likely to be committed, within the jurisdiction.[43]

Special jurisdiction in tort claims when the court is either the *forum delicti* or the *forum damni* is also recognised in most Australian states and territories,[44] New Zealand,[45] Singapore[46] and, still reflecting its Commonwealth inheritance, Hong Kong.[47] This is also the case in the Canadian provinces of Manitoba,[48] New Brunswick[49] and Prince Edward Island.[50]

[37] *Hall v Helicopteros Nacionales De Colombia* 638 SW 2d 870, 872 (1982).
[38] ss 18–19 Common Law Procedure Act 1852 (UK); and see *Jackson v Spittal* (1870) LR 5 CP 542.
[39] O 11 r 1(1) Rules of the Supreme Court 1883 (UK).
[40] The only claims in tort recognised under the earliest rules of special jurisdiction in England and Wales in Order 11(1) Rules of the Supreme Court 1883 (UK), only provided for jurisdiction in suits for an injunction as to any nuisance within England and Wales.
[41] O 11 r 1(1)(ee) Rules of the Supreme Court 1883 (UK), as amended by the Rules of the Supreme Court (No 3) 1920 (UK); *George Munro Limited v American Cyanamid and Chemical Corporation* [1944] KB 432. AB Keith regarded this as a return to the position prior to 1883: AV Dicey and AB Keith, *Digest of the Law of England with Reference to the Conflict of Laws*, 5th edn (Stevens and Sons Ltd 1932) 254–55.
[42] Pt 10, r 1(e) Supreme Court Rules 1970 (NSW).
[43] R 3.1(9) Practice Direction 6B.
[44] R 10.42 Item 5 Federal Court Rules 2011 (Cth); r 6502 Court Procedures Rules 2006 (ACT); Sch 6(a)(ii) Uniform Civil Procedure Rules 2005 (NSW); r 7.01(1)(k) Supreme Court Rules 1987 (NT); r 125(a) Uniform Civil Procedure Rules 1999 (Qld); r 40A(ii) Supreme Court Civil Rules 2006 (SA); r 147A(a)(ii) Supreme Court Rules 2000 (Tas); r 7.02(a)(ii) Supreme Court (General Civil Procedure) Rules 2015 (Vic).
[45] R 6.27(2)(a) High Court Rules 2016 (NZ).
[46] O 11 r 1(f) Rules of Court (Sg).
[47] O 11 r 1(1)(f) Rules of the High Court (HK).
[48] R 17.02 (g), (h) Court of Queen's Bench Rules, Man Reg 553/88 (Man).
[49] R 19.01 (h)–(i) Rules of Court, NB Reg 82–73 (NB).
[50] R 17.02 (g)–(h) Rules of Civil Procedure (PEI).

However, in parts of the Commonwealth special jurisdiction in tort claims remains limited to the *forum delicti*: Northern Ireland,[51] India,[52] Western Australia[53] and every common law country in Africa.[54] It is also the case for most common law provinces in Canada.[55] This is a result partly of the adoption in some provinces of the model Court Jurisdiction and Proceedings Transfer Act and, in others, of the lead given by the common law in Canada – which uniquely for a common law principle presumes that the court for the place of the tort has jurisdiction in tort claims.[56]

At least in the provinces and states of Canada and Australia, there is the possibility of an initial question of the constitutional validity of the legislation or rules of court that give special jurisdiction – as the subnational legislatures in these countries are subject to limits on their power to pass laws with extraterritorial effect.[57] In Canada, the basic principle that the proceedings must have a real and substantial connection with the province is now recognised as both a constitutional limitation and a common law rule,[58] and parallels American minimum contacts limitations on the jurisdiction of US courts.[59] Application of long-arm rules of jurisdiction in Canada may be subject to a similar constitutional enquiry.[60] The Canadian limitation is nevertheless greater, and more clearly stated, than the Australian limitation that the proceedings must have a connection, even if only a remote one, with the state if the assumption of jurisdiction is to be constitutionally valid.[61] This has not prevented doubts emerging around the validity of some Australian tort jurisdictions.[62]

D. Interrelationships

There are plainly some close relationships between the different models. This is most notable in the UK where, before Brexit, the English and Welsh and the Northern Irish courts exercised European jurisdictions when the defendant was domiciled in the EU,[63] but maintained the Commonwealth jurisdictions for all other cross-border litigation. The precise expression

[51] O 11 r 1(1)f) Rules of the Court of Judicature (Northern Ireland) 1981.

[52] ss 19, 20(c) Code of Civil Procedure 1908 (India).

[53] O 10 r 1(1)(k) Supreme Court Rules 1971 (WA).

[54] See generally, RF Oppong, *Private International Law in Commonwealth Africa* (Cambridge University Press 2013) 47–68; r 8(f) Rules of the High Court (Gambia); O 8 r 3(h) High Court (Civil Procedure) Rules 2004 (Ghana); O 5 r 21(f) Civil Procedure Rules 2010 (Kenya); O 11 r 1(f) High Court (Civil Procedure) Rules 2007 (Sierra Leone); O 5 r 22(h) Civil Procedure Rules 1964 (Uganda); O 10 r 15(f) High Court Rules (Zambia). It is also the rule for the Federal High Court in Nigeria: O 13, r 13(e) Federal High Court (Civil Procedure Rules) 2000 (Nigeria).

[55] R 11.25(3)(d) Alberta Rules of Court, Alta Reg 124/2010 (Alta); s 10(g) Court Jurisdiction and Proceedings Transfer Act 2003 (BC); r 6.07(1)(h) Rules of the Supreme Court 1986 (NL); r 47(1)(h) Rules of the Supreme Court of the Northwest Territories, NWT Reg 010-96; s 11(g) Court Jurisdiction and Proceedings Transfer Act 2003 (NS); r 17.02(g) Rules of Civil Procedure, RRO 1990, reg 194 (Ont); s 9(g) Court Jurisdiction and Proceedings Transfer Act, SS 1997, c C-41.1 (Sask); r 13(1)(h) Rules of Court, YOIC 2009/65 (Y).

[56] See text to nn 117–23 below.

[57] *Ashbury v Ellis* [1893] AC 339.

[58] *Morguard Investments Ltd v De Savoye* [1990] 3 SCR 1077, 1109–10; *Hunt v T&N plc* [1993] 4 SCR 289, 324–26; *Club Resorts Ltd v Van Breda* [2012] 1 SCR 572, 589–90, 594; *Chevron Corp v Yaiguaje* [2015] 3 SCR 69, 99–100; and see GD Watson and A Frank, 'Constitutional Limits on Service Ex Juris: Unanswered Questions from Morguard' (2000) 23 *Advocates' Quarterly* 167; J Blom, 'Constitutionalizing Canadian Private International Law – 25 Years Since *Morguard*' (2017) 13 *Journal of Private International Law* 259, 269–81.

[59] See text to nn 16–19 above.

[60] *Muscutt v Courcelles* (2002) 60 OR (3d) 20, [53].

[61] *Flaherty v Girgis* (1985) 4 NSWLR 248; *Mobil Oil Australia Pty Ltd v State of Victoria* (2002) 211 CLR 1.

[62] See above (n 8).

[63] Or in another country that is Party to the Lugano Convention: Convention on jurisdiction and the recognition and enforcement of judgments in civil and commercial matters, Lugano, 16 September 1988 [1988] OJ L319/9.

of the special tort jurisdiction in Practice Direction 6B was nevertheless intentionally aligned with Article 7(2),[64] particularly as the Article had been interpreted since the CJEU's decision in *Mines de Potasse d'Alsace*.[65] The court in England and Wales had from 1987 been given power to assume jurisdiction when it was the *forum damni* as well as when it was the *forum delicti*.[66] This was motivated by Article 7(2) and the decision in *Mines de Potasse d'Alsace*,[67] although it was expressed in the language of the Commonwealth model. Practice Direction 6B therefore also more carefully delineated the alternatives of the place of the tort and the place of damage, and expressly stated Article 7(2)'s power to take preventative measures against a tort that had not yet occurred. After Brexit, a felt need to align English and Welsh special tort jurisdiction with Article 7(2) may weaken. However, Practice Direction 6B to one side, the UK retains a presence in the European model in two ways. First, Scots law largely incorporated the terms of the Brussels Convention and its successors for *all* cross-border jurisdictions, regardless of where the defendant was domiciled,[68] and so Scots special jurisdictions still parallel those of the Brussels Convention with some tweaks. And second, the same position holds for the allocation of jurisdiction *within* the UK.[69] This will be the case where the defendant is domiciled in any of its constituent countries. While the *forum domicilii* will have general jurisdiction in claims against the defendant, there is also a special jurisdiction in tort in the courts of that part of the UK 'where the harmful event occurred or may occur'.[70] The expression of those jurisdictions remains untouched after Brexit.

III. The Grounds of Special Tort Jurisdiction

A close analysis of these three models of special tort jurisdiction identifies three significant connections on which courts are able to assume the power to judge. The place of the tort and the place of damage are shared across the three different models. A place where a court can assume jurisdiction because the defendant has sufficient minimum contacts with the forum state is uniquely American.

A. The Place of the Tort

It is only in those American states in which special tort jurisdiction is determined solely by reference to the minimum contacts test that the rules do not make some explicit reference to the place of the tort. The rules in other places are often expressed in general terms: eg, 'founded on a tort committed within the jurisdiction'.[71] An alternative has been to refer to the place where, more specifically, a wrongful act took place: 'the place where the harmful event occurred'[72] or

[64] Lord Collins of Mapesbury (ed), *Dicey, Morris and Collins on the Conflict of Laws*, 15th edn (Sweet & Maxwell 2012) 453.

[65] *Mines de Potasse d'Alsace* (n 12).

[66] O 11 r 1(1)(f) Rules of the Supreme Court 1965 (UK).

[67] See *Metall und Rohstoff AG v Donaldson Lufkin & Jenrette Inc* [1990] 1 QB 391, 437.

[68] R 2(c) Sch 8 Civil Jurisdiction and Judgments Act 1982 (UK); see generally, P Beaumont and PE McEleavy, *Anton's Private International Law*, 3rd edn (W Green//SULI 2011) 309–17.

[69] s 16 Civil Jurisdiction and Judgments Act 1982 (UK).

[70] R 3(c) Sch 4 Civil Jurisdiction and Judgments Act 1982 (UK).

[71] O 11 r 1(1)(ee) Rules of the Supreme Court 1883 (UK), as amended by the Rules of the Supreme Court (No 3) 1920 (UK).

[72] Art 7(2) Brussels Ia.

'a tortious act within the state'.[73] However the rule is cast, the focus is necessarily on identifying the *locus* of the tort.

Article 7(2)'s reference to 'the place where the harmful event occurred' imports no restriction on what aspects of the tort must have taken place within the place for jurisdiction to be assumed. Neither of the institutional commentators on the Brussels Convention – M Jenard[74] and Dr Schlosser[75] – placed any technical significance on the term, and indeed, Jenard regarded it as a safe restatement of the French and German tort jurisdictions.[76] Jenard's was already an expansive view of the jurisdiction, and was the basis of the CJEU's decision in *Mines de Potasse d'Alsace* that the Article gave jurisdiction to 'the place where the damage occurred or the place of the event giving rise to it'.[77] Although, in general, Brussels Ia is sometimes seen as being more restrictive than the civil jurisdictions that are allowed under the American and Commonwealth models, this is not necessarily so for claims in tort.

The European adjudication on the place where the damage occurred is considered in the next section.[78] So far as 'the place of the event' is concerned, in *Shevill v Press Alliance SA*[79] the CJEU dealt with a claim brought in England against a French newspaper for defamation, although its circulation in England was microscopic compared with sales in France. The distinction made in *Mines de Potasse d'Alsace* between jurisdiction based on 'the place of the event' and jurisdiction based on 'the place of damage' was of significance, because a court that assumed jurisdiction as the *forum damni* could only rule on the injury suffered in that place.[80] The court for the place of the event had jurisdiction 'to hear the action for damages for all the harm caused by the unlawful act'.[81] In *Shevill*'s enquiry into where a libellous 'event' occurred, the CJEU considered that it was the place where the publisher of the newspaper was established.[82] And in a similar vein, in claims for negligent misrepresentation, the CJEU has pushed the *locus* to the place where the misstatement originates; not where the communication is received or acted upon.[83] This strongly contrasts with the approach to communication torts in the Commonwealth.[84] However, it at least gives the claimant the opportunity to bundle all claims for damage suffered across borders into a single court – so long as the court for the publisher's location is prepared to give a remedy at all.[85]

Shevill has been taken as establishing the principle that, under Article 7(2), the *locus delicti* – the place where the event giving rise to the damage occurred – is the place 'where a chain of

[73] § 302(a) Civil Practice Law and Rules (NY).

[74] Report on the Convention of 27 September 1968 on jurisdiction and the enforcement of judgments in civil and commercial matters and to the Protocol on its interpretation by the Court of Justice [1979] OJ C59/26 (Jenard Report).

[75] Report on the Convention of 9 October 1978 on the Association of the Kingdom of Denmark, Ireland and the United Kingdom of Great Britain and Northern Ireland to the Convention on jurisdiction and the enforcement of judgments in civil and commercial matters and to the Protocol on its interpretation by the Court of Justice [1979] OJ C59/111 [134].

[76] Jenard Report (n 74) C59/26; and see Art 59(12) Code of Civil Procedure (France); Art 32 Code of Civil Procedure (Germany); and the discussion of these repealed national rules in M Weser, 'Bases of Judicial Jurisdiction in the Common Market Countries' (1961) 10 *American Journal of Comparative Law* 323, 332.

[77] Jenard Report (n 74) C59/26; *Mines de Potasse d'Alsace* (n 12) 1747.

[78] See text to nn 126–36 below.

[79] Case C-68/93 [1995] ECR I-450.

[80] Ibid, 462 [30].

[81] Ibid, 461 [25].

[82] Ibid, 460–61 [24].

[83] *Domicrest Ltd v Swiss Bank Corp* [1999] QB, 548, 567–68.

[84] See text to nn 110–14 below.

[85] In *Shevill*, it is likely that the claimant would not have succeeded under French law: C Forsyth, 'Defamation under the Brussels Convention: A Forum Shopper's Charter?' [1995] *CLJ* 515, 516.

events which led to a damage had their origin'[86] and, so, tends to be close to the defendant's home. In product liability claims, this means that the event giving rise to the damage occurs where the defective manufacture took place.[87] Qualifications have been made for internet torts, where the CJEU has given juridical significance to the distinction between online communications and the print media. The 'ubiquity of the content' when it is published online means that it is not necessarily possible to quantify its distribution in any given place.[88] Accordingly, for online communications the CJEU 'adapted' *Shevill*[89] – although, really, *Shevill* was abandoned. The *locus* was shifted to the place where the claimant's interests were centred.[90] Although in many cases this would be the place of the claimant's habitual residence, 'other factors, such as the pursuit of a professional activity' may put their centre of interests elsewhere.[91]

In contrast the New York courts did give technical significance to the term 'tortious act within the state' in the CPLR,[92] but have ultimately reached the same position as the CJEU in product liability cases. Soon after the CPLR expressly provided for special tort jurisdictions, it was held that the occurrence of *any* tortious act in the state gave jurisdiction.[93] The New York Court of Appeals soon rejected that in *Feathers v McLucas* and *Singer v Walker*,[94] holding that special jurisdiction on this ground only arose when the tortious acts were 'original'.[95] In his analysis of the product liability claims in *Feathers* and *Singer*, Fuld J brought the relevant 'tortious act' back to the point of manufacture. As both products were manufactured in other states, the New York court had no jurisdiction.[96] The parallels with the European model are evident in *Feathers* and *Singer* but, as also with Article 7(2), the CPLR does not preclude a New York court assuming jurisdiction in product liability claims for defective manufacture outside the state as the *forum damni*.[97]

As an exemplar of the distinctive American policy of protecting expression, the CPLR does not allow the assumption of special jurisdiction in defamation cases unless the defendant is conducting business in New York.[98] This also removes the most significant claims that arise for unlawful online expression. However, the courts' treatment of other communication torts in New York is not entirely consistent. In *Kramer v Vogl*,[99] the Court of Appeals relied on *Feathers* and *Singer* when holding that the tortious act in a case of deceit took place where the false representations were made.[100] Some courts have held that a misrepresentation takes place where the

[86] A Dickinson and E Lein (eds), *The Brussels I Regulation Recast* (Oxford University Press 2015) 162 [4.89].

[87] Case C-189/08 *Zuid-Chemie BV v Philippo's Mineralenfabriek NV/SA* [2009] ECR I-6919, [29]–[30]; Case C-45/13 *Kainz v Pantherwerke AG* EU:C:2014:7 [26]–[27].

[88] Joined Cases C-509/09 and C-161/100 *eDate Advertising GmbH v X* and *Olivier Martinez v MGN Ltd* [2011] ECR I-10302, [45], [46]–[47].

[89] Ibid, [48].

[90] Ibid, [50].

[91] Ibid, [49].

[92] § 302(a) Civil Practice Law and Rules (NY).

[93] See Note, 'Jurisdiction: New York Long-Arm Statute and Products Liability for Out-Of-State Injury' (1964) 64 *Columbia Law Review* 1354; A Homburger, 'The Reach of New York's Long Arm Statute: Today and Tomorrow' (1965) 15 *Buffalo Law Review* 61, 65–66.

[94] 15 NY 2d 443 (1964) (heard together).

[95] Ibid, 466.

[96] Ibid, 464–66 see also *Pilates Inc v Pilates Institute Inc* 891 F Supp 175, 181 (1995).

[97] See text to nn 137–46 below.

[98] § 302(a)(1) Civil Practice Law and Rules (NY); *SPCA of Upstate New York Inc v American Working Collie Association* 18 NY 3d 400, 403–04 (2012); *cf Gary Null & Associates Inc v Phillips* 29 Misc 3d 245 (2010). See RD Nussbaum, 'The Shortcomings of New York's Long-Arm Statute: Defamation in the Age of Technology' (2014) 88 *St John's Law Review* 175, 185–86.

[99] 267 NYS 2d 900 (1966).

[100] Ibid, 903.

communication is received,[101] but *Feathers*, *Singer* and *Vogl* represent the orthodoxy and concentrate on the original wrongful act when identifying the *locus delicti*.[102]

Commonwealth approaches differ significantly. The Privy Council's advice in *Distillers Co (Biochemicals) Ltd v Thompson*[103] has dominated the approach taken by Commonwealth courts when identifying the *locus delicti*, and so whether special jurisdiction in tort can be assumed under rules of court. *Distillers* concerned an action brought in New South Wales on behalf of a child born with deformities after her mother, a resident of the state, had taken a thalidomide compound manufactured in England. The New South Wales court assumed jurisdiction under that state's version of the Common Law Procedure Act 1852 (UK),[104] and so the question was whether 'a Cause of Action' had arisen in the state. In the Privy Council, Lord Pearson considered that there would be jurisdiction when the act that gave the claimant a cause of complaint occurred in the state.[105] 'The right approach is, when the tort is complete, to look back over the series of events constituting it and ask the question, where in substance did this cause of action arise?'[106] In *Distillers* itself the Privy Council held that the negligence was in the defendant's failure to warn in New South Wales that the medication was dangerous, and so the claimant was entitled to complain that the tort arose in the state.

The refusal of the Privy Council in *Distillers* to prioritise a single aspect of the tort, without reference to the context of the case, is in contrast to the approach taken in Europe and New York where the courts concentrate on the earliest 'original' act in the chain of events constituting the wrong.[107] Indeed, when following *Distillers*, the Supreme Court of Canada considered that it was 'unnecessary and unwise, to have resort to any arbitrary set of rules'.[108] *Distillers* has therefore given flexibility in the treatment of product liability cases where, depending on the context of the tort and how it is pleaded, the *locus delicti* can be taken to be the place of manufacture or the place of distribution or marketing. The latter generally reduces the venue risk for claimants, and product liability claims against foreign manufacturers based on the negligent failure to warn of defects or dangers are standard.[109]

However, once again the 'ubiquitous' quality of online communication has challenged the suitability of the open-textured quality of the *Distillers* approach because, with multiple publications in places with different defamation laws, the 'substance' of a libel might differ between places.[110] Commonwealth courts have tended to address communication torts by more specific rules – with an overwhelming preference for the place where the communication was received. The *locus delicti* of misrepresentations is generally the place where the communication was

[101] *Polish v Threshold Technology Inc* 340 NYS 2d 354, 356 (1972); *Leigh Valley Industries Inc v Birenbaum* 527 F 2d 87, 93 (2nd Cir, 1975). The decision in *Abbate v Abbate* 82 AD 2d 368 (1981) that New York was the *locus delicti* is ambiguous as the misrepresentation was given and received in the state: ibid, 385.

[102] *Bauer Industries Inc v Shannon Luminous Materials Company* 383 NYS 2d 80, 80 (1976); *Fox v Boucher* 794 F 2d 34, 37 (2nd Cir, 1986); *Stein v Annenberg Research Institute* 1991 WL 143400, 3 (SDNY).

[103] [1971] AC 458.

[104] s 18 Common Law Procedure Act 1899 (NSW).

[105] Ibid, 468.

[106] Ibid.

[107] See text to nn 79–87, 92–101 above.

[108] *Moran v Pyle National (Canada) Ltd* [1975] 1 SCR 393, 408.

[109] eg, *Jacobs v Australian Abrasives Pty Ltd* [1971] Tas SR 92; *Moran* (n 108); *My v Toyota Motor Co* [1977] 2 NZLR 113; *Castree v ER Squibb & Sons Ltd* [1980] 2 All ER 589; *D'Ath v TNT Australia Pty Ltd* [1992] 1 Qd R 369. Australian adjudication, however, has reinforced that jurisdiction will not be assumed where the claim of negligent failure to warn in the place of distribution is unreal or artificial: *Lewis Construction Co Pty Ltd v Tichauer SA* [1966] VR 341; *Buttigeig v Universal Terminal & Stevedoring Corp* [1972] VR 626; *MacGregor v Application des Gaz* [1976] Qd R 175; *Hall v Australian Capital Territory Electricity Authority* [1980] 2 NSWLR 26.

[110] A Briggs, 'The Duke of Brunswick and Defamation by Internet' (2003) 119 *LQR* 210, 212–13.

received or acted upon,[111] a position that, before Brexit, forced the court in England and Wales to treat misrepresentation claims in Article 7(2) and Practice Direction 6B cases differently.[112] An identical *locus* has been ascribed to defamatory communications,[113] and this has been extended to defamation claims for publications on the internet.[114]

Leaving the more precise pinpointing of the *locus* in communication torts to one side, the emphasis in Commonwealth courts on identifying 'the substance' of the tort has had two additional consequences. First, there is a strong line of authority that, when a question of *forum non conveniens* arises in tort claims, the identification of the place of the tort as the appropriate forum is 'a useful rule of thumb or a prima facie starting point'.[115] It is possible to displace the prima facie position. However, the usual effect is that, if a tort claim is not being heard in the *forum delicti*, the assumption of jurisdiction (whether general or as *forum damni*) may be defeated.[116] Second, a unique emphasis on the *forum delicti* has emerged in Canada at common law and as a constitutional principle. With some reliance on *Distillers*,[117] the Canadian Supreme Court developed a principle that a provincial court could legitimately assume jurisdiction if the proceedings had a reasonable and substantial connection with the province.[118] This is both a common law and a constitutionally directed jurisdiction.[119] In *Club Resorts Ltd v Van Breda*,[120] the Supreme Court gave greater detail to the principle in tort claims by holding that, in addition to traditional common law grounds of general jurisdiction, a real and substantial connection was presumed if '[t]he tort was committed in the province'.[121] As a common law ground of jurisdiction, this is unique in the Commonwealth. It does not help Canadian courts escape the usual problems of identifying the *locus* for communication torts, statutory torts, conspiracy and equitable claims in the penumbra of tort.[122] However, it has helped to give the *forum delicti* a prominence in

[111] *Diamond v Bank of London and Montreal Ltd* [1979] QB 333; *Cordoba Shipping Co Ltd v National State Bank, Elizabeth, New Jersey (The Albaforth)* [1984] 2 Lloyd's Rep 91; *Canadian Commercial Bank v Carpenter* (1990) 62 DLR (4th) 734; *Voth v Manildra Flour Mills Pty Ltd* (1990) 171 CLR 538, 568; *Sedgwick Ltd v Bain Clarkson Ltd* (1994) 56 FCR 578; *Williams v The Society of Lloyd's* [1994] 1 VR 274, 316–17; *Sydbank Soenderjylland A/S v Bannerton Holdings Pty Ltd* (1996) 68 FCR 539; *National Bank of Canada Ltd v Clifford Chance* (1996) 30 OR (3d) 746; *Morin v Bonhams & Brooks Ltd* [2003] 2 All ER (Comm) 36, 46–48; *VTB Capital plc v Nutritek International Corp* [2013] 2 AC 337; *Telesto Investments Ltd v UBS AG* (2012) 262 FLR 119; *Thorne v Hudson Estate* 2017 ONCA 208.

[112] *Domicrest* (n 83) 567–68.

[113] *Bata v Bata* [1948] WN 366; *Eyre v Nationwide News Pty Ltd* [1967] NZLR 851; *Gorton v Australian Broadcasting Commission* (1973) 22 FLR 181; *Pindling v National Broadcasting Corp* (1984) 49 OR (2d) 58; *Australian Broadcasting Corp v Waterhouse* (1991) 25 NSWLR 519.

[114] *Berezovsky v Michaels* [2000] 1 WLR 1004, 1026; *Dow Jones & Co Inc v Gutnick* (2002) 210 CLR 575, 606–07; M Richardson and R Garnett, 'Perils of Publishing on the Internet: Broader Implications of *Dow Jones v Gutnick*' (2004) 13 *Griffith Law Review* 74.

[115] *VTB* (n 111) 358; and see also, ibid, 406–08, 413–14; *The Albaforth* (n 111) 94; *Metall* (n 67); *Schapira v Ahronson* [1999] EMLR 735; *Berezovsky* (n 114) 1014, 1017, 1033; *BHP Billiton Ltd v Schultz* (2004) 221 CLR 400.

[116] As, in international cases, the narrower Australian doctrine of *forum non conveniens* – as stated in *Voth* (n 111) – enables the court to exercise jurisdiction even if there is a clearly more appropriate forum elsewhere, Australian courts have continued to hear tort claims where the foreign court is the *forum delicti*: *Régie Nationale des Usines Renault SA v Zhang* (2002) 210 CLR 491; *Puttick v Tenon Ltd* (2008) 238 CLR 265. This is not the case in questions of interstate jurisdiction: *BHP Billiton* (n 115).

[117] *Morguard* (n 58) 1106; see also V Black, 'Simplifying Court Jurisdiction in Canada' (2012) 8 *Journal of Private International Law* 411, 411–13.

[118] *Morguard* (n 58) 1108.

[119] Above (n 58).

[120] *Club Resorts* (n 58).

[121] Ibid, 618. LeBel J added that tort jurisdiction would be established if '[a] contract connected with the [tort] dispute was made in the province': ibid, 618; and see *Lapointe Rosenstein Marchand Melançon LLP v Cassels Brock & Blackwell* [2016] 1 SCR 851.

[122] S Pitel and V Black, 'Assumed Jurisdiction in Canada: Identifying and Interpreting Presumptive Connecting Factors' (2018) 14 *Journal of Private International Law* 193, 194, 197–202, 2017–19.

Canadian special tort jurisdictions that it does not have in other Commonwealth countries, which have become more reliant on the *forum damni* to exercise jurisdiction in tort claims. It may raise the question whether the court for the province that is merely a place where damage arose can validly assume jurisdiction if the claim does not otherwise have a real and substantial connection with the province.[123]

B. The Place of Damage

The court for the place where damage arose has emerged as an attractive forum for claimants to litigate in as there is a likelihood that it is also the place where the claimant resides.[124] Unless carefully limited, this ground of special tort jurisdiction risks exorbitance because it could simply serve as a substitute for nothing more than the place of the claimant's residence. For commercial claimants in particular, if *any* financial damage that was recoverable according to the applicable law could justify the assumption of jurisdiction, this would effectively create a new ground of tort jurisdiction based on the claimant's place of business.[125] The European and American models have resisted extending tort jurisdiction this far; the Commonwealth has not.

As we have seen,[126] the CJEU has read Article 7(2) as providing that 'the plaintiff has an option to commence proceedings … at the place where the damage occurred'.[127] It has also resisted giving jurisdiction when the connection between the litigation and the place of damage is slim. In *Dumez France SA v Hessische Landesbank*,[128] the CJEU stressed that Article 7(2) should not be interpreted in a way that might see the courts for the place of the claimant's domicile recognised as having special tort jurisdiction.[129] The case involved a claim in France by French companies for damage suffered by the insolvency of German subsidiaries that took place as a result of the cancellation of loans initially made to the subsidiaries by German banks. The CJEU considered that the parent companies suffered only indirect damage,[130] and that special jurisdiction could only arise in the place of damage 'where the event giving rise to the damage … *directly* produced its harmful effects upon the person who is the *immediate victim* of that event'.[131] The French courts therefore had no special jurisdiction.

The jurisprudence on Article 7(2) has subsequently confirmed that the damage must be suffered directly and it must be suffered by the immediate victim. As a result, the CJEU has observed that there is no jurisdiction under Article 7(2) where 'the victim claims financial damage following upon initial damage arising and suffered by him in another [member state]'.[132] The simplest expression of this is in personal injuries cases, where the direct damage is almost always suffered in the place where the injury occurred.[133] The CJEU has also ruled that the place of damage cannot be the place where a commercial victim's assets are located.[134]

[123] *Muscutt* (n 60) [53]; and see text to nn 48–50 above, and *FS Cairo (Nile Plaza) LLC v Brownlie* [2021] 3 WLR 1011, 1060 (*Brownlie II*).
[124] Dickinson and Lein (n 86) 167 [4.105].
[125] *Dicey, Morris and Collins* (n 64) 483.
[126] See text to nn 12–13 above.
[127] *Mines de Potasse d'Alsace* (n 12) 1747.
[128] Case C-220/88 [1990] ECR I-49.
[129] Ibid, [16], [19].
[130] Ibid, [13]–[14].
[131] Ibid, [20] (emphases added).
[132] Case C-364/93 *Marinari v Lloyds Bank Plc* [1995] ECR I-2719, [15].
[133] *Henderson v Jaouen* [2002] EWCA (Civ) 75, [31].
[134] Case C-1168/02 *Kronhofer v Maier* [2004] ECR I-6009, 6031 [20].

Under the European model, the strategic advantage of litigating in the place of the event is that the court then has the power to award a remedy for *all* of the damage suffered, whereas the court for the place of damage is limited to awarding a remedy for the damage suffered only in that place. This gives rise to the 'mosaic theory' relating to claims for damages in multiple numbers of Member States.[135] As was recognised in *Shevill*,[136] when the victim of a communication tort such as defamation suffers direct damage in a number of Member States, the courts for each and all of them may assume jurisdiction as a *forum damni*. The remedy, whether compensatory or an order *in specie*, remains limited to the damage that has arisen or that may arise just in that place.

American special tort jurisdictions modelled on the New York CPLR also allow the assumption of jurisdiction when there is 'injury to person or property' in the state when the tort itself took place outside the state.[137] Although the place of injury brings the jurisdiction closer, in effect, to the claimant's place of residence or domicile, these American rules also demand a more substantial connection between the defendant and the state. In *LaMarca v Pak-Mor Manufacturing Company*,[138] Rosenblatt J, delivering the New York Court of Appeals' opinion, held that, under the CPLR, this ground of jurisdiction had five elements:

> First, that defendant committed a tortious act outside the State; second, that the cause of action arises from that act; third, that the act caused injury to a person or property within the State; fourth, that defendant expected or should reasonably have expected the act to have consequences in the State; and fifth, that defendant derived substantial revenue from interstate or international commerce.[139]

The means by which the *forum damni* jurisdiction under the New York model is narrowed are the commercial connections that *LaMarca*'s fourth and fifth elements require of the defendant. These reflect the requirements of the due process clause.[140] As a result, in an action for wrongful death against a medical practitioner, the New York courts had no jurisdiction when the doctor practised only in Vermont and all of his income was sourced in Vermont.[141] In *LaMarca* itself, the claimant was injured after a loading device on a truck collapsed. The loader was manufactured in Virginia by a Texas corporation. Rosenblatt J held that the requirements of the CPLR were satisfied because the defendant knew that the loader was destined for New York, it earned significant revenue from interstate commerce, and it had a New York distributor.[142] The fifth element of *LaMarca* may require the defendant's sales revenue from out-of-state sources to be compared with its total gross sales revenue.[143] Accordingly, the fifth element was not satisfied by a 2 per cent proportion of cross-border to total revenue;[144] but it was clearly satisfied with a 98 per cent proportion.[145] However, the quantum of revenue may be sufficient in itself to satisfy the fifth element of *La Marca*. A company that earned $9 million in sales from New York satisfied the test even though this was merely 1 per cent of its gross revenue.[146]

[135] Dickinson and Lein (n 86) 169 [4.111]; Beaumont and McEleavy (n 68) 316.
[136] *Shevill* (n 79); and see also *eDate Advertising* (n 88).
[137] § 302(a) Civil Practice Law and Rules (NY).
[138] 95 NY 2d 210 (2000).
[139] Ibid, 214.
[140] See text to nn 190–214 below.
[141] *Ingraham* (n 25) 598–600.
[142] *LaMarca* (n 138) 215.
[143] eg, *Gilmore v Inskip Inc* 54 Misc 2d 218, 221–22 (1967); *Allen v Auto Specialties Manufacturing Co* 45 AD 2d 331, 333 (1974); *Sacco v Reel-O-Matic Inc* NY Slip Op 02613, 6 May 2020, Appellate Division, Second Department.
[144] *Kramer* (n 99) 32.
[145] *Newman v Nathan Inc* 55 Misc 2d 368, 370 (1967).
[146] *Allen v Canadian General Electric Co* 65 AD 2d 39, 41 (1978).

In the Commonwealth, the shift towards grounding special tort jurisdiction on the basis of 'damage suffered wholly or partly' in the place was a consequence of thalidomide cases like *Distillers*,[147] and the perception, which proved to be incorrect, that the *forum delicti* jurisdiction could not deal with claims brought outside the place of manufacture. Although the Privy Council concluded in *Distillers* that the tort took place where distribution occurred, the New South Wales court pre-empted the decision by changing its rules to allow the assumption of jurisdiction when the injury was sustained in the state.[148] In the course of adopting the New South Wales approach,[149] no Commonwealth court qualified the jurisdiction of the *forum damni* along the lines of the New York CPLR or read it down as the CJEU did in *Dumez France*.[150] '[I]ndirect or secondary damage' is sufficient to establish jurisdiction.[151] Commonwealth courts have therefore assumed jurisdiction in personal injuries cases when they are *fora* for the place where pain was suffered,[152] amenities of life were lost,[153] hospital or treatment expenses were incurred,[154] there is loss of care,[155] wages and earning capacity were lost or diminished,[156] an executrix's funeral expenses were incurred,[157] or a widow lost her dependence on her husband.[158] In defamation cases, the *locus damni* is the place where reputation is injured.[159] In commercial tort claims it has been sufficient for a business to show that a loss of profits was suffered in the place,[160] or that equipment there was damaged or impaired.[161] The ideas that the damage must be 'immediate' to the wrongful conduct[162] or must 'complete the cause of action'[163] have also been rejected. Furthermore, the European 'mosaic theory' has also in effect been rejected.[164] Even when only part of the damage has been suffered in the place, courts have been prepared to award remedies for *all* of the damage suffered.[165] The one qualification is that the damage must be significant.[166]

The two *Brownlie* decisions in the UK Supreme Court have strengthened the broad perimeters of this jurisdiction in England and Wales. The English claimant and her husband had stayed at an Egyptian hotel run by a multinational chain. The husband was killed during an excursion

[147] *Distillers* (n 103); and see text to nn 103–06 above.

[148] See the discussion in *Brix-Neilsen v Oceaneering Australia Pty Ltd* [1982] 2 NSWLR 173, 175–76.

[149] See text to nn 42–50 above.

[150] See text to nn 128–32, 137–46 above.

[151] *Pike v The Indian Hotels Company Ltd* [2013] EWHC 4096 (QB) [9].

[152] *Mar v Block* (1976) 13 OR (2d) 422, 424; *Vile v Von Wendt* (1979) 26 OR (2d) 513; *Poirier v Williston* (1981) 31 OR (2d) 320; *Brix-Neilsen* (n 148) 176–77; *Muscutt* (n 60) [28]; *Wink v Croatio Osiguranje DD* [2013] EWHC 1118 (QB) [42]; *Pike* (n 151) [8].

[153] *Vile* (n 152); *Pike* (n 151) [8].

[154] *Mar* (n 152) 424; *Vile* (n 152); *Brix-Neilsen* (n 148) 176–77; *Flaherty* (n 61) 252; *Muscutt* (n 60) [28]; *Cooley v Ramsey* [2008] EWHC 129 (QB) [2]–[10].

[155] *Stylianou v Toyoshima* [2013] EWHC 2188 (QB) [10].

[156] *Vile* (n 152); *Poirier* (n 152); *Cooley* (n 154) [25]; *Wink* (n 152) [42]; *Stylianou* (n 155) [10]; *Pike* (n 151) [8]; *cf Erste Group Bank AG, London Branch v JSC 'VMZ Red October'* [2015] EWCA Civ 379, [104]–[105].

[157] *Booth v Phillips* [2004] EWHC 1437 (Adm) [34]; cf *Erste Group Bank* (n 156) [104]–[105].

[158] *Booth*, ibid, [34].

[159] *Dow Jones* (n 114) 607, 621.

[160] *Skyrotors Ltd v Carriere Technical Industries Ltd* (1979) 26 OR (2d) 207; *Baxter v RMC Group plc* [2003] 1 NZLR 304, 316; *Colosseum Investment Holdings Pty Ltd v Vanguard Logistics Services Pty Ltd* [2005] NSWSC 803, [49]; *PCH Offshore Pty Ltd v Dunn (No 2)* (2010) 273 ALR 167.

[161] *Darrell Lea Chocolate Shops Pty Ltd v Spanish Polish Shipping Co Inc* (1990) 25 NSWLR 568, 577; *Sigma Coachair Group Pty Ltd v Bock Australia Pty Ltd* [2009] NSWSC 684 [124]–[131].

[162] *Brix-Neilsen* (n 148) 179; *Flaherty* (n 61) 266.

[163] *Flaherty* (n 61) 266; *Booth* (n 157) [39].

[164] See text to n 135 above.

[165] *Flaherty* (n 61) 267; *cf* TM Yeo, 'Jurisdiction Issues in International Tort Litigation: A Singapore View' (1995) 7 *Singapore Academy of Law Journal* 1, 15–16.

[166] *Metall und Rohstoff* (n 67) 437.

that had been booked through the hotel. In *Four Seasons Holdings Incorporated v Brownlie*[167] (*Brownlie I*), the claimant had sued the wrong corporation within the hotel chain, so the Supreme Court admitted that any reflections it made on the scope of the *locus damni* were *obiter dicta*.[168] The proceedings came before the Supreme Court again – this time against the correct corporate defendant – in *FS Cairo (Nile Plaza) v Brownlie*[169] (*Brownlie II*). In both appeals, the Supreme Court held by a majority that the English court could assume jurisdiction under Practice Direction 6B on the basis that damage had been sustained in the country. The alleged damage included funeral, repatriation and probate expenses (incurred as executrix); the claimant's own medical expenses; and pain and suffering and loss of amenity of life.[170] In the majority in *Brownlie I*, Baroness Hale concluded that 'damage' was to be given its 'ordinary and natural meaning' and, on the basis of earlier English and Australian decisions, that included 'all the detriment, physical, financial and social which the plaintiff suffers as a result of the tortious conduct of the defendant'.[171] In *Brownlie II*, Lord Lloyd-Jones similarly relied on the 'ordinary and natural meaning' of the term 'damage'.[172] In his judgment, Lord Lloyd-Jones summarised the scope of the damage that could give rise to the assumption of jurisdiction under Practice Direction 6B as 'actionable harm, direct or indirect, caused by the wrongful act alleged', with no need to limit its scope to direct damage.[173] Indeed, he considered the distinction between direct and indirect to be 'obscure'.[174]

In dissent in *Brownlie I*, Lord Sumption preferred to limit the reach of Practice Direction 6B and read it under the glosses of Article 7(2) and *Dumez France*. The 'damage' therefore had to be direct, and had to affect 'bodily integrity, physical property and reputation'.[175] There was a need to show 'some substantial and not merely casual or adventitious link between the cause of action and England'.[176] The risk of reading the rule otherwise was shifting an entitlement to assume jurisdiction to a connection merely with the claimant:

> [A] principle which located damage in the place where the pecuniary consequences of the accident were felt or where any continuing pain, suffering or loss of amenity were experienced would in the great majority of cases confer jurisdiction on the country of the claimant's residence … Personal connections between the parties and England are generally relevant to jurisdiction only in the case of the defendant.[177]

Lord Sumption openly adopted the CJEU's approach to Article 7(2),[178] and justified that by the drafting of Practice Direction 6B specifically to align with Article 7(2).[179] Baroness Hale rejected the view that Practice Direction 6B should be regarded as implementing the Brussels I model and *Dumez France*.[180] Commonwealth cases were a more reliable guide.[181] As the sole dissentient in *Brownlie II*, Lord Leggatt agreed with Lord Sumption's conclusion that only direct damage could establish jurisdiction as the *forum damni* – but disagreed that this was because Practice Direction

[167] [2018] 1 WLR 192 (*Brownlie I*).
[168] Ibid, 202, 210.
[169] *Brownlie II* (n 123).
[170] *Brownlie I* (n 167) 202–03; *Brownlie II* (n 123) 1015–16, 1030–31, 1059.
[171] *Brownlie I* (n 167) 215; see also 218–19 (Lord Wilson) and 219–20 (Lord Clarke).
[172] *Brownlie II* (n 123) 1028, 1038; see also 1016 (Lord Reed, Lord Briggs and Lord Burrows).
[173] Ibid, 1038.
[174] Ibid, 1039.
[175] *Brownlie I* (n 167) 204.
[176] Ibid, 206.
[177] Ibid, 206–07.
[178] Ibid, 207–08.
[179] Ibid, 208.
[180] Ibid, 215.
[181] Ibid, 215. See also, ibid, 221 (Lord Clarke); *Brownlie II* (n 123) 1033–34.

6B should be read to align with Article 7(2).[182] Implicitly disagreeing with Lord Lloyd-Jones, he considered that the adjudication under the European model was only useful to show that it was possible, even 'relatively straightforward in most instances', to draw a line between direct and indirect damage.[183] Rather, Lord Leggatt held that the scope of the *locus damni* had to be limited precisely because the purpose of Practice Direction 6B was to ensure that there was 'a real and substantial connection with England' before jurisdiction could be assumed – and the ground of jurisdiction had to be read accordingly.[184] A claimant cannot call on the power of the court just because she is in England.[185]

An account of the Commonwealth model for jurisdiction in the place of damage uncovers a substantive jurisdiction that is the antithesis of *actor sequitur forum rei*.[186] It takes little to appreciate that damage such as loss of earning capacity or loss of profits may be significant, and because it inheres in the individual or corporate claimant it therefore follows the claimant's location. The *forum damni* approach under the Commonwealth model often serves, in effect, as a proxy for exercising jurisdiction exclusively on the basis of the claimant's residence. As Lord Leggatt put it in *Brownlie II*, the Commonwealth model establishes 'not so much a gateway to bringing proceedings in England against a defendant who is in another country as an open territory with no fence'.[187] It crosses the line of exorbitance,[188] unless the court restrains itself under principles of *forum non conveniens*.[189]

C. Minimum Contacts

All American tort jurisdictions are subject to a minimum contacts enquiry, even if special jurisdiction is exercised under the statutory restrictions of the New York approach.[190] The enquiry is made under the due process clause's guarantee that a person shall not be 'deprived of … property, without due process of law', and therefore concentrates on the sufficiency of *the defendant's* connections with the US or, more commonly, the individual state in question. As will be seen, this means that jurisdiction cannot be assumed on place of damage grounds similar to those allowed under the Commonwealth model.[191]

Professor Borchers considers that, before *International Shoe*,[192] minimum contacts jurisprudence had accepted that the *forum delicti* could validly assume jurisdiction in tort claims.[193] *International Shoe* elevated the need for the defendant's connection with the state, although Borchers suggests that that unnecessarily discounted the claimant's interest in reducing venue risk.[194] As Thomas J said in *Walden v Fiore*,[195] a tortious claim for unlawful seizure of property,

[182] *Brownlie II* (n 123) 1062–63.
[183] Ibid, 1064.
[184] Ibid, 1069.
[185] Ibid, 1066.
[186] See text to n 2 above.
[187] *Brownlie II* (n 123) 1060.
[188] See Mortensen, Garnett and Keyes (n 8) 63–64; and *Courtney v Chalfen* [2020] QSC 195, [70].
[189] In *Brownlie II*, Lord Lloyd-Jones considered that the restraints available under *forum conveniens* principles ensured that claimants could not just bring proceedings because of their residence. Lord Leggatt considered that the reported cases showed that, in practice, *forum conveniens* had never been used as such a restraint: (n 123) 1037–39, 1070–71.
[190] See text to nn 137–46 above.
[191] See text to nn 147–89 above.
[192] *International Shoe* (n 16). See text to nn 15–19 above.
[193] PJ Borchers, 'The Twilight of the Minimum Contacts Test' (2014) 11 *Seton Hall Circuit Review* 1, 24, 26.
[194] Ibid, 24.
[195] 571 US 277 (2014).

'[d]ue process limits on the State's adjudicative authority principally protect the liberty of the nonresident defendant – not the convenience of plaintiffs or third parties'.[196] Ginsburg J's idea that the contacts that the defendant has with the state must be '"so continuous and systematic" as to render it essentially at home in the forum State' reinforces this inclination to minimising venue risk for the defendant.[197]

Having said that, minimum contacts have been satisfied in national defamation cases even when there was no personal connection between the defendant and the state.[198] *Keeton v Hustler Magazine, Inc*[199] was an extreme example of special jurisdiction being assumed by the New Hampshire court as the *forum damni*. The Supreme Court held that due process was satisfied because around 15,000 copies of the defendant's magazine were sold in the state annually. Therefore, said Rehnquist J, it 'has continuously and deliberately exploited the New Hampshire market, it must reasonably anticipate being haled into court there in a libel action based on the contents of its magazine'.[200] The approach taken in US minimum contacts jurisprudence on defamation cases is the closest that American courts come to Commonwealth courts' approach to jurisdiction in defamation cases.[201]

The Supreme Court has, however, qualified its minimum contacts jurisprudence. First, as is evident from cases like *Keeton*, there is a requirement that there must be some act by which the defendant 'purposefully avails itself of the privilege of conducting business activities within the forum State'.[202] Further, the assumption of jurisdiction must be reasonable.[203] In product liability claims, these gave rise in the 1960s to a 'stream of commerce test',[204] which accepts that minimum contacts are satisfied when a defendant business (regardless of its location) places goods into the stream of commerce, and it can be predicted that those goods could be sold or re-sold in the state in question.[205] And while there are suggestions that the manufacturer had to intend that the goods be sold in the state,[206] in *Ford Motor Co v Montana Eighth Judicial District Court*[207] the Supreme Court clarified that the goods which caused injury did not have to be 'designed, manufactured, or first sold' in the state,[208] and that 'regular marketing' in a state will subject it to the jurisdiction of its courts.[209]

J McIntyre Machinery, Ltd v Nicastro[210] exemplifies how, when combined with defendant-based tort jurisdictions, manufacturers can externalise exposure to legal risk through multistate supply chains. In *J McIntyre*, the New Jersey court assumed special jurisdiction in proceedings involving an injury suffered in the state when using machinery manufactured by the English defendant.

[196] Ibid, 284.
[197] *Goodyear Dunlop Tires Operations SA v Brown* 564 US 915, 918, 924 (2011); *Daimler AG v Bauman* 571 US 117, 120 (2014); *BNSF Railway Co v Tyrrell* 137 S Ct 1549, 1554, 1558–59 (2017); *cf* K Bonacorsi, 'Not at Home with "At-Home" Jurisdiction' (2014) 37 *Fordham International Law Journal* 1821.
[198] *Calder v Jones* 465 US 783, 787, 78–79 (1984).
[199] 465 US 770 (1984).
[200] Ibid, 781.
[201] See text to nn 110–14 above.
[202] *Hanson v Denckla* 357 US 235, 253 (1958); and see *McGee v International Life Insurance Co* 355 US 220 (1957).
[203] *Burger King Corp v Rudzewicz* 471 US 462, 477–78 (1985); *Asahi Metal Industry Co v Superior Court* 480 US 102, 112, 114–16 (1987).
[204] *Gray v American Radiator and Standard Sanitary Corp* 22 Ill 2d 432, 441 (1961); *Haldeman-Homme Manufacturing Co v Texacon Industries* 236 F Supp 99, 102 (1964); *AR Industries, Inc v Superior Court* 268 Cal App 2d 328, 333 (1968); *Buckeye Boiler Co v Superior Court* 71 Cal 2d 893, 902 (1969).
[205] *World-Wide Volkswagen Corp v Woodson* 444 US 286, 297–98, 306–07, 316 (1980).
[206] Ibid, 295.
[207] 592 US ___ (2021).
[208] Ibid, 11.
[209] Ibid, 14.
[210] 564 US 873 (2011).

The machinery had been sold by an independent distributor. Although the defendant had directed marketing and sales towards the US market, according to Kennedy J there was no evidence of its engaging 'in conduct purposefully directed at New Jersey'.[211] Although no majority interpretation of the stream of commerce test emerged from the Supreme Court in *J McIntyre*, Roberts CJ and Scalia, Kennedy and Thomas JJ placed greater emphasis on the need for the defendant's purposeful availment of the state.[212]

J McIntyre reinforces the significance in minimum contacts jurisprudence of the defendant's connections with a state, even if that connection is just 'conduct purposefully directed' at the state. It means that, in contrast to the European and Commonwealth models, special jurisdictions grounded merely on the *forum delicti* remain unavailable under the American model. In dissent in *J McIntyre*, Ginsburg J called for a fundamental reconsideration of minimum contacts jurisprudence. Evidently admiring the European model of special tort jurisdiction, she considered that Article 7(2) and *Mines de Potasse d'Alsace* gave a better approach.[213] More recently, the Supreme Court has shown no interest whatsoever in responding to this call.[214]

IV. The Possibility of Unifying Tort Jurisdiction

The HCCH Preliminary Draft Convention proposed that, in addition to places where general jurisdiction may be exercised,[215] an action in tort could be brought in a court for the place where the act or omission that caused the injury had occurred or where the injury arose.[216] The debt to the predecessor to Article 7(2) is evident.[217] However, there are reasons other than its inclusion in the Preliminary Draft Convention for centring the unification of special tort jurisdictions on the *forum delicti*. There is already some international convergence at this point. Even if the slippery *Distillers* approach in the Commonwealth leaves some room for manipulation when identifying the *locus*,[218] there is broad international evidence that the *forum delicti* has a legitimate interest in judging claims that arise there. The same cannot be said for the *forum damni*, despite the Preliminary Draft's contemplating it as an alternative ground of tort jurisdiction.

A comparison of special tort jurisdictions under the European, American and Commonwealth models reveals a cleavage within the common law families – both because *International Shoe*[219] and US minimum contacts analyses have pushed American courts towards a requirement of a connection between the defendant and the state that is paralleled by the policy of the CJEU not to allow the claimant's domicile serve as a basis of special tort jurisdiction,[220] and because of many Commonwealth courts' recognition, in effect, that they can assume jurisdiction on the basis of the claimant's residence. As both Lord Sumption and Ginsburg J differently recognised, the

[211] Ibid, 886.

[212] Ibid.

[213] Ibid, 909; see text to nn 9–70, 65–67 above. For Ginsburg J's other reference to the European model, see *Daimler* (n 197) 141; *cf* RB Ginsburg, 'The Competent Court in Private International Law: Some Observations on Current Views in the United States' (1965) 20 *Rutgers Law Review* 89.

[214] *Ford Motor Co* (n 207).

[215] Arts 3–5 Preliminary Draft Convention (n 3).

[216] Art 10 Preliminary Draft Convention (n 3). The *forum damni* would not be available 'if the defendant establishes that the person claimed to be responsible could not reasonably have foreseen that the act or omission could result in an injury pf the same nature in that State'.

[217] See text to nn 9–14 above.

[218] See text to nn 103–09 above.

[219] *International Shoe* (n 16).

[220] See text to nn 126–34 above.

language of Article 7(2) moderates the extremes that can be found in the common law families.[221] The policies underlying both views merit consideration.

The HCCH Judgments Convention[222] answers the more basic concern that undermined the negotiations for the Preliminary Draft Convention – the terms on which foreign tort judgments, and especially American tort judgments, can be enforced across borders.[223] The Judgments Convention also suggests a more promising approach for negotiating international agreement around suitable adjudicative jurisdictions. Adapting the moderate language of Article 7(2), under the Judgments Convention an enforceable tort judgment arises when

> the judgment ruled on a non-contractual obligation arising from death, physical injury, damage to or loss of tangible property, and the act or omission directly causing such harm occurred in the State of origin, irrespective of where that harm occurred.[224]

It is a *forum delicti* jurisdiction that is already represented in all three models of tort jurisdiction that are discussed in this chapter. It avoids the problematic *forum damni* jurisdiction. If adopted as a common rule of adjudicative jurisdiction, it could not reasonably give rise to any concern when exercised by another country's courts. In focusing on 'the act or omission' causing harm, it is more likely to fix special tort jurisdiction in one place and avoid the slippage of *Distillers*. However, the Judgments Convention's approach to tort jurisdiction does not include a necessary connection between the defendant and 'the State of origin', and in that respect it could not, for American courts, guarantee a constitutionally valid jurisdiction.[225] In practice, without including a connection between the defendant and the place, there could therefore only be a harmonised application of the rule. Even if American states were prepared to adopt it as a rule of special jurisdiction, it would still be subject to *International Shoe* and a minimum contacts enquiry.[226] Similarly, for Canadian courts the rule would also be subject to a *Club Resorts*[227] enquiry, but given the presumption that the *forum delicti* can validly assume jurisdiction it would almost certainly survive.[228] However, agreement on a unified rule of adjudicative jurisdiction will take some time. The adoption of the rule of enforcement jurisdiction by implementation of the Judgments Convention would, in itself, be a welcome first step.

[221] See text to nn 175–79, 213 above.
[222] See above (n 5).
[223] Beaumont (n 4) 77–79, 109; Borchers (n 4) 158.
[224] Art 5(1)(j) Judgments Convention (n 5).
[225] RA Brand, 'Tort Jurisdiction in a Multilateral Convention: The Lessons of the Due Process Clause and the Brussels Convention' (1998) 24 *Brooklyn Journal of International Law* 125, 154–55.
[226] RA Brand, 'Due Process, Jurisdiction and a Hague Judgments Convention' (1999) 60 *University of Pittsburgh Law Review* 661, 701–06; SP Baumgartner, 'The Proposed Hague Convention on Jurisdiction and Foreign Judgments: Where We Are and the Road Ahead' (2002) 4 *European Journal of Law Reform* 219, 229–34.
[227] *Club Resorts* (n 58).
[228] See text to nn 58–60 above.

20

Unjust(ified) Enrichment

ADELINE CHONG AND JAN LÜTTRINGHAUS

I. Introduction

Under Roman law it was considered 'a fundamental principle of natural justice that no one ought unjustly to enrich himself at the expense of another'.[1] This principle pervades the common law, though seeing it as a discrete area of law was much more belated.[2] The concept, role and scope of unjust(ified) enrichment vary across different legal systems, even within those with the same legal tradition.

This chapter analyses unjust enrichment claims from the perspective of both the common law and civil law. It discusses the substantive laws on unjust enrichment (section II), jurisdiction (section III) and applicable law (section IV) from both the common law and civil law perpectives. For the latter, the various private international law instruments of the European Union (EU) are treated as being emblematic of the civil law approach, although of course, the EU Regulations also apply to a small handful of common law countries.[3] Based on this comparative approach, a proposal is made for a global solution to the applicable law for unjust enrichment (section IV.C), before concluding (section V).

II. Substantive Laws on Unjust(ified) Enrichment

Domestic conceptions of a topic are never determinative at the private international law level. However, a brief foray into domestic law is warranted to explain the scope of this chapter. Characterisation of an action as being within unjustified enrichment is difficult at the private international law level due to controversies as to its ambit under domestic law. The conflation of the labels 'unjust enrichment' and 'restitution' has led to uncertainty as to its scope in domestic law. It is now largely accepted that 'restitution' is broader than 'unjust enrichment', the former describes the nature of remedies where the defendant gives up a gain as opposed to remedies focusing on losses incurred by the claimant. Unjust enrichment is one ground on which a restitutionary remedy may lie.[4]

[1] S Meier, 'Unjustified Enrichment' in J Basedow, KJ Hopt and R Zimmermann (eds), *Max Planck Encyclopedia of European Private Law*, Vol II (Oxford University Press 2012) 1742. See D. 12,6,14 and D. 50,17,206.

[2] *Lipkin Gorman* [1991] AC 548; *Pavey & Matthews Pty Ltd* (1987) 162 CLR 221.

[3] Post-Brexit, the only common law countries left in the EU are Ireland and Cyprus, but the UK has retained the Rome I and II Regulations, but not Brussels Ia, as part of its domestic law.

[4] See J Edelman and E Bant, *Unjust Enrichment*, 2nd edn (Hart Publishing 2016) 29.

Actions which are categorised as, in common law parlance, restitution for wrongs and proprietary restitution are not covered in this chapter. There is controversy as to whether restitution for wrongs is based on unjust enrichment; the view that appears to be gaining ground is that restitution for wrongs is a separate category of law.[5] This suggests that for private international law purposes, restitution for wrongs should be subject to different treatment from unjust enrichment actions. Proprietary restitution is generally understood to include actions where the claimant seeks a proprietary remedy. On this, the remedial constructive trust[6] can arise in response to unjust enrichment, but such trusts are not part of all common law systems.[7] Judicial authority is against a similar analysis for the institutional constructive trust[8] and resulting trust.[9] Proprietary restitution also does not appear to have a counterpart in civil law, largely because trusts are generally not part of civil law systems and unjust enrichment only gives rise to personal claims under civil law.[10] Due to the uncertainty as to the extent to which unjust enrichment underlies restitution for wrongs and proprietary restitution, this chapter is confined to unjust enrichment actions.

This foray into domestic laws helps to explain the difference in terminology between the common law and civil law systems. The common law and civil law unjust enrichment frameworks both require that: (1) the defendant was enriched; and (2) this enrichment was at the expense of the claimant. The difference is in relation to the third requirement.[11] Under English law, the claimant has to show that the enrichment was unjust,[12] the so-called unjust factors approach, whereas under civilian systems, it has to be shown that the enrichment was without justification. It is this difference which explains why the subject is generally known as 'unjust enrichment' at common law and 'unjustified enrichment' in civil law. That said, some common law jurisdictions also follow the civilian framework in that it has to be shown that there is an absence of basis for the enrichment.[13] Another variant is the Australian approach, where 'unconscionability' is the underlying principle for restitution.[14] This chapter uses 'unjust enrichment'.

III. Jurisdiction

This section considers the common law service out rules and the grounds of special jurisdiction in the Brussels Ia Regulation[15] relevant to unjust enrichment actions. The two systems have

[5] *Sempra Metals Ltd* [2008] 1 AC 561, 606. See also P Birks, *Unjust Enrichment*, 2nd edn (Oxford University Press 2005) 11–16; G Virgo, *The Principles of the Law of Restitution*, 3rd edn (Oxford University Press 2015) 10–11, 417–18; C Mitchell, P Mitchell and S Watterson (eds), *Goff and Jones: The Law of Unjust Enrichment*, 9th edn (Sweet & Maxwell 2016) 4–5; Edelman and Bant (n 4) 19–21. *cf* A Burrows, *The Law of Restitution*, 3rd edn (Oxford University Press 2011) 9.

[6] *Pettkus* [1980] 2 SCR 834.

[7] Notably, it is not part of English law: *Re Polly Peck International plc (No 2)* [1998] 3 All ER 812 (CA).

[8] *Foskett* [2001] 1 AC 102. *cf* Burrows (n 5) ch 8.

[9] *Westdeutsche Landesbank Girozentrale* [1996] AC 669, 689. *cf* R Chambers, *Resulting Trusts* (Clarendon Press 1997); P Birks, 'Restitution and Resulting Trusts' in S Goldstein (ed), *Equity and Contemporary Legal Developments* (Hebrew University 1992) 335.

[10] A Chong, 'Choice of Law for Unjust Enrichment/Restitution and the Rome II Regulation' (2008) 57 *ICLQ* 863, 867.

[11] For the common law framework, see, eg, *Banque Financière de la Cité* [1999] 1 AC 221, 227. For the civil law framework, see, eg, French Civil Code, Art 1303-1 ('sans cause'); German Civil Code, s 812(1) ('ohne rechtlichen Grund').

[12] *Banque Financière*, ibid, 227.

[13] Canada: *Pettkus* (n 6); Malaysia: *Dream Property Sdn Bhd* [2015] 2 CLJ 453.

[14] *Roxborough* [2001] HCA 68; *Bofinger* [2009] HCA 44 [89]; *Australian Financial Services and Leasing Pty Ltd* [2014] HCA 14. This, however, is argued to be a distinction without a difference from the 'unjust factors' approach: K Barker, 'Unjust Enrichment in Australia: What is(n't) it? Implications for Legal Reasoning and Practice' (2020) 43 *Melbourne University Law Review* 903, 914–15.

[15] [2012] OJ L351/1.

different underlying objectives. The service out rules apply when the defendant cannot be served in the country and identify a connection between the defendant or the action and the forum sufficient to justify the court exercising jurisdiction over the defendant. The grounds of special jurisdiction set out in Article 7 of Brussels Ia are a derogation from the defendant's domicile rule in Article 4.[16] As the rules in the two regimes are formulated against an intricate backdrop of interrelated jurisdiction rules, the aim of this section is not to propose any global solution for jurisdiction in unjust enrichment claims, but rather to outline the existing framework. Unjust enrichment, as an independent branch of the law of obligations standing alongside contract and tort, deserves its own jurisdiction rule.

A. Common Law: Rules on Service Out

The focus is on service out in the English and Welsh Civil Procedure Rules (CPR PD 6B paragraph 3.1(16)) which contains the most comprehensive ground for service out for restitutionary claims compared with the other common law jurisdictions.[17] It is in these terms:

> (16) A claim is made for restitution where –
> (a) the defendant's alleged liability arises out of acts committed within the jurisdiction; or
> (b) the enrichment is obtained within the jurisdiction; or
> (c) the claim is governed by the law of England and Wales.

It is clearly the case that the ground of service out in paragraph 3.1(16) will cover unjust enrichment claims although it is framed wider, ie, in terms of 'restitution'.[18] The other relevant head of service out is CPR PD 63 paragraph 3.1(6) which relates to a claim made 'in respect of a contract', with that phrase being held to be wide enough to cover unjust enrichment claims arising pursuant to a contract or alleged contract.[19] However, the natural home for unjust enrichment claims is paragraph 3.1(16).

In relation to sub-paragraph (a), the gateway can be used when the acts[20] committed within the jurisdiction are those of the claimant.[21] In *Sharab*, it was held that the focus of this gateway 'is principally, although not exclusively, on the acts of the claimant'.[22] This focus on the claimant's acts is misplaced[23] as it is not an adequate basis to assert jurisdiction over the defendant.

Much the same point has been made in relation to sub-paragraph (b): where the enrichment is comprised of services, English domestic law provides that the enrichment is the services that are rendered, not the end product of the services, at least where the services merely 'unlocked' the

[16] A Dickinson and E Lein, *The Brussels I Regulation Recast* (Oxford University Press 2015) para 4.07.

[17] Most of the other common law jurisdictions do not have a ground for service out dealing exclusively with restitution and/or the relevant ground is confined to an approximation of the first limb of CPR PD 6B para 3.1(16). See, eg, The Rules of the High Court, Order 11 r1(p) (Hong Kong); Uniform Civil Procedure Rules 2005 (New South Wales) Sch 6 para (l); Supreme Court Civil Rules 2006 (South Australia) r 40A(l); Supreme Court Rules 2000 (Tasmania) r 147A(l); Court Procedure Rules (Australian Capital Territory) r 6502(l).

[18] Some of the cases cited in this section may more naturally be classified as restitution for wrongs or proprietary restitution but the court's approach towards CPR PD 6B para 3.1(16) remains instructive for unjust enrichment claims.

[19] *Albon (t/a NA Carriage Co)* [2007] EWHC 9 (Ch); *Cecil* [2010] EWHC 641 (Comm) (reversed on other grounds [2011] EWCA Civ 135) (*cf Sharab* [2012] EWHC 1798 (Ch), [58]).

[20] 'Acts' includes 'omissions': *AstraZeneca UK Ltd* [2010] EWHC 1028 (Comm), [65]–[66].

[21] *Gray* [2019] EWHC 1636 (QB), [185]; *Bazhanov* [2017] EWHC 3404 (Comm), [85]; *Sharab* (n 19) [68]. Of course, if the defendant had committed the relevant acts within jurisdiction, this would suffice: eg, *Zumax Nigeria Ltd* [2016] EWCA Civ 567; *Ashley* [2019] EWHC 17 (Ch).

[22] *Sharab* (n 19) [68].

[23] M Hoyle, 'Failures for Consideration: Re-Analysing Jurisdiction in Unjust Enrichment Claims' (2020) 83 *MLR* 1008, 1019.

intrinsic potential value of the defendant's property.[24] This means, again, that the enrichment would be construed in accordance with the claimant's acts, ie, the provision of services within the jurisdiction.[25] This, however presupposes that 'enrichment' is to be construed in accordance with English domestic law, whereas, it is suggested, a better approach would be to interpret it in accordance with English private international law.[26] Thus the assessment of where the enrichment has been obtained requires a prior applicable law analysis.[27]

B. Civil Law: Brussels Ia Regulation

The Brussels Ia Regulation confers exclusive jurisdiction on the court of a Member State in certain situations. Article 24(1) is limited to actions which seek to determine rights *in rem* in the immovable property.[28] Personal claims for unjust enrichment are therefore excluded even if they relate to that property.[29] A claim for unjust enrichment may however be subject to the jurisdiction of a court of a Member State if there is a choice of court agreement for that court pursuant to Article 25. Otherwise claims for unjust enrichment can be made in the defendant's domicile under Article 4[30] or elsewhere using the rules on special jurisdiction in Articles 7(1) and 7(2).

i. Article 7(1) Brussels Ia

Article 7(1) concerns 'matters relating to contract'. A 'contract' requires the establishment of a legal obligation freely consented to by one person towards another.[31] With regard to unjust enrichment some argue that this requirement is not fulfilled because the restitutionary obligation arises *ex lege* rather than from an obligation freely consented to by the parties.[32] However, the word 'relating' suggests that the claim itself need not be contractual in nature. Article 7(1) does not require the conclusion of a valid contract.[33] In *Profit Investment* the European Court of Justice (ECJ) held that

> as regards the link between the action for a declaration of nullity and the recovery of sums paid but not due … (t)hat causal link between the right to restitution and the contractual relationship is sufficient to bring the action for restitution within the scope of matters relating to a contract.[34]

Claims for unjust enrichment are covered by Article 7(1) where they relate to the consequences arising out of an invalid contract,[35] or where the claims are made pursuant to a valid contract such as restitution for overpayment by mistake in performance of a contract.[36]

[24] *Cobbe* [2008] UKHL 55; *cf BP Exploration Co* [1979] 1 WLR 783.
[25] Hoyle (n 23) 1022.
[26] See, eg, A Briggs, *Civil Jurisdiction and Judgments*, 6th edn (Routledge 2015) para 4.62.
[27] See below, section IV.
[28] C-25/18 *Kerr* EU:C:2019:376, para 37. See U Grušić, 'Unjust Enrichment and the Brussels I Regulation' (2019) *ICLQ* 837, 840.
[29] See C-827/18 *MC* EU:C:2019:416, para 18.
[30] *Kleinwort Benson Ltd* [1997] 3 WLR 923, 931 (HL); Cour d'appel de Liège, 13.12.2012 (2013) *Revue critique de droit international privé* 1:61 et seq. See Dickinson and Lein (n 16) para 4.80.
[31] eg, C-334/00 *Tacconi* [2002] ECR I-7357, para 23.
[32] *Kleinwort* (n 30). *Contra* Dickinson and Lein (n 16) para 4.80.
[33] C-419/11 *Česká spořitelna* EU:C:2013:165, para 46.
[34] C-366/13 *Profit Investment* EU:C:2016:282, para 55.
[35] *Profit Investment*, ibid. See Dickinson and Lein (n 16) para 4.41.
[36] C-242/20 *Hrvatske Šume* ECLI:EU:C:2021:985, para 47 et seq. Grušić (n 28) 860; AG Saugmandsgaard Øe C-242/20 *Hrvatske Šume*, EU:C:2021:728, para 49 et seq.

ii. Article 7(2) Brussels Ia

Where the unjust enrichment claim cannot be said to be one 'relating to a contract', the question which arises is if the claimant may rely on Article 7(2). This confers jurisdiction in 'matters relating to tort, delict or quasi-delict' to the 'courts for the place where the harmful event occurred or may occur'.

Given that unjust enrichment is neither a 'tort' nor a 'delict', unjust enrichment claims would only fall within the ambit of Article 7(2) if considered to be a 'quasi-delict'. This is the case if the concept of 'quasi-delict' is a 'catch-all' provision intended to capture 'non-contractual' obligations other than tort and delict referred to in Article 2(1) of the Rome II Regulation[37] (ie, unjust enrichment, *negotiorum gestio* and *culpa in contrahendo*).[38] This has been subject to debate. Unjust enrichment is more naturally associated with the phrase 'quasi-contract' than 'quasi-delict'. However, Article 7(2) does not mention 'quasi-delict' in every language version of Brussels Ia and some versions indicate that *non-contractual* obligations in general may be included.[39] This is the case, eg, in the German ('einer unerlaubten Handlung gleichgestellt') and Portuguese ('extracontratual') versions. Still, Article 7(2) seems to be drafted for claims aimed at the reparation of 'damage' caused by a 'harmful event'.[40] The ECJ held in *Hrvatske Šume* that unjust enrichment does not fall within this category as these claims do not – at least *prima facie* – relate to any damage caused.[41] However, in *Wikingerhof* the ECJ applied Article 7(2) without requiring any damage: rather the ECJ focused on whether there was a 'breach of an obligation imposed by law' as opposed to a contractual obligation.[42] Moreover, the terms used in Article 7(2) are autonomous concepts of EU law that must be interpreted independently from national law and consistent with Rome I[43] and Rome II as suggested by their respective Recitals 7.[44] According to Article 2(1) of Rome II, 'damage shall cover any consequence arising out of tort/delict, *unjust enrichment*'. The ECJ in *Tacconi*[45] decided that claims for *culpa in contrahendo* are covered by the predecessor to Article 7(2); these 'quasi-delictual' claims are on an equal footing with claims for unjust enrichment pursuant to Rome II. The ECJ has repeatedly held that Article 7(2) 'covers all actions which seek to establish the liability of a defendant and which are not related to a contract within the meaning of [Article 7(1)]'.[46] Therefore, there are good grounds to argue that claims for unjust enrichment fall within Article 7(2).[47]

In *Hrvatske Šume* the AG has, however, opposed the placing of unjust enrichment claims within Article 7(2): Not only did the AG base his opinion on the *national* concept of 'quasi delict'

[37] [2007] OJ L199/40.

[38] AG Darmon C-89/91 *Shearson Lehman* [1992] ECR I-164, para 102; P Mankowski, 'Art 7 Brussels I bis Regulation' in U Magnus and P Mankowski (eds), *European Commentaries on Private International Law*, Vol I (Otto Schmidt 2016) para 245; Dickinson and Lein (n 16) para 4.80 et seq.

[39] Where there is a divergence in the wording of a provision of EU law in the different language versions, that provision is to be interpreted 'by reference to the purpose and general scheme of the rules of which it forms part': C-41/09 *European Commission v Kingdom of The Netherlands* EU:C:2011:108, para 44.

[40] *Hrvatske Šume* (n 36) para 53 et seq. AG Wahl C-102/15 *Siemens* EU:C:2016:225, para 59 et seq; *Kleinwort* (n 30); Oberster Gerichtshof (Austria) 13.1.1998, 7 Ob 375/97s and 26.11.2019, 4Ob173/19y. See with regard to the Lugano Convention, Högsta Domstolen (Sweden) 31.8.2009, Ö 1900-08; Corte Suprema di Cassazione (Italy) 29.5.2008 – n 14201/2008.

[41] *Hrvatske Šume* (n 36) para 53 et seq.

[42] C-59/19, *Wikingerhof* EU:C:2020:950, para 33 et seq.

[43] [2008] OJ L177/6.

[44] C-359/14 *ERGO Insurance* EU:C:2016:40, para 43 et seq. The ECJ only deviates from this line of case law where Brussels Ia has a different scope of application or objective; see C-208/18 *Petruchová* EU:C:2019:825, para 63.

[45] *Tacconi* (n 31) para 27 (Art 5(3) Brussels Convention).

[46] eg, C-548/12 *Brogsitter* EU:C:2014:148, para 20.

[47] AG Darmon *Shearson* (n 38). See Dickinson and Lein (n 16) para 4.81; Mankowski (n 38) para 245. *Contra* Grušić (n 28) 861.

under French law but he also ignored the fact that the concept of 'damage' under Article 2(1) of Rome II includes any consequence arising out of unjust enrichment.[48] The ECJ has followed this reasoning and held that an action for restitution based on unjust enrichment does not fall within the scope of Article 7(2).[49] The lack of a ground of special jurisdiction catering for unjust enrichment is out of keeping with its status as an equal partner to contract and tort in the law of obligations and the fact that the Rome Regulations do cover unjust enrichment.

IV. Applicable Law

A. Common Law

Dicey and Morris's old Rule 230[50] sets out that:

(1) The obligation to restore the benefit of an enrichment obtained at another person's expense is governed by the proper law of the obligation.
(2) The proper law of the obligation is (*semble*) determined as follows:
  (a) If the obligation arises in connection with a contract, its proper law is the law applicable to the contract.
  (b) If it arises in connection with a transaction concerning an immovable (land), its proper law is the law of the country where the immovable is situated (*lex situs*).
  (c) If it arises in any other circumstances, its proper law is the law of the country where the enrichment occurs.

Rule 230 is the touchstone applicable law rule for many common law jurisdictions and has been referred to and applied by various courts.[51] This is so even in Australia where the reference to 'unconscionability' in domestic law does not denote that such claims are subsumed under equity[52] and subject to the choice of law rule for equitable claims.[53]

The main point of divergence is on the relationship between the first clause and the sub-rules set out in the second clause. Some courts have emphasised that the applicable law rule for restitution is the proper law of the obligation as set out in the first paragraph and the sub-rules in paragraph 2 are merely illustrations, whereas other courts have focused on identifying which of the sub-rules best fits the facts at hand. The English,[54] Australian[55] and Canadian[56] courts tend to prefer the proper law approach, with varying degrees of reliance on the *Dicey* rule.

[48] AG Saugmandsgaard Øe *Hrvatske Šume* (n 36) para 61 and para 53 et seq.

[49] *Hrvatske Šume* (n 36) para 53 et seq.

[50] L Collins (gen ed), *Dicey, Morris and Collins on the Conflict of Laws*, 14th edn (Sweet & Maxwell, 2006) (*Dicey*). Rule 230 does not appear in the 15th edn, which discusses the restitutionary choice of law provision in the Rome II Regulation instead.

[51] It has been applied not just to unjust enrichment claims, but claims that may more naturally be described as falling within restitution for wrongs and proprietary restitution. Some of the cases cited in this section fall within the latter two categories, but generally illustrate the wide acceptance of Rule 230 in the common law world.

[52] *Pavey & Matthews* (n 2) 256; *David Securities Pty Ltd* [1992] HCA 48.

[53] See discussion in M Davies et al, *Nygh's Conflict of Laws in Australia*, 10th edn (LexisNexis 2020) 554–58.

[54] eg, *Arab Monetary Fund* [1993] 1 Lloyd's Rep 543; *Barros Mattos Junior* [2005] EWHC 1323 (Ch); *OJSC Oil Co Yugraneft (in liquidation)* [2008] EWHC 2613 (Comm); *Fiona Trust and Holding Corporation* [2010] EWHC 3199 (Comm); *OJSC TNK-BP Holding* [2012] EWHC 3286 (Ch); *Dexia Crediop SpA* [2016] EWHC 2824.

[55] eg, *Swiss Bank* (unreported; 9 December 1992; Supreme Court of New South Wales Commercial Division); *Sweedman* (2006) 224 ALR 625; *Huntingdale Village Pty Ltd* [2016] WASC 336; *Benson* (2018) 355 ALR 671.

[56] *Barclay's Bank PCL* 1999 ABQB 110; *Minera Aquiline Argentina SA* 2006 BCSC 1102; *Barrick Gold Corp* 2012 ONSC 3725; *Budget Rent A Car System Inc* 2018 BCSC 1564; *cf Christopher* 2000 BCCA 532.

The Hong Kong[57] and Singapore[58] courts seem to focus more on the sub-rules. Notably, a Scottish[59] court criticised the *Dicey* rule and preferred the application of the proper law of the restitutionary obligation, ie, 'the law of the country with which, in the light of the whole facts and circumstances, the critical events have their closest and most real connection'.[60]

The editors of *Dicey*[61] themselves appear to have regarded the sub-rules as merely examples of the general rule set out in the first clause. The sub-rules give a useful intimation of what may be the law of closest connection.

Generally speaking, unjust enrichment claims could be divided into those arising out of a pre-existing relationship between the parties and those which do not arise out of such a relationship. Sub-rules (a) and (c) are each thought to cover these two categories respectively.

The paradigmatic situation of an unjust enrichment claim arising, where there is a pre-existing relationship between the parties, is where money has been transferred or services rendered pursuant to an ineffective contract such as where the contract is void, frustrated or illegal. *Dicey*'s sub-rule 2(a) points towards the proper law of the contract or putative proper law of the contract, as the case may be.[62]

Where there is no pre-existing relationship between the parties, one could centre the applicable law rule on either the place of the act giving rise to the enrichment or the place where the enrichment is received. The preponderance of judicial authority is correctly in favour of the latter because an unjust enrichment claim focuses on the defendant's enrichment, rather than the claimant's loss. *Dicey*'s sub-rule 2(c) encapsulates this idea. This sub-rule has been judicially approved by the English courts[63] but there is no decision that the sub-rule 'must be treated as a free-standing rule mechanically applying the law of the place [of enrichment] irrespective of the factual circumstances and irrespective of the particular issue'.[64] The Canadian,[65] Hong Kong[66] and Singapore[67] courts have each applied sub-rule 2(c).

Special attention is placed on situations where the restitutionary obligation arises in connection with a transaction concerning immovable property: sub-rule 2(b) suggests that the *lex situs* ought to apply. This can be understood as an extension of the general principle that the *lex situs* applies when one deals with questions of title over immovable property.

B. Civil Law: Rome I and II Regulations

The EU and UK framework splits the applicable law rules for unjust enrichment claims between the Rome I and Rome II Regulations.

Pursuant to Article 12(1)(e) of Rome I, the law applicable to claims for unjust enrichment following a void contract is to be determined by Rome I.[68] Thus, if a void contract is nonetheless

[57] eg, *First Laser Ltd* [2002] HKCU 1484; *Falcon Private Bank Ltd* [2012] HKCU 1414.

[58] eg, *Hongkong and Shanghai Banking Corp Ltd* [1992] SGHC 61; *CIMB Bank Bhd* [2008] SGCA 36; *Bunge SA and another* [2015] SGHC 330.

[59] The Scottish legal system is a mixed system comprising common and civil law elements.

[60] *Baring Brothers & Co Ltd* [1997] CLC 108, 127 (Lord Penrose).

[61] *Dicey* (n 50) paras 34-017, 34-031.

[62] *cf Dexia* (n 54).

[63] *Chase Manhattan Bank NA* [1981] Ch 105; *Re Jogia* [1988] 1 WLR 484; *El Ajou* [1993] 3 All ER 717; *Kuwait Oil Tanker Co SAK*, (unreported, 16 November 1998; affirmed [2000] All ER (Comm) 271 (CA)).

[64] *Barros* (n 54) [117].

[65] *Christopher* (n 56).

[66] *Falcon* (n 57).

[67] *Hongkong and Shanghai Banking Corp Ltd* (n 58); *Thahir Kartika Ratna* [1994] SGCA 105; *CIMB* (n 58); *Bunge* (n 58).

[68] AG Kokott C-185/15 *Kostanjevec* EU:C:2016:397, para 64; J Lüttringhaus, 'Art 1 Rome I Regulation' in F Ferrari (ed), *Concise Commentary on the Rome I Regulation*, 2nd edn (Cambridge University Press 2020) para 24.

performed by one party, the unjust enrichment claim is determined by the parties' choice of law pursuant to Article 3, or, failing that, in accordance with Article 4.

Rome II applies to unjust enrichment claims in general provided, of course, that they fall within the scope of the Regulation.[69] The parties may choose the applicable law within the limits set forth in Article 14. Parties pursuing a commercial activity may freely chose the applicable law before the event giving rise to the unjust enrichment but for others the choice of law may only take place after the event giving rise to the unjust enrichment occurred.[70] In the absence of a choice of law the law applicable to claims for unjust enrichment is, pursuant to Article 10(1), the law that governs a pre-existing relationship between the parties, such as a contract or a tort, provided that the latter is closely connected with that unjust enrichment.[71]

The potential overlap of Article 12(1)(e) Rome I and Article 10 Rome II with regard to unjust enrichment claims arising out of a void contract should be resolved by treating Article 12(1)(e) Rome I as *lex specialis* vis-à-vis Rome II.[72] Whereas in the vast majority of cases, similar results will be reached by these provisions anyway (ie, application of the applicable law to the contract or supposed contract), differences may, at least in theory, arise from the more restrictive approach to choice of law under Article 14(1) Rome II, and the wording of Article 3(3) and (4) Rome I compared with Article 14(2) and (3) Rome II.

Where the applicable law cannot be determined based on Article 10(1), Article 10(2) Rome II points to the law of the parties' common habitual residence. Absent a common habitual residence, the default rule in Article 10(3) is the law of the country where the unjust enrichment was received.[73] Article 10(4) contains an 'escape clause' for cases in which the unjust enrichment is manifestly more closely connected with a country other than that indicated by the relevant rule in Article 10(1)–(3). This escape clause should be used with restraint and its main field of application may be scenarios involving multiple parties. Where, for example, the claimant has paid another person's debt to a third party, Article 10(4) could lead to the application of the law governing the debt paid.[74] The escape clause may also apply where claims for unjust enrichment are closely connected to (immovable) property allowing for the application of the *lex situs*.[75]

Some claims for unjust enrichment are excluded from the ambit of both Rome Regulations: in particular, non-contractual claims based on 'violations of privacy and rights relating to personality, including defamation'.[76] Here domestic applicable law rules apply. In Germany, for example, claims for unjust enrichment arising out of such an infringement to a protected interest are governed by the law of the country where the infringement occurred.[77] However, German conflict of laws rules generally allow for renvoi.[78] Moreover, the parties are free to choose the applicable law after the enrichment occurred.[79]

[69] Art 1.

[70] Art 14(1)(a).

[71] Chong (n 10) 876.

[72] See German Federal Court of Justice, ECLI:DE:BGH:2018:080218UIXZR92.17.0 para. 27; Lüttringhaus (n 68) para 24.

[73] See *Banque Cantonale de Genève* [2015] EWHC 1968 (Comm); Chong (n 10) 882.

[74] P Mankowski, 'Unjust enrichment (restitution)' in J Basedow et al (eds), *Encyclopaedia of Private International Law*, Vol I (Edward Elgar 2017) 1809, 1812.

[75] This might offer a viable solution for claims, such as s 951 German Civil Code, which may be characterised as either unjust enrichment or proprietary claims, see H-P Mansel, *Art 43 EGBGB in Staudinger, EGBGB/IPR* (Sellier-de Gruyter 2015) para 726.

[76] See Rome II, Art 1(2)(g).

[77] See Introductory Act to the Civil Code, Art 38(2) and Art 4. In other cases, claims of unjust enrichment may be governed by the law of the country in which the enrichment took place: Introductory Act to the Civil Code, Art 38(3).

[78] See Introductory Act to the Civil Code, Art 4. *cf* Rome II, Art 24.

[79] See Introductory Act to the Civil Code, Art 42.

C. Global Proposal on Applicable Law

Drawing on the above discussion of the common law and civil law applicable law approaches to unjust enrichment, a proposal is made for the main features of a global applicable law framework.

It can be seen that the common law and EU/UK approaches to applicable law for unjust enrichment have a different structure. Old Rule 230 of *Dicey* sets out a flexible applicable law rule with the sub-rules providing guidance for specific situations, whereas Article 10 of Rome II has specific rules coupled with an escape clause in favour of the law of closest connection. In terms of substance, however, both contain common elements.

Where the claim arises out of a relationship between the parties, both sub-rule 2(a) of *Dicey* and Article 10(1) of Rome II call for the application of the governing law of the relationship. Article 14 of Rome II recognises the principle of party autonomy for choice of law for non-contractual obligations but not for an *ex ante* choice made by parties who are pursuing a non-commercial activity.[80] This restriction is intended to protect the weaker party from a choice imposed by the stronger party,[81] but it is unclear whether the restriction achieves this objective.[82] It is suggested that party autonomy should be unrestricted; the usual fetters on party autonomy such as mandatory rules and public policy ought to afford adequate protection to weaker parties.

That said, criticisms have been levelled against the application of the governing law of the relationship between the parties to the restitutionary obligation.[83] Chiefly, it is argued that this rule undermines the independence of the law of unjust enrichment by reverting to a choice of law founded in contract[84] and that it would be inappropriate or even illogical to give effect to the governing law of an invalid or void contract in relation to the restitutionary aftermath.[85]

On the first criticism, the mere fact that a role is accorded to the governing law of the contract in relation to an unjust enrichment claim does not mean that one is reverting back to discredited quasi-contract reasoning.[86] On the contrary, there are independent reasons for preferring this applicable law rule for unjust enrichment claims. The second criticism has received support from the English court in *Dexia*[87] where it had been argued that English law, as the governing law of the invalid contract, should govern the restitutionary claim. Walker J rejected this and stated that where the restitutionary claim arises because the contract is void *ab initio*,

> the mere fact that the agreement identified a governing law is unlikely in these circumstances to give a close or real connection to that governing law. On the contrary, in my view the invalidity of the parties' agreement at the time that it was made will ordinarily have the consequence that the suggested connection is unreal.[88]

He went on to hold that the same applied for a restitutionary claim which arose because the contract is voidable at the option of the innocent party.[89] This rejection of the (putative) governing

[80] Art 14(1)(b).
[81] COM(2003) 427 final 22.
[82] Chong (n 10) 875–76.
[83] See generally, A Chong, 'Choice of Law for Void Contracts and Their Restitutionary Aftermath: The Putative Governing Law of the Contract' in P Giliker (ed), *Re-examining Contract and Unjust Enrichment* (Brill 2007) 173–75.
[84] S Cohen, 'Quasi Contract and the Conflicts of Laws' (1956) 31 *Los Angeles Bar Bulletin* 71, 74; G Panagopoulos, *Restitution in Private International Law* (Hart Publishing 2000) 147, 263.
[85] J Blaikie, 'Unjust Enrichment in the Conflict of Laws' [1984] *Juridical Review* 112, 127; R Stevens, 'Conflict of Laws' in P Birks and F Rose (eds), *Lessons of the Swaps Litigation* (Mansfield Press 2000) 344.
[86] *Dicey* (n 50) para 34-025; K Zweigert and D Müller-Gindullis, 'Quasi Contract' in K Lipstein (ed), *International Encyclopaedia of Comparative Law, Vol III* (Mohr Siebeck 1974) 12.
[87] (n 54). *cf Deutsche Bank AG London v Comune di Busto Arsizio* [2021] EWHC 2706 (Comm), [411].
[88] *Dexia*, ibid, [164].
[89] Ibid.

law of the contract should not be adopted. If the vitiating factor does not impugn the parties' choice of law, it would neither be inappropriate nor illogical to apply the (putative) governing law to determine the restitutionary consequences as the parties would have reached *consensus* on the governing law of the contract.[90] Further, the parties' expectations are likely for the governing law of the contract to govern all disputes arising out of the contract, including an unjust enrichment claim arising from a failure of the contract or purported contract. In addition, the transfer of wealth occurred pursuant to this 'contract' and its terms have relevance to determine the restitutionary consequences;[91] eg, the court may take its cue on the value of the enrichment from the price stipulated in the agreement.[92] Therefore there are good reasons why the governing law of the relationship between the parties, ought to govern an unjust enrichment claim arising pursuant to that relationship.[93]

It is further suggested that the governing law of the contract should also govern the unjust enrichment claim even if the contract is ineffective because of the application of a law other than the governing law of the contract.[94] For example, it could be that the transfer of the enrichment is *ultra vires* the transferor under the law of its place of incorporation, or the transfer is void as being against the public policy of the forum. It has been suggested that in these situations, the law which strikes down the contract ought to govern the unjust enrichment claim.[95] On the one hand, application of the law which strikes down the contract to the unjust enrichment claim may lead to a more internally consistent outcome. It could be the case that Ruritanian law, which considers the contract to be void, would not grant unjust enrichment in the circumstances of the case, whereas an unjust enrichment claim would succeed under the governing law of the contract. There would be distortion of Ruritanian law should the governing law of the contract apply to the unjust enrichment claim. On the other hand, one could argue that there are two separate, albeit interrelated, questions: first, whether the contract is invalid; and if so, second, whether an unjust enrichment claim pursuant to the invalid contract would be successful. Each of these questions merits its own applicable law. This is supported by *obiter dicta* in *Deutsche Bank*.[96] In addition, the same point on party expectations as to the governing law of the contract, made above, equally applies in this context. It is therefore suggested that the governing law of the contract ought to apply to the unjust enrichment claim even if some other law deems the contract to be ineffective. The fact that there is a prohibition against an unjust enrichment claim under the latter law ought to be irrelevant unless the relevant law is the *lex fori* and the prohibition forms part of the *lex fori's* public policy or is an overriding mandatory rule. It is also possible that the prohibition should also be given effect if it is contained in a law whose overriding mandatory provisions supercede the governing law of the contract.[97]

[90] *Dicey* gives examples of when it would not be appropriate to give effect to the proper law of the contract, eg, where the contract was invalid due to duress which affects the choice of law clause: (n 50) para 34-024. See also *CIMB* (n 58) [54]–57].

[91] See *Baring* (n 60) 126.

[92] See Virgo (n 5) 99–102.

[93] See generally, Chong (n 83) 173–75.

[94] Ibid, 176–81.

[95] This option is supported by R Stevens, 'The Choice of Law Rules of Restitutionary Obligations' in F Rose (ed), *Restitution and the Conflict of Laws* (Mansfield Press 1995) 199, 220; A Dickinson, 'Restitution and the Conflict of Laws' [1996] *Lloyd's Maritime and Commercial Law Quarterly* 556, 571.

[96] (n 87). If the application of Italian law led to a lack of capacity on the part of an Italian local authority to enter into a swaps agreement, Cockerill J would have applied English law (the proper law of the putative contract and the law of the place of enrichment) as the law with the closest and most real connection with the putative transaction to determine the local authority's restitutionary claim for return of sums paid under the agreement.

[97] See, eg, Rome I Reg, Art 9(2) and (3).

The other shared applicable law option is the law of the place of enrichment, which generally applies where the enrichment did not take place against a backdrop of a pre-existing relationship between the parties.[98] One common element amongst all the different domestic conceptions of unjust enrichment is that there must be an enrichment. This in itself strongly suggests that a *locus* associated with the enrichment ought to feature in any applicable law framework for unjust enrichment.[99] However, those who do not favour this applicable law rule often raise the point that the place of enrichment may be difficult to determine. Doubts have also been expressed as to whether its application would provide a just result if the defendant deliberately chose to receive the enrichment in a jurisdiction whose laws were favourable to it.[100] Both are valid concerns but it is suggested that these concerns can be curtailed by carefully considering how the place of enrichment is to be identified.

Identifying the place of enrichment is particularly difficult in relation to electronic fund transfers, where the funds may potentially be transferred from one jurisdiction to another until it is ultimately withdrawn by the defendant.[101] It is suggested that the law of place of immediate enrichment ought to be identified as the applicable law in these sorts of situations. For one, the elements of an action in unjust enrichment usually crystallise at the point of receipt;[102] for another, the initial receipt of the money requires the cooperation of both parties, as opposed to subsequent transfers by the defendant which are effected unilaterally.[103] The last point also reduces the risk of manipulation of this applicable law rule by the defendant.

Where the enrichment does not consist of a transfer of funds or assets, but is of services which results in an end product, identification of the law of the place of enrichment may potentially raise a circular issue. It may be the case that, depending on the context, either the services or the end product is valued as the enrichment according to different laws. For example, the services may be rendered in Ruritania and under Ruritanian domestic law the enrichment is the services rendered, but the end product is received in Utopia which considers the end product to be the enrichment. Identifying either law as the law of place of enrichment is to assume that that law's understanding of 'enrichment' ought to prevail. Short of adopting an autonomous definition of what 'enrichment' means, it is suggested that to break the deadlock, the governing law of the unjust enrichment claim should be the law of closest connection. This solution would be in line with the overarching principle of closest connection in Rule 230(1) and could also be accommodated via Article 10(4) of Rome II.

In terms of differences between the common law and civil law choice of law regimes, Article 10(2) has no counterpart at common law, except insofar as the law of common habitual residence of the parties is found to be the law of closest connection to the restitutionary obligation. If both parties reside in the same place, it is likely that trial will take place there and it would be convenient for the court to apply its own law. The parties would also share similar expectations.[104] Thus, there are practical reasons to support Article 10(2), where the enrichment does not arise out of a pre-existing relationship between the parties.

[98] *Dicey's* sub-rule 2(c); Rome II Reg, Art 10(3). Art 10(3) yields to the law of common habitual residence of the parties in Art 10(2).

[99] See J Bird, 'Choice of Law' in F Rose (ed), *Restitution and the Conflict of Laws* (Mansfield Press 1995) 113–16.

[100] *Swiss Bank* (n 55).

[101] See the scenario posited by Hwang JC in *Hongkong and Shanghai Banking Corp Ltd* (n 58) 500–01.

[102] *Benedetti* [2014] AC 938 (SC), [14]; *BP Exploration Co* (n 24) 836; A Junker, 'Art 10 Rom II-VO' in *Münchener Kommentar zum BGB*, 8th edn (CH Beck 2021) para 28. Even where the cause of action crystallises after receipt, for example where the basis for the transfer fails after receipt, the enrichment is valued at the date of immediate receipt: C Mitchell et al, *Goff & Jones: The Law of Unjust Enrichment*, 9th edn (Thomson Reuters 2016) paras 4-54–4-55.

[103] Chong (n 10) 886–87.

[104] Ibid, 881.

Dicey's Rule 230 refers specifically to the application of the *lex situs*, which does not appear expressly in the Rome II framework. At common law the *lex situs* applies when one deals with questions of title over immovable property. The reasons for this are a mixture of practical and sovereignty concerns. Any judgment which purports to effect title to foreign immovable property will have to be brought before the courts of the country where the property is located for enforcement. This makes it futile to decide the action otherwise than in accordance with the *lex situs*. Party expectations are also likely to be that the *lex situs* will determine whether a transfer of title is good. Sovereignty concerns which arise in relation to immovable property dictate the application of the *lex situs* to title issues.[105]

All these reasons, however, are arguments for the application of the *lex situs* where there is an issue of title to the immovable property. The justifications for application of the *lex situs* do not apply for a personal obligation arising in connection with immovable property. No issue of sovereignty arises in relation to a personal obligation to restore an unjust enrichment, any more than it does in relation to a contractual obligation. Party expectations are more likely to be for the proper law of the relationship between them to govern the restitutionary aspects of an unjust enrichment claim arising in connection with immovable property,[106] similarly to an unjust enrichment concerning a funds transfer, movable property or services rendered. Enforcement of a judgment in relation to unjust enrichment would be sought where the defendant has assets against which the judgment may be realised, which would not necessarily be the *situs* of the subject matter of the claim. One must differentiate between the personal and proprietary aspects of a transaction.[107] Having said that, for unjust enrichment claims relating to immovable property, the *situs* of the immovable property will coincide with the *situs* where the enrichment is conferred. Alternatively, the *lex situs* may be assessed to be the law of closest connection.[108] So situations where it may be appropriate to accord a role for the *lex situs* can still be accommodated without requiring a specific and misleading applicable law rule in favour of the *lex situs*.

Both Rule 230 and Article 10 largely seek to identify the law of closest connection to the unjust enrichment claim. This is clearly so for the general principle enshrined in Rule 230(1) and sub-paragraphs 1, 3 and 4 of Article 10. Article 10(2) has a different focus, ie, the application of a convenient applicable law rule, but as stated above, it can also be supported. Depending on legal tradition, one may feel more comfortable with a flexible applicable law rule with guidelines as what the law of closest connection may be, or with a framework of hierarchical rules which identify specifically what is or ought to be considered as the law of closest connection in various situations.

On balance, it is suggested that the Rome II framework, with its open embrace of party autonomy for unjust enrichment claims in Article 14, represents a modern applicable law approach towards non-contractual obligations.[109] After all, party autonomy is now largely accepted for tort choice of law under both the common law[110] and the civil law,[111] and there do not appear to be

[105] As a matter of common law, the *Moçambique* rule (from *Moçambique* [1893] AC 602) prohibits courts from having subject matter jurisdiction over actions concerning title to foreign immovable property.

[106] Bird (n 99) 118.

[107] Chong (n 10) 895.

[108] See above, text to n 75.

[109] The caveat is that its restrictions on an ex ante choice of law should be disregarded; see text to n 80 et seq.

[110] Under the Private International Law (Miscellaneous Provisions) Act 1995: *Trafigura Beheer BV* [2006] EWHC 1450 (Comm); *Kingspan Environmental Ltd* [2012] EWHC 1147 (Comm). Party autonomy in the context of the double actionability rule for tort has also been obliquely accepted: *Rickshaw Investments Ltd* [2006] SGCA 39, [15] and [44].

[111] See with regard to Dutch private international law and Art 42 Introductory Act to the German Civil Code: COM(2003) 427 final 22. For a global study on party autonomy in tort law see J Basedow, *The Law of Open Societies* (Hague Academy 2015) 168–93.

good reasons why party autonomy should not be extended to unjust enrichment as well. Further, the system of hierarchical rules in Article 10 of Rome II, with an escape clause in favour of the law of closest connection, may engender more certainty compared with the more malleable common law approach.

V. Conclusion

The fact that the domestic laws of unjust enrichment in many countries are still evolving means that the task at the private international law level is not clear-cut. The divergences in approach at the domestic level also add another layer of complexity. Despite this, it is hoped that this chapter has shown that a global framework for applicable law on unjust enrichment which is nimble enough to deal with these issues is well within reach.

21

Property

JANEEN M CARRUTHERS AND MATTHIAS WELLER

I. The Current State of Play Regarding Private International Law and Property

Unified private international law rules pertaining to property are something of a rarity insofar as property comprises an area of law which remains largely untouched by any major harmonisation measure, on either a global or regional level. However, although there is no single, bespoke instrument which purports to deal on an all-encompassing basis with private international law rules concerning property, there is a wide range of instruments which affect, or have the potential to affect, or impinge upon, proprietary rights or interests. To this extent, therefore, there is a mosaic of instruments to which regard must be had when surveying the private international law landscape pertaining to property.

While the recognition and enforcement of judgments relating to property, as with other judgments concerning 'civil and commercial matters', will be subject, in and among Contracting States, to the 2019 Hague Convention on the recognition and enforcement of foreign judgments in civil or commercial matters (HCCH 2019 Judgments Convention), which therefore will serve as a starting point for this contribution, there are, as yet, no bespoke, global rules of direct jurisdiction concerning property.[1]

In addition to this instrument of general ('horizontal') scope and application, there are certain global treaties of more specific subject matter scope, focusing on particular areas of private law – matrimonial property, succession and trusts law in particular[2] – which nonetheless affect proprietary rights or interests and of which account is taken elsewhere in this book.[3]

Similarly, there are various sectoral instruments which affect property and to which regard must be had when assessing the international regulatory landscape. Thus, eg, the 2006 Hague Convention on the law applicable to certain rights in respect of securities held with an intermediary

[1] Contrast, in the EU, the rules of direct jurisdiction for civil and commercial matters (including, subject to Art 1, property), as well as rules on the recognition and enforcement of civil and commercial judgments, set out in Regulation (EU) No 1215/2012 on jurisdiction and the recognition and enforcement of judgments in civil and commercial matters (recast) (Brussels Ia).

[2] See the 1978 Hague Convention on the law applicable to matrimonial property regimes; the 1989 Hague Convention on the law applicable to succession to the estates of deceased persons; and the 1985 Hague Convention on the law applicable to trusts and on their recognition.

[3] See Albert Font I Segura and Jayne Holliday, 'Succession', ch 22; Jonathan Harris, 'Trusts', ch 23; and Rhona Schuz, 'Matrimonial Property', ch 37 in this book.

(HCCH 2006 Securities Convention) concerns a restricted class of property, namely, cross-border holdings and transfers of intermediated securities.

Finally, aside from the work of the Hague Conference on Private International Law (HCCH), institutions such as UNIDROIT,[4] UNCITRAL,[5] and UNESCO[6] respectively, have promulgated measures concerning private international law and property to which consideration will be given.

A. Existing Global Measures for the Unification of Private International Law Rules Pertaining to Property

Unlike the HCCH 2005 Convention on Choice of Court Agreements, which excludes from its scope,[7] tort or delict claims for damage to tangible property that do not arise from a contractual relationship, and rights *in rem* in immovable property, and tenancies of immovable property, the HCCH 2019 Judgments Convention, regarding the recognition and enforcement in one Contracting State of a judgment given by a court of another Contracting State, contains no equivalent exclusions.[8] In order to regulate indirect jurisdiction for recognition and enforcement of judgments in relation to property, the HCCH 2019 Convention takes an innovative approach. First, according to Article 6: '[A] judgment that ruled on rights *in rem* in immovable property shall be recognised and enforced if and only if the property is situated in the State of origin'. Article 6 contains the only exclusive head of indirect jurisdiction within the instrument,[9] thereby even excluding, in derogation from the *favor recognitionis* established by Article 15, recognition and enforcement under more favourable regimes of national law of a Contracting State. Article 6 thereby lays down an absolute exclusive filter for judgments on rights *in rem* over immovable property, as opposed to the large list of non-exclusive filters in Article 5. The rationale is quite clear: since (presumably all) States claim exclusive (direct) jurisdiction for rights *in rem* in immovable property situated on their territory and as these rights generally depend on local public registers and involve local mandatory laws, there is far-reaching, if not global, agreement on this issue, to the extent expressed by Article 6.[10] 'Rights *in rem*' are to be understood – autonomously – as rights that 'directly' concern immovable property and have *erga omnes* effects according to the *lex situs*. Typically, this includes ownership, mortgages, usufructs, and servitudes, etc, but may extend to rights of possession or certain types of long-term leases.[11] '*Erga omnes*' effects is to be taken literally and thus requires effects 'against the world',[12] not merely against some third parties, as may occur under common law.[13] Obviously, rights *in rem* in movables are not covered, nor are claims for transfer of immovable property or from torts

[4] International Institute for the Unification of Private Law.

[5] United Nations Commission on International Trade Law.

[6] United Nations Educational, Scientific and Cultural Organization.

[7] Art 2(2)(k) and (l) HCCH 2005 Convention. For an analysis of the 2005 Convention, see Paul Beaumont and Mary Keyes, 'Choice of Court Agreements', ch 28; and David Goddard and Paul Beaumont, 'Recognition and Enforcement of Judgments', ch 29 of this book.

[8] See Art 2 HCCH 2019 Convention.

[9] F Garcimartín and G Saumier, *Explanatory Report on the 2019 HCCH Judgments* Convention (HCCH 2020) para 231.

[10] Ibid, para 233: 'largely uncontroversial'.

[11] Ibid, para 234.

[12] See also P Nygh and F Pocar, *Report on the Preliminary Draft Convention on Jurisdiction and Foreign Judgments in Civil and Commercial Matters* (HCCH 2000) 65.

[13] From a comparative perspective see, eg, S van Erp, 'Property Law' in M Reimann and R Zimmermann (eds), *The Oxford Handbook of Comparative Law*, 2nd edn (Oxford University Press 2019) 1047.

against immovable property.[14] 'Immovable' is not defined in the text, but the Explanatory Report states that it should include benefits and fixtures, as opposed to chattels.[15] Both the concept of 'immovable property', as well as the exclusivity of the attachment to the *lex situs*, and its scope appear as workable starting points for global private international law.

In addition, the HCCH 2019 Convention offers a sophisticated approach to leases (tenancies), which particularly challenge the distinction between 'contract' and 'property'[16] and thereby result in different characterisations in national legal orders.[17] The Convention reacts by distinguishing between residential and non-residential leases of immovable property and provides for the latter an optional indirect jurisdiction for judgments from the State where the property is located.[18] The optional character of this filter allows use to be made of non-exclusive jurisdiction agreements as an alternative head of indirect jurisdiction under the Convention.[19] In the case of residential leases, the Convention restricts recognition and enforcement to judgments from the State where the property is located, but still allows, in contrast to Article 6 for judgments on rights *in rem*, recognition and enforcement of judgments from different States, if allowed under the national law of the requested State (*favor recognitionis*, Article 15). The same applies to judgments on the registration of immovable property (Article 5(3)). Obviously, Article 5(3) takes into account that mandatory law of the *situs* plays a particularly important role in respect to its two subject matters.[20] The three levels of regulation in Articles 6, 5(3) and 5(1)(h), together with Article 5(1)(i),[21] may be considered as an emerging approach to issues involving and surrounding immovable (tangible) property that may be described as functional and, where possible, attuned to party autonomy – lines of thought and analysis that may appear adequate for global (direct) jurisdiction and applicable law as well. However, no specific filter is offered for judgments on tangible property, eg, from the State in which the property is located,[22] and intellectual property is entirely excluded from the material scope.[23]

Beyond these recent developments, the HCCH has been active in the past in relation to subject-specific measures affecting property. For international sales of goods note must be taken of three Conventions, namely the HCCH 1955 Convention on the law applicable to international sales of goods,[24] the HCCH 1958 Convention on the law governing transfer of title in international sales of goods, and the HCCH 1958 Convention on the jurisdiction of the selected forum in the case of international sales of goods.

[14] Garcimartín and Saumier (n 9) para 235.

[15] Chattels serving the economic function of the immovable property in question, such as, eg, machines used for agriculture run on the property, may be characterised differently in some legal orders, see, eg, s 97 German Civil Code.

[16] Whereas civilian systems tend to characterise leases as contracts but then add 'transsystematic' effects to the contractual position of the lessee vis-à-vis third parties, in particular the acquirer of the object of the lease ('sale does not break lease', see, eg, s 566 German Civil Code, limited to residential leases, or Art 7:226 Dutch Civil Code, extending to movables), English law went further and converted the lessee's position into a kind of right *in rem*. See, from a comparative perspective, van Erp (n 13) 1041.

[17] Garcimartín and Saumier (n 9) para 189.

[18] Art 5(1)(h) HCCH 2019 Convention.

[19] Art 5(1)(m), ibid. Exclusive jurisdiction agreements in principle would be dealt with by the HCCH 2005 Convention, if applicable amongst the involved States, but, as has been mentioned above, tenancies of immovable property are entirely excluded from the material scope. See once more, Art 2(1)(l) HCCH 2005 Convention. Thus, national law applies to such exclusive jurisdiction agreements.

[20] Garcimartín and Saumier (n 9) para 227 et seq.

[21] According to which a judgment is eligible for recognition and enforcement under the Convention if it ruled against the defendant on a contractual obligation secured by a right *in rem* in immovable property located in the State of origin, if the contractual claim was brought together with a claim against the same defendant relating to that right *in rem*.

[22] cp: Art 7(4) Brussels Ia. On this provision see in more detail below (n 57).

[23] Art 2(1)(m) HCCH 2019 Convention, see Paul Torremans, 'Intellectual Property', ch 25 in this book.

[24] See also the HCCH 1980 Declaration and Recommendation Relating to the Scope of the 1955 Convention.

The HCCH 1955 Convention gave priority in Article 2 to party autonomy, failing which in Article 3 to the habitual residence of the seller or, in certain circumstances to the habitual residence of the buyer, but excluded from its scope the transfer of ownership (Article 5(3)) and the effects of the sale on third parties (Article 5(4)). The Convention entered into force in only eight States.[25] It was to be superseded by the HCCH 1986 Convention on the law applicable to contracts for the international sale of goods, but the latter instrument never entered into force. Like the HCCH 1955 Convention, it holds back, per Article 5(c) and (d), respectively, from determining the law applicable to the transfer of ownership or the effect of a sale on third parties.

The HCCH 1958 Convention on the law governing transfer of title in international sales of goods reflected the desire of Contracting States to establish common provisions concerning the law applicable to transfers of title in international sales of goods. However, though signed by Greece and ratified by Italy, this instrument never entered into force. As its name suggests, the scope of the Convention was limited to proprietary issues arising from the sale of goods. It endorsed the *situs* rule, albeit with an unusual temporal application: by Article 3, the transfer to the buyer of title to the goods sold, with respect to all persons other than the parties to the contract of sale, was governed by the internal law of the country where the goods were located at the time when a claim was made concerning them and not, as might have been expected, by the internal law of the country where the goods were located at the time when the transfer of title to the buyer purportedly was effected.[26] However, under the Convention the buyer retained a title which had been recognised as belonging to him by the internal law of one of the countries where the goods sold were previously located. Moreover, in the case of a sale based on documents where the documents represented the goods sold, the buyer retained a title which had been recognised as belonging to him by the internal law of the country where he received the documents.

The rules set out in Article 3 of the HCCH 1958 Convention were subject to elaborate provisions in Articles 4 and 5, providing that, whether the rights of an unpaid seller in the goods sold could be asserted against the creditors of the buyer (such as liens and the right to possession or ownership, particularly through an action of rescission or a clause of reservation of title), was to be governed by the internal law of the country where the goods sold were located at the time of the first claim or attachment concerning such goods (Article 4). Moreover, the rights which a buyer could assert against third persons who claimed title or another real right in the goods sold were to be governed by the internal law of the country where the goods were located at the time of such claim. The buyer, however, retained any rights which had been recognised as belonging to him by the internal law of the country where the goods sold were located at the time when he was put in possession (Article 5). Article 6 made special provision for goods sold which were in transit (*res in transitu*) in the territory of a country, or outside the territory of the State, to the effect that they were considered to be located in the country from which they were sent (*lex loci expeditionis*).[27]

None of the subject-specific instruments delivered by the HCCH in this area of law is notable for its success and for 35 years or so the field has been largely ignored by the HCCH. The failure of these 1950s Conventions (and the unsuccessful follow-up in 1986) is partly

[25] Denmark, Finland, France, Italy, Niger, Norway, Sweden and Switzerland.

[26] On the importance of time, see JM Carruthers, *The Transfer of Property in the Conflict of Laws* (Oxford University Press 2005) paras 1.25–1.26. See also, eg, G Rixen, *Das Sachstatut bei internationalen Verkehrsgeschäften nach der Kodifikation des internationalen Sachenrechtes* (Nomos 2014) 175 et seq.

[27] See, on the complexities of dealing with goods in transit, GA Zaphiriou, *The Transfer of Chattels in Private International Law: A Comparative Study* (Athlone Press 1956) 195, and, with explicit reference to Art 6, v Bar and P Mankowski, *Internationales Privatrecht – Band II: Besonderer Teil*, 2nd edn (CH Beck 2019) § 3, para 106 et seq.

attributable to eurocentric patterns in the proceedings of the HCCH (and other organisations such as UNIDROIT) at the time (insufficient participation of other States, in particular not enough amongst the larger, non-European trading nations and absence of developing States, thus a lack of ownership spirit amongst the latter);[28] partly to superseding developments on the level of UNCITRAL that ultimately resulted in the CISG,[29] as well as developments on the level of the then EC;[30] and partly perhaps to over-inventive solutions.[31]

In addition to specific measures concerning the international sale of goods, the HCCH has produced various instruments focusing on areas of private law which affect proprietary rights and interests and of which account should be taken. Reference has been made already to instruments affecting the laws of matrimonial property, trusts and succession.[32] Most recently, and perhaps most notably in relation to subject-specific interventions, account should be taken of the HCCH 2006 Securities Convention.[33] In view of the global nature of financial markets, and recognising dematerialisation, immobilisation and intermediation as key characteristics of the modern holding and disposition systems in respect of shares and other securities,[34] the HCCH commenced work in 2000 on a project concerning applicable law in relation to securities held with an intermediary (ie, where the securities are credited to a securities account). The purpose of the resultant HCCH Securities Convention was to achieve certainty as to the applicable law in order that market actors might know in advance what law governs securities transactions, thereby keeping legal risk (and, in turn, economic risk) to a minimum.[35] The scope of the Securities Convention is confined to determining the law applicable where securities are held with an intermediary, and does not apply to directly held securities, which continue to be governed by pre-existing, national applicable law rules.

In principle, the HCCH 2006 Securities Convention is testament to the usefulness of international legislative intervention in the cross-border securities market, an area for which national applicable law rules, as traditionally formulated, ie, where the proprietary aspects of transfers of property are governed by the law of the place where the property in question was situated at the time of the purported transaction, viz the *lex situs* or *lex loci rei sitae*, have failed to provide legal certainty and predictability and thereby to boost market confidence or increase market growth. The applicable law problems which are encountered in connection with intermediated securities – the difficulty in localising such securities; in characterising, as proprietary or contractual, the nature of an account holder's rights resulting from a credit of securities to a securities account; and in identifying the law applicable to matters such as the perfection of securities and

[28] The HCCH 1955 Convention was ratified by only a few Western European States, namely Denmark, Finland, France, Italy, Norway, Sweden, Switzerland. Belgium left the Convention in 1999. On these patterns as obstacles to the success of the UNIDROIT (Hague) 1964 Convention relating to a Uniform Law on the International Sale of Goods (ULIS) see (n 69) below; and on the UNIDROIT (Hague) 1964 Convention relating to a Uniform Law on the Formation of Contracts for the International Sale of Goods (ULFC), see R Goode, H Kronke and E McKendrick, *Transnational Commercial Law*, 2nd edn (Oxford University Press 2015) para 8.06.

[29] CISG is a successful uniform law Convention – UN Convention on the International Sale of Goods 1980, available at: uncitral.un.org/en/texts/salegoods/conventions/sale_of_goods/cisg, but Art 4(b) excludes from its scope transfer of title. See also U Schroeter, 'Gegenwart und Zukunft des Einheitskaufrechts' (2017) 81 *Rabels Zeitschrift* 32, 35.

[30] See the Rome 1980 Convention on the law applicable to contractual obligations.

[31] See Art 3 HCCH 1958 Convention on the law governing transfer of title in international sales of goods.

[32] See n 2 above and accompanying text.

[33] In respect of which, see R Goode, H Kanda and K Kreuzer (with the assistance of C Bernasconi), *Explanatory Report on the Hague Convention on the Law Applicable to Certain Rights in Respect of Securities Held with an Intermediary*, 2nd edn (HCCH, 2017) (HCCH Securities Convention – Explanatory Report).

[34] See Carruthers (n 26) paras 7.03–7.05; and M Ooi, *Shares and Other Securities in the Conflict of Laws* (Oxford University Press 2003).

[35] HCCH 2006 Securities Convention – Explanatory Report, Int-33 and Int-34.

priorities among securities – are acute instances of the applicable law problems which arise in relation to intangible movable property generally, and where national applicable law rules typically are opaque or out of step with modern life.[36] At first sight, therefore, in a field of law and practice as technical and specialised as intermediated securities, bespoke rules and/or instruments, rather than, eg, an applicable law rule, or instrument, applicable to intangible property generally, are desirable and probably necessary. But one must doubt the utility and impact of the private international law legislative intervention in this area for, although the Convention is still relatively young,[37] the number of Contracting States is very small (only Mauritius, Switzerland and the USA are Parties),[38] and its moment may have passed. One factor in this development was that the Convention was adopted in the same year as the initial text of the EU's Financial Collateral Directive was issued,[39] combined with conceptual differences in approach between some Members of the EU and the Convention.[40]

Finally, some attention should be given to the UNCITRAL 2016 Model Law on Secured Transactions and the corresponding UNCITRAL 2007 Guide on Secured Transactions. Although only soft law[41] regarding security rights in movable assets, Chapter VIII contains several, rather detailed, recommendations for conflict of laws rules with relevance to general property issues.[42] In order to provide legal certainty, the Model Law selects the law of the *situs* (Article 85(1)) at the time of the putative creation of the security right (Article 91(1) (a)) and, for third-party effectiveness and priority issues, at the time the issue arises (Article 91(1)(b)). In contrast to this rather traditional approach, different connecting factors are suggested for *res in transitu*. At the creditor's choice, either the law of the initial location or the law of the ultimate location applies, provided that the assets reach these destinations within a reasonable time (Article 85(4)). Additionally, according to the UNCITRAL 2007 Guide, registered assets, eg, aircraft, ships and – at least in some States – motor vehicles, are supposed to be governed by the *lex stabuli* or law of registration (recommendation 205).

B. Existing Regional Measures for the Harmonisation of Private International Law Rules Pertaining to Property

In the same way that it is significant to note the absence from output of the HCCH of any single instrument purporting to deal on an all-encompassing or overarching basis with private international law rules concerning property or property interests, so too, in European Union (EU)

[36] Carruthers (n 26) paras 7.57–7.58.

[37] It entered into force on 1 April 2017.

[38] In 2009, the European Commission withdrew an earlier Proposal for a Council Decision concerning the signing of the Convention (COM (2003) 783; [2004] OJ C96/33): 'Withdrawal of Obsolete Commission Proposals' ([2009] OJ C71/17). For detailed background, see P Moffatt, 'The Standardisation of Conflicts of Laws Rules for Intermediated Securities within the EU: Holy Grail or Red Herring?' [2018] *Nederlands Internationaal Privaatrecht* 50.

[39] Directive 2002/47/EC on financial collateral arrangements [2002] OJ L168. See now, addressing issues of substantive law rather than private international law matters, the UNIDROIT 2009 'Geneva' Convention on Substantive Rules for Intermediated Securities (n 73 below).

[40] On these see, eg, Goode, Kronke and McKendrick (n 28) para 15.91 et seq.

[41] For the Model Law, see: uncitral.un.org/en/texts/securityinterests/modellaw/secured_transactions. Legislation based on (partly preceding the Model Law but taking a similar approach), or influenced by, the Model Law has been adopted in eight States (Australia, Colombia, Fiji, New Zealand, Nigeria, Papua New Guinea, Philippines and Zimbabwe). The UNCITRAL 2007 Guide, see: uncitral.un.org/en/texts/securityinterests/legislativeguides/secured_transactions, has influenced some other jurisdictions, eg Belgium, Korea, as well as the World Bank's Secured Transactions Toolkit.

[42] See, eg, E-M Kieninger, 'Das internationale Sachenrecht als Gegenstand eines Rechtsaktes der EU' in K Hilbig-Lugani and D Jakob et al (eds), *Festschrift für Dagmar Coester-Waltjen* (Gieseking 2015) 179 et seq.

law a regulation on the law applicable to proprietary rights and interests is conspicuous by its absence.[43] Given that the EU is something like the world's experimental laboratory for unification and harmonisation of private international law, it is important to note the existence in EU private international law of particular rules of civil and commercial jurisdiction specifically pertaining to immovable property[44] and cultural property,[45] and of harmonised applicable law rules for contracts concerning immovable property.[46]

The rule of exclusive jurisdiction in Article 24(1) of Brussels Ia is that in proceedings which have as their object[47] rights *in rem*[48] in immovable property or tenancies of immovable property, the courts of the Member State in which the property is situated shall have exclusive jurisdiction, regardless of the domicile of the parties.[49] However, in proceedings which have as their object tenancies[50] of immovable property concluded for temporary private use for a maximum period of six consecutive months, the courts of the Member State in which the defendant is domiciled shall also have jurisdiction, provided that the tenant is a natural person and that the landlord and the tenant are domiciled in the same Member State. Article 45(1)(e)(ii) provides that a judgment shall not be recognised or enforced if it conflicts, inter alia, with the rules of exclusive jurisdiction.

Exclusive jurisdiction is mandatory in nature; jurisdiction conferred by Article 24 cannot be excluded by the voluntary submission by a defendant to the courts of another Member State, nor by agreement of the parties. In Brussels Ia there is no equivalent rule of exclusive jurisdiction in relation to movable property. In 2007, a report on the application of the Brussels I Regulation[51] recommended that a rule should be introduced for cases where the object of the dispute is movable property, allocating special, ie, non-exclusive jurisdiction to the courts of the Member State in which the property is situated.[52] Whereas the Commission's Proposal implemented this recommendation,[53] Brussels Ia did not adopt the recommended change.[54]

For applicable law the Rome I Regulation makes bespoke provision, in Article 4, for contracts pertaining to immovable property, but not for those concerning movable property. To the extent that the law applicable to a contract has not been chosen in accordance with Article 3 and without prejudice to the special rules in Articles 5 to 8,[55] a contract relating to a right *in rem* in immovable property or to a tenancy of immovable property shall be governed by the law of the country

[43] For an elaborate proposal for such a Regulation, see Kieninger, ibid.

[44] Brussels Ia, Art 24.

[45] Ibid, Art 7(4).

[46] Rome I Regulation, Art 4(1)(c).

[47] In respect of which, see *Sanders* (73/77); *Barratt International Resorts Ltd* 1994 SLT 434; and *Land Oberösterreich* (C-343/04).

[48] See, eg, *Reichert* (C-115/88); *Webb* [1994] QB 696; and *Weber* (C-438/12). See, on the significance of the distinction between rights *in rem* and rights *in personam*, Carruthers (n 26) paras 2.39–2.50.

[49] eg, *Rosler* [1986] QB 33; *Scherrens* (158/87); *Hacker* [1992] ECR I-1111; and *Jarrett* [1997] 2 All ER 484.

[50] *Sanders* (n 47); and *Klein* (C-73–04).

[51] Regulation 44/2001.

[52] B Hess, T Pfeiffer and P Schlosser, 'Report on the Application of Regulation Brussels I in the Member States', Study JLS/C4/2005/03 (CH Beck-Verlag 2008) para 152 et seq, available at: courtesa.eu/wp-content/uploads/2019/03/study_application_brussels_1_en.pdf. See also, arguing against such a head of jurisdiction, P Franzina, 'The proposed new rule of special jurisdiction regarding rights in rem in movable property: a good option for a reformed Brussels I Regulation?' [2011] *Diritto del commercio internazionale* 789.

[53] COM (2010) 748 final, Art 5(3): 'The following courts shall have jurisdiction: as regards rights *in rem* or possession in moveable property, the courts for the place where the property is situated'.

[54] *cf*, however, Art 98 of the Swiss Act on Private International Law, whereby the courts at the *locus* of the movable are competent.

[55] Pertaining, respectively, to contracts of carriage, consumer contracts, insurance contracts and individual employment contracts.

where the property is situated,[56] demonstrating again the clear interest of the *lex situs* in matters concerning immovable property.

Although the drafters of Brussels Ia eschewed any special jurisdiction rule in respect of movable property generally, a much narrower rule of special jurisdiction, contained in Article 7(4), was adopted providing that a person domiciled in a Member State may be sued in another Member State:

> [A]s regards a civil claim for the recovery, based on ownership, of a cultural object as defined in point 1 of Article 1 of Directive 93/7/EEC initiated by the person claiming the right to recover such an object, in the courts for the place where the cultural object is situated at the time when the court is seised.[57]

This jurisdictional provision favouring the *forum rei sitae* is a natural complement to the pre-existing suite of EU rules concerning cultural objects.[58]

Specific sectoral provision was made in EU law for the protection of cultural objects in 1993,[59] and has been bolstered in subsequent years by various legislative measures on the export of cultural goods and on the return of cultural objects unlawfully removed from a Member State.[60] Directive 2014/60/EU on the return of cultural property does not purport to change national rules concerning transfers of movable property,[61] and Article 13 thereof states that, 'Ownership of the cultural object after return shall be governed by the law of the requesting Member State'. Although international effort has concentrated on the regulation of cultural objects, including export and import control,[62] it is apparent that those rules continue to be subject to private international law property rules.

In addition to specific, sectoral provision, it is important also to note regional provision on areas of private law other than property, which nonetheless has potential to affect proprietary rights and interests, albeit in a tangential manner. Thus, eg, in the same way that HCCH Conventions on matrimonial property and succession may need to be considered, so too one must bear in mind EU Regulations in the realms of family property[63] and succession.[64] In the operation of Regulations such as these, the division between the scope of application of the *lex rei sitae* and the *lex causae* can be a hotly contested issue.[65] Although the nature of rights *in rem*

[56] Art 4(1)(c). Notwithstanding Art 4(1)(c), by Art 4(1)(d), a tenancy of immovable property concluded for temporary private use for a period of no more than six consecutive months shall be governed by the law of the country where the landlord has his habitual residence, provided that the tenant is a natural person and has his habitual residence in the same country. See also, regarding formal validity, Art 11(5).

[57] See also recital 17. See LE Gillies, 'The contribution of jurisdiction as a technique of demand side regulation in claims for the recovery of cultural objects' (2015) 11 *Journal of Private International Law* 295; and M Weller, 'Article 7(4) Brüssel Ia-VO' in B Wieczorek and R Schütze, *Zivilprozessordnung und Nebengesetze, Großkommentar*, Vol XIII/2, 4th edn (De Gruyter 2019) para 117 et seq.

[58] eg, M Weller, *Rethinking EU Cultural Property Law: Towards Private Enforcement* (Nomos 2018) 36 et seq.

[59] Directive 93/7/EEC on the return of cultural objects unlawfully removed from the territory of a Member State. See, subsequently, Directive 2001/38/EC and Directive 2014/60/EU on the return of cultural objects unlawfully removed from the territory of a Member State. See M Weller, 'Cultural objects, protection of' in J Basedow et al (eds), *Encyclopaedia of Private International Law*, Vol I (Edward Elgar 2017) 498, 502 et seq.

[60] eg, Directive 96/100/EC; Regulation 116/2009 on the export of cultural goods; and Regulation 2019/880 on the introduction and the import of cultural goods.

[61] K Siehr, 'The Protection of Cultural Heritage and International Commerce' (1997) 6 *International Journal of Cultural Property* 304, 314 (Directive 93/7).

[62] See further, Carruthers (n 26) ch 5; and C Roodt, *Private International Law, Art and Cultural Heritage* (Edward Elgar 2015) chs 1 and 4.

[63] Regulation 2016/1103 implementing enhanced cooperation in the area of matrimonial property regimes; and Regulation 2016/1104 implementing enhanced cooperation in the area of registered partnerships.

[64] Regulation 650/2012 on succession.

[65] On problems of overlap between subject areas (in this case between the law of succession and property law), see, eg, *Kubicka* (C-218/16); *Mahnkopf* (C-558-16); and *Oberle* (C-20/17). *cf*, on the border between property law and the law of

relating to property is excluded from the scope of each of these Regulations,[66] being a matter which has not been harmonised by the EU, special consideration nonetheless may need to be given, eg, to the effects of such a Regulation on third parties.[67] In addition, as the Court of Justice of the European Union is forced to develop its own conception of property and rights *in rem* as a matter of delineation from regulated issues,[68] it might be tempted to overstretch the scope of matters regulated by EU law, such as matrimonial property and succession.

C. UNIDROIT/UNESCO Measures Affecting Private International Law and Property

Focusing on the modernisation, harmonisation and coordination of substantive private law and on the formulation of uniform law instruments, principles and rules to achieve those objectives, UNIDROIT has finalised various instruments impacting upon property law, including the UNIDROIT 1964 Convention relating to a Uniform Law on the International Sale of Goods (ULIS),[69] the UNIDROIT 1988 Convention on International Financial Leasing,[70] the UNIDROIT 1995 Convention on Stolen or Illegally Exported Cultural Objects,[71] the UNIDROIT 'Cape Town' 2001 Convention on International Interests in Mobile Equipment,[72] and the UNIDROIT 'Geneva' 2009 Convention on Substantive Rules for Intermediated Securities.[73] In addition to these completed projects, work was undertaken to produce, in 1968, a Draft Uniform Law on the Protection of the *Bona Fide* Purchaser[74] and, in 1975, a Draft Convention providing a Uniform Law on the Acquisition in Good Faith of Corporeal Movables.[75]

Similarly, there are various UNESCO measures which affect private international law and proprietary rights and interests, including, notably, the 1954 Hague Convention for the Protection of Cultural Property in the Event of Armed Conflict, with accompanying Protocols,[76] and the 1970 UNESCO Convention on the Means of Prohibiting and Preventing the Illicit Import, Export and Transfer of Ownership of Cultural Property.[77]

contract, Rome I Regulation, Art 14; and see, concerning the third-party effects of the assignment of a claim in the event of multiple assignments of the claim by the same creditor to successive assignees, *Paribas SA* (C-548/18).

[66] Regulation 2016/1103, Art 1(2)(g); Regulation 2016/1104, Art 1(2)(g); and Regulation 650/2012, Art 1(2)(k) (in respect of which, see also recitals 14–19). For detailed commentary, see P Franzina in I Viarengo and P Franzina (eds), *The EU Regulations on the Property Regimes of International Couples: A Commentary* (Edward Elgar 2020) para 1.24; and M Weller in A-L Calvo Caravaca, A Davì and H-P Mansel (eds), *The EU Succession Regulation: A Commentary* (Cambridge University Press 2016) 104.

[67] See, eg, Arts 27 and 28 of Regulation 2016/1103 and of Regulation 2016/1104. See also Regulation 2015/848 on insolvency proceedings, Art 8 ('Third parties' rights *in rem*').

[68] See, eg, CS Rupp, 'The lex rei sitae and its neighbours – debates, developments and delineating boundaries between PIL rules' (2018) 7 *European Property Law Journal* 267.

[69] See: www.unidroit.org/instruments/international-sales/international-sales-ulis-1964. Art 8 excludes from its scope 'the effect which the contract may have on the property in the goods sold'.

[70] See: www.unidroit.org/leasing-ol/leasing-english.

[71] See: www.unidroit.org/instruments/cultural-property/1995-convention.

[72] See: www.unidroit.org/instruments/security-interests/cape-town-convention.

[73] See: www.unidroit.org/instruments/capital-markets/geneva-convention.

[74] DP 1968 – Etude XLV – Doc 37, available at: www.unidroit.org/studies/international-sales-law/373-study-xlv-acquisition-in-good-faith-of-corporeal-movables.

[75] With Explanatory Report by J-G Sauveplanne (*Etude* XLV – Doc 58), available at: www.unidroit.org/english/documents/1975/study45/s-45-58-e.pdf.

[76] See: www.unesco.org/new/en/culture/themes/armed-conflict-and-heritage/convention-and-protocols/1954-hague-convention/.

[77] Weller (n 59) 500 et seq; A Hachmeister, *Gestohlene und unrechtmäßig verbrachter Kulturgüter im Kaufrecht* (Nomos 2012) 56 et seq.

Occasionally, the two organisations have collaborated on specific, sectoral topics, such as in the publication, in 2011, of Model Legislative Provisions on State Ownership of Undiscovered Cultural Objects, which are

> intended to assist domestic bodies in the establishment of a normative framework for heritage protection, [and] to adopt effective legislation for the establishment and recognition of the State's ownership of undiscovered cultural objects with a view, inter alia, to facilitating restitution in case of unlawful removal.[78]

These instruments have been generated on a piecemeal basis and though, in themselves, of intrinsic interest and merit (to varying extents), they do not constitute any overarching regulation of international property law.

II. Working Towards the Progressive Unification of Private International Law in Relation to Property: Opportunities and Challenges

A. Opportunities

Property law is an umbrella term covering several sub-categories, including immovable property, tangible or corporeal movable property, and intangible or incorporeal movable property. The last sub-category itself is extensive and disparate, including intellectual property, and, from a common law perspective, shares and other securities, money debts and rights of action albeit that from a civil law perspective the latter are conceived not as 'property' but as objects with *erga omnes* effects that pose comparable questions to hierarchy, transparency requirements and transfer systems, etc.[79] Any unification of laws project seeking to encompass all of these sub-categories would be extremely wide in scope and ambition, and exceptionally difficult to accomplish. At best, one might consider a horizontal, functional approach in regard to *erga omnes* effects, presumably common to all types of 'property' and rights '*in rem*'.[80] Such an approach would certainly ground on the *lex rei sitae* as a general rule and should particularly focus on its variations, modifications and alterations for specific issues, eg, change of the applicable *lex rei sitae* for movable goods after moving them across borders ('*Statutenwechsel*'), good faith acquisition and adverse possession, *res in transitu*, means of transport, cultural property, and effects of regulation under public law, such as import or export limitations.[81] These issues appear to be those where there is most divergence amongst the legal orders. However, conscious of the likelihood of failure where the scope of a project is too broad, it would be prudent to pursue projects of more limited compass.

[78] See: www.unidroit.org/franchise-2nd-other-lang/474-instruments/cultural-property/cultural-property-model-legislative-provisions/cultural-property-model-legislative-provisions-overview/512-unesco-unidroit-model-legislative-provisions-on-state-ownership-of-undiscovered-cultural-objects-2011. On these see, eg, H Strobl, *Kulturgüterrelevante Verhaltenskodizes* (Nomos 2017) 353.

[79] van Erp (n 13) 1048.

[80] For a recent sectoral initiative of the EU, see the Proposal for a Regulation on the law applicable to the third-party effects of assignments of claims, COM/2018/096 final; see also EGPIL (below at n 88) draft Art 2(a).

[81] For a collection of academic writing on the *lex situs* rule, specialties regarding immovable property, tangible movable property and intangible movable property, conditional sale, security and goods in transit, see JM Carruthers (ed), *Transfer of Property and Private International Law*, Vol 1 (Edward Elgar 2016). On cultural property, see Carruthers, ibid, Vol 2 (Edward Elgar 2016).

In contemplating problems in respect of which global solutions might be explored, one might build modestly on existing regional frameworks and/or existing sectoral provisions. Alternatively, work could be focused on an area where there already exists widespread accord among national legal systems as to the content and substance of rules of law and where, in consequence, international synthesis of the rules would be a goal potentially capable of achievement – eg, in relation to immovable property.[82] From a practical point of view, regard should be had to areas where there is a clear economic need and support from the business community.[83]

With the surge in global mobility, it is increasingly common for individuals to own property outside their home country. Arguably, the growing incidence of ownership of foreign immovable property and the importance of eliminating legal obstacles to sustaining a cross-border property market together would justify commencing work on a project for the progressive unification of rules of private international law pertaining to immovable property. Existing harmonisation measures in civil and commercial matters have been designed to promote effective access to justice and to facilitate mobility through judicial cooperation. To date, however, global harmonisation measures in relation to immovable property have been restricted to the recognition and enforcement of judgments, and so there would be scope for an international project to examine applicable law rules concerning the transfer of immovable property.

The rule of the *lex situs*, whereby any question pertaining to the creation, acquisition, use, disposal or transfer of an interest in immovable property, and its effect on the proprietary rights of any person claiming an interest therein, shall be governed by the law of the place where it is situated, has withstood the climate of change which otherwise has affected private international law, and remains largely the same, and as apparently invincible as it was in the early years of the twentieth century and before.[84] While international consensus as to the appositeness of such a rule probably would be capable of achievement, one reasonably might question the value and utility of any project which merely captures existing consensus, rather than pushing the boundaries or clearly progressing the unification of laws. However, in certain cases (eg, financial provision on divorce, succession to immovable property and the guardianship of property belonging to children and incapable adults), the *situs* rule, in certain respects and to varying degrees has been supplanted, generally because proprietary issues and questions of title have been deemed to be secondary or incidental to the primary legal relationship or obligation in dispute (say, the granting of a divorce or the manner of distribution of an estate), which normally has a closer connection with a legal system other than that of the *situs* of property. To this extent, there are identifiable cracks in the so-called '*situs* monolith'[85] and a project examining the formulation of an applicable law rule in respect of lifetime transfers of immovable property could properly interrogate the matter.

To date, EU private international law has not tackled the subject of international property law in any focused, holistic manner. EU intervention has been fragmented, by way of exclusive jurisdiction in respect of rights *in rem* in and some tenancies of immovable property and the law

[82] See above the approach on the level of recognition and enforcement under the HCCH 2019 Judgments Convention, n 9 et seq and accompanying text.

[83] These factors are usually referred to for explaining the exceptional success (more than 80 Contracting States plus the EU) of the Cape Town 2001 Convention (n 72); see, eg, Goode, Kronke and McKendrick (n 28) para 14.01 et seq, and 14.53; S Huber, 'Transnationales Kreditsicherungsrecht' (2017) 81 *Rabels Zeitschrift* 77, 90 et seq.

[84] See Carruthers (n 26) para 2-06 and 253. For history of the *situs* rule, rooted in territoriality and considerations of public interest, see L d'Avout, 'Property and proprietary rights' in J Basedow et al (eds), *Encyclopaedia of Private International Law*, Vol I (Edward Elgar 2017) 1429–36.

[85] Carruthers (n 26) paras 9.01–9.03; see also B Akkermans and CS Rupp, 'Queen Lex Rei Sitae – Off with her head?' (2018) 7 *European Property Law Journal* 209.

applicable to contracts concerning immovable property, and tangentially by way of regulations on family property, succession and insolvency.

For tangible movable property, EU Member States could revisit the recommendation in the 2007 Report on the operation of the Brussels I Regulation,[86] to address whether, within the EU, there should be an additional ground of special jurisdiction for disputes concerning movable property in the place where the property is situated. Likewise, the terms of Article 4 of the Rome I Regulation could be reviewed to ascertain whether an additional provision ought to be inserted for determining the law applicable to a contract relating to a right *in rem* in movable property. Similarly, it would be possible to instigate a special EU project on applicable law rules in the area of cultural property, as a private international law companion to existing UNIDROIT and UNESCO instruments, and a counterpart to the rule of special jurisdiction in Article 7(4) of Brussels Ia.[87] However, more ambitious plans contemplate the feasibility of a regulation on international property law,[88] encompassing immovable property and tangible movable property. An important part of the EU exercise will be to carefully demarcate between and among the various EU Regulations which already have potential to impinge on proprietary rights and interests.[89] Another aspect will be to connect with – and delineate from – unification and harmonisation of substantive law.[90] On the level of sector-specific projects, the time may have come to work on a specific applicable law rule for cultural property, which would result in a variation of the classical *lex rei sitae*,[91] as has been proposed a number of times for good reasons.[92] All of these issues point to technical challenges that will recur on the global level and will need specific answers there, but should take notice of experiences from the regional level.

Of greater ambition still, it would be an opportune time to consider commencing a global project on the law applicable to proprietary rights, more specifically, concerning the *inter vivos* transfer of title to immovable property and tangible movable property.[93] Widespread international agreement on the general use and application of the *lex rei sitae* principle is a good starting point. In-depth consideration could be given within the framework of such a project to topics such as the characterisation of property, the passing of risk, the difference between static[94] and dynamic conflicts,[95] the significance of the distinction between voluntary and involuntary dispossession, the interests of competing transferees, goods in transit, and the potential role for party autonomy.[96]

[86] Hess, Pfeiffer and Schlosser (n 52) para 152 et seq.

[87] In this direction Weller (n 58) at 69 et seq.

[88] European Association of Private International Law: Project on a future European Regulation on International Property Law (May 2020), available at: eapil.org/2020/05/18/eapil-establishes-working-groups/. See also, European Group of Private International Law (EGPIL), 29th Session of 13–15 September 2019 in Katowice, *Compte Rendu des Seances de Travail, Droit applicable aux droits réels, examen d'un futur règlement européen* 30–38, presenting draft articles of a future EU Regulation and some commentary, based on a *lex rei sitae* approach (draft 'Art 4. General Rule') subject to modifications for *res* in transit (draft Art 5) and means of transport (draft Art 6). Further modifications for certain special situations (stolen goods) or categories of property (cultural property) are contemplated, but not yet worked out.

[89] See Kieninger (n 42) 481 et seq.

[90] See eg, on a general ('horizontal') level B Lurger and W Faber, Study Group on a European Civil Code, Principles of European Law, Acquisition and Loss of Ownership of Goods, Munich 2011. See, on a strictly sectoral level, the core of the Cape Town 2001 Convention (n 72).

[91] Weller (n 58) 72 et seq: '*lex originis*', with reference to Art 90 of the Belgian Code of Private International Law.

[92] eg, M Frigo, 'Circulation des biens culturels, determination de la loi applicable et méthode de règlement des litiges' (2015) 375 *Hague Collected Courses* 217, with further references.

[93] For suggested models, including a draft Convention on the Law Applicable to the Transfer of Property, see Carruthers (n 26) para 9.46 et seq.

[94] Where the *situs* of an asset does not change, but there is a conflict between, eg, the applicable law on contract and the applicable law on property.

[95] Where the *situs* of an asset changes from country X to country Y. See further Carruthers (n 26) 257.

[96] See, eg, R Westrik and J van der Weide, *Party Autonomy in International Property Law* (De Gruyter 2011); see also E-M Kieninger, 'Freedom of Choice of Law in the Law of Property?' (2018) 7 *European Property Law Journal* 221.

Alternatively (or potentially in parallel, as a companion project to one which seeks to build on areas of existing widespread consensus), a new project for the progressive unification of relevant rules of private international law could focus on an area of law where many (if not most) legal systems are undeveloped, or at least under-developed, in respect of a particular subject area and readily could benefit from international collaborative endeavour with other legal systems. A project to address the private international law issues arising in connection with emerging technologies and digitisation would be a bold and ambitious one.[97] There is precedent, in the form of the HCCH 2006 Securities Convention, for the HCCH to embark upon highly specialist projects (albeit that the Securities Convention arguably is an example of where a global project was foiled by regional impasse).[98] Legal systems across the globe are having to react rapidly to regulate new problems deriving from the introduction and use of digital (crypto-) assets and currencies (eg, use of bitcoin and the application of blockchain technology),[99] especially in the context of financial services and/or Fintech,[100] but without any overarching plan in relation to the inevitable private international law dimensions of the subject. Even the recognition, or not, of crypto-assets as property rights is a contentious subject.[101]

In the same way that, in the course of negotiations on the HCCH Securities Convention, the HCCH consulted bodies such as UNIDROIT and UNESCO, a project on digital assets and private international law would be apt for wider collaboration among HCCH, UNIDROIT, UNESCO and even financial services regulatory bodies as well as leading business representatives and organisations.[102] Striving for international certainty and legal consensus, rather than straining for bespoke national solutions, is the most sensible way forward in such a technologically demanding and fast-evolving area of law. Given the importance of technological advances to international commerce, international cooperation to establish clear rules of private international law is essential and countries having an interest in financial services business should lobby for prioritisation of the topic and ratification of suitable instruments.

B. Challenges

Although there is a lacuna insofar as private international law pertaining to property remains largely untouched by any major harmonisation instrument, this is not entirely for the want of trying. Previous attempts to reform applicable law rules concerning property have been largely unsuccessful. However, unlike in parts of the legal landscape of the first half of the

[97] See, for background, B Copigneaux, N Vlasov and E Bani et al, Study on 'Blockchain for supply chains and international trade' (European Parliament 2020), available at: www.europarl.europa.eu/RegData/etudes/STUD/2020/641544/EPRS_STU(2020)641544_EN.pdf.

[98] See text accompanying nn 33–40 above.

[99] See, eg, B Arruñada, 'Prospects of Blockchain in Contract and Property' (2019) 8 *European Property Law Journal* 14; G Dimitropoulos, 'The Law of Blockchain' (2020) 95 *Washington Law Review* 1117. In the English High Court, see *AA v Persons Unknown who demanded bitcoin and others* [2019] EWHC 3556 (Comm); and P Hodge, 'Technology and the Law' (2020), available at: www.supremecourt.uk/docs/speech-200310.pdf. On the subject of cryptocurrencies as property, see *Ruscoe and Moore* [2020] NZHC 728; and for a general overview, compare A de Franceschi and R Schulze (eds), *Digital Revolution: New Challenges for Law* (Beck 2020).

[100] eg, UK Financial Markets Law Committee, 'Issues of Legal Complexity in Fintech' (2018), available at: fmlc.org/wp-content/uploads/2018/06/FinTech_bound.pdf.

[101] See, eg, UK Jurisdiction Taskforce (one of six taskforces of the LawTech Delivery Panel, an industry-led group tasked with supporting the digital transformation of the UK legal services sector), 'Legal statement on cryptoassets and smart contracts' (2019), regarding the status of cryptoassets and smart contracts under the law of England and Wales, available at: technation.io/about-us/lawtech-panel/; summary at: technation.io/news/uk-takes-significant-step-in-legal-certainty-for-smart-contracts-and-cryptocurrencies/. See also, J G Allen, 'Property in Digital Coins' (2019) 8 *European Property Law Journal* 64.

[102] As was the case in the preparation of the Cape Town 2001 Convention (n 72).

twentieth century,[103] private international law is not free from legislative intervention. The global trend towards use of legislation in private international law is clear, whether by way of international treaty or non-binding instrument. Sometimes legislation is confined to one of the three pillars that constitute private international law (jurisdiction, applicable law and recognition and enforcement of foreign judgments), while at other times it seeks to regulate all three – and occasionally more[104] – dimensions of the subject. This metamorphosis, from a situation in which detailed, exhaustive legislative rules on the international level generally were non-existent, to one in which swathes of rules now exist, has taken place in response to the need to contend with the demands and challenges of technological advancement and globalisation. Any project working towards progressive unification of private international law rules pertaining to property law is likely to garner more interest and support than was the case in the mid-twentieth century.

[103] See GC Cheshire, Preface to 1st edn of *Private International Law* (in P Torremans (ed), *Cheshire, North & Fawcett's Private International Law*, 15th edn (Oxford University Press, 2017) vii), '[Private international law] is not overloaded with detailed rules; it has been only lightly touched by the paralysing hand of the Parliamentary draftsman'. For a short historical overview of statutory rules and changing concepts over time, including intangible property, with a stronger focus on continental European jurisdictions see, eg, d'Avout (n 84) 1428 et seq.

[104] eg, international cooperation among Central Authorities and/or the judiciary.

22

Succession

ALBERT FONT I SEGURA AND JAYNE HOLLIDAY

I. Introduction

Private International Law of Succession Law is inherently complex due in part to the historical and cultural diversity among substantive laws which has led to differing legal traditions characterising succession law in different ways.[1] Without the unification of private international law, this diversity can lead to practical difficulties for the international testator to be able to predict which law is to apply to their estate or aspects of their estate and also for heirs, legatees, creditors, executors and legal practitioners dealing with the estate when faced with conflicting rules governing aspects of the succession.[2]

Over the years, the Hague Conference on Private International Law (HCCH) has attempted to unify private international law in the area of succession with varying degrees of success. The 1961 Convention on the Conflicts of Laws Relating to the Form of Testamentary Dispositions (the 1961 Hague Convention) is considered to be a success due to the number of countries that are party to it.[3] Whereas the 1989 Hague Convention on the Law Applicable to Succession to the Estates of Deceased Persons (the 1989 Hague Convention) has yet to be ratified by a single State if we ignore the Netherlands' lonely dalliance.[4] Also the Convention on the Administration of the Estates of Deceased Persons of 2 October 1973 has only three Contracting States (Czech Republic, Portugal and Slovakia) and will not be further considered in this chapter.

Section II of this chapter will therefore critically assess the 1961 Hague Convention and highlight areas for its well overdue first review by the HCCH. Section III will then briefly address the question of personal connecting factors and party autonomy in relation to the applicable law to succession as well as the premature abolition of scission under the 1989 Convention, before setting out an outline for a new Convention on the Law Applicable to Clawback of *inter vivos* gifts from third parties for consideration by the HCCH.[5]

[1] J Holliday, *Clawback Law in the Context of Succession* (Hart Publishing 2020) 1. W Pintens, 'Need and Opportunity of Convergence in European Succession Laws' in M Anderson and E Arroyo i Amayuelas (eds), *The Law of Succession: Testamentary Freedom* (Europa Law Publishing 2011) 6 and 28.

[2] Ibid.

[3] There are currently 42 Contracting Parties to the 1961 Convention at the time of writing (August 2021); see the Status table at: www.hcch.net/en/instruments/conventions/status-table/?cid=40.

[4] The Netherlands was the only Contracting State to ratify the 1989 Convention, but later denounced their ratification to coincide with the 2015 EU Succession Regulation coming into force.

[5] For an in-depth analysis of clawback from third parties in the context of succession and for a suggested draft for a new Convention on the Law Applicable to Clawback from third parties of *inter vivos* gifts, see Holliday (n 1) in particular Annex II.

II. The Current Framework for Private International Law of Succession

A. Introduction

The validity of the will in testate succession is one of the crucial elements to organise the transfer of assets. Such is the importance of the requirements that sometimes a will can be considered null if these conditions are not met (formality *ad solemnitatem*). In such a context, the ultimate goal is to ensure that a will, as a legal act, is free from defects and faults in order to guarantee that the will is the instrument through which the will of the deceased is expressed. It must be noted, however, that formal requirements may be in tension with respect for the real will of the testator.[6]

These formal requirements, however, vary from legal system to legal system.[7] Thus, the need or lack thereof of an authority before which a will is made, and the determination of who can be considered authority, varies depending on the applicable law. Moreover, there are differences regarding the procedure and the language used to make the will. Likewise, divergences can be found regarding the admission of holographic wills, unknown in several countries, as well as the formal requirements that must be met, such as the expression of the place of writing, the date, the inclusion of the name and the signature of the testator. Other differences regarding formal requirements stem from the presence or absence of witnesses and the requirement or not that they be qualified. As a matter of form, it may also include the possibility of accepting an open or closed will, or exceptions provided for in special circumstances, eg, in the event of an epidemic or imminent danger of death. It is worth noting that the possibility of issuing a joint will or concluding succession agreements in accordance with some legal systems also raises important questions regarding the form.

Due to all of the above, the importance of determining the law applicable to the form of the will is paramount in international succession. However, each legal system has its own approach concerning the criteria to determine the law applicable to the form of the will, which causes the issue to be especially complex. Indeed, although it is true that the criterion of the law of the place of the act (*lex loci actus*) has traditionally been used in some jurisdictions to determine the applicable law, in others, the *lex loci actus* has been established as an alternative to another connecting factor, be it nationality, domicile or habitual residence. Conversely, in some jurisdictions no role has been recognised for *lex loci actus* and the rules governing the substantive questions are also applied to govern the formal validity.[8] In sum, in addition to the differences regarding the required solemnities, the differences regarding the criteria to determine the applicable law are also remarkable.

[6] Note that we are referring to the extrinsic or formal conditions required for the document to be valid and effective, and that, therefore, such conditions must be distinguished from the intrinsic conditions of the will of the deceased linked to the legality of its provisions as well as to the freedom, intention and discernment with which those provisions were taken. Succession to property and administration of estates are separate from the issues related to the formal validity.

[7] P Chase, 'The Uniform International Will: The Next Step in the Evolution of Testamentary Disposition' (1988) 6 *Boston University International Law Journal* 317, highlights that within common law can be found two different systems, these differences are 'slight, however, compared to those between the common law and the civil law' (at 321).

[8] To see the evolution of the connecting factors to determine the applicable law, H Batiffol, 'Une succession de méthodes. La forme des testaments en droit international privé' in O Sandrock (ed), *Festschrift für Günther Beitzke zum 70. Geburtstag am 26. April 1979* (De Gruyter 1979) 429–41.

B. International Codification

These differences have not prevented the adoption of Conventions to overcome the difficulties previously exposed. The success of the two Conventions in the field is, however, variable. On the one hand, the 1961 Hague Convention should be highlighted for its general acceptance. This Convention is limited to unifying the rules for determining the applicable law to the form of testamentary dispositions. On the other hand, the 1973 Washington Convention of 23 October 1973, providing a Uniform Law on the Form of an International Will (the 1973 Washington Convention), has had much more limited success.[9] The Washington Convention represents a much more ambitious stage in the process of international unification as it is committed to introducing into the laws of the Contracting States a new form for making a will.

The virtues of the 1961 Hague Convention rely on its non-invasive approach without neglecting the potentialities that can emerge from a unification of the conflict of laws rules. These potentialities are clearly revealed in its two main founding principles: uniformity of decisions and *favor validitatis testamenti*.

The Convention was a milestone at the time it was passed as it was one of the first Conventions adopted at the Hague Conference with a universal scope or, to put it in other words, the Convention has *erga omnes* effect, as it determines the law regulating the form of testamentary dispositions, even if the testator has the nationality of a non-Contracting State or the law to be applied in accordance with the Convention is the law of a non-Contracting State. Thus, the reciprocity principle does not apply (Article 6). The universalist nature of the Convention is also demonstrated by the fact that the signature and ratification is open to States that are not Members of the Hague Conference on Private International Law (Article 16). It can therefore be said that one of the guiding principles of the Convention is that of uniformity in its application.[10] However, the open nature and the broad scope of the Convention is restricted by a wide range of reservations and declarations that restrain its initial universalism. Articles 9, 10, 11, 12 and 13 allow States to make reservations to some of the key questions of the Convention. These reservations can compromise its uniform application as they introduce a heterogeneous factor in some of its rules. A review of the Convention should be aimed primarily at minimising, if not eliminating, the discord caused by these reservations. It must be borne in mind that 19 countries out of 42 have submitted reservations to the Convention. In reality, the above-mentioned Articles embody the difficulties in reaching full consensus. Although none of the countries submitted any reservation based on Article 11, a provision that opens the door to not recognising testamentary dispositions made abroad inasmuch as the conditions cumulatively laid down concur, different countries submitted reservations under Articles 9, 10, 12 and 13. Each of the reservations provided for in these provisions can be analysed taking into account the number of countries that availed themselves of the possibility opened by them.

Thus, of these 19 countries, 13 reserve the right not to recognise testamentary dispositions made orally, save in exceptional circumstances, by one of its nationals possessing no other

[9] See: www.unidroit.org/fr/successions-ol-2/convention-succession-en. At the time of writing, the Washington Convention is in force for 12 States of which six are also party to the 1961 Hague Convention.

[10] See H Batiffol, 'rapport explicative' I.3 (page 144), which is only available in French and we refer here to the pages of the electronic version available as part of the *Actes et documents de la Neuvième session tome III, Forme des testaments* (HCCH) available electronically (in French only) at: assets.hcch.net/docs/99bba174-836b-43f9-aae1-fa93574f5a08.pdf. from 144–59 because a free-standing electronic version of the explanatory report is not available on the HCCH website. All page references to the *Actes* in this chapter are to the electronic version. It would be good if the Permanent Bureau of the HCCH were to prepare an English translation of the explanatory report to enhance the wider adoption of this Convention and ease uniform interpretation of it.

nationality, in accordance with Article 10. Nonetheless, it should be taken into account that there is a misunderstanding about this reservation. It was introduced as an objection to an Austrian law which was an historic relic that had fallen into disuse.[11] However some common law and mixed jurisdictions, such as the UK and South Africa, have submitted reservations under this provision which essentially tilt at windmills. Therefore, it would be advisable to remember the reason that caused the reservation in order not to magnify it.

Ten other countries reserve the right to determine in accordance with the *lex fori* the place where the testator had his domicile, under Article 9. This was a controversial issue whose origin lies in the probate process in common law jurisdictions in which the will must be authenticated and the personal representative – executor or administrator – must be appointed to oversee the probate process and liquidate the inheritance once the letter of probate is obtained, locating and valuing the assets of the deceased, paying the deceased's debts and distributing the remainder of the estate to the heirs and legatees. Given that the probate process usually takes place before the court of the deceased's last domicile and considering the particular conception of domicile in common law jurisdictions, the introduction of the reservation was deemed to be crucial since it had consequences in order to determine which court had jurisdiction over the probate process.[12] This could justify that countries such as Botswana, Eswatini, Fiji, South Africa, Tonga and the United Kingdom, submitted this reservation. However, other countries outside the common law tradition – Luxembourg, the Republic of Moldova, Turkey and Ukraine – also presented this reservation. Consequently, the impact of this reservation should be assessed in a Review Special Commission.

Nine other countries reserve the right to exclude the application of the Convention to any testamentary clauses which, under their law, do not relate to matters of succession, under Article 12. This provision may reduce the broad scope of the Convention as it covers the determination of the law applicable to the form of the clauses contained in a 'will', including the form of the clauses contained in a will that do not relate to matters of succession (ie, the appointment of a guardian or an acknowledgment of filiation). This issue is highly controversial and it seems difficult that a review of the Convention can remove all use of this reservation but perhaps it can persuade States to refine their use of it.

Finally, one single country submitted the reservation established in Article 13 according to which the present Convention only applies to testamentary dispositions made after its entry into force.

A question that draws particular attention is the lack of an autonomous notion of what can be understood by matters of form. However, it is maybe for the sake of the universalism of the Convention that the substantive scope is not clearly defined.[13] There are certainly different aspects that are deemed to be matters of form such as the provisions which limit the permitted forms of testamentary dispositions referring to the age, nationality or other personal circumstances of the

[11] See *Actes*, ibid, 23–24 and 157: 'Il semble d'ailleurs que le seul des Etats signataires dont la loi connaisse le testament oral est l'Autriche, et le Délégué autrichien a indiqué que cette forme de testament est tombée en désuétude, ne constituant plus qu'un vestige historique'.

[12] Ibid, 135–36 and 157. The reservation was included under the pressure of the British delegation with the purpose of facilitating that signatory countries could determine the domicile applying *lex fori*. GAL Droz, 'Les nouvelles règles de conflit françaises en matière de forme des testaments' (1968) 57 *Revue critique de droit international privé* 1, 8; Y Loussouarn, 'La IXe Session de la Conférence de la Haye de Droit International Privé' (1961) 88 *Journal du Droit International* 673; H Batiffol, 'La neuvième session de la Conférence de la Haye de droit international privé' (1961) 50 *Revue critique de droit international privé* 461, 466–67; DG Casswell, 'The Conflict of Laws Rules Governing the Formal Validity of Wills: Past Developments and Suggested Reform' (1977) 15 *Osgoode Hall Law Journal* 165, 188–89.

[13] The 1961 Convention follows a sort of exemplary delimitation of the notion, see H Batiffol, 'Rapport explicatif' in *Actes* 152.

testator or the circumstances that the required witnesses must have for the validity of a testamentary disposition (Article 5). It can be deduced from the very same provision that the possibility to make a holographic will – written, dated and signed entirely by the testator – is not a question linked to capacity to act. However, the Convention does not always provide guidelines regarding what is a matter of 'formal' and what is a matter of 'substantive' validity. Perhaps one of the most controversial issues is joint wills since some authors hold,[14] based on Article 4, that the prohibition to make a will jointly is a matter of form rather than substance. However, Article 4 is clear in its content when stating that the Convention 'shall also apply to the form of testamentary dispositions made by two or more persons in one document', instead of establishing that testamentary dispositions made by two or more persons in one document is a matter of form, which is quite different. Thus, the provision regulates the law applicable to the formal validity of the testamentary dispositions made jointly by two or more people. Therefore, there is no autonomous notion of what a joint testament is in terms of the controversy over whether this is a substantive or a formal matter. This is an aspect to be solved outside the scope of the Convention. The variety of notions from jurisdiction to jurisdiction on what a joint will is, as well as the existence of similar concepts such as mutual wills, should lead to a careful discussion of these issues in a Review Special Commission. An autonomous notion should be developed that would make it possible to overcome divergences in deciding on the boundary between formal and substantive validity, particularly discordant due to the prohibition of making joint wills in certain jurisdictions based on substantive considerations.[15]

A final remark should be made about the scope of the applicable law. Note that the Convention determines the applicable law to the form of 'testamentary dispositions', not to the form of 'wills'. Consequently, it can be raised whether it is possible to apply different laws independently from each of the testamentary provisions to achieve the formal validity of the will. There is no definitive answer, but it seems that from the principle of uniformity of decisions it can be deduced that only one of the laws that can be applied will regulate the formal validity of the entire will.[16]

Returning to the other backbone principle, *favor validitatis testamenti*, the Hague Convention contains a system of alternative connecting factors with the aim of ensuring that the will will be valid in terms of form. The conflict of laws rule has a material orientation given the objective it pursues.[17] In fact, the alternative configuration of the conflict of laws rule is in line with the above-mentioned conception according to which the form requirements are at the service of the substantive regulation of legal acts. Nonetheless, another consideration must be added to ponder the goal of the Convention. The true ratio of the Convention arises from the fact that it is impossible to validate or make the will again due to the deceased's death. Once a will has been declared null and void, it cannot be validated. Therefore, it must be borne in mind the seriousness of considering the formal validity of a will. It is just a 'yes-or-no' question. That is why it embraces an alternative range of connecting factors to preserve the validity of the testamentary dispositions.

[14] E Jayme, 'Identité culturelle et intégration: le droit international privé postmoderne – Cours general de droit international privé' (1996) 251 *Hague Collected Courses* 110; AL Calvo Caravaca and J Carrascosa González, 'Breves observaciones sobre ley aplicable a la forma de las disposiciones testamentarias' (2007) 702 *Revista Crítica de Derecho Inmobiliariot* 1772, 1777.

[15] For an overview about this issue, see A Bonomi, 'Article 27' in A Bonomi and P Wautelet, *Le droit européen des successions: Commentaire du Règlement n° 650/2012 du 04 juillet 2012* (Bruylant, 2016) paras 13–18; for a practical example of the significance this issue may have, see L Nasse, 'The Temporal Scope of the European Succession Regulation and the (in-)Validity of Joint Wills Under Polish Law: Commentary on the Judgement of the Schleswig Higher Regional Court of 25 April 2016, 3 WX 122/15' (October 2018) 10(2) *Cuadernos de Derecho Transnacional* 896.

[16] AE von Overbeck, *L'unification des règles de conflits de lois en matière de forme de testaments* (Universitaire Fribourg 1961) 50.

[17] Batiffol (n 12) 434–35.

In this way, the will of the testator is also preserved.[18] Indeed, Article 1 of the Convention indicates that a testamentary provision is valid in terms of form if it complies with any of the 'internal laws' (no *renvoi* is permitted) of the place where the testator made it, or of a nationality possessed by the testator,[19] either at the time when he made the disposition, or at the time of his death, or of a place in which the testator had his domicile[20] either at the time when he made the disposition, or at the time of his death, or of the place in which the testator had his habitual residence either at the time when he made the disposition, or at the time of his death, or so far as immovables are concerned, of the place where they are situated. However, it must be pointed out that the *lex rei sitae* of an immovable is only applied to the form of testamentary dispositions regarding immovables located within the territory of the State of that *lex rei sitae*.[21] Scission here remains but surely it was the only solution that could be taken. It has to be said that this solution allows overcoming the disadvantages that might be encountered in the registration of the rights *in rem*, although this is a question particularly linked to the substantive effects of the will. The wide range of connecting factors, justified either in a 'reasonable connection with the testator' or in a 'constructive reasonable connection',[22] results in favouring both validity of testamentary dispositions and legal certainty.

The success of the 1961 Hague Convention[23] is so obvious that it definitely inspired the EU legislator to adopt the provision relating to the formal validity of dispositions of property upon death made in writing laid down in Article 27 of the Succession Regulation.[24] The alternative disposition of the connecting factors established in Article 27 of the EU Succession Regulation is virtually identical to that provided for in Article 1 of the Convention. This is quite significant from a global view because not all the Member States bound by the Succession Regulation had ratified the 1961 Convention. It is therefore recommended that the EU encourage their Member States who are not Party to the 1961 Convention to become Party to it in order to meet the EU's stated intention as a Regional Economic Integration Organisation Member of HCCH to support progressive unification of global private international law.

The Washington Convention of 23 October 1973, providing a Uniform Law on the Form of an International Will provides a complementary solution.[25] The relevance of the Washington Convention lies in the annex rather than in the 16 Articles it contains. The essential point is that it introduces a new form – applicable both to international situations and merely domestic situations – within the legal systems of any Contracting State that is the result of the compromise between the civil law and the common law traditions. In this way it is a new form that is not intended to be completely alien to any legal system. The testator can rest assured that the will that follows the form introduced by the Washington Convention will be recognised as valid in all

[18] Ibid, 437.

[19] In case of having different nationalities, any of the laws corresponding to the nationalities possessed may be applied, *Actes* (n 10) 16 and 147; for a general comment, see Droz (n 12) 6. On the other hand, the UK delegation proposed a solution for non-unitary States, *Actes* (n 10) 29 and 39 that was broadly accepted, ibid, 56–59. The provision, see Art 1(2) of the Convention, enshrined the so-called classical solution and inaugurated specific treatment and care for non-unified States.

[20] Casswell (n 12) 189–90.

[21] Batiffol (n 10) 149.

[22] von Overbeck (n 16) 41–43.

[23] C Forsyth, 'The eclipse of private international law principle? The judicial process, interpretation and the dominance of legislation in the modern era' (2005) 1 *Journal of Private International Law* 93, 103, fn 38, who attributes this success to the narrow and specialised scope of the Convention, and to the fact that it does not deal with matters of great principle.

[24] Reg 650/2012 [2012] OJ L201/107.

[25] See the Explanatory Report on the Convention providing a Uniform Law on the Form of an International Will by Mr Jean-Pierre Plantard (1974) I *Uniform Law Review* 91.

Contracting States.[26] Besides, as it is a new form added to and introduced within the legal systems of the Contracting States it may be recognised in non-Contracting States by means of the conflict of laws rules. That is why the Washington Convention can be seen as a complement to the Hague 1961 Convention.[27]

C. Conclusion

From an international perspective the 1961 Hague Convention is a useful tool to regulate international succession. For this reason, its adoption should be promoted by the Hague Conference. In addition, the recommendations set out above: to translate the explanatory report into English to enhance further adoption, to minimise the discord caused by the reservations, to develop an autonomous notion of what constitutes a joint will, and to encourage the EU's role in the progressive unification of private international law, will hopefully form a useful basis for discussion when the Convention is the subject of a Review Special Commission.

III. The Failure of the 1989 Convention and a New Convention on Clawback

In contrast to the success of the 1961 Convention, the Convention of 1 August 1989 on the Law Applicable to Succession to the Estates of Deceased Persons was a remarkable failure. Unfortunately, as the HCCH has neither the funding nor the manpower to formally review failed Conventions the reasons why this Convention failed remain speculative.[28] The following will therefore briefly assess key aspects of the 1989 Convention that may benefit from review should the the HCCH wish to reconsider this topic in the future, before setting out a proposal for a new Convention on a much smaller yet contentious issue related to succession law, that of clawback of *intervivos* gifts from third parties.

A. The Personal Connecting Factor and Party Autonomy

Traditionally, domicile or nationality have been used as the personal connecting factor to determine the law applicable to succession. However, the 1989 Convention chose to use habitual

[26] The Washington Convention has two primary goals: to enable testators to make international wills in jurisdictions where the Washington Convention is in force and to ensure the recognition of an international will in all signatory States as a matter of local law. Chase (n 7) 329. As J-P Plantard pointed out: 'This direct assessment of the formal regularity of an act carried out abroad by reference to national law is an innovation which deserves to be underlined', see the Explanatory Report [3].

[27] M Brandon, 'UK accession to the Convention on the establishment of a scheme of registration of wills and of the Convention providing a uniform law on the form of an international will' (1983) 32 *ICLQ* 742, 746, points out that the inter-effect of the Washington Convention and the Hague Convention is to extend the scope of both of them. See also Plantard, ibid, 4. To complement the 1961 Convention and Washington Convention, the authors recommend that a new Convention on the Registration of Wills would also be beneficial to practitioners and heirs, with the existing precedent available under the 1972 Convention on the Establishment of a Scheme of Registration of Wills (Council of Europe), available at: rm.coe.int/CoERMPublicCommonSearchServices/DisplayDCTMContent?documentId=09000016800730d1.

[28] See Marta Pertegás and Paul Beaumont, 'Hague Conference on Private International Law, ch 7; and Permanent Bureau, 'National Organs and Central Authorities under HCCH Conventions', ch 8 in this book for further explanation of the work of the HCCH and its Permanent Bureau. It is recommended that Conventions should be reviewed in order to ascertain reasons for failure at the earliest opportunity and for accountability for the public funding.

residence as the connecting factor to the applicable law, requiring the deceased who was not also a national of that State, to have resided there for five years before their death.[29] It was held that as habitual residence can be acquired relatively easily, the imposition of a fixed period of residence was needed in order to create a strong connection between the deceased and the new law of succession.[30]

i. Habitual Residence

The ability to determine a person's habitual residence in some cross-border cases is not always straightforward.[31] If we also take into account that the habitual residence of the deceased does not necessarily coincide with the location of the person's assets,[32] this raises the question of just how appropriate habitual residence is for the purpose of identifying the applicable law to succession. The lack of certainty over when a person acquires or loses their habitual residence would imply that its use to determine the applicable law without supplementary rules to strengthen the connection would be inappropriate.

The use of habitual residence on its own may point to a law which may have no relevance to the deceased or may be unclear. This is the antithesis of what is needed for identifying the law applicable to succession.[33] The supplementary rules in Article 3 of the 1989 Convention support the requirements for determining a strong connection between the deceased and the law applicable to the succession. Whether in today's society it is necessary to live in a country for five years before a strong connection is created is for future debate.

ii. Nationality

Nationality became a popular connecting factor for succession as a replacement for domicile towards the end of the nineteenth century as civil law countries codified their law.[34] However, it has faced accusations of being theoretically discriminatory and fallen out of favour.[35] It is argued that it should not be ignored as a valuable connecting factor for flexible global private international law due to its international character.[36]

The 1989 Convention, notwithstanding its use of habitual residence, retained the benefits of nationality as a connecting factor in the objective applicable law (Article 3) and in the law chosen by the deseased (Article 5). The benefit of using nationality as a connecting factor is that it is recognised as a relatively simple rule. Whether it is the nationality of birth or the chosen nationality, in most cases a person will feel connected to that culture.[37] This is particularly relevant for parties who wish to protect the rights of their heirs.[38] The weaknesses lie where the party has

[29] 1989 Convention Art 3(1) and (2).

[30] Proceedings of the Sixteeth Session, Tome II, Succession to Estates – Applicable Law (HCCH 1988) 251 [27] (Proceedings of the 16th Session), available at: assets.hcch.net/docs/6325962d-7e38-4fe1-b4b4-69725ff3c490.pdf.

[31] E Lien, 'A Further Step Towards a European Code of Private International Law: The Commission Proposal for a Regulation on Succession' (2009) 11 *Yearbook of Private International Law* 107, 110.

[32] Holliday (n 1) 137.

[33] Ibid, 134.

[34] P Beaumont and P McEleavy, *Anton's Private International Law*, 3rd edn (W Green/SULI 2011) 151.

[35] Bonomi (n 15).

[36] Ibid.

[37] P Kindler, 'From nationality to habitual residence: Some brief remarks on the future of the EU Regulation on International Succession and Wills' in K Boele-Woelki et al (eds), *Convergence and Divergence in Private International Law Liber Amicorum Kurt Siehr* (Eleven International Publishing 2010) 253.

[38] This was the reason nationality was chosen as a connecting factor for the choice of law within the Succession Regulation, see Holliday (n 1) 145.

more than one nationality or comes from a multi-unit State. On this latter point, Article 19 of the 1989 Convention handles this well and essentially in the same way as Article 1(2) of the 1961 Convention.[39]

However, clear guidance would have to be created for determining the applicable law where the party had dual or multiple nationalities.[40] A current trend in the EU favours the closest connection test.[41] For multi-unit States the closest connection test would also appear to be the most practical rather than looking to the internal private international law rules which may not contain a solution.[42]

iii. Domicile

Domicile is a traditional connecting factor that connects a person with a single system of law.[43] Just as with the concept of habitual residence, there are both strengths and weaknesses surrounding the definition of domicile and how it is obtained.[44] In most cases it is relatively easy to identify a person's domicile. Where it becomes complicated is in cases where domicile is disputed due to a lack of awareness of the person's intentions. In these cases it is for the courts to attempt to ascertain from the evidence the deceased's intention.[45] Although there are weaknesses to using this connecting factor to identify the applicable law, the law of domicile could still prove useful as an option for a person to choose the applicable law as it is still the dominant connecting factor for common law countries.[46]

iv. Conclusion

It is clear that there are arguments for and against the use of each connecting factor to determine the law applicable to succession. For the purpose of cross-border succession it is recommended that the connecting factor needs to provide a strong connection between the testator and the law to be applied to the succession. This is vital for legal certainty needed for estate planning and protecting the legitimate expectations of heirs, third parties and creditors. The ability to expressly choose which law is to govern the estate makes sense for the purpose of estate planning.[47] In order to reflect the intentions of the testator and location of assets, the choice should be realistic and include the testator's habitual residence, domicile or nationality.

[39] (n 19).

[40] Holliday (n 1) 147.

[41] Ibid.

[42] Ibid, 148.

[43] For an account of domicile, see L Collins (gen ed), *Dicey, Morris and Collins on the Conflict of Laws*, 15th edn (Sweet & Maxwell 2012) Rules 4–16.

[44] Ibid.

[45] In relation to a maintenance claim under the Inheritance (Provision for Family and Dependants) Act 1975, Holliday argues that the habitual residence of the dependant would be a more appropriate connecting factor: J Holliday, 'Characterisation within Private International Law: Maintenance or Succession?' in P Beaumont, B Hess, L Walker and S Spancken (eds), *The Recovery of Maintenace in the EU and Worldwide* (Hart Publishing 2014) 443–58.

[46] P Beaumont and J Holliday, 'Private International Law of Succession Scotland' in S Bariatti, I Viarengo and F Villata (eds), *EU Cross-Border Succession Law* (Edward Elgar 2022) 'In 1744, in *Brown v Brown* [(1744) Mor 4604], the Inner House of the Court of Session in Edinburgh was referred to Voet's work for inspiration … The outcome was that the court followed the continental European applicable law rule on domicile of the deceased at the time of death, rejecting the idea that the *lex situs* which applies to immoveables should apply to moveables instead of the *lex domicilii*, a decision which formed the basis of the principle of scission'.

[47] For an account of party autonomy under the EU Succession Regulation, see Beaumont and Holliday, ibid.

B. Scission

The principle of scission is where the law applicable to the transfer of movable property and law applicable to the transfer of immovable property differs.[48] Under this principle, the succession of the immovable property is governed by the law where it is situated, the *lex situs*, and the succession of the movable property by the applicable law to the succession.[49] The 1989 Hague Convention abolished the use of scission and opted for the principle of unity of succession to govern an estate for reasons that scission can create variable outcomes as to how the estate should be divided or point to different heirs which can lead to unfair outcomes.[50] These disadvantages to the principle of scission are not in dispute. However, the decision to solely pursue unity of succession within a global Convention was arguably not a pragmatic one.[51]

The principle of scission is still followed by many States around the world, predominantly those influenced by common law and French law.[52] This position is unlikely to change. There are also many States around the world that follow the unity of succession approach, leading to a clear conflict of laws in this area.[53] One pre-emptive solution to this problem, which has been used by some States that follow a unity of succession approach in their private international law, is to defer to the law of the *lex situs* for immovable property. The reasoning behind this is that it respects the relationship between the property and the State, prevents unenforceable titles[54] due to the *lex situs* for immovable property satisfying the elements relating to transfer of property and contracts relating to a right *in rem*.[55]

Assuming the testator is aware of the rules (which requires receiving appropriate guidance when estate planning) scission creates legal certainty.[56] Unity of succession, whilst theoretically appealing for both testator and practitioner due to its perceived simplicity[57] is simply not practical unless every State adopts the same approach. It does not work when dealing with immovable property if it conflicts with the designated private international law of the forum.[58] This is a problem that is currently being experienced on a daily basis by notaries within the EU following the introduction of unity of succession in the EU Succession Regulation.[59]

[48] Explanatory Report [21]. For authority on the *lex situs* rule, see L Collins (gen ed), *Dicey, Moris and Collins on the Conflicts of Laws*, 15th edn (Sweet & Maxwell 2012) Rule 132, para 23R-062.

[49] Ibid.

[50] Explanatory Report [17].

[51] Holliday (n 1) 152.

[52] A recent and interesting development in French law that could be said to support the principle of scission can be seen in an amendment to Article 913 of the French Civil Code. The amendment aims to protect children in certain situations who do not benefit from a reserved share under the applicable law to the succession, by creating a right of compensation on property that is situated in France. H van Loon update of the G Droz, Questionnaire and Commentary on Succession on Private International Law, Hague Conference on Private International Law (1969) within the HCCH, Proceedings of the 16th Session, 1988 (n 30) 107. Prior to the introduction of the unity of succession within the 2015 EU Succession Regulation, the principle of scission was followed by 'Belgium, Bulgaria, Cyprus, France, Luxembourg, Ireland, Malta, Romana and UK' see J von Hein, 'Conflicts between International Property, Family and Succession Law – Interfaces and Regulatory Techniques' (2017) 6 *European Property Law Jounal* 142, 144.

[53] van Loon, ibid.

[54] von Hein (n 52) 145. This was the approach taken by Germany prior to the EU Succession Regulation and also Israel.

[55] Holliday (n 1) 152. P Torremans (ed), *Cheshire, North and Fawcett: Private International Law*, 15th edn (Oxford University Press 2017) 1255: on the use of the *lex situs* for immovable property, 'This proposition is so clear as scarcely to require authorities'.

[56] Holliday (n 1) 150; von Hein (n 52) 145.

[57] Explanatory Report [18].

[58] von Hein (n 52) 142. For an analysis of the effect of the unity of succession within the EU Succession Regulation on a Scottish testator, see Beaumont and Holliday (n 46).

[59] '[The] main disability' of the EU Succession Regulation 'is that it did not take into account the fact that a significant part of the worlds legal systems observes the principle of the scission system of inheritance in the field of conflict-of-laws

The principle of scission is not going to disappear and future global instruments on applicable law to succession need to be pragmatic and accept its existence.

C. A Recommendation for a New Hague Convention

In the meantime, while the pursuit of a new Convention on the applicable law to succession is highly unlikely, it may prove useful for the HCCH to focus on a much smaller, yet contentious area of law in the context of succession, to see if agreement can be reached at a global level which would create legal certainty for testators and relevant parties where at present there is none.

An issue that has proven to be a thorn in the side of the 1989 Convention and more recently in the EU Succession Regulation due to the 1989 Convention not explicitly excluding it[60] and the EU Succession Regulation including it, is the clawback of gifts made by a person during their lifetime to non-heirs, by their heirs when that person dies for the purpose of satisfying the legitimate portion or maintaining a dependant of the deceased.

i. Clawback and Collation are not the Same Thing

An analysis of the negotiations conducted during the drafting of the EU Succession Regulation revealed an unfortunate misunderstanding that the words 'clawback' and 'collation' were interchangeable.[61] These terms are not interchangeable and to treat them as being the same, especially when creating global private international law on the law applicable to succession is to invite problems where there may be none.

Clawback is a term which refers to the claim to clawback an *inter vivos* gift, gifted by a person who is now deceased, from a third party (a non-heir) for the purpose of satisfying the legitimate portion or to protect against the evasion of the duty to maintain a dependant after death.[62] Collation refers to the reduction of an *inter vivos* gift given to a legitimate heir for the purpose of satisfying the legitimate portion.[63] The donees in cases of clawback and collation are substantively different.[64] The nature of the gifts are different.[65] The nature of the claims are different.[66] They function differently and require different procedures to bring about a claim.[67] These differences dictate that these issues need to be treated separately.[68] There is also a myth that clawback is a problem only for common law countries. This is not accurate. It is also an issue for many civil law countries too and therefore a solution at a global level would be helpful.[69]

The claim for the reduction of an *inter vivos* gift made to a third party in good faith, in a country which does not provide for clawback from third parties to satisfy the legitimate portion,

rules of succession … Such cases occur daily in domestic practice'; see T Szocs, 'The European Succession Regulation from the Perspective of the First Three Years of Its Application' 57. This view was also expressed in F Trémosa, *The state of implementation of the EU Succession Regulation's provisions on its scope, applicable law, freedom of choice, and parallelism between the law and the courts*' a report prepared for the European Parliament (October 2017) 1.

[60] Holliday (n 1).

[61] Ibid, 16. Objections to the concept of clawback of gifts to third parties was one of the main reasons why the UK did not opt into the EU Succession Regulation.

[62] Ibid.

[63] Ibid, 164.

[64] Ibid.

[65] Ibid.

[66] Ibid.

[67] Ibid.

[68] Ibid, 17.

[69] Ibid, 54.

in theory threatens the donee's ability to rely on the gift and is a threat to property and succession law. At present if the law applicable to the succession is not known to the non-heir donee or indeed the testator when they make the gift, then there is no legal certainty as to whether there is a future risk of clawback. At a time when cross-border mobility remains high, the likelihood of a testator knowing where their habitual residence (or indeed domicile or even nationality) at the time of death will be at some unknown time in the future lacks legal certainty, essential in terms of estate planning.

The following recommendations focus on protecting the legitimate expectations of all relevant parties, to support the need for fairness and legal certainty.

ii. Characterisation: The Need for a Sui Generis *Approach*

Clawback cannot be characterised solely as a succession matter as it also has characteristics pertaining to property law, contract law, maintenance law and unjustified enrichment. Therefore to determine the global applicable law, a *sui generis* approach is the more appropriate way forward.[70]

iii. Comparative Law: There is no Common Framework

A comparative analysis of the substantive law in 30 jurisdictions identified that not all countries have rules pertaining to clawback and of those that did, there were few whose frameworks were the same.[71] Although there was no common framework on clawback, it was possible to identify six sub-categories.[72] Broadly speaking, the first category contained countries that have a legitimate portion rule and consider *inter vivos* gifts to be part of the fictive estate and allow for clawback from third parties to satisfy the legitimate portion.[73] This was the most common framework but the rules within the framework varied greatly.[74] Category 2 contained countries which have a legitimate portion rule but do not consider *inter vivos* gifts to be part of the estate and do not provide for clawback from third parties. Category 3 contained countries which have a legitimate portion rule, do not consider *inter vivos* gifts to be part of the estate but do have a discretionary rule for clawback from third parties with the requirement that there needs to be evasion of responsibility to maintain the dependant by the donor.[75] Category 4 contained countries which have a legitimate portion rule, do not consider *inter vivos* gifts to be part of the estate but do have rules to clawback gifts from third parties to prevent the evasion of forced heirship for spouses. The gift has to have been made to specifically diminish the spouse's legitimate portion.[76] Category 5 contained countries which do not have legitimate portion rules, do not consider *inter vivos* gifts to be part of the estate but do have discretionary rules for clawback from a third party if there has been evasion of the duty to maintain a dependant.[77] Category 6 contained countries which do not have a legitimate portion rule, do not consider *inter vivos* gifts to be part of the estate and do not have a discretionary rule for clawback from a third party in cases of evasion of the duty to maintan a dependant.[78]

[70] Ibid, 126.
[71] Holliday (n 1) Annex II.
[72] A detailed explanation of the six categories is found within Holliday (n 1) ch 3.
[73] Ibid, 70.
[74] Ibid.
[75] Ibid, Cyprus.
[76] Ibid, 71, Ireland.
[77] Ibid, 71, England and Wales and Northern Ireland.
[78] Ibid, 71, Australia and South Africa.

Between the analysis of the character of the claim and the comparison of the substantive laws it is possible to distil the legitimate expectations of the relevant parties and take these into account to craft a draft Convention of which a brief discussion of the proposed objective applicable law, subjective applicable law and modal law follows.[79]

D. A Draft Convention on the Law Applicable to Clawback

i. Objective Applicable Law

The decision to use the principle of scission is not fashionable but for global private international law it is pragmatic. Therefore, the *lex situs* should govern a claim against third parties for the reduction of immovable *inter vivos* gifts. There are also many advantages to restricting the connecting factor for movables to habitual residence of the donor at the time the movable gift was made. A flexible escape clause is also appropriate,[80] stating that if at the time the gift is given the donor was manifestly more closely connected to a State of which he was a national then the law of that State will apply. It would be advisable to have a rule obliging the donor to disclose the applicable law for claims which heirs or dependants of the donor may have against third parties to promote legal certainty and manage expectations of the donor's heirs.

ii. Subjective Applicable Law

Party autonomy should be a realistic option in relation to movable gifts.[81] This supports the ability for the donor to plan their estate and manage expectations of heirs.[82] The choice of law should be expressly made so that intentions are clear and the intention should be recorded with a solicitor or notary planning the estate.[83] It is recommended that the donor is able to choose the law of the State whose habitual residence, domicile or nationality he possesses at the time the gift is made.[84] In order to support legal certainty the donee should be made aware of the choice of law at the time the gift is given.[85]

iii. Modal Law

The use of modal law is controversial but in the interest of legal certainty, practicality and fairness in an area of law where the rules vary greatly it is recommended that key terms are clarified, particularly whether habitual residence needs to demonstrate an acceptable level of integration to prevent the donor from arbitrarily choosing the law to apply to the gift, what constitutes an *inter vivos* gift and what constitutes a third party.[86]

In order to support legal certainty for the donor and the donee and clarity for future heirs and creditors, it is recommended that the donor's gift is formally recorded along with the applicable law with their notary or solicitor. A disclosure rule would also protect the donee and allow the

[79] For a detailed draft Convention, see Annex II of Holliday (n 1).
[80] Ibid, 155.
[81] Ibid.
[82] Ibid.
[83] Ibid.
[84] For further detail on this point, see ibid, 155.
[85] Ibid.
[86] For the purpose of the proposed Convention on Clawback, the term third party is understood as someone who is not an heir to the estate or a dependant of the deceased.

donee to make an informed decision on whether to accept the gift or not. An extreme example could be where a donee has received a gift of immovable property, raises a mortgage on that property and later finds that the property is the basis of a claim for clawback which places the donee and lender in a difficult position.[87]

iv. Conclusion

The suggested use of habitual residence at the time the gift is made with the escape clause of the nationality of the donor for movable property and the *lex situs* of the immovable property at the time the gift is made as the pertinent connecting factors recognises the connection that these claims have to succession law, property law, maintenance, contract and restitution. If the law at the time the gift is given is used then both the donor and donee have the ability to know what the law is, in contrast to applying the *lex successionis* as done in the EU Succession Regulation. The decision to revive the principle of scission supports the concept of comity and protects the legitimate expectations of the parties at the time the property is transferred. The legitimate heirs will have certainty if the donor is obliged to record and inform them of any *inter vivos* gifts made and the corresponding law that applies to those gifts.

IV. Conclusion

The 1961 Hague Convention has proven to be successful and should be supported further by the Hague Conference. This Convention has not been the subject of a Review Special Commission by the Hague Conference during its lifetime and therefore it is strongly recommended that this is rectified which in turn should encourage more States to become Party to it.

In the unlikely event that the Members of the HCCH turn their attention once again to the applicable law for succession, it is suggested that aspects of the 1989 Convention such as the definition of the main connecting factor for the objective applicable law, the issue of clawback of *inter vivos* gifts from third parties and the abolition of scission are reconsidered.

Finally, in light of the success of the 1961 Convention which deals with a much narrower area of succession law than the 1989 Convention attempted to, it is recommended that the Members may wish to consider the proposal for a new Convention on Clawback of *inter vivos* gifts from third parties which would provide legal certainty for all relevant parties which at present is lacking.

[87] Holliday (n 1) 160.

23

Trusts

JONATHAN HARRIS

I. Introduction

Amongst all the fields of private international law, that which relates to trusts is in many ways unique. Partly, this is because of the fundamental importance of the trust in many legal systems ('trust States'), especially in common law jurisdictions, and its absence from the domestic law of most civil law States ('non-trust States'). It also straddles the divide between the law of obligations and of property, involving as it does personal duties and accountability on the part of the trustee to beneficiaries for the holding and disposition of property to which they hold legal title. Of course, every trust State also needs to deal with the reality that the trust assets could be located in a non-trust State.[1] The latter may be asked to recognise, and give some meaningful effect to, the trust. Otherwise, the practical utility of a trust may be significantly compromised where the assets themselves are located in, and controlled by, a non-trust State, or where enforcement against such trust assets is required.

It also means that the function of any global rules of private international law is potentially broader than in many fields: for the very possibility of a non-trust State giving effect to a trust that is valid by its governing law entails accepting an institution that does not exist in its domestic law. The acceptance of the trust for private international law purposes in non-trust States may, in due course, provide a catalyst for litigating trusts disputes in such jurisdictions, and, ultimately, perhaps even for the adoption of the trust into the domestic laws of non-trust States.

Against this background, the Hague Trusts Convention[2] was a breakthrough initiative,[3] unlike any attempted before or since at The Hague, designed to build bridges between common

[1] This is clearly not itself an impediment to the validity of the trust (see *Akers v Samba Financial Group* [2017] UKSC 6, [2017] AC 424).

[2] The Hague Convention on the Law Applicable to Trusts and on their Recognition 1985. It entered into force in: Australia; Canada (Alberta, British Columbia, Manitoba, New Brunswick, Nova Scotia Newfoundland and Labrador, Ontario, Prince Edward Island and Saskatchewan; the extension to Ontario was not made until 2018); Cyprus; Hong Kong; Italy; Liechtenstein; Luxembourg; Malta; Monaco; Netherlands; Panama; San Marino; Switzerland; and the United Kingdom. The application of the Convention has been extended by the United Kingdom to Bermuda, British Antarctic Territories, the British Virgin Islands, the Falkland Islands, Gibraltar, Guernsey, the Isle of Man, Jersey, Montserrat, St Helena and Dependencies, South Georgia, the South Sandwich Islands and the Turks and Caicos Islands, as well as to the Sovereign Base Areas in Cyprus of Akrotiri and Dhekelia. Detailed discussion of the Convention can be found in J Harris, *The Hague Trusts Convention* (Hart Publishing 2002) (Harris).

[3] See also *Dicey, Morris and Collins, The Conflict of Laws*, 15th edn (Sweet & Maxwell, 2012) ch 29; P Beaumont and P McEleavy, *Anton's Private International Law*, 3rd edn (W Green/SULI 2011) ch 22; *Underhill and Hayton, Law Relating to Trusts and* Trustees, 19th edn (LexisNexis 2016) ch 25.

law and civil law countries and to facilitate the recognition of trusts for private international law purposes in countries which did not themselves have such a domestic instruction.[4] The Convention aims to 'establish common provisions on the law applicable to trusts and to deal with the most important issues concerning the recognition of trusts'.[5] It requires the recognition of trusts *qua* trusts (rather than by 'translating' the trust into a functional equivalent). Moreover, the Convention's rules are not reciprocal,[6] and apply even if the governing law of the trust is that of a non-Contracting State.

In Contracting States,[7] the Convention has brought clarity[8] and is the dominant instrument concerning applicable law for trusts. The Convention rules emphasise settlor autonomy and the 'obligation' characteristic of the trust, so that they have more in common with the applicable law rules of contract law than those for property transfers. The recognition rules in the Convention facilitate recognition in both trust[9] and non-trust States of trusts otherwise incompatible with that State's domestic law.

As will be seen below, the Convention's scope is far from all-encompassing, and it gives rise to certain difficult questions as to its meaning and ambit. Moreover, important private international law questions fall outside its scope. Nonetheless, the Convention is an invaluable instrument for harmonising applicable law and fostering recognition rules and a crucial step in the search for global rules of private international law. This chapter considers further a number of these issues and the questions to which they have given rise.

II. Meaning of 'Trust' under the Convention

Given the lack of a universal understanding or definition of 'trusts', even in trust States, there was a need to provide guidance as to the Convention's ambit. Moreover, the Convention is not limited to the common law trust and is also intended to cover civil law institutions which exhibit similar core characteristics. To this end, Article 2(1) of the Hague Trusts Convention refers to 'the legal

[4] See *Akers* (n 1) [91] and [99]–[100] (referring to the Official Explanatory Report on the Convention by Professor von Overbeck, paras 12 and 14, available at: www.hcch.net/en/publications-and-studies/details4/?pid=2949&dtid=3) (von Overbeck Report).

[5] Preamble to the Convention.

[6] A State may, however, make a reservation pursuant to Art 21, so that it applies the Convention only to trusts governed by the law of a Contracting State. In the United Kingdom, Art 21 is omitted from the schedule to the Recognition of Trusts Act 1987.

[7] There are, at the time of writing, 14 Contracting States (including Hong Kong. The extension of the Convention to Hong Kong by the United Kingdom was subsequently continued by China).

[8] 'Common-law writing and case law were both fumbling in the dark, and there had been a chorus of complaints about the deplorable state of the law': M Lupoi, *Trusts: A Comparative Study*, trans S Dix (Cambridge University Press 2001) 331. Discussion of the common law principles includes: D Cavers, 'Trusts "Inter Vivos" and the Conflict of Laws' (1930) 44 *Harvard Law Review* 161; W Swabenland, 'The Conflict of Laws in Administration of Express Trusts of Personal Property' (1936) 45 *Yale Law Journal* 438; W Land, *Trusts in the Conflict of Laws; Validity, Construction, Administration and Taxation of Trusts: What Law Governs* (Baker, Voorhis & Co 1940); P Croucher, 'Trusts of Moveables in Private International Law' (1940) 4 *MLR* 111; G Keeton, 'Trusts in the Conflict of Laws' (1951) 4 *Current Legal Problems* 107; V Latham, 'The Creation and Administration of a Trust in the Conflict of Laws' (1953) 6 *Current Legal Problems* 176; R Lafer and A Siegel, 'Trusts of Movables in the Conflict of Laws' [1961] *New York University Law Review* 713; A Lowenfeld, 'Tempora Mutantur – Wills and Trusts in the Conflicts Restatement' (1972) 72 *Columbia Law Review* 382; A Wallace, 'Choice of Law for Trusts in Australia and the United Kingdom' (1987) 36 *ICLQ* 454. See also *American Restatement (2d) on the Conflict of Laws* (American Law Institute, 1971) ch 10.

[9] An example being non-charitable purpose trusts, whose recognition may be required in England when such trusts are permitted by a foreign governing law.

relationships created – inter vivos or on death – by a person, the settlor, when assets have been placed under the control of a trustee for the benefit of a beneficiary or for a specified purpose'.

Certainly, the Convention is not limited to trusts in favour of beneficiaries; both charitable purpose trusts and non-charitable purpose trusts fall within its scope.

At first sight, it is curious that Article 2(1) refers to assets placed under the 'control' of the trustee. A paradigm feature of a common law trust is that legal title is held by the trustee. 'Control' is a far broader concept and could be construed, on one view, to encompass cases of agency or mandate.[10]

Where a settlor declares herself as trustee, it is doubtful whether one can say that 'assets have been placed under the control of a trustee' within the meaning of Article 2(1). This might suggest that declarations of trust are excluded from the Convention. There is, however, no principled reason to exclude declarations by the settlor of herself as trustee from the scope of the Convention (not least since, once the trust is created, its genesis is substantially immaterial) and it is suggested that they fall within its scope.[11]

Article 2(2)(a) states that trust assets constitute a separate fund which is not part of the trustee's own private estate. It is not necessary that the concept of equitable interests be known in a legal system for it to have a 'trust' within the meaning of the Convention. Article 2(2)(b) provides that the trust assets must be held in the name of the trustee or another person on behalf of the trustee. Although the relationship between this provision and the broader description in Article 2(1) of assets being placed under the 'control' of the trust is perhaps not clear, the better view is that the effect of Article 2(2)(b) is that agency and mandate relationships should fall outside the scope of the Convention.

Article 2(2)(c) indicates that a trustee is subject to the powers and duties specified in the trust instrument, and also to duties imposed on her by law. It does not say to whom the trustee is accountable and it appears that trusts might be covered by the Convention, even where the trustee is substantially accountable to the settlor, at least where the court is satisfied that the trust is not a sham trust (ie, that a settlor's intention in setting up a trust is to retain control of his assets but use the trust as a pretence to mislead third parties by hiding his control).[12] The final paragraph of Article 2(2) states that a trustee may himself be a beneficiary, although not the sole beneficiary. The settlor may also be a beneficiary of the trust.

The elusiveness of the quest in Article 2 for an all-encompassing description of the trust has resulted in what has been descripted as a 'shapeless' trust,[13] where the trustee need not be owner of the property and where title could remain in the hands of the settlor, who retains rights and powers and to whom the 'trustee' is accountable. Moreover, Professor Lupoi suggests that, according to this description, very few countries would not have such a 'trust' in their domestic law and that, accordingly, very few are non-trust States within the meaning of the Convention. The result is that an English court would be compelled to recognise such institutions under the

[10] Lupoi (n 8) 334; but see D Hayton, 'The Developing European Dimension of Trust Law' (2000) 11 *King's College Law Journal* 48, 52.

[11] A view supported *obiter* in *Akers* (n 1) [101] (Lord Collins) and implicitly by the judgment of Lord Mance ([10]–[45]), insofar as he considered *obiter* the application of the Convention's rules.

[12] Or that the 'trust' is so under the control of the settlor that she is viewed as having retained the beneficial interest in the assets, so that no valid trust comes into effect. See *JSC Mezhdunarodniy Promyshlenniy Bank & Anor v Pugavchev* [2017] EWHC 2426 (Ch) esp [103]–[169] and [422]–[442]. See further *Underhill and Hayton* (n 3) para 100.60.

[13] M Lupoi, 'The Shapeless Trust' (1995) 1 *Trusts and Trustees* 15. See also M Lupoi, 'The Hague Convention, the Civil Law and the Italian Experience' (2007) 21 *Trusts Law International* 80; contrast Harris (n 2) 111–16. cp: *Investec Trust (Guernsey) Ltd v Glenalla Properties Ltd* [2018] UKPC 7, [2018] 2 WLR 1465; J Robb, 'Personhood and status of legal persons in private international law' (2019) 15 *Journal of Private International Law* 288.

Convention, even if they appear wholly alien to English domestic law. If this view is accepted, then the Convention has made a radical difference to English law and the scope of the Convention is much wider than one might expect. Even so, the intention of the Convention to facilitate the recognition of the trust, and not a range of broader mechanisms for managing property, is clear. The better view is that the Convention should be regarded as concerning only situations where the trustee owns legal title to trust assets directly (or indirectly via a nominee), so that the assets do not form part of his own private estate.[14]

III. Types of Trust Falling within the Ambit of the Convention

Article 3 of the Convention states that it applies to 'trusts created voluntarily and evidenced in writing'.[15] This apparently straightforward statement gives rise to layers of complexity, since it does not describe a coherent or well-recognised category of trusts. Clearly, it covers the paradigm express trust. Moreover, a trust can be sufficiently 'evidenced in writing' even if a trust instrument has not been signed by the settlor, although there must be sufficient written evidence that the settlor intended to create the trust.

The Convention would also seem to cover a trust arising where a trustee continues to hold property after the exhaustion of an express trust.[16] It appears also to cover, eg, other trusts arising by operation of law where a purported disposition on trust is ineffective, or where a trust is imposed to reflect the will of the settlor, provided that it is evidenced in writing.[17] It is uncertain precisely when a constructive trust of property will fall within the Convention.[18] Some such trusts arise so as to give effect to the parties' voluntary actions, such as creating mutual wills, or when a specifically enforceable contract is concluded, and would appear to fall within the Convention's ambit;[19] whereas in other cases (eg, where a trustee renews a lease for himself personally), a trust is imposed irrespective of the will of the parties and should be outside its scope.

Trusts declared by judicial decisions (as opposed to those arising by operation of law) are not included but Contracting States are free to extend the provisions of the Convention to such trusts.[20] A number of States have done so.[21] Indeed, in the United Kingdom, it has been further extended to apply to 'any trusts arising under the law of any part of the United Kingdom or by virtue of a judicial decision whether in the United Kingdom or elsewhere'.[22]

This provision has the effect of applying the Convention to most trusts, save those which are governed by a law outside the United Kingdom and which cannot be said to 'arise' by judicial decision.[23] This has the welcome effect of reducing or eliminating the considerable uncertainty

[14] Hayton (n 10) 53.
[15] Art 3.
[16] See von Overbeck Report (n 4) para 51.
[17] Ibid. See further, D Hayton, 'The Hague Convention on the Law Applicable to Trusts and on their Recognition' (1987) 36 *ICLQ* 260, 263–66.
[18] The personal liability to account as trustee is not within the Convention.
[19] Lupoi (n 8) 342–43.
[20] Art 20 of the Convention, not reproduced in the Recognition of Trusts Act 1987.
[21] In all the common law Canadian provinces, Cyprus, Hong Kong, Luxembourg, Monaco and the UK, see: www.hcch.net/en/instruments/conventions/status-table/notifications/?csid=710&disp=resdn.
[22] s 1(2), Recognition of Trusts Act 1987.
[23] This might exclude institutional constructive trusts and resulting trusts not governed by the law of a part of the United Kingdom, since they are triggered by a set of facts and their existence may simply be *affirmed* by the court. They do not *arise* by the decision of the court.

as to the applicable law rules for the vast majority of trusts.[24] Nonetheless, it extends well beyond the paradigm of voluntarily created trusts, and such an extension may not be palatable for many current or would-be Contracting States.

IV. Preliminary Issues Excluded from the Convention

Article 4 of the Convention states that it does not apply to preliminary issues relating to the validity of wills or of other acts by virtue of which assets are transferred to the trustee:

> The image employed was that of the launcher and the rocket; it will always be necessary to have a 'launcher', for example a will, a gift or another act with legal effects, which then launches the 'rocket' the trust. The preliminary act with legal effects, the 'launcher', does not fall under the Convention's coverage.[25]

Hence, a distinction must be drawn between questions relating to the validity of a will or other instrument which vests property in trustees and the transfer of legal title (which fall outside the ambit of the Convention), and issues relating to the validity and operation of the trust itself (to which the Convention applies). If, in the case of a testamentary trust, the testator had no capacity to make the will or the will is formally invalid, any trust contained therein will fail. But if the will is valid, the trust, once created, will fall within the ambit of the Convention.

In some cases, it is difficult to determine whether a matter falls within the scope of the Convention. The essential distinction to be drawn is between those rules which are applicable to any disposition of property and those which specifically affect the ability to create a trust. The former should be regarded as outside the scope of the Convention; the latter as within the Convention's scope.[26]

Even so, this leaves room for uncertainties as to the boundaries of the Convention. The issue was considered, but not determined, by the Supreme Court in *Akers*.[27] It was stated *obiter* that the Convention applied where a settlor had purported to declare himself trustee of shares. In *Clark and Whitehouse*,[28] Lord Hodge preferred the view expressed in *Dicey, Morris and Collins*,[29] that where a settlor declares itself trustee of property, the question of whether the assets may be alienated at all must first be determined by the applicable law rules for transfers of property outside the ambit of the Convention, and not by the law applicable to the trust and noted that

> otherwise, the results would be startling as a settlor would be able to alienate property which he could not dispose of under the *lex situs*. It would create significant problems for the operation of insolvency law in the jurisdiction in which the asset was located.[30]

If the settlor is able to alienate the property, the question of whether the trust declared is valid is governed by the Convention.

[24] But not as to the question whether the trust arises in the first place (see the discussions of Art 4, and of constructive and resulting trusts, below).

[25] von Overbeck Report (n 4) para 53.

[26] See *Re Barton's Estate, Tod v Barton* [2002] EWHC 264 (Ch).

[27] (n 1) [101]. See J Harris, 'The Hague Trusts Convention after *Akers v Samba*' (2018) 24 *Trusts & Trustees* 346; D Hayton, 'Proprietary Interests in Foreign Property: Equity's Viewpoint' (2016–17) 8 *UK Supreme Court Yearbook*, ch 4. See also *JSC VTB Bank v Skurikhin* [2019] EWHC 1407 (Comm).

[28] [2012] CSOH 55, 2012 SLT 599, [24]; see G Gretton, 'The Laws of the Game' (2012) 16 *Edinburgh Law Review* 414.

[29] (15th edn, Sweet and Maxwell, 2012) para 29-015.

[30] See also *JSC VTB Bank v Skurikhin* (n 27).

The capacity of the settlor is outside the ambit of the Convention.[31] Again, it is suggested that one should distinguish between the capacity of the settlor to alienate property at all and the capacity of the settlor to create the trust structure with that property. Since the transfer of property to a trustee involves a disposition of property no less than an owner who simply gives away or sells his property to another person absolutely, it is suggested that the capacity rules applicable to 'ordinary' transfers of property should be applied to decide whether the settlor may alienate property. There is then a second question as to whether the settlor, who has capacity to alienate property, has capacity to create the trust structure with that property. Here, it has been suggested that the law applicable to the trust should be applied, even if that law has been expressly chosen by the settlor.

V. Applicable Law Rules

The principal applicable law rules themselves in the Convention are somewhat less complex. The settlor may choose the law which governs the trust.[32] It is, however, a fundamental principle that the Convention does not introduce the trust into States which do not presently have it in their domestic law.[33] Accordingly, the settlor may not choose the law of a non-trust State (or of a State which does not provide for the category of trust concerned).[34] If she does so, the Convention provides that the law of closest connection[35] shall instead govern; only if that law does not provide for trusts does the Convention cease to be applicable.

If the settlor has not made a valid, express choice of law, one should then look to see if she impliedly made a choice, which must be determined from the 'terms of the instrument creating the trust or the writing evidencing the trust, interpreted, if necessary, in the light of the circumstances of the case'.

The trust instrument is, accordingly, the primary point of reference. In the case of testamentary trusts, the law applicable to succession is a powerful factor, there being an inference that the settlor intends the same law to govern a trust as governs succession to movables under the will.[36] In the case of *inter vivos* trusts, a jurisdiction clause will be a powerful indicator of the settlor's intention.[37]

If the settlor makes no choice of governing law, Article 7 provides that the trust is governed by the law with which it is most closely connected at the time of creation.[38] This involves considering, in particular,[39] four factors: (a) the place of administration of the trust designated by the settlor; (b) the situs of the assets of the trust; (c) the place of residence or business of the trustee; and (d) the objects of the trust and the places where they are to be fulfilled. There is among these factors 'a certain implicit hierarchy'[40] but also a considerable overlap, since (a) and (c) will usually coincide. Where the place of administration is designated by the settlor, this will be a strong indicator of an implied choice of law pursuant to Article 6, so that it will rarely be

[31] von Overbeck Report (n 4) para 59.
[32] Art 6.
[33] von Overbeck Report (n 4) para 14.
[34] Art 6(2).
[35] As determined by Art 7.
[36] *Att-Gen v Campbell* (1872) LR 5 HL 524; *Saliba v Falzon* [1998] NSWSC 302; but see *Re Barton's Estate* (n 26).
[37] cp: *Att-Gen v Jewish Colonization Association* [1901] 1 KB 123.
[38] *Lady Moon SPV SRL v Petricca and Co Capital Ltd* [2019] EWHC 439 (Ch), [78].
[39] Although the list is not exhaustive.
[40] von Overbeck Report (n 4) para 72.

relevant under Article 7. Depending on the facts, the situs of the assets of the trust may deserve little weight: the movables included in a trust may be intangibles, eg stocks,[41] shares and bonds. That said, one might expect the role of the situs to be stronger where the trust property consists wholly or principally of immovables. The place of residence or business of the trustee may be of little relevance if the original trustees are domiciled in different States, but may be highly significant if, for instance, the settlor sets up a trust company in a certain State.[42] As to the final factor mentioned in Article 7, the objects of the trust and their place of fulfilment, as the search is for the objective law of closest connection, it should only be important where it sheds light on this as, eg, if it indicates where trust assets should be invested, or the trust administered.[43]

Professor von Overbeck suggested that 'one would think that ... the judge will have a tendency to conclude that a trust is most closely connected with a State which has this institution'.[44] Nonetheless, it is suggested that the test of closest connection under Article 7 should be purely objective and no such presumption should operate.[45]

VI. 'Recognition' of a Trust under the Hague Trusts Convention

Pursuant to Article 11, Contracting States are required to recognise the trust. Non-trust States should not do so by attempting to 'translate' the trust into the nearest civil law analogue; they must recognise the trust *qua* trust. Beyond this, there is nothing remarkable about the recognition provisions; they are, essentially, the natural corollary of giving effect to the applicable law rules in the Convention and the content of the governing law. To this end, the statement in Article 11(1) that a trust created in accordance with the law specified in the Convention must be recognised as a trust, is almost tautologous. However, Professor von Overbeck explained that

> judges of civil law countries ... might stand perplexed before the pure and simple affirmation that a trust ... should deploy effects in their countries ... It is necessary that [the Convention should] indicate at least on the principal points, what recognition will consist of and what the effects will be that the trust will deploy.[46]

Accordingly, Article 11 provides that recognition implies

> as a minimum, that the trust property constitutes a separate fund, that the trustee may sue and be sued in his capacity as trustee, and that he may appear or act in this capacity before a notary or any person acting in an official capacity.

Further, insofar as the law applicable to the trust requires or provides, recognition implied, in particular: (a) that personal creditors of the trustee can have no recourse against the trust assets; (b) that the trust assets do not form part of the trustee's estate upon his insolvency or bankruptcy; and

[41] But see *Gorgeous Beauty Limited v Liu* [2014] EWHC 2952 (Ch); *JSC VTB Bank v Skurikhin* (n 27).

[42] *Att-Gen v Jewish Colonization Association* (n 37); *Chellaram v Chellaram* [1985] Ch 409; *Re Carapiet's Trusts, Manoogian (Armenian Patriarch of Jerusalem) v Sonsino* [2002] EWHC 1304 (Ch).

[43] Compare *Chellaram v Chellaram* [1985] Ch 409; *Chellaram v Chellaram (No 2)* [2002] EWHC 632 (Ch), [2002] 3 All ER 17.

[44] von Overbeck Report (n 4) para 61.

[45] Harris (n 2) 161, 208 and 227. *Berezovsky v Abramovich* [2010] EWHC 647 (Comm) [121], [183]. See also *Gorgeous Beauty Limited v Liu* (n 41) [307], [313]. For a view supporting von Overbeck's 'tendency' see *Anton* (n 3) 982–83.

[46] von Overbeck Report (n 4) para 31. See also J Perrin, 'The Recognition of Trusts and their Use in Estate Planning under Continental Laws' (2008) 10 *Yearbook of Private International Law* 629. States may adopt more favourable rules on recognition if they so choose: Art 14.

(c) that the trust assets do not form part of the matrimonial property of the trustee or his spouse nor part of the trustee's estate upon his death. These provisions, like the description of the trust in Article 2, concentrate on the position of the trustee, and arguably deal less than satisfactorily with that of beneficiaries.

The effect of Article 11(3)(d), which deals with the tracing[47] and recovery of assets, is less clear. The first sentence states that 'the trust assets may be recovered when the trustee, in breach of trust, has mingled trust assets with his own property or has alienated trust assets'. The second sentence, however, provides that the rights and obligations of any third-party holder of the assets 'remain subject to the law determined by the choice of law rules of the forum'. This appears to limit a beneficiary's ability to trace trust assets, especially where they are situated in a non-trust State. It has been suggested, however, that this provision should only be invoked where the issue concerns acquisition by a third party and whether she, as a bona fide purchaser, takes free of a subsisting beneficial interest.[48] This matter would be resolved by the applicable law rules governing property transfers. The final sentence of Article 11(3)(d) would not be relevant to the question whether the trust assets or their value could be traced into the third party's hands, which would be determined under the first sentence of that provision by the law applicable to the trust. In *Akers*,[49] the Supreme Court held *obiter* that where a settlor had purported to declare himself trustee of shares located in Saudi Arabia pursuant to certain Cayman law trusts and then transferred those shares to a party in Saudi Arabia, Saudi law, as the law of the situs, would determine whether the effect of the transfer was to defeat the beneficiary's trust rights, in accordance with Article 11(3)(d).

Article 13 provides an important safeguard for non-trust States. It states that no State is bound to recognise a trust the significant elements of which, except for the choice of the applicable law, the place of administration and the habitual residence of the trustee, are more closely connected with States which do not have the institution of the trust or the category of trust involved. This reinforces the fact that the trust is not introduced by the Convention into non-trust States' domestic legal systems.

The application of Article 13 is discretionary. It is, however, striking that courts in non-trust States have not tended readily to reach for it.[50] In part, this may be because the adoption of the Convention is itself something of a leap of faith for non-trust States, which facilitates the use of trusts having material connections to the jurisdiction. Again, this shows the somewhat unique nature of the Convention, whereby recognition of the trust for private international law purposes may serve as a catalyst for increased acceptance of the trust domestically. Indeed, once the trust is admitted for private international law purposes, one might reasonably question why it is possible to achieve a certain result with a trust where there are some connections overseas, but impossible to do so otherwise.[51]

Article 13 was considered to have no useful application in the United Kingdom and was not enacted.[52] This, however, may have considerable ramifications. The broad scope of Article 2 of

[47] ie, the question of whether trust property can be identified when it changes its form through mixture or substitution.

[48] J Harris, 'Tracing and the Conflict of Laws' (2002) 73 *British Yearbook of International Law* 65.

[49] (n 1) [40]–[41] (Lord Mance). See also *Byers v Samba Financial Group* [2020] EWHC 853 (Ch).

[50] For instance, in respect of a trust objectively connected to Italy containing a foreign choice of law clause: see, *Casani v Mattei*, Tribunale di Lucca, reported in English in (1998/99) 1 *International Trust & Estate Law Reports* 925. See also M Lupoi, 'The Civil Law Trust' in R Atherton (ed), *the International Academy of Estate and Trust Law: Selected Papers 1997–9* (Kluwer 2000) 35, 46–49.

[51] See M Lupoi, 'Effects of the Hague Convention in a Civil Law Country' in P Jackson and DC Wilde (eds), *The Reform of Property Law* (Ashgate 1997) 222, 227.

[52] And is omitted from the schedule to the Recognition of Trusts Act 1987.

the Convention means that an English court might, in principle, be faced with analogous civil law institutions ostensibly qualifying for recognition under Article 11. Moreover, the exclusion of Article 13 appears to have the effect of authorising an English settlor, in an otherwise wholly domestic context to create a trust unknown or unauthorised in English domestic trust law, by the simple expedient of choosing a foreign law to govern it. In principle, this could mean that 'pure purpose trusts, variant types of trusts, and so on, can now be formed by Englishmen under the law of, say, Belize or Cyprus, even if all the elements of the trust are connected with England'.[53]

VII. Mandatory Rules and Public Policy

At once both a strength and weakness of the Convention is its provisions on mandatory rules and public policy. Their ostensibly broad scope provides safeguards, especially for non-trust States, against what they may consider unpalatable incidences of recognising trusts and so may encourage ratification, but at the price of uncertainty and potentially undermining some of the benefits of the Convention.

In particular, Article 15 preserves the application of 'rules which cannot be derogated from by voluntary act' in areas related to trusts law. In case of conflict, the law applicable to the trust gives way, but only insofar as the rules in a related area are non-derogable. Article 15 permits the application of the mandatory rules of the State whose law is 'designated by the conflicts rules of the forum' and 'is concerned only to preserve the effect of mandatory rules of a relevant law which may be inconsistent with the recognition of some incidents of a trust'.[54]

The list of areas related to trusts in Article 15 is non-exhaustive.[55] Article 15(1)(a) deals with rules for the protection of minors and incapable parties. Since many such issues are matters of capacity excluded from the Convention, the scope of this provision may be narrow. It might be applied to the capacity to act as a trustee. Article 15(1)(b) concerns the effects of marriage on the trust, especially marital regimes having a form of community of property and the effects to be given to an ante-nuptial contract. Article 15(1)(c) applies to succession rights, testate and intestate, especially the indefeasible shares of spouses and relatives. The scope of Article 15(1)(c) may, however, be somewhat limited because Article 4 may operate to prevent a testamentary trust from arising to the extent that it purports to cover that part of the deceased's estate reserved for the heirs. It is very unlikely that an English court will allow a validly created *inter vivos* trust subsequently to be impugned by foreign forced heirship rules, since an English court should only apply the law applicable to succession to assets which the forum regards as part of the deceased's estate at death.[56] Article 15(1)(d) preserves the application of mandatory rules concerning transfer of title to property and security interests in property. This cannot be concerned with the transfer of property to the trustee, since this is a preliminary issue within the meaning of Article 4 and outside the scope of the Convention. It might be applied to questions of transfer of equitable

[53] Lupoi (n 51) 225. This is subject to the provisions on mandatory rules and public policy.

[54] *Akers* (n 1) [91] (Lord Sumption).

[55] Art 15(2) states that where a mandatory rule is applied under Art 15(1), 'the court shall try to give effect to the objects of the trust by other means'.

[56] See *Pouey v Hordern* [1900] 1 Ch 492. Art 23(2)(i) of the EU Succession Regulation (No 650/2012) states that the *lex successionis* shall determine 'any obligation to restore or account for gifts, advancements or legacies when determining the shares of the different beneficiaries'. This provision was a key reason for the United Kingdom's decision not to opt into the Regulation since it was considered capable of giving rise to claims in relation to assets that had been irrevocably settled on an *inter vivos* trust.

title to the beneficiary,[57] the nature of the beneficiary's interest and the question whether the beneficiary may terminate the trust. In principle, it might also apply to the circumstances in which a good title to trust property might be passed to a third party, although the Supreme Court analysed this question by reference to Article 11(3)(d) in *Akers*.[58] Article 15(1)(e) covers the protection of creditors in matters of insolvency. It is not necessary that a creditor should have acted in good faith.[59] Article 15(1)(e) should only be applied to the protection of creditors upon the beneficiary's insolvency, not that of the trustee. Finally, Article15(1)(f) preserves the application of mandatory rules for the protection of third parties acting bona fide. It is not limited to purchasers and might extend to other third-party recipients of trust property.[60]

Article 16 preserves the application of the mandatory rules of the forum which must be applied even to international situations, irrespective of rules of conflict of laws.

The von Overbeck Report states that:

> Among the laws which fall in this category, mention may be made of those which are intended to protect the cultural heritage of a country, public health, certain vital economic interests, the protection of employees or of the weaker party to another contract.[61]

Article 16(2) permits the application 'in exceptional circumstances' of the overriding mandatory rules of a State of close connection with the case. This may provide further comfort to non-trust States. The United Kingdom did not, however, enact this provision, fearing that it would give rise to undue uncertainty and has made the reservation against it permitted by Article 16(3).[62]

One matter not immediately apparent is the extent to which Articles 15 and 16 can be invoked to negate key requirements for the recognition of a trust under Article 11. Both Articles 2 and 11 seem at first sight to require that the trust assets be treated as a separate fund not forming part of the trustee's personal wealth or available to his creditors. Shorn of that characteristic, it is difficult to imagine an institution as a 'trust' at all. Could it nonetheless be said that a rule of a given legal system that property rights must be undivided and that all assets owned by a person are accordingly treated as part of his personal wealth, is itself a mandatory rule capable of overriding Articles 2 and 11? Although one cannot give a definitive answer, there is a strong argument that only States prepared to accommodate the concept of a fund not forming part of the holder's personal wealth should ratify the Convention; and so far this appears to be the case.[63]

Article 18 allows provisions of the Convention to be disregarded 'when their application would be manifestly contrary to public policy'. This exception may be applied to any or all provisions of the Convention. Although Article 18 does not state that only the forum's public policy may be applied, it is very unlikely that an English court would invoke any other rules of public policy. The robust language of Article 18 suggests an intention that it will be interpreted restrictively. By definition, the recognition of trusts *qua* trusts by non-trust States which ratify the Convention is already something of a leap of faith; and then to regard core characteristics of a trust as contrary to public policy is not a conclusion to be reached lightly.

[57] Where the governing law of the trust recognises an equitable proprietary interest.

[58] (n 1) [40].

[59] von Overbeck Report (n 4) para 145.

[60] Though the decision in *Akers* suggests that such persons are on one view protected by Art 11(3)(d).

[61] See (n 4) para 149.

[62] See the HCCH trusts Status table at: www.hcch.net/en/instruments/conventions/status-table/?cid=59 and click on UK reservations and declarations to come to www.hcch.net/en/instruments/conventions/status-table/notifications/?csid=710&disp=resdn. Other States making the same reservation are Canada (only for Alberta), Luxembourg and Monaco.

[63] See, for instance, the discussion of the position in the Netherlands in Harris (n 2) 319–21 and also M Koppenol-Laforce, *Het Haagse Trustverdrag* (Kluwer 1997) 271.

It is also somewhat unclear in what circumstances a trust State might be justified in invoking Article 18. For instance, in English trusts law, non-charitable purpose trusts are not normally permitted since 'Every trust other than a charitable trust must have a definite object, and there must be someone in whose favour the court can enforce it'.[64] The so-called 'STAR' trust,[65] originating from the Cayman Islands, allows a settlor to create a trust for beneficiaries or for purposes, or for both. Such purposes may be charitable or non-charitable. The beneficiaries do not ordinarily have a right in the trust property itself unless and until it is transferred to them. The trusts are enforced by appointed enforcers. The beneficiary has no right to enforce the trust, unless also appointed as an enforcer. The matter is far from clear, but some commentators have suggested that such trusts should be recognised in England, it being an inevitable incidence of an applicable law Convention on trusts that the English courts will have to uphold trusts that would be invalid under English domestic law.[66] If the objection to non-charitable trusts is that they cannot be enforced, and if, by the governing law, someone can be appointed who can enforce the trust, it may be difficult to see why the trust should be denied recognition on public policy grounds. Even so, it remains doubtful whether an English court would give effect to the trust if it consists principally or substantially of property located in England, or required administration of the trust in England.

If such trusts can be recognised when they are governed by a foreign law, but otherwise wholly connected to England, this shows that the Convention may be a catalyst for reform of domestic law, even in trust States. Why, it might be asked should English domestic law not also permit such trusts to be created and governed by English law, provided that they have an enforcer? Once again, one sees the atypical nature of this area of law, where private international law is capable of influencing the agenda for domestic law reform.[67]

VIII. Sceptical Reaction in Some States

The Convention was a pioneering exercise in fostering a global solution to the private international law issues created by trusts which frequently contained cross-border elements. It has been adopted by a number of non-trust States, whilst not achieving widespread ratification. Nor has it by any means appealed to all trust States. In the United States,[68] some feel that the Convention is not radical enough; that it is insufficiently protective of the settlor's autonomy, contains too many derogations and that it does not do enough to protect 'local' trusts from the claims of forced heirs.[69]

Moreover, a very substantial numbers of trusts are administrated in, and governed by the laws of, offshore jurisdictions. Many such States, far from seeking to preserve the application of mandatory rules of a foreign law relating, for instance, to compulsory heirship or matrimonial

[64] *Lewin on Trusts*, 20th edn (Sweet & Maxwell, 2020) para 5-053.

[65] Originally created in the Cayman Islands by the Special Trusts (Alternative Regime) Law 1997.

[66] D Hayton, 'Developing the Obligation Characteristic of the Trust' (2001) 117 *LQR* 96, 100; Harris (n 2) 395–96. For further discussion, see P Matthews, 'Shooting STAR: The New Special Trusts Regime from the Cayman Islands' (1997) 11 *Trust Law International* 67; A Duckworth, 'STAR Wars: The Colony Strikes Back' (1998) 12 *Trust Law International* 16; P Matthews, 'STAR: Big Bang or Red Dwarf?' (1998) 12 *Trust Law International* 98; A Duckworth, 'STAR Wars: Smiting the Bull' (1999) 13 *Trust Law International* 158.

[67] See further Hayton, ibid, 100.

[68] Which signed the Convention in 1988 but has never ratified it.

[69] See, in particular, J Schoenblum, 'The Hague Convention on Trusts: Much Ado about Very Little' (1994) 3 *Journal of International Trust and Corporate Planning* 5.

property regimes, as does Article 15 of the Hague Trusts Convention, are anxious to ensure that such foreign law rules do not affect local law trusts. Local legislation may provide that no foreign law of forced heirship which confers rights by virtue of a personal relationship to a settlor or beneficiary shall in any way undermine or affect the operation of a trust governed by local law.[70] In this world where the settlor's autonomy is paramount, a State's private international law rules have to be 'competitive'. States such as the Cayman Islands have not wanted to be limited by the terms of the Hague Trusts Convention and have not given effect to it. Since the Convention is open-ended,[71] their trusts might benefit from recognition in non-trust States, but they do not need to take on the burden of the Convention and its choice of law rules. On the other hand, the very individualised positions that they adopt may put their trusts on a collision course with the laws of other States, and their trusts may accordingly have greater difficulty in securing recognition overseas, particularly in States which do have forced heirship or matrimonial property rules.

IX. Trusts Falling Outside the Scope of the Convention: Constructive and Resulting Trusts

It is notable that, for trusts falling outside the Convention's ambit, there is little clarity as to the appropriate applicable law rules, even in trust States. Indeed, underlying this are more profound issues as to whether trusts imposed irrespective of the will of the settlor should be subject to their own applicable law rules at all. For instance, *Dicey, Morris and Collins* note that: 'There seems to be no clear English or Commonwealth authority on the choice of law rules relating to constructive and resulting trusts'.[72] They suggest that: 'The law applicable to a cause of action or issue determines whether a person is required to hold property on constructive or resulting trust'.[73] On this basis, for instance, a trust arising in response to unjust enrichment would be subject to the applicable law rules for restitution; a trust arising pursuant to a transfer of property not treated as a gift would be subject to the applicable law rules in property, and so forth. But even this modest proposition does not command universal acceptance.[74] Equally, considerable challenges remain in 'translating' obligations arising under the laws of non-trust States into constructive trusts in trust States.[75]

Ultimately, a solution to many of these issues requires more Contracting States to extend the ambit of the Convention. As explained above, Article 20 permits a Contracting State to declare, at any time, that the Convention will be applied to any trust declared by judicial decision. But it may be one thing to expect non-trust States to ratify the Convention insofar as it gives effect to trusts arising by virtue of the settlor's autonomy, and quite another to expect them to adopt universal

[70] eg, s 91, Cayman Islands 2020 Revision; s 10, Bermuda Trusts (Special Provisions) Act 1989 (as amended by Trusts (Special Provisions) Act 2020).

[71] Although a State may decide to recognise trusts only when governed by the law of a Contracting State, pursuant to Art 21. To date no State has used this reservation.

[72] At para 29-076. See also J Harris, 'Constructive Trusts and Private International Law: Determining the Applicable Law' (2012) 18 *T & T* 965; D Hayton, '"Trusts" in Private International Law' (2014) 366 *Hague Collected Courses* 70.

[73] Rule 172.

[74] Contrast, for instance, *Lightning v Lightning Electrical Contractors Ltd* (2009) 23 *Trusts Law International* 35 and *Martin v Secretary of State for Work and Pensions* [2009] EWCA Civ 1289, [2010] WTLR 671.

[75] See, for instance, *Arab Monetary Fund v Hashim* (No 9), *The Times*, 11 October 1994; *Kuwait Oil Tanker SAK v Al Bader* [2000] 2 All ER (Comm) 271 (CA); *Grupo Torras SA v Al-Sabah* [2001] CLC 221 (CA).

solutions which may impose a trust upon a non-consenting party. This is particularly so given that, even in trust States, such trusts may straddle the boundaries of cause of action, response and remedy, and generate complex characterisation questions. It is fair to assume that a global solution in respect of such trusts remains a distant prospect.

X. Conclusion

Notwithstanding its limitations, the Hague Trusts Convention remains an important step in harmonising the rules of private international law for trusts. At once, the Convention shows private international law at its most progressive and its most regressive. Given the numerous derogations contained in the Convention, it can, at a minimum, make only fairly minor inroads into the law of non-trust Contracting States. Nonetheless, the ratification of the Convention and the recognition of trusts *qua* trusts is a leap of faith for non-trust States.

Nonetheless, the Convention's flexibility may undermine some of its benefits in the eyes of trust States. Moreover, trust States whose primary concern is to compete within the global trusts market may reject the Convention as insufficiently pragmatic and protective of local trusts from the vagaries of foreign law.

The Hague Trusts Convention is ultimately about pragmatic compromise: it introduces the trust into non-trust States for private international law purposes, but provides flexibility, particularly for non-trust States. Moreover, it excludes a number of difficult issues, and trusts, from the Convention. The Convention is nonetheless a key first stage to the acceptance of the trust in non-trust States.

The Hague Conference has recognised the possibility for further refinement of the Hague Trusts Convention and recently produced a proposal for future work in this area.[76] This recognises 'fundamental differences in the understanding of the sorts of institutions that fall within the scope of the Convention',[77] especially in respect of analogous civil law concepts. Possible topics for future work include:[78] a survey to understand the institutions perceived to fall within the ambit of the Convention; identifying challenges in recognising different types of trust in civil law jurisdictions, and considering whether a distinction in this respect between *inter vivos* and testamentary trusts would assist. Whilst this is certainly to be welcomed, it is hoped that any future work will also encompass other issues (such as the scope of the exclusion of preliminary issues in Article 4), and will seek to identify reasons for the reticence of a number of trusts jurisdictions to ratify the Convention and how any reforms could better meet their needs.

In practice, the Convention represents by far the best and probably the only realistic option for a global solution to the private international law of trusts.[79] In a world where trusts, trust property and parties to the trust relationship are ever more likely to cross borders, the harmonised solution offered by the Hague Trusts Convention offers considerable benefits to trust and non-trust States alike.

[76] *The HCCH 1985 Trusts Convention: Updates and Possible Future Work*, Prel Doc No 15 of December 2020. This followed an invitation from the Council on General Affairs and Policy (CGAP): see C&D No 39 of CGAP 2020.

[77] Para 3.

[78] See para 10.

[79] Moreover, the uncertain state of the law in respect of trusts falling outside its ambit, even in trust States, only reinforces the case for achieving global solutions for trusts where possible.

24

Insolvency and Bankruptcy

FRANCISCO GARCIMARTÍN ALFÉREZ AND SARA SÁNCHEZ

I. Introduction

The growing international physical presence and market activity of companies have made cross-border insolvencies an increasingly common phenomenon.[1] It is thus usual nowadays that in insolvency proceedings some of the assets that form part of the insolvency estate are in a foreign jurisdiction, foreign creditors are involved and/or some liabilities are governed by a foreign law. These situations give rise to conflict of laws problems. Despite the boost of the field's importance, harmonisation of substantive insolvency rules remains rare, and therefore Private International Law (PIL) rules continue to play a key role. Typically, these rules cover four different areas: (i) international jurisdiction to open insolvency proceedings; (ii) law applicable to such proceedings; (iii) recognition and enforcement of decisions and of the powers of the insolvency practitioner; and (iv) coordination and cooperation among proceedings opened in different jurisdictions. These areas mirror the traditional sectors in PIL.

The purpose of this contribution is to describe the core problems raised by cross-border insolvencies and how PIL deals with them. After this brief introduction, section II is mainly normative: it outlines the normative models ('territorialism' and 'universalism') that are usually taken as a reference to cope with cross-border insolvencies. These models are presented as 'ideal models', ie, not referred to the law of any particular State. It describes their main features, their advantages and disadvantages and the ways in which such models can be diluted and moved towards intermediate positions ('modified universalism'). Sections III–VI are based on positive law. Section III examines the EU Insolvency Regulation recast.[2] Sections IV and V the main UNCITRAL soft law instruments on cross-border insolvency: the 1997 UNCITRAL Model Law on Cross-Border Insolvency (the 1997 Model Law), with its 2013 Guide to Enactment and Interpretation;[3] the 2018 UNCITRAL Model Law on Recognition and Enforcement of Insolvency-Related Judgments;[4] and the 2004 and 2013 UNCITRAL Legislative Guides on Insolvency Law (the Legislative Guide)[5] (section V). Section VI briefly mentions other initiatives, such as the Montevideo Treaties,

[1] In this chapter, we use the terms 'insolvency' and 'bankruptcy' interchangeably.
[2] Regulation (EU) 2015/848 of the European Parliament and of the Council of 20 May 2015 on insolvency proceedings [2015] OJ L141/19.
[3] See: uncitral.un.org/sites/uncitral.un.org/files/media-documents/uncitral/en/1997-model-law-insol-2013-guide-enactment-e.pdf.
[4] See: uncitral.un.org/sites/uncitral.un.org/files/media-documents/uncitral/en/ml_recognition_gte_e.pdf.
[5] See: uncitral.un.org/en/texts/insolvency/legislativeguides/insolvency_law.

the Bustamante Code, the Nordic Convention and OHADA Uniform Law on Insolvency Procedures. Throughout sections III–VI we discuss the normative models underlying each instrument, or more precisely, the different versions of modified universalism that they have followed.

II. Normative Models

A. Introduction

Insolvency law deals with debtors who are unable to pay their debts. Its main objective is to maximise the value of the insolvent debtor's estate and to distribute it among his or her creditors in accordance with the ranking of their claims. As can be easily imagined, insolvency law is a complex field both for technical and policy reasons. It entails the liquidation or restructuring of a debtor (or their business) by means of a collective proceeding, where normally somebody has to suffer costs. There are many conflicting interests at stake (eg, creditors, shareholders, employees, tax authorities) and thus a strong presence of public interests. It is private law but with large political repercussions. Even in the case of natural persons, insolvency law requires making policy decisions that affect the socio-economic structure of a country.

In a cross-border scenario, ie, when the insolvent debtor has assets located in foreign jurisdictions and/or foreign creditors and liabilities, the complexity multiplies: countries have very different and conflicting policies to cope with these situations, and to determine who and to what extent is going to suffer the costs that any insolvency proceeding entails. Thus, to explain and understand this part of the legal system, it may be helpful to start with a normative analysis of simple models. Scholars usually commence this analysis by stating that there are two theoretical normative models: territorialism and universalism.[6] Each of these models provides a very different response to the problems presented by cross-border insolvencies. At the core of territorialism is the idea that a court can only exercise jurisdiction over the assets located in that same jurisdiction and, hence, in cross-border insolvency there will (potentially) be as many proceedings as countries where assets are located. Conversely, under the universalist's ideal 'one court, one law', one court would administer the insolvency estate on a worldwide basis, applying the laws of the State of the opening of proceedings. These divergent philosophies are not, however, embraced in practice by States in their 'purest' form. They follow, instead, mixed positions; notably, the so-called 'modified' or 'mitigated universality' model.

B. Territorial Model

The territorial model, in its most radical version, is a perfect reflection of the legal fragmentation which exists in the world: corporate international activity is conducted in a legally fragmented world, a world in which each State has its own legislation and in which each State

[6] The debate between the two models was put forward with special intensity in North American doctrine; by way of introduction, see AT Guzman, 'International Bankruptcy: In Defense of Universalism' (2000) 98 *Michigan Law Review* 2177; LM LoPucki, 'The Case for Cooperative Territoriality in International Bankruptcy' (2000) 98 *Michigan Law Review* 2216; JL Westbrook, 'A Global Solution to Multinational Default' (2000) 98 *Michigan Law Review* 2276. See also, P Omar, 'The Landscape of International Insolvency Law' (2002) 11 *International Insolvency Review* 173, 176–81.

can only guarantee the coercive implementation of rights within its territory. Under this model, insolvency proceedings are understood as collective enforcement proceedings. The result of this in the sphere of international insolvency is easy to deduce: each State where the debtor has assets organises the insolvency according to its own law. This means that: (i) there are as many insolvency proceedings as there are States where the debtor has assets;[7] (ii) each set of proceedings is governed by the law in force in that State; and (iii) only the creditors from the State in question can participate in the proceedings. Both the body of creditors and the estate of the debtor are limited to the territory of each State.

From this starting point, the model can be diluted and move towards intermediate models. Thus, eg: (i) territorial proceedings may be limited to States where the debtor has an establishment, ie, the presence of an asset is not sufficient, but rather the permanent presence of the debtor in that State is required before insolvency proceedings can be opened against him or her; (ii) foreign creditors can form part of the body of creditors, ie, the estate of the debtor remains territorial, but the body of creditors is universal; and (iii) mechanisms of cooperation are established between the different insolvency proceedings in order to ensure, as far as possible, a coordinated winding-up of the company or the international *par condition concurrentium* of creditors (eg, the so-called 'cooperative territorialism').

C. Universal Model

The universal model, on the other hand, stems from the principle of unity and universality:[8] one legal (or natural) person, one patrimony at a worldwide level and thus one universal insolvency proceeding. Even though the economic activity of the debtor is conducted in various markets and, as a result, assets may be located abroad and a plurality of creditors in the different countries are affected by that activity, collective proceedings will be conducted under the authority of a single court and by a single insolvency administration for the entire activity and for all those creditors. This means that: (i) a single procedure is opened in the debtor's 'home country' which encompasses all the assets of the debtor regardless of their location; (ii) a single national law is applied, both to procedural and substantive issues (ie, the *lex fori concursus*); (iii) all creditors, both national and foreign, can participate in the proceedings; and (iv) the decisions made in these proceedings are recognised and enforced in all other States. As someone once said, in the universal model 'one court plays the tune, and everyone else dances'.[9]

Furthermore, as is the case with the territorial model, the universal model can be modified and moved towards intermediate models. Thus, eg: (i) by allowing certain subordinated territorial proceedings to run concurrently alongside the main insolvency proceedings; (ii) by allowing, under certain conditions, the opening of territorial proceedings without the need to open proceedings with universal scope; or (iii) by establishing exceptions to the application of the *lex fori concursus*.

[7] LoPucki (n 6) 'territoriality means that the bankruptcy courts of a country have jurisdiction over those portions of the economy which are within its borders and not those portions which are outside them'.

[8] Westbrook (n 6) 2283.

[9] LM LoPucki, 'Cooperation in International Bankruptcy: A Post Universalist Approach' (1999) 84 *Cornell Law Review* 696, 699.

D. General Policy Considerations

i. Territorial Model

Viewed from the perspective of the policies involved, the territorial model is basically justified for two reasons, one of which is substantive in nature, and the other organisational.[10]

First, it is a suitable model for providing protection for the interest of local creditors. Countries tend to be reluctant to accept the effects of foreign insolvency proceedings when these conflict with the interest of their local creditors, in particular 'unsophisticated and non-adjusting creditors' such as employees, consumers, small suppliers, etc. In the case of 'sophisticated creditors' there are no serious problems: the cost of attending insolvency proceedings abroad is already reflected in the price of the credit they extended to the debtor.[11] When a national bank or a large company enters into an agreement with a foreign firm, it is capable of assessing the associated risks (eg, the need to attend insolvency proceedings abroad or the application of a foreign law), so these risks will be taken into account in the form of a higher or, as the case might be, lower price. However, unsophisticated creditors are unable to make this adjustment. They are unable to adjust the terms of their transaction to reflect the risk they are assuming. This leads to certain inefficiencies arising from the 'moral risk' and from the 'adverse selection' which goes hand in hand with these situations: (i) debtors, insofar as they are not subject to 'close scrutiny' by local creditors, lack any incentive to protect the solvency of the claim; and (ii) it distorts the market of credits: high-risk debtors will borrow too much, while low-risk debtors will borrow too little, which can cause the latter (precisely the more solvent ones) to be driven out of the market.[12]

The same line of argument has been invoked to justify local proceedings with regard to creditors with a privilege over an asset located in the territory of the State in question or with regard to public law claims. In these cases, the problem is not that the creditors ignore the risks they are assuming, but the possibility that the law of the State where the debtor's centre is situated and whose insolvency courts have worldwide jurisdiction (ie, the debtor's 'home country') does not recognise those creditors as having any priority or preferential status. The situation may become even more complicated if we consider the possible strategies open to a debtor in the period prior to insolvency and the incentives to forum shopping inherent in a universal system: as the insolvency court will apply its own law (or at least its own conflict of laws rules), debtors may change their domicile opportunistically after credit has been extended, to take advantage of the differences in the national insolvency laws. The possibility of opening territorial insolvency proceedings operates as a kind of insurance against strategies of this kind.

Second, in certain situations the opening of territorial insolvency proceedings might facilitate the liquidation of assets of the debtor. Thus, eg, when in order to restructure the company it may be sufficient to liquidate some assets located abroad (eg, to sell a division), it may also be sufficient to open territorial insolvency proceedings there, thus saving on the cost of opening universal insolvency proceedings. Just as there are situations where a general anaesthetic is not necessary when operating on a patient, and a local anaesthetic is sufficient, there are situations in which it is not necessary to open universal insolvency proceedings, and in which one (or more) territorial bankruptcies are sufficient. Lastly, there may be cases where it is very costly or complicated to conduct the entire proceedings from a single State and it is preferable to combine the main proceedings with territorial ones. For example, when dealing with rights which have been

[10] LoPucki (n 6).
[11] Guzman (n 6) 2186.
[12] Ibid, 2184.

created according to a law other than the law of the State of opening (*lex fori concursus*), it may prove difficult to transpose them to the insolvency categories recognised by the latter. Or, from the procedural point of view, when the number of local creditors is high, segregating different sub-estates may facilitate the access and participation of local creditors and simplify negotiations. To continue using the same metaphor: when the situation is very complicated, the chief surgeon cannot do everything himself, but requires the assistance of other specialists to operate on different parts of the body.

Nevertheless, the territorial model leads to serious deficiencies. With this model, the position of a creditor in the insolvency may vary depending on where the assets of the debtor are located.[13] This leads to numerous difficulties: (i) the distribution of the assets is difficult to predict, and this increases the price of the credit due to the greater uncertainty associated with it; (ii) the debtor may be tempted, in collusion with certain creditors, to strategically transfer his or her assets from one country to another or to close the establishment which might constitute grounds for jurisdiction; (iii) the costs of conducting the proceedings are multiplied because instead of a single proceeding being held, there are as many as States in which the debtor has assets or establishments; and (iv) it obstructs decisions aimed, not at winding up the company, but at restructuring it. In general terms, it is easier to restructure a company when dealing with the whole than dealing with each individual part.

ii. Universal Model

Set against this, the universal insolvency model reflects the symmetrical advantages: (i) the law applicable is easy to predict; (ii) cross-border relocations of assets are irrelevant; and (iii) proceedings, being centralised, may reduce administrative costs arising from a plurality of proceedings and can therefore be conducted more efficiently. As previously mentioned, this is particularly relevant when the aim of the insolvency proceeding is to restructure the company. The restructuring of any company requires a high degree of cooperation between various parties. The administration and financial rescue of a company must be conducted in a centralised way because the company, from an economic point of view, has to constitute an integrated whole. Only the universal model guarantees that. And the same is true when the liquidation of assets of the debtor proves more efficient through the sale of the company as a going concern. No matter how much cooperation there is between the different territorial proceedings, it is much more difficult to guarantee the efficiency of decisions regarding the maintenance of the going concern value. The universal model increases the winding-up value of the company because it allows it to be sold intact.

Furthermore, (iv) by reducing the uncertainty and the possibilities for opportunism, it allows *ex ante* for a more efficient capital allocation, as it reduces the cost of the credit,[14] and it assigns the capital without distortions external to its economic profitability. (v) *Ex post* it reduces the rush by creditors to request the opening of insolvency proceedings (which can precipitate the insolvency itself). If the creditors know that the debtor can relocate assets to jurisdictions where the enforcement of their claims will be denied ('execution havens'), they will have an incentive to block and realise those assets as soon as possible. If the location of the assets is irrelevant (ie, wherever the assets are located they will be encompassed by the main insolvency proceedings), the incentive no longer applies.

[13] That is why it has been said in these cases that 'international bankruptcy is reduced to a game of musical chairs in which creditors cannot know in advance where the assets of the debtor will be located when the music stops'. Westbrook (n 6) 2309.

[14] Guzman (n 6) 2281.

However, in turn, the universal model also has drawbacks. Together with the fact that there may be cases in which a territorial insolvency may be more efficient in organisational terms, the problem faced by the implementation of the universal model is that it requires a sincere attitude of inter-State cooperation. A State will not be willing to 'sacrifice' its local creditors unless it has a full guarantee that the other States will behave in a reciprocal manner.

Thus, although scholars tend to agree that the best 'ideal' approach to cross-border insolvency is universality, lack of a complete international cooperation impedes a 'full' universalist approach. Instead, pragmatic considerations lead to balanced solutions that, moving towards universalism, make concessions to territorialism. The intermediate step that has become dominant is the so-called 'mitigated universalism'. In the following sections we discuss its different forms in some of the most relevant international insolvency instruments: the EU Insolvency Regulation (recast), the UNCITRAL Model Law and the UNCITRAL Legislative Guide. Although not covered in this contribution, mixed approaches are also taken in other international initiatives, referred to in a final section, eg, the Nordic Convention (below section VI).

III. EU Insolvency Regulation (Recast)

A. Background

On 5 June 1990, the European Convention on Certain Aspects of Insolvency was adopted in Istanbul. The Convention was opened for signature to the Members of the Council of Europe but never attracted sufficient attention, possibly because, almost immediately afterwards, a more ambitious text was adopted in the EU: the Convention on Insolvency Proceedings of 23 November 1995. It was signed by all Member States with the exception of the UK and this is the reason why it never entered into force. This Convention is, nevertheless, the immediate background to EC Regulation 1346/2000,[15] now superseded by the EU Insolvency Regulation recast (EIRr) adopted only a few years later. The EIRr may be considered as the most successful supranational instrument to deal with cross-border insolvencies and thus as a useful reference for any initiative of harmonisation at a worldwide level.

B. Content and Normative Model

In the European Union, the EIRr establishes a common private international law framework for cross-border insolvency, which extends to preventive restructuring procedures.[16] It applies in all Member States, with the exception of Denmark.[17]

[15] Council Regulation (EC) No 1346/2000 of 29 May 2000 on insolvency proceedings [2000] OJ L160. The text remained practically unchanged. This explains why, for the purposes of interpreting the EU Insolvency Regulation, regard was legitimately had to the Explanatory Report which accompanied the 1995 Convention (the so-called Virgós/Schmit Report). See M Virgós and F Garcimartín, *European Insolvency Regulation: Law and Practice* (Kluwer Law International 2004) 7.

[16] For the full reference see (n 2). The scope of application is defined in Art 1(1) and proceedings covered are listed in Annex A. Substantive law issues of preventive restructuring are harmonised at EU level through Directive (EU) 2019/1023 of the European Parliament and of the Council of 20 June 2019 on preventive restructuring frameworks, on discharge of debt and disqualifications, and on measures to increase the efficiency of procedures concerning restructuring, insolvency and discharge of debt, and amending Directive (EU) 2017/1132 (Directive on restructuring and insolvency).

[17] According to the Agreement on the Withdrawal of the United Kingdom of Great Britain and Northern Ireland from the European Union and the European Atomic Energy Community [2020] OJ L29/7 (Withdrawal Agreement), the EIRr

The EIRr lays down common rules on the four areas mentioned in the introduction: jurisdiction, applicable law, recognition and enforcement of judgments, and coordination and cooperation between insolvency proceedings. It also contains a set of uniform material rules on, eg, provision of information to creditors and lodgment of their claims.

The normative model which underlies the EIRr is modified or mitigated universality.[18] It permits the opening of insolvency proceedings in the Member State where the debtor has his or her centre of main interests and gives this process universal scope, on a worldwide basis. In principle, all assets, wherever they are situated, become subject to these proceedings; and all creditors of the debtor, irrespective of their nationality, domicile, residence, or registered office, can participate in them. Furthermore, for conflict of laws purposes, the Regulation is based upon the application of a single law, the law of the State of opening (*lex fori consursus principalis*), to both the procedural and the substantive aspects of the insolvency.

The Regulation establishes a series of rules which correct or mitigate the universality model. Basically, these rules can be divided into two groups.

First, rules which deal with the law applicable and establish exceptions to the application of the *lex fori concursus*. The insolvency effects upon certain pre-insolvency entitlements or rights are not subject to the law of the State where insolvency proceedings are opened, but rather to the national law(s) indicated by the operation of special connecting factors. Second, there are certain material rules for rights over assets located outside the State of opening of insolvency proceedings that provide for immunity vis-à-vis insolvency.

On the other hand, rules whose purpose is to permit the opening of territorial insolvency proceedings. The EIRr places a series of restrictions on the opening of territorial insolvency proceedings in order not to undermine the universality of the main proceedings. Thus: (a) territorial proceedings can only be opened when the debtor has an establishment; (b) the body of creditors is not limited territorially; and (c) the resulting proceedings are, to a certain extent, subordinated to the main proceedings, when both types of proceedings are opened.

C. Main Insolvency Proceedings

The first possibility provided for by the Regulation is the opening of main insolvency proceedings with universal scope. The only courts with jurisdiction to open main insolvency proceedings are those of the Member State where the debtor has its centre of main interests (Article 3 (1)). The Regulation defines the concept of 'centre of main interests' as the place where the debtor conducts the administration of its interests on a regular basis and which is ascertainable by third parties, and includes certain presumptions about its location. Thus, eg, in the case of a company or legal person, the place of the registered office shall be presumed to be the centre of its main interests in the absence of proof to the contrary (Article 3(1) second paragraph).

applied in the UK, and in the Member States in situations involving the UK, to insolvency proceedings provided that the main proceedings were opened before the end of the transition period, 31 December 2020.

[18] M Virgós, 'The 1995 European Community Convention on Insolvency Proceedings: an insider's view' [1998] *Forum Internationale* 6; W Lüke, 'Das europäische internationale Insolvenzrecht' [1998] *Zeitschrift für Zivilprozess (ZZP)* 275, 280–81, who discusses the different interpretations of the term universality in this context; J Taupitz, 'Das (zukünftige) europäische Internationale Insolvenzrecht-insbesondere aus international-privatrechtlicher Sicht-' [1998] *ZZP* 315, 324–25; C Dordi, 'La Convenzione dell'Unione Europea sulle procedure di insolvenza' [1997] 2 *Rivista Di Diritto Internazionale Privato e Processuale* 333, 339; L Fumagalli, 'Il regolamento comunitario sulle procedure di insolvenza' [2001] *Rivista di Diritto. Processuale* 677, 686–87.

There can only be one set of main insolvency proceedings. These proceedings encompass all assets of the debtor, both inside and outside that Member State, and all creditors, both national and foreign, can participate in them. Therefore, both the estate of the debtor and the body of creditors are universal. For these universal proceedings to be effective, the decisions taken in them must be recognised and enforced in the other States. Naturally, in the case of non-Member States, the Regulation is powerless: effectiveness depends on the law of the non-Member State in question, including any international agreement or conventions in force. In the case of a Member State, the Regulation itself ensures the cross-border recognition and enforcement of the decisions of the court of opening (Article 19 et seq). The principle of mutual recognition covers the powers of the insolvency practitioner appointed (Article 20).

In principle, the law of the State of opening will apply to all insolvency issues. This law governs the conditions for the opening of the insolvency proceedings, their conduct and their closure (Article 7). However, there are several conflict of laws rules which follow a different solution (Article 8 et seq): the effects of the insolvency proceedings on specific rights or relationships may be governed by a law other than that of the law of the State of opening. This is the case, eg, of rights in rem over assets located in another Member State (Article 8). The objective of these special rules is two-fold. On the one hand, substantive, as they seek to protect certain pre-insolvency rights or positions vis-à-vis the interference of foreign insolvency rules; and, on the other hand, procedural, since they try to facilitate the administration and management of the estate.

D. Territorial Proceedings

The exception to the idea of single insolvency proceedings with universal scope arises from the possibility provided for by the Regulation of opening territorial insolvency proceedings. These proceedings, however, can only be opened where the debtor has an establishment (Article 3(2)). Unlike the stricter territorial model, the Regulation does not consider the presence of assets of the debtor to be sufficient grounds for permitting the opening of territorial proceedings, but rather requires a more stable and lasting presence. Furthermore, in these cases, even where the 'estate' is strictly territorial (it only encompasses the assets of the debtor located in the State in question), the 'body of creditors' is universal, the proceedings are open to any creditor of the debtor, whether national or foreign, and whether or not their claim has derived from the activities of that establishment.

The reason for allowing a combination of universal proceedings and/or territorial proceedings can be explained in terms of information costs.[19] There may be cases in which a single set of main proceedings is efficient, others in which one or more territorial proceedings are efficient, and cases in which the combination of both is preferable: one size does not fit all. What the Regulation aims at doing is to allow those who possess the necessary information (eg, the creditors or the main liquidator) to choose the model best suited to each specific case while, nevertheless, preventing this choice from being made from purely opportunistic motives. For this reason, it can be said that the Regulation 'does not impose' a specific model, but rather allows those involved to choose one.

These territorial insolvency proceedings can be characterised as either secondary or independent proceedings, depending on whether the main proceedings have been opened or not. Both may be aimed at winding up or restructuring.

[19] Virgós, ibid, 6–7; Lüke, ibid, 282–83.

The Insolvency Regulation permits the opening of territorial insolvency proceedings in Member States, even when no main proceedings are pending. They deal with the insolvency of a part of the company, without the rest of the company being involved. 'Independent' insolvency proceedings can only be opened under two circumstances: either when so requested by 'local creditors' or local public authorities, or when it is not possible to open insolvency proceedings in the State where the debtor's centre of main interests is situated. In this way, the Regulation intends 'that cases where territorial insolvency proceedings are requested before the main insolvency proceedings are … limited to what is absolutely necessary' (recital 37).[20] Furthermore, if main insolvency proceedings are opened at a later point, these territorial proceedings become 'secondary' proceedings.

The Regulation also allows the opening of territorial insolvency proceedings alongside the main proceedings opened in another Member State. In this case, the territorial insolvency proceedings operate as secondary proceedings: they are conditioned by the main proceedings and may be subject to different measures of mandatory coordination, such as the obligation of the insolvency practitioners to cooperate and the directing role given to the liquidator of the main proceedings. Furthermore, the Regulation obliges any surplus assets remaining from the territorial proceedings to be 'transferred' to the main proceedings.

Territorial insolvency proceedings can meet certain needs such as the protection of local creditors or the more efficient administration of the debtor's assets; eg, there may be cases in which the assets of the debtor are too complex to be administered as a single unit or in which the differences between legal systems are so acute that it is preferable to limit the role of the *lex concursus principalis* (see recital 40). However, secondary insolvency proceedings may also hamper the efficient administration of the insolvency estate and therefore the Regulation has established two situations in which the court seised should be able to stay or even refuse the opening of such proceedings (recital 41). These limitations to the opening of territorial proceedings, which have been introduced by the recast of the Regulation, reinforce the role of main insolvency proceedings in the EIRr system.

First, to avoid the opening of secondary proceedings, the insolvency practitioner may give a unilateral undertaking in respect of assets located in the Member State where the debtor has an establishment, according to which the priorities and other rights of creditors will be determined by the law of such Member State when distributing those assets or the proceeds received from their realisation (Article 36). For that purpose, a sub-category of assets is created within the insolvency estate (recital 43). These proceedings, referred to as 'synthetic secondary proceedings', mirror the distribution that would have taken place in secondary proceedings, had they been opened, in the context of the main proceedings; ie, it is 'as if' secondary proceedings were opened. When such an undertaking is granted and if the insolvency practitioner so requests, courts shall refuse the opening of secondary proceedings, if they are satisfied that it 'adequately protects the general interests of local creditors' (Article 38(2)).

Second, where main pre-insolvency proceedings have been opened, in which a stay of enforcement has been granted to allow for negotiations with creditors, the court seised with a request to open territorial proceedings may also stay their opening for up to three months, upon request of the debtor in possession or the insolvency practitioner, 'provided that suitable measures are in place to protect the interests of local creditors' (Article 38(3)).

[20] M Balz, 'Das neue Europäische Insolvenzübereinkommen' [1996] *Zeitschrift für Wirtschaftrecht* 948, 949, who points out that the 1995 Insolvency Convention did not look favourably upon the opening of independent insolvency proceedings; the same is true for the EIRr.

Third, in the cases in which territorial proceedings are opened, the EIRr establishes cooperation and coordination rules which do not only apply to the insolvency practitioners but also to courts. The dominant role of the main insolvency practitioner is ensured by such rules which, eg, give him or her the possibility to intervene in the territorial proceedings. Furthermore, the EIRr has introduced cooperation and coordination rules for insolvency proceedings relating to two or more members of a group of companies (Article 56 et seq). The cooperation between insolvency practitioners may be established through 'agreements or protocols', notions that are not defined in the EIRr and which, as recital 49 states, may take many different forms, eg, written or oral, and may have different scopes. The only limitation is that they should be compatible with the national applicable law (each of the *lex fori concursus*) and be approved by courts 'where necessary'.

In contrast to the model of 'modified' or 'mitigated' universality provided by the Insolvency Regulation, Directive 2001/24/EC regarding the reorganisation and winding up of credit institutions and Directive 2001/17/EC regarding the reorganisation and winding up of insurance undertakings adopt a model of 'full' universality. The reorganisation or winding up is based on a single procedure with universal scope (see Articles 3 and 9, 4 and 8, respectively), and no territorial insolvency proceedings are allowed. Jurisdiction corresponds exclusively to the State of origin or 'home Member State' of the credit institution or insurance undertaking (Article 2 paragraphs 1 and 2, respectively). In both cases, a regime of exceptions to the *lex fori concursus* is established, which is parallel to that of the EIRr.

IV. UNCITRAL Model Laws

The main soft law instruments on international insolvency drafted by UNCITRAL are the 1997 UNCITRAL Model Law on cross-border insolvency, the 2018 UNCITRAL Model Law on recognition and enforcement of insolvency-related judgments and the 2004 and 2013 UNCITRAL Legislative Guides.

The 1997 UNICTRAL Model Law also follows a mitigated universalist model,[21] albeit a weaker form of it. This responds to the fact that the text was negotiated among a larger group of States coming from different traditions and therefore the final draft reflects a compromise among them. As a result, the Model Law's scope is narrower. It does not establish jurisdiction or an applicable law rule. It is more flexible, as a soft law instrument and enacting States are free to implement it as they wish and its own terms leave wide discretion to courts to make certain decisions. Despite the differences with the EIRr, at the Model Law's core is the modified universalist approach. It takes as a point of departure the opening of one set of main proceedings in the country of the debtor's centre of main interests, with the possibility to also open non-main (territorial) ones, and a principle of assistance and cooperation.

A closer look at the Model Law helps to better understand the normative model underlying it. The Model law does not provide for international jurisdiction or applicable law rules and

[21] See G McCormack and Wan Wai Yee, 'The UNCITRAL Model Law on Cross-Border Insolvency Comes of Age: New Times or New Paradigms' (2019) 54 *Texas International Law Journal* 273, 276; I Mevorach, 'On the Road to Universalism: A Comparative and Empirical Study of the UNCITRAL Model Law on Cross-Border Insolvency' (2011) 12 *European Business Organization Law Review* 517, 520; J Pottow, 'Procedural Incrementalism: a Model for International Bankruptcy' (2005) 45 *Virginia Journal of International Law* 935, 963–69; A Walters, 'Modified Universalisms & the Role of Local Legal Culture in the Making of Cross-Border Insolvency Law' (2019) 93 *American Bankruptcy Law Journal* 47, 64; JL Westbrook, 'Chapter 15 at Last' (2005) 79 *American Bankruptcy Law Journal* 713, 716.

therefore enacting States still apply their PIL rules in this regard. Rather, the Model Law focuses on recognition of foreign proceedings and cooperation between countries. Upon application (recognition is not automatic, see Article 15) an enacting State shall recognise (i) a foreign proceeding as main proceeding, if opened in the State where the debtor's centre of main interests is located, or (ii) as non-main, if opened where the debtor has an establishment (Article 17). As is apparent, the Model Law draws inspiration from EU terminology relating to the opening of universal and territorial proceedings, yet for different purposes (ie, recognition of foreign insolvency proceedings).[22]

The recognition of main proceedings triggers certain automatic effects, those essential to ensure the effectiveness of a foreign insolvency proceeding with universal effects (Article 20): stay of individual actions and executions and suspension of the right of the debtor to dispose of its assets. In addition, the courts of the enacting State may grant discretionary relief upon recognition of main or non-main foreign proceedings on some matters (Article 21). Importantly, this includes the handover of assets located in that jurisdiction to the foreign representative, provided, however, the court is satisfied that the interests of local creditors are adequately protected in the main proceedings (see Articles 21(2) and 22). The foreign representative has direct access to courts, including the legal standing to bring avoidance actions once the foreign proceeding has been recognised (Articles 23 and 24). In addition, the Model Law establishes cooperation provisions between national courts and the foreign court or foreign representative, which have a wide scope of application, making cooperation available, for instance, even before an application for recognition (Articles 25–27). The recognition of main foreign proceedings does not hamper the opening of local proceedings. These concurrent proceedings, referred to in Article 28, are only subject to one limitation: the presence of assets in that jurisdiction and that the proceedings' effects are limited to those assets. This provision shows that enacting States have a free hand in determining their jurisdictional rules to open proceedings and thus the mere presence of assets is sufficient. Such jurisdictional ground is not, however, considered for recognition.

The above overview of the Model Law shows a 'modified universalist' approach, even if more modest than that of the EIRr: there are some universalist elements (recognition of main proceedings, with certain automatic effects) and others that mitigate the model (possibility to open territorial proceedings, the fact that relief is discretionary or the protection of local creditors' interests). Yet, the Model Law is a non-binding instrument which needs to be enacted by States and, in so doing, they are free to design the model as they wish. Furthermore, the Model Law does not cover all international aspects of the insolvency. Notably, it is applicable law neutral. In addition, national courts may interpret the domestic instrument and exercise their discretion differently. The manner in which these elements are combined determines whether or not national legislation enacting the Model Law reflects its 'modified universalism' spirit and is operating in practice that way.

As of today, 49 States have enacted the Model Law.[23] Although legislation based on the Model Law and courts' approach vary across jurisdictions, one core feature is that, in principle, courts do recognise foreign proceedings, thus effectively promoting international cooperation

[22] The Guide to Enactment of the 1997 UNCITRAL Model Law expressly acknowledges that both the expression 'centre of main interest', together with the presumption according to which it is the debtor's registered office/habitual residence (paras 81–84 and 141), and the term 'establishment' (paras 88–89) correspond to the formulation in the EC Convention, superseded by the EIRr. Thus, according to the Guide to Enactment, the Virgós/Schmit report and the jurisprudence interpreting such concepts in the EIRr may also be relevant for the interpretation of the Model Law.

[23] See: uncitral.un.org/en/texts/insolvency/modellaw/cross-border_insolvency/status. Few EU Member States have adopted it. The reason may be that they also apply the EIRr *ad extra*. See Westbrook (n 21) 721.

in insolvency matters.[24] Differences arise mainly with regard to the effects of such recognition. Certain States have deviated from the Model Law, and have not established automatic effects upon recognition, eg, Japan.[25] Others, while recognising such automatic effects, take different approaches in relation to the discretionary relief that may be granted by courts and the exercise of avoidance actions by a foreign representative. These differences characterise the orientation of a domestic system towards a stronger or weaker form of modified universalism.[26]

Just by way of example to illustrate the point, US courts, in application of Chapter 15 of the Bankruptcy Code, which enacts the UNCITRAL Model Law in the US, often grant discretionary relief. For example, they entrust the distribution of debtor's assets located in the US to the foreign representative (section 1521), and they do so under foreign law (COMI law).[27] Even if the US courts retain the power to take into consideration the interests of US creditors and in practice frequently impose conditions on the entrustment, they take a stronger universalistic stance towards cross-border insolvency than some other countries which seldom, if ever, grant discretionary relief, eg, Japan.[28] Indeed, US courts go beyond the Model Law, which is applicable law neutral, and apply foreign law in this context, where other States do not, eg, the UK.[29]

The 2018 Model Law complements the 1997 Model Law by providing a regime for the recognition of foreign insolvency-related judgments, defined as those that 'arise[s] as a consequence of or [are] materially associated with an insolvency proceeding' and were 'issued on or after the commencement of that insolvency proceeding' (Article 2d).[30] Under the 2018 Model Law, insolvency-related judgments are recognised, provided that they meet certain requirements (Article 13) and unless there are grounds for refusal of recognition that a court may consider or certain indirect jurisdiction grounds, drafted in wide and flexible terms, are not satisfied (Articles 7 and 14).

V. UNCITRAL Legislative Guide

The Legislative Guide, which covers both substantive and PIL aspects of insolvency, provides a reference to national authorities for the enactment or modification of national insolvency laws for domestic and international situations. For each of the main insolvency issues that an insolvency law needs to cover, the Legislative Guide sets forth a commentary on the principal

[24] Empirical studies reaching this conclusion are, however, based on the available jurisprudence, which is to a large extent that of US courts. See Mevorach (n 21) 533–38; J Leong, 'Is Chapter 15 Universalist or Territorialist? Empirical Evidence form the United States Bankruptcy Court Cases' (2010), available at: papers.ssrn.com/sol3/papers.cfm?abstract_id=1690545, 7.

[25] See Mevorach (n 21) 528.

[26] Indeed, the Model Law has been considered as a step towards universalism. As Walters (n 21) 64–65 puts it, the Model Law is the universalism 'Trojan horse': its neutrality makes it easy to adopt the text and then opens the door for courts to behave 'universalistically'.

[27] See Mevorach (n 21) 543–45.

[28] Ibid, 549. However, see also Leong (n 24), *passim*, in relation to such conditions and qualifications.

[29] See Walters (n 21) 87–88. Given the relevance of the law applicable, the EU has recently submitted a proposal in support of future work by UNCITRAL in this regard. See: undocs.org/A/CN.9/995.

[30] See on the origins of the 2018 Model Law, JAE Pottow, 'The Dialogic Aspect of Soft Law in International Insolvency: Discord, Digression, and Development' (2019) 40 *Michigan Journal of International Law* 479, 483–86. Note that the definition of insolvency-related judgments deliberately differs from that of EU instruments. For status, see: uncitral.un.org/en/texts/insolvency/modellaw/mlij.

approaches to that topic. This is followed by a recommendation of what are considered best practices. In matters relating to cross-border insolvency, it provides recommendations on international jurisdiction and the law applicable. Additionally, it includes the 1997 Model Law in Annex III, whose enactment is recommended (recommendation 5).

The instrument's normative model goes along the same lines as the 1997 Model Law's. The Legislative Guide recommends establishing jurisdiction grounds based on the centre of main interests or on an establishment, as defined in the Model Law (recommendation 10), and the application of just one law, the *lex fori concursus*, subject to a limited number of exceptions (recommendations 31–34). In case of proceedings opened in the debtor's centre of main interests, the insolvency law should specify that the estate should include all assets wherever they are located (recommendation 36). Indeed, the Legislative Guide identifies a trend towards universalism and states that it is increasingly desirable that the estate has a universal scope. However, insofar as divergences in this regard remain, the Model Law provides a regime for recognition and enforcement which is compatible with the different approaches to cross-border insolvency and whose adoption is, as mentioned above, recommended by the Legislative Guide.

VI. Other Initiatives

Although a unilateral response by States is not the ideal approach to deal with competing national views on cross-border insolvency, supranational initiatives to foster cooperation in this area are – beyond those in the EU and the soft law instruments approved by UNCITRAL – still limited. Yet, there are some prominent historical examples.

Among them, first, the Montevideo Treaties of 1889 and 1940 on International Commercial Law, adopted in the First and Second South American Conference of Private International Law, respectively, which establish certain rules on international insolvency.[31] They take as a point of departure the opening of insolvency proceedings in the debtor's domicile, while retaining strong territoriality elements, eg, the opening of other insolvency proceedings where independent establishments ('commercial houses') are located, which are run separately, or the fact that, even if there is only one set of proceedings, local creditors have priority over assets located in that jurisdiction.[32]

Another Latin American instrument, the Bustamante Code, was adopted at Havana in 1928 in the Sixth Conference of American States. Its international insolvency rules show a less protectionist approach.[33] It provides for the opening of just one set of insolvency proceedings in the debtor's domicile (if there is only one domicile) in relation to all assets and liabilities located in Contracting States. The insolvency practitioner appointed can exercise its powers in other Contracting States and decisions made have extraterritorial effects, subject to publicity and other requirements, where appropriate. In case there is more than one domicile (understood as establishments with an entirely separate economic activity), there can be as many insolvency proceedings as independent establishments.[34]

[31] See KH Nadelmann, 'Bankruptcy Treaties' (1944) 93 *University of Pennsylvania Law Review* 58, 69–70. The 1940 Treaty introduced only minor changes to the original treaty. Argentina, Bolivia, Colombia, Uruguay and Peru, are Parties to the 1889 Treaty and Argentina, Paraguay and Uruguay to the 1940 Treaty.

[32] See Arts 35–53. The local creditors' priority was added in the 1940 Treaty.

[33] Nadelmann (n 31) 70; 16 States are Party to it.

[34] Arts 414 et seq Bustamante Code. See Omar (n 6) 188–89.

A contemporary text with the Bustamante Code is the Nordic Bankruptcy Convention, adopted in 1933 by Denmark, Iceland, Norway, Finland and Sweden.[35] The instrument does not establish direct jurisdiction rules but rather indirect jurisdiction rules and it is limited to 'domiciliary bankruptcies', ie, insolvencies opened in the Contracting State where the debtor has its residence or seat. Those proceedings have universal scope, ie, they cover assets located in any Contracting State, the law of the place of the opening of proceedings is generally applicable and decisions have extraterritorial effect. Contracting States are free to establish other grounds of jurisdiction, but in that case the rules on recognition provided by the Convention do not apply.[36]

Other initiatives were pursued at the end of the twentieth century. Notwithstanding some of them never entered into force, they had a decisive influence on later texts. Thus, eg, the European experience offered an important reference for the elaboration of the OHADA Uniform Law on Insolvency Procedures 1998, which includes certain rules on cross-border insolvency.[37]

VII. Concluding Remarks

Territorialism and universalism, as ideal models which provide different answers to problems posed by cross-border insolvency, have inspired international insolvency laws across the globe. At least at a theoretical level, the latter is increasingly considered to be the goal to which legislation should strive. However, large divergences among national laws remain in practice and international cooperation is limited. Driven by practical considerations, the main harmonisation initiatives put forward in the last decades, the EIRr and the UNCITRAL Model Laws and Legislative Guides, have embraced an intermediate model, modified universalism, in which universalism is tempered by concessions to territorialism. Previous instruments paved the way in this direction, eg, the Montevideo Treaties, the Bustamante Code and the Nordic Convention.[38] The dominant modified universalism approach, however, crystallises differently in the various instruments. There is still much work to do at a worldwide level to offer economic actors a sound legal framework on cross-border insolvencies. The next step in this direction will perhaps be the adoption in the context of UNCITRAL of an instrument on applicable law, guided by the principle of modified universalism, which fills the gap that the Model Laws have left in an area where national laws take divergent approaches giving rise to inconsistencies and legal uncertainty.

[35] Note, however, the application of EU insolvency rules, discussed above, in Sweden and Finland.

[36] See M Bogdan, 'Sweden' (1995) 4 *International Insolvency Review* 72, 73–74.

[37] OHADA is the Organization for the Harmonization of Business Law in Africa, of which 17 States are members. See Omar (n 6) 191–92.

[38] 2013 Guide to Enactment (n 3) 22.

25

Intellectual Property

PAUL TORREMANS

I. Introduction

When one thinks of the progressive global unification of private international law the Conventions concluded in the framework of the Hague Conference come to mind immediately. In combination with the request to write a chapter on intellectual property for this book it made me think that I should decline the offer. Intellectual property and private international law do not make for a smooth combination and this applies to such an extent that intellectual property is seen in The Hague as the ultimate troublemaker. Leaving negotiations that ultimately failed aside, it suffices to look at the Convention of 2 July 2019 on the Recognition and Enforcement of Foreign Judgments in Civil or Commercial Matters. At the end of long discussions Article 2(1)(m) excludes intellectual property from the scope of the Convention.[1] The 2005 Convention on Choice of Court Agreements[2] is slightly less radical in its exclusion of intellectual property from its scope in its Article 2(2):

> n) the validity of intellectual property rights other than copyright and related rights;
>
> o) infringement of intellectual property rights other than copyright and related rights, except where infringement proceedings are brought for breach of a contract between the parties relating to such rights, or could have been brought for breach of that contract.

The fact that intellectual property and private international law do not fit together smoothly is better understood if one looks at the roots of the international intellectual property system (that are still very much its main principles). The international intellectual property rights system, as it was conceived in the Paris Convention 1883 and the Berne Convention 1886, shuns the

[1] Not yet in force: www.hcch.net/en/instruments/conventions/full-text/?cid=137. For an explanation of the scope of the intellectual property exclusion in the Convention, see the explanatory report by F Garcimartín and G Saumier, *Explanatory Report on the 2019 HCCH Judgments Convention* (HCCH 2020), available at: www.hcch.net/en/instruments/conventions/publications1/?dtid=3&cid=137, paras 64–65. Some judgments involving intellectual property rights are within the scope of the Convention because the intellectual property questions were not the object of the proceedings (see para 43) or because the judgment is better characterised as contractual than intellectual property: 'The relevant criterion to define the scope of the exclusion is … whether the judgment to be recognised or enforced was mainly based on general contract law or on intellectual property law' (para 65).

[2] In force since 1 October 2015, available at: assets.hcch.net/docs/510bc238-7318-47ed-9ed5-e0972510d98b.pdf. See the Explanatory Report by T Hartley and M Dogauchi, *Explanatory Report on the Convention of 30 June 2005 on Choice of Court Agreements* (Permanent Bureau of the Hague Conference on Private International Law 2005), available at: www.hcch.net/en/publications-and-studies/details4/?pid=3959 especially paras 33–39, 71–81 and 196–201.

creation of transnational intellectual property rights that are valid and apply across borders. Instead, the principle of national treatment, the governing principle in both Conventions, gives rise to a purely territorial system, where national rights are granted on a country-by-country basis and foreign creators and inventors are given access to these national systems in each of the Contracting States. That access is created by treating the foreign author as a national author and in relation to patents and trademarks that is coupled with the right of priority, not merely to allow the applicant to meet the registration requirement country by country, but also to allow the intellectual property right to be held by the same right-holder at the cross-border level.[3] It is also important to point out that intellectual property rights are in essence negative rights, ie, they give their owner the right to stop others from committing certain acts such as reproducing the copyright work or communicating it to the public, using a confusingly similar mark for identical goods or services or making the patented product. That results in rights and their enforcement being two sides of the same coin and it gives a high importance to remedies inside each national intellectual property regime. Add to that the involvement of national registration agencies in patent and trademark law, but not in copyright, and one has a system whose roots seem to operate on a country-by-country basis, whilst ignoring the international element that could trigger the application of private international law.

That territorial country-by-country system stands in sharp contrast to the modern business reality that sees intellectual property rights exploited across borders.[4] Intellectual property rights are often applied for and exploited in many countries. In such cases, many of these rights may be involved in a single infringement action or similar infringing acts may have been committed in the various jurisdictions. And when intellectual property rights are exploited internationally that exploitation may also give rise to transnational litigation. As a result of that combination of national intellectual property rights and remedies and international exploitation, private international law plays an increasingly important role in this area, but the interaction between intellectual property and private international law gives rise to complex issues, both at the jurisdictional level (which court will decide the case)[5] and at the applicable law level (which law will that court apply).[6] The territorial country-by-country approach will also remain a fundamental principle that the rules of private international law need to reflect.

II. Jurisdiction

At first glance, national treatment is about granting rights or, in private international law terms, about applicable law. That means that, in general, the standard private international law rules on jurisdiction can be applied to intellectual property law cases.

[3] L Lundstedt, 'Territoriality in Intellectual Property Law: A comparative study of the interpretation and operation of the territoriality principle in the resolution of transborder intellectual property infringement disputes with respect to international civil jurisdiction, applicable law and the territorial scope of application of substantive intellectual property law in the European Union and United States' (Stockholm University 2016), available at: su.diva-portal.org/smash/get/diva2:972658/FULLTEXT01.pdf.

[4] JJ Fawcett and P Torremans, *Intellectual Property and Private International Law*, 2nd edn (Oxford University Press 2011) 146–49.

[5] L Lundstedt, 'Jurisdiction and the principle of territoriality in intellectual property law' (2001) 32 *International Review of Intellectual Property and Competition Law (IIC)* 124.

[6] See Fawcett and Torremans (n 4). See also European Max Planck Group on Conflict of Laws in Intellectual Property, Conflict of Laws in *Intellectual Property: The CLIP Principles and Commentary* (Oxford University Press 2013) (*CLIP Principles*).

A. Choice of Court Agreements and Exclusive Jurisdiction

The Choice of Court Convention is a good example here. Parties to an intellectual property dispute are free to choose the court before which they wish to bring their case. Examples of this are cases about entitlement to an intellectual property right, ownership cases and cases of copyright infringement. The problem arises when one deals with a registered intellectual property right, such as a patent or a trademark. These are granted by an intellectual property office that is traditionally seen as an organ of the State. The issue of the validity of such a right then becomes a question whether or not an organ of the State made a mistake. National rules on private international law then tend to reserve that matter for the national courts of the State involved. That means that a choice of court by the parties is ruled out when it comes to cases that are concerned with the validity of a registered right and hence the exclusion from the scope of the Choice of Court Convention. These are cases that are essentially brought to invalidate an intellectual property right and to remove it from the register. Matters become more complex when the case is brought as an infringement case and the issue of invalidity is brought up by the defendant (one cannot after all infringe an invalid right). In many countries this can be done in one single case before a single court. The complication that arises then is what the court, which one assumes is not the court of the country of registration, needs to do. Does it lose its jurisdiction merely because the invalidity point is raised? The Choice of Court Convention excludes from its scope infringement of registered intellectual property rights. That indeed avoids the problem, but the exclusion becomes unjustifiably broad. The provision redeems itself marginally by acknowledging that in a contractual setting freedom of choice is the norm and by deriving from that that the exclusion for infringement cases will not extend to cases where infringement proceedings are brought for breach of a contract between the parties relating to such rights, or where proceedings could have been brought for breach of that contract.[7]

But there is even more detail and flexibility to be discovered if one looks in a bit more detail at the exclusive jurisdiction picture. Exclusive jurisdiction for validity cases concerning registered rights takes in the European Union the form of Article 24(4) of the Brussels Ia Regulation.[8]

The way that provision was interpreted by the Court of Justice of the European Union (CJEU) in the *GAT v LUK* case[9] boils down to the extreme suggestion that as soon as validity is raised the exclusive jurisdiction of the court of the country of registration kicks in and any other court needs to stop its proceedings, eg, in an infringement case. This is not the place to repeat all the criticism that has been raised against the *GAT v LUK* decision.[10] Suffice it

[7] See the Explanatory Report (n 2) 79–81.

[8] 'The following courts of a Member State shall have exclusive jurisdiction, regardless of the domicile of the parties:

…

(4) in proceedings concerned with the registration or validity of patents, trademarks, designs, or other similar rights required to be deposited or registered, irrespective of whether the issue is raised by way of an action or as a defence, the courts of the Member State in which the deposit or registration has been applied for, has taken place or is under the terms of an instrument of the Union or an international convention deemed to have taken place'. Other countries adopt similar approaches: *Voda v Cordis* 476 F 3d 887 (2007) (US); *TS Production LLC v Drew Pictures Pty Ltd* [2008] FCAFC 194 (Australia); *Gallo Africa v Sting Music* [2010] ZASCA 96 (South Africa).

[9] C-4/03 *Gesellschaft für Antriebstechnik mbH & Co KG (GAT) v Lamellen und Kupplungsbau Beteiligungs KG (LUK)* [2006] ECR I-6509.

[10] See A Kur, 'A Farewell to Crossborder Injunctions? The ECJ Decisions *GAT v LuK* and *Roche Nederland v Primus and Goldenberg*' (2006) *IIC* 37, 844–55; PLC Torremans, 'The widening reach of exclusive jurisdiction: Where can you litigate IP rights after GAT?' in A Nuyts (ed), *International Litigation in Intellectual Property and Information Technology* (Kluwer 2008) 61–77; PLC Torremans, 'Overcoming *GAT*: The way ahead for cross-border intellectual property litigation in Europe' (2008) 7 *Tijdschrift@IPR.be* 65–79; PLC Torremans, 'The way forward for cross-border intellectual property litigation: Why *GAT* cannot be the answer' in S Leibel and A Ohly (eds), *Intellectual Property and Private International Law* (Mohr Siebeck 2009) 191–210.

to say it is not an example that other countries should follow. It is submitted that the much better way forward is to restrict the exclusive validity jurisdiction to cases that are brought to invalidate a registered intellectual property right and to separate counterclaims to that effect in infringement cases. These scenarios would after all lead to a decision on validity that is valid *erga omnes* and, if invalidated, the right would be deleted in the register. But when the validity point is raised as a mere defence in an infringement case whose outcome will only bind the parties there is no need to apply the exclusive jurisdiction argument. Such an *inter partes* decision on an invalidity defence would after all not bind other parties and the register would not be altered. A separate validity case can be brought and is needed to oblige the registrar to change the register. This is the suggestion made by the CLIP group in Article 2:401 of the CLIP Principles.[11] The most important advantage of this approach is that it allows the consolidation of cases. That means that one court will be able to deal with the (alleged) infringement of various parallel (territorial) intellectual property rights. In turn that reduces the risk of divergent outcomes in parallel cases.

The Choice of Court Convention provides support for this approach, even if the restriction to choice of court agreement scenarios makes the result look a bit opaque. Article 2(3) of the Convention states indeed that the validity of registered intellectual property rights is not excluded from the scope of the Convention where the matter arises merely as a preliminary question and not as an object of the proceedings. In particular, the mere fact that a matter excluded under paragraph 2 arises by way of defence does not exclude proceedings from the Convention, if that matter is not an object of the proceedings. The standard scenario where the parties could nevertheless make a choice of court agreement would then be infringement proceedings, but these are excluded from the scope. That is therefore even more regrettable and, as argued above, it was not necessary. But this is not the end of the story. The Convention may in the end not create the choice of court option in many intellectual property cases, but national private international law systems may. And then Article 10 of the Convention provides a way forward. A national decision based on a choice of court agreement will not be refused recognition, unless separate validity proceedings are brought in the State of registration. This makes a lot of sense, as validity is raised by the defendant in the infringement proceedings. If that stops the infringement proceedings in their tracks that party has little incentive to bring validity proceedings in the court with exclusive jurisdiction. By at least not refusing recognition in those cases where the court dealing with the infringement case also rules on the validity point the Convention reduces that problem. In the words of the Convention the solution is as follows:

> However, in the case of a ruling on the validity of an intellectual property right other than copyright or a related right, recognition or enforcement of a judgment may be refused or postponed under the preceding paragraph only where –
>
> (a) that ruling is inconsistent with a judgment or a decision of a competent authority on that matter given in the State under the law of which the intellectual property right arose; or
>
> (b) proceedings concerning the validity of the intellectual property right are pending in that State.[12]

[11] *CLIP Principles* (n 6) 138 et seq.

[12] See the Explanatory Report (n 2) 198–201.

B. The Pitfalls of the Standard Jurisdiction Rules

This is as far as the Hague Conference originating rules bring us in relation to jurisdiction in intellectual property cases. That brings us to the standard jurisdiction rules that are found in almost any national system of private international law. Their application to intellectual property cases can give rise to issues, so let us take the EU system as an example.

Jurisdiction in the intellectual property area is governed by the Brussels Ia Regulation.[13] The rules of that Regulation apply to intellectual property and that results, outside the areas of exclusive jurisdiction, choice of court and submission, in a standard rule that the defendant can always be sued in the courts of the country where he or she is domiciled (Article 4). That rule does not create particular difficulties for intellectual property cases and neither does the alternative rule for contractual issues which is found in Article 7(1). When it comes to infringement of intellectual property rights, the tort rule in Article 7(2) gives the claimant another alternative. The concept of the place where the harmful event occurred or may occur does cause some problems of interpretation in an intellectual property context. Parallel territorial intellectual property rights may result in damage occurring in several jurisdictions. The court in each of these jurisdictions will only have jurisdiction to hear the case in relation to the local damage as a result of the *Shevill* case[14] (the court of the defendant's domicile under Article 4 is still available to hear the whole case). The latter case also refers to the act leading to the damage and gives jurisdiction to the courts of the place where the defendant has its establishment. It may be better in an intellectual property context to replace that by the place where the infringement takes place.

In the context of Article 7(2) one needs to identify the place where the infringing act takes place and the place where the damage that flows directly from that act occurs. Once that has occurred, the court, which has jurisdiction to hear the case on the basis of Article 7(2), is easily identified and that court can then deal with the matters of substantive law that arise in the case. It therefore makes real sense to reserve points of substantive law for the substantive case and thus leave them out of the jurisdiction debate. Places where acts take place and where damage arises are much more fact related. The CJEU therefore grounds its jurisdiction approach under Article 7(2) in a purely factual analysis. That should improve levels of predictability and legal certainty, and most importantly it should avoid the jurisdiction stage turning into a mini-trial on substance. The approach should save time by disposing quickly and efficiently of the jurisdiction point. The original decision in the *Melzer* case[15] demonstrates that clearly. Mr Melzer and the investment company with whom he dealt were based in Germany, but the money was invested (and subsequently largely lost) by an associate of the latter based in London. Mr Melzer wanted to bring his case for compensation in tort using the first leg of Article 7(2), ie, the place where the act leading to the damage was committed. That was logically speaking England, but Mr Melzer argued on the basis of German national tort law that it could also be in Germany. German tort law contains a rule that states that each of the parties involved is liable for unlawful acts undertaken in common. That rule would cover the German company and its English affiliate

[13] Reg (EU) No 1215/2012 of the European Parliament and of the Council of 12 December 2012 on jurisdiction and the recognition and enforcement of judgments in civil and commercial matters [2012] OJ L351/1.
[14] C-68/93 *Shevill and Others v Presse Alliance SA* [1995] ECR I-415.
[15] C-228/11 *Melzer v MF Global UK Ltd* EU:C:2013:305.

and on the basis of it Mr Melzer wanted to impute the unlawful behaviour of the affiliate, who clearly was the perpetrator who committed the act, on the German defendant and on that basis bring his Article 7(2) case in Germany. That was after all the more cost-efficient option for him. The CJEU refused to consider elements of substantive German tort law and interpreted Article 7(2) in the sense that it does not allow the courts of the place where a harmful event occurred, which is imputed to one of the presumed perpetrators of damage, who is not a party to the dispute, to take jurisdiction over another presumed perpetrator of that damage who has not acted within the jurisdiction of the court seised.[16] Only purely factual elements could be taken into account and these all pointed to England. The rule also applies if one leaves the substantive law element out. In a case with several perpetrators Article 7(2) does not allow one of them to be sued in a country where he or she did not act.[17]

Shortly after the CJEU rendered its judgment in *Melzer*, the *Pinckney* case[18] turned the attention to the second limb of Article 7(2), ie, the place of the damage, in a copyright context. Mr Pinckney had been a singer and he saw CDs that contained recordings of his music for sale via a website accessible from his home in France. He bought these and they were duly delivered to his home, but the royalty payment for the use of his music and the recordings did not follow. By the time the case reached the courts the website had disappeared, leaving Mediatech, the Austrian company which had physically produced the CDs, as the sole defendant. The basis for the jurisdiction of the French court was therefore the fact that the website was accessible in France and that delivery without royalty payment took place there, ie, the place of the damage in the second limb of Article 7(2) was in France. The CJEU endorsed that approach, as it is a logical application of its factual approach with access to the website and failure to pay royalties both located in France. That conclusion applied despite the fact that Mediatech had in no way acted in France, but the somewhat peculiar aspects of copyright liability (and even more so the specific provisions of the French Code de la Propriété Intellectuelle) can be left to one side here.[19] The CJEU applied its *Shevill* doctrine here too and limited the jurisdiction of the court to local damage,[20] but that does not avert the risk that factual access to the website as a basis for jurisdiction potentially grants such 'local damage' jurisdiction to courts in any country around the world. The *Pinckney* case merely dealt with a 'poor' individual musician who wanted to bring a case in a single court, but the impact of the decision is potentially much wider – and much more risky, as Advocate-General Jääskinen pointed out to no avail in the trademark/unfair competition case *Coty Germany*.[21] It is in that respect worth adding that the French Supreme Court applied that same approach at global level outside the Brussels Ia Regulation when it based the jurisdiction of the French courts over a US company on the fact that its website on which it sold T-shirts with a copyright protected photograph printed on them was accessible in France.[22]

The real danger of the CJEU's approach became apparent in the *Hejduk* case.[23] In this case, any hard copy element, such as the delivery of CDs in one location, disappears and the alleged

[16] Ibid, para 41.

[17] C-387/12 *Hi Hotel HCF SARL v Uwe Spoering* EU:C:2014:215 and C-360/12 *Coty Germany GmbH, formerly Coty Prestige Lancaster Group GmbH v First Note Perfumes NV* EU:C:2014:1318.

[18] C-170/12 *Pinckney v KDG Mediatech AG* EU:C:2013:635.

[19] See the decision of the Cour de cassation in case n°10-15.890, available at: www.courdecassation.fr/jurisprudence_2/premiere_chambre_civile_568/33_22_28276.html.

[20] *Pinckney* (n 18) para. 47. See also *Hi Hotel* (n 17).

[21] *Coty Germany* (n 17).

[22] Cour de cassation, Cass 1re Civ, 22/01/2014, case 11-26822 *Korda v Onion/The Onion*, FR:CCASS:2014:C100060.

[23] C-441/13 *Hejduk v EnergieAgentur.NRW GmbH* EU:C:2015:28.

infringement takes place entirely on the internet through a website that is accessible in every single country. Ms Hejduk is an Austrian photographer who specialises in photographs of buildings and the work of specific architects. She had granted EnergieAgentur, a German company, a licence to use some of her photographs in an exhibition, but later found out that they were, or remained, available on the website of EnergieAgentur without her consent. That could have given rise to a case on the basis of breach of contract and the German courts could have been chosen as the courts of the country where the defendant company is based, but Ms Hejduk opted to sue in tort for copyright infringement. The question then arose whether she could use Article 7(2) to sue EnergieAgentur in the courts in Austria. The CJEU answered that question in the affirmative. In doing so it repeated that the place of the damage (where a claim for local damage can be brought) is every place where the website is accessible. In this case both the architect and the photographer were Austrian and if one leaves to one side the concerns surrounding the fact that this is a kind of a *forum actoris*, one is bound to conclude that there is a strong link between the case and Austria, which makes the Austrian courts suitable courts to hear the case. But Ms Hejduk could have sued EnergieAgentur anywhere on the basis of this approach. This turns the CJEU's argument of legal certainty and predictability into a weird form of certainty and predictability, to say the least. One must hope that the claimant will only sue in a jurisdiction where there is sizeable local damage, but the risk of harassment by a claimant that takes a punitive approach cannot be ruled out and the defendant may be forced to defend cases on substance in jurisdictions that have an almost non-existent link with the case. One is almost obliged to ask whether it does not make more sense to require that there is targeting of the jurisdiction by the defendant or serious damage in the jurisdiction before jurisdiction can be established on this basis (whilst that will then in copyright/ubiquitous circumstances allow one to drop the restriction to local damage only).[24] Or one may wish to be reminded of the French case *Samuel v BBC* where the Cour de cassation held that access in the jurisdiction to programmes that another party had put on line via YouTube, despite the fact that the BBC was only accessible via a subscription service, was sufficient to grant the French courts jurisdiction, as the mere factual requirement of access to the website (one way or another and by whichever party) had been met.[25]

Whilst it makes sense to avoid entering into the full detail of substantive law at the jurisdiction stage these cases have demonstrated that an approach relying purely on factual elements is not suitable for intellectual property cases. Trademark and patent cases are less of a risk as the registration requirement stops them from acquiring a global scope, but the combination of copyright infringement and the internet is lethal and could give rise to cases in each and every jurisdiction of the planet. Many of these would ultimately fail or give rise to minimal damages, but the alleged infringer would have to defend the case on substance and the cost and uncertainty associated with that is unacceptable from a sound administration of justice point of view. It also makes a mockery of the much-trumpeted values of predictability and legal certainty. Think about the website of a small local charity in a minority language (ie, impossible to read for the majority of global citizens) that contains a small part of a copyright work covered by an exception in the local copyright law and that charity having to defend cases all over the world as the website is by its nature accessible everywhere. What seemed so logical and sensible in the *Melzer* case achieves exactly the opposite in such copyright cases.

[24] See Art 2:203 *CLIP Principles* (n 6).
[25] Cass 1re Civ, 22/01/2014, case 11-24019, *Samuel v BBC* FR:CCASS:2014:C100039.

C. A Way Forward

Irrespective of the internal EU question whether the case law still allows courts to require that the claimant has an arguable case before taking jurisdiction,[26] requiring an arguable case may well be a way forward to curb the potential excesses of this factual approach. Intellectual property is also in this sense a bit peculiar. The territorial nature of intellectual property rights leads to the conclusion that there can only be infringement of an intellectual property right if both the (allegedly) infringing act and the damage that results from it take place in the same country. Infringement necessarily involves both elements. And one way or another these elements must result from the activity of the defendant. The arguable case threshold therefore translates into what intellectual property lawyers tend to call targeting. In order to understand in detail what that involves it is probably easiest to take the CLIP proposal as an example.

The starting point is the infringement jurisdiction provision that builds in a clause that cuts out the potential excess:

> Article 2:202: Infringement
>
> In disputes concerned with infringement of an intellectual property right, a person may be sued in the courts of the State where the alleged infringement occurs or may occur, *unless the alleged infringer has not acted in that State to initiate or further the infringement and her/his activity cannot reasonably be seen as having been directed to that State.*[27]

That saves the local charity and their website in the example given above. The Article 7(2) Brussels Ia style provision is retained, but the argument is that there will not be an arguable case if the defendant did not act in the State concerned to initiate or to further the infringement and at the same time their activity cannot reasonably be seen to have been directed to that State. Under the first limb there will be both an act and resulting damage in that State, eg, through the unauthorised manufacturing of a patented product, whereas the second limb takes into account that one can target a jurisdiction by merely directing one's activity to that State, eg, by uploading in the UK a copyright work such as a movie in Portuguese without permission onto a website offering access to movies in Portuguese and Spanish. By doing this, one clearly directs one's activity to at least Portugal and Brazil and one targets these markets. In copyright terms there will be an unauthorised act of communication to the public in the UK, but also in Portugal and Brazil, and that act will result in local damage. Similarly, the use of a trademark on a website will amount to unauthorised use in the course of trade in the countries to which activities have been directed (eg, through use of the local language and the option to order from those countries) and there will also be a consequential loss of earnings in these countries. Once more one sees the combination of act and damage in a single jurisdiction.

What flows from such an approach and from the concept of territoriality, is that the extent of the court's jurisdiction is limited to its own country. In an internet infringement scenario that could potentially give rise to cases being brought in all the countries of the planet. That is undesirable. One needs to avoid a scenario where there is an arguable case anywhere and cases are being brought country by country. That would rule out an efficient administration of justice and it could make it virtually impossible for a holder of intellectual property rights to enforce its rights (effectively). Hence the suggestion that a single case can be brought when infringement

[26] *Aspen Underwriting Limited and others v Credit Europe Bank NV* [2018] EWCA Civ 2590. See also P Torremans (gen ed) et al, *Cheshire, North & Fawcett: Private International Law*, 15th edn (Oxford University Press 2017) ch 11.

[27] Art 2:202 *CLIP Principles* (n 6) 69 et seq (italics added).

of intellectual property rights takes place through ubiquitous media. Such an exceptional rule is not necessary if the court of the habitual residence of the defendant is a suitable forum as a result of the infringement of the intellectual property right having a substantial effect there. And one should also not give the claimant the freedom to pick just any jurisdiction. Infringement/tort jurisdiction does after all require a link between the court and the facts of the case. In CLIP terms that results in the following provision:

Article 2:203: Extent of jurisdiction over infringement claims

(1) Subject to paragraph 2, a court whose jurisdiction is based on Article 2:202 shall have jurisdiction in respect of infringements that occur or may occur within the territory of the State in which that court is situated.

(2) In disputes concerned with infringement carried out through ubiquitous media such as the Internet, the court whose jurisdiction is based on Article 2:202 shall also have jurisdiction in respect of infringements that occur or may occur within the territory of any other State, provided that the activities giving rise to the infringement have no substantial effect in the State, or any of the States, where the infringer is habitually resident (Article 2:102) and (a) substantial activities in furtherance of the infringement in its entirety have been carried out within the territory of the country in which the court is situated, or (b) the harm caused by the infringement in the State where the court is situated is substantial in relation to the infringement in its entirety.[28]

III. Applicable Law

Once the court has established that it has jurisdiction to deal with the case it determines the applicable law under its own rules of private international law. There is not merely an absence of Hague Conference originating rules on this point. Most national laws on private international law contain no specific rules on the law applicable to intellectual property related issues. Despite this, there is a relative degree of consistency between the various national approaches.

A. The *lex loci protectionis*

That consistency goes back to the idea of territoriality that is found in the Paris and Berne Conventions. The Berne Convention and the copyright example will clarify this matter. In an era where the main connecting factor was nationality and where entitlement to the benefits of national copyright laws was linked to nationality (or later to first publication in the jurisdiction) the creation of an international copyright system through a full harmonisation of copyright rules and the creation of an international copyright was clearly a goal that was far too ambitious. National treatment was the easier alternative. In essence, one ignores the foreign nationality of the author and gives the foreign author who is a national of one of the Contracting States access to the national copyright system of each of the other Contracting States. That allows these national copyright systems to remain unchanged. That principle is enshrined in Article 5(1) of the Berne Convention 1886 and it leads to territoriality. What interests us, however, more for our current

[28] Art 2:203 *CLIP Principles* (n 6) 85 et seq.

purposes is the somewhat irrational conclusion that Article 5(2) of the Berne Convention drew from it:[29]

> Article 5: Rights Guaranteed:
>
> (1) Authors shall enjoy, in respect of works for which they are protected under this Convention, in countries of the Union other than the country of origin, the rights which their respective laws do now or may hereafter grant to their nationals, as well as the rights specially granted by this Convention.
>
> (2) The enjoyment and the exercise of these rights shall not be subject to any formality; such enjoyment and such exercise shall be independent of the existence of protection in the country of origin of the work. *Consequently, apart from the provisions of this Convention, the extent of protection, as well as the means of redress afforded to the author to protect his rights, shall be governed exclusively by the laws of the country where protection is claimed.*[30]

The territorial country-by-country approach is translated into the application of the local copyright law on a country-by-country basis. Territoriality is turned into an applicable law rule. Arguably, one could satisfy the national treatment requirement by merely granting each author the same applicable law rule, eg, the law of their country of origin. That might be more workable than the sheer endless patchwork of national laws applied on a country-by-country basis.[31] But irrespective of whether one can squeeze this into the constraints of Article 5(2)[32] this is no longer an option. Article 3 of the TRIPS Agreement 1994 copied the national treatment rule and then the draftsmen tried to be helpful and added a footnote that said that it refers to right-holders being granted the same substantive protection. It may not have been intended that way, but in practice it means that in applicable law terms the world is stuck with the law of the country for which protection is sought and that law will be applied on a distributive country by country basis.[33]

The CLIP Principles come to the same conclusion:

> Article 3:102: Lex protectionis
>
> The law applicable to existence, validity, registration, scope and duration of an intellectual property right and all other matters concerning the right as such is the law of the State for which protection is sought.[34]

In turn, that has implications when it comes to the applicable law rule for the infringement of an intellectual property right.[35] Apart from being territorial rights, intellectual property rights are also negative rights. A patent for a new and inventive product does not give its owner the right to make and sell that product. It merely gives its owner the right to stop all others from making the patented product over a 20-year period.

In copyright the right-holder has the right to prohibit the reproduction of the copyright work or its communication to the public by any party that does not have his or her consent. That means that existence and scope of an intellectual property right on the one hand, and the infringement of an intellectual property right on the other, are two sides of the same coin. A negative right

[29] See: wipolex.wipo.int/en/text/283698.

[30] Italics added.

[31] For further details, see Fawcett and Torremans (n 4) ch 12.

[32] P Torremans, 'The Law Applicable to Copyright Infringement on the Internet' [2016] *Nederlands internationaal privaatrecht* 687.

[33] See Fawcett and Torremans (n 4) ch 13.

[34] Art 3:102 *CLIP Principles* (n 6) 229 et seq.

[35] For further details, see Fawcett and Torremans (n 4) ch 15.

needs enforcement and that works through the infringement rules. From a private international law point of view it makes sense to apply the same applicable law rule to existence, scope and to infringement of an intellectual property right as formulated in the CLIP Principles:

> Article 3:601: Basic principle
>
> (1) Unless otherwise provided in this Section, the law applicable to the infringement is the law of each State for which protection is sought.
>
> (2) For the purposes of these provisions, 'infringement' includes
>
> (a) the violation of the intellectual property right,
>
> (b) the remedies, as defined in Article 3:605.[36]

At EU level and in the UK the same approach is found in Article 8(1) of the Rome II Regulation.[37]

B. Issues that Arise and a Way Forward

As a result of territoriality, the world is therefore stuck with a country-by-country distributive application of the local intellectual property law. Such a patchwork of national laws gives rise to a significant burden of proof and associated costs for the claimant and it is hard to see how any court can handle the potential application in a single case of 190 plus national laws (in the extreme copyright on the internet scenario). In the end there may be a denial of justice, as the claimant will not be able to fully enforce their intellectual property rights. At the other end of the spectrum the fact that unregistered rights such as copyright are automatically granted in virtually all countries around the world may lead to the application of laws of countries where there is virtually no impact from the alleged infringing activity. Often there is nothing more than the mere accessibility of a website or a handful of users who (accidentally) clicked on the website. It is hard to justify in those cases that the national law concerned will be applied, that the defendant will have to defend the case, and that valuable court time will be wasted.

This explains why the CLIP group proposed two adjustments that operate at either end of the spectrum. A first adjustment corresponds to the targeting adjustment at the jurisdiction level and avoids the application of national laws with which the case is only connected in a very marginal way. Such an application would in any case either not lead to the establishment of any liability or to the award of very minimal damages, ie, the case is *de minimis*. The proposed provision reads as follows:

> Article 3:602: De minimis rule
>
> (1) A court applying the law or the laws determined by Article 3:601 shall only find for infringement if
>
> (a) the defendant has substantially acted or has taken substantial preparatory action to initiate or further the infringement in the State or the States for which protection is sought, or
>
> (b) the activity by which the right is claimed to be infringed has substantial effect within, or is directed to the State or the States for which protection is sought.
>
> (2) The court may exceptionally derogate from that general rule when reasonable under the circumstances of the case.[38]

[36] Art 3:601 *CLIP Principles* (n 6) 301 et seq.

[37] Reg (EC) No 864/2007 of the European Parliament and of the Council of 11 July 2007 on the law applicable to non-contractual obligations (Rome II) [2007] OJ L199/40. See Fawcett and Torremans (n 4) ch 15.

[38] Art 3:602 *CLIP Principles* (n 6) 308 et seq.

In order to apply a national law one requires either substantial preparatory action from the side of the defendant to initiate or further the infringement in that State or activity directed or targeted at that State, eg, setting up a website dedicated to the public in that State in terms of language and content, or, at the very least, substantial effect in the State concerned irrespective of whether that was the defendant's intention.

At the other end of the spectrum one finds the potentially global case. In essence this is a case dealing with alleged copyright infringement on the internet. One never finds a registered intellectual property right such as a patent or a trademark that is registered in each and every country. What one needs to avoid in such a case is the distributive application of over 190 different national intellectual property laws. It is therefore proposed to apply a single law, even if that goes *stricto sensu* against the wording of the Berne Convention.[39] Whereas the right-holder gets the advantage of the application of a single law, the provision balances that in the first place by suggesting a series of factors that the judge will take into account in determining the single applicable law and that tend to point to the defendant/alleged infringer. In the second place there is a reversal of the burden of proof. The defendant has the option of arguing under another law that his or her activity is either not infringing or benefits from an exception of limitation.[40] A bona fide defendant will have that evidence to hand as part of his or her business plan. That results in the following balanced proposal:

Article 3:603: Ubiquitous infringement

(1) In disputes concerned with infringement carried out through ubiquitous media such as the Internet, the court may apply the law of the State having the closest connection with the infringement, if the infringement arguably takes place in every State in which the signals can be received. This rule also applies to existence, duration, limitations and scope to the extent that these questions arise as incidental questions in infringement proceedings.

(2) In determining which State has the closest connection with the infringement, the court shall take all the relevant factors into account, in particular the following:

- (a) the infringer's habitual residence;
- (b) the infringer's principal place of business;
- (c) the place where substantial activities in furthering of the infringement in its entirety have been carried out;
- (d) the place where the harm caused by the infringement is substantial in relation to the infringement in its entirety.

(3) Notwithstanding the law applicable pursuant to paragraphs 1 and 2, any party may prove that the rules applying in a State or States covered by the dispute differ from the law applicable to the dispute in aspects which are essential for the decision. The court shall apply the different national laws unless this leads to inconsistent results, in which case the differences shall be taken into account in fashioning the remedy.[41]

C. Contract Applicable Law

Contracts relating to intellectual property are omnipresent in our modern economic trading pattern. These highly specialised licence, assignment and joint venture contracts are fortunately 'normal' contracts for applicable law purposes. That means that the parties are free to choose

[39] Avoiding a denial of justice might justify this.
[40] See Fawcett and Torremans (n 4) ch 18.
[41] Art 3:603 *CLIP Principles* (n 6) 314 et seq.

the law applicable to the contract.[42] It is, however, very important that parties make use of that option, as these contracts fit very badly with objective applicable law rules. The best objective applicable law rules for intellectual property contracts rely on the criterion of the closest connection in combination with a set of factors to assist the judge, thereby enhancing predictability and legal certainty.[43]

IV. Conclusion

Intellectual property presents a real challenge for private international law. Its historical national treatment/territoriality roots create specific problems, but these can be overcome and accommodations can be made that allow for legal certainty and a predictable application of jurisdiction and applicable law rules.

The academic efforts of the last couple of decades have shown that it is possible to find common ground and that the remaining divergences are not impossible to overcome. With a bit more political will, the World Intellectual Property Organization, probably with the Hague Conference, could take up this matter in the coming years with a reasonable chance of success.

[42] See Symeon Symeonides, 'Law Applicable to Contracts', ch 14 in this book. See also Reg (EC) No 593/2008 of the European Parliament and of the Council of 17 June 2008 on the law applicable to contractual obligations (Rome I) [2008] OJ L177/6, Art 3; Fawcett and Torremans (n 4) ch 18; Art 3:501 *CLIP Principles* (n 6) 268 et seq.

[43] Art 3:502 *CLIP Principles* (n 6) 272 et seq.

26

Arbitration

GIUDITTA CORDERO-MOSS

I. Introduction

Arbitration is a method for dispute settlement that has enjoyed an exponential growth during the past decades, but is increasingly criticised nowadays. The role of private international law in arbitration seems to have an inversely proportional relationship to arbitration's success – more precisely, to the intensity with which the autonomy and delocalisation of arbitration are advocated.

Ambitions of delocalisation have emerged during the early decades of expansion of arbitration. Arbitration being an international mechanism for dispute settlement that is based on the will of the parties, has increasingly been promoted as the realm of party autonomy, in which national law only plays a marginal role. If national law plays a marginal role, even more so does private international law, which is meant to select the applicable national law. Some arbitration rules deleted any reference to private international law, and left it to the parties or to the full discretion of the arbitral tribunal to determine which law is applicable (if a domestic law is applicable at all).

After decades of asserting delocalisation, the climate is changing. The attention is increasingly shifting from the necessity that arbitration implements the parties' will, to the advisability that arbitration ensures an accurate application of the most important policies protected by national laws.

In this changing climate, private international law may be a useful tool to preserve the legitimacy of arbitration and predictability of the awards. Far from being the retrograde and arbitration-hostile mechanism that it has long been suspected of being, private international law in effect gives instruments to ensure that arbitration maintains its effectiveness.

In the following, I will make a short introduction on the delocalisation of arbitration and the signs of an emerging re-localisation (section II), what delocalisation means for the role of private international law (section III), which private international law is relevant in arbitration (section IV), and how private international law may contribute to the effectiveness of arbitration in light of the emerging re-localisation (section V). I will then ascertain to what extent the existing legal framework for arbitration contains conflict rules (section VI) and will, to conclude, suggest the lines of a uniform body of private international law for arbitration (section VII).

II. Delocalisation and Re-Localisation

The role of private international law in arbitration has been significantly influenced by the understanding of arbitration as an autonomous system, that is detached from national laws. If arbitration is understood as being delocalised and not subject to national law, there is no need for mechanisms to select the applicable law. Hence, private international law, whose task is to select the applicable law, is redundant.

In large part, the understanding of arbitration as delocalised relies on the legal framework of arbitration – particularly, on the 1958 New York Convention on the Recognition and Enforcement of Foreign Arbitral Awards.[1] If parties decide to submit a dispute to arbitration, according to Article II of the Convention, the courts of the 164 States which have ratified the Convention must decline jurisdiction on that dispute. If the arbitral tribunal chosen by the parties renders an award based on the instructions given by the parties and applies the rules chosen by the parties, the courts of all those States have to enforce that award, save only for some few exceptions laid down in Article V of the Convention. This is certainly enhancing the impression that arbitration is an autonomous system, where national laws are allowed to have an impact only to the extent that they have been chosen by the parties.

In part, the delocalisation of arbitration was developed in the context of disputes between foreign investors and the host States, and it can be seen as a step in the process of enhancing investment protection.[2] Perhaps the most significant achievement in this process was the 1965 Washington Convention on the Settlement of Investment Disputes between States and Nationals of Other States (ICSID),[3] which established a special resolution mechanism for investor–state disputes.

While the dedicated legal framework for investment arbitration is the ICSID Convention, which creates a relatively self-contained arbitration system, many investment disputes are carried out under rules of arbitration that are designed for commercial arbitration, such as the UNCITRAL Arbitration Rules. For these investment disputes, the procedural rules are the same as those for commercial disputes. This also includes conflict rules, with the exception that the law applicable to the merits of investment disputes is determined in accordance with the applicable basis for jurisdiction – usually, a Bilateral Investment Treaty on investment protection.

Investment disputes need a legal framework that is wider than the legal system of the host State – to ensure that the host State does not abuse its sovereignty to change the rules of the game to the detriment of the investor. In this context, there are evident concerns in allowing investment disputes to be subject exclusively to the national law of the host State. Hence, the support for delocalisation or internationalisation of investment arbitration.

[1] Convention on the Recognition and Enforcement of Foreign Arbitral Awards (adopted 10 June 1958, entered into force 7 June 1959) UNTS 330 (New York Convention). For an updated status, see: uncitral.un.org/en/texts/arbitration/conventions/foreign_arbitral_awards/status2.

[2] The Resolution of the Institute of International Law's XVIII Commission expressly criticised the assumption that arbitration necessarily takes place within the framework of a national law. See 'Arbitration Between States, State Enterprises, or State Entities, and Foreign Enterprises' *Yearbook – Institute of International Law* (89), II, 324–31, available at: www.idi-iil.org/app/uploads/2017/06/1989_comp_01_en.pdf.

[3] Convention on the Settlement of Investment Disputes between States and Nationals of Other States (adopted 18 March 1965, entered into force 14 October 1966) UNTS 575 (ICSID Convention or Washington Convention), see: treaties.un.org/Pages/showDetails.aspx?objid=080000028012a925. In force for 140 States.

Less evident is the need to emancipate from national laws in purely commercial disputes. However, the delocalisation theory has quickly expanded to also cover commercial arbitration and commercial disputes.[4]

The delocalisation of arbitration, in any case, is not without limits. As will be seen in sections III and VI below, national laws play a restricted, but not insignificant role in arbitration, not the least under the New York Convention.

Furthermore, arbitration is currently under pressure. Among the issues that are increasingly criticised, is the autonomy from national laws. There is an emerging mistrust, both as far as investment arbitration and as far as commercial arbitration are concerned. This development is threatening to reverse the arbitration-friendly trend of the past decades – a trend that had led, among other things, to an ever-growing scope of disputes that could be submitted to arbitration, so-called arbitrability.

Historically, it is customary to consider the US decision in *Mitsubishi*[5] as the one opening an era of arbitration friendliness. Other legal systems have also have undergone a clear shift from an expressed suspicion against arbitration, to an arbitration-friendly attitude – eg, the Swedish system.[6] *Mitsubishi* permitted arbitrability of disputes relating to competition law – which until that time had been considered to involve too important and general interests to be arbitrable. The condition for extending the scope of arbitrability was that courts be permitted to give a 'second look' at the accurate application of the law on the occasion of court control – in particular, through the rule on public policy.

A similar opening was made by the Court of Justice of the European Union (CJEU) with the *Eco Swiss* case.[7] EU competition law was defined as a matter of public policy; nevertheless, disputes involving competition law are arbitrable. The second look approach permits the courts to review the determination of whether important policies (such as, in these cases, competition law) are applicable, and whether they were seriously infringed.

Recently, it has been possible to observe a more restrictive approach.

In commercial arbitration, courts in EU States such as Austria,[8] Belgium,[9] Germany[10] and, formerly, the UK (at least in England and Wales),[11] denied the arbitrability[12] of disputes regarding

[4] See, eg, M Blessing, 'Choice of substantive law in international arbitration' (1997) 14 *Journal of International Arbitration* 39, 39 ff; M Blessing, 'Keynotes on arbitral decision-making, The new 1998 ICC Rules of Arbitration' (1997) *ICC International Court of Arbitration Bulletin* 44, 44 ff; O Lando, 'The new Lex Mercatoria in international commercial arbitration' (1985) 34 *ICLQ* 747, 765 ff; J Paulsson, 'Arbitration unbound: award detached from the law of its state of origin' (1981) 30 *ICLQ* 358, 358 ff, 362 ff and 381; J Paulsson, 'Delocalisation of international commercial arbitration: when and why it matters' (1983) 32 *ICLQ* 53, 53ff.

[5] *Mitsubishi Motors Corp v Soler Chrysler-Plymouth, Inc* 473 US 614, 628 (1985) (United States). The first Supreme Court judgment recognising the arbitrability of matters that previously were deemed to be for the exclusive competence of courts of law, was *Scherk v Alberto-Culver* 417 US 506 (1974). See, for further references, P Carrington and P Hagen, 'Contract and Jurisdiction' (1997) 8 *The Supreme Court Review* 331, 362f, and J Sternlight, 'Panacea or Corporate Tool? Debunking the Supreme Court's Preference for Binding Arbitration' (1996) 74 *Washington University Law Quarterly* 637, 652.

[6] See, eg, the evolution regarding the validity of arbitration clauses entered into in the framework of general conditions of contract, as it appears from the comparison of three Swedish Supreme Court decisions rendered in 1949, 1969 and 1980: L Heuman, *Current Issues in Swedish Arbitration* (Stockholm 1990) 22 ff.

[7] Case C-126/97 *Eco Swiss China Time Ltd v Benneton Int'l NV* [1999] ECR I-3079.

[8] Oberster Gerichtshof 1.3.2017, 5ob 72/16y, Ecolex 520 (2017).

[9] Cour de cassation, 16.11.2006, PAS 2006, I, No 11; Cour de cassation, 14.1.2010, PAS 2010, I, No 12; Cour de cassation, 3.11.2011 PAS 2011, I, No 1.

[10] Bundesgerichtshof, 5.9.2012, *Neue juristische Wochenschrift* (2012).

[11] *Accentuate Limited v Asigra Inc* [2009] EWHC (QB) 2655.

[12] Or they deny the recognition of a contractual choice of forum in favour of a court not located within the EU. This responds to the same rationale, ie, that matters relating to commercial agency shall be decided by courts located in the EU in order to ensure a uniform application of EU law. Therefore, it can be expected that the same courts would also deny arbitrability if the contract contained an arbitration clause.

contracts of commercial agency. EU agency law is deemed to be necessary for the achievement of the internal market. Hence, some courts have affirmed that disputes concerning commercial agency should be decided by courts of EU Member States: choosing a court outside the EU, or choosing arbitration, may endanger the effective enforcement of EU law.

In investment arbitration, concerns are voiced about the ability of arbitrators to understand public interest issues,[13] about the consistency of awards, and about the lack of appeal.[14] For investment disputes based on intra-EU treaties, the CJEU denied arbitrability, arguing that investment arbitration does not give an effective method to control the uniform application of EU law.[15] The decision was based on an unconvincing distinction between commercial and investment arbitration, which gives reason to fear that the distinction may be abandoned, expanding the non-arbitrability also to commercial disputes.[16] For the moment, however, the CJEU, indirectly and as an *obiter dictum*, endorses that commercial disputes regarding the interpretation of EU law may be subject to arbitration, because court control permits the court to review the interpretation of EU law made by the tribunal and, by requesting preliminary rulings, to ensure uniformity of the interpretation of EU law.[17]

There seems to be a growing awareness, in the arbitration community, of the necessity to ensure that the award gives due consideration to the law applicable to the merits.[18] Coupled with the courts' possibility to give a second look at awards to ensure that fundamental principles are not violated, this should be a sufficient basis to ensure the arbitration-friendly attitude opened by *Mitsubishi* continues – although the second look does not provide a perfect system.[19]

The emerging requirement for creditworthiness, particularly in relation to the application of national law, prompts the necessity to determine which law is to be applied. This, in turn, renders the role of private international law in arbitration more important than ever.

III. The Role of Private International Law in Arbitration

In relation to the role of private international law in arbitration, the above described development towards delocalisation had a double consequence: on the one hand, if arbitration is not to apply national laws, there is no need to select the applicable law and therefore there is no need for private international law. This is discussed in this section. On the other hand, if arbitration is delocalised, even when it is necessary to select the applicable law, the arbitral tribunal is not bound to apply the private international law of a specific country. This will be discussed in section IV.

[13] Report of UNCITRAL Working Group III (Investor–State Dispute Settlement Reform) on the work of its thirty-fifth session (New York, 23–27 April 2017), A/CN.9/935, paras 82–88; Report of UNCITRAL Working Group III (Investor–State Dispute Settlement Reform) on the work of thirty-sixth session (Vienna, 29 October–2 November 2018), A/CN.9/964, paras 64–108.

[14] Report of Working Group III on the work of its thirty-fifth session, A/CN.9/935, paras 35, 38; Report of Working Group III on the work of thirty-sixth session, A/CN.9/964, para 30.

[15] C-284/16 *Achmea* EU:C:2018:158.

[16] For a more extensive analysis and references, see G Cordero-Moss, 'Achmea's Distinction between Investment and Commercial Arbitration' in A Calissendorff (ed), *The Future of Arbitration in Europe* (2020 Stockholm Centre for Commercial Law Skriftserie No 36) 17–28.

[17] *Achmea* (n 15) para 54.

[18] L Radicati di Brozolo, 'Mandatory Rules and International Arbitration' (2012) 23 *American Review of International Arbitration* 49, 66 ff.

[19] M Benedettelli, '"Communitarization" of International Arbitration: A New Spectre Haunting Europe?' (2011) 73 *Arbitration International* 583, 597; W Park, 'Private Adjudicators and the Public Interest: The Expanding Scope of International Arbitration' (1986) 12 *Brooklyn Journal of International Law* 642.

In reality, it is not correct that arbitration is not to apply national laws. The legal framework for arbitration provides for restricted, but not insignificant court control. Under certain conditions, courts may set aside an award and can refuse its enforcement. To the extent that the conditions for annulling and refusing enforcement are linked to the application of a certain law, therefore, the arbitration is not autonomous or delocalised.

In the case of a *challenge to the award's validity*, court control is regulated by the arbitration law prevailing in the place of arbitration. National arbitration law differs from country to country; therefore, the court's process in the case of a challenge of the award's validity needs to be analysed on the basis of the national law that is applicable in the specific case. For the sake of simplicity, however, we will assume here that the national arbitration law corresponds to the UNCITRAL Model Law, as it does, more or less literally, in the 85 countries that are considered to be 'Model Law countries'.[20]

This applies to commercial arbitration, and consequently also to the relatively large part of investment disputes carried out under Arbitration Rules that are not designed specifically for investment arbitration, such as the UNCITRAL Rules, the Rules of the Stockholm Chamber of Commerce (SCC) or of the International Chamber of Commerce (ICC). These investment disputes will be subject to the regime applicable to commercial arbitration. For investment arbitration that is carried out under the ICSID Convention, annulment of awards is regulated in Article 52 of the Convention itself, without reference to national law.

In the case of *enforcement of an award*, the applicable law is, in the 168 countries who have ratified it, the New York Convention. For investment arbitration that is carried out under the ICSID Convention, enforcement of awards is regulated in the Convention itself, which creates in Article 54 an obligation to enforce the award as if it was a final court decision rendered in that State.

The court's powers, to the extent that is relevant here, are equivalent in the New York Convention and in the Model Law.[21] Therefore, the analysis can be made without distinguishing between court control carried out in connection with challenge to the award's validity and court control carried out in connection with enforcement of the award. It should be emphasised, however, that if the law applicable in a specific case does not belong to a Model Law country, or if it implements the Model Law with some discrepancies from the original, it will be necessary to verify whether the law applicable to annulment has diverging regulation.

The criteria contained in the New York Convention and the Model Law largely correspond to the criteria contained in Article 52 of the ICSID Convention. These criteria are as follows: an award rendered by an arbitral tribunal whose jurisdiction did not rest on a valid and binding arbitration agreement is not valid[22] and not enforceable.[23] An award rendered as a result of a proceeding that did not give each of the parties the possibility to present its case is not valid[24] and not enforceable.[25] An award rendered in excess of the jurisdiction granted to the arbitral tribunal is not valid[26] and not enforceable.[27] An award rendered by an arbitral tribunal that was

[20] UNCITRAL, 1985 Model Law on International Commercial Arbitration, revised in 2006, see: uncitral.un.org/en/texts/arbitration/modellaw/commercial_arbitration.

[21] This correspondence is intentional, see G Born, *International Commercial Arbitration*, 2nd edn (Kluwer Law International 2014) 3186, 3340; G Cordero-Moss, *International Commercial Contracts* (Cambridge University Press 2014) 224.

[22] Art 34(2)(a)(i) of the Model Law; Art 52(1) (a) and (b) of the ICSID Convention.

[23] Art 36(1)(a)(i) of the Model Law; Art V(1)(a) of the New York Convention; Arts 25 and 26 of the ICSID Convention.

[24] Art 34(2)(a)(ii) of the Model Law; Art 52(1) (d) and (e) of the ICSID Convention.

[25] Art 36(1)(a)(ii) of the Model Law; Art V(1)(b) of the New York Convention.

[26] Art 34(2)(a)(iii) of the Model Law; Art 52(1) (b) of the ICSID Convention.

[27] Art 36(1)(a)(iii) of the Model Law; Art V(1)(c) of the New York Convention.

not constituted in accordance with the parties' agreement or the applicable law, or as a result of proceedings that did not comply with the parties' agreement or the applicable procedural rules, is not valid[28] and not enforceable.[29] An award rendered on a non-arbitrable subject matter is not valid[30] and not enforceable.[31] An award infringing fundamental principles (public policy) is not valid[32] and not enforceable.[33] In addition, in the New York Convention and in the UNCITRAL Model Law there is a rule on public policy which covers not only the procedural public policy, but the substantive public policy. While the ICSID Convention does not mention public policy as a ground to annul an award, it has a specific rule on the necessity that the award be reasoned. Regarding enforcement, ICSID awards are subject to the same regime as final court decisions in the enforcement country. To the extent the enforcement country has a public policy exception, therefore, it will apply also to ICSID awards.

This overview shows that the legal framework for arbitration contains references to national laws. There is no doubt that conflict rules contained in arbitration law apply to arbitration. However, the applicability to arbitration of private international law in general has been questioned, as the next section will show.

IV. Which Private International Law?

The legal framework for arbitration determines whether private international law is applicable by the arbitral tribunal: as was seen above, both the New York Convention and national arbitration law have some conflict rules. In addition, often the parties agree on the applicability of Arbitration Rules. These are procedural rules issued by arbitration institutions. By agreeing to subject the dispute to the administration of a certain institution, the parties also incorporate this institution's Arbitration Rules into their arbitration agreement. If the parties choose ad hoc arbitration, they may agree on Arbitration Rules directly in the agreement, or by making reference to the UNCITRAL Arbitration Rules. The Arbitration Rules thus agreed by the parties will apply to the arbitral proceedings and will prevail over the rules contained in the national arbitration law, if the latter permits derogation from it by agreement of the parties. Often, Arbitration Rules contain provisions on choice of law.

A glance at the above-mentioned sources shows that there is no unitary approach to the question of which private international law an arbitral tribunal shall apply. The range goes from: (i) excluding that national law should be applied by the tribunal (therefore, no need for private international law); to (ii) accepting that the tribunal applies national law, but opening for the free determination by the tribunal of which law to apply (therefore, no need for private international law); to (iii) providing a specific conflict rule for arbitration; to (iv) directing the tribunal to apply conflict rules to determine the applicable law (therefore, a need for private international law, without specifying which one); to (v) determining that the tribunal apply the private international law of its seat.

As far as (i) is concerned, the ICC Rules of Arbitration may be a good example. According to Article 21, 'the arbitral tribunal shall apply the rules of law which it determines to be appropriate'.

[28] Art 34(2)(a)(iv) of the Model Law; Art 52(1) (a) and (c) of the ICSID Convention.
[29] Art 36(1)(a)(iv) of the Model Law; Art V(1)(d) of the New York Convention.
[30] Art 34(2)(b)(i) of the Model Law; Art 52(1) (b) of the ICSID Convention.
[31] Art 36(1)(b)(i) of the Model Law; Art V(2)(a) of the New York Convention; Arts 25 and 26 of the ICSID Convention.
[32] Art 34(2)(b)(ii) of the Model Law; Art 52(1)(d) of the ICSID Convention, with respect to procedural public policy.
[33] Art 36(1)(b)(ii) of the Model Law; Art V(2)(b) of the New York Convention.

By using the term 'rules of law', the ICC Arbitration Rules permit the tribunal to apply not only a national law (which is referred to as 'law'), but any rules of a transnational nature that the tribunal may deem applicable.[34] The intention is to permit the parties to emancipate from the peculiarities of the various national laws and apply a uniform, transnational law. In reality, choice of 'rules of law' does not necessarily exclude the relevance of 'laws': transnational sources (even those which are systematically codified, such as the UNIDROIT Principles of International Commercial Contracts) do not necessarily provide exhaustive regulation and are not necessarily interpreted uniformly.[35] Moreover, 'laws' may not necessarily be disregarded in the context of court control: see section III above.

As far as (ii) is concerned, the same Article of the ICC Rules may be highlighted.[36] Even when the tribunal decides to apply a national law, it can select it applying the so-called *voie directe* and without having to be concerned with the criteria for determining the applicable law contained in private international law.

As far as (iii) is concerned, an example is Swiss law, which has a specific conflict rule for arbitration, based on the principle of the closest connection.[37]

As far as (iv) is concerned, an example is the UNCITRAL Model Law. In a case where the parties have not made use of their party autonomy, the UNCITRAL Model Law directs the arbitral tribunal to select the applicable law on the basis of the conflict rules that the tribunal 'considers applicable'.[38] This flexible version was introduced in the 2006 revision. Originally, the Model Law referred to the conflict rules of the State where the tribunal has its seat. The new version was meant to cater for situations where the place of arbitration has no connection with the dispute, and where it may be appropriate to apply the conflict rules of States with a closer connection.

Those who, in the name of internationality, deem it undesirable to apply national conflict rules, can find the mechanism underlying private international law in transnational sources of soft law, such as the Hague Principles on Choice of Law.[39] Alternatively, they may engage in a comparison of the various private international laws and apply the conflict rule that results from this exercise.

As far as (v) is concerned, an example is Norwegian law.[40] In practice, in many situations, the private international law of the seat is applied even under the approach described under (iv):

[34] More extensively on the distinction, see Cordero-Moss (n 21) 300 ff.

[35] See, more extensively, ibid, 41–80; G Cordero-Moss, 'The UNIDROIT Principles of International Commercial Contracts' in P Butler (ed), *International Commercial Contracts* (Oxford University Press, forthcoming).

[36] See also the LCIA Rules, Art 22(3); the SCC Rules, Art 27(1); and the UNCITRAL Rules, Art 35(1); French Code of Civil Procedure, Art 1511; Swedish Arbitration Act, Art 27a. The eagerness to exclude the applicability of private international law may go too far, eg, sometimes Art 1(2)(e) of the Rome I Regulation on choice of law for contractual obligations is invoked to confirm that private international law does not apply to arbitration. According to this provision, arbitration agreements are excluded from the scope of Rome I. In reality, this provision excludes from its scope arbitration agreements, and not arbitration as such. The same provision also excludes agreements on choice court from the scope of Rome I – yet nobody would induce from this exclusion that the conflict rules of Rome I are not applicable whenever a dispute is decided by a court. Similarly, the exclusion of arbitration agreements should not lead to denying the applicability of the conflict rules of Rome I when a dispute is solved by an arbitral tribunal. This provision says nothing on the question of whether private international law is applicable by the arbitral tribunal. If it is, to the extent Rome I constitutes the applicable private international law, it will apply to arbitration – in the respect, however, of conflict rules specific to arbitration, that will prevail due to the principle of *lex specialis*.

[37] Swiss Private International Law Act, Art 187.

[38] Model Law, Art 28(2).

[39] Hague Conference on Private International Law, Principles on Choice of Law in International Commercial Contracts (2015).

[40] Norwegian Arbitration Act, § 31(2) (2004).

arbitral tribunals may consider their seat as a significant connecting factor and thus apply the seat's conflict rules to determine the applicable law. According to the Model Law, the seat is the proper connecting factor for a series of important aspects, such as the validity of the arbitration agreement, the arbitral procedure, the tribunal's power to issue interim measures, the validity of the award and the applicable public policy – it does not seem unreasonable to consider it also as a proper connecting factor for the conflict rules.

In summary, today the applicability of private international law to arbitration is not uniform. However, with the exception of the *voie directe*, this short overview shows that private international law has still a quite important role in arbitration. Even in those systems that do not expressly refer to, or even exclude, private international law, the arbitral tribunal may desire to turn to private international law criteria to ensure objective and predictable results.[41]

V. How Private International Law Contributes to the Effectiveness of Arbitration

A context in which private international law proves useful to arbitration is the interaction between two of the grounds described in section III above for annulling an award or refusing its enforcement: the ground of excess of power and that of conflict with public policy. As explained below, private international law, by determining the scope of party autonomy, permits tribunals to safeguard public policy without exceeding the power conferred by the parties.

Under the ground of excess of power, an award may be set aside or refused enforcement if it is rendered outside the scope of the arbitral tribunal's power. According to widespread opinion, this ground does not cover the issue of the applicable law.[42] However, the applicable law is relevant to the scope of the dispute: the scope of the dispute is mainly determined by the disputed contract, but the contract does not have legal effects simply by itself – it receives its legal effects from the governing law. The same contract wording may have dramatically different effects depending on which law governs it.[43] It may be argued, therefore, that the scope of the dispute is determined by the contract as construed under its applicable law. An arbitral tribunal that applies legal sources different from the law chosen by the parties in the contract may be equated to a tribunal that applies a contract wording different from the wording contained in the disputed contract. Hence, the tribunal may be deemed to have gone beyond the powers that were conferred on it under the contract.[44] The award may be annulled or refused enforcement.

[41] That the criteria provided by private international law are a useful guideline seems to be recognised even by the authors who do not accept that private international law has a role in arbitration. For more references, see G Cordero-Moss, 'EU Overriding Mandatory Provisions and the Law Applicable to the Merits' in F Ferrari (ed), *The Impact of EU Law on International Commercial Arbitration* (Juris 2017) 317–49, 345–47.

[42] For references, see G Cordero-Moss, 'The Arbitral Tribunal's Power in respect of the Parties' Pleadings as a Limit to Party Autonomy – on Jura Novit Curia and Related Issues' in F Ferrari (ed), *Limits to Party Autonomy in International Commercial Arbitration* (Juris 2016) 289–330, 305 f.

[43] See Cordero-Moss (n 21) 90.

[44] Cordero-Moss, ibid, 282. On the question of whether the arbitral tribunal is expected to restrict its legal reasoning to the sources that were pleaded by the parties, see ibid, 265–307; see also G Cordero-Moss, 'Limitations on Party Autonomy in International Commercial Arbitration' (2015) 372 *Hague Collected Courses* 133; for an extensive analysis of this question in 15 jurisdictions, see G Cordero-Moss and F Ferrari (eds), *Iura novit curia in arbitration* (Juris 2018), with General Report by G Cordero-Moss, 'General Report on Jura Novit Arbiter' 463–87. For further references see, Cordero-Moss (n 42) fns 37–39.

Under the provision on public policy, an award may be set aside or refused enforcement if it conflicts with the court's public policy.[45] An award that seriously infringes important rules of competition law, for example, may be deemed to be against public policy.

The interaction of excess of power and public policy may create a tension that can be solved by private international law. Assume a contract having effects on the EU market, but containing a clause subjecting it to a non-EU law. The arbitral tribunal may need to consider EU competition law for the purpose of avoiding rendering an award that infringes public policy. Usually, competition law would be invoked as a defence by the party who did not comply with the contract, although public policy questions may also be raised *ex officio*. The argument would be that breach of the contractual obligation may not be sanctioned, because an obligation infringing EU-competition law is invalid. However, the choice of law clause subjects the contract to a different law. If the arbitral tribunal applies a law different from the law chosen by the parties, it may be deemed to have exceeded its power. It is, therefore, necessary to verify whether the tribunal has the power to apply a law different from the law that was chosen by the parties.

Under private international law, the parties' choice of law applies only within the scope of contract law (and to a certain extent also tort law). If a dispute implies issues of competition law, the law chosen by the parties is applicable to the contractual issues of the dispute, but not to the aspects of competition law. The same applies if the dispute involves issues in areas in which the State exercises its regulatory powers (overriding mandatory rules or *lois de police*), or if the dispute assumes that preliminary questions are dealt with in areas such as company law or property law, were party autonomy does not apply. The law chosen by the parties will be applied to the obligations between themselves, but the law applicable to the preliminary issues will be selected according to the appropriate conflict rules.[46] Therefore, by considering EU competition law, the arbitral tribunal will not breach the choice of law made by the parties.

It has been suggested that party autonomy in arbitration has a wider scope than party autonomy in private international law.[47] In arbitration law, the parties are often permitted to choose the law applicable not only to the contract, but more generally to the *merits* of the dispute – eg, Article 28(1) of the UNCITRAL Model Law says that the parties may choose the law applicable to the substance of the dispute. This is sometimes interpreted as giving party autonomy a wider scope than the one party autonomy has in private international law: if the dispute has implications that go beyond mere contract law, according to this opinion party autonomy would cover also these aspects. According to this logic, therefore, private international law would not be a sufficient basis to justify the arbitral tribunal's power to consider EU competition law irrespective of the parties' choice: the restrictions to party autonomy would not apply in arbitration.

However, although the wording of arbitration law may seem wider than, eg, the wording of the Rome I Regulation – according to which the parties may choose the law applicable not to the *merits* of the dispute, but only to *contractual obligations* – it may be questioned whether this can be taken as a basis for assuming that the parties in arbitration have the power to choose the law applicable to matters of competition law, company law, property law or regulatory matters.

[45] More extensively on public policy, G Cordero-Moss, 'Article 5(2)(b), Public Policy' in H Kronke, D Otto, P Nacimiento and NC Port (eds), *Recognition and Enforcement of Foreign Arbitral Awards: A Global Commentary on the New York Convention*, 2nd edn (forthcoming).

[46] More extensively, G Cordero-Moss, 'Conflict of laws as a basis to determine the arbitral tribunal's power sections' in F Ferrari and S Kröll (eds), *Conflict of Laws in International Arbitration*, 2nd edn (Juris forthcoming) sections VI, VII and VIII.

[47] L Radicati di Brozolo, 'Party autonomy and the rules governing the merits' in F Ferrari (ed), *Limits to Party Autonomy in International Arbitration* (Juris 2016) 331–62, 341 f.

This is because the choice of law possible in arbitration relates to the merits of the *dispute*. Therefore, it must be interpreted within the scope of the dispute that may be decided by the arbitral tribunal. Generally, arbitration may decide disputes between the parties on rights and obligations that the parties may dispose of, and decides the dispute with effects for the parties. An arbitral tribunal may not render an award with effects for third parties: therefore, an arbitral award will not be empowered to decide that the resolution of a company body is invalid,[48] or that a certain asset of the insolvent debtor is not available to the generality of the creditors. These aspects are outside the dispute; hence, they are not covered by the broad language of the conflict rule for arbitration. A dispute may raise issues of company law, property law or competition law, but these issues will not be the direct object of the claim. They will be preliminary issues that the tribunal may consider in the course of its determination of the claim. For example, a claim for reimbursement of damages due to breach of contract may require that the tribunal examines whether the board resolution upon which the contract was signed was valid, or whether the contract was valid under competition law. The dispute, however, will not become a dispute of company law or of competition law: it will be a dispute of contract law, for the decision of which the tribunal must consider some preliminary issues. The scope of the dispute, and therefore its merits, are defined by the claim, and the claim is, in our example, a contractual claim. The wording of the choice of law rule contained in the Model Law, therefore, does not seem to extend the scope of party autonomy in a significant manner.

If the choice made by the parties is not unlimited, it becomes necessary to find a source regulating the scope of party autonomy. Article 28(2) of the Model Law refers to private international law for the eventuality that the parties have not chosen the law. It is systematically correct to also use the same reference for the purpose of specifying the scope of party autonomy in Article 28(1). Where else should the source regulating the details of party autonomy be found? The Model Law itself does not govern crucial elements such as the parameters for a valid exercise of party autonomy, the specification of its scope, and its effects. All these elements are to be found in private international law, and it is only natural to refer, also for the purpose of Article 28(1), to the private international law that is referred to in Article 28(2).

In summary, a systematic interpretation of the sources applicable to arbitration, including private international law, justifies the arbitral tribunal's power to consider a different competition law, company or property law, to answer preliminary questions, from the law chosen by the parties to govern the dispute to be decided by the arbitral tribunal. The arbitral tribunal may, without exceeding its power, take into consideration sources not chosen by the parties and thus avoid the award violating public policy.

This enables the preservation of both the creditworthiness and the effectiveness of arbitration. If the tribunal does not apply private international law, it lacks a basis to guide its discretion. An unlimited discretion can create issues of legitimacy and predictability.[49]

VI. Conflict Rules in Arbitration Law

An overview of the conflict rules codified in arbitration law shows that only some issues are regulated in a rather uniform way.

[48] Special procedures for company law arbitration are not relevant here, as they do not regard preliminary issues in commercial disputes.

[49] On the disadvantages of giving the arbitral tribunal unlimited discretion, as the *voie directe* does, see Cordero-Moss (n 41) 345 ff.

Selection of the law applicable to the merits of the dispute is regulated in national arbitration law and in the applicable Arbitration Rules, if any. The most important conflict rule is party autonomy. The primacy of party autonomy is generally recognised.

Deserving particular mention here is that most of the applicable sources permit the parties to choose not only a national 'law', as before courts, but 'rules of law': see section IV above.

Party autonomy has a wider scope concerning the sources that can be chosen, but not the issues for which it may be exercised. The parties may not choose the law applicable to preliminary issues such as their own legal capacity (see below) or issues of company law, property law, competition law or other regulatory matters (see section V above). Also in arbitration, these issues are subject to the law applicable according to the relevant connecting factor.

If the parties have not chosen the applicable law, there is no uniform approach, as was seen in section IV. While the traditional approach is that the arbitral tribunal applies conflict rules to determine the applicable law, the delocalised approach permits the tribunal to freely select the applicable rules. This does not prevent tribunals from applying conflict rules when they exercise their discretion. Regarding which conflict rules to apply, the delocalised approach permits the tribunal to freely select them. This does not prevent the tribunal from applying the conflict rules of the seat.

Regarding the selection of the law applicable to procedural issues, the New York Convention and the UNCITRAL Model Law contain rules determining the law applicable to the capacity of the parties (the law determined by the applicable conflict rule),[50] to the validity of the arbitration agreement (failing a choice by the parties, the law of the seat of the arbitral tribunal),[51] to the arbitral procedure (the law of the seat of arbitration),[52] to arbitrability (the law of the enforcement court or of the annulment court)[53] and to public policy (the law of the enforcement court or of the annulment court).[54]

These provisions are sufficiently clear to exclude that the law chosen by the parties to govern the contract also automatically applies to the procedural aspects of the arbitration. Nevertheless, the widespread emphasis on the primacy of party autonomy can sometimes mislead people to assume that the tribunal can only consider the law chosen by the parties, irrespective of the matter at issue. There is case law confirming that the party's choice of law does not cover their legal capacity.[55] There is also case law confirming that choice of the law governing the main contract between the parties does not automatically extend to the arbitration agreement.[56] The parties may choose the law applicable to the arbitration agreement, but they need to do so specifically.

[50] New York Convention, Art V(1)(a); Model Law, Arts 34(2)(a)(i) and 36(1)(a)(i).

[51] Ibid.

[52] New York Convention, Art V(1)(d); Model Law, Arts 34(2)(a)(iv) and 36(1)(a)(iv).

[53] New York Convention, Art V(2)(a); Model Law, Arts 34(2)(b)(i) and 36(1)(b)(i).

[54] New York Convention, Art V(2)(b); Model Law, Arts 34(2)(b (ii) and 36(1)(b (ii).

[55] *State of Ukraine v Norsk Hydro ASA*, Svea Hovrätt, 17 December 2007, T 3108-06. See also *Dallah Real Estate & Tourism Holding Co v Ministry of Religious Affairs, Government of Pakistan* [2010] UKSC 46. This decision was not based on the lack of legal capacity of one of the parties, but on the relevance that that party's law has to the criteria for being deemed bound by an agreement.

[56] See *Enka Insaat Ve Sanayi AS v OOO Insurance Company Chubb* [2020] UKSC 38 in which the majority (3) in the UKSC stated that: 'The assumption that, unless there is good reason to conclude otherwise, all the terms of a contract are governed by the same law applies to an arbitration clause, as it does to any other clause of a contract … An arbitration clause may, however, more readily than other clauses be governed by a different law' (see para 40). 'As a matter of principle and authority there are therefore strong reasons why an agreement on a choice of law to govern a contract should generally be construed as applying to an arbitration agreement set out or otherwise incorporated in the contract' (see para 54). However, 'commercial parties are generally unlikely to have intended a choice of governing law for the contract to apply to an arbitration agreement if there is "at least a serious risk" that a choice of that law would "significantly undermine" that agreement' (see para 109). See in similar terms on these points, paras 229, 230 and 257 of the judgment of the minority (2). However, this last proviso (known as the 'validation principle') does not apply to cases where the issue in dispute is whether the relevant party to the litigation is a party to the arbitration agreement, see *Kabab-Ji SAL (Lebanon) v Kout Food Group (Kuwait)* [2021] UKSC 48, paras 49–52.

VII. Towards a Uniform Private International Law for Arbitration?

This chapter argues that contrary to widespread opinion based on the delocalisation doctrine, private international law is a useful tool that can contribute to the effectiveness and creditworthiness of arbitration. Particularly in view of the emerging criticism against arbitration, it is important that arbitral tribunals are given a basis to render accurate decisions based on predictable and objective criteria, decisions that can resist the scrutiny of court control and that cannot be suspected of contributing to the avoidance of important policies. Private international law provides such a basis. Failing to use private international law affects the legitimacy and predictability of arbitration, exposing it to the risk that the scope of arbitrability is restricted, or that awards are set aside or refused enforcement.

The existing legal framework for arbitration contains several conflict rules. Some of these are widely recognised and quite harmonised, while others are implicit, quite fragmented or could benefit from clarification:

i. Arbitral tribunals apply the law chosen by the parties to the merits of the dispute (the primacy of party autonomy).
ii. Notwithstanding the primacy of party autonomy, the law applicable to preliminary issues is determined in accordance with the applicable private international law.
iii. The parties may choose not only a 'law', but 'rules of law' – even though this does not necessarily exclude the relevance of 'laws'.
iv. In a case where the parties have not made a choice, the applicable law is determined either on the basis of full discretion, or in accordance with the applicable private international law; arbitral tribunals apply the private international law which they deem most appropriate; often, this will be the private international law of the seat.
v. Arbitral tribunals may take into consideration overriding mandatory rules in accordance with the applicable private international law.
vi. Arbitration agreements are subject to the law chosen by the parties specifically for the arbitration agreement (principle of severability); if the parties have not made a choice, the law of the seat applies.[57]
vii. The legal capacity of the parties is subject to the law determined in accordance with the applicable private international law.
viii. The procedure of the arbitration is subject to the parties' agreement, but cannot derogate from mandatory rules of the law of the seat.
ix. The arbitrability of a dispute is subject to the law determined in accordance with the private international law of the annulment or enforcement court.
x. Public policy is subject to the law determined in accordance with the private international law of the annulment or enforcement court.

To develop a coherent body of conflict rules for arbitration, it would be useful to clarify the borders of party autonomy: when do other conflict rules take over, and when can overriding

[57] In *Enka* and in *Kabab-Ji*, ibid, the UKSC was unanimous that generally the law governing the main contract governs an arbitration agreement in that contract when the law governing the main contract has been expressly or impliedly chosen by the parties. In the latter case this was applied at the stage of determining whether or not to enforce a foreign arbitral award under the New York Convention, see paras 35–36 and 39. The majority in *Enka* were of the view that the law of the seat of the arbitration governs the arbitration agreement in the absence of an express or implied choice of another law to govern the main contract (see para 170). The minority (see para 260) would generally apply the law governing the main contract to the arbitration agreement even when the parties have not chosen the law to govern the main contract.

mandatory rules be given effect? It should also be clarified how to select the law, if the parties have not made a choice.

These clarifications could easily be made by confirming that private international law applies to arbitration, and by specifying which private international law applies.

There does not seem to be a need for adjusting the general conflict rules to meet the requirements of arbitration – with the possible exception, reflecting numerous arbitration sources, that the parties be allowed to choose not only a 'law', but 'rules of law'. Such an exception can be applicable anyway as *lex specialis* albeit with the limitations mentioned above.

A transnational instrument of soft law, such as the Hague Principles, would appeal to those who do not consider it appropriate that international arbitration applies national conflict rules. While this has the advantage of making private international law more palatable to the supporters of delocalisation, it has the disadvantage of not enhancing predictability. Confirming the applicability to arbitration of national conflict rules is the most appropriate approach from a systematic perspective. However, it may be seen as turning back the clock. A transnational instrument is more aligned to the current Zeitgeist.

27

Maritime Exceptionalism in Global Private International Law

VERÓNICA RUIZ ABOU-NIGM

I. Introduction

Maritime law and Private International Law (PIL) could be closer allies in the progressive unification of private international maritime law. Maritime law is inherently international; maritime commerce plays a key role in facilitating international trade in the global economy; and shipping litigation lends itself as a fertile field for the development of PIL doctrines that have evolved beyond the sphere of the maritime adventure. Yet, the global normative production of PIL and international maritime law unification have traditionally been the remit of different international fora. The result is less synergetic than arguably possible: recent parallel – rather than interconnected – processes of unification have resulted in excluding some of the most common maritime law scenarios – including the carriage of goods by sea (COGS) – from the scope of application of the latest – potentially – global instruments of unification of general PIL in civil and commercial matters, ie, the 2005 Hague Conference (HCCH) Convention on Choice of Court Agreements and the 2019 HCCH Convention on the Recognition and Enforcement of Foreign Judgments.

This maritime exceptionalism at the global level appears to be one of design, aiming to avoid the conflict of conventions. Maritime law is a highly specialised field, where persistent efforts over centuries to provide a level playing field for maritime commerce globally have resulted in multiple multilateral treaties. Despite these major efforts, broadly speaking, a long-standing bipolarised conflict between shipping and cargo interests has impeded the ultimate success of some of the major unifying projects in COGS. The modern legal landscape is still patchy and intricate, lending itself more to forum shopping and legal expenses than to legal certainty and predictability.

The main argument of this chapter is that this is a field where global PIL methodologies and techniques should be fully explored, moving away from exceptionalism into inter-systemic wayfinding for the optimisation of existing international, regional, national and a-national instruments, providing necessary bridges in the long-standing efforts for private international maritime law unification.

This chapter focuses on COGS, as an illustration of interconnected issues across the sector.[1] The argument is construed as follows: after a succinct overview of salient features of the legal

[1] See W Tetley 'Jurisdiction Clauses and Forum Non Conveniens in the Carriage of Goods by Sea' in M Davies (ed), *Jurisdiction and Forum Selection in International Maritime Law: Essays in Honor of Robert Force* (Kluwer 2005) 183.

landscape (section I.A.), this chapter examines the challenges to global PIL unification, focusing on issues of jurisdiction (section II), and problems of interpretation and application relating to some of the adopted PIL unified rules, with a focus on applicable law (section III). Contemporary exceptionalism is questioned revisiting COGS exclusion from the 2019 HCCH Convention on the Recognition and Enforcement of Foreign Judgments (section IV), with suggestions to approach maritime conflicts in global PIL mores (section V) presented before the conclusion (section VI).

A. Overview

Maritime law is fundamentally transnational, and uniformity is the leitmotif of modern international maritime law.[2] Yet, the modern legal landscape in COGS globally (both substantive and PIL rules) is fragmented and bears the imprint of: (a) the extensive and prolific work of intergovernmental agencies and other expert fora dedicated to providing a level playing field, resulting in a succession of multilateral treaties, none of which have gained global acceptance (the 'legal tower of Babel');[3] (b) the methodological pluralism of these fora, combining substantive provisions with PIL rules in some but not all of these international treaties;[4] (c) the bipolar governance of the shipping industry, historically a considerable hurdle towards more extensive unification; (d) the marked differences between the two most typical and interrelated contracts in this context, charterparty and bill of lading (B/L): the first based on a relatively extended (presumed) equality of bargaining power between the contracting parties; the second without it; (d) the conservatism of maritime law;[5] (e) the tension between the parochialism underpinning the procedural characterisation of several categories relating to maritime proceedings and the 'cosmopolitan nature of the shipping industry';[6] (f) the existence of a web of interlocked obligations between parties from around the globe usually involved in and affected by COGS transactions, requiring a nuanced construction and interpretation of multiple (at times overlapping) legal frameworks;[7] and (g) the extensive use of standardised uniform contracts.

The resulting complexity presents a daunting landscape. Does this justify maritime exceptionalism in PIL, or should this panorama prompt renewed impetus in global PIL mores to promote greater certainty and predictability, as well as sustainable development,[8] in this highly specialised field? Considering the significance of COGS contracts in transnational commercial litigation globally, and moreover, that COGS jurisprudence has contributed to the development

[2] International uniformity in maritime law is the CMI's primary objective, see: comitemaritime.org/.

[3] M Davies 'When Was the Last Time You Were Restrained by a Prince? Conservatism and the Development of Maritime Law' in PK Mukherjee et al (eds), *Maritime Law in Motion* (WMU Studies in Maritime Affairs 8 2020) 153, 154.

[4] W Tetley 'Uniformity of International Private Maritime Law: The Pros, Cons, and Alternatives to International Conventions: How to Adopt an International Convention' (2000) 24 *Tulane Maritime Law Journal* 775, 807–08.

[5] Davies (n 3) 153.

[6] See P Myburgh, 'Conflict of Laws and the Arrest Conventions' in P Myburgh (ed), *The Arrest Conventions* (Hart Publishing 2019) 151, 152.

[7] See V Ruiz Abou-Nigm, 'Choice of court agreements vis a vis third parties' in S Lamont-Black and R Thomas (eds), *Current Issues in Freight Forwarding: Law and Logistics* (Lawtext 2017) 276–97.

[8] 'International shipping is inherently indispensable for economic growth and sustainable development and therefore indirectly plays a role in all of the SDGs': www.imo.org/en/MediaCentre/PressBriefings/Pages/41-SDGS.aspx. A sustainable development lens is appropriate in this context not only because it is part of the HCCH Action Plan 2019–2022, as well as the IMO's, but also because historically some of the hurdles in the journey towards unification of maritime law have been portrayed as deriving from opposed interests in the 'Global North' and the 'Global South'.

of doctrines and techniques of PIL in several legal systems,[9] the proposed argument leans towards the latter, advancing ideas for further inter-systemic coordination between general and specialised instruments. General PIL rules included in multilateral treaties have applied to maritime contracts since the entry into force of the 1889 Montevideo Treaties.[10] Many multilateral instruments include provisions on jurisdiction, applicable law and the recognition and enforcement of foreign judgments that apply to a range of maritime scenarios. That is, PIL rules relevant to COGS claims are not only included in *lex specialis*, but maritime claims are sometimes within the scope of application of general PIL frameworks, eg, in the European Union (EU).

II. Challenges to Global PIL Unification: Focus on Jurisdiction

The availability of concurrent jurisdictions has always been a feature of shipping litigation where there will invariably be a number of reasonably connected *fora* whose PIL rules permit the dispute to be therein entertained.[11] Some of the most fiercely contested conflicts of jurisdiction take place in shipping litigation and copious resources are devoted to solve the jurisdictional dispute.[12] Parallel proceedings and related actions, and PIL doctrines such as *forum non conveniens*,[13] are of daily significance in this context. In COGS most B/Ls include choice of court (and/or arbitration) agreements – usually coupled with choice of law clauses – or incorporate the relevant clauses of the related charterparty to that effect. The widely extended use of standard form charterparties and B/Ls including such clauses is possibly the factor that has contributed the most to 'unification' in this context. However, the result is far from 'global' in more than one sense. First, it is well known that a great number of these clauses provide for the law and/or forum in a few jurisdictions, eg, arbitration in London is provided for in many standard form charterparties,[14] and many B/Ls provide for the exclusive jurisdiction of the High Court in London.[15] Thus, these clauses tend to favour the development of some jurisdictions over others, and benefit the party who can afford to litigate therein, presenting at times an insurmountable hurdle for certain parties, particularly third-party consignees.[16] Limits may be necessary to party autonomy in this context since a contractual clause 'that attributes exclusive jurisdiction to a court … is incompatible with the right of access to a court if that attribution leads to a denial of justice'.[17] Second, there is no global unified PIL response applicable to COGS

[9] Examples include, inter alia, anti-suit injunctions, Mareva injunctions (freezing orders), and notably *forum non conveniens*.

[10] Arts 11–25 of this Treaty refer to maritime law. Currently in force between Bolivia, Argentina, Paraguay, Uruguay, Colombia and Peru. See S Argerich, 'Rol Pionero y Trascendencia del Tratado de Derecho Comercial Internacional de Montevideo de 1889 en Relacion a los Transportes' and V Zorrilla Ferres and H Rau, 'La Regulacion del Transporte Maritimo en el Tratado de Derecho Comercial Internacional de Montevideo de 1889' in C Fresnedo de Aguirre and G Lorenzo Idiarte (eds), *Jornadas 130 Aniversario Tratados de Montevideo 1889* (Fundación de Cultura Universitaria 2019) 263, 279.

[11] See further, V Ruiz Abou-Nigm, *The Arrest of Ships in Private International Law* (Oxford University Press 2011) ch 7.

[12] Ibid, 164.

[13] See, V Ruiz Abou-Nigm, 'Forum Non Conveniens, Forum Conveniens and Forum Arresti: Los aportes de una evaluación integral a la construcción de una visión global' (2015) XLII *Curso de Derecho Internacional* (Organization of American States) 113.

[14] See, eg, NYPE 1946, cl 17; NYPE 1993, cl 45; NYPE 2015 cl 54(b); Gencon 1994, cl 19; Shelltime 4, cl 46.

[15] Y Baatz, 'The Conflict of Laws' in Y Baatz (ed), *Maritime Law* (Informa 2020) 17.

[16] See C Fresnedo de Aguirre, 'The Rotterdam Rules from the Perspective of a Country that is a Consumer of Shipping Services' [2009] *Uniform Law Review* 869.

[17] Draft Resolution on Human Rights and Private International Law, Institute of International Law, Commission No 4, Jürgen Basedow, WD No 11 (September 2018), Draft Resolution, Art 10(1). Consider also, SDG 16, UN 2030 Agenda for Sustainable Development.

in relation to the effectiveness of these clauses,[18] or any global unified PIL response to issues of jurisdiction more broadly in this sphere yet.[19]

There is a confluence of factors that have presented challenges to global unification of jurisdiction rules in COGS. Commonly referred to are the bipolar structure of shipping governance: particularly in container shipping, cargo-owners interests on the one hand, and the shipping industry on the other,[20] and the world divided into countries that are more interested in protecting shippers and others who are more prone to protecting carriers.[21] And developing and least developed countries struggle to protect consignees.[22]

A less *ouvert* tension is that between general and *specialis* unification of private international maritime law explored below.

A. Global/Specialised

The Hamburg Rules[23] (ratified mostly by developing countries)[24] was the first international Treaty aimed at global unification of COGS rules to include jurisdiction provisions, and 'raised hackles in major shipping centres such as London, New York, Rotterdam, Antwerp, and Tokyo'.[25] These Rules give the cargo claimant an option between five jurisdictional bases in which to sue or arbitrate:[26] (i) the principal place of business or, in the absence thereof, the habitual residence of the defendant; (ii) the place where the contract was made, if the defendant has there a place of business, branch or agency through which the contract was made; (iii) the port of loading or the port of discharge; (iv) any additional place designated for that purpose in the contract of carriage by sea, ie, the parties can agree on a different forum via a choice of court agreement in the contract of carriage; however, the parties cannot restrict the jurisdiction grounds stipulated in the Convention;[27] (v) *forum arresti*[28] is also recognised in the Convention, in relation to the carrying ship or a sister-ship, providing that the defendant may request the claim to be pursued in one of the stipulated fora if they provide alternative security for the claim.[29]

[18] COGS is excluded from the scope of application of the HCCH 2005 Convention on Choice of Court Agreements, Art 2(2)(f).

[19] Note the latest report from the HCCH Experts' Group on Jurisdiction, Prel Doc No 3, February 2021, particularly 5(c): 'WG's work proceed in an inclusive and holistic manner, with an initial focus on developing binding rules for concurrent proceedings (parallel proceedings and related actions or claims), and acknowledging the primary role of both jurisdictional rules and the doctrine of forum non conveniens', available at: assets.hcch.net/docs/5fbec58b-d14f-49c6-8719-b1fb68fd6d5b.pdf.

[20] R Taudal Poulsen et al, 'Buyer-driven greening? Cargo-owners and environmental upgrading in maritime shipping' (2016) 68 *Geoforum* 57.

[21] See, inter alia, Fresnedo de Aguirre (n 16).

[22] See, inter alia, UNCTAD, 'Making Trade Work for LDCs: A Handbook on Mainstreaming Trade' (2016), available at: unctad.org/system/files/official-document/aldc2015d5_en.pdf. See also Fresnedo de Aguirre (n 16).

[23] The UN Convention on the Carriage of Goods by Sea 1978. See *The Ratification of Maritime Conventions* (Institute of Maritime Law, University of Southampton 2020).

[24] This international treaty has been ratified by 34 States, mostly developing countries that neither individually nor collectively have a substantial impact on global shipping.

[25] Tetley (n 4) 807–08.

[26] Arts 21 and 22, Hamburg Rules.

[27] A von Ziegler, 'Jurisdiction and Forum Selection Clauses in a Modern Law on Carriage of Goods by Sea' in M Davies (ed), *Jurisdiction and Forum Selection in International Maritime Law: Essays in Honor of Robert Force* (Kluwer 2005) 85.

[28] *Forum arresti* refers to the courts of the country where the ship has been arrested as security for the claim.

[29] Art 22(2), Hamburg Rules.

Chapter 14 of the Rotterdam Rules (not in force) also contains jurisdiction rules. These were at the centre of conflicting views that compromise their broad acceptance.[30] Countries and industry groups supporting carrier interests, along with legal systems that are commonly chosen in choice of court and arbitration agreements, argued that the Rules should not include provisions on jurisdiction or arbitration.[31] Conversely, countries and industry groups supporting cargo interests, along with legal systems that regulate jurisdiction and arbitration domestically or as parties to the Hamburg Rules, insisted that the Rules should follow the lead of the Hamburg Rules to protect a cargo claimant's ability to initiate proceedings in a reasonable forum of her choice.[32] Somewhere in the middle, a number of countries sought a more balanced compromise. The final solution was not only to harmonise the law to the extent possible in separate chapters on jurisdiction and arbitration, but to also accommodate those countries and legal systems unprepared to accept any compromise. Thus, the Rotterdam Rules permit State parties to decide whether to 'opt in' to either of these chapters.[33]

Chapter 14 is very detailed and comprehensive and strives to strike a balance between cargo and carrier interests. It provides the general rules for jurisdiction in relation to actions against the carrier (Article 66); choice of court agreements (Article 67); actions against the maritime performing party (Article 68); arrest and provisional or protective measures (Article 70); consolidation and removal of actions (Article 71); agreement after a dispute has arisen and jurisdiction when the defendant has entered an appearance (Article 72); and recognition and enforcement of decisions by a court having jurisdiction under the treaty (Article 73). The Chapter provides that no additional bases of jurisdiction may be recognised under the Treaty (Article 69), and it establishes the optional character of this Chapter in relation to the Convention as a whole, indicating that a declaration may be made at any time (Article 91) to this effect. The limits around party autonomy in choice of court agreements were the most difficult to agree upon.[34] The general rule (Article 66) is that the claimant has the right to choose a reasonable forum in which to initiate proceedings against the carrier, from a list of *fora* with a reasonable connection to the transaction. The carrier, in turn, is protected from suit in any other forum, providing a balance between the cargo's and the carrier's interests.[35] There is greater freedom of contract to parties to a 'volume contract'[36] to include an exclusive choice of court agreement in their contract that will be valid if certain conditions are met: the choice of court needs to be expressly exclusive; and only a court in a country that is a party to the Convention can be chosen under Article 67(1)(b). Just as a claimant cannot use the general provision on choice of court agreements of Article 66 to force a carrier into a forum that would not apply the Convention, a carrier cannot use Article 67 to force a claimant into a forum that would not apply the Convention.[37]

The Rotterdam Rules negotiation was ongoing at UNCITRAL during the time the Choice of Court Agreements Convention was being prepared at the HCCH. The HCCH adopted a 'no-interference' position, to avoid the clash between these parallel processes.[38] With hindsight,

[30] Fresnedo de Aguirre (n 16).

[31] See MF Sturley, 'Jurisdiction and Arbitration under the Rotterdam Rules' (2009) 14 *Uniform Law Review* 945.

[32] Ibid.

[33] Chs 14 and 15, United Nations Convention on Contracts for the International Carriage of Goods Wholly or Partly by Sea, 2008 (Rotterdam Rules).

[34] See G Yimer, 'Adjudicatory Jurisdiction in International Carriage of Goods by Sea: Would the Rotterdam Rules settle the Controversy?' (2013) 21 *African Journal of International and Comparative Law* 467.

[35] For a detailed analysis of the 'reasonable' connecting factors, see Sturley (n 31).

[36] The special rules for volume contracts are included in Art 80 of the Convention.

[37] A detailed analysis of the jurisdiction chapter exceeds the possibilities of this contribution. For such analysis see, inter alia, Sturley (n 31).

[38] T Hartley and M Dogauchi, *Explanatory Report on the Convention of 30 June 2005 on Choice of Court Agreements* (Permanent Bureau of the Hague Conference on Private International Law 2005), available at:

would it not have been preferable to have COGS within the scope of the HCCH Convention and tackle the (eventual) relationship with the Rotterdam Rules via Article 26 (relationship with other international instruments)?

B. Regional/General

The general EU/EEA PIL regime for jurisdiction (and recognition and enforcement of foreign judgments) in civil and commercial matters, ie, the Brussels Ia Regulation[39] and the Lugano Convention 2007,[40] do not exclude COGS from their scope of application. The basic rule is that a defendant domiciled in an EU/Lugano State must be sued in that State.[41] There are a number of exceptions to this general jurisdiction rule, especially in COGS scenarios where the parties have chosen the court of an EU/Lugano State to have jurisdiction, and the jurisdiction agreement satisfies the requirements of the relevant instrument;[42] when the defendant has submitted to the jurisdiction of the court of an EU/Lugano State without contesting its jurisdiction;[43] or an international convention prevails, as discussed below. Moreover, the claimant may have some additional choices 'in matters relating to a contract, in the courts for the place of performance of the obligation in question';[44] 'in matters relating to tort, delict or quasi-delict in the courts for the place where the harmful event occurred or may occur';[45] 'as regards a dispute arising out of the operations of a branch, agency or other establishment, in the courts for the place in which the branch, agency or other establishment is situated';[46] or 'as regards a dispute concerning the payment or remuneration claimed in respect of the salvage of a cargo or freight, in the court under the authority of which the cargo or freight has been arrested or could have been so arrested but security has already been provided'.[47] Also relevant in this context are provisions for multiple defendants, third-party proceedings and counterclaims,[48] and tonnage limitation proceedings.[49] There are rich and abundant developments of the Court of Justice of the European Union (CJEU) in relation to some complex questions raised by these provisions in the COGS context.[50] Particularly relevant to issues discussed in this chapter, the CJEU held in *TillyRuss*[51] that the reach as regards a third party of a choice of court agreement included in a B/L must be determined by reference to the relationship between the original parties to the contract: if the clause is effective as between the original parties to the contract, it is also

www.hcch.net/en/publications-and-studies/details4/?pid=3959, paras [54]-[58], 'Sub-paragraph (f) excludes contracts for the national or international carriage of passengers or goods, regardless of the means of transport. The exclusion extends to carriage by sea, land and air, or any combination of the three. The international carriage of persons or goods is subject to a number of other important conventions, and this exclusion prevents conflicts arising with those instruments'.

[39] Regulation (EU) No 1215/2012 [2012] OJ L351/1.

[40] Convention on jurisdiction and the recognition and enforcement of judgments in civil and commercial matters [2007] OJ L339.

[41] Art 4 Brussels Ia Regulation (Brussels Ia).

[42] Note the differences between Brussels Ia and the Lugano Convention 2007 in relation to the provision for choice of court agreements: Art 23 of the latter only applies where one of the parties is domiciled in a Contracting State.

[43] Art 26 Brussels Ia; Art 24 Lugano 2007.

[44] Art 7(1)(a) Brussels Ia; Art 5(1)(a) Lugano 2007.

[45] Art 7(2) Brussels Ia; Art 5(3) Lugano 2007.

[46] Art 7(5) Brussels Ia; Art 5(5) Lugano 2007.

[47] Art 7(7) Brussels Ia; Art 5(7) Lugano 2007.

[48] Art 8 Brussels Ia; Art 6 Lugano 2007.

[49] Art 9 Brussels Ia; Art 7 Lugano 2007.

[50] See generally Baatz (n 15) 19–46.

[51] Case 71/83 *Tilly Russ v Nova* [1984] ECR 2417, para 24; Case 159/97 *Castelletti v Trumpy* [1999] ECR I-1597, paras 41–42; and Case 387/98 *Coreck Maritime GmbH v Handelsveem BV* [2000] ECR 1-09337, para 27.

effective between the carrier and a third-party B/L holder who was not an original party to the B/L, provided that the third-party holder succeeded to the shipper's rights and obligations under the applicable national law when it acquired the B/L. If the third-party holder did not succeed to the rights and obligations of the shipper under the applicable national law when it acquired the B/L, it must be established whether it agreed to the jurisdiction clause in accordance with the requirements of the EU general PIL regime.[52] The CJEU has also established that consent is presumed where there is a commercial usage in the relevant branch of international trade or commerce of which the parties are or ought to have been aware.[53] This general principle,[54] developed initially in the COGS context, applies in the EU PIL regime generally: 'The agreement may bind third parties who did not expressly consent to it, if those parties have taken over, in accordance with the applicable law, the rights and obligations of one of the original parties, but not otherwise'.[55] In EU PIL, as well as in some national legal systems like English law, maritime law scenarios have been a fertile field for doctrinal developments that transcend the maritime sphere.[56]

Of particular relevance is Article 71 of the Brussels Ia Regulation providing that the Regulation shall not affect any international conventions to which the EU Member States are parties and which in relation to particular matters govern jurisdiction. The trajectory of this provision in the EU PIL regime has the special jurisdiction rule of *forum arresti* (jurisdiction based on the arrest of ships, as provided for in the international Arrest Conventions)[57] at its core. During the preparatory work pursuant to the accession of the UK, Ireland and Denmark to the Brussels Convention 1968 (Accession Convention 1978),[58] Article 57(1) of the Brussels Convention was amended by Article 25(2) of the Accession Convention, with a view to 'uniform interpretation' enhancing the priority of specialised Conventions. At the time Schlosser remarked that

> it would have been inappropriate to limit the exercise of admiralty jurisdiction to the bases of jurisdiction included in the 1968 Convention in its original form. If a ship is arrested in a State because of an internationally recognized maritime claim, it would be unreasonable to expect the creditor to seek a decision on his claim before the courts of the ship-owner's domicile.[59]

Thus, the fabric of the *lex specialis*[60] provisions of the current general EU/EEA PIL regimes (Brussels Ia/Lugano 2007) bear the imprint of the highly specialised nature of private international maritime claims;[61] however, this has not resulted in exceptionalism but in *coordination*, and the impact has transcended the context of maritime claims. The general principle of the

[52] *Coreck*, ibid.

[53] C-106/95 *Mainschiffahrts-Genossenschaft eG v Les Gravières Rhénanes (MSG)* EU:C:1997:70; *Castelletti* (n 51).

[54] R Fentiman, *International Commercial Litigation*, 2nd edn (Oxford University Press 2015) [2.172].

[55] F Garcimartin, 'Prorogation of Jurisdiction' in A Dickinson and E Lein (eds), *Brussels I Recast* (Oxford University Press 2015) 298.

[56] Sir David Foxton, 38th Donald O'May Lecture (Southampton Institute of Maritime Law, 5 November 2020), available at: www.judiciary.uk/wp-content/uploads/2020/11/Foxton-Donald-OMay-Speech.pdf (2021) *Lloyd's Commercial and Maritime Law Quarterly* (forthcoming).

[57] International Arrest Conventions 1952 and 1999.

[58] [1978] OJ L304/1.

[59] [1979] OJ C59/71, 108. A special section dealing with admiralty jurisdiction was considered but instead a Joint Declaration urging the then Community States to accede to the 'most important of all the Conventions on maritime law, namely the Brussels Convention of 10 May 1952' was signed in Luxembourg on 9 October 1978.

[60] The functioning of Art 71 Brussels I (Reg 44/2001) was assessed in the Brussels I review (see *Heidelberg Report* paras 139–45).

[61] The referred amendment also reflected the importance of other specialised Conventions in the broader carriage context, including air and rail carriage conventions (see further, Schlosser report. para 238 ff.).

lex specialis has a 'long pedigree in international jurisprudence',[62] and the question of 'self-contained regimes' has been examined in relation to normative conflicts in international law.[63] The EU/EEA general PIL regime opens that 'window'[64] expressly in a 'coordination clause'[65] to international conventions that 'in relation to particular matters govern jurisdiction, [or the recognition and enforcement of foreign judgments]' expressly indicating that the *general* regime shall not affect the application of these *specialised* international conventions.[66]

In *The Tatry*[67] a sister-ship had been arrested in England giving the English courts jurisdiction on the merits under the 1952 Arrest Convention. At the time there were pending proceedings on the same claim in the Netherlands and the shipowner argued that the English court, as the court second seised, had to stay its proceedings under the *lis pendens* provision of the Brussels regime. The CJEU held that as the 1952 Arrest Convention does not contain any *lis pendens* provisions there was no conflict and the *lis pendens* provisions of the Brussels regime applied to the effect of negating the jurisdiction of the court second seised (the one based on the 1952 Arrest Convention). That is, the relationship with the Arrest Conventions[68] and others[69] is significant in the case of COGS, not only due to the recognition of *forum arresti*[70] as a special jurisdiction basis for the merits of the dispute, but for what it enables in relation to the normative interaction between general and specialised regimes.[71]

The extent of the normative accommodation between the (regional/general) EU/EEA PIL and (global/specialised) international conventions within and beyond COGS as provided for in the line of cases of the CJEU since *The Tatry* has been subject to critique.[72] An example of an international convention prevailing in COGS would be where the Hamburg Rules apply to a B/L which provides for the exclusive jurisdiction of the courts of an EU/EEA Member State. Article 21 of the Hamburg Rules provides that the cargo claimant can choose from a number of different fora including the court chosen by the parties to the contract, but the parties cannot provide for an exclusive choice of court agreement; this would prevail over Article 25 of the Brussels Ia Regulation which provides a presumption of exclusivity in

[62] M Koskenniemi, 'Fragmentation of International Law – The Function and Scope of the Lex Specialis Rule and the Question of 'Self-Contained Regimes': An Outline' ILC (2001), available at: legal.un.org/ilc/sessions/55/pdfs/fragmentation_outline.pdf.

[63] Ibid.

[64] See J d'Aspremont and F Giglio, 'Windows in International Law' in V Ruiz Abou-Nigm et al (eds), *Linkages and Boundaries in Private and Public International Law* (Hart Publishing 2018) 33–52.

[65] See M Blanca Noodt Taquela and V Ruiz Abou-Nigm, 'The Draft Judgments Convention and its Relationship with Other International Instruments' (2017–18) 19 *Yearbook of Private International Law* 217.

[66] Art 71 Brussels Ia; Art 67 Lugano 2007.

[67] C-406/92 *The Maciej Rataj* (*The Tatry*) EU:C:1994:400.

[68] The International Convention for the Unification of Certain Rules Relating to the Arrest of Seagoing Ships of 1952 and the International Convention on the Arrest of Ships 1999.

[69] eg, inter alia, the Hamburg Rules, and (eventually) the Rotterdam Rules.

[70] See further, Ruiz Abou-Nigm (nn 11, 13).

[71] Since *The Tatry* this provision has enabled doctrinal developments beyond shipping in a line of cases including C-533/08 *TNT Express Nederland BV* EU:C:2010:243; C-452/12 *Nipponkoa Insurance Co (Europe) Ltd* EU:C:2013:858; C-230/15 *Brite Strike Technologies Inc* EU:C:2016:560; C-213/18 *Guaitoli* EU:C:2019:927. See, inter alia, V Lazić and S Stuij, 'Brussels Ibis in Relation to Other Instruments on the Global Level' in V Lazić and S Stuij (eds), *Brussels I bis Regulation* (TMC Asser Institute 2017) 119–50.

[72] See P Beaumont, 'European Court of Justice and Jurisdiction and Enforcement of Judgments in Civil and Commercial Matters' (1997) 46 *ICLQ* 205. Beaumont argued that Art 57 of the Brussels Convention 1968 (Art 71 of Brussels Ia) was therein construed too narrowly, 'distorting the Arrest Convention by adding a rigid *lis pendens* rule that was not provided for by the drafters of that Convention' (211). See also, A Briggs, 'The Brussels Convention Tames the Arrest Convention' [1995] *Lloyd's Maritime and Commercial Law Quarterly* 161. See further Ruiz Abou-Nigm (n 11) 182–88.

choice of court agreements.[73] Beyond the merits of the 'regionalisation' resulting from the manner in which this interaction has been construed in the EU/EEA area of justice, coordination mechanisms of this kind allow for the necessary permeability and flexibility in PIL systemic 'dialogues'.[74]

Before turning to the consideration of applicable law issues,[75] and precisely because of them, it is important to emphasise the weight that the ascertainment of jurisdiction carries in COGS claims. There are a number of reasons why one jurisdiction may be more favourable to one party than the other due to the referred fragmentation, which creates incentives for forum shopping.[76] One key difference in this sector is the applicable law in relation to limitation of liability of the carrier. The main regimes currently in force as provided for in the Hague,[77] Hague Visby,[78] Hamburg Rules, or in national law regimes (some of them a blend between the international regimes)[79] vary considerably in relation to the liability of the carrier – and the resulting amount of compensation due to the cargo claimant;[80] much in relation to the interpretation, construction and application of these rules depends on the PIL rules of the forum.

III. Disparity in Interpretation and Application of Unifying Provisions: Focus on Applicable Law

The interaction between different legal frameworks (national, regional and international) as well as the construction of contractual terms (at times from different but interrelated contracts) incorporating unifying regimes is at the epicentre of interpretation disparities of unified applicable law rules in COGS. Unified applicable law rules are included in international maritime conventions in addition to broader international conventions, such as the 1889 Montevideo Treaty on Commercial Law. In the European system, cargo claims are included within the scope of application of the general rules on applicable law for contractual obligations and non-contractual obligations, respectively.[81] Notably, however, the Rome I Regulation excludes from its scope obligations arising out of the negotiable character of B/Ls.[82] Thus, the Regulation applies only to the obligations between the original parties to the contract, the carrier and the shipper. The extent of the exclusion may present problems of interpretation.[83] In *The Channel Ranger*[84] the English

[73] See also Art 23 of the Lugano Convention; and Baatz (n 15) 2.

[74] E Jayme, 'Identité culturelle et intégration: Le droit international privé postmoderne' (1995) 251 *Hague Collected Courses* paras 60 and 259.

[75] In relation to applicable law issues in COGS, see generally, R Espinosa Calabuig, *El Contrato Internacional de Transporte Maritimo de Mercancias: Cuestiones de Ley Aplicable* (Granada 1999).

[76] Baatz (n 15) 2.

[77] The International Convention for the Uniication of Certain Rules of Law Relating to Bills of Lading, Brussels, 25 August 1924.

[78] The International Convention for the Unification of Certain Rules of Law Relating to Bills of Lading signed at Brussels on 25 August 1924 as amended by the Protocol signed at Brussels on 23 February 1968 and by the Protocol signed at Brussels on 21 December 1979.

[79] eg, in China and the Scandinavian countries.

[80] See, eg, *The Morviken* [1983] 1 AC 565.

[81] Rome I and Rome II Regulations. The provisions of these Regulation continue to apply in the United Kingdom after Brexit as retained EU law (The Law Applicable to Contractual Obligations and Non-contractual Obligations (Amendment etc) (EU Exit) Regulations 2019, SI 2019/834).

[82] Art 1(2) and Recital 9 of the Rome I Regulation.

[83] See Baatz (n 15) 58–59.

[84] *Caresse Navigation Ltd v Ofice National de L'Electricite* [2014] EWCA Civ 1366.

courts applied Article 3 of the Regulation to a negotiable B/L between the original parties to the B/L, and then considered that there was 'no reason why this common form bill of lading should not be transferred to a consignee who (upon becoming a holder of the bill) would succeed to the rights contained therein, which rights were subject to English law'.[85] Party autonomy is the dominant PIL technique[86] in relation to contractual claims in this as in many other contexts.[87] In COGS, limits and safeguards may need to be considered in order to strike a balance between certainty and predictability on the one hand, and flexibility to deal with inequalities that might arise from its application to very dissimilar scenarios on the other.[88]

A quintessentially private international maritime law issue is the effect of *paramount clauses*.[89] Translated into general PIL terms, this relates to the question of whether the parties can contractually extend the scope of application of uniform substantive law, and if so, what are the limits to that prerogative.[90] Two different legal techniques may be applied at once: incorporating the terms of the unifying regime, and doing so by reference to the terms of a related contract. National courts have construed issues of incorporation and reference very differently.[91] One of the technical questions that arises is to what extent the limitation of liability of the carrrier in the Hague, Hague Visby or Hamburg Rules (the unifying regimes in force) could be considered as overriding mandatory provisions (as a safeguard of public interests) in relation to the applicable law to the B/L.[92] Notably for this discussion, in the EU area of justice, insights in relation to the effect of overriding mandatory provisions of a system other than that of the applicable law may be drawn from CJEU decisions in non-maritime cases such as *Greece v Nikiforidis*.[93] This is the other side of the advantages of the inclusion of maritime scenarios within the scope of application of general PIL regimes.

IV. Contemporary Exceptionalism: The Recent Exclusion of Carriage of Goods by Sea Contracts from the HCCH 2019 Convention on the Recognition and Enforcement of Foreign Judgments

Following the formula adopted in the HCCH 2005 Choice of Court Agreements Convention, the HCCH 2019 Convention on the Recognition and Enforcement of Foreign Judgments in Civil and Commercial Matters excludes COGS from its scope. The rationale appears the same as its predecessor:[94] to prevent conflicts with other conventions.[95] In relation to the 2005 Convention,

[85] Ibid, [36].

[86] See R Michaels, 'Party Autonomy in Private International Law – A New Paradigm without a Solid Foundation?' (2013) 15 *Japanese Yearbook of Private International Law* 282.

[87] This is recognised almost universally, not without robust opposition. See, inter alia, C Fresnedo de Aguirre, *La Autonomía de la Voluntad en la Contratación Internacional* (Fundación de Cultura Universitaria 1991).

[88] Fresnedo de Aguirre (n 16) 880.

[89] See J Echebarria Fernández, 'Paramount Clause and Codification of International Shipping Law' (2019) 50 *Journal of Maritime Law and Commerce* 1, 45.

[90] See AWM Struycken, 'Co-ordination and Co-operation in Respectful Disagreement' (2004) 311 *Hague Collected Courses* 380–90.

[91] For the practical effects of the distinction between reference and incorporation see L Collins and J Harris (eds), *Dicey, Morris and Collins: Conflict of Laws*, 15th edn and 5th supp (Sweet & Maxwell 2018) para [32.058] ff.

[92] The rules cannot apply mandatorily to a charterparty although they are often incorporated voluntarily into standard form charterparties. See generally, Baatz (n 15) 68.

[93] C-135/15; EU:C:2016:774, discussed by Trevor Hartley, 'Public Policy and Mandatory Provisions', ch 6 in this book.

[94] See Hartley and Dogauchi, *Explanatory Report* (n 38).

[95] See F Garcimartín and G Saumier, *Explanatory Report on the 2019 HCCH Judgments Convention* (HCCH 2020), available at: www.hcch.net/en/publications-and-studies/details4/?pid=6797, para [54].

the exclusion has been considered a 'missed opportunity', 'to some extent, simply the result of unfortunate timing of parallel negotiations'.[96] The lack of further consideration and discussion of this exclusion is even more unwarranted in the 2019 Convention. The rationale appears to be supported exclusively around the existence (rather than on an assessment of the impact of its functioning) of other (potentially global) conventional structures.[97] Considering the significance of COGS contracts in transnational commercial litigation it is surprising that this exclusion was not debated thoroughly.[98]

The existing global unification instruments in this context are by definition inchoate and selective.[99] Thus, these exclusions based on the avoidance of conflicts of conventions in relation to COGS, in light of the unlikeliness of wide adoption of the Rotterdam Rules – of general knowledge at the time of the adoption of the HCCH 2019 Convention – and considering the fragmentation of COGS global legal landscape more broadly, appears to be yet another missed opportunity. COGS contracts are in some legal systems – notably English law – typical commercial contracts,[100] and litigation involving cargo claims is a considerable part of mainstream international commercial litigation in many jurisdictions around the globe. Moreover, COGS jurisprudence has contributed to doctrinal developments in PIL, commercial law and private law more generally in several legal systems. Excluding COGS from the scope of this Convention may impoverish the strength of the developmental trajectory of this instrument and its overall impact on transnational commercial litigation.

Conversely, cooperation endeavours as well as coordination techniques may offer much more fruitful outcomes for 'leaving no-one behind'. At the time of the UK Accession Convention 1978, the understanding was that the UK would have suffered an unacceptable loss of jurisdiction if the *lex specialis* provision[101] had not been introduced in the EU PIL general regime. The trajectory shows that the benefits of this provision were not exclusive to the UK, and not limited to jurisdiction in maritime claims, but enabled doctrinal developments that allowed EU general PIL rules to interact and integrate specialised conventions, preserving technical specialisation, yet safeguarding the protection of fundamental principles in operation in the EU area of justice. In times of global governance in the pursuit of global goals, PIL methodologies and techniques should be fully explored in the progressive unification of PIL globally.

V. What Bridges for Private International Maritime Law?

PIL unification seeks to provide certainty and predictability in cross-border scenarios while embracing legal diversity. Efforts towards PIL unification have an important role to play in relation to maritime claims.[102] Substantive unification endeavours, no matter how successful, are

[96] C Forrest, 'The Hague Convention on Choice of Court Agreements' (2009) 5 *Journal of Private International Law* 491, 496.

[97] That is, departing from the 2005 Convention, the latest instrument of global PIL unification includes within its scope several maritime scenarios, including emergency towage and emergency salvage, because these matters are not covered by other conventional instruments. See Garcimartín and Saumier *Explanatory Report* (n 95) para [55]. See also, HCCH, Prel Doc No 12 of June 2019, available at: www.hcch.net/en/publications-and-studies/details4/?pid=6642&dtid=61.

[98] *cf* eg, the exclusion of intellectual property, thoroughly explored and debated.

[99] See the list of matters excluded from the scope of application of the 2019 Convention (Art 2). See further, D French and V Ruiz Abou-Nigm, 'Jurisdiction: Betwixt Unilateralism and Global Coordination' in V Ruiz Abou-Nigm et al (eds), *Linkages and Boundaries in Private and Public International Law* (Hart Publishing 2018).

[100] See Foxton (n 56).

[101] Art 57(2) of the Brussels Convention 1968 was amended by Art 25(2) of the 1978 Accession Convention in a way which clarified the priority of specialised Conventions.

[102] C Fresnedo de Aguirre and V Ruiz Abou-Nigm, 'El Derecho Marítimo Internacional y el Derecho Internacional Privado' (2005) XXII *Anuario de Derecho Maritimo* 189.

unlikely to achieve global uniformity.[103] There is general acceptance that the present frameworks do not work as well as they might, particularly in relation to jurisdiction, and that there is global interest in greater coordination. Are there any means of continuing to work towards greater certainty and predictability in this sphere? Detailed mapping of existing PIL rules included in, inter alia, international conventions, regional instruments, widely used standard forms, coupled with thorough empirical research into maritime practice, impact assessments and a review of jurisprudence, including arbitral case law, should provide a robust empirical basis to substantiate further work. So far, however, in the 'who's who of international bodies'[104] that have pursued international maritime law unification in relation to COGS, the HCCH is missing. The HCCH could join efforts with the International Maritime Organization (IMO), the United Nations Commission on International Trade Law (UNCITRAL), the United Nations Council on Trade and Development (UNCTAD), the International Institute for the Unification of Private Law (UNIDROIT) and the Comité Maritime International (CMI), ultimately to support the UN Sustainable Development Agenda 2030.[105]

Arguably, global (general) PIL expertise may be able to provide the missing links, in two possible concomitant directions: (i) exploring means of coordination between existing instruments, which could be built initially via soft-law mechanisms,[106] and could include guidance as to the application of existing general PIL instruments to COGS; (ii) and considering further work in this sphere in the context of the current exploration of jurisdiction issues at the HCCH.[107]

The HCCH is well placed to host collaborative endeavours[108] bringing together the vast experience of these bodies, and has long-standing expertise in developing techniques[109] about relationships between international instruments,[110] to enable systemic dialogues of crucial importance globally in this sector. The experience of the EU where COGS claims are included within the scope of application of EU general PIL could shed some light as to the results in this region,[111] and compared with other regions where there are multilateral (general) PIL treaties in force; and in turn, with the global scenario and its fragmented landscape. CMI[112] endeavours collating judicial and arbitral decisions from a broad range of

[103] See Sturley (n 31).

[104] Davies (n 3) 155.

[105] Support for the UN Agenda 2030 is within the HCCH 2019–2022 Strategic Plan. Access to justice, including access to transnational justice (SDG 16) is a transversal goal for sustainable development, and Private International Law more broadly has an important contribution to make to advance the SDGs. See further, R Michaels, V Ruiz Abou-Nigm and H van Loon (eds), *The Private Side of Transforming Our World: Private International Law and the UN Agenda 2020* (Intersentia 2021).

[106] 'Uniformity' in this sector has seen progress via soft law mechanisms. Could 'the prodigious efforts' that have been made to modernise the law in COGS be somehow made available to the industry via the door of standardised contracts? This is not a novel idea: the UNCTAD/ICC Rules for Multimodal Transport adopted in 1992 were issued in recognition of the fact that the 1980 Multimodal Convention would never come into force (Davies (n 3) 153). That might be a model worth considering in the context of PIL rules in COGS.

[107] Member States of the HCCH approved the constitution of a Working Group under the leadership of Professor Keisuke Takashita (Japan, Chair of the Expert Group) during the first session of the CGAP 2021, 1 March 2021.

[108] The HCCH, UNCITRAL and UNIDROIT are 'sister organisations' with robust collaboration.

[109] Blanca Noodt Taquela and Ruiz Abou-Nigm (n 65).

[110] Both the 2005 and 2019 HCCH Conventions include 'compatibility clauses' to that effect: Art 26 (HCCH 2005); Art 23 (HCCH 2019).

[111] It is a truism to note the limits of coordination endeavours at a global level compared to the rules and processes applicable in the EU area of justice.

[112] See the CMI and the Centre for Maritime Law of the National University of Singapore database, available at: cmlcmidatabase.org/ building on the foundations laid by F Berlingieri in his earlier CMI database of jurisprudence on maritime conventions.

jurisdictions around the world arising from international maritime conventions and other international uniform instruments provide rich empirical evidence. Further research and analysis[113] could unveil to what extent the status quo represents (i) barriers to trade and sustainable development, and (ii) hurdles in the access to justice, revealing also the impact of existing unified rules in (iii) strengthening legal systems and institutions, and (iv) making the overall system of private international maritime law more robust in terms of its doctrinal development. That is, focusing on global private international maritime law for better coordination of the existing normative frameworks to deliver sustainable development, ie, economic, social and environmental benefits for all, including future generations. Moving from exceptionalism to global wayfinding may require swinging from interests to data, from lobbies to researchers, from compromise to inclusive co-design.[114]

VI. Conclusion

'Admiralty is special, everyone knows it'.[115] Yet, maritime exceptionalism in global PIL is not conducive to higher goals.[116] In relation to the 2005 HCCH Convention it has been argued that 'it was simply easier to exclude these from the convention'.[117] There is much to be learnt from the major unification efforts in modern international maritime law; one lesson is that avoiding tackling the most difficult questions does not pay off.[118]

This chapter considers some of the benefits of including COGS in broader processes of progressive unification of global PIL rules in civil and commercial matters. Looking at the degree of specificity included in, eg, the jurisdiction chapter of the Rotterdam Rules, it seems wasteful not to be able to make something more fruitful of all these efforts.

Inclusivity and representation are crucial to the success of any endeavour.[119] The HCCH is well placed to generate such inclusive processes, bringing about the 'colourful tapestry'[120]

[113] HCCH recognises the crucial role of empirical research on the performance of existing instruments and the development of new ones (HCCH CGAP 2021 (Session 2, 2.3.21) however budgetary constraints may prevent this. Academia could support further the work of these organisations.

[114] Promoting greater inclusiveness and universality in the progressive unification of global PIL is a priority of the HCCH Strategic Plan 2019–2022 (strategic priority three), available at: assets.hcch.net/docs/bb7129a9-abee-46c9-ab65-7da398e51856.pdf. Online participation facilitates broader representation.

[115] C Hunter, 'Maritime Exceptionalism – is it justified?' (2019), presentation, 46th Maritime Law Association of Australia and New Zealand.

[116] See HCCH, 'Note' (n 97) referring to the maxim of *lex specialis*: 'the principle was considered to achieve a higher objective in helping to regulate the interactions between the international legal system as a whole and its 'subsystems' (ie, legal branches), because it supports the primacy of legal norms, while also encouraging the development of more specialised subsidiary legal principles'.

[117] Forrest (n 96) 508; referring to A Schulz, 'The Hague Convention of 30 June 2005 on Choice of Court Agreement' (2006) 2 *Journal of Private International Law* 243, 249.

[118] See F Berlingieri, 'The History of the Rotterdam Rules' in MD Güner-Özbek (ed), *The United Nations Convention on Contracts for the International Carriage of Goods Wholly or Partly by Sea* (Beck 2011) 1.

[119] JM Alcantara et al, 'Particular Concerns with The Rotterdam Rules', (https://www.pysdens.com/v2/material/Rotterdam%20Rules%20Paper%20-%20Apr%2010.pdfde;'Declaración de Montevideo', October 2010 (https://www.pysdens.com/wp-content/uploads/DECLARATION-OF-MONTIVIDEO-English-translation.pdf); and J Vicente Guzman et al, 'Una Respuesta Latinoamericana a la Declaracion de Montevideo' (https://comitemaritime.org/wp-content/uploads/2018/05/The-Rotterdam-Rules-A-Latin-American-Response-to-the-Declaration-of-Montevideo.pdf).

[120] Metaphor used by the representative of the Asian-African Legal Consultative Organisation (AALCO) in relation to the universality and inclusiveness of the HCCH, at the first session of the CGAP HCCH 2021, 1 March 2021.

of global PIL. And the CMI has been knocking at the door.[121] The challenge is, thus, to work collaboratively towards global goals. Many major milestones in the unification of maritime law flourished after a big 'disaster'.[122] What else other than the current global pandemic do we need to pull together in pursuit of global goals? Maybe it is time to turn the tide away from exceptionalism to global wayfinding in private international maritime law.

[121] See the response of the HCCH to the CMI proposal in relation to including the judicial sale of ships in the scope of application of the Judgments project, July 2017.

[122] See, inter alia, JM Alcantara, 'La Uniformidad del Derecho Marítimo: Leyenda o Mito?' (2018) 31 *Revista de Transporte y Seguros* 159.

28

Choice of Court Agreements

PAUL BEAUMONT AND MARY KEYES*

I. Introduction

Cross-border commercial activity has become commonplace. This activity is secured by contracts, which now typically include dispute resolution terms. The parties may select from a range of forms of dispute resolution, including litigation, arbitration and mediation. This chapter deals with the parties' selection of litigation as the means of dispute resolution, demonstrated by a choice of court agreement designating the forum in which disputes can be resolved.

The 2005 Hague Convention on Choice of Court Agreements (the Choice of Court Convention) was the first formal outcome of the original Hague Judgments Project, which commenced in 1992.[1] It regulates both jurisdiction and the recognition and enforcement of judgments. This chapter focuses on the jurisdictional provisions of the Choice of Court Convention.[2]

This chapter is structured as follows: section II considers the definition of exclusive choice of court agreements under the Choice of Court Convention, particularly considering whether there is a separate requirement of agreement as a precondition to the operation of the Convention, and the Convention's provisions on formal and substantive validity. Section III addresses the legal effects of exclusive choice of court agreements under the Convention, considering first the effect on the jurisdiction of the courts designated in the choice of court agreement, and then the obligations of the courts which were not designated by the parties. Section IV concludes.

* Paul Beaumont was a member of the Informal Working Group, the Special Commission and the Diplomatic Session representing the UK and served on the Drafting Committee for the Choice of Court Convention. He subsequently represented the EU throughout the various stages of the Judgments Convention (Working Group, Special Commission and Diplomatic Session) and in the Experts' Group (now Working Group) on the Jurisdiction Project. Mary Keyes is representing Australia in the Working Group (previously in the Experts' Group) on the Jurisdiction Project. All views stated here are the authors' personal views and do not necessarily reflect the views of the UK, the EU or Australia.

[1] The Convention's origins are described in its Explanatory Report: T Hartley and M Dogauchi, *Convention of 30 June 2005 on Choice of Court Agreements Explanatory Report* (Permanent Bureau of the Hague Conference on Private International Law 2005) 784–87 (Explanatory Report), available at: www.hcch.net/en/publications-and-studies/details4/?pid=3959.

[2] The recognition and enforcement of judgments given by courts designated in exclusive choice of court agreements (Chapter III of the Convention) are addressed in D Goddard and P Beaumont, 'Recognition and Enforcement of Judgments in Civil or Commercial Matters', ch 29 in this book.

II. Defining Exclusive Choice of Court Agreements

A. Meaning of 'Agreement'

There are those who assert, notably Brand and Herrup,[3] that the concept of 'agreement' in Articles 3, 5 and 6 of the Convention is a free-standing concept. They do not argue that it should be given an autonomous interpretation under the Convention but rather that the existence of an agreement is determined by the 'law of the forum – including its choice of law rules'.[4] The authors argue that:

> An exclusive choice of court agreement requires first that there be an agreement. A case, whether international or not, simply does not get into this Convention unless there has been a meeting of the minds concluded or documented in a way which meets certain formal requirements, and which does certain things (ie designates courts to resolve disputes). Absent the consent of the parties, there simply can be no choice of court agreement. The issue of the existence of an agreement, vel non, which is an essential element to bringing a 'case' within the substantive scope of the Convention under Article 1, is different from the issue of substantive validity of that agreement, which comes into play in Chapter II (Articles 5 and 6) and Chapter III (Articles 8 and 9).[5]

Brand and Herrup accept that the substantive validity of the agreement and the parties' capacity to enter into the agreement are determined by the applicable law rules set out in Articles 5, 6 and 9; respectively the law of the State of the chosen court including its applicable law rules and the law of the forum. They also acknowledge that the formal validity requirements are set out in Article 3(c) and that higher formal validity requirements cannot be established than those set out there. Brand and Herrup rely on the concept of 'exclusive choice of court agreements' being set out in Article 1 – the scope provision – as supporting their argument that the concept has a meaning beyond that of the rules on formal and substantive validity in the Convention. However, in order to determine whether any particular 'exclusive choice of court agreement' falls within the scope of the Convention the only relevant criteria relating to its existence which a court should examine at the scope stage are whether the subject matter of the agreement and the parties fall within the scope provisions in Articles 1 and 2. Brand and

[3] RA Brand and PM Herrup, *The 2005 Hague Convention on Choice of Court Agreements: Commentary and Documents* (Cambridge University Press 2008) 40–41, 79 and 88. See the review article by P Beaumont, 'Hague Choice of Court Agreements Convention 2005: Background, Negotiations, Analysis and Current Status' (2009) 5 *Journal of Private International Law* 125, in which these issues are discussed at 137–40 and 144–46.

[4] Brand and Herrup, ibid, 79.

[5] Ibid 40. Paul Herrup and Ron Brand confirmed to the authors via email that they maintain their position. Paul Herrup reiterated that, 'On its face, [Article 5(1)] requires an agreement as a condition precedent for its operation. The antecedent issue of consent, of a meeting of the minds that brings an agreement into existence, is prior to the operation of the clause and falls outside its scope on its own terms'. One reason Herrup takes this view is to protect weaker commercial parties, who might be unaware of the existence or meaning of jurisdictional provisions in so-called contracts of adhesion, written by the stronger party, and more likely to favour them. The first point is a good one but this literal interpretation was not clearly proffered during the negotiations and must be weighed against the historical interpretation argued for here. Herrup's argument does not lead to the conclusion that the forum should apply its own law to determine whether there is an 'agreement'; it could also support the proposition in the Explanatory Report, quoted below, that the existence of an 'agreement' should be interpreted as a question of fact rather than law. The second point is a policy point with which many will sympathise. However, there is a risk of considerable legal uncertainty in international commercial transactions if the smaller company can dispute contractual provisions that it could have read and rejected but either did not read or did not object to at the time the contract was concluded. The Convention did not create special rules for small and medium-sized enterprises, nor special rules for so-called adhesion contracts, and therefore it is hard to justify a special notion of 'agreement' that overturns 'adhesion' contracts in general or for small and medium-sized enterprises in particular. On the value of upholding boilerplate clauses, including choice of court agreements, in international commercial contracts, see G Cordero-Moss, *International Commercial Contracts* (Cambridge University Press 2014).

Herrup argue that there is a sphere of law not covered by the formal or substantive validity of the agreement or the capacity to enter into that agreement that relates to whether there is an 'agreement'. They treat the question of 'consent' as an independent question that falls outside formal or substantive validity and capacity. This key question of consent is then to be left to the law of the forum.

This approach could potentially undermine the value of the Convention. Such an argument did not feature in the recorded documents of the Informal Working Group that prepared the ground for this Convention.[6] The Minutes of the Special Commissions and of the Diplomatic Session in the Proceedings of the Twentieth Session, Tome III, Choice of Court[7] indicate that delegates believed that 'agreement' is to be established through the combined application of the Convention rules on substantive and formal validity.[8] To be fair, the Minutes of the Diplomatic Session record that the US (supported by Canada) thought that the court seised would have to determine whether there was an 'agreement' in 'difficult cases between issues of form and substance'.[9] The Explanatory Report relevantly states that:

> A choice of court agreement cannot be established unilaterally: there must be agreement. Whether there is consent is normally decided by the law of the State of the chosen court, including its rules of choice of law, though in some circumstances capacity is also determined by other systems of law. However, the Convention as a whole comes into operation only if there is a choice of court agreement, and this assumes that the basic factual requirements of consent exist. If, by any normal standards, these do not exist, a court would be entitled to assume that the Convention is not applicable, without having to consider foreign law. The following is an example. X, who is resident in Panama, sends an unsolicited email to Y, who is resident in Mexico, making an offer on terms that are extremely unfavourable to Y. The offer contains a choice of court clause in favour of the courts of Ruritania (an imaginary State), and concludes: 'If you have not replied within seven days, you will be deemed to have accepted this offer'. The e-mail is deleted by Y's anti-spam software and he never reads it. After seven days, X claims that there is a contract with a choice of court agreement, and brings proceedings in the courts of Ruritania. If, unlike the law of every other State in the world, the law of Ruritania considered that a contract existed and the choice of court 'agreement' was valid, other States, including Mexico, would nevertheless be entitled to treat the choice of court agreement as non-existent.[10]

The key point is that most 'consent' questions are governed by the Convention's applicable law rules for substantive validity of the agreement and capacity to enter into the agreement. The Report suggests that in extreme cases where the applicable law has very bad rules on consent some basic questions of consent can be treated as questions of fact to be determined by the forum.[11] This is different from Brand and Herrup's troublesome suggestion that consent (or the meeting of the minds) is a separate question from substantive validity and therefore subject to the law of the

[6] Andrea Schulz's detailed work in Prel Doc 19, available at: www.hcch.net/index_en.php?act=publications.details&pid=3503&dtid=35 which formed the basis of the discussions of the Informal Working Group, distinguishes 'two sub-groups of substantive validity', namely lawfulness on the one hand and capacity and consent on the other. The Reports of the first and second meeting of the Informal Working Group (Prel Docs 20 and 21, available at: www.hcch.net/en/instruments/conventions/publications1/?dtid=35&cid=98) follow this approach. Consent was always treated as a crucial sub-aspect of substantive validity, like restrictions and limitations for concluding such agreements (the lawfulness/null and void aspect).

[7] (Intersentia 2010).

[8] Ibid, Diplomatic Session, Minutes No 2 statements by Beaumont (UK), Goddard, (New Zealand), the response of the Chair (Bucher) to Kovar (USA) (all at 572) and Beaumont (575).

[9] Ibid, Minutes No 3, 581.

[10] (n 1) paras 94–96.

[11] This 'question of fact' approach is repeated by T Hartley in *Choice-of-Court Agreements under the European and International Instruments* (Oxford University Press 2013) 133–34. He does not engage with other points of view in that text.

forum including its applicable law rules. Hartley pointed out that the passage in the Explanatory Report quoted above was:

> inserted at the request of States participating in the Diplomatic Session in order to clarify what they intended. The final draft of the Report, including this passage was given to all participating delegations for their comments. There were no objections to the passage.[12]

We maintain that is very important for courts to ensure that all the relevant issues surrounding whether there is an 'agreement' between the parties are governed by the law(s) governing questions of capacity to enter into the agreement (the law of the court seised including its applicable law rules and the law of the chosen court including its applicable law rules), the law governing questions of substantive validity of the agreement (ie, the law of the chosen court including its applicable law rules) and the Convention requirements on formal validity. The Convention was carefully crafted to set autonomous standards for formal validity (writing or its technological equivalent) and a hard-fought applicable law rule for substantive validity. Many of the debates about the Convention during its drafting turned on whether it should have an autonomous applicable law rule on substantive validity or follow the precedent of the New York Convention to leave it to the court seised to determine whether the arbitration agreement was null and void, inoperative, or incapable of being performed.[13] The quid pro quo in the negotiations for having a strict applicable law rule, whereby the law of the chosen court governs questions of the substantive validity of the choice of court agreement (strengthening the effectiveness of choice of court agreements by preventing a party running to a forum that does not like such agreements and getting them struck down there on the basis of a forum rule on consent) was the creation of a certain amount of flexibility in the court not chosen to consider whether the choice of court clause would cause a 'manifest injustice'.[14] Our preferred answer to Hartley and Dogauchi's example is to say that the choice of court agreement was valid because it was valid under the applicable law (the law of the chosen court) and meets the Convention's form requirements. The Mexican court seised of the case should decide that giving effect to the agreement would lead to a 'manifest injustice or would be manifestly contrary' to its public policy and not apply it.[15]

[12] Ibid, 134.

[13] The latter solution was originally proposed by the Informal Working Group's draft Convention text: see Prel Doc No 22, Art 4(1) of the Annex and for an explanation of the text see paras 65–67 of the Document, available in the Proceedings (n 7) at 86–89 and 106–07.

[14] This concept was not included in the Working Group's Draft Convention: ibid. Even Kovar (Minutes No 4, Proceedings (n 7) at 589), acknowledged that this provision could deal with non-negotiated commercial agreements that send one party 'to a distant forum with the result that he would effectively be unable to exercise his rights. Given the strict choice of law rule represented, if one did not deal with the situation in the text, it would lead to oppressive results. It was therefore dealt with under paragraph c)' (the draft clause which is now Art 6(c)).

[15] Art 6(c) (discussed below). For clarity on the intent behind 'manifest' being that the injustice or the violation of public policy is both 'serious' and 'clear', see Beaumont, Minutes No 4, Proceedings (n 7) 591, confirmed by the Chair, 592. See also Beaumont, Minute No 8, 616. Paul Herrup's response to this solution, in his email to the authors, is that it 'is inadequate for a global convention operating on a global level. On a global stage, it is both over-broad and not broad enough'. He noted that some States 'have very narrow concepts of public policy which severely limit or even prevent application of the doctrine. And there is little merit to adding – predictably – yet another layer of litigation in some countries over what public policy is and the limits of its adaptability in that country. On the other hand, for states with broad concepts of public policy, reliance on public policy creates a dynamic to appeal to it and a temptation to resort to it and expand it to catch undesirable results … The prospect of interminable argumentation on a case-by-case basis over operations of public policy exceptions should give serious pause'. Herrup is right to warn of an over-extensive use of the manifest injustice or public policy exception. It should not be used to refuse to give effect to adhesion contracts or to protect smaller companies against bigger companies. The example in the Explanatory Report is a clear case of 'manifest injustice' because a party would otherwise be bound by a choice of court agreement they did not know about.

By doing this the text of the Convention and what was broadly agreed in the discussions on the drafting of the Convention are respected.

It is unnecessary to ask the non-chosen court to determine as a question of fact whether or not the choice of court agreement exists. However, if the chosen court is not satisfied with the factual consent to the choice of court agreement, in an extreme case like that posited by Hartley and Dogauchi, it can utilise the passage in the Explanatory Report to decide that the agreement does not in fact exist and therefore that it lacks jurisdiction under the Convention. This solution respects the fact that the passage above in the Explanatory Report was not objected to by the Members of the Hague Conference. It is not a dangerous solution that risks undermining party autonomy because the chosen court will generally want to uphold an exclusive choice of court agreement that is valid under its own law.

The danger is that the passage in the Explanatory Report leaves too much discretion to non-chosen courts to apply their own law of consent by the back door saying they are assessing the issue as a question of fact rather than law. Non-chosen courts should not have this leverage to subtly undermine party autonomy by applying their own standards of consent. Instead, the non-chosen court should determine if there was consent by applying the law of the chosen court to this question of substantive validity. The law of the chosen court is predictable because the parties chose that court. The Convention provides for the non-chosen court which has been seised to take into account the applicable law rules of the law of the chosen court. We contend that they should only take advantage of this opportunity to use renvoi if the parties expressly chose a law to govern their choice of court agreement which is not the law of the chosen court, see II.C below. So, eg, if the parties exclusively chose the English and Welsh courts but made the law of Singapore applicable to the choice of court agreement, then Singapore law should govern the substantive validity of the choice of court agreement whether the matter is heard in the courts of England and Wales or in any other Contracting State. This is the best way to protect party autonomy and legal certainty.

The Convention does permit the non-chosen court to apply, in very extreme cases, its own standards to avert a manifest injustice or a manifest breach of its public policy. The manifest injustice/public policy tool is the correct tool to protect the fundamental interests of the State of the non-chosen court and the fundamental justice requirements of the parties.

B. Formal Validity

The Convention opted for very simple formal validity rules. The agreement must be 'concluded or documented in writing' or 'by any other means of communication which renders information accessible so as to be usable for subsequent reference'.[16] The agreement need not be signed by the parties.[17] The reference to 'documented' means that an oral agreement which is subsequently reduced to writing or any other means of communication which renders information accessible (eg, emails and webpages) is formally valid under the Convention. This is so even if the party benefiting from the oral agreement is the one which documents it.[18] The complex rules in the EU and under the Lugano Convention that allow for choice of court agreements based

[16] Art 3(c). The wording is inspired by Art 6(1) of the UNCITRAL Model Law on Electronic Commerce 1996. See the interventions by Kovar (USA) and Sabo (Canada) in the Proceedings (n 7) 574–75.

[17] Explanatory Report (n 1) para 112.

[18] Ibid, para 114.

on commercial usages or past practice between the parties were not followed.[19] Instead a liberal construction should be given to the Convention's form requirements.[20]

i. Exclusivity

The agreement has to be an 'exclusive choice of court agreement' to fall within the core scope of the Convention.[21] This means that the parties must have selected only the court or courts of one Contracting State to the exclusion of the jurisdiction of any other courts.[22] The Convention has a very important practical provision whereby the agreement is 'deemed to be exclusive unless the parties have expressly provided otherwise'.[23] Thus if the parties confer jurisdiction on the courts of a Contracting State using neutral language, eg, 'disputes under this contract can be resolved in the courts of Singapore', this would be deemed to confer exclusive jurisdiction on the courts of Singapore under the Convention. In order to avoid the application of the Convention the parties need to make it clear that they do not want their agreement to have derogating effects (ie, excluding the jurisdiction of any other courts), eg, 'disputes under this contract can be resolved in the courts of Singapore but not only in the courts of Singapore'.

C. Substantive Validity

The Convention refers the substantive validity of an exclusive choice of court agreement to being 'null and void' under the law of the State of the chosen court including its private international law rules. Article 5(1) states:

> The court or courts of a Contracting State designated in an exclusive choice of court agreement shall have jurisdiction to decide a dispute to which the agreement applies, unless the agreement is null and void under the law of that State.

[19] Hartley (n 11) 163–65. See the critical discussion of the complexity of the European rules in P Beaumont and P McEleavy, *Anton's Private International Law*, 3rd edn (W Green/SULI 2011) 242–49. They argue that: 'the methods relating to practices between the parties and usage of trade are just different formulations of the writing or evidenced in writing requirement' (ibid, 261). So the documented in writing provision in the Hague Convention provides enough flexibility to include oral agreements that are supported by written evidence, without any further references to usages, but does not extend to the rather dangerous European practice of presumed awareness of a commercial usage in a particular sector that then creates presumed consent to a choice of court agreement (ibid, 247–49). See Kovar, Proceedings (n 7) 574–75, saying that 'terms coming from business practice' could be included in a choice of court agreement entered into orally but documented in writing, and affirmed as settled by the Chair (Bucher, 575).

[20] Hartley, ibid 164, says the requirements should not be interpreted 'too strictly' and Brand and Herrup (n 3) 45–46, say the threshold requirement of formal validity is 'low'. See also the statement by Beaumont, Proceedings (n 7) 575, that 'any kind of record of an oral agreement would be sufficient for formal validity. It was not necessary to talk about consent because of the clear separation of the issues of formal and substantive validity. He felt that the only requirement of formal validity was that there is a record, and that we should have a liberal understanding of what that record should be. He was of the view that any person could keep that record, whether a party to the contract or a third party'. For practical examples of oral agreements which are documented in writing (we can thank Bucher for the idea of 'documented' rather than 'evidenced') see Goddard and Kovar (ibid, 576).

[21] The Convention creates a declaration system allowing States to extend the Convention to other types of choice of court agreements but only at the recognition and enforcement stage, see Art 22. No Contracting Parties have taken advantage of this declaration so far. The Hague Judgments Convention 2019, in Art 5(1)(m), comprehensively provides for the recognition and enforcement of judgments based on all other types of choice of court agreements that are not exclusive within the meaning of the Choice of Court Convention, see Goddard and Beaumont (n 2).

[22] Art 3(a). An asymmetric choice of court clause is not an 'exclusive choice of court agreement' for the purposes of the Convention: Proceedings (n 7) 577–78 and Explanatory Report (n 1) paras 105–06.

[23] Art 3(b).

There are various interpretations of the phrase 'null and void'; Brand and Herrup helpfully identify three of them.[24] The first is 'any grounds for declining to give legal effect to a meeting of the minds that has occurred'. The authors give as an example of a situation where the parties have reached a consensus on a choice of court clause but no legal effect should be given to it where the national law prohibits party autonomy in 'certain kinds of contracts (eg, franchise contracts)'. This interpretation is very dangerous as it effectively permits Contracting States unilaterally to remove certain types of contracts from the scope of the Convention without making the declaration required by Article 21. The Article 21 declaration system permits a State to declare that the Convention will not apply to a 'specific matter' but only if it has a 'strong interest' in doing so. It must create transparency by 'clearly and precisely' defining the specific matter in a way that 'is no broader than necessary'. The consequence of making such a declaration is a reciprocal effect in relation to other Contracting States. It cannot therefore be consistent with a contextual interpretation of the Convention to permit 'null and void under the law of that State' in Article 5(1) to include a complete prohibition on all choice of court clauses in a class of contract that is within the scope of the Convention.

Brand and Herrup's second reading of 'null and void' in Article 5(1) is that it is 'coextensive with "lack of substantive validity" or (depending on the concept of "substantive") to refer to any ground of invalidity which is not purely formal'.[25] They find this a 'less compelling reading' but we favour it and it is consistent with the spirit of the negotiations. Support for it can be found in the Explanatory Report which states that:

> The 'null and void' provision applies only to substantive (not formal) grounds of invalidity. It is intended to refer primarily to generally recognised grounds like fraud, mistake, misrepresentation, duress and lack of capacity.[26]

Brand and Herrup's third reading of 'null and void' is that it covers 'some subset of grounds under national law for declining to give effect to a meeting of the minds which has occurred'.[27] This compromise proposal would be slightly less damaging than their first reading but has no support in the *travaux préparatoires* or in the Explanatory Report. It is inherently a very uncertain approach as it is not at all clear which grounds for declining to give effect to an agreement between the parties are permissible and which are not. Brand and Herrup conclude that the 'definition of "null and void" for purposes of the application of Article 5(1) will be a matter resolved through state practice'.[28] The practice should be that the Convention in Articles 5, 6 and 9 refers questions of the substantive validity of an exclusive choice of court agreement to the law of the chosen court, including its applicable law rules, and only if the breach of the substantive validity rules under the law applicable leads to the agreement being 'null and void' under that law will the agreement be disapplied by the chosen court or will a non-chosen court refuse to give effect to it.[29] Any court that is asked to recognise and enforce the judgment of the chosen court cannot refuse to do so on the basis that the agreement was null and void under the law of the chosen court if that court has already decided that the agreement is valid.[30]

[24] (n 3) 80.
[25] Ibid.
[26] (n 1) para 126.
[27] (n 3) 80.
[28] Ibid.
[29] Hartley (n 11) 133–34.
[30] Art 9(a).

The renvoi permitted by a reference to the law of the chosen court (not the internal law of that court) should not be interpreted too broadly. The underlying purpose of the Convention is to protect party autonomy by ensuring the 'effectiveness of exclusive choice of court agreements between parties to commercial transactions' (see the Preamble). Therefore, there is a strong argument for only utilising the renvoi where the reference to the applicable law rules of the State of the chosen court leads to the agreement being substantively valid when it would be substantively invalid under the internal law of the chosen court. Furthermore, in order to protect legal certainty and party autonomy the court should only do this where the parties have expressly chosen a law other than the internal law of the chosen court to govern the choice of court agreement or the contract as a whole. They should not refer to the law selected by the objective applicable law rules of the State of the chosen court.[31] One reason for a reluctance to refer to the objectively applicable law rules of the law of the State of the chosen court is that they are much more unpredictable than the internal law of the chosen court. A decision-maker will only get to those rules when the parties have not expressly chosen the law to govern their agreement (or the contract of which the agreement forms part) and the court has decided that the parties have not impliedly chosen the law of the State of the chosen court even though they have exclusively chosen that court to resolve their disputes and can be deemed to know that applying that law would be more likely to lead to a cost-effective and accurate outcome to the dispute.

III. Effects of Choice of Court Agreements

Choice of court agreements can have both positive (or prorogating) and negative (or derogating) effects. These effects are created by the applicable procedural laws in the relevant forum; this section addresses the positive and negative effects of exclusive choice of court agreements under the Convention.

A. Jurisdiction of the Chosen Court

The Convention provides that 'The court or courts of a Contracting State designated in an exclusive choice of court agreement *shall have jurisdiction* to decide a dispute to which the agreement applies', unless the agreement is null and void under the law of the chosen court.[32] The court designated in an exclusive choice of court agreement cannot 'decline to exercise jurisdiction on the ground that the dispute should be decided in a court of another State.'[33]

The parties sometimes include both an exclusive choice of court agreement and an arbitration agreement in their contract. The Explanatory Report clarifies that '[t]he requirement to hear the case will not be violated where a court declines jurisdiction on the ground that the dispute should be decided by an arbitrator'.[34]

The positive effect of the choice of court agreement applies to 'a dispute to which the agreement applies'. This is a reference to the material, or subject matter, scope of the agreement.[35]

[31] This latter point, but not the former, was made in Beaumont and McEleavy (n 19) 254–55.
[32] Art 5(1) (emphasis added).
[33] Art 5(2).
[34] Explanatory Report (n 1) para 124, fn 155.
[35] See also Art 3(a), which provides that an exclusive choice of court agreement is one which designates a court or courts 'for the purpose of deciding disputes which have arisen or may arise *in connection with a particular legal relationship*' (emphasis added).

Determining whether a dispute comes within the material scope of the choice of court agreement may require interpretation of the agreement, raising the question of the applicable law for the interpretation of the choice of court agreement. There are two possibilities.[36] First, the governing law of the choice of court agreement should be applied. The second is that the law of the chosen court should be applied. The governing law of the choice of court agreement will often lead to the application of the law of the chosen court,[37] so there may not be a conflict in many cases. For consistency with related provisions,[38] the law of the chosen court should be applied, although in principle, it should be determined by the governing law of the choice of court agreement.

The single exception in Article 5(1)[39] is where the choice of court agreement is null and void under the law of the chosen court, which is addressed above.

The jurisdiction conferred by Article 5(1) is subject to two limitations: it does not affect rules 'on jurisdiction related to subject matter or to the value of the claim' or 'on the internal allocation of jurisdiction among the courts of a Contracting State'. These limitations are particularly relevant to non-unitary States in which some courts have limited statutory jurisdiction,[40] and which have rules enabling the transfer of jurisdiction between courts. The first limitation recognises the primacy of subject matter jurisdictional restrictions applicable to the designated court. In relation to the second limitation, the Convention provides that 'where the chosen court has discretion whether to transfer a case, due consideration should be given to the choice of the parties'.[41] If the parties have designated a particular court within a Contracting State, that choice should not 'lightly' be overridden.[42]

Finally, the Convention stipulates that the court designated in an exclusive choice of court agreement cannot 'decline to exercise jurisdiction on the ground that the dispute should be decided in a court of another State'.[43] This excludes the principles of *lis pendens* and *forum non conveniens* and removes any discretion that courts might otherwise have not to enforce an exclusive choice of court agreement designating the forum. This is one of the most important innovations in the Convention which simplified litigation in favour of the courts exclusively chosen by the parties compared with the prior position in both civil and common law countries. The chosen court when it is second seised need not wait for a non-chosen court that was first seised to decide if it has jurisdiction and the defendant in the chosen court cannot argue that the chosen court is *forum non conveniens* because there is a more appropriate forum elsewhere. When combined with the very broad scope of application of the Convention and thus of Article 5 in Contracting States – no connection between the parties and Contracting States is required and the definition of an international case governed by the Convention is any non-domestic element (which includes a choice of law clause) – it means that even parties from non-Contracting States to the Convention can be sure their valid exclusive choice of the courts

[36] Another possibility is that the law of the forum could be applied, but this should be rejected.

[37] This is for two reasons: first, most contracts that include a choice of court agreement also include a choice of law clause, usually nominating the law of the chosen court. Second, if there is no choice of law clause, the choice of court agreement is relevant in determining the contract's applicable law.

[38] Arts 5(1) and 6(a).

[39] Art 19 creates the possibility of a further exception, permitting a State to make a declaration enabling its courts, designated in an exclusive choice of court agreement, to refuse to hear a case if there is no objective connection between that State and the parties or the dispute. As at June 2021, no Contracting State had made such a declaration.

[40] Hartley (n 11) 180–81.

[41] Art 5(3).

[42] Explanatory Report (n 1) para 140.

[43] Art 5(2).

of a Contracting State will be upheld and jurisdiction will not be declined even for 'strong cause' as would have happened under the common law.[44]

B. Obligations of a Court not Chosen

Article 6 establishes the obligations of courts not designated in an exclusive choice of court agreement; ie, the agreement's negative or derogating effects. The court not chosen 'shall suspend or dismiss proceedings to which an exclusive choice of court agreement applies', with five exceptions. The obligation to suspend or dismiss proceedings relates to proceedings 'to which an exclusive choice of court agreement applies'. This refers to the material scope of the choice of court agreement, which should be determined by the applicable law of the choice of court agreement.[45]

i. The Choice of Court Agreement is Null and Void

This exception reflects the lone exception under Article 5(1), already discussed.[46] The law of the chosen court is applied to determine whether the choice of court agreement is null and void, including the relevant applicable law rule.[47] In addition to the grounds discussed above, lack of capacity under the law of the chosen court renders choice of court agreements null and void.[48]

ii. Lack of Capacity

For Article 6(b), the question of capacity is determined by the law of the court seised, including the applicable law rules of that State.[49] The Explanatory Report states that a lack of capacity under the law of the chosen court would also render the agreement null and void.

iii. Manifest Injustice or Manifestly Contrary to Public Policy

Both limbs of this exception are intended to set a 'high threshold'.[50] The first limb justifies the court seised refusing to suspend or dismiss proceedings where doing so would lead to a 'manifest injustice'. The Explanatory Report gives several examples, including where one party would not get a fair trial in the designated courts, 'or where there were other reasons specific to that party that would preclude him or her from bringing or defending proceedings in the chosen court'.[51]

[44] See Art 1(2) and Beaumont (n 3) 149–50 on this issue in the context of the declarations under Arts 19 and 20. For the Commonwealth common law, see case law flowing from *The Eleftheria* [1970] P 94.

[45] Above, text to nn 36–38.

[46] Above, text to nn 25–30.

[47] Explanatory Report (n 1) fn 184.

[48] Ibid, para 149.

[49] Ibid, para 150.

[50] See *Motacus Constructions Limited v Paolo Castelli SPA* [2021] EWHC 356 (TCC) [54]. Judge Hodge QC concluded that: 'The claimant has not satisfied me that it would be contrary to public policy, or unjust, (let alone manifestly so) to require the claimant to enforce its [UK] adjudication award in the courts of Paris, France. There is no good reason why the parties should not be held to the bargain that they freely made' in the exclusive choice of court agreement.

[51] (n 1) para 152.

The second limb, excusing a court from suspending or dismissing proceedings where giving effect to the agreement would be 'manifestly contrary to the public policy of the State of the court seised', is intended to be applied in exceptional circumstances.[52] It does not justify refusal to suspend or dismiss proceedings on the basis that the choice of court agreement would not be enforceable under the domestic law of the State of the court seised, or that the chosen court might not apply a mandatory rule of the law of the State of the court seised.[53] While this clearly applies to domestically mandatory rules of the forum, it is less clear from the drafting history and the Explanatory Report whether the forum's internationally mandatory rules justify non-enforcement of a choice of court agreement.[54]

iv. The Choice of Court Agreement cannot Reasonably be Performed

The fourth exception is where 'for exceptional reasons beyond the control of the parties, the agreement cannot reasonably be performed'. This is based on the idea that the choice of court agreement should not be enforced if it has become frustrated. This exception applies 'where it would not be possible to bring proceedings before the chosen court. It need not be absolutely impossible, but the situation must be exceptional'.[55] Examples are where the designated courts are not operating (eg, because of war), or have ceased to exist either completely or in the form contemplated by the agreement.[56]

v. The Designated Court has Decided not to Hear the Case

This exception seems misconceived. The designated court cannot decide 'not to hear the case'; under the Convention it is obliged to hear the case, and cannot refuse to do so on the basis that another court should hear the case. The only exception under Article 5 is where the choice of court agreement is null and void, which is reflected in Article 6(a). The Explanatory Report suggests that the exception in Article 6(e) ensures the parties' right to a hearing.[57]

Altogether, the Article 6 exceptions only enable non-chosen courts under an exclusive choice of court agreement to refuse to suspend or dismiss proceedings in a narrow range of circumstances. This is an appropriate recognition of the importance of simple and clear rules that provide strong protection for exclusive choice of court agreements. This should in turn be strengthened by the requirement under the Convention that '[i]n the interpretation of this Convention, regard shall be had to its international character and to the need to promote uniformity in its application'.[58] In doing so the courts should give effect to the aim of the Convention in the

[52] See also above, text to n 15.

[53] Explanatory Report (n 1) para 153 only gives examples of what would not be covered under the public policy limb; it does not give examples of what might be covered.

[54] B Marshall and M Keyes, 'Australia's Accession to the *Hague Convention on Choice of Court Agreements*' (2017) 41 *Melbourne University Law Review* 246, 262–65. However, it did not do so in *Motacus* (n 50) [54], where the UK law overriding mandatory provision in favour of compulsory adjudication in the UK of disputes in relation to construction contracts (see s 104(7) of the Housing Grants, Construction and Regeneration Act 1996) was reconciled with giving effect to a French exclusive choice of court agreement under the Convention by saying that the UK adjudicator's award was an interim one (not *res judicata*), lawful under Art 7 of the Convention (and immediately enforceable in the UK), but which could be overturned by the French courts and then the judgment of the French courts would be enforced in the UK under the Convention.

[55] Explanatory Report (n 1) para 154.

[56] Ibid.

[57] Ibid, para 155.

[58] Art 23.

preamble to ensure 'the effectiveness of exclusive choice of court agreements between parties to commercial transactions'.[59]

C. Other Protections of Exclusive Choice of Court Agreements

The explicit protections of exclusive choice of court agreements under the Convention are the requirements that designated courts must exercise jurisdiction, that non-designated courts must suspend or dismiss proceedings, and that judgments of designated courts must be recognised and enforced. This raises the question as to whether the Convention affects, particularly whether it precludes, other means of upholding exclusive choice of court agreements which are available under the national laws of Contracting States, specifically anti-suit injunctions and damages.

i. Anti-Suit Injunctions

The Convention does not explicitly refer to the availability of anti-suit injunctions to restrain the commencement or continuation of proceedings brought in a non-chosen court. Article 7 provides:

> Interim measures of protection are not governed by this Convention. This Convention neither requires nor precludes the grant, refusal or termination of interim measures of protection by a court of a Contracting State and does not affect whether or not a party may request or a court should grant, refuse or terminate such measures.

Although Article 7 is primarily intended to refer to 'measures intended to protect the position of the parties while the proceedings are pending', the Explanatory Report 'suggests that it also covers measures intended to make the choice-of-court agreement more effective', which would include anti-suit injunctions.[60] This applies only to an anti-suit injunction granted by the court designated in an exclusive choice of court agreement.[61]

ii. Damages

The Convention does not explicitly refer to the availability of damages for breach of an exclusive choice of court agreement. Little guidance can be derived from the Convention text, the Explanatory Report or the *travaux préparatoires*. Commentators have suggested that the

[59] In the agreed statement by the drafters of the Convention on the meaning of Art 11 permitting the limitation of recognition and enforcement of judgments to compensatory damages (Explanatory Report (n 1) para 205) the bias towards giving effect to choice of court agreements was reflected in the statement that: 'As in the case for all other grounds of refusal, this provision [Art 11] should be interpreted and applied in as restrictive a way as possible'.

[60] Hartley (n 11) [10.29]. See similarly M Ahmed and P Beaumont, 'Exclusive choice of court agreements: some issues on the Hague Convention on choice of court agreements and its relationship with the Brussels I recast especially anti-suit injunctions, concurrent proceedings and the implications of BREXIT' (2017) 13 *Journal of Private International Law* 386, 397–98. In *Motacus* (n 50) Judge Hodge QC said of Art 7: 'the categories of "interim protective measures" are not closed but are capable of expansion as national courts devise new interim remedies (or measures) to protect the interests of litigants pending the final, substantive resolution of their dispute. The concept extends to any decision that is not a final and conclusive decision on the substantive merits of the case' [57].

[61] Ahmed and Beaumont, ibid, 399. They also note that 'The application of remedies to enforce jurisdiction agreements by some Contracting States may create a rift in the … jurisprudence of the Hague Convention', which could compromise the uniform application of the Convention.

contractual treatment of exclusive choice of court agreements within the Convention[62] is not inconsistent with the designated court protecting an exclusive choice of court agreement by an award of damages,[63] and that a judgment awarding damages might be entitled to recognition and enforcement under the Convention, because the jurisdiction of the court was based on the choice of court agreement.[64] As with all damages awards given by the chosen court, the courts in a State addressed for recognition and enforcement of the judgment have the discretion to reduce the damages to a level which is compensatory rather than penal. It might be particularly difficult to determine what would constitute damages for 'actual loss or harm suffered' in a case where a party has taken the case to a non-chosen court but it should at least cover the legal costs incurred by the other party of having to defend the action in the non-chosen court.[65]

IV. Conclusion

The Hague Choice of Court Convention is one of the most important developments in private international law, because cross-border commercial activity has increased so substantially and choice of court provisions are a common feature of international contracts. The Convention significantly improves upon existing laws, providing better protection of exclusive choice of court agreements. It comprehensively articulates the key principles governing the effects of exclusive choice of court agreements, improving access to justice, facilitating settlement, and reducing the costs of litigation at both the jurisdictional and recognition stages.

In addition to its direct effects in its Contracting States, the Convention has influenced legal developments within the European Union, in bilateral arrangements,[66] and in national laws.[67] It has therefore contributed significantly to the harmonisation of this important aspect of private international law. Together with the 2019 Hague Judgments Convention, the Choice of Court Convention goes a long way towards providing a secure foundation for international commercial litigation, and it is to be hoped that it continues to attract Contracting States.

The Convention regulates only exclusive choice of court agreements. Non-exclusive choice of court agreements are regulated by the laws that are otherwise applicable, derived from regional and bilateral arrangements and national laws. These are diverse in content and complexity,[68] which creates fertile ground for tactical forum shopping. At the date of writing, the Hague Conference on Private International Law was working towards an instrument on jurisdiction,[69] which may address the jurisdictional effects of non-exclusive choice of court agreements, amongst other things. Non-exclusive choice of court agreements are found in a significant number of international contracts, and harmonisation of the law regulating their effects is highly desirable.

[62] Particularly, the description of such provisions as 'agreements' rather than clauses, the Convention's regulation of the substantive validity of exclusive choice of court agreements, and Art 3(d) (providing that 'an exclusive choice of court agreement that forms part of a contract shall be treated as an agreement independent of the other terms of the contract'), See Ahmed and Beaumont, ibid, 396.

[63] Ahmed and Beaumont, ibid 400–01.

[64] A Mills, 'The Hague Choice of Court Convention and Cross-border Dispute Resolution in Australia and the Asia-Pacific' (2017) 18 *Melbourne Journal of International Law* 1, 8.

[65] Explanatory Report (n 1) para 205. Art 11 requires the court addressed to 'take into account whether and to what extent the damages awarded by the court of origin serve to cover costs and expenses related to the proceedings'.

[66] eg, Trans-Tasman Proceedings Act 2010 (Cth) s 20.

[67] eg, Tu and Huang, 'People's Republic of China' in M Keyes (ed), *Optional Choice of Court Agreements in Private International Law* (Springer 2020) 154, 157.

[68] M Keyes, 'General Report' in M Keyes (ed), *Optional Choice of Court Agreements in Private International Law* (Springer 2020) 8.

[69] HCCH Jurisdiction Project, available at: www.hcch.net/en/projects/legislative-projects/jurisdiction-project.

29

Recognition and Enforcement of Judgments in Civil or Commercial Matters

DAVID GODDARD AND PAUL BEAUMONT*

I. Introduction

A truly modern, sophisticated and reasonably comprehensive regime for recognition and enforcement of judgments in civil or commercial matters is now available to all States in the world by becoming Parties to the Hague Judgments Convention 2019 (Judgments) and the Hague Choice of Court Agreements Convention 2005 (Choice of Court).[1] The basic scheme of both Conventions for the purposes of recognition and enforcement involves identifying acceptable bases for exercise of jurisdiction in the State of origin (as assessed by the State addressed, applying the rules of the relevant Convention), no review of the merits in the State addressed, and only a few, well-established grounds for refusal of recognition and enforcement. Both Conventions set a floor rather than a ceiling for recognition and enforcement of judgments within their scope, with one exception found in Judgments.[2] The Conventions should be interpreted uniformly.[3]

II. Objectives of the Two Hague Conventions

At the highest level of generality, the objectives of the two Conventions are:

(a) to promote effective access to justice; and
(b) to facilitate cross-border trade and investment by reducing the costs and risks associated with cross-border dealings.

* David Goddard was a member of the New Zealand delegation and Paul Beaumont of the UK delegation throughout the process of developing the Choice of Court Convention. For the Judgments Convention, David Goddard was the Chair and Paul Beaumont was a member of the EU delegation throughout the process. The views expressed here are personal to the authors.

[1] See RA Brand, 'Jurisdiction and Judgments Recognition at the Hague Conference: Choices Made, Treaties Completed, and the Path Ahead' (2020) 67 *Netherlands International Law Review* 3.

[2] Judgments impose a restriction on recognition and enforcement of judgments in relation to rights *in rem* in relation to immovable property, where the immovable property is not situated in the State of origin. This exception is described in more detail in section IV.B below.

[3] See Art 20 of Judgments and 23 of Choice of Court. For recent exemplary examples of apex courts trying to give a uniform interpretation to an HCCH Convention, see the *Office of the Children's Lawyer v Balev* 2018 SCC 16 and *Monasky v Taglieri* 589 US ___(2020), judgment of 25 February 2020. See PR Beaumont, 'Reflections on the Relevance of Public International Law to Private International Law Treaty Making' (2009) 340 *Hague Collected Courses* 19–33 and J Ribeiro-Bidaoui, 'The International Obligation of the Uniform and Autonomous Interpretation of Private Law Conventions: Consequences for Domestic Courts and International Organisations' (2020) 67 *Netherlands International Law Review* 139.

The two Conventions are designed to advance these objectives in six main ways.

First, and most importantly, the Conventions will ensure that judgments to which they apply will be recognised and enforced in all Contracting States. That enhances the practical effectiveness of those judgments and provides the successful party with better prospects of obtaining meaningful relief. Access to justice is a dead letter if the judgment obtained by a successful party cannot be enforced in practice. Parties to disputes go to court in order to achieve just outcomes that are given practical effect. In today's increasingly globalised world, it is frequently necessary for that practical effect to span borders, if justice is to be effective. The goal of access to justice, in the sense of access to just outcomes that are practically effective everywhere they need to be implemented, is at the heart of the Judgments Project.

Second, and closely related to that goal, at present it is often necessary for a party to a dispute to bring substantive proceedings of the same kind in more than one country in order to obtain the desired practical outcome. Avoiding the need for duplicative proceedings will contribute significantly to access to justice, and to reducing the costs and risks of cross-border dealings.

Third, these instruments enhance the effectiveness of provisions in cross-border agreements prescribing where the parties' disputes may, or must, be resolved. This significantly enhances predictability and reduces risk, both at the time the parties negotiate and enter into the agreement and at the time when a dispute arises.

Fourth, improving the accessibility of law relating to recognition and enforcement of judgments, and improving the certainty and clarity of that body of law, should reduce the costs and time frames associated with obtaining recognition and enforcement of judgments. Access to justice in the context of cross-border disputes is often hindered by the cost of getting an effective result. All litigators are familiar with the challenge, even in the domestic context, of ensuring that justice can be achieved at a realistic cost to participants. When disputes span borders, those costs inevitably increase. If the Conventions reduce the cost and the time frames associated with obtaining a practically effective resolution of a dispute with cross-border elements, that will make a significant contribution to the two broad objectives identified above.

Fifth, as matters stand today a lawyer who is asked to advise on the recognition and enforcement in one State of a judgment given in another State will generally find themselves looking at the national law of the State in which enforcement is sought, and also perhaps a patchwork of conventions in operation between different groupings of States: some well established and very elaborate conventions, and others that are less well known. One of the significant contributions that two successful Conventions will make is to improve the accessibility of the law: to make it possible for those affected, their advisers and also of course the judges who need to decide these cases, to look to one place for a framework that guides the recognition and enforcement of a significant number of foreign judgments. This outcome will not be achieved for all disputes, because the Conventions do not attempt the challenging and almost certainly impossible task of establishing a comprehensive and exhaustive regime for recognition and enforcement of judgments. Rather, they essentially seek to set a floor for the circulation of judgments that is widely accepted and that enables many judgments to circulate among Contracting States. The more widely the Conventions are ratified, the greater their contribution to enhancing the accessibility of the law.

Sixth, a clear, certain and predictable framework for recognition and enforcement of judgments will enable a party deciding where to bring a claim to make more informed choices about where to bring their initial proceedings. If a party has the choice between bringing proceedings in one of two States, and a judgment in one State will circulate under a widely ratified convention while a judgment in another will not, that is an important factor that will guide parties in making informed, efficient choices about where to litigate in the first place. The Judgments Convention does not directly regulate jurisdiction, unlike the Choice of Court Convention, but it does discourage people from breaking their exclusive choice of court agreement by making the obtaining of a judgment in a State contrary to that agreement a ground for refusal of recognition and enforcement of the judgment from the non-chosen State.[4] That ground for refusal also safeguards against breaches of other types of choice of court agreements (not falling within the core scope of Choice of Court) which have derogating effects. It also provides a comprehensive way to recognise and enforce judgments based on other types of choice of court agreements without the need to use the hitherto unused declaration system for such agreements in Choice of Court. That declaration system is inherently haphazard because it only works insofar as two or more States cover the same types of agreements in their declarations. It seems likely that successful conventions on recognition and enforcement of judgments will influence the choices that parties make about where to bring proceedings and will guide them to do so in places which are more, rather than less, productive. All too often a decision to bring proceedings in country A is taken by a party – or that party's lawyers – without thinking about where, ultimately, the judgment will need to be enforced; and without thinking about whether that will be possible. The two Conventions should contribute to the ability of those involved in cross-border disputes to make better decisions about where to bring a claim in the first place.

The extent to which the two Conventions achieve these objectives will of course depend on the Conventions coming into force for a large number of States over time. Only time will tell whether that outcome is achieved. But there are already some promising signs of progress towards that goal.[5]

III. Duty to Recognise and Enforce a Judgment

A. Minimum Standards and No Review of the Merits

Article 4 of Judgments and Article 8 of Choice of Court set out the central obligation imposed on Contracting Parties by the instruments. They provide that a judgment given by a court of a Contracting State (the State of origin) which has effect in that State must be recognised, and

[4] Art 7(1)(d), discussed below, section V.

[5] The final version of the Explanatory Report was approved by the Members of the HCCH and other States that participated in the Diplomatic Session in June/July 2019, see F Garcimartín and G Saumier, *Explanatory Report on the 2019 HCCH Judgments Convention* (HCCH 2020), available at: www.hcch.net/en/publications-and-studies/details4/?pid=6797. Five States have signed Judgments: Costa Rica, Israel, Russia, Ukraine and Uruguay, see the status table, available at: www.hcch.net/en/instruments/conventions/status-table/?cid=137. The EU Commission has made a Proposal for the EU to become a Party to Judgments, see Commission Proposal for a Council Decision on the accession by the European Union to the Convention on the Recognition and Enforcement of Foreign Judgments in Civil or Commercial Matters SEC(2021) 279 final, available at: ec.europa.eu/info/sites/default/files/proposal_eu_accession_judgments_convention_and_annex_en.pdf. If this Decision is adopted by the Council and consented to by the European Parliament, 26 Member States of the EU would become bound by the Convention once at least one other State becomes a Party to the Convention and the EU and that State accept treaty relations between themselves (see section VIII below). Thirty-one States and the EU were Parties to Choice of Court and five other States had signed it, see the status table, available at: www.hcch.net/en/instruments/conventions/status-table/?cid=98.

one which is enforceable in that State must be enforced, in another Contracting State (the State addressed) in accordance with the relevant provisions of the applicable Convention. Importantly, recognition or enforcement of an eligible judgment may be refused *only* on the grounds specified in the Conventions. It is not open to a Contracting State to decline recognition or enforcement on other grounds under national law. Nor is it open to the court addressed to decline to recognise or enforce a judgment based on its own view of the merits of the substantive claim.

The preparatory documents of the Judgments Convention are explicit[6] that the effects of the judgment under that Convention only extend to a strict *res judicata* effect (cause of action estoppel). So the Judgments Convention does not provide for issue estoppel,[7] let alone prevent the reopening of issues that could have been (but were not) addressed in the foreign litigation (competent and omitted or abuse of process).[8]

Choice of Court provides for recognition and enforcement in circumstances that command broad acceptance: where the judgment comes from the courts of the State exclusively chosen by the parties in a prior agreement. The Judgments Convention seeks to identify further cases where recognition and enforcement of a judgment should command broad acceptance. Cases where, if one were to ask 'is it reasonable for this judgment to be recognised and enforced?', a generally positive answer would be expected across the full diversity of global legal systems. The instrument seeks to walk the sometimes delicate line between maximising the scope and impact of the Convention as drafted, and not impairing the objective of commanding widespread acceptance. Even if all Judgments did was restate the obvious, and provide for a 'lowest common denominator' approach to recognition and enforcement of judgments, that would add something to the international legal order because at least it would improve the accessibility of information about the law. But Judgments is more ambitious than that. It seeks to go beyond stating the obvious and enlarges to some extent the classes of judgments that are recognised and enforced under national

[6] See Explanatory Report (n 5) paras 114–115. See also PA Nielsen, 'The Hague 2019 Judgments Convention – from Failure to Success?' (2020) 16 *Journal of Private International Law* 225, 226.

[7] That is, preclusion on an issue of fact or law decided by the foreign court which was necessary for its determination of the case. For an interesting discussion of cause of action estoppel, issue estoppel and wider concerns about issues that could have been addressed in the earlier case but which were not, see *Virgin Atlantic Ltd v Zodiac Seats UK Ltd* [2013] UKSC 46.

[8] See P Beaumont, 'Review of Res Judicata, Estoppel and Foreign Judgments by Peter Barnett' (2002) 118 *LQR* 324, 326: 'If caution is necessary within Europe, then it is all the more necessary in the global context. As Barnett points out, the Nygh and Pocar Report (*Report of the Special Commission* (2000), p 96) on the draft Hague Judgments Convention states that the law of the place where the judgment was granted determines the preclusive effects of any issues decided in that judgment in the countries where that judgment is recognised under the Convention. This is surely the wrong solution. If the draft Hague Convention is ever finalised this part of the Report should be altered. Strict cause of action estoppel (*res judicata*) would seem to be an accepted part of all major legal systems and therefore its recognition is not a problem. However, issue estoppel and any wider doctrine of abuse of process are not features of all major legal systems and therefore it would not be reasonable to apply unknown, and sometimes rather uncertain, foreign doctrines that produce much wider preclusive effects than their own domestic judgments'. The Revised Preliminary Explanatory Report prepared for the Fourth Meeting of the Special Commission of May 2018, Prel Doc No 10, paras 98–99, available at: www.hcch.net/en/publications-and-studies/details4/?pid=6644&dtid=61, shows that the Third Meeting of the Special Commission had decided not to give the effects to the judgment that it has in the State of origin but rather to give a uniform interpretation to the effects of a judgment under the Convention restricted to cause of action estoppel, not issue estoppel or any wider notion of abuse of process. Of course, recognition can go further under national law. This is also the view, in his personal capacity, of one of the co-rapporteurs to the Judgments Convention: 'Probably, the preferable way to interpret this silence is by reference to the 2005 Convention. The parallelism between both instruments calls for a consistent interpretation and therefore an understanding that the main obligation under the Convention is to give *res judicata* effect to the operative part of the judgment; giving other effects further than this is left to national law' in F Garcimartín, 'The Judgments Convention: Some Open Questions' (2020) 67 *Netherlands International Law Review* 19, 27.

law in most States: but not to such an extent that it is seen by States as overly ambitious or problematic when they come to consider whether or not to accept this instrument.

B. Non-Money Judgments

Choice of Court provides for circulation of all final judgments of the chosen court, including both money judgments and non-money judgments. In this it parallels the New York Convention on Arbitration, which does not draw any distinction in relation to enforceability of an award based on the form of relief provided for in the arbitral award. In the arbitration context, States have many years' experience of recognising and enforcing foreign non-money awards. In the context of court judgments, however, recognition of non-money judgments is commonplace but the approach of States to enforcement is more variable. In particular, the traditional common law approach has been to decline to enforce foreign non-money judgments.[9] Instead, the plaintiff who succeeded in State A and obtained (say) an injunction to restrain conduct by a defendant based in State B needs to commence a new substantive proceeding in State B, ask the Court in State B to recognise the foreign judgment as giving rise to a cause of action estoppel (or perhaps, various issue estoppels) and on that basis seek similar injunctive relief in the proceedings in State B.

Judgments, like Choice of Court, provides for recognition and enforcement of non-money judgments. The definition of 'judgment' in Article 3 does not draw a distinction based on the form of relief awarded. The Convention does not require courts of a requested State to enforce forms of order that are not known in that State. As Article 13 confirms, the procedure for enforcement of a judgment is governed by the national law of the requested State. But it is implicit in the Convention that the requested court should grant relief that is as far as possible consistent with the substance of the relief granted in the court of origin, and gives effect so far as possible to the judgment granted by that court.[10]

The inclusion of non-monetary relief is a practically important feature of both Conventions. An increasing proportion of wealth is represented by intangible property that can only be effectively protected by such relief. The ease of dealing across borders, in particular online, means that effective enforcement of non-monetary orders made in one State frequently requires those orders to be practically enforceable in another State where the defendant is situated, and can be made subject to effective practical sanctions to compel performance of the orders.

IV. Bases of Jurisdiction

The model adopted in both Conventions for recognition and enforcement (see Article 8 Choice of Court and Articles 5 and 6 Judgments) is for the courts of the State addressed to apply the Convention standards to determine if the court of origin had an acceptable basis of jurisdiction to give a judgment that can be enforced under the Convention. It does not matter what basis of jurisdiction that court actually used.

[9] But for the Canadian approach, see *Pro Swing Inc v Elta Golf Inc* 2006 SCC 5, [2006] 2 SCR 612.
[10] See Explanatory Report (n 5) para 118.

A. Party Autonomy

i. Prorogation and Derogation Agreements: Articles 8 and 9(a) and (b) Choice of Court and Article 5(1)(m) Judgments

The two Conventions are designed to complement each other in their treatment of party autonomy in the context of recognition and enforcement of judgments. Choice of Court covers 'exclusive' choice of court agreements, ie an agreement to give only the court or courts of one Contracting State jurisdiction to determine disputes covered by the scope of that agreement. It gives effect to party autonomy by requiring the chosen court to exercise jurisdiction (Article 5); requiring non-chosen courts to decline jurisdiction (Article 6); and providing for recognition and enforcement of the chosen court's judgment.[11] All other types of choice of court agreements are covered by Judgments, which provides for recognition and enforcement of a chosen court's judgment. Thus, Judgments covers 'non-exclusive' choice of court agreements where the parties only prorogate the courts of one or more Contracting States but do not derogate from any courts of other Contracting States. It also covers 'multiple exclusive' choice of court agreements where the parties prorogate the courts of more than one Contracting State but derogate from the courts of all other States not listed in the agreement. It also covers 'asymmetric' choice of court agreements where one party to the agreement both prorogates the chosen court and derogates from all other courts whereas the other party to the agreement prorogates the chosen court but does not derogate from all other courts. Finally, Judgments covers any other conceivable type of choice of court agreement in favour of a Contracting State that is not an 'exclusive' one within the meaning of Choice of Court.

ii. Submission and Express Consent: Article 5(1)(e) and (f) Judgments

These provisions are an important supplement to those on choice of court agreements in order to give a comprehensive approach to party autonomy. If a party expressly consents to the jurisdiction of a court, or enters an appearance to contest the merits of a case without, earlier, or at the same time, contesting the jurisdiction or asking the court to decline to exercise its jurisdiction (unless an objection to jurisdiction or a request to decline to exercise jurisdiction would not have succeeded) then this provides a reasonable jurisdictional basis for recognising or enforcing a judgment from that court.[12] These grounds apply even if the parties had previously exclusively chosen another court: their submission or consent to proceeding in the court that delivered the judgment is treated as an agreed departure from their previous choice.

B. Rights *in Rem* in Immovable Property and Leases: Article 5(1)(h), 5(3) and 6 of Judgments

Choice of Court does not cover judgments concerning rights *in rem* in immovable property and leases, because these matters are excluded from its scope (see Article 2(2)(l)). It was particularly

[11] Arts 5 and 6 are discussed by Paul Beaumont and Mary Keyes, 'Choice of Court Agreements', ch 28 in this book.

[12] See G Saumier, 'Submission as a Jurisdictional Basis and the HCCH 2019 Judgments Convention' (2020) 67 *Netherlands International Law Review* 49.

important to regulate these issues in Judgments. Thanks to the willingness of Japan to compromise its position, a major breakthrough was achieved near the end of the Diplomatic Session to create a rational system in relation to these judgments. Non-residential leases (commercial leases) are (appropriately in our view) not subject to any restriction as to where the litigation can take place. Indeed, they could now be subject to any type of choice of court agreement apart from an exclusive one and the judgment of the chosen court would circulate under this Convention. This is a significant breakthrough for international commerce where large commercial leases may be entered into by companies in relation to properties in multiple States.

Article 5(1)(h) of Judgments provides that if a judgment in relation to a non-residential lease is given in the State of the property then it can circulate under the Convention.[13]

Article 5(3) of Judgments provides for recognition and enforcement of judgments ruling on residential leases and registration of immovable property where the judgment was given by a court of the State where the property is situated. These bases are exclusive within the scheme of Judgments, in the sense that such judgments cannot circulate under the Convention on the basis of the other grounds set out in Article 5(1). But they can be augmented by national law rules on recognition and enforcement permitted by the Convention under Article 15.

Finally, Article 6 restricts the circulation of judgments in relation to rights *in rem* in immovable property to judgments from the State where the property is situated. A right *in rem* is a right that, under the law of the State where the property is situated, can be asserted against anyone.

C. Weaker Party Limited Bases for Consumers and Employees: Article 5(2) Judgments[14]

Consumer and employment contracts are excluded from the scope of Choice of Court, see Article 2(1). But consumers and employees can rely on any of the bases of jurisdiction in Judgments if they seek recognition and enforcement of judgments in their favour. Some of the bases of jurisdiction – notably 'home jurisdiction' under Article 5(1)(a) – apply to judgments against consumers and employees. Other bases of jurisdiction are modified in their application to recognition or enforcement against consumers and employees, see Article 5(2).

D. Other Bases

There are too many other bases of jurisdiction in Article 5(1) to be able to analyse them in this chapter. However, the most commercially significant one is the contract jurisdiction in Article 5(1)(g) which is analysed in depth in chapter 15 of this book by two of its framers, Karen Vandekerckhove and Ron Brand. For the tort jurisdiction see chapter 19 by Reid Mortensen.

[13] Although Art 5(1)(h) is on its face of general application, Art 5(3) provides that Art 5(1) does not apply to a judgment that ruled on a residential lease of immovable property.

[14] See N de Araujo and M De Nardi, 'Consumer Protection Under the HCCH 2019 Judgments Convention' (2020) 67 *Netherlands International Law Review* 67.

V. Grounds for Refusal

Both Conventions contain limited and exhaustive grounds for refusing to recognise a judgment from a Contracting State that falls within the scope of the Convention, is still effective and enforceable in the State of origin, and has an appropriate jurisdictional basis under the Convention. There are the usual classical grounds of lack of notice and denial of the right to a hearing (Article 9(c) Choice of Court and Article 7(1)(a) Judgments);[15] procedural fraud (Article 9(d) Choice of Court) or fraud (Article 7(1)(b) Judgments); public policy (Article 9(e) Choice of Court and Article 7(1)(c) Judgments); and conflicting judgments (Article 9(f) and (g) Choice of Court and Article 7(1)(e) and (f) Judgments).[16]

One practically significant provision in Judgments is the new ground for refusal designed to bolster party autonomy by reinforcing any choice of court agreement between the parties that has a derogating effect (Article 7(1)(d) Judgments). If a judgment has been obtained by bringing proceedings in the court of origin contrary to a choice of court agreement that derogated from that court (whether that agreement is exclusive within the meaning of Choice of Court, or multiple exclusive, or asymmetric), the courts of the State addressed have a discretion to refuse to recognise and enforce the judgment. The courts of the State addressed should not do so if the party now relying on the derogative effect of the choice of court agreement expressly consented, or entered an appearance but did not object timeously, to the jurisdiction of the courts of the State of origin. Choice of Court only covers recognition and enforcement of judgments from the exclusively chosen court. It does not expressly give a power to the courts of States addressed to refuse to recognise and enforce a judgment that was granted in violation of a choice of court agreement. Judgments covers this gap both for choice of court agreements within the scope of Choice of Court and derogative choice of court agreements within the scope of Judgments.

Another innovative ground for refusal only found in Judgments is Article 7(2) which is designed to protect proceedings pending in the State addressed where the courts in that State were seised of proceedings between the same parties on the same subject matter before the courts of the State of origin were seised. The courts of the State addressed may dismiss without prejudice the recognition or enforcement of the judgment or postpone the recognition or enforcement proceedings until after the pending proceedings are concluded if there is a close connection between the dispute and the requested State. (This scenario should not of course arise in the Choice of Court context, as under Choice of Court the non-chosen court is required to decline jurisdiction.).

The provision permitting, but not requiring, refusal of any non-compensatory element of a foreign judgment (Article 11 Choice of Court and Article 10 Judgments) is explained in the explanatory reports to both Conventions including quoting a very important explanatory statement that was agreed during the Diplomatic Session on Choice of Court. The provision in Choice of Court was very deliberately mirrored in Judgments. A key point in that statement applies to all the grounds of refusal in both Conventions: 'As in the case of all other grounds for refusal, this provision should be interpreted and applied in as restrictive a way as possible'.[17]

[15] See N Meier, 'Notification as a Ground for Refusal' (2020) 67 *Netherlands International Law Review* 81.

[16] See the insightful attempt to integrate the analysis of some of these grounds for refusal, including the one found in Art 10 of Judgments, into the interpretation of the public policy ground by J Jang, 'The Public Policy Exception Under the New 2019 HCCH Judgments Convention' (2020) 67 *Netherlands International Law Review* 97.

[17] See Explanatory Report (n 5) para 293(b).

One additional safeguard against a foreign judgment not being recognised or enforced that should be welcomed is Article 13(2) of Judgments. This prohibits the court of the State addressed from refusing the recognition or enforcement of a judgment under the Convention on the ground that recognition or enforcement should be sought in another State. This provision is designed to prevent the State addressed creating jurisdiction rules for hearing actions for recognition and enforcement, or indeed declining to hear a case for recognition or enforcement of a judgment under the Convention, because it regards itself as a *forum non conveniens* for a recognition or enforcement application. There has been some evidence of courts and academics in North America putting jurisdictional or *forum non conveniens* hurdles in the way of applications for recognition and enforcement.[18]

VI. Scope and Declarations Reducing the Scope

A. Issues Pertaining to Governments: Articles 1(1) and 2(5) and (6) Choice of Court and Articles 1(1), 2(1)(n), (o) and (q), 2(4) and (5) and 19 Judgments

Both Conventions share the same approach to scope, distinguishing between civil or commercial matters (private law) which are within scope and public law matters which are outside scope. Both Conventions also do not automatically exclude proceedings involving governments from their scope, if the proceedings are civil or commercial in nature, while leaving State immunity rules untouched. Judgments has three further exclusions from scope for the armed forces, law enforcement and unilateral sovereign debt restructuring. And it gives States the option to make a declaration excluding some private law matters from scope in relation to governments, government agencies, and natural persons working for them.[19]

B. Subject Matter Exclusions from Scope: Articles 2(2) and 21 of Choice of Court and Articles 2(1) and 18 Judgments

i. Intellectual Property Exclusion: Article 2(2)(n) and (o) Choice of Court and 2(1)(m) Judgments

One of the most complex and challenging issues for the Diplomatic Session that finalised the text of Judgments was whether to exclude from scope some or all classes of intellectual property matters. The views expressed by delegations and industry stakeholders covered a wide spectrum, from complete inclusion to complete exclusion. Intermediate approaches along the lines of the partial inclusion in Choice of Court were also canvassed.

Ultimately it was not possible to reach agreement by consensus on the inclusion within scope of judgments that have intellectual property matters as the object of the proceedings.

[18] See P Beaumont, 'The Revived Judgments Project in The Hague' (2014) *Nederlands Internationaal Privaatrecht* 532, 538.

[19] For more details on this issue, see P Beaumont, 'Judgments Convention: Application to Governments' (2020) 67 *Netherlands International Law Review* 121.

Article 2(1)(m) excludes from scope 'intellectual property' matters. This is a significant, and in the eyes of some unfortunate, exclusion. It is to be hoped that future work – perhaps by the HCCH in conjunction with the World Intellectual Property Organization – will result in an instrument that governs recognition and enforcement of judgments relating to intellectual property. Until that occurs, the recognition and enforcement of judgments in proceedings concerned with intellectual property matters will continue to be governed by national laws unless the case falls within Choice of Court (ie, the judgment is from a State which the parties had exclusively chosen in writing in a choice of court agreement drafted broadly enough to cover the matter adjudicated upon and it relates to copyright or related rights or to infringement proceedings concerning another type of intellectual property (eg, a patent or a trade mark) which were, or could have been brought, for breach of contract relating to such intellectual property rights).

However, it is important to bear in mind two important limits to the exclusion in Judgments:

(a) A judgment in a contract claim is not within the exclusion merely because the contract contains provisions relating to intellectual property. Suppose for example that a franchisor sues for unpaid franchise fees, and obtains judgment for those fees. The mere fact that the franchise contract provides for licences to be granted in respect of the franchisor's trademarks (or other intellectual property rights) does not mean that the judgment is an 'intellectual property' matter to which Article 2(1)(m) applies.

(b) Article 2(2) provides that a judgment is not excluded from the scope of the Convention merely because a matter to which the Convention does not apply arose as a preliminary question in the proceedings in which the judgment was given, and not as an object of the proceedings. In particular, the mere fact that such a matter arose by way of defence does not exclude a judgment from the Convention, if that matter was not an object of the proceedings. In the example given above of a claim for unpaid franchise fees, the judgment would be within scope even if the franchisee counterclaimed alleging that the franchisor did not hold a valid trademark, so could not grant a valid licence. If that defence was rejected, the ruling on the validity of the trademark would not be enforceable under the Convention, by virtue of Article 8(1). And whether recognition or enforcement of the judgment could be refused would depend on whether the judgment was based on the trademark validity ruling, pursuant to Article 8(2).

ii. Defamation and Privacy Exclusions: Article 2(1)(k) and (l) of Judgments

Judgments relating to defamation and privacy were discussed at some length in the Special Commission meetings, and at the Diplomatic Conference on Judgments. These were not exclusions from Choice of Court because it is rare for such disputes to come within agreements between two commercial parties. Nor are there significant human rights and public policy concerns in the context where the parties consented to the forum to resolve their disputes. In the context of Judgments, however, differences between national laws and policies, and the evolving nature of the law in these fields in many States, gave rise to understandable concerns and sensitivities about the scenario where one party (not necessarily a commercial party) had not consented to the dispute being resolved in the court of origin.[20] The ultimate result is the exclusion of these

[20] These issues are discussed in C North, 'Note on the possible exclusion of privacy matters from the Convention as reflected in Article 2(1)(k) of the February 2017 draft Convention', available at: assets.hcch.net/docs/ff125c57-c85a-467d-ab5e-8acc3a50e2eb.pdf and Cara North, 'The Exclusion of Privacy Matters from the Judgments Convention' (2020) 67 *Netherlands International Law Review* 33. See Explanatory Report (n 5) paras 60–63.

matters from the scope of Judgments in Article 2(1)(k) and (l). The latter exclusion is broadly expressed, to accommodate current differences in national laws concerning the scope of privacy claims and to ensure that the exclusion can accommodate the evolution of national laws in this fast-developing field. But as with intellectual property, the privacy exclusion does not mean that a judgment with some connection to privacy issues, however tenuous, is excluded from the scope of the Convention. For example, the exclusion would not apply to a judgment obtained by a data holder against an IT service provider for losses caused by a failure to meet contractual standards for data security, merely because the data are personal data and the data subjects might also have claims against the data holder or the IT provider for breach of privacy laws. Claims of this kind are in substance contract claims between commercial entities, not privacy claims; the resulting judgment will be within scope and will circulate under Judgments.

iii. Competition/Antitrust Partial Exclusion in Judgments but Complete Exclusion in Choice of Court: Article 2(2)(h) Choice of Court and Article 2(1)(p) Judgments

Another scope issue that attracted detailed discussion in Judgments was the proposed exclusion of competition/anti-trust matters. These matters are excluded from Choice of Court. The concern expressed by some participants and stakeholders was that this is an area with a large policy component, and cross-border enforcement could give rise to sensitivities. Others considered that these concerns are not so great as to justify the wholesale exclusion from scope of such matters, and that it would be unfortunate to exclude this important class of proceeding from the scope of the Convention. They emphasised that few of the Article 5 filters will apply to such claims – in particular, the Article 5(1)(j) non-contractual obligation filter, which is confined to physical injuries, will not apply – and that any significant public policy concerns in the State addressed can be addressed under Article 7(1)(c), or perhaps by a declaration under Article 19.[21] The outcome was a compromise,[22] intended to ensure that judgments against participants in hard-core cartels are enforceable under the Convention, but other competition/anti-trust judgments are outside scope with enforcement left to national laws. Article 2(1)(p) excludes from scope:

> [A]nti-trust (competition) matters, except where the judgment is based on conduct that constitutes an anti-competitive agreement or concerted practice among actual or potential competitors to fix prices, make rigged bids, establish output restrictions or quotas, or divide markets by allocating customers, suppliers, territories or lines of commerce and where such conduct and its effect both occurred in the State of origin.

The language is based on an OECD Recommendation concerning hard-core cartels.[23] That document is likely to be of considerable assistance in interpreting and applying Article 2(1)(p).

[21] These issues are described in more detail in C North, 'The possible exclusion of anti-trust matters from the Convention as reflected in Article 2(1)(p) of the 2018 draft Convention', available at: assets.hcch.net/docs/dcd7c92a-d3fd-46a5-bae5-627ff1636003.pdf. See Explanatory Report (n 5) paras 69–73. See also ch 17 in this book.

[22] This compromise could not have been achieved without the help of China who were willing to show some flexibility on their position on this issue at the end of the Diplomatic Session and having shown that flexibility actively persuaded other doubting States to shift to including judgments against hard core cartels in order to reach a consensus based on partial exclusion rather than complete exclusion (the default position where there is no consensus to include something within the scope of a Convention).

[23] OECD Competition Committee (1998) Recommendation of the OECD Council concerning effective action against hard core cartels, available at: www.oecd.org/daf/competition/2350130.pdf.

iv. Specific Subject Matter Declarations: Article 21 Choice of Court and 18 Judgments

Article 21 Choice of Court is a novel provision introduced to allow States to carve out from scope specific subject matters in relation to which they were not comfortable assuming obligations under the Convention. This provision was relied on by the EU to exclude some insurance contracts from the scope of their obligations when acceding to Choice of Court. In doing so the EU interpreted Article 21 (correctly, in our view) to allow the declaration to be restricted to part of a subject matter rather than all of it.[24] That view has now been expressly confirmed in Article 18 of Judgments.

C. Arbitration: Article 2(3) Choice of Court and Judgments

Both Choice of Court and Judgments favour a clear and complete exclusion for arbitration which ensures that arbitral awards circulate under the New York Convention and court judgments circulate under the two Hague Conventions. In the unusual event of a conflict between a court judgment and an arbitral award on the same subject matter between the same parties the arbitral award would prevail (see Article 23(2) Judgments).[25] The exclusion of arbitration and related proceedings also makes clear that the two Conventions have no relevance to issues such as whether court proceedings should be stayed or dismissed by reference to an arbitration agreement, or whether recognition and enforcement of a judgment should be declined because the proceedings in the court of origin were brought in contravention of an arbitration agreement.

VII. Minimum Harmonisation: Article 15 of Judgments and Chapter III of Choice of Court

Article 15 of the Judgments Convention makes explicit an important structural feature of that Convention: it expressly allows national law to go further in recognising and enforcing foreign judgments, with the one exception found in Article 6 which prohibits recognising and enforcing a judgment on a right *in rem* in immovable property from a State other than the State where the property is located. An example from Australasia provides a helpful illustration of the way in which Articles 5, 6, 7 and 15 of the Judgments Convention operate to set a floor for enforcement of judgments. Suppose Australia and New Zealand both become Parties to Judgments. Under the trans-Tasman scheme for recognition and enforcement of judgments, most judgments are enforced without any jurisdictional prerequisites being applied.[26] The only defence available in

[24] See Beaumont (n 18).

[25] The point is not so clear in Choice of Court but of course should not arise in that context because the parties should not agree to an exclusive choice of court agreement and to arbitration in relation to the same dispute.

[26] There are a handful of exceptions to the scheme: one such exception is that it does not require recognition and enforcement of a judgment given in a proceeding in the other country where the subject matter of the proceeding was immovable property that was not situated in that country. See Art 5(8)(a) of the Agreement between the Government of New Zealand and the Government of Australia on Trans-Tasman Court Proceedings and Regulatory Enforcement (signed 24 July 2008, entered into force 11 October 2013) 2013 NZTS 6; and s 61(2)(c) of the New Zealand Trans-Tasman Proceedings Act 2010. Thus, there is no inconsistency with Art 6: any judgment to which Art 6 applies falls outside the scheme.

the court addressed in most cases is that recognition or enforcement would be contrary to public policy: any other challenge to the validity or enforceability of the judgment must be raised in the court of origin. That scheme could continue to operate as between Australia and New Zealand without any inconsistency with Articles 5, 6 and 7 of Judgments. New Zealand would enforce a wide range of Australian judgments that do not qualify for recognition and enforcement under Articles 5 and 6 of Judgments. In proceedings in New Zealand for the enforcement of an Australian judgment, none of the grounds for refusing recognition and enforcement in Article 7 of Judgments would apply except Article 7(1)(c). Indeed there are some grounds for refusing enforcement that fall within Article 7(1)(c) that would not be available in the trans-Tasman context, eg, where the proceedings in the court of origin are inconsistent with the principles of procedural fairness. That issue would need to be raised in the relevant Australian court.

Chapter III of Choice of Court regulates the terms by which a Contracting Party must ensure that a judgment given by a court of a Contracting State designated in an exclusive choice of court agreement shall be recognised and enforced under the Convention. It does not prevent a Contracting Party from recognising and enforcing a judgment from a Contracting State under national law when the exclusive choice of court agreement does not meet the formal validity requirements in the Convention, eg, an oral agreement on the exclusive choice of court which is not documented in writing but based on a practice between the parties or on a trade usage.[27]

Consistent with this approach, Contracting States will be able to include provisions in implementing legislation that prescribe in more detail how certain provisions in the two Conventions will be applied by the courts of that State. For example, Article 7(1) of Judgments and Article 9(1) of Choice of Court provide that recognition or enforcement *may* be refused in certain circumstances. Implementing legislation could omit some of these grounds for refusal. Conversely, legislation could require refusal in some or all of these cases. Or it could confer a discretion on the court addressed. Any of these approaches would be consistent with the architecture of the Conventions. Similarly, implementing legislation could take a number of different approaches to Article 7(2) of Judgments and Article 8(4) of Choice of Court, which provide that recognition or enforcement *may* be postponed or refused in certain circumstances, including where an appeal is pending in the State of origin. Implementing legislation could mandate a stay rather than a refusal in such circumstances, or vice versa, or could confer a discretion on the court addressed.

VIII. Bilateralisation

The topic of bilateralisation is political. No such system applies in Choice of Court, which is completely open to all States (Article 27). It is less politically sensitive than Judgments because it is predicated on commercial parties choosing a court, and Article 6 allows a non-chosen court to hear a case where giving effect to the agreement would lead to a manifest injustice (perhaps due to systemic failings in the justice system of the courts chosen by the parties in their agreement). Judgments creates obligations on States to recognise and enforce judgments from States

[27] Arguably, however, the terms of Art 5(1) of Choice of Court mean that the courts of a Contracting State are not at liberty to recognise and enforce a judgment from a Contracting State based on those courts having jurisdiction under an exclusive choice of court agreement if the courts of that State have already decided that the exclusive choice of court agreement is substantively invalid.

where the defendant in those proceedings may have consistently opposed the courts of that State exercising jurisdiction.

Participants rejected at an early stage the option of adopting some sort of 'positive' bilateralisation process, under which judgments from one Contracting State would be recognised and enforced in another Contracting State only if both States had made positive declarations to that effect. Concerns were expressed about the practical reality of such an approach. If, eg, there were 50 Contracting States, an approach of this kind would require each of those States to declare their willingness to recognise and enforce judgments from each of the others – some 2,450 treaty actions. That seems impracticable. The 1971 Hague Convention on the Recognition and Enforcement of Foreign Judgments in Civil and Commercial Matters has only a handful of parties and has not come into operation. It required 'positive' bilateralisation, and that approach was not seen by States as workable.[28]

The solution that was ultimately seen as workable is set out in Article 29. A State that becomes a party to the Convention can notify the depositary that its ratification, acceptance, approval or accession will not have the effect of establishing relations with an existing Contracting State. Each existing Contracting State can notify the depositary that the ratification, acceptance, approval or accession by the new party will not have the effect of establishing relations between them. The Convention applies between two States only if neither has given such a notification vis-à-vis the other. Such notifications can be withdrawn at any time.

This mechanism ensures that a State will not enter into a treaty relationship with another State that requires it to recognise and enforce that other State's judgments without first having an opportunity to decline to accept such treaty obligations.[29] Once a State has accepted such treaty obligations it cannot a subsequently opt out of them in relation to a particular State, eg, because that State's judicial system becomes much worse. But its courts can use the public policy exception to refuse to recognise a judgment from that State which is tainted by corruption or other very serious injustices.

IX. Conclusion

We are optimistic that the two Conventions have succeeded in walking the fine line between breadth of scope and impact, and acceptability to States considering becoming Parties. We hope that the Conventions will enhance access to justice and facilitate cross-border trade, investment and mobility by creating a strong framework for the recognition and enforcement of judgments in civil or commercial matters.

[28] See, eg, 'Some reflections of the Permanent Bureau on a general convention on enforcement of judgments' (Prel Doc No 17 of May 1992) in *Hague Conference on Private International Law, Proceedings of the Seventeenth Session* (1993) Vol I, 231; Brand (n 1).

[29] See also Nielsen (n 6) 242–45, chair of the Informal Working Group at the Diplomatic Session on Final Clauses; and Explanatory Report (n 5) paras 407–16.

30

Conflicts of Jurisdiction

ARDAVAN ARZANDEH AND MATTHIAS LEHMANN

I. Introduction

The litigation of private international law disputes presents many challenges to courts worldwide. These challenges range from contending with questions that concern the substance of the dispute, to ruling on how the trial process should be conducted. Given that these disputes have elements that are linked to more than one territory, one of the first issues that must be settled before engaging with other procedural and substantive matters, is whether the court has jurisdiction to entertain the dispute. To this end, each system of law has developed its own set of 'jurisdiction rules'. The wider structural and substantive similarities between the jurisdiction rules of different legal systems mean that it is possible to place them into broader categories. Two of these categories are the common law and civil law rules of jurisdiction. They are the most significant for two reasons. First, almost all major centres for the litigation of cross-border private disputes are based in States with common law and civil law systems. Second, these legal traditions are in operation in many countries around the world.

In the context of private international law disputes, it is possible for courts of more than one country, based on their respective rules, to have jurisdiction over the same claim. In other words, there could be 'conflicts of jurisdiction' between courts of different States. These conflicts can manifest regardless of whether the rules in force in the relevant jurisdiction have common law or civil law roots. Where conflicts of jurisdiction exist, significant problems would arise if each court were to proceed to entertain the matter. Chief among these is the risk of the initiation of multiple proceedings concerning similar (if not identical) legal issues in different fora, which is bound to result in wasteful and costly litigation. Moreover, it is conceivable that conflicting judgments could be rendered at the conclusion of each set of proceedings, thus creating confusion regarding which judgment should subsequently receive recognition or enforcement. Even where the risk of multiple proceedings is minimal (or, indeed, non-existent), the availability of more than one forum for entertaining the disputes can encourage 'forum shopping' on the part of the litigants. This is a phenomenon whereby a litigant bypasses the forum with close connection to the dispute and, instead, initiates proceedings in a venue from which it expects to receive the most favourable judgment, notwithstanding that the forum has little (or no) connection with the claim.[1]

[1] *Boys v Chaplin* [1971] AC 356 (HL) 401 (Lord Pearson). On the importance of venue in the context of cross-border commercial litigation, see, eg, AS Bell, *Forum Shopping and Venue in Transnational Litigation* (Oxford University Press 2002); F Vischer, 'General Course on Private International Law' (1992) 232 *Hague Collected Courses* 224–28; and P de Vareilles-Sommière (ed), *Forum Shopping in the European Judicial Area* (Hart Publishing 2007).

In short, conflicts of jurisdiction can lead to the creation of serious problems in the litigation of cross-border claims. In order to pre-empt these problems, civil law and common law jurisdiction rules include measures based on which courts may (or, in some instances, must) relinquish their otherwise soundly established jurisdiction in favour of another foreign court. The discussion in this chapter begins, in section II, by briefly outlining these responses. It then proceeds, in section III, to evaluate the civil law and common law approaches to conflict of jurisdiction problems. This section in the analysis seeks to highlight that the differences in the responses to conflicts of jurisdiction under these legal regimes are largely due to the differences in the broader values which civil law and common law traditions have historically pursued. Finally, in section IV, the chapter examines whether, by drawing on the rules in both civil law and common law traditions, a 'global' approach to conflicts of jurisdiction can be developed. Given the importance and influence of these bodies of laws, attempts at forming a global response to problems that arise due to conflicts of jurisdictions should seek to draw on both systems. It is argued that, by and large, the Preliminary Draft Convention on Jurisdiction and Foreign Judgments in Civil and Commercial Matters, adopted in The Hague in 2001,[2] provides a potentially fruitful starting point for designing a global approach to conflicts of jurisdiction.

II. Civil Law and Common Law Responses to Conflicts of Jurisdiction: An Introduction

Before identifying the main responses which civil law and common law traditions have developed to conflict of jurisdiction problems, the reasons why these problems might arise in the first place must be explained. In this respect, it is helpful to assess briefly the jurisdiction rules within these systems of law.

Jurisdiction rules under civil law are predominantly codified, meaning that statutory instruments are the primary sources for the courts' assumption of jurisdiction in cross-border disputes. Courts in civil law countries often have some room for manoeuvre in interpreting these instruments. The majority of jurisdiction rules at civil law are phrased in a general and abstract way – such as 'place of performance' of a contractual obligation or 'place of harm' in tort claims – thus affording courts some leeway in interpreting those provisions. But, compared with their common law counterparts, courts in civil law countries have considerably less discretion in how jurisdiction rules are applied. Consequently, there is limited scope in fashioning new rules concerned with jurisdiction at civil law beyond what is included within the statutory instruments. Where courts are persuaded that they have competence over the dispute, they must entertain the claim.

At civil law, the starting point for assumption of jurisdiction is the well-known Roman adage *actor sequitur forum rei*: the claimant has to sue the defendant at the latter's domicile.[3] This principle, which is enshrined in the Brussels Ia Regulation,[4] as well as in national laws in a number

[2] Summary of the Outcome of the Discussion in Commission II of the First Part of the Diplomatic Conference 6–20 June 2001 Interim Text Prepared by the Permanent Bureau and the Co-reporters, available at: assets.hcch.net/docs/e172ab52-e2de-4e40-9051-11aee7c7be67.pdf.

[3] On the historical origins of *actor sequitur forum rei*, see, eg, A von Mehren, 'Must Plaintiffs Seek Out Defendants? The Contemporary Standing of Actor Sequitur Forum Rei' (1997–98) 8 *King's College Law Journal* 23.

[4] Regulation (EU) No 1215/2012 of the European Parliament and of the Council of 12 December 2012 on jurisdiction and the recognition and enforcement of judgments in civil and commercial matters (recast) [2012] OJ L351/1, Art 4.

of civil law jurisdictions,[5] requires a much more meaningful connection between the defendant and the forum, before the court can assume jurisdiction, than is envisaged at common law. In this way, it serves to protect defendants against the initiation by claimants of frivolous or purely speculative proceedings.

However, civil law jurisdiction rules do not merely confine the claimants to commencing proceedings in the defendants' place of domicile. In many instances, claimants have the option of bringing their claim in a forum other than the defendant's place of domicile. For example, special jurisdiction rules at civil law allow claimants to initiate proceedings, in a contractual dispute, at the place of performance of the contract, or, in a tort claim, where the harmful event occurred.[6] In some areas, courts are granted exclusive jurisdiction, to the detriment of all other courts, including those at the defendant's place of domicile. For instance, in disputes concerning rights *in rem* over immovable property, exclusive jurisdiction is conferred on the court of the place where the property is located.[7] In addition, recent years have witnessed the introduction of jurisdiction rules that seek to afford greater protection to vulnerable parties such as consumers[8] and employees.[9] For the most part, these rules are based on a combination of optional jurisdiction (for claims by the vulnerable party) and exclusive rules of jurisdiction (for claims against the vulnerable party).[10]

Although certain aspects of civil law jurisdiction rules could be described as 'exorbitant',[11] by and large, the existence of a real connection between the defendant or the dispute and the forum is essential to founding jurisdiction. As such, it is generally rare for civil law courts to find that they have competence over a claim that has little (or no) connection with the forum. Nevertheless, it is possible for a civil law court to have jurisdiction over a claim, for instance, where the defendant is domiciled in the forum, when proceedings involving the same (or related) parties and/or issues are pending in another foreign forum where the cause of action happened. As stated earlier, the existence of multiple proceedings in more than one venue could lead to myriad problems. These problems exist both at the litigation stage, but also after the conclusion of the hearings, when, in the event that there are conflicting judgments, there is likely to be confusion over which of them should be recognised or enforced.

In response to this conflicts of jurisdiction problem, civil law courts rely on the doctrine of *lis pendens*.[12] An especially strict version applies inside the European Union (EU). In conflicts of jurisdiction between the courts of two EU Member States, the court second seised must relinquish its jurisdiction where proceedings involving the same cause of action and between the

[5] eg, French Code of Civil Procedure, Art 42; German Code of Civil Procedure, §§ 12–13; Swiss Federal Private International Law Act (PILA) Art 2.

[6] eg, Brussels Ia Regulation, Art 7(1) and (2); German Code of Civil Procedure, §§ 29 and 32; French Code of Civil Procedure, Art 46 nos 1 and 2; and Swiss PILA, Art 113 and Art 129 phrase 2.

[7] Brussels Ia Regulation, Art 24(1); German Code of Civil Procedure, §§ 29 and 32; French Code of Civil Procedure, Art 42; Swiss PILA, Art 113 and Art 129 phrase 2.

[8] Brussels Ia Regulation, Arts 17–19; Swiss PILA, Art 114.

[9] Brussels Ia Regulation, Arts 20–23; Swiss PILA, Art 115.

[10] See Brussels Ia Regulation, Arts18, 21 and 22. The Swiss PILA merely provides the first limb, ie, optional jurisdiction for claims by the consumer, see Swiss PILA, Art 114, while allowing different fora for claims by the other party. The latter rule is, however, limited to consumers domiciled in States that have not adhered to the Lugano II Convention. Consumers domiciled in Switzerland and the other signatory States are protected by the exclusive forum provided for claims against them under the Lugano II Convention, Art 16(2); see A Bonomi in A Bucher (ed), *Loi sur le droit international privé. Convention de Lugano* (Helbing & Lichtenhahn 2011) Art 114, margin no 17.

[11] Such as nationality- or asset-based jurisdiction: see Arts 14–15 French Code civil; s 23 German Code of Civil Procedure.

[12] See Brussels Ia Regulation, Arts 29–34; Swiss PILA, Art 9.

same parties are already pending before the court first seised.[13] This rule of temporal priority is applied strictly without the court second seised having the right to second-guess the first court's jurisdiction.[14] It is only where 'related actions' are ongoing before courts in two different EU Member States that the court second seised has discretion whether to decline its jurisdiction.[15] Related actions are those that are 'so closely connected that it is expedient to hear and determine them together to avoid the risk of irreconcilable judgments resulting from separate proceedings'.[16] In exercising this discretion, the court second seised assesses the connection of the disputes, the risk of conflicting judgments, and whether, overall, it is (im)prudent to allow the action before it to proceed.[17] Second seised EU courts also have discretion to stay the proceedings in favour of courts of a third State, ie, a non-Member State.[18] Factors to take into consideration in making this decision include the question whether the court in the third State will give a judgment capable of recognition in the EU and that the stay is necessary for the proper administration of justice.[19] A rejection of a stay is indicated, inter alia, where the proceedings in the third State are unlikely to be concluded within a reasonable time.[20]

As far as common law jurisdiction rules are concerned, conflict of jurisdiction problems tend to occur predominantly where the courts' competence is rooted in the defendant's presence in the forum. In many common law countries, it has long been established that, no matter how fleeting, the defendant's presence in the forum at the commencement of the proceedings is sufficient to establish jurisdiction.[21] In essence, a common law court's jurisdiction is 'based upon the principle of territorial dominion, and that all persons within territorial dominion owe their allegiance to its sovereign power and obedience to all its laws and to the lawful jurisdiction of its courts'.[22] It is immediately apparent that this basis for assuming jurisdiction could confer competence on courts in situations where, other than the defendant's presence, there is little (or no) real connection between the litigation and the forum.

In such an instance, a defendant can apply to the common law court to relinquish its (otherwise) soundly established jurisdiction under the *forum non conveniens* doctrine. Although the doctrine is now a well-known feature of common law jurisdiction rules, it was first 'invented' in Scotland,[23] a legal system encompassing elements of both common and civil legal traditions. The Scots doctrine helped to shape similar doctrines across the common law world. In the case of

[13] Brussels Ia Regulation, Art 29.

[14] See C-351/89 *Overseas Union Ltd et al v New Hampshire Insurance Co* [1991] ECR I-3342, [25]. An exception was only recently introduced in cases where the court second seised was chosen by the parties in a manner consistent with Brussels Ia Regulation's Art 25 to have jurisdiction over the dispute: see Brussels Ia Regulation, Art 31(2).

[15] Brussels Ia Regulation, Art 30(1).

[16] Ibid, Art 30(3).

[17] See, eg, C-406/92 *Owners of Cargo Lately Laden on Board the Ship Tatry v Owners of the Ship Maciej Rataj* [1994] ECR I-5439.

[18] See Brussels Ia Regulation, Arts 33 and 34.

[19] Ibid Arts 33(1)(a) and (b) and 34(1)(b) and (c).

[20] Ibid, Arts 33(2)(b) and 34(2)(c).

[21] In England, see, eg, *HRH Maharanee Seethadevi Gaekwar of Baroda v Wildenstein* [1972] 2 QB 283 (CA). For a detailed account on the provenance and development of this basis for assuming jurisdiction at common law, see A Dickinson, 'Keeping up Appearances: The Development of Adjudicatory Jurisdiction in the English Courts' (2016) 86 *British Yearbook of International Law* 6. As for the United States, see, eg, *Burnham v Superior Court of California* 495 US 604 (1989); *Grace v MacArthur* 170 F Supp 442 (1959).

[22] *Carrick v Hancock* (1895) 12 TLR 59, 60 (Lord Russell of Killowen CJ).

[23] P Beaumont and P McEleavy, *Anton's Private International Law*, 3rd edn (W Green/SULI 2011) para 8.405. For an in-depth analysis of the doctrine's genesis in Scotland, see A Arzandeh, 'The Origins of the Scottish *Forum Non Conveniens* Doctrine' (2017) 13 *Journal of Private International Law* 130.

England, eg, Lord Goff of Chieveley, in articulating the current basis for the doctrine's application, in *Spiliada Maritime Corporation v Cansulex Ltd*,[24] drew on leading Scottish judgments.[25]

The approaches to the application of the *forum non conveniens* doctrine vary across the common law world. The English version of the doctrine – known as the 'more-appropriate-forum test' – has been adopted by courts in a number of common law territories, including Hong Kong,[26] Singapore,[27] New Zealand,[28] Ireland,[29] Brunei[30] and Gibraltar.[31] In the United States, the *forum non conveniens* doctrine is applied by assessing a number of 'private-' and 'public-interest' considerations.[32] In Australia, courts opted not to embrace the more-appropriate-forum test. Instead, in private international law disputes in Australia, the *forum non conveniens* doctrine enables courts to stay their proceedings if they are satisfied that Australia is a 'clearly inappropriate forum' for entertaining the dispute.[33] Express or implied statutory limitations could affect the doctrine's scope. In the United Kingdom, eg, the doctrine cannot be deployed where the court's jurisdiction is rooted in the provisions in the Warsaw Convention for the Unification of Certain Rules Relating to International Carriage by Air 1929. While the Brussels Ia Regulation was in force in the United Kingdom, its courts could not rely on the doctrine to relinquish jurisdiction which was rooted in the provisions within that instrument. In the event of the United Kingdom's accession to the Lugano II Convention,[34] the doctrine will remain unavailable to UK courts in the context of cases where their jurisdiction is based on the provisions in that Convention.

Under the more appropriate forum test, the court has discretion to stay its proceedings if it concludes that another foreign forum, which would assume jurisdiction over the dispute, is more appropriate for hearing the case. The test is applied in two stages.[35] At the first stage, the onus is on the defendant to convince the common law court that another foreign forum is available and more closely connected to the dispute.[36] Availability is established if the defendant can show that the foreign court would assert jurisdiction over the case.[37] In deciding whether the foreign forum is more closely connected to the dispute, various factors are considered. For example, if the parties and/or the claim are more closely connected to the foreign forum, then, all else considered, this would point in favour of granting a stay in favour of that forum.[38] Similarly, the fact that the dispute is governed by the law of State A would make it more likely for the common law court to stay its proceedings in favour of State A, if the case turns on a question of law and there are

[24] [1987] AC 460.

[25] eg, *Sim v Robinow* (1892) 19 R 665.

[26] *The Adhiguna Meranti* [1988] 1 Lloyd's Rep 384.

[27] *Brinkerhoff Maritime Drilling Corp v PT Airfast Services Indonesia* [1992] 2 SLR 776.

[28] *McConnell Dowell Constructors Ltd v Lloyd's Syndicate 396* [1988] 2 NZLR 257.

[29] *Analog Devices BV v Zurich Insurance Company* [2002] IESC 1.

[30] *Syarikat Bumiputra Kimanis v Tan Kok Voon* [1988] 3 MLJ 315.

[31] *The Waylink and Brady Maria* [1998] 1 Lloyd's Rep 475.

[32] *Gulf Oil Corporation v Gilbert* (1947) 330 US 501.

[33] *Voth v Manildra Flour Mills Pty Ltd* (1990) 171 CLR 538.

[34] Convention on jurisdiction and the recognition and enforcement of judgments in civil and commercial matters [2007] OJ L 339/3. On 8 April 2020, the United Kingdom applied to join the Lugano II Convention. As of 7 June 2021, the final outcome of the UK's application remains unclear.

[35] This is where the test applicable in England is different from the one in operation at federal level in Canada. Under the Canadian *forum non conveniens*, courts examine whether a foreign forum is more appropriate than them based on a one-stage test: see, principally, *Amchem Products Inc v Workers Compensation Board* [1993] 1 SCR 897.

[36] *Spiliada* (n 24) 476.

[37] *Connelly v RTZ Corporation* [1998] AC 854 (HL).

[38] eg, *The Lakhta* [1992] 2 Lloyd's Rep 269 (English proceedings were stayed as the court in Russia was found to be the natural forum for the dispute).

marked differences between the two legal systems.[39] The existence of parallel or related proceedings in a foreign court – *lis alibi pendens* – too can be a consideration at this stage in favour of granting a stay, particularly where the foreign proceedings are far advanced or the court is about to render its judgment.[40] It should be noted that none of these factors is, without more, definitive in winning the argument in support of a stay. But where the common law court concludes that the foreign court is better placed to hear the case, it can give up its jurisdiction.

If, after its enquiry under the first limb of the more appropriate forum test, the common law court arrives at the conclusion that the foreign court is not available or is not more closely connected to the dispute, then the defendant's stay application will fail. Otherwise, the second stage of the test becomes relevant. At this point, the claimant can seek to resist a stay order on the basis that the foreign forum would be unable to dispose of the claim justly.[41] To this end, the claimant can adduce evidence that highlights

> [a] risk that justice will not be obtained by a foreign litigant in particular kinds of suits whether for ideological or political reasons, … inexperience or inefficiency of the judiciary, … excessive delay in the conduct of the business of the courts or the unavailability of appropriate remedies.[42]

If the court concludes that, notwithstanding that another available foreign forum is more closely connected to the dispute, it is not in the interests of the parties and the ends of justice for the case to be heard there, then it would reject the stay application.

It must be highlighted that there is one area in which the jurisdiction rules of the common law and the civil law converge. This area is where the parties have chosen the competent court through agreement. The validity of choice of forum clauses is admitted in both common and civil law jurisdictions. This is reinforced by international agreements, like the Hague Choice of Court Convention 2005.[43] Although the emphasis of this study is on the areas in which the jurisdictional rules diverge, this important convergence is not to be forgotten.

III. Civil Law and Common Law Responses to Conflicts of Jurisdiction: An Evaluation

Having outlined the responses at civil law and common law to conflicts of jurisdiction, this section of the discussion sets out to evaluate their effectiveness. To begin with, it is important to touch on the broader criteria against which this evaluation should be conducted. In this respect, two criteria are especially relevant. The first criterion for evaluating the efficacy of the civil law and common law responses to conflicts of jurisdiction is certainty. In general, the question of whether a particular court would assert and exercise jurisdiction over a cross-border commercial dispute should be predictable to the litigants from the outset. If the principles for resolving conflicts of jurisdiction are overly open-ended or fluid, then parties are liable to expend considerably more time and resources in identifying the forum that would entertain the claim. Furthermore, uncertainty in this context could create wider difficulties for the parties, by forcing

[39] eg, *VTB Capital plc v Nutritek International Corpn* [2013] UKSC 5; [2013] 2 AC 337 (in England); and *Seereederei Baco Liner GmbH v Al Aliyu* [2000] FCA 656 (in Australia).

[40] *de Dampierre v de Dampierre* [1988] AC 92 (HL).

[41] *Spiliada* (n 24) 478, citing Lord Diplock in *The Abidin Daver* [1984] 1 AC 398 (HL) 411.

[42] *The Abidin Daver*, ibid (Lord Diplock).

[43] The Convention of 30 June 2005 on Choice of Court Agreements, available at: assets.hcch.net/docs/510bc238-7318-47ed-9ed5-e0972510d98b.pdf. See Paul Beaumont and Mary Keyes, 'Choice of Court Agreements', ch 28 in this book.

them to take steps – such as requiring collateral at the time of the contract's conclusion or settling a claim on less advantageous terms after a dispute has arisen – which they would not have taken had the rules been clearer.

The second basis for assessing the suitability of the responses to conflicts of jurisdiction within civil law and common law traditions is the appropriateness of the court designated as competent in terms of its close connection to the dispute. There is an innate attraction in settling the question of which of the two fora with jurisdiction over a case should hear it in favour of the one that, on balance, has closer links to the dispute. By and large, a court with more meaningful connection with the litigation is better placed to perform efficiently the various aspects of the trial process. Moreover, if conflicts of jurisdiction are resolved by promoting connectedness, then that is likely to discourage attempts at forum shopping.

Against the yardstick of certainty, the civil law approach to conflicts of jurisdiction fares well. Despite their abstract nature, the statutory rules on jurisdiction provide relatively clear guidance on the competent court. In cases where parallel proceedings are brought concerning the same cause of action and the same parties in different fora, the *lis pendens* doctrine – interpreted as a strict rule of temporal priority – leaves little room for doubt about which court has to stay the proceedings. Any remaining doubts are solved by case law.[44] The clarity of the position on conflicts of jurisdiction in cases of this type enables parties to have a reasonably clear sense as to which of the competing fora in which the matter may be brought would proceed to hear it. By removing a major source of uncertainty regarding which court would exercise jurisdiction, the *lis pendens* doctrine helps to reduce the costs associated with identifying the place in which the case should be brought.

However, as far as the promotion of connectedness when responding to conflicts of jurisdiction is concerned, the civil law approach seems less effective. Although civil law rules, with their hard-edged nature, enlist jurisdictional bases that signify points of connection that are generally strong, they do not always allow the forum with a stronger connection with the claim to entertain the case. As a result, under a civilian system for allocating jurisdiction, it is entirely possible for a court to have competence over a dispute that is more strongly connected to a competing foreign forum. In this respect, the following hypothetical example is illustrative:

> A is domiciled in Arcadia, a civil law jurisdiction. While on holiday in Narnia, A suffers serious injuries that he attributes to the actions of B and four other parties. B is an Arcadian domiciliary; the others are domiciled in Narnia. The overwhelming majority of evidence and witnesses are in Narnia. A commences proceedings against B and the other defendants in Arcadia. The Arcadian court has jurisdiction over B, as he is domiciled in the forum. A has been able to add the other four accused parties to his claim against B to the Arcadian proceedings. Narnian law is the dispute's governing law. The Narnian court would assert jurisdiction, were a claim brought before it.[45]

On these facts, civil law jurisdiction rules prescribe that the Arcadian court must exercise jurisdiction over the claim, even though the court in Narnia appears to be much better placed to hear it. This rigidity in the approach to conflicts of jurisdiction at civil law is largely due to the absence of a doctrinal measure that seeks to promote connectedness when addressing instances of conflicts of jurisdiction. Even in the context of related actions within the Brussels regime, the discretion afforded to the court second seised to decline its jurisdiction is to be exercised

[44] In the context of the Brussels regime, see, eg, 144/86 *Gubisch Maschinenfabrik KG v Palumbo* [1987] ECR 4861.

[45] Although hypothetical, the circumstances outlined in the example bear strong resemblance to the facts in C-281/02 *Owusu v Jackson* [2005] ECR I-1383.

chiefly to avoid the risk of irreconcilable judgments resulting from separate proceedings.[46] Furthermore, under the Brussels regime, a litigant can abuse the *lis pendens* rule by commencing 'negative-declaration proceedings' in a court that has a slow civil litigation system. These are actions where one party pre-emptively initiates a claim against the other, to obtain a declaration that it is not at fault on the facts. The engagement in delaying tactics of this nature allows litigants to frustrate their opponents, not least because they force any subsequent action in another EU Member State that involves the same cause of action and the same parties to be stayed. Indeed, until relatively recently the textual reading of the *lis pendens* doctrine under the Brussels I Regulation[47] meant that, even where the parties' express agreement was the basis for the court second seised's jurisdiction, it still had to decline jurisdiction until the court first seised ruled that it lacked jurisdiction to hear the case.[48]

By comparison, the common law's approach to conflicts of jurisdiction, through the application of the *forum non conveniens* doctrine, is liable to give rise to outcomes that are less certain. The reason for this observation is because the more appropriate forum test is open to the charge of affording courts a disproportionately broad discretion when deciding whether to exercise jurisdiction. This drawback in the common law's response to conflicts of jurisdiction is well known and has been openly recognised within the academic commentary.[49] The breadth of discretion can, in turn, result in courts arriving at different judgments in cases which seem to involve broadly similar facts and issues.[50] Accordingly, parties can find themselves lacking the desired level of certainty, from the outset, about where their case will be heard. Additionally, because of the breadth of the discretion available to the courts, parties, especially in high-value disputes, tend to resort to adducing large volumes of evidentiary material to substantiate their claims regarding whether proceedings should be stayed.[51] Consequently, trials involving *forum non conveniens* pleas – which are, in essence, hearings about where the case should be entertained – can be drawn out and costly.

But when it comes to ensuring that conflicts of jurisdiction are resolved by allowing litigation to be heard in a forum which has stronger connection to it, the approach at common law has much to commend it. While mere presence as a basis for assuming jurisdiction could lead to courts asserting competence over cases with little (or no) connection to the forum, the *forum non conveniens* doctrine ensures that the common law court in question can give up its

[46] Brussels Ia Regulation, Art 30(3) and Lugano II Convention, Art 28(3).

[47] Brussels I Regulation on jurisdiction and the recognition and enforcement of judgments in civil and commercial matters (Reg (EC) No 44/2001; [2001] OJ L12/1.

[48] C-116/02 *Erich Gasser v MISAT Srl* [2003] ECR-14693, [54]. This position is now reversed, following the introduction of Brussels Ia Regulation, Art 31(2).

[49] See, eg, DW Robertson, '*Forum Non Conveniens* in America and England: "A Rather Fantastic Fiction"' (1987) 103 *LQR* 398; AG Slater, 'Forum Non Conveniens: A View from the Shop Floor' (1988) 104 *LQR* 554; J Hill, 'Jurisdiction in Civil and Commercial Matters: Is There a Third Way?' [2001] *Current Legal Problems* 439 449–50; and A Arzandeh, 'Should the *Spiliada* Test Be Revised?' (2014) 10 *Journal of Private International Law* 89, 96–97 (focusing mainly on the shortcomings with the doctrine's second limb).

[50] See, on the one hand, *Cherney v Deripaska* [2009] EWCA Civ 849; [2009] 2 CLC 408 and *Altimo Holdings and Investment Ltd v Kyrgyz Mobil Tel Ltd* (also known as, *AK Investment CJSC v Kyrgyz Mobil Tel Ltd*) [2011] UKPC 7; [2012] 1 WLR 1804, both service-out cases, where it was held that England was the appropriate forum, and, on the other hand, *OJSC Oil Company Yugraneft (in liquidation) v Abramovich* [2008] EWHC 2613 (Comm) and *Pacific International Sports Clubs Ltd v Soccer Marketing International Ltd* [2010] EWCA Civ 753 where the foreign forum was deemed to be more appropriate.

[51] For judicial criticisms of the volume of material presented before the courts, which concern the application of the *forum non conveniens* doctrine, see Lord Collins of Mapesbury's in *Altimo Holdings* (ibid) 1808, Lord Neuberger of Abbotsbury PSC in *VTB Capital plc v Nutritek International Corp* [2013] UKSC 5; [2013] 2 WLR 398, [82]–[83], and Lord Briggs in *Lungowe v Vedanta Resources plc* [2019] UKSC 20; [2019] 2 WLR 1051, [6]–[14].

jurisdiction in favour of a more suitable forum elsewhere. As noted by Dr Bell,[52] the *forum non conveniens* doctrine creates

> a neutral and objective solution to clashes between parties relating to the venue for the resolution of a transnational dispute – something of a tie-breaker in cases of contested jurisdiction and at the same time a corrective to the phenomenon of forum shopping.[53]

As touched on earlier, the set of considerations which courts can examine when applying *forum non conveniens* is not exhaustive. Whether the existence of a particular factor would lead to a finding that stay of proceedings should be granted depends on the facts of the given case. A main consequence of this flexibility is that common law courts can decide to stay their proceedings if they are satisfied that it is in the interests of the parties and the ends of justice. Moreover, the different versions of *forum non conveniens* in operation across the common law world make important strides towards minimising instances of forum shopping by ensuring that disputes are litigated in fora with real connection to them.

IV. Responding to Conflicts of Jurisdiction: A 'Global' Solution?

The discussion thus far has highlighted that the responses to conflicts of jurisdiction at civil law and common law are varied. They are the product of different historical origins and legal cultures. Today, their survival is due to diverging policy preferences and values. Upholding legal certainty is the main preoccupation of the civil law rules of jurisdiction. The judges' power to exercise discretion in addressing conflicts of jurisdiction is highly limited. By contrast, the common law courts' principal concern, in this context, is to promote connectedness. Their approach, as set out under *forum non conveniens*, is much more flexible than the one under the *lis pendens* doctrine. Whereas civil law rules leave judges with much less room for manoeuvre in cases involving the same cause of action and parties, common law rules afford judges considerable discretion in how to address conflicts of jurisdiction.

In these circumstances, trying to develop a uniform approach in this area of law, by drawing on the approaches at both civil law and common law, may appear especially challenging. Nevertheless, it is possible to find at least one serious attempt, in recent times, to realise this aim. This attempt was made, towards the end of the twentieth century, when the Members of the Hague Conference on Private International Law embarked on negotiating a worldwide Convention on jurisdiction and judgments in civil and commercial matters. At the turn of the twenty-first century, a Preliminary Draft Convention emerged from the negotiations, which contained wide-ranging and detailed provisions on different aspects of civil jurisdiction and judgments. After failing in subsequent meetings to reach consensus on all the components of the Preliminary Draft Convention, the Members of the Hague Conference on Private International Law chose to proceed to finalise conventions concerning the aspects in relation to which the negotiators could find agreement. To this end, in 2005, the Hague Choice of Court Convention was concluded. More recently, in July 2019, the delegates of the twenty-second Diplomatic Session of the Hague Conference on Private International Law adopted the Judgments Convention.[54]

[52] Now, the Honourable Justice Andrew Bell, the President of the New South Wales Court of Appeal.

[53] Bell (n 1) para 3.89.

[54] The 2019 Convention on the Recognition and Enforcement of Foreign Judgments in Civil or Commercial Matters, available at: assets.hcch.net/docs/806e290e-bbd8-413d-b15e-8e3e1bf1496d.pdf. See David Goddard and Paul Beaumont, 'Recognition and Enforcement of Judgments in Civil or Commercial Matters', ch 29 in this book.

One of the aspects of the Preliminary Draft Convention, regarding which no further progress has been achieved, concerned conflicts of jurisdiction. Be that as it may, a sensible starting point in examining the scope for developing a uniform, global response to conflicts of jurisdiction should pick up the discussion where it was left by those provisions. The record of the negotiations preceding the conclusion of the Preliminary Draft Convention highlights much debate and disagreement, among the representatives of the different civil law and common law countries, on the contents of the global approach in this particular area of private international law. In the end, the negotiators settled on what became Preliminary Draft Convention, Articles 21 and 22. Limitations in space prohibit a detailed discussion of all the different components of those Articles. Instead, the chief aim is to set out a broad overview of the key features of these provisions, and to examine whether they provide a viable starting point for designing a uniform approach to conflicts of jurisdiction.[55]

In many respects, the *lis pendens* rule under Article 21 represents some notable improvements on the equivalent doctrine at civil law. At least two examples can be cited in support of this observation. First, the provision takes away priority from the court first seised in negative-declaration claims.[56] As stated earlier, these are claims where one party, in a forum of its choosing, pre-emptively commences a claim against the other to obtain a no-fault declaration. The *lis pendens* rule within the Brussels regime is open to being abused by litigants who initiate negative-declaration claims as a delaying tactic to frustrate their opponents. By forcing any court other than the one first seised to decline jurisdiction, where the dispute is between the same parties and involves the same cause of action, defendants in negative-declaration claims can find themselves with little choice but to agree to settle on unattractive terms.[57] Consequently, by stating that the court first seised will not be deemed as such if the action before it concerns a negative declaration, Article 21 addresses one of the major shortcomings of the *lis pendens* rule at civil law.[58]

The second example which supports the claim that the *lis pendens* rule under the Preliminary Draft Convention represents an enhancement on the version in operation across the civil law world is that it allows the court *first* seised to stay its proceedings if persuaded that the court second seised is clearly more appropriate to resolve the dispute, as defined under Article 22.[59] It signifies a far more relaxed attitude to the application of the *lis pendens* rule than the one presently available at civil law. This flexibility, in turn, allows greater scope for the claim to be heard by a court in the forum that is essentially its home. As a result, in addition to being concerned with ensuring certainty in cases involving multiple proceedings between the same parties and concerning the same cause of action, the *lis pendens* rule under the Preliminary Draft Convention also gives some prominence to connectedness.

[55] See similarly P Nygh and F Pocar, *Report on the Preliminary Draft Convention on Jurisdiction and Foreign Judgments in Civil and Commercial Matters* (HCCH 2000) 89–98, available at: assets.hcch.net/docs/638883f3-0c0a-46c6-b646-7a099d9bd95e.pdf; M Stuckelberg, '*Lis Pendens* and *Forum Non Conveniens* at the Hague Conference' (2001) 26 *Brooklyn Journal of International Law* 949; WE O'Brian Jr, 'The Hague Convention on Jurisdiction and Judgments: The Way Forward' (2003) 66 *Modern Law Review* 491, 501–02; and P Beaumont, '*Forum non conveniens* and the EU rules on Conflicts of Jurisdiction: A possible global solution' (2018) *Revue Critique de Droit International Privé* 447.

[56] Preliminary Draft Convention, Art. 21(6).

[57] As stated earlier, the scope for the execution of this tactic has been removed for choice of court agreements having derogatory effects in the context of the Brussels Ia Regulation, following the introduction of Art 31(2).

[58] See, also, O'Brian Jr (n 55) 501.

[59] Preliminary Draft Convention, Art 21(7).

Article 22 outlines the 'exceptional circumstances' in which a Contracting State may decline its jurisdiction.[60] The rapporteurs of the Preliminary Draft Convention were at pains to emphasise that Article 22 and *forum non conveniens* were distinct concepts.[61] However, the two do have some important similarities. Under both common law *forum non conveniens* and Article 22, stays are granted at the application of the defendant. Moreover, to secure a stay by virtue of Article 22 and *forum non conveniens*, the defendant has to establish that the alternative foreign forum will assert jurisdiction over the matter.[62] At the same time, there are noteworthy differences between the approaches to discretionary staying of proceedings under Article 22 and at common law. For example, although there is some overlap in the types of factors which are examined in determining the stay applications, the range that is to be considered for the purpose of Article 22 seems to be narrower.[63] In particular, there is no explicit requirement under Article 22 for the court that has been asked to relinquish its jurisdiction to enquire whether the forum elsewhere would be able to entertain the relevant claim justly. More importantly, to grant a stay under Article 22 the court has to be persuaded that it is 'clearly inappropriate' to exercise jurisdiction, and that the court in another State which has jurisdiction is 'clearly more appropriate' to resolve the dispute. In their report on the Preliminary Draft Convention, Professors Nygh and Pocar stated that 'the fact that another forum may be "clearly more appropriate" does not necessarily mean that the forum seised is itself "clearly inappropriate"'.[64] In these circumstances, it has been observed that stays under Article 22 are 'strictly limited to exceptional cases'.[65]

But, on a closer inspection, these requirements seem to place two hurdles where one would suffice. In practice, the finding that a forum is clearly (in)appropriate to hear a claim hinges on whether the alternative foreign forum is a more appropriate venue for entertaining it. Put differently, it is virtually impossible to test the inappropriateness of the local forum without taking account of the appropriateness of the forum elsewhere.[66] Therefore, insisting that defendants must show that the forum before which the case is brought is clearly inappropriate, *and* that the foreign forum is also more appropriate, is liable to create unnecessary complications in deciding the stay question. In these circumstances, parties are likely to seek to adduce substantial body of evidence to support their respective claims. This can be a considerably costly exercise for the parties. Moreover, a disproportionate amount of trial time is likely to be occupied by the examination of the evidence. Separately, more clarity is likely to be needed as to how exceptional the circumstances must be to warrant issuing a stay under Article 22. The need for clarity in this context is especially acute, not least because of the absence of a court that would act as the ultimate body for deciding the scope of Article 22.

In sum, the proposed approach to conflicts of jurisdiction, as outlined in the Preliminary Draft Convention, captures many positive attributes of the *lis pendens* and *forum non conveniens* doctrines. While there are certain areas where the relevant provisions concerned with addressing conflicts of jurisdiction in this instrument could be further improved, overall,

[60] The power to grant a stay under this provision is unavailable where the jurisdiction of the court in the Contracting State is rooted in Preliminary Draft Convention, Art 4, Art 7, Art 8, or Art 12.

[61] Nygh and Pocar (n 55) 93.

[62] Preliminary Draft Convention, Art 22(1). At common law, see, eg, *Connelly v RTZ Corporation* [1998] AC 854 (HL).

[63] Preliminary Draft Convention, Art 22(2).

[64] Nygh and Pocar (n 55) 94.

[65] eg, Stuckelberg (n 55) 972. See, similarly, O'Brian Jr (n 55) 501.

[66] This point is illustrated in the comparison between the approaches to discretionary (non-)exercise of jurisdiction in England, under the more-appropriate-forum test, and Australia, based on the clearly inappropriate forum test: see, A Arzandeh, 'Reconsidering the Australian *Forum (Non) Conveniens* Doctrine' (2016) 65 *ICLQ* 475, 486–88.

the provisions represent a well-balanced symbiosis of the civil and common law approaches. If a significant number of States could agree to use these measures in addressing conflicts of jurisdiction, it could indeed provide the nucleus of a global solution to this aspect of private international law.

V. Conclusion

This chapter has examined conflicts of jurisdiction within civil law and common law rules of jurisdiction. If left without adequate response, this private international law phenomenon can create numerous problems for litigants and courts. The discussion began by outlining the various responses to conflicts of jurisdiction which are available within civilian and common law traditions. In *lis pendens* and *forum non conveniens*, civil law and common law courts have largely distinct principles for determining which of the two or more courts with competence over the claim should entertain it. This difference has much to do with the diverging policy preferences and values, which themselves are products of different historical origins and legal cultures, within these legal systems. In responding to conflicts of jurisdiction, civil law courts are mainly concerned with upholding legal certainty, while common law courts are chiefly focused on identifying the forum, among the ones with competence, which is more strongly connected to the claim. Consequently, both approaches exhibit strengths and limitations of their own.

The obvious differences in the approaches at civil law and common law might make it seem all but impossible to fashion a response to conflicts of jurisdiction that draws on the relevant practices in these systems of law. However, the provisions articulated in the Preliminary Draft Convention on jurisdiction and judgments in civil and commercial matters show what such a global approach to conflicts of jurisdiction could look like. As the discussion illustrated, while the conflict of jurisdiction provisions within the Preliminary Draft Convention can be further refined, they nonetheless provide a realistic starting point for any serious attempt at finding a worldwide solution to the problem of more than one court having competence to entertain the dispute. Of course, in practical terms, garnering the desire to develop a global response to conflicts of jurisdiction is sure to be a difficult task, not least because, in recent years, nationalism has been on the rise, and globalism in retreat. However, the successful conclusion of the Judgments Convention in 2019 could trigger a move towards a serious examination of whether problems arising from conflicts of jurisdiction, too, could be tackled with a global approach. Indeed, it seems the HCCH is making progress in the field of conflicts of jurisdiction with its Council in March 2021 elevating the work of the Experts' Group on Jurisdiction to a Working Group mandated to

> proceed in an inclusive and holistic manner, with an initial focus on developing binding rules for concurrent proceedings (parallel proceedings and related actions or claims), and acknowledging the primary role of both jurisdictional rules and the doctrine of *forum non conveniens*.[67]

It is to be hoped that this development will eventually lead to the articulation of a harmonious approach at the global level to the problems arising from conflicts of jurisdiction which incorporates the key benefits of both the common law and the civil law rules.

[67] See para 9(b) of the Conclusions and Decisions of the Council, available at: assets.hcch.net/docs/94e2d886-1cbf-4250-b436-5c1899cb942b.pdf.

31

Collective Redress

KOJI TAKAHASHI AND ZHENG SOPHIA TANG*

I. Overview

Collective redress refers to relief sought by a large number of claimants sharing broadly the same cause of action against the same defendant by means of a collective procedure. There is a wide variety of collective procedures:[1] typically a representative action of opt-in or opt-out type resulting in a judgment or settlement. Though collective redress is usually pursued in a domestic setting,[2] its transnational dimensions are assuming growing importance as exemplified by the recent 'Dieselgate' affairs.[3]

Collective procedures have both merits and drawbacks[4] and opinion is divided whether they should be promoted. Certain procedural features embraced or encouraged by some States are unpalatable to others. For example, the opt-out style representative actions are deemed contrary to public policy in many States in Europe and elsewhere.[5] Due to the profound controversy surrounding the procedures, it seems premature to attempt a fully-fledged unification of private international law in this field. Several aspects of it will be outlined in the next section.

II. Aspects of Private International Law

A. Applicable Law and Direct Jurisdiction

Collective procedures presuppose that the bundling of claims of similarly situated persons is possible. It would be helpful if such claims could be brought in the same forum and adjudicated under the same legal system. It is debated whether and to what extent jurisdictional rules

* Sections II and IV were primarily authored by Koji Takahashi and Section III by Zheng Sophia Tang, with sections I and V jointly authored.

[1] Zheng Sophia Tang, 'Consumer Collective Redress in European Private International Law' (2011) 7 *Journal of Private International Law* 101, 103.

[2] KM Clermont, 'Solving the Puzzle of Transnational Class Actions' (2015) 90 *Indiana Law Journal Supplement* 69, 71.

[3] M Celis, 'The Volkswagen (VW) emissions scandal – The saga continues: Now it's the turn of the Netherlands, France and Belgium', available at: conflictoflaws.net/2020/the-volkswagen-vw-emissions-scandal-the-saga-continues-now-its-the-turn-of-the-netherlands-france-and-belgium.

[4] European Commission, 'Towards a European horizontal Framework for Collective Redress' COM(2013) 401/2; Zheng Sophia Tang, *Electronic Consumer Contracts in the Conflict of Laws*, 2nd edn (Hart Publishing 2015) 267–69.

[5] Even in the United States, some states prohibit class actions in their statutes: See TA Dickson, *Class Actions: The Law of 50 States* (Law Journal Press 2003) Appendix C, A-49.

will permit the consolidation of such claims and whether applicable law rules will result in the same law governing such claims.[6] It is, however, doubtful whether the unification of such rules at an international level is useful.

Where the collective procedure of the given forum requires the commonality of claims in the sense that they are subject to the same governing law, it is arguable that the applicable law rules should be tailor-made for the procedure to ensure that the same law is applicable to the claims to be bundled. Where, on the other hand, the collective procedure of the given forum permits the bundling of claims even if they are not subject to the same governing law, there will be less need for such tailor-made applicable law rules. Applicable law rules are, therefore, a matter for which the autonomy of each State should be respected.

The same may be said of the rules of direct jurisdiction. Take, eg, the rules for protecting weaker parties such as consumers and employees. Whether these rules should be available when a representative entity seeks collective redress on behalf of such persons is a question which each State should decide autonomously by considering whether the litigation power of the parties still needs to be rebalanced in a collective procedure.[7]

B. Coordination of Parallel Proceedings

Collective redress is particularly prone to give rise to forum shopping and abusive litigation.[8] Coordination may be attempted by each court individually exercising its power to stay proceedings or decline jurisdiction. A more centralised coordination may be possible where parallel proceedings occur in a domestic setting (eg, transfer by the federal judicial panel of multi-district litigation in the United States[9]). Such a top-down approach seems, however, unfeasible at an international level as there is a wide variety of collective procedures.

C. Cross-Border Recognition of the Standing of Representative Entities

In the European Union, there have been efforts to facilitate the cross-border recognition of the standing of representative entities by setting out the minimum qualification which such entities must possess to represent potential claimants in a foreign forum.[10] It may be useful to extend this approach from the regional level to the international level, though considerable difficulties will be encountered as there is a greater diversity in the underlying collective procedures.

D. Cross-Border Recognition and Enforcement of Judgments and Settlements

Clarity in the rules for cross-border recognition of judgments and settlements is critically important for the smooth functioning of collective procedures in an international setting.

[6] See Tang (n 1) 115–20, 138–40; DL Bassett, 'US Class Actions Go Global: Transnational Class Actions and Personal Jurisdiction' (2003) 72 *Fordham Law Review* 41.

[7] Tang, ibid, 106–15.

[8] Tang, ibid, 124–29.

[9] 28 USC § 1407.

[10] Art 6 of Directive 2020/1828 on representative actions for the protection of the collective interests of consumers.

In an opt-out procedure, a class certification may rely on the assessment of how likely the eventual judgment is to be recognised in the State where the absent plaintiffs reside. In the context of a settlement negotiation, the allegedly responsible party would be reluctant to agree to the terms covering potential claimants residing in a foreign State unless there is a good likelihood that the settlement will be recognised in that State.

The Hague Conference has created two Conventions for the cross-border recognition and enforcement of judgments and settlements: the 2019 Hague Judgments Convention and the 2005 Hague Choice of Court Convention. Collective redress is not excluded from the scope of either of them.[11] They are, however, awkward to apply to collective procedures as they do not appear to be drafted with such procedures in mind. Consequently, it is necessary to either come up with creative interpretations or take some legislative steps (by amending the existing text or creating a new instrument) to deal specifically with collective redress. Generally, the rules for cross-border recognition and enforcement could be harmonised even if there is no consensus on direct jurisdiction or applicable law and even if there is a wide divergence in the underlying procedures. The remainder of this chapter will, therefore, focus on this aspect of private international law, examining first the recognition and enforcement of judgments (section III) and then settlements (section IV).

III. Recognition and Enforcement of Foreign Judgments Arising from a Collective Procedure

A. Classification

Classification concerns whether collective actions are covered in the scope of the existing international instruments. Both the Judgments Convention and the Choice of Court Convention apply to 'civil and commercial matters'. Some collective actions are brought by a public authority, such as a consumer ombudsman or competition authority. These actions, nevertheless, shall not be classified as exercising public law power. The nature of the representative action shall not be determined by the identity of the representative entity, but by the subject matter of the proceedings, ie, whether it concerns exercise of public power, or private law matters between private parties.[12] It is also relevant to consider the relationship between the parties, ie, whether the representative is exercising public power of regulation, or simply seeking to enforce the private rights assigned to it by a private party in relation to a private relationship. A collective action that seeks to enforce the private rights between private parties, irrespective of the representative's identity, should be classified as 'civil and commercial matters'.

The second issue concerns whether a collective action brought on behalf of consumers or employees to enforce their rights under contracts should be classified as proceedings on consumer or employment contracts, which are treated differently to protect the interests of the weaker party. The

[11] F Garcimartín and G Saumier, *Explanatory Report on the 2019 HCCH Judgments Convention* (HCCH 2020) para 95, states '"A decision on the merits" … includes … judgments in collective actions' (Garcimartín/Saumier Report). T Hartley and M Dogauchi, *Explanatory Report on the Convention of 30 June 2005 on Choice of Court Agreements* (Permanent Bureau of the Hague Conference on Private International Law 2005) is silent on this matter (Hartley/Dogauchi Report).

[12] C-167/00 *Verein für Konsumenteninformation v Henkel* [2002] ECR I-08111, paras 25–30. See also, Garcimartín/Saumier Report, ibid, paras 35 and 82.

Choice of Court Convention excludes consumer contracts and employment contracts from its scope.[13] Although consumer and employment contracts are covered in the Judgments Convention, they receive different treatment in indirect jurisdiction.[14] This issue has been discussed by the Court of Justice of the European Union (CJEU) in relation to the Brussels Ia Regulation, which provides protective jurisdiction for consumer contracts. The CJEU made it clear that the protective jurisdiction rules do not apply to collective redress, either for collective injunctive relief led by consumer associations, or a representative action for damages.[15] Consumer contracts are treated differently from ordinary contracts due to the necessity to correct the inequality of the bargaining power and litigation power between the parties.[16] While consumers assign the right to sue to an association, this association does not have the same unequal litigation power in contrast to the business and there is no need to continue to apply the protective rules for jurisdiction.[17] Furthermore, when a consumer acts as a representative on behalf of other consumers in a collective action, his litigation status is on an equal footing with the defendant. The CJEU has stated under the Brussels Ia Regulation that protective jurisdiction only applies to the direct parties to a consumer contract, and a representative is not a 'direct' party to all the claims.[18] It is suggested that classification of collective actions does not depend on the identity of individual claimants that have assigned their claim to the representative. As a result, collective redress on behalf of consumers or employees to assert their claims on consumer or employment contracts should not be treated as consumer contract or employment contract actions in the Judgments Convention and the Choice of Court Convention.

B. Indirect Jurisdiction

The Hague Judgments Convention provides indirect jurisdiction as a basis to recognise and enforce foreign judgments.[19] Under the Hague Choice of Court Convention, a valid exclusive choice of court agreement serves as a basis of indirect jurisdiction.[20] Some of the jurisdictional bases in the Judgments Convention would facilitate the bundling of all claims under collective procedures, as in the cases where the defendant against whom recognition and enforcement is sought was habitually resident, had its principal place of business, or maintained an establishment the activities of which have given rise to the claim, in the State of origin.[21]

Indirect jurisdiction that may facilitate international collective actions also includes jurisdiction by consent or submission.[22] There may be a contract binding on both the defendant and each of the represented claimants in which there is a choice of court agreement in favour of the court of origin. It is also possible for the representative and defendant to enter into a choice of court agreement to bring the collective action. Since indirect jurisdiction has the purpose to protect the person against whom recognition and enforcement is sought, it is questionable whether

[13] Art 2(1) of the Choice of Court Convention.

[14] Art 5(2) of the Judgments Convention.

[15] C-89/91 *Shearson Lehmann Hutton Inc* [1993] ECR I-00139; *Henkel* (n 12). JURI Committee, 'Collective redress in the Member States of the European Union', available at: www.europarl.europa.eu/RegData/etudes/STUD/2018/608829/IPOL_STU(2018)608829_EN.pdf, para 3.1.2.3.

[16] *Shearson Lehmann*, ibid, para 18.

[17] Ibid; *Henkel* (n 12) para 33.

[18] C-498/16 *Schrems v Facebook* EU:C:2018:37, para 49.

[19] Art 5.

[20] Art 8.

[21] Art 5(1)(a), (b) and (c).

[22] Art 5(1)(e), (f) and (m) of the Judgments Convention, and Art 8 of the Choice of Court Convention.

an agreement between the representative and the defendant on an *ex post* basis is binding on the represented claimants. The represented claimants could assign their rights and obligations, including the right to choose the competent forum, to the representative. In an opt-in procedure, this does not need to be explicit and the action to participate in a collective action would be considered a constructive consent for the representative to choose the appropriate forum for the action. In an opt-out procedure, however, the absent claimants do not need to adopt any active actions to be bound by the collective procedure. Whether or not a constructive consent to the jurisdiction exists depends on whether they receive sufficient notice of the procedure and the information on jurisdiction, and they have opportunities to opt out. The key factor is whether the consent is given and whether any approach to find constructive consent meets the due process or procedural fairness requirements. This question is closely connected to due process for the represented claimants, discussed below.

The indirect jurisdiction based on the defendant's habitual residence or the defendant's consent or submission facilitates international collective actions that could bind all claims in one set of proceedings. However, they should not be the only basis for collective redress. If the defendant's home State does not adopt collective procedure or does not permit collective procedure to consolidate claims of overseas claimants, and the defendant with this knowledge refuses to enter into an agreement to choose another court, a single-forum collective action is impossible. The Judgments Convention thus provides other bases, under which a partial bundling of claims would likely be possible, eg, jurisdiction of the courts for the place of performance of contracts,[23] or the place where tortious activities causing damages occurred.[24] The jurisdiction is based on contested activities in individual claims. In a transnational collective action, which includes potential claimants from multiple countries, the place of performance of individual contracts or the place of wrongful acts that lead to damages may occur in different countries. A strict interpretation means the court of the place only has jurisdiction to hear collective actions concerning activities that occurred in its territory. This approach may result in parallel collective proceedings. A flexible approach is to permit any of these places jurisdiction over claims internationally raised, which, however, would mean uncertainty for the defendant and may lead to a court with insufficient proximity to hear international collective proceedings. Both are inappropriate.

So a centralisation approach may be applied to give these jurisdiction grounds a more purposive interpretation to satisfy the needs of collective procedures. The State that is the centre of gravity of the contractual performance or tortious activities should be eligible for international collective procedure. This base, in most cases, would coincide with the home State of the majority of the potential claimants. It enables consolidation of claims and may not unreasonably harm certainty and predictability, as the defendant usually should be able to predict the consequence of its activities and could determine which States to target.

C. Grounds for Refusal

Under the Hague Conventions, recognition and enforcement may be refused on the grounds of due process, fraud, public policy and conflicting judgments.[25] Collective procedures generate

[23] Art 5(1)(g).
[24] Art 5(1)(k).
[25] Art 7 of the Judgments Convention; Art 9 of the Choice of Court Convention.

specific problems for application of some refusal grounds. Since collective procedures are not considered when drafting the two Hague Conventions, the refusal grounds that are provided to protect the person against whom recognition and enforcement is sought, are not compatible with collective procedures.

i. Lack of Sufficient Notice

Due process for claimants is the special problem for collective redress, where the represented claimants are not named parties to the collective procedure, and usually have no opportunities to present their cases or comment. Due process protects the parties' procedural rights, which mainly include sufficient notice and the opportunity to be heard. Both Conventions provide that recognition and enforcement may be refused if the procedure

> was not notified to the defendant in sufficient time and in such a way as to enable them to arrange for their defence, unless the defendant entered an appearance and presented their case without contesting notification in the court of origin, provided that the law of the State of origin permitted notification to be contested.[26]

However, the literal reading suggests that the right to sufficient notice only applies to the 'defendant'. It is suggested 'defendant' here may need to be interpreted to include anyone against whom recognition and enforcement is sought, which may include absent claimants.

When is an absent claimant sufficiently notified in a collective action? In an opt-out action, absent claimants are not required to give active consent. Whether sufficient notice is given is particularly important. 'Sufficiency' depends on the method and content of notice.[27] Notice may be given by mail, email, or through mass media, such as newspapers and websites. Although some countries may deem notice through mass media sufficient,[28] consideration should be given to the region of distribution, language and access data of these mass media in particular countries. Second, the content of notice is important. Notice in opt-out procedures should cover the nature of the action in detail, inclusion of the recipient as someone meeting certain criteria in the class, the effect of the action on the recipient's legal rights, and instructions as to how to opt out. The method of opt out should also be convenient and feasible. Failing to achieve any of the above would render notice 'insufficient'. The lack of notice can also be raised in the opt-in procedure, where an opt-in claimant may argue the content of the notice is unclear, lacks detail, or fails to fully inform of the legal consequences, especially the preclusive effect, of the collective judgment.

ii. Infringement of Public Policy

Public policy is an ambiguous concept and the Judgments Convention permits public policy to be determined differently in individual States.[29] Although no uniform definition is provided, the concept should be interpreted strictly and can only be applied if the judgment is 'manifestly

[26] Art 7(1)(a)(i) of the Judgments Convention; Art 9(c)(i) of the Choice of Court Convention.

[27] TJ Monestier, 'Transnational Class Actions and the Illusory Search for Res Judicata' (2011) 86 *Tulane Law Review* 1, 39–40.

[28] Tang (n 4) 297; XE Kramer, 'Securities Collective Action and Private International Law Issues in Dutch WCAM Settlements' (2014) 27 *Pacific McGeorge Global Business and Development Law Journal* 235, s IV.B.3.

[29] Garcimartín/Saumier Report (n 11) para 264.

incompatible with the public policy of the requested State'.[30] Therefore, a State cannot refuse to enforce a collective judgment simply based on the fact that there is no similar procedure available in its domestic law. However, the State may rely on the underlying reasons why it rejects adoption of all or certain types of collective action to refuse to enforce foreign collective judgments, if these reasons concern fundamental principles of law or fundamental social, cultural and economic interests.

Both Conventions specifically mention 'specific proceedings leading to the judgment were incompatible with fundamental principles of procedural fairness' of the requested State as an instance of the case of public policy infringement.[31] A potential argument is that a defendant should have the right to 'present every available defence'.[32] In collective actions, potential claimants generally have common issues to bring the same claim, but there are usually small differences in individual situations. In other words, it is hard to find two completely identical claims. Collective actions aggregate these claims in one set of proceedings based on the commonalities. However, it is argued that a defendant has the right to 'individualised adjudication of liability when plaintiffs differ in any meaningful way'.[33] The collective judgment simply imposes 'mass' liability on the defendant without permitting the defendant to contest each individual claim fully. This argument suggests only claims raising completely identical factual and legal issues may be aggregated.[34] It may specifically challenge the enforcement of collective judgments against the defendant in an opt-out procedure where the class members are certified in a fictional or statistical way, without any assessment of the same factual and legal bases.[35] This ground may not be enough to refuse enforcing all collective judgments but indirectly imposes requirements on the mechanism used to certify the class members.

Another potential argument is the European conception that individuals are the only right holders, and the compensation should be based on the individual assessment of each claimant's injury or damage.[36] This argument prevents enforcement of collective judgments in cases where the factual and legal bases for liability to individual claimants are highly similar, while damages may differ for individual claimants,[37] and the need to be assessed according to individual circumstances, including the severity of injury, age, earning capacity and the living standards of the habitual residence.[38] Fictional damages, or punitive damages, that are not based on individual assessment may not be enforced.

Another potential procedural unfairness relates to the distribution of damages. Collective action notices sometimes do not include details on how damages may be calculated and distributed[39] whereby opted in or decided not to opt out, class members did not know the potential damages that they could receive. After a favourable judgment, they realised that actual damages were inadequate. While absent members have no way to comment or refuse the amount allocated to them, it violates procedural fairness to deprive them of their right to remedies.

[30] Art 7(1)(c) of the Judgments Convention; Art 9(e) of the Choice of Court Convention.

[31] Art 7(1)(c) of the Judgments Convention; Art 9(e) of the Choice of Court Convention.

[32] JA Rosenthal, 'The Case Against Constitutionalized Commonality Standards for Collective Civil Litigation' (2013) 32 *Yale Law & Policy Review* 309, 311.

[33] Ibid, 310.

[34] Ibid, 312.

[35] Marcy Hogan Greer, *A Practitioner's Guide to Class Actions* (American Bar Association 2011).

[36] JURI Committee (n 15) 104.

[37] LJ Ball, 'Damages in Class Actions: Determinations and Allocation' (1969) 10 *British Columbia Law Review* 615, 617–18.

[38] Ibid, 617.

[39] This practice was permitted by some courts. See *Gottlieb v Wiles* 11 F3d 1004, 1013 (10th Cir, 1993).

However, pursuant to Article 4(2) of the Judgments Convention the requested court should not be expected to assess whether the damages are adequate as this inevitably requires the review of the merits.[40] The procedural matters, including notice and procedure to calculate and distribute damages, should be considered. Inadequate damages can only be relied on to refuse to recognise foreign collective judgments if it resulted from procedural unfairness. If the notice does not include the details on how damages are calculated/distributed, and the damages are equally distributed to putative claimants without considering claimants' personal situation, procedural unfairness is likely breached. On the other hand, if putative claimants consented to the formula to calculate damages, or actively claimed their share after judgments were made, no procedural unfairness is present.

iii. Violation of Dispute Resolution Agreements

A judgment may not be recognised if it violates a dispute resolution agreement between the parties.[41] In collective actions, some putative claimants may have entered into *ex ante* agreements to submit disputes to arbitration or to a particular court. If collective procedures are brought in a different jurisdiction and these claimants fail to opt out, given the effect of dispute resolution agreements, these claimants should not be included as absent claimants and not be bound by the collective judgments. In opt-in procedures, these claimants may not be entitled to opt in without the consent of the defendant. Exceptions may be found in special contracts involving inequality of bargaining power, such as consumer contracts and employment contracts, in which the dispute resolution agreements may not be valid. Consumers or employees thus may be bound by the negative effect of foreign collective procedures. The protection granted to consumers and employees in validating jurisdiction agreements under their contracts is to their disadvantage in this respect, but such a consequence is appropriate to balance the interests of relevant parties. Anyway, consumers and employees could still rely on other grounds, such as due process, to refuse recognition of collective judgments.

iv. Inconsistency with Other Judgments

A collective redress judgment may not be recognised if it is irreconcilable with a judgment given between the same parties in the requested court,[42] or it is irreconcilable with an earlier judgment rendered by another country involving the same cause of action between the same parties that could be recognised in the requested court.[43] In collective procedures, it depends on the interpretation of the 'same parties'. A 'litigating party' approach only deems the representative entity as the party and suggests a court may recognise a collective judgment even if there is an inconsistent judgment concerning one represented consumer and the same defendant on the same subject matter. It clearly does not meet the legislative purpose and harms transnational collective procedures. It is suggested that the 'legal effect' approach should be adopted. This refusal ground should apply to judgments on the same cause of action between anyone who is bearing the legal effect of an action, or is bound by the judgment.

[40] Art 4(2) of the Judgments Convention provides: 'There shall be no review of the merits of the judgment in the requested State'.

[41] Art 7(1)(d) of the Judgments Convention.

[42] Art 7(1)(e) of the Judgments Convention; Art 9(f) of the Choice of Court Convention.

[43] Art 7(1)(f) of the Judgments Convention; Art 9(g) of the Choice of Court Convention.

IV. Cross-Border Recognition and Enforcement of Court-Approved Collective Settlements

Collective actions typically end in a settlement, usually with the approval of a court.[44] Since such actions are difficult to manage due to the involvement of diverse interests, there is something to be said for encouraging settlements. Yet, currently there is a lot of uncertainty whether court-approved collective settlements will be recognised and enforced across borders.

Under the Judgments Convention and the Choice of Court Convention, judicial settlements enforceable in the State of origin are eligible for cross-border enforcement in the same manner as judgments (Article 11 of the Judgments Convention and Article 12 of the Choice of Court Convention). Applying the Hague Conventions to court-approved collective settlements, however, encounters three difficulties. First, while collective settlements are often concluded out of court,[45] there is uncertainty whether the notion of 'judicial settlement' under the Choice of Court Convention covers an out of court settlement approved by a court. Second, both Conventions lack provision for the cross-border recognition, as distinguished from enforcement, of judicial settlements. And third, the provisions setting out the bases for indirect jurisdiction and the grounds for the refusal of recognition and enforcement are ill-equipped to deal with the features of court-approved collective settlements. We will examine these points in turn below.

A. Whether an Out of Court Settlement Approved by a Court Constitutes a 'Judicial Settlement'

Under the Choice of Court Convention, the Explanatory Report considers that an out of court settlement which is subsequently approved by a court does not constitute a 'judicial settlement'.[46] The opposite position is taken by the Judgments Convention,[47] which is applicable to '[j]udicial settlements (transactions judiciaires) which a court of a Contracting State has approved, or which have been concluded in the course of proceedings before a court of a Contracting State' (Article 11). In this sentence, the words 'in the course of proceedings' are placed in the suitable part to indicate that those words do not function as a qualifier with respect to the court's approval of a settlement but only with respect to the conclusion of a settlement. Accordingly, the notion of 'judicial settlement' covers a court-approved settlement irrespective of whether the approval is given in the course of proceedings.

In the EU context, an out of court settlement was not a 'court settlement' (Article 58) under the Brussels I Regulation.[48] This reading was derived from the English text which stated that a

[44] See, eg, Rule 23(e) of the United States Federal Rules of Civil Procedure. For the rules of Scandinavian countries, see A Stadler, 'Conflicts of Laws in Multinational Collective Actions – A Judicial Nightmare?' in D Fairgrieve and E Lein (eds), *Extraterritoriality and Collective Redress* (Oxford University Press 2012) para 11.38. *The Dutch Act on the Collective Settlement of Mass Damage Claims* (Wet Collectieve Afwikkelingen Massaschade – WCAM) provides for a binding declaration by the Amsterdam Court of Appeal in Art 907 of Book 7 of the Civil Code and Art 1013 of the Code of Civil Procedure.

[45] As is the case under the Dutch WCAM procedure: See H van Lith, 'The Dutch Collective Settlements Act and Private International Law' (2010), available at: citeseerx.ist.psu.edu/viewdoc/download?doi=10.1.1.369.7966&rep=rep1&type=pdf, para 5.2.2. It is also not uncommon in the United States for a settlement to occur before class certification.

[46] See Hartley/Dogauchi Report (n 11) para 207, stating that 'judicial settlements' are restricted to settlements putting an end to proceedings.

[47] See also Garcimartín/Saumier Report (n 11) para 297.

[48] Regulation (EC) No 44/2001 on jurisdiction and the recognition and enforcement of judgments in civil and commercial matters.

'court settlement' had to be approved by a court in the course of proceedings and the French and German text which stated that a 'court settlement' had to be concluded before a court in the course of proceedings. The Brussels Ia Regulation[49] now provides for the definition of 'court settlement' (Article 2(b))[50] in terms capable of embracing an out of court settlement approved by a court, with the German text[51] most clearly indicating that the qualifier 'in the course of proceedings' does not apply to the approval by a court.

It is suggested that the notion of 'judicial settlement' under the Hague Choice of Court Convention should also be interpreted as covering out of court settlements approved by a court. That interpretation is not inconsistent with the current text.[52] Furthermore, such settlements are intentionally excluded from the scope of the Singapore Convention[53] to avoid overlaps with the Hague Conventions.

B. Possibility of Cross-Border Recognition

The Hague Conventions provide for the cross-border enforcement, but not recognition, of judicial settlements (Article 11 of the Judgments Convention and Article 12 of the Choice of Court Convention).

i. Classification as a 'Judgment' Rather than a 'Judicial Settlement'?

Under the Hague Conventions, it is considered that a consent order known in common law countries, ie, an order made by the court with the consent of both parties, constitutes a 'judgment'.[54] Then, does a court-approved settlement constitute a 'judgment'?

Interestingly, a similar issue is discussed in the EU context. Like the Hague Conventions, the Brussels Ia Regulation provides for the cross-border enforcement, but not recognition, of a 'court settlement'. It has been argued that a collective settlement which the Dutch court has declared binding under the WCAM procedure should be regarded as a 'judgment' rather than a 'court settlement' due to the considerable degree of control that the court has on the substance of the settlement.[55] This interpretation may not, however, be consistent with the ruling of the European Court of Justice in *Solo Kleinmotoren v Boch*.[56] In that case, the Court held that the word 'judgment' referred solely to judicial decisions actually given by a court (paragraph 15) and observed that a settlement, even if it brought legal proceedings to an end, did not come

[49] Regulation (EU) No 1215/2012 on jurisdiction and the recognition and enforcement of judgments in civil and commercial matters.

[50] It is defined as 'a settlement which has been approved by a court of a Member State or concluded before a court of a Member State in the course of proceedings'.

[51] The corresponding part reads, 'einen Vergleich, der von einem Gericht eines Mitgliedstaats gebilligt oder vor einem Gericht eines Mitgliedstaats im Laufe eines Verfahrens geschlossen worden ist'.

[52] Garcimartín/Saumier Report (n 11) para 296 (fn 216) makes the same observation.

[53] 2019 United Nations Convention on International Settlement Agreements Resulting from Mediation, Art 1(3)(a)(i).

[54] Hartley/Dogauchi Report (n 11) para 207; Garcimartín/Saumier Report (n 11) para 296.

[55] See, eg, van Lith (n 45) paras 5.2.1 and 5.2.3 and A Halfmeier, 'Recognition of a WCAM settlement in Germany' (2012) *Nederlands Internationaal Privaatrecht* 176, 180. The first author rested this interpretation partially on the fact that an out-of-court settlement was not a 'court settlement' under the Brussels I Regulation (as seen above). The same interpretation is, however, still taken under the Brussels Ia Regulation by T Bosters, *Collective Redress and Private International Law in the EU* (Asser Press 2017) para 12.2.

[56] C-414/92 EU:C:1994:221.

within that definition since their terms depended first and foremost on the parties' intention (paragraph 18). If the classification of 'judgment' depends on the extent of judicial control, drawing a clear line between 'judgment' and 'court settlement' would be difficult since there is a spectrum of control exercised by the court approving a settlement.[57] For example, some courts may merely check to see whether the settlement complied with local procedure; some may go a little further to ensure that the settlement represents the parties' true consensus; some may assess whether the settlement represents an appropriate or proportionate outcome in light of the merits of the claims;[58] and some may even propose and discuss the terms of settlement with the parties.[59]

Under the Hague Conventions, a 'judgment' is defined as 'any decision on the merits given by a court' (Article 3(1)(b) of the Judgments Convention and Article 4(1) of the Choice of Court Convention). It implies contentious judicial proceedings in which a court disposes of the claim.[60] It seems to follow that a court-approved settlement is not a 'judgment'.[61] This will be so even if the terms of the settlement are initially proposed by the court, since the settlement is not a 'decision on the merits' but an agreement of the parties.

ii. Recognition of Procedural Effects as Opposed to Contractual Effects

A settlement agreement is a contract. The formation of a settlement agreement as a contract is subject to the governing law of the agreement. Thus, where the parties' consent is vitiated by mistake or undue influence, that legal system will determine whether the settlement is invalid. The contractual effects of a settlement agreement are also determined by the governing law of the agreement. Accordingly, a settlement agreement is binding on third parties to the extent the exceptions to the principle of privity of contract are accepted.

Where a settlement agreement is approved by a court, its procedural effects are determined by the *lex fori* (law of the forum). The procedural effects may be more extensive than the contractual effects. Thus, like a judgment a court-approved settlement agreement may have *res judicata* effect[62] and may be binding on a wider range of interested persons than those who are bound by it under contractual principles.

The omission of reference to 'recognition' in the Hague Conventions means that the procedural effects which a judicial settlement has under the law of the State of origin is not recognised in other States. Accordingly, such effects may not be invoked as a procedural defence to a contradicting claim. The Conventions' silence on 'recognition' does not, however, preclude the recognition of contractual effects. A judicial settlement may be adduced as evidence like any other contract and invoked as a contractual defence to a contradicting claim.[63]

[57] R Fentiman, 'Recognition, Enforcement and Collective Judgments' in A Nuyts and N Hatzimihail (eds), *Cross-Border Class Actions: The European Way* (Sellier 2013) 85, 99.

[58] See, eg, Rule 23(e)(2) of the United States Federal Rules of Civil Procedure, which provides that the court may approve a proposed settlement only on finding that it is fair, reasonable and adequate.

[59] According to Halfmeier (n 55) 179, this is the practice of German court settlements.

[60] Garcimartín/Saumier Report (n 11) para 95.

[61] See also H Muir-Watt, 'Collective redress' in J Basedow et al (eds), *Encyclopedia of Private International Law*, Vol I (Edward Elgar 2017)374, § IV.3.

[62] See, eg, P Mayer, 'L'existence d'une transaction entre les parties ne fait pas obstacle à la reconnaissance du jugement' [1998] *Revue critique de droit international privé* 326 on French law; Halfmeier (n 55) 179 on the Dutch WCAM procedure; and more generally, T Hartley, *Civil Jurisdiction and Judgments in Europe* (Oxford University Press 2017) para 19.03.

[63] Hartley/Dogauchi Report (n 11) para 209.

iii. Particular Importance of 'Recognition' for Collective Settlements

In the case of an ordinary settlement, it will usually be sufficient if the agreement is binding on the immediate parties and their successors in accordance with contractual principles. The contractual effects would not, however, be sufficiently extensive in the case of a collective settlement. The latter is submitted to a court for approval with the specific aim of making the agreement binding on potential claimants. Only the procedural rules of the *lex fori* may grant preclusive effects covering all such persons.

The effectiveness of collective settlements may be undermined by the omission of reference to 'recognition' in the Hague Conventions. Suppose that a collective settlement agreement is concluded under which the allegedly responsible party agrees to pay a sum of money to a defined group of potential claimants. Suppose further that the settlement is submitted to the court of a Contracting State and approved. If one of the potential claimants in the defined group nevertheless brings a new action in another Contracting State seeking payment on the same cause of action, the allegedly responsible party cannot rely on the Conventions to invoke the settlement in defence of the action.

iv. Good Reasons for the Omission of 'Recognition'?

The Judgments Convention does not preclude the recognition of judicial settlements under national law.[64] Are there, then, any good reasons for not providing for recognition in the Convention? Possible reasons may be gleaned from the Nygh/Pocar Report[65] as well as the Hartley/Dogauchi Report.

The Nygh/Pocar Report states that in some jurisdictions, judicial settlements do not have the force of *res judicata* and therefore cannot be recognised in another State. The correctness of this statement is evident. It does not, however, mean that where judicial settlements do have such effects, they should not be entitled to cross-border recognition. In fact, the 1999 Draft Convention, for which the Nygh/Pocar Report was prepared, provided for the cross-border recognition of settlements where they had the force of *res judicata* in the State of origin (Articles 25(2) and 36).

The Hartley/Dogauchi Report[66] states that the Choice of Court Convention does not provide for recognition mainly because the effects of settlements are different in different legal systems. This concern may be addressed by requiring the party seeking the recognition of a settlement to produce a certificate of the court of the State of origin[67] giving the details on the preclusive effects of the settlement in that State, including those on the range of persons bound by it. In addition, a recommended form of the certificate may be prepared.[68] If this is done, the diversity of effects would not be a sufficient reason to deny cross-border recognition.

The omission of 'recognition' in the current text could not be rectified by interpretation. It is suggested that some legislative action should be taken (by either amending the existing text or creating a new instrument) to provide for the cross-border recognition of judicial settlements.

[64] Garcimartín/Saumier Report (n 11) para 298.

[65] P Nygh and F Pocar, 'Report on the Preliminary Draft Convention on Jurisdiction and Foreign Judgments in Civil and Commercial Matters' (Prel Doc No 11 of August 2000) para 123.

[66] (n 11) para 209.

[67] For the purpose of enforcement, see Art 12(1)(d) of the Judgments Convention and Art 13(1)(e) of the Choice of Court Convention.

[68] See Art 12(3) of the Judgments Convention; Art 13(3) of the Choice of Court Convention.

C. Conditions for Cross-Border Recognition and Enforcement of Judicial Settlements

Under the Hague Conventions, the cross-border enforcement of judicial settlements is subject to the same conditions as judgments (Article 11 of the Judgments Convention and Article 12 of the Choice of Court Convention). In general, the court of origin must have indirect jurisdiction as set out in the Judgments Convention or be designated by an exclusive choice of court agreement in accordance with the Choice of Court Convention, and judicial settlements are subject to the same grounds for the refusal of enforcement as those for judgments (Article 7 of the Judgments Convention and Article 9 of the Choice of Court Convention). This scheme for cross-border enforcement should be extended to recognition if it is thought, as argued above, that judicial settlements should be given cross-border recognition.

i. Jurisdiction of the Court of Origin (Indirect Jurisdiction)

The Garcimartín/Saumier Report states[69] that because settlements are essentially consensual, the issues of indirect jurisdiction will not arise. Under the Brussels Ia Regulation, the jurisdiction of the court of origin may not be reviewed[70] since the infringement of public policy is the only permitted ground for refusing the enforcement of a court settlement (Articles 58(1) and 59). In principle, however, it is doubtful whether cross-border recognition and enforcement should be granted without ensuring the legitimacy of the court of origin. A particular challenge with judicial settlements lies in working out the approach of reviewing the jurisdiction of the court of origin.

Where the settlement is concluded before a court in the course of proceedings, indirect jurisdiction should be reviewed by reference to the underlying proceedings. If the proceedings are based on a collective procedure, the bases of jurisdiction should be the same as those for collective judgments (for which, see the discussion at section III.B above).

Where, on the other hand, the settlement is concluded out of court before it is presented to a court for approval, the parties submitting the settlement may be deemed to have submitted to the jurisdiction of the court. Accordingly, if the settlement is an ordinary two-party settlement, the jurisdictional issue will be practically irrelevant. What if it is a collective settlement? Suppose that a collective settlement is presented to a court of a State which has no substantive connection with the dispute. Even if the absent claimants have been notified of the terms of the settlement in sufficient time and in such a manner as to enable them to opt out from the settlement or file an opposition to the terms, they would be deterred from filing an opposition if they have to appear in an inconvenient forum. In a few cases decided under the WCAM procedure,[71] the Dutch court affirmed its jurisdiction to grant an out of court settlement a binding declaration by relying on what was then Article 6(1) of the Brussels I Regulation. To apply this provision,

[69] (n 11) para 299.

[70] See, eg, the judgment of the German Oberlandesgericht Koblenz (Judgment of 04/05/2004 – 11 UF 43/04). In this case, the German court enforced a settlement approved by an Austrian court without reviewing the latter's jurisdiction notwithstanding that the debtor contested it: B Hess, T Pfeiffer and P Schlosser, 'Report on the Application of Regulation Brussels I in the Member States' (Study JLS/C4/2005/03) (2007) para 623.

[71] eg, the *Shell* decision on 29 May 2009 by the Amsterdam Court of Appeal (case no 106.010.887), available at: globalclass-actions.stanford.edu/content/royal-dutch-shell-decision-decision-amsterdam-court-appeal-2009 with a sworn translation into English; and the *Converium* decision on 12 November 2010 by the same court (case no 200,070,039-01), available at: uitspraken.rechtspraak.nl/inziendocument?id=ECLI:NL:GHAMS:2010:BO3908&showbutton=true.

which set forth jurisdiction for the consolidation of closely connected claims against multiple defendants, the court treated the absent claimants as if they were defendants. This interpretation is doubtful,[72] because it would allow jurisdiction to be extended to all potential claimants solely on the basis of the domicile of one of them in the forum State. It is suggested that the court approving an out of court settlement should be considered to have indirect jurisdiction if, assuming that a collective action had been brought before that court, it would have indirect jurisdiction. For this analysis, the bases of indirect jurisdiction should be the same as those for collective judgments (see the discussion at section III.B above).

ii. Grounds for the Refusal of Recognition and Enforcement

The Garcimartín/Saumier Report[73] states that in practice, the most relevant ground for refusing the enforcement of judicial settlements will be the infringement of public policy of the requested State (Article 7(1)(c) of the Judgments Convention). It is without doubt that this ground of refusal would be of particular importance especially where the settlement is a collective settlement. While many public policy concerns are shared with collective judgments (for which see the discussion at section III.C.ii above), settlements could give rise to unique concerns. Thus, it frequently happens that a defendant is forced by fear of the risk of bankruptcy to settle even if it has no legal liability. Conversely, it could happen that a defendant is smart enough to conduct a sort of 'reverse auctioning' to the detriment of the claimants' interests.[74] Since public policy is a flexible notion, it should be possible to deal with concerns arising from such situations under the present text.

The Garcimartín/Saumier Report further observes[75] that because settlements are essentially consensual, other grounds for refusal such as insufficient notification will not be invoked. Interestingly, the infringement of public policy is the only permitted ground for refusing the enforcement of a court settlement under the Brussels Ia Regulation (Articles 58(1) and 59). It means that a court settlement, which may be seen as something less than a judgment, enjoys a higher degree of enforceability than a judgment. This is difficult to justify since other refusal grounds could also have relevance.[76]

Where the settlement is a collective settlement, the lack of sufficient notification (Article 7(1)(a) of the Judgments Convention and Article 9(c) of the Choice of Court Convention) would be a particularly important refusal ground. In the cases of ordinary two-party settlements, insufficient notification will be a practically irrelevant refusal ground since the consent to a settlement implies that the parties have waived the right to contest notification. In the cases of collective settlements, the interest of the absent claimants could only be protected by sufficient notification.[77] The current text is, however, not suitably drafted for collective settlements. It refers to the notification

[72] See, eg, Tang (n 1) 101, 123; Halfmeier (n 55) 178; A Pato, *Jurisdiction and Cross-Border Collective Redress: A European Private International Law Perspective* (Hart Publishing 2019) 171. See also, van Lith (n 45) para 2.4.1, for an argument supporting this interpretation and para 2.8, for a discussion on other possible bases of jurisdiction.

[73] Garcimartín/Saumier Report (n 11) para 299.

[74] B Hay and D Rosenberg, 'Sweetheart and Blackmail Settlements in Class Actions: Reality and Remedy' (2000) 75 *Notre Dame Law Review* 1377, 1391.

[75] (n 11) para 299.

[76] See Hartley (n 62) paras 19.04 and 19.26.

[77] See, eg, Rule 23(e)(1) of the United States Federal Rules of Civil Procedure. Under the Dutch WCAM procedure, notification is required at two stages: prior to the court's binding declaration to give potential claimants an opportunity to file an objection and subsequent to the binding declaration to give them a chance to opt out. See van Lith (n 45) para 1.1.

of the 'document which instituted the proceedings' to the 'defendant' to arrange for his 'defence'. A lot of linguistic gymnastics would be needed to construe it as referring to the notification of the 'settlement agreement' to the 'absent claimants' to allow them to 'opt out' from the settlement or 'object to the terms'. It would be useful to take some legislative action to provide that an absent claimant may resist the recognition of a court-approved settlement if he has not been provided with sufficient notification enabling him to opt out from the settlement or object to its terms.

V. Conclusion

The aspect of private international law for which international harmonisation seems most useful and promising in the area of collective redress is the recognition and enforcement of judgments and settlements. The two Hague Conventions do not exclude collective redress from their scope but the texts are ill-equipped to deal with the features of collective procedures. Consequently, it is necessary to either come up with creative interpretations or take some legislative action (by amending the existing texts or creating a new instrument).

Multiple indirect jurisdiction bases should be available for collective procedures, including jurisdiction based on the defendant's habitual residence, *ex post* jurisdiction agreements between the representative and the defendant, the centre of gravity of contracts and torts, and the home State of the majority of the potential claimants. The combination of different bases and the centralisation approach helps to encourage an international solution and also protect the right to pursue collective procedures if not available in the defendant's home State.

The refusal ground for recognition and enforcement of judgments in individual actions can equally apply to collective procedures, though special issues arise in public policy. The Conventions or new instruments, however, should pay more attention to recognition of collective judgments against represented claimants, which raises innovative questions on due process, procedural fairness, inconsistent judgments and breach of dispute resolution agreements. Although collective procedures, especially the opt-out style, face due process challenges, the conventional concept of due process can be interpreted in a way to promote collective redress. The explanatory material of the Conventions or any new international instrument would need to squarely address what methods of fictional notice would be tolerable and to what extent, and what content should be covered in the notice.

Collective actions typically end in a settlement, usually with the approval of a court. Sometimes a settlement is reached out of court before being presented to a court for approval. Such a settlement as well as a settlement concluded before a court in the course of proceedings should be interpreted as falling within the notion of 'judicial settlement' under the Hague Conventions. Both Conventions provide for cross-border enforcement of judicial settlements but neither provide for cross-border recognition. Given the particular importance of recognition for collective settlements, the regime for enforcement should be extended to recognition. The Conventions lack clarity on how the indirect jurisdiction of the court approving settlements should be reviewed, an issue of particular importance to collective settlements. Clarity is also lacking on whether an absent claimant may invoke insufficient notification to resist the recognition of a collective settlement. It would be useful to take some legislative action to remedy these inadequacies.

PART V

Family Law

32

Divorce

MÁIRE NÍ SHÚILLEABHÁIN AND JAYNE HOLLIDAY

I. Introduction

This chapter explores divorce jurisdiction and recognition from a global perspective. Section II will analyse the 1970 Hague Convention on the Recognition of Divorces and Legal Separations (1970 Convention) and section III will consider the possibility of a new global Convention on conflicts of jurisdiction in divorce matters.

The global divorce landscape has been transformed since the 1960s when the 1970 Convention was being negotiated.[1] At that time, some of the States participating in the negotiations did not allow for divorce within their domestic legal orders (Italy, Spain and Ireland), and in those States where divorce was sanctioned, its availability was typically conditional on proof of fault or mutual consent before a judge.[2] This very formal treatment of divorce (in most of Europe and in North America), contrasted with the situation in some other parts of the world whereby men could divorce their wives by private repudiation as a matter of religious personal law.[3]

In the early 2020s, Europe and North America are moving towards a model of unilateral divorce on demand,[4] with a trend towards non-judicial divorce[5] and digitisation[6] (and this pattern is repeated elsewhere).[7] This reflects a wider deregulation of family law, and an orthodoxy of private-ordering in divorce matters.[8] In States applying Islamic personal law, by contrast, there has been an *increased* formalisation of divorce, with mandatory involvement of religious or State authorities now much more common, and with new requirements of notification in many countries.[9]

[1] On the ideological and philosophical roots of this change, see M Antokolskaia, 'Objectives and Values of Substantive Family Law' in J Meeusen et al (eds), *International Family Law for the European Union* (Intersentia 2007) 54 ff.

[2] See P Bellet and B Goldman, *Explanatory Report on the 1970 Hague Convention on the Recognition of Divorces and Legal Separations* (English translation) (1971) 17 (Explanatory Report); and M Antokolskaia, 'Divorce Law in a European Perspective' in J Scherpe (ed), *European Family Law, Volume III: Family Law in a European Perspective* (Edward Elgar 2016) 69–72.

[3] J Tucker, *Women, Family and Gender in Islamic Law* (Cambridge University Press 2008) 86–92.

[4] A Laquer Estin, 'Marriage and Divorce Conflicts in International Perspective' (2017) 27 *Duke Journal of Comparative & International Law* 485, 486–87; and L Trinder et al, *Finding Fault? Divorce Law and Practice in England and Wales* (Nuffield Foundation 2017) 151–54.

[5] See Trinder, ibid, 13 and the reports on European national divorce practice, available at: e-justice.europa.eu/content_divorce-45-en.do.

[6] See S Aggarwal, 'Online Divorce Petitions' [2019] *Family Law* 985.

[7] eg, in Australia, see ibid; also E Nash and A Parker, 'No Fault Divorce: the Australian Experience' [2016] *Family Law* 261.

[8] Estin (n 4) 486–87; J Singer, 'The Privatization of Family Law' [1992] *Wisconsin Law Review* 1443.

[9] N Moosa, 'An Overview of Divorce and Dispute Resolution in Islamic Law' [2004] *International Family Law* 225; Tucker (n 3) 116–17; *H v S (Recognition of Overseas Divorce)* [2012] 2 FLR 157, [18]–[19] (HC).

These changes in domestic divorce practice have impacted private international law. In Europe, the easing of domestic restrictions allowed for the adoption of an EU Regulation harmonising divorce jurisdiction and recognition (Regulation 2201/2003, the Brussels IIa Regulation).[10] Elsewhere the increased formalisation of religious divorce has improved the prospects of cross-border recognition.[11] The contractualisation of domestic family law has led to a wider acceptance of party autonomy in devising tailored solutions to cross-border family disputes.[12]

The 1970 Convention has attracted 20 Contracting States so far and in the wake of the United Kingdom's withdrawal from the EU, it is possible that it may attract further ratifications.[13] Section II analyses some of the key provisions in the 1970 Convention and considers its long-term viability. Section III considers how the 1970 Convention can be revitalised (and the necessity for this) and also examines the advantages and feasibility of a new Convention on conflicts of jurisdiction.

While the original challenges facing the negotiators of the 1970 Convention have mostly receded (in particular, State interests in restricting divorce),[14] different challenges have emerged for those seeking to reinvigorate the 1970 Convention and/or to develop a new global instrument on conflicts of jurisdiction.

The advent of same-sex marriage and registered partnership have led to new political divides on divorce.[15] Human rights norms (now increasingly relevant to the development of private international law) may pull in different directions.[16] Even with increased formalisation, the

[10] Council Regulation (EC) No 2201/2003 of 27 November 2003 concerning jurisdiction and the recognition and enforcement of judgments in matrimonial matters and the matters of parental responsibility, repealing Regulation (EC) No 1347/2000 [2003] OJ L338/1.

[11] See P Torremans (ed), *Cheshire, North & Fawcett Private International Law*, 15th edn (Oxford University Press 2017) 1015; M Ní Shúilleabháin, '"A Peculiarly Pointless Line of Division": Recognition of Proceedings and Non-Proceedings Divorces under the Family Law Act 1986' in A Dickinson and E Peel (eds), *A Conflict of Laws Companion* (Oxford University Press 2021) 273: under the UK Family Law Act 1986, the more formal the foreign divorce process, the more likely recognition is.

[12] In Europe there is strong support for choice of court agreements in divorce matters, although this policy has yet to receive legislative sanction at EU level: see T Kruger and L Samyn, 'Brussels II *bis*: Successes and Suggested Improvements' (2016) 12 *Journal of Private International Law* 132, 143–45; J Borg-Barthet, 'Jurisdiction in Matrimonial Matters – Reflections for the Review of the Brussels IIa Regulation' (Study for the JURI Committee of the European Parliament, 2016) 13–14; also the 2019 GEDIP Proposal for a Regulation on jurisdiction, applicable law and recognition of judgments and decrees with regard to divorce and legal separation, Arts 5 and 6, available at www.gedip-egpil.eu/reunionstravail/2019_Katowice/divorce/DIV-Txt-ENG-27.11.19.pdf.

[13] See N Lowe and D Hodson, 'The UK's Family Law Prospective Position on Fully Leaving the EU' [2018] *Family Law* 1391 expressing hope that the EU Member States which are not currently Party to the 1970 Convention might be persuaded to join; also EU Commission, 'Notice to Stakeholders: Withdrawal of the United Kingdom and EU Rules in the Field of Civil Justice and Private International Law' (27 August 2020) 8 noting that '*currently* only 12 EU Member States are contracting parties' (emphasis added).

[14] See Explanatory Report (n 2) 3; AE Anton, 'The Recognition of Divorces and Legal Separations' (1969) 18 *ICLQ* 620, 620, 625. Only two countries in the world, the Philippines and the Vatican, continue to view marriage as indissoluble: see D Coester-Waltjen, 'Divorce and personal separation' in J Basedow et al (eds), *Encyclopedia of Private International Law*, Vol I (Edward Elgar 2017). In February 2020 the Committee on Population and Family Relations in the Philippine House of Representatives approved a bill to legalise divorce see: perma.cc/8TDT-G82N.

[15] The EU Commission abandoned its plans for reform of divorce jurisdiction under the Brussels IIa Regulation (n 10) because of disagreement over same-sex marriage: see the Commission Staff Working Document Impact Assessment SWD (2016) 207 final, 19–21; also S Kraljić, 'Same-Sex Partnerships in Eastern Europe: Marriage, Registration or No Regulation?' in K Boele-Woelki and A Fuchs (eds), *Same-Sex Relationships and Beyond*, 3rd edn (Intersentia 2017) 55–75.

[16] See nns 69, 71 and 113 below.

treatment of religious divorces remains highly contested.[17] Party autonomy pushes against the imposition of mandatory connecting factors where there is party agreement on the obtaining of the divorce.[18]

Cooperation on jurisdiction poses particular challenges. In the modern era, State authorities may often have much less appetite for restricting the availability of divorce, or even recognition of foreign divorces[19] – but sovereign interests are significantly implicated by any instrument affecting the exercise of jurisdiction and access to publicly funded legal services.[20] Also, insofar as the court seised of divorce very often tends to serve as the 'anchor' court for ancillary financial proceedings and proceedings concerning children, the designation of that divorce forum can vitally affect party interests, child welfare and the public purse.[21] This emerged clearly in the wake of the EU harmonisation of divorce jurisdiction: on the face of it, the Brussels IIa Regulation only regulated jurisdiction to pronounce divorce, and jurisdiction in ancillary financial matters was excluded, but in practice the allocation of divorce jurisdiction was often contested because of its implications for ancillary financial relief.[22]

There is widespread recognition that conflicts of jurisdiction present significant difficulties for families divorcing in a cross-border context,[23] and in an ideal world one might aspire towards international harmonisation of the grounds for jurisdiction. However, cultural differences[24] – and differing views on the appropriate accommodation of party autonomy[25] – make global agreement on direct jurisdiction extremely unlikely.[26] Therefore, in line with recent developments in the Hague Jurisdiction Project on civil and commercial matters,[27] it is proposed that any new instrument on divorce jurisdiction should focus on the management of conflicts of jurisdiction and the avoidance of concurrent proceedings.

[17] See nn 68–71 below.

[18] See Kruger and Samyn (n 12) 145 and T de Boer, 'The Second Revision of the Brussels II Regulation: Jurisdiction and Applicable Law' in K Boele-Woelki and T Sverdrup (eds), *European Challenges in Contemporary Family Law* (Intersentia 2008) 322, 324–25 arguing (in the EU context) for the freedom to agree on any divorce forum.

[19] Estin (n 4) 486–87, 505.

[20] See F Maultzsch, 'Party Autonomy in European Private International Law: Uniform Principle or Context-Dependent Instrument?' (2016) 12 *Journal of Private International Law* 466, 468 discussing the sovereign interest in jurisdiction in a different context.

[21] M Ní Shúilleabháin, *Cross-Border Divorce Law: Brussels II bis* (Oxford University Press 2010) 165 ff.

[22] Ibid.

[23] See L Walker, 'Party Autonomy, Inconsistency and the Specific Characteristics of Family Law in the EU' (2018) 14 *Journal of Private International Law* 225, 240, 261; P Beaumont and G Moir, 'Brussels Convention II: A New Private International Law Instrument in Family Matters for the European Union or the European Community?' (1995) 20 *EL Rev* 268, 274; Ní Shúilleabháin (n 21) 167–71, 216–21.

[24] Some countries (typically those with a civil law tradition) favour nationality-based jurisdiction, while others see habitual residence as the most appropriate basis for divorce jurisdiction: see Estin (n 4) 501–04; Anton (n 14) 630; G Cuniberti, *Conflict of Laws: A Comparative Approach* (Edward Elgar 2017) 467–69.

[25] eg, as to whether the choice should be restricted to particular connected fora, or whether previously agreed jurisdiction clauses should be binding, see (n 18 above); also Maultzsch (n 20) 476; Walker (n 23) 250–53; Ní Shúilleabháin (n 21) 79.

[26] See A von Mehren, 'Drafting a Convention on International Jurisdiction and the Effects of Foreign Judgments Acceptable World-wide: Can the Hague Conference Project Succeed?' (2001) 49 *American Journal of Comparative Law* 191, 194–98 arguing that direct jurisdictional harmonisation is very difficult to achieve in the context of non-convergent legal orders.

[27] See Report on the Jurisdiction Project, Prel Doc No 3 of February 2021, available at: www.hcch.net/en/projects/legislative-projects/jurisdiction-project.

II. The 1970 Hague Convention on Recognition of Divorces and Legal Separations

A. Introduction

In Alexander Anton's introduction to his report on the negotiation of the 1970 Convention, he compared its potential benefits to 'a glittering prize'.[28] This rather emotive language by a member of the UK delegation to the negotiations expressed belief both in the aims of the Convention and its content. Now, over 50 years since it was drafted, and in light of the Hague Conference's recent decision to prepare a questionnaire on this Convention, the following will critically assess the 1970 Convention to see whether it remains of value.[29]

B. Development of Global Private International Law on Divorce

The 1970 Convention was not the first time the Hague Conference had considered the issue of divorce.[30] A Convention on the settlement of conflicts of law and jurisdiction on matters of divorce and separation was drafted by the Hague Conference in 1902 but it was not a success.[31] By the mid-twentieth century, almost half of the 12 Contracting States to that Convention had denounced it, leaving private international law on divorce in a state of 'virtual anarchy'.[32] As Anton noted, this had

> serious social inconveniences because the validity of second marriages, the legitimacy of the children of such marriages, and rights deriving from the law of matrimonial property or of succession may all depend on whether, from system to system, recognition is accorded to a divorce.[33]

Therefore, in 1964, in their next attempt to minimise 'limping marriages',[34] the Hague Conference decided to draft a Convention on the Recognition of decrees of divorce, legal separation and the nullity of marriage.[35] In doing so they chose to focus their efforts on negotiating a single Convention[36] on the basis that it was considered easier for States to accept indirect grounds of jurisdiction which do not bind the State where the judgment was made,[37] than for States to reach agreement on a double Convention which would require them to potentially agree to abandoning their own grounds of jurisdiction.[38] This decision to focus on recognition remains one of the Convention's major strengths.

[28] Anton (n 14) 620.

[29] In March 2021, the HCCH, Council on General Affairs and Policy, 'Conclusion and Decisions', para 33 agreed to 'the circulation of a brief questionnaire on the 1970 Divorce Convention with a view to developing a better understanding of the current operation of the Convention and why more States have not become party to the Convention', available at: assets.hcch.net/docs/94e2d886-1cbf-4250-b436-5c1899cb942b.pdf.

[30] Explanatory Report (n 2) 2.

[31] Ibid. Anton (n 14) 622.

[32] Ibid. Anton (n 14) 622. The text of the Convention of 12 June 1902 for the settlement of conflicts of law and jurisdiction on matters of divorce and separation can be found at: www.hcch.net/en/instruments/the-old-conventions/1902-divorce-convention.

[33] Anton (n 14) 622; Explanatory Report (n 2) 2.

[34] 'Limping marriages' is a term used to describe a situation where a person is regarded as simultaneously married in one State whilst divorced in another.

[35] Explanatory Report (n 2) 2. The final text excludes nullity of marriage.

[36] Anton (n 14) 624; Beaumont and Moir (n 23) 268–88, 271.

[37] Beaumont and Moir, ibid, 271.

[38] Anton (n 14) 624; Beaumont and Moir, ibid, 271.

Unfortunately for the Hague Conference and its pursuit of progressive unification of private international law rules,[39] out of the 25 States who were involved in the drafting of the 1970 Convention, 10 were simultaneously negotiating a purely civil law instrument on divorce.[40] Out of those 10 States, only four would go on to ratify the 1970 Convention, which would suggest that the pursuit of a truly global private international law solution to this issue was not a primary concern for some.[41]

C. The Current Status

Since its entry into force in 1975, and contrary to Anton's initial optimism, the 1970 Convention has only attracted 20 Contracting Parties.[42] However, to determine whether it can be considered a 'success' it is necessary to dig deeper than this. If we unpack the status table, not all Contracting Parties have accepted the accessions of other Contracting Parties and therefore the number of States that a Contracting Party can rely on to recognise its divorces are fewer than might be imagined at first glance.[43] This low reciprocity rate within the Convention is a concern. The last country to accede to the Convention was Albania in 2013.[44] Yet, since then, Albania's accession has only been accepted by five States, most recently by the UK in October 2020.[45]

If this Convention is to be successfully revived, this hitherto accepted non-engagement by Contracting States needs to change. The Convention is based on reciprocity.[46] The benefit of reciprocity for the Contracting Parties is that their divorces are recognised by other Contracting Parties which in turn protects divorcees and their families from the consequences of limping marriages.

Some Members of the Hague Conference on Private International Law (HCCH) are not Parties to the Convention but have, at least in part, modelled their private international law rules on it. This can be seen in the laws of Canada, New Zealand and South Africa.[47] However, this unilateral approach is short-sighted compared with becoming a Party to the Convention as it does not guarantee that their own divorces will be recognised by a Contracting State and therefore it fails to protect vulnerable parties or provide those parties with legal certainty.

[39] Statute of The Hague Conference on Private International Law, Art 1.

[40] The Commission Internationale de l'Etat Civile Convention was signed in 1967. Professor RH Graveson called for an independent approach to be conducted at the Hague due to the incompatibility of the Convention with common law, see Anton (n 14) 621 and 622.

[41] Beaumont and Moir (n 23) 273.

[42] Albania, Australia, China (Hong Kong), Cyprus, the Czech Republic, Denmark, Estonia, Egypt, Finland, Italy, Luxembourg, the Netherlands, Norway, Poland, Portugal, Republic of Moldova, Slovakia, Sweden, Switzerland and the United Kingdom.

[43] Out of the Contracting Parties that have acceded to the Convention, Albania has five connections, Australia 14, Cyprus 15, Poland 10 and Republic of Moldova four.

[44] Ibid.

[45] Ibid. See 'Albania: Acceptance of Accessions', available at: www.hcch.net/en/instruments/conventions/status-table/acceptances/?mid=1205. J Holliday, 'The urgent need for the UK to accept the accessions of EU and Non-EU Contracting Parties to the 1970 Hague Convention on Recognition of Divorces and Legal Separation' (Working Paper 2019/1), available at: www.stir.ac.uk/about/faculties/arts-humanities/law-and-philosophy/law-research/law-working-papers/.

[46] Art 1, 1970 Convention.

[47] Canada (was present at the XI Session of the Hague Conference in 1968) see s 22(3) of the Divorce Act RSC 1985; New Zealand see s 44 of Family Proceedings Act 1980; South Africa see s 13 of the Divorce Act 1979 where it is implicit that the divorce granted is effective under the law of the country where it was granted, see: uk.practicallaw.thomsonreuters.com/6-566-4825?transitionType=Default&contextData=(sc.Default)&firstPage=true#co_anchor_a359839.

Another possible explanation for the low number of Contracting Parties could be that the automatic recognition of divorce decrees under the various iterations of the Brussels II Regulation may have detracted from the need for EU Member States to press for attention to be given to this Convention.[48] If this is the case then this is contrary to the aim of the EU to promote the unification of global private international law in its position as a Regional Economic Integration Organisation at the Hague Conference.[49] Unfortunately, the method for EU Member States to ratify or accede to the Convention is not straightforward as it currently requires a unanimous EU decision for all Member States to join the 1970 Convention or to permit those Member States who have not joined to do so.[50] On a positive note, as the Brussels II direct jurisdictional framework was influenced by the 1970 Convention indirect jurisdictional framework, EU divorces would stand to benefit from recognition in Contracting States outside the EU if they come from EU Member States that are Contracting States to the Convention.[51] It is strongly recommended that the EU Commission encourages the EU Member States to agree to the remaining Member States becoming Parties to the 1970 Convention.[52] This could also serve to encourage other States to become Parties to the Convention.[53] The contemporary justifications for supporting the Convention and avoiding limping marriages will be discussed in more detail later in this chapter (section III).

D. A Brief Assessment of the Key Articles within the 1970 Hague Divorce Convention

The ability to recognise a foreign divorce (or legal separation) under the Convention requires, in broad terms, two conditions. The first is for it to have been 'obtained' in, and effective under the law of, a Contracting State and the second is for one or both parties to have had a personal connection with that jurisdiction.[54]

i. *Article 1*

The test as to whether a divorce or legal separation falls within the scope of the Convention is found within Article 1 which provides for the

> recognition in one Contracting State of divorces and legal separations obtained in another Contracting State which follow judicial or other *proceedings officially recognised* in that State and which are *legally effective* there.[55]

[48] (n 10). P Beaumont and P McEleavy, *Anton's Private International Law*, 3rd edn (W Green/SULI 2011) 16.23. See also P Beaumont, 'Interaction of the Brussels IIa and Maintenance Regulations' in I Viarengo and F Villata (eds), *Planning the Future of Cross Border Families* (Hart Publishing 2020) 338, which puts forward the argument for the EU to encourage its Member States who are not yet Members of the 1970 Convention to become Contracting States – which will in turn encourage non-EU Members to join.

[49] Statute of the Hague Conference on Private International Law, Art 3.

[50] Holliday (n 45).

[51] P Franzina, 'The Interplay of EU legislation and International Developments in Private International Law' in P Franzina (ed), *The External Dimension of EU Private International Law After Opinion 1/13* (Intersentia 2017) 183, 197–98. Beaumont and McEleavy (n 48) 16.23.

[52] Beaumont (n 48) 338.

[53] Ibid.

[54] Arts 1–5, 1970 Hague Convention.

[55] Emphasis added.

Article 1 should be interpreted in a way which upholds the aim of the Convention to minimise limping marriages. The Convention does not provide a definition of 'divorce'.[56] This was a conscious decision by the negotiators so that 'legislative, administrative and religious acts' would fall within its scope.[57]

In order to ascertain whether there have been 'proceedings officially recognised' two factors need to be considered.[58] First, there has to have been 'proceedings'. The term 'proceedings' was given a very broad interpretation: 'a minimum of acts, steps or formalities required to be taken by established rules and carried out by an authority or at any rate with the agreement of such authority or in its presence'.[59] This is an objective test.[60]

Second, the proceedings must be officially recognised, ie, the Contracting State of origin must recognise the proceedings as a method of obtaining a divorce within their jurisdiction.[61] If proceedings have taken place, then there is an expectation that the parties will have been given reasonable notice and will have had a reasonable opportunity to participate in them.[62]

Some case law has focused on 'proceedings' other than judicial proceedings.[63] The term was left deliberately open to allow the courts to decide what would fall within the Convention. It was thought that a religious divorce ought to be recognised under the Convention if it 'involves the intervention of the public or religious authorities and can be regarded as proceedings'.[64]

a. The Religious Divorce

Religious divorces are frequently denied recognition in European and American courts, in particular the Islamic *talaq*,[65] although the increased formalisation of Islamic divorce appears to have increased the scope for recognition.[66] Of the Contracting States to the 1970 Convention, only Egypt has a family law system based on religious law, but Israel also participated in the negotiations, and the Convention allowed for recognition of religious divorces obtained following 'proceedings', it being accepted that defences could be invoked to protect women denied due process.[67] Aside from Israel and Egypt, a number of other Hague Conference Members allow for religious divorce (including India, Saudi Arabia and Morocco) and so it is important to explore the potential for recognition of religious divorces under the 1970 Convention.

[56] Explanatory Report (n 2) 6, para 12.

[57] Ibid. Anton (n 14) 626.

[58] Explanatory Report (n 2) 6, para 13.

[59] Ibid. During the negotiations, the UK wanted to amend Art 1, to remove the term 'proceedings', so that the Convention was more clearly inclusive of all legally effective divorces, including repudiation, to prevent limping marriage, see *Actes et documents de la Onzième session (1968) – Divorce* 100.

[60] Ibid (Explanatory Report) para 13.

[61] Ibid, para 13.

[62] Art 8, 1970 Convention. *Joyce v Joyce* [1979] Fam 93 recognition was refused as the wife had not had a reasonable opportunity to participate in proceedings in Canada. *Mamdani v Mamdini* [1984] FLR 699 recognition refused as the wife had not had a reasonable opportunity to participate in proceedings in Nevada due to lack of financial means.

[63] *Quazi v Quazi* [1980] AC 744; Ní Shúilleabháin (n 11) 284–90. In Australia in *Maider and Carrigan* [2008] FamCA 862 [12] a decree arising from a religious court or through a non-judicial procedure like an Islamic *talaq* will be recognised under the Convention if recognised and effective in the State it arose in. In this case the Pakistani authority had cancelled the certificate and therefore the judge held that the divorce was not legally effective in accordance with the law of Pakistan.

[64] Explanatory Report (n 2) 7.

[65] See Estin (n 4) 505; also nn 68 and 70 below.

[66] See n 11 above.

[67] Explanatory Report (n 2) 4, 7.

Religious divorces are often denied recognition for human rights reasons including gender equality and due process.[68] It is also arguable that the mandatory application of religious law (with no right to opt out) is a violation of the right of free self-identification.[69] On the other hand, however, a per se denial of recognition for religious divorces (or particular classes of religious divorces)[70] is difficult to justify: this brings about large-scale discontinuity of status for certain migrant groups and there is arguably a violation of cultural and religious rights in such an uncompromising position.[71] It is to be hoped that a flexible interpretation of the 1970 Convention would allow for recognition of many overseas religious divorces at least where a wife who was denied due process or equal treatment is herself demanding recognition.[72]

b. *Talaq*

The *talaq* without any further formalities or the 'bare' *talaq* was not a permitted method of divorce under the internal laws of the States that drafted the Convention. At the time of drafting although both Israel and Egypt were delegates to the Eleventh Session only Egypt explained its experience of the *talaq*.[73] The UK was in favour of permitting a unilateral divorce without proceedings under the Convention in order to avoid a limping marriage and to allow the wife to remarry in any Contracting State and proposed an amendment which said:

> The present Convention shall apply to divorces and legal separations obtained in a Contracting State in accordance with its internal law. It shall apply whatever the form or methods of divorce which the State provides or permits.

This amendment was supported by Germany, Japan, Switzerland, United Arab Republic (Egypt), United Kingdom and United States against 15 rejections.[74] The States who were in favour of the amendment still partially achieved their aim through the broad interpretation of the term 'proceedings'.

An example of a *talaq* with proceedings which falls under the scope of the Convention can be seen in *Quazi v Quazi*.[75] In this case a Pakistani *talaq*, which complied with the Muslim Family Laws Ordinance 1961's requirement to notify a public authority, who did not have the power to veto the divorce but was there to encourage conciliation, was held to be 'proceedings' for the purpose of the Convention.[76]

[68] Estin (n 4) 505; K Kaesling, 'The Recognition of Religious Private Divorces in Europe' in K Boele-Woelki and D Martiny (eds), *Plurality and Diversity of Family Relations in Europe* (Intersentia 2019).

[69] See *Molla Sali v Greece* App no 20452/14 (ECtHR, 19 December 2018) [156]–[158] dealing with the right to opt out of Sharia law in a succession context. Within Europe, the ECHR allows spouses to demand non-recognition of decrees issued in third-country matrimonial proceedings in non-compliance with the due process standards of Art 6 ECHR: see *Pellegrini v Italy* (2002) 35 EHRR 2 (mandating non-recognition of a Vatican annulment).

[70] In Belgium only *talaqs* sanctioned by a judge in the court of origin are entitled to recognition – so overseas 'bare *talaqs*', effective without any court involvement, are not recognised at all: see C González Beilfuss, 'Islamic Family Law in the European Union' in J Meeusen et al (eds), *International Family Law for the European Union* (Intersentia 2007) 432–33. Similarly, in Ireland, it appears that bare *talaqs* are refused recognition in all circumstances: see *MY v AA* [2017] IEHC 227 [93].

[71] See J Fawcett, M Ní Shúilleabháin and S Shah, *Human Rights and Private International Law* (Oxford University Press 2016) 680 ff.

[72] This is already the position in some European countries: see González Beilfuss (n 70) 433.

[73] Eleventh Proceedings (n 59) 99.

[74] Ibid, 101.

[75] *Quazi v Quazi* [1980] AC 744.

[76] Ibid.

It should be noted that a bare *talaq* is not expressly included or excluded in the Convention.[77] Arguably if the act of *talaq* takes place in a Contracting State which 'agrees' to that act as a method of divorce (satisfying the standard in the Explanatory Report quoted above if the authorisation of the legislature is treated as 'agreement of an authority')[78] and a Convention jurisdictional test is met, then it is difficult to see why it could not be recognised by another Contracting State, especially if it is the woman who is requesting recognition.[79] This point would benefit from further discussion at The Hague in a Review Special Commission on the 1970 Convention.

c. *Gett*

Under the Convention a Jewish *gett* will be regarded as 'other proceedings' due to the required involvement of the rabbinical courts.[80] Under Jewish law a *gett* is considered valid wherever it is done if it follows certain formalities.[81] This can lead to a *gett* being initiated in one State and obtained in another.[82] The status of 'transnational' divorces needs to be clarified at a Review Special Commission on the 1970 Convention. As Dicey observes, the transnational nature of certain religious divorces was 'imperfectly appreciated by those who drafted the [1970] Hague Convention'.[83] The Convention refers to the 'institution of the proceedings' (Article 2) in the Contracting State where the divorce was 'obtained' (Article 1) and it can be argued that this envisages all 'steps' in the divorce being taken in that State of origin. We support a more flexible interpretation whereby the focus is on where the divorce was 'obtained' and it does not matter where it began.[84] With increased privatisation and digitisation of secular divorce, there will be more and more transnational divorces and the uncertainty surrounding their status will have an ever broader impact (beyond the domain of *getts* and religious divorces).[85]

ii. *Indirect Jurisdiction*

The second condition for a divorce to be recognised is if it complies with the jurisdictional 'tests' contained within Articles 2–5.[86] The choice of connecting factors – habitual residence, domicile and nationality of one or both parties sometimes coupled with time requirements – was deemed necessary when dealing with States with 'divergent conflict rules'.[87] It should be noted that not

[77] Explanatory Report (n 2) 7.

[78] See text to n 59 above. (It might, however, be contended that this interpretation conflates the requirements of 'proceedings' with those of official recognition and legal effectiveness under Art 1.)

[79] See Swiss case – BBG 88 I 48 described in T Einhorn, *Private International Law in Israel* (Wolters Kluwer 2009) 66, where a Swiss wife who wanted to be recognised as a divorcee in Switzerland had her divorce which was obtained by her husband by *talaq* in Egypt not recognised as it was considered contrary to Swiss public policy. It was pointed out that the court should have passed judgment on the result not the rule.

[80] Explanatory Report (n 2) 7.

[81] L Collins (ed), *Dicey, Morris & Collins, The Conflict of Laws*, 15th edn (Sweet & Maxwell 2012) 1034.

[82] *Berkovits v Grinberg* [1995] Fam 142 In this case a husband initiated a *gett* in England, but the divorce was obtained in Israel where it was served on and accepted by the wife who was living and habitually resident there (satisfying Art 2(1)). Israel officially recognised the divorce and regarded it as effective (satisfying Art 1). However, the English court did not recognise the divorce on the basis that as the husband had written the *gett* in England the divorce was 'transnational' in nature and therefore did not fall within the scope of the Convention-inspired provisions of the UK Family Law Act 1986. (This Act extended the same recognition criteria to divorces obtained in non-Contracting States.)

[83] *Dicey, Morris & Collins* (n 81) 1034.

[84] Ibid, 1037; B Berkovits, 'Transnational Divorces: The Fatima Decision' (1988) 104 *LQR* 60.

[85] Ní Shúilleabháin (n 11) 294.

[86] Anton (n 14) 629.

[87] Ibid. The choice of jurisdiction test was intended to discourage forum shopping and balance fairness to the defender against convenience to the petitioner, see Beaumont and McEleavy (n 48) 16.23.

all foreign divorces are to be recognised irrespective of their jurisdictional basis.[88] This is arguably one of the Convention's strengths insofar as it allows for ratification by those countries which continue to restrict or delay access to divorce. The Convention aims to reduce, not eradicate, the number of limping marriages by reaching for a solution which acknowledges differing conflict rules, respects cultural differences and is in accord with the reasonable expectations of the parties.

iii. The Right to Remarry: Priority of Recognition of Divorce Over Capacity to Marry Rules

Outside the 1970 Convention, the effect of recognition of the divorce does not automatically give the right to remarry if there are impediments under the general private international law rules of the recognising State.[89] This was a cause of concern for the drafters who agreed to change this technical obstacle to the ability to remarry.[90] The priority of the recognition of divorce rules over the applicable law rules for capacity to marry is found in Article 11: 'A State which is obliged to recognise a divorce under this Convention may not preclude either spouse from remarrying …'.[91]

iv. Indirect Limitations to the Public Policy Exception

Article 6 contains indirect limitations to the public policy clause in Article 10.[92] At the time of drafting it was thought that reviewing the facts or merits in a case based on the internal law of the recognising State could lead to non-recognition of the divorce and to a limping marriage which was contrary to the aim of the Convention.[93] The drafters did not want a divorce to be unrecognised on these grounds and therefore they created indirect limitations.[94] These limitations are still a cause of current concern for some countries who are not yet Party to the Convention and do not recognise a foreign divorce when it is based on a ground they do not themselves apply or in cases where 'a law was applied other than that applicable under the rules of private international law of that State'.[95] However the reservation in Article 19(1) permits States to

> refuse to recognise a divorce or legal separation between two spouses who, at the time of the divorce or legal separation, were nationals of the State in which recognition is sought, and of no other State, and a law other than that indicated by the rules of private international law of the State of recognition was applied.

[88] Ibid. Arts 7–10.

[89] Anton (n 14) 640.

[90] Ibid.

[91] See further, Explanatory Report (n 2) para 54; and Anton (n 14) 640. This does not mean that obstacles to remarriage in the general private international law of the recognising State that do not relate to recognition of divorce should not be taken into account.

[92] Anton (n 14) 634, 635. Art 6 states that the 'recognition of a divorce or legal separation shall not be refused (a) because the internal law of the State in which such recognition is sought would not allow divorce or, as the case may be, legal separation upon the same facts, or, (b) because a law was applied other than that applicable under the rules of private international law of that State'.

[93] Anton (n 14) 635–36.

[94] Ibid.

[95] VC Govindaraj, '*The Conflict of Laws in India: Inter-Territorial and Inter-Personal Conflict*', 2nd edn (Oxford Scholarship Online 2019). This book raises concerns about Art 6(a) and (b) which Govindaraj suggests would discourage India from becoming a Party to the Convention but omits discussion of the reservation.

This should soothe this point of concern, as it allows Contracting Parties to reduce the effects of Article 6(b).

v. *Reservations*

There are several reservations within the Convention found in Articles 19, 20, 21 and 24. The Explanatory Report criticises these reservations for reducing the unification of private international law.[96] Yet, it could be argued that these reservations were at the time, and indeed remain, a pragmatic solution to enable States with less liberal divorce laws to get on board.[97]

The need for most of these reservations is clear from the status table. Out of the 20 Contracting States, eight have an Article 19 reservation (see above), six have an Article 24 reservation,[98] and two have an Article 21 reservation.[99] No States have an Article 20 reservation.

E. New Issues

As discussed earlier, in the 1960s the global attitude to divorce between heterosexual couples was very different from today.[100] There were still many States where heterosexual divorce was not legal.[101] Today, outright prohibitions on heterosexual divorce are no longer an issue. However, another issue which has the capacity to divide States once again concerns recognition of same-sex divorce.[102] The statistics for same-sex divorces show that numbers are rising.[103] The terminology within the Convention is not gendered and therefore it is suggested that same-sex divorce could be supported, at least in Contracting States with no public policy objection to it, through the adoption of a good practice guide to interpreting the Convention.

Even without that option, States who permit same-sex divorce will find that Article 17 of the 1970 Convention allows for flexibility. Article 17 allows Contracting States to apply rules which are more favourable than the Convention, leaving them free to recognise *talaqs* as they see fit, and same-sex divorces, and divorces granted by a court nominated in a choice of court agreement (even if the court did not have jurisdiction under Articles 2–5). It does not guarantee recognition in another Contracting State, but it does allow for societal changes without making the Convention redundant.

[96] Explanatory Report (n 2) 3. Beaumont and Moir (n 23) 273 also see these as a set-back.

[97] See n 95.

[98] Art 24: 'reserve the right not to apply this Convention to a divorce or to a legal separation obtained before the date on which, in relation to that State, the Convention comes into force'.

[99] Art 21: 'reserve the right to refuse to recognise a legal separation when, at the time it was obtained, one of the spouses was a national of a Contracting State whose law did not provide for legal separation'.

[100] (n 2).

[101] Ibid.

[102] See (n 15). Other issues such as non-gendered divorce and divorces in polygamous marriage also need to be considered but are beyond the scope of this chapter.

[103] 'Same-sex couples have been able to marry in England and Wales from March 2014. Since then, the number of divorces of same-sex couples increased each year from very small numbers in 2015 when the first divorces took place, to more than 800 in 2019, reflecting the increasing size of the same-sex married population in England and Wales' see: www.ons.gov.uk/peoplepopulationandcommunity/birthsdeathsandmarriages/divorce/bulletins/divorcesinenglandandwales/2019.

F. Conclusion

The Convention has stood the test of time well. There is balance in this Convention to protect cultural and religious diversity. Article 6 is balanced with the reservation in Article 19 as well as the public policy exception in Article 10. In contrast, for those States who wish to go beyond the scope of the Convention, the flexibility in Article 17 allows for societal change, meaning that a bare *talaq*, same-sex divorce or divorce jurisdiction agreement could be recognised by a Contracting State to this Convention if that is permissible within their own law.

A minimum harmonisation approach makes sense for a global instrument on divorce. The Convention was skilfully drafted with flexible terminology like 'proceedings' and 'obtained', allowing the Convention to evolve with societal changes. Apart from encouraging new Contracting States and the acceptance of accessions by existing State Parties it is also recommended that the Conference creates a best practice guide to enhance uniform interpretation of the Convention, including on what constitutes 'proceedings' and the accommodation of religious, transnational and same-sex divorces. As will be discussed in section III below, the 'glittering prize' of recognising foreign divorces to minimise limping marriages is one which is still worth striving for. This Convention has the potential to operate well, and it is encouraging to see it on the HCCH's radar.[104]

III. Necessity for a Renewed Focus on the 1970 Divorce Convention and a Complementary Convention on Conflicts of Jurisdiction

A. Introduction

Double and mixed conventions requiring harmonisation of direct rules of jurisdiction are notoriously difficult to agree[105] and therefore a realistic proposal is for the HCCH to focus on encouraging the widespread adoption of the 1970 Convention (a single Convention), along with guidance on how it should be interpreted, and to consider creating a new Convention on Conflicts of Jurisdiction on matters of Divorce.[106] The value of revitalisation of the existing Convention, and the feasibility and utility of a new Convention on Conflicts of Jurisdiction, are considered below.

B. Contemporary Relevance of the 1970 Convention: Necessity for a Renewed Commitment to its Goals

The 1970 Convention was presented as a response to limping marriages as a result of increased migration in the aftermath of the Second World War.[107] By this metric, the need for international

[104] See n 29 above.

[105] See nn 26 and 37 above.

[106] It seems from the Council Conclusions and Decisions of March 2021 (n 29) para 9(b) that the best prospect of success in the Jurisdiction Project on civil or commercial matters is on conflicts of jurisdiction. See also Ardavan Arzandeh and Matthias Lehmann, 'Conflicts of Jurisdiction', ch 30 in this book.

[107] Anton (n 14) 622.

cooperation on divorce recognition is even more acute now than it was then. The advent of globalisation has brought about migration levels far beyond those in contemplation in the late 1960s – and it is estimated that in 2019, the number of persons residing outside their country of birth was four times higher than it was in 1960.[108] These levels of movement and displacement are likely to lead to a much higher incidence of limping marriages. Although it is true that (ex-) cohabitees are gaining legal rights and protections in many jurisdictions,[109] and there is a growing tendency to focus on 'fact' rather than 'form' in family law,[110] marital status still matters a great deal – and many rights and obligations may be contingent on the existence of a valid marriage (and therefore on the recognition of a prior divorce). Further, while there has been a widespread relaxation of domestic divorce restrictions since the 1960s, recognition policies do not necessarily keep step, and many countries retain relatively stringent recognition rules alongside liberal internal laws on divorce.[111]

A renewed focus in The Hague on the 1970 Convention might energise State authorities to lift the 'heavy burdens' of limping marital status from the shoulders of 'real people already struggling with the human cost of marital breakdown'.[112]

The European Court of Human Rights has been giving increasing emphasis to the need to secure cross-border continuity of personal status as an obligation under Article 8 of the European Convention on Human Rights (ECHR) (the right to respect for family life), both with respect to family decrees issued in ECHR Contracting States and those issued in third countries[113] – and it is possible that the elevation of cross-border status-recognition into a human rights obligation may assist in focusing political minds on the desirability of ratifying the 1970 Convention.

C. A New Convention on Conflicts of Jurisdiction in Divorce

There appears to be broad agreement on the undesirability of split actions (in which different aspects of the divorce are dealt with in different fora),[114] and on the need to combat the 'rush to court' whereby one party steals a march on the other and anchors the proceedings in an objectively inappropriate forum which serves the applicant's own interests.[115] The difficulties entailed in any direct harmonisation of jurisdiction have been discussed above; however, it may be possible to develop conflict of jurisdiction rules to tackle forum shopping and fragmentation of proceedings.

[108] See J Chamie, 'International Migration amid a World in Crisis' (2020) 8 *Journal on Migration and Human Security* 230, 232.

[109] Estin (n 4) 486; J Scherpe, *The Present and Future of European Family Law* (Edward Elgar 2016) 69–76.

[110] D Martiny, 'Objectives and Values of (Private) International Law in Family Law' in J Meeusen et al (eds), *International Family Law for the European Union* (Intersentia 2007) 78.

[111] See, eg, Estin (n 4) 504, 517 referring to the non-recognition in the US of divorces obtained by US residents in the jurisdiction of nationality; also A Dutta, 'Brexit and International Family Law from a Continental Perspective' (2017) 29 *Child and Family Law Quarterly* 199, 204 anticipating UK divorces facing potential non-recognition on the European continent post-Brexit. (For an overview of the often complex criteria applied by EU Member States in determining the recognition of third-country divorces, see the Annex to the Asser Institute Report on *Cross-Border Proceedings in Family Law Matters Before National Courts and CJEU* (2018) 99 ff, available at: www.asser.nl.)

[112] See *H v H* [2015] IESC 7 (O'Donnell J) [4]; also Estin (n 4) 517: 'the limping divorce … has the potential to cause enormous difficulty'.

[113] See *Wagner v Luxembourg* [2007] ECHR 1213 (adoption); *Negrepontis-Gianissis v Greece* [2013] ECHR 1239 (adoption); *Mennesson v France* [2014] ECHR 664 (order of parentage following surrogacy); *Orlandi v Italy* [2017] ECHR 1153 (same-sex marriage).

[114] See n 23.

[115] EU Commission (n 15) 14.

i. Declining Jurisdiction

State Party agreement on the declining of jurisdiction may assist in steering the spouses towards a court which is *forum conveniens* for divorce and all satellite proceedings. As far as the declining of jurisdiction is concerned, civil law countries traditionally lean in favour of a *lis pendens* doctrine which prioritises the court first seised, while common law countries prefer a flexible *forum non conveniens* discretion, and this divergence of legal tradition can inhibit international cooperation. However, the interim text of the Judgments Convention from 2001 illustrates how it is possible to marry these two approaches, by giving priority to the court first seised but allowing it to decline jurisdiction in favour of the court second seised where it is clearly a more appropriate forum.[116] The 1970 Convention includes a *lis pendens* provision in Article 12 but this tends to favour the court first seised as per the civilian tradition[117] and does not provide a robust mechanism for the management of parallel proceedings. The inclusion of a transfer mechanism in Articles 8 and 9 of the 1996 Hague Protection of Children Convention (and Article 15 Brussels IIa) illustrates the capacity for compromise on this question and perhaps a recognition of the need for flexibility in responding to the complex needs of international families[118] It is also noteworthy that the 2019 GEDIP proposal for a Regulation on divorce jurisdiction, recognition and applicable law includes a provision on transfer.[119] A Hague Convention on Conflicts of Divorce Jurisdiction might also allow for direct communication between courts in participating fora[120] and for a mandatory time-frame for any stay in favour of the court second seised (to avoid excessive delay).[121] In the divorce context, where ancillary satellite proceedings are perhaps more common than in the commercial sphere,[122] it might be advisable to avoid the language of 'exceptionality' in describing the circumstances in which the court first seised might grant a stay.[123]

ii. Privatisation of Divorce

Negotiations will also be complicated by the shift towards administrative or private divorce, since in this context it is not meaningful to speak of a court exercising or declining jurisdiction. It is difficult to see how a *lis pendens* or transfer mechanism can function in the absence of court involvement. This question was not satisfactorily resolved in the recent negotiations on the Recast of the Brussels IIa Regulation: while the new Regulation 2019/1111 makes special provision for EU mutual recognition of extra-judicial divorces,[124] the implications for jurisdictional verification

[116] P Beaumont, '*Forum Non Conveniens* and the EU Rules on Conflicts of Jurisdiction: A Possible Global Solution' [2018] *Revue Critique de droit international privé* 447, 450–52. This solution is, once again, under active consideration in the context of the Hague Jurisdiction Project (in civil or commercial matters): see Report on the Jurisdiction Project (n 27) 6–7.

[117] Explanatory Report (n 2) 25, para 50.

[118] See Costanza Honorati and Mary Keyes, 'Parental Responsibility, Custody and Access', ch 33 in this book.

[119] See Art 10 GEDIP proposal (n 12).

[120] See Report on the Jurisdiction Project (n 27) 19–20.

[121] See Beaumont (n 116) 452.

[122] Ní Shúilleabháin (n 21) 216.

[123] The use of an exceptionality criterion has also been challenged in the civil/commercial context of the Hague Jurisdiction Project: see Report on the Jurisdiction Project (n 27) 8.

[124] Arts 64–68 of Council Regulation (EU) 2019/1111 of 25 June 2019 on jurisdiction, the recognition and enforcement of decisions in matrimonial matters and the matters of parental responsibility and on international child abduction [2019] OJ L178/1.

and *lis pendens* are not fully worked out. Those negotiating any future HCCH Convention on conflicts of jurisdiction in relation to divorce would have to consider whether the transfer mechanism could come into play at the point where judicial authorities do get involved, even if it is only to regulate the financial aspects of the divorce.

IV. Conclusion

The Hague Conference has succeeded in establishing a successful system of international law where children are concerned but the same is not yet true of adult relationships and divorce.[125] As it stands, the 1970 Convention, which has been sorely neglected by both Contracting States and until recently the Hague Conference, remains effective and should not be dismissed due to its age and the low number of Contracting States. If a new international instrument is to be considered, then it is recommended that a new Convention on conflicts of jurisdiction relating to divorce would be a complementary and helpful addition to the 1970 Convention on Recognition of Divorces and Legal Separation.

[125] Estin (n 4) 485–86.

33

Parental Responsibility, Custody and Access

COSTANZA HONORATI AND MARY KEYES

I. Introduction

Disputes about cross-border parental responsibility, custody and access[1] have become common due to the substantial increase in family mobility. Diversity in national laws that determine the outcome of cross-border parental responsibility disputes incentivises parallel proceedings, which inhibit the amicable, timely, efficient and effective resolution of disputes. The need for a more coordinated, simple, clear and consistent legal response has led to significant developments at the multilateral level in the 1996 Hague Convention on Jurisdiction, Applicable Law, Recognition, Enforcement and Cooperation in Respect of Parental Responsibility and Measures for the Protection of Children (1996 Convention).[2]

The 1996 Convention has brought about significant changes to private international law in the area of parental responsibility. This Convention gives prominence to the child's habitual residence in terms of jurisdiction, recognition of foreign measures and the applicable law. Like other modern Hague children's Conventions,[3] it requires substantial cooperation between the authorities of Contracting States.

This chapter focuses on the 1996 Convention and is structured as follows: section II describes the 1996 Convention, considering its provisions relating to jurisdiction, recognition of foreign measures and the applicable law. Section III addresses the European Union (EU) regime, as established by the Brussels IIa Regulation and its 2019 recast, focusing on some analogies and differences between the Convention and the EU regime. Section IV concludes that the 1996 Convention and the EU regime significantly improve many aspects of private international law in the area of parental responsibility.

[1] A range of terms is used to describe the concepts of parental responsibility. Recently, the term 'parental responsibility' has been widely adopted to encompass both custody and access.

[2] The Convention entered into force on 1 January 2002 and as at November 2021 it is binding on 53 States: www.hcch.net/en/instruments/conventions/status-table/?cid=70.

[3] eg, Hague Convention on the Civil Aspects of International Child Abduction (1980 Convention); Hague Convention on Protection of Children and Co-operation in Respect of Intercountry Adoption 1993 (1993 Convention).

II. The 1996 Child Protection Convention

The 1996 Convention[4] is comprehensive for private international law, in that it contains provisions relating to jurisdiction, applicable law and the recognition and enforcement of 'measures of protection' in relation to a child.[5] The Convention generally uses the term 'parental responsibility', which is defined broadly in Article 1(2) to include: 'parental authority, or any analogous relationship of authority determining the rights, powers and responsibilities of parents, guardians or other legal representatives in relation to the person or the property of the child'. The Convention does not define 'measures of protection', but Article 3 gives examples of the kinds of measures which are within the Convention's scope,[6] and Article 4 identifies 10 issues which fall outside its scope.[7] The Convention's scope is broad: it 'covers just about everything that affects a child and almost every aspect of parental responsibility, with some limited exceptions',[8] including rights of custody and rights of access (Article 3(b)).

The 1996 Convention forms part of a set of Hague children's Conventions, with which it was designed to integrate. For example, its scope excludes adoption and maintenance, each of which is the subject of specific conventions.[9] The priority that it gives to the courts of the Contracting State in which the child is habitually resident as the presumptively appropriate courts to determine disputes concerning children supports the scheme of the 1980 Convention;[10] and its provisions allocating jurisdiction in child abduction cases (Article 7) are consistent with the 1980 Convention. Like the other modern Hague children's Conventions, it encourages the amicable resolution of disputes (Article 31(b), and it mandates and sets the main frame for cooperation between Central Authorities of the Contracting States (Article 29 and Chapter V).[11]

[4] For detailed analysis, see P Lagarde, *Explanatory Report on the Convention of 19 October 1996 on jurisdiction, applicable law, recognition, enforcement and co-operation in respect of parental responsibility and measures for the protection of children, Proceedings of the Eighteenth Session (1996), Tome II – Protection of children* (Hague Conference on Private International Law 1996) (Explanatory Report); and Hague Conference on Private International Law, *Practical Handbook on the Operation of the 1996 Hague Child Protection Convention* (The Hague 2014) (Practical Handbook), both available at the HCCH Child Protection section: www.hcch.net/en/instruments/conventions/specialised-sections/child-protection). See also N Lowe and M Nicholls, *The 1996 Hague Convention on the Protection of Children* (Jordan 2012).

[5] The 1996 Convention covers measures of protection of the child's person and of the child's property. As this chapter concerns parental responsibility, we shall not address issues relating to the child's property. The 1996 Convention applies to children 'from the moment of their birth until they reach 18 years': Art 2.

[6] Orders for the return of children to, or prohibiting the removal of children from, their habitual residence are 'measures of protection' for this Convention: *In re J (A Child) (Reunite International Child Abduction Centre intervening)* [2015] UKSC 70, [23].

[7] These include the determination of parental status, adoption and maintenance obligations: Art 4(a), (b) and (e).

[8] M Nicholls, 'Australia and the 1996 Hague Child Protection Convention' (2013) 3 *Family Law Review* 123, 123. See likewise, L Silberman, 'Co-Operative Efforts in Private International Law on Behalf of Children: The Hague Children's Conventions' (2006) 323 *Hague Collected Courses* 263, 398.

[9] The 1993 Convention; Hague Convention on the International Recovery of Child Support and Other Forms of Family Maintenance 2007.

[10] The 1980 Convention requires children to be returned to the place where they were habitually resident at the time of the wrongful removal or retention: Art 12 (subject to the Art 13 exceptions). See Maria Caterina Baruffi and Jayne Holliday, 'Child Abduction', ch 34 in this book.

[11] Contracting States are required to designate a Central Authority (Art 29) which is responsible for taking, recognising and enforcing measures under the Convention (Ch V). Cooperation between judicial authorities is facilitated by the International Hague Network of Judges as well as by the Convention's provisions requiring cooperation between Central Authorities. Direct judicial communication has also been used, eg, in *Bunyon & Lewis (No 3)* [2013] FamCA 888, [207]–[210] (between the courts of Australia and the Netherlands).

A. Jurisdiction

The jurisdictional principles are the foundation for the Convention's principles of recognition and enforcement and the applicable law. The jurisdictional principles focus almost exclusively on the child's connections, particularly of habitual residence. The courts of the place of the child's habitual residence have pre-eminent jurisdiction to take measures, including those dealing with parental responsibility, with very limited exceptions. The Convention contains a *lis pendens* provision, and enables the transfer of proceedings between the authorities of Contracting States.

i. Grounds of Jurisdiction

The principal jurisdictional provision of the Convention is Article 5. Article 5(1) provides that 'The judicial or administrative authorities of the Contracting State of the habitual residence of the child have jurisdiction to take measures directed to the protection of the child's person or property'.[12] There are only two exceptions.[13] The first recognises a jurisdiction of necessity for authorities of the Contracting States of the place in which children are present in three limited circumstances: children who are refugees; or who are 'internationally displaced'; or whose habitual residence cannot be established (Article 6).[14]

The second exception recognises the jurisdiction of the authorities of the Contracting State exercising jurisdiction in an application for divorce or legal separation, if at least one parent who has parental responsibility habitually resides in the place where the application is being determined, and both parents (or any other person who has parental responsibility) accept the jurisdiction of those authorities to take measures directed to the person of the child (Article 10).

Article 11(1) provides that the authorities of the Contracting States of the place where the child is present have a limited jurisdiction in case of urgency to take emergency measures.[15] The UK Supreme Court has held that when a court exercises this jurisdiction, it should be used to support the primary jurisdiction of the authorities of the child's habitual residence, and that it should not 'interfere in issues that are more properly dealt with in the home country'.[16] This jurisdiction may also be used by the courts of refuge in cases of international child abduction to order measures that will safeguard children's best interests on return to their place of habitual residence,[17] pending any decision on custody by the authorities of that place.

Although the principal jurisdictional provision is simple and clear, it relies on the concept of 'habitual residence'. As for other Hague Conventions, the 1996 Convention does not define

[12] Unlike Brussels IIa, this Convention does not state the time at which the child's habitual residence is to be determined, except in cases of wrongful removal or retention of the child, in which case, the relevant time is 'immediately before' the removal or retention: Art 7(1). It has been held that otherwise the relevant date is the date of the hearing: *In re NH (A Child)* [2015] EWHC 2299, [24] (citing Explanatory Report (n 4) paras 38–43), *Bunyon & Lewis* (n 11) [185].

[13] In addition, the authorities of Contracting States which are not competent under Arts 5 and 6 may acquire jurisdiction if proceedings are transferred to them under Arts 8 and 9. See below, section II.A.ii.

[14] Rarely, it may be impossible to establish a child's habitual residence: eg *In re NH (A Child)* (n 12).

[15] This includes where children are present because they have been wrongfully removed to or retained in a Contracting State: eg *Bunyon & Lewis* (n 11) [117]. Such emergency measures lapse when the courts designated under the primary jurisdictional provisions take relevant measures: Art 11(2).

[16] *In re J (A Child)* (n 6) [34].

[17] Ibid, [38]; Lowe and Nicholls (n 4) para 3.31.

this term. The Practical Handbook states: '[i]t is an autonomous concept and should be interpreted in light of the objectives of the Convention'.[18] There is surprisingly little jurisprudence or commentary on the meaning of habitual residence in the context of the 1996 Convention, in comparison to the 1980 Convention. Within the EU, habitual residence is interpreted uniformly within Brussels IIa which regulates both child abduction and parental responsibility.[19] It is not settled that the same applies for the Hague family Conventions. There are two competing views. The first is that habitual residence should be interpreted consistently for all the Hague family Conventions, which are designed to interact coherently.[20] It would frustrate the operation of the 1980 Convention if a child was held to have a different habitual residence for the purposes of the 1996 Convention. The second view is that 'habitual residence may be subject to different considerations depending on whether the vantage point is from the 1996 Convention or the 1980 Convention',[21] given the different contexts in which the term is used in these Conventions.[22] Although some commentators and judges support the second view, such statements of support simply suggest that different considerations might be relevant to the interpretation of habitual residence for these two Conventions without identifying those considerations, or explaining how they might lead to different results. This view ignores the fact that both Conventions can be relevant in cases of child abduction: it would be problematic if the term was interpreted differently in the same case, for the purposes of the different Conventions.

It is difficult to see in principle why the context of the 1996 Convention *should* lead to a different result, and difficult to envisage in practice situations in which a child might have different habitual residences for the purposes of the two Conventions. Applying the same interpretation to both contexts is preferable because it is easier to understand and simpler to apply. In our view, the term should be interpreted consistently for both Conventions, and the substantial jurisprudence and commentary on the meaning of habitual residence in the context of the 1980 Convention should be used for the 1996 Convention.

The determination of a child's habitual residence is a question of fact which depends on the circumstances of each case. There is a growing consensus that determining a child's habitual residence requires reference to objective factors indicating the extent of the child's integration into the 'social and family environment',[23] and that the parents' intentions are not determinative, but rather constitute 'an "indicator" capable of complementing a body of other consistent evidence'.[24] The jurisprudence of the EU Court of Justice, interpreting the term in the context of the Brussels IIa regime, has been influential in developing a uniform international interpretation of the term 'habitual residence'.[25]

[18] Practical Handbook (n 4) 40, para 4.5.

[19] See below, section III.A.i.

[20] See *A v A (Children: Habitual Residence)* [2013] UKSC 60, [35], [54].

[21] Lowe and Nicholls (n 4) [3.7] (referred to with approval in *Bunyon & Lewis* (n 11) [188]). See also *Practical Handbook* (n 4) 40, para 4.6; Nicholls (n 8) 127.

[22] Practical Handbook (n 4) 173, para 13.84.

[23] C-111/17 PPU *OL v PQ* EU:C:2017:436, [42] (CJEU), cited with approval by the Supreme Court of Canada in *Office of the Children's Lawyer v Balev* [2018] 1 SCR 398, [51] and by the US Supreme Court in *Monasky v Taglieri* 589 US __, 8 (2020).

[24] *OL*, ibid, cited with approval by the Supreme Court of Canada in *Balev* ibid, [45]. See also *A v A* [2013] UKSC 60, [54]. Nonetheless, the intention of the parents could be decisive when they have recently agreed on where the child should be habitually resident and the child is present there: Permanent Bureau, 'Revised draft Practical Guide: Cross-border recognition and enforcement of agreements reached in the course of family matters involving children' (2019), available at: assets.hcch.net/docs/97681b48-86bb-4af4-9ced-a42f58380f82.pdf, Annex, Explanatory Note, paras 130–31.

[25] See above (nn 23–24).

ii. Lis pendens *and Transfer of Proceedings*

While the 1996 Convention 'is intended to centralise jurisdiction in the authorities of the State of the child's habitual residence and avoid all competition of authorities having concurrent jurisdiction',[26] there may be cases where the authorities of more than one Contracting State will be competent. In general, jurisdictional conflicts are resolved by *lis pendens*. The competent authorities of a Contracting State 'must abstain from exercising this jurisdiction' if, at the time proceedings were commenced, a request for corresponding measures of protection was under consideration by the competent authorities of another Contracting State (Article 13).

The Convention also enables the transfer of proceedings from the competent authority of one Contracting State to an authority of certain other Contracting States.[27] The transfer can be initiated either by the authority which is competent under Articles 5 and 6, or by an authority of another Contracting State which regards itself as better placed to resolve the dispute.

Article 8(1) provides that an authority which is competent under Articles 5 or 6 which

> considers that the authority of another Contracting State would be better placed in the particular case to assess the best interests of the child, may either
>
> – request that other authority, directly or with the assistance of the Central Authority of its State, to assume jurisdiction to take such measures of protection as it considers to be necessary, or
> – suspend consideration of the case and invite the parties to introduce such a request before the authority of that other State.

The Contracting States the authorities of which may be requested are those of the child's nationality; or the courts of which 'are seised of an application for divorce or legal separation of the child's parents, or for annulment of their marriage'; and 'with which the child has a substantial connection' (Article 8(2)). If the authority requested considers that it is in the best interests of the child for it to assume jurisdiction in place of the authority which has jurisdiction under the principal provisions, it may do so (Article 8(4)).

Under Article 9(1), authorities of the States listed in Article 8(2), if they 'consider that they are better placed … to assess the child's best interests' can initiate a request to the competent authority of the place of the child's habitual residence to be authorised to exercise jurisdiction,[28] or can invite the parties to make such a request. If the request is accepted, the requesting authority may exercise jurisdiction in place of the authority of the child's habitual residence (Article 9(3)).

The provision on transfer of proceedings may be used to balance the limited scope of party autonomy in the Convention.[29] For example, parents may agree to confer jurisdiction on one of the Contracting States listed in Article 8(2) in order to have the case decided in a court other than that of the child's habitual residence. But even so, the parents' autonomy is constrained as transfer is subject to strict requirements. These are that either the transferring authority determines that the authority of the Contracting State agreed upon by the parents is better placed to assess the child's best interests and that such authority assumes jurisdiction; or that the authority of the

[26] Explanatory Report (n 4) para 37.
[27] Ibid, para 52.
[28] *Kubat & Kubat* [2019] FamCA 671 (Australian court initiated a request to Turkish courts); *Re M & L (Children)* [2016] EWHC 2535 (English court initiated a request to Norwegian courts); *Bunyon & Lewis* (n 11) (Australian court refused to initiate a request to Dutch courts).
[29] As already noted, party autonomy is relevant under Art 10 (see above section II.A.i).

Contracting State to which the proceedings is to be transferred determines that it is better placed to assess the child's best interests and that the authority of the Contracting State of the child's habitual residence accepts the request to transfer jurisdiction.[30]

B. Recognition and Enforcement of Foreign Decisions

The Convention contains a simple scheme for recognition and enforcement which has been described as the 'real core of, and the real force of, the 1996 Convention'.[31] It requires the authorities of Contracting States to recognise (Article 23(1)) and enforce (Article 26(1)) measures taken by authorities of other Contracting States under the Convention, with limited exceptions, set out in Articles 23(2) and 26(3) respectively. Indirectly, therefore, the Convention upholds the jurisdiction of the authorities of the child's habitual residence.

Under Article 23(1), foreign measures are automatically recognised 'by operation of law'; but Article 24 also enables 'any interested person' to request a decision from the competent authorities of a Contracting State about whether a foreign measure will be recognised. If measures require enforcement in a Contracting State other than that in which they were made, an interested person can request a declaration of enforceability, or registration, of the measures (Article 26),[32] and Contracting States are obliged 'to apply to the declaration of enforceability or registration a simple and rapid procedure'.[33] The declaration procedure is often used in relation to urgent measures taken in child abduction cases.

The party against whom the measure is invoked must establish the exceptions to recognition and enforcement of a foreign measure. The exceptions are where:

- The authority which took the measure lacked jurisdiction (Article 23(2)(a)).
- Except in cases of urgency, the child (Article 23(2)(b)),[34] or a person asserting parental responsibility (Article 23(2)(c)),[35] was denied an opportunity to be heard.
- Recognition would be 'manifestly contrary to the public policy of the requested State, taking into account the best interests of the child' (Article 23(2)(d)).[36]
- The measure conflicts with a later measure taken in a non-Contracting State of the child's habitual residence (Article 23(2)(e).
- The procedure in Article 33 was not followed (Article 23(2)(f).[37]

These grounds are exhaustive, but not mandatory: the authorities of the requested State are not obliged to refuse recognition on any of these bases.[38] Merits review is not permitted (Article 27).

[30] See Revised draft Practical Guide (n 24), para 135.

[31] Nicholls (n 8) 129.

[32] One difficulty with declarations of enforceability is that courts of different countries express measures differently: see *Merrick & Wellington* [2014] FamCA 514, [34].

[33] In some cases, it has been noted that the State of recognition or enforcement has not established a simple and rapid procedure: *State Central Authority & Shanli* [2018] FamCA 715.

[34] The requirement that the child should have the opportunity to be heard must be part of the 'fundamental principles of procedure' of the requested State: *NG v OG* [2014] EWHC 4182 (Fam).

[35] This exception only applies at 'the request of any person claiming that the measure infringes his or her parental responsibility' (Art 23(2)(c)). See *Uhd v McKay* [2019] EWHC 1239 (Fam), [103].

[36] See *U (Children)* [2014] EWHC 4535 (Fam), [18]; *Uhd v McKay* [2019] EWHC 1239 (Fam), [78], [104].

[37] Art 33 sets out requirements that the competent authority must follow, if it considers placing 'the child in a foster family or institutional care, or the provision of care by kafala or an analogous institution' in another Contracting State.

[38] Explanatory Report (n 4) para 121; *F v M* [2018] EWHC 2106 (Fam) [63].

C. Applicable Law

In general, the Convention designates the internal law[39] of the forum as the applicable law (Article 15(1)). The jurisdictional rules will usually lead to the application of the law of the place of the child's habitual residence.

The general rule is subject to two exceptions. First, the competent authority 'may exceptionally apply or take into consideration the law of another State with which the situation has a substantial connection' if the protection of the child requires it (Article 15(2)). Second, the competent authority may disapply the applicable law if it 'would be manifestly contrary to public policy' (Article 22). Although the general choice of law rule designates forum law, Articles 16 and 17 provide that the law of the place of the child's habitual residence applies for the attribution or extinction of parental responsibility by operation of law, and for the exercise of parental responsibility.

The Convention is universal for applicable law: its provisions in relation to the applicable law apply even if the law designated is that of a non-Contracting State (Article 20).

III. The Impact on the EU: The 2003 Brussels IIa Regulation and its 2019 Recast

The 1996 Convention has promoted greater harmonisation of private international law in the area of parental responsibility, including because of its influence in the EU. In this section, we address some of the more prominent similarities and differences between the Convention and the Brussels II regime.

A. Twofold Impact on EU Law

The 1996 Convention has had a significant impact on EU law, showing its influence in two ways. First, it had an impact on the drafting of the EU rules in the field of parental responsibility and family matters. The Convention's negotiation history corresponds in time with the negotiation of the old Brussels II Regulation,[40] then repealed in the Brussels IIa Regulation on jurisdiction, recognition and enforcement of judgments in matrimonial matters and on parental responsibility matters.[41] This instrument was recently recast through the Brussels IIb Regulation, in force as

[39] In the Convention's chapter on applicable law, 'the term "law" means the law in force in a State other than its choice of law rules' (Art 21(1)). But note the exception in Art 16(2).

[40] Council Regulation (EC) 1347/2000 of 29 May 2000 on jurisdiction and the recognition and enforcement of judgments in matrimonial matters and matters of parental responsibility for children of both spouses [2000] OJ L160/19–36).

[41] Council Regulation (EC) 2201/2003 of 27 November 2003 [2003] OJ L338/1–29). Literature on Brussels IIa, which has been applicable for more than 15 years in 28 States, is immense. For general overviews, see N Lowe, M Everall and M Nicholls (eds), *The New Brussels II Regulation. A Supplement to International Movement of Children* (Jordan 2005); K Boele-Woelki and C Gonzalez Beilfuss (eds), *Brussels II bis: Its Impact and Application in the Member States* (Intersentia 2007); C Honorati (ed), *Jurisdiction in Matrimonial Matters, Parental Responsibility and International Abduction* (Giappichelli-Peter Lang 2017); U Magnus and P Mankowski (eds), *Brussels II bis Regulation, European Commentaries on Private International Law*, 2nd edn (Sellier 2017).

from 1 August 2022,[42] which will substantially improve the overall coordination with the 1996 Convention. Although indirect, such impact has been substantial. Because of the parallel drafting history, similar solutions are to be found in the two instruments and the core of the two instruments – jurisdiction in parental responsibility matters – is indeed very similar. It should, however, be recalled that Brussels IIa also covers decisions on matrimonial matters (divorce, separation and annulment), as well as international abduction of children.

In principle, the 1996 Convention applies also to EU Member States, albeit with a limited scope, as will be seen. Following the treaty-making power of the EU in private international law matters, over which the EU has exclusive competence, EU Member States require a formal authorisation by the EU to become Parties to a Convention (where the EU cannot become a Party to the Convention as an REIO).[43] Today, all 27 EU Member States, which amounts to more than half of the 53 Contracting States, are Parties to the 1996 Convention. However, its practical application is to a large extent reduced because, following the principle of primacy of EU law, the above-mentioned Regulation has priority over any other legal rule, including international conventions.[44] Brussels IIa and IIb therefore in principle displace the 1996 Convention in their own scope of application.

The peculiar relation to the 1996 Convention is highlighted by a specific provision, Article 61 of the Brussels IIa Regulation, which provides a simple and straightforward rule. In regard to jurisdiction rules, the Regulation will only apply when the child is habitually resident in the territory of an EU Member State. Accordingly, EU courts will apply the residual rule envisaged by the 1996 Convention (Article 6) to children who find themselves in the EU both when they are resident in a State which is a Party to the 1996 Convention, as well as when they are neither resident in an EU Member State nor in a State Party to the 1996 Convention.[45] Recent case law has also clarified that when a child, originally resident within the EU, was abducted to a third State Party to the 1996 Convention and has acquired his or her habitual residence in such State, the 1996 Convention applies.[46]

Brussels IIb seeks a better coordination with the 1996 Convention and provides for other cases where, as an exception to the general rule, the Convention shall prevail notwithstanding that the child's habitual residence is within the EU. In fact, Article 10 of the Convention shall apply to any agreement which confers jurisdiction on a State which is a Party to the 1996 Convention (and not an EU Member State); similarly, Articles 8 and 9 of the Convention shall apply in regard to the transfer of proceedings from an EU court to any court of a State Party to the 1996 Convention; finally, Article 13 of the Convention shall apply when proceedings relating to parental responsibility are pending before a court of a State Party to the 1996 Convention, which was instituted before parallel proceedings were brought in a court of an EU Member State.

[42] Council Regulation (EU) 2019/1111 of 25 June 2019 on jurisdiction, the recognition and enforcement of decisions in matrimonial matters and the matters of parental responsibility, and on international child abduction (recast) [2019] OJ L178/1–115.

[43] See Council Decision of 5 June 2008 [2008] OJ L151/36-48. It will therefore be for the EU to decide if its Member States will object, or not, to the accession of a new Contracting State under Art 58(3) of the 1996 Convention. Accession, or the objection thereto, will then produce its effects against all EU Member States.

[44] Mention should be made of the special relation to the 1980 Convention. Indeed Art 11 of Brussels IIa makes express reference to this Convention in regard to the application for the return of an abducted child. The conventional regime is then complemented and reinforced by a set of special rules (see Art 11(2–8)) which modify the Convention in intra-EU abduction cases.

[45] This leaves very little room for the application of Art 13 of Brussels IIa, a provision for refugee and internationally displaced children which mirrors Art 6 of the Hague Convention, which is consequently limited to displaced children who were resident in a different EU Member State. Brussels IIb clarifies this point at recital 25.

[46] See C-603/20 PPU *SS v MCP* EU:C:2021:231.

The Regulation shall apply to recognition and enforcement of all decisions that are given by a court of a Member State, irrespective of where the child's habitual residence is, and therefore also when this is in a Contracting State of the Convention. The 1996 Convention will instead be applicable when the State of origin is a Party to the Convention (and not an EU Member State).

Finally, the Convention regains its full operational scope in regard to the applicable law, given that this matter is not dealt with by Brussels IIa or Brussels IIb.

B. The Same Ground of Competence: The Child's Habitual Residence

As previously mentioned, the two instruments have a similar approach and structure. As in the 1996 Convention, also in Brussels IIa the main criterion is the habitual residence of the child, irrespective of his or her nationality. This is no surprise, given that the child's habitual residence expresses the quest for proximity and is regarded as the procedural expression of the principle of the best interests of the child. As is often the case within EU law, such notion is to be given an autonomous interpretation, which excludes any reference to national law. Although not defined by the legislature, the child's habitual residence has acquired an acceptably clear meaning through the many decisions of the Court of Justice of the European Union (CJEU). Interestingly, preliminary rulings have been made mainly in the context of parental responsibility cases and much less in the context of child abduction cases.[47] The CJEU does not seem to attach any weight to the different occasion and procedural background, which looks reasonable as jurisdiction lies by the very same rule.

The child's habitual residence thus corresponds to the place which reflects 'some degree of integration by the child in a social and family environment'.[48] Similarly to what happens within the Convention, the criterion is construed as a factual notion, to be established on the basis of the circumstances specific to each individual case. The physical presence of the child in the territory of a Member State, although a necessary requisite, is to be complemented by other factors which show that such presence is not temporary or intermittent, such as the duration, regularity, conditions and reasons for the stay in the territory of such State, the child's nationality, the place and conditions of attendance at school, the linguistic knowledge of the child and the family and social relationships of the child in that State. The list is however not exhaustive and other objective factors may acquire weight.

While the basic features of this notion are very similar to what is envisaged in the framework of the 1996 Convention, a difference between the two attains to the weight to be given to the intention of the parties, whether of the child or the parents. Because of the strong quest for predictability and certainty, the intention of parents within the EU is granted a residual role and will acquire relevance only if it is manifested by tangible steps. In other words, 'mere' intention is not decisive in itself, being mainly construed as a clue for a better understanding of more tangible elements.[49]

[47] Of the eight decisions taken by the CJEU regarding a child's habitual residence as at the date of writing (September 2020), only three of them (C-497/10 PPU *Mercredi* EU:C:2010:829; *OL* (n 23); and C-376/14 PPU *C* EU:C:2014:2268) arose from an alleged international abduction case.

[48] See, among many, C-523/07 *A* EU:C:2009:225, paras 37–38; *Mercredi*, ibid, paras 44–49; and *OL*, ibid, paras 42–43.

[49] *A*, ibid, para 40; *C* (n 47) para 52; *OL*, ibid, para 47; and C-512/17 *HR* EU:C:2018:513, para 64. See Susanne Gössl and Ruth Lamont, 'Connecting Factors', ch 4 in this book for a critique of this approach.

C. Prorogation of Competence: Wider Scope for Party Autonomy

A head of jurisdiction of great practical importance is the so-called prorogated competence, which, under strict conditions and based on a (limited) party autonomy, allows parental responsibility issues to be brought before a court other than that of the child's habitual residence. While in some respects reflecting Article 10 of the Convention, Brussels IIa goes a step further and Brussels IIb even further in the direction of providing flexibility.

The first part of Article 12 (ie, paragraphs 1 and 2), is indeed similar to what is envisaged by the 1996 Convention and aims to favour concentration of proceedings and procedural economy in family crises. It is clearly connected to divorce proceedings and extends the competence of such court to hear parental responsibility issues.

Although the rationale of the two rules is similar, there are significant differences between the two. First, while the Convention does not create a new ground of competence and limits itself to recognising a competence which is founded on national law, Brussels IIa sets a common, uniform, rule which applies also if national law does not provide for concentration of proceedings. Second, under the Convention, prorogation is conditional on one of the parents having their habitual residence in the chosen forum, while the Regulation has no such limitation as it refers to the wider range of grounds for divorce and separation used by Article 3 of Brussels IIa. The latter rule indeed provides for a very broad range of criteria: the parents' common habitual residence, habitual residence of one of the parties in connection with other requirements, or common nationality of both parties. By choosing an appropriate divorce forum, parties are also able to choose where to litigate on parental responsibility.[50]

Even more far-reaching is the second part of Article 12 (ie, paragraphs 3 and 4), which is not linked to matrimonial proceedings and allows for prorogation in other cases, and even when no other proceeding is pending,[51] provided that the forum has a 'substantial connection' with the child. The rule provides a few examples of what is meant under 'substantial connection'.[52] A similar rule is missing in the Hague system, and it is inspired by the dual need to respect party autonomy and to gain some flexibility.

Interestingly, the new Brussels IIb has gone another step further and has disconnected prorogation from the existence of matrimonial proceedings. The future Article 10 allows a wider scope for party autonomy – albeit not in its full potential and putting into place guarantees for the child's interests – and will probably set a new standard, opening the door to party autonomy in regard to parental responsibility. It is noteworthy that prorogation will also apply in abduction cases, thus allowing parents to agree on bringing before the court of the State of refuge issues regarding parental custody which may, eg, have been the subject of a mediated agreement. The Hague system currently lacks a satisfactory set of rules to deal with this situation.[53]

[50] Competence may extend to claims on maintenance obligations pursuant to Art 3(c) of Reg No 4/2009 on Maintenance Obligations.

[51] See, in this respect, C-656/13 *L v M* EU:C:2014:2364.

[52] Art 13(3)(a) clarifies that a substantial connection with a Member State may exist if one of the holders of parental responsibility is habitually resident in, or if the child is a national of, that Member State. These are however only examples and do not exhaust the range of possibilities, eg, factors considered for transfer of proceedings by Art 15 may usefully be argued to express a substantial connection.

[53] See the project on-going in the frame of the Hague Conference for cross-border recognition of agreements involving children, available at: www.hcch.net/en/projects/legislative-projects/recognition-and-enforcement-of-agreements; and Paul Beaumont and Nieve Rubaja, 'Family Agreements Involving Children', ch 38 in this book.

Article 10 strikes a reasonable balance between respect for party autonomy and safeguarding the child's interests. In fact, an agreement between the parents – which shall be expressed, before or at the time of the proceedings[54] – will not suffice to constitute a valid prorogation. Only courts which have a 'substantial connection' with the child may be prorogated. Furthermore, the parents' agreement will not be binding on such court, as the judge is required to critically assess whether the exercise of competence serves, from a procedural point of view, the best interests of the child. Such assessment is not different from that which is required in regard to the transfer of proceedings. And indeed, while the rule undoubtedly is a step forward in regard to meeting families' needs, its functioning resembles the scheme of transfer of proceedings, subject as it is to the court's full scrutiny of the child's interests.

D. Transfer of Proceedings

Transfer of proceedings is indeed a genuine novelty in European family law, one which owes greatly to the 1996 Convention. Transfer is functional to a proper operation of the Regulation, as it aims to counterbalance the rigidity of the criterion of the child's habitual residence and to introduce some flexibility in particular cases by giving weight to special circumstances to be assessed *ex post* by the court. Although this may lead to some unpredictability, proximity is especially important in cases relating to minors, as the best interests of the child requires that all decisions are taken by the court which is closer to the child.

For a transfer of proceedings to be considered, three requirements must be fulfilled. First, one of the relevant connections mentioned by Article 15(3) must exist between the child and the court (which includes the previous or new residence of the child; the child's nationality; residence of one of the parental responsibility holders; the location of the child's assets). Second, the court to which the proceedings are to be transferred must be better placed to hear the case. Third, the transfer to such court must be in the best interests of the child. According to the EU Court of Justice, the latter is a separate, autonomous test requiring the court to assess any negative effects that such a transfer may have on the familial, social and emotional attachments of the child, or on his or her material situation.[55] In this context, the best interests of the child test is only related to the procedure and should not involve the final outcome of the case.

Brussels IIb has doubled the rule on transfer of proceedings (now Articles 12 and 13), splitting the current provision into two, depending on whether the request for transfer is initiated by the competent (and already seised) court or triggered by the court having a substantial connection with the child but otherwise lacking competence under the Regulation. The future Brussels IIb will thus sensibly mirror the parallel provisions under the 1996 Convention (Articles 8 and 9). This is probably to be approved, although the new provisions do not seem to answer a specific need in the European arena, especially given that any transfer between EU courts and courts of other Contracting Parties who are not EU Member States will in any case be governed by the 1996 Convention's rules pursuant to Article 97(2)(b).

[54] Under the current Brussels IIa it is debated whether the defendant who appears without contesting the lack of competence is considered as having accepted the jurisdiction. Such ambiguity is now cleared by Brussels IIb which provides that, if the agreement is made in the course of the proceedings, the court shall ensure that all parties have been informed of their right not to accept the jurisdiction (see Art 10(1)(b)(ii)).

[55] C-428/15 *Child and Family Agency v JD* EU:C:2016:819.

IV. Conclusion

Cross-border disputes on parental responsibility have become very common. International and regional harmonisation of private international laws which determine such disputes, in the 1996 Convention and in the Brussels IIa regime, have significantly improved many aspects of the law in the area of parental responsibility. There is a high degree of consistency between the 1996 Convention and the Brussels IIa regime, due to the influence of the Convention on the Brussels II scheme, and the recast of Brussels IIa has led to an even greater degree of consistency. This is clearly desirable and sets an interesting and important example for other regions, in enhancing cooperation and harmonisation of the law in this area.

It must be acknowledged that there also are differences between the schemes, which are mainly due to the different – regional or potentially universal – contexts in which the two instruments operate. Nonetheless, they have a similar structure, pursue similar aims and are indeed tightly related. Furthermore, many of their provisions are parallel and similarly inspired by the best interests of the child doctrine.[56] It is here maintained that both instruments would benefit from a closer look at the interpretation and application of the other.

Whereas the EU legislator has repeatedly looked to the 1996 Convention when drafting or recasting the Brussels II Regulation, national courts and practitioners of States Party to the 1996 Convention could profit from the abundant and generally consistent case law generated by the application of the Regulation within Europe. This would seem appropriate especially when the wording of the relevant instruments is similar.

The more intense and more consistent application of the rules set by the Brussels IIa Regulation, as given by the courts of EU Member States under the supervision of the EU Court of Justice, constitutes a very useful – and perhaps as yet underutilised – source of guidance for the interpretation of terms and concepts in the Convention that are similarly expressed and pursue similar aims.[57] The Convention has only relatively recently entered into force,[58] so although the jurisprudence on its effect is growing, it remains at a relatively early stage of development.[59] We wholeheartedly endorse the statement of Watts J of the Family Court of Australia that it is 'permissible, when construing the meaning of the Child Protection Convention, to also have reference to the Brussels II Regulation, and supplementary material available in relation to the Brussels II Regulations [*sic*]'.[60]

The endorsed cross-fertilisation between the two instruments appears to have high potential and calls for further attention from scholars and lawmakers. We mention two aspects where such an approach could be of use, by way of example. The first is in relation to the definition of habitual residence, a term which is crucial to the operation of both schemes. As we have noted, for the 1996 and 1980 Conventions, there are far fewer cases which have considered the meaning of this term in the context of parental responsibility than in the context of child abduction, although interestingly the opposite is true for Brussels IIa. We have suggested that the approach taken in

[56] This is true, eg, in regard to the general ground of habitual residence, as well as to the rules on transfer of proceedings, and on prorogation of competence of the court for divorce.

[57] See, eg, *Bunyon & Lewis* (n 11) [245].

[58] The Convention entered into force in 2002. It has only entered into force in the last 10 years in 31 of its 53 Contracting States.

[59] Ten years after it entered into effect in Australia, an Australian court noted that 'There has to date been virtually no experience in this country, or indeed to the best of our knowledge in any country, with the operation of the Child Protection Convention': *Cape & Cape* [2013] FamCAFC 114, [73]. See also *Re J (A Child)* [2014] EWCA Civ 1661, [13]. Since then, the number of cases has grown.

[60] *Zegna & Zegna* [2015] FamCA 340, [41].

the European Union, in which the term is defined consistently in these two contexts, should also be followed for the 1996 Convention, not just because this is defensible in principle, but because it is important in order to ensure that the 1980 and 1996 Conventions operate coherently.

The second is in relation to the child's right to be heard in proceedings relating to parental responsibility. While this is universally recognised as a fundamental right of the child, which is clearly upheld in many international instruments binding a large majority of States,[61] its practical implementation would greatly benefit from clear guidance and normative support. Once again, direction is available in, and should be drawn from, the Brussels system, specifically from Article 21 of Brussels IIb, which requires that the child should be given 'a genuine and effective opportunity to express his or her views, either directly, or through a representative or an appropriate body'.

While the 1996 Convention has been relatively successful,[62] many countries have not yet adopted it, and it does not have universal application. Its provisions on jurisdiction only address the allocation of jurisdiction amongst authorities of Contracting States and its provisions on recognition only require the authorities of Contracting States to recognise and enforce measures taken by authorities of other Contracting States. Outside the EU, where the Brussels II regime applies to most cases, this leaves considerable scope for the application of what remain often diverse national laws, some of which are parochial in effect, and others which rely on the unpredictable exercise of judicial discretion. It is obviously desirable that the private international laws regulating disputes about parental responsibility should be both as simple and as consistent as possible, to minimise the costs and complexity of resolving such disputes, and to reduce the possibility of parallel proceedings. For those reasons, adoption of the 1996 Convention should be strongly encouraged.

[61] See especially, the UN Convention on the Rights of the Child, Art 12, available at: www.unicef.org.uk/wp-content/uploads/2010/05/UNCRC_united_nations_convention_on_the_rights_of_the_child.pdf.

[62] As mentioned above (n 2), 53 States are Contracting Parties to the Convention, of which 27 are EU Member States which apply the Convention only partially and 11 others are from Europe (Albania, Armenia, Georgia, Monaco, Montenegro, Russia, Serbia, Switzerland, Turkey, Ukraine and the UK). The Convention has been adopted by some Central (Barbados, Costa Rica, Cuba, Guyana, Honduras and Nicaragua) and South American (Ecuador, Paraguay and Uruguay) States. It has been less popular in other regions, but it does reach into Africa (Lesotho and Morocco) and the Asia-Pacific Region (Australia and Fiji). Argentina, Canada and the US have signed the Convention – their ratifications would make a huge difference to the impact of the Convention on children's lives.

34

Child Abduction

MARIA CATERINA BARUFFI AND JAYNE HOLLIDAY

I. Introduction and Aims of the 1980 Convention

Cross-border parental child abduction is where a parent or guardian unilaterally takes their child(ren) to, or retains them in, a country other than the child's habitual residence without the permission of the other parent. This type of abduction which was brought to the attention of the Hague Conference in the 1970s was attributed to the increased ease of international travel, the increase in international relationships and the breakdown of relationships.[1] The 1980 Convention on the Civil Aspects of Child Abduction (1980 Convention) was drafted in response to the fact that at that time there was no 'viable legal remedy' available for the left behind parent when faced with a cross-border parental abduction, and also in order to protect children against the long-term harm they face as a result of being abducted/retained.[2]

The 1980 Convention framework works on the principle of restoring the status quo immediately prior to the wrongful removal or retention, by ensuring the prompt return of the abducted or retained child to the State of their habitual residence.[3] For the removal or retention to be considered wrongful, the left behind parent has to have had custody rights, and has to have been exercising those rights at the time of the removal or retention.[4] Where the application for return is brought within one year of the wrongful removal or retention, only the exceptions in Articles 13 and 20 apply. Where the application for return is brought more than one year after the wrongful removal or retention, those exceptions may still apply and the child may not be returned if they are settled in their new environment.[5] The Convention does not require that the child is returned to the left behind parent, but only that the child is returned to their habitual residence.[6]

[1] P Beaumont and P McEleavy, *The Hague Convention on International Child Abduction* (Oxford University Press 1999) 2.

[2] Ibid, 3. M Freeman, 'International Child Abduction: Research on the Effects of Abduction and Reunification', slide 12–19, available at: www.mofa.go.jp/files/000495491.pdf. The full text of the 1980 Convention is available on the HCCH website: assets.hcch.net/docs/e86d9f72-dc8d-46f3-b3bf-e102911c8532.pdf.

[3] E Pérez-Vera, *Explanatory Report on the 1980 HCCH Child Abduction Convention*, para 16 (Explanatory Report), available at: assets.hcch.net/docs/a5fb103c-2ceb-4d17-87e3-a7528a0d368c.pdf. Beaumont and McEleavy (n 1) 31. It is possible to return the child to a third State, see *Re B* [2020] EWCA Civ 1187.

[4] See Art 3 of the 1980 Convention on the Civil Aspects of Child Abduction (1980 Child Abduction Convention), available at: assets.hcch.net/docs/e86d9f72-dc8d-46f3-b3bf-e102911c8532.pdf. The abductor may be a parent, guardian, or close family member.

[5] Art 12 of the 1980 Convention.

[6] Ibid.

The child's habitual residence is considered to be the appropriate forum for determining custody and access cases.[7]

The most recent 1980 Convention statistics gathered by Lowe and Stephens in 2015 show that the initial increase in the global numbers of return orders that occurred in the years following the introduction of the Convention is starting to slow down, but the need for this Convention remains vitally important.[8] In the 2015 data, out of the 2,997 children at the centre of the 1980 Convention return orders, the majority of the children abducted or retained were between the age of three and seven years.[9]

Contrary to the initial expectations of the sociologists (whose data informed the drafting of the Convention) that the majority of abducting parents would be fathers, by the late 1980s the predominant abducting parent had switched to become the custodial mother.[10] This global trend brought a somewhat unexpected dimension to the academic debate surrounding the gender of the abductor and related gendered issues such as domestic violence.[11] In 2000, Silberman wrote that all unlawful unilateral abductions harm children irrespective of whether it has been conducted by the mother or the father,[12] and that the Convention 'does not contain double standards' as to whether the abductor is the mother or the father.[13] From the wording of the negotiations in the Fourteenth Proceedings, the drafters worked from the premise that either parent could be the abductor and designed the Convention accordingly;[14] leaving matters such as domestic violence to be dealt with on a case-by-case basis by the courts.[15] This, unsurprisingly led to differences in interpretation and outcomes.[16] In 2020, the Hague Conference on Private International Law (HCCH) published the Guide to Good Practice Part VI Article 13(1)(b), which is a valuable tool for encouraging uniformity of interpretation in difficult cases.[17]

[7] Explanatory Report (n 3) para 16.

[8] N Lowe and V Stephens, Part I – A statistical analysis of applications made in 2015 under the Hague Convention of 25 October 1980 on the Civil Aspects of International Child Abduction – Global report produced for the Seventh Meeting of the Special Commission on the Practical Operation of the 1980 Hague Child Abduction Convention and the 1996 Hague Child Protection Convention (October 2017) 6, available at: assets.hcch.net/docs/d0b285f1-5f59-41a6-ad83-8b5cf7a784ce.pdf.

[9] Ibid, 9.

[10] See Beaumont and McEleavy (n 1) 8; Lowe and Stephens (n 8) 7. Joint custody is becoming more common and therefore the Convention needs to be viewed through this lens rather than through a primary care giver versus non-custodial parent lens.

[11] Beaumont and McEleavy (n 1) 9. R Schuz, *The Child Abduction Convention. A Critical Analysis* (Hart Publishing 2013) 58. R Lamont, 'Mainstreaming Gender into European Family Law? The Case of International Child Abduction and Brussels II Revised' (2011) 17 *European Law Journal* 366.

[12] L Silberman, 'The Hague Child Abduction turns twenty; Gender Politics and other issues' (2000) 33 *New York University Journal International Law and Politics* 221, 225.

[13] Ibid.

[14] Hague Conference on Private International Law, *Actes et documents de la quatorziéme session*, example in the foundational *Dyer Report*, Prel Doc No 1 August 1978 (19–23), available at: assets.hcch.net/docs/05998e0c-af56-4977-839a-e7db3f0ea6a9.pdf (electronic pages 17–21 in the *Actes*). See also the sociological findings by ISS showing 'that fathers were abducting more than mothers' (electronic page 134 in the *Actes*) but giving examples of abductions by both (ibid 137–41). See also para 13 of the Explanatory Report (n 3).

[15] Under Art 13(1)(b). Mr Jones of the UK during the Diplomatic Session clearly envisaged what became Art 13(1)(b) being used in a situation of prior domestic violence between the parents constituting an 'intolerable situation' for the child justifying non-return (*Actes*, ibid, 300).

[16] O Momoh, 'The interpretation and application of Article 13(1) b) of the Hague Child Abduction Convention in cases involving domestic violence: Revisiting *X v Latvia* and the principle of "effective examination"' (2019) 15 *Journal of Private International Law* 626.

[17] HCCH, *Guide to Good Practice Part VI Article 13(1)(b)*, available at: assets.hcch.net/docs/225b44d3-5c6b-4a14-8f5b-57cb370c497f.pdf. Momoh's recommendations for process in the context of domestic violence are also helpful on this point (ibid).

The Convention should be interpreted purposively.[18] This does not mean that the child should be returned at all costs. The drafters were aware that there were instances where it might not be in a particular child's interests to be returned and set out important exceptions to their return.

This chapter will therefore briefly set out some of the key features of the 1980 Convention before considering ways to improve the effectiveness of the Convention to support the success of this global private international law instrument. Section I of this chapter will set out the aims and scope of the Convention. Section II will briefly consider the tension between repudiatory retention and the need to reconsider the weight to be placed on parental intention when determining the child's habitual residence. Section III will provide an overview of the exceptions to the return of the child under the Convention.

A. Aims of the 1980 Convention

The aims of the 1980 Convention are to protect children from the harm caused by cross-border parental abduction or retention, to protect the child's right to a meaningful relationship with both parents, and to protect the left behind parent's custody rights and right of access.[19] The Convention therefore protects the best interests of 'children' and the rights of those with the legal responsibility to care for the child.[20]

The qualified summary return mechanism within Article 1 of the 1980 Convention, which provides for the prompt return of the child to their habitual residence immediately prior to their wrongful removal or retention, is a good example of pragmatism within private international law.[21] At the time of drafting the Convention, it was accepted that traditional private international law rules would not work and a decision was made to focus on custody rights rather than decisions.[22] As time was of the essence, four experts worked together to arrive at this novel solution.[23] This flexibility in the working methods at the Hague Conference contributed to their arrival at this novel and practical solution.

This Convention was also the first time that an extensive role was given to Central Authorities to ensure the expediency of the process and to facilitate international cooperation.[24] The benefits of centralisation (both for administrators and courts) is that a manageable number of people can benefit from gaining expertise in how the Convention operates which is invaluable for all concerned. This innovative approach to tackling the problem of child abduction has since

[18] Art 1 of the 1980 Convention.

[19] Preamble to the 1980 Convention. Beaumont and McEleavy (n 1) 29.

[20] Beaumont and McEleavy, ibid, 13. In order to understand how this Convention operates and to interpret it appropriately it is necessary to appreciate the fundamental difference between the 'best interests of children' and the 'best interests of the child' principles, see *X v Latvia* no 27853/09 (2014) 59 EHRR 100, [97], where the Grand Chamber acknowledged that restoring the *status quo ante* under the Convention was in the best interests of children, ie, to protect children as a whole from the harm caused by abduction, while the exceptions to return protected the interests of individual children. This process is not contrary to the rights of the child.

[21] AE Anton, 'The Hague Convention on International Child Abduction' (1981) *ICLQ* 537.

[22] Ibid, 541.

[23] Explanatory Report (n 3) para 3. The experts were Anton, Leal, Pérez-Vera and Dyer.

[24] See Arts 6 and 7 of the 1980 Convention. Prior to the 1980 Convention the 1965 Convention on the Service Abroad of Extrajudicial Documents in Civil and Commercial Matters was the first Convention to make use of Central Authorities. Beaumont and McEleavy (n 1) 242.

been rewarded not only by the number of States who have joined this Convention,[25] but by the numbers of children who have been assisted by it.[26]

However, it should be noted, that assessing the success of a Convention requires deeper analysis than simply counting how many Contracting Parties it has attracted. This Convention, like the 1970 Divorce Convention, suffers with non-engagement by Contracting Parties.[27] For example, in November 2020, the Secretary General of the HCCH, raised concerns about the UK's non-acceptance of several accessions to the 1980 Convention. Subsequently Beaumont recommended that the UK 'should exercise its regained external competence in this field' and accept these accessions 'in order to make the Convention effective between the UK and those States'.[28] It is clear from the status table that many other Contracting States who have acceded to the Convention are not benefiting from it to the extent that should be possible due to the inaction of other States. This needs to be addressed.

i. Habitual Residence

The qualified summary return mechanism uses habitual residence as its sole connecting factor.[29] Therefore the court needs to identify where the child was habitually resident immediately prior to the abduction or retention as it is the law of the child's habitual residence which ascertains whether the applicant has custody rights, and it is also the country to which the child is returned if the application is upheld. The habitual residence of the child immediately prior to the wrongful return or retention was chosen as it is the most appropriate forum to hear the custody and access dispute.[30] Taking into account that the 1980 Convention works for the best interests of children, it is not for the court in the Contracting State hearing the return application to conduct a full merits test assessing the best interests of the child, but rather to limit themselves to an effective examination of the exceptions to return which are pleaded before them.[31] If a return is upheld a full welfare test assessing the best interests of the child can be conducted in the *forum conveniens*.

The agreement by Contracting States to work towards the HCCH's aim of uniform interpretation requires courts to consider the relevant decisions made by Supreme Courts in other Contracting States.[32] The recent convergence of the world's leading courts in adopting a hybrid approach to the interpretation of habitual residence, which seeks to balance the parental intention approach and the child-centric approach, is encouraging.[33] However, much remains to be

[25] At the time of writing there are 101 Contracting Parties to the 1980 Convention.

[26] Lowe and Stephens (n 8).

[27] See Máire Ní Shúilleabháin and Jayne Holliday, 'Divorce', ch 32 in this book.

[28] See P Beaumont, 'Some reflections on the way ahead for UK private international law after Brexit' (2021) 17 *Journal of Private International Law* 1, 9. At the time of writing the UK has still not accepted the accessions by Barbados, Bolivia, Cuba, Gabon, Guatemala, Guinea, Guyana, Iraq, Jamaica, Lesotho, Nicaragua, Pakistan, Paraguay, Philippines, Sri Lanka, Thailand, Trinidad and Tobago, Tunisia, Zambia.

[29] Beaumont and McEleavy (n 1) 88. The use of the term 'home' to describe the child's habitual residence is seen throughout the Explanatory Report. *Monasky v Taglieri* 589 US___(2020)[10] 'that custody is adjudicated in what is presumptively the most appropriate forum – the country where the child is at home'.

[30] See Susanne Gössl and Ruth Lamont, 'Connecting Factors', ch 4 in this book.

[31] Beaumont and McEleavy (n 1); P Beaumont, K Trimmings, L Walker and J Holliday, 'Child Abduction: Recent Jurisprudence of the European Court of Human Rights' (2015) 64 *International and Comparative Law Quarterly* 39; Momoh (n 16); HCCH, 1980 Child Abduction Convention Guide to Good Practice, Part VI Article 13(1)(b) (HCCH 2020) 53 sets out what is required for 'effective case management'.

[32] Art 1 of the Statute of the Hague Conference on Private International Law.

[33] P Beaumont and J Holliday, '"Habitual residence" in child abduction cases: hybrid approach is now the norm but how much weight should be given to parental intention?' in M Pfeiffer, J Brodec, M Zavadilová and P Bříza (eds),

done to agree on how much weight should be given to parental intention(s) in determining the habitual residence of an allegedly abducted child.[34]

The parental intent of a child's custodial parent(s) is particularly significant in determining the habitual residence of young children.[35] Beaumont and Holliday put forward that if enough weight is given to the parental intention of the custodial parent(s) of a newborn child then physical presence should not be required to establish habitual residence.[36] The Court of Justice of the European Union has recently committed to 'presence' being an absolute requirement of the child in a country before that child can be habitually resident there.[37] The courts in the rest of the world do not need to follow this approach, at least in relation to newborn children and where all the holders of custody are agreed about where their child should have their home (their habitual residence).[38] It is suggested that the HCCH Special Review Commission on the Abduction Convention could recommend the appointment of an Experts' Group comprising a mixture of judges, lawyers and academics to prepare a Good Practice Guide on the Meaning of Habitual Residence under the 1980 Convention.[39]

ii. Custody and Access

The 1980 Convention is not concerned with the merits of any custody rights.[40] For a left behind parent to rely on the Convention, their custody rights must exist, and those rights must have been breached by a wrongful removal or retention.[41] Article 5(a) contains a semi-autonomous definition of custody rights. It states that 'rights of custody' shall include rights relating to the care of the person of the child and, in particular, the right to determine the child's place of residence.[42] To ascertain whether the left behind parent has custody rights for the purpose of the Convention, the rights of the left behind parent are first considered under the domestic law of the child's habitual residence,[43] and then in light of Article 5(a).[44] Uniform interpretation of custody rights under Article 5(a) is important for the success of the Convention. The prevailing approach to interpreting custody rights was endorsed by the US Supreme Court decision in *Abbott v Abbott*.[45] It is sufficient that someone has the right to prevent the child from leaving a jurisdiction.[46] This may not be classified as a 'custody right' in domestic law but for the purpose of the Convention it is sufficient.

Liber Amicorum Monica Pauknerová (Wolters Kluwer 2021) 27. For cases discussing how the child's habitual residence should be identified, see Case C-497/10 *Mercredi* [2012] Fam 22 [56]; *Office of the Children's Lawyer v Balev* 2018 SCC 16 (for analysis of the different approaches to habitual residence); *Monasky* (n 29); and *Re M (Children) (Return Order: Habitual Residence)* [2020] EWCA Civ 1105.

[34] Beaumont and Holliday, ibid.

[35] Ibid, 29–31.

[36] Ibid, 32–35.

[37] Case C-393/18 PPU *UD v XB* [70].

[38] Beaumont and Holliday (n 33), 35–36.

[39] Ibid, 36.

[40] Explanatory Report (n 3) para 9. Art 19 of the 1980 Convention.

[41] Explanatory Report, ibid. Art 3 of the 1980 Convention.

[42] Schuz (n 11) 59.

[43] Ibid, 147. Beaumont and McEleavy (n 1) 46, point to the circularity of logic in Art 3 where the custody rights are determined by the child's habitual residence which is determined by those with the custody rights.

[44] Schuz (n 11) 147.

[45] *Abbott v Abbott* 176 L Ed 2d 789 (2010). Schuz (n 11) 148. P Beaumont and P McEleavy, *Anton's Private International Law*, 3rd edn (W Green/SULI 2011) 83.

[46] Schuz (n 11) 150.

iii. The Age of the Child

The Convention applies to children from birth to the age of 16.[47] The decision to cap the age of the child at 16 was in part due to the 'conviction that from a certain age the child has a will of his own which cannot be ignored by his parents or the authorities'.[48] The drafters found it impossible to determine a minimum age to hear the child as every age 'seemed artificial, even arbitrary'.[49] At the time of drafting, some States wanted the Convention to be restricted to children up to the age of 12.[50] However, as the Convention gave the judges' discretion to take the child's views into account, it was agreed that setting an age limit which included relatively mature children was not an issue.[51]

iv. An Expeditious Process

The need for States to act expeditiously due to the impact any delay has on these cases is heavily emphasised within the Convention.[52] The guideline in Article 11 is that a decision concerning the return of the child should be made within six weeks from the start of proceedings. If a relevant authority has not made a decision within six weeks of the proceedings starting, the requesting State is then able to ask for an explanation. The EU turned the guideline for an expeditious process into a legal requirement in the Brussels IIa Regulation and in Brussels IIb has clarified that each legal instance should be concluded within six weeks. This is an example of good practice and to be commended.

II. Wrongful Removal or Retention of the Child

The removal to or retention of a child in a place other than the child's habitual residence is wrong if it occurs in breach of another's custody rights and those custody rights were being exercised at the time.[53] The date at which the removal or retention took place can be key to determining whether the act was wrongful or not. The relevant date at which a child is removed from a State is usually easy to ascertain. Indeed, the relevant date at which a retention occurs is also relatively easy if, eg, a parent retains a child after a two-week holiday abroad. But it is less easy to identify when the retention occurs during a period of agreed time abroad which may be for many months.[54]

A. The Balance between Repudiatory Retention and Parental Intention

If a child is taken to a new State by one parent with the agreement of the other parent for a certain time but the taking parent renegues on that agreement before that time has ended, the

[47] Art 4 of the 1980 Convention. Beaumont and Holliday (n 33).
[48] *Actes* (n 14) 184.
[49] Explanatory Report (n 3) para 30.
[50] *Actes* (n 14).
[51] Ibid. For discussion of Art 13(2) and the child's objection to return see below.
[52] Preamble and Arts 1, 2, 7 and 11 support the aim of the Convention for the prompt return of the child.
[53] Art 3 of the 1980 Convention.
[54] *Re H (Abduction: Custody Rights)* [1991] 2 AC 476.

child may already have acquired a habitual residence in the new State. This situation leaves the left behind parent without a remedy under the 1980 Convention and does not respect the aims of the Convention.[55] Controversially, in the view of the UK Supreme Court, the breach of the agreement to return does not have to be relayed to the left behind parent for the wrongful retention to start.[56] From one perspective this means that the court can look to any behaviour that might amount to repudiatory retention to ascertain the date of wrongful retention[57] before the habitual residence of the child has changed, but from another it could leave the left behind parent in a weak position as they are not aware that the start of the 12-month period to bring the return application under Article 12 has already begun.[58] The decision by the courts to allow the child's habitual residence to change to the new State at any time before the original parental agreement expires (particularly if that agreement expressly states that the child's habitual residence will not change during the child's agreed period in another country) can be viewed as rewarding the retaining parent's unilateral act and undermining the aims of the Convention and needs to be reconsidered.

Contracting States need to raise public awareness on this point as the left behind parent, by exercising their custody rights, eg, to allow the other parent to take the child to another State to visit the child's grandparents or for medical treatment risks losing the ability to invoke the Convention if the child's habitual residence changes in the interim period. In cases where the parents had an agreement that allowed one parent to take the child out of the child's habitual residence for a limited period it is recommended that weight should be given to the original joint parental intention.[59] The outcome of this approach would be that the child's habitual residence would not change for the purpose of the 1980 Convention unless both parents agreed to this change and the aims of the Convention would be upheld.[60]

In order to protect the child and the custody rights of both parents, the Contracting States to the 1980 Convention should aim to reduce the need for this Convention.[61] This could be done by increasing public awareness of its qualified summary return mechanism in order to improve its effectiveness as a deterrent and to reduce the number of children who are harmed by their abduction or retention.[62] 'Current practices in family relocation' is a possible topic for the 2023 Special Commission Meeting. It is strongly recommended that the HCCH takes this topic forward and develops this further by producing principles on relocation which would in turn benefit children at risk of parental abduction.[63] Where appropriate, Central Authorities and other support groups should also work towards successful agreement between the parties by mediation to reduce the length of time the case takes and costs for the parties, including where legal aid is available.[64]

[55] *Re A (Hague Convention: Wrongful retention)* [2021] EWHC 1204 Fam – a demand to return the child during the agreed period did not make the retention unlawful.

[56] *In the matter of C (Children)* [2018] UKSC 8 [51iii].

[57] Ibid.

[58] See Susanne Gössl and Ruth Lamont, 'Connecting Factors', ch 4 in this book.

[59] Beaumont and Holliday (n 33).

[60] Ibid.

[61] HCCH, Guide to Good Practice, Part III – Preventive Measures (2005) x.

[62] Ibid.

[63] Schuz (n 11) ch 4. HCCH, '1980 Child Abduction/1996 Child Protection Conventions: Planning for the next Special Commission meeting', Prel Doc No 5 of December 2020, available at: assets.hcch.net/docs/f2c6d534-d7cf-4ae0-a016-874b07d88ba2.pdf, para 9.

[64] For access to best practice guides to implementing mediation within the 6-week time frame of the 1980 Convention, see: www.amicable-eu.org/.

III. Exceptions to the Return of the Child under the 1980 Child Abduction Convention: An Overview

The 1980 Convention framework rests on the principle of restoring the *status quo ante* before the removal or retention considered wrongful within the meaning of Article 3 thereof, namely by ensuring the prompt return of the child to the State of his or her habitual residence. The main operational rule to pursue this aim is found in Article 12(1) of the Convention, requiring the authorities of the Contracting State where the child is (State of refuge) to order the return when the proceedings were initiated within one year from the date of the wrongful removal or retention. This mandatory return mechanism is based on the one-year time limit that was conventionally adopted in order to presume the return of the child as being in his or her interests.[65]

Against this stringent background, a degree of flexibility is nonetheless allowed by means of exceptions provided in the 1980 Convention itself, whereby the competent authorities are afforded discretion to refuse the return of the child under the circumstances described in the relevant provisions (ie, Articles 12(2), 13 and 20). Each exception is assessed below in more detail with a view to identifying approaches and trends of good interpretation throughout the different jurisdictions bound by the Convention that can further contribute to the development of a true 'global jurisprudence'[66] of this instrument.

A. The Exceptions Concerning the Child

i. *Article 12(2) of the 1980 Convention: The 'Settled-In' Exception*

The exception in question is closely connected with the mandatory return mechanism regulated by Article 12(1) of the 1980 Convention. Indeed, it envisages that return proceedings be initiated one year or more from the wrongful removal or retention, to which a cumulative condition is added, that is the settlement of the child in his or her new environment. Unlike the other exceptions provided in Article 13, this rule does not specify the party on which lies the burden of proof, but it seems reasonable to allocate it upon the person opposing the return (usually the abductor) for reasons of internal coherence.[67]

Regarding the temporal requirement, Article 12(1) clarifies both the *dies a quo* and the *dies ad quem* of the one-year time limit, respectively fixed on the date of the wrongful removal or retention and on the date of the commencement of the return proceedings. Notwithstanding the clear wording of the provision, the case of concealment of the child occurring after the removal or retention may pose interpretative difficulties in relation to its potential impact on the passage of time towards the expiry of the time limit. From the relevant case law, it appears that the evidence of concealment requires the judicial authority to conduct a critical assessment of the factual circumstances with a view to ascertaining whether the alleged settlement of the child is genuine

[65] As clarified in the Explanatory Report (n 3) para 107, this time limit is the result of the drafters' attempts to find an objective rule in order to establish the level of integration of the child in his/her new environment following the wrongful removal or retention. More precisely, the one-year term 'although perhaps arbitrary, nevertheless proved to be the "least bad" answer' to the difficulties in finding such a rule.

[66] LJ Silberman, 'Interpreting the Hague Abduction Convention: In Search of a Global Jurisprudence' (2005) 38 *University of California Davies Law Review* 1049; and LJ Silberman, 'United States Supreme Court Hague Abduction Decisions: Developing a Global Jurisprudence' (2014) 9 *Journal of Comparative Law* 49.

[67] In this sense, see the Explanatory Report (n 3) para 109.

and stable.[68] Therefore, it may be possible that in these cases a finding of settlement cannot be made even after a significant amount of time has run between the removal or retention of the child and the subsequent discovery.[69] Nevertheless, the application of a clear-cut rule according to which the time gained by concealment should be subtracted when determining whether the one-year time limit has elapsed (following the US doctrine of 'equitable tolling') has generally been rejected in the context of the Article 12(2) defence as being too narrow and in conflict with the Convention's objectives.[70]

As to the child's settlement in the new environment, the relevant point in time for the court's evaluation is the date of the hearing of the return application, which should be preferred to the date of the commencement of the proceedings to prevent possible delays and to take into account further developments in the child's situation. When it comes to the circumstances upon which the settled-in exception can be grounded, it requires there to be an emotional and psychological element that qualifies the settlement of the child as more than a 'mere adjustment to surroundings'.[71] However, the literature has contended that this standard of proof should not be higher than that employed to establish, for instance, a change in habitual residence.[72] Indeed, the possible conflation of the circumstances relied upon for a determination of a child's habitual residence under Article 3 of the Convention and for a finding of settlement pursuant to Article 12(2) thereof, has found support also in the case law, pointing out that the differentiation resides in the point in time in which those circumstances are to be assessed (in the former case it is prior to the date of the alleged removal or retention of the child, while in the latter case it is after that date).[73] Furthermore, specific situations such as the concealment of the child in the new environment or his or her young age should not necessarily limit the court when establishing the settled-in exception. It is rather the child's connection to the location where he or she is living that becomes decisive in the determination of settlement and should always be considered from the child's perspective even where he or she is very young.[74]

But perhaps the most debated issue in relation to the settled-in exception is whether the judicial authority enjoys a discretionary power to make a return order despite the two cumulative conditions set out in Article 12(2) being met.[75] Also in this regard, the exception in question differs from the others regulated by Articles 13 and 20 of the Convention insofar as the wording of the

[68] eg, *Cannon v Cannon* [2004] EWCA 1330; *C v C* [2008] CSOH 42.

[69] eg, in *C v C*, ibid it was after two-and-a-half years from the removal that the location of the children was discovered and return proceedings were initiated, then concluded with a return order.

[70] Equitable tolling is a well-established principle of US case law and is applied to federal statutes of limitations, whereby the common law principle of equity allows the running of a statute of limitations to be extended when an applicant is prevented from bringing a timely action due to extraordinary circumstances. Its applicability to the one-year time limit envisaged in Art 12(1) of the 1980 Convention in cases of concealment of the child (thus, to a provision of an international treaty and not of domestic law) was ultimately ruled out by the US Supreme Court on the ground that the given time limit is not a statute of limitations and the equitable tolling principle is not required by the Convention provisions: see *Lozano v Montoya Alvarez* 134 SCt 1224 (2014). The decision was also influenced by the interpretation given in other jurisdictions, which consistently refused to subject the one-year period to equitable tolling when the abductor conceals the child from the other parent: eg, England and Wales (*Cannon v Cannon* (n 68)); Hong Kong SAR (*AC v PC* [2004] HKMP 1238); Canada (*Kubera v Kubera* [2010] BCCA 118).

[71] According to the wording used in *Re N (Minors) (Abduction)* [1991] 1 FLR 413, in which the narrow approach to the definition of settlement was first proposed.

[72] As underlined by Beaumont and McEleavy (n 1) 207.

[73] *Balev* (n 33) paras 66–67, where the habitual residence of the child was determined following a 'hybrid approach', that is on the basis of all the evidence at the disposal of the court, and this was not deemed to be in conflict with the settled-in exception. In the same sense, also *Ludwig v Ludwig* 2019 ONCA 680, paras 54–59.

[74] Schuz (n 11) 230–32.

[75] See N Lowe and M Nicholls, 'Revisiting Article 12(2) of the 1980 Hague Abduction Convention' (2019) *International Family Law* 31.

latter provisions expressly confers discretion to order the return of the child.[76] Notwithstanding this textual differentiation, a widespread view in the case law has read the existence of discretion also into the situations envisaged by Article 12(2): in some jurisdictions, it was inferred from the provision itself in order to make it consistent with the other exceptions,[77] whereas a different position has derived it from Article 18 of the Convention according to which the rules of Chapter III thereof (ie, including the exceptions) do not limit the power of the competent authority to order the return 'at any time'. In this latter regard, it should be specified that Article 18 has been interpreted broadly as a Convention means to afford the court discretion to make provisions for the child's return.[78]

Neither of these approaches, however, appears to fully respect the original drafting of the Convention rules. As already mentioned, on the one hand the textual interpretation of Article 12(2) would rather support the absence of any discretionary power of the court whenever the return proceedings have been commenced after the expiry of the one-year time limit and the chid has settled in his or her new environment. On the other hand, a more correct interpretation of Article 18 would vest the judicial authority with power to order the return by resorting to provisions outside the Convention, eg, under the domestic laws.[79] In addition, the 'discretion' approach may run the risk of misuse insofar as a return order of a settled child taken in compliance with the general policy objective of the Convention would ultimately override the competing interests of protecting the child's wellbeing that underlie the Article 12(2) exception.[80]

ii. Article 13(1)(b) of the 1980 Convention: The 'Grave Risk' Exception

Article 13(1)(b) aims at providing a margin of appreciation of the welfare implications of returning a child wrongfully removed or retained while preserving the summary nature of Convention proceedings. When drafting the Convention, the balance between these conflicting interests was found in the narrow wording that allows the judicial authority to refuse the return in those cases where 'there is a grave risk that his or her return would expose the child to physical or psychological harm or otherwise place the child in an intolerable situation'.[81] The provision in question lists

[76] More precisely, the first paragraph of Art 13 stipulates that the judicial or administrative authority 'is not bound to order the return' where either of the exceptions applies, while the second paragraph thereof states that it 'may refuse to order the return' if the child objects to it. Similarly, Art 20 provides that the return 'may be refused' if it implies a violation of human rights and fundamental freedoms in the requested State. See also the Explanatory Report (n 3) para 113.

[77] Particularly in the UK: see *Re M. (Children) (Abduction: Rights of Custody)* [2007] UKHL 55, in which the House of Lords held, 'not without considerable hesitation', that Art 12(2) 'does envisage that a settled child might nevertheless be returned within the Convention procedures', thus introducing flexibility in the concept of settlement.

[78] Such is the position in the USA: see *Fernandez v Bailey* 909 F 3d 353 (11th Cir, 2018), in which the return of a settled child pursuant to Art 18 of the Convention was nonetheless described as 'an infrequent occurrence'.

[79] This interpretation of Art 18 of the Convention finds support also in the Explanatory Report (n 3) para 112, where it is clarified that such rule authorises the competent authorities to issue a return order 'by invoking *other provisions* more favourable to the attainment of this end' (emphasis added). See, however, Lowe and Nicholls (n 75) 49–50, who point out the inevitable drawback of having diverging laws that allow the court to order the child's return and, consequently, advocate for an interpretation of Art 18 within the Convention system 'in the interests of promoting a global approach'.

[80] In this sense, see Schuz (n 11) 237–39. The 'no discretion' approach has been espoused by the Full Court of the Family Court of Australia (*Secretary, Department of Family and Commentary Services & Magoulas* [2018] FamCAFC 165), following previous decisions that did not adopt a consistent position. It is worth mentioning that the 1980 Convention has been given effect in the Australian legal order by means of the Family Law (Child Abduction Convention) Regulations 1986, therefore these decisions have addressed the issue of discretion in the context of the settled-in exception in the light of this domestic legislation.

[81] The Explanatory Report (n 3) para 116, underlines that each of the terms used in this provision 'is the result of a fragile compromise reached during the deliberations of the Special Commission'.

three types of risk to the child that can ground the defence, either separately or taken together, and each of them must be qualified as 'grave' in the sense that they have to be characterised as sufficiently real and serious according to the specific circumstances of the case. Furthermore, this exception is 'forward-looking', taking into account the situation as it would be following the return of the child to the State of habitual residence, although circumstances that occurred prior to the wrongful removal or retention may also form part of the overall assessment of the competent authority as to the existence of a grave risk.[82]

From a practical perspective, the approach to establish whether the defence is successful requires the court to perform a step-by-step analysis. First, it should be determined whether the allegations made by the person (or institution or body) opposing the return are sufficiently detailed and substantiated to constitute a grave risk within the meaning of Article 13(1)(b). Then, on the basis of the collected evidence and considering whether protective measures available or put in place in the State of habitual residence can mitigate the harm to the child, the exception to the return is established or not. Even in the positive, the court would still enjoy discretion to make a return order, but the case law has reasonably deemed this possibility as merely theoretical.[83]

As mentioned above, the grave risk exception constitutes the most relevant instance that allows the welfare of the child, and more broadly his or her interests, to be taken into account in the framework of the Convention. It is generally accepted that Article 13(1)(b), as well as the other exceptions to return, should be interpreted 'in a restrictive fashion'.[84] An 'effective examination' of the grounds for refusal of return should be conducted in order to uphold the aims of the Convention. This is consistent with the European Convention on Human Rights (ECHR) as interpreted by the Strasbourg Court.[85] In the context of Article 13(1)(b), the evaluation to determine whether the return would expose the child to one or more of the grave risks, after having considered the information and evidence available,[86] should be focused on the adequacy of the protective measures arranged in the State of habitual residence.[87]

Among the factual circumstances that can fall within the scope of the grave risk exception, allegations of domestic violence towards the abductor and/or the child have attracted a lot of attention. In both cases, the existence of the grave risk of harm is in relation to the child in order for the defence to be argued.[88] In particular, the case of domestic violence may pose significant difficulties to the judicial authority in balancing the needs for an effective case management in

[82] As clarified by the Permanent Bureau of the HCCH in the Guide to Good Practice under the Convention of 25 October 1980 on the Civil Aspects of International Child Abduction. Part VI. Article 13(1)(b) [2020], at: www.hcch.net, para 37.

[83] See *Re S (A Child) (Abduction: Rights of Custody)* [2012] UKSC 10, para 5: '[i]n reality … it is impossible to conceive of circumstances in which, once [the grave] risk [identified in Article 13(1)(b)] is found to exist, it would be a legitimate exercise of the discretion nevertheless to order the child's return'.

[84] According to the well-known wording used in the Explanatory Report (n 3) para 34.

[85] See, in particular, *X v Latvia* (n 20). In the extensive literature, eg, Beaumont et al (n 31) 39; P McEleavy 'The European Court of Human Rights and the Hague Child Abduction Convention: Prioritising Return or Reflection?' [2015] *Netherlands International Law Review* 365.

[86] In the words of Beaumont et al (n 31) 45, the effective examination standard should be construed as to require a 'moderate level of due diligence that can be done in a few weeks'.

[87] This approach has been endorsed by the UK Supreme Court in *Re E (Children) (FC)* [2011] UKSC 27 and *In the matter of S (a Child)* [2012] UKSC 10. For further insights from that jurisdiction, see MacDonald J, 'Article 13 Exceptions – Return and Best Interests of the Child in the Jurisdiction of England and Wales' (Winter 2018–Spring 2019) 23 *The Judges' Newsletter on International Child Protection* 17, 21–22.

[88] See, eg, Tribunal fédérale, IIe Cour de droit civile (Switzerland), judgment of 30 January 2017, 5A_936/2016: in a case of domestic violence, it was reiterated that the intolerable situation within the meaning of Art 13(1)(b) has to be found with respect to the child and not the taking parent.

summary proceedings with the requirement of an effective examination of the allegations made by the taking parent. However, it seems that a sensible approach should favour a non-stereotyped assessment in order to establish the veracity of those allegations,[89] otherwise the subsequent focus on the effectiveness of the protective measures put in place in the State of habitual residence may run the serious risk of being ill-advised.

iii. Article 13(2) of the 1980 Convention: The 'Child's Objections' Exception

The defence laid down in Article 13(2) of the Convention is meant to ensure an effective participation of the child in the abduction proceedings, which would subsequently be generalised as the fundamental right to participation in all proceedings enshrined in Article 12 of the 1989 United Nations Convention on the Rights of the Child (CRC). More precisely, the child's views can amount to an explicit objection to being returned to his or her State of habitual residence upon condition that the judicial authority is satisfied that the child has attained an age and maturity at which it is appropriate for those views to be taken into consideration. Following this first stage, the court can then exercise its discretion in ordering or refusing the return against a wider range of considerations, particularly the overarching objectives of the Convention as well as welfare concerns.[90]

Despite this exception being rooted in human rights considerations, its practical operation is subject to domestic laws and procedures concerning the modalities through which the child's views are presented to the court, or the child's representation and qualification as a party to the proceedings, with the consequence that the relevant practices vary significantly between jurisdictions.[91] This may also explain the different figures at the national level with regard to the number of judicial refusals to return a child based on the Article 13(2) defence,[92] which nonetheless amount only to a relatively low number from a global perspective.[93] As it has been noted, these findings confirm that the child's objections exception has not been perceived as an 'escape mechanism'[94] to the obligation to return the child, but it is rather carefully employed and its requirements narrowly interpreted. Indeed, judges seem to be mindful that they should not superimpose their own evaluation of the circumstances and the parent–child relationship upon the views expressed by the child,[95] while also acknowledging that a

[89] In this sense, Momoh (n 16) 650.

[90] See, eg, *M (A Child)* [2007] EWCA Civ 260, 80, where the approach followed by the Court involved 'balancing the nature and strength of [the child's] objections against both the Convention considerations … and general welfare considerations'.

[91] Beaumont et al (n 31); HCCH, *The Judges' Newsletter on International Child Protection* Volume XXII (Summer–Fall 2018) 'The Child's Voice – 15 Years Later', 11.

[92] eg, Mexico has a consistent proportion of judicial refusals based on the child's objections (five out of 11 judicial refusals, amounting to 45% of the total), while in several EU Member States there were none (such as in Belgium, Poland, Italy) or only a few (for instance one each in the UK – England and Wales, and in Spain): see N Lowe and V Stephens, *Part III – A statistical analysis of applications made in 2015 under the Hague Convention of 25 October 1980 on the Civil Aspects of International Child Abduction – National Reports* produced for the Seventh Meeting of the Special Commission on the Practical Operation of the 1980 Hague Child Abduction Convention and the 1996 Hague Child Protection Convention (July 2018), available at: assets.hcch.net/docs/6ca61ff3-5ca6-4fbe-a79a-cb6e7485f4b0.pdf.

[93] Namely, only 15% of all judicial refusals at the global level relied upon Art 13(2) as sole or combined ground for refusal and the trend is downwards as compared to the previous statistical analyses: see Lowe and Stephens (n 8) table, 16.

[94] N Lowe and V Stephens, 'A statistical analysis of the child objections exception' (Summer–Fall 2018) 22 *The Judges' Newsletter on International Child Protection* 12, 13.

[95] See Cassazione civile, sezione I, judgment of 26 September 2016 no 18846, which reversed the lower court's decision on the ground that it had made a value judgement concerning the objections to return expressed by the child. In the Italian case law, it is worth mentioning a significant *revirement* of the Supreme Court jurisprudence concerning precisely the relevance of the child's objections, which was recognised as an autonomous ground for refusal of the return and not merely having a subsidiary function: Cassazione civile, sezione I, judgment of 4 March 2014 no 5237.

degree of influence from the parents over the child is generally understandable but does not necessarily undermine the genuineness of the child's views taking into account their level of maturity and understanding.[96]

B. The Exceptions Concerning the Person having the Care of the Child

i. *Article 13(1)(a) of the 1980 Convention: The 'Consent/Acquiescence' Exception*

Article 13(1)(a) lists three different defences that all find their background in circumstances which call into question the wrongful character of the removal or retention within the meaning of the Convention. On the one hand, the party opposing the return can raise the exception of non-exercise of custody rights by the person (or institution or body) having the care of the child and on the other hand, it can contend that the same person has consented or acquiesced to the removal or retention.

As is well known, the difference between consent and acquiescence resides in the point in time where the two conducts occur: the former is given before the removal or retention and the latter takes place afterwards. Both defences, however, pursue the same aim of preventing that the left behind parent, notwithstanding an initially consensual behaviour, may subsequently take advantage of the Convention provisions against the other parent.[97] In relation to consent, it is necessary that its giving or withdrawing be made known by words and/or conduct to the removing parent, otherwise it cannot be effective.[98]

Since both conducts of consent and acquiescence relate to a person having custody rights in relation to the child, the relevant question becomes to assess the impact of this exception on the abducted child and his or her return to the State of habitual residence. The obvious stage at which these considerations must come into play is the subsequent exercise of discretion by the competent court once the consent or acquiescence has been established. In this regard, it seems appropriate that the case law has supported a wide reading of this discretion allowing consideration of many aspects,[99] especially the welfare of the child and the policy objectives of the Convention. This exercise of discretion, however, is highly case-specific, requiring the court to identify all the relevant factors and to attach to them appropriate weight depending on the circumstances of each case. Where there has been consent to the removal or retention of a child, it may be the case that the policy considerations of deterring abduction and favouring return are 'relatively slight', with the consequence that giving them a predominant importance without conducting a detailed welfare analysis results in an error of approach in the balancing exercise by the competent court.[100]

[96] See, eg, *X v Y & Ors* [2012] EWHC 2838 (Fam).

[97] For an example of a decision confirming the wrongful removal of the child, having found that the parent having custody rights had not consented, either expressly or implicitly, to the child's relocation, see Audiencia Provincial A Coruña, secciòn 6ª, judgment of 30 January 2020, ES:APC:2020:778A. In contrast to the lawful removal or retention of the child on the grounds of consent or acquiescence for a certain period of time that becomes 'wrongful', see section II.A above on repudiatory retention.

[98] See *Re G (Abduction: Consent/Discretion)* [2021] EWCA Civ 139, para 26: 'what is required is an act or actions and not just an internal state of mind'.

[99] A list of possible considerations for the purposes of the court's discretion has been provided, for instance, in *W v W (Child Abduction: Acquiescence)* [1993] 2 FLR 211.

[100] As held in *Re G (Abduction: Consent/Discretion)* (n 98) paras 42, 49–50, 'The removal of the children was wrongful in name only, the children's current situation gives rise to no obvious concerns, and there is no advantage (and considerable

C. The 'Fundamental Rights' Exception

Article 20 of the Convention has been described as 'a ghost'[101] given its limited relevance in practice. The provision refers to the return being refused on the ground that it would be in contrast 'with the fundamental principles of the requested State relating to the protection of human rights and fundamental freedoms', therefore having a broad scope insofar as the person whose human rights are breached is concerned.

One of the fundamental issues with the practical operation of this exception is the overlap with the grave risk defence provided by Article 13(1)(b) of the Convention. The situations covered by the latter would arguably entail also a violation of fundamental rights of the child, and vice versa. In this regard, commentators have proposed a distinction based on the subject matter of the claims on which the two defences are based: Article 20 would come into play whenever they concern the legal context of the requested State, while Article 13(1)(b) would rather address factual matters.[102] Despite this proposed classification, it seems more likely that a party opposing the return would rather plead both defences, with the consequence that the boundaries between them remain blurred from a practical perspective.

IV. Conclusion

The current success of this Convention is due to its pragmatic summary return mechanism and the invaluable involvement of Central Authorities. To improve on the current position, it is recommended that Contracting States should be encouraged to accept the accessions of other Contracting States to maximise the Convention's effectiveness. Central Authorities also require additional support both in terms of staffing and available technology to support cross-border cases.[103] Cases should not be held up by inadequate access to video conferencing facilities.[104] In addition, to support the need for expediency, Contracting States should consider adopting the six-week guideline in Article 11 of the Convention into their domestic law.

The HCCH is to be commended for putting interpretation of habitual residence for the purpose of the 1980 Convention on to the list of possible topics for the next Special Commission meeting in 2023.[105] It is recommended that the HCCH appoint an Experts' Group comprising a mixture of judges, lawyers and academics to prepare a Good Practice Guide on the Meaning of Habitual Residence under the Abduction Convention, inter alia, in order to find the appropriate weight to be given to parental intention in determining a child's habitual residence, in particular for cases involving family agreements, newborns and cases involving coercion.[106]

disadvantage) in them being moved from where their father had agreed they should be in order for a decision to be taken about their future' [50].

[101] C Honorati, 'Cross-border Parental Child Abduction in the EU. Is there Room for a Human Rights Exception?' in E Bergamini and C Ragni (eds), *Fundamental Rights and Best Interests of the Child in Transnational Families* (Intersentia 2019) 243.

[102] See Beaumont and McEleavy (n 1) 174.

[103] P Beaumont, L Walker and J Holliday, 'Conflicts of EU courts on child abduction: the reality of Article 11(6)–(8) Brussels IIa proceedings across the EU' [2016] *Journal of Private International Law* 211, 235.

[104] Ibid.

[105] HCCH (n 63) para 1.

[106] For an example of coercion see *In the matter of A (Children)* [2013] UKSC 60 in P Beaumont and J Holliday, 'Recent Developments on the meaning of "Habitual Residence" in Alleged Child Abduction Cases' in M Župan (ed), *Private International Law in the Jurisprudence of European Courts – Family at Focus/Međunarodno privatno pravo u praksi europskih sudova – obitelj u fokusu* (Faculty of Law JJ Strossmayer University of Osijek 2015).

The exceptions to return are an integral part of the Convention essential to achieving its aims, notably safeguarding the best interests of children. However, there are still elements that have yet to be settled at a global level such as the impact of concealment of the whereabouts of an abducted child on the time constraints within Article 12 and the lack of uniformity in practice under the Convention in relation to the age at which a child will be heard and the impact of the child's views on when Article 13(2) should be upheld.

When agreement can be reached on interpretation it is heartening to see the HCCH produce Guides to Good Practice such as the recent one on Article 13(1)(b). The numbers of children around the world affected by abduction remain significant. This Convention is vital for protecting children from the harm caused by wrongful abduction/retention, for protecting their right to maintain a meaningful relationship with both parents, and for protecting the custody rights of the left behind parent. Anything that can be done to improve the Convention's efficacy is worth doing.

35

Adoption of Children

LAURA MARTÍNEZ-MORA*,[1]

I. Introduction

'Adoption'[2] is a legal institution which creates a permanent social and legal relationship between a parent and a child.[3] It is one of the possible alternative care solutions present in the child protection systems of many States.[4] It provides a permanent family solution for children deprived of parental care where the efforts to keep them in, or return them to, the care of their family have failed.[5]

Adoption can be domestic, where the child and the prospective adoptive parents are habitually resident in the same State, or intercountry, where the child and the prospective adoptive parents are habitually resident in different States and the child has been, is being or is to be moved to the receiving State.[6]

While there is no global instrument in force dealing with the private international law (PIL) aspects of domestic adoptions,[7] there is a Convention that deals specifically with intercountry adoptions, namely the 1993 Convention on the Protection of Children and Cooperation in Respect of Intercountry Adoption (1993 Adoption Convention; 1993 Convention; or simply

* The views expressed herein are those of the author alone and should not be attributed to or be understood to reflect the views of the HCCH. The author is grateful to Hans van Loon, former Secretary General of the HCCH and one of the fathers of the 1993 Adoption Convention, Nigel Cantwell, Capucine Page and Keith Loken, for their helpful comments on an earlier version of this chapter.

[1] All HCCH documents mentioned in this chapter are available on the HCCH website at: www.hcch.net under 'Adoption'.

[2] The 1993 Adoption Convention does not include a definition of adoption due to the lack of consensus among the drafters, see G Parra-Aranguren, 'Explanatory Report on the Convention of 29 May 1993 on Protection of Children and Cooperation in Respect of Intercountry Adoption' in HCCH, *Proceedings of the Seventeenth Session (1993), Tome II, Adoption – cooperation*, para 87 (Explanatory Report). For a historic view of adoption, see JHA van Loon, '*Report on Intercountry Adoption*' in HCCH, *Proceedings of the Seventeenth Session (1993), Tome II, Adoption – cooperation*. The adoption of adults falls outside the scope of this Convention and this chapter.

[3] Adoption creates a permanent parent–child relationship (Art 2(2) 1993 Convention) but may or may not terminate the relationship with the birth parents. If it terminates the relationship with the birth parents it is a 'full' adoption; if not, it is a 'simple' adoption.

[4] Excluding many States where Islamic law prevails, and which prohibit adoption. See also UN 1989 Convention on the Rights of the Child (UNCRC) Art 20(2) and (3).

[5] See UN 2010, *Guidelines for the Alternative Care of Children*, para 2(a).

[6] This distinction is based on Art 2(1) of the 1993 Convention.

[7] See HCCH Permanent Bureau (PB), *Report on the cross-border recognition of domestic adoptions*, Prel Doc No 12 of December 2018 for the attention of the Council on General Affairs and Policy of the HCCH.

Convention). This chapter (section II) presents briefly this Convention; (section III) identifies the challenges that existed to unify private international law rules at the time of its drafting; (section IV) describes some concerns with its content and interpretation; (section V) presents some remaining gaps; and (section VI) concludes with a summary of the main achievements of this Convention and some ideas for the way forward.

II. The 1993 Adoption Convention: More than a PIL Convention

The 1993 Adoption Convention contains a rule on recognition of adoptions established in conformity with the Convention.[8] However, it does not include rules on direct jurisdiction of authorities (but 'some jurisdictional problems are dealt with indirectly, for example by making a distribution of responsibilities between the State of origin and the receiving State') nor does it determine the law applicable to the granting of the adoption or its effects.[9]

Importantly, this Convention goes further than creating a rule for the recognition of intercountry adoptions as:

- Unlike other Hague Conference on Private International Law (HCCH) Conventions, it includes substantive rules: it establishes minimum standards and safeguards to ensure that adoptions take place in the best interests of the child and with respect for his or her fundamental rights (Article 1(a)). Only adoptions made in accordance with the guarantees and safeguards of the Convention shall be recognised by operation of law in the other Contracting States.[10]

  These safeguards are a floor, not a ceiling, and Contracting States are encouraged to do their utmost to raise them. For example, according to the Convention, a birth mother can only consent after the birth of her child (Article 4(c)(4)). However, many Contracting States have raised this standard by establishing a longer period after birth[11] that allows the mother to fully consider her decision which will have an impact for the rest of her life, even if the circumstances in which she decides to consent to the adoption are specific to a certain time and situation in her life.
- The Convention establishes a system of cooperation between Contracting States to facilitate the implementation of its safeguards and procedures. Cooperation also aims *indirectly* at preventing the abduction, sale of and trafficking in children for adoption (Article 1(b)) and other abuses because 'it is expected that the observance of the Convention's rules will bring about the avoidance of such abuses'.[12]
- The Convention is mandatory as 'all intercountry adoptions granted by the Contracting States must comply with the conventional rules'.[13]

[8] In most States, adoption is a judicial decision but in some States it is an administrative decision (eg, China (by the respective Provincial department of civil affairs) and Peru (by the Central Authority, Decreto Legislativo 1297/2016, Art 139)). Exceptionally, in some cases it can be by a contract (eg, for step-parent adoptions in Guatemala, 2007 Law on Adoptions, Art 39). See also, HCCH, *Guide to Good Practice No 1: The Implementation and Operation of the 1993 Adoption Convention* (Jordan Publishing Limited 2008) para 444 (Guide to Good Practice No 1).

[9] Explanatory Report (n 2) para 65.

[10] Arts 2(1) and 23(1).

[11] Six weeks (2008 European Convention on the Adoption of Children, Art 5(5)); two months (Belgium (Civil Code, Art 348(4)); Finland (Adoption Act 22/2012, Art 15); Germany (Civil Code, Art 174(7)); three months (Denmark (Danish Adoption (Consolidation) Act, Art 8(2)); Haiti (Loi d'adoption, Art 43)).

[12] Explanatory Report (n 2) para 52.

[13] Ibid, para 70.

- States should put the emphasis on proper cooperation *en amont* and on applying all the standards. The Convention is not intended to solve *fait accompli* situations where a child has been adopted without respect for safeguards and procedures. On the contrary, it goes much further in the protection of children's rights with an *a priori* system, whereby safeguards and procedures need to be satisfied throughout the adoption procedure, for the adoption to be recognised. Therefore, if problems are identified during the adoption procedure, the adoption should not proceed[14] until those problems have been resolved (if it is possible to address them).
- Finally, the Convention also includes a mechanism (Article 24) to refuse recognition but 'only if the adoption is manifestly contrary to [the] public policy'. This clause is, in its turn, subject to the child's best interests (to avoid cases where non-recognition would be more harmful to the child than the recognition of the adoption). When taking such decisions, authorities should consider the short-term consequences for the child (recognition may be seen as an advantage for the child as he or she would have secure legal parentage) but also the long-term consequences[15] (adoptees need to build their identity, and it is extremely difficult to do so if the adoption was not done according to legal and ethical standards).

III. Challenges to Unification

The work of the HCCH on a new instrument on intercountry adoption started in 1988, when the secretariat of the HCCH, the Permanent Bureau, presented a proposal to work on this topic,[16] followed by a proposal made by Italy in support of the Permanent Bureau's proposal.[17] The desirability to work on this issue was clear as there were at that time very serious abuses,[18] an increasing number of intercountry adoptions and no international multilateral instrument which could deal with this matter.[19]

However, the feasibility of drafting an instrument was more complicated. One of the challenges was that both receiving States and States of origin needed to participate in the negotiations to have a meaningful discussion and a balanced and objective result but most of the Member States of the HCCH at that time were receiving States. Fortunately, as the principle that non-Member States may participate in the work of the HCCH had been accepted some years before, these States could and did participate, as invited States with a right to vote, in the negotiations.[20]

[14] See Art 17(c) of the Convention, for cases where the child has not been entrusted. Other actions should also be available for illicit practices discovered after the Art 17(c) agreement, see HCCH Working Group on Preventing and Addressing Illicit Practices in Intercountry Adoption, Report of the July 2020 meeting, para 18.

[15] Ibid, para 22.

[16] JHA van Loon, 'Note on the desirability of preparing a new Convention on international co-operation in respect of intercountry adoption' in HCCH, *Proceedings of the Sixteenth Session* (1988) Tome I, *Miscellaneous Matters* 165–85.

[17] Explanatory Report (n 2) paras 1 and 2.

[18] Many such scandals are currently being investigated in more detail, eg, by the Committee Investigating Intercountry Adoption in the past in the Netherlands, by the Conseil Fédéral in Switzerland, and specific cases by the judiciary in several other States.

[19] Explanatory Report (n 2) para 6. The 1965 Convention on Jurisdiction, Applicable Law and Recognition of Decrees relating to Adoptions could not answer the serious problems existing at the end of the 1980s. It only had three States Parties (Austria, Switzerland and the United Kingdom) which subsequently denounced the Convention between 2003 and 2004.

[20] Explanatory Report (n 2) paras 2, 8 and 11. An extensive effort was made by the HCCH PB to motivate and invite States of origin, and to provide for Spanish interpretation for Spanish-speaking States.

Another challenge to unification was that in order to provide a meaningful response to the existing problems, there was a need to go further than simply unifying traditional private international law rules: substantive principles, rules and procedures and a legal framework of cooperation between States of origin and receiving States were thus included to better protect children. In fact, the first part of the title of the 1993 Convention reflects this broader approach: 'Convention on the Protection of Children'. In addition, the 1993 Convention expands the guarantees established in the UN Convention on the Rights of the Child (UNCRC).[21]

This new Convention also meant moving intercountry adoption from the private sphere – where actors (eg, adoption agencies, medical and legal professionals, religious organisations, interpreters) had long-standing experience, powerful interests and had found a way to make the system 'financially' stable – to the public sphere[22] – where, in many cases, especially at the beginning, both experience and necessary resources were lacking. There were extensive negotiations regarding whether some of the functions of the Convention could be performed by private actors, including some which pursued profit objectives. The Convention aimed at changing this situation as permitting profits to be made from adoption – a child protection measure – is contrary to children's rights and is very dangerous as it spawns or enables many abuses. A compromise was found to include adoption agencies that would need to be accredited and pursue non-profit objectives ('adoption accredited bodies'), and persons and bodies that would only need to be 'approved (non-accredited)' and could pursue profit objectives, but subject to a number of restrictions and safeguards.[23] In practice, only very few States allow 'approved (non-accredited) persons or bodies' to act in their States, and the number of such approved persons or bodies is extremely limited.[24]

Finally, an issue which could have been an obstacle when negotiating the Convention is that States prohibiting adoption (eg, some States governed by Islamic law) could have decided to try to block the negotiations but did not do so. On the contrary, eg, the Egyptian delegate suggested that the Convention should also apply to methods of child protection other than adoption, such as *kafalah*. However, due to the structural legal differences between adoption and *kafalah*, this proposal was not considered due to lack of support.[25]

IV. Problems with the Content and Interpretation of Unifying Laws

After more than 25 years of implementation of the 1993 Adoption Convention, which as of June 2021 has 104 States Parties,[26] it can be said that the Convention has had a very important 'effect on domestic socio-legal policies', and it has been a basis for increased support to birth families

[21] Preamble of the 1993 Convention.

[22] HCCH PB, '20 years of the 1993 Hague Convention – Assessing the impact of the Convention on laws and practices relating to intercountry adoption and the protection of children', Prel Doc No 3 of May 2015 for the attention of the Special Commission of June 2015 on the practical operation of the 1993 Adoption Convention, para 27.

[23] See Art 22. See also HCCH, *Guide to Good Practice No 2: Accreditation and Adoption Accredited Bodies* (Jordan Publishing Limited 2012) para 619 (Guide to Good Practice No 2).

[24] eg, in the USA, as of 30 July 2020, out of 116 adoption service providers, 112 were accredited bodies and only four were approved (non-accredited) persons or bodies.

[25] Explanatory Report (n 2) paras 42 and 90. However, *kafalah* falls under the scope of the 1996 Convention on Jurisdiction, Applicable Law, Recognition, Enforcement and Co-operation in Respect of Parental Responsibility and Measures for the Protection of Children.

[26] See '20 years of the 1993 Convention' (n 22); HCCH, Brochure: *1993 Adoption Convention – 25 Years of Protecting Children in Intercountry Adoption*, 2018. The list of Contracting Parties is available at: www.hcch.net under 'Adoption'.

and efforts to find appropriate family solutions in the State of origin.[27] The Convention has also helped to establish a safer, 'clear, ethical, transparent, and smooth adoption procedure' and to promote 'effective regulations, more controls, more rigorous procedures, and the processing of ICAs through competent authorities, all of this contributing to mobilising political will to increase efforts to prevent and address illicit practices'.[28]

The main challenge is to ensure that States Parties implement the Convention properly, so that if a child needs to be adopted intercountry, such adoption takes place 'in the best interests of the child and with respect for his or her fundamental rights as recognised in international law' (Article 1(a)). Regrettably, some States lack proper implementing legislation, resources, expertise or the political will to implement it adequately.[29] To help such States overcome some of these challenges, States with good practices, UNICEF, the HCCH and the International Social Service (ISS), as well as other organisations, may and do provide technical assistance. In addition, the HCCH and ISS have developed materials which provide specific guidance on how the Convention should be implemented.[30]

Adoption needs to be rooted in a functioning child protection system.[31] If the child protection system is very basic and there is neither comprehensive legislation[32] nor adequate resources, it is very difficult to implement the Convention properly.[33]

The Convention sets out basic and clear rules that are now commonly accepted by most States. It uses several broad terms and principles which provide some degree of flexibility and thus take into account some specificities of the relevant State and its culture.[34] This has facilitated ratification or accession by a broad number of States Parties, but nonetheless has created some difficulties regarding the interpretation of certain terms, such as those presented below.

The first such term is 'habitual residence' which, as in other HCCH Conventions, is not defined in the Convention. For example, it can be challenging to determine the habitual residence of adoptive candidates who are only living temporarily in a State for work. In other cases, adoptive candidates who are nationals of the State of origin but live permanently in the receiving State will still be considered habitually resident in the State of origin by that State. The HCCH has published a note on habitual residence and the 1993 Adoption Convention which, using case scenarios, presents a common understanding of the factors which might be considered when determining the habitual residence of the adoptive candidates and the child, as well as recommended practices to address cases of non-compliance with the Convention.[35]

[27] JHA van Loon, 'The Global Horizon of Private International Law' (2016) 380 *Hague Collected Courses* 71; N Cantwell, *The Best Interests of the Child in Intercountry Adoption* (Innocenti Insight – UNICEF 2013) 74 (UNICEF, *Best Interests*).

[28] HCCH Brochure (n 26) 14–15.

[29] '20 years of the 1993 Convention' (n 22) paras 25–28; Conclusions and Recommendations adopted by the Fourth Meeting of the Special Commission on the practical operation of the 1993 Adoption Convention (8–12 June 2015) C&R No 4.

[30] See Guide to Good Practice No 1 (n 8) Annex 2.8; Guide to Good Practice No 2 (n 23) section 12.4; and HCCH Brochure (n 26) for a list of materials.

[31] 2015 Special Commission (n 29) C&R No 3.

[32] eg, Cambodia approved in 2009 a Law on Intercountry Adoption. However, family support, alternative care and domestic adoption are regulated in other legal instruments. This makes the implementation further complicated as a smooth and clear procedure is lacking, which makes coordination among different authorities and bodies challenging. See Ministry of Social Affairs, Veterans and Youth Rehabilitation, *Capacity Development Plan for family support, foster care and adoption* (Cambodia 2018).

[33] See van Loon (n 27). In contrast, if the child protection system is very well developed, intercountry adoption is usually not needed.

[34] UNICEF, *Best Interests* (n 27) 6.

[35] HCCH, Note on Habitual Residence and the Scope of the 1993 Adoption Convention, 2018.

The principle of subsidiarity in intercountry adoption is one of the cornerstones of the Convention (Article 4(b)).[36] It means that

> States Party to the Convention recognise that a child should be raised by his or her birth family or extended family whenever possible. If that is not possible or practicable, other forms of permanent family care in the country of origin should be considered. Only after due consideration has been given to national solutions should intercountry adoption be considered, and then only if it is in the child's best interests.[37]

In practice, it is not easy to determine if 'due consideration' has been given or not, and views differ regarding whether domestic temporary family measures should have preference over international permanent family measures. In any case, what is clear is that, if possible, children should be able to live in a family, as a permanent solution, and within their State. As statistics show, the Convention has contributed to the proper implementation of this principle.[38]

There are also differing views on the interpretation of the principle of the best interests of the child.[39] For example, even if poverty should *never* be the only justification for the removal of a child from parental care,[40] some believe that intercountry adoption is always in the best interests of the child because it is a way of 'saving' children living in poverty in a State of origin and ensuring that they are adopted by rich families living in receiving countries.[41] However, the 1993 Adoption Convention provides clear guidelines on the essential factors that must be taken into consideration in determining what is in the best interests of a child being considered for an intercountry adoption. These are, among others: the principle of subsidiarity; ensuring that the child is adoptable; ensuring that the adoptive candidates are eligible and suitable; preserving information about the child's origins (right to identity); access to origins; professional matching; and protection from all forms of abuse.[42]

Another broad term is 'adoptability': a child must be declared adoptable (ie, it must be ensured that the child's status permits adoption to be considered and that he or she can be expected to benefit from that measure) from a legal, medical, psychological and social perspective before the adoption procedure can start. According to the Convention, each State can determine when a child can be considered adoptable. From the legal point of view, adoptable children are usually:

- Children whose birth parents have given their consent to adoption: very specific safeguards – substantive rules – were introduced in the Convention regarding consent (Article 4(c) and (d)). Among others, consent must be informed (given after proper counselling and information about the effects of the consent),[43] given freely (ie, not induced by any type of payment or compensation), given in the required legal form, expressed or evidenced in writing, not have been withdrawn, and for mothers, given only after the birth of the child.[44] One achievement

[36] 2015 Special Commission (n 29) C&R No 2. See also B Mezmur, 'Intercountry Adoption as a Measure of Last Resort in Africa: Advancing the Rights of a Child Rather than a Right to a Child' in (2009) 6 *International Journal on Human Rights* 83.

[37] Guide to Good Practice No 1 (n 8) para 47.

[38] P Selman, *Global Statistics for Intercountry Adoption: Receiving States and States of origin*, 2020. See also '20 years of the 1993 Convention' (n 22) ch 3.1.

[39] UNICEF, *Best Interests* (n 27) 5.

[40] *Guidelines on Alternative Care* (n 5) para 15.

[41] eg, s 199 of the Civil Code of Nepal (2017) includes a 'fast track' rule for adoptive candidates who are renowned foreign citizens, including heads of state, chiefs of international organisations and persons having an annual income of more than 300,000US$.

[42] UNICEF, *Best Interests* (n 27) 60; Guide to Good Practice No 1 (n 8) Glossary.

[43] eg, providing false advice to the birth parents in order to obtain their consent (eg, making a false promise that the child will receive education and/or medical treatment and then come back) should be considered an illicit practice.

[44] Regrettably, in some States, it is possible to give consent before birth for domestic adoption.

of the Convention is that due to more effective implementation of legislation and the development of good practices regarding consent, today an increasing number of birth mothers, after proper counselling and information, decide to keep and raise their child themselves.[45] Yet, a challenge is to provide long-term support to the birth family in order to avoid situations where the child re-enters the child protection system.

- Orphans: today the vast majority of orphans live with members of their extended family[46] and, contrary to widespread belief, children with no living parents make up only a minority of those adopted abroad.[47]
- Children whose origin is unknown:[48] such children are usually found living on the street, or in police stations, child institutions, religious buildings or baby boxes. The competent authorities should do their best to search for the birth family. One concern, however, is that sometimes no active search is carried out during the time frame allocated for tracing. Today, DNA testing can help find the birth family, but often the authorities do not have the necessary resources to do this, and it may also raise privacy issues.
- Children whose birth parents have had their parental rights and responsibilities withdrawn following abuse and/or neglect: in these cases, the competent authorities have determined that the birth parents should no longer exercise parental care because they are unable or unwilling to take proper care of the child. In some instances, this may occur despite the objections of the birth family to the adoption of their child. This issue has created much controversy in several countries.[49] Today, an increasing number of adoptable children have been abused, neglected and institutionalised before adoption.

While the Convention provides procedural rules (Article 16(1)) for all children above, it only provides specific substantive rules for cases following consent. Further guidance is therefore needed in this area for all other cases.

In determining adoptability, there is a difficult balance to strike between (1) supporting the birth family (if known) to overcome its problems and assist it in being able to take care of the child; and (2) the need to provide a domestic family solution – preferably permanent – for the child. Taking a timely decision is crucial: if the adoption decision is taken too quickly it may lack guarantees, while if authorities are too slow in making a decision, the child may end up being too old making it more difficult to find an adoptive family, and for him or her to bond properly with the new family.[50]

The authorities must ensure that, having regard to the age and maturity of the child, children consent to their adoption after being properly informed and counselled (Article 4(d)). This has special relevance today because many children adopted intercountry are older. However, this fundamental right of children is not always respected and, even in the most child-friendly scenarios, it is by no means a given that a child or adolescent will be able to measure the full implications of his or her decision. The consequences of not obtaining proper consent can be disastrous for the adoptee and both families and may eventually cause a breakdown of the adoption.

[45] eg, Guatemala (*Memoria de Labores del Consejo Nacional de Adopciones (CNA)*: eg, in 2019, 90% of birth mothers decided to keep their children after counselling and support.

[46] See UNICEF 'Children in Alternative Care', 2021 and UNICEF Press Centre – 'Orphans', 2018.

[47] See responses to question 9 of HCCH Country Profile.

[48] In some countries, this is the case for many adoptable children (eg, China when there was the one-child policy).

[49] eg, Colombia (Sentencia T-844/11 de la Corte de Constitucionalidad); UK (for domestic adoptions: European Parliament, DG for Internal Policies, *Adoption without consent*, 2015).

[50] This is the case in some receiving States. According to the Convention, authorities must act expeditiously to prevent unnecessary delays, while respecting the Convention (Art 35).

With respect to prospective adoptive parents, the Convention establishes that they must be declared eligible (ie, legal criteria) and suitable (ie, psycho-social and medical criteria) to adopt, and have been appropriately counselled (Articles 5 and 15).[51] Again, the Convention provides flexibility as it leaves it to each individual State to decide when adoptive candidates should be considered suitable and eligible. It also means that there are differences between States on the requirements to be considered for eligibility and suitability,[52] and how counselling is provided.[53] In practice, candidates from States with more comprehensive laws and procedures, and who receive proper support and counselling before, during and after the adoption procedure, are usually better prepared to adopt.

Matching ensures 'the identification of the adoptive parents from among the approved applicants who can best meet the needs of the child'.[54] It should be done by a multidisciplinary team of professionals. Therefore, adoptive candidates should not first identify a child (eg, by visiting a childcare institution) and then ask to declare the child adoptable, nor take a child under their care informally, and years later attempt to regularise the situation by requesting to adopt the child.[55]

After the matching process and the agreements under Article 17 have been given, it is in the best interests of the child and the prospective adoptive parents to have a probationary (socialisation) period supervised by professionals. If this probationary period is successful and after ensuring that all guarantees have been respected, then the relevant competent authority may issue the adoption decision. This adoption decision, if done according to the Convention, should be recognised by operation of law (ie, automatically) in all other States Parties. However, in certain States Parties this is not the case, and issuance of the Article 23 certificate confirming that the adoption was done in conformity with the Convention does not lead to automatic recognition because, departing from the Convention, these States require additional procedures for the adoption to be recognised.[56]

Lastly, another general term is 'improper financial and other gain' (Article 32(1)). While the prohibition against such gain is clear, it is sometimes challenging to differentiate between transparent and reasonable costs and between fees to be paid to professionals and improper financial gain. At what point do such payments become improper? This needs clarification as many problems that occur in intercountry adoption are linked to financial issues. For instance, while the Convention only mentions costs, expenses and professional fees (Article 32(2)), actors in the adoption process have found other ways to 'make money': initially through donations (which, paradoxically, in some countries are considered as 'mandatory'), contributions, and cooperation or development projects[57] (notwithstanding that adoption accredited bodies generally do not have expertise regarding developmental aid), and, more recently, child maintenance and

[51] Guide to Good Practice No 1 (n 8) para 400.

[52] See responses to question 14 of HCCH Country Profile. Different requirements may include status (eg, married, single, registered partnership) and age (minimum age, maximum age, difference in years between the adoptee and the adoptive candidates).

[53] See responses to question 15 of HCCH Country Profile: there may be mandatory (in many States) and non-mandatory courses, different number of hours (from just a couple of hours to 40 hours in Croatia, Ireland, Latvia, or 48 in Czech Republic), and content.

[54] Explanatory Report (n 2) para 318.

[55] This is done in domestic adoption cases in Latin America ('*niño puesto*'), and in some cases to circumvent adoption rules.

[56] '20 years of the 1993 Convention' (n 22) para 46. This is the case, eg, in Belgium, France and Italy.

[57] eg, Cambodia (2009 Law on Intercountry Adoption, Art 25); Italy (Law 184/1983, Art 39ter); and Vietnam (2010 Law on Adoption, Art 7).

health costs.[58] But the question remains 'on what children's rights basis the child protection system, including the adoption system, in a country should be partially funded by prospective adoptive parents or adoption accredited bodies through contributions, donations and / or cooperation projects'?[59]

On the positive side, many Latin American States, among others, have been able to ensure that some costs and fees involved in intercountry adoption are covered by the State,[60] as is the case with other child protection measures. The 'international' nature of intercountry adoption should not mean increased costs. Adoption should incur costs similar to those of other child protection measures. In this respect, the HCCH has developed several tools to guide stakeholders on how to interpret all those terms, and how to achieve transparency and reasonableness.[61]

V. Remaining Gaps to be Rectified

The Convention is silent on certain matters because, in many cases, the drafters were not able to reach an agreement or it was thought that the matter could be resolved at the domestic level.

For example, the Convention says that there shall be no contact between the prospective adoptive parents and the child's parents or any other person who has care of the child before matching (Article 29). However, the Convention does not prohibit contact between the prospective adoptive parents and the child because this situation 'does not have the potential for abuse that contact with the parents has, and may normally be both desirable and unavoidable'.[62] In retrospect, this can be considered a gap in the Convention text. Many States have been able to raise the standards and include the prohibition of contact between the prospective adoptive parents and the child before matching.[63] The HCCH *Guide to Good Practice No 1* is also clear that '[m]atching should not be done by the prospective adoptive parents, … by selecting an appealing child in person'.[64]

Nonetheless, there is a situation that is supported by a few States of origin to permit such contact: according to their experience, adoptable children who have the opportunity to meet with adoptive candidates at hosting programmes or summer camps[65] tend to have a better chance to be adopted. These programmes are targeted at older children and children with health problems for whom it may be more difficult to find a family. Still, these programmes create a loophole for bypassing some of the safeguards and procedures of the Convention, and they also have other issues (eg, children who are not adopted may feel rejected).[66]

[58] Between matching and before the child is entrusted to the adoptive family, some States require that the adoptive parents pay maintenance costs for the child who is at that time living in a child institution. See responses to HCCH Tables on Costs (eg, Burkina Faso, Haiti, Vietnam).

[59] HCCH Working Group on Preventing and Addressing Illicit Practices, Conclusions and Recommendations of the May 2019 meeting, para 9.

[60] See the responses to the Table on Costs associated with Intercountry Adoption (eg, Brazil, Chile, Colombia, Dominican Republic, Honduras, Peru).

[61] eg, HCCH, Note on the Financial Aspects of Intercountry Adoption, 2014.

[62] Explanatory Report (n 2) paras 496 and 499. However, there was considerable discussion about this as many States wanted to prohibit such contact.

[63] See responses to question 66 of the HCCH 2020 Questionnaire on the Practical Operation of the 1993 Adoption Convention, eg, Australia, Brazil, Burkina Faso, Canada, Chile, Dominican Republic, Ecuador, France, Haiti, Honduras, Lithuania, Luxembourg, Mexico, Monaco, Montenegro, Norway, Peru, Poland, Romania, Senegal, Slovenia, South Africa, Spain, Sweden, Switzerland, Turkey, United States of America and Vietnam prohibit such contact before matching.

[64] Guide to Good Practice No 1, para 65.

[65] eg, Colombia and Latvia (see responses to the 2020 Questionnaire (n 63).

[66] See Guide to Good Practice No 1 (n 8) section 8.8.9 about respite care abroad leading to the adoption of a child.

A similar but more recent phenomenon that is also proving to be difficult to deal with is voluntourism in child institutions[67] (ie, activities that support child institutions by individuals who are primarily, or were initially, tourists on vacation). Voluntourism in child institutions allows adoptive candidates to meet with children, get attached to them and then want to adopt them.[68] This is very problematic as it goes against many of the principles of the Convention.

The Convention does not include a provision on which nationality(ies) the child should have after being adopted. Many States of origin provide expressly that the adoptee should retain his or her country's nationality.[69] Still, in some cases this is not the case,[70] and adoptees (often adults) who want to regain their nationality of origin face difficult and expensive procedures to do so.[71] In the case of receiving States, in most instances the nationality is accorded automatically to the adopted child, provided that at least one of the adoptive parents has the nationality of the receiving State.[72] However, there are some cases where adoptees do not acquire that new nationality as, eg, the adoptive parents do not complete the necessary paperwork or are not well counselled on what has to be done. In such cases, if an adult adoptee commits an offence he or she may be subject to deportation to the State of origin.[73] Returning to the State of origin can be very difficult for the adoptee as he or she may not speak the language, know the culture or have any known relatives in that country.[74]

Another of the criticisms of the Convention is that it no longer applies once the child is adopted and it only includes a very general rule requiring States to take all appropriate measures to promote post-adoption[75] services in their States (Article 9(c)). While the number of intercountry adoptions has decreased sharply in recent years (from 45,483 in 2004 to 6,520 in 2019),[76] there are still a large number of adoptees.[77] Adoptees should have access to counselling and support not only immediately after adoption, but throughout their lifetime. However, this is not always the case, and it may not be clear which authority or body should provide these services and how they should be financed.[78]

[67] This practice is sometimes known as 'orphanage voluntourism'. However, as most children living in child institutions are not orphans, the term orphanage has not been used here. UNICEF and other bodies are organising campaigns to prevent this (Orphanage Voluntourism in Nepal and Volunteering in orphanages).

[68] See responses to questions 69 and 70 of the 2020 Questionnaire (n 63): Brazil, Canada, Colombia, Dominican Republic, Haiti, Honduras, Norway, South Africa, Spain and United States of America have experienced this recently, and in most cases the applications were rejected and/or the children were not adoptable.

[69] Guide to Good Practice No 1 (n 8) para 496. See responses to questions 26 and 27 of the 2020 Questionnaire (n 63) (eg, nowadays, adoptees from Brazil, Colombia, Dominican Republic, Ecuador, Honduras, Lithuania, Panama, Peru, Senegal, United States of America, retain their nationality upon adoption).

[70] eg, in Brazil, when male adoptees turn 18 they need to present themselves to the Brazilian Consulate in the receiving State for military enlistment abroad. If they do not do so, they may lose their nationality (see response to question 26 of the 2020 Questionnaire, (n 63)); in the Republic of Korea, an adoptee may recover his/her Korean nationality through the reinstatement of nationality. Several States of origin indicate that if the adopted child takes the nationality of a State that does not allow dual citizenship, that receiving State may not recognise the child's State of origin nationality (see responses to HCCH Country Profile, eg, Benin, Burkina Faso, Romania, United States of America).

[71] See ICAV, 'ICAV Perspective Paper Illicit Intercountry Adoptions', 2020.

[72] Guide to Good Practice No 1 (n 8) para 497.

[73] eg, United States of America (see US Department of State website). At the time of finalising this chapter, a bill to extend the Child Citizenship Act retroactively to adult adoptees who did not automatically naturalise as US citizens when the law came into effect is in the US Congress.

[74] Guide to Good Practice No 1 (n 8) para 499.

[75] Ibid, ch 9.

[76] See Selman (n 38).

[77] A rough estimation by Selman is that there are at least one million since 1948 (approximately half of them were adopted to the United States). It has to be noted that not all adoptees have been adopted under the Convention.

[78] See ICAV Paper (n 71), and EurAdopt, Statement Post Adoption Services, 2019.

While the Convention is very clear on the need to collect and preserve information, the access to origins is subject to the laws of each State (Articles 9(a) and 30). Many adoptees (independently if they have experienced problems due to their adoption), as well as their descendants, do search for their origins. Some States have developed specific programmes;[79] yet, in some cases it has proven difficult to search for information as prior to the Convention's existence, information was not always kept[80] and even if it is available there is no clear system to access the information. In addition, a few States have some limitations for access.[81]

In some cases, the search for origins leads to the discovery of illicit practices.[82] Competent authorities have to inform their Central Authority if they find that any provision of the Convention has not been respected or there is a serious risk that it may not be respected, and Central Authorities have to ensure that appropriate measures are then taken (Article 33). Recently, illicit practices – in many instances concerning cases before the Convention or outside its scope – have been discovered[83] and authorities do ask for guidance on how to prevent, but also how to respond to, such abuses. The HCCH Working Group on Preventing and Addressing Illicit Practices in Intercountry Adoption[84] was established to develop tools to assist States in this matter as the Convention indirectly prevents abuses but does not have a mechanism on how to address them.

The Convention is silent on cases of problems, or a breakdown, after the adoption is issued.[85] In such instances, the child protection system of the receiving State is responsible for the child, as is the case for any other child in that country.[86] Today many intercountry adoptions concern older children and/or children with health problems and this increases the possibility of breakdowns. While some Central Authorities continue to cooperate after the adoption has taken place, others say that it is no longer under their competence or that they do not have information on breakdowns. In any case, it is of the utmost importance to analyse the circumstances that triggered the problems and ensure that cooperation between States continues. In addition, the HCCH 1996 Child Protection Convention may be useful to resolve some of the problems after the adoption has been issued.[87]

Is the Convention adaptable for use in the new technological era, where most of the procedures and exchanges of information take place online? The Convention is silent on such matters as the environment in which it was drafted was very different and the situation has changed drastically due to rapid technological developments. However, the spirit and the letter of this

[79] eg, Colombia, Peru, Philippines. See responses to question 3 of the 2020 Questionnaire (n 63).

[80] See ICAV Paper (n 71).

[81] In most States, the adoptee needs to be 18 years old. In a few States there are other restrictions, eg, Benin ('in case of vital need'); Bulgaria ('only if solely when significant circumstances impose'). See responses to question 31 of the HCCH Country Profiles.

[82] See responses to question 7 of the 2020 Questionnaire (n 63): eg, Belgium, Chile, Panama, Spain, United States of America.

[83] Regrettably, there have been some abuses and allegations of abuses under the Convention (see responses to question 29 of the 2020 Questionnaire (n 63)), some of which are currently being investigated (eg, in Armenia, the Netherlands, etc (n 18)).

[84] See WG Illicit Practices (2020) and (2019) (nn 14 and 59).

[85] The Convention includes a provision to deal with the breakdown of placements of the child with the prospective adoptive parents in the receiving State *before* the adoption has been issued (Art 21). Today, a minority of States have this system (eg, the Philippines), as most States prefer that the adoption takes place in the State of origin (see Art 28) and the child leaves the country of origin with secure legal parentage. See further, Explanatory Report (n 2) para 74.

[86] Guide to Good Practice No 1 (n 8) section 9.4.

[87] See HCCH, *Practical Handbook on the Operation of the 1996 Child Protection Convention*, 2014, 156 and, more generally, on the 1996 Convention, see Costanza Honorati and Mary Keyes, 'Parental Responsibility, Custody and Access', ch 33 in this book.

Convention should not constitute an obstacle to the use of modern technologies.[88] In fact, modern technologies have improved the intercountry adoption process by making communications easier and the process more expeditious, eg, most of the communications take place by email; short videos of the child may be used for the matching done by a multidisciplinary team; the child and the prospective adoptive parents may be in contact after the matching through online platforms; and DNA testing can be used in the search for families.[89] The COVID-19 pandemic has also led to an increased use of many of these technologies. Nevertheless, there is a need to raise awareness of the risks associated with the use of modern technologies, including social media, in particular for photo-listing and during the search for origins. In this regard, giving training to professionals and providing counselling to families is of vital importance.[90]

Knowing that many of the issues presented in this section are of key importance, most of them are scheduled to be discussed at the next meeting on the practical operation of the 1993 Adoption Convention in 2022,[91] in order to provide further guidance on how to prevent and address them.

VI. Conclusion: A Convention which Protects Children

The 1993 Adoption Convention is still fit for purpose almost 30 years after its conclusion. It is the HCCH Convention which has attracted the most States Parties in the shortest period of time; its flexibility makes it adaptable to current times and the 'theory' of the Convention is increasingly better known (although some still see adoption as a way to 'save orphaned' children). More importantly, the Convention has helped to raise awareness about the importance of better supporting birth families and finding domestic permanent family solutions as a priority (ie, the principle of subsidiarity);[92] it has also helped drastically to stop abuses, eg, by establishing moratoria, in some States.[93] These are some of the reasons behind the global decline in intercountry adoptions mentioned above. The Convention has also promoted far better preparation – of the birth family, the child and the prospective adopters – for intercountry adoption thereby ultimately reducing the risk of abuse and failure of the adoption.

States Parties should ensure that they have the necessary political will and human and material resources to implement the Convention, but with a focus on the child protection system as a whole and not just on adoption. A good system of adoption must always be properly integrated into the child protection system.

The 1993 Adoption Convention does not aim at promoting or banning intercountry adoptions. Its purpose is to ensure that if intercountry adoptions are done, they are done with all the safeguards and guarantees. As its title anticipates: the Convention is there to protect children.

Although the Convention establishes only minimum rules, and while there may be some gaps as shown by this chapter, this is not an excuse for deficient implementation. The Convention should not be implemented in a vacuum, but with the assistance of Guides to Good Practice and

[88] This is also the case for other HCCH Conventions; see eg, HCCH, *Practical Handbook on the Operation of the Service Convention*, 2016, 169; and David McClean, 'Service of Process', ch 12 in this book.

[89] DNA testing is becoming cheaper. Public DNA databases with appropriate guarantees should be encouraged.

[90] 2015 Special Commission (n 29) C&R Nos 38–40. See also ISS, *New Technologies and Adoption*, 2015.

[91] See the Adoption Section of the HCCH website.

[92] eg, Chile, China, Republic of Korea, Vietnam. See Statistics on the HCCH website.

[93] Guide to Good Practice No 1 (n 8) section 8.2.4.

other materials developed by States, the HCCH, ISS and other organisations which provide the necessary guidance to implement the Convention properly. Technical assistance to new States Parties is also a way to develop promising practices and avoid problems.

In addition, States have to be co-responsible in implementing the Convention: even if the Convention establishes different responsibilities for States of origin and receiving States, they must work together and cooperate; it is too easy to simply blame the other party for any problems that may arise. For example, a State of origin may be overwhelmed with applications from adoptive candidates of receiving States. In such circumstances, some receiving States prefer that the State of origin establishes a *moratorium*, instead of the receiving States themselves having to inform their adoptive candidates that further applications will not be taken for that specific State of origin.

There is of course always room for further improvements; while many abuses took place before the Convention entered into force or are occurring outside the scope of the Convention, States Parties to the Convention should be vigilant as they are not immune to contravening the letter and/or spirit of the treaty. A critical first step is becoming a Party to the Convention, but, more importantly, States must implement its safeguards properly. If not, abuses can still occur.[94] Cooperation between Central Authorities – a key objective of the Convention – has been and is key to stop, prevent and address illicit practices.

Today, there are stories in the media focusing on adoptions that are illicit but many of these situations are not per se adoptions as no procedures or laws were followed. It is true that a single abuse is one too many. However, intercountry adoption has been, is and can be a solution for certain children if it is in their best interests. In fact, if well organised and done with appropriate guarantees, intercountry adoption has many chances to be successful.[95] Taking into consideration the new developments in certain States regarding legal parentage where it is possible to have more than two legal parents, one may wonder if in the future simple and open adoptions will be more common as they allow contact with the birth family.[96]

Finally, the UNCRC establishes that intercountry adoption should enjoy safeguards and standards equivalent to those existing in the case of national adoption (Article 21(c)). The reality is that in some States the Convention's standards are higher than those for domestic adoptions, and practices in intercountry adoption have also positively informed the development of many domestic adoption systems.

[94] See above (n 83).

[95] See J Palacios et al, 'Adoption in the Service of Child Protection: An International Interdisciplinary Perspective' (2019) 25 *Psychology, Public Policy and Law* 57.

[96] See above (n 3); open adoptions are full adoptions where some type of contact takes place between the adoptive family and the birth family after the adoption.

36

Maintenance

PAUL BEAUMONT AND LARA WALKER

I. Introduction

The Hague Convention on the International Recovery of Child Support and other Forms of Family Maintenance (the Convention),[1] represents a pragmatic approach to the global recovery of maintenance. The Convention's core is on the recovery of child support and spousal support.[2] It contains indirect rules on jurisdiction and other provisions on recognition and enforcement, and provisions on cooperation through Central Authorities (CAs). Under the core Convention the provisions on CAs do not apply where the application is purely for spousal support but currently they apply in the majority of Contracting States because of Declarations.[3]

The Convention entered into force on 1 January 2013. Forty-three States (including 26 EU Member States) and the EU are bound by the Convention.[4] The Convention applies in a variety of countries around the world, such as Albania, Brazil, New Zealand, Norway, Turkey, UK and the USA, highlighting its appeal to countries of diverse legal traditions and socio-economics.

The aim of the drafters of the Convention was, as far as possible, to create a global minimum standard (replacing the earlier Hague Conventions and the UN 1956 Convention) for obtaining cross-border maintenance, encompassing the Commonwealth scheme and allowing deeper cooperation bilaterally or regionally. This chapter focuses on the Convention as the key to global private international law of maintenance, advocating that all States become a Party to it.

The Hague Protocol on Applicable Law 2007 is not part of the core global private international law as it was negotiated by the civil law States in the Hague Conference on Private International Law (HCCH) and has no prospect of being applied by the common law States in the world (other than the very few in the EU).[5]

[1] Of 23 November 2007. See: www.hcch.net/en/instruments/conventions/specialised-sections/child-support for the text of the Convention, the *Explanatory Report* by A Borras and J Degeling (Explanatory Report) and the status table.

[2] Art 2(1). Under Art 2(3) States can extend the application of the whole or any part of the Convention to any maintenance obligation arising from a family relationship, parentage, marriage or affinity. Brazil and Turkey have used this very broadly and Ukraine quite broadly while excluding spousal support.

[3] Art 2(1)(c). The provisions on CAs have been extended to spousal support by Albania, Brazil, EU apart from Denmark, New Zealand, Nicaragua, Norway, Turkey and the UK.

[4] The Convention does not apply to Denmark. The Convention applied to the UK through EU approval up to 31 December 2020. Further to a ratification on 28 September 2020 by the UK in its own right, the Convention continues to apply to the UK after 31 December 2020 and its entry into force for the UK remains 1 August 2014.

[5] See P Beaumont, 'International Family Law in Europe – The Maintenance Project, the Hague Conference and the EC: A Triumph of Reverse Subsidiarity' (2009) 73 *Rabels Zeitschrift* 509; P Beaumont, B Hess, L Walker and S Spancken (eds), *The Recovery of Maintenance in the EU and Worldwide* (Hart Publishing 2014); and L Walker, *Maintenance and Child Support in Private International Law* (Hart Publishing 2015).

The Convention has been signed but not yet ratified by North Macedonia,[6] Canada[7] and Burkina Faso.[8] The Convention also appeals to non-Member States of the Hague Conference.[9] It is hoped that more States continue to become Parties to the Convention, so that it attracts the numbers now seen by the Hague Abduction and Adoption Conventions.[10] The more States that apply the Convention, the more global it will be. This should make it easier for maintenance creditors to recover maintenance from debtors who live in a different country from them.

The recovery of maintenance and child support is an important method of solving poverty. Single parents are far more likely to live in poverty than couples who are parents,[11] but the effective recovery of child support can help to lift these families out of poverty.[12] Therefore, an aspect of fundamental importance to the United States (US), was that maintenance creditors should not be prevented from claiming maintenance in cross-border cases because of prohibitive costs for assistance and high legal fees.[13] The Convention had to provide real solutions to practical problems, and it would not be successful in doing this unless the services provided under the Convention were cost free, including when establishing maintenance in the residence of the maintenance debtor.[14] This was particularly important in a context where the residence of the maintenance creditor or of the child are not, in themselves, a valid basis of jurisdiction in the US. Consequently, the Convention contains detailed provisions on administrative cooperation, legal aid and requests for specific measures to assist creditors with the recovery abroad of maintenance.

This chapter considers applications, CAs, legal aid, jurisdiction and recognition and enforcement, highlighting the pragmatic approach which resulted in enough flexibility to make the Convention attractive to States.

II. Applications

The Convention is not a traditional Convention on recognition and enforcement of maintenance judgments, like its predecessors in 1958 and 1973. It was drafted to include maintenance decisions by administrative authorities because some of the most successful cross-border systems are administrative rather than judicial, eg, Australia and Norway.[15] It was the brainchild of the then

[6] 9 December 2019.

[7] 23 May 2017.

[8] 7 January 2009.

[9] Guyana and Honduras.

[10] Abduction Convention 101 and Adoption Convention 104 Contracting States (at 15 November 2021).

[11] See Joseph Rowntree Foundation, *UK Poverty 2019/2020 Report*, 7 February 2020, available at: www.jrf.org.uk/report/uk-poverty-2019-20; J Browne and A Hood, 'Living Standards, Poverty and Inequality in the UK: 2015–16 to 2020–21' (Institute of Fiscal Studies 2016); J Levine, 'The plight of international child support enforcement' (2017) 22 *Child and Family Social Work* 617; and L Walker, 'Child support and the Government's children's socio-economic rights obligations' (2020) 28 *International Journal of Children's Rights* 860.

[12] See L Cuesta, M Hakovirta and M Jokela, 'The antipoverty effectiveness of child support: Empirical evidence for Latin American Countries' (2018) 52 *Social Policy Admin* 1233; M Hakovirta, C Skinner, H Hiilamo and M Jokela, 'Child poverty, child maintenance and interactions with social assistance benefits among lone parent families: a comparative analysis' (2019) 49 *Journal of Social Policy* 19; and C Skinner, M Hakovirta and J Davidson, 'A Comparative Analysis of Child Maintenance Schemes in Five Countries' (2012) 14 *European Journal of Social Security* 330.

[13] MH Carlson, 'United States Perspective on the New Hague Convention on the International Recovery of Child Support and other forms of Family Maintenance' (2009) 43 *Family Law Quarterly* 21.

[14] Carlson, ibid, and W Duncan, 'The New Hague Child Support Convention: Goals and Outcomes of the Negotiations' (2009) 43 *Family Law Quarterly* 1.

[15] See Art 19(1) and (3) and paras 431–32 of the Explanatory Report (n 1). For the success of Australia and Norway, two administrative systems, see the high volume of cross-border cases recorded in 2019 (n 26); and see J Saue,

Deputy Secretary General of the HCCH, William Duncan, to ensure that the Convention covers a wide number of maintenance applications, see Article 10. In particular, establishment actions fall within the scope of the Convention if they are brought through CAs. The maintenance creditor gets free help with the application for child support from the CA in their own residence and in the place where the claim is made, coupled with free legal aid in the latter place.[16] Furthermore, if States have a reservation against recognising and enforcing a decision from a State where the child was habitually resident at the time the proceedings in that State were commenced, then the State has a duty to facilitate the establishment of child support if it cannot recognise the decision on the basis of one of the other grounds of indirect jurisdiction available under the Convention.[17] This duty includes accepting that the foreign decision has established that child's eligibility for maintenance in the State addressed.[18] Under the Convention, creditors can apply for establishment, modification, recognition and enforcement, and enforcement of decisions;[19] whilst debtors can only apply for modification or recognition of a decision, or for a procedure limiting enforcement.[20] The focus on creditors as the sole party for issuing establishment applications, where the application is made through the CA, helps to protect creditors against the risk of conflicting decisions, and the direct rules of jurisdiction for modification proceedings seek to provide creditors with further protection.[21]

III. Some Recent Statistics on Applications

Brazil has reported that a large number of cases are being processed under the Convention; near the end of 2019 the country had around 1,200 active cases (800 outgoing and 400 incoming).[22] It is impossible to tell how many cases are being processed under the Convention as only 21 other States were able to give statistics to the Permanent Bureau by October 2020[23] in preparation for an HCCH Review Special Commission (originally scheduled for June 2020 but postponed due to Covid-19 to between March and June 2022).[24] This lack of commitment to the

F de Jongh Bekkali, E Soettem and B Rustad, 'Administrative Establishment and Enforcement of Child Support in Norway' in P Beaumont, B Hess, L Walker and S Spancken (eds), *The Recovery of Maintenance in the EU and Worldwide* (Hart Publishing 2014) 161–81.

[16] See Arts 9–17 of the Convention.

[17] See Arts 10(1)(d) and 20(3)–(4).

[18] See Art 20(5).

[19] Art 10(1).

[20] Art 10(2).

[21] See section IV.B below.

[22] See Brazil's response to the questionnaire on the practical operation of the Child Support Convention (HCCH, Prel Doc No 1 of August 2019), available at: www.hcch.net/en/publications-and-studies/details4/?pid=6676&dtid=33.

[23] The number of active Convention cases near the end of 2019 reported in response to the questionnaire, ibid, was as follows (total or outgoing/incoming): Austria – 42; Belarus – 51/7; Bulgaria – 1; Croatia – 18/28; Cyprus – 1/2; Finland – 31/14; France – 45/119; Germany – 356/86; Hungary – 20/5; Latvia – 26/3; Lithuania – 61/8; Luxembourg – 4/0; Netherlands 30/28; Norway – 200/73; Poland – 134/144; Portugal – 50/62; Romania – 9/8; Slovenia – 35/15; Sweden – 1807; Ukraine – 221/179; UK (just England and Wales) – 13/185. The Swedish number is so high that it might be an error.

[24] See CGAP of March 2021 Conclusions at: assets.hcch.net/docs/94e2d886-1cbf-4250-b436-5c1899cb942b.pdf. It is disappointing that the USA is not able to give statistics on its caseload because it is dealt with by states and the Federal Government cannot compel them to provide statistics on Convention cases. It is poor that the UK statistics are incomplete because the Scottish and Northern Irish CAs did not return the questionnaire or enable the UK Government to supply UK-wide data. Even more worrying is the fact that many Contracting States did not respond to the questionnaire at all – even after the CGAP extended the deadline for submissions – Albania, Bosnia and Herzegovina, Belgium, Czech Republic, Estonia, Greece, Honduras, Ireland, Italy, Malta, Montenegro, Slovakia, Spain and Turkey.

processes of developing the Convention by such significant States as Belgium, Czech Republic, Italy, Kazakhstan,[25] Spain and Turkey is deeply worrying for the successful operation of the Convention and for the successful payment of maintenance across borders. The responses to the questionnaire show that as the Convention is nowhere near universal in its scope yet, and as the EU Maintenance Regulation and Nordic instrument displace the Convention for cases between Parties to those instruments, a lot of cross-border maintenance cases are still processed under the UN New York Convention 1956, or the Hague Convention 1973, or the Commonwealth scheme, or bilateral agreements.[26] So a complete understanding of global private international law of maintenance still requires a knowledge of lots of legal instruments.

By adding incoming and outgoing cases together and dividing by two we can get a rough idea of how many international maintenance cases, that can be accounted for by CAs, there were in the reporting States that were Parties to the Convention in late 2019: Convention – 2,661; non-Convention – 17,832.[27] The balance will shift towards the Convention, now that it applies between the UK and the EU,[28] by several thousand cases while reducing non-Convention cases by the same amount. Clearly the overall balance will only change when more States become Parties to the Convention and keep statistics on Convention and non-Convention cross-border maintenance cases going through CAs. A significant number of Convention cases will not go through CAs and statistics will be difficult if not impossible to keep.

IV. CAs and Legal Aid

CAs have a key role to ensure that child (and spousal) support is paid across international borders between Contracting States. The Preamble to the Convention repeats the aim of the UN Convention on the Rights of the Child that States should enter into an international agreement 'to secure the recovery of maintenance for the child from the parent(s) or other responsible persons'. Article 1 of the Convention contains the object of the Convention which is 'to ensure the effective international recovery of child support and other forms of family maintenance'. Article 1(a) notes that this object can 'in particular' be achieved by 'establishing a comprehensive system of co-operation between the authorities of the Contracting States'. CAs are the key

[25] The Convention does not apply between Kazakhstan and the US because the latter objected to the former's accession, see: www.hcch.net/en/instruments/conventions/status-table/notifications/?csid=1375&disp=resdn.

[26] See the responses to the questionnaire (n 22). Australia, not a party to the Convention, had 27,495 active outgoing cases and 12,695 incoming cases as at 30 June 2019 (Australia said: 'The reciprocating jurisdictions with which Australia has the most cases are New Zealand (bilateral agreement), the United Kingdom (1956 Convention, 1973 Hague Convention and Commonwealth arrangements), the United States of America (bilateral agreement), the Philippines (1956 Convention) and Canada (Commonwealth arrangements)'. Belarus – 38 outgoing cases under the 1956 Convention; Brazil – 400 outgoing and 200 incoming non-Convention cases coming through its CA; Bulgaria – 3 outgoing and 26 incoming such cases; Canada, not a party to the Convention (excluding some of its most populous provinces, ie, British Columbia, Ontario and Quebec) – 720 outgoing and 525 incoming cases in March 2018; Croatia – 495 outgoing and 174 incoming; Cyprus – 23 and 76; Finland – 217 and 510; France – 587 and 1,600; Germany – 2,016 outgoing (UN Convention 588, EU Reg 1,406 and bilateral 23) and 7,164 incoming (UN Convention 1,860, EU Reg 5,264 and bilateral 40); Hungary – 531 and 260; Latvia – 1134 and 98; Lithuania – 721 and 106; Luxembourg – 245 and 29; Mexico, not a party to the Convention – 2,186 and 178; Norway – 1,151 and 41 (plus several hundred cases for establishment not under an international instrument); Poland – 4,660 and 949; Portugal – 975 and 234; Romania – 27 and 32; Slovenia – 120 and 47; Sweden – 665 and 80; Switzerland, not a party to the Convention – 1,199 and 1,554; Ukraine – 71 and 162; and UK (only for England and Wales) – 1,112 and 8,924.

[27] There were another 25,052 non-Convention cases in the non-Convention States that gave statistics (Argentina, Australia, Canada, Chile, Mexico and Switzerland).

[28] Following the end of the Brexit transition period on 31 December 2020.

competent authority under the Convention in each State and must cooperate with foreign CAs and the competent authorities in their own State to 'achieve the purposes of the Convention'.[29] In addition CAs are tasked with being the Convention's troubleshooters as they have to seek 'solutions' to 'difficulties which arise in the operation of the Convention' within the realm of what is 'possible'.[30] They have a core role of transmitting and receiving Convention applications and of instituting or facilitating the institution of proceedings in relation to incoming applications.[31] So they are there, at no cost to applicants, to facilitate establishing, modifying and enforcing maintenance.

CAs have a long list of matters in relation to applications where they are to take 'all appropriate measures'. That phrase is a term of art in Hague Conventions in relation to CAs.[32] All the obligations on CAs are mandatory but the ones noted above must be delivered 'comprehensively' whereas the functions prefaced by 'all appropriate measures' need only be delivered: 'to the extent permitted by their powers and resources and their internal law'.[33] However, one must not be distracted by the limited nature of the obligations on CAs in Article 6(2) of the Convention because the unlimited binding nature of the obligations in Articles 5 and 6(1) mean that CAs must seek solutions to ensure that child support (and spousal support when accompanying child support) is recovered, not just that a decision awarding it is given or is recognised and made enforceable but that recovery of the amount awarded is achieved (ie, effective enforcement).

A. CA Composition and Staffing

CAs usually have responsibility for the whole State[34] but in multi-unit States there may be CAs for each unit within a State whilst one CA has to be designated as being able to receive incoming applications from other States when the applicant is not sure which CA is best placed to deal with the application.[35]

For the effective recovery of maintenance CAs need to be well enough resourced.[36] The recent HCCH questionnaire on the Convention reveals the following data on full-time equivalent (FTE) numbers of staff in CAs dealing with international maintenance cases:

Austria – 2
Belarus – 2
Brazil – 7
Bulgaria – 1
Croatia – 2[37]

[29] See Art 5(a). Note the similarity to Art 7(1) of the Abduction Convention.

[30] See Art 5(b). The positive nature of the obligation to 'seek solutions' is highlighted in para 102 of the Explanatory Report (n 1).

[31] See Art 6(1). CAs can delegate these functions to other public bodies but remain responsible to ensure that these mandatory tasks are carried out, para 96 of the Explanatory Report, ibid.

[32] See Art 6(2) of this Convention; Art 7(2) of the Abduction Convention; and Art 9 of the Adoption Convention.

[33] See para 96 of the Explanatory Report (n 1). See also Practices of Central Authorities under Arts 5 and 6 of the 2007 Convention (HCCH, Prel Doc No 8 August 2020) available at: assets.hcch.net/docs/08e33460-cacf-41b0-97fb-c7f73533b46a.pdf.

[34] See Art 4(1).

[35] See Art 4(2).

[36] See the work on this by Walker (n 5) 236–40.

[37] See Prel Doc No 1 (n 22). The Croatian CA has seven employees in the Central Authority but only two are dealing with maintenance full time.

Cyprus – less than 1[38]
Finland – 2[39]
France – 9
Germany – 70
Hungary – 9
Latvia – 32
Lithuania – 2
Luxembourg – 2
Netherlands – 4
Nicaragua – 2
Norway – 22[40]
Poland – 31[41]
Portugal – 8
Romania – 2
Slovenia – 2
Sweden – 40[42]
Ukraine – 3
United Kingdom (England and Wales only) – 21

The troubling figures here are the heavily populated countries that should be or are handling a large volume of cases with relatively few FTEs in their CAs, notably Brazil, France and Ukraine. CAs do not always perform the same functions. Some of them only transmit applications to private lawyers and play little or no role in the transfer of funds or the enforcement of orders. Indeed, some of them only keep an active file in relation to bad debtors whereas others keep all cases as ongoing even where maintenance payments are being made correctly because those CAs are involved in the transfer of funds.[43] One sign that CAs may be understaffed is that some CAs have reported a lack of response from the receiving State in regard to applications,[44] indicating a lack of cooperation under the Convention. The absence of figures on how many FTEs are handling international maintenance cases in other Contracting States, notably for Italy, Kazakhstan, Spain, Turkey and the US, is worrying as it may hide some very poor data. There are encouraging signs of best practice from Germany, Norway and Sweden and, even before becoming a Contracting State to the Convention, Australia, which has 106.4 FTEs working on its large number of international maintenance cases. Having enough staff is only a start; it is necessary to have enough well-qualified (some lawyers) and well-trained staff with the necessary language skills. No assessment of these issues was attempted by the HCCH questionnaire.

[38] The Cypriot response to the questionnaire, ibid, does not reveal the total number of FTEs in the Central Authority but it does reveal that it is embedded in the Ministry of Justice.

[39] Ibid. Finland has 10 FTEs in the CA but only 2 FTEs dealing with maintenance. The Finnish Social Insurance Institution deals with EU maintenance cases and has 3 FTEs handling those cases.

[40] Ibid. Plus 5 FTEs in their transmitting agency.

[41] Ibid, 5 in the CA and 26 in the Regional Courts.

[42] Ibid, 9 of which are dealing with Convention cases.

[43] See Prel Doc No 8 (n 33).

[44] Prel Doc No 1 (n 22). See the responses of Brazil and Norway to Q3.8. The US has reported inconsistencies, occasional delays and lack of cooperation.

B. The Provision of Legal Aid

The responses to the HCCH questionnaire,[45] do not indicate any problems with the delivery of legal aid to natural person maintenance creditors (usually mothers) seeking to establish a decision on child support in relation to a child under 21 in another State Party or to recognise and enforce such a decision from one State Party in another State. There can be a problem when the claim is made in the name of the child as the maintenance creditor (a common practice in Germany), but the receiving State can only process a claim if it is made in the name of the relevant parent of the child or of the State body recovering maintenance that has already been paid to the child by the State (as seems to be required in many US states). This can be overcome by a simple change in the name of the applicant. Another problem noted in several responses is the difficulty of ensuring that, where the person for whom child support has been ordered is now over 21 and is entitled to arrears of child support for the period when the person was under 21, the matter is dealt with as an application under the Convention and that free legal aid is granted. It is clear that an application for arrears falls within the scope of the Convention.[46] It should also be clear that the obligation to provide free legal assistance in Article 15(1) of the Convention applies to claims brought by a maintenance creditor who is now over 21 to get arrears of maintenance due to him when he was under 21 because it is 'in respect of' an available application under Article 10 of the Convention 'concerning maintenance obligations arising from a parent–child relationship towards a person under the age of 21 years'. The key is that the maintenance obligation to pay the arrears 'arose' from a parent–child relationship when the child was under 21. This should be the correct interpretation of the Convention even though the Explanatory Report in relation to Article 15(1) could be misconstrued: 'Reflecting the scope provision (Art 2(1)), this obligation applies only in respect of "a person" below the age of 21 years'.[47] The scope provision in Article 2(1), like Article 15(1), is carefully drafted not to limit the scope of application of the Convention to creditors who are under 21. The Convention applies to 'maintenance obligations arising from a parent–child relationship towards a person under the age of 21 years'. Therefore, the Convention applies in respect of a maintenance obligation owed by a parent to his child when the child was under 21. However, the question whether a child can under the Convention establish the maintenance obligation in relation to the period before he is 21 after he is 21, retroactive maintenance, is different from whether he can enforce a decision granted before he was 21 on which arrears have accumulated. However, both should be treated in the same way as they arise out of an obligation on a parent in relation to their child when he was under 21 years old.[48]

Another problem highlighted very forcefully by the German Institute for Youth Human Services and Family Law (DIJuF) in their separate response to the HCCH questionnaire is the difficulty for public bodies to successfully use the Convention to recover maintenance from a debtor in another State Party when the State body has already paid the maintenance to the creditor. In such situations the public body is entitled to free legal aid when it is seeking to enforce a

[45] Ibid.

[46] See Explanatory Report (n 1) para 436.

[47] Ibid, para 381.

[48] The Explanatory Report, ibid, para 436, says that an Art 19 'decision' can cover both arrears and retroactive maintenance: 'a requirement to pay arrears, retroactive maintenance or interest may also be included. It is clear that arrears are included in the scope of the Convention. The difference between "arrears" and "retroactive maintenance" is that retroactive maintenance means maintenance for periods prior to the application for a decision while arrears refer to the unpaid maintenance for periods after the decision'.

judgment from the courts of its own country in another Contracting State.[49] If such a judgment cannot be enforced in that country because of a reservation and Article 20(4) applies, the public body is entitled to free legal aid to establish a maintenance decision in that country.[50]

The fact that the focus of attention is now on whether legal aid can be claimed in cases where the child is now over 21 but the claim relates to maintenance obligations when the child was under 21, or on the precise scope of free legal aid for public bodies who are maintenance creditors, is testimony to what was revolutionary in the Convention – an obligation to provide free legal aid for maintenance creditors in cross-border child support cases achieved after long negotiations[51] – now being uncontested and commonplace.

V. Jurisdiction

A. Indirect Jurisdiction

The Convention does not contain positive direct rules on jurisdiction for the establishment of a decision. Instead it contains indirect rules, which means that jurisdiction can be reviewed at the recognition and enforcement stage. There is a risk of conflicting decisions arising because direct jurisdiction and conflicts of jurisdiction are largely unregulated by the Convention. This could put maintenance creditors in a precarious position because they may have already undergone lengthy and costly proceedings in the State of origin, only to find out that their maintenance order cannot be enforced in the State where the debtor lives.[52] However, the pragmatic approach taken by the HCCH is to only make the progress achievable by consensus so that Conventions can secure a large number of ratifications to achieve global reach. Consensus was possible on indirect, rather than positive direct, rules of jurisdiction[53] with some degree of flexibility for potential Contracting States through a reservation system.[54]

The Convention contains six bases of indirect jurisdiction:[55] the respondent was habitually resident in the State of origin at the time the proceedings were instituted;[56] the respondent submitted to the jurisdiction, either expressly, or by participating in the proceedings without objecting to the jurisdiction at the first available opportunity;[57] the creditor was habitually resident in the State of origin at the time the proceedings were instituted;[58] the child for whom the maintenance was ordered was habitually resident there at the time proceedings were instituted (this base is only available where the respondent had already lived with the child in that State, or

[49] See Arts 10(1)(a) and (b), 15(1) and 36. See the Explanatory Report (n 1) para 384 saying: 'The Diplomatic Session resolved that Article 15(1) should only apply to applications by creditors including public bodies'.

[50] See, ibid, and Art 36(1). See also D Martiny, 'Jurisdiction, Recognition and Enforcement in cases of Reimbursement Claims by Public Bodies' in Beaumont et al (eds) (n 5) 485.

[51] See Beaumont et al (eds) (n 5).

[52] This is also possible if jurisdiction is harmonised but rules on conflicts of jurisdiction are not harmonised or are only partially harmonised, see P Beaumont, 'Interaction of the Brussels IIa and Maintenance Regulations with (Possible) Litigation in Non-EU States: Including Brexit Implications' in I Viarengo and F Villata (eds), *Planning the Future of Cross Border Families* (Hart Publishing 2020) 331, 332–33.

[53] See, eg, Duncan (n 14) and Walker (n 5).

[54] Duncan, ibid.

[55] Art 20(1) and (2). Contracting States can make a reservation in relation to the bases in sub-paras (c), (e) and (f).

[56] Art 20(1)(a).

[57] Art 20(1)(b).

[58] Art 20(1)(c).

had lived in the State and provided support for the child there);[59] there is a jurisdiction agreement in writing (this provision does not apply in disputes relating to children);[60] the decision was made by an authority exercising jurisdiction on a matter of personal status or parental responsibility, unless that jurisdiction was based solely on the nationality of one of the parties.[61]

The Convention does not define habitual residence even though the possibility of doing so was discussed.[62] The Explanatory Report emphasises that the case law on habitual residence under the Abduction Convention should not be automatically followed, because the context is significantly different,[63] but case law sensitive to the context of the Convention should be developed.[64] It is hoped that there is a relatively low threshold for establishing that a residence is 'habitual' in the context of maintenance, to enable maintenance creditors to easily establish decisions at their habitual residence, or their child's habitual residence or the debtor's habitual residence.

The respondent's habitual residence and submission were both relatively unproblematic grounds at the time of the negotiations. Both these bases appeared in the Hague Maintenance Convention 1973,[65] they are widely accepted across the world,[66] and therefore no reservations can be made in relation to these bases of jurisdiction. The other base where no reservations can be made is the habitual residence of the child at the time the proceedings were instituted provided that the respondent has lived with the child in that State or has resided in that State and provided support for the child there. It will not apply where the mother and the child move to a new State and attempt to establish a maintenance decision there, or where the mother moves while she is pregnant with the child. Migration patterns are often interconnected with divorce, separation and cohabitation,[67] and following relationship breakdown the mother will often return to the State of her nationality.[68] The move is designed to provide the mother and child with emotional support, to try and make the family more financially stable as the childcare will be more cost effective and assist with return to work. Therefore, the provision is beneficial, but it may not help in all cases and it is not a complete substitute for creditor-based jurisdiction.

In many States the habitual residence of the maintenance creditor is an accepted base of jurisdiction in order to protect the weaker party,[69] eg, the EU Maintenance Regulation provides this as a key ground of direct jurisdiction.[70] However, creditor-based jurisdiction is not acceptable in all States, in particular the US.[71] This created a problem because it was in the global

[59] Art 20(1)(d).
[60] Art 20(1)(e).
[61] Art 20(1)(f).
[62] Explanatory Report (n 1) para 62.
[63] Ibid, para 444.
[64] Ibid.
[65] Convention of 2 October 1973 on the Recognition and Enforcement of Decisions Relating to Maintenance Obligations.
[66] Explanatory Report (n 1) paras 446–51.
[67] See S Morano-Foadi, 'Problems and Challenges in Researching Bi-National Migrant Families Within the EU' (2007) 21 *International Journal of Law Policy and the Family* 1.
[68] This migration pattern can be seen in child abduction cases. See, eg, N Lowe, 'A Statistical Analysis of Applications Made in 2008 Under the Hague Convention of 25 October 1980 on the Civil Aspects of Child Abduction' (2011) and the 'Statistical Analysis of 2015 Applications' (2018), both available at: www.hcch.net/en/instruments/conventions/publications1/?dtid=32&cid=24; L Silberman, 'The Hague Child Abduction Convention Turns Twenty: Gender Politics and Other Issues' (2000) 33 *New York University Journal of International Law and Politics* 221;and L Walker, 'The Potential Effects of Brexit on the Cross-Border Circulation of Private Family Law Judgments with a Particular Focus on Questions relating to Gender' in M Dustin et al (eds), *Gender and Queer Perspectives on Brexit* (Palgrave Macmillan 2019) 125.
[69] See above (nn 17–19).
[70] Reg 4/2009 [2009] OJ L7/1.
[71] See, eg, Duncan (n 14) s IX; Carlson (n 13) s III, A.2; and R Keith, 'Ten Things Practitioners Should Know about the Hague Convention of 23 November 2007 on the International Recovery of Child Support and Other Forms of Family Maintenance' (2017) 51 *Family Law Quarterly* 255.

interest to design a Convention that the US could agree to – 'many delegates told the US delegation that the global community did not need another child support Convention that the United States did not join'.[72] Therefore a special approach was needed in order to produce a Convention which could provide a truly global solution to the recovery of child support. Keith has described this solution as the 'grand compromise'.[73] States, such as the US, can make a reservation in relation to this indirect jurisdiction ground[74] but this does not mean that a decision made on this base of jurisdiction has no effects. The Convention takes a nuanced approach to protect creditors.

The Convention minimises any harm to creditors by providing further provisions for judges to consider when they are deciding whether to refuse to recognise and enforce a decision on the basis of inadequate jurisdiction in the State of origin.[75] The Convention first requires that even where a reservation has been made, the Contracting State shall recognise and enforce a decision if its law would in similar factual circumstances confer or would have conferred jurisdiction on its authorities to make such a decision.[76] The reservation is not in itself sufficient to ignore the order, the enforcing court must look to the factual circumstances on which the jurisdiction is based, and recognise the order if that court would have accepted jurisdiction in similar circumstances. Where this is not possible, the Convention provides that where the debtor is habitually resident in the State addressed that State must take all appropriate measures to establish a maintenance decision in that State.[77] If the decision to be enforced relates to child support (and the reservation as to jurisdiction is the only issue preventing enforcement) then that decision establishes eligibility for child maintenance in the State addressed. An award for child support should now be established in that State.[78] Therefore, the creditor should still end up with a maintenance order that is enforceable in the State where the debtor lives. In accordance with Articles 15 and 16, the authorities in the State of enforcement should not charge the creditor for any costs relating to the establishment of the new decision where Article 20(4) applies. Therefore, the creditor should not face any additional financial hardship where the original decision cannot be enforced and a new decision has to be established due to a reservation in relation to creditor-based jurisdiction.

B. Direct Rules on Modification

The Convention contains direct rules on jurisdiction in the context of modification. These are useful and restrict the debtor's ability to modify a decision in a new State. This rule applies where the decision was given in the State of the creditor's habitual residence, and the creditor continues to live in that State. If the decision is established under Article 20(4) and/or (5), discussed in the previous paragraph, the creditor would unfortunately not be able to benefit

[72] Carlson, ibid.

[73] Keith (n 71) s X.B.

[74] The USA is the only State to have made a reservation in relation to all the grounds it is permitted to do so under Art 20(2), ie, in respect of Art 20(1)(c), (e) and (f). Brazil has a reservation in relation to Art 20(1)(e) for agreements in relation to 'incapacitated adults and elderly persons'. Nicaragua also had a reservation in relation to Art 20(1)(e) but then withdrew it on 12 November 2020.

[75] Art 20 (3)–(5).

[76] Art 20(2).

[77] Art 20(4). It is envisaged that this provision would apply in most cases, because the decision is most likely to be enforced in a State where the debtor is actually present (unless the decision relates to the transfer of assets, rather than simple child support); it should be relatively simple to establish habitual residence for the purpose of maintenance.

[78] Art 20(5).

from Article 18, because the decision was not given in the State of her habitual residence. Therefore, where the debtor relocates he may be able to apply for modification in his new State of habitual residence (but that State is not likely to form an acceptable indirect basis of jurisdiction under the Convention (unless the requirements for submission are fulfilled) so any resulting modification is not likely to be recognised and enforced in any Contracting State). But in rare cases this may create an additional problem for creditors where the original decision cannot be recognised in accordance with Article 20(1)(c) or (d).

In cases where the decision was made in the State of the creditor's habitual residence and the creditor still remains there, there are a number of exceptions to the prohibition on the maintenance debtor bringing proceedings elsewhere. Two of these exceptions are designed to protect the parties. First, where the competent authority in the State of origin cannot, or refuses to, exercise jurisdiction to modify the decision or to make a new decision.[79] Second, where the decision made in the State of origin cannot be recognised or enforced in the State where the debtor is contemplating modification.[80] The retention of the original jurisdiction would not be helpful for the parties in either of these scenarios. The third exception is where the decision concerns adult maintenance and the parties have a jurisdiction agreement to go to another forum.[81] Here the debtor can apply for modification in the place provided for in the jurisdiction agreement thus protecting party autonomy. The final exception is where the creditor submits to the new jurisdiction.[82] This is done where the creditor either expressly accepts the jurisdiction or does not defend any proceedings on this basis at the first available opportunity. Unfortunately, the creditor may appear without being able to receive competent legal advice and unwittingly submit to the jurisdiction.[83] It is hoped that where the application for modification goes through the CAs, creditors are informed by their CA that the modification does not need to be done in a new State, provided that the other exceptions do not apply. Although the absence of rules on conflicts of jurisdiction means that the Convention does not address the problem of conflicting proceedings in all applications, the provisions in Article 18 help to resolve this problem in relation to modification proceedings.

VI. Recognition and Enforcement

The first part of the recognition and enforcement procedure concerns the indirect jurisdiction requirements (see section V.A above). These are positive requirements for recognition and enforcement in the sense that the order can only be recognised and enforced where the decision was established in relation to one of the rules on jurisdiction. There are also negative provisions where the authorities may refuse to recognise and enforce the decision if it conflicts with an important issue, such as where it is manifestly incompatible with the public policy of the enforcing State.[84] Recognition and enforcement can also be refused where the decision was obtained by fraud in connection with a matter of procedure,[85] the respondent has neither appeared nor

[79] Art 18(2)(c).
[80] Art 18(2)(d).
[81] Art 18(2)(a).
[82] Art 18(2)(b).
[83] See L Walker, 'New (and old) problems for maintenance creditors under the Maintenance Regulation' in P Beaumont, M Danov, K Trimmings and B Yüksel (eds), *Cross-border Litigation in Europe* (Hart Publishing 2017) 770.
[84] Art 22(a).
[85] Art 22(b).

was represented in the proceedings in the State of origin,[86] or where the decision was made in violation of Article 18.[87] The latter provision is useful because it serves to protect the direct jurisdiction rule under Article 18. This is not the case under the EU Maintenance Regulation where jurisdiction is covered by direct rules and it cannot be reviewed at the recognition and enforcement, or enforcement, stage.[88]

The final two provisions aim to assist with the problem of conflicting decisions, which may occur in establishment proceedings, due to the lack of rules on direct jurisdiction in this area. The first of these provisions gives priority to any proceedings pending in the State addressed for enforcement purposes, where those proceedings were commenced first.[89] In most child support cases conflicting decisions should not be a problem, and in the rare situation that proceedings have been issued in two Contracting States this should be picked up early on by the cooperating CAs. The issue of conflicting decisions is likely to be more prevalent in applications that are not directed through CAs. The second provision applies where the decision to be enforced is incompatible with another decision given for the same purpose between the same parties, either in the State addressed or a third State, and that decision is capable of being recognised and enforced in the State addressed.[90] In this situation there is no priority in time rule. As the Explanatory Report says this was a deliberate decision of the Diplomatic Session: 'It would be left to the wisdom of the judge or the authority to decide in each individual case which of the incompatible decisions has priority'.[91] This was to allow for discretion to refuse to recognise and enforce the decision that is being sought to be enforced – either by the maintenance creditor or the maintenance debtor – if there is a fairer decision of the State addressed or of a third State. In exercising that discretion, the authority or judge should take account of the object of the Convention to secure the effective international recovery of maintenance as guided by the language of the Preamble.

Once it has been established that a decision is capable of recognition and enforcement in the State of enforcement (normally the debtor's habitual residence), actual enforcement is a matter for the national law of the State addressed.[92] However, national laws on the calculation of child support and maintenance vary considerably. This means that a decision given in one Contracting State, which is capable of recognition and enforcement under the Convention, may prove difficult to enforce under national law if the content of the decision is not clear enough. One issue that was reported by CAs is where the decision provides for a percentage of the debtor's income, but no exact figure is provided. In these situations it can be unclear which income is included or whether the percentage applies to net or gross income.[93] 'States have the most difficulty in enforcing percentage of income orders if the order contains references to undefined terms such as the country's minimum standard of living'.[94] Authorities resolve these issues by asking for further clarification then altering the maintenance or creating an order that can be enforced. This is not seen as modification but rather providing clarification to the original order so that it can be enforced. Percentage of income orders normally relate to child support. The most important

[86] Art 22(e).

[87] Art 22(f). For a full analysis of these provisions see, eg, Explanatory Report (n 1) paras 477–89; Walker (n 5) 156–65; and P Torremans et al, *Cheshire, North and Fawcett Private International Law* (Oxford University Press 2017) 1084–86.

[88] Most decisions that circulate under the Maintenance Regulation do not require a declaration of enforceability, due to the abolition of exequatur (Art 17).

[89] Art 22(c).

[90] Art 22(d).

[91] (n 1) para 485.

[92] Art 32.

[93] See the responses of Germany, Norway and the USA to question 5.1. Latvia overcomes the problem by requiring an indexation table.

[94] Response of the USA.

thing is that orders are enforced promptly to provide for children and improve their standard of living. National authorities need to find the most effective way of ensuring this outcome.

VII. Conclusion

The Convention provides an excellent framework for global private international law on maintenance that is already in force in a number of key States that were unable to ratify the earlier Hague Maintenance Conventions. Its core scope deals with the essential issue of child support and encompasses spousal support in a more nuanced way. It would be excellent if all Contracting States were to cover all spousal support applications fully within the Convention.

The Convention creates a framework for ensuring that children get maintenance without harmonising direct jurisdiction rules. This is achieved by making establishment of maintenance available in the residence of the maintenance debtor with the free assistance of CAs and free legal aid, if it proves impossible or undesirable to recognise and enforce a decision there from the jurisdiction where the maintenance creditor is habitually resident. Indeed, for States with a reservation against certain indirect grounds of jurisdiction this turns into a duty to establish maintenance, with an acceptance of the maintenance creditor's eligibility for maintenance, when the lack of the reserved indirect ground of jurisdiction prevents the recognition and enforcement of the foreign decision. The Convention provides a number of solutions for protecting maintenance creditors, particularly in the context of child support, thereby providing socio-economic benefits for children and some other poor adults.

For establishing maintenance, the Convention turns on the efficacy of the work of CAs and free legal aid. The early data from the recent HCCH questionnaire indicates no problems with legal aid in the countries that have responded but does indicate a number of countries with relatively few employees in their CA. Of concern is the significant number of Contracting States not supplying any data and the still relatively small number of States that have become Parties to the Convention.

The Convention does have comprehensive provisions on recognition and enforcement of maintenance decisions which are not dependent on the efficiency of the CAs. So public bodies can bypass inefficient CAs to get maintenance decisions enforced in other Contracting States. However, all States need to be Parties to the Convention with well-resourced CAs to make global private international law of maintenance effective.

37

Matrimonial Property

RHONA SCHUZ

I. Introduction

Applicable law in relation to matrimonial property has become more relevant in the modern age due to the greater number of 'international couples', increasing international mobility and higher incidence of marriage breakdown. Attempts at harmonising applicable law rules in relation to matrimonial property have met with limited success. Only three States ratified the Hague Conference on Private International Law's (HCCH's) 1978 Convention on the Law Applicable to Matrimonial Property Regimes (Hague Convention).[1] More recently, an EU initiative for harmonisation in this area has failed to command universal support. Accordingly, the Council Regulation on jurisdiction, applicable law and the recognition and enforcement of decisions in matters of matrimonial property regimes (EU Regulation)[2] is not binding on all EU States, but only on the 18 who have chosen to participate in the enhanced cooperation.[3]

This chapter will discuss the main differences between the applicable law rules in relation to matrimonial property in different legal systems[4] and consider possible directions for global harmonisation. Particular attention will be paid to the question of the extent to which the EU model might serve as a basis for such harmonisation.

To understand the significance of applicable law rules in relation to matrimonial property, it will first be necessary to consider very briefly the impact of the differences between the prevalent matrimonial property regimes (section II). The subsequent sections will deal with the central aspects of applicable law in matrimonial property, in relation to which there is divergence: personal connecting factor (section III); party autonomy (section IV); effect of migration (section V); and law applicable to division of property on divorce (section VI). Each section will set out and analyse the various approaches to the issue in question found in different legal systems

[1] Text of the Convention at: www.hcch.net/en/instruments/conventions/full-text/?cid=87. Status table showing ratification by France, Luxembourg and the Netherlands, available at: www.hcch.net/en/instruments/conventions/status-table/?cid=87.

[2] Council Regulation 2016/1103 [2016] OJ L183/18 implementing enhanced co-operation in the area of jurisdiction, applicable law and the recognition and enforcement of decisions in matters of matrimonial property regimes (EU Regulation).

[3] Ibid, paras 10–13 of the Recitals and: e-justice.europa.eu/content_matters_of_matrimonial_property_regimes-559-en.do.

[4] These differences are illustrated within Europe by the TMC Asser Institute in The Hague in their Final Report (2003), available at: www.asser.nl/upload/ipr-webroot/documents/cms_ipr_6_1_Final%20Report%20EU%20Commission%20030703.pdf (2003 Final Report), which was prepared for the EU Commission. This report analyses national reports, which set out the substantive and conflict of laws position in relation to matrimonial property in 16 jurisdictions.

and in the harmonisation instruments. Section VII will summarise the conclusions and briefly discuss the major obstacles which stand in the way of increased harmonisation.

II. Matrimonial Property Regimes

Matrimonial property regimes[5] may be divided into four broad categories: community;[6] deferred community/participation of assets;[7] equitable distribution regimes;[8] and pure separate property regimes,[9] and variations exist within each type of regime.[10] Thus, the exact outcome in any given case may be significantly different, depending on the applicable law.[11] However, all the regimes, apart from separate property, are based on the same policy objectives (equality, fairness and the need to find an appropriate balance between autonomy and family solidarity)[12] and share a degree of commonality on the functional level.[13] Accordingly, there will usually not be any difficulty of principle in applying a foreign regime.

In contrast, the prospect of applying a foreign separate property regime, which does not share the same objectives, is problematic and this may influence the approach to choosing the applicable law. For example, Israeli courts by means of creative interpretation effectively neutralised the statutory immutability regime, to avoid application of separate property regimes on immigrants from Islamic States.[14] Indeed, it seems to be only a matter of time until European States will have

[5] Detailed information about domestic marital property law in European countries can be found in the 26 national reports written as part of the Commission on European Family Law (CEFL) harmonisation project. These are based on the law as it stood in 2008 and are available at: ceflonline.net/property-relations-reports-by-jurisdiction, and in K Boele-Woelki, B Braat, and I Curry-Summer, *European Family Law in Action, Volume 4: Property Relations Between Spouses* (Intersentia 2009). For an overview of the regimes in each of the 26 countries, see table in K Boele-Woelki et al (eds), *Principles of European Family Law Regarding Property Relations between Spouses* (Intersentia 2013) (Boele-Woelki et al, *Principles*) 12–16.

[6] The property which is in the community is owned jointly throughout the duration of the marriage. Liability for debts is also joint. Thirteen of the jurisdictions surveyed by the CEFL have a community of property regime operating as a default regime (Boele-Woelki et al, *Principles*, ibid, 219). In the US there are community regimes in nine states.

[7] During the marriage, the assets acquired by each spouse are treated as his separate property and only upon termination of the marriage by death or divorce does the community or the right to participate equally in the relevant assets of the other crystallise. The mechanism for sharing varies between regimes. (Boele-Woelki et al, *Principles* (n 5) 140 ff). Countries which have such regimes include Germany, Israel, the Nordic States and British Columbia.

[8] Property is owned separately by the parties during the marriage, but the court has wide discretion to divide the property between the parties on dissolution. This approach is adopted in most common law jurisdictions, including England and Wales, the US 'separate property' states, Australia and most Canadian provinces.

[9] Each party owns his own property and can deal with it as he sees fit, subject to the general law of property and trusts, and on dissolution the parties do not have any rights in relation to the property of the other. Very few modern States have pure separate property as a default regime, although many allow parties to opt for such a regime by agreement, either prior to or during the marriage (Boele-Woelki et al, *Principles* (n 5) 141). However, pure separate property is the default regime in Islamic States and some developing countries.

[10] eg, in relation to the assets covered by the regime.

[11] M Antokolskaia, *Harmonisation of Family Law in Europe: A Historical Perspective* (Intersentia 2006) 474; *Impact Assessment Study on Community Instruments concerning matrimonial property regimes of unmarried couples with transnational elements, Final Report* (5 March 2010) 39 (stating that there are vast differences between substantive and procedural rules in EC States).

[12] Antokolskaia, ibid, 473 ff; B Bratt, 'Matrimonial Property Law: Diversity of Forms, Equivalence in Substance' in M Antokolskaia (ed), *Convergence and Divergence of Family Law in Europe* (Intersentia 2007) 237, 243 ff.

[13] eg, most systems provide some degree of discretion to correct any injustice arising out of equal division of property, B Restar, 'Matrimonial Property in Europe: A Link between Sociology and Family Law' (2008) 12 *Electronic Journal of Comparative Law* 9, available at: www.ejcl.org.

[14] For detailed discussion, see R Schuz, 'Choice of Law in Relation to Matrimonial Property in the 21st Century' (2019) 15 *Journal of Private International Law* 1, 20 ff.

to address the implications of the recent mass immigration from Islamic States on their applicable law rules in relation to matrimonial property.

An additional challenge for private international law which arises from the different types of regimes relates to equitable distribution regimes. It is not clear whether these regimes should be characterised as matrimonial property regimes for the purpose of applicable law. Some authors have taken the view that since the court's powers to redistribute property take into account the parties' needs, resources and behaviour, they should be treated as issues of maintenance rather than of matrimonial property.[15] This position is based largely on the Court of Justice of the European Union decision in *Van den Boogaard v Laumen*,[16] in the context of jurisdiction.

There are cogent reasons for rejecting this approach. First, characterising schemes as maintenance simply because needs and resources are taken into account ignores the fact that a major objective of equitable distribution regimes is to reflect the parties' financial and non-financial contributions during the marriage, in the same way as do participation and community regimes.[17] Second, many immediate and deferred community/participation regimes provide the court with discretion to deviate from the equal sharing principle. It seems clear that a court applying such a foreign scheme would, if appropriate, invoke this discretion,[18] which would usually involve taking into account needs, resources and behaviour. It is difficult to justify treating these schemes as a completely different category from those schemes which allow discretion *ab initio*, particularly in relation to jurisdictions where in practice equal sharing is the starting point. Accordingly, this chapter proceeds on the basis that equitable distribution regimes are to be treated as matrimonial property regimes for the purposes of applicable law.

III. Personal Connecting Factor

A. The Different Approaches

In most civil law systems, there is a unitary approach under which the applicable law applies to all the property of the parties, irrespective of where it is situated, and no difference is made between movables and immovables.[19] Whilst the position in common law systems is not uniform,[20] English academic opinion supports a unitary approach.[21] Accordingly, it seems reasonable to

[15] eg, T Hartley, 'Matrimonial (Marital) Property Rights in Conflict of Laws: A Reconsideration' in J Fawcett (ed), *Reform and Development of Private International Law Essays in Honour of Sir Peter North* (Oxford University Press 2002) 215, 232. For a more nuanced approach, see CMV Clarkson, 'Matrimonial Property Law on Divorce: All Change in Europe' (2008) 4 *Journal of Private International Law* 421, 428.

[16] Case C-220/95 *Van den Boogaard v Laumen* [1997] ECR I-1176.

[17] R Schuz, *A Modern Approach to the Incidental Question* (Kluwer 1997) 143–44; M Hook, 'A first principles approach to couples' property in the conflict of laws' (2019) 15 *Journal of Private International Law* 257, 269 ff.

[18] eg, *Vladi v Vladi* 39 DLR (4th) 563 (1987).

[19] See 2003 Final Report (n 4) 117.

[20] English case law appears to indicate that where the immovables are abroad, the foreign *lex situs* will apply, but where they are in England, the matrimonial domicile will apply (CMV Clarkson et al, *2003 English National Report* 25–26 on file with the author). In British Columbia, it has been held that the *lex situs* of immovables determines the applicable matrimonial property regime, rather than that of the matrimonial domicile (*Tezcan v Tezcan* (1992) 62 BCLR (2d) 344) and this rule has been adopted by statute in Nova Scotia (Matrimonial Property Act, RSNS 1989, c 275 s 22) and Newfoundland (Family Law Act RSNL 1990). In the US, whilst in theory the *lex situs* of the immovables seems to apply, in practice its operation is severely limited by the tracing rule that marital rights in assets used to buy the land will be recognised (P Hay, P Borchers, S Symeonides and C Whytock, *Conflict of Laws*, 6th edn (West 2018) 605).

[21] eg, L Collins (ed), *Dicey Morris and Collins, Conflict of Laws*, 15th edn (Sweet & Maxwell 2012); Hartley (n 15) 225; Clarkson (n 15) 440.

assume that the question of which law should apply in relation to immovables is not a serious obstacle to harmonisation.[22]

Under most systems, in the absence of an express agreement between the parties, marital property relations concerning movables will, at least initially, be governed by the personal law of the parties at the time of the marriage. As is well known, the personal law is usually that of the domicile in common law countries and that of the nationality in civil law countries.[23] Whichever personal law is chosen, a problem will arise where the parties do not have a common personal law at the time of the marriage and a secondary rule will be required to determine which of the two personal laws should apply or that some third law is applicable. Three main approaches to cases where there is no common personal law can be identified.[24] The first is the US approach, under which the domicile of the party who acquired the property should be applied.[25] The second is that advocated by some English scholars, under which the applicable law should be that of the country to which the parties and the marriage have the closest connection,[26] although it is not entirely clear to what extent the test is objective or subjective.[27] The third is that found in some modern European private international law codifications, of a hierarchy of alternative connecting factors.[28]

B. Harmonisation Instruments

Both the Hague Convention and the EU Regulation adopt the unitary approach and do not make a distinction between movables and immovables, but the Hague Convention does allow parties to designate in relation to immovables the law of the place where the immovables are situated.[29] The EU Regulation does not allow such a choice.

In the absence of choice of the applicable law,[30] both the Hague Convention and the EU Regulation adopt the spouses' first common habitual residence after the marriage as the primary connecting factor.[31] This choice accords with the routine adoption of habitual residence as the main personal connecting factor in Conventions drawn up under the auspices of the HCCH, inter alia, because it is seen as 'neutral' and so acceptable both to common law and civil law systems.[32] In the relatively unusual situation in which the parties never have a common habitual residence, both instruments provide for the law of their common nationality to apply.[33] Where

[22] Although, in Scotland, a different rule for immovables (the *lex situs*) was entrenched in statute in 2006, see P Beaumont and P McEleavy, *Anton's Private International Law*, 3rd edn (W Green/SULI 2011) 916.

[23] *cf* some civil law States apply common residence, eg, Belgium and Latvia, *Impact Assessment Study* (n 11) 40; Sweden has its own concept of domicile, J Shiratzki, 2003 Swedish National Report 28 (on file with the author).

[24] Additional approaches can be found, eg, in Ontario, in the absence of a common habitual residence, the law of the forum (s 15 Family Law Act 1990); and in New Brunswick, the law of the habitual residence of the applicant (s 44(1) Marital Property Act 1980).

[25] Restatement Second (Conflict of Laws) para 257.

[26] Clarkson et al (n 20) 25.

[27] Hartley (n 15) 226, whilst referring to the centre of gravity of the marriage, states that the aim is to ascertain the reasonable expectations of the parties. In Israel, it has been held *obiter* that in the case where the parties do not share a common domicile, the law of the intended matrimonial home should apply, provided that the parties move there within a reasonable time, CA 7687/04 *Sasson v Sasson* PD 59(3) 596 (2005).

[28] See, eg, Art 9(2) of Spanish Civil Code (as amended in 1990); C Martinez, Spanish 2003 National Report 18, available at: citeseerx.ist.psu.edu/viewdoc/download?doi=10.1.1.193.9063&rep=rep1&type=pdf.

[29] Arts 3 and 6.

[30] See below, section III.

[31] Hague Convention (n 1) Art 4; EU Regulation (n 2) Art 26(1).

[32] LI De Winter, 'Nationality or Domicile?' (1969) 128 *Hague Collected Courses* 347.

[33] Hague Convention (n 1) Art 4(3); EU Regulation (n 2) Art 26(1). The Hague Convention, Art 4 provides for application of the law of the nationality in additional situations.

there is no common nationality, both instruments provide for a closest connection test,[34] but the Hague Convention refers to connection with the matrimonial property regime, whereas the EU Regulation refers to connection with the spouses jointly.

C. Analysis

Given the prevalence of the connecting factor of habitual residence in private international law conventions, it has to be assumed that this would be the basis of any future harmonisation attempts.[35] However, it should be borne in mind that the concept of habitual residence is more problematic than appears to have been anticipated[36] and that habitual residence may not in fact be the State most closely connected with the parties, eg, in cases of temporary or recent relocations.[37] The most feasible solution to this problem would be to create an exception which could be invoked where it could be shown that the parties were manifestly more closely connected to a country other than that of their habitual residence. The use of an exception rather than an open-ended connecting factor *ab initio*[38] substantially reduces the uncertainty inherent in the closest connection approach.[39]

IV. Party Autonomy

A. The Different Approaches

There is lack of consensus in relation to the extent to which parties should be allowed to choose the law applicable to their matrimonial property. Whilst generally in domestic law there appears to be an increased willingness to enforce pre-marital agreements,[40] most States have enacted procedural requirements for such agreements[41] and some limit the parties' freedom of contract[42] or provide substantive fairness requirements.[43] Moreover, in the applicable law context, most

[34] Ibid.

[35] Although, it should be noted that global conventions, in which habitual residence of adults (as opposed to children) has been the connecting factor determining applicable law (as opposed to jurisdiction or recognition of foreign judgments), have not been widely ratified, eg, Hague Conventions on Matrimonial Property and Succession.

[36] See A Briggs, *Private International Law in the English Courts* (Oxford University Press 2014) 76–81; and P Rogerson, 'Habitual Residence: the New Domicile' (2000) 49 *ICLQ* 86.

[37] Clarkson (n 15) argues that the law of the first common habitual residence should only apply where it has endured for a period of time, say three years.

[38] As advocated by Hook (n 17) 281 ff.

[39] As in torts, Art 4(3) the Rome II Regulation (Reg 864/2007EC of the European Parliament and of the Council of 11 July 2007 on the law applicable to non-contractual obligations [2007] OJ L199/40).

[40] In relation to the US, see generally, LJ Ravdin, *Premarital Agreements, Drafting and Negotiation*, 2nd edn (American Bar Association 2017). In England and Wales, see the landmark case of *Radmacher (formerly Granatino) v Granatino* [2010] UKSC 42.

[41] Ravdin, ibid, chs 2–4; JT Oldham, *Divorce, Separation and Distribution of Property* (Law Journal Press 2017) (release 59) para 4.03. For summary of the requirements in each US state, see J Halloran and McLaughlin, 'Should Marital Property Rights be Inalienable?' [2003] *Nebraska Law Review* 460, 499–507; for Europe, see Boele-Woelki, Braat and Curry-Summer, *European Family Law in Action* (n 5) 1151–60 and 1171–81.

[42] In relation to Europe, the comparative overview in Boele-Woelki et al, *Principles* (n 5) 100–16 shows considerable differences in the ways in which States restrict party autonomy.

[43] Halloran and McLaughlin (n 41). In England and Wales, the extent to which effect will be given to a pre-nuptial agreement depends on whether it is seen as causing unfairness, *Radmacher* (n 40) [75].

European States limit the parties' freedom to choose the law applicable to their matrimonial property to laws which have one of a number of specific connections with them.[44] There is no parallel restriction at common law.[45]

B. The Harmonisation Instruments

Both the Hague Convention and the EU Regulation restrict the parties' choice of applicable law to that of the State of habitual residence or nationality of at least one of the spouses at the time the agreement is concluded.[46]

Both instruments provide that the agreement should be in writing, dated and signed by the parties.[47] In addition, the Hague Convention provides that the designation of the applicable law should comply with the form prescribed either by the internal law designated by the spouses or by that of the place where it is made.[48] In contrast, under the EU Regulation, it is necessary to comply with the formal requirements of the country of habitual residence of either party, unless only one party is habitually resident in a Member State of the EU, in which case the requirements of that State have to be met.[49]

The Hague Convention provides that requirements relating to consent of the parties shall be determined by the law chosen[50] and the EU Regulation provides that the material validity of the agreement is governed by the law chosen.[51]

C. Analysis

In accordance with the principle of party autonomy both in domestic law and in relation to applicable law, agreements concerning the law applicable to matrimonial property law should be honoured,[52] provided that parties give informed consent, fully understanding the implications of such an agreement.[53] Models which restrict the choice of the parties to the laws of certain prescribed States are not consistent with modern day principles of autonomy and do not give effect to the parties' reasonable expectations. Whilst it might be argued that parties would not reasonably expect the application of any law other than those listed, since it would not be sufficiently closely connected to them,[54] the very fact that they have chosen some other law suggests

[44] See 2003 Final Report (n 4) 118–21.

[45] *Dicey, Morris and Collins* (n 21) 1473.

[46] Hague Convention (n 1) Art 3 (providing additionally for designation of the law of a new State where one of the spouses establishes a new habitual residence after the marriage and for the law of the place where immovables are situated in relation to such assets) and EU Regulation (n 2) Art 22.

[47] Hague Convention (n 1) Art 13; EU Regulation (n 2) Art 23.

[48] Hague Convention (n 1) Art 13. This accords with the general rule in relation to contracts. See, eg, *Dicey, Morris and Collins* (n 21) 1848; and EU Regulation 593/2008 on law applicable to contractual obligations (Rome I) Art 9.

[49] EU Regulation (n 2) Art 23.

[50] Hague Convention (n 1) Art 10.

[51] EU Regulation (n 2) Art 24. However, a party who claims that he did not consent can rely on the law of his habitual residence at the time the court is seised if it would not be reasonable to determine the effect of his conduct in accordance with the law chosen.

[52] Briggs (n 36) 775.

[53] See recital 47 to the EU Regulation (n 2), but the requirement of a signature in Art 23 does not ensure informed consent. *cf* Recommendation in Law Commission's Report on Matrimonial Property, Needs and Agreements No 343, paras 9.16–9.21 requiring material disclosure of the other party's financial position and independent legal advice.

[54] See Proposal for Council Regulation 2016/0059 (CNS), available at: eur-lex.europa.eu/legal-content/en/ALL/?uri=CELEX%3A52016PC0106, commentary on Art 22.

otherwise. In particular, there may be good reasons for choosing the law of another State, eg, if they expect to move there in the future or if a substantial proportion of their assets are situated there. Any concern that the choice of an unconnected law is designed to provide an unfair advantage to one party could be met by providing for more stringent formal requirements, which will enable verification of informed consent, in cases where the parties wish to choose a law other than that of a State of habitual residence or nationality. Such formal requirements should ensure that the parties are aware of the relevant provisions of the chosen law and the implications of their choice if they move to another country.[55]

In relation to formal validity, the approach of the EU Regulation is to be preferred. In the light of the importance of formal requirements in order to protect the more vulnerable party, by ensuring voluntary and informed consent, it would seem reasonable to expect the law of the State with which their relationship is closely connected to determine the necessary requirements. Thus, satisfaction of the formal requirements of the place of contracting should not suffice, where that State was not the habitual residence of either of them or perhaps their intended habitual residence. Similarly, in relation to substantive validity, overriding mandatory rules of the laws of the habitual residence(s) of both parties should apply, in addition to those of the chosen law.

V. Effect of Migration During Marriage

A. The Different Approaches

It has been claimed that the question of the effect of a change in the personal law of one or both of the parties during the marriage on their matrimonial property relations has taxed lawyers for 900 years.[56] Indeed this issue still seems to be the crux of the disparity between different systems. Traditionally, three models have been identified.

Under the first, referred to as the doctrine of immutability, the personal law at the time of the marriage continues to govern the property relations at all times and thus the applicable law is frozen at the date of the marriage.[57] The key advantage of immutability is certainty and predictability. The main disadvantage is that the applicable law may be a law with which the parties have not had any connection for much or even most of their married life and so it is questionable whether, in such circumstances, this accords with their reasonable expectations.[58]

In contrast, under the doctrine of mutability, the applicable law changes with the personal law of the parties, effectively meaning that the most recent personal law governs. This approach is consistent with the fact that usually the State which has the strongest interest in application of its law is that in which both parties are habitually resident at the time when the dispute arises, inter alia, because its rules in relation to property relations between spouses reflect social norms, which it wishes to promote among those who now form part of its society, and because it has an interest

[55] The Law Commission (n 53) para 7.59 recommended that where a person with a foreign nationality or domicile or owning property abroad is entering into a nuptial agreement, he should be advised to obtain advice from a lawyer from the relevant foreign jurisdiction.

[56] M Davie, 'Matrimonial Property in English and American Conflict of Law' (1993) 42 *ICLQ* 855, 858.

[57] Ibid.

[58] Schuz (n 14) 32; A Bonomi, 'The Proposal for a Regulation on Matrimonial Property, A Critique of the Proposed Rule on the Immutability of Applicable Law' in K Boele-Woelki, N Delthoff and W Gephart (eds), *Family Law and Culture in Europe: Developments, Challenges and Opportunities* (Intersentia 2014) 231, 243.

in fostering cohesion between its residents by providing them with a uniform legal framework.[59] Conversely, a State in which the parties lived previously, but have now left would not seem to have any real interest in the application of its law.[60] An additional advantage of mutability is that, in cases where questions of matrimonial property arise on death, the applicable law will often be the same as that applying to succession, thus reducing the risk of 'over-protection' or 'under protection' of the surviving spouse.[61] Moreover, mutability is more likely to result in application of forum law and so reduce the need to prove foreign law, which will invariably increase uncertainty and the cost of litigation.[62] The major disadvantage of the mutability approach is that it effectively ignores vested rights and means that parties cannot predict which law will apply.

Under the third approach, known as partial mutability, changes in personal law do not affect property previously acquired. In other words, the parties' personal law at the time of the acquisition of each asset governs the ownership of that asset. This approach maximises the advantages of the first two. Its main drawback is that it is liable to lead to different laws applying to different assets and so complicates the task of division of property, especially where there has been more than one move.

Examples can be found of all three models. Traditionally the immutability doctrine has been the prevailing approach in civil law systems[63] and was adopted by the Israeli legislature.[64] The mutability approach has now been adopted in some European countries[65] and some Canadian provinces.[66] The partial mutability approach prevails in the US.[67] The position at common law in England and Wales is far from clear and depends on the interpretation given to two cases decided by the House of Lords more than a century ago.[68] Some commentators take the view that these cases support the doctrine of immutability,[69] whilst others consider that they are consistent with the doctrine of partial mutability.[70]

B. The Harmonisation Instruments

Harmonisation attempts have created a fourth model,[71] allowing for the application of the law of a new common habitual residence instead of the previously applicable law, where certain additional

[59] A Buchler, *Islamic Law in Europe* (Ashgate 2011) 38.

[60] Thus, there appears to be a false conflict. For the need to take into account State interests in devising choice of law rules (as opposed to US-style judicial ad hoc interest analysis in individual cases) see, eg, English Law Commission WP 89 on Choice of Law in Marriage, 30–31; and P Torremans (ed), *Cheshire, North and Fawcett's Private International Law*, 15th edn (Oxford University Press 2017) 37.

[61] JG Miller, 'Family Provision on Death – The International Dimension' (1990) 39 *ICLQ* 261, 263.

[62] Impact Assessment Study (n 11) 98.

[63] eg, Austria, Germany, Hungary, Estonia and Romania, *Impact Assessment Study*, ibid, 93; Quebec, Davie (n 56) 859.

[64] Spouses (Property Relations) Law, Laws of the State of Israel, vol 27, 313, s 15. However, via the construct of a deemed agreement, the courts have effectively introduced a mutability regime, at least in relation to couples immigrating to Israel, see Schuz (n 14) 20 ff.

[65] eg, Malta, Lithuania, Slovenia and Poland (*Impact Assessment Study* (n 11) 93) and Switzerland Art 55, Private International Law Act 1987; see generally A Samuel, 'The New Swiss Private International Law Act' (1988) 37 *ICLQ* 681, 693.

[66] Which provide for the application of the last common habitual residence of the spouses. See, eg, Ontario Family Law Act 1990 s 15; New Brunswick Marital Property Act 1980 s 44(2). Similarly, in New Zealand, the Property Relationships Act 1976 (which allows for making of matrimonial property orders) applies in relation to movables where one of the parties is domiciled in New Zealand at the date of the application or at the date of an agreement between the spouses relating to division of their property.

[67] Hay et al (n 20) 461; T Oldham, 'Conflicts of Laws and Marital Property Rights' [1987] *Baylor Law Review* 1255, 1273. However, some states adopt a full mutability approach, S Symeonides, *American Private International Law* (Kluwer 2008) 259.

[68] *Lashley v Hog* (1804) Paton 581 (an appeal to the House of Lords in a Scottish case); *De Nicols v Curlier* [1900] AC 21.

[69] eg, Hartley (n 15) 224; *Dicey, Morris and Collins* (n 21) 1478–82.

[70] eg, Clarkson (n 15) 28; *Cheshire, North and Fawcett* (n 60) 1370.

[71] A few modern applicable law codes have also adopted this model. See, eg, J Shiratzki, 2003 Swedish National Report 28; and E Gottberg, 2003 Finland National Report 30, both on file with the author.

criteria are met, which are based on convergence of connecting factors or on passage of time. The Hague Convention provides that the applicable law will change where the parties are both nationals of the State of their new common habitual residence or where the new habitual residence has endured for 10 years.[72] The EU Regulation provides that a court may decide, on the application of either spouse, that the law of the parties' last common habitual residence is the applicable law where the parties had their habitual residence there for a significantly longer period of time than in the country whose law would otherwise be applicable and the parties had relied on that law in planning or arranging their property relations.[73] Thus, whilst under the Hague Convention the change of applicable law is automatic, the EU Regulation provides for an escape clause, which can only be activated by judicial proceedings. The Hague Convention provides that the law of the new State will not apply to property belonging to the parties before the change of applicable law.[74] In contrast, the EU Regulation provides that the law of the new State will apply from the conclusion of the marriage, unless one spouse disagrees, in which case it will apply from the date of establishment of habitual residence there.[75]

It can be seen that despite the differences between the two instruments, they also have much in common. Both provide for conditions which will trigger a change in applicable law and in such cases, at either spouse's request, the originally applicable law will continue to apply to previously acquired property. Accordingly, the regimes introduced by these instruments might be appropriately described as ones of 'modified partial mutability'.

C. Analysis

The via media of 'modified partial mutability', adopted in the Hague Convention and EU Regulation seems to be the most likely basis for any future harmonisation initiative. Its main advantage, compared with the mutability approach, is that it recognises that change of habitual residence per se does not necessarily indicate a strong connection with the new State. However, further thought needs to be given to the criteria for triggering the change in applicable law and whether it should apply retrospectively.

First, the fact that both parties are nationals of the new State should not be sufficient by itself to lead to a change in the applicable law, particularly where the parties still retain nationality of the old State. Second, whilst a threshold time-period is preferable to a purely arithmetical comparison of the time spent in each State,[76] a five-year period[77] is deserving of legal recognition.[78] Third, the additional requirement in the EU Regulation that both parties had relied on the law of the new State in arranging or planning their property relations goes too far and may defeat the couple's reasonable expectations. Fourth, the EU Regulation's requirement of judicial proceedings

[72] Hague Convention (n 1) Art 7. In addition, in cases where they did not have a common habitual residence after the marriage and the law of their common nationality applied, when they do become habitually resident in the same State, that law will now apply.

[73] EU Regulation (n 2) Art 26(3).

[74] Hague Convention (n 1) Art 8.

[75] EU Regulation (n 2) Art 26(3).

[76] The only situation in which a comparative test might be appropriate would be where the time spent by the parties in the old State, including that before marriage, was less than the threshold period.

[77] Clarkson also supports a five-year period (n 15) 439. In Israel, an unpublished reform proposal made by the Ministry of Justice in 1995, based on the Hague Convention, adjusted the time period to five years.

[78] Perusal of residence periods required for naturalisation from over 80 States reveals that five years is the most common period and that most of the States require a period of five years or less, see: en.wikipedia.org/wiki/Naturalization.

in order to trigger the change of law creates unnecessary uncertainty. The change in applicable law should occur automatically, but on the application of either party, a court could by way of exception hold that the original law continues to apply, where application of the new law would create injustice. An example of such a situation would be where it can be shown that the parties continued to rely on the law of the previous State of habitual residence or that one of them did so, to the knowledge of the other.

Finally, the EU Regulation's default provision that the new law applies to all the parties' property, unless one spouse disagrees, avoids the complexity involved in applying more than one law, whilst protecting a spouse who would be prejudiced by such retrospective application.

VI. The Law Applicable to Property Division on Divorce

A. The Different Approaches

Disputes about matrimonial property may arise during the subsistence of the marriage, on divorce or on death. Traditionally, there was perhaps little need to make any distinction between these different contexts both because the two original matrimonial regimes – separate property and immediate community – did not make any such distinction and because divorce was rare. However, today the main importance of applicable law in relation to matrimonial property is in cases of divorce.[79] Whilst in most European countries no distinction is made between the applicable law rules in each context, in the UK a clear distinction is made between the law applicable to division of property on divorce and that in other contexts, with the law of the forum applying to property division on divorce.[80] Similarly, in the US, equitable distribution states apply the law of the forum to division of matrimonial property on divorce.[81]

B. The Harmonisation Instruments

Both the Hague Convention and the EU Regulation adopt the continental European approach and do not make any distinction between the different contexts. The EU Regulation provides expressly that the applicable law governs the dissolution of the matrimonial property regime and the partition, distribution or liquidation of the property.[82] Thus, the law of the forum cannot be applied unless the applicable foreign law 'is manifestly incompatible with public policy'[83] or, under the EU Regulation, insofar as the law of the forum contains mandatory overriding provisions.[84]

[79] Clarkson (n 15) 421–23.

[80] This approach applies even where the financial relief is being awarded following a foreign divorce, Matrimonial and Family Proceedings Act 1984 Part III, in accordance with the Law Commission's recommendations, Law Com WP 77, para 56. In relation to Scotland, see Beaumont and McEleavy (n 22) ch 20.

[81] Hay et al (n 20) 601–02. See, eg, *Day v Day* 137 Ore App 264 (1995). In Texas and some other US community property states, for the purposes of division on divorce, property acquired whilst the parties were domiciled in a separate property state is characterised as quasi-community property and so can be divided on divorce, but some community states apply the law of the earlier domicile (referred to as 'the borrowed-law approach') and Louisiana has a hybrid regime, Symeonides (n 67) 260–63.

[82] EU Regulation (n 2) Art 27.

[83] Hague Convention (n 1) Art 14; EU Regulation, ibid, Art 31.

[84] EU Regulation ibid, Art 30.

C. Analysis

Whilst it is difficult to defend the application of the *lex fori* per se,[85] there are convincing arguments which support adopting a full mutability approach on divorce and applying the law of the common habitual residence at the time of the divorce, which will usually be the *lex fori*.

First, in the context of divorce, the parties' expectations may well take into account the fact that division of property is an integral part of the divorce process and that under many types of regime, marital property rights do not ripen until divorce.[86] Moreover, as seen above, in many jurisdictions, the court's powers to divide property on divorce are wider than simply determining the parties' respective rights, often including some kind of discretion to adjust the way in which the property is shared between the parties. Thus, even if couples do not expect that mere change of habitual residence would lead to a change in the law governing the ownership of their property, they might well expect that, if they get divorced in the State of their new habitual residence[87] in accordance with its law,[88] this law will also apply to the division of all their property, unless they have a nuptial agreement. Second, on divorce, the law of the State of common habitual residence often has a strong interest in regulating the division of property between the parties, as well as applying to the divorce and other ancillary matters.[89] In particular, that State may be directly influenced by the outcome, if one of its residents is not adequately provided for.[90] Third, in most States there exists some mechanism via which a court can compensate for any unfairness caused by the change in the applicable law.[91]

Despite the above, in light of the fact that relatively few jurisdictions have adopted such an approach and the general lack of support from commentators,[92] it does not seem to be a feasible option for any harmonisation initiative. Accordingly, where application of the law of habitual residence at the time of the marriage to all or some of the assets on divorce would cause serious injustice, which cannot be remedied by exercise of discretion within the applicable law, it will be necessary to invoke the public policy exception.

The most likely scenario where this will be appropriate will be cases where the law of the parties' habitual residence at the time of the marriage provides for separation of property and the wife owns little or no property. If the law of that State applies to the parties' assets or most of them,[93] the wife will not receive any share of the husband's property, unless the foreign law is held to contravene the forum's public policy. The principle of ensuring equal treatment of spouses is

[85] Inter alia because it is likely to encourage forum shopping where jurisdiction can be based on a connection created by one party unilaterally.

[86] Halloran and McLoughlin (n 41) 472.

[87] In accordance with the familiar adage 'when in Rome do as the Romans do'. Where both spouses are no longer habitually resident in the country of their last common habitual residence, see Schuz (n 14) 35.

[88] It should be noted that under Art 8 of Council Regulation (EU) No 1259/2010 of 20 December 2010 implementing enhanced cooperation in the area of the law applicable to divorce and legal separation (Rome III), in the absence of agreement, the law to be applied to divorce is the last common habitual residence of the parties, so long as one party is still resident there at the time the court is seised and no more than a year has passed since the other spouse ceased to reside there.

[89] See, eg, per Supreme Court of California in *Addison v Addison* (1965) 62 Cal 2d 558, 566: ('Clearly the interest of the state of the current domicile in the matrimonial property of the parties is substantial upon the dissolution of the marriage relationship').

[90] Oldham (n 41) para 4.08.

[91] Bonomi (n 58) 246–47.

[92] Ibid, 242.

[93] Either because the criteria for triggering change of applicable law have not been met or most of the assets were acquired prior to that date and the husband does not agree to retrospective application of the new law.

now recognised as a principle of international law, by virtue of the Convention on the Elimination of all forms of Discrimination against Women (CEDAW), which has been ratified by 189 States.[94] As has been made clear by the CEDAW Committee, default separate property regimes discriminate against women since social and economic factors invariably impair the capacity of women to increase their property during marriage.[95] Thus, a foreign default separate property regime can be seen as offending external public policy,[96] unless the wife had a real opportunity to choose an alternative or was in an equal position to acquire property.

VII. The Way Ahead

The failure of the Hague Convention and the limited success of the EU Regulation do not bode well for any future harmonisation initiatives. The via media between immutability and mutability in the Hague Convention does not seem to satisfy the supporters of either approach. Those who oppose automatic change in applicable law are not appeased by the lengthy 10-year habitual residence requirement. Yet, this is insufficient for those who are concerned about proximity between the parties and the applicable law. Whilst the EU Regulation's formula does seem to have been an acceptable compromise to two mutability States[97] as well as a significant number of immutability ones, it has to be borne in mind that there are more incentives for harmonisation within the EU than globally. In any event, it seems unlikely that many common law States will be prepared to agree to the application on divorce of the State of first habitual residence, at least not unless the conditions for triggering a change of applicable law are significantly broader than those in the EU Regulation.

The crux of the problem would seem to be a lack of consensus about policy objectives. The EU initiative is predicated on the prime importance of predictability and stability of couples' matrimonial property regimes, inter alia, in order to provide legal security for the spouses and their creditors. However, the value of this stability may be more illusory than real, since many couples are not aware of the matrimonial property regime which applies to them and are not able to predict how it will impact on them in the future. Similarly, the need to protect third-party creditors does not preclude changes in the applicable law, since creditors' rights can be safeguarded by providing that a law may not be invoked against them unless they had actual or constructive knowledge that it governed the spousal property[98] or by general internal rules of property law protecting bona fide third parties who enter into transactions without actual or constructive notice of the rights of an owner of the property.[99]

[94] See: www.ohchr.org/en/professionalinterest/pages/cedaw.aspx.

[95] General recommendation No. 29 on Article 16 of the Convention on the Elimination of All Forms of Discrimination against Women (Economic consequences of marriage, family relations and their dissolution) of the CEDAW Committee (30 October 2013), available at: tbinternet.ohchr.org/_layouts/treatybodyexternal/Download.aspx?symbolno=CEDAW/C/GC/29&Lang=en, paras 43–44; R Halperin-Kaddari and M Freeman, 'Economic Consequences of Marriage and Its Dissolution: Applying a Universal Equality Norm in a Fragmented Universe' [2012] 13 *Theoretical Enquiries in Law* 323.

[96] See, eg, *Aleem v Aleem* 947 A 2d 489 (2008) (refusal to apply Pakistani separate property system, inter alia, because policy of allowing the husband to retain all the property accumulated during the marriage was in violation of important State policies) and Canadian case of *Vladi v Vladi* 39 DLR (4th) 563 (1987) (Iranian law held to be archaic and repugnant to ideas of substantial justice in the province of Nova Scotia).

[97] Malta, Slovenia (n 65).

[98] EU Regulation (n 2) Art 28.

[99] See, eg, Italian law, as applied in *Winkworth v Christie* [1980] Ch 496.

The emphasis should be on predictability at any given time, rather than future predictability *ab initio*. It is not realistic at the time of the marriage to expect to anticipate the impact of unforeseen future events, in the absence of an agreement. However, parties should be able to know with certainty the repercussions of an impending migration to a particular State and which law applies once a dispute has arisen.[100] Often, the latter type of certainty is best provided by rules which increase the likelihood of application of the law of the parties' current or last common habitual residence, which is where the litigation will usually take place.

Moreover, there are additional policy and applicable law objectives which support application of the law with which the parties are now clearly more closely connected, where they have not agreed otherwise. In particular, this is more likely to accord with the parties' reasonable expectations and with States' interests in protecting their residents and fostering social cohesion by providing a uniform legal framework.

On a more optimistic note, the EU Regulation can perhaps be seen as a first step in the right direction, since it means that 18 States, most of whom were immutability States, have accepted the possibility of a change in the applicable law, albeit by way of escape clause and in limited circumstances. It is to be hoped that over time, immutability States will realise the need to promote a wider range of policy objectives and that all States will appreciate the advantages of harmonisation and be prepared to make a real effort to find an acceptable via media.

One way of making progress towards such an objective might be by starting off with a soft law approach at the HCCH, involving formulation of non-binding guiding principles.[101] The advantages of such an approach are twofold. First, it would avoid the controversy as to whether the applicable law rules should apply to same-sex marriages, which is liable to be a major obstacle to any work on a hard law instrument.[102] Second, there is a greater likelihood of obtaining agreement to general principles, which leave State Parties with some leeway to fill in the details. For example, there could be a principle that provision should be made for a change in the applicable law, subject to protection of vested rights, where conditions are satisfied which indicate that the parties are now clearly more closely connected to a new State, without specifying the conditions.[103] Similarly, there could be a principle that party autonomy to choose the applicable law should not be restricted more than is necessary to ensure informed consent, without specifying permitted restrictions. Whilst this approach does not amount to full unification, it would represent some degree of alignment between the different legal systems. Moreover, focusing on common ground and weakening the mutability versus immutability dichotomy might pave the way for a global hard law instrument in the future.

[100] See the examples given in the *Impact Assessment Study* (n 11) 95 ff.
[101] As in the Hague Conference's Principles in Choice of Law in International Commercial Contracts.
[102] This seems to be one of the reasons that some States did not join the EU Regulation.
[103] Although examples might be given of recommended options.

38

Family Agreements Involving Children

PAUL BEAUMONT AND NIEVE RUBAJA

I. Introduction

In the context of International Family Law, as well as at a domestic level, amicable solutions are widely commended since they let parties solve their own problems and organise their family life. In general, parties are more likely to comply with agreed solutions than those imposed by judicial or administrative authorities, and agreed solutions provide more stability and foreseeability.[1] Internationality creates challenges for enforcing agreed solutions. In the first place, different subject matters are involved, eg, arrangements about custody, contact, maintenance and payments for travel of the children between the holders of parental responsibility, in these family or 'package' agreements.[2] In the second place, the different legal systems that could be involved may offer different private international law rules on jurisdiction (including the extent of the parties' autonomy), applicable law and recognition and enforcement.[3]

All the modern private international law family instruments foster amicable agreements[4] and some provide mechanisms for their recognition and enforcement. These instruments

[1] A Bonomi, 'Explanatory Report on the Hague Protocol of 23 November 2007 on the Law Applicable to Maintenance Obligations' (Permanent Bureau) 54, 55.

[2] Packages may also include: costs of education, property of the child, separation of property in the context of divorce, particular aspects in international child abduction cases, among others.

[3] Notwithstanding the increasing extension of party autonomy in family matters, it has been underlined that States have not completely abandoned the concept of legal paternalism, according to which the State's interference in the decision-making processes of private parties is legitimate whenever sensitive matters, relevant to the society as a whole, are at stake including in matters involving children's rights. N de Araujo and D Trejos Vargas, 'The cross-border recognition and enforcement of private agreements in family disputes on debate at the Hague Conference of Private International Law' in JA Moreno Rodríguez and C Lima Marques (eds), *Jornadas de la Asadip 2014* (Cedep 2014) 490–91.

[4] Amicable solutions are also encouraged by other areas, eg, the ASADIP Principles on Transnational Access to Justice (TRANSJUS), Buenos Aires, 2016. Art 1.1. 'In proceedings initiated pursuant to transnational litigation, judges and other State authorities should seek to ensure, in a reasonable manner, adherence to the following principles: b.- Principle of "favoring amicable solutions": States and judges shall promote, facilitate and favor the amicable resolution of disputes through negotiation, mediation, conciliation or any other mechanism of alternative dispute resolution'. See: www.asadip.org/v2/wp-content/uploads/2018/08/ASADIP-TRANSJUS-EN-FINAL18.pdf. In the EU, 'Amicable' is a co-funded project which has the overarching aim of improving the situation of children in cross-border parental responsibility disputes and child abduction cases within the EU. The project started in March 2019 and continued for a period of 24 months. See: www.amicable-eu.org. Besides, there are several institutions which employ this resource as the best solution in these cases, eg, 'REUNITE' in UK; 'International Mediation Centre for Family Conflict and Child Abduction, MIKK', in Germany; 'Mediation Bureau – IKO' in the Netherlands; '*Miission d'aide à la médiation internationale pour les familles*', in France.

represent an extremely important resource for family agreements but those providing for recognition and enforcement are not in force in enough countries and they deal with each subject matter individually leaving a complex scenario when it comes to ensuring children's rights. The need to clarify, and hopefully simplify, this complex scenario has been the origin of the work that the Hague Conference on Private International Law (HCCH) has been developing in this area.

The Council on General Affairs and Policy (CGAP) established an Experts' Group at its 2012 meeting, with the following mandate:

> Council … decided to establish an Experts' Group to carry out further exploratory research on cross-border recognition and enforcement of agreements reached in the course of international child disputes, including those reached through mediation, taking into account the implementation and use of the 1996 Convention. Such work shall comprise the identification of the nature and extent of the legal and practical problems, including jurisdictional issues, and evaluation of the benefit of a new instrument, whether binding or non-binding, in this area.[5]

The Experts' Group has held six meetings (November 2013, December 2015, June 2017, June 2018, September 2021 and a drafting meeting of the whole group in November 2021). After the second meeting it recommended to CGAP to further explore the development of two instruments:

(1) A non-binding navigation tool to provide best practices on how an agreement made in the area of family law involving children can be recognised and enforced in a foreign State under the 1980, 1996 and 2007 Hague Conventions; and
(2) a binding legal instrument that would establish a 'one-stop shop' for agreements in a cross-border context pertaining to custody, access, child support and other financial arrangements (including property issues) and provide more party autonomy by giving parents the possibility of selecting an appropriate authority. The instrument would allow for the conferral of jurisdiction exclusively on one court or authority for the approval of such agreements and would provide for simple mechanisms for recognition and enforcement of the decision of that court or authority. It will build on and supplement the 1980, 1996 and 2007 Hague Conventions.[6]

In 2016 CGAP mandated the Permanent Bureau 'to develop a non-binding "navigation tool" to provide best practices on how an agreement made in the area of family law involving children can be recognised and enforced in a foreign State under the 1980, 1996 and 2007 Conventions'.[7] Regarding the proposed binding instrument, CGAP concluded that the need for and feasibility of developing that kind of instrument would be revisited based on further information which would result from work on the navigation tool.

In the first part of this chapter the non-binding instrument (navigation tool) will be analysed; in the second part, the focus will be on the need for and feasibility of a binding instrument.

[5] See 'Conclusions and Recommendations of the Council on General Affairs and Policy of the Conference (17–20 April 2012)', available at: www.hcch.net under 'Governance' then 'Council on General Affairs and Policy', para 7.

[6] 'Report of the Experts' Group meeting on cross-border recognition and enforcement of agreements in family matters involving children (The Hague, 2–4 November 2015)', Prel Doc No 5 of January 2016 for the attention of the Council of March 2016 on General Affairs and Policy of the Conference, available at: www.hcch.net under 'Governance' then 'Council on General Affairs and Policy', para 32.

[7] See 'Conclusions and Recommendations of the Council on General Affairs and Policy of the Conference (15–17 March 2016)', available at: www.hcch.net under 'Governance' then 'Council on General Affairs and Policy', paras 16–18.

II. How the Current Hague Conventions Work for Family Agreements

The Experts' Group's navigation tool is designed to assist legal advisers, judges, mediators and others involved in helping families to arrive at amicable solutions in cross-border family disputes involving children, particularly in the practical use of the Hague Convention of 25 October 1980 on the Civil Aspects of International Child Abduction (the 1980 Convention), the Hague Convention of 19 October 1996 on Jurisdiction, Applicable Law, Recognition, Enforcement and Co-operation in Respect of Parental Responsibility and Measures for the Protection of Children (the 1996 Convention), and the Hague Convention of 23 November 2007 on the International Recovery of Child Support and Other Forms of Family Maintenance (the 2007 Convention). The goal is that amicable solutions reached within the scope of these instruments should be effectively recognised and enforced in Contracting States whilst protecting the rights of children. The navigation tool covers three typical scenarios in which family agreements can be used to achieve a good solution if their enforceability is ensured: cross-border relocation; and return and non-return agreements in international child abduction cases. The navigation tool is drafted on the assumption that the 1980, 1996 and the 2007 Conventions are applicable between the States concerned and that the family agreements deal with issues contained within the scope of those instruments.[8]

The draft of the navigation tool (Practical Guide) was submitted to the Members of the HCCH for approval at the 2019 meeting of CGAP. In the light of some reservations that were expressed, the draft was recirculated to allow Members to provide additional comments. By November 2021 the Experts' Group reached consensus on the wording of a revised navigation tool described as a Practitioners' Tool.

Three main aspects covered by the navigation tool will be analysed: (A) the role that party autonomy has in the modern Hague Family Conventions; (B) whether or not the amicable solution must be embodied in a decision, or in an equivalent measure, in order to be recognised; and (C) the strategic importance of deciding where and how the agreement should be made enforceable initially.[9]

A. Party Autonomy

The HCCH Conventions in family matters encourage amicable solutions.[10] In this regard, it is important to take into account that on the one hand, each of the aforementioned instruments allows party autonomy to varying degrees, but on the other hand all of them show, especially among the Central Authorities' functions, that there is a spirit of promoting agreed solutions in order to end disputes more expeditiously and with less economic and emotional costs.

[8] The in-depth narrative part of the 2019 version of the navigation tool is the 'Explanatory Note on how an agreement made in the area of family law involving children can be recognised and enforced in a foreign State under the 1980 Hague Child Abduction Convention, the 1996 Hague Child Protection Convention and the 2007 Hague Child Support Convention' in Prel Doc No 4 of January 2019, available at: www.hcch.net under 'Projects', then 'Legislative Projects', then 'Family agreements involving children' ie: assets.hcch.net/docs/97681b48-86bb-4af4-9ced-a42f58380f82.pdf, para 2.

[9] These aspects are analysed in Chapters III and IV of the 'Explanatory Note' (n 8).

[10] Moreover, in the post-legislative work of the Hague Conference on Private International Law (HCCH) significant work has been done to promote mediation and other forms of amicable settlements.

i. The 1980 Convention

The successful 1980 Convention shows remarkable foresight in its recognition of the potential for family agreements to solve some of the most difficult of family conflicts in the midst of an international child abduction. Much post-legislative work has been done in this context to promote such agreements.[11] The Convention itself promotes family agreements in several ways.

First, agreements on rights of custody are recognised under Article 3 of the Convention if the agreement has 'legal effect' under the law of the child's habitual residence at the time when the child is abducted. Thus, if the child is removed from his or her habitual residence or retained away from that residence without the consent of the holder of the custody rights under the 'agreement', the custody right holder can seek the return of the child to the child's habitual residence utilising the provisions of the Convention.

Second, one of the grounds upon which there is no obligation on the judicial or administrative authorities to return the child to his or her habitual residence is the 'consent or acquiescence' of the holder of custody rights to the child being taken to or remaining in the State he or she is now present in (see Article 13(1)(a)). This shows that if the holders of custody rights can reach an agreement (either before or after the abduction) they are in principle free to authorise the change of residence of the child and by doing so bring about a change in the child's habitual residence. In particular, the 'acquiescence' by the left behind custody right holder to a removal or retention in the course of the return proceedings allows the custody right holders (usually the parents) to agree through an amicable solution the non-return of the child to the State of his or her habitual residence, among other possibilities. The question that remains is how this kind of agreement can be given effect to without violating Article 16 of the Convention, which blocks jurisdiction on the merits of custody while the return proceedings are still pending (see below, section II.C).

Third, Article 13(2) shows prescience by the drafters of the Convention in seeing that the rights of the child mean that children's views should be heard before deciding whether or not to order their return to their habitual residence. Clearly the weight to be given to those views depends on the age and maturity of each child and on the strength with which each child holds their views. This provision is a signal that the custody right holders should create an opportunity for their children to express their views before finalising a family agreement. If they do not do so and simply agree that the children should be returned to their habitual residence it is possible that the court where the child is present might refuse to give effect to the agreement and refuse to order the return of the children under Article 13(2). Of course, such an outcome is unlikely as it will be a rare case where it is in the best interests of children to stay in the country where they are present if the custody right holders both want the children to return to their habitual residence. The point is that Article 13(2) sends an important signal that an agreement between custody right holders on where their children should live should be a 'family agreement' in which the custody right holders have given appropriate weight to the views of their children.

Finally, Article 7(c) of the 1980 Convention imposes a duty on Central Authorities, either directly or through an intermediary, to take all appropriate measures 'to secure the voluntary

[11] The work includes the elaboration of a Guide to Good Practice on Mediation under the 1980 Convention (2012) and the Principles for the Establishment of Mediation Structures. See 'Working Party on mediation in the context of the Malta Process. Principles for the Establishment of Mediation Structures in the Context of the Malta Process', drawn up by the Working Party with the assistance of the Permanent Bureau, November 2010, available at: www.hcch.net under 'Instruments', then 'Conventions, Protocols and Principles', then 'Convention of 25 October 1980 on the civil aspects of international child abduction', then 'Mediation'.

return of the child or to bring about an amicable resolution of the issues' in child abduction cases. It is this duty on Central Authorities which provides a strong basis for Contracting States to put in place systems which will quickly enable parties to reach a return or non-return agreement, often resolving their underlying custody dispute in a way that the courts making a return or non-return order under the Convention cannot do.[12]

ii. The 1996 Convention

The 1996 Convention encourages agreements to establish rights of custody and to settle disputes on matters falling within its scope.[13]

First, the provision on jurisdiction applying in cases of child abduction, Article 7, preserves the position in relation to custody agreements provided for by Article 3 of the 1980 Convention, discussed above. Article 7(2) of the 1996 Convention allows for the possibility that a Contracting State's law may permit custody rights to be created by an agreement having legal effect under that State's law. If that State is the habitual residence of the child at the time of the abduction, then the actions of any custody right holder under the agreement have to be taken into account under Article 7 before the jurisdiction of the courts of the habitual residence of the child prior to the abduction can be lost.[14]

Second, the applicable law provisions in the 1996 Convention, in particular, Article 16(2) confirm that the law of the habitual residence of the child determines whether the attribution or extinction of parental responsibility by agreement has legal effect. Article 16(3) provides that a change of habitual residence does not lead to the loss of a person's parental responsibility due to a different legal situation in the new State. Thus, an agreement validly attributing parental responsibility in accordance with the law of the State of the child's habitual residence at the time when the agreement takes effect is given force in any new State of habitual residence of the child which is a Contracting State to the 1996 Convention.

Third, regarding jurisdiction, the 1996 Convention creates a relatively narrow scope for party autonomy. The principle is that jurisdiction corresponds to the authorities of the State of the child's habitual residence (Article 5); but Article 10 allows the parents of a child, in certain conditions, to agree that the court dealing with their divorce or legal separation may have jurisdiction on measures of child protection. According to Article 10(1)(b) the choice of jurisdiction by the parents must be in the 'best interests of the child' in the view of the divorce court. However, the Convention indirectly facilitates a broader notion of party autonomy, beyond the divorce jurisdiction, to any State with which the child has a 'substantial connection' through invoking the transfer provisions in Articles 8 and 9 of the Convention. However, in these cases party autonomy is limited because it requires the support of the courts of two States.

Fourth, this instrument also promotes amicable solutions; among the duties of the Central Authorities, either directly or through public authorities or other bodies, is to take 'all appropriate steps' to 'facilitate, by mediation, conciliation or similar means, agreed solutions for the protection of the person or property of the child in situations to which the Convention applies' (Article 31(b)).

[12] See S Vigers, *Mediating International Child Abduction Cases: The Hague Convention* (Hart Publishing 2011).
[13] 'Explanatory Note' (n 8) para 99.
[14] Ibid, paras 100 and 101.

iii. The 2007 Convention

The 2007 Convention does not have positive direct rules of jurisdiction but in the context of recognition and enforcement it has rather generous provisions with regard to foreign maintenance agreements and decisions arrived at through party autonomy.[15] Two possibilities are available for the recognition and enforcement of agreements: (a) an agreement that is included in a decision or court settlement, or that has been concluded before or approved by an authority of a Contracting State (Article 19(1));[16] (b) an agreement that is drawn up or registered as an authentic instrument or has been authenticated by, or concluded, registered or filed with a competent authority ('maintenance arrangements' in the sense of Article 3(e)) can be recognised or enforced in all Contracting States that have not entered a reservation in relation to such arrangements (see Article 30(5)).[17]

Also, Central Authorities should assist in this regard. Article 6(2)(d) provides that in relation to applications for maintenance made through Central Authorities under the Convention they have to 'take all appropriate measures … to encourage amicable solutions with a view to obtaining voluntary payment of maintenance, where suitable by use of mediation, conciliation or similar processes'.[18]

B. Recognition and Enforcement of Agreements Whether they are Embodied in a Decision or Not

Family agreements falling within the scope of the 1996 and 2007 Conventions can be enforced in Contracting States to those Conventions. The former Convention requires that the agreement (or its content) be embodied in a 'measure of child protection'. The latter admits two possibilities as described above.

It should be taken into account that both Conventions provide a number of grounds for non-recognition. Among these, the most relevant requirements of the 1996 Convention are those regarding indirect jurisdiction (the measure can be refused recognition if it was taken by an authority that had no international jurisdiction under the Convention); the failure to give an opportunity for the child to be heard, except in urgent cases; and if such recognition is manifestly contrary to public policy of the requested State, taking into account the best interests of the child (Article 23(2)(a), (b) and (d)).[19] The grounds for non-recognition in the 2007 Convention differ, depending on whether the agreement is embodied in a decision (or equivalent) or not. In the first case, the main grounds will be indirect jurisdiction – according to the bases provided by the

[15] The 2007 Hague Protocol introduces the possibility of a choice of law for maintenance matters (except for child maintenance).

[16] Furthermore, the parties can take their agreement to the courts of any Contracting State and their agreement to that jurisdiction will be the basis for recognition and enforcement of the decision in all Contracting States except in disputes relating to maintenance obligations in respect of children, see Art 20(1)(e). However, Brazil and the US have made a reservation in relation to Art 20(1)(e). See ch 36, n 74, in this book.

[17] The only States with such a reservation, provided for by Arts 30(8) and 62, are Brazil (for minors, incapacitated adults and elderly persons), Turkey and Ukraine.

[18] In the 'Explanatory Note' it is also underlined that the Convention text indicates the readiness to accept party autonomy concerning jurisdiction. See the exception for party autonomy to the rules limiting the direct jurisdiction for maintenance debtors in Art 18 and in the indirect rules of jurisdiction in Art 20 the reference to 'agreement on jurisdiction' (n 18). See 'Explanatory Note' (n 8) para 111.

[19] In addition, the 1996 Convention provides an advanced recognition mechanism in accordance with Art 24.

Convention – (Article 20(1)) and manifest incompatibility with public policy (Article 22 (a)). In the second case, the main difference is that the indirect jurisdiction rules do not apply (Article 30).

Finally, if the countries involved in a case are not Parties to these Conventions, the analysis would include the possibility that another binding tool in force between them in some of the subject matters is applicable;[20] also domestic regulations, safeguards and requirements for the recognition and enforcement of this kind of agreement should be taken into account.

C. The 'Starting Point' of the Agreements or Decisions in which they are Embodied: The Strategic Path

Among the guidelines that the navigation tool provides, a question of paramount importance is the consideration of the 'starting point' of the agreements. The 'starting point' is not necessarily the place where the agreement was reached but the jurisdiction in which it would be presented to be made enforceable. This aspect should be analysed strategically in order to meet the requirements of validity of the agreements in the legal system in which they shall be first rendered binding and enforceable. In addition, all the legal systems in which the agreement is expected to be enforced should be taken into account. This means that any applicable international, regional or bilateral private international law instruments, as well as the domestic private international law rules regarding recognition and enforcement, need to be considered, especially international jurisdiction conditions, other procedural safeguards or grounds for non-recognition.[21]

In the Explanatory Note, the 'starting point' of the agreements is analysed in depth, in particular according to the rules provided by the 1996 and 2007 Conventions. In addition, the 'starting point' for 'package agreements' is also studied, whether the subject matters fall fully within the scope of the two Conventions or not.

For analysing the 'starting point' of agreements within the 1996 Convention, it is important to have in mind that this instrument, 'centralise[s] jurisdiction in the authorities of the State of the child's habitual residence [to] avoid all competition of authorities having concurrent jurisdiction'.[22] Therefore, as the agreement should be embodied into a decision or equivalent, the 'starting point' to enforce such an agreement generally will be the Contracting State of the habitual residence of the child, where the measure of child protection should be obtained. This jurisdiction will also be acceptable for the requested State under the Convention (Article 23(2)(a)).

This analysis in the 2007 Convention should take into account whether: (a) the agreement is included in a decision or court settlement or has been concluded before or approved by an authority of a Contracting State – in the sense of Article 19(1); or (b) the agreement is rendered enforceable abroad as a 'maintenance arrangement' under Article 30.

In the former scenario, the 'starting point' should be a Contracting State with international jurisdiction over the subject matter in light of the indirect rules of jurisdiction under the 2007 Convention, considering the possible reservations that are allowed in this regard (Article 20(2)).

[20] eg, the Inter-American Convention on Support Obligations, which is in force between 13 American States, provides in Art 11 a mechanism for the recognition and enforcement of maintenance decisions. As the recognition and enforcement of agreements are not regulated as such they would need to be embodied in a judicial decision.

[21] 'Explanatory Note' (n 8) para 48.

[22] See P Lagarde, 'Explanatory Report on the 1996 Hague Child Protection Convention' in *Proceedings of the Eighteenth Session (1996), Tome II, Protection of children* (SDU 1998) 535–05, para 37.

As a consequence the safest options would be: seising the court in the State of the habitual residence of the respondent (the maintenance debtor); seising the court of another State which the respondent submits to the jurisdiction of; or seising the court in the State of habitual residence of the child given the respondent has lived with the child in that State or has resided in that State and provided support for the child there.[23] Note that the 'starting point' for subject matter within the 1996 Convention (habitual residence of the child) might not be a proper 'starting point' within the 2007 Convention when the child and the debtor do not have the same habitual residence.

In the latter scenario, a 'maintenance arrangement', the grounds for non-recognition related to indirect jurisdiction do not apply. Nevertheless, it should be considered that Article 30 admits of reservations to the recognition and enforcement of maintenance arrangements which are enforceable in other Contracting States.[24] Also a check should be made to see if the country intended as a starting point accepts under its own law the enforceability of 'maintenance arrangements', as defined in Article 3(e), as required by Article 30(1) of the Convention.

The navigation tool seeks to gather the best practices that these instruments offer and show the 'best case scenario' to take advantage of them together.[25] Nevertheless, the situation can be very complex when the two instruments need to be applied simultaneously and the 'starting point' may not be the same State. This complexity increases when subject matters outside the scope of the Conventions are included in the 'package agreement' or one or both of these Conventions is not in force between the relevant States.

These possibilities are addressed in the navigation tool in three typical scenarios: (a) agreement in the context of cross-border relocation; (b) return agreement in international child abduction cases; and (c) non-return agreement in international child abduction cases.

In the first case (a), the agreement is likely to address matters on the exercise of parental responsibility, child maintenance, spousal/ex-spousal maintenance, and travel and education costs, among others. It should be first considered whether the 1996 and 2007 Conventions apply in the relevant States; if so, their rules for recognition and enforcement of agreements/decisions as were described above can be followed. Those aspects that exceed their scope will be governed by any other international instruments in force between the States involved or by private international law rules at the domestic level. Difficulties may appear in contact cases in which one of the parents habitually resides in one State and the other parent in another. Therefore, if the 1996 Convention is in force between all States, the ideal 'starting point' jurisdiction for the agreement in the contact context is the State of habitual residence of the child. However, if the agreement also includes maintenance aspects, the ideal option would be to use the habitual residence of the child if that State accepts an agreement as a 'maintenance arrangement' under the 2007 Convention (Articles 3(e) and 30), paying attention to possible reservations made by the other State(s) involved. In that latter case, the parts of the agreement concerning maintenance must be made part of a decision as foreseen in Article 19(1) of the 2007 Convention in a State which meets one of the indirect grounds of jurisdiction in Article 20 of the Convention. The problem is that the child's habitual residence is only an acceptable basis of indirect jurisdiction for child support (never for spousal support) if 'the respondent has lived with the child in that State or has

[23] These grounds sought in Art 20(1)(a), (b) or (d) of the 2007 Convention do not allow for any reservation.

[24] See above (n 17).

[25] The 'Explanatory Note' refers to these cases when the 1996 and the 2007 Conventions are in force between all States concerned by the dispute, all matters treated in the agreement fall within the scope of either Convention and the same authority in the 'starting point' legal system is in accordance with national procedural law competent to give the necessary force to the agreement under both Conventions. To complete the 'best case scenario', the competent authority acts expeditiously and free of charge or imposes reasonable charges only. 'Explanatory Note' (n 8) para 143.

resided in that State and provided support for the child there' (Article 20(1)(d)) and therefore checks need to be made to see if there is an acceptable basis of indirect jurisdiction under one of the other grounds in Article 20(1).[26]

In international child abduction cases the enforcement of the agreements could be even more complex because of the urgency of these cases (expeditiousness of the procedures) and the complications caused by Article 16 of the 1980 Convention. According to this provision, the courts in the State to which the child was taken cannot decide on the merits of custody while the Hague return proceedings are pending. In addition, the 1996 Convention provides that international jurisdiction for matters falling within its scope remains with the authorities of the State where the child, immediately before the abduction, habitually resided until the conditions for a shift of international jurisdiction are met (Article 7). Thus, for the return agreement (b), the court where the child was taken will not have international jurisdiction to render a decision on the merits of custody and contact while the return proceedings are pending. Even though Article 11 of the 1996 Convention grants jurisdiction for measures of protection to the authorities of any Contracting State in whose territory the child is present in cases of urgency it cannot assist in rendering the agreement fully binding; it only may play a role in the context of return proceedings when it comes to ensuring the safe return of the child with certain measures of protection.[27] The Explanatory Note pointed out that the ideal 'starting point' legal system to render the agreement legally binding and enforceable will be the State of habitual residence of the child immediately before the wrongful removal or retention.[28] Also, it is noted that some difficulties may arise regarding the speed of proceedings, or the need for the presence of both parties in that State, but the use of direct judicial communications or the participation of the International Hague Network of Judges are noted as important resources in this regard. If agreements in this context include maintenance issues, the analysis should follow the rules foreseen in the 2007 Convention that were mentioned above, considering jurisdictional aspects independently.[29]

The situation is in some respects similar in a non-return agreement (c), since the courts in the State to which the child was taken cannot decide on the merits of custody while the return proceedings are pending (Article 16 of the 1980 Convention) and until then the international jurisdiction remains with the authorities of the State where the child was habitually resident before the abduction. The Explanatory Note underlines that a more appropriate solution can be offered to parents who conclude a non-return agreement when the courts of the State hearing the Hague return proceedings can end the return proceedings and simultaneously give effect to the 'family agreement' not to return the child. They can do this because a shift of international jurisdiction on matters of custody and contact under the 1996 Convention has occurred in accordance with Article 7 of the 1996 Convention, as the non-return agreement means that the left behind custody holder has 'acquiesced' in the removal or retention, and both custody holders want the child to be habitually resident in the country where the child is present.[30] A detailed discussion regarding

[26] Ibid, para 151.

[27] These measures are considered 'temporary' and presuppose a situation of urgency. Ibid, para 157.

[28] Ibid, para 160.

[29] Ibid, para 161.

[30] Ibid, para 164. The policy of the Experts' Group in relation to this issue has been followed by the EU Council in its Regulation 2019/1111 on jurisdiction, the recognition and enforcement of decisions in matrimonial matters and the matters of parental responsibility, and on international child abduction [2019] OJ L178/1 (referred to as the Brussels IIb Regulation). So, for intra-EU cases, recital 22 states that: 'Member States which have concentrated jurisdiction should consider enabling the court seised with the return application under the 1980 Hague Convention to exercise also the jurisdiction agreed upon or accepted by the parties pursuant to this Regulation in matters of parental responsibility where agreement of the parties was reached in the course of the return proceedings. Such agreements should include agreements

this issue of a change in habitual residence was held within the Experts' Group and the consensus in the group is carefully reflected in the Explanatory Note. The final consensus on habitual residence (and on a number of other issues) in the 'Practitioners' Tool' agreed by the Experts' Group in November 2021 is noticeably different from that agreed by the Experts' Group in June 2018 in the 'Practical Guide'. This can be explained by the addition of some new members of the Experts' Group in 2021 to reflect the concerns of the Members of the HCCH who were not ready to adopt the Practical Guide in 2019.

The Experts' Group also agreed on how to interpret Article 16 of the 1980 Convention in this context. The Article only prevents a court from 'deciding on the merits of rights of custody until it has been determined that the child is not to be returned under this Convention'. That has been understood as a consequence of a systematic and teleological interpretation of Article 16 of the 1980 Convention, which aims to avoid the misuse of custody proceedings by the taking parent in the State to which the child was taken bringing about conflicting custody decisions and circumventing the Convention's return mechanism. Finally, it was noted that where the court seised with the Hague return proceedings ends the proceedings by approving a parental agreement on non-return, this is a correct use of the 1980 Convention and not a circumvention of it.[31] Another possibility that was discussed is the transfer of jurisdiction provided in Articles 8 and 9 of the 1996 Convention but this may take a lot of time in order to give an urgent solution. Maintenance could also be a part of the 'package agreement' and the same considerations as in the previous two scenarios have to be considered.

Evidently, the existing Hague Conventions provide effective solutions for the recognition and enforcement of amicable solutions, but they were designed to respond particularly to the problems that fall within their scopes individually. Reality shows that amicable solutions and package agreements are increasingly frequent and they do not always fall within 'the best case scenario'.[32] Lack of effectiveness of such agreements impacts directly on children's rights and on their best interests. This complex scenario requires an efficient response and it is the HCCH that should provide it. Meanwhile international cooperation between national authorities of the States involved may help in finding effective solutions.[33]

III. Binding Instrument

In March 2020 the Council on General Affairs and Policy received an Information Document from the Permanent Bureau, prepared in consultation with the Chair of the Experts' Group, giving an overview of the findings of that Group in relation to the development of a normative

both on the return and the non-return of the child. If non-return is agreed, the child should remain in the Member State of the new habitual residence and jurisdiction for any future custody proceedings there should be determined on the basis of the new habitual residence of the child'. The new broad jurisdiction based on the agreement of the parties is found in Art 10.

[31] 'Explanatory Note' (n 8) paras 165–67.

[32] See above (n 25). In addition to the difficulties described, it might occur that in cases where a State was chosen as a 'starting point' its authorities are not considered to have international jurisdiction in accordance with applicable private international law rules in force; that the authorities with jurisdiction for each subject matter might differ in both the State of origin and the requested State according to their domestic rules, among other things. It was also noted that besides legal difficulties, there might be practical obstacles (eg, access to legal aid in other States, mediators or advisers with knowledge in Private International Law, language issues, etc): I Goicoechea, 'Acuerdos de familia que involucran a niños' in C Fresnedo de Aguirre and G Lorenzo Idiarte (eds), *Jornadas 130 Aniversario de los Tratados de Montevideo de 1889* (Fundación de Cultura Universitaria 2019) 617.

[33] The administrative and judicial cooperation has also been working as a resource to facilitate access to justice. Ibid, 634.

instrument.[34] The Experts' Group has a very diverse membership – in 2018 it was comprised of 25 experts in the field drawn from 21 States and an REIO,[35] eight men and 17 women, five judges, seven legal practitioners, six government officials and seven academics. It reached its conclusions by consensus.

The Experts' Group has made four recommendations for a new binding instrument on family agreements:[36]

1. Build on and supplement the existing HCCH Conventions

It is crucial that States promote family agreements by ratifying the 1980, 1996 and 2007 Conventions. These Conventions are irreplaceable for a variety of reasons – not least because they provide an excellent framework for solving many cross-border family disputes that cannot be resolved by 'agreement' between the relevant parties. But the existing Conventions do not cover all substantive matters covered by family agreements and do not provide a unified and simple approach to handling such agreements.

2. Provide a 'one-stop shop' for voluntary agreements

In policy terms it is clearly more efficient and conducive to encouraging amicable settlements if the parties to the agreement know that they can get the whole of their agreement rendered enforceable in one State (either because such agreements in and of themselves are enforceable or because there is one competent court or authority able to make the agreement enforceable). The Experts' Group considered the feasibility of States being willing to do this within the framework of a new Convention. It noted that this 'may prove difficult but the problems … are not insuperable given the appropriate political will'.[37]

3. Provide for simple rules for recognition and enforcement

The family agreement should be able to be registered or given a declaration of enforceability in one court in each Contracting State. This avoids the problem of having to go to different courts, in many Contracting States, to get enforcement of agreements/decisions under the 1996 and 2007 Conventions and opens up the possibility of widening the material scope of recognition and enforcement of family agreements, at least on an opt-in or opt-out basis, beyond the scope of those two Conventions. Recognition of a family agreement should be possible as a defence or as an answer to a preliminary question in any court in a Contracting State.

4. Provide for greater party autonomy

As noted above one of the weaknesses of the current system is the relative lack of party autonomy in the context of the 1996 Convention which can only be overcome with the consent of one court in a divorce case or with the consent of two courts in a transfer case. A new Convention should build on the flexibility conceded in principle through the transfer system of the 1996 Convention that it can be in the best interests of a child for a case to be heard in any court with which the 'child has a substantial connection'.[38] This is an area where global private international law could

[34] See Info Doc No 2, available at: www.hcch.net under 'Projects', then 'Legislative Projects', then 'Family agreements involving children', ie: assets.hcch.net/docs/3cd99dea-d087-4999-8016-57f738854e90.pdf.

[35] Argentina, Australia, Austria, Brazil, Chile, China, Dominican Republic, EU, Finland, France, Germany, Ireland, Israel, Netherlands, New Zealand, Japan, Russia, Spain, South Africa, Switzerland, UK, USA.

[36] Info Doc No 2 (n 34) para 14.

[37] Ibid, para 17.

[38] Ibid, para 14(d). The Experts' Group showed that such increased party autonomy would not be in violation of the 1980, 1996 and 2007 Conventions, see ibid, paras 19–25.

follow the example of EU law. The Brussels IIb Regulation provides in Article 10 for prorogation of jurisdiction in matters of parental responsibility where the child has a 'substantial connection' with the chosen State and the courts of that State regard the exercise of jurisdiction as being in the best interests of the child.[39]

In June 2018, the Experts' Group acknowledged that there was some hesitancy from certain Members of the HCCH regarding the development of a binding instrument. The Experts considered the need for additional research with a view to gaining a more in-depth assessment of the benefits of a binding instrument and to conclude its work on its feasibility. Against this background, the Experts' Group made the following recommendations in regard to a possible binding instrument for the attention of the 2019 meeting of CGAP:

> The Experts' Group recommends that the Project of cross-border recognition and enforcement of agreements in family matters involving children be kept on the work programme of the Hague Conference and that the Permanent Bureau continue to monitor developments in this area, including the impact of the Practical Guide. The Experts' Group is willing to assist, without cost implications for the Organisation, the Permanent Bureau in its monitoring role until further steps have been decided by Council. The Permanent Bureau would consult with the members of the Experts' Group, at least once a year, through video and telephone conference. Finally, the Experts' Group recommends that the Permanent Bureau explore with the members of the Experts' Group the possibility of applying for funded research to investigate further the problems and good practice associated with enabling cross-border family agreements to be made enforceable in different legal systems. In the light of the research findings the Experts' Group will consider whether to uphold its recommendation to develop a binding legislative instrument.[40]

Thus, it can safely be said that any legislative developments in the HCCH on family agreements are a long way off. However, the Experts' Group adopted the Practitioners' Tool by consensus in November 2021, which in turn was adopted by consensus by the Members of the HCCH at the Council in March 2022.[41] The HCCH could at some point conclude that a non-binding instrument is not enough to overcome the obstacles to making cross-border recognition and enforcement of family agreements successful. Experts who had participated in the Experts' Group are also not precluded from seeking, hopefully with the Permanent Bureau, funding for empirical research on cross-border family agreements. It can only be hoped that the findings of such research will persuade the small number of States in the HCCH that are sceptical about the value of a new instrument to support working on such an instrument or at least to not block consensus in CGAP for allowing it to go ahead.

[39] See above (n 30) for the full reference. This is another area where the work of the Experts' Group may have encouraged the EU Council to make this change in intra-EU cases.

[40] See 'Conclusions and Recommendations of the meeting of 28–29 June 2018 for the attention of the Council on General Affairs and Policy of March 2019', available at: www.hcch.net under 'Projects', then 'Legislative Projects', then 'Family agreements involving children', paras 2–3.

[41] Conclusions and Decisions of the March 2022 Council record that:

> '12. CGAP approved the Practitioners' Tool: Cross-Border Recognition and Enforcement of Agreements Reached in the Course of Family Matters Involving Children, subject to editorial amendments, for publication.
>
> 13. With the conclusion of the Experts' Group's work, CGAP expressed its gratitude to the Chair, Professor Paul Beaumont, and to the members of the Group. In preparing for the next meeting of the Special Commission on the practical operation of the 1980 Child Abduction and the 1996 Child Protection Conventions, CGAP noted that HCCH Members and the PB may wish to consult the experts who had participated in the Group, who may provide feedback, on a voluntary basis, on the use of the Practitioners' Tool.' available at: www.hcch.net under 'Governance' then 'Council on General Affairs and Policy'.

Finally, a new Convention is needed to ensure children's rights and their best interests are safeguarded within a context of greater party autonomy providing an easy and cheap system to secure the effectiveness of cross-border family agreements. Complex scenarios require special solutions and the HCCH has the experience;[42] this is the time to face this challenge.

[42] As Hans Van Loon affirmed 'The "Hague model" of treaty based institutional – administrative and judicial – direct transnational co-operation regarding private crossborder relationships … has proven to be an effective tool to assist families and children in overcoming some major hazards that globalization may cause to their mutual relationships', H Van Loon, 'The global horizon of Private International Law' (2016) 380 *Hague Collected Courses* 87.

39

The Protection of Adults

PIETRO FRANZINA

I. The Protection of Adults: An Overview

A. Adults' Protection Defined

Persons aged 18 or over may find themselves unable, permanently or temporarily, to protect their interests due to an impairment or insufficiency of their personal faculties. This may concern, among others, persons experiencing intellectual disability since birth or from a very young age, older persons suffering from neurodegenerative diseases resulting in cognitive decline, and persons with attention or memory difficulties after a stroke or brain surgery.

While in this condition, the individuals in question may need support to take decisions regarding their health, welfare and other personal matters, as well as their property and affairs. Without appropriate support, they are exposed to a risk of abuse and neglect.

B. A Legal Landscape Marked by Diversity

Support may come in different forms, depending on the circumstances of the case and the applicable law. Generally speaking, a distinction may be made in this context between voluntary and non-voluntary measures of protection.

Non-voluntary measures involve the appointment, by a public authority (judicial or administrative), of a person (the adult's 'administrator') charged with assisting and/or representing the adult with respect to a given set of decisions. The conditions for appointing the administrator, the nature and scope of his prerogatives and the extent of the supervisory powers vested in the competent authorities vary from one legal system to another.[1]

Voluntary measures rest, instead, on the self-determination of the adult concerned. While still in a position to protect their interests, the person in question appoints one or more attorneys to

[1] For an overview of the rules on adults' protection in a broad selection of countries, see R Frimston, A Ruck Keene, C van Overdijk and A Ward (eds), *The International Protection of Adults* (Oxford University Press 2015). See also R Dinerstein, E Grant Grewel and J Martinis, 'Emerging International Trends and Practices in Guardianship Law for People with Disabilities' (2016) 22 *ILSA Journal of International & Comparative Law* 435; AF Johns, 'Person-Centered Guardianship and Supported Decision Making: An Assessment of Progress Made in Three Countries' (2016) 9 *Journal of International Aging Law & Policy* 1; AD Ward, 'Legal Protection of Adults – An International Comparison' [2017] *Elder Law Journal* 147.

act on their behalf, or assist them, in the event of a loss of capacity. The instruments established for this purpose are known as 'lasting (or enduring, or durable) powers of attorney' in English-speaking jurisdictions. In this chapter, they will be referred to as 'private mandates'. The rules governing private mandates, including their formal requirements, the manner of exercise of the powers granted thereunder and the conditions for their coming into effect, also vary from country to country.[2] It is worth adding that private mandates are a relatively recent creation. The law of several jurisdictions does not contemplate this kind of arrangement, and rather sticks to the rule whereby powers of attorney cease to be effective as soon as the granter loses capacity.[3] Unless exceptions are provided to the latter rule, planning for incapacity may prove extremely difficult under those laws.[4]

C. The Impact of Measures of Protection on Capacity

Voluntary and non-voluntary measures of protection tend to affect the concerned adult's capacity to enter into a contract or other juristic acts. The impact of measures of protection on capacity depends on the applicable law and on the content and features of the particular measures adopted in the circumstances.

In the past, the protection of adults typically involved a deprivation of the concerned adult's capacity. This affects, in principle, all aspects of life. Decisions relating to the personal welfare or the property of a protected adult had to be taken, systematically, by somebody else on their behalf. The picture has since significantly evolved. Reforms have been enacted in several countries, in particular since the 1990s, which implemented, or at least promoted, a transition from substitute to supported decision-making.[5] Supported decision-making refers to the process whereby one or more persons assist the adult in question by collecting information, giving explanations and helping the adult concerned express their will.[6] Such assistance, too, may have an impact on the scope and manner of exercise of the adult's capacity. In fact, transactions performed without the prescribed support are often void, or voidable, in basically the same way as transactions concluded by a person lacking capacity.[7] That said, assistance remains fundamentally different from incapacitation because its purpose is to preserve, and strengthen, the self-determination of the adult in question, not (just) to manage the implications of the lack of it.

[2] See, again, the contributions referred to in the previous footnote.

[3] See, eg, Art 223 of the Greek Civil Code: C van Overdijk, M Maousmouti and H Meidanis, 'Greece' in R Frimston, A Ruck Keene, C van Overdijk and A Ward (eds), *The International Protection of Adults* (Oxford University Press 2015) 523, 529.

[4] Trusts, too, may be used for incapacity planning, at least in trust countries. A trustee, however, may only be charged with the management of the concerned adult's property or affairs, not with the task of deciding on the adult's welfare or health. See generally DJ Feder and RH Sitkoff, 'Revocable Trusts and Incapacity Planning: More than Just a Will Substitute' (2016) 24 *Elder Law Journal* 1.

[5] See generally, K Booth Glen, 'Changing Paradigms: Mental Capacity, Legal Capacity, Guardianship, and Beyond' (2012) 44 *Columbia Human Rights Law Review* 93 and L Series, 'Comparing Old and New Paradigms of Legal Capacity' (2014) *Elder Law Journal* 62.

[6] See, among others, KA Shogren, ML Wehmeyer, J Martinis and P Blanck, *Supported Decision-making – Theory, Research, and Practice to Enhance Self-determination and Quality of Life* (Cambridge University Press 2019); and A Stewart, *Supporting Vulnerable Adults – Citizenship, Capacity and Choice* (Dunedin Academic Press 2012).

[7] See, for instance, Art 412 of the Italian Civil Code.

II. Adults' Protection as a Human Rights Concern

A. The New Paradigm of Disability

The move towards supported decision-making in national legislation reflects a broader development in law, politics and society which occurred over the last few decades of the twentieth century.[8] Central to this development is a renewed understanding of disability.[9] Disability is no longer viewed as the result of a deficit which prevents the individual concerned from performing certain functions or activities. It is understood, instead, as the outcome of a dynamic interaction between the person concerned and their social and cultural environment. This means that disability arises and persists because, and insofar as, a person's environment fails to enhance the latter's enablement.

Alongside the described evolution, and in connection with it, scholars and policymakers have begun approaching disability (and adults' protection) from a human rights perspective.[10] By supporting those unable to take care of their interests, States no longer provide 'care' to 'dependent' people. They rather fulfil their obligations towards the individuals concerned and realise the fundamental rights of the latter.

B. Universal and Regional Instruments on the Rights Relating to Disability

The key universal legal instrument regarding the fundamental rights associated with disability is the UN Convention on the Rights of Persons with Disabilities (UNCRPD), of 13 December 2006. The Convention is currently in force in more than 180 States as well as one international organisation, the European Union (EU).[11]

The principle of respect for the dignity, autonomy and independence of persons, the principle of non-discrimination, and the principle of full and effective participation and inclusion of disabled persons in society are among the tenets of the Convention.[12]

Against this backdrop, the Convention imposes a number of obligations that have an impact on the way in which States provide for the protection of those unable to protect their interests.

Specifically, Article 12 of the UNCRPD stipulates that 'persons with disabilities enjoy legal capacity on an equal basis with others', and prescribes that States 'take appropriate measures to provide access by persons with disabilities to the support they may require in exercising their legal capacity'.[13] The measures relating to the exercise of capacity must 'provide for appropriate and effective safeguards to prevent abuse'; they must also 'respect the rights, will and preferences of the person, [be] free of conflict of interest and undue influence, [be] proportional and tailored

[8] See, in general, V Lipp and JO Winn, 'Guardianship and Autonomy: Foes or Friends' (2011) 5 *Journal of International Aging Law & Policy* 41.

[9] J Herring, *Vulnerable Adults and the Law* (Oxford University Press 2016) 97 ff.

[10] P Gooding, *A New Era for Mental Health Law and Policy* (Cambridge University Press 2017).

[11] See: www.un.org/development/desa/disabilities.

[12] See Recitals 1, 3 and 15 of the Convention, together with Art 3.

[13] As observed by the United Nations Committee on the Rights of Persons with Disabilities (CRPD) in its General Comment No 1, dated 11 April 2014, UN Doc CRPD/C/GC/1, legal capacity is understood by the Convention as referring to 'the capacity to be both a holder of rights and an actor under the law' (para 12).

to the person's circumstances, apply for the shortest time possible and [be] subject to regular review by a competent, independent and impartial authority or judicial body'.[14]

Regional organisations dealing with the protection of fundamental rights have also played an important role in shaping the duties of States as regards the protection of persons lacking the ability to protect their interests. The Council of Europe and the Organization of American States have been particularly active in this field, elaborating both binding and non-binding instruments relating, inter alia, to legal capacity and measures aimed to support their exercise. The work of the above organisations, which in part predates the adoption of the UNCRPD, basically rests on the assumption that the personal autonomy and social inclusion of persons with disabilities are crucial to the realisation of the latter's fundamental rights, as enshrined in the relevant regional and universal texts.[15]

C. The Contribution of Civil Society

International civil society, too, contributed to shaping and implementing the new approach to disability and the protection of adults. One remarkable expression of advocacy in this field is the declaration adopted by the First World Congress on Adult Guardianship Law in 2010, known as the Yokohama Declaration,[16] which reaffirms and further develops the principles stated in the UNCRPD and the regional instruments mentioned above.

III. The Role of Private International Law in the Realisation of the Fundamental Rights of Adults

A. The Right to Obtain Support in Cross-Border Cases

The States' obligations outlined in the previous section apply regardless of whether support to exercise capacity is sought in a domestic or in a cross-border scenario.

Nothing is said in the UNCRPD as to the role that private international law may play in the realisation of the fundamental rights of disabled persons. However, the concern for the effective protection of the rights enshrined in the UNCRPD implies that those be safeguarded in any circumstances (ie, including in international situations), by any appropriate means (ie, including through private international law rules, as the case may be).

B. The Instrumentality of Private International Law

Private international law rules may enhance the rights of the adults concerned. The provisions governing the recognition of foreign measures of protection, for example, are crucial to providing

[14] For detailed analysis, see L Series and A Nilson, 'Article 12' in I Bantekas, MA Stein and D Anastasiou (eds), *The UN Convention on the Rights of Persons with Disabilities* (Oxford University Press 2018) 339.

[15] As regards the Council of Europe, see, among other documents, Recommendation (99)4 of 23 February 1999, on Principles Concerning the Legal Protection of Incapable Adults, and Recommendation (2009)11 of 9 December 2009, on Principles Concerning Continuing Powers of Attorney and Advance Directives for Incapacity, available at: www.coe.int. With respect to the Organization of American States, see the Inter-American Convention on Protecting the Human Rights of Older Persons of 15 June 2015, available at: www.oas.org.

[16] The Declaration, as revised and amended by the Fourth World Congress on Adult Guardianship Law of 2016, is available at: www.international-guardianship.com.

the adult in question with a spatially continuous protection, ie, one available wherever the interests of the adult in question may need to be safeguarded. As a matter of fact, the protection of adults moving from one country to another (eg, to enjoy the company of relatives living abroad, or to benefit from healthcare opportunities unavailable in their home country), and that of adults with property located in two or more States, would hardly be effective without rules ensuring – subject to appropriate safeguards – the cross-border portability of measures of protection.

Private international law has in fact an important role to play in the realisation of the fundamental rights of disabled adults. To exploit the potential of private international law in this field, two conditions must be satisfied. First, the applicable private international law rules should be designed (and interpreted) with the policies of the UNCRPD in mind. Second, States should make sure that their courts are in a position to exchange and cooperate with the courts and authorities of other States whenever joint or concerted action proves beneficial to the protection of the adult in question.[17]

IV. The Hague Adults Convention

A. Origins and Principal Orientations of the Convention

In the 1990s, when the new paradigm of disability had not yet obtained the widespread recognition it enjoys today, the Hague Conference on Private International Law engaged in a project aimed precisely to enhance, in international situations, the protection of those unable to take care of their interests.[18]

The project resulted in the Convention of 13 January 2000 on the International Protection of Adults.[19] The Convention applies, in cross-border cases, to situations involving persons aged 18 or over who are unable, because of their physical or mental state, to properly manage their assets and/or to care about their personal and health interests. Protection comes within the scope of the Convention no matter whether the impairment or insufficiency of the concerned adult's faculties is temporary or permanent, acquired or congenital, reversible or irreversible, and regardless of the remaining degree of self-determination of the adult themselves. The term 'protection' is understood by the Convention to encompass any measure the purpose of which is to protect the adult concerned, no matter whether (and the manner in which) they affect the adult's capacity, and no matter whether they entail that the adult is represented by an administrator on a continuous basis, or is rather assisted or advised in relation to specific acts.[20]

[17] Several international instruments in the field of human rights, including those of disabled persons, require that Contracting States cooperate for the realisation of the purpose and objectives of such instruments: see, in particular, Art 32 of the UNCRPD. Cooperation may be needed in a broad range of situations. Arguably, these include the handling by the authorities of one State of cases with a cross-border element.

[18] A Hague Convention on guardianship and similar measures of protection had already been adopted on 17 July 1905. Its success has been limited. Nine States ratified the Convention, but five of them subsequently denounced it. Though still in force for Italy, Poland, Portugal and Romania, the 1905 Convention is apparently no longer applied in any of these States.

[19] The text of the Convention is found at: hcch.net, with information on ratifications and declarations, and an explanatory report drawn up by P Lagarde (Lagarde Report). Regarding the Convention see, generally, in English language literature, E Clive, 'The New Hague Convention on the Protection of Adults' (2000) 2 *Yearbook of Private International Law* 1, and AR Fagan, 'An Analysis of the Convention on the International Protection of Adults' (2002) *Elder Law Journal* 329. See also Frimston et al (n 1) 77 ff.

[20] As regards the scope of the Convention, see generally, the Lagarde Report (n 19) para 8 ff.

A Study commissioned by the UN Special Rapporteur on the rights of persons with disabilities, acknowledged that the Convention is not, as such, inconsistent with the UNCRPD, and that there are a number of ways in which the Hague Convention is capable of evolving to reflect the 'operationalisation' by both current and future Contracting States of the UNCRPD within their domestic legal systems.[21]

The Hague Adults Convention entered into force on the international plane on 1 January 2009. Thirteen States are currently bound by the Convention, namely Austria, Belgium, Cyprus, the Czech Republic, Estonia, Finland, France, Germany, Latvia, Monaco, Portugal and Switzerland. The United Kingdom, too, is a Party to the Convention, but, so far, only with respect to Scotland.

The Convention has close ties with the Hague Convention of 19 October 1996 on Jurisdiction, Applicable Law, Recognition, Enforcement and Co-operation in Respect of Parental Responsibility and Measures for the Protection of Children. In fact, the two instruments have basically the same structure, and several provisions of the Convention of 2000 resemble, in both their rationale and the wording, the corresponding provisions of the Convention of 1996.

These similarities reflect the fact that the two texts basically pursue a protective function, namely the protection of the adult or the child concerned. While the language of the two texts is not always identical, the view is generally accepted that the goal of enhancing the protection of children and adults affects, in general, the design and the interpretation of both the 1996 and the 2000 Convention.[22]

B. Some Key Features of the Convention

The concern for the effective protection of those unable to care for their interests explains most of the key features of the Adults Convention.

i. An 'Integral' Regime

The Convention brings together rules on direct jurisdiction, applicable law and the recognition and enforcement of protection measures. Such a one-stop shop approach is common to the 1996 Convention on the protection of children. This is in itself remarkable, since most of the texts adopted within the Hague Conference on Private International Law address no more than one or two issues. For instance, the Convention of 14 March 1978 on the Law Applicable to Agency only deals with conflicts of laws, while the Convention of 1 June 1970 on the Recognition of Divorces and Legal Separations is merely concerned with recognition, and does not regulate either direct jurisdiction or the applicable law.[23]

'Integral' regimes are particularly effective at facilitating the international circulation of decisions. By harmonising the rules on jurisdiction and those on applicable law, integral instruments create a climate of mutual trust which makes it easier for States to display an open attitude towards the work of foreign authorities and their measures, insofar as such authorities belong to

[21] S Rolland and A Ruck Keene, 'Interpreting the 2000 Hague Convention on the International Protection of Adults Consistently with the UN Convention on the Rights of Persons with Disabilities' (3 June 2021), available at the website of the Office of the UN High Commissioner for Human Rights: www.ohchr.org.

[22] For a discussion on the meaning and use of the 'interest of the adult' formula in the Adults Convention, see J Long, 'Rethinking Vulnerable Adults' Protection in the Light of the 2000 Hague Convention' (2013) 27 *International Journal of Law, Policy and the Family* 51, 58 ff.

[23] See, for both instruments: hcch.net.

States involved in the same climate and their measures are consistent with the policies on which that climate is built.

Article 22 immediately translates the Convention's concern for the portability of protection measures. It stipulates that the measures issued in a Contracting State 'shall be recognised by operation of law in all other Contracting States'. Recognition may only be denied on one or more of the grounds enumerated in the provision. A denial is justified, in particular, where it is established that the measure in question does not deserve the trust that the Contracting States accord each other as a matter of principle, notably because the measure 'was taken by an authority whose jurisdiction was not based on, or was not in accordance with, one of the grounds provided for by the [Convention]', or where the authorities of the State of origin failed to provide the fundamental rights of the adult in question with appropriate protection (eg, because the measure 'was taken, except in a case of urgency, in the context of a judicial or administrative proceeding, without the adult having been provided the opportunity to be heard, in violation of fundamental principles of procedure of the requested State'). Instead, the authorities of the State requested are not authorised to review the law applied in the State of origin.[24] In an area of law marked by the diversity of domestic rules, the harmonisation of the rules on jurisdiction and the applicable law increases mutual trust and helps provide the adults concerned with a spatially continuous protection.[25]

The one-stop shop approach followed by the Convention also improves the effectiveness of the protection in another way. Cases exist where various concerns arise and need to be accommodated. They call for balanced answers. A fair balance, however, cannot always be struck on the basis of the rules on jurisdiction alone, or the rules on the applicable law alone. Sensible answers may rather be provided through the combined operation of the two sets of rules.

The Convention's provisions on private mandates are particularly illustrative. Pursuant to Article 15(1), mandates are governed, in principle, by the law of the State of the adult's habitual residence at the time the mandate was entered into. This implies that the powers granted under a mandate made in accordance with the latter law may in principle be relied upon in any other Contracting State.

Occasionally, however, the spatial continuity thus achieved can raise concerns. What if the powers conferred are not exercised in conformity with the fundamental rights of the granter? Where a similar concern is raised, the adult themselves, or anyone else interested, should be able to apply for the necessary court orders or directions. But the courts of which State should have jurisdiction to give such directions? If the Convention were only concerned with applicable law, the answer would be left with the domestic rules of the individual Contracting States. Positive and negative conflicts of jurisdiction would likely ensue, which would defeat the benefits of the unification of applicable law rules. The Convention avoids this risk by laying down rules of direct jurisdiction. Article 16 of the Convention provides that the powers conferred under a private mandate may be withdrawn or modified through judicial or administrative measures 'taken by an authority *having jurisdiction under the Convention*' (emphasis added). This ultimately mitigates the risk of negative and positive conflicts of jurisdiction.

An additional issue, however, may arise in a scenario like the one described, ie, based on which law should the competent court decide whether to modify or withdraw the powers conferred under a mandate.

[24] Lagarde Report (n 19) para 118.

[25] On the challenges posed by the diversity of domestic rules regarding the protection of adults, see K Karjalainen, 'Fragility of Cross-Border Adult Protection: The Difficult Interplay of Private International Law with Substantive Law' (2018–19) 20 *Yearbook of Private International Law* 439.

Article 13(1) of the Convention stipulates that, in exercising their jurisdiction under the Convention, the authorities of a Contracting State generally apply their own law. The problem is that, if the *lex fori* were to apply in all and any circumstances, Article 15(1), which provides for the application of the law of the adult's habitual residence at the time of the mandate, would lose much of its practical effect. In fact, the court with jurisdiction to supervise the attorney's conduct might well sit in a State other than the State where the adult had his or her habitual residence when the mandate was originally entered into. Thus, powers granted under the law of country X could be withdrawn or modified in accordance with the law of country Y. This is something the granter could hardly foresee, and – worse – something the granter will often be unable to redress in person (for, when the problem arises, the adult will most probably be unable to correct, adapt or clarify the power of attorney).

The opposite solution, ie, the systematic application of the law specified in Article 15, may not lead to sensible results, either. The supervising court might in fact have to apply a foreign law, which could make supervision difficult to carry out and time-consuming. Article 16 of the Convention helps strike a balance between the above concerns by providing that, where powers of representation are withdrawn or modified, 'the law referred to in Article 15 should be taken into consideration to the extent possible'.[26]

All in all, the combined harmonisation of rules on jurisdiction and on applicable law allows the supervision of a private mandate to be done in a manner which ensures a high degree of predictability, the efficiency of the concerned courts' action and a rapid response to the needs of the adult concerned.

ii. The Choice of Habitual Residence as the Main Connecting Factor

The Hague instruments dealing with family relations and the law of persons invariably use habitual residence as the main connecting factor. The Adults Convention is no exception. Article 5, the general rule on jurisdiction, provides that the authorities of the Contracting State of the habitual residence of the adult 'have jurisdiction to take measures directed to the protection of the adult's person or property'. In case of a change of residence to another Contracting State, jurisdiction lies with the authorities of such State.

The choice of habitual residence echoes the central place occupied by the interests of the adult among the policies of the Convention and contributes to the realisation of the fundamental rights of the adults concerned. By conferring jurisdiction on the courts of the State of the habitual residence of the adult, the Convention intends to ensure that measures of protection are taken, in principle, by such courts as are normally best placed to assess the needs of the adult and shape the latter's protection accordingly. Generally speaking, the courts at the adult's habitual residence are better placed to appraise the views, habits and preferences of the protected person, and to direct the work of those involved in his or her protection. They are also the most easily accessible by the adult concerned. In fact, an adult's right to be heard is easier to enforce in the State where the centre of the adult's interests are situated rather than elsewhere.

The use of habitual residence as a connecting factor facilitates States in complying with their obligations under the UNCRPD to make sure, inter alia, that measures be adopted that are tailored to the adult's circumstances, apply for the shortest time possible and are subject to regular review.

[26] On the rationale of this provision, see further Lagarde Report (n 19) para 108.

One additional advantage of the use of habitual residence is that it promotes social inclusion. This is so because habitual residence itself rests on the concerned person's ties and relations.[27] In fact, the protection afforded by the courts of the State of the habitual residence of the adult (rather than, say, the courts of the adult's State of nationality) builds on those ties and is, as such, well suited to safeguard and consolidate the adult's relations.

Finally, the choice of habitual residence as a connecting factor helps avert the risk of discrimination. The rule in Article 5 of the Convention implies in fact that all adults whose habitual residence is in a Contracting State are granted equal access to the support they may require to exercise their capacity, regardless of any other personal circumstances, such as their nationality.[28]

Interestingly, the Convention does not rule out the possibility that jurisdiction be asserted in a Contracting State on a ground other than the adult's habitual residence, notably if that proves beneficial to the adult in question in the circumstances. In fact, other grounds of jurisdiction are contemplated, which operate concurrently with the habitual residence of the adult. For instance, Article 7 provides that the courts of a State of which the adult is a national have jurisdiction to take measures of protection if they consider that they are 'in a better position to assess the interests of the adult'. This entails a need for inter-jurisdictional (dialogue and) coordination. The Convention provides that the courts of the State of nationality may claim jurisdiction only after advising the authorities of the State of habitual residence of the adult, and add that the former must cease to exercise their jurisdiction as soon as the latter authorities have informed them that they are dealing with the situation, or that no measures should be taken. In any case, the measures taken by the 'national' courts lapse as soon as the authorities of the State of habitual residence have taken measures required by the situation or have decided that no measures be taken.

iii. The Respect for, and Promotion of, the Adult's Self-Determination

Another noteworthy feature of the Hague Adults Convention is the importance it accords to the will and preferences of the adult. This, too, is in line with the human rights-based paradigm of disability underlying the UNCRPD, and is reflected in the Preamble to the Hague Adults Convention itself, which affirms that the adult's dignity and autonomy are to be treated as 'primary considerations' when it comes to his or her protection.

The Convention fosters self-determination in various ways. The provisions regarding private mandates are, of course, particularly significant in this regard, since mandates are, in essence, instruments of self-determination. As noticed above, Article 15(1) makes private mandates subject, in principle, to the law of the State where the adult concerned habitually resided when the mandate was made. The stated irrelevance of any subsequent change of habitual residence is itself a way to reinforce the adult's ability to plan for incapacity, in that it shields the effects of the mandate under the law of the original habitual residence from any subsequent change in the concerned adult's residence.

Significantly, the Convention goes as far as to establish that the law applicable to a private mandate may be chosen by the parties, provided the chosen law is either the law of the State of

[27] *cf* with reference to other normative texts using habitual residence as a connecting factor, T Kruger, 'Habitual Residence: The Factors that Courts Consider' in P Beaumont, M Danov, K Trimmings and B Yüksel (eds), *Cross-border Litigation in Europe* (Hart Publishing 2017) 741.

[28] According to Art 6(1), jurisdiction to rule on the protection of refugees and internationally displaced persons rests with authorities of the Contracting State on the territory of which these adults are present. The same rule applies, under Art 6(2), to adults whose habitual residence cannot be established.

the adult's nationality, the law of the State of a former habitual residence of the adult, or the law of a State in which property of the adult is located (but only with respect to the said property). The provision ultimately makes it easier for the adult concerned to plan reliably in contemplation of a loss of capacity, including in complex situations where the objective rule in Article 15(1) might prove too rigid or otherwise unsuited to fulfil the needs of the granter.

Article 8(2)(d) of the Convention further contemplates the possibility that the adult chooses the Contracting State whose courts are to protect them. Clearly, this further expresses the Convention's concern for self-determination. The practical importance of the provision, however, is limited. The adult's choice under Article 8 does not itself confer jurisdiction on the courts of the chosen State. In fact, the provision merely states that the courts at the adult's habitual residence, 'if they consider that such is in the interests of the adult', may request the authorities of the State chosen by the adult (or those of other States with which the case is connected, as listed in Article 8 itself) to take measures for the protection of the person or property of the adult. In fact, the adult may make known their wish that their protection be dealt with in a given Contracting State, but the courts of that State are not entitled to deal with the matter unless the courts which would ordinarily be in charge of the case so provide.

iv. Adults' Protection Outside Judicial or Administrative Proceedings

Adults who need support to exercise their capacity mostly require support on an ongoing basis. Actually, measures of protection are often organised in such a way as to cover a broad range of decisions, including day-to-day decisions and transactions of limited importance. Courts are only involved in particular circumstances, notably when a protection regime is set up or terminated, or where a decision of particular importance is contemplated, which requires prior authorisation.

The Adults Convention applies in any context in which the protection of an adult may be at issue, including in situations outside judicial or administrative proceedings. Some provisions of the Convention are designed to enhance the protection of adults in the latter situations. Article 38 is among them. It stipulates that the authorities of a Contracting State where a measure of protection was taken, or a private mandate was confirmed, may deliver a certificate indicating the capacity in which the person entrusted with protection is entitled to act on behalf of the adult in question and the powers conferred. The capacity and powers resulting from the certificate 'are presumed to be vested in that person as of the date of the certificate, in the absence of proof to the contrary'.

The purpose of the certificate is, basically, to improve legal security by making it easier for those in charge of the adult's protection to make use of their powers outside the State where the powers originated, eg, the State where a bank account of the adult is located. The adult's administrator should in principle be able to provide evidence of his powers as regards the money deposited in the account by presenting the bank manager with an Article 38 certificate. This should make support more readily and more efficiently available, thereby increasing the effectiveness of the protection of the adult concerned.

v. The Promotion of Inter-Jurisdictional Dialogue and Cooperation

The Convention is not merely a collection of uniform rules of private international law. In fact, the goal of the Convention is also to create a permanent framework of international cooperation between the Contracting States. The idea is that, in international situations, the interests of the adult are often best served through the joint or concerted action of the authorities of two or more States, or based on a shared assessment of the relevant circumstances.[29]

As a matter of fact, some provisions of the Convention would hardly achieve their potential if dialogue proved impossible, or difficult, between the authorities of the States concerned. The aforementioned Article 8 is one such provision. As observed, Article 8 contemplates the transfer of a case from one Contracting State to another when the authorities seised of the matter consider that their counterparts in another State are better placed to rule on the adult's protection. In practice, a transfer can only be conceived of where the authorities of the two States are in a position to exchange their views on the transfer itself. The authorities of the State to which the transfer is contemplated must themselves be convinced of the benefits of the move and must be willing to engage in the protection of the adult. They do not have to accept the transfer.[30]

The cooperation that the Convention aims to foster may refer to any aspect of protection and benefit the operation of any provisions. Cooperation may unfold at different levels. Each Contracting State is required to appoint a Central Authority for the purposes of the Convention. The task of Central Authorities, according to Article 29, is twofold. They must cooperate with each other and must promote cooperation among the competent authorities in their respective States to achieve the purposes of the Convention.

Dialogue, however, may also take place at a decentralised level, ie, in the form of direct (judicial) communications.[31] Individual Contracting States may declare that certain requests for assistance will not be considered unless they are channelled through their Central Authorities, but apart from such declarations, nothing in the Convention prevents the authorities of Contracting States communicating directly between them where this is conducive to the protection of the adults concerned.

V. The International Protection of Adults in Prospect

The Adults Convention is almost unanimously praised by scholars and practitioners as providing a comprehensive set of balanced and workable answers to the issues surrounding the international protection of adults.[32]

However, the interpretation of the Convention may in some cases prove problematic (for instance, when the determination of the habitual residence of an adult lacking capacity is at issue, namely where the latter's move from one State to another does not appear to accord with his or her preferences).[33] Moreover, some of the provisions of the Convention – Article 38, among others – are only seldom used and ultimately fail to provide all the benefits they could.

[29] Dialogue between courts is in fact regarded, more generally, as a tool to enhance the protection of fundamental rights: see generally the contributions collected in A Müller and HE Kjos (eds), *Judicial Dialogue and Human Rights* (Cambridge University Press 2017).

[30] If they do not accept it, the courts originally seised will retain their jurisdiction: Art 8(3).

[31] The Hague Conference has been promoting direct judicial communications in various fields, notably the protection of children. See, in general, P Lortie, 'Les Lignes de Conduite Émergentes et les Principes Généraux de la Conférence de La Haye Relatifs aux Communications Judiciaires Directes' in S Menétrey and B Hess (eds), *Les Dialogues des Juges en Europe* (Larcier 2014) 285.

[32] Several authors advocated a broad ratification of the Convention. See, recently, among others: R Frimston, 'Cross-Border Incapacity: Hague 35, the Only Life Raft Available in Choppy Waters' (2015) *Elder Law Journal* 166 ff; M Álvarez Torné, 'Current Issues in the Protection of Adults from the Perspective of Private International Law' (2016) 32 *Revista Electrónica de Estudios Internacionales* 1, 17; M Drventić, 'The Protection of Adults in the European Union' (2019) 3 *EU and Comparative Law Issues and Challenges Series* 804, 805.

[33] See, for an illustration, the cases discussed in GR Ashton, J Baker and M Marin (eds), *Mental Capacity: Law and Practice*, 4th edn (LexisNexis 2018) 520 ff.

These shortcomings should not be overestimated. The main problem with the Convention is that it is in force only for a limited number of States. In fact, the pace of ratifications has been, so far, rather slow. Eight ratifications occurred during the 15 years following the adoption of the Convention. After that, the Convention attracted one ratification in 2016, one in 2017, two in 2018, none in 2019 and again one in 2020.

The concerns that the Adults Convention addresses are regarded as important by a large number of States. Most of them, however, appear to prioritise other topics.

In this respect, it would be unfair to compare the Adults Convention with the 1996 Convention on the protection of children, which is in force for more than 50 States. The 1996 Convention is, indeed, a very successful instrument, but the reasons behind its success are specific to the protection of children. Child protection is a subject of high political relevance and regularly attracts the attention of media. The interest of the general public in the protection of adults is more discrete. In addition, while several advocacy groups exist which are concerned with the fundamental rights associated with disability, only some of them appear to be fully aware of the potential of private international law for the realisation of those rights.

One explanation for the relatively slow rhythm of ratifications is that several States regard the ratification of the Convention as one component of a broader strategy aimed at enhancing the protection of adults, the other element being the modernisation of the domestic rules that govern the substance and procedure of adults' protection. This is a sensible approach in itself. The modernisation of the internal rules on the protection of adults, however, often comes at the price of demanding legislative efforts, which eventually affect the timing of the ratification of the Convention. Belgium, for example, only ratified the Convention in 2020, in the aftermath of a comprehensive reform of its internal legislation on adults' protection.

All in all, the promotion of the Hague Convention of 2000 appears to be more difficult than that of many other Hague instruments.

The Hague Conference is actively working at the promotion of the Convention. Various initiatives have already been taken to this end, including a conference held in Brussels in 2018, organised by the Permanent Bureau of the Conference jointly with the European Commission. The 2018 conference witnessed the growing interest of States and other stakeholders in the Convention and provided evidence of the Convention's added value.[34] Other initiatives are currently being prepared and will materialise in the relatively near future. The single most notable step in this direction was taken in 2019, when the Council of the General Affairs and Policy of the Conference decided that a Special Commission be convened in 2022 to discuss the practical operation of the Convention.[35] The event is expected to provide a unique opportunity to assess the functioning of the Convention, illustrate the best practices developed thereunder and address the doubts or difficulties surrounding the interpretation of some of its provisions.

The Special Commission will also be an occasion to attract further ratifications of the Convention, and hopefully extend its current geographical reach. Today, the 13 States that are bound by the Adults Convention are all from Europe. Ten of them are also Member States of the EU. In spite of some notable exceptions, such as Canada and Mexico, most of the States with a known interest in ratifying the Convention (Luxembourg and Sweden, among others) also come from within the European region.[36]

[34] The Conference's conclusions and recommendations can be found at: hcch.net.

[35] See the conclusions and recommendations adopted by the Council at its meeting of 5–8 March 2019, para 34, available at: hcch.net. See also the Council's conclusions and decisions adopted at the meeting of 3–6 March 2020, para 31, ibid.

[36] See the mentioned States' replies to the questionnaire drafted by the Permanent Bureau to assess the need to convene a Special Commission, available at: hcch.net.

Various factors explain this state of affairs. One such factor is the high rate of international mobility that exists in Europe. Specifically, EU citizens enjoy freedom of movement throughout the Union, regardless of whether their movement is prompted by economic rather than personal reasons (such as retiring in a country with a milder climate and a lower cost of living). Additionally, EU citizens are more likely than others to hold assets located in different (European) States, because of the free movement of goods and capital they enjoy under EU law. All of this increases the likelihood that they may require support in the exercise of capacity in situations featuring a cross-border element, which in turn prompts a special interest in harmonising the law and fostering cooperation.[37]

That said, the mobility of persons and their assets being a global phenomenon, States in all regions of the world arguably have an interest in enhancing the international protection of adults, and should consider ratifying the Hague Adults Convention accordingly.

VI. Concluding Remarks

Adults lacking the ability to protect their interests because of an impairment or insufficiency of their personal faculties have a fundamental right to obtain the support they may require to exercise such capacity as well as the right to be protected from abuse and neglect. The enforcement of such rights involves that measures be taken by States to enhance the autonomy and social inclusion of those concerned, and shield them from undue influence.

Where a foreign element is present, all this involves the enactment of appropriate private international law rules. These rules effectively advance the respect for the above rights where they ensure the spatial continuity of the concerned adults' protection, without hindering otherwise their fundamental rights (eg, the right to have their views and preferences considered), and minimise the extra costs and uncertainties that the internationality of the situation could entail.

The Hague Adults Convention is intended to achieve precisely those goals. It is consistent with a human rights-based approach to disability and appears to work efficiently in practice. While some of its rules call for review for possible enhancements, the Adults Convention ranks among the finest products of the Hague Conference, and provides an example of how private international law can effectively contribute to the realisation of fundamental human rights.

[37] In 2017, the European Parliament asked the Commission to present a proposal for a regulation on the protection of adults in cross-border situations: Resolution of 1 June 2017 with Recommendations to the Commission on the Protection of Vulnerable Adults (2015/2085(INL)) OJ C 307, 30.8.2018, 154. The Commission replied that it would rather keep promoting the ratification of the Adults Convention by Member States: see Follow up to the European Parliament Resolution of 1 June 2017 with recommendations to the Commission on the protection of vulnerable adults, SP(2017)510. In the aftermath of the Resolution, the European Law Institute (ELI), an independent organisation, launched a project aimed at identifying the measures that the EU might take to enhance the protection of adults in cross-border cases. The project's final report, adopted in 2020 (*The Protection of Adults in International Situations*, rapporteurs: P Franzina and R Frimston) suggest that the EU request remaining Member States to ratify the Convention and enact legislation intended to enhance the operation of the latter between Member States (eg, through the creation of a European Certificate designed to improve the certificate provided for by the Convention): the report is available at: www.europeanlawinstitute.eu. On 7 June 2021, the Council of the EU approved a political document titled *Conclusions on the Protection of Vulnerable Adults across the European Union* (OJ C 330I of 17 August 2021, p 1), where it stressed the importance of the Hague Adults Convention and invited Member States that have not yet done so to ratify it.

40

International Surrogacy and International Parentage: Hopes for a Global Solution

GIACOMO BIAGIONI

I. The Emerging Need for Uniform Private International Law Rules on Parentage

At least since Greek antiquity, a very strong emphasis has been placed on the establishment of parentage as a complex process as several myths show.[1] However, in the context of myth, determination of parentage is not the consequence of the assessment of legal issues but rather of the mere discovery of relevant facts. In subsequent legal traditions, a set of substantive rules, connected to the principles of *mater certa* and *pater est quem nuptiae demonstrant*, became well settled and a common core of substantive law principles is still shared by many countries.[2] In that context, the specific rules enacted in every legal system may vary, but for a long time the existence of such divergences in national legal systems was not considered to give rise to important practical inconveniences in cross-border cases.

Probably for this reason, unlike most matters of family law, parentage matters were the subject of an extraordinarily small number of international conventions, which have a very narrow scope of application and enjoyed a limited success among States.[3] In addition, those instruments usually do not touch upon private international law issues, which are accordingly left to the domain of domestic law.

A different attitude towards problems connected to parentage, especially in its cross-border dimension, arose only in recent years, when the impact of new technologies on procreation processes, on the one hand, and the practice of surrogacy, on the other, called for a reconsideration of the very foundations of the law of filiation.[4] Those social developments resulted in the

[1] For a re-evaluation of myth as a crucial notion to a system of law, see P Fitzpatrick, *The Mythology of Modern Law* (Routledge 1992).

[2] See Prel Doc No 3C of March 2014, A Study of Legal Parentage and the Issues Arising from International Surrogacy Arrangements, Permanent Bureau of the Hague Conference, paras 11–13.

[3] See, in particular, the 1962 Convention on the establishment of maternal descent of natural children; the 1975 European Convention on the Legal Status of Children Born out of Wedlock; and the 1980 Convention on the voluntary acknowledgment of children born out of wedlock (never entered into force).

[4] On the plurality and diversity of family concepts and family laws in the contemporary world, see C Kohler, 'Unification of Private International Law in Family Matters in the European Union: Cultural Issues' in I Viarengo and F Villata (eds), *Planning the Future of Cross Border Families. A Path Through Coordination* (Hart Publishing 2020) 3.

enactment of divergent legislation in different countries and in a consequential recourse to forum shopping by individuals willing to evade limitations imposed by their national legal systems.

Unsurprisingly, it was in the wake of the variable response of domestic authorities and judiciaries that the need for uniform rules of private international law was first envisaged. As a consequence, since 2010 the organs of the Hague Conference on Private International Law (HCCH) devoted their attention to issues concerning the status of children and, in particular, filiation, placing a special emphasis on surrogacy.[5] In 2015, an Experts' Group charged with the task 'to explore the feasibility of advancing work in this area' was established.[6] The mandate of the Group was later extended in order to include the drafting of two instruments, namely 'a general private international law instrument on the recognition of foreign judicial decisions on legal parentage' and 'a separate protocol on the recognition of foreign judicial decisions on legal parentage rendered as a result of an international surrogacy arrangement'.[7]

The respective scope of application of the two instruments has not been clearly defined yet,[8] but the underlying idea seems to be that surrogacy displays some distinctive features that require the adoption of different provisions. The suggestion to include also children born through assisted reproductive technologies in the separate protocol was advanced by the Experts' Group at a preliminary stage,[9] but it appears to have been later discarded because of the risk of discrimination between children.

While the work of the Group is continuing and no draft text of future instruments has been circulated to the public, it is possible to evaluate the efforts undertaken by the HCCH and to develop some thoughts about the capability of the proposed instruments to provide viable solutions.

II. The Interplay between Private and Public Values in Matters of Filiation

Private international law rules in parentage matters are expected to take into consideration general principles stemming from substantive rules of the law of filiation, which can be influenced by several factors. While the needs and expectations of the private individuals concerned by the parent–child relationship are closely intertwined with each other, they also have to be reconciled to the general interests of the community. However, in the last decades, the notable impact exercised by the protection of human rights brought about a clear shift of the balance between those factors and urged, in particular, an enhanced appreciation of the position of the child in the establishment of parentage.[10]

[5] Conclusions and Recommendations adopted by the Council on General Affairs and Policy of the Conference of 7–9 April 2010, 3–4.

[6] Conclusions and Recommendations adopted by the Council on General Affairs and Policy of the Conference of 24–26 March 2015, para 5.

[7] See Conclusions and Recommendations adopted by HCCH Council at its meeting of 5–8 March 2019, paras 7–12.

[8] See, however, Prel Doc No 2A of July 2021, referring to the relevance of domestic adoptions in the scope of application of the proposed instruments.

[9] Report of the Experts' Group on Parentage/Surrogacy Project, Meeting of 31 January–3 February 2017, para 28.

[10] On the role of the HCCH in the promotion of human rights, see M Groff, 'The Hague Conventions: Giving Effect to Human Rights through Instruments of Private International Law' in J Handmaker and K Arts (eds), *Mobilising International Law for 'Global Justice'* (Cambridge University Press 2018) 89–118.

The way for this development was paved by the interpretation of Article 8 of the European Convention on Human Rights (ECHR), as the European Court of Human Rights underlined that respect for private and family life encompasses the legal parent–child relationship as a key element of the fundamental right of the latter to identity:[11] in that context, the establishment of details of one's identity as an individual human being must be ensured by Contracting States also by complying with positive obligations, eg, with regard to voluntary acknowledgments[12] or to proceedings for the establishment of maternity or paternity.[13]

The centrality of human rights considerations in the law of filiation has also gained strong impetus from the principles enshrined in the 1989 UN Convention on the Rights of the Child. The existence of specific provisions closely connected to the legal relationship between a child and its parents and regarding the right of the child to registration and to name, the right to identity 'as recognised by the law' and the right to family life can certainly exert influence on the legal framework of filiation. But the driving force of the principle of the best interests of the child under Article 3 of the Convention proved to be the main element to be taken into consideration even with regard to parentage.[14] The deference due to that principle implies that children's rights as to their legal status of filiation will usually gain primacy over the possibly conflicting rights of their parents (eg, the right of the biological father to privacy).[15]

In any event, the necessity to focus on the protection of fundamental rights does not exhaust the range of factors that should be considered, as the parent–child relationship does not have a merely inter-individual nature. Accordingly, as is common in family law, the rules governing parentage matters tend to reflect social customs or ethical and even religious beliefs, that vary from one country to another. For this reason, in cross-border cases private international law provides mechanisms that may allow domestic legal systems to ensure the compatibility of the status granted to the child with their fundamental principles.

In addition, one should not forget the paramount importance of the principle of legal certainty in matters of personal status. In the light of this principle, private international law rules in matters of filiation should primarily serve the purpose of preventing limping relationships, which are inconsistent both with the individual right to identity and with the general interest of every legal system, requiring the coherence and the cross-border continuity of a civil status, it being a condition for several rights and obligations established by law.[16] In this regard, State authorities are called upon to play the role of 'guardians' of legal certainty, as they are usually empowered to give publicity to the legal parent–child relationship and are expected to take action in order to avoid possible inconsistencies.

Nonetheless, in cross-border cases such inconsistencies may arise from several sources. On the one hand, private international rules are confronted with the fact that concurring methods for the establishment of parentage are usually contemplated in domestic legal systems. In most

[11] On the 'negative' and 'positive' obligations arising from Art 8 ECHR, see F Salerno, 'The identity and continuity of personal status in contemporary private international law' (2019) 395 *Hague Collected Courses* 33 ff.

[12] European Court of Human Rights, *Marckx v Belgium* (application no 6833/74) paras 36–37.

[13] *cf* eg, European Court of Human Rights, *Mikulić v Croatia* (application no 53176/99); *Boljevic v Serbia* (application no 47443/14).

[14] R Baratta, 'La reconnaissance internationale des situations juridiques personelles et familiales' (2010) 348 *Hague Collected Courses* 265 ff, esp 338 ff.

[15] S Besson, 'Enforcing the Child's Right to Know Her Origins: Contrasting Approaches under the Convention on the Rights of the Child and the European Convention on Human Rights' (2007) 21 *International Journal of Law, Policy and the Family* 137.

[16] P Franzina, 'Some Remarks on the Relevance of Article 8 of the ECHR to the Recognition of Family Status Judicially Created Abroad' [2011] *Diritti umani e diritto internazionale* 609.

countries legal presumptions about the identity of the father can be rebutted, in accordance with the need to consider the biological and social reality:[17] as a consequence, the establishment of parentage may require in many cases the coordination of those presumptions with the content of voluntary acknowledgments or with the results of judicial determination.

On the other hand, it must also be borne in mind that the impact of new technologies may give rise to further difficulties for the establishment of parentage, because they can create a divergence between the biological reality and the intended family life. As the recent practice of national courts shows,[18] the problem may be especially serious in cross-border cases, as the approach of different legal systems to the so-called assisted reproductive technology (ART) may be deeply divergent.

III. The Possible Features of a General Instrument in Parentage Matters

A tentative analysis of the proposed general Hague instrument about parentage must first consider the possible scope of application. In this regard, the mandate of the Council has clearly referred to a convention in matters of recognition of judgments, but from the reports of the Experts' Group a strong suggestion in favour of a more comprehensive instrument, including rules on jurisdiction, applicable law and recognition of judgments and of public documents, clearly emerges.

That suggestion appears to be justified, in the light of the peculiar characteristics of parentage matters, as in a majority of cases parentage is not established by judicial determination. Judicial proceedings are usually resorted to when there is a dispute about the identity of one of the parents.[19] Accordingly, an instrument exclusively devoted to the recognition of judgments would not cover a significant number of cases.

For the same reason, it is correct to assume that the conflict rules aimed at the designation of the law governing the establishment of parentage may play a pivotal role in the future instrument. As the legal parent–child relationship is usually enshrined in the birth certificates issued by the competent authorities of each State or in voluntary acknowledgments made before them, cross-border continuity of that status is more likely to be achieved if the authorities of different States apply the same law to establish parentage, with a view to ensuring legal certainty.[20]

In the light of the same principle, it would be useful to clarify in the future instrument that its provisions would be relevant for the establishment of parentage even when the determination of the parent–child relationship constitutes a preliminary question, eg, in proceedings concerning maintenance or parental responsibility.[21] This could prevent the risk of a merely incidental assessment and ensure that any decision about the existence of the status be governed by the same applicable law, whatever the context in which the question may arise.

The suggestions that were advanced by the Experts' Group as to the contents of the conflict rules to be included in the future instrument show full awareness of the role of legal certainty in

[17] European Court of Human Rights, *Kroon and Others v Netherlands* (application no 18535/91) para 40.

[18] See, eg, Italian Constitutional Court, judgment no 230/2020, concerning the rectification of the birth certificate of a child born through assisted reproductive technologies.

[19] See Prel Doc No 3C (n 2) para 13.

[20] Salerno (n 11) 162 ff.

[21] On the relevance of filiation as an incidental question, *cf* S Corneloup, 'Les questions préalables de statut personnel dans le fonctionnement des règlements européens de droit international privé' in *Travaux du Comité français de droit international privé, Années 2010-2012* (Pedone 2013) 189–222.

filiation matters. The Experts' Group mentioned the place of birth as the main objective connecting factor but with two exceptions:

i. When neither of the parents are habitually resident in the State of birth, the law of the State of the habitual residence of the person who gave birth should apply; and
ii. when parentage is established at some point after the child's birth, the law of the habitual residence of the child may be applied, if it is beneficial to the child itself.[22]

The use of the connecting factor of the place of birth in a general conflict rule in a future Convention has clear advantages:

(a) This is the approach shared by many States, both of civil law and common law tradition, and therefore widespread adoption of the Convention would be easier; and
(b) as Article 7 of the 1989 UN Convention on the Rights of a Child provides that the State of birth is under an obligation to register the child, such a conflict rule would provide a simple and practical solution for carrying out that obligation in comparison with other traditional connecting factors (eg, the nationality of the child or the habitual residence of the child[23] or of the parents)[24] and it would avoid possible difficulties in the application of foreign law.

While the proposed solution in principle rules out the possibility of applying foreign law in the State of birth, this would not remove the danger of limping relationships, if a different State, closely connected to the parties (for instance, because of their habitual residence or of their nationality), considers that the law of the State of birth is incompatible with its public policy or that its application should be complemented with existing mandatory rules of the *lex fori*. Such a reaction by States other than the State of birth could be encouraged because the parties would be granted some degree of law-shopping through the choice of the place of future birth. In this regard, the safeguard clause envisaged by the Experts' Group and based on the habitual residence of the parents does not appear to be capable of preventing any possible attempt at law-shopping, as the practice in family matters shows that the determination of the habitual residence may sometimes rest on very thin evidence.[25]

This scenario may arise especially when recourse is made to assisted reproductive technologies, given the wide diversity of approaches across different countries. Accordingly, the application of the general provision subject to the intervention of the public policy clause would entail the danger of creating limping status for this category of children, eg, if they are nationals of or habitually resident in a State prohibiting the recourse to certain assisted reproductive technologies. In this regard, an ad hoc conflict rule covering the situation of children conceived through those technologies, when they imply the use of genetic elements coming from a third-party donor, could certainly mitigate such difficulties.

Conversely, the positive dimension of the public policy clause may be called into question in accordance with the need to protect the fundamental right of the child to identity and to take

[22] Aide-Memoire annexed to the Report of the Experts' Group on Parentage/Surrogacy Project, Meeting of 12–16 October 2020, para 3.

[23] The use of the connecting factor of habitual residence at the time of birth was initially considered by the Experts' Group; however, it was subsequently concluded that it could give rise to uncertainty due to the possible divergences in the determination of the habitual residence of a new-born baby: Report of the Experts' Group on the Parentage/Surrogacy Project, Meeting of 6–9 February 2018, para 26.

[24] On possible shortcomings arising from the use of those connecting factors, *cf* M Bogdan, 'The EC Treaty and the Use of Nationality and Habitual Residence as Connecting Factors in International Family Law' in J Meeusen et al (eds), *International Family Law for the European Union* (Intersentia 2007) 303–17.

[25] *Rapisarda v Colladon (Irregular Divorces)* [2014] EWFC 35.

into consideration his or her best interests:[26] for instance, the principle of equality of children born out of wedlock is by now considered in several countries a fundamental principle of family law.[27] For this reason, the proposal to depart from the approach based on the use of the same connecting factor, irrespective of the method and timing for the establishment of parentage, is to be welcomed, as it would leave room for an evaluation of the compatibility of the applicable law with the best interests of the child. The subsidiary conflict rule envisaged by the Experts' Group reserves a broad margin of discretion for the competent court to evaluate when the application of a law other than the law of the place of birth is beneficial for the child. However, there seems to be no need to restrict this discretion to permitting only the alternative application of the law of the habitual residence of the child. Moreover, this solution, possibly requiring domestic courts to apply foreign law, would be subject to the intervention of the public policy clause; allowing domestic courts to apply, as an alternative, their own law could be a more viable option when parentage must be established by judicial decision.

Of course, the acceptance of the latter option could be facilitated if the future instrument contains rules on direct grounds of jurisdiction. It is more likely, however, that only indirect grounds of jurisdiction will be agreed as acceptable bases for the circulation of judgments in Contracting States. The Experts' Group considered that the habitual residence of the child and the habitual residence of the defendant should be included in a possible list.

Those grounds of jurisdiction find their basis in the proximity principle, which requires the existence of a real and substantial connection between the parties and the competent court: accordingly, the reference to the habitual residence of the child may help to achieve the best interests of the child, making his or her access to court easier;[28] on the other hand, the reference to the habitual residence of the defendant may be suitable for the need to collect the necessary evidence, usually through genetic testing undergone by the child and by the presumed father.

The necessity to strike a proper balance between opposite goals is especially conspicuous here. For this reason, when the child (or a person acting on their behalf) is the claimant,[29] the identification of a broader range of grounds of jurisdiction could be convenient, as access to a tribunal for the establishment of parentage contributes to the protection of the right of the child to identity and to family life.

While the proposed model in matters of recognition of judgments is very similar to other Hague instruments on family matters, one crucial point will be the circulation of public documents.[30] The Experts' Group is aware that, given the peculiar features of filiation, special rules dealing with that issue are needed. The category of public documents relevant to the establishment of parentage include both birth certificates and acts of voluntary recognition, which pose, however, different challenges.

The circulation of foreign public documents should not be sought merely for administrative simplification,[31] but it should imply that the acceptance of a foreign public document may ensure the cross-border continuity of the legal status of the child.[32] Two approaches to the circulation of

[26] On the notion of 'positive public policy', see SL Gössl, 'The public policy exception in the European civil justice system' [2016] *European Legal Forum* 85.

[27] See C Cicero, 'The Italian Reform of the Law of Filiation and Constitutional Legality' [2016] *Italian Law Journal* 237.

[28] S Maya Bouyahia, *Le principe de proximité en droit international privé de la famille* (Pedone 2015) 31.

[29] See the Report of the Experts' Group, Meeting of 31 January–2 February 2017, para 23.

[30] Salerno (n 11) 138 ff.

[31] See, by contrast, Regulation (EU) 2016/1191 of the European Parliament and of the Council of 6 July 2016 on promoting the free movement of citizens by simplifying the requirements for presenting certain public documents in the European Union and amending Regulation (EU) No 1024/2012 [2016] OJ L200/1–136.

[32] The Opinion of AG Kokott in Case C-490/20 *Stolichna obshtina, rayon 'Pancharevo'* EU:C:2021:296 seems to point in the opposite direction, as it is stated that: 'Article 21(1) TFEU must be interpreted as meaning that a Member State may not refuse to recognise the family relationships, established on the birth certificate issued by another Member State,

foreign public documents other than judgments may be identified to achieve this aim. The first, defined as the 'recognition approach', tends to assimilate foreign public documents to foreign judgments and to ensure that they enjoy cross-border the same effect as they have in the State of origin, provided that they were validly issued there and subject to possible limitations (in particular, a public policy review).[33] The second, defined as the 'applicable law approach', ensures the circulation of foreign public documents, insofar as the legal relationship enshrined therein is in accordance with the outcome resulting from the application of the conflict rules of the forum; in this context, a foreign public document recording the parent–child relationship will mainly be used as evidence under the substantive applicable law.

The set of rules envisaged in the reports of the Experts' Group are particularly well suited for the circulation of birth certificates, which are issued by the State where the child is born and in accordance with the local law. Thus, even if the 'applicable law approach' is chosen, the legal situation of the child as recorded on the birth certificate will usually correspond to the parent–child relationship as established by the ordinarily applicable law, ie, the law of the State of birth. This would ensure a smoother circulation of administrative acts, granting, in principle, that the child be recognised abroad as having the same status since the date of their birth, at least on a rebuttable presumption. In this context, the legal status of the child as documented by the birth certificate could be superseded only subsequently by a voluntary recognition or by a judicial decision or, in exceptional cases, if the law of the State of birth is discarded in a foreign State as being incompatible with its public policy. In the light of these considerations, the advantages of adopting a 'recognition approach' (or of an optional standard form for birth certificates) do not appear to be of great relevance.

The situation can be different when a voluntary recognition is at stake, as it cannot be taken for granted that the law of the State in which it is made will also govern the establishment of parentage. The solution of the use of a different connecting factor for the establishment of parentage when it relies on a private act is common to several domestic legal systems[34] and is likely to be accepted also under some conditions in the future instrument. This would probably necessitate the enactment of two uniform conflict rules relating to the formal validity, on the one hand, and to the substantive validity, including capacity and consent requirements, on the other.

However, even though such rules are usually influenced by the principle of *favor recognitionis* and may thus list multiple connecting factors,[35] the benefits of a 'recognition approach' for the continuity of the status so acquired would be clear: provided that the voluntary act is validly performed abroad in accordance with substantive and formal requirements under local law, it could be immediately accepted in foreign States, except for a public policy review. Nonetheless, in that case a major cause for concern could arise from the inherent risk of forum shopping,

between one of its nationals, her wife and their child for the purpose of exercising the rights conferred on that national by secondary EU law on the free movement of citizens … Reliance on national identity within the meaning of Article 4(2) TEU may justify the refusal to recognise that a married couple of two women are the parents of a child, as established on the birth certificate issued by the child's Member State of residence, for the purpose of drawing up a birth certificate in the child's Member State of origin or the Member State of origin of one of those two women, determining the parentage of that child for the purposes of the family law of that Member State'. This solution, subsequently upheld by the CJEU (see Judgment of 14 December 2021 EU:C:2021:1008), may lead to an unnecessary division between the legal condition of the child for the purpose of EU rules on free movement of persons and the status of the same child as a matter of domestic family law.

[33] See P Kinsch, 'Recognition in the Forum of a Status Acquired Abroad – Private International Law and European Human Rights Law' in K Boele-Woelki et al (eds), *Convergence and Divergence in Private International Law – Liber Amicorum Kurt Siehr* (TMC Asser Press 2010) 259 ff.

[34] *cf* Prel Doc No 3C (n 2) para 82.

[35] The consequences of a principle of *favor* on the contents of a conflict rule are broadly discussed in JD González Campos, 'Diversification, spécialisation, flexibilisation and matérialisation des règles de droit international privé' (2000) 287 *Hague Collected Courses* 363 ff.

unless it is possible to agree on uniform rules clarifying the conditions in which the authorities of a State are competent to receive acts of voluntary recognition. In any event, the safeguards due to the principle of the best interests of the child and the need to respect concurring rights of other interested parties would still require that a voluntary act establishing parentage be recognised cross-border on the condition that contestation remains possible. In this respect, the combination of the 'recognition approach' with the 'applicable law approach' is an option that should be given serious consideration to ensure proper evaluation of the best interests of the child.

IV. The Challenges of Surrogacy: National Fragmentation and Intervention of Supranational Courts

Turning to surrogacy, one could argue that, insofar as it is connected to the establishment of legal parentage, the same issues should come into consideration. This is partially true, because the focus should be kept on some of the same general objectives, including the role of legal certainty in preventing limping relationships, preserving the right to identity, and ensuring recognition of foreign public documents (birth certificates) as well as judgments.

Notwithstanding that, the necessity of a separate Protocol to govern conflict of laws issues concerning international arrangements in those matters, as foreseen by the Council of the HCCH in accordance with clear suggestions from doctrinal debate,[36] stems from different reasons.

First, it must be considered that, while in parentage matters an overarching system of shared principles exists and in similar legal systems the variations in the applicable regime mainly concern its operative provisions, substantive rules governing surrogacy and the status of children born from a surrogate mother are very fragmented among countries, even within the same geographical area or within the same federal state (as the US experience demonstrates), and may lead to opposite outcomes.[37] In fact, several States enacted a full prohibition against surrogacy, declaring void and unenforceable every arrangement between surrogate mothers and intended parents; the prohibition is often assisted by criminal sanctions.[38] In addition, even within the category of States allowing surrogacy arrangements in their legal system a distinction must be drawn between those which only permit altruistic surrogacy and ban the possibility of charging any fee for surrogacy or for intermediation services, and those in which commercial activity concerning surrogacy can be legally performed.

In the light of the existing contrast between irreconcilable approaches, some States may be reluctant to adhere to a global instrument containing private international law rules on surrogacy, probably on account of the possible undesired influence on domestic cases. For this reason, if they were contained in a general instrument concerning every aspect of parentage, it would probably be doomed to failure, at least in the short run. On the contrary, by splitting the topic into two different instruments, the risk exists that States prohibiting surrogacy under domestic law could be reluctant to adhere to the separate Protocol, as it could lead them, in the long run, to also

[36] The reference is especially to the seminal study by P Beaumont and K Trimmings (eds), *International Surrogacy Arrangements* (Hart Publishing 2013) in which a broad comparative analysis of domestic regimes about surrogacy can also be found.

[37] R Pol, 'Proposing an International Instrument to Address Issues Arising out of International Surrogacy Arrangements' (2017) 48 *Georgetown Journal of International Law* 1309.

[38] On the criminalisation of surrogacy in EU Member States, see L Brunet et al, *A comparative study on the regime of surrogacy in EU Member States*, PE 474.303, commissioned by the European Parliament.

allow domestic surrogacy arrangements (eg, in order to prevent discrimination).[39] However, this would leave the door open for a future ratification, if the attitude of those legal systems towards surrogacy varies over time.

Second, it must be considered that surrogacy, despite being subject to various regimes in different countries, does not fit into the traditional model of parentage, as it presupposes the presence of a mother giving birth to the child, but not entering into a legal relationship with the child. This clear departure from the principle of *mater certa* that is inherent in most national systems makes the use of general conflict rules on filiation unsuitable for surrogacy. This is clearly the case when the intended parents are neither nationals of the State of birth nor habitually resident in that State because the most common connecting factors (nationality or habitual residence of the parents or of the child; use of *lex fori*) lead to the application of a domestic law prohibiting surrogacy and thus precluding the establishment of the legal parent–child relationship. But the issue would remain unsolved even if the law of the State of birth were applicable, as legal systems banning (or even criminalising) surrogacy would certainly consider the establishment of parentage as incompatible with their public policy.

In addition, a third point can be made as to the usefulness of a separate regime for surrogacy in the context of an international regulation of private international law issues concerning parentage. In international surrogacy arrangements, unlike traditional filiation cases, the legal relationship between the child and the intended parents is at the core of the problem, but other issues must be considered, like the possible relationship of the child to the surrogate mother or the contract between the latter and the intended parents. It is then clear that the scheme of surrogacy shows some similarities to the framework of intercountry adoption, as it, though revolving around parentage, encompasses multiple legal relationships and requires active cooperation between different States.

The greater complexity of international surrogacy arrangements also explains the urgent need for a global instrument dealing with those matters. In this regard, it is worth noting that the heterogeneous attitude of domestic legal systems towards surrogacy gives rise to obvious difficulties especially in cross-border cases, as no special restrictions are usually applicable to non-nationals or non-residents willing to have recourse to surrogacy in countries that consider it as legal. Accordingly, in those countries no possible obstacle may arise as to issuing public documents mentioning only the intended parents according to the local law. Conversely, in most States in which surrogacy is banned domestically the private international law system also lacks any express provision dealing with cross-border cases and this may lead to the result that a legal vacuum exists for intended parents who are nationals of those States or habitually reside there.

The absence of a clear legislative framework in domestic legal systems, often including mechanisms aimed at indirectly restricting parents from resorting to surrogacy in other jurisdictions,[40] has encouraged judicial activism in several countries,[41] for instance through mechanisms of adaptation of the status to local regimes, and is requiring the frequent intervention of supranational

[39] See, on the relevance of domestic surrogacy arrangements and domestic adoptions in the context of surrogacy arrangements, Prel Doc No 2A (n 8).

[40] C Fenton-Glynn, 'International Surrogacy Before the European Court of Human Rights' (2017) 13 *Journal of Private International Law* 545.

[41] K Boele-Woelki, '(Cross-Border) Surrogate Motherhood: We Need to Take Action Now!' in The Permanent Bureau of the Hague Conference on Private International Law, *A Commitment to Private International Law. Essays in Honour of Hans Van Loon* (Intersentia 2013) 47–58.

courts, especially in order to take into account the protection of fundamental human rights involved in those cases.[42]

Since the cases of *Mennesson v France* and *Labassee v France*,[43] the European Court of Human Rights has dealt with cross-border surrogacy cases several times (and others are in its docket). Those cases presented very similar features, as they concerned couples having their habitual residence in States that prohibit surrogacy, facing there a public policy-based refusal of recognition of their parentage of a child born abroad through surrogacy.

The European Court, in its findings in the 2019 advisory opinion concerning the follow-up to the *Mennesson* case,[44] strongly emphasised the necessity to consider the best interests of the child as paramount and to protect the right of the child to private life, with special regard to their right to identity and the right of the child itself and of the intending parents to family life, especially when the de facto family relationship lasted for a long time.

In this context, the Court marked the importance of a possible genetic link with one of the intending parents (usually, the father),[45] which requires that parentage be clearly established in that case:[46] such a principle has a bearing both on substantive law, obliging Contracting States to adjust their domestic family law, and on private international law, as a foreign law could be considered as incompatible with public policy in a Contracting State if it does not take into consideration the existence of the mentioned genetic link.

However, the criterion of the so-called 'biological reality', being closely connected to the right of the child to identity, could give rise to new difficulties, for instance concerning the position of the surrogate mother,[47] and for children born through assisted reproductive technologies with the use of biological material of a third-party donor. Also, in the light of the right of the child to know their origins, possible situations of conflict about parentage could be envisaged, so endangering the principle of legal certainty.

The situation is different for intending parents who are not genetically related to the child, at least from the point of view of private international law. In that situation, the domestic legal system is still required to afford the opportunity to establish legal parentage to the other intended parent, even if no biological tie exists with the child, to abide by the principle of the best interests of the child. Nonetheless, as Contracting States enjoy a wider margin of appreciation in this regard, they remain free to choose the most suitable means in order to achieve this result: accordingly, the European Court clarified that no violation of the right to private and family life can occur if the State refuses to register the birth certificate issued abroad and requires intending parents to go through special proceedings for adoption complying with the requirements enshrined in the ECHR. In addition, even non-recognition of the legal parent–child relationship may be an acceptable option in the light of the specific circumstances of the case, that may allow a Contracting State to refuse to recognise the status validly established abroad on public policy

[42] R Blauwhoff and L Frohn, 'International Commercial Surrogacy Arrangements: The Interests of the Child as a Concern of Both Human Rights and Private International Law' in C Paulssen et al (eds), *Fundamental Rights in International and European Law* (Springer 2015) 211–41.

[43] European Court of Human Rights, *Mennesson v France* (application no 65192/11); *Labassee v France* (application no 65941/11).

[44] European Court of Human Rights, Advisory Opinion of 10 April 2019 (request no P16-2018-001).

[45] See, recently, European Court of Human Rights, *Valdís Fjölnisdóttir and Others v Iceland* (application no 71552/17).

[46] P Beaumont and K Trimmings, 'Recent Jurisprudence of the European Court of Human Rights in the Area of Cross-Border Surrogacy: Is There Still a Need for Global Regulation of Surrogacy?' in F Ippolito and G Biagioni (eds), *Migrant Children: Challenges for Public and Private International Law* (Editoriale Scientifica 2016) 109–36.

[47] On the importance of the rights of the surrogate mother, N Bala, 'The Hidden Costs of the European Court of Human Rights' Surrogacy Decision' (2019) 40 *Yale Journal of International Law Online* 11.

grounds.[48] This may happen especially when, there being no real connection between the intending parents and the State of birth, surrogacy is in clear circumvention of important domestic rules; but States are still under a duty to assess the consequences of the establishment or non-establishment of legal parentage in compliance with the principle of the best interests of the child.

Two implications arise from the above summarised principles. On the one hand, a violation of the obligations concerning the protection of human rights can result from the existence of a legal vacuum or from the failure to provide adequate mechanisms that take into consideration the special characteristics of surrogacy cases and ensure that all the involved interests are weighed. However, neither domestic case law with its possible fluctuations nor the jurisprudence of the European Court of Human Rights can substitute for express provisions concerning cross-border surrogacy cases, which require the development of a comprehensive regime.[49] On the other hand, private international law is not confronted with a completely open choice as to the available mechanisms in order to deal with the consequences of children born abroad through surrogacy: their identification, though left within the margin of appreciation of States,[50] is expected to ensure clear and predictable solutions, an objective in conformity with the traditional goals of private international law and, at the same time, in conformity with the protection of the fundamental rights of the parties.

V. International Surrogacy Arrangements: The Cautious Approach of an Optional Instrument

Even though the scope of the future Protocol concerning international surrogacy arrangements will focus on the establishment of parentage,[51] its contents are as yet very summarily outlined in the reports of the Experts' Group, as the general approach is still to be determined.[52] In this regard, two different techniques, both implying a broadening of the scope of the instrument as envisaged by the Council, are under consideration, namely recognition of judgments and of other foreign public documents, possibly connected to a certification process, or the enactment of special conflict rules.

However, the conflict of laws technique does not seem to be particularly helpful in matters of cross-border surrogacy. On the one hand, if the future Protocol recalls the same connecting factor of the place of birth that is likely to be used in the general Convention, this would be a clear stand in favour of 'surrogacy-friendly' States, hindering the accession of other States to the Protocol or increasing the number of cases in which the public policy clause is likely to be activated. On the other hand, the option to resort to connecting factors referring to the nationality or to the habitual residence of the parties involved would imply that the law of a State prohibiting surrogacy would very often be applicable, depriving the Protocol system of its purpose. Accordingly, should the future instrument be based on the enactment of conflict rules, it could be advisable to insert a provision like Article 5 of the 1985 Hague Convention on the Law Applicable to Trusts and on

[48] European Court of Human Rights, *Paradiso and Campanelli v Italy* (application no 25358/12).

[49] Beaumont and Trimmings (n 46) 133.

[50] The relevance of the doctrine of the margin of appreciation in private international law matters is discussed in LR Kiestra, *The Impact of the European Convention on Human Rights on Private International Law* (TMC Asser Press 2014) 42.

[51] On the suitability of the separation between contract issues and parentage issues, *cf* Blauwhoff and Frohn (n 42) 237.

[52] See Prel Doc No 2B of November 2021.

their Recognition,[53] precluding the application of the Protocol whenever the applicable law does not provide for surrogacy (or prohibits it altogether).

But even the so-called 'recognition approach' does not appear to be able to solve all the difficulties arising out of the lack of uniformity in the acceptance of cross-border surrogacy among different States, if based on the traditional method, requiring the requested State to ascertain *ex post* whether the conditions for recognition are met. The existence of possible safeguards for international surrogacy arrangements would probably not be sufficient to induce States prohibiting surrogacy to ratify the Protocol: such a mechanism could be seen by States as an unnecessary restriction on their margin of appreciation, which allows them to exercise a deeper control, for instance requiring the intending parents to go through the adoption procedure.

In any event, as the fundamental rights and the best interests of the child are at stake, there is a strong necessity to ensure that in as few cases as possible recognition is refused, because such a refusal brings about a situation of uncertainty for the child about their status and a prejudice to their enjoyment of private and family life. However, the 'recognition approach' would not overcome those shortcomings, insofar as the requested State would be confronted with a legal parent–child relationship already established abroad, that it may only recognise or refuse to recognise.

An alternative option would be to follow more closely the existing model of the 1993 Hague Inter-Country Adoption Convention,[54] in the light of the coincidence of the objectives stated in its Preamble with those pursued by the proposed Protocol, ie: facilitating the possibility to 'offer the advantage of a permanent family to a child' and the recognition of the legal parent–child relationship established in one State; complying with the principles of the best interests of the child and of the protection of the child's, the intending parents and the surrogate mother's fundamental rights; and avoiding the risk that cross-border surrogacy may acquire a purely 'commercial' nature.[55]

Such a system would imply establishing a cooperation mechanism between the State of origin and the requested State, administered by national Central Authorities discharging procedural functions, to ensure *ex ante* that parentage be established with legal effects in both countries. To this aim, the future Protocol should set forth clear obligations for Contracting States as to the evaluation, on an *a priori* basis, of the necessary conditions to permit a lawful cross-border surrogacy arrangement. These include consideration of the (best) interests of the child, the suitability of the surrogate mother and of the intending parents, the free consent of all the parties involved and the absence of coercion during the entire process, the appropriateness of possible intermediaries, and the fair terms of the contract(s). The existence of detailed requirements accepted by Contracting States, to be subject to previous verification, could also lead to a restriction of the scope of application of public policy review, that should be relevant only in truly exceptional cases calling into question the best interests of the child as in Article 24 of the Adoption Convention.

An approach analogous to the Adoption Convention, while in itself consistent with the requirements suggested by the European Court of Human Rights,[56] would not remove all and every point of contention, starting with the challenge of its smooth functioning. In addition,

[53] See Jonathan Harris, 'Trusts', ch 23 in this book.

[54] See H Baker, 'A Possible Future Instrument on International Surrogacy Arrangements: Are there "Lessons" to be Learnt from the 1993 Hague Intercountry Adoption Convention?' in P Beaumont and K Trimmings (eds), *International Surrogacy Arrangements* (Hart Publishing 2013) 361–75.

[55] See also Conclusions and Recommendations No 11 of HCCH Council on General Affairs and Policy at its 2019 meeting.

[56] See European Court of Human Rights, *D v France* (application no 11288/18).

one should not forget that other significant issues – the legal position of the surrogate mother, the right of the child to find their origins, the consequences of the impossibility to establish legal parentage when an international surrogacy arrangement does not fit into the system provided by the proposed Protocol – may require clarification, with a view to building a comprehensive framework. From a different point of view, the risk of an all-encompassing instrument could be its reduced attractiveness, at least in the short run, for those States in which commercial surrogacy is legal, as they could be less inclined to accept a restriction on the freedom of their nationals to provide cross-border surrogacy services.

VI. Concluding Remarks

It appears from the preparatory works of the Hague Parentage Project that the initiative to draft a Convention concerning private international law rules in parentage matters and an optional Protocol concerning cross-border surrogacy was prompted by the perceived necessity to react to an undesired fragmentation in the response of States and to the contrast between opposite approaches towards surrogacy.

In that context, it is hardly questionable that the existence of a system based on the cooperation between the largest possible number of States would improve legal certainty and thus the protection of fundamental rights of interested parties. The way forward on parentage can be successfully based on traditional private international law solutions. However, in relation to surrogacy this chapter has shown that traditional private international law solutions will not work. The example of the Hague Adoption Convention, which has been widely adopted by States that are enthusiastic about intercountry adoptions and those that are more sceptical about their benefits,[57] by insisting on proper regulation, the best interests of the child and respect for their fundamental rights, gives hope for uniting a divided world through similar regulation of international surrogacy. The Hague Conference needs to rediscover the vision and boldness of those who were concerned about 'sale of children' (Preamble to the Adoption Convention) to solve the problem of international surrogacy.

[57] See Laura Martínez-Mora, 'Adoption of Children', ch 35 in this book.

PART VI

Conclusion

41

Conclusion: Mapping of the Strength of Global Private International Law

PAUL BEAUMONT AND JAYNE HOLLIDAY

This book set out to be a guide to the state of the art on global private international law. It shows where global private international law is strong, developing strongly, has great potential, is weak but could be revived, and is non-existent but could be created. It even has areas where creation of global private international law is not advised in the near future. This conclusion will attempt to briefly map each of these areas.

I. Strong

Laura Martínez-Mora (chapter 35) has shown that even a highly controversial area like Intercountry Adoption can be tackled by the Hague Conference on Private International Law (HCCH) in an inclusive way with ambition to protect the best interests of children and the rights of the other people involved in cross-border adoptions. The HCCH was wise to adopt a highly regulated approach ensuring screening of the suitability of adopting parents, no exploitation of the natural parents or of the potential adopted child, good record-keeping and some flexibility for a less regulated approach that still guarantees appropriate minimum standards in the process. The latter was important to bring on board one of the key players in achieving truly global private international law (the US) but it is good to note from Martínez-Mora's chapter that even in the US this less regulated approach has become a small minority of US adoptions under the Convention. Martínez-Mora makes the very significant conclusion that:

> The 1993 Adoption Convention does not aim at promoting or banning intercountry adoptions. Its purpose is to ensure that if intercountry adoptions are done, they are done with all the safeguards and guarantees.

Martínez-Mora's chapter shows that as the key official in the HCCH in charge of developing the Intercountry Adoption Convention 1993 and making sure it remains fit for purpose she is full of ideas for issues that should be discussed and clarified at the next Review Special Commission in 2022. These 'Review' Special Commissions are one of the jewels in the HCCH crown and when driven forward well by knowledgeable and enthusiastic Permanent Bureau staff can create a global private international law community of people involved in making a Convention work (staff of Central Authorities, government officials, judges, academics and specialised agencies – in this case adoption agencies) who can create and drive best practice and uniform interpretation.

Post-Covid 19 it will be important for these actors to meet in person in The Hague to build that sense of 'community' commitment to making an international instrument work on the ground. There are many tools at the disposal of Review Commissions to try to create uniform interpretation of Conventions and best practice in their implementation and operation. They can adopt Recommendations and Conclusions – a form of soft law which should be given significant attention as it is arrived at by consensus with many of the key players in the field present, ask for Experts' Groups to be set up to do specialist work on a particular issue (eg, as the 2011–12 Special Commission on the Child Abduction and Child Protection Conventions did in relation to family agreements), and ask for Practical Handbooks and Good Practice Guides to be prepared. As Marta Pertegás and Paul Beaumont note in their chapter on the HCCH (chapter 7) these Review Special Commissions and the potential soft law instruments that flow from them to improve the operation of existing Conventions are strengthened when HCCH Members and the Permanent Bureau ensure a high level of expert involvement, in particular of academics. There is a danger that the cult of the generalist in some modern civil services leads to Special Commissions being dominated by government officials (including members of Central Authorities) who may not have the expertise (or even interest) in private international law to drive forward creating and drafting all the tools that can be used to maximise the utility of that Convention. Ignacio Goicoechea and Brody Warren for the Permanent Bureau very helpfully set out in chapter 8, two of the other jewels in the HCCH crown – the idea of national organs and Central Authorities – and show the advantages of them having sufficient expertise (ie, amongst the employed government officials) but also drawing on outside expertise, including academics, to help drive forward coherent national policies on the development of global private international law.

Furthermore, in terms of the future work of the Conference there is a risk that Members no longer have the vision to take risks in developing major new Conventions that would be good for the world (like the 1993 Intercountry Adoption Convention did to try to stop the exploitation of children in developing countries by adopting parents in developed countries) but which might not reflect their current national interest (see chapter 40 by Giacomo Biagioni pleading with the Conference to regulate international surrogacy in the same bold way it regulated intercountry adoption whether a Member is for or against international surrogacy). Some Members use the fact that HCCH takes decisions by consensus as a means of vetoing any progress on any topic (eg, on private international law for cohabitants) or potentially reducing any soft law instrument to the lowest common denominator (a danger shown in chapter 38 on family agreements by Paul Beaumont and Nieve Rubaja in relation to what is likely to be called a 'Practitioners' Tool' – a new innovation in the pantheon of HCCH soft law instruments which is aimed primarily at legal advisers in cross-border cases). For the HCCH to be strong it needs consensus to be used to drive up standards (eg, the US persuading the rest of the world to agree to non-means tested, free legal aid under the Maintenance Convention for child support applications and then implementing the Convention – see chapter 36 on maintenance by Lara Walker and Paul Beaumont), to boldly state best practice (even if it means Members will have to invest more resources in staffing their Central Authorities with more and better qualified people – see the chapters by Walker and Beaumont, Pertegás and Beaumont and the Permanent Bureau), and to allow States who wish to do so to go ahead with a topic at the HCCH even though it cannot at the moment command global support (eg, as was done by the common law world in relation to the Hague Maintenance Protocol on Applicable Law and could be done in the future on family agreements involving children).

The Hague Convention on International Child Abduction (1980) like the Intercountry Adoption Convention has over 100 Contracting States and is clearly a strong pillar of global private international law. The creativity and foresight of its drafters is commendable. It is the HCCH Convention that has generated the most case law and so far is the only one that the

HCCH has created a dedicated case law database for (INCADAT). Uniform interpretation of this Convention is key and has been advanced by the internationalist outlook of some of the world's leading judges in the US, UK and Canadian Supreme Courts. Maria Caterina Baruffi and Jayne Holliday conclude (chapter 34, footnotes omitted) that:

> The current success of this Convention is due to its pragmatic summary return mechanism and the invaluable involvement of the Central Authorities. To improve on the current position, it is recommended that Contracting States should be encouraged to accept the accessions of other Contracting States to maximise the Convention's effectiveness. The Central Authorities also require additional support both in terms of staffing and available technology to support cross-border cases.
>
> …
>
> It is recommended that the HCCH appoint an Experts' Group comprising a mixture of judges, lawyers and academics to prepare a Good Practice Guide on the Meaning of Habitual Residence under the Abduction Convention in order to find the appropriate weight to be given to parental intention in determining a child's habitual residence, in particular for cases involving family agreements, new-borns and cases involving coercion.
>
> The exceptions to return are an integral part of the Convention essential to achieving its aims, notably safeguarding the best interests of children. However, there are still elements that have yet to be settled at a global level such as the impact of concealment of the whereabouts of an abducted child on the time constraints within Article 12 and the lack of uniformity in practice under the Convention in relation to the age at which a child will be heard and the impact of the child's views on when Article 13(2) should be upheld.

The 1980 Child Abduction Convention is not the only Convention whose global efficacy is negatively impacted by Contracting States not engaging with later accessions. Other Conventions, such as the 1970 Hague Taking of Evidence Convention and the 1970 Hague Divorce Convention, which require Contracting States to be proactive rather than passive when accepting accessions, also suffer from this problem.[1] This demonstrates that there is a need to encourage Contracting States to take an active role in supporting Conventions throughout a Convention's lifespan.

Brooke Marshall and Nadia de Araujo (chapter 13) brilliantly show how the Hague Taking of Evidence Convention is working. It is undoubtedly one of the strengths of global private international law given the large number of Contracting States. It is also being made to work in the modern era of videoconferencing showing the adaptability of well-drafted Conventions even from a different era (1970). However, the chapter also exposes the very different approaches to the gathering of evidence in civil and commercial litigation between the US, the Commonwealth common law world and the civil law world. The Convention works for each of these systems but in different ways and there is an ongoing risk that the more liberal approach to taking evidence from other countries, seen in many common law countries, leads to the Convention being bypassed. They end on an optimistic note:

> [T]here is hope that the Convention will help to foster internationalism, tolerance and the administration of justice, and that comprehension of its procedures, coupled with technology, might help.

The Taking of Evidence Convention is a good example of pragmatic private international law (a theory explained in chapter 2 by Abubakri Yekini and Paul Beaumont). It allows Contracting States to protect their sovereign interests through formal processes set out in the Convention

[1] P Beaumont, 'Some reflections on the way ahead for the UK private international law after Brexit' (2021) 17 *Journal of Private International Law* 1, 8.

(civil law States) while at the same time not preventing other Contracting States from using more informal processes to obtain evidence abroad without using the Convention and keeping the Convention for the hard cases where those informal processes do not work (common law States). Both sets of States need to see their interest in making the Convention processes work well because even litigants in the common law world may have to rely on it to get a vital witness statement or document. States need to engage with this Convention more to ensure that they are accepting the accessions of other States and to drive forward best practice. As Marshall and de Araujo point out the civil law States may in fact protect their sovereignty better by giving a more flexible interpretation to the way the Convention can be used by foreign judges to take evidence in their country than by sticking to a rigid interpretation and encouraging common law States to simply ignore the Convention.

Another highly successful older Convention on Service of Documents (1965) is explained eloquently by one of the doyens of the HCCH, David McClean (one of the negotiators of the Child Abduction Convention 1980). He concludes (chapter 12) that, although the Convention has stood the test of time remarkably well and is made to work in the electronic era through soft law mechanisms guiding its application:

> [A]lmost 60 years after its negotiation there seems to be a need to revisit it and explore how the various regional arrangements can be brought into a global system.

Careful thought should be given by the Permanent Bureau in the run-up to the next Special Commission on Taking of Evidence and Service of Documents in 2023 as to how these two key pillars of global private international law can be strengthened and possibly even added to in order to make international litigation proceed more efficiently and fairly, well into the twenty-first century.

Although it is not the work of the HCCH, it is important to acknowledge that some very important aspects of the private international law of arbitration are harmonised globally through the UN (New York) Convention on the Recognition and Enforcement of Foreign Arbitral Awards (1958) (169 Contracting States), and the UNCITRAL Model Law on International Commercial Arbitration (1985, revised in 2006) (implemented in 85 States). Giuditta Cordero-Moss advocates in chapter 26 that some of the gaps in the coverage of these two instruments in relation to the private international law of arbitration could be addressed:

> To develop a coherent body of conflict rules for arbitration, it would be useful to clarify the borders of party autonomy: when do other conflict rules take over, and when can overriding mandatory rules be given effect. It should also be clarified how to select the law, if the parties have not made a choice.
>
> These clarifications could easily be made by confirming that private international law applies to arbitration, and by specifying which private international law applies.
>
> There does not seem to be a need for adjusting the general conflict rules to meet the requirements of arbitration – with the possible exception, reflecting numerous arbitration sources, that the parties be allowed to choose not only a 'law', but 'rules of law'. Such an exception can be applicable anyway as *lex specialis* albeit with the limitations mentioned above.
>
> A transnational instrument of soft law, such as the Hague Principles, would appeal to those who do not consider it appropriate that international arbitration applies national conflict rules. While this has the advantage of making private international law more palatable to the supporters of delocalisation, it has the disadvantage of not enhancing predictability. Confirming the applicability to arbitration of national conflict rules is the most appropriate approach from a systematic perspective. However, it may be seen as turning back the clock. A transnational instrument is more aligned to the current Zeitgeist.

The reference in the above quotation to 'overriding mandatory rules' shows the importance of understanding the technical vocabulary of private international law. The chapter in this book by Trevor Hartley (chapter 6) on public policy and mandatory provisions helps readers to get to grips with the difference between overriding mandatory rules and domestic mandatory rules. It also explains the key concept of public policy and shows that 'mandatory' rules and 'public policy' are concepts utilised in many HCCH Conventions and Principles:

> The purpose of international instruments dealing with private international law is to unify the law internationally so as to increase certainty and ensure that the result will be the same irrespective of the court in which proceedings are brought. However, by their very nature, the theories of public policy and mandatory provisions introduce – and are intended to introduce – an element of unpredictability. The whole idea behind them is that in some situations certainty and predictability have to be sacrificed in order to protect important values and interests of one of the countries involved. Moreover, if a distinction is drawn between the application of forum law and that of foreign law, the result will necessarily be different depending on which court is hearing the case.
>
> How is this to be reconciled with the objectives of certainty and predictability? In general, there is not a great deal that can be done except by using restrictive language. Thus, most international instruments insert a word like 'manifestly' in the phrase 'contrary to public policy'. For example, Article 11(3) of the Hague Principles says that a provision of the law chosen by the parties may be refused application 'only if and to the extent that the result of such application would be manifestly incompatible with fundamental notions of public policy (*ordre public*) of the forum'. Similar language is used in other instruments.
>
> …
>
> The theories of public policy and mandatory provisions by their very nature run counter to the ideal of certainty and predictability. However, they are essential in any system of private international law. The important issues are to ensure that they are not applied too widely and that the interests of foreign countries are not forgotten (footnote omitted).

Symeon Symeonides (chapter 14) uses his unparalleled knowledge of comparative law on the law applicable to contracts when chosen by the parties to demonstrate the global nature of private international law in this field. This came about through national law reforms and the development of common law by judges rather than by the adoption of an international treaty. Indeed, the fact that it had been achieved by such divergent routes meant that the HCCH thought it best just to confirm and reinforce this development globally through the adoption of Principles on Choice of Law in International Commercial Contracts (2015).

An area where there is almost universal agreement is that the law applicable to rights in property in relation to immovables is the law of the place of the immovable property (the *lex situs*) but this is not codified in any international treaty. Janeen Carruthers and Matthias Weller (chapter 21) discuss whether codification of this (possibly) universally recognised rule is worthwhile and say that 'a project examining the formulation of an applicable law rule in respect of lifetime transfers of immovable property' could consider whether there should be any exceptions to the basic rule. This possible project could be considered alongside the suggestion made by Albert Font i Segura and Jayne Holliday (chapter 22) that the HCCH should consider applicable law rules on which law applies to the clawback of lifetime transfers of property by way of gifts to non-heirs – where the writers propose the application of the *lex situs* in relation to the clawback of gifts of immovable property.

Finally, it is appropriate to refer to the most successful HCCH Convention – Apostille (1961) – which has over 120 Contracting States. It is at the margins of the core of private international law (jurisdiction, applicable law and recognition and enforcement of foreign decisions) but it has practical significance in many countries (mainly civil law) where historically a foreign document (eg, a marriage certificate) had to be legalised in each country where the holder wants that document to be relied on. The Convention simplifies this process by allowing a document to circulate based on the apostille certifying certain aspects of its authenticity in the country where the document was produced. Of course, the apostille only proves those aspects of the authenticity of the document; it does not mean that the other States party to the Convention have to accept all aspects of the authenticity of the document, far less the underlying status testified to in the document (eg, the validity of the marriage which the marriage certificate relates to).

II. Developing Strongly

The Child Protection Convention (1996) is well on the way to being a strong example of global private international law with over 50 States party to it. It needs more States to become Parties to it and it needs to develop a stronger body of case law but undoubtedly there is every chance of a strong level of unification of global private international law on parental responsibility (including questions of custody, access and the care of a child's property). Costanza Honorati and Mary Keyes (chapter 33) skilfully outline its key provisions and make excellent suggestions as to how the extensive practice of the intra-EU regime in this field (Brussels IIa and b Regulations) can be used to benefit the interpretation and application of the Child Protection Convention notably on habitual residence and the right of the child to be heard. In relation to habitual residence a uniform interpretation of the term between the Child Abduction Convention and the Child Protection Convention is, as Honorati and Keyes say, highly desirable. Exactly what that interpretation should be is more controversial. Readers of the book will want to compare and contrast the approach of these authors in this chapter with that of Ruth Lamont and Susanne Gössl in chapter 4 on connecting factors. The editors of this book are very sympathetic with the views of Lamont and Goessl in advocating a much stronger role for parental intention in determining 'habitual residence' under the Child Abduction and Child Protection Conventions than has been given to it hitherto by the Court of Justice of the European Union. Indeed, this echoes the views of the HCCH Experts' Group on Family Agreements involving Children in their draft Practical Guide (2019) that the recent shared parental intention as to the habitual residence of their child (formalised in a family agreement) should be determinative where the child is present in the place nominated by the parents.

As noted by Holliday and Font i Segura in their chapter on succession, the Hague Form of Wills Convention 1961 is still fit for purpose and has been relatively widely adopted by States (either by becoming a Party to it (42) or copying its ideas in their own law). The HCCH could give this a boost by holding a Review Special Commission and ascertaining how many States conform to it in their own law or agree with its policy and therefore could become a Party to it. The Permanent Bureau could also prepare an English text of the explanatory report on the 1961 Convention which is currently only available in French. There is no reason why, with proper promotion by the HCCH, the 1961 Convention could not be the standard for formal validity of wills everywhere given the breadth of applicable law options that it permits to maximise the chance of a person's will being formally valid. It was ahead of its time in using all relevant connecting factors (nationality, domicile, habitual residence, and the *lex situs* for immovables).

The Hague Maintenance Convention 2007 is developing well (42 States and the EU bound by it) and will get its first major review by the Special Commission in 2022. Walker and Beaumont in their chapter take advantage of the opportunity to analyse the responses of the HCCH Members to the questionnaire prepared by the Permanent Bureau for the Special Commission. They also highlight the current state of play in relation to the key reservations and declarations under the Convention which shows that the negotiators were wise to build in some flexibility but that the core of the Convention has not been diluted by many reservations and indeed declarations have brought spousal support fully into the Convention for many States (a trend which should be followed by other States when becoming Parties to the Convention). Walker and Beaumont note that:

> For establishing maintenance, the Convention turns on the efficacy of the work of Central Authorities (CAs) and free legal aid. The early data from the recent HCCH questionnaire indicates no problems with legal aid in the countries that have responded but does indicate a number of countries with relatively few employees in their CA.

In the area of insolvency there is already a good level of soft law agreed globally for certain cross-border issues thanks to the UNCITRAL Model Laws. The 1997 UNCITRAL Model Law on cross-border insolvency has been implemented in 49 States. The 2018 UNCITRAL Model Law on Recognition and Enforcement of Insolvency-Related Judgments has not yet been implemented in any States. The implementation of the 1997 Model Law is developing strongly, and the 2018 Model Law has great potential. There are, however, important gaps in the private international law framework for insolvency and bankruptcy globally. One of these gaps is currently being addressed as work is under way in UNCITRAL on applicable law with the support of the HCCH Permanent Bureau. Francisco Garcimartín and Sara Sánchez are supportive of this work in chapter 24 concluding that:

> The next step in this direction will perhaps be the adoption in the context of UNCITRAL of an instrument on applicable law, guided by the principle of modified universalism, which fills the gap that the Model Laws [on insolvency matters] have left in an area where national laws take divergent approaches giving rise to inconsistencies and legal uncertainty.

III. Great Potential

The Hague Choice of Court Convention (2005) has over 30 Parties and a number of signatories. Paul Beaumont and Mary Keyes (chapter 28) are strong advocates of its key rules. It has the benefit of a simple and clear rule on formal validity of exclusive choice of court agreements, a sophisticated applicable law rule on substantive validity, a clear rule requiring the chosen court to hear the case and not to decline jurisdiction, a balanced rule generally requiring the non-chosen court to decline jurisdiction in favour of the chosen court with limited exceptions to protect against manifest injustices. They conclude that:

> The Convention significantly improves upon existing laws, providing better protection of exclusive choice-of-court agreements. It comprehensively articulates the key principles governing the effects of exclusive choice-of-court agreements, improving access to justice, facilitating settlement, and reducing the costs of litigation at both the jurisdictional and recognition stages.

David Goddard and Paul Beaumont, two of the architects of the Judgments Convention (2019), in their chapter on recognition and enforcement of judgments in civil or commercial matters (chapter 29) strongly advocate the potential for that Convention as an excellent minimum harmonisation solution for global private international law on recognition and enforcement of judgments in civil or commercial matters. They conclude in relation to the Judgments Convention and the recognition and enforcement provisions in the Choice of Court Convention:

> We are optimistic that the two Conventions have succeeded in walking the fine line between breadth of scope and impact, and acceptability to States considering becoming Parties. We hope that the Conventions will enhance access to justice and facilitate cross-border trade, investment and mobility by creating a strong framework for the recognition and enforcement of judgments in civil or commercial matters.

Pietro Franzina wrote the chapter (chapter 39) that analyses the Hague Convention on the International Protection of Adults (2000). Although it has a relatively disappointing number of Parties at present (13) this is an excellent modern Convention that should be seen as the companion to the Child Protection Convention (1996) to create a just and efficient international regime for the protection of vulnerable adults. At a time when the spotlight of the world has been on the legal regime in the US applied to Britney Spiers, it can only be hoped that the often-forgotten category of adults who need some form of help or protection in making legal decisions becomes much more centre stage in the minds of policymakers. Hopefully more governments and campaign groups will fight for State time and resources to be devoted to implementing and operating the HCCH Adults Convention. Franzina concludes that:

> Adults lacking the ability to protect their interests because of an impairment or insufficiency of their personal faculties have a fundamental right to obtain the support they may require to exercise such capacity and, more generally, the right to be protected from abuse and neglect. The enforcement of that right involves, among other things, that measures be taken by States to enhance the autonomy and social inclusion of those concerned, and shield them from undue influence.
>
> Where a foreign element is present, all this involves the enactment of appropriate private international law rules. These rules effectively advance the respect for the above rights where they ensure the spatial continuity of the concerned adults' protection, without hindering otherwise their fundamental rights (eg, the right to have their views and preferences considered), and minimise the extra costs and uncertainties that the internationality of the situation could entail.
>
> The Hague Adults Convention is intended to achieve precisely those goals. It is consistent with a human-rights based approach to disability and appears to work efficiently in practice. While some of its rules call for review for possible enhancements, the Adults Convention ranks among the finest products of the Hague Conference, and provides an example of how private international law can effectively contribute to the realisation of fundamental human rights.

It can be hoped that more States become Parties to the Convention. Best practice and uniform interpretation of the Convention should begin to be shaped at the first Review Special Commission on the Convention to be held in 2022. It is very good that a Working Group has been established to develop a Practical Handbook on the Operation of the Protection of Adults Convention.

IV. Weak but could be Revived

The Hague Divorce Convention (1970) is a jewel in the Hague's crown which needs to be brought into the light so that it can be more widely appreciated. Máire Ní Shúilleabháin and Jayne Holliday (chapter 32) convincingly demonstrate that it is still fit for purpose and should be much more widely adopted. Although it only has 20 Contracting States after existing for more than 50 years it is still fit for purpose and able to allow for the recognition of divorces and legal separations of a very wide variety (judicial, administrative, religious, etc) provided that such a divorce is legally effective in the Contracting State where it was obtained, and that a minimum level of 'proceedings' were involved in obtaining the divorce. The next step is a questionnaire to be prepared by the Permanent Bureau, but this should lead to a Review Special Commission and a renewed awareness that this Convention works well and has been applied successfully in judicial decisions in Contracting States. The authors conclude that:

> As it stands, the 1970 Convention, which has been sorely neglected by both Contracting States and until recently the Hague Conference, remains effective and should not be dismissed due to its age and the low number of Contracting States. If a new international instrument is to be considered, then it is

> recommended that a new Convention on conflicts of jurisdiction relating to divorce would be a complementary and helpful addition to the 1970 Convention on Recognition of Divorces and Legal Separation.

Jonathan Harris (chapter 23) eruditely outlines the key provisions of the Hague Trusts Convention (1985) and shows that it is still a very sound basis for harmonisation of global private international law in this area. Trusts are a very important legal tool, widely used in common law systems and in some mixed and civil law systems. This tool of legal ownership of property is significant across a wide range of contexts (from family law, through succession law, charity law to commercial law). There is every reason to believe that it should be ratified by many more States than the current number of 14. The Permanent Bureau's report on the Convention for the March 2021 Council was noted but really this Convention, when the busy round of Review Special Commissions postponed because of Covid 19 has passed, deserves the high profile it would gain from its first Review Special Commission.

Michael Hellner (chapter 18) scrutinises the Hague Conventions relating to Applicable Law in Torts – Traffic Accidents (1971) and Products Liability (1973). They are in force in 21 and 11 States respectively. He concludes that these Conventions would need to be overhauled in order to become more widely ratified suggesting that:

> Important aspects of their modernisation would include a simplification …, the introduction of explicit rules on party autonomy, and regard to the interplay with choice of law in contract.

There are three other HCCH Conventions not separately analysed in this book which fall into this category. Perhaps in a future edition of this book they will be the subject of separate chapters. The first is the International Access to Justice Convention (1980), the second is the Celebration and Recognition of the Validity of Marriages Convention (1978), and the third is the Law Applicable to Certain Rights in Respect of Securities held with an Intermediary (2006). Access to Justice has 28 Contracting States, Marriages has three Contracting States, and Securities has three Contracting States.

V. (Largely) Non-Existent but could be Created

In the area of unjustified enrichment Adeline Chong and Jan Lüttringhaus (chapter 20) convincingly argue that this is an area ripe for development at the HCCH. They carefully dissect the best of the rules on applicable law in relation to unjustified enrichment in the EU and UK under the Rome II Regulation and in leading common law countries to show that a broad consensus is possible in this field with party autonomy at the heart of it.

Johan Meeusen (chapter 16) suggests following the example of the Hague Principles on Choice of Law in International Commercial Contracts by creating Hague Principles on the Law Applicable to Companies. In his chapter he concludes that:

> This search for coordination, rather than unification, could be a promising path at the international level. Why indeed not lower the ambitions to a more realistic level, one that would be within reach, and aim at agreement on a number of 'principles of coordination' to enhance smooth cross-border corporate activities?
>
> …
>
> Such Principles could be an interesting instrument to reach some international consensus on corporate applicable law. Putting the focus first on practical solutions, adopted on the basis of reciprocity, coupled with flexibility as to the precise principles that interested States would adopt, could be the basis for a step-by-step approach to generate trust and reach international agreement.

> At the basis of these Principles should be the idea that whatever approach States follow with respect to the valid constitution of companies governed by their own law, it is only the cross-border action of these companies that is of interest to other States. Moreover, the Principles should recognise that the involvement of companies in another State's legal system can be more or less extensive: access to its courts, the capacity to conclude contracts, the transfer of its real seat or that of its statutory seat – all raise different concerns and therefore may be subject to different legal treatment.

In the field of competition law, the level of global private international law is very small, just some judgments in relation to hard core cartels will be able to circulate under the Judgments Convention (2019) when it enters into force. Mihail Danov and Carmen Otero García-Castrillón (chapter 17) suggest that this is an area where more could be achieved. They advocate starting with a soft law measure like a model law:

> Model laws, which set out principles or even guides (addressing predominantly procedural issues concerning parallel and consecutive related proceedings), can be a feasible and successful approach. Such a soft legal instrument could set the scene for a more effective framework for international cooperation which would provide injured parties better access to adequate and effective regulatory and compensatory remedies, generating broader societal impacts. In other words, once such model laws have been successfully advanced, an appropriate regime for judicial cooperation on competition law enforcement may be devised. It would be important to consider issues of regulatory and adjudicatory jurisdiction including the interaction between regulators and courts (footnote omitted).
>
> Moreover, given the public interest safeguarding role of competition law, promoting an appropriate level of international cooperation is linked to the question: how could a PIL mechanism be advanced to safeguard the interests of claimants and defendants, as well as the various legitimate regulatory interests, by involving foreign regulators in the proceedings before appropriate national courts?

In relation to intellectual property some global private international law has been created in the context of the Choice of Court Convention (2005) particularly for copyright issues. However, this was an area that was highly controversial in the Judgments Convention (2019) negotiations and was ultimately excluded from the scope of that instrument. Paul Torremans (chapter 25) advocates cooperation between the World Intellectual Property Organization and the HCCH to achieve progress in this area building on the Conflict of Laws in Intellectual Property Principles.

As regards property law Carruthers and Weller (chapter 21) identify a new area where private international law requires to be developed to cope with technological innovations:

> A project to address the private international law issues arising in connection with emerging technologies and digitisation would be a bold and ambitious one … Legal systems across the globe are having to react rapidly to regulate new problems deriving from the introduction and use of digital (crypto-) assets and currencies (eg, use of bitcoin and the application of blockchain technology), especially in the context of financial services and/or Fintech, but without any overarching plan in relation to the inevitable private international law dimensions of the subject. Even the recognition, or not, of crypto-assets as property rights is a contentious subject (footnotes omitted).

Veronica Ruiz Abou-Nigm (chapter 27) advocates that aspects of private international law of maritime law could be developed involving the HCCH in cooperation with other specialist international organisations. She argues in her chapter that:

> The HCCH could join efforts with the International Maritime Organization (IMO), the United Nations Commission on International Trade Law (UNCITRAL), the United Nations Council on Trade and Development (UNCTAD), the International Institute for the Unification of Private Law (UNIDROIT) and the Comité Maritime International (CMI), ultimately to support the UN Sustainable Development Agenda 2030.

> Arguably, global (general) PIL expertise may be able to provide the missing links, in two possible concomitant directions: (i) exploring means of coordination between existing instruments, which could be built initially via soft-law mechanisms, and could include guidance as to the application of existing general PIL instruments to [carriage of goods by sea] COGS; (ii) and considering further work in this sphere in the context of the current exploration of jurisdiction issues at the HCCH (footnotes omitted).

Koji Takahashi and Sophia Tang (chapter 31) acknowledge that the Choice of Court Convention (2005) and Judgments Convention (2019) can be relevant for collective redress but that they are not well designed for such matters. They argue for a new Convention on recognition and enforcement of judgments coming from collective redress proceedings with the following indirect grounds of jurisdiction:

> Multiple indirect jurisdiction bases should be available for collective procedures, including jurisdiction based on the defendant's habitual residence, *ex post* jurisdiction agreements between the representative and the defendant, the centre of gravity of contracts and torts, and the home state of the majority of the potential claimants. The combination of different bases and the centralisation approach helps to encourage an international solution and also protect the right to pursue collective procedures if not available in the defendant's home State.

In relation to the role of States and governments in private international law litigation Uglješa Grušić, Paul Herrup and Lucian Martinez (chapter 11) conclude that:

> In the case of State litigation concerning cross-border enforcement of regulatory laws, State practice shows that States tend to observe public international law limits of State power and are increasingly willing to cooperate in the enforcement of regulatory laws protecting shared interests. Presently, however, jurisdictional rules of public international law and most domestic law rules defining the limits of State power are unsettled. Given the importance of protecting shared interests and a degree of convergence of State practice, international unification appears desirable and possibly feasible in the form of a model law or international principles.

Conflicts of jurisdiction is an area where the HCCH is currently considering a new Convention. The Working Group on Jurisdiction will doubtless find chapter 30 by Ardavan Arzandeh and Matthias Lehmann interesting. They are strong advocates of the broad balance already achieved between *forum non conveniens* and *lis pendens* in the Preliminary Draft Convention Interim Text 2001, Articles 21 and 22. For example they say that Article 21:

> [A]llows the court *first* seised to stay its proceedings if persuaded that the court second seised is clearly more appropriate to resolve the dispute, as defined under Article 22. It signifies a far more relaxed attitude to the application of the *lis pendens* rule than the one presently available at civil law. This flexibility, in turn, allows greater scope for the claim to be heard by a court in the forum that is essentially its home. As a result, in addition to being concerned with ensuring certainty in cases involving multiple proceedings between the same parties and concerning the same cause of action, the *lis pendens* rule under the Preliminary Draft Convention also gives some prominence to connectedness (footnote omitted).

The Working Group on Jurisdiction is also tasked with considering suitable jurisdiction rules either as part of minimum harmonisation of direct jurisdiction rules or as part of guiding rules in the context of prioritising courts in an instrument on conflicts of jurisdiction. Reid Mortensen (chapter 19) analyses the suitability of the tort indirect ground of jurisdiction under the Judgments Convention (2019) as a possible direct ground of jurisdiction. He is of the view that:

> The Judgments Convention also suggests a more promising approach for negotiating international agreement around suitable adjudicative jurisdictions. Adapting the moderate language of Article 7(2), under the Judgments Convention an enforceable tort judgment arises when:

> the judgment ruled on a non-contractual obligation arising from death, physical injury, damage to or loss of tangible property, and the act or omission directly causing such harm occurred in the State of origin, irrespective of where that harm occurred (footnote omitted).
>
> It is a *forum delicti* jurisdiction that is already represented in all three models of tort jurisdiction that are discussed in this chapter. It avoids the problematic *forum damni* jurisdiction. If adopted as a common rule of adjudicative jurisdiction, it could not reasonably give rise to any concern when exercised by another country's courts. In focusing on 'the act or omission' causing harm, it is more likely to fix special tort jurisdiction in one place and avoid the slippage of *Distillers*.

Ron Brand and Karen Vandekerckhove (chapter 15) discuss the indirect contract jurisdiction in the Judgments Convention. The editors of this book believe it could form the basis for a direct ground of jurisdiction in any future Jurisdiction Convention and should at least be used as a priority basis of jurisdiction in any new Hague Convention on Conflicts of Jurisdiction.

Another area or areas where the Hague Conference is already working on developing a new instrument or instruments is legal parentage and international surrogacy. Doubtless the Experts' Group will be inspired by Giacomo Biagioni's chapter (chapter 40). In relation to their work on parentage he is very supportive of their approach saying:

> A tentative analysis of the proposed general Hague instrument about parentage must first consider the possible scope of application. In this regard, the mandate of the Council has clearly referred to a convention in matters of recognition of judgments, but from the reports of the Experts' Group a strong suggestion in favour of a more comprehensive instrument, including rules on jurisdiction, applicable law and recognition of judgments and of public documents, clearly emerges.
>
> That suggestion appears to be justified, in the light of the peculiar characteristics of parentage matters, as in a majority of cases parentage is not established by judicial determination. Judicial proceedings are usually resorted to when there is a dispute about the identity of one of the parents. Accordingly, an instrument exclusively devoted to the recognition of judgments would not cover a significant number of cases.
>
> For the same reason, it is correct to assume that the conflict rules aimed at the designation of the law governing the establishment of parentage may play a pivotal role in the future instrument. As the legal parent–child relationship is usually enshrined in the birth certificates issued by the competent authorities of each State or in voluntary acknowledgments made before them, cross-border continuity of that status is more likely to be achieved if the authorities of different States apply the same law to establish parentage, with a view to achieving legal certainty.
>
> In the light of the same principle, it would be useful to clarify in the future instrument that its provisions would be relevant for the establishment of parentage even when the determination of the parent–child relationship constitutes a preliminary question, eg, in proceedings concerning maintenance or parental responsibility (footnotes omitted).

This last point on preliminary questions shows the importance, in drafting private international law conventions, of understanding some of the technical issues that have to be grappled with. This book benefits from a truly outstanding analysis of the role of preliminary questions and renvoi in making international conventions by Maria Hook (chapter 5) who concludes on preliminary questions that:

> This leaves a choice between the *lex fori* approach and the (whole of the) *lex causae* approach. This choice is often framed as one between internal (domestic) consistency and international harmony. If the former approach is adopted, a person's status will be the same domestically for all purposes, regardless of whether the main question (such as the existence of maintenance obligations) is governed by foreign law or not; but in the context of resolving the main question, the person's status may differ from country to country. If the latter approach is adopted, then for the purposes of the particular 'main' question, a

> person's status will be the same in all states that have adopted the uniform applicable law rule (eg, all contracting parties to the Hague Maintenance Protocol would apply the conflict of laws rules of the particular *lex causae* that has been designated as applicable by the Protocol).
>
> …
>
> an appropriate compromise may be to leave contracting states to apply the *lex causae* approach [to the preliminary question] as they see fit (which would be consistent with Article 12 of the Hague Marriage Convention). After all, the problem arises only in cases where the conflict of laws rules of the *lex causae* differ from those applicable in the forum court. The more harmonisation (or unification) there is of applicable law rules for issues that are likely to arise incidentally [or preliminarily] (eg, the validity of marriage), the less likely it is that courts will need to worry about their approach to the incidental [or preliminary] question. From this perspective, therefore, the unification of conflict of laws rules on questions of status would be a priority (footnote omitted).

Biagioni's views on international surrogacy are to encourage boldness by the HCCH Experts' Group in taking a regulatory approach that will protect the rights of all concerned, notably of the child (often as yet unborn) and of the surrogate mother, and ensure the suitability of the intended parents:

> Such a system would imply establishing a cooperation mechanism between the State of origin and the requested State, administered by national Central Authorities discharging procedural functions, to ensure *ex ante* that parentage be established with legal effects in both countries. To this aim, the future Protocol should set forth clear obligations for Contracting States as to the evaluation, on an *a priori* basis, of the necessary conditions to permit a lawful cross-border surrogacy arrangement. These include consideration of the (best) interests of the child, the suitability of the surrogate mother and of the intending parents, the free consent of all the parties involved and the absence of coercion during the entire process, the appropriateness of possible intermediaries, and the fair terms of the contract(s). The existence of detailed requirements accepted by Contracting States, to be subject to previous verification, could also lead to a restriction of the scope of application of public policy review, that should be relevant only in truly exceptional cases calling into question the best interests of the child as in Article 24 of the Adoption Convention.

Work is currently stalled in the HCCH on any future hard law instrument on family agreements involving children pending the adoption of a Practitioners' Tool on how the existing HCCH Conventions work in relation to such agreements (Child Abduction (1980), Child Protection (1996) and Child Support (2007)) and then some monitoring by the Experts' Group and Permanent Bureau of how well the Guide helps to facilitate the international circulation of such agreements. Rubaja and Beaumont argue in their chapter that in due course a new hard law instrument (a Convention) is justified for family agreements involving children to secure a one-stop shop for family agreements being made enforceable in States where the agreement itself is not enforceable, easy recognition and enforcement in other Contracting States of the agreement and of a decision based on that agreement, increased party autonomy in the selection of a place to make the agreement and to make the agreement enforceable by a decision of a court or other competent authority where that is required by the relevant national law. They conclude that:

> [A] new Convention is needed to ensure children's rights and their best interests are safeguarded within a context of greater party autonomy providing an easy and cheap system to secure the effectiveness of cross-border family agreements.

There is an HCCH Convention on the Law Applicable to Matrimonial Property Regimes (1978) (3 Contracting States) but Rhona Schuz (chapter 37) does not believe that it is fit for purpose as it stands to persuade other States to become Parties to it. Instead, she argues in her conclusion that:

> One way of making progress towards such an objective might be by starting off with a soft law approach at the HCCH, involving formulation of non-binding guiding principles. The advantages of such an approach are two-fold. First, it would avoid the controversy as to whether the applicable law rules should apply to same sex marriages, which is liable to be a major obstacle to any work on a hard law instrument. Second, there is a greater likelihood of obtaining agreement to general principles, which leave State parties with some leeway to fill in the details (footnotes omitted).

Font i Segura and Holliday note that matters relating to succession, apart from the Form of Wills discussed above, have not been successfully dealt with in the HCCH. The Convention on the Law Applicable to Succession (1989) is not fit for purpose with no Contracting States. They advocate moving forward with new work at the HCCH on the niche area of clawback in the context of succession building on Holliday's earlier monograph on that topic. This is an area that highlights the importance and difficulty of determining which area of law is being dealt with from a private international law perspective so that the correct private international law rules can be applied – the problem of characterisation. The significance of getting characterisation right in the context of uniform private international law instruments is also skilfully set out in chapter 3 on characterisation by Chiara Goetzke and Ralf Michaels. They conclude that:

> At the global level the HCCH provides guidance on the interpretation of its instruments in the explanatory reports on each Convention, and in Guides to Good Practice, Practical Handbooks, and recommendations and conclusions of Review Special Commissions in relation to all the successful HCCH Conventions, etc. Such interpretations … should serve as well-reasoned focal points for courts to take account of and for academics to propagate when addressing characterisation issues in relation to HCCH Conventions.
>
> Altogether, international instruments provide specific opportunities for characterisation that is on the one hand explicitly comparative and on the other explicitly regulatory. Such processes are best done in cooperation between courts and academics. Lawmakers should indeed interfere where it is possible to resolve difficult characterisation issues or where the implications of specific policy decisions are important. Beyond that, a very detailed regulation of specific issues threatens to deprive private international law of its necessary flexibility in view of new and unexpected situations and undermine the chance for a successful comprehensive international system (footnote omitted).

VI. Not the Time to Act on a New Global Instrument (but Some Practical Suggestions for Application of Foreign Law)

Symeon Symeonides concludes in his chapter (14) on the law applicable to contracts that the area of private international law concerning the law applicable to a contract in the absence of a choice of law by the parties is one where

> the commendable efforts of the Hague Conference can be put to better use on other subjects for which the need for uniformity or approximation is more obvious.

On the very important dichotomy between substance and procedure in private international law (the former is subject to applicable law rules in many areas of law and can therefore be governed by a foreign law whereas the latter is subject to the law of the forum) Richard Garnett (chapter 9) does not propose any kind of global instrument on this issue but concludes that:

> While it would be premature to suggest that there has been a global unification of the principles in this area of private international law, there is undoubtedly evidence of increasing convergence.

Marta Requejo Isidro (chapter 10) does not argue for a new global instrument on the application of foreign law as it was not many years ago that this was removed as a possible legislative project from the work schedule of the HCCH. However, she does encourage a practical approach to the issue in which the HCCH can play a role:

> The Hague Conference supports judicial dialogue in a number of ways; the task should continue with a dedicated focus on the application of foreign law. Judicial seminars and training on the cooperation tools could be organised or promoted by the Permanent Bureau. The publication of guidelines on complex aspects, such as how to formulate questions on the applicable law, would also be helpful.
>
> The creation of a global network of institutions and experts for complex questions on foreign law, facilitated by the Permanent Bureau, was mentioned in 2012 but left for study at a later stage; it was never taken up. The value of establishing mechanisms to identify experts to assist in the ascertainment and understanding of the foreign law was also acknowledged. Both initiatives should be resumed; to the extent that they focus on technical devices, they should not be hindered by political considerations.

VII. Final Remark

We would like to finish the book by saying that it has been an absolute privilege to work with so many extremely capable and enquiring minds, and we would like to take the opportunity, once again, to show our appreciation and thank them all for their hard work and support.

INDEX

www.ingramcontent.com/pod-product-compliance
Ingram Content Group UK Ltd.
Pitfield, Milton Keynes, MK11 3LW, UK
UKHW050418051026
15470UKWH00022B/1589